THE INFORMATION NEEDS OF COMMUNITIES

The changing media landscape in a broadband age

Steven Waldman

and the Working Group on Information Needs of Communities

Federal Communications Commission

Table of Contents

4

Executive Summary

In most ways today's media landscape is more vibrant than ever, offering faster and cheaper distribution networks, fewer barriers to entry, and more ways to consume information. Choice abounds. Local TV stations, newspapers and a flood of innovative web start-ups are now using a dazzling array of digital tools to improve the way they gather and disseminate the news—not just nationally or internationally but block-by-block. The digital tools that have helped topple governments abroad are providing Americans powerful new ways to consume, share and even report the news.

Yet, in part because of the digital revolution, serious problems have arisen, as well. Most significant among them: in many communities, we now face a shortage of local, professional, accountability reporting. This is likely to lead to the kinds of problems that are, not surprisingly, associated with a lack of accountability—more government waste, more local corruption, less effective schools, and other serious community problems. The independent watchdog function that the Founding Fathers envisioned for journalism—going so far as to call it crucial to a healthy democracy—is in some cases at risk at the local level.

As technology offered consumers new choices, it upended traditional news industry business models, resulting in massive job losses—including roughly 13,400 newspaper newsroom positions in just the past four years. This has created gaps in coverage that even the fast-growing digital world has yet to fill. It is difficult to know what positive changes might be just around the corner, but at this moment the media deficits in many communities are consequential. Newspapers are innovating rapidly and reaching new audiences through digital platforms but most are operating with smaller reporting staffs, and as a result are often offering less in-depth coverage of critical topics such as health, education and local government. Many local TV news broadcasts remain excellent, and, on average, they actually produce more hours of news than a few years ago—but too few are investing in more reporting on critical local issues and some have cut back staff. Beyond that, a minority are exhibiting alarming tendencies to allow advertisers to dictate content. In most communities, commercial radio, cable, and satellite play a small role in reporting local news. Public TV does little local programming; public radio makes an effort to contribute but has limited resources. Most important, too few Internet-native local news operations have so far gained sufficient traction financially to make enough of an impact.

On close inspection, some aspects of the modern media landscape may seem surprising:

> An abundance of media *outlets* does not translate into an abundance of *reporting*. In many communities, there are now more outlets, but less local accountability reporting.

> While digital technology has empowered people in many ways, the concurrent decline in local reporting has, in other cases, shifted power away from citizens to government and other powerful institutions, which can more often set the news agenda.

> Far from being nearly-extinct dinosaurs, the traditional media players—TV stations and newspapers—have emerged as the largest providers of local news online.

> The nonprofit media sector has become far more varied, and important, than ever before. It now includes state public affairs networks, wikis, local news websites, organizations producing investigative reporting, and journalism schools as well as low-power FM stations, traditional public radio and TV, educational shows on satellite TV, and public access channels. Most of the players neither receive, nor seek, government funds.

> Rather than seeing themselves only as competitors, commercial and nonprofit media are now finding it increasingly useful to collaborate.

This report looks not only at the changing face of media, but at the relevant policy and regulatory situation, including the FCC's own track record. Our basic conclusion: with the media landscape shifting as fast as it has been, some current regulations are out of sync with the information needs of communities and the fluid nature of modern local media markets.

In crafting recommendations, this report started with the overriding premise that the First Amendment circumscribes the role government can play in improving local news. Beyond that, sound policy would recognize that government is simply not the main player in this drama.

However, greater transparency by government and media companies can help reduce the cost of reporting, empower consumers, and generally improve the functioning of media markets. And policymakers can take other steps to remove obstacles to innovation and ensure that taxpayer resources are well used.

Our specific recommendations follow six broad principles:

> Information required by FCC policy to be disclosed to the public should, over time, be made available online.

> Greater government transparency will enable both citizens and reporters to more effectively monitor powerful institutions and benefit from public services.

> Existing government advertising spending should be targeted more toward local media.

> Nonprofit media need to develop more sustainable business models, especially through private donations.

> Universal broadband and an open Internet are essential prerequisites for ensuring that the new media landscape serves communities well.

> Policymakers should take historically underserved communities into account when crafting strategies and rules.

It is a confusing time. Breathtaking media abundance lives side-by-side with serious shortages in reporting. Communities benefit tremendously from many innovations brought by the Internet and simultaneously suffer from the dislocations caused by the seismic changes in media markets. Our conclusion: the gaps are quite important, but they are fixable. In other words, we find ourselves in an unusual moment when ignoring the ailments of local media will mean that serious harm may be done to our communities—but paying attention to them will enable Americans to develop, literally, the best media system the nation has ever had.

Overview

IS IT POSSIBLE TO CAPTURE how much the information revolution has changed our world? Eric Schmidt, former CEO of Google, certainly conveyed the gist when he estimated that humans now create as much information in two days as we did from the appearance of Homo sapiens through 2003.[1] Or, we could consider that Facebook did not exist in 2003—and now reaches more people than all other major U.S. media outlets combined.

Or we might contemplate the pigeons of Paul Julius Reuter.[2] In 1851, the businessman used a fleet of carrier pigeons to carry stock market quotations and news between London and Paris.[3] It worked well (pigeons beat the train-carried news by seven hours). But as technology improved, his company, Reuters, changed its approach, each time with techniques more mind-boggling than the last.[4] In the course of its life, the company has gone from distributing news by attaching a little packet of information to the feet of a bird to pushing electromagnetic bursts through cables under the sea to cramming voice data into radio waves in the air to bouncing data off a satellite in outer space—to transmitting little "packets" of information in the form of ones and zeros over wireless Internet networks.[5]

And if the company, now called Thomson Reuters, were to bring back the pigeons, each could clutch a 256-gigabyte flash drive holding roughly eight million[6] times the amount of information that one of the original Reuters pigeons could comfortably haul.

These comparisons only begin to convey a sense of the scale of changes that have occurred. The digital revolution has utterly transformed how information is created, distributed, shared, and displayed. But we are just beginning to wrestle with the implications of these changes, including what they mean for journalism, the profession that Paul Julius Reuter practiced and that the Founders viewed as a cornerstone of American democracy.

Thomas Jefferson, who loathed many specific newspapers, nonetheless considered a free press so vital that he declared, "Were it left to me to decide whether we should have a government without newspapers or newspapers without a government, I should not hesitate a moment to prefer the latter." If he were alive today, Jefferson would likely clarify that his dedication was not to "newspapers" per se but to their *function*: providing citizens the information they need to both pursue happiness and hold accountable government as well as other powerful institutions.[7]

That sense of the vital link between informed citizens and a healthy democracy is why civic and media leaders grew alarmed a few years ago when the digital revolution began undercutting traditional media business models, leading to massive layoffs of journalists at newspapers, newsmagazines, and TV stations. Since then, experts in the media and information technology spheres have been debating whether the media is fulfilling the crucial role envisioned for it by the Founders. In 2008 and 2009, a group that was both bipartisan (Republicans and Democrats) and bi-generational ("new media" and "old media") studied this issue at the behest of the John S. and James L. Knight Foundation. The group, the Knight Commission on the Information Needs of Communities in a Democracy, concluded:

> "America is at a critical juncture in the history of communications. Information technology is changing our lives in ways that we cannot easily foresee.

> "The digital age is creating an information and communications renaissance. But it is not serving all Americans and their local communities equally. It is not yet serving democracy fully. How we react, individually and collectively, to this democratic shortfall will affect the quality of our lives and the very nature of our communities."[8]

The Knight Commission's findings, as well as those of other blue-ribbon reports, posed a bipartisan challenge to the FCC, whose policies often affect the information health of communities. The chairman responded in December 2009 by initiating an effort at the FCC to answer two questions: 1) are citizens and communities getting the news, information, and reporting they want and need? and 2) is public policy in sync with the nature of modern media markets, especially when it comes to encouraging innovation and advancing local public interest goals?

A working group consisting of journalists, entrepreneurs, scholars, and government officials conducted an exploration of these questions. The group interviewed hundreds of people, reviewed scores of studies and reports, held hearings, initiated a process for public comment, and made site visits. We looked not only at the news media but, more broadly, at how citizens get local information in an age when the Internet has enabled consumers to access information without intermediaries.

This report is intended both to inform the broad public debate and help FCC Commissioners assess current rules. It is divided into three sections.

In Part One, we assess the "media and information landscape," ultimately providing diagnoses on which sectors are healthy and which are not. Part One is divided into four sections. The report looks first at commercial media sectors (TV, radio, Internet, newspapers, etc.) and how well each medium is currently ferreting out and presenting civically important information and news. It then examines nonprofit media, including public broadcasting, nonprofit websites, state public affairs networks (SPANs), low-power FM (LPFM) radio stations, and other nonprofit entities. Next, it looks at ways that consumers get information that are not reliant on journalistic intermediaries. We focus particularly on libraries, emergency alert systems, digital literacy efforts in schools, and the crucially important move by governments to become more transparent. In the final chapters of Part One, we step back from the platform-by-platform analysis and look at key cross-cutting, cross-platform trends. When one considers both the losses of old media and the additions from new players, which media markets are healthy and which are not?

Throughout Part One, we attempt to make this report not only a description of problems but also a resource— a reliable history of these industries and information sources, a non-ideological description of how things work, and a catalogue of some of the efforts underway to improve communities. Our hope is that laying out this information in one place will be useful and stimulating, even to those who disagree with our conclusions.

In Part Two, we look at the current policy and regulatory landscape, considering some of the main laws and regulations—including those issued by the FCC—that directly and indirectly shape the news media. This should be understandable to the broad public, not just to a small group of communication law experts.

In Part Three, we make recommendations. Some are directed to the FCC, some to the broader community of policymakers, philanthropists, and citizens.

We are well aware that a report crafted by staff at a government agency about the media could be met with suspicion. The media, after all, should be examining the government—not vice versa. But we also believe that it would be public policy malpractice for the Federal Communications Commission to simply assume that the current (voluminous) set of public policies about communications—some crafted before there was an Internet—are well suited for the 21st century. It is impossible to understand the information needs of communities—a clear statutory focus of the FCC—without taking a holistic look at all media. When the media landscape changes so rapidly and so dramatically, the Commission must understand whether its assumptions and rules are still operating, as the Commission is legally required to do, in service of the "public interest, convenience, and necessity" and in furtherance of "localism, competition, and diversity." The Commission has not only the authority but the affirmative duty to look at these issues.[9]

It is also important to realize that just because this report points out a particular problem does not mean that we believe the FCC has the responsibility or authority to solve it. We do not view the government as the main player in this drama. In some cases, the role of this report is simply to describe things—to stimulate discussion and to suggest new paradigms for understanding local media markets.

We started with a view that there has never been an ideal age of journalism. Reports far thicker than this could document the failures of traditional journalism to uncover or understand important stories, sufficiently shed its biases, emphasize the important stories over the frivolous, cover all constituencies with sufficient rigor, and live up to the highest ideals and ethical standards of the profession. But we place those hard truths in a practical context by also noting two other ideas: 1) just because something is imperfect does not mean it cannot get worse, and 2) for every instance of journalistic neglect there are many more in which the media have performed exactly the functions a democracy needs. Or, as James Madison, put it, "Some degree of abuse is inseparable from the proper use of everything; and in no instance is this more true than in that of the press." Yet despite the press's "abuses," Madison argued that efforts to restrain the bad actors would hurt the good:

"It is better to leave a few of its noxious branches to their luxuriant growth, than, by pruning them away, to injure the vigor of those yielding the proper fruits. And can the wisdom of this policy be doubted by anyone who reflects that to the press alone, checkered as it is with abuses, the world is indebted for all the triumphs which have been gained by reason and humanity over error and oppression?"[10]

We share Madison's grand vision about the importance of the press. If the United States does not have healthy media markets, communities will suffer real harm. Yet despite the serious challenges, we are optimistic: while the problems are serious, they are manageable. If citizens, entrepreneurs, nonprofit groups, and businesses work collectively to fill the gaps and continue to benefit from a wave of media innovation, the nation will end up with the best media system it has ever had.

PART ONE: THE MEDIA LANDSCAPE

Attempting to convey a clear picture of the modern media landscape is like trying to draw a hurricane from within the storm. In our review of the industry's history, we note that leaders of each medium believed that the latest new technology would doom them, yet many survived and adapted. And yet this sense that the future is unknowable cannot be used as an excuse for failing to attempt to understand what is happening around us now—especially when history has shown that in transformative moments like this, decisions made by policymakers and industry leaders reverberate for decades. So in approaching this analysis, we faced two opposing challenges: fully describing the current media landscape is impossible; failing to try is irresponsible.

Certainly there can be no doubt that the traditional media business has been significantly shaken, with potentially serious consequences for communities:

> Newspaper advertising revenue dropped 47 percent from 2005 to 2009.[11]

> Between 2006 and 2009, daily newspapers cut their annual editorial spending $1.6 billion per year, or more than a quarter, according to the Poynter Institute's Rick Edmonds.[12]

> Staff at daily newspapers has shrunk by more than 25 percent since 2006, with some major newspapers seeing half their staffs disappear in a matter of a few years. There are about as many journalists working today as there were before Watergate.[13]

> Television network news staffs have declined by half from the late 1980s.[14]

> Newsmagazine reporting staffs have dropped by almost half since 1985.[15]

> The number of all-news local radio stations has dropped from 50 in the mid-1980s to 30, which reach a third of the country.[16]

> Only about 20 to 30 percent of the population has access to a local all-news cable channel.[17]

> There are 520 local TV stations that air no local news at all (258 commercial stations and 262 noncommercial stations). Considering those, along with stations that air less than 30 minutes of local news per day, 33 percent of commercial stations currently offer little or no local news.[18]

Hyperlocal information is better than ever. Technology has allowed citizens to help create and share news on a very local level—by town, neighborhood, or even block. These sites mostly do not operate as profitable businesses, but they do not need to. This is journalism as voluntarism—a thousand points of news.

But these statistics in traditional media, alarming as they are, tell us only part of the story and leave many unanswered questions. How significant has the impact of these cuts been? Are the effects entirely negative? Have the losses been offset by efforts in other media?

To get a handle on this, it is useful to recall that in a typical community, each medium has played a different role. To oversimplify: with larger staffs, newspapers carried the heavier burden of reporting—especially of investigative, enterprise, and beat reporting—while local TV and radio "cast" the news to a "broad" audience. Thus, changes in the health of one medium—newspapers—ripple through the entire local news economy, prompting recalibrations among all media.

Local Newspapers

This report's truncated history of newspapers includes an examination of how new technologies have repeatedly forced change over the industry's 200-plus-year lifespan. We also look at the evolving role of independent journalism; the rise of corporate chains; and why, precisely, the Internet has proved so devastating to traditional newspaper business models.

We then turn to the key question: What are the repercussions when newspapers lay off large numbers of reporters? A major report commissioned by the Columbia Journalism School in 2009 concluded, "What is under threat is independent *reporting* that provides information, investigation, analysis, and community knowledge, particularly in the coverage of local affairs." [19]

We concur. A handful of case studies conducted in U.S. cities helps quantify the effects:

Baltimore: The *Baltimore Sun* produced 32 percent fewer stories in 2009 than in 1999—and 73 percent fewer than in 1991, according to a study by the Pew Center for Excellence in Journalism. [20]

Philadelphia: A study comparing sample weeks in 2006 and 2009 found, "Available news about Philadelphia public affairs issues has dramatically diminished over the last three years by many measures: news hole, air time, story count, key word measurements." [21]

Raleigh-Durham, North Carolina: In 2004, the *Raleigh (NC) News & Observer* had 250 employees. By February 2011, the newsroom headcount was down to 103. The beats that lost reporters included: courts, schools, legal affairs, agriculture, environment, and state education. [22]

Across the country, the number of reporters covering essential beats has diminished:

Statehouse: From 2003 to 2008, while state government spending rose substantially, the number of statehouse reporters dropped by one-third, according to the *American Journalism Review*. [23] In New Jersey, the number of statehouse reporters dropped from 35 to 15. [24] In California it fell from 40 to 29; [25] in Texas, from 28 to 18; [26] and in Georgia, from 14 to 5. [27]

Investigative: There is no reliable direct count of investigative reporters, but indirect measures indicate a decline. Membership in the Investigative Reporters and Editors association dropped from 5,391 in 2003 to 4,000 in 2010. [28] From 1984 to 2010, submissions to the Pulitzer Prize "public service" category declined by 43 percent. [29]

Environment: The Society of Environmental Journalists had 430 newspaper reporter members in 2004; now, it has 256. [30]

The impact of national policy on communities: Twenty-seven states have no Washington reporters, according to Pew's Project for Excellence in Journalism. The number of papers with bureaus covering the Capitol has dropped by about half since the mid-1980s. [31]

In other cases, hard numbers are unavailable, but experts on the ground describe distressing changes:

Religion: "Religion news at the local level is nearly gone," reports Debra Mason, executive director of the Religion Newswriters Association. [32]

Health: The number of health reporters has declined, while interest in the topic has remained strong, leading to fewer reporters doing more work and "a loss of in-depth, enterprise and policy-related stories," according to a study by the Kaiser Family Foundation. [33]

Education: Schools reporters are overextended. Responsible for covering more ground than ever, they are unable to do so adequately. Richard Colvin, former director of the Hechinger Institute, put it this way:

"Local coverage has likely not dropped in volume. But it has certainly dropped in ambition.... [T]hose who [cover education] may not do so full time and don't have the leeway to write much of substance. They also have very little capacity to think about broader issues."[34]

Business: Andrew Lack, CEO of Bloomberg Multimedia, says that local business journalism is suffering today: "It's not a market that's well served."[35]

The consequences of journalistic shortages can be seen in places like Bell, California, a working class suburb, where the city's chief administrative officer was drawing a salary of $787,637, and the police chief, $457,000. The *Los Angeles Times*, to its credit, broke the story in June 2010—and won a Pulitzer Prize for its efforts—but the scandal had been unfolding since at least 2005. No reporters regularly covered the Bell city government during that period. Had there been even a single regular reporter, there is a reasonable chance that taxpayers would have saved much of the $5.6 million the officials pocketed. Such examples also help explain why David Simon, a former reporter for the *Baltimore Sun*, who went on to create the HBO show *The Wire*, said in a 2009 Senate hearing: "It is going to be one of the great times to be a corrupt politician."[36]

Reporters and editors have told us and other researchers that they are spending more time on reactive stories and less on labor-intensive "enterprise" pieces. An editor in Tennessee pointed to a story list on a conference room white board. There was an "X" next to a story he wanted to do about the failures of a state board that regulates incompetent doctors, but because the paper had laid off one of its health reporters it could not afford to let the remaining health reporter conduct a labor-intensive investigation.[37] A reporter in another town described a tip he had received about local authorities being overly restrictive in issuing gun permits, but explained that he has not had time to look into it.[38]

It is hard to know exactly what gets lost when reporters devote less time to enterprise stories, but clues can be found by looking at the journalism that has occurred *after* recent catastrophes. Several publications brilliantly documented that the Upper Big Branch mine in West Virginia had "1,342 safety violations in the past five years"—but it requires no stretch of the imagination to think that the 29 people who died in the 2010 mine explosion might have been spared had more journalists aggressively reported these safety problems *before* the accident.[39]

We were especially struck by the testimony of non-journalists who rely on good information to solve community problems. In Michigan, coverage of juvenile courts has gotten "smaller and smaller over the years," according to Vivek Sankaran of the University of Michigan, an expert on family courts; the result is "parents whose rights are terminated who shouldn't be terminated. It just takes somebody to go down there to get the story, but nobody is ever down there."[40]

Given that polls show the public has a low opinion of journalists, it is easy to forget that when reporters have less power, other institutions tend to end up with more. The Pew study of Baltimore concluded that governmental institutions increasingly drove the stories—not reporters:

"As news is posted faster, often with little enterprise reporting added, the official version of events is becoming more important. We found official press releases often appear word for word in first accounts of events, though often not noted as such.... Government, at least in this study, initiates most of the news. In the detailed examination of six major storylines, 63 percent of the stories were initiated by government officials, led first of all by the police. Another 14 percent came from the press. Interest group figures made up most of the rest."[41]

Bill Girdner, owner and editor of Courthouse News Service, notes that as it has become harder for reporters to get information about cases, "the court bureaucracy has gotten stronger and stronger.... When journalists don't have presence, others control the information process."[42]

Many newspapers have responded to the challenges with tremendous creativity, trying to use their remaining staffs as effectively as possible. Some papers actually have been placing a greater emphasis on "accountability journalism"—beat and investigative reporting about powerful institutions such as schools, city hall, and courts. Most papers are embracing new technological tools to try to maximize their remaining reporters' impact—often making especially good use of data put online by local or national government. In most communities, the number one online local news source is the local newspaper, an indication that despite their financial problems, newspaper newsrooms are still adept at providing news.

But the broader trend is undeniable: there are fewer full-time newspaper reporters today, and those who remain have less time to conduct interviews and in-depth investigations. In some ways, news production today is more high tech—there is nary a reporter in America who does not know how to tweet, blog, and use a flip video camera—but in other ways it has regressed, with more and more journalists operating like 1930s wire service reporters—or scurrying on what the *Columbia Journalism Review* calls "the hamster wheel" to produce each day's quota of increasingly superficial stories.[43] They can describe the landscape, but they have less time to turn over rocks. They can convey what they see before their eyes—often better and faster than ever—but they have less time to discover the stories lurking in the shadows or to unearth the information that powerful institutions want to conceal.

This study starts with newspapers because traditionally they fielded the most reporters in a community and set the agenda for the rest of the local media. But a reduction in newspaper reporters need not mean an overall shrinkage of journalism—if the slack were to be taken up by other journalists in town, such as those on TV, radio, and the Internet. So, we next turn to TV.

Local TV News

Most Americans still get their news from the local TV news team—and many stations do an extraordinary job informing their communities. Increasingly, they are offering news through multiple platforms, giving consumers more ways to get the bread-and-butter news they need. Though local TV stations are not as financially robust as they were five years ago, most are profitable. Indeed, for now, local TV news may have the strongest business model for providing local news.

In many cases, local TV news teams have increased productivity. Over the last seven years, the number of hours of local TV news has risen by 35 percent. Stations offer more newscasts, additional multicast digital channels, mobile apps, and increasingly popular websites. Many have been creative in using new technology—from citizens' cell phone photos to eyewitness Twitter reports—to improve the quality of their offerings. Many serve their communities with genuine passion for making the news available, for free, to an impressively broad audience. In many ways, local TV news is more important than ever.

Unfortunately, many stations are not where they need to be if they are going to plug the reportorial gaps left by newspapers.

For starters, most local TV stations have increased the volume of news production, while *reducing* staff—which generally weakens a station's capacity for depth. Matthew Zelkind, news director of WKRN in Nashville explains: "Long-form stories are dying because they're not financially feasible.... It's all economically driven."[44] Fred Young, a long-time TV executive, echoed the view that investigative reporting at most stations is shrinking: "Investigative [stories], in the eyes of some of the people who looked at the bottom line of those stations, were not as productive as the reporters turning a story a day. Investigative has suffered."[45]

Topics like local education, health care, and government get minimal coverage. In a 2010 study of Los Angeles TV news by the Annenberg School of Communications, such topics took up just a little over *one minute* of the 30 minute broadcast. Only one out of 100 lead stories was about the ongoing budget crisis.[46] In another study—of local broadcasters in 175 cities—coverage of city government was found to be about one-third as common as crime stories. Other studies have discovered the same pattern.[47]

More stations are increasingly relying on "one-man bands"—reporters who interview, shoot, and edit. In some cases, this is a powerful and sensible efficiency that stations could use to increase the number of reporters in the

A cross-subsidy system had developed: a consumer who bought the newspaper for the box scores was helping to pay the salary of the city hall reporter. Today, a reader can get a mobile app that provides only box scores (with second-by-second updates!). The bundle is broken—and so is the cross-subsidy.

field. But in many communities, that is not what has happened. "Let's face it—it is what it is, and it is economic," says Con Psarras, former news director at KSL in Salt Lake City. "It is an ability to cut heads and it is a full-time equivalent-reduction campaign. It does not make the pictures better, it does not make the stories better—it does not make the coverage on the web better. That's a mythology—it just saves money."[48] One typical TV reporter said that while he was one-man banding, he was so busy tweeting, shooting, and editing, he had less time for interviews. "It's the research. When I was one-man-banding, if I had interviewed one or two people, I'd say, hey, that's enough to get on the air."[49]

Perhaps most disturbing is the persistence of cases in which local TV news programs have allowed advertisers to determine on-air content. In Wisconsin, a news director resigned over the station's "pay-for-play" arrangement with a local hospital that had agreed to advertise in exchange for a commitment from the station to air health stories twice a week—from a list of ideas provided by the hospital.[50] A hospital in Ohio paid local TV stations $100,000 or more to air "medical breakthrough" segments that benefited the hospital.[51] A Florida morning show was soliciting $2,500 fees in exchange for guest slots.[52] In other cases, stations are airing video press releases as if they were news stories created by news staff. Though we have no way of knowing how many stations have adopted these egregious practices, the trend-line is worrisome: "The evidence we've seen suggests that this is much more widespread than a few years ago," says Tom Rosensteil, the director of the Pew Project on Excellence in Journalism.

There are about as many journalists working today as there were before Watergate. Television network news staffs have declined by half from the late 1980s. Newsmagazine reporting staffs have dropped by almost half since 1985.

This is not meant to be a blanket indictment of local TV news. Some stations have done more than maintain their reporting capacity; they have improved it. But the evidence indicates that in many communities if local TV news continues on its *current* path, it will not fill the gaps in accountability reporting left by newspapers. In fact, 64 percent of broadcast news executives believe that their profession is headed in the wrong direction; they are even more pessimistic than newspaper editors.[53] We emphasize the word "current" because local TV news has the capacity to play a different—more journalistically significant—role in the new ecosystem. The question is whether the industry will seize that opportunity. (Chapter 3, Television.)

Radio

Though commercial radio offers a dazzling range of programming options, in most cities local journalism is not one of them. While the news-talk format is thriving, it has relied largely on nationally syndicated shows, rather than locally produced ones. Eighty-six percent of the news and public affairs programming broadcast on news-talk radio is national rather than local. Though there are still some extraordinary local news efforts—from WINS in New York to the Rubber City Radio group of Akron, Ohio—they are more rare than they used to be. The number of commercial all-news stations has dropped from 50 in the mid-1980s to 30 today—with only 30 to 40 percent of the population living in an area that has an all-news station.

Low-power FM was created by Congress to provide community broadcasting, and some of the 800 LPFM stations provide excellent hyperlocal programming. A bill that was signed into law in January 2011 is intended to help spawn more stations, but it is too early to know what its effects will be. (Chapter 2, Radio.)

Cable TV

Financially, cable TV is thriving.[54] The industry's two-revenue-stream model—advertising and subscriber fees—has proved more durable than broadcast TV's traditional reliance on advertising alone. The growth of national cable news networks has helped make up for some of the reportorial losses broadcast network news has suffered—but, as with radio, cable news is vibrant on a national level, and weaker on a local level. Some cable operators, such as Time Warner and Cablevision, offer excellent all-news local channels. But other cable companies view such operations as unprofitable and unlikely to grow. Currently, only about 20 to 30 percent of the population can watch a local or regional cable news show.

Some cable operators offer state public affairs networks (SPANs) modeled after C-SPAN, a particularly valuable service given the cutbacks in statehouse reporting. By broadcasting state legislatures and governmental bodies in action, even if these state SPANs are not generating big ratings, they add a measure of accountability since politicians know that they *might* be observed. But 27 states do not have them—and in only 4 states does the cable industry support them as they do C-SPAN.

Since the early days of cable, there has also been a system of local public, educational, and governmental access (PEG) channels. Often set up to offer citizens a way to express themselves, PEG channels—roughly 5,000 of them—have recently been working to find a new mission in an era when self-expression opportunities abound online. Some have become important venues for teaching digital literacy skills, and a few have begun to focus on citizen journalism. At the same time, cities and states have been cutting back significantly on their funding, causing scores of PEG channels to go dark. This is a time of both great promise and peril for PEG stations. (Chapter 3, Television; Chapter 7, Public Access Channels; and Chapter 27, Cable Television.)

Satellite

Satellite technology is not particularly conducive to local programming, but the FCC requires satellite service providers to set aside 4 percent of the channels they carry for educational programming; currently, some of these channels focus on public affairs. Some educational channels—including those providing religious, public affairs and foreign language programming—have had great success. But in recent years, satellite operators have been turning away prospective channels for lack of capacity. Some educational programmers also found it too expensive: unlike the PEG system, in which programmers *get* paid, nonprofit programmers must, by law, pay satellite operators significant fees. (Chapter 9, Satellite.)

Internet and Mobile

The enormous challenges facing traditional media would be of less concern if the vibrant new digital media were filling the gap. Is it?

It is important to appreciate that the Internet has not only allowed for new forms of self-expression but has improved news in many ways. Lower barriers to entry and the vast amount of available space online have led to a greater diversity of voices, increased depth of some types of coverage, more consumer choices.

Technology has reduced the costs of gathering, producing and distributing news, in some cases substantially. Reporters can use computerized databases to pull together stories in hours that would have previously taken weeks. The cost of producing and publishing images, sound, and text has fallen sharply. And most obviously, and most dramatically, the search-engine-driven Internet has made it infinitely easier to find a wide range of information rapidly.

Citizens are more empowered than ever. They choose where to get their content, how to share it, and are reporting it themselves. Billions of hours of volunteer labor have helped bring important information online and make it accessible on a grand scale. With 76 percent of cell phone owners using their phone to take pictures, we may conclude that, as remarkable as it is that most Americans now carry around a minicomputer, it is just as significant that most now carry a camera. Indeed, it has become a staple of modern news coverage to include photos and videos from citizens who captured images with their phones. Perhaps the most important piece of citizen journalism in this new era was the video taken by an Iranian doctor on his cell phone of a woman named Neda Agha-Soltan being murdered on the street in Tehran.

Citizens can customize what news they want and when. There is not a topic that does not have aggregators providing headlines from around the world. We can get it on demand (when we're ready to consume) or in real time; through desktop, tablet, phone, or TV; in text, video, still images, audio or an infinite combination. Even data has become infinitely customizable. For instance, the Texas Tribune, a news startup in Austin, Texas, offers online readers the ability to sort through data about Texas lawmakers, prisoners, and public employees. Readers can set the parameters as they wish, based on their particular interests—say, information about their particular town—and the gizmo tailors the results to them. Built as one feature—a database—from a consumer perspective it actually provides thousands of different "stories."

Citizens can now play a much greater role in holding institutions accountable. Whether it's snapping photos of potholes that the city hasn't fixed and posting it to a website, or scouring documents to help a news website uncover a scandal, a broad range of Americans can now more easily scrutinize government, companies and other powerful organizations.

These attributes are not just enriching born-on-the-Internet websites but the digital operations of traditional media as well. Newspapers and TV stations are now, on their websites or other digital platforms, making use of citizen submissions of reporting, images, and video; statistical databases; photo galleries; crowd-sourcing; interactive maps; user-comment areas; aggregation of information from around the web; Twitter feeds; live video streaming; and many other information tools.

Perhaps no area has been more dramatically transformed than "hyperlocal"—coverage on the neighborhood or block by block level. Even in the fattest-and-happiest days of traditional media, they could not regularly provide news on such a granular level. Professional media have been joined by a wide range of local blogs, email lists, websites and the proliferation of local groups on national websites like Facebook or Yahoo! For the most part, hyperlocally-oriented websites and blogs do not operate as profitable businesses, but they do not need to. This is journalism as voluntarism—a thousand points of news.

The number and variety of websites, blogs, and tweets contributing to the news and information landscape is truly stunning. Yet this abundance can obscure a parallel trend: the shortage of full-time reporting.

For instance, the Pew case study of Baltimore revealed a profusion of media outlets. Between new media (blogs and websites) and traditional media (TV, radio, newspapers), researchers counted 53 different outlets—considerably more than existed 10 years ago. But when Pew's researchers analyzed the content they were providing, particularly regarding the city budget and other public affairs issues, they discovered that 95 percent of the stories—including those in the new media—were based on reporting done by traditional media (mostly the *Baltimore Sun*).[55] And those sources were doing less than they had done in the past. Several other studies have had similar findings.

This is not a criticism of citizen media or web-based news aggregators and commentators. Even when they are working primarily with the reporting of others, they often add tremendous value--distributing the news through alternate channels or offering new interpretations of its meaning. But we are seeing a decline in the media with a particular strength—gathering the information—and seeing it replaced by a media that often exhibits a different set of strengths (for instance, distributing and interpreting it).

This problem became evident several years ago, prompting a flood of former newspaper journalists and concerned citizens to start web operations dedicated to serious reporting, especially about local civic affairs. More than a hundred impressively creative websites—such as MinnPost in Minneapolis, voiceofsandiego.org, the Texas Tribune, the Bay Citizen in San Francisco, the Sacramento Press, and the Chicago News Cooperative—now populate the cyberscape. Some are nonprofits, some for-profits—and many have brought new energy to the local journalism scene. Some are even becoming profitable and self-sufficient.

Over the last seven years, the number of hours of local TV news has risen by 35 percent. Stations offer more newscasts, additional multicast digital channels, mobile apps, and increasingly popular websites.

But so far these new websites are not large enough or self-sustaining enough to fill the gaps left by newspaper layoffs. In a recent survey of 66 local news websites, half reported that their organizations drew in annual income of less than $50,000, and three-quarters reported annual income of less than $100,000. That is not a typographical error; it is *annual* income for the whole website.

The nonprofit online news sector may be vibrant, but it is small in scale. The Knight Foundation hosted a recent gathering of leaders from 12 of the most influential and well-funded websites. Together they employ 88 full-time staffers, which seems quite encouraging until one remembers that more than 15,000 journalists have left the newspaper industry in the last decade (and 13,000 left in the last four years alone.)[56] Another point of reference: while newspapers have been suffering an estimated $1.6 billion drop in editorial spending per year, foundations have contributed an estimated $180 million to fund new online ventures *over a period of five years*. Billions out, millions in.[57]

In addition to the local websites, there are a handful of national Internet companies making major efforts to serve local communities. Examiner.com has sites in 233 cities, deploying 67,000 "examiners" to write on local topics. But these part-timers focus on lifestyle topics, such as entertainment, retail, and sports—not on hard news.[58] AOL's Patch has created local websites in 800 communities, hiring a reporter-editor in each location—meaning that

Patch has likely hired more reporters than any other media organization in the past two years. In the wake of the AOL merger with HuffingtonPost, founder Arianna Huffington maintained that a major reason for her interest in this deal was to do more for local news and information. On the other hand, AOL executives in the past have stressed that to succeed financially, they must focus their efforts on affluent areas. And a single editor wearing many hats, even working with volunteer contributors, will usually not have time to do full-time enterprise reporting on par with the best of traditional urban dailies—though he or she may well match or better the efforts of local community newspapers. In other words, Examiner, Patch, and companies like them add tremendous value to the media ecosystem, but they also leave many crucial gaps unfilled.

Michele McLellan, who has studied the digital news scene comprehensively for the University of Missouri journalism school, writes, "The tired idea that born-on-the-Web news sites will replace traditional media is wrongheaded, and it's past time that academic research and news reports reflect that."[59]

Why has the Internet not so far spawned business models that can sustain large numbers of reporters? To answer that, we review some of the most important ways that the digital revolution has changed the economics of news production.

The great unbundling: During the news media's most profitable days, in many towns, there was only one newspaper, leaving consumers with limited choice. And, though we may not have thought of it this way, purchasing a paper meant having to buy a bundle of goods, even if readers only wanted certain parts. A cross-subsidy system had developed, in which a consumer who bought the paper for the box scores was helping to pay the salary of the city hall reporter. Today, however, a reader can get a mobile app that provides *only* box scores (with second-by-second updates!). The bundle is broken—and so is the cross-subsidy.

Advertisers have benefited from unbundling, too. Remember the saying attributed to department store executive John Wanamaker: "Half the money I spend on advertising is wasted; the trouble is I don't know which half"? On the Internet, the executive *can* know which half is wasted, and spend it elsewhere.

Downward pressure on online advertising rates: It is a myth that local newspapers suffered because they did not grow traffic online. From 2005 to 2009, newspapers' online traffic skyrocketed—from 43.7 million unique monthly users to 70 million, from 1.6 billion monthly page views to 3 billion page views.[60] But in financial terms, that growth was shockingly meaningless. During that period, online advertising revenue—for the entire newspaper industry—grew $716 million, while the print advertising side of the business lost $22.6 billion.[61] This led to the saying in the newspaper world that "print dollars were being replaced by digital dimes." The constant growth of Internet page views—fueled in part by social media—has resulted in online advertising rates that are a fraction of TV and newspaper ad rates.

Advertising is increasingly disconnected from content: While billions of ad dollars have shifted from TV and newspapers to the Internet, many of those dollars do not go to websites that produce their own content, like newspaper and magazine sites. In 2000, one percent of online ad dollars went to the purchase of advertising units appearing in search engine results. In 2009, 47 percent did. On mobile devices, advertisers can increasingly geo-target ads based on where the consumer is located at a particular moment. Through social media and direct-to-consumer discount services like Groupon, advertisers can reach consumers without having to search for an appropriate editorial context for their ads. To reach consumers, advertisers need content less and less.

Mobile has brought huge innovation to news distribution, but not to news media business models: The fastest growing platform for accessing news and information is the mobile device. Fifty six percent of all mobile device users, and 47 percent of the population, now use such devices to get local news via an Internet connection.[62] Increasingly, the mobile device is a news media platform—just like a newspaper or a TV set—as much as it is a two-way communication device. Publishers have expressed some optimism about the iPad and other tablets fundamentally altering the economics of digital news, making it far more likely that consumers will pay to access content. But the jury is still out

Databases created by governments provide information directly to citizens, and make it possible for reporters to conduct investigative research in days that previously would have taken months.

regarding whether they, or other mobile devices, will have that impact. An October 2010 review of Apple's App Store A May 2011 review of Apple's App Store revealed that approximately 72 percent of iPad news apps and 71 percent of iPhone news apps were available for free.[63]

The nature of news as a public good: To some degree, the struggles of traditional media flow from fundamental economic principles related to certain types of news that are essentially "public goods." Economists say that many people simply will not pay for news, since they know they can "free ride" and still get the benefits of the news. If you want an apple, you have to pay for it, and the benefits go only to you. By contrast, education reporting can generate stories that benefit an entire community, and yet people get the benefits of better schools even if they do not subscribe to the paper. The result: lots of apples sold, but few education reporters employed.

Consider: In a three-day December 2008 series about the probation system, the *Raleigh (NC) News & Observer* established that 580 North Carolina probationers had killed people since the start of 2000. The series occupied several staff over six months, costing roughly $200,000 to produce. It prompted the governor to try to fix the program. In the future, there will probably be people walking the streets of Raleigh who were not murdered because of the reforms. But local residents have no way of knowing who among them is alive due to the newspaper series. To have benefited from it, one did not need to have read the series or subscribed to the *News & Observer* (which was available for free on the Internet). It is a terrific deal for citizens: tremendous benefit, without the cost or even the bother of reading. (Chapter 4, Internet.)

> In Los Angeles, stories about local civic issues like transportation, community health, the environment, education and taxes, took up one minute and 16 seconds of the half hour

Of course the catch is that if too many people free ride, media outlets cannot pay the salaries of the reporters who painstakingly gather the information. One of the most famous phrases of the Internet era is "Information wants to be free." There is some truth to that. People want to distribute and receive information for free. But what that leaves out is reality that in some cases the information will not come to the fore without the work of professional reporters. And while information may want to be free, labor wants to be paid.

Nonprofit Media

While most analysis of the new information and news landscape has focused on commercial media, it has become clear that nonprofit media, broadly defined, are trying to play an increasingly significant role. This is a welcome development. But there is much confusion about the nature of the nonprofit media sector, what it does, and what it needs to succeed.

For starters, the nonprofit media sector has become quite diverse. On TV and radio, it includes not only public TV and radio but also state public affairs networks (SPANs), low-power FM (LPFM) stations, PEG channels, and nonprofit programming. In digital media, it includes local news websites (like those previously mentioned), national organizations that fund investigative journalism, programmers who code in "open source" languages, and a full range of blogs, wikis, and citizen journalism vehicles. It includes millions of volunteers who contribute information, expertise, and reporting to websites throughout the Internet.

Some nonprofit media receive government subsidies; most do not. Some are one-person operations; others are sizeable institutions, such as Wikipedia, the Associated Press, *Consumer Reports*, NPR, *National Geographic*, and AARP. In this section, we look at the state of the current nonprofit media sector, which we view as a crucial element in the media landscape.

Nonprofit Websites and News Services

Hundreds of nonprofit websites have sprung up, and have made significant contributions in the realm of hyperlocal news, national investigative journalism, international coverage, and citizen journalism. Within its first year, ProPublica, a national group focused on investigative reporting, won a Pulitzer Prize jointly with *The New York Times* for a magazine piece about the agonizing decisions made by medical personnel at Memorial Hospital in New Orleans as the flood waters rose during Hurricane Katrina. The *St. Petersburg Times*, run by the Poynter Institute, launched PolitiFact.org, while the Annenberg Public Policy Center of the University of Pennsylvania launched FactCheck.org.

The Sunlight Foundation uses new technology to collect and disseminate government data. These organizations have joined several long-standing nonprofits that promote investigative, or enterprise, reporting, including the Center for Public Integrity and the Center for Investigative Reporting, which also runs California Watch. Several of these organizations not only execute important journalistic projects but also maintain databases that enable other entities to create localized versions of a story.

Nonprofit news organizations have launched to improve coverage of a number of niche sectors, such as health (Kaiser Health News), schools (Public School Notebook, the Hechinger Report, Education News Colorado), and foreign coverage (Pulitzer Center on Crisis Reporting and the International Reporting Project). Many have been created specifically to cover local affairs, sometimes launched by laid-off journalists, sometimes by citizens concerned about information gaps in communities. The Texas Tribune has pioneered the use of government databases, NJ Spotlight uncovered a scandal that had been costing the state millions, MinnPost has forged new business models, and scores of others have worked tirelessly to provide what they see as crucial information their communities wouldn't otherwise have. The creativity in this sector is inspiring, though it is not yet clear which entities will be able to survive and grow in the long run. (Chapter 12, Nonprofit News Websites.)

Public TV

In general, studies indicate that public television stations, which are licensed by the FCC, have offered high-quality educational, cultural, and national news and public affairs programming. PBS is currently the most trusted and neutral source for news, according to polls. However, public TV plays a minimal role in providing local programming, including news and accountability journalism. About 94 percent of local public TV stations offer less than 30 minutes of local news per day—a much lower percentage than the commercial market. In a 2004 survey, 79 percent of the public television licensees indicated, "the amount of local programming they currently produce is not sufficient to meet local community needs."

Public Radio

Public radio in 2010 deployed more than 1,400 reporters, editors, and producers in 21 domestic and 17 foreign bureaus—more than any of the broadcast TV networks.[64] Public radio also has proven far more interested in supporting local journalism than the commercial radio sector. From 2004 to 2009, the number of public radio stations reporting that they carried local news or talk programming rose from 595 to 681, with hours aired each week increasing from 5,182 to 5,693.[65] There are 185 self-described "all-news" public radio stations.[66] But while public radio does more than public TV and more than commercial radio, theirs are mostly small-scale operations.[67]

Other local nonprofit institutions that may play a role in filling local journalism gaps include:

State public affairs networks (SPANs): The best not only provide coverage of legislatures but also of candidate debates and other public affairs issues that are not being covered elsewhere.

Public, educational, and government (PEG) channels: The mission of PEG channels is evolving, with some working to promote digital literacy and others to help with local news and information.

Educational programming on satellite systems: Religious, ethnic, and some public affairs channels take advantage of the set-aside requirement to expand their reach, but satellite companies also have been rejecting many such channels due to a lack of satellite capacity.

Low-power FM (LPFM) stations: There are already 800 in existence, and a new law has increased the likelihood that hundreds more hyperlocal radio stations will be established.

Journalism schools: There is a growing movement among J-schools to not only teach journalism, but also to have students practice it by contributing to local websites and publications.

The nonprofit media sector is miniscule compared with the commercial sector, but its members are focusing on exactly the areas that have been abandoned by commercial media. In this sense, we can see an important new paradigm developing in which nonprofit media plays a greater role in these specific areas—and in which nonprofit and for-profit media work symbiotically in local communities.

However, there are also obstacles to nonprofits expanding. A handful of foundations have been underwriting tremendous innovation, but most others have been reluctant to support local reporting. Tax restrictions may make it difficult for nonprofit websites to create sustainable business models and for newspapers to convert to nonprofit status. There is insufficient collaboration among nonprofit media entities, many of which view other such entities as competitors for scarce donor dollars. For those offering online video and audio, the cost of streaming the material is growing rapidly. And government funding for public broadcasting is under threat.

In sum, the nonprofit sector has the ingenuity and spirit to fill many of the gaps left by the contraction of traditional commercial media but it faces many challenges.

Non-Media Sources of Civically Important Information

Americans have always received critical information from sources outside the media. The PTA newsletter, a flier on the bulletin board at work, gossip over the hedge, the Sunday sermon, the National Weather Service, campaign advertisements, public health announcements—these are just a few of the myriad ways we learn about issues that affect our lives. The digital revolution has opened up new channels through which Americans can access civically important information outside the flow of the news media. In this section, we look at four providers of such information: government, libraries, emergency alert systems, and schools.

Greater government transparency is already serving to empower citizens and journalists. Databases created by local and national government provide information directly to citizens—and they make it possible for reporters to conduct investigative research in days that previously would have taken months. In this way, transparency reduces the cost of journalism. Indeed, having government make more information available online is a crucial ingredient to improving the general health of local media systems and the vitality of reporting. However, the transparency movement has a long way to go, and even at its best does not obviate the need for journalists to prod, question, and verify. (Chapter 16, Government Transparency.)

Surprisingly, far from being made obsolete by the Internet, public libraries are becoming more important. Forty-four percent of people living in households below the federal poverty line use the library to access the Internet. Yet many librarians report they cannot keep up with the demand of these patrons. (Chapter 18, Libraries.)

While the media plays a crucial role during emergencies, government entities must also establish and operate basic emergency communications systems. Efforts are currently underway to upgrade from outdated broadcast-based systems to new ones that take advantage of digital technology and social media. (Chapter 17, Emergency Information.)

Most of this report deals with the production and supply of information, but the "demand side"—what consumers and citizens want and ask for—is tremendously important, as well. Many Americans do not know how to find what they need online and are not sophisticated consumers of news. A movement has developed to get America's schools to teach digital literacy (how to use new technology), media literacy (how to assess online media in general), and news literacy (how to consume news in a sophisticated manner). (Chapter 19, Schools.)

Key Cross-Cutting Trends

The lines between these sectors are becoming increasingly blurred. In this world of converging media, TV is on the phone, the Internet is on the TV, and the newspaper is on the tablet. This section looks at the media landscape through different lenses. Rather than looking at individual market sectors—such as "newspapers" or "mobile"—it examines trends that cut across many platforms.

Consumer Trends

As the media systems have offered more choices, consumer behavior has changed:

More choice, more news consumption: The contraction of some media has stimulated an expansion in the number of media outlets available to consumers. As a result, Americans are spending more time consuming media.

There has been an explosion of local news entrepreneurship. Sometimes started by laid off newspaper reporters, sometimes by concerned citizens, sometimes created as nonprofits, sometimes as for-profit ventures, hundreds of new local news websites have been born in the last few years.

More are going "newsless": However, the percentage of Americans going without any news the day before they were surveyed rose from 14 percent in 1998 to 17 percent by 2009, according to Pew. The percentage is highest—31 percent—among 18 to 24 year olds.[68] One possible explanation is that while the opportunities to consume news have grown, so too have the opportunities to consume entertainment, sports, and all manner of other content, so those who had been only marginally interested in news have abandoned it for other alternatives.

Spending more on media: Though we think of the 21st century as the moment the information economy went from "paid" to "free," in many ways the opposite is true. We pay more money to access media than ever before—largely due to the fees we must pay for cable and Internet service in order to get to our "free" content. From 2003 to 2008, the average annual spending per person on media and information rose from $740 to $882.[69] (Chapter 20, News Consumption.)

Types of News

After looking at these broad trends, we then turn to a central question of this report: when you take into account both the advances and setbacks in the media industry, which *functions* traditionally performed by "news media" are being carried out adequately and which are not being fulfilled?

Our assessment, categorized by region of coverage, is as follows:

Hyperlocal (neighborhood-based) information is better than ever: Technology has allowed citizens to help create and share news on a very local level—by small town, neighborhood, and even block.

Local (municipal and state) information is struggling mightily—with a measurable decline in certain types of accountability reporting: As noted earlier, newspaper staffs have shrunk while other media have not yet been able to employ enough reporters to make up for the loss. But there is an interesting twist: while traditional media have not been able to support robust reporting staffs, they have made headway in expanding their online audiences. In an FCC analysis of three cities (Toledo, Seattle, and Richmond), the local newspaper or TV station emerged as the dominant provider of online local content.

National news is vibrant and dynamic: There are certainly many areas of concern; for instance, we describe the distressing gaps in coverage of regulatory agencies and the changes in the reporting capacity of newsmagazines. But national newspapers have increased their reach, and websites operating on a national level—ranging from HuffingtonPost to Politico to the Daily Caller—are showing the potential to develop business models that will sustain a variety of types of national news, information, and journalism. The national news market is far from perfect, but it is dynamic. (Chapter 21, Types of News)

International is a mixed picture: The contraction of newspapers, newsmagazines, and network news severely undercut traditional ways of getting foreign news. But other media organizations—including Bloomberg, the *Wall Street Journal*, and NPR—have expanded their overseas presence, and a few nonprofit organizations are funding international reporting. Just as important, the Internet, cable, and satellite now offer Americans access to an increasing number of foreign news sources, such as the BBC and Al Jazeera. (Chapter 21, Types of News.)

Diversity

For ethnic minorities, it is a real best-of-times-worst-of-times story. Minority ownership of broadcast TV stations, already too low, has now declined further, as has the number of minorities employed as journalists. On the other hand, digital media provide such low barriers to entry that minorities who have been shut out of mainstream media now have infinitely greater potential to create content and reach audiences. Without gatekeepers, minority viewpoints are freer to find their audiences. Also, the high usage of mobile phones among minority populations positions wireless broadband to surpass efforts by other media to reach historically underserved communities with news and information. (Chapter 23, Diversity.)

People With Disabilities

People with disabilities have benefited from new tech developments as well, but much more needs to be done in that area. Digital media makes it infinitely easier to present content in multiple formats; any given text story can be accompanied by audio, video, and captions, making it accessible to people with visual and hearing impairment. However, not all content creators exercise those options, and new technologies continue to be designed without taking the needs of people with disabilities into consideration. (Chapter 24, People with Disabilities.)

Will Commercial Media Markets Evolve to Fill Gaps?

Although we acknowledge that this gap we have been referring to cannot be measured with true precision, we offer a rough estimate: It would take the media universe as a whole—commercial and nonprofit sectors—somewhere between $265 million and $1.6 billion annually to bridge the gaps we now see in the provision of civically important information.

Signs that commercial markets are evolving in ways that could lead to healthier local information sectors include:

Local advertising is growing; targeting is improving: Predictions are that local advertising will double to $42.5 billion between now and 2015, which can only help local media models that rely on advertising. Ad targeting is getting more sophisticated which might help raise advertising rates. As broadband penetration increases, more businesses will go online, increasing local ad spending.

Experimentation with pay models is growing: Scores of traditional media companies—from the The Wall Street Journal to the Augusta Chronicle—are experimenting with charging for digital content. Google and Apple have unveiled new systems allowing publishers to sell subscriptions and charge for content in other ways. Firms, such as Journalism Online, have sprouted to help newspapers and other content creators figure out the right strategy to meet their particular goals. In addition, several small news services now cover state government, using a different kind of paid model: expensive subscription price with smaller circulation. As more people go online, the number of potential paying customers could continue to rise as well.

New forms of bundling may arise: Although the Internet has broken up bundles, there are new ones forming. Netflix, Hulu, and Pandora offer bundled content—access to a variety of different types of content for a single subscription price. The Huffington Post is a general interest website in which popular entertainment content in some ways subsidizes less popular content. News Corp. has created a daily news publication available only on the iPad by paid subscription without the costs of printing and delivery trucks. In fact, many content creators are hoping that the pleasure of consuming a print magazine or newspaper as a unit can be recreated on tablets, and thereby help re-establish the bundle and cross-subsidy model.

Says Esther Dyson, "News start-ups are rarely profitable and, by and large, no thinking person who wanted a return on investment would invest in a news start-up, not that they don't sometimes work."

Technology continues to drive down the cost of many types of information gathering and dissemination: Technology developments have made capturing video, distributing it, researching, publishing text, transmitting photos, editing audio, and many other processes for gathering and disseminating information easier, cheaper, and more accessible to a broader range of people. The trend is continuing along those lines.

It is early: It is only in the last three years that a wave of citizens began experimenting with new local news models. In many cases, the first wave of innovation was led by journalists, some of whom had limited business skills. Learning by trial and error takes time.

At the same time, we found compelling evidence that while evolving commercial markets will fill many needs, some fundamental characteristics of the digital news economy bode ill for the prospects of local accountability reporting quickly and sufficiently being supported by new commercial business models. The evidence for *that* view:

Media companies will struggle to create new bundling models, because metrics are increasingly precise and corporate prioritization decisions will inevitably steer away from low-ROI products: In the olden days, newspaper managers had a general sense that they were probably losing money on their overseas coverage, but they had no way to gauge this with any precision. Now, managers know in agonizing detail how many page views a foreign article generates. Each piece of content can now be subject to return-on-investment (ROI) analysis. To be sure, companies can decide to sustain money-losing propositions in the service of some greater corporate goal—improving prestige or brand, for instance—

On the one hand, the study showed Baltimore had a booming collection of news and information outlets. But 95 percent of the stories—including those in the new media—were based on the reporting done by traditional media (mostly the Baltimore Sun). And those organizations were doing fewer stories.

but each time the CEO or the finance department assesses the performance of the company's products, the ones that lose money will have bull's-eye on their backs.

Local media companies will face their own obstacles in charging for content and creating bundles that could cross-subsidize expensive journalism: While there has been some limited success for national media companies charging—the *Wall Street Journal, Consumer Reports*—the track record for local media is discouraging. *Editor & Publisher* declared:

> "2010 was supposed to be the Year of the Paywall for newspapers. But consumers overwhelmingly repudiated the efforts of the few publishers who dared to demand payment for access to the news, leaving newspaper content about as widely and freely available on the Web at year's end as it has been for the past one-and-a-half decades."[70]

Those attempting to make it on a free, ad-supported model will face all of the aforementioned forces suppressing Internet advertising rates—plus a new one: on the Internet, one does not have to be a local content creator to be a venue for local advertising. National Internet companies can attract local advertisers with their ability to geographically target messaging to local consumers, regardless of whether the content (or context) is locally oriented.

Most trends point to an even more challenging advertising picture in the future: Relatively few local web-native businesses that create original content have succeeded financially, in part because advertisers have less and less need to place their ads in an editorial context. This became apparent when advertising dollars began to flood into search. And the trend is continuing, as the most popular new ad vehicles—social media and coupons—can thrive without being associated with content. Currently only 20 percent of digital marketing spending goes to legacy media companies (TV, magazines, radio, billboards, etc.), and that is projected to decline to 13 percent by 2020.

More shoes still to drop: For people without easy access to the Internet, it still may be easier today to read classifieds or clip coupons in the local newspaper than to shop or sell on Craigslist. Eventually, broadband will reach these audiences—and the old media business models in their towns will suffer, too. Similarly, as Internet radio arrives in cars, traditional broadcast may suffer; as IPTV (Internet TV) becomes more common form of TV watching, local TV stations may suffer. In each case, more consumers may be reached, but traditional media's higher ad rates will likely be undercut by the lower ad rates on the Internet. One survey found that 58 percent of print newspaper subscribers who also use their iPad a lot "said they were very likely to cancel their print subscriptions within the next six months."

The shifting power of "distributors" and "content creators": In the past, content distributors and creators were one and the same (e.g., the newspaper company wrote the articles and hired the paperboys). They could use the profits generated by distribution to subsidize the creation of content. In the new media universe, there is currently a greater divide between distributors and content creators. Most Internet service providers, for instance, charge for access to content without sharing the proceeds with the creators of that content. The separation of these functions may have benefits but it also makes cross-subsidization between distribution and content-creation arms less likely.

News as a public good: The free-rider problem has not gone away. If anything, technology innovations often make it easier for consumers to get information without paying for it or even seeing advertisements.

A shift in thinking?: Furious debates still erupt between "new media" and "old media" advocates. But in the last two years, we have noticed a subtle shift. Traditional media leaders no longer mock the pajama-clad practitioners of the new craft quite as much as they used to. Digital media advocates have become convinced that while the digital revolution has improved many, if not most, types of information gathering, commercial Internet businesses may not solve all problems.

> Clay Shirky, a highly respected advocate for digital media, believes most of the contraction of old media will be replaced, and then some, by new media—yet he also believes there is an important exception: "One function that's hard to replace is the kind of reporting that comes from someone going down to city hall again today, just in case. There are some in my tribe who think the web will solve that problem on its own, but that's ridiculous."[71]

> Hal Varian, Google's chief economist, concluded that the "online world reflects offline: news, narrowly defined, is hard to monetize."[72]

> Esther Dyson, chairman of EDventure Holdings and an Internet pioneer, explains, "News start-ups are rarely profitable and, by and large, no thinking person who wanted a return on investment would invest in a news start-up."[73] She believes that when it comes to accountability journalism, the nonprofit sector will need to play a bigger role.[74]

> And then there is John Hood, president of the John Locke Foundation, a market-oriented think tank in North Carolina. The Foundation's *Carolina Journal* finances nonpartisan investigative journalism, in part because the number of reporters covering the statehouse had plummeted over the years. "In North Carolina, several TV stations [in towns outside the Capitol] had reporters. None has a bureau now. We were responding to changes in the market," Hood says. He is skeptical that commercial markets will fill all the gaps in local accountability reporting. "When you get to the state and local level, the collapse of the traditional business models imperils the delivery of sufficient public interest journalism—and we do believe that donor driven journalism can be a very important model."

Given the speed and magnitude of change, anyone in the media or information technology space has to be pretty humble about making predictions. However, we conclude that at a minimum it is not a certainty that commercial markets alone will fill the reporting gaps—and that even if they eventually do, that transition period could be long and, for communities, quite painful. (Chapter 25, How Big is the Gap and Who Will Fill It?)

The New Relationship Between the For-Profit and Nonprofit Sectors

For-profit commercial entities are increasingly partnering with nonprofits to supplement their news operations. Examples include: the web venture Texas Tribune providing reporting for *The New York Times*; a variety of journalism schools providing content to local newspapers; San Diego's NBC station collaborating with voiceofsandiego.org. In each case, the commercial media entity benefits from a level of labor-intensive accountability reporting that the commercial model cannot sustain, and the nonprofit benefits from the massive distribution networks the commercial entity has built up over time. Even better, in some cases, the commercial media outlets pay cold, hard cash, opening up a new revenue stream—fee-for-service journalism—for the nonprofits. In other words, we are beginning to see a new model arise on the local level in which commercial media outsources certain types of labor-intensive but civically important journalism to the nonprofit sector, and the commercial sector turbocharges the nonprofits' distribution efforts.

> **Advertising is increasingly disconnected from content. In 2000, one percent of online ad dollars went to the purchase of advertising units appearing in search engine results. In 2009, 47 percent did.**

The Relationship Between Old and New Media

Although old and new media advocates have spent some time in the past few years attacking one another, it is clear now that the new and old forms complement each other. Parents and retirees can attend the school board meeting and write about what happened, and a well-sourced journalist can report what went on behind the scenes; then parents can spread the word through social media, and they can continue to pursue the issue after the reporter has moved on to other stories. Professional reporters can go where volunteers do not have the time or access to go—for instance, prisons, war zones, the restricted corridors of city hall—and citizen reporters can, through their numbers, be in more places than reporters possibly can.

If a community does not have a critical mass of full-time professional journalists, it will not harness the benefits of this new system. Indeed, it will be worse off than it has been in years. Full-time journalists are not just useful parts of this new machine—they are essential components. The digital media innovations—citizen journalism, crowd-sourcing, public databases, blogs, social media—are not ancillary. They are at the heart of the new system. Without both, a community will not get the information it needs. With both, it can thrive as never before.

PART TWO: THE POLICY AND REGULATORY LANDSCAPE

In the second part of the report, we explore the major public policies that have shaped the news media. We pay special attention to those policies administered by the FCC, but in order to gain a holistic understanding, we also look at information-related laws and regulations more broadly.

FCC Rules About TV and Radio

This section reviews and offers assessments on FCC policies touching on commercial TV and radio—broadcast, cable, and satellite:

The Fairness Doctrine: We believe that re-instituting the Fairness Doctrine would chill debate and harm local news. (Chapter 26, Broadcasting Rules.)

Sponsorship Identification Rules: These rules require broadcasters to publicly disclose if elements that appear to be news are actually content dictated or are sculpted by advertisers. The rules require stations to disclose such relationships on air. But the penalties have not been updated in years, the FCC does not make it sufficiently easy for whistleblowers to report infractions, and, most important, stations are not required to post the information online.

The public interest obligations of broadcasters: We focus in detail on the history of local stations' obligations to broadcast news and public affairs. Because when the taxpayers gave some of their limited spectrum to broadcasters, they were promised something in return: that those broadcasters would serve the community. Originally, the FCC established detailed rules outlining what broadcasters were required to air. Over time, court rulings, constitutional concerns, and FCC decisions have left a system that is unclear and ineffective. The current system of public interest obligations for broadcasters is broken: TV stations are required to maintain programming records and other such paperwork, which FCC staff and members of the public rarely read. (Some provide detailed descriptions of substantive news programming; others list the sponsorship of an *America's Next Top Model* tryout as fulfilling the obligation to provide issue-responsive programming.) Licenses are routinely renewed, regardless of whether a station is investing huge sums in local reporting or doing no local programming at all. Over the FCC's 75-year existence, it has renewed more than 100,000 licenses. It has denied only four renewal applications due to the licensee's failure to meet its public interest programming obligation. No license renewals have been denied on those grounds in past 30 years. The current system operates neither as a free market nor as an effectively regulated one; and it does not achieve the public interest goals set out by Congress or the FCC.

Enhanced disclosure: In 2007, the Commission approved an "enhanced disclosure" policy that attempted to fix the licensing system by requiring stations to publish significant amounts of information about their programming. Our assessment: the "enhanced disclosure" rule was overly bureaucratic and cumbersome.

Ownership rules: The FCC's quadrennial ownership review will come out later this year, and it will be informed by new, more sophisticated academic studies commissioned specifically for the purposes of the review. Hence, we restrict ourselves to a few broad observations:

> The nature of the "diversity" calculus may have changed. In an earlier day, it was reasonable to assume that a diversity of "voices" indicated general media health. Now, a media market can simultaneously have a diversity of voices and opinions and yet a scarcity of journalism.

> More is not necessarily better. Another assumption of past regulatory efforts was that more choices lead to greater benefits for consumers. But changes in the media market can sometimes call this assumption into question. For instance, it might be better to have nine TV stations in a market than 10, if consolidation leads the remaining stations to be economically healthier and therefore more able to invest in local journalism.

Minority and small business ownership: The Commission currently has few operating programs designed to encourage ownership of small businesses, including minority-owned and women-owned businesses. Moreover, the FCC is not collecting enough information to understand the nature of the changes in minority ownership and employment in media.

Leased access: Cable operators were supposed to provide up to 15 percent of their capacity to independent programmers. Currently they provide less than one percent. The leased access system appears to be dysfunctional.

Satellite radio: FCC regulations prohibit satellite radio operators from creating and airing locally originated programming. It is not clear whether this rule has diminished the likelihood of local news and public affairs programming on radio.

Nonprofit Media

Although, for the most part, the public broadcasting system has been a major success, we see rules and strategies that might be updated to fit the new times. (Chapter 31, Nonprofit Media.)

Funding rules limit digital innovation: CPB is required by law to provide a fixed percentage of its funds to TV stations and a certain amount to radio. Little is left over for digital innovation, or to help fund other nonprofit media.

Policies do not encourage local programming: The economics of public TV make it hard for stations to do much local programming, and neither CPB nor the FCC require stations to do local programming.

Restrictions on business models: Rules set up by the FCC, Congress, and the Corporation for Public Broadcasting (CPB) restrict the ability of public TV stations to raise revenue. There are regulations that limit advertising, the extent to which stations can merchandize public TV characters, and whether they can seek payment from cable and satellite operators that air their shows. Public broadcasters themselves have tended to agree with these restrictions, believing that revenue generation could taint their noncommercial identity and undermine public support. (Chapter 32, Advertising Policy.)

Streaming costs loom as a potential problem: Current policies do not address the threat that rising audio and video streaming costs pose to public broadcasters. (Chapter 6, Public Broadcasting.)

Policies that affect other types of nonprofit media include:

State public affairs networks get insufficient help: In 23 states cable operators provide carriage for SPANs, though they provide financial support in four states. Satellite providers offer state SPAN in only one state: Alaska.

Confusion about current tax law may hinder nonprofit media development: Some nonprofit media feel they get mixed signals from the IRS. Some nonprofit websites fear that publishing commentary about public affairs could cost them their nonprofit status. The confusion may hinder the ability of nonprofit news entities to become sustainable. There are similar concerns about accepting advertising.

Satellite TV: Congress required the FCC to set aside between 4 and 7 percent of its carrying capacity for educational programming. Reluctant to put undue pressure on the fledgling satellite industry, the FCC opted for 4 percent. Today, satellite companies, which are now profitable, provide carriage for dozens of religious and educational channels. But they also turn away many nonprofit programmers on the grounds that they have hit the 4 percent set-aside target. In other cases, nonprofit programmers end up walking away because the cost of carriage is prohibitively high—because, unlike PEG channels, which get paid by local governments, educational programmers on satellite pay fees to the operators).

A telling statistic: during the over 75-year existence of the FCC, there have been easily more than 100,000 license renewals—and only four cases in which a renewal application was denied because the licensee failed to meet its public interest programming obligation.

PEG Channels: State and local changes have reduced the funding and, in some cases, the prominence on the cable dial, of public, educational, and government channels (PEG) at a time when the need for local programming is especially urgent.

Religious broadcasters: Religious broadcasters feel restricted by government underwriting rules, including an FCC rule that limits a station's ability to raise money for charities on the air.

Other Policy Areas

Government entities other than the FCC set policies and engage in practices that affect the health and development of media. Significant examples include:

The federal government spends significant amounts of money on advertising but does not attempt to guide those funds toward local media: The federal government in 2005 spent roughly $1 billion on advertising, but much of it appears to go to national rather than local media entities. (Chapter 32, Advertising Policy.)

U.S. Postal Service policies may inadvertently and indirectly hurt local newspapers: Because postal rates are so favorable to bulk advertisers ("junk mailers"), it is likely that they spend less money on newspaper insert ads. (Chapter 33, Print.)

Decisions in copyright lawsuits stand to have a big impact on the media industry: Court battles on copyright and intellectual property could affect the economics of news media. (Chapter 34, Copyright.)

Policy in an Era of Local Reporting Shortages

Due to constitutional constraints and long-standing policy decisions, most media-related regulations are not addressing the gaps in local programming:

> Broadcast licenses are renewed whether or not a station offers coverage of the community.

> Cable operators are required to carry the signals of TV broadcasters—whether or not they provide local programming.

> Government spends billions of dollars on advertising (for military recruitment, public health messages, and other campaigns), but there is no requirement that any of those funds be spent on local media.

> The Corporation for Public Broadcasting spends a few hundred million dollars annually, but there is no requirement that a minimum amount be spent on local programming.

> Satellite TV companies are required to carry educational programming but not local programming.

> Satellite radio companies are prohibited from airing locally originated programming.

> Leased access rules have not succeeded in encouraging local programming.

Neither public policy nor private philanthropic emphases are sufficiently targeted at the areas of greatest need: local programming in general, and accountability journalism in particular.

Policy in a Digital Era

Many of the existing FCC policies were created to address issues inherent to a particular medium. But because content no longer lives within just one platform there are many policy inconsistencies. A nonprofit TV show gets funding from the Corporation for Public Broadcasting if it is using over-the-air broadcast spectrum but not if it is using satellite spectrum—and not if it is being streamed online. Broadcasters have more public interest obligations than cable or mobile service providers, even though they compete with each other.

Ignoring the ailments of local media will mean serious harm is done to our communities—but paying attention to them will enable citizens to develop, literally, the best media system the nation has ever had.

The seemingly infinite capacity of the Internet does not negate the need for policy or regulations, but it does necessitate a rethinking of the best approaches.

There is one area in which technology actually makes it easier for policymakers to offer sensible prescriptions: transparency. The FCC and other government agencies have long relied on disclosure rules to ensure the public's access to information it has a right to—but often that information ends up sitting in media company files where it is difficult for the public to utilize. The Internet makes it easy to post such information online, where it can be readily found, digested, and analyzed.

PART THREE: RECOMMENDATIONS

The following findings from Parts One and Two should inform decisions made by policymakers and philanthropists:

> Government is not the main player in this drama, and the First Amendment circumscribes government action to improve local news.

> Nonetheless, greater transparency by government and media companies can help reduce the cost of reporting, empower consumers, and foster innovation.

> When measuring the information health of a community, one must look not only at the number of media outlets, access, diversity, and competition, but also at resources invested, including the number of reporters.

> Although there is tremendous innovation in the commercial sector, and it is difficult to predict what will come next, it is not inevitable that commercial media markets will solve all the problems we face, especially the provision of relatively unprofitable, labor-intensive accountability reporting.

> The nonprofit media sector is increasingly diverse, and now includes nonprofit websites, state-level C-SPANS, public access channels, low-power FM stations, journalism schools, and public TV and radio stations. These entities, many of which are not government funded, need to play a bigger role and be better understood.

> Collaborations among media—including between for-profit and nonprofit media—will and should be an important ingredient in the new system.

With those points in mind, we believe government policy changes should focus on three primary goals: making better use of the public's resources, increasing transparency, and, in the words of the National Religious Broadcasters, "fertiliz[ing] the conditions under which the media does its work."[75]

In Part Three, we lay out a detailed set of recommendations. What follows is a summary of some of the key items.

Emphasize Online Disclosure as a Pillar of FCC Media Policy

Actions the FCC should consider taking:

> Eliminate unnecessary paperwork and move toward an online system for public disclosures. Specifically, the FCC should eliminate the long-standing requirement that local TV stations keep, in a paper file on the premises, a list of issues-responsive programming for the year. This should be replaced with a streamlined, web-based form through which broadcasters can provide programming information based on a composite or sample week. Information could include: the amount of community-related programming, news-sharing and partnership arrangements, how multicast channels are being used, sponsorship identification disclosures (see below) and the level of website accessibility for people with disabilities. Over time, move to an online system for most disclosures, while ensuring that the transition is sensitive to the needs of small broadcasters, focusing, for instance on TV rather than radio.

> Replace the burdensome "enhanced disclosure" rule, terminate the localism proceeding and repeal the remnants of the Fairness Doctrine still on the books.

> Require that when broadcasters allow advertisers to dictate content, they disclose the "pay-for-play" arrangements online as well as on the air.

> Consider allowing noncommercial broadcasters that do not receive Corporation for Public Broadcasting funding, including religious broadcasters, to devote up to one percent of their on-air time to fundraising for charities.

> Require satellite operators to post their disclosure forms online.

> Conduct a comprehensive study on the effectiveness of the leased access program to determine whether it is meeting the goals set out for it by Congress. Policymakers should consider whether to give regulatory relief from leased access requirements to cable operators that support local cable news networks or SPANs.

Make It Easier for Citizens to Monitor Their Government by Putting More Proceedings, Documents, and Data Online

To improve accountability and reduce the cost of reporting:

> Every state should have a state public affairs network similar to C-SPAN. On a voluntary basis, multichannel video programming distributors (MVPDs) should do more to ensure that SPANs can thrive. Congress should consider regulatory relief through the leased access program for those that do.

> Governments at all levels should collect and publish data in forms that make it easy for citizens, entrepreneurs, software developers, and reporters to access and analyze information.

> Government should aspire to make proceedings and hearings available online, and to keep them in a publicly accessible archive.

Consider Directing Existing Government Advertising Spending Toward Local Media

> The federal government should consider targeting some of the money it already spends on advertising to local news media, both commercial and nonprofit, traditional and online. (That amount was roughly $1 billion in 2005). Such efforts must include measures to guard against political bias and manipulation and ensure that government marketing goals are not compromised.

Make It Easier for Nonprofit Media to Develop Sustainable Models

> Tax experts and nonprofit leaders should recommend to the IRS and policymakers clarifications or changes in tax rules that would make it easier for nonprofit news operations to develop sustainable business models.

> Local foundations, philanthropists, and ordinary Americans should consider increasing donations to organization that provide reporting, especially at the local level.

> The Corporation for Public Broadcasting should have more flexibility to fund *local* programming and innovation, including efforts by media entities that are not traditional broadcasters.

> Journalism schools should continue to increase their role in providing local journalism through the "medical residency" model (practicing local journalism as they teach it).

> Community media centers that run public, educational, and governmental access (PEG) channels can be important players in the local media ecosystem. They should consider shifting their mission toward teaching digital literacy; partnering with other institutions that provide nonprofit programming; and working to increase the transparency of government and other civic institutions.

> The FCC should make sure that the Local Community Radio Act is implemented in a way that allows low-power FM stations (LPFMs) to gain traction throughout the country.

Ensure that Broadband Access and Use is Widespread Enough to Help Fuel Digital Media Innovation

> Universal broadband and an open Internet are essential prerequisites to media innovation and will make it more likely that digital media will be able to develop sustainable business models.

> Should Congress give the Commission authority to conduct incentive auctions, local public TV stations should be able to participate on the same terms as commercial stations.

> If policymakers use any auction proceeds to invest in innovation, they should consider supporting the development of information technology that could increase government transparency, fuel local media innovation, stimulate entrepreneurship.

Ensure that Modern Media Policy Works for People in Historically Underserved Communities

Actions the FCC should consider taking:

> Require stations to disclose whether and in what ways their websites are accessible to people with disabilities.

> In areas where TV channels 5 and 6 are not currently utilized for TV broadcasting, there exists potential to expand TV and radio opportunities to new small businesses, including those owned by minorities and women.

> Proactively disseminate information about local LPFM broadcast opportunities to minority communities.

> Continue to collect industry data on minority ownership. Resolve outstanding confidentiality issues related to the collection of employment data, and then resume the collection of such data.

> Continue to educate would-be entrepreneurs about financing opportunities in both traditional and new media.

Congress should consider:

> Restoring the tax certificate program to encourage media ownership by small businesses and new entrants, including minorities and women.

Conclusion

Although each citizen will have a different view on which information is important—and who is failing at providing it—Americans need to at least come together around one idea: that democracy requires, and citizens deserve, a healthy flow of useful information and a news and information system that holds powerful institutions accountable.

There are many legitimate disagreements in the realm of media policy, but it is time to move past some of the false dichotomies. Do we need professional or citizen reporters? Obviously, we need both. Do we need old media or new media? Again, both. Objective or advocacy journalism? Commercial or nonprofit? Free or paid? Both, both, and both.

Our biggest fear is a slow, steady lowering of standards and expectations regarding what kinds of information Americans are entitled to. It is easy to see how this could happen. A shortage of reporting manifests itself in invisible ways: stories not written, scandals not exposed, government waste not discovered, health dangers not identified in time, local elections involving candidates about whom we know little. And, at first glance, our media landscape does not seem barren at all. News is all around us—more than ever before. This illusion of bounty has the danger of making us passive. Why would we worry about shortages in the midst of such abundance?

To switch metaphors, one can imagine an old-fashioned bucket brigade, each citizen passing water to the next to put out a raging fire. In many cases, we now have more citizens, more buckets, and less water. It is gratifying that we have more citizen involvement, and more vessels for passing along the water. But we cannot forget: if we have less water, the fires will burn.

And yet, consider this: If we can figure out a way to get more water into the bucket line, the fires will not only be put out—they will be put out faster than ever before. That is why we are conditionally hopeful. With concerted action, a bad situation can be transformed into not merely a tolerable one but a great step forward.

the media landscape

commercial media

NEWSPAPERS

RADIO

TELEVISION

CABLE

SATELLITE

INTERNET

MOBILE

1 Newspapers

NEWSPAPERS ACROSS THE COUNTRY have experienced severe cutbacks during the past decade, which has undermined their ability to perform their role as the nation's watchdog. Ad revenue dropped nearly 48 percent between 2005 and 2010,[1] and with it the industry's annual spending on reporting and editing capacity dropped by $1.6 billion, from 2006 to 2009, a reduction of more than 25 percent, according to the Pew Research Center's Project for Excellence in Journalism and Rick Edmonds of the Poynter Institute.[2] The number of full-time journalists at daily newspapers fell from a peak of about 56,900 in 1989 to 41,600 in 2010, a level not seen since before the Watergate era.[3]

Early History: Cheap Paper, the Telegraph, and the Rise of the Independent Press

The Founding Fathers believed newspapers to be so important to the development of the young country that they facilitated the creation of a robust distribution network. They provided newspapers with subsidized postal rates that were far below the actual costs of fielding, feeding, and caring for that day's distribution technology: (horses).

These policies changed the economics of newspapers, reducing publication costs and enabling publishers to expand beyond the confines of their hometowns. (Typical were the *Mansfield Gazette* and *Ashtabula Sentinel* in Ohio: a study found that in the 1820s a majority of their subscribers lived outside the central circulation area.)[4] Laws also enabled newspapers to swap copies with one another free of charge, which led to the frequent appropriation of content from other newspapers. By the 1840s the average newspaper received 4,300 exchange copies each year.[5]

In the early days of the republic, newspapers were usually aligned with a political faction. This did not just mean that newspapers had ideological proclivities; they often received money from, and coordinated with, political sponsors, usually through printing contracts or the placing of "official notices" in the papers as advertisements. In 1830 in New York State, for example, 22 editors served as postmasters.[6] Under President Andrew Jackson, 59 journalists received government appointments.[7] Without support from political parties, many of the partisan newspapers would not have survived. The one redeeming feature of this otherwise highly questionable system of partisan press was that both parties engaged in it, which ensured a diversity of voices.[8]

By the 1830s, technology began to change newspaper economics, which in turn profoundly affected newspaper content. As the cost of ink and paper declined,[9] some publishers dropped the price of an issue from around six cents to one penny, allowing them to reach a wider market. With a larger readership, they could reap greater advertising revenue—and influence.[10] But to hold that larger audience, they needed to be independent and avoid political affiliation. Papers in this era, according to Paul Starr, became more focused on local news and "independent newsgathering."[11] In the *New York Herald*'s first edition in 1835, founder James Bennett wrote, "We shall support no party—be the organ of no faction or coterie, and care nothing for any election or any candidate from president down to constable."[12] (The partisan press called the independent papers' coverage of current events, such as crimes and trials, sensational.)

By 1844, another new technology—the telegraph—changed the business and the editorial content once again. Previously, because information tended to travel by horse or boat, up to 28 percent of newspaper items reported on events a month or more after they occurred. The telegraph allowed newspapers to be more up to date.[13]

The role of advertising increased markedly from the 1870s through 1900. Railroads made it possible for companies to create national brands. Advertisers saved time and money dealing with a few large papers instead of a bevy of small ones.[14]

Newspaper publishing increasingly became a big business rather than an independent trade. While a new press in the 1840s could cost from $4,000 to $5,000, the more sophisticated presses in the 1880s cost $80,000 each. The barriers to entry had risen.[15]

The First Technological Challenges: Radio and TV

As radio grew in popularity in the 1930s, newspapers lost significant audience to the airwaves. Along with readers went advertisers. Between 1929 and 1941, newspaper ad revenue dropped 28 percent overall and national advertising fell 42 percent.[16]

Foreshadowing some of the concerns heard today, print journalists complained that radio stations often lifted copy directly from newspapers, aired stories that didn't go into depth, and hired inexperienced reporters. Newspaper executives tried to undermine competition from radio. The Associated Press, created by the newspaper industry, vowed in 1933 not to sell wire copy to radio stations. David Culbert, in his book *News for Everyman*, describes how the radio networks responded:

> "The networks agreed to a humiliating 10-point program. News could not be sold commercially. There would be only two five-minute summaries daily, and late enough in the morning and evening so as not to interfere with newspaper sales. The [American Newspaper Publishers Association] would provide bulletins—which urged listeners to purchase a newspaper for details. Radio commentators could not present headlines. They would confine themselves to 'generalizations and background of general news situations.' In return, the newspapers promised to continue publishing daily radio schedules."[17]

DAILY NEWSPAPER PAID CIRCULATION (1940–2009)	
Year	Total Paid Circulation
1940	41,132,000
1945	48,384,000
1950	53,829,000
1955	56,147,000
1960	58,882,000
1965	60,358,000
1970	62,108,000
1975	60,655,000
1980	62,202,000
1985	62,766,000
1990	62,328,000
1995	58,193,000
2000	55,773,000
2005	53,345,000
2009	45,653,000

Source: Newspaper Association of America and U.S. Census[20]

These efforts merely delayed the major radio networks' use of news bulletins. Eventually, radio networks were able to buy news from the wire services, cultivate their own reporters, *and* have their program listings published in newspapers.

While papers tried to resist the spread of news to radio, some complained that newspapers imitated the entertainment programming offered on radio. In the 1944 book *The Disappearing Daily,* Oswald Garrison Villard saw newspapers attempting to "add to their readership by printing pages and pages of comics, hints to the lovelorn, canned advice to parents, syndicated recipes for the housewife, widely marketed cuts of coming fashions for women young and old."[18]

With the arrival of television, Americans further split their time among news sources. TV viewership spread rapidly, with penetration in some markets jumping from zero to 70 percent within five years of being introduced into a community.[19] Although raw readership numbers continued to grow along with the population, the percentage of Americans reading newspapers gradually declined. With a smaller percentage of households subscribing to newspapers—and fewer households buying more than one paper—the number of newpapers being published also decreased.

The Rise of the Lucrative Monopoly Newspaper

In 1920, 42.6 percent of U.S. cities had two or more newspapers competing with each other. By 2000, only 1.4 percent did, mostly because afternoon newspapers had disappeared. The increasing competition from early news on television, the shift away from a manufacturing work schedule of 7 a.m. to 4 p.m., and the flight of readers from the central city into the suburbs had made delivery of an afternoon paper less profitable.[2]

The rise of the monopoly newspaper coincided with another development: the growth of the newspaper chain. Large companies and Wall Street investors saw profits in local newspapers, profits that would grow through the efficiencies of chain management. At the same time, the federal government's imposition of inheritance taxes had prompted some families that owned local papers to sell in order to avoid having their heirs pay substantial inheritance taxes. In 1920, 92 percent of newspapers were independent. Eighty years later, 23.4 percent were.[22]

For American journalism, the growth of the newspaper chain was a blessing and a curse. Chains introduced efficiencies that helped newspapers thrive despite circulation declines. For example, chain newspapers could share

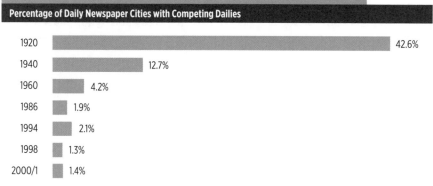

CHANGES OVER TIME IN DAILY NEWSPAPER COMPETITION

Percentage of Daily Newspaper Cities with Competing Dailies

Year	Percentage
1920	42.6%
1940	12.7%
1960	4.2%
1986	1.9%
1994	2.1%
1998	1.3%
2000/1	1.4%

Source: Eli M. Noam, *Media Ownership and Concentration in America,* 142 (Oxford University Press, 2009).

marketing, human resource management, and distribution costs. Papers could share advertising sales and negotiate ads for multiple papers with clients hoping to reach regional or national audiences. Chain newspapers could also share content, lowering the cost of news production by using the same copy across multiple markets.

But chains also led to the corporatization of newspapers.[23] Unlike family newspaper owners, who had long histories with their papers and were rooted in the communities they served, newspaper chain executives oversaw properties in many cities and towns across the country. They often lacked a connection to their readers and to the journalists who reported the news, and they focused more on overall corporate financial performance.[24]

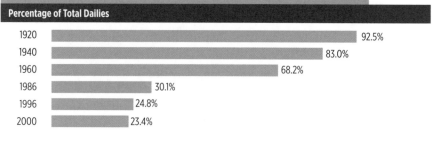

PERCENT OF DAILY NEWSPAPERS INDEPENDENTLY OWNED

Percentage of Total Dailies

Year	Percentage
1920	92.5%
1940	83.0%
1960	68.2%
1986	30.1%
1996	24.8%
2000	23.4%

Source: Eli M. Noam, *Media Ownership and Concentration in America* 139 (Oxford University Press, 2009)[25]

Newspapers managed to convert stagnant readership into increased profits—profits that far exceeded those of other industries. In the late 1990s, after years of circulation declines, the industry's average cash flow margins were 29 percent, according to newspaper industry analyst Lauren Rich Fine.[26] As competition disappeared, surviving newspapers raised ad rates. Between 1965 and 1975, ad rates rose 67 percent (remaining below the inflation rate); but between 1975 and 1990, as more newspapers became monopolies, rates skyrocketed 253 percent (compared with 141 percent for general consumer prices).[27]

Newspaper consolidation in the 1990s involved the sale of many smaller newspapers, which often were rearranged into regional clusters. "Of the 564 U.S. newspapers sold from January of 1994 through July of 2000, about two-thirds had circulations of less than 13,000. One hundred and eleven of these small papers were sold two, three, or even four times during this six-and-a-half year period."[28]

For all the controversial aspects of consolidation and profit taking, it could be argued that the high profit margins of the late 1980s led to high employment levels for journalists. In 1989, newspapers employed more editorial personnel than at any time during the previous 30 years.[30] However, journalism jobs began to disappear in the 1990s and early 2000s, as corporations, responding in part to Wall Street investors, squeezed higher profit margins out of newspapers. The papers themselves began to shrink in physical size (many used smaller paper and ran fewer pages) and in editorial scope.[31]

CASH FLOW MARGINS OF SELECTED NEWSPAPER COMPANIES (NEWSPAPER DIVISION ONLY) (1988–2008)

Year	AH Belo	Central Newspapers	Community Newspapers	Gannett	Journal Register	Knight Ridder	Lee Enterprises	McClatchy	Media General	New York Times	Pulitzer	EW Scripps	Times Mirror	Tribune	Wash. Post
1988	13%	16%	23%	27%	—	20%	—	20%	—	21%	14%	18%	19%	21%	23%
1990	18%	16%	19%	27%	—	20%	—	20%	—	16%	9%	18%	13%	16%	22%
1992	19%	18%	19%	26%	29%	20%	36%	22%	12%	12%	15%	16%	12%	26%	20%
1994	24%	21%	20%	28%	33%	21%	35%	24%	16%	17%	17%	26%	15%	28%	21%
1996	26%	23%	21%	27%	34%	21%	31%	22%	19%	20%	18%	26%	20%	27%	18%
1998	29%	27%	25%	31%	34%	23%	29%	28%	30%	25%	22%	30%	23%	31%	23%
2000	29%	—	31%	34%	34%	30%	31%	30%	31%	27%	26%	28%	—	28%	20%
2002	27%	—	30%	32%	28%	27%	28%	30%	29%	24%	25%	34%	—	26%	18%
2004	18%	—	30%	31%	26%	—	27%	29%	27%	20%	—	35%	—	25%	19%
2006	13%	—	24%	27%	22%	—	28%	27%	25%	15%	—	28%	—	24%	15%
2008	–1%	—	n/a	20%	n/a	—	21%	19%	14%	10%	—	14%	—	n/a	2%

Source: Lauren Rich Fine[29]

Profit expectations became unrealistically high, leading to changes in newspapers' priorities, many experts have argued. In his 1991 book *Preserving the Press: How Daily Newspapers Mobilized to Keep Their Readers,* Leo Bogart, longtime executive vice president and general manager of the Newspaper Advertising Bureau, explained:

> "During the years of the bull market on Wall Street, corporate managements were impelled to maximize current earnings as a way of boosting the price of the stock…. The price of the stock not only was the accepted index of management's success, but also could represent a large part of its compensation. Growth targets were set and achieved in a variety of ways: by acquiring additional properties, expanding sales, cutting costs, and raising prices….
>
> "Since public companies reported their earnings quarterly, their management focus tended to be on the here and now of the 'bottom line.'… Even in privately held companies, management bonuses were often based on quarterly earnings performance, so the short-run mentality prevailed there as well."[32]

Certainly family owners wanted to make money, too, but their timelines were different. "To preserve the institution he could afford to think long range," Bogart writes. "Besides, an improvement in quality might provide the publisher with deeper, non-financial satisfactions: an awareness of accomplishment, the admiration of associates and of the public."[33] In *The Vanishing Newspaper*, Philip Meyer argued that, having become fabulously wealthy already, family-owned-newspaper moguls moved on to psychic rewards:

> "Jim McClatchy expressed such a personal sense of mission when he said his family's newspapers were pitted against 'the exploiters—the financial, political, and business powers whose goal was to deny the ordinary family their dreams and needs in order to divert to themselves a disproportionate share of the productive wealth of the country.' John S. Knight showed where his heart was by keeping the title of editor or editor emeritus to the very end of his life. 'There is no higher or better title than editor,' he said…. Katherine Graham's support of her editors and reporters who uncovered the Watergate crimes was not motivated by profit but by her sense of civic duty."[34]

During World War II, with paper rationing in place, *New York Times* publisher Arthur Hays Sulzberger turned down advertising to maximize the news hole. That decision led to an increase in circulation and allowed the paper to thrive in the long run.[35]

By the 1990s, as corporate profit goals rose, editors at papers across the country became increasingly frustrated that editorial decisions were being made not in order to keep the papers afloat, but to propel profit levels ever higher. The former editor of the *Des Moines Register*, Geneva Overholser, recalled:

"The budget process for that year had begun with a memo from Gary Watson, Gannett newspaper division president, saying…:

"'Don't allow yourself or your team to be lulled into some false sense of reality by thinking you can plan for 1995 as if the newsprint price increase didn't really exist. Newsprint prices will be going up, and we still have the responsibility to produce a return for our shareholders….'

"Thus having already removed heart, soul, and giblets, we cut some more—another $63,000 in newsroom spending. Very shortly thereafter, by January, we learned that during the months we were engaged in these hope-withering negotiations, Gannett earnings were up 22 percent over the previous year's fourth quarter.

"The *Register's* plan for 1995, the year newsprint prices were soaring, was for a 23.4 percent profit margin before taxes—compared to the previous year's 21-plus percent with low newsprint prices."[36]

John Carroll, who served as editor of the *Lexington (KY) Herald-Leader,* the *Baltimore Sun,* and the *Los Angeles Times,* became convinced that owners were sacrificing the long-term financial health of their newspapers for short-term gain:

"I first heard the phrase 'harvest strategy' in the nineties, when it was briefly mentioned in a board meeting at the *Baltimore Sun.* I was the *Sun's* editor then, and merely hearing those two words gave me the willies.

"I sensed what they meant. They meant milking a declining business for all the cash it can produce until it dies….

"For the record, I am unaware of any formal decision to harvest the *Sun* or any other paper…. And yet, symptoms of harvest are staring us in the face. They include a low rate of investment, fewer employees, fewer readers, falling stock prices and, most especially, high profit margins.

"In 2005, our troubled industry reported operating margins averaging 19.3 percent. That's double the average among Fortune 500 companies. These high profits were achieved by relentless cost-cutting, which is rendering newspapers less valuable to their readers each year, and less able to compete."[37]

Later, it also became clear that many buyers were financing consolidation and growth by taking on huge amounts of debt. That made newspapers extraordinarily vulnerable during the economic downturn—particularly to competition from the Internet and emerging technologies. Mark Contreras, senior vice president of newspapers for the E. W. Scripps Company, estimated that by 2010, 14.9 percent of daily newspapers were owned by lenders or private equity firms, and those papers accounted for 20.4 percent of daily newspaper revenue.[38] (Predictions are that by mid-2011, seven of the 25 largest papers will be owned by private equity firms.) The 2011 Pew State of the Media report declared: "As a result of bankruptcies, private equity funds now own and operate a substantial portion of the industry. The era of newspapers being dominated by expanding publicly traded corporations is now winding down." The impact of private equity ownership is not black-and-white, with some predicting further staff cuts and others holding out hope that the new owners can help newspapers reinvent themselves for the digital era. Pew concludes:

"The firms have not made radical changes in the content or format of papers once they take over. Some cuts have followed, but not necessarily deeper ones than those by established companies like Gannett and McClatchy.

While the private equity owners are undoubtedly in the newspaper business motivated by a chance to make money rather than for public service, they appear to be betting that these distressed properties will bounce back after several years. There is no market right now to strip the organizations down and sell the pieces….

All this leaves the funds an important player in the industry's future, but still a wild card in where they will take the newspaper organizations they own."[39]

About as many Americans subscribe to newspapers today as did in 1945, even though the number of households is three times larger.

DAILY NEWSPAPER INDUSTRY FIGURES—BY OWNERSHIP TYPE

Category	Percentage of Daily Newspaper Revenue	Percentage of Daily Newspapers Owned
Public	44.2%	24.8%
Lender-Owned	18.1%	11.2%
Corporate-Group	18.0%	21.1%
Family-Owned Group	7.5%	21.4%
Independent	6.5%	13.8%
Private Equity	2.3%	3.7%
Corporate—Single Paper	1.8%	0.4%
Nonprofit	1.1%	0.4%
Entrepreneur	0.5%	3.3%

Source: Mark Contreras, Scripps[40]

The Next Technological Challenge: The Internet

By 2005, the Internet had begun seriously undercutting newspaper revenue. In 2000, total newspaper print advertising amounted to almost $48.7 billion. Ten years later, it had plummeted to $22.8 billion, a loss of more than 50 percent.[41]

Although newspapers gained audience—and a flood of new ad dollars—on the Internet, they were unable to make up for the loss in profits from their print products. Online traffic at newspaper websites did, indeed, skyrocket between January 2005 and April 2010—from 43.3 million unique viewers a month to 69.1 million, from 1.6 billion page views to 2.9 billion.[42] Online ad revenue for the entire newspaper industry grew by a billion between 2005 and 2010. But print advertising lost $24.6 *billion*. This led to the saying in the newspaper world that "print dollars were being replaced by digital dimes." That turns out to be a rather cheerful way of phrasing it. More accurately: each print dollar was being replaced by four digital pennies.

Faced with economics like this, newspapers were reluctant to shift resources from their print editions to their web operations. As a purely practical matter, it made great short-term sense to buck up the traditional business.

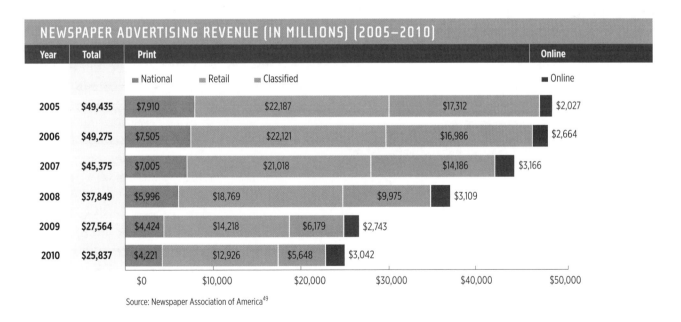

Source: Newspaper Association of America[49]

Classified advertising was hit the hardest, as consumers and advertisers found themselves with an array of much cheaper, faster, and more efficient alternatives. In 2000, revenue from ads for employment, real estate, vehicles, and the sale of smaller items and services accounted for 40 percent of newspaper's print advertising revenue, but by 2010 it had fallen 71 percent, from $19.6 billion to $5.6 billion, amounting to just 25 percent of total print ad revenue.[44] As the Internet grew, some of that money went to Google, where small businesses could advertise easily and efficiently. Some went to specialty sites for jobs (including Monster.com and CareerBuilder.com),[45] cars (AutoTrader.com and Cars.com),[46] and real estate (Realtor.com, Yahoo Real Estate, and Zillow.com),[47] and some went to Craigslist, which runs ads in all those categories and more. Consider how the economics of classified advertising has changed the market for ads in a city served by Craigslist, such as Kansas City: the price for a garage sale ad in the *Kansas City Star* is $22.95, an employment-listing package starts at $419, and an apartment rental ad package starts at $79.[48] The cost to place those same ads on Craigslist is zero. Craigslist charges for only a few categories of ads, including brokered apartment rental listings in New York City and job postings in fewer than 20 U.S. metro areas. More than 47 million people in the U.S. visit Craigslist each month.[49]

CLASSIFIED ADVERTISING (IN MILLIONS OF DOLLARS) BY TYPE

Year	Real Estate	Automotive	Employment	Other	Total
2000	$3,117	$5,026	$8,713	$2,703	$19,609
2010	$1,239	$1,106	$756	$2,550	$5,648

Source: Newspaper Association of America[50]

Declines in national and retail advertising compounded problems. National advertising expenditures in newspapers reached a high of $8 billion in 2004, while local advertising peaked at $22 billion in 2005. Both declined in 2006 and 2007 and then plummeted during the recession the following two years. By 2010, national advertising expenditures in newspapers were only $4.2 billion, and retail advertising had dropped to $12.9 billion.[51] It was a double whammy: just as classified advertisers migrated to the Internet, national advertisers cut spending and shifted some resources to other media, including cable television, niche publications, and the Internet.[52]

The sharp drop in ad revenue meant that some newspapers could not pay back their loans. In some cases, they defaulted even though they were making money, because their profits were not substantial enough to cover the debt service. This led to an unusual corporate development, as *profitable* newspapers like the *Philadelphia Inquirer* and the *Minneapolis Star Tribune* declared bankruptcy.[53] Some newspapers managed to survive by declaring bankruptcy and reorganizing, but many just disappeared. The table below shows the newspapers, large and small, that stopped publishing print editions from 2007 to 2010. Those marked with an asterisk switched to online-only editions. The vast majority of them have ceased to exist in any form.[54]

The loss of revenue precipitated a more than 25 percent reduction in newsroom staffs, affecting reporters, editors, online producers, photographers, artists, and videographers.[55] The drop between 2006 and 2010 is particularly striking: in just four years, newspaper employment fell from 55,000 to roughly 41,600—about where it was before Watergate.[56]

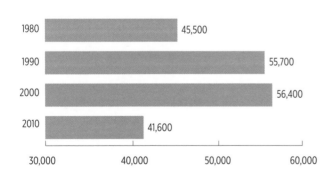

TOTAL U.S. DAILY NEWSPAPER NEWSROOM WORKFORCE (1980–2010)

Year	Workforce
1980	45,500
1990	55,700
2000	56,400
2010	41,600

Source: Pew State of the Media 2011; American Society of Newspaper Editors, Newsroom Employment Census, 2010[57]

Cuts at many newspapers far exceeded the national average. After seven rounds of layoffs in four years, the *San Diego Union-Tribune* newsroom staff in 2010 was half what it had been in 2006. In 2008, the paper closed its Washington Bureau—just two years after its reporters had won a Pulitzer Prize for stories that put a member of Congress behind bars.[58] More than half of Seattle's newspaper reporters lost their jobs.[59]

In October 2008, the *Newark (NJ) Star-Ledger* announced a staff reduction of about 45 percent through voluntary buyouts. This came after the paper had generated losses for at least three years in a row.[60] In April 2009, the *Chicago Tribune* announced the departure of 53 editorial

The Adit

The Advance Leader, Penn Hills Progress and Woodland Progress

Albuquerque Tribune

Algonquin Countryside, Cary-Grove Countryside and Wauconda Courier

American Fork Citizen, Lehi Free Press, Lone Peak Press, Orem Times and Pleasant Grove Review

Americké Listy

Ann Arbor News*

The Argus Champion

Arlington Heights Post, Elk Grove Times, Hoffman Estates Review, Palatine Countryside, Rolling Meadows Review, Schaumburg Review and Wheeling Countryside

Art Review & Preview

AsianWeek*

Baltimore Examiner

Batavia Sun, Bolingbrook Sun, Downers Grove Sun, Geneva Sun, Glen Ellyn Sun, Lisle Sun, St. Charles Sun, Wheaton Sun

Bay State Banner

Bedford Sun, Euclid Sun Journal, Garfield-Maple Sun, Nordonia Hills Sun, Sun-Press and Twinsburg Sun

Bellevue Business Journal

Berkeley Daily Planet*

The Bethel Beacon, The Brookfield Journal, The Kent Good Times Dispatch and The Litchfield Enquirer

Big Sky Sun

The Birmingham Eccentric, West Bloomfield Eccentric, Troy Eccentric, Rochester Eccentric, and Southfield Eccentric

Bloomfield Free Press*

Bloomfield Journal, Windsor Journal, Windsor Locks Journal

Boca Raton News*

Boulder City News

Branford Review, Clinton Recorder, East Haven Advertiser, Pictorial Gazette, Shelton Weekly, Shore Line Times, Stratford Bard and Wallingford Voice

Brick Township Bulletin, Woodbridge Sentinel

The Bridge*

Bridgeville Area News

The Bulletin

Business Journal of Corpus Christi

Business Times of the Rio Grande Valley

California Real Estate Journal

The Capital Times*

Carson Times

Chicago Free Press

Christian Science Monitor*

Cincinnati Post and Kentucky Post*

The City Star

The Clarke Courier

The Clinton News

Coatesville Ledger

Connecticut Valley Spectator

Coral Gables Gazette*

Coraopolis-Moon Record

The Daily Reporter

Dakota Journal

Danville Weekly*

Delaware Valley News

The Democrat

Denmark Press

Dennis Pennysaver and Yarmouth Pennysaver

Des Plaines Times and Mount Prospect Times

Detroit Daily Press

El Dia

The District Weekly

Door Reminder

Donegal Ledger

Douglas Times

Downingtown Ledger

Doylestown Patriot

Eagle-Times

East Bridgewater Star, West Bridgewater Times and Whitman Times

East Hartford Gazette

East Iowa Herald

East Side Herald

El Nuevo Dia Orlando

Elizabethtown Chronicle

Encino Sun, Sherman Oaks Sun and Studio City Sun

Eureka Reporter

Fallon Star Press

Farmer City Journal

Fitchburg Star*

Fort Collins Now

The Franklin Chronicle

La Frontera

Gazette Advertiser

Germantown Courier and Mount Airy Times Express

Greenville Press

Greenwood Lake and West Milford News

Gooding County Leader

Grapevine Sun

Hamden Chronicle

Hanson Town Crier

Hardee Sun

Harlem Valley Times, Millbrook Round Table, Voice Ledger

Henderson Home News

The Hershey Chronicle

Heyworth Star and LeRoy Journal

Hill Country View

Homer Sun, Lincoln-Way Sun, Plainfield Sun

Hopi Tutuveni

Hoy

Hyde Park Townsman

The Independent

Iraan News

Island Breeze*

Jeanerette Enterprise

The Journal-Messenger

Kansas City Kansan*

Kitsap Free Daily

LA City Beat

La Palma

La Tribuna

Lake Elmo Leader

Lake Highlands People, Lakewood People and West Plano People

Lake Norman Times

Lakota Journal

The Leader

Leadville Chronicle

The Lemoore Advance

Lincoln County Journal

Los Gatos Weekender and West San Jose Resident

Loudon Easterner

Main Street News

Maricopa Tribune

McCamey News

McKnight Journal and North Journal

The Message for the Week

The Milford Observer

Ming Pao New York

Ming Pao San Francisco

Minidoka County News

The Monitor-Herald

NASCAR Scene*

New Hope Gazette

New York Blade

The New York Sun

News Gleaner, Northeast Breeze and Olney Times

The Newton Record

Nichi Bei Times

Noblesville Daily Times

North Haven Post

North Side News

Northern Star

Oak Cliff Tribune

Orfordville Journal & Footville News

Oxford Tribune, Parkesburg Post Ledger and Solanco Sun Ledger

Pawling News Chronicle

Peoria Times-Observer

Petoskey Citizen-Journal

The Phoenicia Times and The Olive Press

Pinellas News

Placer Sentinel

Plymouth Bulletin

Pocono Business Journal

The Post-Crescent

Putnam County Courier

Quakertown Free Press

Register Herald

Rhinoceros Times*

Rocky Mountain News

Rumbo de San Antonio

Rumbo del Valle

San Juan Star

Seattle Post-Intelligencer*

Selah Independent

The Sentinel

Stillwater Courier

South Florida Blade

Southern Idaho Press

Southern Voice

Spotlight

Suffolk Life

The Sun

Sun Post

Sun Tribune

Thomasville Times

Today Newspapers

The Town Meeting

Tucson Citizen*

Ulster County Townsman

Vail Sun

Vail Trail

Valley Journal

Washington Blade

The Weekly Almanac

The Western Tribune

Whitehorse Community News

Wood River Journal

Wrightstown Post-Gazette

Source: Erica Smith, Paper Cuts (March 3, 2011)

*Switched to online edition only

employees, a move that left a newsgathering team of about 430 at a paper whose newsroom had numbered about 670 just four years earlier.[61]

In 2009 alone, the website Paper Cuts counted 34 papers that had laid off more than 100 employees each.[62] Meanwhile, journalists across the country who managed to hang onto their jobs often were forced to accept unpaid furloughs, pay cuts, or both.[63]

Was the decline of newspapers inevitable?

On one hand, the dominance of newspapers has been diminishing for a long time. From 1940 to 2010, the number of daily newspaper subscriptions in America rose by 2 million—but the number of households increased by 83 million.

From 2005 to 2010 online ad revenues for the newspaper industry grew more than $1 billion—but print advertising declined $24.6 billion.

Here is another way of looking at it: about as many Americans subscribe to newspapers today as did in the early 1940s, even though the number of households is more than three times larger.[64]

While large metro dailies have struggled, smaller papers have not faced the same level of financial assault. Community newspapers, often defined as weekly or daily newspapers with circulations of 15,000 or less, account for about 80 percent of the newspapers in the U.S.[65] Among the approximately 8,000 community newspapers operating, about 7,000 do not publish daily.[66]

The Inland Press Association reports that from 2004 to 2008 the smallest daily newspapers suffered less significant financial losses than larger papers.[67]

In a 2007 piece entitled "News Flash: Small-Market Papers Prosper," for the fedgazette, a publication of the Federal Reserve Bank of Minneapolis, Joe Mahon noted that many smaller newspapers were doing very well due to their unique market position:

> "While this drama was playing out, Lee Enterprises was quietly going about its business of making money from newspapers. The Iowa-based holding company specializes in mid-size and small-market papers, including the *Billings Gazette, Bismarck Tribune* and nine others in the district. In the third quarter of 2006, when most companies were reporting slumping circulation and revenue, Lee saw circulation increase at 37 of its 51 dailies. Lee's revenue grew about 38 percent in the last year, helping the company post a 20 percent average operating profit (more than 5 percentage points higher than the industry average) over the past five years....

> "The chief basis for the success of small-town newspapers is simple: market penetration. Less competition in smaller communities for readers and advertising dollars means that newspapers still dominate their markets to a degree that metro dailies cannot. The technologies that have plagued the big-city papers, primarily cable television and Web news, might eventually have dire consequences for their small-town cousins, but so far they have been sheltered."[68]

Future trends that might reduce the advertising advantages of community newspapers include the expansion of hyperlocal websites, the development of mobile advertising that targets phones based on geography, the extension of websites such as Craigslist into smaller cities and towns, and the advancement of strategies by search engines to capture local advertisers. The timing and impact of these trends on community newspapers, however, remain very open questions.

In one sense, the response of large newspaper owners to the drop in revenue has proved successful: cost cutting has largely stemmed financial losses. Writing for the Nieman Journalism Lab, analyst Ken Doctor wrote:

> "Across the board, the reporting of public news companies reflects a new, if unsteady reality. In short, that reality is one of profit. Not the big profit of 20-percent-plus profit margins—the envy of many other industries—that were a truism as recently as five years ago. Now, the profit's more tepid, mostly in single digits: the *New York Times*, 8 percent; Gannett, 8 percent, McClatchy, 1.5 percent. Expectations run that news companies will show a five to 10 percent profit for the year, absent unforeseen calamity."[69]

In the fourth quarter of 2010, newspaper stocks led all media with an increase of 22 percent (though many remained down for the year as a whole).[70] Media analyst Douglas Arthur of Evercore Partners attributed the fourth-quarter rebound to signs that print advertising was bottoming out, setting the stage for positive growth in 2011. Arthur said he not only expected growth in traditional newspaper advertising, but that he was optimistic about the impact of the iPad.[71] On the other hand, the cost of newsprint is rising, insert advertising is declining, and many companies still spend significant sums on servicing their debt.[72] Doctor concluded that the profits were fragile and unlikely to result in much greater investment in "product."

The Price of Newspaper Cuts

When they were faced with shrinking budgets, newspaper editors had some tightening they could do without hurting critical functions. Many editors consider their local beat reporters indispensable: those who cover schools and city councils, police and courts, suburban developments and urban neighborhoods, local elections and statehouses, for instance, are thought to provide information that is crucial to the functioning of the community—and even democracy itself.[73] On the other hand, reporters who provide the kind of coverage that can be found elsewhere are considered less essential. When layoffs began, arts reporters, for instance, were among the first let go. Undoubtedly, some talented local voices lost their platform, but the truth is, readers can find national arts news and reviews on a number of websites; the aggregation site Rotten Tomatoes, to name but one, links to more than 200,000 movie reviews.[74]

But cutting "nonessential" beats alone did not save enough money. In paper after paper, local accountability journalism is down, according to several studies. Developments at newspapers in three cities illustrate the trend:

Baltimore: In January 2010, the Pew Project for Excellence in Journalism released a study of journalism in Baltimore. It concluded that although newspapers in the area still provided the bulk of news content, coverage had diminished considerably. During 2009, the study reported, the city's dominant paper, the *Baltimore Sun*, produced 23,668 stories, down 32 percent from the 34,852 stories it published in 1999—and down 73 percent from 1991, when competing staffs generated morning and evening newspapers, and ran a total of 86,667 stories.[75]

Significantly, with fewer reporters on the job, governmental institutions drove much of the coverage. "As news is posted faster, often with little enterprise reporting added, the official version of events is becoming more important," the PEJ study said. "We found official press releases often appear word for word in first accounts of events, though often not noted as such.... Government, at least in this study, initiates most of the news. In the detailed examination of six major storylines, 63 percent of the stories were initiated by government officials, led by the police. Another 14 percent came from the press. Interest group figures made up most of the rest."[76]

> "Official press releases often appear word for word in first accounts of events, though often not noted as such.... Government, at least in this study, initiates most of the news," reported a Pew study about Baltimore.

Philadelphia: In the 1970s, while the *Washington Post* rode the Watergate wave to worldwide notoriety, a large group of regional and big-city newspapers around the country was beginning to produce some of the best journalism in American history. One of the most respected of these regional powerhouses was the *Philadelphia Inquirer*, which won 17 Pulitzer Prizes from 1975 through 1990.[77] In addition to operating bureaus in six foreign countries, the paper managed to cover Philadelphia as it had never been covered before. Along with its prize-winning work on poor conditions at a local mental hospital and corruption in Philadelphia courts, the paper covered the many ethnic parades held in the city, from Polish to Irish, Italian to Puerto Rican. This was a newspaper deeply engaged with its city and with the world.[78]

But as Knight Ridder, like other newspaper chains, began to push for higher profit margins, cost-cutting pressures rose in the *Inquirer* newsroom. Foreign and domestic bureaus closed, and staff was reduced through a series of layoffs and buyouts. A newsroom staff that once numbered 680 was down to 280 by 2010, and according to the *American Journalism Review*, shrinkage reflected in the coverage.[79] In 2006, Knight Ridder was purchased by the McClatchy Company, which sold the *Inquirer* to Philadelphia Media Holdings LLC, a local business consortium.[80] In 2009, almost $400 million in debt, the paper's owners declared Chapter 11 bankruptcy.[81] In April 2010, the *Inquirer* was sold to a group of creditors in a bankruptcy auction.[82]

J-Lab: the Institute for Interactive Journalism, a center that funds journalism innovation, studied the Philadelphia news "ecosystem" during sample weeks in 2006 and 2009. In a report on its findings, author Jan Shaffer, formerly an editor at the *Inquirer*, concluded that "available news about Philadelphia public affairs issues has dramatically diminished over the last three years by many measures: news hole, air time, story count, key word measurements."[83] She summarized interviews she did with civic leaders: "People in Philadelphia want more public affairs news than they are now able to get. They don't think their daily newspapers are as good as the newspapers used to be. They want news that is more connected to their city."[84]

Raleigh-Durham, North Carolina: When Leonard Downie Jr. and Robert Kaiser published the *News about the News* in 2002, they lavished special praise on the *Raleigh (NC) News & Observer*:

> "The *News & Observer* stands out from most American newspapers because of its ambition and its execution.... Raleigh, its region and the state of North Carolina are all better communities because the *News & Observer* is their paper. The paper challenges resident officials to confront serious issues. It creates a sense of shared experience that strengthens the connections among individuals and institutions in its area. Not incidentally, it enables readers to know what's happening that could affect their lives."[85]

But the *News & Observer* is no longer the same paper. Professor James Hamilton of Duke University (a consultant to the Future of Media project) studied changes at the *News & Observer* and found that its newsroom of 250 employees in 2004 had been reduced to 132 in 2009.[86] By February 2011, the newsroom headcount was down to 103.[87] Among the beats the paper stopped covering full time: Durham courts, Durham schools, legal affairs, agriculture, science, environment, and statewide public education. And among the losses in staff were a "workplace reporter" who once produced stories on illegal immigrants in North Carolina, visa violations, and companies that evaded unemployment tax payments; a full-time banking reporter who had written about predatory lending in the state and about Fannie Mae and Freddie Mac's mortgage ties in the Research Triangle Park, a well-known high-tech research and development center; a full-time tech reporter who had covered the many high-tech companies in the Research Triangle Park; and a pharmaceutical reporter who covered local drug and health companies. "With all those full-time reporters gone, the odds of similar series and stories being written have declined," Hamilton concluded.[88]

While legacy newspapers used to lag in innovation, some have become quite creative in their use of social media, database journalism, and community engagement.

Repercussions like those Hamilton observed in North Carolina are evident at newspapers throughout the country: Many staff cutbacks have occurred on beats that had enormous civic impact but lacked sexy, marketable stories. As editors prune beats to leave only those that generate buzz—or, in the case of websites, traffic—they are tempted to serve fewer portions of "broccoli journalism," i.e. stories that might be both unpopular but good for you.

"What you tend to cut is the day in, day out, beat reporting—or the city council meeting, or doing three days of reporting on the immigration bill instead of one," says Mark Silverman, editor of the *(Nashville) Tennessean*. "There's less time to invest in in-depth coverage."[89]

The cutbacks have touched many areas of coverage but experts have raised particular concerns about about a few crucial areas:

State Government: States spent more than $1.2 trillion in fiscal year 2008, compared with $977 billion in 2003—and yet the number of reporters covering statehouses has fallen sharply.[90] A comprehensive survey by the *American Journalism Review* found that the number of statehouse reporters has dropped by one-third—from 524 in 2003 to 355 in 2009.[91]

The story is the same in state after state.

During a time when New Jersey government has been beset by scandals, the number of journalists covering the capitol has fallen from 39 in 2003 to 15 in 2009.[92]

In California, which is battling one of the nation's worst budget crises, 29 newspaper reporters covered the statehouse in 2009, down from 40 six years earlier.[93]

Georgia had 14 full-time statehouse newspaper reporters in 2003; in 2009 it had five.[94]

In 1989, 83 people covered the state legislature, governor, or executive agencies in Texas. In 2009, 53 did, according to the *Houston Chronicle*.[95]

In 2001, Albany, New York, had 51 journalists and 29 news organizations covering the statehouse. By 2008, the numbers had fallen to 42 journalists and 27 news organizations.[96] The *Staten Island Advance*, the *Schenectady Daily Gazette*, the *Troy Record*, the *Jamestown Post Journal*, and the Ottaway News Service are among those that have eliminated their statehouse bureaus entirely.

In Pennsylvania, Jeanette Krebs, editorial page editor for the *Harrisburg Patriot News*, remembers more than 40 correspondents crowding the Capitol's pressroom in 1987 when she was an intern. In 1994, when she was president of the Pennsylvania State Legislative Correspondents Association, there were 35. Now, 19 reporters cover the statehouse, including some who come only when the legislature is in session.[97] "Our state Capitol used to be bustling with the media," said Matthew Brouillette, president of the Harrisburg-based Commonwealth Foundation. "Now, you can swing a dead cat and not hit anybody in the state Capitol newsroom."[98]

Nine journalists—print and TV—covered the Nevada legislature in 2010. In better times, according to Ed Vogel of the *Las Vegas Review-Journal*, more than 20 would have been there. As the coverage has shrunk by half, the state has more than tripled in size.[99] "If you're not there, it changes how legislators look at it," says Vogel, the lone remaining reporter from his newspaper. "The oversight, the watchdogs won't be there. It's a benefit to society that won't exist anymore."[100]

In many cases, smaller newspapers have abandoned statehouses altogether. For years, the *Champaign (IL) News-Gazette* had a reporter in the Capitol, in Springfield, to cover topics of particular importance to Champaign-Urbana—home to the University of Illinois' largest campus—such as higher education bills and state pension issues. In 2010, legislative coverage was done from the Champaign newsroom. "We miss the in-depth coverage and the perspective and nuance that having a reporter there every day provides," editor John Beck says. "What we're missing more is the enterprise coverage…the investigative coverage. As newsrooms have lost staff members, which we have like all other newsrooms, it makes it harder to do these kinds of stories."[101]

For nearly five years, Aaron Chambers was the statehouse bureau chief for the *Rockford (IL) Register Star*. At one point, he broke the story that the executive branch was improperly managing government contracts, potentially risking millions of taxpayer dollars. In 2008, his paper eliminated its statehouse bureau; Chambers went into public relations.[102]

In all, a survey by the *American Journalism Review* published in the spring of 2009 found that more than 50 newspapers and news companies nationwide had at that point stopped covering their statehouses entirely since 2003. They include the *Anniston (AL) Star*, the *East Valley (AZ) Tribune*, the *Stockton (CA) Record*, the *Bakersfield Californian*, Copley News Service (CA), Lehman Newspapers (CO), the *Daily Camera (CO)*, the *New Haven (CT) Register*, the *Pocatello Idaho State Journal*, the *Nampa Idaho Press-Tribune*, the *Rockford (IL) Register*, the *Bloomington (IL) Pantagraph*, the *Champaign (IL) News-Gazette*, Gannett Company Inc. (IN), the *Covington Kentucky Post*, Community Newspaper Company (MA), the *Lawrence (MA) Eagle Tribune*, the *Pontiac (MI) Oakland Press*, the *Duluth (MN) News Tribune*, the *St. Cloud (MN) Times*, the *Mankato (MN) Free Press*, the *Cape Girardeau Southeast Missourian*, *Foster's Daily Democrat (NH)*, the *Trenton (NJ) Times*, the *Trentonian (NJ)*, the *Staten Island (NY) Advance*, the *Schenectady (NY) Daily Gazette*, Ottaway News Service (NY), the *Troy (NY) Record*, the *Jamestown (NY) Post Journal*, the *Durham (NC) Herald-Sun*, *Wilmington (NC) Star News*, *Grand Forks (ND) Herald*, the *Minot (ND) Daily News*, Gannett Company Inc. (OH), GateHouse Media (OH), Community Newspaper Holdings Inc. (OK), the *York (PA) Daily Record*, Ottaway News Service (PA), Calkins Media (PA), the *Wilkes-Barre (PA) Times Leader*, the *Myrtle Beach (SC) Sun News*, McClatchy Newspapers (SC), the *Charlotte (NC) Observer*, the *Argus (SD) Leader*, the *Rapid City (SD) Journal*, Scripps Newspapers (TX), Valley Freedom Newspapers (TX), the *Danville (VA) Register Bee*, the *Morgantown (WV) Dominion Post*, and Lee Enterprises Inc. (WI).[103]

A reader recently complained about the arbitrary way concealed weapons permits are handled, possibly denying gun permits to those who deserve them. Great idea, Hamlin thought—but he no longer has time to pursue it.

Recent efforts to fill these gaps have come largely from the nonprofit sector. For example, the web-based Texas Tribune, California Watch, and NJ Spotlight, which are financed largely by foundations, provide substantial coverage of their respective statehouses.[104] The Associated Press has made a commitment to keep at least one reporter in each statehouse.[105]

Municipal Government: In doing triage, many big-city newspapers have held on to their primary city hall reporters and cut back on coverage of neighboring towns and cities, according to Rick Edmonds, of the Poynter Institute.[106] Perhaps the most infamous and instructive case is in Bell, California. For years, residents of Bell, population 37,000, wondered how their town officials managed to live like the rich and famous. Bell is a working-class, largely immigrant suburb of Los Angeles with a median household income of around $30,000. But the town manager, Robert Rizzo, owned a mansion by the beach and a 10-acre horse ranch outside Seattle.[107]

"For a long time there's been evidence that they were paying themselves big salaries," says Christina Garcia, a community activist and teacher, "but no one knew how much."[108] In July 2010, *Los Angeles Times* reporters gave Garcia and the rest of the country a shocking answer: Rizzo was earning $787,637 a year. The police chief, Randy Adams, was earning $457,000—about 50 percent more than the Los Angeles police chief or county sheriff, and more than the president of the United States.[109]

In 1993, when council members hired Rizzo to be interim chief administrative officer, his starting salary was $72,000.[110] By September 2004, he was drawing down $300,000 annually.[111] Ten months later, his salary jumped an additional 47 percent to $442,000.[112] Rizzo's large and regular raises continued until the *L.A. Times* wrote about Bell, at which point the city council ordered a staff report on city salaries.[113] In September 2010, the Los Angeles County district attorney filed charges against eight Bell officials, alleging that they stole $5.5 million in public funds. Rizzo was charged with 53 felony counts, 44 of which pertain to misappropriation of Bell's municipal coffers.[114]

"What you tend to cut is the day in, day out, beat reporting—or the city council meeting, or doing three days of reporting on the immigration bill instead of one," says Mark Silverman, editor of the (Nashville) Tennessean. "There's less time to invest in in-depth coverage."

Why did it take so long for the financial scandal to be exposed? "A lot of residents tried to get the media's attention, but it was impossible," Garcia says. "The city of Bell doesn't even have a local paper; no local media of any sort."[115]

The closest television stations are in L.A., but they rarely cover Bell. There are six newspapers operating within a 10-mile radius of Bell (the *Los Angeles Times*, the *Los Angeles Daily News*, the *Los Angeles Downtown News*, the *Torrance Breeze*, the *Whittier Daily News*, and the *South Pasadena News*); and 19 within 20 miles (including the *Long Beach Press Telegram*, the *Orange County Register*, and papers in Burbank and Pasadena). But the *Bell, Maywood, Cudahy Community News*, which used to be the local watchdog, was sold in 1998, just five years after Rizzo was hired, and it eventually went out of business.[116]

The demise of smaller papers in the region has left the *Los Angeles Times* pretty much on its own to cover 88 municipalities and 10 million citizens.[117] Metro editor David Lauter laments that his staff is "spread thinner and there are fewer people on any given area.... We're not there every day, or even every week or every month. Unfortunately, nobody else is either."[118]

While the *Times* has a policy against disclosing specifics, Lauter wrote in an email that "the metro staff is just slightly less than half the size it was in September 2000 and about 30 percent smaller than in January 2008.... largely as a result of eliminating separate staffs in our far-flung suburban regions."[119] *Times* reporters Jeff Gottlieb, Ruben Vives, and Catherine Salliant learned about the unusually high salaries of Bell officials while investigating possible wrongdoing in the nearby community of Maywood.[120] Gottlieb says Bell residents have been effusive in their thanks. "They come to newspapers to have their wrongs overturned."[121]

Without adequate media coverage, citizens have a tough time taking on city hall. Filing documents for public access is expensive. Bell's demographics added another layer of complication. Many of its residents are legal immigrants, not citizens. Others are undocumented immigrants. Most do not have the language, skills, education, cash, or, frankly, the time to fight the system.

Terry Francke, Voice of OC's (Orange County) open government consultant and general counsel for Californians Aware, summed up the problem this way:

"In short, the Bell spectacle is what happens to communities without their own old-fashioned diligent news coverage by veteran newspaper reporters, or at least smart reporters led by veteran newspaper editors. The result need not be on paper, but it must be done with the community memory and professional savvy almost unique to newspaper-trained journalists with experience watching small-town politics."[122]

The shrinking coverage of municipal government around the country raises the risk of corruption and wasted taxpayer dollars. And local officials know it. Garcia, the Bell activist, says, "The city has done everything they can to suppress communication. They did the minimum they could by law."[123] They held meetings in the middle of the workday, sometimes adjourning after one minute.

In more rural areas, the coverage is likely to be even thinner, with citizens more dependent on government itself to provide accurate and honest information. Jerry Black, a Republican state senator in Montana, told the Knight Commission:

"Local news coverage is mainly up to city and county governments, civic groups, and local organizations to contact the local papers and radio station with information and news they need and what those providing the information want released. This has an upside and a downside. Some city and county governments are better than others in providing information and unless they have someone in the media asking 'hard questions' or probing for more information, the public may never know what they really should or need to know."[124]

Longtime investigative reporter Mark Thompson, now of *Time* magazine, summarized: "Government responds to pressure, whether it be two or three reporters at the local city hall demanding a filing or reporters at the local cop shop demanding police reports." But someone has to be there to ask, he says.[125]

Crime and Criminal Justice: Given that local TV news tends to focus on the latest murder or fire, it is tempting to think that we will never have a shortage of crime coverage. And on a superficial level that is true. But cutbacks at newspapers have meant that coverage of underlying issues—how well the criminal or civil justice systems work—has suffered. In most cases, newspapers have not entirely eliminated their coverage of courts, but instead send so few reporters to do so much that reporting has become more reactive and shallow, and less enterprising.

Consider Vacaville, a small northern California town between mountains and farmland, 55 miles inland from San Francisco and 33 miles southwest of Sacramento. Ten years ago, the *Vacaville Reporter* had 27 staffers; now it has fewer than 14.[126] Five news reporters cover the roughly 900 square miles and 400,000 people of Solano County, as well as some neighboring counties. Brian Hamlin, who covered courts in Solano and parts of two other counties for the *Reporter* and its sister paper, the *Vallejo Times,*[127] said he had time for little besides spot news. For instance, a reader recently complained about the arbitrary way concealed weapons permits are handled, possibly denying permits to those who deserve them, because the local police chief has wide discretion (more than in other states). The reader suggested investigating the process. Great idea, Hamlin said. "Firearms and weapons permits always are a hot-button issue and are frequently misunderstood and/or misapplied." But he could not work on it, as he was frantically busy keeping up on coverage of ongoing trials in the various courts.

The previous time Hamlin was able to tackle an enterprise story was about two years ago, when he investigated the problems faced by mentally incompetent criminal defendants. California had built just one new mental health prison facility in the 1980s and 1990s, and it did not have enough space to house this growing population. As a result, many inmates languished in county jails for weeks, and because they were not receiving state mental-health care, their competency to stand trial could not be evaluated. "We'd like to be able to devote more time to longer, more in-depth pieces as we once did on a regular basis," Hamlin said. "But we have neither the time nor the staff to do so."[128]

The problem is not limited to small suburban papers. "Trial coverage by newspapers has all but vanished," reports Bill Girdner, owner and editor of Courthouse News Service, a California-based wire service that publishes le-

"Our state Capitol used to be bustling with the media," said Matthew Brouillette of the Pennsyvlvania-based Commonwealth Foundation. "Now, you can swing a dead cat and not hit anybody in the state Capitol newsroom."

gal stories and distributes them to newspapers. At a recent Los Angeles trial in which police officers were accused of beating journalists covering a public protest, Girdner saw no reporters from major newspapers. "They've abandoned the pressroom. They rely on the local wire service."[129]

Ironically, while the Internet has made many reporting tasks easier, it also at times has added to the bureaucracy that can make information difficult to access. In most courthouses, for instance, reporters of years past could find out about pending cases by rifling through boxes or baskets of paperwork and transcripts that were made available. Girdner says that courts have tightened access to information, citing digital technology as an excuse. In the Riverside County courthouse, he explained, the old wooden box is gone, ostensibly replaced by online postings—which often take days to process: "You would think information would flow faster, but it's quite the opposite."[130]

This has, in effect, led to a power shift from the public to government bureaucracies, according to Girdner: With fewer, and less experienced, reporters in the courts, "the court bureaucracy has gotten stronger and stronger.... And they do what bureaucracies do: they control the process of access more and more, and they push reporters back in time." If it takes two to three days to access court documents, "the press just walks away. They just give up."[131]

"When journalists don't have presence," Girdner says, "others control the information process."

Several court experts say the mere presence of reporters would change the behavior of judges and other court personnel. Assistant prosecuting attorney Steven Kaplan in Macomb County, Michigan, northwest of Detroit, says that because the *Detroit News* and *Detroit Free Press* have one reporter each covering the entire court system, they cannot keep tabs on incompetent judges: "Maybe you have a judge who is chronically tardy or absent, someone who says at 11:30, 'All right, everyone be back at 1:30,' and he doesn't come back until 3 p.m. Maybe he would be more on time if he thought a reporter would write about it." Kaplan equates the watchdog effect of journalists to the presence of patrol cars on highways: people might perform at a higher level in order to avoid embarrassment: "A reporter is a conscience of the community; he or she holds up a periscope for the public to see."[132]

Who suffers from the lack of court coverage? Often, those who most need someone to look out for them. Consider child welfare cases. In the 1990s and 2000s, the *Detroit Free Press* had a full-time beat reporter, Jack Kresnack, covering family courts. His pieces about the child abuse death of a boy at the hands of his parents led to changes in guardianship laws; his series about the murder of a child by his foster parents led to criminal charges. But Kresnack left in 2007 and has not been replaced.[133] In Michigan, coverage of juvenile and family courts has become "smaller and smaller over the years," according to Vivek Sankaran, director of the new Detroit Center for Family Advocacy.[134] Without scrutiny, he says, mistakes are made that have a life-changing impact: "Parents whose rights are terminated who shouldn't be terminated," he says. "It's that type of story. It just takes somebody to go down there to get the story, but nobody is ever down there."[135]

Advocates are particularly concerned that papers are paying less attention to wrongfully convicted prisoners, some of whom are on death row. "Over the years, the work of investigative journalists has been extremely helpful in... helping to prove that people have been wrongly convicted," says Paul Cates, communications director of the Innocence Project in New York, an organization dedicated to exonerating wrongfully convicted prisoners.[136] He pointed, for instance, to a 14-part series in the *Columbus Dispatch* that uncovered flaws in Ohio's DNA testing system. Seth Miller of the Innocence Project of Florida says, "Stories that were getting written three, four years ago that supplemented the legal work the [I]nnocence [P]rojects were working on, are just not happening."[137]

In a 2009 opinion piece in the *Washington Post*, David Simon, a former police reporter for the *Baltimore Sun* (who later became a screenwriter), gave this particularly vivid account of the need for journalistic persistence on criminal justice beats:

> "[Baltimore] was a wonderland of chaos, dirt and miscalculation, and loyal adversaries were many. Among them, I could count police commanders who felt it was their duty to demonstrate that crime never occurred in their precincts, desk sergeants

who believed that they had a right to arrest and detain citizens without reporting it and, of course, homicide detectives and patrolmen who, when it suited them, argued convincingly that to provide the basic details of any incident might lead to the escape of some heinous felon. Everyone had very good reasons for why nearly every fact about a crime should go unreported.

"In response to such flummery, I had in my wallet, next to my *Baltimore Sun* press pass, a business card for Chief Judge Robert F. Sweeney of the Maryland District Court, with his home phone number on the back. When confronted with a desk sergeant or police spokesman convinced that the public had no right to know who had shot whom in the 1400 block of North Bentalou Street, I would dial the judge.

"And then I would stand, secretly delighted, as yet another police officer learned not only the fundamentals of Maryland's public information law, but the fact that as custodian of public records, he needed to kick out the face sheet of any incident report and open his arrest log to immediate inspection. There are civil penalties for refusing to do so, the judge would assure him. And as chief judge of the District Court, he would declare, I may well invoke said penalties if you go further down this path.

"Delays of even 24 hours? Nope, not acceptable. Requiring written notification from the newspaper? No, the judge would explain. Even ordinary citizens have a right to those reports. And woe to any fool who tried to suggest to His Honor that he would need a 30-day state Public Information Act request for something as basic as a face sheet or an arrest log.

"'What do you need the thirty days for?' the judge once asked a police spokesman on speakerphone.

"'We may need to redact sensitive information,' the spokesman offered.

"'You can't redact anything. Do you hear me? Everything in an initial incident report is public. If the report has been filed by the officer, then give it to the reporter tonight or face contempt charges tomorrow.'"[138]

In the piece, entitled "In Baltimore, No One Left to Press the Police," Simon went on to say that his appeals eventually became less successful, in part because the *Sun* and other papers had fewer reporters pressing for public documents.

Health: A March 2009 report, entitled *The State of Health Journalism in the U.S.*, produced for the Kaiser Family Foundation, found that the number of health reporters has declined even though reader interest in the topic remains strong. Fewer reporters are doing more work, resulting in "a loss of in-depth, enterprise and policy-related stories."[139] The report, by Gary Schwitzer, an associate professor of journalism at the University of Minnesota, concluded:

"Interest in health news is as high as it's ever been, but because the staff and resources available to cover this news have been slashed, the workload on remaining reporters has gone up. Many journalists are writing for multiple platforms, adding multimedia tasks to their workload, having to cover more beats, file more stories, and do it all quicker, in less space, and with fewer resources for training or travel. Demand for 'quick hit' stories has gone up, along with 'news you can use' and 'hyper-local' stories.

"As a result, many in the industry are worried about a loss of in-depth, enterprise and policy-related stories. And newsrooms with reduced staff who are facing pressure to produce are more vulnerable to public relations and advertising pressures. Health news may be particularly challenged by the issues of sponsored segments, purchased stories, and [video news releases] VNRs."[140]

While specific figures are not available to track newspapers' reduction in health reporters, the Kaiser report said that, in a survey of members of the Association of Health Care Journalists, 94 percent of respondents said that "bottom-line pressure in news organizations is seriously hurting the quality of health news."[141] Further, 40 percent of journalists surveyed said that the number of health reporters at their outlets had gone down during their tenure there, and only 16 percent said the number had increased.[142] In addition, "39 percent said it was at least somewhat likely that their own position would be eliminated in the next few years."[143]

Losing journalists who cover such a specialized beat as health is significant. Reporters often spend years building up an expertise in the intricacies of medicine. They must learn how to decipher, explain, and put in context complex, confusing, and often controversial developments in treatment and cures, breakthroughs and disappointments. They need to translate medical speak into plain English. They need to be on top of developments in such areas as pharmaceuticals, clinical testing, hospital care, infectious diseases, and genetics. Theirs are not the kinds of stories that other reporters can easily produce.

In 2009, Ferrel Guillory, director of the University of North Carolina's Program on Public Life, explained in a *North Carolina Medical Journal* article how the latest staff reductions had impacted health reporting at one paper. "Only a few years ago," he wrote, "the *News & Observer* in Raleigh had as many as four reporters assigned to various health-related beats. They covered the big pharmaceutical industry in Research Triangle Park, Chapel Hill-based Blue Cross Blue Shield, the medical schools of the University of North Carolina at Chapel Hill and Duke University, and local hospitals. As of August 2009, the *N&O* has only one reporter with a primary focus on health."[144] Guillory concluded that, although the appetite among the public for health stories remained high, "dependable, continuous" health coverage had diminished.[145] Further, he wrote, journalists (in particular, those on television), focus more on emergencies, public health "scares," and the announcements of new "cures" and technologies than on important policy matters and major trends in health and health care.[146]

Mark Silverman, editor of the *(Nashville) Tennessean* recalls the day he stood with a staff researcher in front of a blackboard listing major stories he had hoped the paper would produce in the coming months. One line listed a story about how the state medical board was allowing incompetent doctors to mistreat patients, be disciplined by local hospitals, and then continue practicing medicine at other locations. But that story idea had an "X" next to it, meaning it would not get done, because the paper now had one health reporter instead of two.[147]

While doing research for a book, Maryn McKenna, a former health writer for the Atlanta Journal Constitution, made an astonishing discovery: The "flesh-eating disease"—MRSA, or methicillin-resistant Staphylococcus aureus—

27 states have no Washington reporters, reports Pew. The number of Washington reporters working for regional papers dropped from 200 in the mid-1990s to 73 at the end of 2008.

was rampant at Folsom Prison in California.[148] In an average year, the highly contagious skin infection kills 19,000 Americans, puts 370,000 in hospitals, and sends an estimated seven million to doctors or emergency rooms. "Some guards are getting infected, seriously infected," McKenna says. "When prison guards go home, they take MRSA with them."[149] Now, families and friends, wives and children, the convenience-store clerk who hands over change or a lottery ticket are susceptible to the infection, which easily spreads outside the prison into the general and unwitting population. At the time, MRSA had been described in the national and specialty press, but no one had written about the situation at Folsom. "I just kept thinking, 'I can't believe nobody's written about this,'" McKenna says. "Why hasn't it been in the L.A. papers, in the San Francisco papers? It's not like those are lazy institutions." She then realized that, as at many newspapers large and small, deep staff cuts had left them unable to cover the story. The crisis went unnoticed until McKenna wrote about it.

Even when they are able to cover a medical story, time-strapped reporters often miss significant pieces of information. In the Kaiser study, more than 75 percent of the 500 stories reviewed concerning treatments, tests, products, or procedures failed to adequately discuss cost.[150] And more than 65 percent failed to quantify the potential benefits and dangers, according to HealthNewsReview.org, a website created by Schwitzer, the author of the Kaiser study.[151]

In the report and on HealthNewsReview.org, complaints abound from seasoned reporters who lament the growth of "press release reporting" and the lack of time they have to check out the veracity of information contained in a press release.[152] Twenty eight percent of health reporters said that they personally get story ideas from public relations firms or marketing outreach somewhat or very often.[153] Among those who work on at least some web content, half said that having to work across different media has resulted in less time and attention for each story, and 59 percent said it meant that they work longer hours.[154]

In an attempt to replace some of the health coverage that disappeared from newspapers, the Kaiser Family Foundation in late 2008 created a nonprofit news service that would produce in-depth coverage of the policy and politics of health care.[155] Kaiser Health News (KHN) hires seasoned journalists to produce stories for its website, KaiserHealthNews.org, and for mainstream news organizations.[156] Drew Altman, president of the Kaiser Family Foundation, explained to the *New York Times* why Kaiser Health News was a top priority: "I just never felt there was a bigger need for great, in-depth journalism on health policy and to be a counterweight to all the spin and misinformation and vested interests that dominate the health care system," he said. "News organizations are every year becoming less capable of producing coverage of these complex issues as their budgets are being slashed."[157] In addition to KHN, a number of smaller nonprofits have emerged to provide health care reporting in various states.[158]

Education: Coverage of schools long has been crucial to most American communities. That is why many papers, in the past, assigned several reporters to the task. That has changed. Few newspapers have eliminated education coverage entirely, but many have assigned larger swaths of the beat to fewer people. The Brookings Institution, which has produced three recent papers on the quality of education reporting, concluded:

> "The most basic problem is a broad decline in the number of education beat reporters. As news organizations have cut budgets, news rooms have seen their beat reporters' responsibilities stretched to general assignment reporting, and their general assignment reporters covering stories that once constituted a beat."[159]

The *News Tribune* in Tacoma, Washington, is typical. "Where we once had two full-time K–12 reporters, a half-time higher ed reporter and another handful of reporters (maybe three) who covered education in the small cities they also covered, we now have—me," reporter Debbie Cafazzo wrote.[160] Cafazzo is responsible for covering 15 school districts, two private liberal arts colleges, a public university, and four community colleges. Private schools are last on her list of priorities. "I spend a lot of time putting out fires, lurching from crisis to crisis, with little time left for deeper level reporting on broad education issues or the humanizing features on great teachers or great kids that I used to do more of in the past," Cafazzo said in her email. "I have a strong personal philosophy that we have an obligation not just to report on the problems in public education (and they are legion), but on the solutions. It's mighty hard, most weeks, to get to the latter."

In Michigan, coverage of juvenile and family courts has become "smaller and smaller over the years," one expert says. "Parents whose rights are terminated who shouldn't be terminated.... It just takes somebody to go down there to get the story, but nobody is ever down there."

Ironically, Cafazzo and every other education reporter and editor interviewed for this report said their editors-in-chief considered education coverage to be central to their paper's mission. They simply do not have the staff to do the job the way they used to. Richard Colvin, former director of the Hechinger Institute, put it this way: "Local coverage has likely not dropped in volume. But it has certainly dropped in ambition.... The beats are not being eliminated and in many places there may be more people writing about schools. But those who do may not do so full time and don't have the leeway to write much of substance. They also have very little capacity to think about broader issues."[161]

The number of education editors at newspapers appears to have declined too, Colvin said. "We used to do a seminar every year and have 30 or 40 education editors come. We abandoned that two years ago because there aren't enough people whose job is education editor anymore. They can't assign more sophisticated stories because they themselves don't understand [educational trends]."[162]

Education reporters interviewed by *Education Next*, a nonpartisan journal of opinion and research on education policy and school reform, described a loss of accountability:

> "They are pushed to write shorter articles, leaving little space for in-depth reporting.... What is lost is that the superintendent will bring in a new program, and nobody will be there to explain to the community whether similar programs have worked or failed in other places." (Richard Whitmire, past president of EWA)

> "We hear from superintendents that the coverage is worse than ever.' All the reporters seem to want is a 'couple of quotes' for a 'sensationalist' story." (Richard Colvin)

> "Those with a vested interest—the teachers unions, realtors—will continue to get their message out. But there will be no one to counter these self-serving opinions." (Jim Bencivenga, former education editor of the *Christian Science Monitor*.)

On the other hand, some of the changes hitting newsrooms may have improved coverage. Although the *Washington Post* has fewer education reporters, long-time journalist Jay Matthews says that by blogging he has gotten closer to real-world classroom issues: "I think that on balance—and this is a very contrarian view—our education coverage is better in the new era than in the old, because we have more contact with readers. Blogs allow us to be in contact with readers—it creates a debate and a back and forth." He mentions a local story he covered about teachers who no longer return graded exams to students. Parents were upset because they could not help their children learn from their mistakes. Matthews said the blog version of his story received about 50 comments from readers all over the country. "Clearly this is something teachers are doing everywhere," he says.[164]

As in other areas, the cutbacks in education reporting have spurred the establishment of a number of non-profits that hire seasoned journalists to cover stories that newspapers miss. Dale Mezzacappa reported on education for the *Philadelphia Inquirer* for 20 years before going to work for the *Philadelphia Public School Notebook*, where she is a contributing editor. Launched as a quarterly in 1994 to cover "underserved" communities in Philadelphia, the *Notebook* is now available on the web. It cannot begin to replace large daily newspapers, Mezzacappa says, but it can fill in some of the gaps.[165] Alan Gottlieb, a former reporter for the *Denver Post*, launched Education News Colorado in January 2008.[166] The website, financed by local foundations, started by focusing on school-related legislation in the state capitol, "because nobody does that anymore," Gottlieb says.[167]

Nonetheless, another Brookings survey reported that Americans still rely heavily on newspapers for school coverage. It concluded:

"Americans want more media coverage of their local schools. In particular, they want more information than they now receive about teacher performance, student academic achievement, crime, and violence in their schools—and more as well about curricula, finances and reform efforts. While there is a great interest in receiving this information through new technological sources more so than ever before Americans however, continue to rely on traditional media, particularly newspapers, for information on their schools."[168]

Local Investigative: Investigative Reporters and Editors (IRE), a national nonprofit aimed at improving the quality of investigative journalism, had 4,000 members in 2010. In 2003, it had 5,391. "There is certainly less investigative reporting and watchdogging occurring than there was a few years ago," says executive director Mark Horvit.[169] Longtime journalist Mary Walton recently assessed the state of investigative journalism for the *American Journalism Review*. While citing several national newspapers that have retained, or even increased, their commitment to investigative journalism, she concluded that the norm was a decline in investigative reporting. "Kicked out, bought out or barely hanging on, investigative reporters are a vanishing species...." Walton wrote. "Assigned to cover multiple beats, multitasking backpacking reporters no longer have time to sniff out hidden stories, much less write them."[170]

One measure of the decline cited by Walton is the drop in submissions for investigative journalism awards. Between 1984 and 2010, submissions to the Pulitzer Prize investigative category fell 21 percent; in the "public service" category, entries dropped 43 percent.[171] IRE contest entries dropped from 563 in 2004 to 455 in 2009, and submissions to the Selden Ring Award, presented by the USC Annenberg School for Communication & Journalism, fell from 88 in 2005 to 64 in 2010.

Gauging the level of investigative reporting can be difficult. Some papers have dedicated "investigative units," while others rely more heavily on stories that develop during the course of normal beat reporting. In 2006, Arizona State University students surveyed the 100 largest newspapers in the country and concluded that 37 percent had no full-time investigative or projects reporter, the majority had two or fewer, and only 10 newspapers had four or more investigative or projects reporters. Of the newspapers participating in the survey, sixty-two percent did not have a single editor specifically designated to work on investigations.[172]

Walton's reporting for *AJR* suggested that a handful of papers and one chain have retained strong investigative teams: the *New York Times*, the *Washington Post*, the *Wall Street Journal*, the *Dallas Morning News*, the *Philadelphia*

"Religion news at the local level is nearly gone," reports Debra Mason, executive director of the Religion Newswriters Association.

Inquirer, the *Milwaukee Journal Sentinel*, the *Oregonian*, the *Seattle Times*, and Gannett. What is more, it is clear that computer-assisted reporting techniques, combined with increased availability of government data, has enabled the smaller cadre of investigative reporters to do valuable work (See Chapter 16, Government Transparency.)

But the norm among local newspapers has been to cut their investigative teams, Walton concluded. She assembled a depressing litany of what has been lost:

> "At the *Palm Beach Post*, an era of fat budgets was dissolving like lard in a hot frying pan. In a single month in 2008, the staff of roughly 300 was reduced to 170, greased by a buyout offer that included health benefits for life. [Tom] Dubocq's prize-winning probes of local corruption had put three county commissioners and assorted others in jail. He had his eye on a fourth commissioner, but instead signed up for the buyout. He was, he says, making too much money. 'I knew ultimately I would get laid off. It was time to make the move.'
>
> "What happens, I ask Dubocq, when people like him vanish from the newsrooms of America?
>
> "'The bad guys get away with stuff.'"[173]

In truth, there is some debate within the profession about whether it is better to assign reporters to investigative units or to beats where they can gather tips as part of a daily routine. When Janet Coats became editor of the *Tampa Tribune* in 2005, she disbanded the investigative team. As Walton reported in *AJR*:

> "Coats' solution was to pair former I-Team members with reporters who could profit from their expertise, but her plan backfired when the Florida housing bubble broke, the economy skidded downward and the *Tribune* newsroom staff shrank from 300 to 180. 'From a practical standpoint,' Coats says, 'someone would get sick, we didn't have enough bodies, so those people got pulled into the breaking news.'"[174]

The dearth of investigative journalism at newspapers has spurred some foundations to finance nonprofits intended to hold feet to the fire. In late 2006, Herb and Marion Sandler made a commitment to donate $10 million a year to fund ProPublica, a nonprofit newsroom pursuing investigative reporting.[175] Led by former *Wall Street Journal* managing editor Paul Steiger, the New York–based outfit has a staff of 32 journalists who produce investigative, public interest stories. In 2010, one of its stories, which was published in the *New York Times Magazine*, won a Pulitzer Prize for Investigative Reporting.[176] "Investigative journalism is at risk," ProPublica's website declares. "Many news organizations have increasingly come to see it as a luxury." Moreover:

> "Profit-margin expectations and short-term stock market concerns, in particular, are making it increasingly difficult for the public companies that control nearly all of our nation's news organizations to afford—or at least to think they can afford—the sort of intensive, extensive and uncertain efforts that produce great investigative journalism.
>
> "More than any other journalistic form, investigative journalism can require a great deal of time and labor to do well—and because the 'prospecting' necessary for such stories inevitably yields a substantial number of 'dry holes,' i.e. stories that seem promising at first, but ultimately prove either less interesting or important than first thought, or even simply untrue and thus unpublishable.
>
> "Given these realities, many news organizations have increasingly come to see investigative journalism as a luxury that can be put aside in tough economic times."[177]

In Chicago, James O'Shea, former managing editor of the *Chicago Tribune* and former editor of the *Los Angeles Times*, created the Chicago News Cooperative. His reasons were similar to Steiger's.[178] At an FCC hearing, O'Shea reflected on the importance of being able to pursue public service journalism over an extended period of time:

"In a series of projects that lasted for more than five years, [*Chicago Tribune* reporters] documented numerous cases of misconduct by prosecutors, torture-induced confessions, violence in the Cook County Jail, defense lawyers who slept through court hearings and judges who were oblivious to the wobbly scales of injustice in their own courtrooms. Thanks in no small part to their work, state officials eventually found that 17 people on death row had been wrongly convicted. After reading the coverage, a Republican Illinois governor slapped a moratorium on capital punishment in Illinois.

"I saw public service journalism in Los Angeles, too, when three reporters from the *Los Angeles Times* documented scandalous conduct in a public hospital just south of Watts. They showed that instead of caring [for] and curing the poor and the sick, the hospital had a long history of killing or harming those it was meant to serve. Their stories chronicled how nurses neglected dying patients; how hospital staffers withheld crucial drugs for patients or administered toxic ones by mistake; and how guards used Taser stun guns on psychiatric patients."[179]

These are not the only beats or functions being harmed. Many kinds of specialty beats have suffered:

> Although there are still dozens of reporters covering the big stories about Congress, there are far fewer covering Congressional delegations—especially their work on local issues. Twenty-seven states have no Washington reporters, according to a study by the Pew Research Center's Project for Excellence in Journalism. The number of papers with bureaus in the capital has dropped by about half since the mid-1980s; the number of reporters working for regional papers dropped from 200 in the mid-1990s to 73 at the end of 2008.[180] The Down East website in Maine, which has no Washington reporters, described well the implications: "In place of having someone on the scene, Maine news organizations rely on interviews with delegation members to determine what they're up to. This method has several obvious drawbacks, the most glaring being that our elected officials in the nation's capital aren't likely to tell us anything they don't want us to know. Maine voters are dependent on the delegation's assessment of itself."[181]

> "Religion news at the local level is nearly gone," reports Debra Mason, executive director of the Religion Newswriters Association. Although religion has taken root in a few national online venues—the Washington Post, USA Today, CNN, and the Huffington Post—newspapers have mostly dropped local religion coverage. "At smaller papers—100,000 circulation or less—the religion beat, even as a half-time beat, is nearly extinct," she says. Larger papers that used to have multiperson reporting teams are mostly down to one. Mason believes that nonprofits will need to step in to help provide local religion coverage.[182]

> Local business reporting has often suffered despite its importance to the local economy. "It's not a market that's well served," says Andrew Lack, CEO of Bloomberg Multimedia.[183] What is more, Lack says, the drops in statehouse reporting hinder the ability of private businesses to get a rich feel for economic trends and conditions: "There isn't anyone covering the bond issue that's destroying the state economy." Not surprisingly, a study by Michigan State University found more coverage in newspapers of crime and disasters than local business.[184]

> Coverage of border crime and immigration has suffered at a time when concern about both topics has risen. At one time, the *Dallas Morning News* had 13 reporters in its Mexico City bureau; now it has one. When Michel Marizco began covering border issues for the *Arizona Daily Star* in 2003, he says, there were nine border reporters at six newspapers in Arizona. Now there is one.[185]

> The Society of Environmental Journalists had 430 newspaper reporters as members in 2004. Six years later, there were 256.[186] "In a topic like environment, people spend a lot of years building up a knowledge base, and when you lose that, you have to rebuild it over a long time," says Beth Parke, executive director of the Society

"I think that on balance—and this is a very contrarian view—our education coverage is better in the new era than in the old because we have more contact with readers," says Jay Mathews of *The Washington Post.*

of Environmental Journalists."[187] Tim Wheeler, who reports on the environment for the *Baltimore Sun,* says, "The work cycle here has changed.… We're much more like wire service reporters than we were before. My job is to feed the beast."[188]

Finally, there is an intangible factor: when a town ends up with only one reporter covering a particular beat, the reporter no longer has the fear of being scooped by the competition. It is impossible to quantify the impact, but there is no doubt that for some reporters competition spurs greater quality.

Hamsterization

As newsrooms have shrunk, the job of the remaining reporters has changed. They typically face rolling deadlines as they post to their newspaper's website before, and after, writing print stories. Some are required to blog and tweet as well, some to produce videos. The good news is, they can write shorter, more focused stories for the print edition of the paper and provide longer, more detailed versions online that can be enhanced and updated as events progress. However, these additional responsibilities—and having to learn the new technologies to execute them—are time-consuming, and come at a cost. In many newsrooms, old-fashioned, shoe-leather reporting—the kind where a reporter goes into the streets and talks to people or probes a government official—has been sometimes replaced by Internet searches.

Newspapers have tried to become more like the new medium—emphasizing speed and dissemination through multiple platforms. But that drive can take a toll on quality. In an article in the *Columbia Journalism Review* in the fall of 2010, Dean Starkman likened newspaper reporters to hamsters on a wheel:

> "The Hamster Wheel isn't speed; it's motion for motion's sake. The Hamster Wheel is volume without thought. It is news panic, a lack of discipline, an inability to say no.… But it's more than just mindless volume. It's a recalibration of the news calculus. Of the factors that affect the reporting of news, an under-appreciated one is the risk/reward calculation that all professional reporters make when confronted with a story idea: How much time versus how much impact?

> "This informal vetting system is surprisingly ruthless and ultimately efficient for one and all. The more time invested, the bigger the risk, but also the greater potential glory for the reporter, and the greater value to the public (can't forget them!). Do you fly to Chicago to talk to that guy about that thing? Do you read that bankruptcy examiner's report? Or do you do three things that are easier?

> "Journalists will tell you that where once newsroom incentives rewarded more deeply reported stories, now incentives skew toward work that can be turned around quickly and generate a bump in Web traffic.…

> "None of this is written down anywhere, but it's real. The Hamster Wheel, then, is investigations you will never see, good work left undone, public service not performed."[189]

Going Forward

Though we have spoken of "newspapers" and "the Internet" as two separate things, the distinction is becoming less meaningful. When experts talk about the decline of "newspapers," they really mean the decline of paper-based newspapers and the traditional business models that enabled them to hire large staffs. In fact, from a traffic perspective, newspapers have come to dominate the Internet on the local level. An analysis conducted in early 2010 by the Project for Excellence in Journalism and the Pew Internet & American Life Project concluded that the websites of "legacy" news organizations—mainly major newspapers and cable television stations—dominate online news space in both traffic and loyalty. "Of the top 199 sites in our analysis, 67 percent are from legacy media, and they account for 66 percent of the traffic. In all, 48 percent are from newspapers, and 19 percent from all other legacy media," the study reported.[190] The Future of Media project's analysis of online local news sources in three cities—Toledo, Richmond, and Seattle—came to the same conclusion. In each city, the number one online source for news was the website of the city's long-standing newspaper.

The Internet has clearly increased the reach of some newspapers. In May 2010, NYTimes.com had 32 million unique visitors, equivalent to nearly one-quarter of the 123 million individuals who visited all newspaper websites. By contrast, daily circulation of the *New York Times* print edition was 876,638 in September 2010.[191]

What is less clear is whether newspapers will be able to carry their online advantage in brand and reach into business models that can sustain substantial newsrooms. In the Internet section, (see Chapter 4, Internet) we explain why ad-only models have not gotten them there. As a result, a number of newspapers have spent much of the past decade experimenting with other revenue models.[192] In 2010, Gannett implemented pay walls at the websites of three papers and announced plans for the creation of page design hubs for its community newspapers in five cities.[193] The *New York Times* website, generally considered the most innovative newspaper site, erected a metered pay wall in 2011.[194] (See Chapter 5, Mobile and Chapter 25, How Big is the Gap?) The *Times* and the *Wall Street Journal* have introduced beefed up local editions, raising the possibility that some of the local reporting gap will be filled by national newspapers attempting to increase their circulations in certain cities. Some papers, such as the *Tampa Tribune*, are trying to recoup classified ad money by creating coupon businesses through mobile platforms.[195] Many newspapers are offering iPad and phone apps, and News Corp. has launched TheDaily, an iPad-only newspaper.[196] It is too early to say whether these experiments will pay off, but it is worth noting that most of the newspaper apps offered for the iPad are free. (See Chapter 5, Mobile.)

What is more, while legacy newspapers used to lag in innovation, some have become quite creative in their use of social media, database journalism, and community engagement. For instance, the Journal Register Company had its papers create new web operations using free, publically available tools, enlisting community members in the news creation process.[197] Many have made great strides in using web tools and reader contributions to beef up "hyperlocal" coverage of neighborhoods. "There is a new formula typically relying on some professional news staff, editing and coordinating, but with most of the content coming from volunteer or semi-professional writers based in the communities they cover," Pew's *State of the News Media 2011* reported.[198] Blogs, crime maps, user generated video and photos, social networking, photo galleries—many of them innovations pioneered by independent websites—can now be found on most newspaper sites.

From a traffic perspective, newspapers have become dominant sources of online local news.

Bankrupt newspapers are expected to re-emerge soon, with less debt. Others are expected to stabilize or, at the very least, shrink at a slower pace. As the nation climbs out of the recession, most newspapers that have survived will continue to do so, at least for the time being. The real question is how much in-depth local reporting will they be able to sustain.

Conclusions

Throughout the history of this nation, newspapers have provided the bulk of the civically important functions that democracy requires. Good TV, radio, and web operations do this, too, but traditionally, and currently, broadcast and Internet media rely heavily on newspapers to provide original reporting on topics that matter.

In this section, we reviewed the evolution of newspapers and the causes of the newspaper collapse. We noted a peculiar phenomenon: despite the financial collapse, many newspapers in the past decade still managed to break even or make profits. This raises a provocative thought: Perhaps we have not gone from an era when newspapers could be profitable to one in which they cannot, but rather from an era when newspapers could be wildly profitable to one in which they can be merely moderately profitable or break even. It is an important distinction, because it means that certain public policy remedies—for instance, making it easier for newspapers to reestablish themselves as non-profit entities—might be more fruitful than in the past. Or it may mean that wealthy individuals—entrepreneurs and philanthropists—will view newspaper ownership in a different light than most corporate leaders have: not as a profit-making venture, but as a way to provide an important civic benefit that will help to sustain democracy.

In the second part of this section, we attempted to answer the question, "So what?"

Compared with job-loss rates in other industries, the number of out-of-work journalists does not in itself constitute a national crisis. The real question is, what damage is their absence from newsrooms doing to communities and citizens? Surely, there was a great deal of duplication at these fat-and-happy newspapers. And surely some editors, when instructed to cut, tried to preserve their papers' most important functions. In addition, we make no claims that all stories of importance were covered during the "golden age" of journalism; there always were holes in coverage, important matters neglected in favor of sexier stories. But just because a system has serious problems does not mean it cannot get worse—and that is exactly what happened.

Proving a negative (i.e. what is *not* being covered now) is hard, but we believe that the material presented above—based on a wide range of independent studies, journalistic accounts, and interviews by researchers for this report—gives a glimpse of the severity of the problem. Although in most cases newspapers have not gone from massive coverage of a topic to no coverage of it all, now stretched reporters and editors not only have to do more with less, they have to do it *faster*, with fewer checks and balances. The combination of time pressures and the influence of the web has led a stunning 62 percent of newspaper editors to say that "the Internet" has caused "loosening standards" for journalism.[199]

Experts tell us that these days, much of reporters' time is taken up on reactive stories, describing what happened on a more superficial level, rather than digging deep into the causes and implications of a development. They have less time to investigate, to question, to take a story to the next level. Fewer newsrooms than ever can afford to deploy reporters to work on labor-intensive stories. That means not only fewer investigative stories, but, more commonly, less daily beat reporting about municipal government, schools, the environment, local businesses, and other topics that impact Americans' future, their safety, their livelihood, and their everyday life.

In very real ways, the dramatic newspaper-industry cutbacks appear to have caused genuine harm to American citizens and local communities.

2 Radio

WHEN RADIO TRANSMISSION WAS FIRST PROPOSED more than 100 years ago, even Thomas Edison was skeptical. Upon hearing that his former assistant, Reginald A. Fessenden, thought it was possible to transmit voices wirelessly, Edison replied, "Fezzie, what do you say are men's chances of jumping over the moon? I think one as likely as the other."[1]

For his first transmission, in December 1906 from Brant Rock, Massachusetts, Fessenden broadcast a Christmas-themed speech and music. It mainly reached radio operators aboard ships, who expressed surprise at hearing "angels' voices" on their wireless radios.[2] But the medium vividly demonstrated its power in 1912, when the sinking *Titanic* used radio to send out one of the first SOS signals ever sent from a ship. One nearby ship, the *Carpathia*, heard the distress call through its wireless receiver and rescued 712 passengers from the ocean. When the *Titanic* survivors arrived in New York City, they went to thank Guglielmo Marconi, regarded as the "father of radio," for their lives.[3]

But it was a boxing match in 1921 between Jack Dempsey and Frenchman George Carpentier that transformed radio from a one-to-one into a one-to-many medium. Technicians, according to one scholar, connected a phone with "an extremely long wire that ran out of the stadium and all the way to Hoboken, New Jersey, to a giant radio transmitter. To that transmitter was attached a giant antenna, some six hundred feet long, strung between a clock tower and a nearby building." The blow-by-blow coverage was beamed to hundreds of thousands of listeners in "radio halls" in 61 cities.[4] As the *Wireless Age* put it: "Instantly, through the ears of an expectant public, a world event had been 'pictured' in all its thrilling details.... A daring idea had become a fact."[5]

The Birth of Radio News

Radio boomed after World War I, as department stores and manufacturers of receivers used broadcasts to promote radio sales. Commercial broadcasting began in 1922, and between 1922 and 1923 the number of licenses issued by the Department of Commerce rose from 30 to 556. The number of radios sold rose from 100,000 to over 500,000.[6]

As the number of stations grew and programming became more varied, news began to play a role, initially with broadcasters reading newspapers aloud as filler. Then news and political coverage expanded to include emergency news alerts, presidential speeches, and special news events like the Scopes "Monkey Trial" in Tennessee.[7] But in 1925, news and political coverage still made up only 2.5 percent of programs broadcast.[8]

> Radio audiences in general have declined little over the last decade. But the number of people who said that they listened to news on the radio dropped from 54 percent in 1991 to 34 percent in 2010.

The 1930s saw the rise of broadcast networks, fueled by advertising. This in turn increased pressure to develop new programming.[9] In the fall of 1930, NBC-Blue, one of the four major radio networks of the period, became the first to introduce news as a regular feature in radio programming when it launched a 15-minute, five-day-a-week newscast by Lowell Thomas.[10]

At first, newspapers did not feel threatened, in part because they owned or were affiliated with between 50 and 100 of the nation's 500 stations.[11] Beginning around the time of the Great Depression, however, the print media came to believe that radio news was in fact undercutting their business by using news from the Associated Press (AP), United Press, and International News Service—the same wire services they relied on.[12]

Newspapers saw their combined ad revenue decrease from $800 million before October 1929 to $450 million in 1933.[13] Meanwhile, radio revenues expanded despite the Depression, from $40 million in 1929 to $80 million in 1932.[14] After the 1932 election, a survey of AP's newspaper membership found that 70 percent opposed giving AP news services to any radio stations under any circumstances. These tensions were further aggravated in 1933, when

President-elect Franklin D. Roosevelt was nearly assassinated in Miami and a CBS radio reporter got the story first.[15]

In December 1933, newspaper stakeholders banded together around what would become known as the Biltmore Agreement. Under pressure, the major radio networks, with their affiliates following suit, agreed to stop gathering their own news, to air news bulletins no more than five minutes in length, and to air morning news only after 9:30 a.m. and evening news only after 9 p.m. so as not to impact newspaper sales.[16]

But the independent stations continued to use the wire services, and newspapers became increasingly interested in radio as a profitable opportunity, so within a few years the Biltmore Agreement fell apart.[17] Soon after, the number of radio stations owned by or affiliated with newspapers doubled from 15 percent to 30 percent, leaving J. R. Knowland, publisher of the *Oakland Tribune* to concede, "We cannot hope to sweep back the ocean with a broom…. Radio is here to stay."[18]

During World War II, radio news took center stage as Americans sought reliable, up-to-the-minute information on developments in Europe. In response to the demand for instantaneous updates, CBS's news chief pioneered a broadcasting practice in which reporters were stationed in different locations around the world to give real-time commentary directly from the site of a news event.[19] Both NBC and CBS set up foreign news bureaus for this purpose. In 1944, CBS scheduled 1,497 hours of news programming, and NBC aired 1,726 hours. Americans could follow the war live from their living rooms, from events like the D-Day invasion to Japan's final surrender.[20] For those who bemoan the role of amateur journalists in today's Internet startups, it is worth noting that one of that era's big new stars of radio, Edward R. Murrow, had little real journalism experience when he started broadcasting from the rooftops of London for CBS radio.[21]

A national poll conducted in 1944 found that over 50 percent of Americans cited radio as their most accurate source of political information, while only 25 percent chose newspapers.[22] Stations grasped the significance of radio's new role and dramatically increased news programming. After World War II, one poll found that 13 percent of radio programs broadcast in 1946 included news and politics, a sharp increase from 1932, when only 2.6 percent of radio programs did.[23]

> **Mel Karmazin, former CBS Station Group President:**
> "A lot of these larger companies abandoned what had made these radio stations enormously successful, which was local, local, local."

After World War II ended, consumers' appetite for goods (such as radio and phonograph equipment), suppressed during wartime, surged, resulting in an overwhelming demand for new AM, FM, and television licenses. The FCC was faced with competing requests for spectrum from FM radio inventor Edwin Armstrong, on the one hand, and television stations, on the other. The FCC ultimately decided to take away Armstrong's FM frequencies and give them to television broadcasters. FM was reassigned to different bands on the VHF spectrum, rendering between 400,000 and 500,000 existing FM receivers obsolete.[24] The public, advertisers, and investors lost confidence in FM, and it would not be until the 1960s that FM radio would capture the public's interest.

Since radio stations could no longer rely on war news to fill airtime, news directors began to focus on local and regional stories. This trend was further encouraged by the release of an FCC report, *Public Service Responsibility of Broadcast Licensees*, which stated that the FCC would consider the inclusion of local news programs to be a positive factor when deciding whether to grant or renew licenses.[25]

TV stations began to lure talent away from radio, forcing radio stations to develop new programming strategies in order to better appeal to listeners—for instance, shifting emphasis from prime time to "drive time" to reach people during their commute to and from work.[26]

During the 1960s, some stations experimented with all-news formats. Radio pioneer Gordon McLendon introduced all-news programming on Mexican station XETRA in the early 1960s and then brought it to WNUS in Chicago in 1964. Impressed with his success, several major-market stations, including WINS-AM in New York, converted to all-news a year later.[27] At about the same time that all-news was taking off, KGO-AM in San Francisco launched the first news/talk format, in which conversation was scheduled between lengthy news blocks. By the 1970s this hybrid approach became more popular than its all-news predecessor, and similar stations sprang up in other cities, including KYW in Philadelphia and WMAL in Washington, D.C.[28]

Although they initially focused on national news, many all-news stations soon found a niche covering local events. For example, in the 1950s WMAL's broadcasting consisted of 75 percent national news and 25 percent local news, but by 1960 it was 90 percent local. Andy Ockershausen, WMAL's general manager, explained, "No one else was doing it and it gave us a reason to exist.... It helped us better serve the community and our advertisers loved it." They were fortunate, Ockershausen said, that the *Evening Star* newspaper, the owner of WMAL at the time, allowed them to make this commitment to local news.[29]

Other all-news stations, such as Chicago's WLS-AM in the 1970s, carried news around the clock, with five-minute newscasts at night and two-minute casts from 6 a.m. to 6 p.m. daily. To comply with the FCC's "ascertainment" requirements (See Chapter 26, Broadcast Radio and Television.), WLS broadcast a half-hour agricultural report every morning at 5 a.m. to serve farmers in rural areas of the Midwest.[30]

Meanwhile, music was becoming increasingly popular on the airwaves. Largely because FM stations aired music with higher fidelity sound (and in part because the FCC had stopped issuing AM licenses),[31] FM radio became the fastest-growing segment of American broadcasting.[32] In 1976, FM listeners made up 40 percent of the U.S. radio audience, and FM stations earned 20 percent of all radio income; by 1986, FM listeners made up 70 percent of the audience, and FM stations earned 70 percent of radio income. As a result, many AM stations switched from music to more specialized formats, such as news, talk, and sports.[33]

Even many stations that were not "all-news" offered some news and public affairs—typically an average of five minutes of news per hour, which focused heavily on local stories or the local angle of national and worldwide headlines.[34] During this period, most radio stations producing news hired a news director to manage the news staff, supervise the news budget, deal with the radio technologies involved in news operations, and, in general, oversee the station's news coverage.[35]

Deregulation

The FCC's deregulatory policies reshaped the radio landscape in the 1980s. Up until that time, radio stations had been offering extensive news and public affairs programming, in part because that's what was encouraged—and to some extent required—by regulators. While local news radio, unlike local television news, was not a guaranteed profit center, stations that offered news benefited from FCC guidelines that guaranteed fast-track processing of station license renewals if the stations offered a certain amount of non-entertainment (i.e., news and public affairs) programming. However, in 1981, the FCC eliminated the guidelines, specifying that news and public affairs should account for 8 percent of programming for AM stations and 6 percent of programming for FM stations. Optimistically, the FCC concluded, "We are convinced that absent these guidelines significant amounts of non-entertainment programming of a variety of types will continue on radio."[36]

At least in terms of local news programming, this prediction proved to be wrong. Seventeen percent of major-market stations—those serving populations of one million or more—experienced cutbacks in news programming, while only 2.1 percent reported increases, according to a 1987 study. Among large-market stations—those serving populations between 250,000 and one million—13.5 percent said that deregulation had caused cutbacks in news programming, while 3.8 percent reported gains.[37] Scholars, such as John Kittross of Temple University, argued that public affairs programming, including debates, documentaries, and discussions, had substantially declined due to deregulation.[38]

Additionally, since the FCC no longer required stations to air news programming, many station executives de-

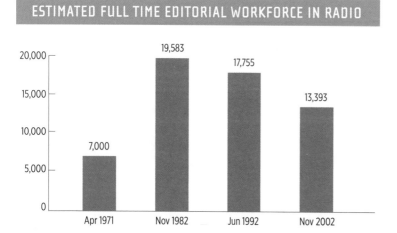

ESTIMATED FULL TIME EDITORIAL WORKFORCE IN RADIO

Source: David H. Weaver, Randal A. Beam, Bonnie J. Brownlee, Paul S. Voakes, and Cleveland G. Wilhoit[41]

manded that news operations show profits, which made it difficult to sustain local news programming.[39] At most stations, news coverage was cut to fit into a one-to-four-minute slot, in which one or two major stories were highlighted. Some FM music stations relied on their DJs to provide commentary on current events; others outsourced news reporting to distribution services.[40] News staff positions, which had risen from 1971 to 1982, declined by several thousand from 1982 to 2002, as the chart at left illustrates.

In 1989 and 1992, the FCC loosened the ownership rules.[42] In 1996, Congress enacted the Telecommunications Act of 1996, which lengthened radio license terms to eight years, revised the process for reviewing license renewals, and dramatically expanded the number of radio stations an entity could own, eliminating the nationwide cap altogether and setting local limits based on the size of the market. These new ownership provisions had an immediate impact. Rapid consolidation yielded a sharp rise in profits and station valuations as corporations like Clear Channel combined facilities and staff under one roof. Merger and acquisition activity was intense. According to one industry publication, 2,045 stations were sold the year the act went into effect.[43] Clear Channel grew from 196 stations in 1997 to a total of 1,183 stations (AM and FM) in 2005. (The second largest radio station owner, Cumulus Broadcasting, had 297 stations.)[44]

John Hogan, Clear Channel's CEO, says that radio is not the highly consolidated industry many people believe it to be:

> "We are the largest radio company in the country—we own 857 [FM] radio stations, which sure sounds like a lot—but in fact radio is the least consolidated medium that I can think of. There are well over 10,000 radio stations in the country, and we own less than 1,000. There isn't anybody who's an 800-pound gorilla, despite what people have been led to believe.

> "There are enormous economic challenges, there are enormous technological and, in turn, competitive challenges, and while I think radio is a terrific medium and important medium, I think it is as challenged today as it has ever been."[45]

Other radio industry executives, like Jeff Smulyan, CEO of Emmis Communications, argue that consolidation was necessary for firms to survive—and keep pace with the rest of the economy.[46]

Whether or not consolidation was imperative, its impact has been to make the industry much more bottom-line focused. Analyst Zemira Jones argues:

> "This new breed of group owner was much more focused on efficiency and bottom-line performance and top-line growth of audience and revenue. In the 1990s top-line growth was being taken for granted by many of these operators as well as their investors who encouraged the mind-set of leverage, expansion, and quarter-to-quarter growth."[47]

The Current State of Radio

In many ways, radio seems surprisingly healthy. Audiences have declined very little over the last decade and almost 240 million Americans—more than 90 percent of the population over age 12—listened to at least some radio during an average week in the fall of 2010.[48]

It is true that radio revenues declined in 2008 and 2009 due to the recession, but those declines came after growth in revenues over the prior decade, as the chart on the next page demonstrates.

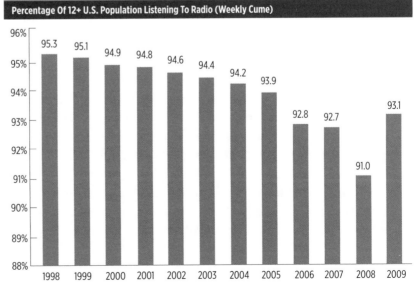

RADIO AUDIENCE 1998–2009

Percentage Of 12+ U.S. Population Listening To Radio (Weekly Cume)

Year	Percentage
1998	95.3
1999	95.1
2000	94.9
2001	94.8
2002	94.6
2003	94.4
2004	94.2
2005	93.9
2006	92.8
2007	92.7
2008	91.0
2009	93.1

Source: Arbitron. Radio Today Report: General Listening Series 1998–2010.[49]

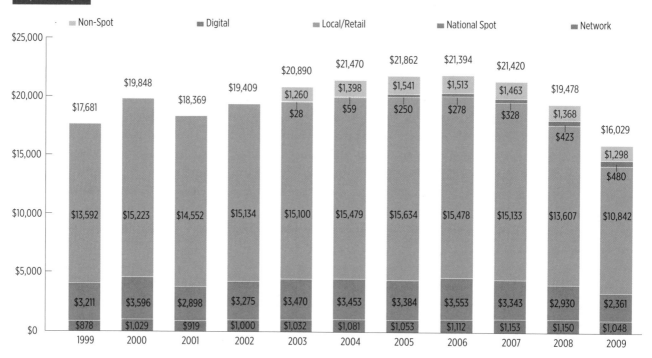

Source: SNL Kagan 10-Year Historical Broadcast Revenue Report: June 29, 2010

With respect to profits, a 2007 FCC staff paper concluded that radio companies earn higher gross profits but lower net profits than the average S&P 500 firm, often because they carry high debt loads and pay high levels of interest on that debt.[50] Still, radio station profits have remained over 20 percent (with a couple of exceptions) in the last few years.

Local News Radio

But while radio in general has fared reasonably well, local news radio has not. In the mid-1980s, the Radio Information Center reported that there were 50 commercial all-news stations throughout the United States,[51] but in 2010 there were only 30 all-news stations.[52] Commercial all-news stations serve no more than 30 to 40 percent of the nation's listeners.[53]

Whether this is the result of consolidation or other factors—such as the growth of the Internet or the economics of news versus entertainment—it is clear that fewer people are relying on radio for their news. The number of people who said that they listened to news on the radio dropped from 54 percent in 1991 to 34 percent in 2010, according to a Pew Research Center study.[54]

This is a much sharper decline than that seen in overall radio listenership, which remained above 90 percent, during the same period.[55] (Only newspaper readership suffered a greater decline, from 56 percent in 1991 to 31 percent in 2010; while TV news viewership fell from 68 percent to 58 percent during the same period.)[56]

In a recent interview, one of the major architects of radio consolidation, former president of CBS Station Group, Mel Karmazin, explained how competitive pressures led to the decline in local news programming:

> "The last thing I wanted to do was commoditize radio. Every station was different, had a different audience, a different fabric, and by putting all these things together you're going to homogenize and not make it successful standing alone. So, long story short—CBS goes in the same direction as Clear Channel, as ABC, as every other company, and in the course of that consolidation and the course of trying to figure out how to save money—well, gee, you don't need this many reporters on the street and you don't need as many people doing public affairs programming…. A lot of these larger companies abandoned what had made these radio stations enormously successful, which was local, local, local."[58]

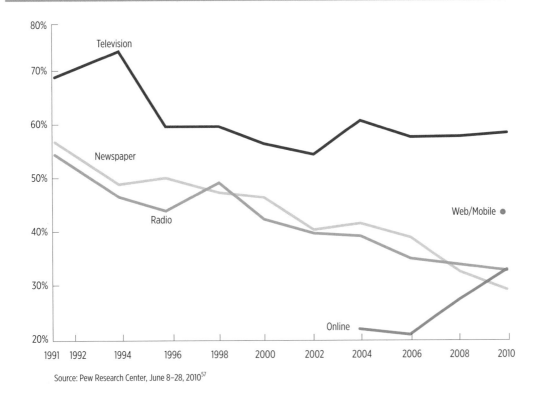

Source: Pew Research Center, June 8–28, 2010[57]

Longtime radio consultant Paul Jacobs, a partner at Jacobs Media, says consolidation has hurt local programming:

"You could almost measure the impact of deregulation [by] reading the trades and headlines. [The headlines about radio] went from content-based stories about great content and great personalities to Wall Street–based stories on radio. All of a sudden, the trades were filled with companies buying others, consolidation, and everything else. The conversations we had to have with [our clients], radio owners, changed dramatically because we had to help them figure out how to completely re-integrate their operations, bring competition into their buildings, and, from a programming standpoint, how to take advantage of owning a lot of stations.... The headcount at radio stations decreased dramatically. Local content, especially news, has disappeared. In a lot of cases, local programming and local focus have deteriorated and have been replaced by a lot of syndicated programming."[59]

The "hub-and-spoke" system enables large radio conglomerates to have their urban stations produce and package local news stories for sister stations in distant markets. Lee Hood, an assistant professor at Loyola University Chicago's School of Communication, found that by 2007 more than 40 percent of all radio stations were outsourcing news.[60] When Clear Channel owned a station in Casper, Wyoming, its news was produced in Denver, more than 200 miles away, and just 4 percent of the stories related to Casper. When the station was sold, however, the news was no longer produced remotely and 41 percent of the stories were local. Hood explained:

"If you listened to Casper news that came out of Denver, you would have thought Casper was a very different place from what I was experiencing on the ground. I was there when they had a parade, and it was like a local holiday with people standing three deep on the sidewalk, and not a single bit got on the newscasts. In addition, there was a forest fire outside of town, and that did not make the local newscast produced out of Denver. I was astonished as to how different my experience in Casper was compared to what I was hearing on the remotely produced newscast."[61]

On the other hand, John Hogan, Clear Channel CEO, explains that radio station owners use the hub-and-spoke system to tailor the news for local audiences.

"I am not sure where the whole notion of hub-and-spoke or that nomenclature comes from, because I don't think of it that way at all. What I think of is connectivity between markets.

"What we do is gather news from any one of our markets, and we have a number of locations where we have better, more qualified readers of the news. We become more efficient: instead of having news gatherers and anchors in every market, we have news gatherers and anchors in some markets. It's a way for us to make sure we have the highest-quality presentation of the news. The economy has gotten tougher and tougher and tougher, and we've had to stretch to be able to be as innovative as we can, and that's one of the things that we use."[62]

J. P. Skelley, a reporter for KORN-AM in Mitchell, South Dakota—a station that has retained its commitment to locally produced news through several changes of ownership—says:

"From what I have seen, the larger groups such as Clear Channel are focused on the bottom line, [and] when those companies acquire stations, the first thing they want to do is see how much they can get away with."[63]

But Clear Channel's Hogan notes that the content that is of most interest to local listeners is not always local news. When it comes to radio news, he says, often the Clear Channel stations are giving the audience exactly what they want:

"The way that we view local is you've got to give the people what is compelling or interesting for them. [A]nd sometimes it might be the school board and sometimes it might be something about Britney Spears and sometimes it might be something about what's happening in Washington, D.C. We can't possibly provide resources [enough to] have somebody from every market in D.C. or somebody from every market focused on these entertainment pieces, so we use content from our stations in Los Angeles, which are closer to entertainment. We use content from [our] stations in Washington, and we share those things that are most interesting and most compelling and those things get repurposed. So that way, we have the widest variety in the biggest menu of choices for our listeners. People want to be informed and entertained, and they don't particularly care where it comes from as long as it connects with them—that's what they're really interested in."[64]

Whether driven by user interest or management preference, radio news staffing has declined sharply. Robert Papper, director of the Radio Television Digital News Association's RTDNA/Hofstra University Annual Survey, says that the survey sample size makes it difficult to use precise numbers, but the trend is clear: "I can say this without a doubt—there are far fewer stations doing news than 10 years ago, there are far fewer people hired by commercial radio to work in the newsrooms, and the median number of people employed in a commercial radio newsroom has been 'one' for quite a few years."[65]

The latest surveys of commercial radio newsroom staffing indicate, similarly, that most radio newsrooms, if they exist, are small. In 2009, the typical median-size radio station had just one employee working on the news. At the same time, the typical radio news director was overseeing news on three stations, and more than 80 percent of news directors surveyed said they were stretched thinner with station responsibilities that extend well beyond the news.[66] In 2009, 30.7 percent of news directors oversaw the news on more than three stations, while in 2010, 48.5 percent did. In markets where more than one related station runs news, almost two-thirds (66.2 percent) share a centralized newsroom.[67]

The decline in local news coverage is sharply evident in minority-owned radio stations, as well. As one news commentary noted, "Black-oriented radio journalism in the nation's capital has plummeted from 21 reporters at three stations, 30 years ago, to four reporters at two stations [in 2003]."[68] (See Chapter 23, Diversity.)

In the words of one of radio's harshest critics, Andrew Jay Schwartzman, professor of communications at Johns Hopkins University and senior vice president and policy director of the Media Access Project:

"It [local radio] has largely abdicated its responsibility to generate local news coverage to public radio."

The aggregate numbers would be even lower if it weren't for a few extraordinary stations that continue to employ larger news staffs to produce local programming, and thus skew the numbers upward. For the past ten years, one such station, 95.9 WATD-FM in Marshfield, Massachusetts, has earned the Associated Press "Bay State Award," which honors the state's best local news operation. Station owner, Ed Perry, and his dozen staffers, plus a squad of volunteers, produce from 15 to 20 original news stories a day. Perry describes his station's niche in the local market:

> "In certain times, we would be lucky to have 500 people listening, and that would be when we do special locally serviced things, say a high school football game where we are just doing one community in the area. Then, there will be times when we have 50,000 people listening because there is a storm coming, or something has happened to cause people to turn on the radio, and we are one of the few local voices that has the capacity to really get people out in the field."[69]

Perry explained that he finances the radio station by renting broadcast towers on his property to cellular telephone operators and other tenants.[70]

Dan Dillion, news director at KFDI-AM/FM Radio in Wichita, Kansas, says each of his six full-time reporters is expected to be a general assignment reporter and news anchor, in addition to covering particular beats (e.g. county government, the courthouse, sports):

> "This year, more of our reporters are taking video and posting it on our website and posting still photos.... More listeners are going to digital devices such as Blackberries and iPhones, but we still have a number of people, especially in South Central Kansas, who rely on getting the newscast at the top of each hour."[71]

Dillon says the entire focus of his newsroom is local news, and it generates good ratings for the station, which has been in business for 50 years.[72]

Local ownership helps, says Edward Esposito, vice president of information media for Rubber City Radio Group in Akron, Ohio:

> "We are owned by a local guy, who lives up the road. We have nine people full time in my news department, down from a high of 16, which I had last year [and] most of whom I got rid of were the part-timers. It's still very important to [the owner] for us to be a creator of content so he can make those individual decisions and say, ' You know what, I'm good at taking less profit margin' or 'I'm willing to stomach a loss in this line item as long as I can generate revenue in another item.' Every time Akron City Council meets, we are there.... We also cover the school board meetings."[73]

Esposito says it costs in the range of $600,000 to $700,000 a year to run a middle-market-size radio newsroom in America, and that in his case the highest cost is personnel.[74]

Many of the successful all news station are located in the largest markets —not surprising given the high fixed costs of creating a news operation. Many of them are CBS affiliates. In big cities, "all-news radio is stronger than it has ever been, in terms of popularity," says Harvey Nagler, vice president at CBS News Radio.[75] They often rank among the top ten radio stations in the markets. WTOP-FM, in Washington, D.C. is the highest-billing radio station in the nation even though the station services the ninth-ranked market.[76] "We do this by pushing out useful news and information on FM radio, on HD radio, on streaming audio, on podcasts, text messages, email alerts, tweeters, and tweets," says Jim Farley, vice president of news for Bonneville International, which owns the station.[77] Other successful all-news stations

"The way that we view local is you've got to give the people what is compelling or interesting for them," says Clear Channel's Hogan. "[A]nd sometimes it might be the school board and sometimes it might be something about Britney Spears and sometimes it might be something about Washington, D.C."

"Local content, especially news, has disappeared," says Paul Jacobs of Jacobs Media. "In a lot of cases, local programming and local focus have deteriorated and have been replaced by a lot of syndicated programming."

include KCBS in San Francisco, WCBS in New York, KYW in Philadelphia, WBZ in Boston, and WBBM in Chicago,[78] which draws up to a million listeners a week.[79]

One big-city station, CBS-owned KRLD-AM in Dallas, announced in September 2010 that it would be abandoning its news/talk format for all-news programming. The last time a Dallas station attempted all-news was in February 1996, but the station—94.9 KEWS-FM—dropped the format before the year's end.[80] Though the number of all-news stations has risen from 27 in 2009 to 30 in 2010, CBS' Nagler said he did not believe this development signified future growth in the number of all-news stations beyond the large metropolitan areas. The stations that are currently succeeding have been building brand and audience for a long time, and starting an all news station from scratch would be quite difficult, says Dan Mason of CBS Radio. "Longevity is key factor," he said. "It is not easy to build a news radio on day one."[81]

Radio's defenders, like Barbara Cochran, president emeritus of RTDNA, argue that some radio stations with local news reporting infrastructure do make an attempt to provide information in local communities, especially in times of crisis, like the 2010 snowstorm in the Washington, D.C., area. "If you were one of the thousands who were without electric power for several hours or days, you could still keep informed with your battery-operated radio, thanks to all-news station WTOP," she says.[82]

According to an Arbitron study, radio played a critical role during the hurricanes that hit Florida and the Gulf Coast in September 2004: "In many cases, while millions of people were without electricity, radio proved to be their only source of information."[83]

Ham radio operators and Low Power FM (LPFM) stations also have played a major role in serving communities during emergencies. In New Orleans, after Hurricane Katrina struck, "of the 42 radio stations in the area, only four of them stayed on the air during or right after the storms," says Prometheus Radio Project founder, Pete Tridish, "and two were LPFM stations, providing vital local service on the power of a car battery."[84]

The Rise of News/Talk

While the prevalence of traditional local news radio has declined, the news/talk format has exploded. "News/talk allowed stations to provide news around the clock without the expense," says Zemira Jones, a former radio station executive. "Talk was cheaper and helps hold audiences longer than all-news did. In other words, an operator could get higher ratings with news/talk than all-news."[85]

This new type of programming was a boon for struggling AM stations that had been unable to compete with the higher-quality sound that drew listeners to FM. By 2009, an estimated 53 million people were listening every week to news/talk radio, which includes all-news, sports talk, and other talk shows.[86] Most talk shows use news headlines mixed with selected details of news stories to drive discussion, and the stations broadcasting them tend to have a much higher proportion of formal newscasts than stations with other formats.[87] Currently, as is noted in Pew's *State of the News Media 2010* report, "News-and-talk remains the most popular category in broadcast radio, and it [has grown] in both audience and number of stations."[88] As seen in the chart below, the number of news/talk stations trended sharply upward, increasing from 2,634 in 2009 to 3,446 in 2010—to make up 24 percent of the country's more than 14,000 commercial radio stations.[89]

News/talk radio serves an important function in a democratic society by giving voice to millions who use the medium to express their support for or opposition to what the government is doing. But while the increase in news/talk programming means that there are now more stations broadcasting current events, there is an important caveat: the shows tend to be national, not local in their focus. According to a survey done for the FCC's Localism Task Force in 2005, news/talk radio stations aired 67 minutes of local news and public affairs and 428 minutes of non-local

NEWS-TALK RADIO STATION GROWTH (1990–2009)

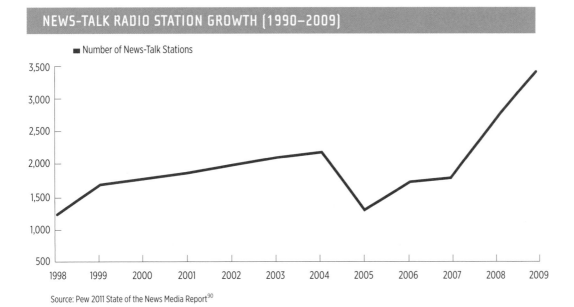

■ Number of News-Talk Stations

Source: Pew 2011 State of the News Media Report[90]

news and public affairs every day.[91] Because it spreads fixed costs, national programming often is more cost-effective for stations than local.

DAILY MINUTES OF LOCAL VS. NON-LOCAL NEWS (2009)

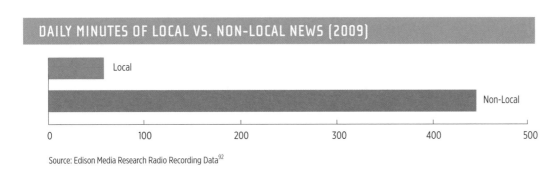

Source: Edison Media Research Radio Recording Data[92]

The Changing Radio Market

Public Radio

Public radio has stepped in to fill some of the gaps in local news left by commercial radio. As Kenneth P. Stern, former CEO of National Public Radio, explained:

> "The consolidation of commercial radio and the very significant reductions in local news [on the radio] created an open playing field for NPR and local public radio. The big local news all-news stations like WCBS-AM and WTOP-AM/FM still draw very large audiences but there are fewer and fewer of those stations, and the demise of serious local and national radio news created a real opportunity and mission for NPR and public radio. We decided to go at it hard to fill this growing vacuum, because we saw both a marketplace and public service opportunity."[93]

Public radio now deploys more than 1,400 reporters, editors, and producers in 21 domestic and 17 foreign bureaus, more than any of the broadcast TV networks. There are 185 self-defined all-news public radio stations. From 2004 to 2009, the number of stations carrying local news or talk programming rose from 595 to 681, and the number of hours such programming aired each week increased from 5,182 to 5,693.[94] But while public radio does more local news and public affairs than public TV, and more than commercial radio, these are mostly small-scale operations. Only 15 percent of local public radio stations have three or more reporters; only 4 percent have more than three editors.[95] (See Chapter 6, Public Broadcasting.)

Radio played a critical role during the hurricanes that hit Florida and the Gulf Coast in September 2004: "In many cases, while millions of people were without electricity, radio proved to be their only source of information."

Low Power FM (LPFM), a non-commercial service which beams signals short distances, has spawned several hundred stations, and some believe it can become a source for hyperlocal audio. (See Chapter 10, Low Power FM.)

Satellite Radio

Satellite radio got its start in 1997 when American Mobile Radio Corporation (the predecessor of XM Radio) paid $89,888,888, and Satellite CD Radio (the predecessor of Sirius Radio) paid $83,346,000, as the winning bids in an auction to operate a digital audio radio service in the 2320 to 2345 MHz spectrum band.[96] The companies planned to use state-of-the-art satellite technology to provide CD-quality music and information to a nationwide audience.[97] As a condition for authorization to use terrestrial repeaters, the licensees agreed not to use them for locally originated programming that was not also carried on their satellites or to seek local advertising revenue.[98] In 2002, shortly after satellite radio's debut, the service was seen as a niche offering that would serve long-distance truckers and music aficionados but not threaten the existing radio market. Soon, though, XM Satellite Radio began to install hundreds of terrestrial radio repeaters that could enable it to transmit local programming to local subscribers, raising fears in the radio industry that XM's intention was to become more than a national service. When XM and Sirius merged in 2008, at the request of the broadcasters, the FCC reaffirmed the prohibition on satellite radio offering locally originated programming and seeking local ad revenue.[99]

After years of losing subscribers and revenues, satellite radio appears to be in stronger shape: In 2010, Sirius XM subscriptions grew 7.5 percent to 20 million and revenues rose 12 percent to $2.8 billion.[100] Increased public awareness of satellite radio may explain the turnaround.[101]

Sirius XM CEO, Mel Karmazin, is upbeat about the future of satellite radio, noting that his company has long-term agreements with the automobile manufactures to put satellite radio in every car. He also cites an Arbitron study that found that more than 35 million people listen to Sirius XM in the car.[102]

Internet Radio

As with written content, the Internet has transformed both the user experience and business models for audio. The Internet nullifies one of the fundamental characteristics of terrestrial radio—its boundedness to geography. Up until the digital revolution, a radio station's reach was physically constrained by the power of its transmitter. Now, the Internet makes it possible for every piece of audio content, whether created by a tiny LPFM station or a national network, to find a national or international audience. Listeners who have a particular passion that might be unusual in their community, can find audio that originates in another region. The fly fisherman who lives in a big city, the New York Yankees fan who lives in Iowa, the soldier from Montgomery, Alabama, the only Cambodian in a Midwestern town— they can all access audio on the Internet that speaks to their interests and that they cannot get through terrestrial radio. What is more, every local radio show has the potential to be national, to reach audiences far and wide.

Radio critic Alan Hoffman described Internet radio's appeal:

"Internet radio explodes the boundaries of radio broadcasting, opening up a universe of stations offering far more diversity than what is available on the traditional radio dial. Once you start listening to Internet radio, the limits of AM and FM—a limited number of stations, within a limited geographic area—seem like a throwback to another era. Net radio provides possibilities for listening well beyond the advertising-soaked sameness of the commercial stations available."[103]

Although only a small number of Americans (17 percent) reported listening to online radio in 2010, the major shift in their listening choices is of significance. For the first time ever, more Americans (55 percent) listened to online-*only* radio (like Pandora or Slacker Radio) than to online streaming from an AM or FM radio station (40 percent).[104] And an increasing number say that they are hoping to get Internet radio in their car.[105]

"On-demand audio" has been with us—in significant volume—for quite a while, in the form of podcasts and other types of downloadable audio. Twenty-three percent of surveyed Americans said they downloaded podcasts in 2010, compared with 11 percent in 2006.[106] However, only 4 percent said they downloaded a news podcast "yesterday."[107]

RADIO STATION DIGITAL AD REVENUE PROJECTIONS

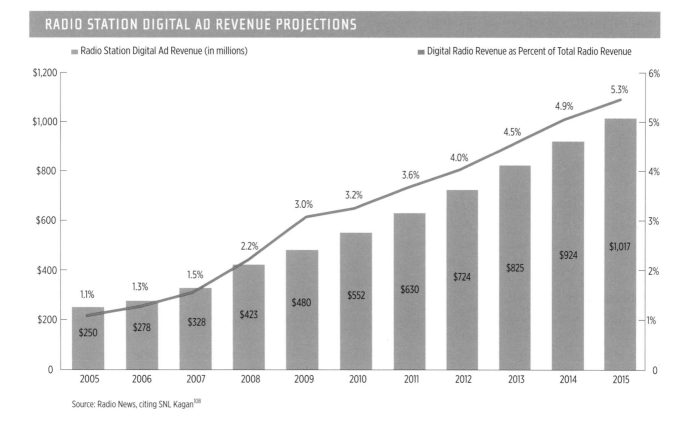

- ■ Radio Station Digital Ad Revenue (in millions)
- ■ Digital Radio Revenue as Percent of Total Radio Revenue

Source: Radio News, citing SNL Kagan[108]

As of November 2010, there had been only 1,110 "news and politics" podcasts created—compared with 48,984 in the "general" category, 10,524 in "music," and 2,991 in "business."[109]

Each new technology development brings more ways to listen to audio online. Pandora, the service that allows users to create their own Internet-based music program, is widely used on computer desktops and newer smartphones, and the Pandora application is one of the five most popular on all smartphone platforms.[110] Also attracting listeners is Stitcher, which provides a similar service for online news and podcasts.[111]

But while publishing text online is invariably less expensive than doing it in print, publishing audio online in many cases is *more* expensive than broadcasting it. As Bill Kling of American Public Radio explained:

> "We can reach 14 million people in Los Angles with a transmitter that runs on 600 watts of power. If we tried to reach 14 million people with broadband…we'd be bankrupt. We spend now $500,000 a year in our company alone on broadband spectrum in order to serve the audiences, and I don't think everybody realizes that every time you download a podcast or stream audio…it's a collect call to us."[112]

Another difference between Internet audio and broadcast radio relates to local advertising. Currently, if a local business wants to reach a local radio audience, they have little choice but to go to a local radio station. As Internet radio gains popularity, they will have another option: to place ads on websites that target local listeners without necessarily offering local content. This may be good for local businesses but could harm the business models of local radio.

In addition, it is not yet clear whether ads associated with online content—whether they're presented before, during, after, or alongside the audio itself—will be able to garner comparable rates to those for broadcast ads or whether revenue from them will be enough to make up for the increased costs of streaming.

The Internet nullifies one of the fundamental characteristics of terrestrial radio— its boundedness to geography.

Internet companies have experimented with a range of business models—including advertising, per-download fees, and monthly subscriptions—to try to make the business of providing online audio content financially viable. As in other Internet industries, it remains to be seen which models will take hold and how they will evolve. SNL Kagan projects that online radio revenue will rise from $552 million in 2010 to $1 billion in 2015.[113]

Perhaps journalist Peter Goodman best captured the uncertainty and hope in radio today, in this description:

> "Radio is under assault—from the sky, from the computer, even from tiny low-powered stations that threaten to sneak in under the radar…. It may still be called radio in 10 years, for lack of a better word, but that familiar world of transmitters, antennas, and frequency and amplitude modulation…appears to be going through changes that will add up to a revolution in how we get food for our ears."[114]

Radio, like other media platforms, is struggling to find a new revenue model ideal for the Digital Age. "The digital channels and the evolution of technology and how people are getting their information from so many different sources is the biggest challenge the industry has ever faced," says Harvey Nagler, vice president at CBS News Radio.[115]

Conclusions

Given its origins as a fundamentally local medium, it is ironic that radio now excels at national programming. On the one hand, the industry seems economically healthier than might have been expected. On the other hand, regulatory and economic changes have dramatically reduced radio's role in delivering local news. Satellite radio was blocked from trying locally originated programming, but far fewer commercial radio stations do homegrown local reporting, anyway, and the number of all-news stations has dropped sharply. It is possible that local news will, over time, become the province of public radio, which now has six times as many stations doing local news as the commercial broadcasters. But their resources are limited, and it is unclear whether they will be able to sufficiently fill the breach.

In some ways, radio should have an easier time adapting to the Internet economy than TV. It is far cheaper and faster to transmit audio online or through a phone than video. In that sense, the question is not whether audio will be popular in the new media world. It already is. What is less clear is whether commercial business models will emerge that will once again make local "radio journalism" seem profitable.

3 Television

BROADCAST TV

THE FCC BEGAN LICENSING EXPERIMENTAL television stations as early as 1937, but sponsorship of programs by advertisers was forbidden during this testing phase. Almost immediately after World War II war ended, the FCC was hit with 158 new applications, many of them from newspaper and radio companies trying to head off anticipated competition. By 1948 there were 34 stations operating in 21 different cities, broadcasting to over one million television sets.[1] Newspaper companies owned over 33 percent of those stations, and by 1952 that figure had climbed to 45 percent.[2]

The *New York Daily News* applied for an ownership license in 1946, despite New York's already having three stations. Its managers had hit on an idea for differentiation: feature *local* news instead of the 15-minute national and international news broadcasts shown by the network stations. "Our plan was for a people's newscast," explained Leavitt Pope, an executive of Channel 11. It aired in the form of *Telepix Newsreel*, two local nightly newscasts filling a 10-minute slot at 7:30 p.m. and a 15-minute slot at 11 p.m., after the prime-time shows had finished. Channel 11 grew popular, particularly because it allowed viewers to see events hours after they occurred, rather than having to wait for national and international footage to reach stations days later.[3] Successful local newscasts sprouted in Chicago and Los Angeles at around the same time.[4]

Stations that were owned and operated by networks (O&Os)[5] began to add their own local news segments: New York's WNBC in 1954, followed by CBS's WTOP in Washington, D.C., WBBM in Chicago, and WCAU in Philadelphia. Initially, their coverage was limited to a "man-on-camera" format—an anchor reading telegraph announcements.[6] Then New York's WPIX began to enliven its newscast by including extensive interviews; and WBAP's *Texas Newsreel* experimented by doing away with the anchor altogether.[7]

Between 1945 and 1952, television's audience grew from being almost nonexistent to including more than 33 percent of American households. Advertising spending rose, too. In 1952, 6 percent of all advertising spending, or $454 million, went to television ads; by 1960, $1.6 billion, or 13 percent, did. During that period, advertising consisted of one-minute commercials, infomercial-like programs that were 15 to 30 minutes in duration, and sponsorship of whole shows. National advertising made up more than half of all television advertising between 1949 and 1952.[8]

While many newspapers have been printing fewer pages, the average number of hours of news aired by local TV stations has increased by 35% in the last seven years.

Television journalism did not truly find its stride until the 1950s when national news gained widespread popularity. NBC and CBS were each producing 15-minute newscasts that ran once a day: *Camel News Caravan* with John Cameron Swayze and *Douglas Edwards with the News,* respectively. Beginning in 1951, CBS's *See It Now,* hosted by Edward R. Murrow, devoted 30 minutes to in-depth coverage of a news event or controversial public figure.[9] The popularity of such programs prompted NBC and CBS to lengthen their news slot to an hour in 1963, devoting a half hour each to local and network news.[10]

The networks began offering special events coverage, as well. Broadcasts of Queen Elizabeth II's coronation, Soviet ruler Nikita Khrushchev's 1959 visit to the United States, and other such events drew audiences fascinated by the chance to see history for themselves. When the networks dedicated airtime to the McCarthy hearings, their daytime ratings increased by about 50 percent.[11] And, in an early indication of TV news' potential influence, *See It Now*'s extensive coverage helped turn public opinion against McCarthy.[12] During the four days of nearly nonstop coverage following President John F. Kennedy's assassination in 1963, the average home had the TV on for over 13 hours a day, and 93 percent of American homes tuned in during his burial.[13] By the end of the decade, two-thirds of Americans said TV was their most-viewed, most-believed medium for newsgathering.[14]

TV networks valued their news operations. Why they did is open to debate, but former newsman Ted Koppel argues:

> "To the degree that broadcast news was a more virtuous operation 40 years ago, it was a function of both fear and innocence. Network executives were afraid that a failure to work in the 'public interest, convenience and necessity,' as set forth in the Radio Act of 1927, might cause the Federal Communications Commission to suspend or even revoke their licenses. The three major broadcast networks pointed to their news divisions (which operated at a loss or barely broke even) as evidence that they were fulfilling the FCC's mandate. News was, in a manner of speaking, the loss leader that permitted NBC, CBS and ABC to justify the enormous profits made by their entertainment divisions....
>
> "On the innocence side of the ledger, meanwhile, it never occurred to the network brass that news programming could be profitable.... Until, that is, CBS News unveiled its '60 Minutes' news magazine in 1968. When, after three years or so, '60 Minutes' turned a profit (something no television news program had previously achieved), a light went on, and the news divisions of all three networks came to be seen as profit centers, with all the expectations that entailed."[15]

At the local level, there is no dispute that news has long been profitable for TV stations. In the 1950s, local stations would typically air their own half-hour news, weather, and sports programming directly before the network newscast, and deliver a short local summary directly following the network news.[16] By the 1960s and 1970s, many stations were airing more of their own news programming than of that provided to them by networks.[17] Local news was inexpensive to produce compared with entertainment programming, and it proved even more profitable, because local stations could sell and retain all the revenue from advertising during their local segments, rather than having to return a significant portion to networks, as they did during network programming.[18] As local news programs became more common, television stations relied on their two to three half-hour newscasts for more than half of their profits.[19]

The Changing Economics of Modern Local TV News

Local TV news continued to grow and prosper over the next four decades, but by 2008 signs that the industry was entering a new era became apparent. At first, it seemed that perhaps the only difference between the economics of local TV news and local newspapers was a few years—that the economic forces that had devastated newspapers would soon take a toll on the revenue of local TV stations, and therefore their newsrooms. The broadcast audience continued its drift to cable, satellite, and the Internet.

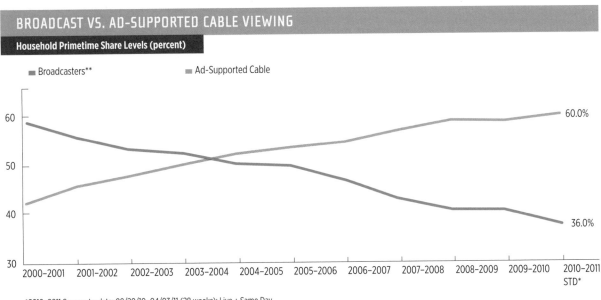

BROADCAST VS. AD-SUPPORTED CABLE VIEWING

Household Primetime Share Levels (percent)

■ Broadcasters**   ■ Ad-Supported Cable

*2010–2011 Season-to-date: 09/20/10–04/03/11 (28 weeks); Live + Same Day.

**Broadcasters included: ABC, CBS, CW, Fox, Ion, MNT & NBC.

Source: Cable Advertising Bureau (CAB) analysis of Nielsen data.[20]

The economic changes from 2005 to 2008 hit local news-producing stations especially hard.

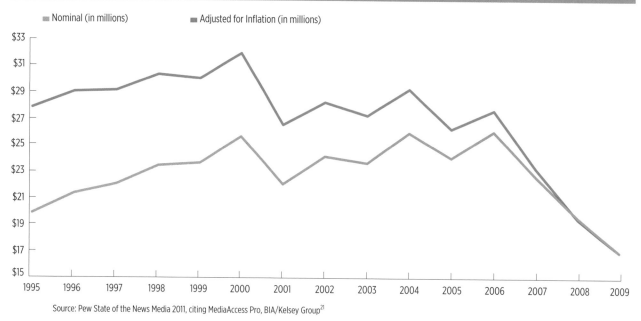

AVERAGE STATION REVENUE OF NEWS-PRODUCING STATIONS (1995–2009)

Source: Pew State of the News Media 2011, citing MediaAccess Pro, BIA/Kelsey Group[21]

In comments filed with the Future of Media project, the National Association of Broadcasters said local TV news pre-tax profits declined 56.3 percent from 1998 to 2008—and that the drop was even sharper, 62.9 percent, in smaller cities (media markets number 150–210).[22]

But many local TV stations remain highly profitable. According to survey data compiled by the National Association of Broadcasters, a local TV station in 2009 with average net revenues and cash flow would have a cash flow margin of nearly 23 percent of revenues.

And local TV news had a strong year in 2010. While the rest of the economy was struggling, local TV stations' revenue rose. Ad spending on local TV in the first three quarters of 2010 was up 27 percent from the same period in 2009, according to a TVB analysis of Kantar Media data. Total local TV 2010 ad revenue was up 17 percent from 2009, reported BIA/Kelsey.[24] The reasons, according to industry analyst SNL Kagan:

FINANCIAL PERFORMANCE OF LOCAL TV STATIONS (2005–2009)

| | National Average | | |
Year	Net Revenues	Cash Flow	Pre-Tax Profits
2005	$15,418,056	$5,484,728	$3,512,208
2006	$16,849,704	$6,290,389	$4,210,359
2007	$16,147,873	$5,258,288	$3,320,667
2008	$15,837,222	$4,703,953	$2,686,481
2009	$13,453,516	$3,071,995	$1,125,630

Source: NAB, Television Financial Reports, various years[23]

"TV station revenue has been going gangbusters in 2010 thanks to the return of auto ad spending, a strengthening of core categories and influx of political dollars."[25]

Indeed, news seems to be playing an increasing role in TV stations' overall finances. Pew's *State of the News Media 2010* report notes that the high percentage of income derived from news—44.7 percent in 2009—is "increasingly significant when considering the average television station that produces news airs an average of just 4 hours and 36 minutes of news per weekday. Advertising from the rest of the day—more than 19 hours—represents the remaining 56 percent of revenues."[27]

There are several reasons that the economic prospects for local broadcast stations and their news operations remain brighter than the outlook for local newspapers:

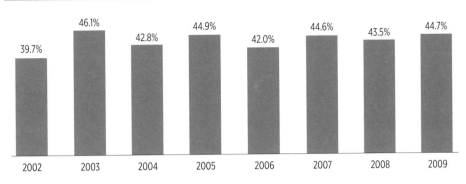

AVERAGE PERCENT OF TV STATION REVENUE PRODUCED BY NEWS

39.7% | 46.1% | 42.8% | 44.9% | 42.0% | 44.6% | 43.5% | 44.7%
2002 | 2003 | 2004 | 2005 | 2006 | 2007 | 2008 | 2009

Sources: Pew Project for Excellent in Journalism, 2010 Report[26]

People are watching as much TV as ever. The average amount of time Americans spent consuming major media rose from 10.6 hours in 2008 to 11 hours in 2010, with the portion of time devoted to TV remaining fixed at 40 percent.[28]

With viewing habits more fragmented, broadcast TV has retained some clout as an effective way to reach large numbers—not to the extent that it has in the past but still more than most cable networks. As a result, significant ad spending on broadcast TV will continue.

MEDIA SHARE OF U.S. ADVERTISING (1949–2009)

Share of total

◼ Newspapers ◼ TV and Cable ◼ Radio ◼ Internet

Source: Martin Langeveld at Nieman Journalism Lab; data from NAA, TVB, IAB, McCann

A significant element that contributed to newspapers' gloomy fate does not exist in the local TV drama: classified advertising. While the lion's share of newspapers' revenue drop resulted from classified ads fleeing to free or low-cost online venues, classifieds were never important to local TV's bottom line. (See Chapter 1, Newspapers.)

Political advertising is soaring and is expected to grow in the future. In January 2010, in *Citizens United v. Federal Election Commission*, the U.S. Supreme Court struck down portions of a national campaign finance law, making it far easier for corporations to spend unlimited amounts of money on political campaigns. Borrell Associates, a consulting firm that focuses on local media and advertising, estimates that the court ruling generated additional political advertising totaling $400 million in the 2010 elections.[29] This created a windfall for local TV stations: in 2010, political advertisers spent an estimated $2 billion to $3 billion on local TV stations, which may be as much as 100 percent more than in 2008—despite that 2008 was a presidential election year and 2010 was not.[30]

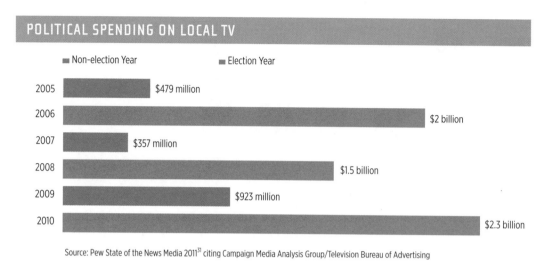

POLITICAL SPENDING ON LOCAL TV

■ Non-election Year   ■ Election Year

2005	$479 million
2006	$2 billion
2007	$357 million
2008	$1.5 billion
2009	$923 million
2010	$2.3 billion

Source: Pew State of the News Media 2011[31] citing Campaign Media Analysis Group/Television Bureau of Advertising

Broadcasters are demanding and getting higher payments for their programming from cable operators in the form of "retransmission" fees. That means that the loss of local TV advertising as more viewers switch to cable will be at least partly offset by an increase in the fees that the highly profitable cable operators pay to local TV stations for broadcast programming.[32]

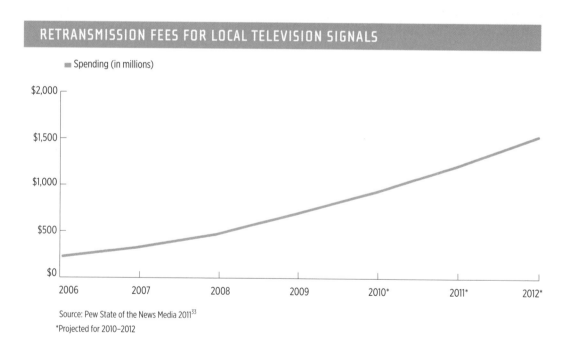

RETRANSMISSION FEES FOR LOCAL TELEVISION SIGNALS

■ Spending (in millions)

Source: Pew State of the News Media 2011[33]
*Projected for 2010–2012

The Current State of Local TV News

Today, the most popular source for local news is television. On "a typical day," 78 percent of Americans say they get news from their local TV news station—more than from newspapers, the Internet, or the radio.[34] Fifty percent of all Americans watch local TV news "regularly." Viewership rates have been declining over the years—along with consumption rates for all other non-Internet news sources—but they still remain higher than those for any other single news source.[35]

In addition, evidence is growing that, after a slow start, local TV stations are becoming important sources for news online. In fact, local TV news sites rank among the most popular news websites (those with at least a half a million monthly unique visitors), along with newspaper sites.[36]

In other words, neither the ongoing migration of viewers to cable TV nor the growth of the Internet has changed the basic fact that most Americans turn to their local TV news team for local news.

Indeed, it could be argued that the "media food chain" has changed in a way that presents an historic opportunity for local TV news.

There Is More Local TV News

While newspapers have been printing fewer pages, the average number of hours of news aired by local TV stations has increased by 35 percent in the last seven years, according to the *RTDNA/Hofstra University Annual Survey*, conducted by Robert Papper for the Radio Television Digital News Association and Hofstra University, where he is a professor.

HOURS OF LOCAL NEWS (WEEKDAYS)

Year	Hours
2003	3.7
2004	3.6
2005	3.8
2006	4.1
2007	4.1
2008	4.6
2009	5.0

Source: Radio Television Digital News Association (RTDNA)/Hofstra
Surveys based on survey responses of news directors[37]

In 2009, despite the depressed economy, 28.6 percent of all local stations—and almost 40 percent of those in the largest markets—*added* newscasts.

CHANGES IN LOCAL NEWSCASTS (2009 VS. 2008)

All News Stations, Big 4 Affiliates and Other Stations

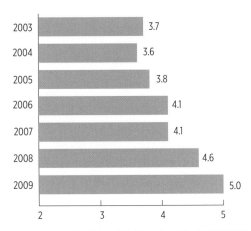

All Local TV News

- Added a Newscast 28.6%
- Cut a Newscast 13.7%
- No Changes 57.7%

Changes	Big Four Affiliates: ABC, CBS, NBC, Fox	Other Commercial Broadcast TV Stations
Added a Newscast	28.2%	42.9%
Cut a Newscast	12.5%	18.2%
No Changes	59.3%	38.9%

Station Market Size

	Station Market Size				
Changes	1–25	26–50	51–100	101–150	151+
Added a Newscast	39.6%	22.6%	41.9%	19.7%	12.5%
Cut a Newscast	20.8%	16.1%	13.5%	10.0%	8.3%
No Changes	39.6%	61.3%	44.6%	70.3%	79.2%

Source: RTDNA/Hofstra 2010 Annual Survey

In 2009, news directors said they expected to increase the amount of news they offered in the coming year.

All TV Local News

- "Not Sure" 8.2%
- 32.6% Increase
- 1.8% Decrease
- 57.4% Same

Changes	Big Four Affiliates: ABC, CBS, NBC, Fox	Other Commercial Broadcast TV Stations
Increase	31.6%	50.0%
Decrease	1.7%	0%
Same	57.9%	41.7%
"Not Sure"	8.8%	8.3%

Station Market Size

Changes	Station Market Size				
	1–25	26–50	51–100	101–150	151+
Increase	34.9%	26.2%	32.6%	34.9%	30.6%
Decrease	1.6%	4.8%	1.1%	1.2%	1.6%
Same	54.0%	59.5%	56.2%	56.6%	62.9%
"Not Sure"	9.5%	9.5%	10.1%	7.2%	4.8%

Source: RTDNA/Hofstra 2010 Survey. 38

The main reason for the increased hours: stations are adding or expanding "early-bird" morning news shows, beginning at 4:30 A.M. or even earlier.[39] Brian Bracco, vice president of news for Hearst Television Inc.'s 29 stations, suggests that these shows fill useful niches for the local viewer:

"They are starting their day earlier and are working harder and longer, and they are not at home at 5 or 6 P.M.—so that's where their source of news is…. [Consumers] need to know the weather, the traffic, get around the traffic jam…. [The mentality is] 'I want to be smart when I go to work and want to know the latest.'"[40]

Post-Newsweek Stations, the *Washington Post*'s broadcasting division, which added early-bird news to many of its stations, believes that both additions draw in more revenue and make it more likely that viewers will tune in to later broadcasts. Deborah Collura, vice president and managing director of news at Post-Newsweek's seven television stations, says:

"Yes, it generates more revenue when you have these…. They [the sales department] need more inventory. I also think it gives you a jumpstart, a head start on your other newscasts. You are setting the plate earlier."[41]

As an economic matter, adding more newscasts is often cheaper than using syndicated programming. A Midwestern medium-market local TV station can acquire a syndicated show like *Oprah* for a half a million dollars a year, or *The Ellen DeGeneres Show* or *Rachael Ray* for a third of that cost. But adding a newscast can involve simply shifting resources and adding one show producer.[42] Steve Schwaid, director of news and digital content at WGCL-CBS in Atlanta, anticipates that adding a newscast will bring many advantages, including economic ones: "We'll add some staff, it won't be as expensive as syndication, but we'll create a greater local footprint for ourselves on the market, and [it] creates more ad revenue."[43]

In addition to adding newscasts, many local TV stations have become major online sources of news. (See Chapter 4, Internet.) And, if they broadcast in high definition on their primary channel, they typically have several additional, multicast channels available to program. Some station groups are using those new digital channels to air less expensive programming or as a way to repurpose existing news and programming content. Some are using them for weather reports, Spanish-language broadcasts, or live breaking news coverage when an emergency in the station's community calls for around-the-clock coverage.

The bottom line: while newspapers are producing less news, local TV stations are producing more newscasts and news content.

While the Volume of News Has Risen, Staffs Have Shrunk

Rather than adding staff to sustain this increase in news, TV stations on average have actually cut personnel—"with the median full-time staff dropping from 32 in 2006 to 29 in 2009," according to Pew's *State of the News Media 2011* report.[44] Nearly two-thirds of local TV news directors reported staff cuts in 2009, according to the *RTDNA/Hofstra Annual Survey.*[45] And two-thirds of news directors said that despite the expanded number of hours of news, their budgets had decreased.[46]

Most news directors in 2009 reported that they had decreased their staff size.

AVERAGE LOCAL NEWS STAFF (2009 VS. 2008)		
	All TV News	**Big Four Affiliates: ABC, CBS, NBC, Fox**	**Other Commercial Broadcast TV Stations**
Increased	11.5%	11.4%	15.2%
Decreased	64.1%	64.0%	60.6%
Same	24.1%	24.2%	24.2%
"Don't Know"	0.3%	0.3%	0%

Source: RTDNA/Hofstra Surveys based on survey responses of news directors[47]

When asked about their planned hiring in 2010, however, news directors were optimistic, with those planning to hire outnumbering those planning to make staffing cuts.

PLANNED STAFF CHANGES IN 2010		
	All TV News	**Big Four Affiliates: ABC, CBS, NBC, Fox**	**Other Commercial Broadcast TV Stations**
Increase	22.7%	23.0%	27.3%
Decrease	7.1%	7.8%	3.0%
Same	60.8%	60.8%	54.5%
"Don't Know"	9.4%	8.4%	15.2%

Source: Radio Television Digital News Association (RTDNA)/Hofstra 2010 Annual Survey
based on survey responses of news directors[48]

Excellence in Local TV News

Have these productivity gains—more hours of news with fewer staff—helped or hindered quality? Of course, it is difficult to generalize. Despite the industry's problems, the best of the local TV stations are still producing high-quality broadcast journalism of tremendous value to the community—while reaching a far broader audience than newspapers in terms of size, diversity, and socioeconomic status. It is hard to overstate the importance and value of these broadcasts.

During emergencies, the local TV station is often considered to be as vital a part of the local community as the police and fire departments, and despite cutbacks most local TV reporters and managers believe they still are able to excel in the midst of a crisis. Mike Devlin, president and general manager of WFAA-TV in Dallas, Texas, asked:

> "Does the FCC know that WWL-TV [a Belo-owned New Orleans station] stayed on for 16 days straight without a commercial during Hurricane Katrina? Or that KHOU in Houston stayed on for Hurricane Ike down there…for 60 hours? When I look at that WWL coverage, there were people that, if they didn't have WWL, would not have had a connection to the outside world or have known what was going on."[49]

When Nashville suffered major floods in May 2010, the national press gave it little attention, but WKRN-TV stayed on for 16-hour stretches, airing both heart-wrenching human-interest stories and practical information. "These stations were lifelines," says Matthew Zelkind, WKRN news director. "We told them where to get water, where to get shelter, how to get the water in drinkable condition." The station used its website to stream its broadcast and solicited and aired information from users via email, Twitter, and by phone. Zelkind praised the staff's dedication during such times, noting one case in which a photographer rushed to the office to deliver video, even though part of his own house had burned down. "His duty was to his profession. That guy's a hero."[50]

A group of the nation's largest local television groups including Gannett, Belo Corp., and Raycom Media, have written that their stations provide around-the-clock coverage of severe weather events at a significant cost in resources and lost advertising revenue. In a filing with the Future of Media proceeding, they noted the example of WFMY-TV in Greensboro, North Carolina, interrupting its coverage of the highly popular Sweet 16 round of the NCAA basketball tournament to provide viewers with critical information about tornados that entered the region. The station moved its coverage of the basketball game to a multicast channel and used its primary signal to bring critical safety information to viewers. They also pointed to WPEC in West Palm Beach, Florida, and KFDM in Beaumont, Texas, which both routinely air half-hour hurricane preparation programs before emergencies occur (and offer print and online hurricane survival guides), in addition to extensive coverage when emergencies do happen.[51]

In March 2010, Jane Mago, general counsel for the NAB, testified at an FCC workshop:

> "Just this past weekend for example, stations in Hawaii helped local residents prepare for the tsunami predicted to strike the Islands as a result of the massive earthquake in Chile, which fortunately did not come to pass. Stations in the mid-Atlantic and Northeast have been assisting their viewers for months now during this record-breaking snow season."[52]

Local Stations Are Becoming More Creative Online

For many years, local television stations invested very little in their websites or digital strategies, using them primarily as promotional vehicles or to list programming schedules. Today, however, stations and station groups are paying full attention to the second and third of the "three screens" available to news programmers: TV, the Internet, and mobile devices. WWL in New Orleans, for instance, relied on its website to stay connected to its community during Hurricane Katrina. Even when weather conditions relegated its news crews to back-up studios in Baton Rouge and to the station's transmitter site, information was consistently available on its website. WWL.com offered forums where friends and relatives impacted by the storm could search online for each other, and its streaming coverage allowed displaced storm victims as far away as Georgia and Tennessee to learn about their community and their homes.[53] The station received awards for exemplary television and web coverage.[54]

Salt Lake City's KSL-TV serves a market of over 3 million people, and its website consistently ranks as one of the nation's top broadcast sites, drawing an audience of more than 3 million monthly unique visitors. The station was one of the first in the country to launch local classified ads, and though 70 percent of its traffic is driven by classified ads, its news and traffic is also among the top ten in the country.[55]

KING-TV in Seattle found wasted funds in the ferry system; 9NewsKUSA in Denver uncovered mortgage fraud; and WTHR in Indianapolis did an eight-month investigation into how state officials inflated job statistics.

During historic snowstorms in the winter of 2010, crews at Hearst Television–owned WGAL in Lancaster, Pennsylvania, could not navigate around the viewing area due to road closures and snow. So the station enlisted viewers to help report the news, encouraging them to upload video, pictures, and information on the WGAL website to help alert the community to hazardous areas and other safety issues. Viewers responded in large numbers.[56]

Social media can sharpen coverage, bringing in new information and nuance. KDFW (FOX4) in Dallas has 200,000 Facebook fans for the station or individual reporters, an asset it actively uses in its on air reporting and to strengthen their bond with viewers. For instance, FOX4 recently was seeking examples of people who had mortgage foreclosure problems and found relevant interview subjects from among their Facebook fans. And News director

Maria Barrs noted that after the station recently ran a piece about drinking among some area Lockheed workers, viewers pointed out that two of the workers recorded were contractors not employees—a distinction that the station then made in the follow-up piece. Then other Facebook fans suggested if they checked out a different parking lot, they'd find workers smoking drugs, a tip that also turned out to be true "Social media is a really powerful tool and we use it all the time," Barrs says. "I've never seen our job as being a one way street. But now there are intersections all over the place."[57]

Perhaps the most widespread new web initiative among local stations is the development of "hyperlocal" community websites, which allows for more granular coverage. In Charlotte, North Carolina, alone, Raycom Media has launched 60 community websites that will offer neighborhood-based hyperlocal websites.[58] DataSphere, the company building the sites for Raycom, is also launching 160 neighborhood sites for other broadcasters, including Fisher Communication.[59] In June 2010, Gannett Broadcasting launched hyperlocal sites in 10 markets.[60] Belo Corp. has partnered with Broadcast Interactive Media (BIM), which has over 90 affiliates in 73 markets. BIM's products, such as the user-generated content platform YouNews, allow Belo stations' website users to upload videos, photos, and stories to local websites and also enables online contests, and content exchange.[61]

> "Does the FCC know that WWL TV [in New Orleans] stayed on for 16 days straight without a commercial during Hurricane Katrina?" says Mike Devline of WFAA in Dallas. "Or that KHOU in Houston stayed on for Hurricane Ike down there...for 60 hours?"

These efforts have been rewarded, in part, with increased online ad revenue. Local TV online revenue was $1.34 billion in 2010 compared with $1.08 billion in 2008.[62] FOX Television Stations CEO, Jack Abernathy, has beens particularly bullish on the future of local TV news on tablets: "I think you can assume a younger generation that's going to expect to see television on portable devices soon. If it can be scaled properly, it could be very, very big business."[63]

Currently, the most popular content on TV station websites is weather, followed by local newws. Some stations have launched specialized sites, like KWCH in Wichita whose Catch it Kansas covers high school sports statewide. In Oklahoma, Griffin Communications' OKBlitz.com handles sports for the entire state and was projecting profits in 2010.[64]

Although newspapers still produce the number one websites in most large markets, local TV stations lay claim to the top local sites in 14 markets, including Minneapolis, Pittsburgh, Raleigh-Durham, and Salt Lake City.[65] An FCC analysis of three cities—Toledo, Richmond, and Seattle—revealed that the dominant online sources of local news were either local TV stations or newspapers. (See Chapter 21, Types of News.)

The 2010 *RTDNA/Hofstra University Annual Survey* of news directors found that staffing for television websites on average has gone up by as much as one full-time employee and one-part time employee over the last year.[66] As more stations invest meaningful dollars into building up their hyperlocal web coverage, it will be important to see whether they will also invest in additional reporters to help provide this more granular coverage.

Although most of the discussion about charging for content has been driven by newspaper companies, some local TV executives are mulling over the idea of paid products for their stations, as well. Rich Boehne, CEO of the E.W. Scripps Company, says that they will experiment with charging for certain premium services in the coming year. In general, he believes that the cookie-cutter nature of many local TV stations hinders their ability to develop and adapt to successful new business models. "Turn on the local news and it all looks the same, times four," he says. Audiences will therefore have no compelling reason to stick with a particular station, or that medium in general, over time. He argues that the contraction of newspapers creates opportunities for local TV stations, but only if they seriously invest in creating original content: "Our job depends on great original content and agenda setting."[67]

A Few Are Trying Innovative Collaborations With Independent Digital Ventures

A small but increasing number of local TV stations have begun partnering with digital news operations to bolster coverage of their communities. San Diego's KNSD-TV, owned and operated by NBC, has joined forces with voiceofsandiego.org—one of a growing number of nonprofit online news outlets that have emerged at the community level across the country—to produce two regular segments: "San Diego Fact Check," a roughly five-minute piece analyzing the statements or assertions of local officials, and "San Diego Explained," which tackles difficult subjects like public pensions. "They had depth of reporting that we could benefit from," says Greg Dawson, vice president of news at KNSD. "It gives us something very strong that's unique to that show."[68] Scott Lewis, voiceofsandiego.org CEO, views the arrangement as "fantastic," as it gives the site significant exposure and they get paid a retainer for their services.[69] The partnership became the basis for a commitment made by Comcast as part of its merger with NBC to attempt to create partnerships "similar in approach and level of involvement and support to the arrangement" in four other cities.[70] Additionally, NBC recently solicited proposals to participate in local news-sharing partnerships from nonprofit online news organizations in New York, Los Angeles, Chicago, Miami, Philadelphia, San Francisco, Dallas-Ft. Worth, Washington, and Hartford-New Haven, Connecticut.[71]

In Spokane, Washington, KXLY-TV has partnered with the *Inlander*, a weekly alternative newspaper, in an exclusive cross-promotional agreement that allows the station first-run rights on the paper's long-form investigative stories. Also in Spokane, KREM plans to partner with a for-profit website called Tributes.com to offer online and on-air obituaries and share revenue with funeral directors. Collaborations are even happening between long-time competitors. In Seattle, KING 5 has teamed up with the *Seattle Times* to create a local online ad network that potentially will offer revenue to local blogs and hyperlocal sites.[72]

But these are only isolated examples of local stations trying to enhance their coverage through partnerships with other journalistic outfits. There are more opportunities. Newspapers are struggling to have more impact with fewer resources. Hundreds of new local news websites are producing good local journalism but lack a sufficient audience. Local public radio has begun to invest in local news. All of them have content—and need exposure. Meanwhile, local TV stations are producing more and more hours of news, with fewer people. They have airtime but lack sufficient content. It seems obvious that local TV stations could vastly improve their service to their community by pursuing local partnerships in ways they have not yet explored.

Mobile and Local TV

Local TV stations are also attempting to capitalize on opportunities presented by the mobile phone. While many have developed applications ("apps") for phones, local TV stations are also experimenting with a very different idea: beaming *broadcast signals* directly to the phone. In April 2010, 12 of the major broadcast groups—Belo Corp., Cox Media Group, E.W. Scripps Company, FOX Broadcasting Company, Gannett Broadcasting, Hearst Television Inc., ION Television, Media General Inc., Meredith Corporation, NBCUniversal Media, Post-Newsweek Stations Inc., and Raycom Media—announced plans for a stand-alone joint venture that would utilize their existing broadcast spectrum to deliver content to mobile devices. On November 18, 2010, the Mobile Content Venture (MCV) announced that by the end of 2011 it would be delivering mobile video service to markets serving more than 40 percent of the U.S. population. In early 2010, an experiment was conducted in which consumers were given phones equipped to receive broadcast signals. The most viewed type of programming: local news.[73]

> KNSD-TV in San Diego has a partnership with the nonprofit local website Voice of San Diego. "They had depth of reporting that we could benefit from" says Greg Dawson oft KNSD. "It gives us something very strong that's unique to that show."

Investigative Powerhouse Stations

Local television news has broken numerous important, high-impact stories in the last decade. In 2000, KHOU in Houston broke the Bridgestone/Firestone tire story, which resulted in a federal investigation and forced the Ford Motor Company and Bridgestone/Firestone to recall 6.5 million potentially defective tires at a cost of $300 million. WBBM in Chicago blew the whistle on dangers at Chicago's O'Hare airport, and KMOV in St. Louis chronicled the failures of the East St. Louis school system. In fact, the 2010 Alfred I. duPont-Columbia University Awards, the top honors for broadcast journalism, gave more awards to local TV than in recent years. Recipients included KING-TV in Seattle, for its four-month investigation of wasted funds in the ferry system; 9NewsKUSA in Denver, for its six-month investigation of mortgage fraud; WKOW in Madison, for its eight-month investigation of the Wisconsin Bureau of Consumer Protection; and WTHR in Indianapolis, for its eight-month investigation into how state officials inflated job statistics.[74]

In comments filed with the FCC, broadcasters pointed to WHAS in Louisville, Kentucky, whose investigation of sexual conduct between prison guards and inmates led to a new state law. In explaining the role TV stations play in promoting public health, the broadcasters cited the ways in which, during the 2009 H1N1 flu epidemic, stations offered community-specific information about vaccinations and how citizens could obtain them.[75]

RTDNA, which represents news directors, declared in its written comments that most broadcasters are good stewards of their licenses and go to great lengths to be reliable, dynamic sources of local news and information.[76] They cited KHOU in Houston, which won a regional Edward R. Murrow Award for its two-year investigation of the Texas National Guard. The station's investigation, which began with an inquiry into allegations

> Early experiments conducted in mobile TV on phones indicate that local news was the most viewed programming category.

of harassment and discrimination against female officers, then uncovered instances of corrupt practices and misappropriation of funds by the Texas National Guard's commanding officers. Ultimately, Governor Rick Perry relieved the Texas Guard's top officers of their command and installed new leadership, which for the first time in Texas history included a female commander.[77]

Evidence shows that, while many stations have cut back on in-depth and beat reporting, quite a few have preserved their "investigative team." The Pew Research Center's Project for Excellence in Journalism found that "although the substance of this enterprise reporting can vary widely by station, stations appear to have protected their spotlight and investigative teams as important to their brand." In some cases, this is more than merely semantics. Schurz Communications Inc. owns six television stations, including KWCH in Wichita, Kansas, and KY3 KYTV in Springfield, Missouri. Marci Burdick, senior vice president of news for Schurz, explains why both stations have kept their award-winning investigative units:

> "Unless we are doing news and information that people can get nowhere else, we are nothing but a commodity. I think companies covering car wrecks and traffic accidents are kidding themselves if they think they are going to survive the Internet Age because that information can be gotten by anyone with an iPhone. So we have always preached in our company—and it is in our core values—serving our communities with deep information."[78]

Mike Devlin, general manager for Belo Corp.'s flagship station, WFAA in Dallas, Texas, says Belo senior management supports the decision to keep a strong investigative operation:

> "There's a company culture that holds great value in that for the impact it has on local communities. The cable companies are not going to do it, [nor are] the telephone companies, the satellite companies.... The only people who can do this type of reporting are local television stations or local newspapers."[79]

Several top local television groups, including Belo, Gannett, Post-Newsweek, and Raycom Media, have stated that they understand the importance of investigative reporting. They pointed to WPLG in Miami, which broke the news that inmates, many of whom did not have licenses to drive, were permitted to drive county vehicles while on work release. After these TV reports, Florida enacted a new law banning the practice.[80] At KHOU in Houston, the station's executive producer for investigations is optimistic:

> "From the standpoint of my own company and station, not only have we not reduced our investigative reporting efforts, but we now have an additional group of newsroom reporters selected to focus on generally shorter-turn investigations. Those efforts—in conjunction with the unit I have been a part of for the past 13 years (where we tend to focus on long-term, large-scope investigations)—has definitely increased the enterprise/investigative output of our station."[81]

Although most discussions of the fate of local news focus on newspapers, the number one source for local news today is actually television. On "a typical day," 78 percent of Americans say they get news from their local television news station—more than newspapers, the Internet or radio.

At small-market station KBCI in Boise, Idaho, two reporters uncovered a trail of financial corruption by Boise's mayor and his chief of staff that led to the resignation and indictment of both officials. Even a station in Monroe, Louisiana, was celebrated for its investigation of corruption within the local National Guard in the aftermath of Hurricane Katrina.[82]

However, while many stations excel, several trends in local news are discouraging.

Scant Coverage of Important Local Issues

Topics like education, health care, and local government get relatively small amounts of coverage these days. A study of Los Angeles newscasts over 14 randomly selected days between August 1 and September 30, 2009, conducted by the Norman Lear Center at the USC Annenberg School for Communication & Journalism, found that stories about local civic issues impacting L.A. residents' lives, like transportation, community health, the environment, education, taxes, activism, and fundraisers took up *one minute and 16 seconds* of the monitored half-hour broadcasts. Stories about local government led the newscasts only 2.5 percent of the time. Only one out of 100 newscast leads was about the developing budget crisis.[83]

A 2009 Michigan State University study of local media serving 98 metropolitan central cities and 77 suburban cities revealed that city government received about one-third less television coverage than crime stories did.

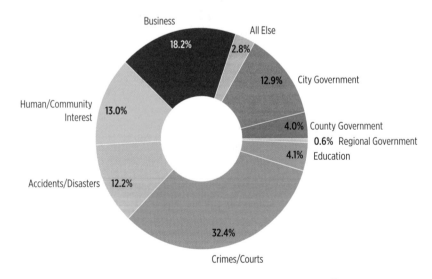

LOCAL TV NEWS COVERAGE ANALYZED BY TOPIC (2009)

Business 18.2%
All Else 2.8%
City Government 12.9%
County Government 4.0%
Regional Government 0.6%
Education 4.1%
Crimes/Courts 32.4%
Accidents/Disasters 12.2%
Human/Community Interest 13.0%

Source: Data Adapted from News Media Coverage of City Governments in 2009-Michigan State University[84]

Local election coverage on commercial television stations is particularly lacking. In 2004, a study of local TV news coverage in 11 media markets found that only 8 percent of the 4,333 broadcasts during the month before the election had stories that even mentioned local races. During the run-up to the elections, the stations produced eight times more coverage on accidental injuries than on local races, according to the Lear Center at the USC Annenberg

LOCAL MEDIA NEWS COVERAGE BY TOPIC AND MEDIA TYPE (2009)

By Media Types

Story Topic	Newspaper	Television	Radio	Citizen Journalism
City Government	24.5%	12.9%	16.6%	16.5%
County Government	2.0%	4.0%	5.7%	6.1%
Regional Government	0.4%	0.6%	0.7%	0.5%
Education	8.7%	4.1%	5.3%	3.3%
Crimes/Courts	17.8%	32.4%	29.3%	14.6%
Accident/Disasters	4.1%	12.2%	9.9%	3.3%
Human/Community Interest	24.1%	13.0%	12.2%	27.4%
Business	16.8%	18.2%	17.3%	23.6%
All Else	1.7%	2.8%	2.9%	4.7%
N	3185	2870	543	212

Source: Data Adapted from News Media Coverage of City Governments in 2009-Michigan State University[84]

School. Meanwhile, the stations were flooded with TV ads about local races. In states with competitive Senate races, four times as many hours were given to advertisements as to coverage of the race. Yet less than one percent of the political stories that were done critiqued the ads. Among the examples cited in the Lear report:

> "In Seattle, where there was an extremely close gubernatorial race, 95 percent of the half-hours captured in that market in the month before the election contained no stories at all about the race for governor. Time spent on teasers, bumpers and intro music in Seattle outnumbered time covering the Washington gubernatorial race by 14-to-one.

> "Ten of the 11 markets in the sample had a race for U.S. Senate, yet 94 percent of the broadcasts analyzed in these markets failed to contain a single story about a Senate race.

> "In Denver, where there was a highly competitive U.S. Senate race, 88 percent of the half-hours of news studied contained no stories about the Senate race. Six times as much time was devoted to crime, and twice as much time was devoted to stories about accidental injury, than to stories about the Senate race.

> "Los Angeles stations collectively devoted less time to the Senate race in a month than they collectively gave to bumper music and teasers in a single night.

> "Not one story about a race for the U.S. House appeared in the Los Angeles stories captured during this period….

> "Non-candidate races—stories about ballot or bond initiatives—accounted for about four-and-a-half percent of all campaign stories captured in the 11 markets….

> "Local races accounted for just 6 percent of all stories aired about elections in the 11 markets, compared to 61 percent devoted to the presidential election, but stations aired a sizable number of stories about the voting process….

> "Only 3 percent of the campaign stories on the six local Spanish-language stations studied (in New York, Los Angeles and Miami) focused on local races."[85]

It is unlikely that matters have improved since then. In 2006, viewers of local news in the Midwest got 2.5 times more information about local elections from paid advertisements than from newscasts, according to a University of Wisconsin study. The average length of a political piece was 76 seconds (down from 89 seconds in 2002), and "most of the actual news coverage of elections on early and late-evening broadcasts was devoted to campaign strategy and polling, which outpaced reporting on policy issues by a margin of over three to one."[86]

Although there is no directly comparable study regarding the 2010 election, it seems that local coverage fared no better and may have fared worse: Writing in PoliticsDaily.com, veteran political reporter Walter Shapiro described a campaign rally of a candidate in a highly contested gubernatorial primary in South Carolina just 72 hours before Election Day:

"[T]here was one thing missing from the picturesque scene—any South Carolina newspaper, wire service, TV or radio reporters. What we are witnessing in this election cycle is the slow death of traditional statewide campaign journalism. I noticed the same pattern (and the same nearly reporter-free campaign trail) in Kentucky last month as I covered libertarian Rand Paul's decisive defeat of the state Republican establishment in the GOP Senate primary."[87]

It is not only politics that gets limited coverage. So do local business and economic matters. The University of Wisconsin study indicated that 47 seconds out of a typical half-hour broadcast related to "business/economy," while another study by Wisconsin and USC Annenberg, in 2004, of over 8,000 hours of programming on 4,082 broadcasts in 44 markets, also found that only 47 seconds per half hour were devoted to business and economy.[88]

Less Depth

Tom Rosenstiel, director of the Pew Research Center's Project for Excellence in Journalism, testified at an FCC hearing that the amount of in-depth accountability journalism on many local TV newscasts has been declining for a while. From 1998 to 2001, Rosenstiel said, the percentage of stories generated by "enterprise reporting" (for example, digging into the details of city, county, or state records; asking bold questions of elected officials or corporate leaders) as opposed to stories based on press releases, chasing the action on the police scanner, or following a story already in the local newspaper, fell by 30 percent. Pew researchers also found an increase in instances of cameras being sent to events without correspondents, a higher percentage of "tell" stories (those narrated by the anchors), and greater use of material from press releases and syndication. The percentage of syndicated stories (that came from a national or regional feed) rose by 62 percent during that period. "And there is every reason to believe that this phenomenon of stretching resources thinner has continued through this decade," Rosenstiel concluded.[89]

In Washington, D.C., the Media Policy Initiative team of the New America Foundation has conducted reviews of several local news markets as part of its Information Community Case Study Project and concluded that local television news programming—even in the nation's capital—does not regularly address hard news subjects in the same depth as other media does.[90]

One cause (and effect) of the thinning coverage over the years is that fewer TV newsrooms now maintain a beat system. Traditional beats in local TV newsrooms included education, health, business, religion, government/politics, and crime/courts. Some stations have ad-

"Companies covering car wrecks and traffic accidents are kidding themselves if they think they are going to survive the Internet age," says Marci Burdick of Schurz Communications.

opted hybrid models in which reporters do both general assignment and some specialties. Howard Finberg, director of interactive learning at the Poynter Institute says, "The basic beat reporting in a local TV newsroom is under a huge amount of stress. The institutional knowledge [of a beat reporter] is the ability to sort the wheat from the chaff, and that is disappearing."[91] Wally Dean, a longtime news executive, coauthor of *We Interrupt This Newscast,* and currently director of training for the Committee for Concerned Journalists, says he is seeing stations refer to people as "beat reporters" when they are more accurately described as the point person for press releases on a particular topic. "Frequently the so-called 'health reporter' fronts the heath news but is using hand-outs from the health industry or using material from one of the feeds coming into the TV station," Dean says.[92]

TV news reporters appear to have less opportunity than they once did for time-intensive journalism. Two-thirds of news leaders responding to the Annenberg *Institutions of Democracy Media Survey* in 2005 said that profit pressures had reduced the number of stories they could assign that take time and money to report. Fifty-six percent said profit pressures had in fact increased the number of "quick and dirty stories" they ran. Watchdog journalism, the study reported, suffered the most.[93]

Many also see a growing emphasis on performance and aesthetics. "The criteria for hiring has changed," says Mathew Zelkind, station manager of WKRN in Nashville. "The Walter Cronkites and John Chancellors are a dying a breed. In many cases, you don't have journalists, you have performers. Aesthetics matters a lot. There are a lot of people on TV who wouldn't have been 26 years ago. A lot of it is economically driven." He added that his station has about one-third fewer reporters than it did 15 years ago. "We have fewer people, less specialization. Just fewer people on the street."[94]

Despite Notable Exceptions, Investigative Reporting Is Declining at Many Stations

The investigative operations mentioned earlier are important but increasingly rare. Investigative Reporters and Editors (IRE), a non-profit organization devoted to "improving the quality of investigative reporting," states that submissions from local TV stations for its top awards have fallen by more than half since 1999.[95] Broadcast membership in IRE has also dropped, from 874 broadcast members in 2000 down to 648 in 2010.[96] Longtime news executive Fred Young says investigative units have become financially hard to justify: "Investigative people, in the eyes of some of the people who looked at the bottom line of those stations, were not as productive as the reporters turning a story a day. Investigative has suffered."[97]

The *Columbia Journalism Review* reports that when it comes to making personnel cuts, investigative teams often are among the first casualties:

> "Their reporters [the investigative unit] tend to be some of the newsroom's most experienced and highly paid, and in some cases the unit is assigned a dedicated producer and photographer. That adds up to the kind of money that many cash-strapped stations well might decide to save or reallocate—no matter how prestigious the unit."[98]

Roberta Baskin, a longtime investigative reporter, won a duPont-Columbia award for a series she did for WJLA in Washington, D.C., called "Drilling for Dollars," about a chain of dental clinics doing unnecessary and painful root canals on children in order to collect money from Medicaid.[99] The day after she received the award, she and the rest of the station's I-team were laid off.[100] Baskin, now working in the federal government, says:

> "There is no longer any investigative reporting to speak of in Washington, D.C. It breaks my heart to see the shift toward doing more crime, fires, weather stories, instead of spending the time and resources to tell the public what they really need to know."[101]

Bill Lord, the station manager who cut Baskin's team, says that letting his I-team go was a painful decision purely based on the economic downturn and the timing of contracts.

> "It really wasn't a decision so much about the I-team as much as it was…a year and a half ago…we were, like every other station in the country, faced with a complete fall-off in revenues, and we had to adjust the expense line.…It was the timing of contracts, which caused us to go that direction to save money. The investigative people tended to be higher paid than the others, but they also had contract windows that allowed us to do it in a timely fashion. As difficult as that was, we had to make that call."[102]

Matthew Zelkind of WKRN in Nashville offers a similar description of the financial pressures that squeeze investigative reporting: "Investigative definitely suffers. One hundred percent. Long-form stories are dying because they're not financially feasible."[103] In previous years, Zelkind's staff produced long pieces on homeless children, problems with the water treatment system, and a high school that had more than a dozen pregnant teens. He said he was told, "not to do it anymore."[104] After a recent change in general managers, though, the station is doing more long-form pieces again, he said.

In some cases, critics argue that stations have continued to employ the "I-team" label while producing increasingly frivolous "exposés." Former WBZ-TV Boston investigative reporter Joe Bergantino, now director of the New England Center for Investigative Reporting (NECIR), a nonprofit based at Boston University, laments the trend:

> "Exploding picnic tables, dangerous department store hooks, the kind of scare-tactic stories that really, I think, have cheapened the whole meaning of what investigative reporting is.… They are using 'investigative reporting' more as a label rather than

Nearly a fourth of the crime leads in the Los Angeles stations were about crimes that did not take place in the LA media market.

a real thing. The trend is that stations call promotable stories 'investigative,' while shrinking or disbanding their investigative units. Serious, in-depth investigative reporting happens on rare occasions in local television news."[105]

Bergantino left his 27-year career in TV news two years ago when he was told that his station would have to start doing fewer "in-depth projects." He believes that these cutbacks in substantive reporting are "costing the viewers, the citizens, a lot…in that they're not getting the kind of information they need from television news to hold the government accountable, and the powerful accountable, and to be informed citizens in a democracy."[106] Byron Harris of WFAA, who broke the savings and loan crisis story in the 1980s, says "Allowing public officials, corporate leaders, and community leaders to go unprobed, unchallenged, and unquestioned is a big problem."[107]

One way that a number of TV stations have managed to preserve some investigative capacity is by teaming up with nonprofits. Such collaborations were pioneered at the network level. For instance, ProPublica, a nonprofit investigative entity, has partnered on various projects with ABC, CNN, CNBC, and CBS's *60 Minutes*. . However, to work, nonprofit groups must figure out ways of earning money. New England Center for Investigative Reporting, another nonprofit, has produced a dozen multimedia investigative pieces in the last 18 months. Bergantino, the group's director, says, "There's an opportunity for television stations in all the major cities where centers like ours exist, to essentially boost the quality and quantity of investigative reporting by connecting with our centers and paying them something for our work…to look to us to help fill that void."[108] However, he noted that his organization has had difficulty getting paid for its work. Investigative News Network (INN), an umbrella organization of 51 nonprofit news organizations,[109] has produced several series (including "Campus Assaults," which uncovered rapes at university fraternity houses that administrators were hiding or ignoring), but CEO Kevin Davis says, "Local TV and radio outlets see it as a cheap way to get investigative reporting, and while we want to push the content to a wide audience, we [INN members] have to receive money for the work."[110]

> A study of local TV news coverage in eleven media markets found that only 8 percent of broadcasts in the month before an election had stories even mentioning local races.

Bleeding Is Still Leading

For several decades, a popular saying about local TV news has been "If it bleeds, it leads," referring to the tendency of local stations to emphasize more sensational incidents, particularly crime stories. Recent studies show that this tendency is alive and well, and may even be increasing.

> - One out of three Los Angeles TV broadcasts *led* their newscast with a crime story, according to the USC Annenberg study.[111]

> - In Baltimore, Maryland, crime was the number one topic on local TV news, representing 23 percent of stories, twice as many as other subjects, including city government, and schools, according to the Pew Project for Excellence in Journalism.[112]

> - More than 44 percent of all stories aired by local television stations in the Michigan State study were about crimes, accidents or disasters—twice the level found in newspapers serving the same area.[113]

> - An earlier Pew study of 2,400 newscasts and 30,000 stories that aired from 1998 to 2002 indicated that an even higher percentage of *lead* stories involved crime. "While crime, disasters and accidents make up 36% of all stories studied in our 1998–2002 study, they made up 61% of all lead stories, those given the most time and reporting resources on the air. And in subsequent, smaller 2005 studies crime, fires and disasters made up 77% of lead stories."[114]

Some news managers say that they emphasize crime because viewers want it. "If I had a penny for every person that says 'I do not watch that kind of stuff,'" says Steve Hertzke, former news director of KUTV in Salt Lake

Viewers of local news in the Midwest got 2.5 times as much information about local elections from the paid advertisements than from the newscasts.

City. "Really? Well, the ratings say different."[115] Clearly, crime stories are engaging and important to viewers, and easier to make visually compelling.

But others in the industry are not persuaded that the ratings demand quite this dominance of crime stories. Charles Gibson, the former anchor of ABC World News Night News and Good Morning America, and a former local TV journalist, told a gathering of news directors in 2006:

> "What truly matters to people are their local schools, garbage collection, road repair, water quality, hometown healthcare. Those things are much more important to people than our regular fare on Good Morning America or World News Tonight. So why don't you cover those things? Why do you lead night after night with crime and fire?"

He suggested that station managers were overly influenced by consultants and small, short-term movements in ratings, instead of long-term ratings and reputation.

> "I know you all love the minute-by-minutes. They're like news director crack. Seductive and addictive. But the reputation and eventually the ratings of your newscasts don't depend on a minute. They depend on the weeks and the months and the years of good solid civic coverage of your city.   More Americans get their news from local newscasts than from any other source. And that makes what you do important."[116]

The economic crunch may be increasing the emphasis on crime stories, because they are less expensive to produce. Al Tompkins, group leader for broadcast and online at the Poynter Institute, and formerly a news director there, explains:

> "Back in our day we led with it because we thought that's what people wanted and we thought that was really important and exciting. Now the reason to do it is it's by far the cheapest thing to cover. It's principally driven by manpower and economics whereas once it was more driven by an editorial decision that, you know, 'We're action news, this is who we are.' We could cover other stuff, we just don't want to."[117]

With advances in technology, TV stations now have cheap, easy access to sensational footage through daily national feeds from the network they are affiliated with. This allows them to air crime stories even when the crime did not occur in their coverage area. Nearly a fourth of the crime stories that led the Los Angeles newscasts in USC's Lear Center study involved crimes that did not take place in the L.A. media market.[118]

"One-Man Bands" Are Increasing

Many local TV stations are opting for "one-man bands," defined by local TV news managers as journalists who do it all: conduct interviews, shoot video, and edit their own stories. As recently as five years ago, the typical production approach was to have crews of two people: a reporter and a camera person. Sometimes in a larger local market and at the network news level, a producer would also be part of the team. The replacement of that system with one-man bands has been rapid. About 31.7 percent of newsrooms "mostly use" one-man bands (compared with 22.3 percent three years ago), and another 29 percent "use some," according to the 2010 RTDNA/Hofstra University survey. The highest incidence was in small markets, but even in big markets the practice is widespread, and 43.1 percent of news directors expect to use one-man bands in the near future.[119]

In some cases, this is clearly a wise efficiency and potentially even a journalistic improvement. Cameras are now smaller and lighter, which makes it easy for a reporter to carry one while out on a story. And video-editing software has become much more user-friendly, so reporters can readily be trained to edit their own material. Scripps

Television Station Group is requiring all their reporters and photojournalists to morph into multimedia journalists, as part of their "Newsroom of the Future" initiative, launched in 2009. Vice president Bob Sullivan says:

> "We have moved from one strand [of content] coming out of the stations to three: mobile, web, and broadcast. How do we better prepare our broadcast journalists to service these three platforms? Can we do it under the existing format? The decision was 'no.' We had to reexamine the overall structure, the editorial processes of our newsrooms, and our production processes internally, as well as the processes of what a journalist is when they go out on the street."[120]

Hearst Television Inc. launched one of broadcasting's first multimedia training projects for newsroom staff, called the "Next Generation Newsroom Project." Hearst's Brian Bracco says news gatherers are equipped with laptops, smartphones, webcams, flip cams, and air cards. Reporters, photographers, and producers were trained in field editing, using Skype, and other new technological innovations. During a recent tornado, a reporter from Hearst's Omaha TV station, with a laptop and a web camera mounted on the dashboard of the news car, was able to chase the funnel cloud, broadcasting live as the tornado headed down the road.[121]

Sullivan says that Scripps staffers must adapt to the changing circumstances: "It is all an ongoing process to get the Literal Larrys and Literal Lindas, accustomed to doing things one way, to understand that newsroom personnel must adapt, learn, and change with the times and technology."[122] Susan Schuler, vice president of news at Raycom Media, which owns 31 television stations, had a similarly blunt message: "Each person needs three to five to six skill sets as opposed to the one or two they have now. Over the next few years it will be a requirement to keep your employment."[123]

"Frequently the so-called 'health reporter' fronts the health news but is using hand-outs from the health industry," says industry veteran Wally Dean.

Without question some of these changes have reduced costs and sharply increased productivity per person. "We used to assign reporters one story a day. Now, under the right circumstances, they're doing more and the quality isn't suffering," says Andrew Vrees, news director at WCBV in Boston. "We just need to be more efficient."[124]

In theory, with the money saved from laying off no-longer-needed staff, stations could put more one-man bands on the ground. Multimedia journalist Ben Winslow, himself a one-man band in Salt Lake City, hopes that instead of a newsroom filled with 20 photographers and 20 reporters, "there will be 40 people who can do both. I hope we will have more resources of people to go out and practice journalism, do quality journalism."[125]

But at many stations, that is not what has happened. On average, most stations have not used the savings to hire more reporters. "Let's face it. It is what it is, and it is economic," says Con Psarras, former news director and now vice president of editorials and special projects at KSL-TV in Salt Lake City. "It is an ability to cut heads, and it is a full-time-equivalent-reduction campaign. It does not make the pictures better. It does not make the stories better. It does not make the coverage on the web better—that's a mythology. It just saves money."[126]

The main consequence is simple: reporters who once just reported the news now have many other tasks, and more newscasts to feed, so they have less time to research their stories. At KREM in Spokane, Washington, a young, energetic reporter named Othello Richards says that on an average day he might be doing two separate packages on a double homicide-suicide to lead the 5:00 and 6:00 P.M. newscasts—operating his own live truck, shooting his own live stand-up on-camera, and shooting, writing, and editing the packages. He is also responsible for contributing to the station's website.[127] KREM's news director, Noah Cooper, has the smallest staff in town with 34 employees— down from 48 in 1999/2000—including seven reporters, all of them multimedia journalists (one-man bands). Each reporter is expected to be able to turn in two separate stories a day.[128] That level of daily production leaves very little time for in-depth research and investigation.

In a research study done at the Annenberg School for Communication at the University of Pennsylvania, Mary Angela Bock interviewed 65 video journalists (VJs) and found some subtle but important trends in how they cover stories. "Instead of the smaller cameras and simpler software making it easier to take chances, television VJs see themselves as having *less freedom* to take chances with their stories," she says.[129]

"Many expressed concerns that news stories become preplanned, mapped out, and even written in advance; they have time for fewer interviews, and fewer video shots. They were asking themselves, 'What can I do in one or maybe two shoots that will allow me to get back to my shop—my edit point is by about three o'clock—so I can cut my story, maybe shoot my own stand-up, and feed the darn thing by deadline?'"[130]

VJs who work for television organizations and must deliver a package each day said that deadline pressures make them more likely to pursue "easy, one-location features stories" than more labor-intensive pieces.[131]

Marco Villarreal, who has worked as a reporter at several local TV stations, said that at one station he worked at, he was so busy tweeting, shooting, and editing that he simply had less time to conduct interviews. The common casualty was the depth of reporting: "It's the research. When I was one-man banding, if I had interviewed one or two people, I'd say, 'Hey, that's enough to get on the air.'" He feels the system can work quite well for many kinds of breaking news but not for "in-depth reporting."[132]

Mike Daniels, who currently works at KESQ/KDFX in Palm Springs, California, previously worked as a one-man band in Grand Junction, Colorado. He describes a typical day of reporting for a VJ:

"Because I was one-man banding I couldn't take the time that I would have liked in order to really cover the story. Shooting was rushed, interviews were rushed, and writing and editing was as well. It made me a quick writer and editor, but the quality wasn't as good because of that. It was nerve-racking because I was always worried about shooting the right video and making sure the audio was correct."[133]

To be clear, the invention of the one-man band could still end up being a positive development when employed thoughtfully and when VJs are equipped with journalistic training, so they know how to cover a story, how to ask bold questions, and how to push beyond the surface of a story in pursuit of enterprising and needed information for the viewer. Video journalist Ben Winslow of FOX 13 in Salt Lake City says he refuses to shoot his own live stand-ups. "I had a story the other day on the oil spill, and the kids are all flashing gang signs behind me.... There are certain things you cannot control, so you need a photographer."[134] Bill Lord, station manager at Albritton Communications–owned WJLA in Washington, D.C., limits one-man bands to stories happening in one place, such as a Boy Scout anniversary parade at the National Mall. But he decided send a full crew to cover a recent thunderstorm. "You need a couple of sets of eyes.... You want to divide up the work of shooting, writing, editing, and feeding in such a way that you get a better product."[135]

"Investigative people, in the eyes of some of the people who looked at the bottom line of those stations, were not as productive as the reporters turning a story a day. Investigative has suffered."

It seems worth reiterating the point that the efficiencies enabled by new technology would be even more clearly a plus for journalism if the savings from creating one-man bands were used to increase the overall number of reporters or invested in bolstering enterprise and accountability journalism in local television newsrooms. But if it is simply a way to have fewer bodies producing more news, more superficially, TV news will have stepped backward. Jill Geisler of the Poynter Institute, which trains journalists and media leaders, says that asking people to do multiple stories a day harms the quality of the reporting: "There is only so much water you can put in the soup."[136]

Advertisers Too Often Dictate Content Through "Pay-for-Play" Arrangements

For TV news veterans and the audience as well, one of the most worrisome developments in local TV journalism is the rise of "pay-for-play" business deals in which news coverage is directly shaped by advertisers.

For many years, local television stations maintained a strict separation—sometimes called the "ad-edit wall" or the "church-state wall"—between the sales department and the newsroom, similar to the system at most newspapers. Those in the newsroom were told little or nothing about the deals made between the TV sales department and advertisers, so they would not feel pressured to direct coverage toward anything other than what was in the best interest of viewers. But financial pressures have often broken down the wall, according to Stacey Woelfel, who chaired the RTDNA Ethics Committee for seven years and is now news director at KOMU-TV in central Missouri. "Pay-for-play is still an issue," he says. "It's the station looking for a dollar here or there where they did not have to worry about it before. What do they have to offer? Well…airtime."[137]

In January 2008, Glen Mabie resigned from his position as news director at WEAU in Eau Claire, Wisconsin, over a coverage deal in which a local hospital would pay the station to air two health stories twice a week on topics selected from a list provided by the hospital. The only people the reporters could interview for those stories were personnel at that hospital, which would also have first crack at interviews for any other health stories the station did. Mabie says that station management removed the exclusivity provision after he and other staffers complained.[138] But he maintains that the executives told them to "wipe the big J for Journalism off their sweaters because that is not the way it is anymore." The station later abandoned the plan, and the president of the company that owns the station made a personal appearance at the station to announce that they would not implement the deal.[139]

Trudy Lieberman, a professor at Baruch College at the City University of New York, conducted a two-year study on the crumbling ad-edit wall. She reported:

> "In Austin, Texas, KTBC-TV viewers heard the morning news anchor Joe Bickett introduce a new electronic rehabilitation system for injured kids. Bickett then pitched to reporter Sharon Dennis who would have more on that story. Sharon Dennis presented a report on the computer-guided rehab program at Cleveland Clinic in Cleveland, Ohio. Dennis does not work for KTBC and there was no mention made of the fact that Dennis—a former veteran TV reporter—worked for the Cleveland Clinic. In fact, Dennis's pre-packaged stories go out to local TV stations all over the country distributed to, among others, Fox News Edge, a service for Fox affiliates that in turn distributes to 140 Fox stations."[140]

According to Lieberman, "The hospital had controlled the story. In some cases the hospitals pay for the airtime, a sponsorship, and in others they don't but still provide expertise and story ideas at a cost. Viewers think they are getting health news but they are getting a form of advertising."[141] KTBC news director, Pam Vaught, says the station has a policy mandating that viewers be informed when a story originated from and is reported by the Cleveland Clinic, but on that particular day a young producer was on duty in the KTBC newsroom and neglected to follow station policy.[142]

In 2007, an award-winning story by Steph Gregor in Columbus, Ohio's *The Other Paper* reported that the Ohio State University Medical Center was paying local TV stations $100,000 or more to air so-called "Breakthroughs in Medicine" segments that benefited the hospital—and the stations had not disclosed that the content was paid for by the Medical Center. One station vice president maintained that the segments were not ads but "vignettes," and that he did not see anything wrong with them.[143] Ike Walker, news director at WCMH-TV in Columbus, Ohio, says he was not the news director at the time and that the anchorwoman who did the spots is no longer there. He also says that there is now a clear wall between sales and news departments. For instance, the station has run a special promoting good breast health that is paid for by a consortium of non-profit Ohio hospitals and healthcare organizations, but the consortium has no editorial voice or role in selecting the content, Walker says.[144]

Roberta Baskin won the top award for a series about dental clinics doing unnecessary root canals on children to collect Medicaid dollars. The next day, she was laid off.

Pay-for-play arrangements with the health care industry have prompted an outcry from journalists in the field. The Association of Health Care Journalists and the Society for Professional Journalists issued a joint statement urging local broadcast stations to avoid arrangements that improperly influence health coverage. The statement said that even if such deals are disclosed, handing over editorial decision making to hospitals violates the principles of ethical journalism and betrays the public trust.[145]

These advertising relationships are not limited to the health care sector. Forest Carr, a former ethics fellow at the Poynter Institute and longtime local television news director, says he has seen many manifestations of what he calls "stealth advertising" over the years—including an incident in which one TV station curiously decided to cover a food special at a shopping mall during a local flood. Carr explains:

"It's pretty obvious the station was getting paid to do that at the mall. It wasn't disclosed as such, and I asked the producer what was that about, and I was told that it was part of a deal where the mall paid the station to do it. And it was not disclosed to the viewer. It had serious adverse effect on the station's ability to serve the public when the lives of the public were in jeopardy from bad weather moving through, and they had their weather guy tied up doing a commercial."[146]

In many markets, shows not necessarily affiliated with the news department are being created just for the purpose of attracting pay-for-play partnerships. Steve Hertzke, then news director at KUTV in Salt Lake City, explained that station management came to him and wanted to create a "value-added show"—as such programs are now being called—that would be built around the station's noon newscast. The 90-minute show would open with 30 minutes of news produced by the news department, which would be followed by an hour-long "value-added show" anchored by different talent drawn from the station's programming department. In this latter hour, pay-for-play would be welcome.[147] But with a news show leading directly into the pay-for-play segments, how would audiences know to make a distinction between the two? Hertzke said that the plan was to use talent from the morning show rather than the news shows to host pay-for-play segments. Asked why the station was adding an additional show just for pay-for-play, Hertzke responded that they "need revenue because it is revenue that hasn't been tapped."

Some managers submit that pay-for-play is more acceptable if it is done on morning news shows, which generally have less hard news, or on a morning program that is built for entertaining. In Tampa, Florida, according to a *Washington Post* report, WFLA's *Daytime* invited guests to pay to appear on the show, charging $2,500 for a four-to-six-minute interview. The general manager defended the practice, saying that *Daytime* is not a news show nor is it operated by the news department.[148] After a public outcry, *Daytime* began more clearly labeling sponsored interviews.

How common are these practices? In a 2010 Pew survey, 24 percent of local TV news executives reported "a blurring of lines between advertising and news." Several anonymously offered examples; a Pew summary of these comments stated:

> "Sponsored segments have in some cases become paid content that looks like news. One executive described 'news time paid for by a local hospital with hospital having approval over content.' Another station executive, similarly, mentioned a daily paid interview with the local hospital.

> "One broadcast executive described how 'ask-the-expert segments' are sold by sales people and then the news department is strongly encouraged to validate the expertise of these people by interviewing them for legitimate news stories. Others described the same thing. 'We have an interview format newscast. Our sale staff has "sold" some interviews to our online experts. They don't always offer great content, but a guest appearance is part of their sales package.'

> "Said another news executive, 'Our sales department comes to the newsroom with story ideas they've already "sold." They just need a reporter to do the story.'"[149]

For the most part, TV station news directors and journalists dislike these arrangements, viewing them as unprofessional and harmful to quality. There is some disagreement about whether the bad situation is merely persisting or getting worse. Stacey Woelfel, former chair of the RTDNA Ethics Committee, says, "It has not gotten any better and it has not gotten any worse over the last five years or so." Tom Rosensteil, director of the Pew Project on Excellence in Journalism, states: "The evidence we've seen suggests that this is much more widespread than a few years ago. That's what I'm hearing from news directors."[150] James Rainey, media reporter for the *Los Angeles Times*, recently won a prestigious press criticism award for his articles about at least three different pay-for-play cases. In an article about a woman who appears on local TV stations as an objective expert on toys—even though she's actually paid by the toy manufacturers whose products she touts—Rainey concluded, "Local television news has become a hotbed for pay-to-play promotions." He explained why the problem seems to be growing:

> "The trend promises to continue and grow. TV news producers must fill an expanding news hole, particularly in the mornings, where many news programs have been extended from three to four, five and even six hours. And advertisers, fearful of being blocked by viewers with video recorders and mute buttons, don't mind paying for promotional appearances that make them more visible and credible."[151]

Some news managers continue to resist pay-for-play. KSL in Salt Lake City so far has been able to hold the line against any pay for play invading the newsroom, but it has not been easy, according to former KSL news director, Con Psarras: "There was a time when our sales staff was hoping to circulate a list of our preferred vendors so if we had a story about consumer electronics we could go to one place over another. Whenever they give me that list it is guaranteed we will not go to that place."[152]

Some advertisers use pay-for-play to pit one station against another for their business. Marci Burdick, senior vice president of news for Schurz Communications Inc., says that some advertisers have shown her proposals from other stations supposedly guaranteeing that the advertiser's experts will be interviewed in exchange for an ad sale. Burdick says she rejected the deals and that "it is a fireable offense in our company. Our sales manager will be the first to tell our advertisers our integrity is not for sale."[153]

Another more subtle form of advertiser intrusion into newscasts involves product placement of the sort routinely accepted in movies but previously considered unethical in news operations. A 2006 survey found that out of 251 television news directors, 12.4 percent said they were either already doing or considering doing product placements within their newscasts.[154] Fairness and Integrity in Telecommunications Media also provided research on embedded advertising (including references to McDonald's coffee being placed on local newscasts and Starbucks paying for product placement on an MSNBC cable newsmagazine show).[155] NAB and others responded that the station provides disclosures through on-air announcements and on-screen graphics.[156]

In 2008, the *New York Times* reported that KVVU Las Vegas had been paid to place cups of McDonald's iced coffee on the news desk as anchors reported the news-and-lifestyle portion of the morning show.[157] The six-month promotion for the fast food chain was expected to "shore up advertising revenue" for KVVU, "[and would] not influence content," the station said.[158] The station also noted that the cups "appeared in the 7:00–9:00 a.m. segment of the program, when the news was lighter, and did not affect content."[159] A May 2010 article in *Broadcasting & Cable* magazine, entitled "Your Ad Here…and Here," revealed that "insiders say an advertiser might pay $350,000 annually to sponsor a leading midsize station's sports reports. Branded props on the set of that station might go for around $300,000, though that sum would include traditional spots, too."[160]

The Airing of Video News Releases

Video News Releases are video packages created by companies, governments or others hoping to influence the news. Sometimes they take the form of a fully-formed "news story," sometimes they offer interview sound bites, and sometimes provide just B-roll (generic video) for video use in a real news story. Some VNRs feature actors playing reporters and include a suggested script to introduce the story. Some TV stations run them as full stand-alone pieces, others use snippets in other stories.

Some of the first VNRs were created by the automotive industry, which hired crews to film new model rollouts and news conferences in the 1960s. The U.S. government produced VNRs, the source of some controversy in 2005.[161] By 1999, the largest VNR producer was Medialink, with $27 million worth of sales in 1997. Today VNRs can be distributed to local stations through satellites, the Internet, and major network news feeds, such as PR Newswire, CNN Newsource, CBS Newspath, and Pathfire.[162]

In 2006, the media and consumer watchdog group the Center for Media and Democracy (CMD) released a report entitled *Fake TV News: Widespread and Undisclosed*, which found that over a 10-month period 77 broadcast stations and cable outlets ran 98 separate instances of 36 VNRs, without disclosing to viewers that these were video press releases rather than journalism independently created by local news teams."[163] In 2007, the FCC proposed fining Comcast $20,000 for airing portions of VNRs without proper disclosure of the source. The VNRs in that case

In some cases, "one man bands" improve journalism and efficiency. During a recent tornado, a reporter from the Omaha Hearst TV station was able to chase a tornado with a laptop and a web camera mounted on the dashboard of the news car, broadcasting live as the tornado headed down the road.

"Let's face it—it is what it is and it is economic," says Con Psarras of KSL-TV about one-man-bands. "It is an ability to cut heads and it is a full-time-equivalent-reduction campaign. It does not make the pictures better. It does not make the stories better. It does not make the coverage on the web better, that's a mythology. It just saves money."

were produced for Nelson's Rescue Sleep, General Mills's Wheaties, Allstate Insurance, and Trend Micro. They were aired in cablecasts on a regional Comcast channel.[164] Public relations executive Joe Loveland has argued that even PR professionals shouldn't support the use of VNRs without proper disclosure: "The use of PR people mimicking the dress and conventions of news reporters without real time disclosures of their mimicry crosses the line from briefing reporters to impersonating reporters."[165]

In a 2005 Radio and TV Digital News Association survey of news directors, most said that they rarely used VNRs and that when they did they disclosed it properly to their viewers.[166] But more recently Stacey Woelfel, former chair of the RTDNA Ethics Committee and currently news director at KOMU, said that heavy use of VNRs continues today: "There is a lot of time to fill and not as many people to fill it as you would like to have. Sources of video that show up in the newsroom that are fun or interesting…still are attractive to TV newscast producers."[167]

Indeed, on March 24, 2011, the FCC issued two Notices of Apparent Liability against TV stations for violating sponsorship identification rules. In one case, the FCC proposed to fine KMSP-TV $4,000 for airing a VNR produced for General Motors without identifying the sponsor. In the other, the FCC proposed to fine WMGM-TV $4,000 for airing a VNR produced for Matrixx Initiatives, the makers of Zicam Cold Remedy, without a sponsorship identification announcement. The piece featured medical experts talking about travelers catching colds, with one doctor adding, "But there are some things you can do to get better. Especially in the first 48 hours. To cut down on the severity and duration of symptoms. You can take an intranasal zinc preparation, like Zicam."[168] The piece closed with a reporter saying, "To see this report again or to find out more about zinc as a treatment for the common cold, go to our website." The stations argued that they should not have been fined because they did not accept payment for running the news releases and that the FCC action constituted an infringement on their First Amendment rights.[169]

Some defend the partial use of VNRs, or at least of the footage contained in them, as long as their provenance is disclosed to consumers. Longtime executive Fred Young says that the demand for content—"feeding the Hoover"—results in producers "sweeping stuff up." "Today if you clearly identify where [the VNR] came from," he says, "I have no problem with it. It is the people who are taking it and passing it off as news that bothers me."[170]

News 8 Austin, a 24-hour local news station owned by Time Warner Cable—and the recipient of numerous awards for excellence in journalism, including a Walter Cronkite Award and a Regional Edward R. Murrow Award—is among the local cable news stations that sometimes use VNRs, under certain circumstances. News 8's news director, Kevin Benz, talked about his station's policy:

> "There are video news releases produced by the Texas Parks and Wildlife Department. They are outdoors related and related to hunting, fishing, enjoyment of the outdoors, camping, parks, and those kinds of things. We fully vet them. We are completely transparent about where we get them and who gives them to us, both on air, and online.… If there is something that we feel is overly promotional, or only promotional, we don't air it."[171]

Some station managers say that attention from public interest groups, Congress, and the FCC has reduced their usage of VNRs. The Post-Newsweek Stations Group's six local television stations do not use VNRs at all.[172] Steve Schwaid, former senior vice president of news for all 30 NBCUniversal television stations and current director of news and digital content at the local CBS station in Atlanta, is also leery of VNRs:

> "We don't use VNRs. Okay, they're not allowed on my air, period. We have no control over them. The only exception will be if there is a recall on a pharmaceutical drug and [this is] the only video from inside the factory and we clearly label where it came from. But we do not take VNR handouts, period."[173]

Some of the large television station groups have not banned VNR usage but, in the wake of the FCC's Comcast fine and the CMD report, they have designed and written new policies. Hearst Corporation vice president of news, Brian Bracco, described Hearst's current guidelines: "We do not use VNR stories as a whole, but if we use generic [VNR] video we have to identify it then, and identify it at the end of the newscast, as well. And we have to be clear where the VNR came from."[174] Renai Bodley, news director at FOX 13 in Salt Lake City, says her station often gets VNRs from such places as a local radioactive waste company, which supplies the station with video and audio they choose rather than inviting the local station to come and shoot a story themselves. Bodley has a policy with her newsroom staff: a "Courtesy of" marker must be burned into the videotape before they even review it in order to prevent it from being used later as B-roll (generic video) for another story without being identified as a VNR.[175]

The trailblazing VNR producer Medialink is now called Synaptic Digital,[176] and Brian Schwartz, director of client solutions in its Los Angeles office, says that his company does not use the term "video news release" much any more. But he says that news stations continue to use the video and interviews Synaptic sends out (from clients that include Siemens, General Motors, KIA, Land Rover, the Gates Foundation, and UNICEF), because it is free content, and stations complain that they do not have the resources to gather such material themselves.[177] Another big player in the field is DS Simon Productions Inc., credited with distributing the Rescue Sleep VNR, one of the four videos that led to Comcast's being fined $20,000 in total by the FCC. When contacted for an interview, Douglas Simon, the company's president, responded emphatically: "I can tell you that despite the proliferation of third-party video, and the near-death experience of TV news, VNRs aren't a relevant communications tool anymore. I don't have anything else to add."[178]

Many Stations Now Outsource Their News Operations

Some stations have dealt with cost pressures by getting out of the news production business altogether—literally outsourcing their entire newscast to another party.[179] Nearly one-third of TV stations say they are running news produced by another station, according to the 2010 RTDNA)/Hofstra University Annual Survey. Professor Robert Papper, who conducts the study, says in his latest survey that there are 762 stations originating local news and another 224 that get news from one of those 762 stations. Some involve common ownership, some joint operating agreements.[180]

Communications Workers of America (CWA) and Media Council Hawaii say they have identified at least 25 television markets in the U.S. where stations have entered into "shared services agreements" (SSAs), in which one station effectively takes over the news operation of a second. CWA claims the SSAs reduce the diversity of local voices in a community by replacing independent newscasts with those of the brokering stations and invariably lead to reductions in news personnel.[181]

The Honolulu, Hawaii, market is the focus of an official complaint with the FCC by the Media Council of Hawaii, alleging that Raycom Media, the licensee of two Honolulu stations, entered into an SSA with a third station and is now operating a consolidated news service that provides programming to all three: the NBC affiliate, the CBS affiliate, and the MYNetworkTV affiliate. The plaintiffs charge that the SSA led to 68 layoffs—more than one-third the combined news staffs of the three participating stations.[182] Raycom has said the SSA was necessary to ensure its economic survival, no FCC approval was required because there was no change in ownership or control of the stations, and the FCC has approved similar arrangements in the past.[183] The matter is pending.

Another cost-saving strategy some stations have adapted is to contract out to a company that bills itself as a local news service—even though significant portions of the "local" news programming are created far from the markets it serves. The Independent News Network (INN; not to be confused with the Investigative News Network, mentioned above), produces anchored newscasts from its base in Davenport, Iowa, that are designed to look and feel local to viewers in its clients' markets. As the company explains on its website, "This service is delivered by experienced anchor and reporter teams at a fraction of the cost to produce it internally!"[184] Five days a week, INN produces a four-anchor news, weather, and sports program with anywhere from 26 to 28 minutes of

> A local hospital paid the TV stations $100,000 or more to air so-called "Breakthroughs in Medicine" segments that benefitted the hospital, according to one report.

airtime. Stations can save anywhere from $40,000 to $150,000 of monthly overhead, depending on the market size and how much local newsgathering capacity they opt to retain.[185] They have the option of feeding some local elements to Iowa to be inserted into the newscast, and INN encourages them to retain at least two reporters for that purpose. But if locally produced pieces are not up to INN standards, INN produc-ers discard the material, and there are no local segments that day.

When asked if INN will grow into a company doing journalism that includes investigative reporting, enterprise news, and beat report-ing, CEO Dave McAnally said, "That's for somebody else to do. Frankly, the margins in that stuff, they aren't there."[186] The company outsourced its first news show in April 2001, and it now produces newscasts for at least a dozen stations, in locations that include Springfield, Missouri; Cheyenne, Wyoming; Columbus, Georgia; Waterloo, Iowa; Omaha, Nebraska; Reno, Nevada, Gainesville, Florida; Jef-fersonville, Indiana; Alexandria, Louisiana; Montgomery, Alabama; as well as for a block of Spanish-language, Azteca America–affiliate stations in Atlanta, Las Vegas, Dallas, Houston, Denver, San Diego, and San Antonio.[187]

> "When I was one-man-banding, if I had interviewed one or two people, I'd say, 'Hey, that's enough to get on the air.'"

Local stations do not always disclose to viewers that some of the seemingly local talent is actually delivering the news from across the country. For instance, on its website, WLTZ in Columbus, Georgia, lists the INN anchors in Iowa as part of its local news team.[188]

Competing Stations Increasingly Collaborate to Save Money

Another significant and controversial trend in local news involves competing stations sharing news reporting and production resources. More than 60 percent of stations say they are involved in some sort of cooperative newsgather-ing or coverage agreement with another station or medium.[189]

A common form of cooperation is "pooling." Stations can save money and eliminate duplication by pooling their resources and sharing coverage of certain events. On November 13, 2008, NBC and FOX affiliates announced a plan to begin sharing cameras crews in order to slash costs in markets like Philadelphia, Los Angeles, New York, Washington, Dallas, and Chicago—creating what they called "a local news service (LNS)."[190] CWA says it knows of 19 markets where two or more stations participate in an LNS.[191]

In a typical LNS, two or more stations contribute camera crews to a jointly run assignment desk that decides which stories to cover and feeds video back to individual newsrooms to be produced internally. FOX Television Sta-tions CEO, Jack Abernathy, explained:

> "Four [stations] are covering the same five stories every day. We bring the same pictures back every day. This venture will just
> cover those four or five stories in a pooling situation. And it has nothing to do with homogenization. It's, 'Gee, why don't we
> take our limited resources and have them focus on independent reporting?'"[192]

In the Los Angeles market the FOX, NBC, and Tribune stations are members of the LNS, which is housed on the same lot as KNBC, the local NBC station. There is an LNS managing editor, financed by the three members. Each station donates an assignment editor and three crews in a rotating arrangement. Each morning, the LNS assignment-editor-of-the-day informs the stations what the LNS will be covering. Often in Los Angeles, it is a sporting event or a press conference with a local official.

In a written submission to the FCC, a group of some of the top local television station owners, including Belo Corp., Barrington Broadcasting Group, and Raycom Media, argued that LNS arrangements enable them to share and reduce costs for events such as press conferences and court hearings that do not require multiple cameras to capture almost identical feeds. The broadcasters said that the common element in all of these LNS arrangements is that they provide creative mechanisms for local stations to redeploy journalistic resources in the most effective manner pos-sible for service to their local communities.[193]

In practice, enhanced service to local communities is not always the result. The June 2010 opening of a new Veterans Home in California provides a typical example: Various elected officials and veterans gathered for an event in Los Angeles, a substantial homeless veterans problem. The lone cameraman in attendance was from the LNS. He placed his camera on the platform set up for the press, recorded video of the ribbon cutting, and when the event was over he packed up his camera and left. There was no reporter with him to ask questions of top elected officials, to ask questions of the veterans, or to pursue any enterprise stories that might have come to mind in the course of the event.[194]

Increasingly, cooperative news services are not only sharing footage from official events but also interviews, so stories on three different stations might feature the same newsmaker interview. And, as noted above, when a pool sends only a camera person, not a reporter, it is less likely to get the story behind the story—or an angle other than the one officials choose to show the public. Marci Burdick, senior vice president of news for Schurz Communications, says:

> "What I think you lose then is what has been the value of the traditional journalism, which is…the reporter getting in there and finding out what the real story is and dig[ging] down beyond the spray coverage and get[ting] into the issues about what really affects consumers in the school and city government."[195]

Some stations have decided not to participate in pooling arrangements. Bill Lord, station manager at WJLA in Washington, D.C., explains:

> "I don't want to share my coverage plans for the day with the other stations; I don't want to give up a couple of photographers to go do generic things that will play on all of the news stations."[196]

Lord says there are some stories where pool agreements do make sense and have existed among competing stations for years.

> "If you're talking about a trial when the camera's in the courtroom recording the testimony of a witness—that makes sense for a pool. But when it's a story about the summer jobs program that the mayor is going to be talking about, it's not just the head bite of the mayor you're talking about, it's all the ancillary information. It's about going out and talking to the people who have the jobs. It's about being relevant to an audience."[197]

Rebecca Campbell, former president and general manager of WABC in New York and now president of the ABC-owned Television Station Group, agrees: "Our crews are our ambassadors. The minute you take that away, you lose that voice…. The money savings should be in technology not the voices."[198]

Less controversially, increasing numbers of stations are sharing helicopters. A news helicopter costs at least two million dollars to buy, not even counting the expensive camera and transmission equipment. Four stations in Washington, D.C., now share one helicopter, an economically driven arrangement that even WJLA's Bill Lord, who is not part of the pool for on-the-ground coverage, finally had to agree to:

> "We held out for a long time—we kept our own chopper, because we had an inexpensive chopper deal—but in the end, it just made more sense to be a part of this, because the economics are such that nobody can afford a full-time helicopter for over a million dollars a year per station."[199]

Even sharing helicopters can mean a compromise in coverage and diversity of information. Deborah Collura, vice president of news for Post-Newsweek Stations, finally sacrificed her Detroit station's helicopter to a pooling agreement in order to maintain her investigative unit, and she spoke to this point:

"When I was in Miami, we were the first with our chopper over the Value Jet crash. You know, you send up a veteran reporter, and they talk from the chopper for hours. In Houston last year we sent our chief meteorologist over the devastation of the hurricane and it was fabulous. He went up for a couple of days and did these tours and it looked like a war zone…. When you are in a pool situation, you cannot do that…. It's a missing element from the show."[200]

CWA argues that LNSs undermine the FCC's long-standing public interest goals of diversity, competition, and localism, as well as "evade the letter or spirit" of the FCC's local television ownership rules.[201] In 2010, it called on the FCC to "tighten up the rules for attributing local marketing agreements and joint service agreements" and urged the commission to "revise its reporting and disclosure requirements so both the Commission and the public know about these agreements and can better assess their effect on diversity, competition, and localism."[202]

Finally, while pooling and sharing costly equipment like helicopters can be justified as a way of being able to afford more reporters in the field, TV executives generally have continued to order staff cuts per the mandates from station owners at the same time that they're embracing these efficiencies. For some news directors, entering into pooling agreements may have helped prevent *deeper* cuts, but there is no sign that pooling, or other economies like shared helicopters and one-man bands, have led to an increase in investigative or enterprise reporting, particularly not at the multitude of stations that never invested in this kind of reporting to begin with.

Some Stations Use Their New Digital Channels for News, Many Do Not

When Congress required broadcasters to switch from analog to digital spectrum, the efficiencies of digital transmission allowed each station to provide more programming streams. Typically, they could fit four channels onto their spectrum instead of one. At the time, broadcasters suggested that many of these new channels—known as "multicast channels"—would serve the local community with news and information. But according to the 2010 RTDNA/Hofstra University survey, only 4.1 percent of the stations created all-news programming on these channels, whereas 22.2 percent set up a 24-hour weather service, another 22.2 generated programming that fell into the category "other"[203]—which includes weather radar, sports, and other news programs—and 46.6 percent offered programming that was not overseen by a news director at all.[204]

NBC Local Media began rolling out new local 24/7 news channels on formerly unused multicast spectrum; the first such broadcast was in New York in 2009; Miami, Dallas, and a joint Los Angeles–San Francisco–San Diego channel followed in May 2011; and Philadelphia, Washington, D.C., and Chicago are slated for late 2011.[205] Each of the new channels will include a nightly, weekday newscast "complementing and expanding" on the newscasts already airing on the stations' primary channels. According to local media president, John Wallace, "These new offerings continue our ongoing effort to expand our local news and information programming in our ten O&O markets."[206]

A Raycom-owned station in Savannah, Georgia broadcasts high school graduations on its digital channels and streams the ceremonies on the station website to enable deployed U.S. soldiers to watch their children graduate.

Some news directors say they expect to be more involved in programming their stations' multicast channels in the coming year. Plans for what those channels may provide include more news, more weather, more sports, and possibly some foreign-language programming—but this is no indication that stations intend to dedicate bandwidth or staff time to additional in-depth reporting. The Belo Corp., which says it uses its multicast channels to enhance local coverage, currently operates 17 multicast channels and plans to launch more soon. Its Boise station, KTVB, has dedicated its multicast capacity almost exclusively to local news, information, and public affairs, with one of its channels offering 16 hours of local news on weekdays and more than 25 hours of local news on weekends.[207]

Gray Television Inc., owner of 36 television stations across the country, has 39 digital channels up and running with syndicated programming from MyNetworkTV, CW, and This TV, which syndicates the film and television archives owned by MGM. Gray stations' digital lineup also includes several local news and weather channels. Plus, some of its channels air local high school sports, and according to Robert Prather, chief operations officer and a director at Gray, they're pushing to do more:

> "When there is a natural disaster or weather in our markets, we will run 24 or 36 hours straight sometime[s] on news with no breaks—no commercial breaks. We did that for that Fort Hood tragedy, our Waco station did, when the guy shot all those people in Fort Hood—36 straight [hours of] programming. We moved our CBS programming over to our digital channel and ran a crawl on our regular station, 'If you want to watch your local station turn to the digital channel.'"[208]

Some stations in Texas are using their digital channels for Spanish-language broadcasting and high school football.[209] A Raycom Media–owned station in Savannah, Georgia, that serves a large military community, broadcasts

> **"'We have an interview format newscast. Our sales staff has 'sold' some interviews to our online experts. They don't always offer great content, but a guest appearance is part of their sales package.'"**

high school graduations on its digital channels and streams the ceremonies on the station website to enable deployed U.S. soldiers to watch their children graduate.[210] Another Raycom station in Montgomery uses its digital channel when the legislature is in session to air special programming on issues and candidates. Raycom vice president of news, Susanna Schuler, says sports are also big on the digital channels:

> "We have been using that to cover not only high school football and basketball—that gets a lot of coverage you know—but volleyball and swimming and track and things that don't get that amount of coverage. And we partner with local colleges and [in] some cases those really aggressive high schools to let those kids run the cameras and let those kids field produce."[211]

A Large Number of Stations Do No News at All

Historically, when considering the public service performance of local TV stations, the FCC highlighted local news and public affairs (see Chapter 26, Broadcast Radio and Television), which could lead one to assume that all or almost all broadcast stations carry local news. That is not the case.

Three different studies have assessed this issue and come to similar conclusions.

First, a 2011 FCC staff analysis of data from Tribune Media Services, found that 520 local stations air no local news at all—258 commercial stations and 262 noncommercial stations. Adding in those stations that air less than 30 minutes of local news per day, 33 percent of commercial stations currently offer little or no local news. Most of those that do not offer local news are independent stations with no affiliation with a broadcast network. About 44 percent of the no-news stations are in the top 50 markets.[212] For instance, Los Angeles has 27 TV licensees. Fourteen of its stations provided 30 minutes or less of local news (including seven that provided none at all).

PERCENTAGE OF COMMERCIAL STATIONS AIRING LOCAL NEWS (MINUTES PER DAY)

All Commercial Stations

Big 4 Affiliates Only

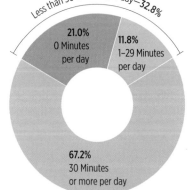

Less than 30 minutes per day—*32.8%*

21.0% 0 Minutes per day

11.8% 1-29 Minutes per day

67.2% 30 Minutes or more per day

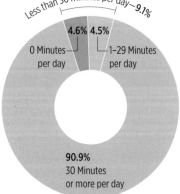

Less than 30 minutes per day—*9.1%*

4.6% 0 Minutes per day

4.5% 1-29 Minutes per day

90.9% 30 Minutes or more per day

Source: FCC analysis of Tribune Media Services data[213]

Although large markets have more stations with no news, they also have more stations that *do* offer local news. Los Angeles also has 13 stations that offer at least a half hour of local news, including eight that offer more than two hours per day.

Conversely, medium and smaller markets tend to offer less news. A disproportionate number of markets with two or fewer local newscasts are small- or medium-size.

TV MARKETS AIRING 30 MINUTES OR MORE OF LOCAL NEWS PER DAY (BY MARKET SIZE)

Market Size Range	Number of Markets			
	0–2 Stations	3 or 4 Stations	5 or more Stations	Total
1 to 50	0	10	40	50
51 to 100	0	32	18	50
101 to 150	6	41	3	50
151 to 200	34	15	1	50
201 to 210	10	0	0	10
Total	50	98	62	210

Source: FCC analysis of Tribune Media Services data

In terms of the raw volume of local news, citizens in medium and small markets clearly get less than their big-city counterparts. There were 92 markets that produced 500 minutes or less of local news (when combining all the stations); 91 of them were from medium or small markets (markets 101–210 in the chart).

AVERAGE NUMBER OF LOCAL NEWS MINUTES OFFERED, BY MARKET SIZE

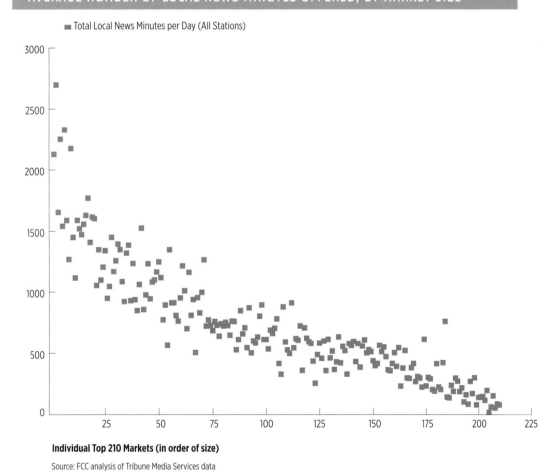

■ Total Local News Minutes per Day (All Stations)

Individual Top 210 Markets (in order of size)

Source: FCC analysis of Tribune Media Services data

The FCC's Industry Analysis Division looked at the same question by reviewing TV listings for all stations. The approach yielded comparable results: in the top 100 markets, 35.7 percent of commercial stations air no local news. Among stations in all size markets, 30.6 percent do not air local news.

Finally, the 2010 RTDNA/Hofstra University survey found that 790 TV stations—about 44 percent—do not air news at all. It is important to note that the 986 stations that do offer news *include* 224 stations that are contracting for local news shows from other stations.[215] Some involve common ownership, some joint operating agreements, and some are paid—with either party paying the other depending on the arrangement. With that factored in, it appears that fewer than half the local TV stations in the U.S. actually have local newsrooms, according to the RTDNA data.

One station that dropped its news coverage is WYOU in Scranton, Pennsylvania, a CBS affiliate owned by Mission Broadcasting. The station had been airing the newscast of WBRE, an NBC station owned by Nexstar. According to a study by the New America Foundation:

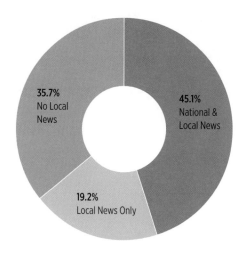

LOCAL NEWS ON COMMERCIAL TV (2010)

35.7% No Local News

45.1% National & Local News

19.2% Local News Only

Sources: FCC Industry Analysis Division.[214]

"On April 4, 2009, due to lagging ratings, Nexstar abruptly pulled its newscast from WYOU and laid off 14 news and production staff. Mission Broadcasting replaced the news with the syndicated programming *Judge Joe Brown*, *Judge Judy*, *Access Hollywood* and *Entertainment Tonight*. Representatives at Nexstar Broadcasting stated the company would save $900,000 annually by ending the WYOU newscast. 'By offering a broad range of popular entertainment choices to our Wilkes-Barre/ Scranton viewers, WYOU can provide additional attractive business solutions to our advertisers and as such we believe this is a win-win situation for our entire community,' Louis Abitabilo, Vice President and General Manager of WBRE, said in a press release on the programming changes."[216]

Network News

At Columbia University's May 2010 "Transitioned Media Conference," senior vice president of NBC News, Adam Jones, projected a slide with the blunt sentence: "Network news viewership is in irreversible decline...[and the] traditional network news business model is broken."[217] As is documented in greater detail in the Cable section of this chapter, the audience is shifting away from broadcast television to cable and the Internet, both of which are drawing off viewers and advertisers.

Given that the newcasts produced by ABC, CBS, and NBC were, for many years, the nation's dominant source of news, their decline is of some significance. In its heyday, network news provided both original reporting and, just as important, a common "place" where much of the population got the news. During the 1970s, the three network evening news broadcasts enjoyed a 75 percent audience share of TV-owning households. Since audience numbers dictate advertising rates—the industry's lifeblood—broadcast news aimed to appeal to the largest number of viewers possible. The networks' economic motivations meshed well with long-standing journalistic principles: news programs aimed for the appearance of balance and objectivity. Network news divisions hired large teams of best-in-the-field correspondents who sought out credible sources of information, maintained bureaus around the world, and offered the public anchors like "the most trusted man in America," Walter Cronkite, whose credibility with large numbers of viewers, for better or worse, helped establish a common cultural understanding of news events.[218]

At first, entertainment programming subsidized the networks' news divisions in much the same way classified sections of newspapers paid for the reporting on the front page. Legendary CBS owner and CEO, William Paley, instructed his news reporters not to worry about costs, assuring them: "I have Jack Benny to make money."[219] The era of news divisions oblivious to costs came to a definitive end in the 1980s, when GE bought NBC, Capital Cities purchased ABC, and Laurence Tisch took over CBS.[220]

With the rise of cable news 30 years ago, the audience for network news began to erode. Today the combined audience for ABC, CBS, and NBC's evening news broadcasts is less than 20 percent of the overall television audience—and trends show a continuing loss of about one million viewers per year.[221] Network newscasts still reach a much larger audience than any particular cable news shows, but the abundance of choices has and will continue to erode the reach of network news.[222] As with newspapers, says TV news consultant Andrew Tyndall, "It is not the case that a single new type of news presentation has superseded the old format. Rather, the phenomenon is fragmentation."[223]

BROADCAST NETWORK EVENING NEWS HOUSEHOLD RATINGS

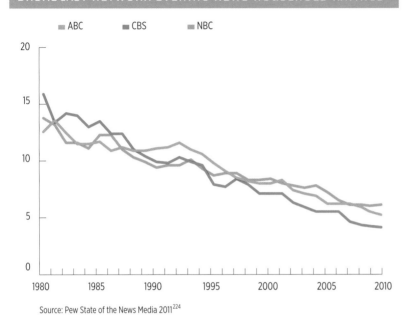

Source: Pew State of the News Media 2011[224]

Meanwhile, broadcast news' remaining viewers are getting older. The median age watching network newscasts is 62.3 and rising. That makes these programs less appealing to advertisers who prefer to target younger viewers (ages 25 to 54) on the theory that they are more fluid in their consumer choices.[225]

MEDIAN AGE OF NIGHTLY NETWORK NEWS VIEWERS (2004–2009)

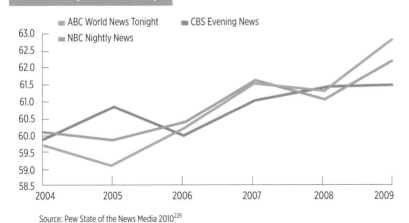

Source: Pew State of the News Media 2010[226]

The long-term financial trend is downward, but in 2010 news programs saw rising revenue resulting from the overall recovery in ad spending. Pew estimates that all three were in the black, with ABC and MSNBC generating meaningful profits.[227] Tellingly, NBC News earns more from its cable channels, MSNBC and CNBC, than it does from its national broadcast channel; almost 60 percent of NBC News's $1.8 billion in total revenue (cable and broadcast) came from the two cable channels.[228] Media industry analysts have quickly come to understand that CBS News and ABC News cannot survive (or pay for newsgathering) on their own. The two news divisions already have alliances with CNN and Bloomberg News, respectively. They could substantially increase their partnerships in the future or be absorbed by their cable partners in order to spread the cost of newsgathering.

Traditional network news has always been an expensive operation. In their years of media dominance, the networks spent lavishly on footage that might not have added much to the story—such as expensive helicopter aerial photography of the White River during the Whitewater controversies of the Clinton administration. Even now, Disney, which owns ABC News, estimates that it takes 3.8 million labor hours to produce the network's 1,600 hours of news annually.[229]

Like their newspaper and local TV counterparts, all of the network news divisions have tried to boost their viability by cutting costs. Pew's *State of the News Media 2010* report estimates that network news has cut news division resources by more than half since their height in the late 1980s.[230] But network managers argue that recent cuts eliminated duplication and wasteful spending and should not harm coverage. "The time has come to re-think how we do what we are doing," wrote David Westin, then president of ABC News, in an internal memo in February 2010. As part of that rethinking, Westin said ABC would "dramatically" expand its use of "digital journalists" (one-man bands) who report, shoot, and edit their own pieces. He also said that the newsmagazine shows, *20/20* and *Primetime*, would replace many of their full-time employees with freelancers.[231]

With the Internet's explosion in popularity, network news divisions are devoting more of their resources to websites, social media, digital products, and mobile offerings. CBS News led the group with 1.62 million Twitter followers, followed by ABC with 1.18 million. But their website traffic has lagged behind that of the cable networks' websites: ABC and CBS attract 19.3 million and 15.3 million unique monthly viewers, respectively, compared with 48.7 million for MSNBC and 67.8 million for CNN.com.[232]

For all their problems, each of the network news divisions still employs more than 1,000 people, and they continue to do extraordinary journalism. ABC and CBS News both won 2011 duPont-Columbia awards, the former for a series about sexual misconduct among swim coaches and the latter for an investigation of the causes of the Deepwater Horizon disaster.[233] And despite their declining audience, the three network evening newscasts still draw 22 million viewers—five times the number tuning in to the three major cable networks (CNN, FOX, and MSNBC) during primetime.[234] The truth is, network news is not a horrible business; it's just not as robust as cable.

CABLE TELEVISION

In June 1948, John Walson Sr., a lineman for the power company, erected a 70-foot antenna on New Boston Mountain in Mahoney City, Pennsylvania, and brought residents up the hill to watch TV programs they had been unable to receive in their homes. Because the town lay in a bowl of land surrounded by hills, they'd had no broadcast reception up to that point. Walson later ran a twin-lead wire down the hill, connected it to the power company poles, and boosted the signal into six homes at an installation charge of $100, plus a $2 monthly fee. On the other side of the country, in Astoria, Oregon, Ed Parsons, installed an antenna on top of a hotel to intercept the signal from a Seattle TV station broadcasting from across several mountain ranges and beamed it into his penthouse for the viewing pleasure of his wife and awestruck neighbors.[235] American ingenuity found ways to overcome topographical limitations in order to bring the newest media craze into homes in remote hamlets. A thankful Montana state senator later said, "Until the advent of cable TV, we in small places were isolated from many of the finer things in life. Now it is a different picture."[236]

Though in its early years, cable was a niche business—70 cable systems served 14,000 customers in 1952—pioneers like retired naval commander Bill Daniels grasped its potential to grow. Daniels rented a microwave relay from

In 1992, CNN, CNN Headline News, and CNBC had a combined audience of approximately 680,000 households. In 2010, Fox News's median audience was 1.9 million, MSNBC was 747,000, CNN was 564,000 and CNN Headline News was 434,000.

New England Cable Network won awards for its one-hour program on a 40-year-old woman with advanced breast cancer who opted for home hospice care instead of radical medical treatment.

the Bell System at $8,000 a month and transmitted a signal from Denver to Laramie, Wyoming. Customers paid $150 for the connection, plus $7.50 a month for the service, and voted to pick the programs they wanted to watch: "If more people wanted to watch *I Love Lucy* than Sid Caesar, then that's what we showed," Daniels said.[237]

By 1964, bigger investors stepped in, like Jack Kent Cooke, a retired publisher (and the future owner of the Washington Redskins), who dropped $22 million into cable systems,[238] and by 1968, the cable industry had grown to include 3.5 million subscribers (6.4 percent of the population) and logged $240 million in annual revenues.[239]

As broadcasters awakened to the threat cable posed, an alarmed official from the National Association of Broadcasters stated the issue starkly:

"What we have here is a completely unregulated business competing against a regulated industry, using as its major weapon the very product which its competitor turns out, and paying nothing for the product."[240]

Broadcasters sought to stifle competition from cable operators through regulatory means. The FCC, which had in 1959 adopted a policy supporting the growth of cable TV, in 1966, took the side of the broadcasters. Specifically, the FCC imposed two conditions on cable systems: (1) a cable system *must carry* the signals of all local stations, and (2) a cable system was not permitted to carry the programs of a distant station when they duplicated the programs of a local station 15 days before or after the local broadcast (the "blackout rule").[241]

Two developments in the 1970s "forever divided cable from broadcast TV in viewers' minds," according to the author of a book on the cable industry's origins.[242] With the advent of Home Box Office (HBO)—the first network to offer subscribers "uncut, uninterrupted, and commercial-free movies direct to living rooms"—city viewers, who generally got good broadcast reception and thus had no need for cable, now had a reason to subscribe. Gerald Levin, a former divinity student who took over HBO in 1972, advanced the ball even further in 1975 when he leased space on an RCA satellite (six years for $7.5 million) to deliver programming faster and more efficiently than was possible through the existing practice of using microwave towers or shipping videotape. Levin's signature event: the "Thrilla in Manila" heavyweight fight between Muhammad Ali and Joe Frazier, broadcast live to pay-TV viewers on September 30, 1975.[243]

Satellite-delivered programming took another leap in 1977 when the Supreme Court blocked the FCC from enforcing rules that prevented cable from offering choice programming like movies and sporting events.[244] This opened the way for entrepreneur Ted Turner to operate his Atlanta-based facility as a superstation (WTBS) with national reach that could provide desirable programming to cable operators across the country.[245]

For the next 25 years, cable viewership grew, finally surpassing the broadcast TV stations' combined total day (24-hour) viewership in the 2001/2002 season and surpassing its prime-time viewership two years later.[246]

Cable News Networks

With the launch of Ted Turner's Cable News Network (CNN) in 1980, a new era for news unfolded. Before that, major news stories often broke on broadcast TV with a "We interrupt this program" announcement. Now news was available 24 hours a day.[247]

In the early 1990s, NBC-owned CNBC and MSNBC followed CNN's lead.[248] FOX News launched in 1996, after its owner, Rupert Murdoch, gave cable operator TCI a $200 million loan and an option to buy 20 percent of the network in exchange for carriage to 10 million homes. Murdoch also spent $100 million to create the news network.[249] Today, there are at least 13 cable news channels, including those mentioned above, plus Bloomberg TV, HD News, and The Weather Channel.[250]

These news networks have grown exponentially over the past two decades. In 1992, CNN, CNN Headline News, and CNBC had a combined audience of approximately 680,000 television households during an average quarter-hour. In 2010, FOX News's median audience in prime time was 1.9 million, MSNBC's was 747,000, CNN's was 564,000 and CNN Headline News's was 434,000.[251]

Unlike the broadcast networks, which depend on advertising as their sole revenue source, cable networks have the benefit of subscriber fees in addition to advertising dollars.

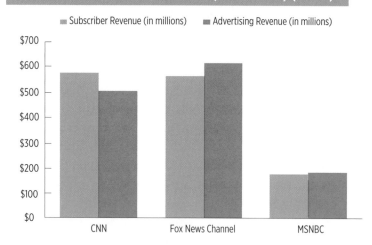

CABLE NEWS REVENUE STREAMS (ESTIMATED) (2009)

Source: SNL Kagan, a division of SNL Financial LLC, as discussed in The Pew Project for Excellence in Journalism, The State of the News Media 2010[252]

Audience actually declined in 2010—the biggest year-over-year decline ever—with combined viewership in prime time dropping 16 percent to 3.2 million.[253] Nonetheless, each cable news network projected increases in operating profits, continuing a long-term trend.[254]

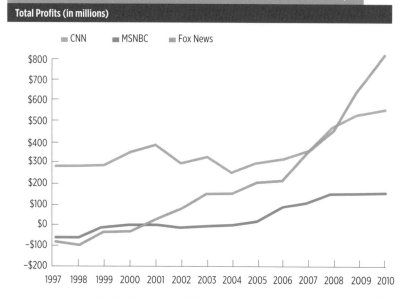

CABLE NEWS PROFITABILITY BY CHANNEL (1997–2010)

Source: Pew State of the Media 2010 and 2011 Reports, citing SNL Kagan, a division of SNL Financial LLC[255]
Note: All figures are estimates.

All three cable news networks increased their investment in news. In 2010, overall spending at FOX News surpassed that at CNN and MSNBC, although CNN still has more staff and bureaus.

Though not a big moneymaker, the cable industry has contributed mightily to the flow of public affairs by sustaining C-SPAN (See Chapter 8, C-SPAN.), which, like most commercial cable channels, receives a fee based

CABLE NEWS STAFFING (2010)

Channel	Total Staff	Change in Total Staff
CNN	4,000	no reported change
Fox News Channel	1,272	+72
MSNBC	600*	no reported change

Source: Pew State of the News Media 2011[256] *Note: MSNBC's staff was last reported in 2007.

CABLE NEWS BUREAUS (2010)

Domestic Bureaus			Foreign Bureaus		
CNN	Fox News	MSNBC	CNN	Fox News	MSNBC
Atlanta (HQ)	Atlanta	Atlanta	Abu Dhabi	Baghdad	Baghdad
Boston	Boston	Burbank	Amman	Islamabad	Bangkok
Chicago	Chicago	Chicago	Baghdad	Jerusalem	Beijing
Dallas	Dallas	Dallas	Bangkok	Kabul	Beirut (new)
Denver	Denver	New York (HQ)	Beijing	London	Cairo
Los Angeles	Los Angeles	Miami (new)	Beirut	Moscow (closed)	Frankfurt (new)
Miami	Miami	Washington	Berlin	Rome	Havana
Minneapolis	New York (HQ)		Bogotá		London
New Orleans	San Francisco		Buenos Aires		Islamabad
New York	Seattle		Cairo		Kabul
Orlando	Washington		Chennai		Moscow
San Francisco*			Dubai		Tehran
Seattle			Havana		Tel Aviv
Washington			Hong Kong		Tokyo
			Islamabad		
			Istanbul		
			Jakarta		
			Jerusalem		
			Johannesburg		
			Kabul		
			Lagos		
			London		
			Madrid		
			Mexico City		
			Moscow		
			Mumbai		
			Nairobi		
			New Delhi		
			Paris		
			Rome		
			Santiago		
			Seoul		
			Tokyo		

Source: Pew State of the News Media 2011[257] *CNN transitioned its San Francisco bureau into a new Silicon Valley bureau in January 2011

on the number of subscribers signed up by a local cable operator. Cable's business model of bundling a package of programs for subscribers, rather than permitting them to choose individual programs a la carte, may be a factor in explaining how C-SPAN and the news networks were able to survive, and even thrive. As *New York Times* "Talking Business" columnist, Joe Nocera, explains:

> "[U]nmoored from the cable bundle, individual networks would have to charge vastly more money per subscriber. Under the current system, in which cable companies like Comcast pay the networks for carriage and then pass on the cost to their customers—networks get to charge on the basis of everyone who subscribes to cable television, whether they watch the network or not. The system has the effect of generating more money than a network 'deserves' based purely on viewership. Networks also get to charge more for advertising than they would if they were not part of the bundle."[258]

Local Cable News

Cablevision Systems Corporation launched the first 24-hour local cable news channel on New York's Long Island in 1986.[259] Other cable operators, including Time Warner Cable, Comcast Corporation, Bright House Networks, and Cox Communications, as well as television broadcast station owners Tribune Broadcasting, Hearst-Argyle Television, and Belo Corp., also launched local cable news channels in the 1980s and 1990s.[260]

In May 2011, there were approximately 39 local and regional cable news channels originating varying amounts of local news content. Roughly 20 to 30 percent of the population has access to these local cable news networks.[261] Of the 39 channels, 11 are owned by or affiliated with traditional news sources—such as a newspaper, broadcast TV station, or network—but typically they also have some association with a cable operator providing carriage.[262] One such entity is Chicagoland, a Chicago-area cable news channel operated by the Tribune Company, which also owns the *Chicago Tribune* and *Red Eye* newspapers, WGN-TV, WGN-AM, and *Chicago Magazine*.[263] On May 2, 2011, NBC announced the launch of new multicast 24/7 local news channels in Miami, Dallas, San Francisco, Los Angeles, and San Diego that would also be carried on its local cable outlets.[264] An additional 28 local or regional cable news channels are owned and operated by cable operators themselves.[265] For example, NY1, seen in 1.6 million homes, is owned by Time Warner Cable and provides a model for that company's seven other news channels in New York State.[266]

Offering local news to retain subscribers is a key element of the company's business strategy. Steve Paulus, a Time Warner Cable official, says that a popular attraction like NY1 helps reduce the "churn factor" and keep subscribers from switching to satellite or other telco providers.[267] "Subscribers won't leave cable if they think they'll lose NY1," he says. Time Warner launched News 8 Austin in 1999 in the hope that "News 8 would provide a community service and help differentiate cable from those rat bastards in satellite, who were stealing their customers at an alarming rate," according to Kevin Brass at the *Austin Chronicle*.[268] Kevin Benz, News 8's news director, says, "These stations were not meant to be ad-revenue producers."[269]

There are also regional news channels, such as New England Cable News (NECN), owned by Comcast, which reaches 3.7 million subscribers in more than 1,050 cities and towns in six New England states.[270]

By focusing on high-interest local issues, local cable news channels have driven up audience ratings. "We did 90 hours of live, continuous coverage during 9/11, because two of the airplanes came out of Boston," says Charles Kravetz, station manager and vice president of news at NECN. "When there's major news, weather, snowstorms, blizzards, our viewership is off the charts."[271] For NY1, a big boost came from a hotly contested mayoral race between David Dinkins and Rudolph Giuliani in 1993. "The local papers routinely credit NY1 as a source for political information, much more than our broadcast competitors," Paulus says. "Politicals acknowledge readily that NY1 is the only station that cares about covering politics."[272]

In a move that goes against the bare-bones norm of local 24-hour news stations, NECN has become a producer of award-winning documentaries. In 1997, the station won a prestigious George Foster Peabody Award for its one-hour program *Look For Me Here: 299 Days in the Life of Nora Lenihan*, the poignant story of a 40-year-old woman with advanced breast cancer who opted for home hospice care instead of radical medical treatment. NECN also conducted an 11-month investigation into the sexual abuse scandal by priests in the Boston archdiocese, airing its findings in December 2003 and January 2004 in an hour-long program, *Who Can Fathom the Human Heart? Father Shanley and the Church Crisis*.[273]

As local news networks have become established in their communities, they have become increasingly popular with viewers. In Florida's Tampa Bay market, Bright House Networks' Bay News 9 emerged as the third-most-watched morning show in a February 2006 survey—even though it is available to only 60 percent of the local television market. News 12 Networks has seven local cable news channels, five weather and traffic channels, interactive TV channels, and an expanding array of online and mobile ventures.[274]

Local cable news channels use the Internet in different ways. For example, on its website, News 12 Networks (which operates in the New York metropolitan area) asks prospective users if they are cable television subscribers before allowing them to access its news and information pages. If would-be users are not cable subscribers, the site allows registration and access for a subscription fee of $4.95 a month, or $48 per year.[275] By contrast, Tampa's baynews9.com provides immediate access to its news and information to anyone who chooses to use its website.[276]

However, until NBC announced its decision in May 2011 to create new local news operations in five major metropolitan areas, the overall number of local cable news networks had not grown, and may even have declined in some areas. Most cable operators have not invested in local cable news and had no plans to do so. These stations generally set a goal of breaking even, rather than making a profit, according to cable industry officials interviewed by FCC staff.[277] Since 2003, several cable news channels affiliated with local, over-the-air broadcasters, newspapers, and cable operators have either stopped operations, or in some cases switched from broadcasting independent newscasts created by in-house staff to merely rebroadcasting news from an associated network channel. There are two exceptions to this general trend. One is Time-Warner, which plans to expand its local cable news stations because the company believes that local cable channels pay off in the long run, by reducing subscriber churn. The second is NBC, which is starting new local news outlets to fulfill promises it made to do so during the FCC's review of its proposed merger with Comcast—although it is unclear how much new local news reporting these entities will do. If they evolve into full-fledged local all news channels, the percentage of the population with access to local all-news cable programming will rise to roughly 29 percent.

Cable Trends

Cable is an extraordinarily popular medium. The number of cable subscribers increased steadily for 25 years, from 9.8 million in 1975 to 66.25 million in 2000, and they declined only slightly over the next nine years, to 62 million in 2009.[278]

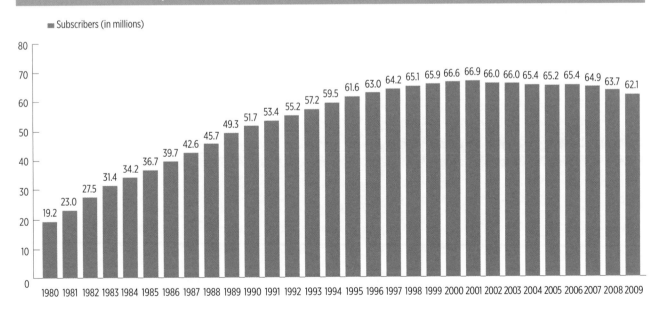

CABLE SUBSCRIBERS (1980–2009)

Subscribers (in millions)

Source: SNL Kagan, U.S. Cable Industry Historical Projections, Volume 1 (1980–2009)

In recent years the growth story has become murkier. With the exception of a modest rebound in subscribers in 2006, the cable industry has been losing customers since 2003.[279]

In the view of industry analysts, cable continues to face threats from the growth of satellite TV, Internet video services (including free video websites such as hulu.com), the broadcast resilience, and the introduction of Internet TVs, which give consumers the capability to watch online content on a full-size TV without a computer.[280] Some analysts predict that pay-TV services (like cable) are likely to experience significant disruption by the end of 2015 in the form of 4 million to 5 million customers canceling their subscriptions.[281] Since this trend will inevitably increase the demand for broadband, cable companies are focusing on developing their broadband segments as subscribers cut the cord.[282]

Cable has a strong financial engine. Even though subscriptions declined in recent years, revenues have risen every year, from $883 million in 1975 to $84.3 billion in 2009.[283]

CABLE MULTIPLE SYSTEM OPERATOR REVENUES (1980–2009)

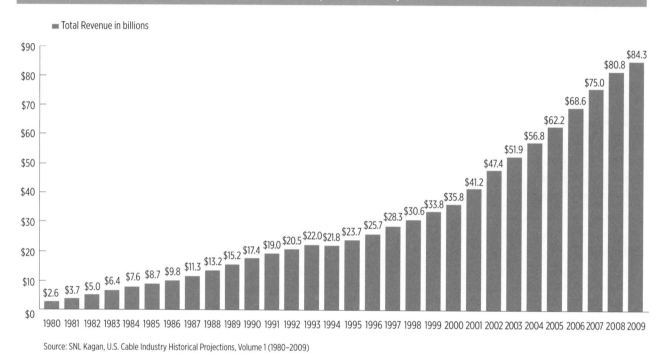

Source: SNL Kagan, U.S. Cable Industry Historical Projections, Volume 1 (1980–2009)

Income per subscriber has also increased, from $5 or less in the early years to between $30 and $40 or more for many cable systems in the 1990s.[284] Cable operators have earned profits that exceeded 30 percent in each of the past several years. Finally, while cable offerings have increased so have prices. The FCC's 2011 Cable Price Survey notes that a typical subscriber pays $92.10, if they sign up for video, Internet access, and phone service; and $63.92 if they get only video service.[285]

CABLE RATES—AVERAGE MONTHLY BASIC SERVICES (1980–2009)

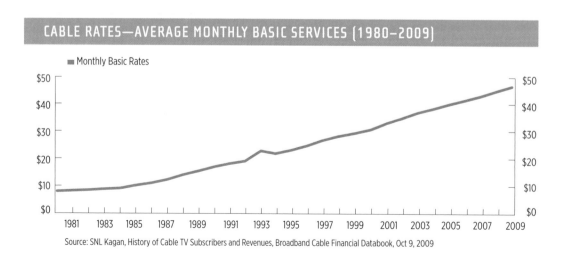

Source: SNL Kagan, History of Cable TV Subscribers and Revenues, Broadband Cable Financial Databook, Oct 9, 2009

SATELLITE TV

In a 1945 article in *Wireless World* magazine, science fiction writer Arthur C. Clarke laid out the blueprint for the global satellite communications industry. Clarke proposed launching space stations that would orbit Earth at 22,300 miles above the equator. Signals would bounce from an uplink on Earth to the satellites and then down to "small parabolas perhaps a foot in diameter." Clarke never sought to patent this idea, which led to a multibillion-dollar industry. Though credited as the "Godfather of Satellite Communications," he remained modest: "I suspect that my early disclosure may have advanced the cause of space communications by approximately 15 minutes. Or perhaps 20."[286]

Twenty years later, on April 6, 1965, Clarke watched from a Washington, D.C., studio as the COMSAT Corporation, a government-created monopoly, launched its first satellite. His idea was on its way to becoming reality.

By 1982, the FCC concluded that DBS would provide high-quality television service to as many as 11 million people in rural areas who had no on-air reception or got fewer than three channels.[287] The FCC authorized DBS service, amended the Table of Frequency Allocations to permit DBS downlink operations in the 12.2 to 12.7 GHz band and uplink operations in the 17.3 to 17.8 GHz band, and adopted rules to prevent harmful interference to DBS operators from terrestrial licensees in the 12 GHz band.[288]

Despite the FCC's push, intended to promote competition, the market was slow to follow.[289] None of the initial licensees survived, sunk by the high cost of launching satellites (estimated at $700 million for the first year) and the lack of programming that differentiated DBS from on-air television. Given the prevailing rate of $300 for equipment and $39.95 a month for programming, few customers signed up.[290] DBS, at least initially, was seen as a major flop.[291]

Congress then stepped in to try to help DBS overcome obstacles it faced in getting subscribers. In 1988, Congress enacted the Satellite Home Viewer Act, which carved out a narrow exception to copyright laws in order to allow satellite carriers to deliver broadcast programming to satellite viewers without getting the copyright holder's permission. This provision enabled DBS to target its service to the small number of households that did not receive broadcast programming ("unserved households").[292] Even more critically, in 1992 Congress went further and enacted the "program access" requirements (section 628), which essentially prevented cable companies from denying popular programming to DBS and enabled DBS to begin offering this content to its viewers.[293] This boost was sufficient to get DBS off the ground.

Pent-up demand for an alternative to cable was huge. On June 17, 1994, DirecTV began providing high-power DBS service, transmitting over 50 channels of subscription and pay-per-view programming. Within a year, DirecTV had sold over a million systems, "far more than the number of VCRs, CD players and TVs sold in the same time frame when they were introduced," according to author Stephen Keating.[294]

A satellite company has the option of providing local broadcast station programming—also known as "local-into-local service"—but is not required to do so. A satellite company that elects to provide local-into-local service is required to provide subscribers with all the local broadcast TV signals assigned to that designated market area (DMA) that ask to be carried on the satellite system and are otherwise eligible.[295] DISH Network provides local-into-local service in all 210 designated markets in the U.S. and DirecTV to 175 of them.

Local PBS stations and other noncommercial stations are generally included among the "local" stations offered.

In addition, satellite operators are required to set aside 4 percent of their capacity for "educational programming." (See Chapter 28, Satellite Television and Radio.)

Current State

DirecTV, the largest DBS provider and second largest multichannel video programming distributor (MVPD) in the U.S., serves 19.2 million subscribers and offers over 285 channels, more than 160 of which are in high definition (HD).[296] DISH Network, the second largest DBS provider and third largest MVPD, has 14.3 million subscribers[297] and offers over 315 channels of programming.[298]

From 1996 to the present, the number of DBS subscribers has risen every year.

SATELLITE TV SUBSCRIBERS (1994–2009)

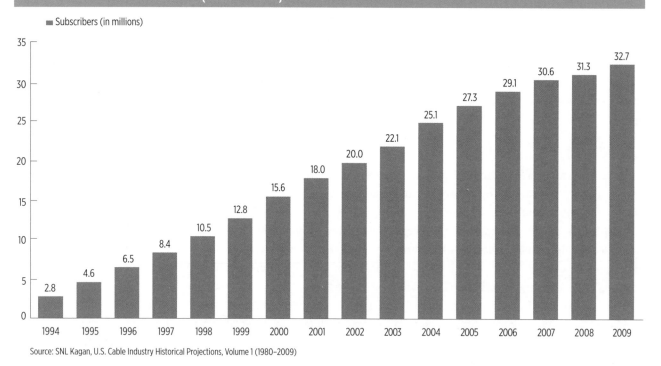

■ Subscribers (in millions)

Source: SNL Kagan, U.S. Cable Industry Historical Projections, Volume 1 (1980–2009)

Revenues have also continued to grow, from $2.2 billion in 1995 to $30.3 billion in 2009.

SATELLITE TV REVENUES (1997–2009)

■ Revenues (in billions)

1997	1998	1999	2000	2001	2002	2003	2004	2005	2006	2007	2008	2009
$2.3	$3.5	$5.7	$7.7	$10.2	$11.9	$14.3	$16.5	$20.2	$23.2	$26.3	$28.9	$30.3

Source: SNL Kagan, History of DBS Subscribers and Revenues (1997–2009)

In 2010, both DBS operators reported strong profits. DirecTV netted $2.198 billion, up from $942 million in 2009,[299] and DISH Network saw a $985 million profit, up from $636 million in 2009.[300]

DBS has grown to become a significant provider of video services and a vibrant competitor to cable.

Conclusions

The decline of newspapers created an opportunity for local TV news. Has it filled the void they left?

The best of the local TV stations prove day in and day out that local TV news can be great—not only performing the great functions of journalism, but doing so in a way that is accessible to a broad cross-section of the community.

Many newsrooms have begun trying to adapt creatively to the new realities, having reporters learn new skills and digital production techniques. Many have sought ways to squeeze out what they see as inefficiencies by cooperating with other stations or forming new partnerships. And some continue to offer high-quality local news.

Unfortunately, the evidence is strong that many local TV stations have not stepped up to meet the challenges of the moment and in too many cases may even have moved backward. On average, local news has become thinner, not deeper. The amount of coverage dedicated to important public issues—like education, health, or government—remains tiny, according to several studies. The amount dedicated to crime seems as high, if not higher, than ever. In-depth, investigative, and beat reporting are declining.

We found instances in which local stations appeared to sell their news time, and reputation, to advertisers—in some cases literally allowing sponsors to buy their way into news segments. Too many local TV station executives and managers have responded to financial pressures from owners by allowing advertisers to dictate—and in some cases to create—content, undermining long-standing journalistic standards.

Some cost efficiencies, like resource pooling and "one-man bands," that could have freed money to finance more journalism—seem rarely to have led to that result. In some cases, they have instead resulted in less diversity of reporting.

Instead of using the money saved by new technologies and production efficiencies, and the additional money that poured into local TV stations from the historic levels of political advertising in the 2010 election season, to increase the pool of reporters who could cover their communities and more effectively monitor institutions and government agencies, many stations have opted to let those dollars simply flow to the bottom line. In today's multitasking news operations, reporters given broadened production responsibilities have less time to do the labor-intensive reporting that can provide vital information to the local viewer and hold local institutions and leaders accountable.

All of these factors together may help explain why, in a recent survey by the Pew Project for Excellence in Journalism, 64 percent of TV news executives said that they believe their profession is headed in the wrong direction, compared with 35 percent who believe it is headed in the right direction. Amazingly, despite being relatively better off financially, TV news executives are significantly more pessimistic than even newspaper editors.[301]

Finally, we note that while we offer these criticisms of some local news operations, they are at least doing something. A study by the FCC Media Bureau found that 258 commercial stations do no local news at all. Another study found that of those stations that do air news, a good third of them are airing the broadcasts of other stations—meaning that as many as half the nation's TV stations do not have a local news room.

It would be overly alarmist to declare that these changes have crippled the ability of local TV newsrooms to cover their communities. Some stations continue to provide extraordinary programming. And in general, local TV news is still capable of handling, sometimes brilliantly, many types of basic news—local weather emergencies, crimes, fires, earthquakes, and news that piggybacks off the shrinking news operation of local newspapers. What many local TV stations seem increasingly unable to do is enterprise reporting, investigative pieces, in-depth reporting, beat coverage of important local institutions, and stories that require reporters to do more than a few interviews.

The challenge to local TV news posed by the Internet will continue to be formidable. But local TV stations are well positioned to convert their strong local brands into digital businesses. In most communities, the leading websites for local news are those run by the TV stations and newspapers. In fact, it could be argued that local TV news is, based purely on the numbers, the best business model currently operating for sustaining local news. Given the current local media landscape, having the best business model may be viewed by some as akin to having the best sleeping berth on the *Titanic*, but local TV news operations have great opportunities to expand their reach and influence.

What about cable television? Cable television is doing financially even better than broadcast TV, since cable operators generate revenue from subscriptions, not just advertising. But so far, this relative health has not led the cable industry to invest heavily in news and public affairs in their communities. Currently, only about 25–30 percent of the population can watch one of the 39 local or regional cable news shows. And, with a few exceptions, cable operators view these as unprofitable and have no plans for expansion. While C-SPAN thrives, it is unclear whether state public affairs networks will.

Satellite TV does carry many local TV stations but the system of providing carriage for "educational programming," including public affairs, has shown strains. For instance, only one state SPAN has managed to get satellite carriage. (See Chapter 8, C-SPAN and State Public Affairs Networks.)

Relative to the problems of local news, we feel no great concern about the quantity of national TV news. That is not to say that the national TV news system is fine as is. There are important ongoing debates about the quality and emphasis of network versus cable news. But the national news markets seem dynamic and fluid, with gaps created by market change currently being filled by innovation from existing or new media.

Local TV news remains the public's number one source of news. Even though a small percentage of people get local news through the original method—an over-the-air signal—these channels are all carried on cable and satellite systems. And local TV news teams remain popular. Just as NBC radio became NBC television, which became MSNBC.com, we expect local news operations to have some staying power if they adapt to the changing terrain. What is less clear is how many will adequately perform the civic functions that their licenses require of them and their communities need.

So far, despite many outstanding news operations, it appears that many local TV news operations have not seized the opportunity presented them by the changing media landscape. So far, they have not filled the gaps left by newspapers.

4 Internet

FROM ITS EARLIEST DAYS, IT WAS CLEAR that the Internet would be, in some important ways, fundamentally different from other communication system breakthroughs. The printing press, the telegraph, and broadcasting each dramatically improved the efficiency of information distribution, but they nonetheless relied on (and allowed) a relatively small number of people to produce content and send it on its way.

The Internet was created by government-financed researchers to allow for the easy sharing of information and resources among academics. It was designed to be decentralized, with power and control diffuse. Same with the World Wide Web that developed on the Internet. As Tim Berners-Lee, inventor of the World Wide Web,[1] explained in a December 2010 *Scientific American* article:

> "The primary design principle underlying the Web's usefulness and growth is universality. When you make a link, you can link to anything. That means people must be able to put anything on the Web, no matter what computer they have, software they use or human language they speak and regardless of whether they have a wired or wireless Internet connection....
>
> "Decentralization is another important design feature. You do not have to get approval from any central authority to add a page or make a link. All you have to do is use three simple, standard protocols: write a page in the HTML (hypertext markup language) format, name it with the URL naming convention, and serve it up on the Internet using HTTP (hypertext transfer protocol). Decentralization has made widespread innovation possible and will continue to do so in the future."[2]

Decentralization and universality—these principles insured that the Internet and the web would revolutionize not only the dissemination of news and information but how it was gathered and packaged and by whom. This would radically democratize publishing, make "sharing" an essential fuel to the new media, and along the way upend traditional business models that had sustained journalism for years.

Not surprisingly, news has been an important part of the Internet since its earliest days, when Usenet newsgroups provided places for users to discuss and share news and information. Small content websites proliferated in the early 1990s, and toward the end of the decade venture capitalists financed the creation and expansion of a wave of new businesses that published original content. Venture capital investment grew from $595 million in 1995 to $15.6 billion in 2000.[3] Content companies that launched during those heady days include WebMd, MarketWatch, Salon, Beliefnet, and Slate.[4] AOL, CompuServe, and Yahoo!—among the largest online communities at the time—expanded their content offerings.

But in late 2000 and early 2001, the Internet bubble burst.[5] Venture capitalists began pulling back their investment in existing companies that were not profitable and investing less in content firms in general. Despite a movement of ad dollars from print publications to the web, new-media pioneers found it challenging to cover the costs of content creation using traditional business and staffing models.

A few years later, web innovation and investment began to accelerate again—this time fueled by social media, or what came to be known as "web 2.0." The new generation of websites that emerged had two economic advantages over conventional content sites: First, since the bulk of their content was created by the users themselves, their content-creation costs were lower. Second, although ad rates were lower on social-media sites, they could generate page views far more efficiently than content sites could. One reason: users tended to dive into these sites more deeply— often visiting them more often and staying longer. For instance, the average reader spends 20 minutes a month on the *New York Times* website, compared with seven hours on Facebook.[6]

Within the universe of content-based websites, so-called news aggregators became increasingly significant. Google News, for instance, provides links to the most popular news stories, using computer algorithms that weigh factors like where and how often stories appear as text or hot-linked headlines in order to determine how prominently they will be displayed on the site.[7] Digg and Delicious rely on user votes to elevate stories on their list, in effect allowing the "wisdom of the crowds" to decide which stories are recommended. Other sites combine automated algorithms with editorial judgment to select stories to feature. The Drudge Report became enormous and influential, largely by linking to a variety of columnists and news sites. Some aggregators summarize the articles in addition to providing links. The Huffington Post added original bloggers into the formula but relied most heavily on linking to and summarizing other websites' content.

Some time in 2010, a milestone was hit: more Americans were getting their news online than from traditional printed newspapers. Among younger consumers, more were getting news online than through newspaper *or* TV, according to a 2010 survey.[8]

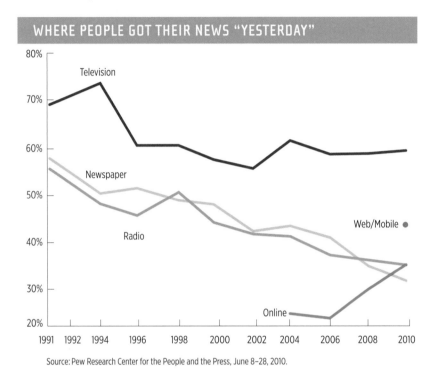

WHERE PEOPLE GOT THEIR NEWS "YESTERDAY"

Source: Pew Research Center for the People and the Press, June 8–28, 2010.

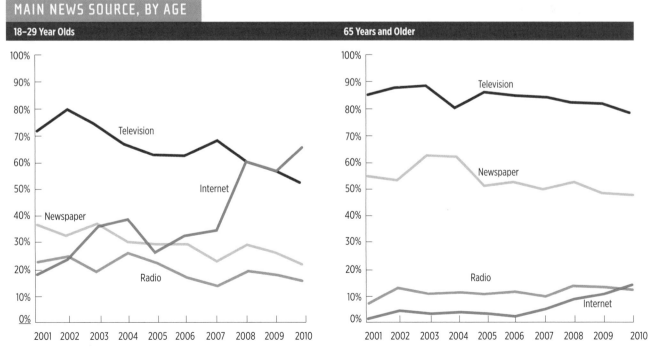

MAIN NEWS SOURCE, BY AGE

Source: Pew State of the News Media 2011, citing Pew Research Center Dec. 1–5, 2010. Figures add up to more than 100% because respondents could volunteer up to two main media sources.[9]

Meanwhile, the advent of free, simple-to-use blogging software was making it possible for every American to be a publisher, reporter, and pundit. By May 2011, one of the most popular blogging platforms, WordPress, was hosting 20 million blogs.[10] Though only a few bloggers have audiences large enough to place them among the top 100 websites, their contribution to news and commentary online has been revolutionary. The "long tail" came into view: instead of information being provided primarily by a few large players, the ecosystem now could support millions of smaller players each serving a small but targeted audience.[11] The democratization of content creation caught on quickly. Wikipedia and other "wikis" enabled readers to collaborate in the creation of content; YouTube allowed a full range of users—from creative geniuses to proud parents to freaks—to "broadcast" their own videos; and Facebook gained national dominance as an all-purpose platform for self-expression and communication. Millions of people became not only consumers of information but creators, curators, and distributors. Remarkably, WordPress, Twitter, Wikipedia, YouTube, and Facebook offered these publishing tools to users for free.

It is hard to overstate the significance of these changes. In just a few years, the cost of publishing went from being relatively expensive to almost free—at least in terms of the publishing technology.[12]

The digital world continues to change by the minute. Smartphone applications, tablet apps, e-Readers, and other new services now make it easy to access news and information on-the-go, using the Internet as a pipeline but bypassing the need for a web browser to display it. As consumers increasingly gravitate to applications and services that make use of the Internet through more closed systems, such as smartphones, some even question the viability of business plans built on the current search-based, website-centric Internet.[13]

The crop of news and information players who gained prominence on the web 2.0 landscape—bloggers, citizen journalists, and Internet entrepreneurs—was initially mocked by traditional media leaders as being inferior, worthless, and even dangerous. Famously, Jonathan Klein, then-president of CNN, declared, "Bloggers have no checks and balances. [It's] a guy sitting in his living room in his pajamas."[14]

Hardly. It is important to appreciate the extraordinary positive effects the new media—including those contributing while in pajamas—has had, not only in the spread of freedom around the world, but specifically in the provision of news, reporting, and civically important information.

How the Internet has Improved News and Information

More Diversity and Choice

Traditional media limited the number of voices that could be heard, not (usually) for conspiratorial reasons but because of something less sinister: space was limited. Column inches in a newspaper and minutes in a newscast are finite. Many editors choose wisely, some do not—but they do have to choose. A local newspaper editor putting together a package on abortion might appear fair-minded by including one spokesperson from a pro-life group and one from a pro-choice group, even though there are variations of opinion within and outside those movements. Now, on the

Internet, an editor can provide—and a reader can search for—a much wider range of perspectives.[15]

The Internet has the luxury of unlimited space and a cost-of-publication that approaches zero, which means that it is no longer only—or primarily—editors who get to decide which voices are heard. Consider how the Internet has transformed a staple of the traditional newspaper: the letter to the editor. On a typical recent Sunday, the *New York Times* published nine letters to the editor in its print edition. By contrast, the comment area on just the home page of The Huffington Post included 73,234 reader comments.[16] Think of those as instantaneous letters to the editor, and one can understand how much more easily a typical citizen can now reach a large audience with her viewpoint.

> By 2010, a historic milestone had been hit: more Americans got their news online than through newspapers.

When one considers both online and offline media, most communities have seen a rise in the number and diversity of outlets. A study of news outlets in Baltimore by the Pew Center for Excellence in Journalism found 53 different news and information sources, not including occasional bloggers.[17] On the national level, choice is even greater, because consumers can tap into newspapers and publications that may have been difficult or expensive to access in the past. In 2009, only 17 percent of *The Washington Post*'s print circulation went to readers outside the Washington, D.C., metro area—but 91 percent of the newspaper's *online* readers live outside the D.C. area.[18] Along similar lines, a conservative living in liberal Berkeley can find refuge online at NationalReview.com; a liberal in Orange County can join the DailyKos.com community; an African-American in an all-white town can explore TheRoot.com; and an evangelical in a secular enclave can bond with believers on ChristianityToday.com.

And individuals can personalize their information flow with amazing precision. There is not a topic area that does not have aggregators providing headlines from around the world. News about Ultimate Frisbee? USA Ultimate provides that.[19] News about Geocaching?[20] Groundspeak has that.[21]

Greater Depth

Consider how a typical newspaper might have covered a speech by the president before the Internet. In about 750 words, a reporter could include six or seven quotes from the president, some context on the issue at hand, and two or three quotes from people reacting to the speech. By contrast, today's online experience might start with an article similar to the newspaper piece. Then, the reader can examine the speech itself, in excerpts or in its entirety, through video, audio, or transcript. And, in addition to the brief sound-bite quotes from three experts, one can now get detailed analysis from dozens—even hundreds—within a few hours of the event, rather than the next day. After all that information is absorbed, one can scour the web for even more, perusing instantaneous fact-checking efforts and connecting with others online who share an interest in the speech.

Traditional media companies can now offer much of this additional information themselves and in doing so make a story more relevant to viewers and readers. In a pre-Internet age, the network news shows might have simply reported on a problem regarding federal regulation of toxic waste dumps, for instance. But now they can also post a list of the dumps to their website and update it as new information becomes available; viewers can see if any are near their home, and experts can use the data to create maps of the hazards.

The ability of websites to sort and store data easily makes large volumes of information customizable in ways that makes it far more relevant to individuals. For instance, the Texas Tribune, a news startup in Austin, Texas, offers online readers the ability to sort through data about Texas lawmakers, prisoners, and public employees. Readers can set the parameters as they wish, based on their particular interests, and the gizmo tailors the results to them. Built as one feature—a database—from a consumer perspective it actually provides thousands of different "stories."

More Diversity in Commentary and Analysis

The commentary business is far more open to new players. In the past, there were a handful of well-worn paths to pundit-hood, usually requiring work as a big-time newspaper reporter or a top level government official. The Internet allows for more newcomers. Markos Moulitsas, a former army sergeant, was a web developer when he created the Daily Kos, which has become the leading liberal blog. Glenn Reynolds, one of the top libertarian bloggers, is a professor at University of Tennessee. Matt Drudge was a telemarketer before he created the pioneering conservative aggregation site, the Drudge Report, and Andrew Breitbart, a leading conservative media entrepreneur, got his start in the online news world while working for Drudge.

The best web analysts have used the technology to improve the quality of their offerings. Andrew Sullivan was among the first to use the interactivity of the Internet to hone his argument in public, putting out an initial viewpoint and then adapting it, as new ideas or information challenged him. The best bloggers write with the knowledge that shoddy reporting or thinking will be caught in a matter of minutes.

Some of these commentators perform the same function as the best newsmagazine and newspaper reporters: connecting dots (recognizing the links between seemingly isolated events) and finding inconsistencies in publicly available information. A handful of conservative bloggers, for instance, figured out that a key document in Dan Rather's controversial *60 Minutes* report on George W. Bush's military service must have been fake, in part by noticing that the typeface on an ostensibly 30-year-old letter was suspiciously similar to a modern Microsoft Word font.[22]

> In just a few years, the cost of publishing has gone from quite expensive to almost free.

The ease of sharing content—by emailing a link or posting news to a social network—has transformed the process of news storytelling. Posts on Twitter, Facebook, and Ustream, for instance, can be read in raw, flowing form or sifted through by editors or writers and shaped into a cohesive story. Both processes played a key role in keeping the world informed during the revolutions in Iran and Egypt.

Editors or citizens can see broad national patterns far more easily. For years, local newspapers wrote occasional stories about cases of priests abusing children and being protected by church hierarchies. When the *Boston Globe* ran such a story in 2002, however, something different happened: The story was passed around via email to editors at other newspapers and activists around the country. The editors called on their own reporters to investigate whether cases of abuse existed in their towns, and before long, it became clear that this was a crisis for the entire Catholic Church.

Enabling Citizen Engagement

With 76 percent of cell phone owners using their phone to take pictures,[23] we may one day conclude that, as remarkable as it is that most Americans now carry around a minicomputer, it is just as significant that most now carry a camera. News organizations can rely on not only a stable of professionals but also on a much larger corps of amateurs; it has become a staple of modern news coverage to include photos and videos from citizens who captured images with their phones. Perhaps the most important piece of citizen journalism in this new era was the video taken by an Iranian doctor on his cell phone of a woman named Neda Agha-Soltan being murdered on the street in Tehran.

The term "citizen journalism" has come to include any instance when a non-professional contributes not just opinions but facts, sounds, or images to a developing news story. In Egypt and Iran, citizens used social media not only to organize each other but to report—providing real-time information that both educated citizens and fed the work-product of professional journalists. Shrewd reporters have come to view social-media content neither as frivolous froth nor "the truth" that should be passed on without question, but rather as comprising invaluable eyewitness accounts, tips, and ideas, as well as manifestations of raw emotion.

In some cases, web journalists have enlisted their own readers to help report a story. Joshua Marshall, editor and publisher of the award-winning TalkingPointsMemo website, asks readers to help scour government "document dumps" and report to him on behavior at local polling places on Election Day.

Citizen reporting works not only in the case of disaster but also in more pedestrian aspects of civic life. The website SeeClickFix.com enables citizens anywhere in the world to report and track non-emergency issues in their community; for instance, they can photograph a pothole and forward the geographically tagged image to other citizens and to city officials.[24] Even Internet-based message boards and community forums, which many people dismiss as places for bloviation and social chatter, often become venues where citizens share important information with one another—about which schools in the area have the best principals, which clinic has the shortest line for vaccinations, and which hotels have bedbugs. In the words of New York University professor Jay Rosen, "When the people formerly known as the audience employ the press tools they have in their possession to inform one another, *that's* citizen journalism."[25]

Web scholar Clay Shirky estimates that the citizens of the world have one trillion hours of free time annually—what he refers to as a "cognitive surplus"—that could be devoted to shared projects and problem solving.[26] Technology has enabled some of this time to be spent on frivolous enterprises ("lolcats," perhaps?), but some has been applied to civically important communal digital projects, as well. Shirky cites this example: Ory Okolloh, a blogger in Kenya, was tracking violence in the aftermath of her country's December 2007 elections when the government imposed a news blackout. She appealed to her readers for updates on what was happening in their neighborhoods but was quickly overwhelmed by the flood of information she received. Within 72 hours, two volunteer software engineers had designed a platform called "Ushahidi" to help her sort and map the information coming in from mobile phones and the web, so readers could see where violence was occurring and where there were peace efforts. This software has since been used "in Mexico to track electoral fraud, it's been deployed in Washington, D.C., to track snow cleanup and most famously in Haiti in the aftermath of the earthquake," Shirky says.[27]

In other words, the technological revolution has not merely provided a flood of cool new gizmos. It has also democratized access to the world's vast storehouse of knowledge and news.

Speed and Ease

The most obvious change brought by the Internet is speed. Once an article is done being edited for a print newspaper, it must then be laid out, printed, and physically delivered—a process that could take at least half a day. Online, that same article can come before a reader within seconds of being edited. *The Daily Show* correspondent Jason Jones captured the essence of the shift when he pointed to a print edition of the *New York Times* and challenged an editor: "Give me one thing in there that happened today."[28]

The new media's fixation on getting news published quickly has its downside, as reporters and editors may take less time to analyze and contemplate the information they have gathered. But if a hurricane is approaching, the ability to have real-time updates can be lifesaving.

Expanding Hyperlocal Coverage

In order to maximize revenue, news operations that rely on advertising have traditionally sought to appeal to a broad range of consumers. But the larger and more diverse the region of coverage, the more difficult it is to address the full spectrum of issues that matter to its citizens. An individual reading a big-city metro section or watching the local TV news will rarely see stories about his or her neighborhood. Community newspapers may offer more local content, but they are typically published weekly or monthly (rather than daily) by tiny staffs covering an entire town. The new-media universe, however, is rife with ways for people to share information about events in their community and on their block—including Listserv® and other email groups, blogs, and social-media sites. For example: Arlington Virginia's ARLNOW blog in May, 2011 had a discussion of a zoning debate regarding whether live music can be offered at a local outdoor pub.[29] Universal Hub, a community news and information website for the Boston area, features contributions from hundreds of local residents

> Since everyone now can, in effect, publish his or her own opinion, it is tempting to suggest that the Internet is all about lowering the bar. But it likely has made pontificating more meritocratic.

and bloggers; in its "Boston Crime" section, crime data are plotted and made searchable by neighborhood.[30] Though many hyperlocal sites do not make much money, they do not need to, because they function more as civic organizations than businesses, relying on volunteer efforts rather than cash.

Among businesses that aggregate news, there are some that focus specifically on hyperlocal news, such as Topix, Outside.In, Placeblogger, and MSNBC.com's Everyblock.[31] Without the burden of the infrastructure required to produce and distribute a newspaper, hyperlocal websites—whether run by an individual or a large corporation—can keep costs low. Executives of Patch, a network of hyperlocal sites owned by AOL, say that a Patch site costs 4.1 percent of what a comparable print daily community newspaper does to operate.[32]

With 76 percent of cell phone owners using their phones to take pictures, we may one day look back and conclude: society was changed as much by the fact that most Americans now carry around a camera as that they now carry around a mini-computer.

Serving Highly Specific Interests

The traditional mass-media model often left content providers struggling to lend expertise to a broad range of niche topics. A TV station might have a city hall reporter but be unable to afford to have someone cover every community board. Now, citizens, activists, and experts (professors, consultants, retired officials, etc.) can receive and contribute information through their own blogs or through any number of sites devoted to highly specialized topics. For instance, Irish Philadelphia focuses on music, dance, art, food, genealogy, and other local news and culture for Philadelphia's Irish American community.[33] Bikeportland.org collects information on biking news and personalities in Portland, Oregon.[34]

Cheaper Content Distribution

As costly as content creation (reporting, writing, developing expertise, etc.) can be in the traditional mass-media model, distribution is an even greater expense. Indeed, for newspapers, 33 percent of spending goes into distribution and production versus 14 percent for editorial.[35]

In the new-media world, the cost of distribution is dramatically lower—not only because publishers can bypass the printing process but because they can rely on informal networks to spread news from one person to another, through email, texting, or social media. In fact, a Pew Internet Project survey found that 32 percent of Internet users in Philadelphia, Pennsylvania; Macon, Georgia; and San Jose, California, use social-networking sites to get local news.[36]

Cheaper Content Creation

Researching an investigative story often entails accessing and reading through piles of documents. Previously, only the biggest news organizations had the resources to sustain comprehensive reference libraries; now everyone has access to massive numbers of online documents and research sources, often regardless of where they are located. Bill Allison, a veteran investigative journalist and editor, recently recounted how he used to "spend days and days" going from the Securities and Exchange Commission to the Office of the Clerk of the House of Representatives to the Senate Office of Public Records to the Justice Department to track down Freedom of Information Act records.[37] "Now," he says, much of that information can be obtained online "with one search," making for huge savings of time.[38]

Technology has reduced the cost of reporting in a variety of less obvious ways. Finding sources is far easier and less time-consuming. A reporter can supplement her Rolodex with web searches or by reaching out to people through social networks. Cheaper video cameras have made it possible for more people to shoot footage; cheaper editing software has lowered the cost of pulling together video into a coherent story. In some cases, information is put in the public domain, and someone in the general public finds an inconsistency or error—and so contributes to the reporting effort, without getting paid or raising a media company's labor costs.

Direct Access to Community and Civic News

Consumers can now obtain relevant information without journalistic intermediaries. Previously, residents of New York who wanted to know which local schools had gotten positive evaluations would hope that a local newspaper reporter would ferret out the information *and* mention that one particular school they were interested in out of the hundreds. Now, those same New Yorkers can go to the Department of Education website and see reviews of every school in the city[39] or go to one of several citizen-run websites that link to the government's evaluations.[40] Government offices now use new media to directly interact with and provide information to citizens. Legislative representatives announce their votes to their Facebook followers. Presidential contenders answer questions submitted on YouTube. Various new apps allow citizens to track issues of importance to them.(See Chapter 16, Government Transparency.)

However, the Internet Has Not Solved Some of Journalism's Key Problems

Given the dazzling ways the web has improved information dissemination—and the continuing arrival of a new innovation seemingly every day—one might expect the Internet to have already solved all of the reporting gaps left by the contraction of newspapers. It has not.

Abundance of Voices Does Not Necessarily Mean Abundance of Journalism

There is no question that the Internet has brought consumers a profusion of choice: It offers countless news *outlets* (newspaper websites, TV news websites, web-only news sites, national and local news sites, news aggregators), a variety of *formats* (video, audio, text) that can be accessed by computer or phone, and ever-expanding *options for sharing* news (email, Twitter, Facebook, etc.).

But how does the Internet rank when it comes to local accountability reporting?

The Pew Center for Excellence in Journalism conducted a study in Baltimore to evaluate how the entire media ecosystem was working in a single city.[41] For one week, researchers tracked every piece of content supplied by every local news operation—"from radio talk shows, to blogs, specialized news outlets, new-media sites, TV stations, radio news programs, newspapers and their various legacy media websites."[42] On one hand, the study showed that Baltimore had a booming collection of news and information outlets. But Pew did not stop there. It analyzed the content, looking particularly at coverage of critical civic issues (e.g., the city budget), and found that 95 percent of the stories—including those generated by new media—were based on reporting done by traditional media (mostly the *Baltimore Sun*).[43] Yet, at the same time, those traditional media organizations were doing less than they had in the past. In 2009, the *Baltimore Sun* produced 32 percent fewer stories on any subject than it did in 1999, and 73 percent fewer stories than in 1991.[44] So, the original reportage being chewed over by these secondary outlets was likely thinner and not as well researched as it would have been previously. (See Chapter 1, Newspapers.)

Other studies have demonstrated the same phenomenon: the growing number of web outlets relies on a relatively fixed, or declining, pool of original reporting provided by traditional media.

> In 2009, Michigan State University researchers studied media coverage of municipal government in 98 major metropolitan cities and 77 suburban communities.[45] After evaluating 6,811 stories by 466 news outlets, they concluded that "citizen journalism" was doing a marginally better job covering local government than local cable television, but both were at the bottom of the heap—with most of the original news still being created by the traditional media: "For all cities, the dominant providers of news and opinion about city government were daily newspapers, weekly newspapers and broadcast television."[46] Traditional media sources were responsible for 88.6 percent of the news about city governments and 93 percent about suburban governments.[47] "This finding," the researchers warned, "should give significant pause to those who believe that the 'new media' will fill any gaps left by the 'old media.'"[48]

> Nate Silver, a statistician and blogger at the *New York Times*, recently did a search in Google News and Google Blog Search for the phrase "reported" after the name of a news outlet—as in, "the Chicago Tribune reported"—to see who was providing the underlying information chewed over by the rest of the Internet. Of the top-30 most-cited sources, 29 were traditional news-media outlets (the one exception being gossip site TMZ).[49]

> In Philadelphia, a study by J-Lab: the Institute for Interactive Journalism, which funds innovative web journalism start-ups, found a plethora of new blogs, hyperlocal sites, and budding collaborations—including 260 new blogs (at least 60 with some "journalistic DNA") and as many as 100 people working part time or full time to produce news about Philadelphia.[50] Yet despite that explosion of news "outlets," J-Lab researchers concluded that overall, "the available news about Philadelphia public affairs issues has dramatically diminished over the last three years [from 2006 to 2009] by many measures: news hole, air time, story count, key word measurements."[51]

> Researchers at Harvard's Nieman Journalism Lab looked at 121 distinct stories listed on Google News about attempts to hack into Google from China. They found that only 13 "contained some amount of original reporting" and only "one was produced by a primarily online outlet."[52] The other 100-plus stories were essentially rewrites, summaries, and links to or rehashes of reporting done by a handful of outlets.[53]

> The Knight Foundation's New Voices initiative found that most of its 55 local web-based news projects were providing (often very useful) hyperlocal coverage that had never been offered by metropolitan dailies before. But a study assessing these programs concluded that, "Rarely did they replace coverage that had vanished from legacy news outlets—or even aspire to."[54]

> A snapshot of the Huffington Post home page on January 8, 2009, illustrated a similar phenomenon: of 29 news stories, 23 were copies or summaries of journalism produced by mainstream media outlets. The others were based on public domain information (e.g., public press conferences, TV shows, etc.).[55]

Disappointing Financial Track Record for New Local, Online, Labor-Intensive Accountability Journalism

There has been an explosion of impressive local news websites in the last few years. Some were started by laid-off newspaper reporters, some by concerned citizens. Some are for-profit ventures, including the Alaska Dispatch, the Batavian, and the Arizona Guardian. (See Chapter 25, How Big is the Gap and Who Will Fill It?) Some are nonprofits, such as MinnPost in Minneapolis,[56] voiceofsandiego.org,[57] and the Texas Tribune. Several have broken even or appear to be on their way to doing so. (See Chapter 12, Nonprofit Websites.) In trying to get a head count, Michele McLellan of the Reynolds Journalism Institute at the University of Missouri compiled a list of more than 140 local news websites.[58]

Yet while journalistically many of the local news start-ups have soared, financially most have not gained traction. A 2010 survey of 66 of the most exciting online news start-ups—a mix of nonprofit and for-profit—delivered this sobering news: half of the organizations had annual revenue of less than $50,000, and three-quarters had annual revenue of less than $100,000.[59]

Even those that are breaking even are doing so on a scale that makes them unlikely candidates to fully fill the reporting gaps left by newspapers. A 2010 gathering of leaders of the top 12 local nonprofit news sites revealed that together they employed only 88 staff reporters. (Recall, more than 13,000 jobs in newspaper newsrooms have disappeared in just the last four years.) While foundations have contributed more than $180 million to local news start-ups over five years,[60] the Poynter Institute's Rick Edmonds estimates that budget cuts in traditional media have constituted a $1.6 billion drop in newspaper editorial spending *per year*.[61] The uneven math tells the story: billions out, millions in.

Part of the problem is that the new sites have not been able to generate enough page views to attract sufficient ad dollars. An FCC staff examination of three cities—Toledo, Ohio; Richmond, Virginia; and Seattle, Washington—found that not one of their local web-based start-ups cracked the top 10 websites visited by local residents. (See Chapter 21, Types of News.) In a paper on the economics of online news, the Pew Internet & American Life Project concluded that: "even the most established citizen sites are not in a position to take on the job of traditional news outlets."[62]

> One study of 6,811 stories concluded that most of reporting came from traditional media. Another study looked at 121 distinct stories about attempts to hack into Google from China. They found that only 13 "contained some amount of original reporting."

The venture capital world—which funded much early and current Internet innovation—has been cool to local news start-ups. Esther Dyson, chairman of EDventure Holdings and an Internet pioneer, explains, "News start-ups are rarely profitable and, by and large, no thinking person who wanted a return on investment would invest in a news start-up."[63] She says that investors are more interested in low-cost ways of drawing communities together: "The way to attract their attention is to talk about a 'local Craigslist'—not local content. They're looking at things that revolve around user reviews."[64]

What about national Internet companies attempting to offer local coverage? AOL's Patch service has hired more local editor/reporters than any other media company in recent years: as of March 2011, its 800 sites employed about 800 reporter/editors.[65] Examiner.com, founded by entrepreneur Phillip Anschutz, has sites in 233 cities, employing 67,000 "examiners" who write on local topics. In November 2010, Examiner.com sites counted 24 million unique visitors and generated 68 million page views.[66] Both companies have spread their technology costs across the entire country, so local content contributors can post material without have to bear the cost of creating a new website.

But while these sites offer tremendously useful content, it seems unlikely that they will fill the gaps in labor-intensive accountability reporting at the city and state level. Examiner.com president, Rick Blair, says that to work financially the sites tend to focus on lifestyle topics, such as entertainment, retail, and sports, not investigative reporting.[67] And it is possible that the Patch formula is only commercially viable when it is applied to affluent towns of a certain size, its focus so far. (An AOL marketing page boasts, "Patch & AOL Local is in 800 of the most affluent towns across the US, where 70% of all big box stores are located.") [68]

In fact, AOL has said that since its business model would not sustain a more varied socio-economic range of Patch sites, it created a noncommercial adjunct, the Patch.org Foundation, "to partner with community foundations and other organizations to fund the operation of Patch news and information sites in communities that need them most: inner-city neighborhoods and underserved towns."[69] It remains to be seen whether AOL's approach will change with its acquisition of the Huffington Post, which also has been diving into the local space, using an effective formula relying on unpaid bloggers, news links, and summaries of news from other media outlets.

Having studied the new breed of news websites, Michele McLellan wrote that those websites often offer hyperlocal services that traditional media never did but, on the other hand, do not fill the gaps in reporting left by the newspapers, "The tired idea that born-on-the-Web news sites will replace traditional media is wrong-headed, and it's past time that academic research and news reports reflect that."[70]

Why Has the Internet Not Filled the Reporting Gaps Left by Newspapers?

The Great Unbundling (Consumer Choice)

Before the advent of the Internet, readers had limited say in how they received their news. For one thing, most of them lived in cities or towns with only one local newspaper. And for another, although they tended not to think of it this way, purchasing a newspaper meant buying a whole bundle of goods, even if they only wanted certain parts. Readers who only cared about box scores got a lot more, including articles about health, education, and city hall. This was not an onerous burden since the paper was so cheap—25 cents for a newspaper produced by hundreds of people each day was an incredible bargain—and consumers and society alike benefited from readers tripping over the occasional story about the mayor.

Newspaper editorial spending dropped $1.6 billion per year. Meanwhile, foundations have contributed $180 million toward the creation of local nonprofit journalism startups over *five* years.

Most consumers were not conscious of it, but by selling all types of content in a bundle, newspapers had developed a cross-subsidy system. Readers buying the paper for the box score helped pay the salary of the city hall reporter. Ann Landers funded the Bagdad bureau. The horoscope helped pay for a cub reporter to attend every school board meeting.

Today, a reader can go to a website, or get a phone app, that only delivers box scores (and does so with the added value of pitch-by-pitch updates), never coming into contact with that article about city hall—let alone being drawn inadvertently into reading it. The bundle is broken—and so is the cross-subsidy. When people go to a sports website instead of buying a print newspaper, they have stopped contributing to a jerry-rigged system in which profitable topics subsidize unprofitable coverage. Some cross-subsidies still occur—websites still sometimes post articles they know will not attract much traffic (see Chapter 25, How Big is the Gap and Who Will Fill It?)—but web editors are exquisitely sensitive to which articles draw eyeballs, and resources typically shift toward those areas.

Free Riding

Unbundling makes apparent which articles or video clips are not carrying their own weight financially. It challenges us to consider why consumers are not more inclined to click on or pay for a certain type of content.

Markets usually respond to consumer demand. But what happens if consumers don't demand something they essentially need? Economists have long argued that certain types of goods are valuable to consumers, regardless of whether that is reflected in their spending.[71] News is one such "public good," meaning that it has certain characteristics:

It is deemed "nonexclusive," in that people can consume it, whether or not they pay for it. It is also "non-rival," meaning that one person's consumption of a news item does not make it unavailable for others to consume, as well. Public goods often confer benefits to society that are in excess of what the producer of those goods stands to gain—which economists refer to as "positive externalities."[72] A city hall reporter watching over budget spending may save taxpayers money, for instance. And a story about a school being torn down might spur citizens to act collectively to solve problems that led to the decision. The Knight Commission on Information Needs of Communities in a Democracy summarized the public benefits of local news and information as: contributing to the coordination of community activity, collective problem solving, public accountability, and public connectedness.[73] But, alas, economists teach us that people do not like to pay much for public goods. And when consumers do not pay, the market may respond by not providing.

Why would consumers not want to pay for goods that are so beneficial? The short answer is: because they do not have to. They can receive the information or the benefit of the information's creation regardless of whether they have paid for it, essentially getting a "free ride." Newspaper journalism that helps prevent corruption by aggressively covering city hall contributes to civic health, benefiting those who do not buy a newspaper just as much as the people who do.

Just because they have not paid for it, does not mean they do not value it. Consider a December 2008 series in the *Raleigh (NC) News & Observer* on the state's probation system. The three-part series established that 580 North Carolina probationers had killed people since the start of 2000,[74] which prompted the new governor to expand funding and fix the program.[75] The series occupied several staff over six months, costing in the range of $200,000 to produce.[76] The benefits of this accountability coverage were widely distributed across the residents of the Research Triangle area— yet the benefits were, by their nature, mostly unrecognized. Some citizens of Raleigh are walking around today, not murdered, but they will never know who the lucky ones were, let alone make the connection to why they were spared.

It has always been a struggle in American society to sustain certain types of journalism. Fear that pure consumer demand would not be sufficient to support a newspaper industry prompted the Founding Fathers to offer postal subsidies. (See Chapter 33, Print.) This is also evidenced by the fact that many American political magazines in the 20th century lost money, because they were unable to find enough paying customers to underwrite journalism about civic affairs.

Free riding has always been possible—with minor inconveniences, like having to get your friend to Xerox that interesting article he mentioned and hoping your neighbor watched enough of the evening news tell you what you want to know. But the Internet has made free riding far easier: most news websites are free; friends can send links to you with a click of the mouse; news headlines appear before our eyes, unsolicited, on portals like Yahoo or AOL; free news apps on mobile devices find and display news from around the Internet. It should come as no surprise, then, when young people these days say they do not feel the need to seek out news sources, because if something important happens "the news will find me."[77]

The problem is that if everyone gets the news without paying for it, media outlets do not make enough money and are therefore less likely to employ the reporters producing the information. Among new-media mavens, one of the most famous phrases of the Internet era is "Information wants to be free."[78] True, people want to distribute and receive information for free. But what this leaves out of the equation is the small matter of what it costs to dig out certain types of information.

Information may want to be free, but, it turns out, labor wants to be paid.

Some kinds of information will be provided to the public even without paid reporters making it happen. Movie listings will be posted by theaters, the mayor's ribbon cutting will be publicized by the mayor's staff. Other types of information—for instance, information that the mayor *does not* want publicized — may only come to light as a result of persistent reporting by a full-time professional.

And there's the problem in a nutshell: civically important content often costs a lot to produce; yet relatively few readers want to consume or pay for the material. High cost, low revenue—an economic model that will excite few publishers.

The Great Unbundling (Advertiser Choice)

Along with consumers, advertisers have benefited from the unbundling of content. Remember the saying attributed to department store executive John Wanamaker: "Half [the money I spend on] advertising is wasted; [the trouble is] I just don't know which half."[79] On the Internet, in most cases the executive *can* know which half he is wasting, and stop the foolishness. The media world has been transformed by the simple fact that web advertising is far more measurable than TV, radio, or newspaper advertising. Advertisers can see precisely how many people looked at a page with their message on it and how many clicked on that ad.

Google embraced this fact—and turned the advertising business model upside-down. Instead of asking advertisers to take the chance that enough readers will see their ad to make what they spend worthwhile, Google assumes the risk, offering a stunning promise to advertisers: you only pay us if someone clicks on the ad.[80] Imagine if the newspapers had said to car dealers, you only have to pay if someone comes to your car lot.

So what is the problem? The new advertising reality has commoditized advertising placement opportunities, driven ad rates down, and attracted dollars away from the sites that create the most labor-intensive types of content.

Downward Pressure on Internet Advertising Rates

As noted earlier (see Chapter 1, Newspapers), from 2005 to 2009, newspaper print advertising revenue dropped from $47.4 billion to $24.8 billion.[81] One might wonder whether newspapers could have offset this loss with online ad revenue if they had only grown their web traffic more rapidly. Well, during that same period, newspapers' online traffic *did* skyrocket—from 1.6 billion page views to about 3 billion page views,[82] leading to a $716 million increase in online ad revenue.[83] But, alas, print ad revenue dropped $22.5 billion during that time.[84]

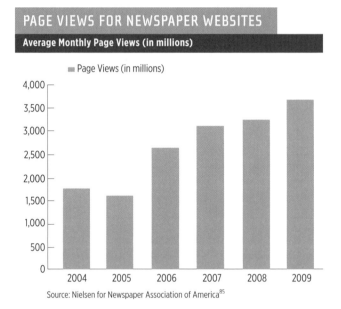

PAGE VIEWS FOR NEWSPAPER WEBSITES

Average Monthly Page Views (in millions)

Source: Nielsen for Newspaper Association of America[85]

Online advertising rates mostly pale in comparison with ad rates for other media. In May 2010, a typical online ad cost about $2.52 per 1,000 viewers (CPM, or cost per 1,000 impressions).[86] If a blog has three ads on a page (a typical number), and generates 100,000 page views per month, those ads may produce $756 in monthly income. By contrast, the average CPM for broadcast television networks (primetime) was $19.74 in 2010.[87] In 2008, the average CPM for newspapers in larger markets was $19.72.[88] If that blog could charge TV or newspaper rates instead of Internet rates, monthly revenue would go from under $1,000 to around $6,000—from sustaining a hobby to creating a paying job. Newspapers' transition from print to online would have been much less painful if they could have replaced their print dollars with even digital dimes or quarters, instead of pennies.

RELATIONSHIP BETWEEN TRAFFIC, CPM AND REVENUE

Monthly Page Views	Average CPM (assumes 3 ads per page view)							
	$1.00	$2.52	$5.00	$7.50	$10.00	$15.00	$20.00	$25.00
100,000	$300	$756	$1,500	$2,250	$3,000	$4,500	$6,000	$7,500
500,000	$1,500	$3,780	$7,500	$11,250	$15,000	$22,500	$30,000	$37,500
1,000,000	$3,000	$7,560	$15,000	$22,500	$30,000	$45,000	$60,000	$75,000
5,000,000	$15,000	$37,800	$75,000	$112,500	$150,000	$225,000	$300,000	$375,000
10,000,000	$30,000	$75,600	$150,000	$225,000	$300,000	$450,000	$600,000	$750,000

Source: Flatiron Media ; CPM=Cost per 1,000 impressions

The general softness of digital ad rates is compounded by a challenge those in the news business have always faced: advertisers generally do not want their products associated with controversy. That holds true on the Internet just as in traditional media. As Hal Varian, Google's chief economist, observed, "online world reflects offline: news, narrowly defined, is hard to monetize."[89]

There is some silver lining, however: Although the average ad rate on the Internet is $2.52 CPM, the average rate for large newspaper websites is $7—still a fraction of the ad rates for their print editions but at least higher than the Internet average.[90] Certain topics are so attractive to advertisers that websites that focus on them can fetch even higher rates. This is especially true for health and financial content, which is why a disproportionate number of the successful content websites have been in those sectors (e.g., WebMD, Everyday Health, CBS MarketWatch, the Motley Fool).

Persistently limp online ad rates were not what experts anticipated in the early days of the Internet. Some predicted that online ad rates would rise over time.[91] It was not a crazy theory. As consumers spent more time online, advertising dollars would follow them there, driving rates upward.[92] The theory turned out to be partly true: consumers do spend significantly more time online, and the amount of ad dollars has indeed grown steadily. (In fact, in 2010, advertisers spent more money online than in print newspapers.)[93]

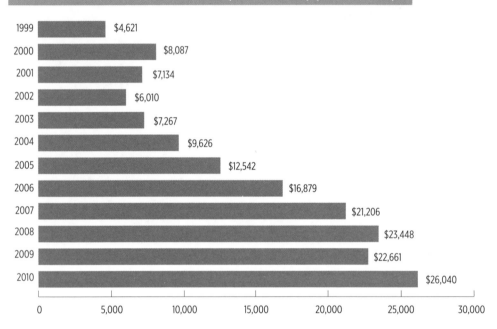

INTERNET ADVERTISING REVENUE (IN MILLIONS) (1999–2010)

1999	$4,621
2000	$8,087
2001	$7,134
2002	$6,010
2003	$7,267
2004	$9,626
2005	$12,542
2006	$16,879
2007	$21,206
2008	$23,448
2009	$22,661
2010	$26,040

Source: Internet Advertising Bureau (IAB) Internet Advertising Revenue Report 2010[94]

But those who believed that this would lead to a windfall for content websites did not count on two factors.

First, the volume of web pages grew exponentially. Google, the most popular search engine during the last decade, had an index of 26 million pages in 1998.[95] In mid-2008, Google indexers counted one trillion "unique URLS on the web."[96] More web pages, meant advertisers had more places to park their ad dollars, and the small number of media entities could not get away with charging higher rates.

Second, a huge and growing portion of online ad dollars went to search engines instead of to content sites. In 2000, search advertising generated one percent of online ad dollars.[97] By the first half of 2010, it brought in 47 percent of the total.[98]

Advertising Is Less Dependent on Content

In traditional media, advertisers always have been strategic about placing ads in a particular editorial context. To some extent, the editorial quality of a publication would have a "halo" effect: if a reader trusted and respected the local news-

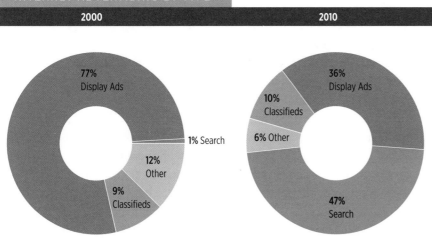

2000

77%
Display Ads

1% Search

12%
Other

9%
Classifieds

2010

36%
Display Ads

10%
Classifieds

6% Other

47%
Search

Source: Internet Advertising Bureau (IAB) 2010 Revenue Report[99]

paper, he would trust the car dealer advertising in its pages. But mostly, advertisers wanted to appear in proximity to certain types of editorial content in order to reach particular readers. An advertiser that wanted to market to 30-year-old women would advertise in *Glamour*, *Elle*, or another magazine catering to that demographic. A local advertiser would have few options but the local newspaper to reach residents of that community.

But using content as a proxy for reach was always a rougher science than publishers wanted to admit. The hardware store might well get its message in front of the man thinking of buying a lawnmower but it would be inadvertently marketing to many other people who had no interest in lawnmowers. The advent of directed search on the Internet has removed much of the uncertainty, allowing advertisers to get directly in front of the desired consumer at the optimal moment.[100] Where, in the past, car dealers would run TV promotions, knowing that only a small fraction of viewers were actually shopping for a car, now they can advertise on car websites or associate their ad with search phrases like "best subcompact car." This targeting ability is becoming more finely tuned by the day. Google places ads next to searches not only on the basis of the exact words in the search but also on the basis of patterns in consumers' previous behavior online—purchases made, websites visited, searches conducted.[101]

Thus, advertisers now can reach consumers more expediently without placing their message in an editorial context. Currently, only 36 percent of online advertising spending goes to display advertising (such as banner ads), the sort most likely to benefit content creators.[102] And of this relatively small amount, an even smaller portion goes to the sites that invest in content creation: about 16 percent of online display ads run on TV station, newspaper, and news and current events websites.[103]

Search engines have had a mixed hand in the fate of news websites, making them the subject of much debate. On the one hand, there is no question that they send significant amounts of traffic to news sites: between 35 and 40 percent of news sites' traffic comes from search engines.[104] In that way, they help news providers mightily. On the other hand, 44 percent of online news consumers look at Google News headlines—and then do not click to read the full stories.[105] They get the gist of the news, without visiting the site that employed the people who created that gist. In the olden days, when a consumer bought a newspaper, he or she would both scan headlines and dive deeply into a smaller number of articles. But it was fine with the newspaper if a reader only scanned some, since they'd purchased the whole newspaper. Hence, the paper would derive value from both scanners and deep divers. On the Internet, news sites only capture financial value from the deep divers (i.e. those who click).

Google has made some efforts to help newspapers and other content creators better monetize their efforts—for instance, the company worked with newspapers to create "flip pages" that allow readers to view newspaper content in a visually appealing bundle. On the other hand, consumers have many ways to avoid ads if they choose. For instance, a popular third-party application on Google's browser product Chrome strips out ads from sites that Chrome users visit, thereby depriving the destination sites of this crucial way of monetizing the content.[106] Several popular iPad apps create virtual magazines, displaying content from a variety of publications, while stripping out the ads. (See Chapter 5, Mobile.)

It Is Easier to Generate Page Views Without Investing in Journalism

Some of the ad dollars that media experts expected to shift from offline content creators to online content creators have instead gone to websites that repackage content but generally do not bear the main cost of its creation. Of the top-20 news sources online, as measured by Hitwise, a leading online metrics firm, seven are either pure aggregators (sites that primarily draw traffic by summarizing news unearthed by other publications or posting links to content on other sites) or hybrids (which summarize news and link out to stories).[107]

Consider the economics from the perspective of the newspaper: The publication might pay a reporter to work on a story that takes several weeks to research and write. When the story runs, it may or may not turn up as a top link in search engine results—most often it will not. (Items that are listed on the first page of search engine results, especially those at the top, get the vast majority of clicks.) At the same time, hundreds of other sites can list the headline, summarize the story, and comment on the original material and do quite well in search results if they meet other search engine criteria (such as the number of other sites linking to them). They then draw clicks and the associated ad revenue.

It is easy to see how, from a purely economic perspective, one could conclude that it is preferable to be the company telling others about content than the company creating it. On the web, it is extremely difficult for the company that invests in the creation of content to capture enough ad dollars or subscriber fees to pay for the labor-intensive journalism required. When *Rolling Stone* broke the story about General Stanley McChrystal criticizing Obama administration officials in the summer of 2010, it was big news.[108] AP ran a story about it, which was "tweeted" by NBC; soon Politico.com and Time.com printed the entire *Rolling Stone* story, prompting *New York Times* columnist David Carr to note, "a PDF of the piece the magazine had lovingly commissioned, edited, fact-checked, printed and distributed, was posted in its entirety on not one but two web sites, for everyone to read without giving *Rolling Stone* a dime."[109]

> If that blog could charge TV rates instead of Internet rates, monthly revenue would go from under $1000 to almost $6,000—from sustaining a hobby to creating a paying job.

Search engines, summarizers, and aggregators are not the only operations that have managed to generate page views—and attract ad dollars—without investing in costly, labor-intensive journalism. "Content farms," such as Associated Content and Demand Media, pay small fees to writers who produce content on topics that appeal to advertisers—and rarely involve enterprise reporting.[110] Demand Media content generates 621 million page views per month globally,[111] and, prior to its acquisition by Yahoo! in May 2010, Associated Content (now Yahoo! ContributorNetwork) drew "about 16 million unique visitors per month, according to comScore numbers," and generated "1.75 billion page views" between its launch in 2005 and its sale in 2010.[112] Some of this content is quite useful; *USA Today* has begun using Demand Media for its travel tips section.[113] But it is rarely the sort of civically important reporting that newspapers previously did—and because writers are paid only a small stipend, the cost-per-page-view basis is a small fraction of what it would be for the content a newspaper produces.

To their credit, these companies—aggregators, summarizers, and content farms—have managed to build sustainable business models for at least some types of content creation. That consumers flock to their sites indicates that they are offering a valued service. Even when they pay writers little or no money, they are providing them other benefits, such as the opportunity to share their expertise and ideas with a large readership. But there may be an unintended casualty: this drives down pay rates for professional freelance writers, producers, photographers, and journalists. A Kaiser Family Foundation study about the declining coverage of global health issues reported:

> "Arthur Allen, a former AP staff writer and now an author and freelancer, said a prominent online publication recently dropped its rate from $1,000 to $500 a story. Another pays $300 a story. 'I asked why they are decreasing payment and they say, "Some people are writing for nothing,"' Allen said. 'It's a hobby for people who have other gigs…Certainly doctors and lawyers have a lot to say about things, but it's difficult for people like me who are journalists.'"[114]

Allen said that although *The Washington Post* will pay him up to $1,000 for a piece (and some publications pay even more), those stories can take two or three weeks to complete, so when you break it down to a per-hour basis, the higher fee still does not amount to much. So, Allen thinks hard about story selection: "My journalism has become over the last year or two, picking low-hanging fruit and grabbing something that I feel I can do a relatively quick kill on," he said. Some freelancers who do not want to limit themselves to "quick kill" pieces try to supplement their income with money from foundations or advocacy groups, but both are in limited supply and the latter may come with ideological strings attached.[115]

Social media will continue to generate advertising-ready page views inexpensively. Facebook's 500 million users spend over 700 billion minutes per month on the site.[116] The Internet marketing and metrics company comScore concluded that if it were not for the sheer volume of page views on Facebook and MySpace, ad rates online would be 18 percent higher now.[117] Facebook and MySpace are doing nothing wrong. They attract the audience, and the ad dollars, because they are providing a highly desired service. But the easier it becomes for advertisers to reach online audiences without subsidizing content created by full-time reporters and writers, the harder it will be to sustain business models in which journalists and others involved in the content creation process actually get paid.

Then, there is the issue of outright copyright violation. Search engines don't automatically distinguish between a website that steals another website's content—copies it and pastes it into a new template without attribution—and the site where it originated (unless the violation is reported to the search engine, which will then remove it from search results). So, the site that stole the content can easily rank high in search results and monetize the content using ad networks or Google AdSense. A recent study found that 70,101 online news articles generated 400,000 cases of articles being printed without permission[118] — and, of course, none of the sites involved initially shared their revenue with the entity that had invested in creating the content.[119] In December 2010, Google announced that it was taking measures to crack down on content farms[120] and make it easier for content creators to notify them about piracy and less likely that such content could be monetized through AdSense.[121]

Hal Varian, Google's Chief Economist, concluded that the "online world reflects offline: the news, narrowly defined, is pretty hard to monetize."

When it comes to pirated video, Google has offered an intriguing solution. If a content creator notifies YouTube (which is owned by Google) that a pirated video appears on its service, YouTube then diverts any ad revenue generated from the pirating company to the original content creator.[122] This is even better than taking the material down, since the content creator earns some revenue. But, implementing such a system outside of YouTube would be far more complex. So far Google has not taken such action when it comes to pirated text-based articles that generate AdSense revenue when they come up in its search engines.

In sum, pre-Internet, most advertising spending went to businesses that created content—newspapers, magazines, radio, and TV shows. The majority of ad spending online goes to entities that do not create the content—search engines, summarizers, and aggregators. The earlier media system rewarded both the distributors and the creators of content; the new one primarily rewards those who find and distribute content. This does not mean that aggregators or search engines are evil or parasitic. It simply means they have found a way to make money locating and distributing content rather than creating it. They are not the villains of this new world; they are simply its main beneficiaries.

Fragmentation Slices the Pie into Smaller Pieces

On a local level, a handful of websites capture a majority of the traffic, and yet often they still do not attract enough ad revenue to sustain their business. Our analysis of the local sites in Toledo, Richmond, and Seattle indicates the difficulty of reaching a critical mass on a local level. The number-one site in Toledo, ToledoBlade.com, generated 2 million page views per month. A typical site with two million page views generates $15,000 per month, assuming an average effective CPM of $2.52 and three ads per page.[123] The number-four site, FOX Toledo, drew 73,408 page views, which typically would generate under $1,000 per month. Even if both sites succeeded in sustaining ad rates at double or triple the average, it would be extremely difficult to operate a newsroom on that kind of revenue. In addition, because they don't have the marketing clout of a traditional media company behind them, it is especially difficult for independent web sites to reach scale.

What is more, the ad departments of local news sites must now compete not only with each other but with national Internet companies that run local ads—even when they do not offer local content. If someone from Toledo

Pre-Internet, most advertising spending went to businesses that created content—newspapers, magazines, radio and TV shows. Now, the majority goes to entities that do not create the content—search engines, summarizers and aggregators.

visits Yahoo! News to read a national story, they may see a local ad. The ad market in Toledo is now split not only among the local content creators, but the national players capable of targeting local ads. Indeed, this is part of the reason that the lion's share of digital ad dollars is spent on a relatively small percentage of websites. According to the Interactive Advertising Bureau, since at least 2001, the top-10 companies have received at least 70 percent of online ad revenue.[124] These leaders include Google, Yahoo!, Microsoft, AOL, and Facebook.[125]

Newspapers' share of online ad revenue has actually fallen in the past few years, from 16.2 percent in 2005 to 11.4 percent in 2009, and PricewaterhouseCooper projects that their portion will shrink to 7.9 percent in 2014.[126]

Conclusions About the Internet

We disagree with those who claim that the Internet has provided us with a world of pajama-clad bloviators and parasitic aggregators as opposed to real reporters. In fact, the Internet has brought *improvements to* news and information ecosystems in a variety of ways:

> Unlimited space and lower barriers to entry have led to a greater diversity of voices and more choices for consumers.

> Links make it possible for any piece of content to point toward huge numbers of additional sources of information, allowing an interested reader to access a far greater depth of information.

> The everyone-is-a-publisher economy has allowed for the rise of a new commentariat, and a system that is arguably more meritocratic than before.

> Citizen contributions have enhanced the coverage of important topics, including weather events, disaster recovery, local zoning decisions, scheduling of community events, and the quality of public transportation.

> The cost of some types of reporting has dropped dramatically.

> Thanks to volunteer contributions, database-driven tools, and low-cost publishing platforms, hyperlocal reporting and news is now able to thrive like never before.

Yet it is also possible that while the Internet is doing all of the above, it is doing something else as well: undermining the business models that enabled legacy journalism firms to employ reporters, especially on beats that are costly to maintain. One can appreciate the incredible benefits of the web while still confronting head-on some of its more unfortunate repercussions:

> As of now, in many cases, communities now have more news distribution outlets and, simultaneously, less accountability journalism.

> So far, relatively few new websites have been able to create sustainable business models that would support significant hiring of reporters on a local level.

> Revenue from advertising has, up to this moment, not been sufficient to replace losses in print advertising revenue or sustain news start-ups because:

>> Rates are low and showing no signs of rising.

>> Ad dollars are getting scooped up by a small group of advertising venues.

>> Advertisers have less and less need to advertise next to content as a way of reaching their targeted audience.

>> Internet companies (and would-be investors) can generate monetizable page views in far more cost-effective ways if they avoid hiring of large numbers of reporters and expensive freelance writers.

These limitations do not nullify the benefits, but it does mean that while the Internet solves many problems, it does not solve all of them.

This still leaves us with a crucial question: even if the new-media system has not filled all of the gaps so far, does that mean it will not or cannot? With digital technology and business models changing rapidly, is it not possible—even likely—that the problems existing today will be solved tomorrow? In the next chapter, on mobile platforms, we look at some of the new ways that publishers are trying to charge for content and improve their advertising businesses. And in Chapter 25 (How Big is the Gap and Who Will Fill It?), we look holistically at the likelihood of the commercial sector evolving in ways that will lead to the gaps in accountability reporting getting filled.

5 Mobile

THE FASTEST-GROWING MEANS for accessing news and information is the mobile device.[1] Fifty-six percent of all mobile device users, and 47 percent of the population, now use them to get local news via an Internet connection.[2] Increasingly, mobile phones, e-Readers and tablets are news media platforms—just like a newspaper or a TV set—as much as they are two-way communications tools.

This section focuses on the ways in which mobile technology has become a major delivery mechanism for news—with the potential to provide consumers, including minority and low-income populations, greater access to digital news and information content. The section also explores the financial impact of mobile technology on the news industry, finding that the delivery of content over mobile devices is not yet proving to be a major source of revenue for news outlets, although, early returns suggest that e-Readers and tablets may offer more financial upside.

For purposes of this report, "mobile" refers to wireless communications technologies designed to be used while in motion or from different fixed points, as opposed to technologies designed to be used from a single fixed point. In this section, we focus on news consumption over *handheld* devices that use mobile technologies—such as cell phones, smartphones, tablets (such as the iPad), and e-Readers, such as Kindle and nook.

History

The cellular phone was invented by Martin Cooper at Motorola in 1973 and became commercially available in the United States a decade later. First-generation cell phones were primarily used for voice traffic. The transition from analog to second-generation (2G) digital transmission technology, primarily during the 1990s, brought about better sound quality, increased spectral efficiency, and enhanced features like mobile voice mail.[3]

From 1994 to 2000, the FCC auctioned a large number of licenses to use the Personal Communications Service (PCS) spectrum, more than tripling the stock of spectrum available for commercial mobile devices and vastly increasing the capacity to carry digital signals—including voice —over commercial cellular networks.[4] The mobile industry responded with a new wave of innovation and investment, which brought about dramatic change. From 1994 to 2000:[5]

> The per-minute price of cell phone service dropped by 50 percent.

> The number of mobile subscribers more than tripled.

> Cumulative investment in the industry more than tripled from $19 billion to over $70 billion.

> The number of wireless providers increased significantly in most markets.

Then came the development and expansion of "mobile broadband." Colloquially, "mobile broadband" refers to "high-speed, wireless Internet." More precisely, the term "mobile broadband" refers to advanced network technologies, usually at speeds and latencies (amount of delay in sending and receiving data packets) that allow for Internet access and the use of mobile applications ("apps"). The growth of the mobile broadband industry has been driven by a number of factors, including the development of smartphones and other mobile computing devices, the availability of additional suitable spectrum, and the deployment of mobile wireless broadband networks.[6] In the years since the FCC auctioned PCS licenses, the FCC increased the total spectrum available for mobile services by threefold again—largely through the auction of spectrum in the 700 MHz and 1.7/2.1 GHz bands and the rebanding of spectrum at 2.5 GHz—and this spectrum is coming online for mobile broadband deployment today.[7] Most of the major mobile wireless service providers are currently rolling out or planning to deploy new technologies which, by supporting even higher data throughput rates and lower latencies, will facilitate a broader range of mobile applications, such as the viewing of large volumes of video.[8] Industry analysts project substantial continued growth of mobile wireless, with data traffic forecasted to increase 35 times 2009 levels by 2014.[9]

In June 2010, approximately 71.2 million mobile wireless Internet access service subscriptions were reported to the Commission on its Form 477, an 85 percent increase from the 38.4 million reported in June 2009.[10]

The Mobile News Audience

A recent article described mobile as a "critical…news delivery platform."[11] According to a smartphone-user study conducted by Google with Ipsos OTX in late 2010, 57 percent of "mobile searchers" are looking for news—a higher percentage than that of users looking for dining (51 percent), entertainment (49 percent), or shopping (47 percent) information.[12] In addition, 95 percent of users have used their smartphone to look for local information.[13]

What kind of news do people access through their mobile devices? Weather was the most popular topic accessed (42 percent), followed by local restaurants/businesses (37 percent), general local news (30 percent), local sports scores/updates (24 percent), local traffic/transportation (22 percent), local coupons/discounts (19 percent), and news alerts (15 percent).[14]

The increase in the mobile consumption of news is fueled in part by the proliferation of smartphones. While there is no industry standard definition of a smartphone, the distinguishing features of a smartphone generally include: an HTML browser that allows easy access to the full Internet; an operating system that provides a standardized interface and platform for application developers; and a larger screen size than on a traditional handset.[15] Other types of cell phones—sometimes referred to as "feature phones"—may offer more limited Internet access without a standardized platform for applications.[16] And there are some cell phones—sometimes referred to as "basic phones"—that do not provide Internet access at all. Smartphones are outselling PCs worldwide—101 million to 92 million in the fourth quarter of 2010.[17] Nielsen predicted that "by the end of 2011, [there will be] more smartphones in the U.S. market than feature phones."[18]

One study found that the top 10 mobile devices used for "news and information access" were either smartphones or high-end feature phones.[19] This is in part because accessing news websites and applications is far easier on smartphones.

Significantly, low-income earners, African-Americans, and Hispanics had high cell phone use.[20] Although it is difficult to generalize, data from 2008 and 2011 indicate that these populations have relatively *high* rates of mobile Internet usage and local information consumption via mobile devices,[21] even though they consume print news and news through desktop computers at lower rates than white Americans.[22]

According to the Pew Internet & American Life Project study, *Mobile Access 2010*, an estimated 54 percent of African-Americans and 53 percent of English-speaking Hispanics access the Internet on a handheld device.[23] And while 18 percent of African-Americans and 16 percent of English-speaking Hispanics gain access to the Internet only through wireless mobile, only 10 percent of white Americans do.[24] The study also found that mobile data application usage is higher among African-Americans and Latinos than whites.[25] Hispanics use wireless mobile devices for news with special frequency. Among those who go online using a handheld device, 55 percent of English-speaking Hispanics do so several times a day.[26] The study observed that "minority Americans lead the way when it comes to mobile access…using handheld devices"—a trend that the Pew Internet & American Life Project "first identified in 2009" in its *Wireless Internet Use* report.[27]

In addition, it appears that smartphone usage is spreading within the African-American and English-speaking Hispanic communities faster than in white communities in the U.S.[28] Daily mobile Internet access by African-Americans increased by 141 percent, from 12 percent at the end of 2007 to 29 percent at the beginning of 2009, roughly double the rate of increase among the general population.[29] In addition, in Pew's *Mobile Access 2010* report, only 19 percent of white cell phone owners said they "use a social networking site" on their device, while 33 percent of African American respondents and 36 percent of English-speaking Hispanic respondents said they did.[30]

> Fifty-six percent of all mobile device users, and 47 percent of the population, now use such devices to get local news via the Internet.

135

It is too early to tell the implications of the high usage of phones for news among African-Americans and Latinos. For instance, will heavy minority use of mobile devices lead to more news apps or services targeted at, or run by, members of those groups? At a minimum, since new technologies sometimes get to minorities late in the game, it is at least heartening that the uptake of this new technology among minorities is robust.

Different Types of Mobile News Platforms

Google's former CEO Eric Schmidt predicts that "in five or 10 years, most news will be consumed on an electronic device of some sort. Something that is mobile and personal, with a nice color screen."[31] He envisions a mobile news platform that "is smart enough to show you stories that are incremental to a story it showed you yesterday, rather than just repetitive"; a platform intertwined with social networking, that "knows who your friends are and what they're reading and think is hot"; and one that is conscious of locale, that "has a GPS and a radio network and knows what is going on around you."[32] Schmidt expects this future to be realized financially through a business model "involving both subscriptions and ads."[33]

"Minority Americans lead the way when it comes to mobile Internet access using handheld devices."

Electronics giants are already developing flexible and folding monitors that can be used with mobile devices[34] so that accessing the Internet over a mobile phone will not always necessitate reading from a small screen. Some industry experts predict that with more powerful central processing units (CPUs) in the works for smartphones—which will allow the basic mobile unit to be supplemented with a "docking station" that includes a keyboard, full-size display, and camera[35]—mobile devices may well replace PCs.[36] The mobile advertising industry, meanwhile, to further enhance revenue potential, is developing new software to make it easier for local businesses to geo-target advertisements in order to reach consumers based on where they, and their phones, stand at any given moment.[37]

The market for smartphones, tablet computers, laptops, PCs, and TVs is evolving rapidly, as the distinctions between these devices become increasingly blurred. Right now, wireless mobile devices offer a few different ways for consumers to access news.

Mobile News Sites vs. Applications

Users can visit news sites by using a web browser on their phone, just as they might on their personal computer. Or, they can use special mobile applications, designed specifically for use on a phone. Despite all the buzz about "apps," Americans so far still rely more on Internet browsers to access news websites, even when they are using a phone. In June 2010, comScore reported that over a three-month period ending in April 2010, an average of 26 million people consumed news content via browser access each month, while an average of approximately 9.3 million accessed news content via mobile applications.[38]

However, use of news mobile applications is growing rapidly: that 9.3 million represented a 124 percent increase from a year before.[39] Data from the Associated Press (AP) suggests that what mobile applications lack in audience share they may make up for in total usage time. For example, users of the AP mobile website spent an average of just 2.7 minutes per month on the site, while users of the AP BlackBerry application spent 16.6 minutes per month on it.[40]

Many news organizations offer mobile-specific Internet content, including versions of their websites optimized for mobile devices' smaller screens and mouseless navigation. Generally, a mobile user who navigates to a standard website on a mobile Internet browser is routed automatically to a simplified, faster-loading mobile website if one exists.

Building mobile websites can be a costly and complex process, particularly if the mobile website features multimedia elements. Building multiple websites for different mobile devices and operating systems is even more expensive. While the cost of building a rudimentary mobile website might run under $10,000, corporations frequently spend over $25,000 building more sophisticated ones.[41]

Virtually every major news organization in print, television, and radio operates a mobile website.[42] A recent survey of newspaper publishers revealed that in mid-2010, the majority of newspapers surveyed were formatting their websites for mobile devices[43]—among them, 58 percent of newspapers with circulations under 25,000.[44]

"Mobile applications" are generally defined as software programs designed to run on a mobile device. They provide a user-friendly window into website content, real-time alerts, and a dizzying array of other features, and they are typically designed to be used with one or more of the mobile operating systems, including: Apple's iOS, Google's Android, RIM's BlackBerry OS, Nokia's Symbian OS, Microsoft's Windows Mobile, and Palm's OS. Some apps may be native to, or "pre-loaded" on, a device; others can be "side-loaded" from a personal computer. Many apps do *not* require that a mobile device be connected to a wireless network or the Internet when used. News-related apps can be used without an Internet connection, but, in such instances, do not contain the latest updated information. It is expensive to develop professional-quality mobile apps. In 2009, the technology research firm Forrester Research Inc. estimated that building a professional-quality mobile app "without frills" would cost at least $20,000.[45]

Mobile apps are available—some for free, some for a fee—through the application stores of the smartphone operating systems with which given apps are compatible. The level of control exerted over developers by Microsoft, RIM, Apple, Nokia, Google, and other firms owning mobile operating systems varies.[46]

The number of apps specifically devoted to news is relatively small. According to Morgan Stanley, in December 2009, news applications accounted for approximately 2 percent (or about 2,700 applications) out of a total of more than 118,000 apps available for Apple iPhone and iTouch devices.[47] News ranked 14th in a tally of the number of applications offered by category.[48] A scan of the BlackBerry App World catalog reveals a similar percentage of news applications—1057 news applications out of 30,962 applications total, or approximately 3.4 percent—which makes news 6th out of 20 categories.[49] (The news category includes "soft" news topics such as Hollywood gossip, fashion trends, sports, and automobiles.)

News—with the exception of weather—rarely makes the top-10, top-50, or top-100 lists of most-downloaded apps. According to a survey conducted in January 2011 by the Pew Research Center's Project for Excellence in Journalism, while nearly five in 10 adults consume local news on a mobile device, only one in 10 have downloaded an app to do so.[50] Furthermore, only 10 percent of adults who use mobile apps to connect to local news and information use apps that require a fee.[51] This amounts to just one percent of the total U.S. adult population.[52] In an August 2010 survey, however, Nielsen found that 36 percent of smartphone users, and 24 percent of feature phone users, had used news apps in the previous 30 days.[53]

Nearly every major print, television, and radio news organization offers at least one mobile application. Some news organizations also offer separate mobile applications for popular shows and supplements from their print product.

Increasingly, smaller and more locally oriented news organizations are offering mobile applications, as well. For example, LSN Mobile has created a free app that offers local breaking news, video clips, weather, sports scores, movie show times, and school-closing notices from a network of more than 250 local media outlets.[54] Application developer DoApp reports that it has developed applications for 120-plus local media organizations, and a total of 185 local media outlets have signed up to build them.[55] Alternative weeklies, such as *L.A. Weekly, Philadelphia Weekly, Charleston City Paper,* and the *Village Voice,* offer apps, as well.[56] A number of local radio stations have created apps that facilitate consumption of radio news content, even by those using mobile devices that do not feature tuners.[57]

Some of the most innovative news-related mobile apps aggregate news produced by multiple sources. For example, Newsy's app[58] compiles video coverage of a given story produced by many different news organizations and offers viewers "all sides and sources of each story," in the words of one reviewer.[59] The Zen News app uses what is known as "tag cloud navigation."[60] Such navigation "takes the most prevalent topics or keywords and organizes them by size, with the larger words being more important."[61]

The popularity of social-media services like Twitter and Facebook on smartphones presents another important way of disseminating news, each serving, in effect, as a customized news service that relies on the judgment of the consumer's network of friends or followers.

Users of the AP mobile website spent an average of just 2.7 minutes per month on the website, while users of the AP BlackBerry application spent 16.6 minutes per month.

Are Americans more likely to consume different types of news content on a mobile device than they would via traditional media (newspapers, TV, radio) or on a desktop computer? Particular technologies can lend themselves more to certain types of content: For instance, the moving image on a TV makes it more conducive to capturing emotion and drama than print is. Mobile phones would seem particularly good at short-and-fast. Mobile's ability to push content through a phone (as opposed to waiting for someone to seek out a website) makes it ideal for news bulletins and emergency notices.

Does this mean that, along with the remarkable increase in mobile news consumption taking place, ushering in what for the moment appears to be a move "[f]rom 17-inch displays to 3-inch displays,"[62] we should expect a corresponding decline in the actual quantity and depth of news content consumed by Americans? The available data is inconclusive. One 2010 study asked university students, "What percentage of a news article do you typically read on your smartphone?" The results: 9 percent said "headline only," 47 percent read "only three paragraphs," 31 percent read "25 to 50 percent," and 13 percent read "100 percent of the article."[63] The Digital Media Test Kitchen at the University of Colorado, which conducted the study, also observed that "the small screen of a smartphone is not ideally suited for lengthy reading sessions, and the majority of mobile users tend not to view much of long videos or listen to long sessions of audio."[64] The organization resists the conclusion that the results of its study establish "that smartphones…are not a good medium for news presentation beyond short articles and brief snippets of video and audio," suggesting that news consumption off of larger desktop screens fares no better.[65]

Advertisers spent $202 million on display ads for mobile devices in 2010, up 122 percent from a year before.

An important dataset concerning *desktop* consumption of news, dating from 2007, challenges this. The Poynter Institute's extensive 2007 research using eyeball tracking reached the rather surprising conclusion that people "read *further* into stories online than in print" and found that this was "true for stories of all lengths."[66] In the Poynter study, "[o]nline participants read an average of 77 percent of story text they chose to read," in contrast to those reading from non-tabloid print newspapers, who "read an average of 62 percent of stories they selected."[67]

Common sense tells us that consumers may end up using some devices for shorter bursts of content and others for longer pieces or clips. The Pew Internet Project's studies indicate that mobile news consumers use a greater number of news platforms than other adults:[68] 55 percent of mobile news consumers use at least four different news platforms on a daily basis, and they are 50 percent more likely than other adults to read a print version of a national newspaper.[69] That is why the Digital Media Test Kitchen envisions news consumers reading the same content over time on both their smartphone and on devices with larger screens, depending on whether they are in transit, at the office, or at home:

"Especially for in-depth and enterprise packages, news providers can expect a portion of their audience to go back and forth between devices. The bus commuter might begin a compelling enterprise news package on a smartphone during the ride, then pick it up again later on an office PC, home laptop, or iPad tablet, for example…. Portability of content across various systems and interfaces increasingly will be critical for news providers seeking to reach the largest audience possible."[70]

Software facilitating cross-device bookmarking has already been developed for some devices.[71]

A number of state and federal government entities offer mobile-specific Internet content, including versions of their websites optimized for mobile devices' smaller screens, and mobile apps. For example, in 2010, the state of Rhode Island launched a free iPhone app that provides quick access to Rhode Island government news and resources, including photos and maps, and allows users to search for online government services.[72] The Arkansas Game and Fish Commission's free Game Check iPhone app allows hunters to report hunted game to the Arkansas Game and Fish Commission through their smartphones.[73] Usage of the app rose 330 percent during 2010's hunting season, compared with the 2009 season.[74] The federal government offers optimized websites and mobile apps that allow people to, for example, search for a federal job,[75] check for product recalls,[76] search the Smithsonian's collection,[77] run the FCC's mobile broadband speed and quality test,[78] and view the FBI's most-wanted lists on the FBI's Most Wanted app.[79]

Accessing News Content via Tablets and e-Readers

Many print news organizations sell electronic versions of their content that can be downloaded wirelessly and read on a tablet or an e-Reader.[80] For example, the Amazon Kindle Store offers monthly subscriptions to more than 70 U.S. newspapers.[81] Of the 25 largest-circulation newspapers in the United States, at least 20 are available on the Kindle, including more than 40 of the 100 most popular.[82] Several smaller-market papers—including the *Lewiston (ID) Tribune*, the *Charlottesville (VA) Daily Progress*, and the *Manistee (MI) News Advocate*—are available, as well.[83] So are subscriptions to many of the most popular blogs and U.S. newsmagazines.[84]

Publishers are particularly optimistic about the potential impact of the iPad. In a May 2010 ChangeWave survey, 50 percent of iPad owners said that they read newspapers on the device (versus 14 percent of respondents using e-Readers other than the iPad), and 38 percent of iPad owners said that they read magazines on it (versus 11 percent on other e-Readers).[85] In a December 2010 Reynolds Journalism Institute survey of iPad owners, 84.4 percent said that the most popular use of their iPad is to follow breaking news and stay updated on current events.[86] One 2010 study confirms that iPad owners are using the device to access desktop-oriented websites, rather than or in addition to mobile websites.[87]

How will tablets alter mobile news economics? Among the questions that are already arising: Are consumers more likely to pay a subscription fee for a publication on a tablet than on a phone? Will advertisements perform better (i.e., get noticed by consumers more) and therefore enable publishers to charge higher rates? Further discussions about the impact of tablets and e-Readers are below, in the "Revenue Models" and "Track Records" sections.

Local TV News Experiments with Hyperlocal Mobile

Mobile platforms are providing local television stations with new opportunities. In 2009, TV stations made $29 million from mobile, about 12 percent of the year's total local mobile advertising expenditure.[88] While others are not quite as bullish, one analyst states: "I expect that figure to skyrocket into the billions within two years as the transition from desktops and laptops to hand-held devices takes off."[89]

Local television stations are seeking to develop "hyperlocalized" mobile news platforms that focus on the concerns of individual neighborhoods and even more narrowly defined communities. For example, LIN TV Corporation, owner of 28 local TV stations,[90] is partnering with News Over Wireless "to bring local text and video updates to mobile phones," and local NBC affiliates are partnering with "the neighborhood site Outside.In to provide information about local news, events and other things."[91] More than 230 iPhone apps were offered by local TV stations in 2010.[92]

In contrast to the general experience with mobile display advertising, prominent publishers are expressing optimism about the iPad.

While the most common way of watching local TV news video is through apps or web browsers making use of the Internet, broadcasters have also been promoting a different technology—one that beams a traditional broadcast signal directly into the phone rather than over the Internet pathway. In November 2010, the Mobile Content Venture (MCV) announced its plans to "upgrade TV stations in New York, Los Angeles, Chicago, San Francisco, and 16 other markets to a standards-based digital TV system," which will allow viewers to watch locally based programming on their mobile devices.[93] Currently, there are more than 50 mobile DTV stations on-air, according to the Harris Corporation, which supplies equipment required for mobile DTV broadcasting.[94] A recent test of the devices found that one of the most common ways mobile TV is being used is for news access. (See Chapter 3, TV.)

Equipment for mobile DTV broadcasting typically costs a local station in excess of $100,000.[95] It is not entirely clear whether consumers will tune in to live local broadcast news on their phone when they can access so many other news sources via the Internet, also on their phone. The business model has not yet been decided either. "Broadcasters are still grappling with whether to offer free, ad-supported television or a subscription model, and the number of U.S. TV stations streaming a mobile digital signal has increased slowly," the *Wall Street Journal* reported in October 2010.[96] Consumers must use specialized devices to view mobile DTV.[97] These devices include mobile phones with mobile DTV reception capability, accessory USB dongles, netbooks, portable DTV players, and in-car displays.[98]

Mobile Radio

There are several ways that consumers can access audio online. One in three Americans say they listen to online radio—and this figure does not include podcasts, which are an increasingly popular way for consumers to get audio programs.[99] Consumers essentially use the Internet as if it's a radio tuner, listening live to audio from around the web. Advertising and subscription revenues associated with mobile radio could reach into the hundreds of millions within the next five years.[100] Already the Public Radio Player—a free application, developed by Public Radio Exchange for iPhone and Android devices, that plays shows and stories broadcast over public radio—has had over 3 million unique downloads for iPhone since its December 2008 launch.[101] The player has been the number-one free app in iTunes, and it has largely remained among the top-25 free music apps.[102]

Podcasts are audio or video files downloaded via an Internet connection and enjoyed directly from a PC or transferred to a mobile device and listened to on-the-go. Numerous news organizations, ranging from the largest TV and radio networks to small-town affiliates, provide news content in the form of podcasts.

Another technology that can be used to bring consumers news and information in an audio format is the FM chip—a small receiver placed in the phone that allows the headset to act as an antenna, so the phone can function as an FM radio. (See Chapter 29, Internet and Mobile.)

Text and SMS

Services utilizing SMS (short message service) text messaging provide another way for consumers to access news and information content on mobile devices. According to survey data from comScore, 32.4 million people—or more than half of the total number of mobile news and information consumers—used SMS to access news and information in January 2009.[103] Typically, a user can sign up for "mobile alerts" by texting a brief message to a specified "short code" (an abbreviated phone number created for easy use). According to Pew's Project on the Internet and American Life, "11% of cell phone owners have alerts sent to their phones via text or email."[104] Given the nature of SMS—messages are limited to roughly 160 characters—these alerts are limited to headlines.

"MOJO": Mobile Journalism by Citizens

Because smartphones can capture still images—and many can record digital video footage—they are becoming critical to the distillation of newsworthy events. Mobile phone videos, recorded by witnesses to the 2009 shooting of Oscar Grant in a Northern California subway station by a police officer, became a focal point of news coverage of the event and the later criminal trial. Major news organizations relied on mobile phone images during the early 2011 pro-democracy protests in Egypt, the January 2010 earthquake in Haiti, and the summer 2009 uprisings in Iran in their coverage of events for which conventional broadcast video was unavailable. Individuals posting social media "status updates," with text and images, also play a part in informing the world of events they have witnessed and disasters they have survived. During the earthquake in Haiti, the number of Facebook status updates rose to 1,500 per minute.[105]

"Mobile Voices" is an effort to allow immigrant workers in Los Angeles to "create stories about their lives and communities directly from cell phones."

There are numerous venues through which news content produced by smartphone-wielding nonprofessional journalists can be distributed. CitizenTube, YouTube's "news and politics blog," provides a feed of the latest breaking news videos on YouTube.[106] Individuals with a Twitter account who record news footage on their mobile device can "tweet" such footage, along with related text, to CitizenTube's Twitter address, @citizentube. CitizenTube then posts the material on its feed. News outlets are increasingly offering ways for citizens to share images directly with editors, as well, and some use Facebook to post the images that people share.[107]

Mobile phones can enable citizens to contribute to and receive news in lower-income areas that do not have widespread computer usage. *Grocott's Mail*, based in Grahamstown, South Africa, uses SMS technology to distribute news and gather community opinion, which is then published in the print edition of the newspaper. The paper sends SMS alerts and headlines to 500 low-income subscribers; it has trained 100 citizen journalists; and it published 188 citizen-journalist-authored stories on its website in 2010.[108] "The inspiration for the whole project is trying to democratize news and information and put it into the hands of more people, give people more access to it, and create more participation—not just one-way, top-down communication," says professor Harry Dugmore of Rhodes University, director of the Knight Foundation–sponsored program called "Iindaba Ziyafika" (or "The news is coming!").[109]

Consumers in the United States are using mobile communications platforms to participate in civic life and foster community engagement. Pew Research Center's Project for Excellence in Journalism's January 2011 survey found that people who use their mobile phone or tablet to get local news are more enthusiastic in some respects about their community and the role they play in it.[110] A late 2009 survey found that 22 percent of all American adults had signed up to receive alerts about local issues—such as traffic, school events, weather warnings, and crime alerts—via email or text messaging.[111]

Among owners of all e-Readers (including the iPad) 18 percent were reading newspapers, and 14 percent were reading magazines.

Innovative efforts have sprouted throughout the country to empower citizens to use mobile phones to receive and help shape the news. Mobile Voices, a collaboration between the USC Annenberg School for Communication & Journalism and the Institute of Popular Education of Southern California, was designed to enable people with limited computer access to participate in digital media.[112] Immigrant workers in Los Angeles are invited to "create stories about their lives and communities directly from cell phones."[113] Some blog by sending photos with descriptive text messages to a Mobile Voices email address; users can also simply send text messages or call a local number to leave an audio message.[114]

VoteReport, another civic media project, used Twitter and eight volunteers to gather 17,000 user reports of conditions at U.S. polling places on election day 2008.[115] People could submit reports to Twitter by texting to a dedicated number through iPhone and Android apps, or by phoning a dedicated number.[116] Smartphone features like cameras and GPS have brought about new opportunities for civic engagement.[117] SeeClickFix creates and distributes mobile applications that empower citizens to report "non-emergency" events, problems, and issues in their community—for example, a pothole or fallen power line—to government entities and interested groups and neighbors.[118]

Revenue Models and Track Record

Advertising

Many news outlets have tried to monetize their content through mobile advertising, which can take several forms. Ads can be displayed on mobile websites ("display ads"), and they can be embedded in mobile applications as text, video, or a software instruction that sends the user to their Internet browser where they can see the ad ("in-app ads"). Advertisers spent $202 million on display ads for mobile devices in 2010, up 122 percent from a year before.[119] According to eMarketer, between 2009 and 2010, U.S. mobile ad spending was up 79 percent, from $416 million to $743 million.[120] It hit $1.1 billion in 2011 and is projected to reach $1.5 billion in 2012.[121]

However, despite the rapid rise in mobile ad spending, the Pew Project for Excellence in Journalism points out that "the dollars here are still small relative to other online advertising—browser-based search alone is around $12 billion."[122] And, on closer examination, this revenue increase appears to be due to the explosion of mobile sites on which ads appear more than to an increase in mobile advertising rates. Mobile ad rates are in the $10-to-$15 CPM (cost per 1,000 views) range[123]—but, factoring in all the mobile impressions that do not have ads on them would lower the average effective CPM dramatically.

Mobile content providers typically attract advertisers and advertising revenue through mobile advertising networks such as AdMob (purchased by Google in 2009), Quattro Wireless (purchased by Apple in 2010), Millennial Media, and Jumptap, which take between 15 and 50 percent of revenue.[124]

Prominent publishers are expressing more optimism about advertising via the iPad than through phones.[125] Gannett reports that it is currently charging Marriott a $50 CPM for Marriott ads embedded in its *USA Today* iPad application, more than five times the average CPM advertisers pay for ads placed on the *USA Today* website.[126] (Chapter 25, How Big is the Gap and Who Will Fill It?)

Local newspapers are attempting to reach residents through the iPad, too. A review of Apple's App Store in May 2011 found more than 200 iPad apps offering local U.S. news content.[127] Fifty-seven percent of newspaper publishers surveyed by the Audit Bureau of Circulations said that they "have plans to develop an iPad app in the next six months."[128] According to Pew's *State of the News Media 2011* report, local mobile advertising revenue is growing rapidly.[129] It is quite possible that as the market matures, the cost of developing iPad apps will drop, allowing a greater number of smaller media companies to get in the game.

Just how much media companies will benefit from these revenue streams depends in part on how big a share ends up going to the companies that control the phones. For example, according to the *Wall Street Journal*, Apple charges advertisers one penny every time a consumer views a banner ad in an iPhone app and two dollars every time a person clicks on the ad.[130] *PC World* reported that, after purchasing AdMob, Google shares 68 percent of its ad revenue.[131]

If aggregator apps that are not created by news organizations continue to grow in popularity, they too could have a significant impact on how news organizations fare. "Aggregator" apps pull news from a variety of sources, allowing users to customize how it is displayed on their device. Often, ads do not appear next to the content. Consumers can absorb much of the content without seeing an ad or clicking through to the site that created the content—which may make it a better experience for the user but makes it harder for media companies to monetize the experience. News aggregators and news readers appear in significant numbers on lists of the most-downloaded news-related apps (both paid and free) designed for the iPhone and Android devices.[132] In June 2010, Pulse, a relatively simple iPad app that displays RSS feeds (regularly updating news feeds) drawn from a variety of sources, was the number-one paid app sold on Apple's iTunes store when it was selling for $3.99 (it is now available for free).[133] Pulse allows users to see headlines, chunks of text, and in some cases the full text of articles—all without any advertising appearing alongside it. Typically developers/owners of news reader and aggregator apps earn revenue from the sale of the app and from in-app advertising—without passing on any portion to the digital news producers upon whose content their products rely. Because media organizations have control over what goes through RSS feeds, they can tailor, say, their Pulse RSS feeds to offer less content, making it somewhat more likely that a reader might click back to the original site for more information. The technology underpinning these news feeds makes it possible for publishers to insert ads to accompany their content, but so far most content producers have not done so. Some large news organizations have been able to strike special deals with aggregator app developers to get more financial value out of providing content.[134] Even more controversial are products such as Flipboard and Zite that do not rely on RSS feeds but rather "scrape" content from the publishers' websites, leaving content producers with little control over how the material is used.[135] One company, Readability, drew praise when it announced a program to charge for its content-reading app and then share the revenue with content creators, based on what content consumers read.[136]

> In the BlackBerry App World catalog, 238 of the 269 news applications were free. Approximately 62 percent of news apps for the iPhone were free.

Charging for Content

When smartphones started to grow in popularity, publishers began to express optimism that they would offer a new, better way to charge customers and reduce reliance on advertising. But, tellingly, so far most of the news apps for mobile phones are free. Among the news organizations offering free mobile applications are ABC news, Associated Press, CBS News, FOX News, MSNBC, NPR, Reuters, *Time*, *USA Today*, and the *The Wall Street Journal*.[137] In May, 2011, the BlackBerry App World catalog listed only 71 paid news applications out of a total of 1,079 news applications, which amounted to less than 7 percent.[138] A May, 2011, review of Apple's App Store revealed that approximately 71 percent of news apps for the iPhone were available for free.[139]

However, some news organizations have attempted to charge for their apps . . . with varying success. Major news producers such as CNN, *Newsweek*, *The Washington Post*, and the *L.A. Times* developed "premium" apps for which they charged relatively low prices (in these cases, $1.99). These producers' apps included special features not available on the related free mobile websites. For instance, in December, 2009, "[i]n an era where nearly everyone has grown accustomed to reading news online for free, CNN made a bold move by deciding to charge $1.99 for its offering", which allowed purchasers to access news, weather and traffic reports for any location they chose, and its "iReport" feature invited and aggregated user-submitted content.[140] Then in December, 2010, with the launch of its free iPad app, CNN made its iPhone and iPod Touch applications free as well.[141] Similarly, when the *L.A. Times* launched its premium paid app in June, 2010, purchasers could save content (e.g., photos and articles) for later review and share stories on social-networking sites.[142] As of May, 2011, however, the application is available for free with the same features.[143] The *New York Times'* smartphone and tablet apps, however, allow purchasers to access the paper's "Top News" section, but other sections are only accessible if they have a digital or home-delivery subscription.[144]

Although it does not necessarily offer much promise of substantial funding to local news operations, this revenue model has led to at least one modest success story. Public Radio Exchange developed an app containing content from a highly popular program produced by Chicago Public Media: *This American Life*.[145] The $2.99 app allows users to search for and sample every episode of the program that has aired since 1995. It has earned revenue in the "low hundreds of thousands," which has helped offset production costs associated with the program, whose overall budget is about $2 million, according to Chicago Public Media.[146]

Moreover, of the 29 percent of paid news applications for the iPhone (2,719 out of 9,233), most offer little in the way of hard or breaking news and instead provide very soft "news"—auto news, entertainment news, and sometimes no news at all, just cartoons and entertainment.[147] Those that do charge split the revenue earned with the owners of the operating system. Apple, Google, RIM, and Nokia manage the app purchases on devices that use their operating system and usually retain approximately 30 percent.[148]

> Gordon Crovitz, founder of Journalism Online, believes subscriptions, rather than one-time apps or pay walls, are the most promising revenue source.

On the iPad, too, most news apps are free: A February 2011 survey of Apple's iPad App Store revealed that only about 29 percent of apps were available for free[149]—yet nearly all of the *news* apps were free.[150] For instance, NPR, BBC, AP, and Reuters offer free iPad apps[151]—as does *USA Today* (its app ranked sixth in popularity in June 2010 among free iPad apps).[152] The 537 paid iPad apps designated by Apple as "news" apps are primarily news aggregator and news reader apps, foreign news apps, and apps focusing on soft news items like sports, entertainment, and cartoons—but they also include apps published by the *New York Post* and *60 Minutes*.[153] And in our own May 2011 survey of Apple's App Store, we found a number of U.S. newspapers, radio stations, and TV stations offering iPad apps for free—more than 200 at present, including the *Oklahoman*, the *Virginian-Pilot,* and the Boston Pilot.[155]

However, publishers are constantly experimenting with new ways of making money from their apps. Several publishers are experimenting with a hybrid model that offers apps for free *if* consumers are paid subscribers to either the print or online editions of their publication. For example, the *Wall Street Journal* app, downloadable without charge, provides access to content for consumers who already have signed up for a $3.99 per week subscription.

Some premium magazines have developed, or are in the process of developing, paid apps for the iPad that include the content of a specific issue along with additional special content. Some simply put their print magazine into a digital format. For example, Conde Nast's *Vanity Fair* offers an iPad version of its current issue each month through Apple's iTunes store for $1.99 for a one-month subscription or $19.99 for the year.[156] *Time, Popular Science,* and *Wired* also have developed publication issue apps for the iPad.[157]

Pay Wall/Subscription Models

For content providers hoping to generate non-advertising revenue through mobile devices, the most promise seems to be in charging an ongoing monthly subscription fee—particularly with tablets and e-Readers (as opposed to phones).

In March 2010, prior to the iPad launch the following month, only one major newspaper, the *Wall Street Journal*, offered a digital subscription (as opposed to a paid app). Though consumers express antipathy to the idea of paying for content, Apple's Steve Jobs argues that consumers will be willing to pay for content that has "more value than just a webpage."[158] In March 2011, the *New York Times* switched to a metered pay system in which readers who are not home delivery subscribers get access to 20 free digital articles per month, but have to pay for a digital subscription

Several publishers are experimenting with a hybrid model that offers apps for free *if* consumers are paid subscribers to either the print or online editions of the publication.

to exceed that limit on their computers, smartphones, or tablets.[159] Within the first three weeks of launch, the *Times* had 100,000 paying subscribers, but it is not yet clear how lucrative this set-up will ultimately be.[160] Another closely watched experiment is News Corp.'s launch of *The Daily*, a newspaper available exclusively on the iPad with no print companion.[161] It will test whether newspaper economics can work better when they no longer have to carry the cost of trucks, ink, and paper.[162]

Some publications have been charging for monthly subscriptions through Kindle and nook e-Readers. Newspapers with e-Reader subscription plans include the *St. Petersburg Times* (at $9.49 per month); the *Orlando Sentinel* ($5.99); the *Atlanta Journal-Constitution* ($5.99); the *Charlottesville (VA) Daily Progress* ($4.49); the *Big Rapids Pioneer (MI)* ($6.75); the *Lewiston Tribune* (serving counties in Washington and Idaho, $3.99); the *Arizona Republic* ($9.99); the *San Jose Mercury News* ($5.99); the *Orange County Register* ($5.99); and the *Austin American-Statesman* ($5.99).[163] Gordon Crovitz, founder of Journalism Online, a venture to help publishers charge for content, says that in the past year he has become convinced that subscriptions, rather than one-time fees for apps or pay walls, show the most promise as a revenue source.[164]

Annual subscriptions for newspapers and magazines are beginning to be offered through iTunes. But some publishers have complained that because Apple is retaining all of the information about customers, their ability to fully monetize the subscriptions is limited. Google has entered the fray, offering a deal that it says is better for publishers.[165] According to press reports, issues being discussed in the negotiations include "who controls data about users and how to split subscription revenue,"[166] as well as how subscriptions will be priced.[167]

Donation Models and Mobile Technology

The devastating earthquake in Haiti in early 2010 provided an opportunity to demonstrate the particular effectiveness of mobile fundraising. Concerned people could offer a donation by texting a designated number; the American Red Cross earned $800,000 within 48 hours of the earthquake this way.[168] These fundraising efforts necessitated the participation of wireless service providers.[169] As new, low-cost payment methods designed specifically for mobile devices are developed, opportunities for conducting more technologically sophisticated forms of mobile fundraising will no doubt emerge. Given the ability mobile technology provides to reach a broad range of consumers, mobile fundraising has the potential to benefit not only charities but also nonprofit media, such as public radio, which rely on donations as their primary revenue source. As mobile fundraising methods evolve, the procedures and policies adopted by various entities in the mobile ecosystem—including service providers, phone makers, application store operators, and application developers—likely will have an impact on the effectiveness of mobile donations as a revenue source for nonprofit media.[170]

Mobile Industry Finances

Total annual service revenues for the mobile wireless industry reached approximately $159.9 billion in 2010, up 5 percent from $152.6 billion in 2009.[171] Earnings before interest, taxes, depreciation, and amortization (EBITDA) margins for the four nationwide mobile wireless service providers in 2010 (Q3) ranged from approximately 17 percent to 47 percent.[172]

Conclusions

With mobile wireless changing rapidly, predictions are difficult. Even the definition of "mobile" is evolving: when tablets get smaller and start to have phoning capability, will they be tablets or phones?

But here are several trends that can be identified:

First, mobile is becoming a major delivery mechanism for news. We see no reason that this will abate. The phone is a pocket-size way of getting bulletins quickly and so lends itself to news. Trends suggest that, increasingly, those news bursts will be personalized to individual users' interests and locales.

Mobile news distribution has the potential to make digital news and information more accessible to populations that previously lacked access to personal computers or were simply less likely to look for news and information online. Mobile Internet usage is disproportionately high among members of those populations, including minority and low-income consumers. (See Chapter 23, Diversity.)

So far, mobile devices have not proved to be a major source of revenue for news outlets, neither through advertising nor paid applications, but news organizations are still experimenting with different business models. While some news organizations are giving away their mobile apps for free, others (e.g. the *Wall Street Journal* and the *New York Times*) are requiring a digital or home delivery subscription for access to mobile applications. The mobile advertising market is also changing. Advertisers spent $202 million on display ads for mobile devices in 2010, up 122 percent from a year before.

It is too early to determine whether content published on e-Readers and tablets like the iPad will be more lucrative for publishers. Most news apps on the iPad are free. On the other hand, people are proving more likely to buy media subscriptions on e-Readers than they have been on phones or websites. E-media revenue for magazines is expected to grow by double digits next year. Annual subscriptions for newspapers and magazines via the iPad are beginning to be offered through the Apple Store. The launch of *The Daily*, a newspaper available exclusively on the iPad with no print companion, brings an opportunity to observe newspaper economics with the cost of trucks, ink, and paper removed from the equation.

nonprofit media

Throughout American history, the vast majority of news has been provided by commercial media. For the reasons described in Part One, the commercial sector has been uniquely situated to generate the revenue and profits to sustain labor-intensive reporting on a massive scale. But nonprofit media has always played an important supplementary role.

While many nonprofits are small, community-based operations, others are large and some have developed into institutions of tremendous importance in the information sector. The Associated Press is the nation's largest news wire service, AARP: The Magazine is the largest circulation print magazine in the country, NPR is the largest employer of radio journalists, and Wikipedia is one of the largest information sites on the Internet.

Technological changes have transformed noncommercial media as much as they have commercial media. Public TV and radio are morphing into multiplatform information providers. Even before the Internet, nonprofit programming was emerging independent of traditional public TV and radio on satellite, cable television, and low-power FM stations. And now, with the digital revolution, we see an explosion of new nonprofit news websites and mobile phone applications. What is more, our perception of the nonprofit sector must now expand to include: journalism schools that send students into the streets to report; state-level C-SPANs; citizen journalists who contribute to other websites or Tweet, blog and otherwise communicate their own reporting; and even sites born of or shaped by software developers who create "open source" code, free to the public for use and open to amendment by other developers. This has led to countless programs and software languages including Mozilla Firefox, Linux, Drupal, and WordPress.

Therefore, to understand the full media landscape—especially when it comes to news, journalism, and information—we must consider not only the still-important realm of public broadcasting and its digital extensions, but also the wider range of nonprofit media whose primary mission is to serve the public's information needs.

Several factors have prompted media watchers to focus more intensely on the role of nonprofit media. First, as noted in Chapter 4, Internet, the types of information that are in decline are those that have always been challenging for the commercial sector to produce profitably. Business models from the past that relied on more profitable types of information to subsidize the production of less profitable types have crumbled in the digital age, making the challenge of providing those less profitable types even greater. Among the products the commercial sector seems to be under-producing are local labor-intensive beat reporting; investigative reporting; so-called broccoli journalism (about topics important to individual and communal health, but not always popular); and foreign coverage.

Commercial enterprises have struggled to find business models that would sustain such journalism, in part because of the "free rider" problem: many Americans find these topics important in theory, but figure they will find out about them without having to pay for the content. (See Chapter 4, Internet), The value of such "public goods" to a healthy society is not always readily apparent. And there is the fact that most advertisers do not like to associate their brands with controversial or less popular content, so they are unlikely to pay premium rates to help sustain the content production.

Most American media outlets are now owned by publicly held corporations traded in the equity markets. This structure has many advantages, providing operational efficiencies and drawing massive amounts of private capital into the media system. But it has drawbacks, too. These companies have a fiduciary responsibility to maximize profit, making it sometimes difficult for them to do what nonprofit media or some family-owned businesses did in the past: accept lower short-term profit margins in order to invest in the community, either for psychic rewards or a longer-term financial payoff.

The persistence of gaps in the markets for information has led many to wonder whether the role of nonprofit organizations in the media ecosystem should become different or larger, especially in regard to local news. Indeed, some nonprofits seem inclined to step up their contributions to local information, news, and journalism, but they face many obstacles in doing so.

6 Public Broadcasting

THE AMERICAN PUBLIC BROADCASTING SYSTEM is the product of two historic moments, one in the 1930s, when spectrum was first set aside for noncommercial broadcasters, and the other in 1967, when Congress created the modern system of public TV and radio. Many experts believe that we now sit at a third such critical juncture. This is a "1967 moment" for public broadcasting, says Ernie Wilson, former chairman of the Corporation for Public Broadcasting (CPB) board of directors and current dean of the USC Annenberg School for Communications & Journalism.[1]

Today's pivotal decisions concern, in part, how public TV and radio will adapt to the same changes that are buffeting commercial media: the rise of the Internet and mobile, the proliferation of consumer choices, the economic downturn's impact on revenue, and the disruptions of digital technology. But, the soul-searching goes further. What should the public media mission be? Some suggest they should increase their educational content and their work with schools, as districts everywhere seek to improve educational services. Others urge public media to focus more on local content, especially news, information, and journalism. In "The Reconstruction of American Journalism," an October 2009 report for the *Columbia Journalism Review*, Leonard Downie Jr. and Michael Schudson recommended that public broadcasters increase their production of local information:

> "The CPB should declare that local news reporting is a top priority for public broadcasting and change its allocation of resources accordingly. Local news reporting is an essential part of the public education function that American public radio and television have been charged with fulfilling since their inception."[2]

Picking up on policy proposals for CPB reform,[3] Steve Coll, a Pulitzer Prize–winning journalist and head of the New America Foundation, recommends a new "strategic direction" for CPB, which he thinks should be renamed the "Corporation for Public Media." The funding regime for the restructured entity, Coll says, "should be measured by whether or not it will produce more serious, independent, diverse, public-minded reporting."[4] On the other hand, the political problems that arise whenever public broadcasters make a controversial decision with respect to programming or staffing raise questions about whether a focus on journalism would not simply exacerbate concerns about the use of taxpayer dollars in media.

Whether public broadcasters (or an expanded group of public media participants) will play a more central role in the provision of news and information, especially at the local level, depends on many factors, including whether the current public broadcasting culture, structure, and rules can adapt to new realities, and how legacy and emerging public media entities define their missions.

History

Public broadcasting had its origins in American universities. In 1917, the University of Wisconsin in Madison launched 9XM,[5] the first educational radio station, which aired shows like *The Friendly Giant*, a precursor to *Sesame Street*.[6] Four years later, the Latter-Day Saints University in Salt Lake City, Utah, received an official federal government license for a station[7] that broadcast educational lectures, basketball games, and musical concerts.[8] By the mid-1930s, there were 202 such "educational" stations in existence.

But in 1936, the bottom fell out. Universities discovered that their stations did not stimulate greater enrollment or publicity, and that those who staffed them lacked the time and expertise to produce compelling shows. Struggling economically through the Depression, most universities let their licenses expire or transferred them to commercial enterprises.[9] Meanwhile, commercial radio stations were attracting large audiences, and they coveted the spectrum held by educators.[10]

As increasing numbers of educational stations turned their licenses over to commercial operations, a wide range of organizations began to fear that their interests would be neglected under this new regime. Agrarian stations worried that farm extension programs would be lost; church leaders and religious broadcasters were concerned about programming for the disadvantaged and working class; the growing labor movement was afraid that it would be unable to reach the people. Many feared that a wholly commercial system would squelch free speech by reserving the airwaves for majority viewpoints.[11] University of Wyoming president, Arthur G. Crane, called the commercial system "an almost incredible absurdity for a country that stakes its existence upon universal suffrage, upon the general intelligence of its citizens, upon the spread of reliable information…and then consigns a means of general communication exclusively to private interests, making public use for general welfare subordinate and incidental."[12] A coalition of noncommercial stations pressed the newly created Federal Communications Commission (FCC) to reserve channels for educational broadcasting.[13]

The commercial broadcasting industry fought back. Broadcasters feared that spectrum set-asides would deprive businesses of lucrative markets and that new noncommercial entrants would siphon off audience and support. To address the interests of educational broadcast supporters, the National Association of Broadcasters offered instead to increase the amount of commercial broadcast time its members dedicated to educational programming.[14]

In 1938, the FCC decided that educational programming merited a dedicated capacity, so it took the historic step of reserving spectrum for noncommercial broadcast use.[15] In 1945, the Commission reserved the 88–92 MHz band for noncommercial educational FM stations.[16] By 1952, there were 90 stations, with regional networks developing to foster the exchange of programming among stations.[17] The birth of television renewed the debate over noncommercial channels. Frieda B. Hennock, the FCC's first female commissioner, argued that even though educational institutions might not yet be equipped to create TV programming, spectrum should be reserved for when the capability arose.[18] To do otherwise, she said, would "result in a tragic waste from the standpoint of the public interest if, at the outset of development in this field, adequate provision were not made for the realization of almost limitless possibilities of television as a medium of visual education."[19]

A 2010 Roper Survey found that PBS outranked courts of law as the single most trusted institution in the United States.

In 1952, the FCC reserved 242 television channels for noncommercial educational (NCE) television stations—and in May 1953, the University of Houston's KUHT (now HoustonPBS) became the first educational TV station to operate on a reserved channel.[20] These early stations aired mostly instructional programs, such as university telecourses in psychology, how-tos on flower-arranging, and high-minded discussions of current events. Popular programs included in-studio concerts, Japanese brush painting (which sparked a national fad), an award-winning set of poetry readings by Robert Frost, and half-hour conversations with philosopher Eric Hoffer.[21]

During this period, noncommercial broadcasters emphasized localism and experimentation, giving rise to programming that did not fit the traditional educational model. The Pacifica Radio Network, for example, aired controversial and political material, discarding educational and commercial broadcast conventions.[22] Where other newscasters tended to air short news pieces, Pacifica offered continuing and in-depth reporting on the civil rights movement in the 1960s and took on legal cases to protect news sources in the 1970s.[23] Over time, a broader community radio movement developed that included ethnically targeted foreign-language broadcasters, volunteer-driven radio networks, and stations that were financially supported by their listeners, rather than by educational institutions.[24]

Despite some success stories, noncommercial stations entered the second half of the 20th century short on money and organizational competence—essentially failing. By the 1960s, educational radio had declined dramatically. When, at this time, foundation funding shifted away from general station support to directed programming grants, public TV stations were forced to make massive cuts.[25] Some were kept afloat only by grants from the Ford Foundation.[26] Leaders from educational TV stations asked that a national commission be formed to address the crisis, a goal President Lyndon Johnson endorsed.[27]

The resulting Carnegie Commission on Educational Television (financed by the Carnegie Corporation), issued an influential report in January 1967, entitled *Public Television: A Program for Action*. It called for a new system of public television that would provide national programming, yet retain its local roots. And it called for two key changes: (1) an increase in federal support for noncommercial broadcasting, and (2) the establishment of a private corporation that would coordinate public broadcasting operations. The report foresaw a broad mission for public television, arguing that the service had the potential to "deepen a sense of community in local life," "be a forum for debate and controversy," and "provide a voice for groups in the community that may otherwise be unheard."[28] Congress incorporated many of the recommendations into the Public Broadcasting Act, which was signed into law by President Johnson that same year.

The Act established the Corporation for Public Broadcasting (CPB), an organization that would provide regular funding through a process relatively insulated from politics.[29] Though appointed by the U.S. president with the advice and consent of Congress, CPB's board of directors can have no more than a bare majority from one political party and must be composed of non-governmental officials barred from involvement in political campaigns.[30] To ensure that it would not control public broadcasting content, CPB was prohibited from producing or distributing programs. Its purpose was to dispense funds to individual stations and to the independent, nonprofit national networks created in 1970: the Public Broadcasting Service (PBS) and National Public Radio (NPR).[31]

Over the next 40 years, PBS and NPR evolved in very different ways. Unlike national commercial networks, PBS does not own stations or programming. It is supported and governed by its member stations, and its primary purpose is to aggregate and brand programming produced by local outlets and other programmers. In the early years of the public broadcasting system, federal funding was allocated for television alone; to the extent that radio received funds at all, it was at the will of television entities.

> While in other countries the "public" in public broadcasting means "government," in the U.S., most of the funding for public broadcasting comes from non-governmental sources.

That changed in the late 1970s through an act of Congress that specifically allocated funding to local public radio stations. These stations have, like their TV brethren, formed a national network. Like PBS, NPR does not own stations and is governed, and largely financed, by its member stations. However, because of the lower political profile of radio when the networks were established, NPR was allowed to produce its own news and cultural programming for distribution across the member stations' network. (There is a full discussion of CPB structure, rules and policy in in Chapter 31, Nonprofit Media.) Also, in part because radio is cheaper to produce and in part because of legal interventions, there are competing national networks in public radio (e.g., Public Radio International and American Public Media) that don't exist in public television.

In terms of audience reach and appreciation, the Public Broadcasting Act must be deemed a success. Before 1967, there were only 292 educational FM stations; today there are more than 900.[32] Before the Act, there were 124 educational TV stations on the air;[33] today there are 365.[34] Together, they reach nearly 281 million individuals.[35] Public radio's audience in particular is substantial and growing. NPR reached 34 million people over the airwaves of member stations in 2010, its best year ever, and millions more downloaded its podcasts.[36] In 2010, NPR had a reported 1.8 million followers on Twitter and 700,000 fans on Facebook;[37] its smartphone applications had been downloaded 2.5 million times since 2008, and its iPad application had been downloaded on one out of every five iPads sold.[38] PBS. org's iPad app hit number one in Apple's iTunes store within 24 hours of its release.[39]

Though subject to occasional controversy, public broadcasters have generally achieved a high level of respect among the public, according to polls. Public television in particular seems to occupy a special place of honor for a wide swath of Americans. A 2010 Roper Survey found that for the seventh consecutive year, PBS outranked courts of law as the single most trusted institution in the United States among every measured age group, ethnicity, income, and education level of the public.[40]

Business Models

The economics of public broadcasting are often misunderstood. While in other countries the "public" in public broadcasting means "government," in the U.S. most of the funding for public broadcasting (referred to in the following charts as "revenue") comes from non-governmental sources.[41]

In 2008, about 60 percent of public broadcasting revenue came from private sources, including grants from corporations, colleges, universities, foundations, and individual subscribers.[43] Individual donors comprise the largest

TOTAL PUBLIC BROADCASTING SYSTEM REVENUE BY SOURCE

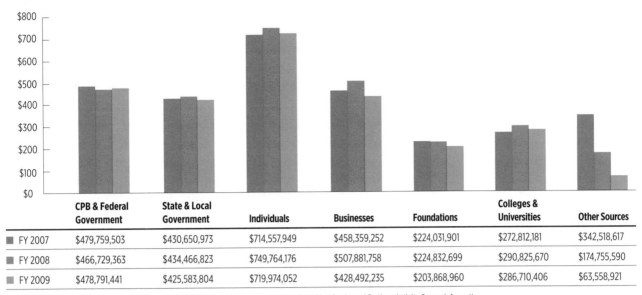

	CPB & Federal Government	State & Local Government	Individuals	Businesses	Foundations	Colleges & Universities	Other Sources
■ FY 2007	$479,759,503	$430,650,973	$714,557,949	$458,359,252	$224,031,901	$272,812,181	$342,518,617
■ FY 2008	$466,729,363	$434,466,823	$749,764,176	$507,881,758	$224,832,699	$290,825,670	$174,755,590
■ FY 2009	$478,791,441	$425,583,804	$719,974,052	$428,492,235	$203,868,960	$286,710,406	$63,558,921

Source: Corporation for Public Broadcasting Annual Financial Report, Station Activities Benchmarking Study, and Stations Activity Survey Information

PUBLIC BROADCASTING REVENUE BY SOURCE (FY 2008)
Public Radio and Public Television

Total Revenue: $2.85 billion

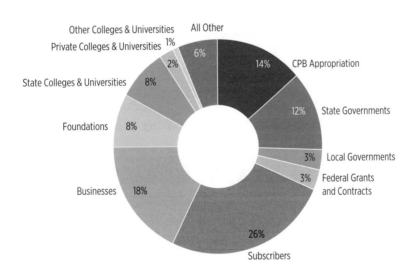

Source: Corporation for Public Broadcasting Appropriations Request[42]

single source, accounting for nearly $750 million, or 26.3 percent of revenue.[44] Mid-size and larger stations rely even more heavily on individual donations. For example, individual contributions accounted for 46 percent of the revenue of WHYY in Philadelphia in 2010[45] and provided 52 percent of the support for the local operations of WETA in Washington D.C.[46] For public stations overall, businesses provide 17.8 percent (about $508 million) and foundations 7.9 percent (about $225 million).[47]

The broad base of public broadcasting funding is an underappreciated attribute of the system. It is what public broadcasting systems in other countries strive for: a system rooted in local connections, civil society partnerships (e.g., universities, local sponsors), and diverse financial support. This structure also has some of the features that commercial entities seek. Indeed, in some ways the public media business model has proven more stable during the past few years than existing commercial media models. For-profit entities have responded to the drop in advertising by searching for ways to draw more money from viewers, listeners, and readers. Public broadcasters have spent decades refining techniques to appeal directly to listeners and viewers for support, and they have built strong relationships in many communities. Public broadcasting also relies heavily on volunteers; a 2010 survey indicated that 46 percent of the local public broadcasting news workforce is made up of nonprofessionals.[48]

But the economic recession was a blow to public broadcasting, forcing budget cuts on even the most popular programs and forestalling investment in new ones. For example, *PBS NewsHour*'s budget for June 2010 through July 2011 was expected to fall by about $200,000 from the previous fiscal year as a result of reductions in corporate underwriting.[49] From 2008 to 2009, non-federal support for public television stations declined an estimated $260 million. Public radio and television stations estimated that their revenue declined 14 percent between 2009 and 2010.[50] During the same period, individual donations fell by $30 million or 4.5 percent. Individual donations dropped from $653.6 million to $624 million from 2008 to 2009, after a steady annual growth since 2006.[51] Foundation support dropped from about $225 million in 2008 to $204 million in 2009. And, in 2009, the stations "project[ed] a $307 million loss in non-federal revenue through FY 2010."[52]

About 14 percent of public broadcasting revenue comes from the federal government through CPB, and 13.6 percent more comes from other forms of government support (including state colleges, local governments, and federal grants and contracts). For rural and small stations, the share of federal support is significantly higher than 14 percent. Stations that operate with less than $1 million of non-federal financial support rely on CPB funding for nearly half (47.5 percent) of their revenues.[53] In 2009, the two-year advance federal appropriations for CPB were approximately $400 million.[54] The advanced appropriation in 2011 (for FY 2012 and 2013) is $445 million.[55] The size of this federal allocation puts the U.S. in stark contrast to most other developed countries, which spend significantly more per capita of taxpayer dollars on public broadcasting. (See Chapter 15, The Evolving Nonprofit Media.)

By law, the federal funds that pass through CPB are allocated (1) by distribution platform (radio and TV) and (2) by a formula that rigidly dictates how much money goes to stations themselves and how much is available for program producers. Almost 67 percent goes to TV and 22 percent to radio. Of the money that goes to TV, about 73 percent goes to stations for general station support, with the rest going directly to programming. The ratio of general station support to direct programming support is about the same for radio. Funding for noncommercial stations themselves (as opposed to national networks or programmers)—the lion's share of the federal CPB appropriation—is distributed through Community Service Grants (CSG) according to formulae that consider the size of a station, the amount of non-federal dollars the station is able to raise, the extent to which the station provides sole service to a community, and other factors, including programming differentiation.[56] CSG funding can be used for programming, whether for

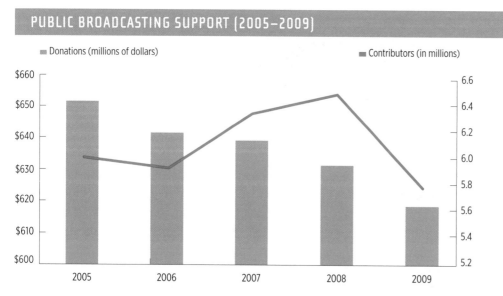

PUBLIC BROADCASTING SUPPORT (2005–2009)

■ Donations (millions of dollars)   ■ Contributors (in millions)

Source: Corporation for Public Broadcasting, Public Broadcasting Membership and Donation Data, Fiscal Years 2005–2009

local productions or national programming, but it goes in equal part (at least for TV stations) to support broadcast infrastructure and ancillary station operations. It is difficult for the public to get a sense of the distribution of public broadcasting funds across the system. While CSG funds are allocated for seven categories of expenses (including "programming and production," and "broadcasting, transmission and distribution"), and stations must report expenditures in these categories annually to CPB, CPB does not make the data public in a way that facilitates data analysis.[57]

Over the years, in addition to the CPB appropriation, the federal government has provided money for basic public broadcasting infrastructure, such as transmitters, radio towers, studio space, production equipment, and satellite interconnection, which gives individual stations the ability to acquire and distribute national programming through high-power satellites. More recently, Congress appropriated additional funds to help public broadcasters transition to digital TV.

> When it comes to news and public affairs, public television's great strength has historically has been national, programming—from Frontline to Firing Line with William F. Buckley to News Hour.

Funds appropriated to help new noncommercial stations build out their facilities (through the Public Telecommunications Facilities Program) and funds appropriated for noncommercial broadcast digital initiatives have been zeroed out.[58] In March 2011, the House of Representatives passed a bill that would have ended federal funding for NPR and for all other noncommercial radio programming, but it was not passed into law.[59]

Public Broadcasting's Mission

The broad mission of public broadcasting has been to help promote civil discussion, take creative risks, serve the underserved, and supply educational programming. In economic terms, the goal has been to serve the public with media content that is not sufficiently profitable for commercial broadcasters.[60] It has been left largely up to local public broadcasters to define what this means, with each creating its own mix of educational, music, cultural, talk, and public affairs programming.[61] CPB now articulates public broadcasting objectives in terms of "the three D's"—"diversity, digital, and dialogue": meeting the information needs of a diverse nation, innovating in digital media and emerging technologies, and strengthening public media's role as a resource and partner in the dialogue of local communities.[62] Others, looking to the language of the Public Broadcasting Act and to emerging needs in the digital era, have emphasized the importance of creating content that is under-produced by the commercial market, curating content, and connecting communities with content that is of use to them.[63]

Education and Culture: A Record of Leadership

Public television has been widely acclaimed for consistently producing high-quality educational and cultural programming—from *Sesame Street* to Ken Burns's documentaries (e.g., *The Civil War* and *Baseball*) to *NOVA*. In many cases, public television has produced and broadcast content that never would have made it on commercial TV; in other cases, it has provided a laboratory for experimental programs that became popular on public TV and then moved to commercial networks. For example, children's programming began on PBS with *Sesame Street* and the Children's Television Workshop, as did the first reality TV show, *An American Family*. Science programming, serious historical documentaries, independent films, and arts programming all began on public television. Public television was also first to develop closed captioning for the hearing impaired, offering it initially in 1972 and as a regular service by 1980.[64] And public television was an early leader in the production of original high-definition digital programming, as well.

PBS has received more Emmy Awards in children's programming than all the broadcast and cable networks combined.[65] According to a recent Nielsen study, PBS KIDS had four of the top ten programs among kids 2–5. It also had six of the top 10 shows, including five PBS KIDS shows tying for first place, among mothers aged 18–49 with children under the age of 3.[66] A study comparing 10 randomly selected PBS shows with commercial programs found that public television episodes were, on average, higher in quality in terms of their focus on cognitive-intellectual content.[67] Some of this programming emerges from PBS's Ready to Learn initiative, funded by a grant from the Department of Education, which seeks to promote literacy and reading skills, with an emphasis on serving the needs of children of low-income families.[68]

Public broadcasters also have been successful in using digital platforms and tools to serve children. More than 9 million children visit the PBS KIDS website each month.[69] It is the most popular children's site for video, with more than 100 million video streams viewed per month.[70]

Several PBS kids programs are notable for their appeal across a wide spectrum of family demographics. Programs such as *Clifford the Big Red Dog*, for example, are as watched in households with incomes of less than $20,000 as they are in households with incomes above $60,000 per year.[71] Other programs, such as *Sesame Street*, have higher viewership among more affluent and well-educated families.[72]

In addition to its work in children's television, PBS provides voluminous materials directly to educators, and this is a growing focus. Eighty-five percent of its member stations offer educational content to their communities aligned to applicable education standards and 95 percent offer structured learning as part of their educational services.[73] Public television has been one of the largest suppliers of K–12 instructional programming for schools. PBS operates the website, TeacherLine, which offers over 130 professional development courses for pre-K–12 educators and has had more than 50,000 enrollments.[74] PBS is ranked among the top three sources of online K–12 content and has been ranked by teachers as a top source of video in the classroom.[75]

PBS has received more Emmy Awards in children's programming than all the broadcast and cable networks combined.

PBS Education is currently working on the Digital Learning Library (DLL), an initiative to create a repository of "purpose-built" digital learning objects (currently nearing 10,000 and still growing) available to teachers nationwide.[76] It strives to unlock the archives of data, photos, video, and other media held by potential partners, such as the Smithsonian Institution and the National Science Foundation, by putting them into digital forms suitable for teaching.[77]

PBS also pioneered long-distance learning for adults. A study conducted over a decade ago found that more than two-thirds of America's 3,000 colleges were using PBS adult learning services.[78] LiteracyLink offers basic education and GED preparation tools, using technology for underserved and hard-to-reach adults.

When cable television matured, there was some question as to whether new commercial, kid-oriented channels would obviate the need for public television's children's programming. Few make that argument now, as it has become evident that commercial outlets tend to excel at entertainment programming, while public broadcasting emphasizes educational content, content geared toward younger children, and content designed specifically to improve cognitive functioning and school performance.[79]

Both public television and radio also offer significant amounts of cultural programming. *Masterpiece*, the longest-running prime-time drama program in American television; *Great Performances*, the only continuing prime-time performance showcase on American television; and the history series *American Experience* are all multiple Emmy award–winning series. *From the Top at Carnegie Hall*, an Emmy Award–winning children's series, showcases young musicians. Public broadcasting has historically enjoyed high levels of support among rural state lawmakers, in part because PBS has offered music and other cultural programming that is otherwise unavailable in more remote regions of the country.[80]

PBS is ranked among the top three sources of online K–12 content, and has been ranked by teachers as a top source of video in the classroom.

PBS has tried to attract broader audiences by featuring more contemporary programming. *Austin City Limits*, for example, features music legends and innovators across all genres and is now the longest-running music series in American television history.[81] It is also the only TV program to receive the nation's highest award for artistic excellence: the National Medal of Arts.[82] Despite its efforts, PBS has been fairly criticized for failing to broaden its appeal further and showcase an even wider range of cultural expression.[83]

Public radio has not played as prominent a role as has public TV in producing educational and children's content. However, its cultural programming is probably more diverse, in part because there is beneficial competition among different national public radio networks, unlike in TV. In addition to NPR, there is Public Radio International (PRI), which distributes the enormously popular *This American Life* and *A Prairie Home Companion*, and American

The latest economic crisis in some cases has made a bad situation worse. WLVT–PBS 39 in Lehigh Valley, Pennsylvania has won an Emmy for its news and public affairs programming, but recently had to drop its documentary team, cut its production budget 70 percent, and cancel two of three shows which focused squarely on local news and public affairs.

Public Media, which produces the syndicated program *Being* (formerly called *Speaking of Faith*) for 230 stations on a wide range of spiritual issues. Overall, these outlets, plus Pacifica and a variety of local stations and independent distributors, contribute to the diversity of programming available on public radio.[84]

Music accounts for about one-third of all public radio listening and 8 percent of public radio formats.[85] More than 100 stations have full-time music formats.[86] Public radio has helped spur efforts to preserve and enhance important American musical genres such as bluegrass and Celtic music.[87] Public radio provides most of today's classical and jazz music programming, as well.[88] The two largest NPR members are classical music stations. *From the Top*, a showcase for exceptional young musicians, has over 700,000 weekly listeners via nearly 250 stations.[89]

News and Public Affairs

Public broadcasting advocates have long argued that noncommercial media should strengthen democracy by promoting participation in the public sphere.[90] The Carnegie Commission report stated:

> "Public Television can extend our knowledge and understanding of contemporary affairs. Its programming of the news should grow to encompass both facts and meaning, both information and interpretation. It should be historian, in addition to being daily journalist. Its programs should call upon the intellectual resources of the nation to give perspective and depth to interpretation of the news, in addition to coverage of news day by day."[91]

A 1993 report by the Century Foundation asserted that public television should "enlarge the horizons of the American people and inform them of the issues—past, present, and future—that affect their society."[92] In more recent years, numerous media commentators have called on public media to play a more prominent role in providing news and information.

To accurately assess public broadcasting's performance in these areas, we distinguish between public TV and radio, and between national and local activity below.

Public Television

When it comes to news and public affairs, public television's great strength historically has been national programming. A recent public survey rated PBS news and public affairs programming as the most fair and unbiased, surpassing NBC, ABC, Fox, and MSNBC in the public's trust.[93] This programming has often filled a gap in the news and information business by providing more in-depth coverage of significant issues than commercial networks do. *PBS NewsHour*, for example, dedicated about two times more coverage to international news in 2009 than did average commercial broadcast networks and more than twice the airtime on the health care debate of 2009.[94]

PBS also airs some of the best journalistic documentaries on TV. *Frontline* has been "one of the most honored series in television history,"[95] repeatedly receiving the rarely awarded Gold Baton from the Alfred I. duPont-Columbia University Awards for Excellence in Broadcast Journalism. The *American Experience* series runs documentaries that focus on events and figures of the recent past, providing, for example, biographies of U.S. presidents and histories of epochal events in American life. Other national public affairs shows over the years have included *Washington Week in Review, Bill Moyers Journal*, William F. Buckley Jr.'s *Firing Line*, and *Nightly Business Report*.

But public television has placed a much smaller emphasis on *local* news. A 2011 FCC study of data from Tribune Media Services found that 68 percent of noncommercial TV stations provided no local news in the course of three weeks, and 94 percent provided 30 minutes or less per day.[96]

In another study, researchers who examined 170 PBS-affiliated stations listed on PBS.org found that only 14 of them—about 8 percent—produced a local newscast five or more nights per week.[98] Local commercial TV news has

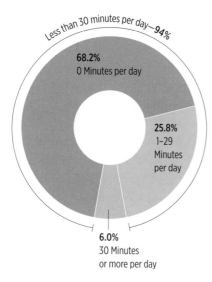

Less than 30 minutes per day ~94%

68.2%
0 Minutes per day

25.8%
1–29 Minutes per day

6.0%
30 Minutes or more per day

Source: FCC analysis of Tribune Media Services Data[97]

often been criticized for its insufficient coverage of serious issues—but the unfortunate reality is that local public TV has produced even less.

In a 2004 survey of public TV stations conducted by the General Accounting Office, "79 percent of the licensees responding…indicated that the amount of local programming they [were] currently produc[ing was] not sufficient to meet local community needs." A majority of responding licensees said that it was because they lacked adequate funds, and several said that "they have had to ignore local issues and turn away programming opportunities" for lack of funding.[99]

The recent cutbacks in newspapers and local TV have only heightened appeals, both within and outside of public broadcasting, for public television and public radio to become more active locally. Serving needs for local information is particularly important for public broadcasters because, according to respondents in a PBS survey, "public television stations are rapidly becoming the only locally owned and operated television broadcast medium."[100]

William Baker, president emeritus of WNET, has argued that creating serious local news programming in the public interest "would be a powerful new way for public broadcasters to fulfill their ongoing commitment to public service."[101] Others put it more bluntly: "There's a crying need for serious reporting at the local level," says Jim Lehrer, anchor of *PBS NewsHour*. "Public media has a responsibility to meet that need."[102]

Many PBS stations are experimenting with new models. CPB has recently created Local Journalism Centers, drawing together local public TV and radio to do original reporting.[103] Some local public television stations are creating hyperlocal websites for neighborhoods in their markets.[104] Jim Lehrer is traveling the country trying to convince local stations to team up with newspapers to provide local newscasts. He noted that KLRN is working with the *San Antonio Express* to create a local news show.[105] In some cases, stations have attempted to use national content to spur local engagement. For example, the PBS documentary *Not in Our Town*, which told the story of how a small Montana town successfully responded to an increase in local hate crimes, launched community efforts to respond to hate crimes across the country.[106] In *Facing the Mortgage Crisis*, St. Louis public station KETC provided an online social network and information on housing, health care, financial counseling, and emergency services for residents impacted by the financial crisis.[107] The station then created a locally adaptable model that is now being used by public stations in "32 of the hardest-hit [financial] markets [in] the country."[108] As part of its efforts to link with other noncommercial media entities, the station is also providing office space for a local nonprofit website, the Beacon.[109]

Some have focused on lower-cost public affairs shows. In St. Louis, Amy Shaw is vice president of Education and Community Engagement at KETC, now called "the Nine Network," which includes four public broadcasting channels (some digital) in the St. Louis area. One of its programs, *Donnybrook*, is a live in-studio forum in which media pundits get together to talk about community issues and events of the week. In addition, the network produces a weekly public affairs show, *Jeff City Journal*, which is broadcast statewide and discusses issues facing the state legislature. The station has also done a series on immigration and the regional economy. Shaw says, "We are evangelizing to get local public stations all over the country to connect more closely with the community…and find a way to create local programming around the issues."[110]

There are significant financial obstacles standing in the way of more local public TV news and information programming. The director of Television Programming Projects for PBS, Lynda Clarke, says that producing local news is too expensive:

"Doing production, even a small production at a public television station requires space, it requires lighting, and technical equipment and people...especially nowadays when people are accustomed to a certain level of quality on the air. You end up not wanting to duplicate what is on the commercial airwaves if it is already there and...it is very expensive."[111]

In some cases, the recent economic crisis has made a bad situation worse. The experience of PBS 39/WLVT in Lehigh Valley, Pennsylvania, an Emmy award winner for news, is illustrative. The station recently lost $1 million in state funding. Amy Burkett, vice president of production at WLVT, reports that while local commercial television news was doing a high volume of crime stories, her news team was covering economic development and the enormous amount of unemployment in the region—giving community issues five to 30 minutes of airtime each night on a news and public affairs show called *Tempo InDepth*. According to Burkett, WLVT also aired local documentaries that showcased community issues and helped educate viewers on how to find jobs and create new businesses. Due to the loss of funding, the station has had to drop its documentary team, cut its production budget 70 percent, and cancel two of three shows that focused squarely on local news and public affairs. Burkett's remaining staff of four is seeking new reporting models. The station is attempting to partner with 10 colleges and universities in its viewing area, offering video production classes and to run some of the student work on air.[112]

After a 15-year run, *Life and Times*, a nightly news and public affairs program in Los Angeles, went off the air in 2007 for lack of resources. For years, *Life and Times* had been dispatching reporters into the field to cover topics of interest to the local community that get little or no attention from the commercial nightly news programs in the L.A. market—including immigration, county commissioners, and the troubled school system. The show was expensive to produce, and over the years had gradually cut back on costly field production.[113]

Most local PBS and public radio stations do not have the money to provide more local reporting, and doubt their capacity to raise the money, for what has typically been high-cost programming. "The economics of doing local are beyond most local TV stations," says Laura Walker, head of WNYC, a major New York City public radio station.[114] Local broadcasters that have tried to launch a locally produced half-hour broadcast have struggled, primarily because of an inability to attract underwriters.[115] Particularly in the markets that already have several commercial local newscasts, it may be difficult for public stations to allocate scarce resources to producing competing local news—at least in its traditional format.[116]

Generally speaking, for news and for other programming, stations have not thus far found it economical to produce high-cost content that cannot be syndicated nationally and therefore generate revenue across a larger audience base. The programming that does go national is produced by a small group of stations. In 2008, the top three content producers—New York's WNET, Boston's WGBH, and Los Angeles' KCET—generated about 60 percent of all public television programming.[117]

94% of public TV stations offer 30 minutes or less of local news.

The economics of local programming production may change as new models for sourcing content are developed. One Los Angeles public TV station, KCET, is currently experimenting with new models, having withdrawn from the PBS network in October 2010 to escape the financial burden of member dues. It plans to replace PBS favorites like *NOVA* and *Sesame Street* with locally produced programming.[118]

Public Radio

Public radio's approach to local news and information has been somewhat different.

Unlike PBS, which is prohibited from producing its own programs, NPR produces more than 100 hours of original programming each week—including popular news and information programs such as *All Things Considered*, *Morning Edition*, and *Talk of the Nation*. American Public Media produces *Marketplace*. NPR's listenership has grown steadily, with 27.2 million weekly listeners in 2010.[119] The reach of its three top shows grew from 19.9 million in the fall of 2000 to more than 28.8 million in the fall of 2009.[120] In many communities, NPR has become one of the most listened to news sources on radio.[121] News consumption accounts for four of every 10 hours of public radio listening, with the all-news format being the most-listened-to of public radio formats.[122] About 185 stations are dedicated full time to news, and another 480 stations feature news as part of a mixed format.[123] With 17 international bureaus, NPR now has more overseas correspondents than NBC, CBS, Fox, or MSNBC. Its total editorial staff, including digital editors and traditional on-air reporters, grew 8 percent in 2010, to 335 people.[124] Overall, public radio deploys more than 1,400 reporters, editors, and producers in 21 domestic and 17 foreign bureaus.[125]

The investment NPR has made in establishing itself in the digital world seems to be paying off in terms of audience penetration.[126] Its iPhone applications were downloaded 2.5 million times from 2008 to May 7, 2010, making them among the most popular news applications.[127] According to its internal measures, NPR.org averaged 15.7 million unique visitors across all digital platforms in 2010, up more than 5 million from 2009, putting it on par with CBS News, according to Nielsen figures.[128]

In an attempt to deepen its newsgathering capacity, NPR recently created an investigative team that would work with beat and field reporters.[129] It has launched partnerships with independent nonprofit reporting outfits, as well, including one with the Center for Public Integrity to produce a multipart series on the problem of sexual assault on college campuses, and another with the Center for Investigative Reporting to examine law enforcement's use of confidential informants.[130] This year, NPR produced *Going Radical*, a multipart investigative series that documented the life, background, and radicalization of Christmas Day bomber Umar Farouk Abdulmatallab.[131]

Public radio stations often have well-staffed newsrooms in the major radio markets, but skeletal crews in the medium and small markets.[132] From 2004 to 2009, the number of stations that carried local and regional news or talk programming increased from 595 to 681, with hours aired each week increasing from 5,182 to 5,693.[133] In all, one-third of total public radio programming is locally produced.[134] Similarly, 74 percent of stations now produce segments that air as part of the national newscasts of *Morning Edition* and *All Things Considered*.[135]

The Station Resource Group is an alliance of public media organizations that operate public radio stations across America, many of which have built substantial local news operations.[136] Its co-chief executive, Tom Thomas, describes the local public radio landscape:

> "About a half a dozen stations are at the apex of the pyramid and most are in the largest metropolitan areas that have successful, well-established, high-impact local news operations and are ambitious to make them bigger and stronger. Below those stations, there are probably another 15 to 20 public radio operations [whose] local newsrooms might be on the order of seven to 15 reporters and editors and producers, and they are in the next tier down in market size. They are in places like St. Louis or are part of regional services like Vermont Public Radio or Wisconsin Public Radio or New Hampshire Public Radio."[137]

Beyond those leaders, Thomas says there is a more significant drop-off in local newsgathering capacity. Most stations in the medium and small markets have little or no staff to produce local radio news and public affairs programming, even though there are often no commercial stations doing local news either.

In the larger markets and with some of the bigger state public radio services—local news and public affairs programming initiatives have been around for a while. WBEZ, Chicago Public Radio, produces *Eight Forty-Eight*, a one-hour weekday program with a distinctive focus on local news, views, people, and culture.[138] Wyoming Public Radio's *Open Spaces* is a weekly news magazine that provides in-depth coverage of issues affecting Wyoming residents. Other examples include: *Charlotte Talks* on WFAE in Charlotte, North Carolina; WNYC's Peabody Award–winning daily program, *The Brian Lehrer Show*; and Minnesota Public Radio's *The UBS Forum*, which hosts community discussions and public debates.[139]

Although large numbers of public radio stations are involved in some kind of local news and public affairs programming, for most, these news efforts have been small-scale operations. Fewer than 15 percent of local radio stations have four or more reporters; only 4 percent have three or more editors. One-third of stations have no full-time reporters; 22 percent have one; 30 percent have two to three.[140] Only 25 percent of stations have any full-time producers.[141] As a result, many produce little enterprise journalism. In Colorado, for example, the single public radio station devoted to news airs 22 hours of national programming every weekday, but only two hours of state-specific news programs.[142]

At the other end of the spectrum is Minnesota Public Radio (MPR), based in St. Paul and owned by American Public Media Group. MPR operates 41 radio stations in Minnesota and surrounding states and has a regional news staff of about 90. American Public Media also operates KPCC, Southern California Public Radio, in Los Angeles, with a news staff of 42 and an $8.5 million news and public affairs programming budget.[143]

In *Facing the Mortgage Crisis*, St. Louis public station KETC provided information on housing, health care, financial counseling, and emergency services for residents impacted by the financial crisis.

Because public radio can produce news at less cost than TV, public radio leadership in recent years has made a major push to bolster local news. With the help of several CPB grants, NPR has intensified its efforts to help local stations improve their coverage on air and online. In October 2009, NPR launched Project Argo to expand the reporting capacity of public radio stations on environmental policy, rural economic diversification, public health, and other issues that tend to get overlooked or under-addressed by commercial media.[144] Project Argo offers support to stations that are developing expertise on specialized subjects, relevant to their regions, and it equips them with resources to develop in-depth original reporting and share online content.[145] For instance, KPLU in Seattle focuses on the global health industry, while WGBH in Boston focuses on global warming. KQED in San Francisco specializes in technology in education, while WXPN in Philadelphia focuses on local music.[146] The intent is to produce content that is web-friendly first, and then to integrate it as appropriate into the broadcast.

Public broadcasting news initiatives have attracted some foundation support. The Knight Foundation awarded New York City's WNYC a $2 million grant in 2008 to create *The Takeaway*, a morning news program, produced in partnership with WGBH in Boston, the BBC World Service, and the *New York Times*, and designed to provide an alternative to NPR's *Morning Edition*. Knight also gave NPR $1.5 million in 2007 to train 600 staff in the use of digital media technology.[147] And in October 2010, NPR announced that it had received a $1.8 million grant from the Open Society Foundation that will, if NPR is able to raise enough additional funds, place at least 100 journalists at NPR member radio stations in all 50 state capitols to increase coverage of state government.[148] Several of the largest stations in major cities have made a move to increase their journalistic footprint dramatically. In October 2010, leaders of several large public radio stations—led by American Public Radio founder, Bill Kling—announced a $100 million fundraising target that would allow them to triple the news staffs in New York, Chicago, Los Angeles, and Minnesota.[149] As part of that effort, Laura Walker of WNYC says she hopes to raise money to field 100 reporters, which would transform the station into a major journalistic presence in New York. She says this is only likely to happen with foundation or government support. "I'm not sure we can sustain the journalism from listener-supported radio," she explains. "It doesn't pay. People value it but don't value it at the level it costs."[150] So far, the $100 million campaign has not gotten much traction with foundations.

As public radio seeks to expand its news operations, it faces criticism for its audience composition. Some say that public radio appeals too narrowly to the affluent, white, and well educated, and this criticism has some empirical support. According to the Pew Project on Excellence in Journalism, the median household income of an NPR listener in 2010 was $86,114, compared with the national median of $55,462; 40 percent of NPR listeners have a household income of more than $100,000, compared with 22 percent of the general population.[151] Educationally, 69 percent of NPR listeners have a college degree or higher, compared with only 26 percent of the general population.[152]

Collaboration

Whatever the strengths (and weaknesses) of public broadcasting's news efforts, it has become increasingly clear that the nonprofit news sector will not thrive without a significant increase in cost-efficient collaborations among public broadcasting outlets, and between public broadcasters and other nonprofit entities.

CPB has taken steps to encourage multimedia collaboration among public radio and TV stations. In 2010 it launched seven Local Journalism Centers (LJCs),[153] each run jointly by television and radio stations that hire reporters, editors, and community outreach managers to report on topics of regional interest in their area and then distribute the content over multiple platforms, including TV, radio, mobile, and Internet.[154] The LJCs are (or will be) operating in the Southwest, the Upper Midwest, the Plains, Upstate New York, Central Florida, the Northwest, and the South.[155] The Southwest center will focus on border and immigration issues, while the Midwest center will focus on agribusiness. WVIZ in Michigan, together with Michigan Radio and Chicago Public Radio, has already staffed its first project, Changing Gears: Remaking the Manufacturing Belt. And the Healthy State Collaborative Local Journalism Center, a partnership of several Florida public media stations, is operating with a dedicated staff of six focusing on issues of importance to the state's large population of older residents.[156] The center recently launched a website to promote its mission of "super serv[ing] the residents of [the] region with an intense journalistic commitment to the unifying topic of health care."[157]

CPB also is co-sponsoring NewsWorks.org, a website produced by the Philadelphia PBS- and NPR-affiliate, WHYY, that emphasizes hyperlocal reporting and teams community members with station editors to produce content for multiple platforms (TV, radio, Internet, and mobile). Focusing on seven distinct neighborhoods, the website also features a discussion forum, where community members can "exchange ideas around the clock."[158]

In St. Louis, a nonprofit online newspaper, the *St. Louis Beacon,* has partnered with local PBS-affiliate KETC on local reporting and "public awareness projects." *KQED News* in San Francisco dramatically expanded its news coverage with a website that combines content from KQED Public Radio, KQED Public Television, and KQEDNews.org. These synergies have helped KQED to increase the local newscasts it broadcasts from six to 16.[159] KQED represents one of more than 50 media outlets (online, broadcast, and print) that carry reports from the nonprofit investigative website California Watch for a fee, and the station has ongoing partnerships with at least 25 other news outlets, as well.[160] Other stations have teamed up with local libraries, universities, journalism schools, and other nonprofits to act as "anchor institutions" within their community's media ecosystem.[161]

News consumption accounts for 4 of every 10 hours of public radio listening, with the all-news format the most-listened-to of public radio formats.

New technology platforms have been instrumental in facilitating collaboration. A watershed moment came in July 2008, when NPR released an open API (Application Programming Interface)[162] that allows different public media entities and third parties to share, remix, and distribute public media content.[163] Individual stations can use this API easily to post NPR stories, audio segments, and photos on their websites. NPR reports that the API served some 1.1 billion stories in one month alone, and in the first half of 2010 nearly five billion NPR stories were distributed to a host of different websites.[164]

However, collaboration can be expensive and time-consuming, at least in the short term.[165] Stations do their own fundraising and jealously guard their membership relations. CPB has made some efforts to incentivize collaboration among public broadcasting stations, in part by establishing new networks, as discussed above. However, the funding formulas that it administers do not compel collaboration. Indeed, because funding is so significantly station-based, grantees may be encouraged to maintain duplicative operations within a community "(to be discussed in Chapter 15, The Evolving Nonprofit Media).

Political Pressure and Local News

Even if public broadcasters *can* do more local journalism, there are some who argue that they should not. There are two conflicting concerns: that public media will be too dependent on government and, conversely, that they will be too independent. If public media entities were to offer more accountability journalism, for instance, would they be able to withstand political pressure from those who disagree with the content? Could politicians use the leverage of tax dollars to manipulate coverage? Opponents, such as writer Adam Theirer, argue that significantly expanding government funding for newsgathering would "dampen the incentive for aggressive reporting on government activities or abuse, and invite political meddling in the news that is ultimately…disseminated to the public."[166]

The first thing to note is that federal government contributions usually make up only a small percentage of station revenue, at least for stations in larger markets. At KPCC in Los Angeles, for instance, 45 percent of revenue comes from individual contributions, 40 percent from corporate underwriting—overwhelmingly from local hospitals, universities, museums, and arts institutions—and just 7 percent comes from the federal government.[167] That is not to say that the federal contribution is unimportant. It often provides critical funding for operations—basic transmission and administrative costs—that members and foundations are less interested in funding. It also provides seed money to launch programs that stations later sustain through outside sources.[168]

With respect to federal influence, the funding structure was designed to keep legislators and the White House from influencing public broadcasting programming choices. CPB, as a relatively passive pass-through for federal dollars, should serve as a firewall between the funders and the funded. This structure has been tested with respect to particular programming choices. In 1980, the Carter administration reportedly tried to pressure PBS to cancel the airing of *Death of a Princess,* a drama-documentary "about a Saudi princess executed for an affair with a commoner."[169] Pressure also came from Mobil Oil, "a major PBS underwriter." PBS president, Larry Grossman, refused to cancel the program, but many PBS affiliates became unwilling to air it, anyway.[170] In 2002, PBS promised to keep an HIV-positive Muppet off *Sesame Street* after congressional conservatives wrote to PBS to remind the network of its financial dependence on federal dollars. In 2005, PBS pulled an episode of *Postcards from Buster* that included a family with two moms after the Bush administration called for PBS to return federal funds dedicated to the show.[171] On balance, however, the public broadcasting system structure—and the CPB firewall—has been relatively effective in protecting programmers from program-specific political intervention. Although these examples are worrisome, they are small in number.

But political pressure also can impact programming and content in ways that are not easy to detect. Broadcasters may skew coverage or avoid controversy to forestall political criticism. A condition of CPB funding is that public stations must demonstrate "objectivity and balance" in their coverage of controversial matters[172]—and it is up to CPB to ensure that this is done. This stipulation has lead public broadcasters to strive for a disciplined nonpartisanship, a role that increasingly distinguishes them from the many other media entities that have grown more partisan. On the other hand, some argue that the drive for balance has made public broadcasters more tentative when it comes to tackling controversial issues. NPR news programs like *All Things Considered,* for example, have been criticized for being too cautious and unwilling to challenge the conventions of mainstream journalism.[173] Moreover, "objectivity and balance" are inherently subjective terms, open to a variety of interpretations depending on who is managing the organizations at any given moment.[174]

Whatever the strengths and weaknesses of the CPB firewall, there is also a question as to whether it will be adequate should local stations begin to do more aggressive journalism. In addition, the dynamics of political and corporate pressure might be different on the local level. For instance, UNC-TV, licensed to the University of North Carolina, recently was forced by the North Carolina General Assembly to turn over the notes and video footage from one of its reporters on a story that cast the corporation Alcoa in a negative light. Internal emails show that station management wanted to fight the lawmakers' request and protect the reporters and sources, but the decision was up to University of North Carolina.[175]

Then there is the other criticism: that public media journalists already are *too* independent of public mores and taxpayer inclinations. Conservative groups have argued that public radio programming espouses a liberal agenda and does not serve the interests of the public at large.[176] NPR's autumn 2010 firing of Juan Williams reinvigorated the accusations of liberal bias. In the aftermath of that event, FOX News Channel's Bill O'Reilly said:

> "The news-based programming on PBS and NPR is heavily tilted to the left. In fact, as far as their news analysts are concerned, there are 18 liberal-leaning individuals on the air and one moderate, David Brooks. There are no conservative voices heard in the national public broadcasting precincts."[177]

Others have argued that this criticism of NPR is out of date. *New York Times* columnist and *PBS NewsHour* commentator, David Brooks, says:

> "The damaging thing to me is NPR has really worked hard over the past 10, 20 years to become a straight-down-the-middle network. I'm not sure they were decades ago. But now they really are."[178]

Is it possible for public media to be—or be viewed as—a neutral ground? Steve Coll, president of the New America Foundation, wrote:

> "In this time of niche publications and cable networks that thrive on ideological anger, we should be seeking to strengthen NPR's role as a convener of the public square, a demagogue-free zone where all political and social groups—including conservatives and others opposed to federal funding of public media—should be welcome on equal terms."[179]

Randolph May of the conservative Free State Foundation thinks public media, by its nature, cannot play this role:

"[G]overnment's involvement tends to exacerbate public tensions in a way that makes civil discourse more difficult. This is because government content decisions are seen by many as tilting the public policy playing field in a way inconsistent with their beliefs."[180]

Impact of the Internet and Digital Technology

When it comes to Internet realities, commercial and noncommercial broadcasters face similar challenges. Both compete for mindshare with the myriad other choices Americans have. And both are impacted when viewers switch from watching a program on TV to consuming content online. The blow to the commercial broadcaster may be worse, however, because advertising rates online are much lower than those on broadcast TV. While noncommercial programmers must contend with the same circumstances regarding corporate underwriters, they also have the ability to solicit audience donations on either medium.

Like commercial media, public broadcasting has had to adapt to the changing landscape. Although to date, only 3 percent of public broadcasting news professionals work exclusively online, public broadcasters in general have tried to expand their audience by offering increasing amounts of web content.[181] PBS's *Frontline* streams its programs online in their entirety, with links to relevant resources.[182] The PBS KIDS' website offers full-length episodes and educational games.[183] *PBS NewsHour* produces regular online webcasts, for which the audience more than doubled from 2008 to 2010, reaching 1.4 million unique monthly views in 2010.[184] PBS also places its content on Hulu, YouTube, digital multicast channels, mobile smart phones, and social-networking sites.[185]

PBS recently launched free iPad and iPhone applications, which quickly became the number one downloaded applications.[186] Public radio podcasts are downloaded by the millions each month; one program, WBUR's *On Point*, is downloaded as many as 500,000 times weekly.[187] Nashville Public Television's *Next Door Neighbors* uses an online interactive immigration data map to raise awareness of cultures

Overall, public radio deploys more than 1400 reporters, editors, and producers in 21 domestic and 17 foreign bureaus.

that would otherwise be unfamiliar to local residents.[188] Its programming on Nashville's Kurdish community has reportedly gone viral in Kurdistan. Public TV in Atlanta created LENS on Atlanta, an Internet destination with tools that allow users to create and share content, engage in online dialogue, and even connect with local government leaders.[189] KPBS in San Diego made early use of Twitter to alert community members about forest fires that affected the region in 2007.[190]

Several PBS stations have made creative use of their digital multicast channels.[191] The Orlando station uses a multicast signal to carry The Florida Channel, a public affairs television network covering legislative and judicial proceedings in the state, as well as meetings of the governor, his cabinet, and other local electoral and public affairs programming. The South Carolina Channel, also carried on a multicast channel, provides coverage of the State House of Representatives, local sports, and other local programming. The Minneapolis station carries The Minnesota Channel, broadcasting programming created by and for Minnesota and neighboring audiences.[192] Public radio stations across the country are also doubling and tripling their offerings by using digital subchannels to broadcast local community events, town hall meetings, hearings, and legislative floor sessions, in addition to using these new streams to display song information, weather, traffic updates, and local news.[193]

The development of smartphone applications has also been a tremendous success for NPR and Public Radio Exchange (PRX), a nonprofit that distributes independently produced noncommercial radio programs and facilitates content exchanges among consumers, producers, and public radio stations. The Public Radio Player—a free application developed by PRX for the iPhone—has been downloaded 2.5 million times since 2008.[194] After the release of the iPhone, iPad, and Android apps, mobile traffic rose from 5 percent to at least 27 percent of NPR's total digital traffic.[195]

Public media companies are also trying to leverage their reputations and brands in the social-media space in various ways. Public Insight Journalism, a project pioneered by American Public Media (APM) and funded by the Knight Foundation, brings together a network of nearly 100,000 sources, who contribute information to a database of topics and stories in order to guide journalists and connect them with resources. This "curated crowdsourcing" is being used for national programs such as *Marketplace* and *On Being*, and by radio stations in major markets, such as New York City and Los Angeles, as well as in smaller markets, like Charlotte, North Carolina, and St. Louis, Missouri.[196]

The Problem of Streaming Costs and Digital Distribution

Public broadcasters have a significant problem in the digital world that commercial broadcasters do not face. Since many commercial broadcasters put ads on their archived clips, they make money each time a video or audio clip is played online. The sponsorship deals of public stations are not tied to viewership in the same way, so each time someone watches a video clip on a public TV website it adds to the station's broadband streaming costs—without bringing in additional revenue. The more popular the clip, the less financially beneficial it is to the public station. For all the justified excitement about the Internet as a means of conveying video and building audience, for public media the Internet has thus far been a more expensive way to transmit content on a per capita basis than broadcast has been. Bill Kling of APM puts it this way:

> "[W]e can reach 14 million people in Los Angles with a transmitter that runs on 600 watts of power. If we tried to reach 14 million people with broadband…we'd be bankrupt. We spend now $500,000 a year in our company alone on broadband spectrum in order to serve the audiences and I don't think everybody realizes that every time you download podcast or stream audio…it's a collect call to us."[197]

He estimates that in Los Angeles, it costs the local public radio station $3,000 per year for the electricity to run its radio transmitter but almost $300,000 to stream audio over the Internet.[198] The alternative music public radio station in Philadelphia, WXPN, spends about 2 cents per unique listener each year for ordinary radio transmission.[199] But to stream to its online audience of approximately 45,000, WXPN spends about $9,000 annually on bandwidth costs—amounting to $2 per user.[200]

The costs of streaming are significantly higher when video is involved. In May 2010, PBS streamed approximately 1.3 million hours of video to users, running up a tab of roughly $20,000 for that month alone. This is all in addition, of course, to the broadcast costs.[201] PBS projects that number of hours streamed will increase by 17 to 25 percent each year over the next 10 years.[202]

Another factor likely to drive up costs is consumer demand for better quality. PBS currently delivers its online video at transmission speeds well below those of industry leaders like Netflix and Hulu. As access to high-speed broadband continues to grow, PBS anticipates that it will need to put additional resources toward enhancing its streaming quality.[203]

All of these costs are expected to skyrocket as demand grows. PBS considered three different scenarios to try to gauge just how much content delivery costs might rise over the next 10 years: Using a conservative growth model, in which usage and quality increase while streaming prices drop, annual costs could reach $14 million. Imagining a more moderate situation, in which prices do not drop as quickly as usage increases, the estimate was $27 million. And, assuming a 50 percent jump in online video usage, as some industry analysts have predicted, annual costs could reach in excess of $100 million. In other words, PBS could be looking at an eight-fold to 60-fold increase in content delivery costs between now and 2020.[204]

PBS emphasizes the speculative nature of these projections, noting that new business deals and technological advances could impact costs dramatically. As the volume of streams grows, the cost-per-stream declines. But clearly, at this point, the potential cost burden of online streaming is cause for concern.

What is more, these models assume that broadband providers will not begin charging some content providers more than others (sometimes referred to as "paid prioritization"). But, as demand for high-bandwidth content (such as video or even 3-D video) increases, providers of broadband capacity may turn to content providers as well as to consumers to pay for the "pipes," or transmission capacity, required to serve up the content.[205] As more and more content moves to broadband, content providers could face additional access costs, as well. These concerns have led some public broadcasters to call for policy interventions that assist noncommercial providers in establishing ownership of their own broadband infrastructure and accessing third-party broadband infrastructure at low cost.[206]

Streaming poses yet another business model challenge, in that it potentially shifts viewer allegiance from local stations to national public media brands. In the old system, the only way consumers could listen to NPR or watch PBS was through a local public TV or radio station, which would then attempt to garner revenue by asking them to donate. Now, people can go straight to NPR.org and PBS.org and listen to national content without developing a relationship with the local station. National and local public broadcasting leaders have worked out ways of splitting the revenue but that tension will likely not disappear.

Membership Support

The mechanics of collecting member contributions has grown more complex. If collaborations with other nonprofit organizations or among public media broadcasters are to thrive, public media organizations will need to be able to distribute funds to multiple partners. The news collaboration between a nonprofit digital media entity, the local public radio station, and a journalism school will flourish only if the membership donation to one can be channeled to others in the partnership. Some public media officials believe membership contributions would grow if Apple were to allow one-click donations, using the iTunes store, within iPad and iPhone applications.[207]

Other Challenges Facing Public Broadcasting

Inflexible or Inappropriate Government Funding Streams

In Chapter 31, Nonprofit Media, we explore the Corporation for Public Broadcasting (CPB) funding system in more detail, but here are key points relevant to this discussion: 1) by law, about 67 percent of the total annual appropriation to CPB is earmarked for TV infrastructure and programming, and about 22 percent is earmarked for radio—an allocation that made sense before the Internet but now is overly rigid and restrictive; 2) most of this funding is allocated according to a formula, with CPB having little ability or inclination to tie funding to quality standards or to policy goals (such as increasing local programming); 3) CPB can direct only a relatively small amount of its budget to digital innovation. Most of the innovative digital projects funded by CPB to date were supported by a temporary allocation of between $30 million and $40 million dollars that was earmarked for the conversion of stations to digital broadcasting, as well as for content and services associated with the conversion.[208] This funding stream has now ended.

Intra-Broadcast Collaboration

Fifteen markets in the U.S. are considered "multi-provider" markets by CPB, meaning that most of the market is served by more than one CPB-eligible public television station.[209] This creates inefficiencies. First, stations typically fail to collaborate optimally on the use of spectrum capacity, infrastructure, and administrative functions, the result of which is duplicated effort and wasted resources. Second, these stations often provide redundant services, failing to give the public sufficient value for the amount of spectrum and resources allocated to them. According to CPB data collected from stations, the cost of merely broadcasting content (that is, getting it from the satellite out to the broadcast consumer) can be as high as that of producing content. Public TV stations spend between $2.9 million and $27.3 million each on the broadcast delivery of content annually.[210] If they could consolidate broadcast distribution onto shared channels, share master control and other functionality, and take other steps to economize on distribution and back office functions, they would free up resources for content production.

Some have criticized public radio for appealing too narrowly to the affluent, white, and well-educated.

For example, Boston's WGBH acquired WGBY of Springfield, Massachusetts, as a sister station, and the paired PBS stations were able to invest more in content with what they saved on broadcast operations. The national nonprofit, Public Radio Capital (PRC), provides capital to public broadcasters seeking to operate additional stations so that they can spread content investments and operational expenses over more platforms. PRC helped Denver's Colorado Public Radio purchase a second noncommercial FM station in 2008, resulting in a revenue boost for the station and additional service to the public (news on one channel and classical music on the other).[211]

One of the benefits of station consolidation and joint operation is better management. Direct governance, meaning direct oversight of media operations by a nonprofit board, plays a critical role in establishing more efficient, well-run station operations (governance issues are discussed in the next section). After responsibility for the operations of Los Angeles station KPCC shifted from a university to a high-powered community board that directly oversaw station operations, the station morphed from a failing station with a $1 million budget and a $135,000 annual deficit into one with $16 million in revenue, a balanced budget, and the largest news audience of any public media company in Los Angeles.[212]

With the current national need to ensure that spectrum is put to the best use—especially by providing universal high-speed Internet—tolerance for inefficient use of spectrum will decrease. For many years, CPB has tried to get multi-provider markets to consolidate as many operations as possible and to differentiate programming as much as possible. It has offered financial incentives for stations to combine master control operations, which amount to $11,000 to $72,000 in monthly expenses.[213] To date, these efforts have not been terribly successful. CPB set up an incentive fund in 2010 to encourage more collaboration among stations in and between markets.[214]

Collaborations often are more difficult than it might seem. In some cases there is uncertainty about what is legally permissible for stations with regard to joint operation.[215] Different licensees may have incompatible goals and management structures. In some cases, stations competing with each other for membership dollars are wary about sharing information and resources. Finally, unlike in the private sphere—where there is a pool of investors to finance roll ups—the public media world has less capital to finance such mergers.[216]

Institutional Licensees

Twenty-three percent of all public TV licenses and 31 percent of all radio licenses are held by colleges and universities.[217] The percentages are larger for CPB grantees, with 33 percent of all television grants and 48 percent of radio station grants in the hands of colleges or universities.[218] In the early days of public radio and TV, universities played a crucial role in providing educational programming. But there is debate today in public media circles about whether so many stations should be operated by universities.

The Public Broadcasting Act requires community licensees—that is, private nonprofit licensees—to have community advisory boards to ensure high quality and responsiveness to communities. However, the 1,053 university-owned NCE (noncommercial educational) licensees are exempt from this requirement, as are government licensees. Perhaps more important, community licensees are typically governed by boards whose only responsibility is the station's operation. By contrast, university and government licensees are governed by institutions that typically have many other responsibilities and are concerned with outcomes that go beyond (and may be at odds with) the public's interest in information.[219]

Some argue that when a station lacks a governing board that is directly and exclusively responsible for the performance of the station, performance is suboptimal.[220] Oversight of the station's operations may fall to the university's board of regents or board of trustees, which may have little interest in the station's performance, little expertise in media matters, and little desire to exercise authority over station management.[221]

Despite these issues, some of the most respected public TV stations in the country are owned by universities. Public Radio News Directors award winners in 2010 included WAMU, run by American University; WKYU, run by Western Kentucky University; and WGCU, run by Florida Gulf Coast University.[222]

The need for good governance extends, of course, beyond stations licensed to universities.[223] According to Terry Clifford, co-chief executive of Station Resources Group, "Good governance is a combination of…strong leadership at the top, vision, mission, strategy, a financial model that supports that core mission, and a sense of responsibility, accountability, and transparency to the community."[224] Some "advisory boards" are merely ceremonial. "They come together and talk about things they care about relative to programming content—and then they leave," Clifford says, contrasting this to "governing boards," which have the power to hire and fire, "decide how much financial risk they can take, open doors, raise money, approve, and contribute to strategy."

At least one public broadcast organization, American Public Media, has recommended that, "as a condition of holding an FCC broadcast license, all noncommercial stations or networks that have a combined population under signal of more than 500,000 people be required to have a Direct or Independent Board of Directors."[225] While not disagreeing with the principle that direct governance could improve station functions, another public broadcaster notes that power over a station will always be wielded by the entity that holds the license.[226]

Diversity

Serving diverse audiences is a core mission of public broadcasting. CPB currently provides financial programming support to at least 75 stations that are minority owned.[227] CPB also funds the National Minority Consortia, which consist of the Center for Asian American Media, National Black Programming Consortium, Native American Public Telecommunications, Native Public Media, Pacific Islanders in Communications, and Latino Public Broadcasting.[228] The Consortia fund, produce, and distribute radio and television programming about their ethnic communities, and they "award grants for program production, training, exhibition, and outreach activities."[229]

Nevertheless, public television and radio have faced sharp criticism for failing to provide programming that more accurately reflects the populations of the communities their stations serve.[230] Station Resource Group's Grow the Audience project reports that many people of color do not believe that current public radio content adequately addresses their daily concerns. African-Americans are about 80 percent, and Hispanics only 42 percent, as likely to listen to public radio as the population as a whole.[231] Only 5 percent of NPR's audience is African-American (compared with 12.2 percent of African-Americans in the overall U.S. population).[232] The latest 2010 data shows that NPR listeners are, on average, older, more affluent, more likely to be male, and more likely to describe themselves as "middle of the road" politically—though those who describe themselves as liberal are slightly more liberal than the general U.S. population.[233]

PBS, on the other hand, reports that its audience demographics increasingly align with the U.S. population. It says that the nearly 115 million people who watch their local PBS stations reflect "the overall U.S. population with respect to race/ethnicity, education and income."[234] Specifically, as of 2008, 11.8 percent of its audience was African-American (compared to 12.1 percent in the overall population). Similarly, 10.9 percent of its audience identified as Hispanic (compared to 10.8 percent in U.S).[235] The demographics of PBS's online audience are also quite diverse. Both PBS.org and PBSKids.org report that African-Americans, Asians, and Hispanics make up a larger share of their audiences than of the general population.[236] Excluding PBSKids.org visitors, the average visitor to PBS.org is 35 years old, 10 years younger than the national average.[237]

Public broadcasting stations have struggled to employ sufficient numbers of minority staffers and managers. By 2010, the number of minority public broadcast news professionals overall was at 20 percent,[238] while the total minority population in the United States was approximately 28 percent.[239] In comments to the FCC, the National Federation of Community Broadcasters, which is an alliance of stations, producers, and others committed to community broadcasting, encouraged the Commission to collect race and gender data about public broadcasting governing boards to facilitate policies to promote diversity in broadcasting.[240] They also recommended that the Commission collect data about local news and cultural programming production by noncommercial radio stations and other outlets in order to better assess the connection between programming and the resources needed to support those efforts.[241] Commenters argued that understanding whether minority groups are being well served is consistent with the law creating public TV and radio, which included among its goals addressing "the needs of unserved and underserved audiences, particularly children and minorities."[242]

Measurement Gaps

Public broadcasting has always had trouble measuring its value. Commercial ratings do not work for public media companies because they are supposed to be providing an alternative to commercial fare—an alternative that does not

"Government's involvement tends to exacerbate public tensions in a way that makes civil discourse more difficult," says Randolph May of the conservative Free State Foundation.

168

necessarily draw large audiences. Public media entities emphasize factors such as the ability of programming to meaningfully engage citizens in civic and public life, but achievement of those goals are hard to quantify.[243] Ellen P. Goodman, a law professor at Rutgers-Camden and Distinguished Visiting Scholar at the FCC, summarizes the dilemma:

> "At the same time that public broadcasting is supposed to supplement the market, it is also expected to reflect existing audience preferences for particular kinds of media products—the very task at which the market excels. If public broadcasting invests too heavily in programming that is not widely consumed, some deem it irrelevant."[244]

Members of the public service media community hunger for a more appropriate analysis of the influence, engagement, reach, and effectiveness of public media activities.[245] Researchers at the American University Center for Social Media are working to develop common standards to assess social returns on media investments, much as has been done in the business world with "triple bottom line" standards for socially responsible businesses.[246] NPR, in an attempt to assess the real impact of its programming, has found that two out of three NPR listeners typically do further research after listening to a story and nearly 25 percent have become involved with a local or national political issue.[247] KETC in St. Louis has tried to define and measure the impact of its series *Facing the Mortgage Crisis* in terms of whether its work causes people to "take action" about a problem or discuss it with others.[248]

Better, or at least more widely shared, metrics for measuring the value of public service media would make it easier to demand certain performance levels.

Should "Public Broadcasting" Become "Public Media"?

As media have converged across multiple platforms, public broadcasting leaders have had to wrestle with what it means to be "public media" or "public service media" that makes use of a full range of platforms, as opposed to "public broadcasting," based on traditional TV or radio.

Of course, public broadcasters are increasingly reaching their audiences through non-broadcast means, especially Internet and mobile, and as they enter new production and distribution modalities, they find that they share the field with other nonprofits. There has been a proliferation of content creators that do not have public broadcasting licenses but closely resemble public broadcasters in mission and spirit. Yet they do not receive funds from CPB, which almost exclusively funds traditional broadcast licensees. For instance, there are an estimated 5,000 PEG stations (public, educational, and governmental access channels; see Chapter 7, Public Access Channels) that operate on a local level to provide highly localized content.[249] None of them gets CPB money. There are 23 states in which cable TV operators air state equivalents of C-SPAN (i.e., state public affairs networks or SPANs; see Chapter 8, C-SPAN and State Public Affairs Networks), covering state government activities[250]—but the National Association of Public Affairs Networks has identified only four such networks (in Alaska, Florida, Ohio, and South Carolina) that are affiliated with a public broadcaster[251] and none that directly receives CPB funding.[252]

Most important, the newly created nonprofit websites provide local news and journalism outside the boundaries of the traditional public broadcasting system. As noted in in Chapter 12, Nonprofit Websites, these websites are testing innovative approaches to local funding but have struggled mightily to develop sustainable business models.

Five of the top ten audio podcasts on iTunes were from public radio.

Some have suggested reconstituting the Corporation for Public Broadcasting (CPB) as the Corporation for Public Media or the Corporation for Public Service Media to reflect today's wider range of nonprofit content.[253] Former CPB board chairman Ernie Wilson argues that what should define "public service media" is not platform or funding model, but the "embrace [of] our evergreen mission of seeking out and providing information in the public interest."[254]

7 Public, Educational, and Governmental (PEG) Access Channels

IN DECEMBER 1968, DALE CITY, VIRGINIA, launched what would be America's first community access cable channel, DCTV.[1] Broadcasting for one hour every Tuesday night, the station aired such programs as *Ex Cons Tell It Like It Is*, in which inmates of the nearby prison were interviewed; *The Fire*, an interview with the local fire chief after a devastating fire; a Fourth of July parade and carnival; and local sporting events such as Little League baseball, Little League football, and a soapbox derby.[2]

Around the same time, George Stoney, considered the "father" of public access television, was in Canada, working on a program called *Challenge for Change*. He filmed low-income citizens talking about their lives and then showed the films to local communities and government officials to raise awareness.[3] Impressed by the quality and impact of this first effort, Stoney returned to New York, where he helped found the Alternate Media Center at New York University.[4] Funded by local cable companies and the National Endowment for the Arts, the center trained "public access interns" from around the country and then sent them back to establish local community media access centers in their own neighborhoods.[5]

As more cable companies began to seek local franchises to create infrastructure in a community, many local franchising authorities (LFAs)—most often local governments—began to require cable operators to set aside public, educational, and governmental (PEG) access channels.[6] Today, about 75 percent of franchises charge cable operators franchise fees, some of which may be allocated to support one or more of the three types of PEG operations at the LFA's discretion. A 1998 survey reported that only 18 percent of cable systems have public access channels; 15 percent have educational access channels; and 13 percent have governmental access channels.[7] There are thought to be as many as 5,000 PEG channels nationwide.[8] The Alliance for Community Media, which represents over 3,000 PEG access centers (some operating several channels) across the nation, estimates that at least 375,000 organizations use PEG services every year, and that local PEG programmers produce on average over 20 hours per week of local original programming, amounting to over 2.5 million hours a year.[9]

PEG services are unevenly distributed across the country. States in the Northeast, the Midwest, and on the West Coast tend to have more PEG activity than states in the South or the Rocky Mountain region.[10] MappingAccess.org, which compiles a list of PEG channels, lists none in Alabama or Mississippi.[11] Massachusetts has more PEG channels per capita than any other state.[12]

The scale of PEG access center operations varies widely, with some having multimillion-dollar budgets, but most having a paid staff of just one or two people.[13] With about a third of public access centers operating on budgets of less than $100,000 per year, many are staffed almost entirely by volunteers.[14]

Public access channels (the "P" in PEG) are usually controlled by nonprofit groups, which must first petition LFAs for a contract to manage one or more channels. They must meet certain competency and eligibility requirements. In many cases, the group not only runs the distribution channel itself, but also a community media or access center that trains local citizens in media production.[15]

If public broadcasting has historically focused on the delivery of information, nonprofit cable access channels have focused on providing a platform for public expression. In 1984, Congress spelled out its hope for the PEG system:

"Public access channels are often the video equivalent of the speaker's soap box or the electronic parallel to the printed leaflet. They provide groups and individuals who generally have not had access to the electronic media with the opportunity to become sources of information in the electronic marketplace of ideas. PEG channels also contribute to an informed citizenry by bringing local schools into the home, and by showing the public local government at work."[16]

Today, the question is whether PEGs can evolve to retain, or increase, their relevance in a digital world, in which many other "soap boxes" now exist online.

What PEG Channels Do

Although there has never been a comprehensive study of PEG channel performance, anecdotal evidence suggests that quality varies widely. At their best, PEG channels provide essential local programming not provided by other media.[17] "For many rural locales and suburban and exurban areas that are in the 'shadow' of larger metro areas where commercial and public broadcasters have little time and incentive to cover local events," says the Alliance for Community Media, "PEG access entities are the only electronic media."[18] For instance, CCTV in Salem, Oregon, is one of the only local broadcast television stations serving the state's capital city; other television stations, though licensed in Salem, tend to serve the larger media markets in Portland and Eugene.[19] CCTV has televised more than 2,200 local government meetings, 2,000 programs with local public schools and colleges, and 1,000 other programs with community groups. The station serves 150 groups in six languages through its 9,400-square-foot nonprofit information center.[20] In Pikeville, Kentucky, the local commercial TV stations are based more than 50 miles away in Hazard or across the border in West Virginia, so the public access channel, PikeTV, is the one that regularly covers high school sports and other community events.[21]

PEG channels reflect the special interests and character of each local community. For instance, a typical day's programming on the PEG channel in Franklin, Tennessee, includes *Army Newswatch*, *Today's AirForce*, *Sharing Miracles*, and Board of Mayor and Alderman meetings. In Palm Beach County, Florida, the lineup includes: *Naturescope*, *Everything Animal*, *Green Cay Wetlands*, *Positive Parenting Today*, and *Film Festival Review*. Other examples of PEG channels include:

> Mount Prospect Television in Mount Prospect, Illinois, provided disaster coverage and assistance when an 80-to-90-mile-per-hour wind tore through town in 2007.[22]

> Chicago Access Network television, on five PEG channels, offers coverage of town hall meetings and other community events, and has worked with health care organizations to disseminate basic education about AIDS prevention through live call-in programs.[23]

> In Minnesota, the Saint Paul Neighborhood Network (SPNN) offers eight programs for the growing Somali population in the area.[24]

> Cambridge Community Television (CCTV) in Cambridge, Massachusetts, has provided more than 22,000 hours of programming on three community cable channels, including *BeLive*—a weekly call-in program, featuring artists, poets, comedians, and neighborhood activists.[25]

> In Cincinnati, more than 80 churches use the Media Bridges community access center to reach out to those unable to leave their homes.[26]

> Across the country, multilingual channels provide programming in Greek, Czech, Hungarian, Albanian, German, French, Portuguese, Vietnamese, Chinese, Korean, Hmong, Farsi, Arabic, Hebrew, and Swahili.[27]

PEG advocates note that their media access centers do not just broadcast programs, but also serve as community centers, providing training and production services. For instance, the Grand Rapids Community Media Center (GRCMC) houses a full-power FM radio station, two PEG channels, an online citizen journalism platform, a vintage theater, and full-service information technology (IT) services—including web design, networking, database creation, and web hosting—to some one hundred nonprofit entities across the state and nation.[28] GRCMC's IT department built websites for the Reentry Resource Center to help those released from incarceration integrate back into the local community.[29] Through its Mobile Online Learning Lab for Information Education, GRCMC offers skilled trainers and digital video production equipment to schools and community organizations for special projects.[30] Other examples of PEG community centers include:

> In Cincinnati, Media Bridges[31] operates three public and one educational access channels, a low-power FM radio station (WVQC), and a community media facility. It offers space for classes (in graphic design, IT, web design, video and audio production) and meetings by such groups as the Genesis Men's Program, Women Writing for (a) Change, the Literacy Network, and the World Piano Competition.[32]

> The Boston Neighborhood Network's Beard Media Center offers "state-of-the-art connectivity and interactivity," two television studios, digital field production and editing equipment, a multimedia lab, a mobile production truck, and media training classes.[33]

> In Saint Paul, SPNN partnered with AmeriCorps to launch the Community Technology Empowerment Project, which teaches digital literacy skills, providing over 250,000 hours of community service to libraries, workforce centers, and media centers.[34]

> The Public Media Network in Kalamazoo, Michigan, offers "vocational courses in radio broadcasting and digital video production to high school students."[35]

> Lewisboro Community Television in New York State trains volunteers from local community organizations and, as almost all PEG centers do, allows them to borrow equipment.[36]

In general, a medium-sized PEG access center can train anywhere from 100 to 200 community video producers each year.[37]

Unfortunately, because there has been no comprehensive study of the quality or audience size of PEG channels, it is hard to tell whether these inspiring examples are the exception or the rule. The small budgets and first-come-first-serve ethos for programming have inevitably led to some dubious programming choices—fictionalized in the movie *Wayne's World*, depicting two slackers with a cable access show filmed from their basement.[38] An extreme real-life case occurred in 1989, when Kansas City attempted to shut down its public access station in order to bar the Ku Klux Klan from airing its program, *Race and Reason*.[39] Proponents assert that this kind of controversial programming largely ended in the 1990s, and even then comprised only one percent or less of all public access programming.[40]

Where PEG channels have weak reputations, it is sometimes because they spend many hours airing electronic bulletin boards with community information,[41] often in conjunction with a local radio station or a radio reading service for the visually impaired.[42] For instance, the public access station in Bellhaven, North Carolina, runs its bulletin board most hours of most days, going live only for special events on Halloween, Christmas, and the Fourth of July.[43] PEG supporters argue that such electronic bulletin boards provide an essential community service, informing residents of school closings, health screenings, job postings, and government meeting schedules, but there are no solid audience numbers.[44]

Factors Affecting Quality

At their best, PEG channels and community media centers help a community develop its ability to communicate. PEG channels can approximate a kind of hyperlocal blogging with higher production values, cable distribution, and community connections. The community access centers can provide media production and literacy training, increasing the ability of community members to communicate effectively. In a recent poll conducted for PEG proponents, 74 percent of respondents said local community programming is important and nearly 60 percent think that one dollar or more of their "monthly cable bill[s]" should be "set aside and used" to create this programming.[45]

At their worst, however, PEG channels provide an unnecessary platform for self-expression, as it is now available in abundance on the Internet, and thus take up cable capacity and funding that could be used for more valuable or worthwhile programming.

What distinguishes the high-quality PEGs from the rest? PEG advocates often say the key is "money." And they have a point. Cable operators pay fees to local franchising authorities for the use of public right-of-way facilities.

These franchise fees can generate huge sums for municipalities—for instance, as much as $142 million for Dallas in 2007 and $140 million for New York in fiscal year 2010.[46] While in the past, a substantial portion of these fees were used to support PEG channels and other public communications needs, the law does not require that any of the money go to PEG channels[47]—and today, very little does.[48]

In California, new laws that allow cable operators to drop certain public access obligations altogether have eliminated $590,000 in PEG support.[49] In San Francisco, only about 8 percent of the roughly $10 million to $12 million cable operators pay in franchise fees goes to public access each year.[50] After the city of Dallas took over PEG funding from the cable provider in 2000, it reduced PEG allocations from $700,000 in 2001 to $246,000 in 2008, and in 2009 it eliminated all funding.[51]

The financial situation is getting worse. A variety of FCC rulings and state and local law changes—described in greater detail in in Chapter 27, Cable Television—have left many PEG stations in dire straits.[52] Many states have adopted "state franchising," in which the state determines franchise fees and other cable obligations and dictates how franchise fees are spent (often after allowing local authorities to weigh in). In a survey of 165 PEG centers, half said that their funding dropped between 2005 and 2010, and among those reporting a decline, the average loss was 40 percent. The survey stated that 100 community media centers had to shut down during that period.[53] The American Community Television Association estimates that by 2012, over 400 PEG channels could be lost across six states—including Wisconsin, Florida, Missouri, Iowa, Georgia, and Ohio.[54] In 2006, California adopted a law allowing cable operators to drop long-standing obligations to provide free studios, equipment, and training to the public, which led to the closure of at least 12 public access studios in Los Angeles alone.[55] At least 45 PEG access centers have shut down around California because of cable company responses to the change in the state law.[56] Kansas, South Carolina, Missouri, and Nevada do not require new cable operators to provide any PEG support.[57]

PEG leaders also say that cable operators are treating PEG channels progressively worse as the environment becomes more competitive. AT&T has placed all PEG outlets on a single channel—

> In Cincinnati, more than 80 churches use the Media Bridges community access center to reach out to those unable to leave their homes.

channel 99.[58] A drop-down menu allows viewers to select their community, and then a second drop-down menu allows them to select channels within that community. AT&T argues that "U-verse TV is based on an all-IP architecture totally unlike that of traditional cable operators" and that the "[m]ethod of delivering PEG should not be frozen in time."[59] American Community Television, Inc. observes that Charter Cable has moved PEG channels to the 900 range, "off the basic tier of service and into the digital stratosphere."[60] Some cable operators are moving their PEG channels from analog to digital tiers, but not all cable subscribers have the equipment necessary to view the digital channels.[61]

Reduced funding and terms of cable carriage are not PEG channels' only problem. Media funders and others in local journalism report that PEG operations are difficult to support and to partner with, in part because they often lack stable leadership and staffing. They are largely volunteer-run, in keeping with the spirit of public access and also out of financial necessity. Yet, as volunteers come and go, it is hard for PEG centers to sustain programs, engage in long-term planning, and bring good ideas to fruition.[62]

Some suggest that PEG channels are too bound to their studios and don't source programming from a large enough pool of contributor throughout the community. PEG operators have bristled at new laws that require them to air a minimum number of hours of non-repeat programming per week.[63] However, they might have an easier time complying with these requirements if they expanded the types of content they used, offering sporting events, flip-cam videos, and commentary or other shows produced in the field.

In addition, PEG operators could improve quality, and impress state lawmakers, by collaborating with other nonprofit entities. As a report from the Benton Foundation noted, "Perhaps the most promising trend on the horizon for community media is the emergence of new highly integrated organization structures and collaborative processes."[64] Enlightened PEG leaders realize that their industry has to innovate to remain relevant, especially given the competition for cable channels and the ability the Internet provides for anyone to speak their mind. As Media Bridges in Cincinnati noted in its comments to the FCC, "PEG channels have evolved over time to retain their effectiveness and must continue to evolve to ensure effectiveness in the digital future."[65]

Tom Glaisyer of the New America Foundation and Jessica Clark of American University's School of Communication summarized the areas where PEG channels can have the most positive impact:

> *"Digital and civic literacy training:* Community media organizations can help to foster civic engagement and broadband adoption among underserved populations, and to serve as hubs for access to not only broadcast, but broadband and wireless.

> *"Vocational training:* PEG access TV stations and community media centers have traditionally provided youth and adults with access to vital job training skills and other educational opportunities that may not be available to them anywhere else in the community. In this way, they are often closely aligned to the services provided by public libraries and other trusted community anchors.

> *"Government transparency:* Community media organizations can foster oversight, broadcasting gavel-to-gavel coverage or hold politicians to account via interviews.

> *"Making local and national connections:* The organizations in which community media is created have to operate with a collaborative, boundary spanning approach. Community media are important in the development of digital literacy training, citizen journalism, hyperlocal civic agency, and collaboration with local communities and nonprofits. There is currently some collaboration happening between public and community media; more should be encouraged.

> *"Providing open access to communications infrastructure:* Historically this has been achieved through PEG channels, though equally important opportunities exist around radio and other community anchor institutions."[66]

Based on interviews with PEG organizations and small-market PEG operators across the country,[67] and a survey of existing research,[68] it appears that, in addition to sufficient funding, the common features of high-performing PEG operations include:

> a board that reflects the community and internalizes the purpose, importance, and openness of PEG

> sound management practices that ensure adequate bookkeeping and accountability, reasonable openness to the public, and the ceding of editorial control to producers

> the embrace of new technologies that allow PEG production capabilities to be distributed throughout the community, using wireless connectivity, handheld cameras, digital networks, and mobile studios

> access to community fiber networks and high-speed connections to other public institutions

> community support through membership and other means

> partnerships with other nonprofits and public media that can produce high-quality content

PEG, Local News, Information, and Journalism

Intriguingly, some recent PEG endeavors aim to help fill gaps in local journalism. The Grand Rapids Community Media Center started an online newspaper, *The Rapidian*, a citizen journalism project "intended to increase the flow of local news and information in the Grand Rapids community and its neighborhoods."[69] It has 180 community-based reporters and 60 to 70 nonprofit contributors.[70] Stories from *The Rapidian* have been heard on Michigan radio and picked up by the *Grand Rapids Press.*

One of the most promising templates for the future of public access centers seems to be emerging in the San Francisco Bay Area. In September 2009, the Bay Area Video Coalition (BAVC)—a long-standing community media center—took control of San Francisco's public access television station,[71] and is now working with municipal and noncommercial entities to produce a neighborhood news network, called "n3," which will link PEG channels to 15 community sites throughout the city using an existing fiber network. Like *The Rapidian*, n3 is designed to be a bottom-up network, providing residents with the skills and equipment necessary to share "relevant, timely, and hyperlocal news and information with each other." Each n3 program will be broadcast on BAVC's cable channels, reaching up to 200,000 San Francisco households, and also made available online as a "channel" on BAVC's local video website.[72] These sites can then be used to broadcast live and pre-recorded community events and programs from cultural centers and schools around San Francisco.

Other local entities are enlisting PEG channels to help with local journalism. The Saint Paul Neighborhood Network in Minnesota has partnered with independent newspapers to produce public affairs content. It has also joined forces with an independent African-American newspaper, *Insight News*, to produce 20 hours of public affairs programming on important issues in the Minnesota African-American community.[73] The Boston Neighborhood Network produces a nightly *Neighborhood Network News* program with a three-person staff and assistance from Boston University students.[74] And the Manhattan Neighborhood Network, the oldest PEG operation, is planning to launch a "mini-C-SPAN" to cover city elections and public affairs.[75]

While the Internet has somewhat reduced the importance of PEG channels as a platform for expression, it is important to remember that as long as there is not universal broadband, digital distribution will not match the reach of PEG. At the same time, the digital revolution may increase the importance of the educational function PEG can serve.

Doing journalism was never really a primary goal of the PEG system, but in the new media climate it is not inconceivable to imagine that these groups could play a role, in cooperation with other entities and with improved management. After all, public access channels have been doing "citizen journalism" since before the Internet was born.[76]

Government Channels

The "G" in PEG refers to government channels, which broadcast government or public meetings.[77] According to one report, government access television is available in approximately 2,800 communities in at least 19 states.[78]

Government access channels have been broadening their content in recent years. Many now offer field coverage of public policy forums, third-party-sponsored policy events, and a range of public affairs programming, including call-in programs, issue discussions, interviews, neighborhood news, and news-in-review programs.[79] For example, the Seattle government's Seattle Channel, founded in 2002, offers cultural programs that explore the local art scene, showcase films from the Seattle Municipal Archive, and display the charms of Seattle's "sister cities" around the world.[80]

Government operators often act as content editors and gatekeepers, creating their own programming and selecting externally produced programming to air.[81] These channels tend to play it safe. According to one commentator, they broadcast little more than "safety tips from government departments such as police, fire, and transportation,"

In Pikesville, Kentucky, it is the public access station that regularly covers high school sports and other community events.

to avoid charges of political bias.[82] Even so, government channels are susceptible to charges of propaganda.[83] A reporter in St. Petersburg, Florida, has accused the local government access channel of "trying to influence public opinion" with respect to the state budget.[84]

Other government access channels are administered by independent, nonpartisan organizations, usually led by political appointees. The use of an intermediary administrative body helps to shield the channel from political influence, and channels that are administered in this way tend to be more likely to provide diverse and inquisitive coverage, according to writer J.H. Snider.[85]

Whatever their management structure, most government access channels are supported by public funds.[86] This leads to two contradictory criticisms: 1) governmental bodies that control PEG funding have an economic incentive to underfund government access channels in order to decrease political accountability;[87] and 2) government may overfund government access channels at the expense of public access channels.[88] Critics have called for the creation of an equitable funding mechanism that would guarantee a proportion of funding to public access and ensure that "government speakers won't displace the public."[89]

The City of San Francisco came up with a potentially promising solution when it awarded a public access channel contract to an operator that is working to preserve public access services in the city. Under this contract, the operator, the Bay Area Video Coalition (BAVC), receives only 20 percent of what the previous operator received in annual operations funding, but can obtain up to three times more capital funding for equipment and facilities that are distributed throughout the city.[90]

8 C-Span and State Public Affairs Networks

IN 1979, BRIAN LAMB, then *Cablevision Magazine*'s Washington, D.C., bureau chief, pitched an idea to a cable conference about a nonprofit network that would provide gavel-to-gavel coverage of the House of Representatives. No talking heads, no analysis, just the speakers on the floor, and the chance for voters to decide for themselves. One early cable pioneer, Bob Rosencrans, liked the idea and wrote a $25,000 check.

The cable television industry launched C-SPAN (the "Cable-Satellite Public Affairs Network") in 1979 as a private, nonprofit organization.[1] The industry's financial support for C-SPAN has always been voluntary.[2] It currently awards C-SPAN fees of about 10 cents per subscriber. These subscriber fees make it possible for the network to avoid dependence on government funding, which might compromise its objectivity or reputation for fairness.[3] In 1980, C-SPAN covered its first presidential election and pioneered the nationwide viewer call-in program. By 1982, C-SPAN's schedule had expanded to 24 hours a day, seven days a week. Today, the network has a staff of 275, and its round-the-clock programming is available to 86 million TV households via nearly 7,900 cable systems.

In addition to live coverage of House and Senate proceedings and local and general elections, the three C-SPAN channels air government hearings, full candidate speeches and debates, press conferences, space shuttle launches, conferences, and series such as *Road to the White House, Booknotes, Washington Journal,* and *American Presidents.* A 2009 survey found that 21 percent of cable TV households, an estimated 39 million Americans, watch C-SPAN "sometimes" or "regularly."[4] Another survey showed that C-SPAN's audience is politically active, nearly equally liberal and conservative, and geographically diverse. Ninety percent of its viewers say they voted in 2008.[5]

The channel has earned a reputation for fairness and neutrality. In granting Brian Lamb one of its highest awards, the American Historical Association declared, "Many Americans—including a fair share of the American Historical Association's membership—rightfully value C-SPAN as an achievement of historic significance."[6]

As newspapers have pulled back on statehouse coverage, it is arguably more important than ever that the basic proceedings of state government be televised, just as the U.S. Congress is on C-SPAN. Currently, state public affairs networks (SPANs) air on cable TV systems in 23 states and the District of Columbia, delivering gavel-to-gavel coverage of state legislative, executive, judicial, and agency proceedings, as well as public policy events, supplemented with a wide variety of produced public affairs programming.[7] Furthermore, the National Conference on State Legislatures has found that live webcasts (audio, video, or both) of legislative proceedings are available from at least one chamber (House, Senate, or both) in all 50 states, the District of Columbia, Puerto Rico, and the Virgin Islands.[8] Although many of these webcasts are available to the public via broadcast or online links, in 29 states or territories they are not carried on cable.[9] To date, satellite providers have not carried SPANs in any state except Alaska.[10]

In several states, SPANs have played a key role in providing statehouse and other political coverage. For example:

> During the lead-up to the 2010 elections, Connecticut's public affairs network, CT-N, aired 96 hours of debates, which included 10 gubernatorial debates, eight between U.S. Senate candidates, and others between candidates for attorney general, secretary of state, and comptroller.[11] In 2003, CT-N chronicled the governor's entire impeachment investigation, from the legislature's Select Committee of Inquiry to the state Supreme Court.[12] In 2005, when the Federal Base Realignment and Closure Commission sought to close Connecticut's New London Submarine Base, CT-N provided detailed coverage of public strategy sessions held by Governor Rell, the Connecticut Congressional Delegation, and other state leaders aimed at building a case for saving the base and the tens of thousands of Connecticut jobs that came with it.[13]

> WisconsinEye's 2010 election coverage included 300 programs about the elections, including interviews with more than 100 of the candidates for state legislature.[14] During the 2009 state budget-making process, Wisconsin citizens had access to a verbatim record of the entire public process from WisconsinEye, including all legislative floor activity and all meetings of the Joint Committee on Finance, both in the Capitol and in a series of public field hearings the joint committee held statewide.[15]

> TVW in Washington State was nominated for a regional Emmy Award for a series of programs that spotlighted high school and middle school students involved in the public policy process.[16] As the *Seattle Times* noted, "Once expected to be the haven for policy wonks and insomniacs, TVW has emerged as a versatile forum for Washington citizens' participation and monitoring of state government and other institutions," allowing citizens to follow state proceedings on TV, streaming video, and podcasts.[17] In the 2010 elections, TVW aired 15 debates, 10 of which were for congressional seats and were not covered by local broadcasters. It provided particular focus on the state's 11 ballot initiatives—and even created a video voters guide about the substance of these initiatives.[18]

> Pennsylvania Cable Network (PCN) covered the 2010 elections by airing 20 gubernatorial debates, eight of which involved closely contested races. In the course of the year, PCN covered a grand total of 47 election-related events, only three of which ran on local broadcast stations.[19]

"We're a non-biased and unedited-surveillance form of journalism," says Chris Long of WisconsinEye. Newspapers, TV stations, and websites "don't have enough reporters to look around the corner. Increasingly, we're the eyes and ears of the people, in state Capitals."[20]

As noted earlier, national C-SPAN was set up as an independent nonprofit, financed by the cable industry itself, in part because Brian Lamb and other creators of C-SPAN believed it was important that the service not be government funded, lest its independence and objectivity be compromised. "I'm a huge believer that I don't want government anywhere near me," says Lamb.[21]

> "Many Americans...rightfully value C-SPAN as an achievement of historic significance."

In contrast, cable operators have provided significant financing to state SPANs in only four states: California, Michigan, Wisconsin, and Pennsylvania.[22] In 12 states, SPANs are funded by the state government.[23] Washington State's TVW, which reaches only 60 percent of the state via cable, receives 85 percent of its operating funds from state appropriations, and only 15 percent from private interests. In addition, private interests have donated space to the channel, valued at an estimated $9 million.[24]

The median annual operations budget among SPANs is $953,000, although more established SPANs (e.g., in Pennsylvania) may have up to $4.5 million in operating expenses.[25] Each SPAN has its own operational and budgetary structure.

> Founded in 1979, PCN broadcasts statewide 24/7 on cable as well as on Verizon's FiOS service and the Internet. It has 36 full-time employees and an annual operating budget of $4.5 million derived primarily from fees paid by the cable operator.[26] The network gets no funding from the state government; it receives "84 percent of its revenues from cable subscriber fees, and the remainder comes from a variety of sources including corporate underwriting, DVD sales, and paid programming."[27]

> CT-N, founded in 1999, is available statewide 24/7 on expanded basic cable, AT&T U-verse, and the Internet. It provides gavel-to-gavel coverage of the three branches of state government, in addition to other public policy programming, with an approximate staff of 25 and an annual operating budget of $2.2 million provided by the state legislature.[28] CT-N is technically owned by the Connecticut General Assembly, but is managed as a 501(c)(3) nonprofit organization and receives nearly 100 percent of its operational and capital funding through a revenue-intercept from the gross receipts tax assessed on cable and satellite television subscribers.[29]

> Michigan Government Television (MGTV), launched in 1996, is a part-time network, broadcasting 20 hours of state government and other public affairs programming weekly, with six full-time employees and $900,000

in annual operating expenses funded by the state's cable industry.[30] The cable operators carrying these 20 hours of MGTV programming fill the remainder of their schedules with programming of their choice, including infomercials and public access programs.[31]

> The Ohio Channel, a 24/7 service operating since 1996, is offered over-the-air, as a channel multicast by Ohio public television stations, and on some cable systems. It is also carried on some cable television PEG channels and has a robust website with streaming and video on demand. The Ohio Channel airs state legislature sessions, Supreme Court of Ohio cases, and events that take place at the State Capitol.[32] The contracts with the state that fund this programming are administered by a public television station in Cleveland, with additional programming on the channel provided by Ohio's other public broadcasting stations.[33] Although CPB does not directly fund the Ohio Channel, it provides indirect support in the form of grants to the public TV stations that carry the Ohio Channel.[34]

> WisconsinEye, a 24/7 statewide public affairs network, is wholly privately financed. It is a 501(c)(3) organization[35] that receives neither direct nor indirect funding from the state.[36] Although it is carried on Charter Cable's system, Time Warner Cable's refusal to enter into a long-term carriage agreement with the channel has prevented it from serving the Green Bay and Greater Milwaukee markets; as a result, its distribution revenue for 2010 was approximately half of what it expected.[37] Four-fifths of its million-dollar operating revenue currently comes from donations and other sources, including programming sponsorships, DVD sales and other paid services.[38]

> Alaska's public affairs network, 360 North, was launched in 1995 and has grown to become a 24/7 channel, multicast on three public TV stations as well as by the state's largest cable operator and by both direct broadcast satellite companies.[39] The network is operated by the public television station in the state capital and funded by a grant from the City of Juneau and by private companies and organizations.[40]

Christopher Long, president and CEO of WisconsinEye, says that "a pure-private financing model, and organizational separation between governance and operations, is the surest way to establish editorial independence of SPANs from state government. For example, independent SPANs are best situated to provide unfettered coverage of state election campaigns, and in particular, of the platforms of those challenging incumbents, without facing pressure from those incumbents in the state government."[41]

Brian Lockman, president and CEO of PCN, says that PCN was well positioned to cover all aspects of Pennsylvania's pay raise controversy in 2005:[42] "[PCN's] funding model gave [it] the editorial independence to cover the issues in a balanced fashion as opposed to just from the legislators' point of view."[43] PCN is funded wholly by cable interests and receives no funding from the state. However, Paul Giguere, president of the National Association of Public Access Networks (NAPAN) and CEO of the CT-N, has said that he knows of no instances in which coverage has been compromised by state funding in Connecticut.[44] Giguere further explains that:

"In states where SPANs have been operational for some time, legislatures have found the experience to be positive. There is frequently hesitation at the outset, rooted in the concern that such a network could be made into a political tool by the majority party. However, in states where networks with independent and nonpartisan operating models (like CT-N) have launched and had the opportunity to prove themselves, those concerns quickly dissipate."[45]

The success of these independent SPANs[46] raises an obvious question: why do more states *not* have such independent SPANs?

Lack of Support from Cable Operators

SPAN channels are not "must-carry" channels. In order to get statewide coverage, they must forge carriage agreements with each and every local operator in the state.[47] Typically, there is not a statewide entity with whom a network can contract for carriage throughout the state. Giguere describes the difficulty CT-N had obtaining carriage:

"In 1998, prior to CT-N's launch, the position of the Connecticut cable television industry…was that the MSOs [cable multiple system operators] were all channel locked, with no capacity to spare for carriage of CT-N. Also, we were told that since CT-N was not defined as a must-carry, there was no compelling reason to provide us with free bandwidth to carry the channel. By

2005, the importance of the project both to the Connecticut General Assembly and Connecticut consumers was clear enough that MSOs in our state were ultimately willing to provide 24/7 channel capacity for CT-N on their expanded basic tier. But it took seven years of pushing the issue to get there. We would hope that since the case is now made for carrying a state public affairs network, it shouldn't have to be re-made elsewhere, state-by-state."[48]

SPANs, unlike public broadcasters, are allowed to receive payment for carriage of their programming, which offers one potential revenue stream. But only in four states do local cable operators follow the model set by the national cable operators with respect to C-SPAN, providing a portion of subscription fees to support SPAN operations.[49]

Lack of Support from Satellite Providers

Section 335(b) of the Communications Act,[50] as implemented in section 25.701(f) of the Commission's Rules,[51] requires direct broadcast satellite (DBS) providers to set aside 4 percent of their channel capacity for use by qualified programmers for noncommercial programming of an educational or informational nature.[52] The nature of satellite technology leads the service to emphasize national programming. Though satellites carry local programming, there are technological and cost limitations to the amount of local or regional programming that can be carried.

To date, only one SPAN, Alaska's, is carried on satellite, and none receives funding from satellite providers. Giguere has described the difficulties in obtaining carriage via satellite:

> "The direct broadcast satellite providers would not even return our phone calls for many years and were not willing to negotiate carriage whatsoever until the Connecticut General Assembly began exerting pressure about the carriage of CT-N three years ago. Even though a bill was passed out of a legislative committee mandating carriage of CT-N on satellite, the industry maintained…[that it is] not subject to state jurisdiction and would offer us no consideration beyond the [federal set-aside requirement]. We have participated in that application process with no success to date, but the expense involved and the likelihood that a network designed to serve a single state would be selected for nationwide channel capacity makes this an untenable solution for one public affairs network, let alone 50 of them."[53]

Paying for carriage on satellite can cost as much as $10,000 per month or $120,000 per year, a figure that SPANs find prohibitive given their small budgets.[54] Because it would be difficult to replicate a C-SPAN-type model today, most SPANs agree that some form of carriage assistance from satellite and telcos is needed if the system is to flourish.[55] Satellite carriage of all or even many SPANs is, to be sure, a heavy lift, because satellite is principally a platform for national distribution. However, as discussed below, satellite operators do carry many local broadcast signals in every market.

Lack of Support from the Corporation for Public Broadcasting

Although a few public TV stations have made deals directly with individual SPANs, the Corporation for Public Broadcasting (CPB) does not currently provide direct funding to SPANs, nor does it have the budget to do so. As noted above, in 12 states, the state government provides funding to support the local SPANs, but with budgets tightening there has been little interest from lawmakers in adding a new budget line for SPANs. Furthermore, some SPAN advocates dislike the notion of state funding because of its potential to undercut broadcast independence.[56]

At a time when in-depth state news coverage by newspaper and local TV is declining, expanded state public affairs networks can play a highly important role. According to Giguere:

> "In an era of declining news coverage of state government, it is more important than ever that all citizens have direct access to this type of primary source 'surveillance journalism.' The benefit of a better educated electorate is, not to overstate, a healthier democracy.… State governments are where increasing amounts of public policy are set, and the arenas where much of the battles between the federal government and the states are fought, and we allow the current transparency vacuum to exist in states where these initiatives have been unable to flourish at our collective peril as a nation."[57]

9 Satellite

WHEN DIRECT BROADCAST SATELLITE (DBS) transmission became commercially available in the early 1990s, policy-makers wrestled with what role noncommercial programming might play. Satellite providers were using scarce spectrum, so policymakers decided that, like broadcast and cable providers, they should be required to make some airtime available for "noncommercial programming of an educational or informational nature."[1] (Full regulatory history in Chapter 28, Satellite Television and Radio.)

Congress gave the FCC the power to set aside from 4 to 7 percent of capacity for public interest programming, and in 1998 the FCC opted to set aside just 4 percent.[2]

To qualify for carriage on this reserved capacity, programmers must be a noncommercial entity offering non-commercial programming of an educational or informational nature. And most must be willing and able to pick up half the costs incurred by the DBS operator in making the programming available.[3] The two major DBS providers in the U.S., DirecTV and DISH Network list the noncommercial programming offered over the DBS set-aside channels in their public files. DirecTV has reserved 23 channels based on its 2009 capacity calculations, and DISH Network has reserved 40 channels for noncommercial programming offered over the DBS set-aside channels.[4] The difference in channel numbers is due to the architecture of the networks.

> Congress gave the FCC the power to set aside four to seven percent of capacity for public interest programming. The FCC chose to set aside four percent.

Congress designed the noncommercial satellite set-aside requirement to mimic the obligation of cable to provide PEG channels. But because of technological and market differences between satellite and cable, the PEG and the satellite set-aside requirements were destined to function very differently. First, satellite technology—beaming to the entire country—meant that these set-aside channels would be national, not local.

Second, there was no provision for the satellite operators to subsidize the programmers. Indeed, the financial exchange goes the other way. The channels pay the satellite operator (albeit at reduced rates) for carriage. Of the public interest programmers awarded capacity on DISH Network, for example, only two have zero charges per month, while the remaining 19 each pay $10,371 per month. Similarly, for DirecTV, five public interest programmers have zero charges, the three newest programmers pay $6,756 per month, and the remaining 15 each pay $6,350 per month.[5]

DirecTV and DISH Network have a two-tier rate system for the set-aside channels. Most channels pay 50 percent of costs. In a limited number of cases (e.g., C-SPAN, NASA), the satellite providers carry channels at no charge, based on a determination that there is some "business value" in doing so.[6]

Many set-aside channels are religion-based. Of DirecTV's 23 set-aside channels, 11 are Christian and one is Jewish. Of DISH Network's 40 set-aside channels, six are Christian. The Christian channels air talk shows, call-in shows, and youth-oriented programming from a biblical perspective.[7]

Very few religion-oriented DBS public interest channels produce their own local news, but many air newscasts produced by the Christian Broadcasting Network, such as *The 700 Club* and *CBN Newswatch*. BYUtv produces a weekly program focused on the activities and interests of Brigham Young University (*BYU Weekly*), and EWTN produces *The World Over*, a weekly digest of interviews, investigative reports, and live coverage of special events and cultural news.[8]

Some set-aside channels are educational. ONCE TV México, a university-owned channel in Mexico City that describes itself as the oldest public television network in Latin America,[9] produces three daily news programs focused on Mexico, including *Everything*, a program for young people on politics, fashion, alternative arts and entertainment.[10] Other education-oriented channels include NASA TV, The Pentagon Channel, and The Health and Human Services Television Network, which offers health and emergency preparedness information.[11] Through its Florida Education

Channel, the Panhandle Education Consortium provides educational programming for K–12 students.[12] The Northern Arizona University House Channel does the same, and also offers accredited university courses.[13]

Other multicultural and Spanish-language channels include the Hispanic Information and Telecommunications Network (HITN) and V-me.[14] Geared toward the American Latino community, V-me airs news and current affairs programming (*V-me Noticias*), along with educational, how-to, and lifestyle programs; telenovelas, such as *Hay Alguien Ahi*; and a nightly talk show, *Viva Voz*.[15] CoLours TV is another multicultural channel, producing such news programs as *The Arabic Hour, Northwest Indian News*, and *The White House Report*.[16]

Finally, several channels are dedicated solely to news and information. C-SPAN is carried on both DirecTV and DISH Network. Free Speech TV airs documentaries and original productions, along with such popular news and current affairs programs as *Democracy Now, Al Jazeera English*, and *GRITtv with Laura Flanders*.[17] Other news channels aggregate news and information programs from a variety of international broadcasters. For instance, Link TV airs news and current affairs programs such as *Mosaic, Global Pulse*, and *Pulso Latino*, along with *Al Jazeera English World News*.[18] MHz Worldview on DirecTV similarly offers programming from such international broadcasters as Al Jazeera English, Beijing Television, Deutsche Welle, euronews, France 24, NHK World, and SABC News International.[19]

In general, both DISH Network and DirecTV group their public interest channels together in the channel lineup, and many programmers complain about their placement in the distant reaches of the program guide. For instance, on DISH Network, public interest channels can typically be found between channels 9400 (The Research Channel) and 9418 (Florida Educational Channel). There are notable exceptions, with C-SPAN occupying channel 210, NASA TV occupying channel 212, and Trinity Broadcasting Network occupying channel 260.[20] On DirecTV, most public interest programmers are similarly clustered between channels 348 (Free Speech TV) and 448 (Enlace Christian Television). As with DISH Network, there are exceptions, with NASA TV occupying channel 289 and MHz Worldview occupying channel 2183.[21]

The satellite providers decide which channels to carry and which to reject. In 2009, DISH Network rejected 10 out of 10 new applicants for set-aside channels on the grounds that it had insufficient capacity to carry them.[22] Among the stations rejected for lack of capacity since 2007 are numerous religious stations (including CatholicTV, God TV, and Almavision Hispanic Network), CT-N, The Documentary Channel, Classic Arts Showcase, Free Speech TV, New Abilities Television (a station for people with disabilities), TV Japan, CoLours TV, American Public Television, and California State University.[23] Although satellite providers offer little local programming, they do include stations that promote education, programming for minorities and the disabled, and channels providing international information.

Noncommercial channels carried on DBS complain of a lack of security due to the short-term nature of their contracts, which are either month-to-month or annual.[24] One programmer remarked that the "terms of DBS public interest carriage are difficult and tenuous."[25] Some in the nonprofit media world complain that the system is inhospitable to the provision of consistently good noncommercial programming. Pat Aufderheide and Jessica Clark of American University's Center for Social Media criticize the failure to fund programming. By not providing support for nonprofit programmers, and indeed by charging programmers for carriage, the set-aside system all but guarantees that the programming on these channels will be weak. The programming entities "have no funding for staff or content, have marginal audiences, depending either on the organizations that back them or on the kindness of strangers who donate in response to on-air pleas, to let them limp from year to year."[26]

Nonetheless, those noncommercial programmers that have gained satellite carriage through the set-aside requirement say it has given them real opportunities. Jose Luis Rodriguez, founder and CEO of HITN, says that his network fills "a critical gap" in the video landscape by providing needed educational and instructional programming to the Latino community.[27] The satellite industry points to examples like HITN to argue that the system "effectively serves the public interest."[28] Representatives of DISH Network and DirecTV say:

> Satellite operators argue that the program has been a success: "For more than 10 years, the DBS Providers diligently have recruited, evaluated, and selected qualified, noncommercial programmers for carriage on their systems."

"[F]or more than 10 years, the DBS Providers diligently have recruited, evaluated, and selected qualified, noncommercial programmers for carriage on their systems. In doing so, each DBS Provider annually evaluates applicants for its set-aside channels; assesses key measures such as program quality, signal quality, and genre; and strives to ensure a diverse, non-repetitive mix of educational and informational programming."[29]

There is very little data available regarding the audience size of the set-aside channels or their impact. Viewership is too low for Nielsen ratings, and DBS providers do not seem to collect audience information for these services.

Could satellite be playing a greater role in providing local programming, including news and information? Since the advent of local-into-local service (providing local TV station signals via satellite), DBS operators have offered packages of channels consisting of nationwide programming, as well as hundreds of local television broadcast channels. To the extent possible, the local channels are carried on "spot beams" that focus coverage on a particular region of the country. The use of spot beams, along with channel compression, creates capacity for the carriage of local channels. Indeed, DBS operators must carry the signals of *all* local broadcasters in any market that they choose to serve with *any* local signals.[30] At last count, DISH Network offered local-into-local service in more than 210 markets, and DirecTV offered such service in 175 markets.[31]

Jose Luis Rodriguez says the Hispanic Information and Telecommunications Network fills "a critical gap" in programming to the Latino community.

The allocation of channel capacity and spot-beam configuration for local programming is not especially dynamic, because operators must make this allocation in the satellite design, before the satellite is launched into space. As a result, changes in the relative capacity devoted to national and local programming take years to implement. Moreover, these changes must be synchronized to the cycle of satellite launches, which is typically once every year or two.[32]

Given the difficulties of planning for and then implementing satellite carriage of local signals, the FCC has in the past decided that requiring satellite providers to include more local or state programming would be too burdensome. (See Chapter 28, Satellite Television and Radio for full discussion.) This conclusion may well remain valid, though it is fair to periodically re-evaluate given that technology has changed and the industry matured.

As noted in Chapter 29, Satellite Television and Radio, a law was enacted in 2010 that allows satellite providers to reduce their public interest carriage obligations to 3.5 percent if they provide retransmission of SPANs in at least 15 states.[33] However, the organization representing these networks says the law will likely have no impact, because most satellite providers are already meeting their 4 percent set-aside requirement by carrying noncommercial educational stations—and they are unlikely to voluntarily substitute state SPANs for any of those because of the disruption it would cause.[34]

10 Low Power FM (LPFM)

IN JANUARY 2000, THE FCC CREATED the low-power FM category of radio station that reaches only a few miles with power of 100 watts or less. The FCC hoped that these new stations would draw "new voices on the airwaves and to allow local groups, including schools, churches, and other community-based organizations, to provide programming responsive to local community needs and interests."[1] There are already 860 low-power FM stations (LPFMs).[2] Many, if not most, of these stations are operated by volunteers.[3] These stations have the advantage of offering an inexpensive way for aspiring broadcasters to get a radio station.

Although we have no systematic data on LPFM performance, anecdotal evidence suggests that many LPFM stations can, and do, play an important role in reaching underserved communities.

In many cases, LPFM provides a key source of news and information for non-English-speaking communities.[4] In Oroville, California, KRBS-LP offers programs for its Latino, Hmong, Laotian, and other Southeast Asian communities.[5] Immokalee, Florida's WCIW-LP is part of a larger community center that offers one of the only public Internet access points for the community's migrant workers.[6] In addition, several LPFMs offer public affairs programs produced by and designed for senior citizens, a population segment with low digital access and adoption.[7]

In some cases, LPFMs emphasize religious programming. Prometheus Radio, the primary organization pushing community radio, describes WBFC in Boyton, Georgia: "When the station first went on the air, it received dozens of calls from listeners overjoyed to find Southern Gospel on their local airwaves. The station broadcasts three hours a day of Christian-oriented youth programming, as well as local Christian music provided by local churchgoers."[8] Some LPFM stations provide media and civic training. In Spokane, Washington, law students pair with local attorneys on *Radio Law* to inform listeners about locally relevant legal issues, such as regulation of toxins in the Spokane River and Washington's assisted-suicide laws.[9] KKDS-LP in Eureka, California, runs a Teen Platform program that provides hands-on training for area high school students.[10] Other stations train news reporters and program engineers. WSCA-LP in New England broadcasts more than 25 hours of locally produced arts, public affairs, and music per week, providing otherwise unavailable airplay to amateur local musicians.[11]

> LPFM advocates say stations are invaluable in times of crisis—as when they sent emergency messages for trapped victims of severe snowstorms in Colorado and alerted Florida migrant workers of an approaching hurricane in their native languages.

LPFMs sometimes partner with other news sites, media outlets, and community organizations to share volunteers and other resources across platforms. In the Urbana-Champaign area, for example, WRFU-LP operates a Community Media and Arts Center that trains volunteers to cover and distribute news across broadcast and digital platforms. KDRT-LP in Davis, California, partners with Davis Media Access to share content and programming with public access radio and television stations.[12]

Finally, the low wattage and strong local ties of LPFM stations make them particularly useful during emergencies. LPFM stations can be powered by small generators or car batteries, and since many households have battery-

When Hurricane Katrina hit local power lines, WQRZ–LP Station Manager Bryce Phillips in Mississippi swam to the station with a battery pack to continue broadcasting.

operated radio receivers, they are able to reach residents even when power lines and cell towers fail. LPFM advocates say that these traits have made them invaluable in times of crisis: They were used, for example, to send emergency messages to trapped victims during severe snowstorms in Colorado, to alert Florida migrant workers in their native languages of an approaching hurricane, and to provide critical information and reports for hurricane victims in East Texas who lost electricity for a week. In 2005, when Hurricane Katrina knocked out local power lines, WQRZ-LP station manager, Bryce Phillips, swam to the station with a battery pack to continue broadcasting emergency information for the Bay St. Louis, Mississippi, area. LPFM stations have been so effective during emergencies that in several cities, including Richmond, Virginia, and Davis, California, they serve as official emergency response outlets.[13]

For a variety of reasons, LPFM stations have been limited to rural areas. (See Chapter 26, Broadcast Radio and Television.) But the Local Community Radio Act, enacted in early 2011, is expected to significantly expand LPFM licensing opportunities in larger markets. The FCC is currently working on rules to implement the law and allow for the creation of hundreds of new LPFM stations.

11 Religious Broadcasting

ALTHOUGH DISCUSSION OF PUBLIC BROADCASTING rarely focuses on religious programming, religious broadcasters have a significant and valuable presence on the airwaves. Approximately 42 percent of noncommercial radio stations have a religious format, though that may understate the number since some religious broadcasters operate mixed format stations, which count in a different category).[1] Eighty percent of the 2,400 Christian radio stations and 100 full-power Christian TV stations are nonprofits.[2] As noted above, more than half of the channels set aside for educational programming by DirecTV go to religious stations and almost a third of DISH Network's educational set-aside capacity is used by religious stations.

According to FCC regulations, religious broadcasting entities are permitted to hold noncommercial educational (NCE) licenses if their station is "used primarily to serve the educational needs of the community" and "for the advancement of educational programs."[3] As with secular public radio programming, the FCC has traditionally let stations determine what constitutes educational programming.[4] In 1999, the FCC attempted to narrow the definitions, stating that "religious exhortation, proselytizing, or statements of personally-held religious views and beliefs" would generally not qualify as general educational programming.[5] Given that such a definition could be read to eliminate much religious programming, a firestorm of criticism arose, and the Commission returned to its earlier position, saying that it would not narrow eligibility for NCE licenses.[6]

Forty percent of Christian TV and radio programs are "news and information," according to the National Religious Broadcasters.

Forty percent of Christian TV and radio programs are categorized as "news and information," according to the National Religious Broadcasters association.[7] The Christian Broadcasting Network employs international and domestic journalists to create its professional-standard newscasts. The Total Living Network, viewed in more than 30 states, produces programs on current events and personal life issues, and won an Emmy for its original documentary, *Acts of Mercy*, "about the humanitarian work of mercy ships, which are floating hospitals, staffed by volunteer doctors who perform extreme plastic surgery for hideously deformed individuals in West Africa."[8]

Although most religious broadcasters do not focus on news in the traditional sense, many do offer public affairs programming tied to issues of concern for their audience. Generally speaking, it has been the popular national ministries that have had the resources for original programming, and their focus has been more on issues of national concern than local.

CPB rules prohibit the provision of federal Community Service Grants to noncommercial stations that "further the principles of…religious philosophies."[9] Religious broadcasters have not sought to have that changed, but have suggested that government restrictions on fundraising and sponsorships might leave noncommercial broadcasters to "languish."[10] (See Chapter 31, Nonprofit Media.) The FCC prohibits all noncommercial broadcasters from devoting time to fundraising for third parties[11] in an attempt to keep public TV from becoming too commercialized, but some claim this has limited religious broadcasters' ability to fundraise for religious charities. (See Chapter 31, Nonprofit Media for full discussions.)

The Total Living Network won an Emmy for its original documentary, Acts of Mercy, "about the humanitarian work of mercy ships, which are floating hospitals, staffed by volunteer doctors who perform extreme plastic surgery for hideously deformed individuals in West Africa."

12 Nonprofit News Websites

FROM THE EARLY DAYS OF THE INTERNET, nonprofits have played a critical role. Most of the researchers who invented the Internet were working for universities, under government contracts. Many parts of the web now operate on open source software, often created outside the commercial realm by volunteer programmers who share code freely to help build applications rather than to generate profit. Most people who blog do it as a personal avocation, not as a commercial enterprise. Massively popular online services that are set up as nonprofits include Wikipedia, WordPress, Mozilla, and BBC.co.uk.

Some significant national efforts to sustain journalism also have been set up as nonprofits. ProPublica was created by Paul Steiger, former managing editor of the *Wall Street Journal*, to finance labor-intensive investigative journalism. In its first years, the site won two Pulitzer Prizes, including one for a collaboration with the *New York Times* on the agonizing decisions made by medical personnel at Memorial Hospital in New Orleans as the flood waters rose during Hurricane Katrina. The Investigative News Network, a consortium of independent publications, was formed to promote and distribute enterprise reporting. The *St. Petersburg Times*, run by the Poynter Institute, launched PolitiFact.org, while the Annenberg Public Policy Center of the University of Pennsylvania launched FactCheck.org. These organizations joined several long-standing nonprofits that promote investigative and enterprise reporting, including the Sunlight Foundation, the Center for Public Integrity, and the Center for Investigative Reporting, which also runs California Watch. They have shown extraordinary commitment to labor-intensive and sometimes costly accountability efforts. For instance, California Watch ran a series about whether schools could withstand an earthquake—the sort of preventive journalism that could save many lives. It found 1,100 schools in need of repair. The series cost $550,000 to produce.[1]

> California Watch ran a series about whether schools could withstand an earthquake— the sort of preventive journalism that saves lives. They found 1,100 schools in need of repair. The series cost $550,000 to produce.

Nonprofit news organizations have sprung up to fill reporting gaps in a number of sectors, including health (Kaiser Health News), schools (Public School Notebook, The Hechinger Report, Education News Colorado), and foreign coverage (Pulitzer Center on Crisis Reporting and the International Reporting Project), among others. The John Locke Foundation, a libertarian/conservative think tank in North Carolina, publishes the *Carolina Journal* on state and local policy. Advance Publications, owners of Newhouse newspapers, recently decided to convert its for-profit Religion News Service into a non-profit, with support from the Lilly Endowment. In its new form, RNS hopes to support local religion reporting.[2]

Hundreds of nonprofit websites and blogs have arisen to provide local news. The creativity and spirit of these new efforts is inspiring. Michele McLellan, a fellow at the Missouri School of Journalism, who has done a comprehensive survey of local sites, estimates that just under half of the 66 most promising sites she studied were set up as nonprofits. An even higher percentage of the larger sites were set up as nonprofits.[3] McLellan identifies one group of websites as the "new traditionals," describing them as ventures that focus predominantly on original content produced by professional journalists.[4] Her list and descriptions (paraphrased) include these nonprofits:

> Chicago News Cooperative, founded by the former editor of the *Chicago Tribune*, focuses on public policy and politics in the Chicago metro area.

> CTMirror focuses on the Connecticut statehouse.

> Gotham Gazette, operated by New York's Citizens Union Foundation, uses interactive games to engage viewers in solving civic problems.

> The Lens, an initiative of the Center for Public Integrity, does investigative news and journalism about New Orleans and the Gulf Coast states.

> MinnPost, founded by refugees from struggling Minneapolis newspapers, hired a Washington correspondent to cover the Minnesota delegation, and offers multifaceted coverage of the state. Headlines include: "Twin Cities–Area Schools More Segregated Than Ever," "The Big Question for Economic Recovery: Which Stresses Are Merely Cyclical and Which Indicate a Cold, New Reality?," "New Stadiums Raise a Big Question: Is Minnesota's Sports Industry Sustainable?," and "The Coen Brothers Talk—Reluctantly—About Talking."[5]

> The New England Center for Investigative Reporting was founded by Boston journalists Joe Bergantino and Maggie Mulvihill. Based at Boston University's College of Communication, it uses student journalists to develop investigative projects.

> The New Haven Independent is a professionally staffed local news site in Connecticut, edited by Paul Bass and sponsored by the Online Journalism Project.

> NJ Spotlight in its first week online broke a story about how an affiliate of the state's gas company had failed to pay $47 million it owed the state.[6]

> The New Mexico Independent, with a small staff of five, covers news from around the state.

> The St. Louis Beacon was founded and is staffed by professional journalists. It is a member of the Public Insight Network, which solicits citizen perspectives and experiences to inform journalism.

> The Texas Tribune, with a staff of 25, has drawn attention to the overuse of passive restraints on disabled children and to the mismanagement of the workers compensation system. The site also offers databases of important and useful information, such as voting records, political contributions, and details of Texas's sprawling prison system.

> voiceofsandiego.org has done exposés on San Diego's social safety net, a major real estate swindle, and other civic issues.

> WyoFile provides public interest news about the state of Wyoming.

McLellan identifies a second group of "community news sites,"[7] which she says "often rely on professional journalists, but they tend to be bootstrappers who also focus on community building—actively seeking user feedback and content…and fostering civic engagement…."[8] Among those nonprofits she lists:

> Chicago Talks is run by Columbia College and gets most of its content from Columbia students who focus on local stories that other outlets are not covering, including Chicago's poorer neighborhoods.

> The Florida Independent, published by the American Independent News Network, covers news and politics in the state of Florida.

> Intersections: The South Los Angeles Report, publishes local news from a variety of contributors, including college students. It is supported by the USC Annenberg School for Communication & Journalism.

> NOWCastSA.com recruits community journalists to cover San Antonio, Texas.

> Oakland Local covers environment, food, development, identity, arts, and education and has been praised for its strategic use of social media to create community buzz.

> Open Media Boston reports local news with a small professional staff supplemented by citizen journalists.

> Twin Cities Daily Planet covers neighborhoods and communities, work, and economy, politics and policy, arts and lifestyle, and immigrants and immigration.

> VTDigger.org covers Vermont with "citizens contributing the news and journalists verifying it."[9]

Nonprofit organizations have assisted journalism in other ways. At Spot.us, a journalist with an idea posts a description of the proposed project, and individuals are invited to donate money through the website to help finance the reporting. The website ensures that "the reporter is not beholden to any individual donor" by "limit[ing] how much an individual can donate."[10] As of March 3, 2011, Spot.us had financed about 165 stories,[11] including some that were picked up by Wired.com, the *Epoch Times*, and the *Texas Observer*, among others.[12] The Sunlight Foundation has created both web and mobile apps to help track data in government. Its Congress Android App allows citizens and journalists to read up on their representatives, follow them in the news, and even engage them on Twitter.[13] Sunlight Foundation's Labs have also produced a number of ongoing government data projects, including the Fifty States Project for tracking state legislatures and the National Data Catalog for government data across all levels.[14] In some cases, local foundations and think tanks have actually created news operations devoted solely to covering state government. The John Locke Foundation in North Carolina created *Carolina Journal* to cover the statehouse and undertake non-partisan investigative journalism, in part because the number of reporters covering the statehouse had plummeted over the years. "In North Carolina, several TV stations had reporters. None has a bureau now. We were responding to changes in the market," says president and CEO John Hood. Although politically conservative, Hood is now skeptical that the commercial markets will fill the gaps in certain types of local accountability journalism: "When you get to the state and local level, the collapse of the traditional business models imperils the delivery of sufficient public interest journalism—and we do believe that donor driven journalism can be a very important model."[15]

Beyond these organizations, there are hundreds if not thousands of hyperlocal bloggers covering their blocks, neighborhoods, and communities that can be categorized as nonprofit sources of information, even though they may not have formally established themselves as either a business or a nonprofit.

Why the boom in nonprofit websites?

First, some of the social entrepreneurs who created these organizations believed that the types of journalism most lacking in the commercial sector—such as accountability journalism targeted at municipal government—were not likely to be re-invigorated by the commercial media. These were the so-called broccoli beats—important to the health of the body politic, but not necessarily the first thing people choose to read nor the most likely to make money for commercial media. Michael Stoll, executive director of the SF Public Press explains the rationale for his venture:

"There had been 25 reporters assigned to city hall from various different news organizations. Last year, there were five on a very good day who could be found in and around [the] city hall pressroom. At the same time, a lot of other topics such as entertainment, food, and travel have really maintained their levels of coverage, in part because those are the most lucrative areas and most tied into [the] advertising industry. The areas of core civics reporting, business reporting in terms of producers of consumer goods and retailers and [the] financial industry, people in those industries have a lot fewer eyes on them."[16]

Editor Margaret Wolf Freivogel at the St. Louis Beacon recalls:

"The number of reporters has shrunk dramatically. The [Beacon's] founders included several who worked at the *St. Louis Dispatch*. After we took buyouts, we said, 'Wait a minute, overall reporting capacity is shrinking.' That was the initial impulse. Just trying to increase [the] amount of reporting. We think of ourselves as [a] means for people to engage issues in community."[17]

Many of these websites were started with foundation support, particularly from the Knight Foundation, which has provided grants to 200 since 2006.[18]

Although many are small operations, a few have attracted significant donations. ProPublica drew $30 million, mostly from philanthropists Herb and Marion Sandler.[19] In 2010, MinnPost ran a surplus, in part because of an increase in advertising and sponsorship revenue. The revenue breakdown: $309,508 in sponsorship and advertising, $466,350 in foundation grants, $380,724 in individual and corporate donations, $101,466 in gross receipts from MinnRoast, and $20,742 in other revenue.[20] The success of MinnPost likely offers lessons to all nonprofit websites: survival requires the development of multiple revenue streams. By December 2010, the Bay Citizen had drawn more than $11 million,[21] five million of which was donated by Warren Hellman's family foundation as seed funding.[22] The

Although a free-market conservative, John Hood is skeptical that commercial markets will fill all gaps. "When you get to the state and local level, the collapse of the traditional business models imperils the delivery of sufficient public interest journalism—and we do believe that donor driven journalism can be a very important model."

Texas Tribune raised nearly four million dollars during its first year and has made significant progress in creating a sustainable model.[23]

A few websites have forged successful partnerships with traditional media companies, both commercial and nonprofit. As part of its application to the FCC for its merger with NBC, Comcast promised to create similar models in four other cities in which NBC owns and operates local TV stations. The Texas Tribune, the Chicago News Cooperative, and the Bay Citizen are providing content for the *New York Times*. Journalists from voiceofsandiego.org regularly appear on the local news station, NBC 7, to discuss local issues. This could be a promising model: the local TV station gets an infusion of high-quality local journalism and the web start-up gets invaluable exposure.

In some cases, nonprofit advocacy groups have decided to produce journalism. Both liberal groups (such as Human Rights Watch) and conservative groups (such as the Franklin Center for Government and Public Integrity) have financed reporting, especially on the state level. In many cases, the quality is excellent. But at the same time, some experts worry that the advocacy missions—advancing a particular cause—could sometimes conflict with the goal of providing the most accurate or fair-minded reporting.[24]

The proliferation of nonprofit local news websites—and the success of a handful of them—has led some to believe that the gap in journalism left by the contraction of newspapers will be filled quickly. But while there are some notable and exciting exceptions, nonprofit websites have not fully filled the gap. First, there is a problem of scale. The Poynter Institute estimated that cuts in traditional media constituted a $1.6 billion drop in journalism spending *per year*.[25] J-Lab has estimated that foundations put a little over $180 million into local nonprofit journalism outlets since 2005.[26] So foundations are not funding enough new journalism to replace what has been lost from traditional media.

A 2010 gathering of the leaders of 12 websites funded by the Knight Foundation featured perhaps the most innovative and sophisticated new players in the field. But together these organizations employ a mere 88 full-time journalists. That is a crucially important contribution but it is worth remembering that employment in newspaper newsrooms dropped by almost 15,000 in the last decade (with 13,000 leaving in just the last four years).[27]

A recent survey of 66 of the most exciting new online news start-ups delivered sobering news: half reported annual income of less than $50,000, and three-quarters had annual income of less than $100,000. Asked what percent of Knight Foundation journalism grantees could survive if (and when) their grants disappeared, Eric Newton of the Knight Foundation estimated 10 percent.[28]

The Knight Foundation's New Voices initiative, which funded 55 hyperlocal projects, found that sites were offering great content but that most relied on volunteer labor. Jan Shaffer, who studied the projects, observed, "There is a mismatch between instilling sustainable civic demand for local news information and developing sustainable economic models. While most of the New Voices sites are exploring hybrid models of support, none is raising enough money to pay full salaries and benefits."[29]

Most of the existing local news websites are not large enough to generate sufficient advertising revenue.[30] An analysis for the Future of Media project of Toledo, Richmond, and Seattle indicates that no nonprofit start-ups had broken into the top five (or even the top ten) in terms of traffic in those cities. (See Chapter 25, How Big is the Gap and Who Will Fill It?) For instance, in mid-December 2010, the St. Louis Beacon, praised for its quality, was attracting approximately 50,000 monthly unique visitors and generating 118,000 monthly page views.[31] By one measure, that is impressive—a larger audience than most community newspapers draw—but at an average Internet ad rate, that would generate less than $2,000 a month in revenue. Confusion also exists as to whether nonprofits can retain their nonprofit status if they accept advertising.[32] (See Chapter 31, Nonprofit Media for full discussion of this issue.)

In all, independent nonprofit websites are providing exciting journalistic innovation on the local level—and a handful have created sustainable business models—but most either are struggling to survive or are too small to fill the gaps left by newspapers.

13 Foundations

FOUNDATIONS HAVE TRADITIONALLY BEEN major funders of public TV and radio, both through direct support to stations and by financing individual shows. In 2009, foundations gave $203,868,960 to public broadcasting.[1]

A 2009 study conducted on behalf of Grantmakers in Film + Electronic Media (GFEM) determined that public and private grantmakers collectively contributed an estimated three billion dollars toward the support of media content, infrastructure, and policy in 2008.[2] But that includes grants to filmmakers, social-networking media, games with a social focus, and scholarly research and writing.[3]

The amount of foundation spending on local reporting and news has been growing in the last few years, though it still represents only a tiny percentage of foundation spending overall. As noted in Chapter 12, Nonprofit Websites, according to J-Lab, between January 2005 and February 2011, 272 foundations contributed more than $180 million[4] to U.S. news and information projects—less than 0.1 percent of total foundation spending.[5] And that figure includes many projects that focus on national, not local journalism.[6] "Some foundations fund only national reporting on subjects of particular interest to their donors or managers—such as health, religion, or government accountability," Michael Schudson and Len Downie Jr. concluded in a report for the Columbia School of Journalism. "Grants for local news reporting are much smaller and usually not high priorities for foundations, many of which do not make any grants for journalism."[7]

> The Knight News Challenge has received 10,000 applications—and funded about 100.

Still, the increased focus on this topic by foundations is an important development. Many of the most promising nonprofit startups have foundation support. Among those that have financed journalism projects are the John S. and James L. Knight Foundation, Carnegie Corporation of New York, Gates Foundation, Atlantic Philanthropies, MacArthur Foundation, Ford Foundation, Open Society Institute, McCormick Foundation, Ethics and Excellence in Journalism Foundation, Omidyar Network, Skoll Foundation, Belo Foundation, Scripps Howard Foundation, Hewlett Foundation, William Penn Foundation, California Endowment, Annenberg Foundation, Irvine Foundation, Pew Foundation, Kaiser Family Foundation, Arca Foundation, Herblock Foundation, Annie Casey Foundation, Benton Foundation, and Rockefeller Foundation.[8]

> "The flow of local news is as important as the flow of jobs, or the flow of traffic, or electricity," Alberto Ibarguen, the Knight Foundation's CEO.

The Knight Foundation, whose money principally came from the Knight family that built the Knight-Ridder newspaper chain, has funded 200 different community news projects, often providing[9] small grants to "innovative ideas for using digital media to deliver news and information to geographically defined communities."[10] Knight leaders have said that they believe they are funding only a small fraction of what needs to be funded. The Knight News Challenge, for instance, has received 10,000 applications—and funded about 100.[11] When the Grantmakers in Film + Electronic Media asked, "Do you consider the amount/proportion of resources your organization devotes to media to be sufficient?" one executive responded, "The magnitude of the challenge—the 'creative destruction' of the media ecosystem brought about by the digital age—is much greater than anything one foundation can cope with. The 10,000 traditional newspaper reporters recently unemployed, for example, represents something along the order of magnitude of between $300 million and $400 million worth of lost journalism each year in the U.S. alone."[12]

Foundation leaders are also the first to point out that they provide seed money and hope not to provide ongoing operational support. Though this sounds sensible—all foundations should aspire toward creating self-sufficient organizations—it creates a problem for local news start-ups. Public broadcasting can combine project-by-project grants from foundations with a baseline of operational funding from the Corporation for Public Broadcasting, but local news websites do not have that option.

One possible source of funding for local news and journalism projects is local "community foundations," sometimes known as "placed-based" foundations because their focus on a particular geographical locale. With combined assets of $31 billion, the 650 local community foundations in the U.S. make grants of approximately $2.6 billion annually.[13] In 2008, in an effort to stimulate more activity, the Knight Foundation created the Knight Community Information Challenge, a five-year initiative that gives matching grants to local foundations that finance journalism projects. "The flow of local news is as important as the flow of jobs, or the flow of traffic, or electricity," Alberto Ibarguen, the Knight Foundation's CEO, told a group of local foundation leaders. "It is a resource essential to a properly functioning community—a resource we can no longer take for granted."[14]

Four years ago, after extensive consultation with local leaders, the Community Foundation for Greater New Haven (one of the nation's oldest and largest community foundations) reorganized to allow for greater flexibility in the hope of spurring innovation. Subsequently, it gave the *New Haven Independent* news site a two-year, $21,600 grant. After the site showed initial results, the foundation followed up with more funding, enabling the staff of three full-time and two part-time journalists (plus a number of stringers) to further develop and sustain the site.[15]

As J-Lab's Jan Shaffer points out, given the relatively low costs for digital media start-ups, a small amount of money can go a long way. NewCastleNOW.org, Westchester New York's News and Opinion Weekly, serves as an example of the big impact a relatively small grant can have. Three longtime community volunteers, all empty-nesters with experience in local government affairs, founded the site with a $17,000 grant from J-Lab. NewCastleNOW.org covers issues in New Castle and the surrounding Westchester County communities, and now attracts a wide array of community funding, including advertising revenue.[16]

One cautionary note: local foundations often get their money from companies and influential individuals in the area. Some may not want the foundations associated with controversy. And what happens when the local journalism efforts investigate some of the institutions affiliated with donors or their friends? As the publisher of one local online news start-up put it, "Community foundations don't get money from poor folks. Investigative reporting puts the community foundation in great jeopardy if news stories offend donors."[17]

> 46 percent of community foundations said they have increased their funding for media projects. So far, though, a minority of the money goes to developing "credible professional news sources."

Community foundations appear to be increasing their commitment to local news. Of 154 foundations that responded to a recent Knight Foundation survey (out of an estimated 700 nationwide), 46 percent said that their funding of information and media projects has increased over the past three years, and 59 percent said that they expect their funding of these projects to continue to increase.[18]

However, it is important to note that the local foundations were *not* giving the lion's share of their funds to efforts to develop "credible professional news sources," such as investigative reporting and hyperlocal news. Only 33 percent reported giving in this area, while 73 percent gave instead to campaigns to create awareness about community issues (e.g., the need to reform local education policy); 50 percent funded platforms for civic engagement and action (e.g., online social-networking sites aimed at engaging young people in a region); 31 percent funded efforts to share news and information, such as citizen-journalist blogs and virtual town squares; and 35 percent aided digital and media literacy training programs.[19]

14 Journalism Schools

FAR FROM BECOMING OBSOLETE, many journalism schools have been flooded with applicants—in part because would-be journalists realize that new skills are needed with each passing day. It is no longer sufficient to report and write; today's journalists also need video shooting and editing skills. It is no longer sufficient to be a great news photographer; photojournalists now have to know how to conduct interviews, and set up a website. Modern journalism schools not only teach the five W's (who, what, where, when, and why) but also crowdsourcing, computer-assisted reporting, and a wide variety of digital-era skills.

As the good journalism schools retool themselves, a big question has arisen: can they play a significant role not only by teaching journalism, but by actually doing it? Increasingly, the eyes of journalism school deans have turned to a model they can see across campus: teaching hospitals. In an April 2010 letter to the FCC, 13 deans of journalism schools explained that some schools are becoming "more like the communications equivalent of university teaching hospitals, by partnering with local news outlets to undertake journalistic work that also emphasizes pedagogical and professional best practices."[1] Columbia School of Journalism professor Michael Schudson elaborated: "This system has been very successful in simultaneously providing real-life training for medical students, medical care for patients and staffing for hospitals at the center of medical research."[2]

> The Cronkite School of Journalism at Arizona State University produces a half-hour newscast that airs three nights a week on the local PBS station.

Commercial entities are far more open to student labor than they once were, says Chris Callahan, dean of the Cronkite School of Journalism at Arizona State University.[3] In 2007, his school created the Cronkite News Service (CNS), which enlists students to work on stories about state issues and lawmakers. In December 2009, the students examined the financial filings of Arizona members of Congress and discovered that seven members had paid a total of $300,000 in bonuses to their staff at the height of the recession in 2008.[4] The story ran in newspapers throughout the state and appeared on websites.

The school also produces a half-hour newscast that airs three nights a week on the local PBS station. According to Callahan, his students' 30-minute program is a "wonderful alternative" to the "cops and robbers" broadcasts aired by the commercial stations in Phoenix.[5] Students work two days a week in the CNS newsroom. Their editor, Steve Elliott, says he teaches his students to "[identify] what newspapers aren't covering" so they can offer material that's non-duplicative, and to do stories that "the AP doesn't have time to do."[6]

Some journalism schools have been using this approach for years. The University of Missouri's journalism school helps runs KOMU-TV8, the NBC TV affiliate in Columbia, Missouri. Students have been reporters, producers, and writers for the station since 1970.[7]

One of the more ambitious new partnerships began earlier this year in San Francisco. Warren Hellman provided five million dollars in seed money to the Bay Citizen, which is partnering with the Berkeley Graduate School of Journalism and the *New York Times*, to produce two pages of content twice a week for the *Times*'s San Francisco edition. Students serve as paid interns at the Bay Citizen, and some even go on to full-time jobs there. The goal, says Berkeley dean, Neil Henry, is "to be front and center in figuring out a way to give news to local communities at a time when the industry is losing its ability to do that kind of work."[8]

Some journalism schools have focused on providing hyperlocal information and reporting. New York University, City University of New York (CUNY), and the University of California–Berkeley all run websites featuring writing by students and neighborhood residents on hyperlocal issues. CUNY's journalism school, for example, took over full-time management of The Local, a *New York Times* blog that covers a section of Brooklyn.[9] On a typical day, the site published articles about a rally for community gardens and changes in local bus routes that had been confusing area residents.[10] The site features an events calendar and links to relevant blogs, and also uses digital-era information-gathering processes such as crowdsourcing to collect data on, among other things, broken car windows in a particular neighborhood.[11]

At NYU's journalism school, Professor Jay Rosen created a hyperlocal site about the East Village with the *New York Times.*

If these models succeed, it could be of considerable help in some communities. There are approximately 483 colleges and universities in the U.S. and Puerto Rico that have journalism and/or mass communications programs. In the fall of 2008, U.S. journalism and mass communication programs enrolled 216,369 students (201,477 undergraduate, 14,892 graduate).[12] An estimated 50,850 students earned bachelors degrees, and 4,480 students earned master's degrees in journalism in the 2008/09 academic year.[13]

The most frequent criticism of the teaching hospital model is that student journalists are a source of cheap labor and actually end up displacing their professional counterparts. The students are willing to work for "free," earning course credit at a time when professional newsrooms are eliminating staff to cut costs. One former editor, Peter Scheer, wrote, "Does it make sense for [J-schools] to be subsidizing the accelerated dislocation of one generation of their graduates to make room for a younger generation of their graduates? In the investment world this is called a Ponzi scheme."[14] But Nicholas Lemann, dean of the Columbia University Graduate School of Journalism, responded that students are doing journalism that newspapers no longer can. "With the typical metro news editor looking at a half-empty newsroom, the question isn't whether to cover local issues with journalism students or veteran reporters, it's whether to cover local issues with journalism students or not at all," Lemann says.[15] CUNY's dean, Steve Shepard, admits that his students are "very cost effective," but adds that without them the hyperlocal journalism in Brooklyn's Fort Greene and Cobble Hill neighborhoods "wouldn't get done."[16]

These programs work only if they can maintain high quality. The managing editor of the *Milwaukee Journal Sentinel*, George Stanley, says he will not use University of Wisconsin students anymore, because he had to run a correction on the one student-produced article he published. These collaborations "are much more of a service to

"With the typical metro news editor looking at a half-empty newsroom, the question isn't whether to cover local issues with journalism students or veteran reporters, it's whether to cover local issues with journalism students or not at all," says Columbia's Nick Lemann.

students than they are to the professional media," he says.[17] Quality control is "a legitimate concern," Shepard confirms. "They all need editing and oversight," he says of his students.[18] The Cronkite School's Chris Callahan says that without a high-level editor who treats the students' work as his or her own, these partnerships won't work.[19] The Cronkite News Service's editor, Steve Elliott, acknowledges that he spends a lot of time rewriting student copy to bring it up to professional standards.[20]

These programs' ability to fill journalistic gaps is also constrained by the academic calendar; most cannot provide news content during the summer break, and because students graduate and new ones arrive each year, they lack institutional knowledge about the subjects they are covering. It is only the full-time faculty like Elliott who can bring institutional knowledge to these journalistic efforts. With a class of approximately 50 students, Berkeley's journalism school is the biggest news operation in the region according to its dean, Neil Henry. "The problem," according to Henry, is that the students "don't hit the ground running and there is tremendous changeover."[21] The University of California at Berkeley pays students to work during holidays to update digital news sites in Oakland, the Mission District, and Richmond. Henry believes that if he could finance one full-time journalist as an anchor, he could make the schedule work. The Cronkite School's Chris Callahan is exploring how to go from a three-night-per-week, 30-week-per-year operation, to a year-round one. (He estimates that it would cost two million dollars over three years—approximately $600,000 per year—to expand their public TV show to five nights a week and make it year-round).[22]

Teaching hospitals also offer venues for medical research, and journalism schools expect the new breed of J-schools to offer high quality research. CUNY established a Center for Entrepreneurial Journalism initially capitalized at $10 million (largely funded by foundation gifts) to train students how to create new journalism enterprises. At NYU's journalism school, Professor Jay Rosen created a hyperlocal site about the East Village with the *New York Times*. "Deciding how to launch the site, how it should operate, and how to make it effective in the East Village community are ideal tasks for students," Rosen says. The students are "immersed in the innovation puzzle in journalism."[23] Clients actually pay the Cronkite School to develop media products for them. For instance, the *Arizona Guardian*, a web publication devoted to state politics and government, commissioned the school to develop an iPhone application that provides background material on lawmakers and allows users to immediately contact their representatives using the phone's GPS.[24] Several schools have created joint efforts with other divisions within their universities. A recent article in the Columbia Journalism Review suggested that J-schools and law schools team up to provide legal help for journalists who want to press for access to government information.[25]

Most, if not all, of the journalism (and the expense) is being shouldered by the schools, not their collaborators, often with the help of foundations. CUNY's production of The Local is financed by the Carnegie Corporation of New York, with additional funding from the McCormick Tribune Foundation and the John S. and James L. Knight Foundation.[26] The Cronkite School raised $18 million in three years from national foundations to help finance its new facility in downtown Phoenix.[27] The Berkeley journalism school's digital news sites have been funded by grants from the Ford Foundation. The two-year, $500,000 grant (which was recently renewed for another two years) has been used to hire two multimedia professionals to teach the students.[28]

15 The Evolving Nonprofit Media

IT IS CLEAR THAT THE NONPROFIT SECTOR holds great potential here to help fill the gaps in news, information, and journalism left by the depleted commercial media sector. It is therefore imperative that we gain a more nuanced understanding of what exactly is meant by nonprofit media. For instance, the biggest player in this sector is "public broadcasting," which has become a confusing term. It is intended to mean "supported by the public" as opposed to advertisers. But since "public schools" and "public housing" receive most of their money from taxpayers, some have come to think of public broadcasting as largely taxpayer supported, even though only about 15 percent of public radio's money comes from the taxpayer-financed Corporation for Public Broadcasting (CPB). The digital age has further complicated the terminology. Public TV and radio stations are moving well beyond "broadcasting," aggressively using mobile and digital platforms.

Moreover, there is a large and growing world of nonprofit media unaffiliated with traditional public broadcasting—including state public affairs networks; low-power FM stations; public access, educational, and governmental channels; nonprofit programmers carried by satellite TV; and, now, a burgeoning world of nonprofit websites.

More accurate than "public broadcasting," the term "nonprofit media" better captures the full range of not-for-profit news and media organizations. Some nonprofit media groups are affiliated with public broadcasting, some not; some receive government funds, most do not. But what these groups have in common is this: they plow excess revenue back into the organization, and they have public-interest missions that involve aspirations toward independent journalism.

Two (contradictory) concerns have been expressed about the size of the nonprofit sector: a) that it is too small to have an impact and b) that it could be so big it would hurt commercial media. (Some have argued that the power of the BBC, underwritten by British taxpayers, has stymied commercial media there.) But in the U.S., almost no nonprofit media—not even NPR or PBS—receive the majority of their money from the government (as the BBC does). Congress would need to increase the budget of CPB by more than 600 percent to equal that of the BBC in dollar terms, and by 6,000 percent to equal it in terms of per capita contribution. The amount the federal government spends on public broadcasting is a small fraction of what other national governments do: U.S. taxpayers give about $1.35 to public broadcasting each year, compared with $22.48 in Canada, $58.86 in Japan, $80.36 in the United Kingdom, and $101 in Denmark, based on appropriations (for the U.S.) and license fees (for the other countries) for 2007.[1] But since the American public broadcasting system receives a larger percentage of its funds from private donations, a more accurate comparison would be to look at private and public spending combined. Even then, total 2009 spending for public broadcasting in the U.S. from *all* sources—private and government—is less than half the fiscal year 2009/10 operating expenditure of the BBC.[2] It seems unlikely that the nonprofit sector will grow enough to become a true threat to the commercial sector.

That raises a different question: Is it possible that that nonprofit sector growth will never be significant enough to have a notable impact?

Within the nonprofit media world, there are giants and pipsqueaks, too. While public broadcasting is a mere speck compared to commercial media, nonprofit websites are collectively a mere speck compared to public broadcasting.

On the other hand, looking at the "nonprofit" sector more expansively, it is clearly possible for substantial institutions to take root. In addition to the Associated Press, AARP, Wikipedia and NPR, major nonprofit media organizations include: *National Geographic*, C-SPAN, *Consumer Reports*, WordPress, and the *St. Petersburg Times*.

Moreover, it is hard to overstate the importance of the noncommercial element in the development and flowering of the Internet, itself the product of government-funded research and development. The most vibrant media distribution networks—social media—are for-profit entities fueled by private citizens voluntarily sharing material with their friends, without desire for monetary gain. Any website making use of reader reviews or volunteer message board moderators is employing the unpaid voluntary contributions of readers to help make commercial business models sing. Wikipedia and other communal information ponds rely on millions of hours of volunteer labor.

Perhaps even more important is the under-appreciated contribution of open source computer programming. Since the beginning of the web, large numbers of software developers have written and shared programming code freely, to be used, manipulated, improved, and shaped by anyone who chooses to. Rather than seeking patents or protection, the open source community offers its creations, free of charge, to the rest of the world. This has led to the development of countless programs and software languages including Mozilla Firefox, Linux, PHP, Apache, and Drupal. WordPress, the most popular blogging software, is an open source platform. One need not be a computer geek to realize that the open source movement—a nonprofit model—has fundamentally enhanced the digital revolution, with incalculable benefits for private enterprise as well as consumers.

Nonprofit organizations are both hindered and aided by the tax and financial rules that govern their operations. They can receive tax-deductible donations, but cannot raise funds by promising to provide profits or dividends in return for investments. They compete with each other, and with for-profits. Like commercial players, they rise and fall based on whether they can provide useful services to consumers. Most important, they can focus their energies on long-term missions rather than short-term profits, but they may also lose the benefits of market discipline as a result.

As in the commercial sector, the new and old media in the nonprofit sector complement one another. Collaboration is key. Vivian Schiller, former president of NPR, applauds the quality content produced by online news sites and sees potential synergies: "We have a massive audience, but we never have enough content. So the notion of us partnering is really compelling."[3] Several cross-platform collaborations have shown great promise: the Berkeley Journalism School is working with the Bay Citizen; voiceofsandiego.org collaborates with Channel 4; the Cronkite School provides a newscast for a local PBS station; the Chicago News Cooperative offers local coverage for the *New York Times*. In Oklahoma, four different foundations have teamed up with a mix of for-profit and nonprofit media organizations, including the Tulsa World, the *Oklahoman*, two major state universities, and local public TV and radio stations to create Oklahoma Watch, a statewide journalism organization.[4]

But collaborations face hurdles too. Many entities seek money from the same sources, so there may be reticence among them about helping a potential competitor. With more nonprofits entering the media landscape, there will be more entities chasing what has so far been a relatively static pool of donors. The economic recession that exacerbated the problems of the commercial media also led to a drop in donations for nonprofits. Other factors that can deter groups from collaborating include cultural differences, concerns about quality, disparate missions, and a more primal sense of protectiveness.

Although the nonprofit sector offers great promise, we see several obstacles to its necessary evolution:

> Current tax and corporate policies restrict the ability of nonprofits to develop sustainable business models. (Fuller discussion in Chapter 31, Nonprofit Media.)

> Commercial entities are not contributing enough. By law, satellite and cable operators are supposed to be helping to support local nonprofit media but the ineffectiveness of the regulatory systems have meant less success for nonprofit media groups than there could be.

> The economics of online video streaming may severely impact some nonprofits. Most have neither the business model nor the capacity to generate per-stream advertising revenue. This means that the more people access audio and video online, the more the costs for nonprofits will rise.

> Current funding is insufficient. Foundations do not currently make local journalism a high priority. Government funds only one part of the nonprofit media landscape (public broadcasting).

> Foundations have always focused on seed funding, but to survive, nonprofits will need to develop ongoing sources of revenue, especially from members.

On the other hand, the nonprofit sector has the ingenuity and spirit to fill many of the gaps left by the contraction of traditional media. If some of these obstacles can be removed, these organizations will likely play a crucial, and growing, role.

non-media players

GOVERNMENT
TRANSPARENCY

EMERGENCY ALERT
SYSTEMS

LIBRARIES

SCHOOLS

Americans have never relied solely on the media as their source for critical information. The PTA newsletter, a flier on the bulletin board at work, gossip over the hedge, the weekly sermon, the National Weather Service, campaign advertisements, public health announcements—these are among the myriad ways we learn about events that impact our lives. The digital revolution has not only transformed traditional media but also has created new ways for Americans to get civically important information from outside the flow of the news media. In this chapter, we look at four areas we expect will become increasingly important sources for information: government, libraries, emergency alert systems, and schools.

16 Government Transparency

GOVERNMENT HAS LEGITIMATE REASONS to want to preserve secrecy when it comes to national security and other private matters—but when it comes to matters that directly affect the lives of citizens, transparency and accessibility are crucial. And the weaker the traditional journalism sector is, the more crucial these become: By making relevant data available online, information that previously might have taken weeks to track down can be found in hours through a computer-assisted search. This reduces the expense of accountability journalism, and it empowers citizens to act on their own behalf. Greater government transparency has been recommended by the Knight Commission in *Informing Communities: Sustaining Democracy in a Digital Age*,[1] the Columbia Journalism School in *The Reconstruction of American Journalism*,[2] the Federal Trade Commission, and many others.[3]

In previous chapters we touched on some efforts that have enabled citizens to observe the workings of government, including state public affairs networks, local governmental access channels on cable TV, and C-SPAN. In this section, we will take a broader look at the developing movement for government transparency, we will discuss ways to improve transparency in the future, and we will talk about the limitations of transparency as a strategy for meeting public information needs.

The Three-Stage Open Government Movement

The contemporary open government movement traces its roots to the 1966 enactment of the federal Freedom of Information Act (FOIA).[4] FOIA significantly expanded the obligations of federal agencies to publish fundamental government information and disclose specific records upon public request.[5] FOIA's enactment also spurred a nationwide revolution in open government law. Every state now has its own version, and Congress has repeatedly amended the federal FOIA, almost always in the direction of greater openness. In addition, Congress enacted the Electronic Freedom of Information Act Amendments of 1996,[6] which directed agencies to use new technologies to further realize FOIA's promise of government transparency.

More recently, a second branch of the open government movement has blossomed, promoting the sharing of government databases. President Obama's January 21, 2009, Memorandum on Transparency and Open Government stated: "Executive departments and agencies should harness new technologies to put information about their operations and decisions online and readily available to the public."[7] The Office of Management and Budget then issued an Open Government Directive,[8] requiring agencies to "identify and publish online in an open format at least three high-value data sets"[9] and develop "an Open Government Plan that will describe how it will improve transparency and integrate public participation and collaboration into its activities."[10]

Perhaps the most visible national spokesperson for this trend is Vivek Kundra, the White House's chief information officer, who, as chief technology officer for the District of Columbia, created what many consider the gold standard in online data sharing by local government. Among its 29 databases,[11] the DC.gov site enables citizens to search:

> *Campaign Contributions*—by amount, contributor, date, location, or recipient

> *Citywide Calendar*—for information on events in D.C.

> *D.C. Parks*—for information on swimming pools, basketball courts, before- and after-school care, and other programs at parks and recreation centers

> *Local and Small Businesses*—for listings of small, local, minority, and disadvantaged businesses in D.C.

> *Grants*—for information on current competitive federal, city, and foundation grant opportunities for local organizations

> *Health Professionals*—to find Department of Health licenses for practitioners, including chiropractors, dentists, psychologists, and social workers

> *Property Sales*—for sale prices and other information about D.C. properties

> *Public Library Catalog*—for book information and availability

> *Reference Materials*—for online access to magazines, newspapers, and reference materials on a wide variety of subjects

> *Public School Demographics*—for D.C. Public Schools data on racial composition, Stanford-9 scores, attendance rates, and more

> *Free Internet Access*—to find organizations offering free or low-cost Internet access

> *Meeting Facilities*—to find places to hold a convention or meeting in D.C.

> *Property Assessments*—for D.C. property tax assessments

> *Surplus Property Auctions*—for sales of surplus assets through online auctions

> *Public Land Records*—by grantor, grantee, document number, lot/square, or document type

> *Zoning Maps*—for maps of neighborhood zones

Other impressive local efforts include San Francisco's DataSF and NYCStat, which describes itself as "New York City's one-stop-shop for all essential data, reports, and statistics related to City services."[12]

A third frontier in the drive for government openness is a growing engagement with social media. Nearly three-quarters of local government jurisdictions around the country use Twitter to push news to citizens and the media, especially with regard to emergency and public safety alerts. About the same number are using Facebook to communicate with citizens, frequently targeting users demographically or by interest.[13] In addition, governments are involving residents interactively in the gathering and reporting of civic information. "Many cities and counties have developed web-based applications that encourage citizens to submit pictures of potholes in need of repair, garbage needing pick-up, or graffiti that needs to be erased,"[14] says Alan Shark, executive director of the Public Technology Institute, a nonprofit group that supports city and county government. Examples include:

> Boston developed the Citizens Connect application to allow residents and visitors to gather information about the physical state of the city and send that information directly to the appropriate city department through their iPhone. Citizens can attach a photo and capture system-generated Geographic Information System (GIS) coordinates. The Boston Globe reported that, "City officials say the iPhone application is being used mostly by younger residents who have not previously called the hot line."[15]

> The City of Mesa, Arizona, developed a Citizen Dashboard for Bond and Capital Improvement Projects, keeping citizens apprised of public projects financed by their bond votes.[16]

> Pittsburgh's iBurgh application for the iPhone debuted in August 2009 and reportedly had 8,000 users in its first five months.[17]

> San Jose launched a complaint app called the San Jose Mobile City Hall.[18]

> One private site, SeeClickFix, recently reported the posting of its 50,000th city maintenance issue to be resolved.[19]

These apps can aid journalists, who track posts as sources for stories.[20] And these records-and-data-sharing initiatives will likely have a public impact that goes beyond stimulating information flow. Their very existence has the potential to reduce corruption and promote accountability in the same way that publicity typically does. A team of scholars working through the École des Hautes Études Commerciales (EDHEC) Business School examined the disclosure practices of the national legislatures of 126 countries and compared them to corruption scores indicated by the International Country Risk Guide. Their conclusion: greater public access to financial disclosure by public officials correlated to lower levels of corruption.[21]

Boston's Citizens Connect application allows residents to gather information about the physical state of the city and send it directly to the appropriate city department through their iPhone.

How Transparency Fosters an Informed Public

Government transparency improves information flow three ways: directly to citizens themselves, through "information entrepreneurs," and through journalists.

Direct Access

Many governments have found that citizens value the access they have to information, and they put it to good use. On the federal level, a list of Data.gov's top-10 most downloaded datasets of all time can be found at http://www.data.gov/metric/visitorstats/top10datasetreport. In May 2010 (a sample month), four of the 10 most popular datasets were from the Geography and Environment category, among them a worldwide listing of real-time earthquakes and an inventory of sites subject to environmental regulation. The dataset on U.S. Overseas Loans and Grants was frequently accessed, too.[22]

There is great variety in the city datasets that prove popular. In May 2010, San Franciscans searched most often for traffic accident data, school dropout data, information on library books available in the San Francisco Public Library, and information on Treasure Island development plans.[23] In Seattle, neighborhood maps, crime statistics, active building permits, and a list of the locations of the city's public toilets were among those most-frequently accessed.[24] The District of Columbia's most popular datasets are those on juvenile arrests and charges, crime incidents, purchase orders, and public space permits.[25] In Ann Arbor, Michigan, the most downloaded datasets are the city boundary data, records of checks or fund transfers issued to the city, and a graphic representation of land use planning parcels.[26]

A 2010 study by the Pew Internet & American Life project found that 35 percent of Internet users have researched official government documents or statistics.[27] Citizens access the information through a variety of devices. As the Pew study noted, "[Four percent] of cell phone owners who use text messaging signed up to receive text messages from a government agency or official."[28] Use of phones for these purposes is small but growing. In 2009, the Brookings Institution found that 2 percent of federal government websites and 3 percent of state government websites offer PDA (personal digital assistant—or mobile device) access. Although these rates lag behind the corporate sector—10 percent of corporate web sites offer PDA access—the numbers are slowly increasing.[29] For many Americans, mobile phones and hand-held devices provide the most attractive means of accessing the Internet—and are especially popular among African-Americans and Latinos as primary tools for reaching the Web.[30] Governments can thus maximize the utility and inclusiveness of their transparency initiatives by making web sites compatible with mobile devices and enabling the development of free smart phone applications that give users easy access to government information.

One study of 126 countries found that good financial disclosure by public officials correlated with lower levels of corruption.

Information Entrepreneurship

Not only do open government initiatives support direct citizen access to information, they support private sector and nonprofit entrepreneurs who create applications to organize and structure government data so that it can be searched and utilized.

Both New York City and the District of Columbia have enhanced the value of their datasets by wooing developers to create applications. New York held a "BigApps" competition, which selected 10 winning applications from a pool of more than 80 submissions that included "a resource for better navigating the City and its cultural resources, a guide to New York City schools, a live-feed commentary on New York City taxis, and an application that helps users locate books at Public Libraries."[31]

In the case of D.C., the Apps for Democracy program, "which offered a cash prize to the developer who could produce the most user-friendly applications based on government data—ultimately led to the development of 47 different applications (with an estimated value to the city of $2.3 million) at a cost of just $50,000 in prize money."[32] Examples include DCCrimeFinder, which uses citizens' phone locations to inform them of crimes that have occurred nearby; Achieve D.C., which shows both poverty and achievement rates for D.C. elementary, middle, and high schools; and PointAbout, which allows citizens to use their iPhones to find nearby embassies, vacant properties, banks, and a variety of other community assets, based on their location.[33]

This trend shows every sign of continuing. Sunlight Labs, part of the D.C.-based nonprofit, nonpartisan Sunlight Foundation is "an open source community of thousands dedicated to using technology to transform government," chiefly by advancing transparency.[34] Its two "Apps for America" contests elicited the development of dozens of open source applications designed, in one way or another, to advance government accountability through data.[35] The winner of Apps for America 1, Filibusted, aggregates data compiled by Sunlight Labs and GovTrack to reveal the rate

DCCrimeFinder uses citizens' phone locations to inform them of crimes that have occurred nearby.

at which different Senators vote against cloture motions that would cut off floor debate and permit Senate votes on pending legislation.[36] A runner-up, Legistalker, aggregates all online activity by members of Congress including news stories, "tweets," and YouTube videos.[37] The winner of Apps for America 2, DataMasher, enables users to analyze data sets in tandem. For example, a user could take data on federal spending by state and divide it by the data for each state's population to create a data mashup of federal spending per person per state.[38] The runner-up, GovPulse, makes it possible to track the frequency of federal agency appearances in the Federal Register and to search and digest Federal Register entries more easily.[39]

In April, 2011, the John S. and James L. Knight Foundation partnered with the FCC to establish an "Apps for Communities" competition. Its goal "is to create apps that use publicly available data to help people in communities across the country," even if those communities lack the big population base (or municipal budgets) of a New York or D.C.[40] The formal challenge urges programmers: "Using hyper-local government and other public data you should develop an app that enables Americans to benefit from broadband communications—regardless of geography, race, economic status, disability, residence on Tribal land, or degree of digital or English literacy—by providing easy access to relevant content."[41]

Of course, nonprofit institutions may foster increased transparency through their own direct initiatives, as well. Among national nonprofits, the Sunlight Foundation, mentioned above, has played an especially important role in making government data available in formats useful for both journalists and the general public. For example, RealTimeCongress, developed by its Sunlight Labs, is a mobile phone app that gives updates on live floor debates and votes, information on key documents as they are published, and access to "whip" notices and hearing schedules.[42] An example of state-level initiative is the Texas Tribune, a nonprofit public media organization that hosts several state government datasets.[43] Its compilation of government employee salaries is the most popular. Other highly

Nearly one out of five print stories were based on public records.

demanded datasets include a directory of all elected officials in Texas, data on Texas prisons, education-related data (such as school rankings, superintendent comparisons, and student demographics), a list of red-light cameras, campaign finance data, and county-by-county election results.

Information Serving Journalism

Journalists have long considered access to government records central to effective journalistic practice. In December 2001, the Society of Professional Journalists, looked at 4,000 individual news stories in 20 different media outlets and found that nearly one out of five print stories was based on public records, as were 11 percent of broadcast stories.[44] *Uplink* is the online magazine of the National Institute for Computer-Assisted Reporting (NICAR). Reviewing the issues of *Uplink* between January 2009 and June 2010, the FCC Future of Media team found that much of the data journalists and reporters were interested in during that time fell into four distinct categories: 1) Spending and tax-related datasets, including information on state loans, economic recovery spending, and local stimulus spending; 2) Environmental datasets, which included data tracking violations and enforcement of the Clean Air and Clean Water Acts as well as air pollution by geographical region, logging practices, and the level of trace pharmaceuticals in water supplies; 3) Crime data, including crime in schools, crime stories, and statistics on Taser usage by local police departments; and 4) Census data, which—when viewed in combination with other datasets—can reveal how social and economic trends are affecting Americans taking into account such variables as race, income, and place of residence. NICAR's database library, available only for investigative reporters, offers information on federal spending, crime, and campaign spending. Other crime-related datasets, such as airport crime statistics and data on violations of Federal Aviation Administration regulations, also are available.[45]

To the extent that government databases reveal the behavior of private entities, they can support greater accountability in the private as well as the public sector. One of the most innovative government-initiated transparency efforts is the Securities and Exchange Commission requirement that corporations use XBRL (Extensible Business Reporting Language) in submitting financial disclosure forms. A company's reports (including footnotes) can be tagged with metadata so that facts and numbers can be searched and analyzed. The XBRL reporting requirement makes information easy to mine and convert into structured data for rapid analysis.[46] Given that government agencies routinely require information submissions on subjects as disparate as workplace safety, environmental compliance, and the finances of tax-exempt nonprofit organizations, one can see how attention to submission format on a government-wide basis could facilitate deeper journalistic analysis across every sector of social and economic activity.

A comparison of two recent Pulitzer Prize–winning projects illustrates two impressive uses of records research. In 2010, Barbara Laker and Wendy Ruderman of the *Philadelphia Daily News* received a Pulitzer Prize for Investigative Reporting. Their "Tainted Justice" series exposed the corrupt practices of a police narcotics squad. Laker and Ruderman read through thousands of search warrants by hand and verified the addresses listed on them. Then they went looking for the drug dealers named in the warrants, knocking on scores of doors in the process. Through this painstaking effort Laker and Ruderman proved that the information contained in the warrants did not match bystander and other nonpolice accounts of the drug raids. This type of work required extensive resources. *Philadelphia Daily News* editor, Gar Joseph, said that his "back of the envelope" calculation was that the series cost $164,000, an amount that factors in the salaries of the two reporters and the time spent editing.[47]

In contrast, the Pulitzer Prize for Public Service was awarded to the *Bristol (VA) Herald Courier* in 2010 for Daniel Gilbert's investigation of payments owed to local mineral-rights owners by gas corporations. The publisher of the *Herald Courier* sent Gilbert to a workshop on computer-assisted reporting held at the University of Missouri's journalism school, where he learned how to analyze the data he had obtained. According to managing editor J. Todd Foster, "Gilbert used two sets of data: the monthly gas production numbers that companies report to the state for an online database, and the monthly escrow statements generated by Wachovia Bank, data obtained from the Division of Gas and Oil through a Freedom of Information Act request" for his exposé.[48] The Gilbert investigation could not have been done without computerized records and data-mining techniques.[49]

Journalists are receiving assistance from information entrepreneurs, especially in the nonprofit sector, who use government datasets to create relevant, accessible databases designed to match likely reporter interests. For example, ProPublica, a 501(c)(3) investigative journalism organization, has compiled government stimulus data from Recovery.gov and other sources to create a database journalists can use to track the distribution of economic stimulus money. This data has been used in reports by sources that range from the *New York Times* to National Public Radio to the *Salt Lake Tribune* to the *Bozeman (MT) Daily Chronicle*.[50]

The Sunlight Foundation has created Congrelate, a data-rich website that provides information about legislators and their districts, including their voting history, their top donors, and fundraising efforts—all in tables that can be manipulated to display data in the way a given researcher finds most useful.[51] TransparencyData, another Sunlight Foundation project, allows users to explore data on federal campaign contributions, lobbying, grants, and contracts.[52] Poligraft, a third Sunlight Foundation project, enables users to cross-reference TransparencyData information with the text of articles (that the user can submit in a field on the site).[53] The site then displays political contributions re-

> The Sunlight Foundation created Congrelate, a data-rich website that provides information about legislators and their districts, including voting history, top donors, and fundraising efforts.

ceived and made by organizations and individuals described in the article. For example, if an article mentions the National Rifle Association (NRA) or the National Organization for Women (NOW) and a particular senator, Poligraft would display the campaign contributions made by the NRA or NOW to that senator.

The journalistic use of such tools is not limited to the employees of conventional media organizations. The Sunlight Foundation's PolitiWidgets allows bloggers to easily embed a wide range of information about elected officials into blog posts.[54]

Computer-assisted reporting is increasingly finding its way into mainstream media through the efforts of independent groups. Bill Buzenberg, executive director of the Center for Public Integrity (CPI), told a workshop of the Federal Trade Commission how CPI downloaded information on 350 million mortgages from the Home Mortgage Disclosure Act database and used it to identify the top-25 subprime lenders.[55] CPI found that nine of the top-10 lenders were based in California and that at least 21 of the top-25 subprime lenders were financed by banks that received bailout money.[56]

The Current State of Government Transparency

President Obama made government transparency the central theme of several initiatives on his first full day in office. These included an executive order expanding access to the presidential records of prior Administrations,[57] a memorandum directing the Office of Management and Budget to create an Open Government Directive setting transparency requirements for all executive departments and agencies,[58] and a memorandum on Freedom of Information Act implementation.[59] The last of these prescribed that "[a]ll agencies should adopt a presumption in favor of disclosure… to all decisions involving FOIA."[60] On March 19, 2009, Attorney General Holder issued a new policy,[61] setting narrower grounds for defending the withholding of government records than had been adopted in 2001.[62]

The Obama Defense Department lifted the prior administration's ban on photographing the coffins of the war dead returning from Iraq and Afghanistan,[63] and the White House agreed to post its visitor logs online, making public all but a few narrow categories of visitors to the president or vice president.[64] In December 2009, President Obama created a National Declassification Center in the National Archives, whose goal is to make all properly declassified records within a backlog of over 400 million pages of records publicly accessible by December 31, 2013.[65] In January 2010, the Administration released the names of detainees at the Bagram AirBase in Afghanistan.[66]

> Most websites created by local or state governments did not offer the most essential civic information, such as budgets, audits, contracts, and tax documents.

However, independent assessments[67] still give the federal bureaucracy mixed reviews for achieving the President's transparency goals. For example, the Federal Funding Accountability and Transparency Act, passed by Congress in 2006, required the Office of Management and Budget (OMB) to create a public website with data on federal contracts, grants, loans, and spending.[68] The Government Accountability Office (GAO) was to determine the extent of OMB's compliance with the requirements of the Act.[69] In March 2010, GAO reported that "of nine requirements [GAO] reviewed, OMB has satisfied six, partially satisfied one, and has yet to satisfy two." GAO also raised concerns about data quality.[70]

Efforts to obtain information through the Freedom of Information Act also continue to be stymied by obstacles. The federal Freedom of Information Act ordinarily requires agencies to determine within 20 days how they will respond to records requests.[71] But in 2009, only eight of the 29 largest federal agencies had an *average* response time on "simple requests" of 20 days or less; the average for all 29 was over 32 days.[72] And this was an improvement over 2008.[73] In other words, over two-thirds of federal agencies handling the overwhelming majority of FOIA requests do not even average a response time in compliance with the law.[74]

The 2010 reports filed by the Chief FOI officers of every federal agency specify the steps taken within each agency to promote proactive disclosure and implement the presumption of openness that President Obama called for.[75]

Though not required to do so by law, agencies releasing data should also include an Application Programming Interface (API) that allows the data to be shared easily with other computers and applications. These approaches can not only allow citizens to participate but make the services and analysis of government more effective. For instance, the FCC recently undertook to document the broadband speeds in different parts of the country. Instead of sending out, say, a half dozen researchers to report on the variations, they built an application that allowed citizens to perform tests themselves and report the data to the FCC. Two million submissions resulted.[76]

Of course, transparency at the federal level involves not only the executive branch, but also Congress. Federal legislation is frequently both lengthy and complex. Requiring the House and Senate, as urged by transparency advocates both within and outside Congress, to post all non-emergency bills online for 72 hours before adoption would enable not only legislators, but reporters and the general public to analyze and critique Congress' handiwork more effectively.[77]

The degree of government openness on a state and local basis varies widely. In 2009, a survey of government websites in 48 states revealed how many states (see numbers in parenthesis below) provide online records in various categories:[78]

> Department of Transportation projects and contracts (46)
> Statewide school test data (46)
> Political campaign contributions and expenses (45)
> Disciplinary actions against doctors (43)
> Audit reports (42)
> Disciplinary actions against attorneys (38)
> Environmental citations/violations (36)
> Teacher certifications (32)
> Fictitious business name registrations (29)
> Nursing home inspection reports (28)
> Database of local government expenditures (25)
> Consumer complaints (25)
> Bridge inspection and safety reports (23)
> Personal financial disclosure reports of elected or appointed officials (22)
> Child care center inspection reports (22)
> Hospital inspection reports (18)
> School inspection/safety records (9)
> School bus inspections (11)
> Death certificates (8)
> Gas pump overcharge records (8)

The only state to provide online data in all 20 categories was Texas; New Jersey was right behind with 19; and the state with the least information online was Mississippi.[79]

In a similar vein, Pew's Center on the States grades states on how well they use data and technology to make decisions and communicate with the public.[80] Only five states earned an A: Michigan, Missouri, Utah, Virginia, and Washington.[81] New Hampshire and South Dakota ranked the lowest, both receiving a D+.[82] The average across the states was a B-.[83] The criteria taken into account include the state's information technology planning, the state's and state agencies' use of cost and performance information, and the public's ability to access information about the performance of state programs.[84]

A number of states have undertaken initiatives similar to the Federal Funding Accountability and Transparency Act of 2006, which requires OMB to post federal spending data online.[85] In March 2010, Sunshine Review, an independent group,[86] announced the results of its evaluation of over 5,000 government websites, including those of 3,140 counties, 805 cities, and 1,560 school districts, through "crowdsourcing"—inviting participants around the country to use a "transparency checklist" to "collaboratively determine the extent to which government-managed websites contain the information people need."[87] According to the findings, in 2010 there were 41 websites created by local or state governments that made available the most essential civic information needed by citizens, such as budgets, audits, contracts, tax documents for public officials, and contact information for the person charged with fulfilling local FOIA requests.[88] In 2011, that number had risen to 112 local and state government websites.[89]

In terms of local news, the relative lack of openness regarding the courts and the criminal justice system is cause for special concern. According to David Cuillier, FOI chair of the Society of Professional Journalists, journalists commonly have a difficult time procuring records regarding law enforcement; agencies tend to be overly secretive and deny valid public records requests.[90]

Journalists seeking court records at the federal level have the great advantage of the PACER (Public Access to Court Electronic Records) web site.[91] PACER includes case and docket information for all district, bankruptcy, and appellate courts, and it currently hosts 500 million case file documents. However, only the U.S. District and Bankruptcy Courts provide searchable transcripts, and personal identifiers are removed before the records are made public. Transcripts from the U.S. Courts of Appeals are not made available. As of May 2010, PACER added digital audio recordings of court proceedings to its public offerings.

Access to electronic *state* court records is uneven. The Reporters Committee for Freedom of the Press (RCFP) maintains an online state-by-state summary of which court records are available online, along with links to websites where more details can be obtained and a summary of laws governing remote electronic access to court information.[92] The RCFP found that, at the Supreme Court and appellate level, most states have made at least some information available online. Most Supreme Court and appellate court opinions are online, with calendars and docket sheet information sometimes available as well, but briefs are less often accessible. At the trial court level, information is generally less available; some amount of docket sheet information is provided, but full access to filed court documents is rare. Even in states where the judicial system aims to make such information available, a lack of resources and expertise on electronic access capabilities often limits the scope of the initiative. The following states charge fees for online access to court records: Colorado, Delaware, Florida, Kansas, Oregon, Utah, and Washington.[93] Transcripts can often be obtained directly from a court, and many courts offer electronically viewable and searchable transcripts, though often there is a fee for transcription services.[94]

> The Center for Public Integrity downloaded information on 350 million mortgages from the Home Mortgage Disclosure Act database and used it to identify the top-25 subprime lenders.

Access to police records is yet more problematic. The laws governing public access to law enforcement records differ significantly from state to state. No studies have been found that compile these differences.[95] In the wake of recent political scandals, Illinois strengthened its Freedom of Information law, enhancing the powers of public access counselors (PAC). Illinois's PAC system could easily become a model for the country.[96]

Journalism professor Ira Chinoy, also a prize-winning journalist, has found that public employees are sometimes resistant or even antagonistic to public records requests. They are often uninformed about public records laws and the ease with which they could actually comply with them. Agencies may have legal authority to waive fees—if the request is in the public interest—but may be reluctant to do so when they are obligated to pay a contractor for the labor entailed in responding to the request.

In some cases, public authorities may be wrestling with computer systems that impede easy access.[97] In other cases, jurisdictions are working with systems designed by an outside contractor and then turned over to government employees not well versed in their operation.[98] And some record systems make databases especially difficult to copy.

The persistence of these problems underscores the need for a critical mass of full-time professional journalists. As the press is weakened by dwindling numbers and less experienced reporters "the court bureaucracy has gotten stronger and stronger," says Bill Girdner, editor and publisher of Courthouse News Service in Pasadena, California. "When journalists don't have presence, others control the information process."[99]

Girdner also points out that electronic court filings have, in some cases, made gaining access to judicial information *more* difficult. Traditionally, hard-copy filings were maintained in a wooden box in the clerk's office in every court around the country. Courthouse reporters typically thumbed through the filings in the wooden box for good stories. When the Riverside County courthouse was renovated, however, a wall went up—literally—from floor to ceiling, and the wooden box disappeared in favor of electronic documents. Filing documents are now available only as quickly—or as slowly—as the staff uploads them, which can mean a delay of days. "The time that they take to get this stuff done and online…by that time, a story is old news," Girdner says.

> "As we lose resources, we lose our ability to fight Freedom of Information suits," says Doug Guthrie, court reporter for the Detroit News. "We try to fake them out with stern letters, but they know we don't have it."

Girdner's concerns are echoed by Doug Guthrie, court reporter for the *Detroit News*:[100] "As we lose resources, we lose our ability to fight Freedom of Information suits. We try to fake them out with stern letters, but they know we don't have it." Girdner corroborates the point. He cites an instance in which Courthouse News Service (CNS) sued the Houston court clerk for denying access to documents, in one case, for nine days. CNS won an award of $253,000, but spent $1.2 million in attorney's fees last year.[101]

Guthrie believes that, as journalistic resources thin and access to records is denied or withheld, stories are going untold.[102] As a consequence, violations of citizen rights may go unchecked. He says that crime statistics have been "spun and polished" to show that crime has decreased. But, meanwhile, police and courts "seem to be more busy.… Big cities need newspapers to overcome big problems, big issues," he says. "We don't do it anymore."[103]

Even if public officials have the best of intentions, they may put forth data in a way that emphasizes a particular story line. Kerry O'Brien, who directs the NYC school survey for the New York City Department of Education, does not regard the Department's extensive survey and data-sharing initiatives as a substitute for independent reporting, as proud as she is of those initiatives.[104] Although her office provides an annual report, its intention is to motivate friendly coverage; the picture presented may well be a fair one but is not necessarily balanced. "People in any organization," O'Brien said, "will want to put their best foot forward in any public presentation."[105]

Limitations to Transparency Strategies

As important as government transparency is, it is not in itself a sufficient strategy toward the goal of an informed citizenry.

Ongoing Government Resistance to Disclosure. Ira Chinoy at the University of Maryland reports that his students almost invariably meet resistance in their first attempts to acquire digital copies of databases that are subject to mandatory disclosure under the Maryland Public Records Act. The reasons given for noncompliance "range from legitimate [antiquated computer systems or even high-end computer systems not designed with transparency in mind] to ludicrous, and a large middle of crankiness instead of helpfulness."[106] In short, despite recent efforts to improve government transparency, extracting significant information from the government often requires skill at framing questions, persistence, and significant resources of time and money.[107]

Data Does Not Interpret Itself. Data requires analysis. For example, the National Highway Traffic Safety Administration Office of Defects Investigation maintains a "safety complaints search engine," that allows users to find all complaints filed with the agency based on the make, model, and model year of any vehicle sold in the United States.[108] It does not appear that anyone used this application prior to the major Toyota recalls of 2009 to sound the alarm on Toyota safety issues. Analysis requires some sophistication.[109]

Transparency Without Reporting Can Promote Misunderstanding. In a 2009 essay, Professor Lawrence Lessig bemoaned the fact that certain kinds of public disclosure can unjustifiably undermine public trust by facilitating quick, cynical, unjustified conclusions about what influences government behavior.[110] Consider, for instance, a theoretical example in which an "exposé" reveals that a member of Congress received contributions from a certain industry and also voted in support of that industry. That correlation, by itself, proves little. It may be that the House member is voting in the way he or she hopes will be rewarded by contributors in the future, or it may be that contributors are rewarding House members whose views match those of the industry. Similarly, if a reporter should uncover a year-to-year reduction in the number of public school students achieving math or verbal "proficiency" for a particular jurisdiction, it would be important to investigate whether the measure of "proficiency" used by the testing agency had changed during the relevant time span.[111] If there were an increase in the number of crime reports on a university campus, it would be important to determine whether it reflected an increase in crime or improvements in the ease of reporting. In short, data poses questions as much as it answers them; the more data government shares, the more questions there are to be answered.

Data Manipulation by Government. In the hands of a skilled practitioner, data can be made to lie or mislead. For example, if a government finds that its average rate of something puts it in a bad light, it can simply change the quantity being averaged. Sort states by "average household income" and you will get one ranking; sort by "average family income" and the list will be different. For this reason, it is important to have available journalists trained in analysis to police the accuracy of data. Politicians and bureaucrats may knowingly falsify data, but even inadvertent errors can be misleading—and are unlikely to be detected by persons unaccustomed to data-based argument.

Corporations and Nonprofit Groups Require Monitoring, Too. Much of the data currently being disclosed shines light on government performance. But cutbacks in the number of journalists have also affected news organizations' ability to hold other powerful institutions accountable, such as large hospitals, major corporations, trade unions, and universities.

Unequal Recourse. The social divide among Americans who pay attention to government information and those who do not is significant. The 2010 Pew study of Internet users found that people who access information on government sites most often have substantially higher levels of income and education than those who interact with government websites only occasionally. Compared with light users, heavy and moderate users are also slightly more likely to be middle-aged (30 to 49 years old) and less likely to be younger than 30 or older than 65.[112] There is a danger that, unaccompanied by accessible journalistic analysis, government transparency initiatives may further skew the "informed electorate" toward a narrow slice of the wealthiest, best-educated, most technologically sophisticated Americans.

17 Emergency Information

DURING SNOWSTORMS, FLOODS, EARTHQUAKES, terrorist attacks, and other emergencies, most broadcasters mobilize their news teams.[1] They also, at times, turn over the airwaves to government-generated alerts.[2] The government is currently in the middle of a major effort to transform its emergency alert systems to make them more effective and in line with the media platforms of the 21st century.[3]

The Emergency Alert System (EAS) was established in 1994 to provide the president a way to use broadcast, satellite, and cable platforms to deliver vital messages to Americans in times of national emergency,[4] and to provide state and local emergency personnel similar tools. However, the EAS has never been used to deliver a presidential alert; it has been used, almost exclusively, to deliver state and local public emergency messages, such as weather bulletins and AMBER alerts about missing children.[5] The system's track record for local disasters has been mixed.

The adequacy of the EAS was much discussed after a January 2002 freight-train crash and derailment in Minot, North Dakota. The derailment took place in the middle of the night. Neither news broadcasters nor the EAS notified those in the immediate area that a deadly cloud of anhydrous ammonia was heading their way. Local authorities had attempted, unsuccessfully, to trigger the EAS at KCJB, the radio station designated to feed the initial EAS signal to other stations within its coverage area.[6] They then called KCJB and other radio stations in Minot, but no one answered the calls.[7] For an hour after the train derailment, not one of the six local radio stations, all of which are owned by Clear Channel, reported on the event.[8] Meanwhile, the local 911 system was jammed with phone calls, creating dispatch problems.[9] The police department ultimately had to contact a local TV news director at his home to arrange emergency broadcasts.[10]

Subsequent investigations revealed that local government and law-enforcement officials had failed to properly install, test, and train their personnel in the use of EAS equipment and so were unprepared for this crisis. The night of the incident, after emergency personnel realized that their EAS equipment was not working, they tried to use obsolete Emergency Broadcast System equipment. Although the local radio stations may be faulted for not having news staff available, the EAS equipment at the local radio stations was working and could have transmitted the alert automatically, if local officials had known what to do. The author of a 2005 study comparing various local emergency alert system responses to hazardous freight derailments concluded that Minot's emergency alert system failed because of a basic lack of understanding as to how the system works and poor coordination between emergency communication hubs.[11]

According to one study, during three incidents similar to the Minot derailment, emergency personnel never even attempted to activate the EAS.[12] Apparently, it was not used effectively during Hurricane Katrina, either. According to Lieutenant Lawrence McLeary, a public information officer for the Louisiana State Police, the EAS was ineffective during Hurricane Katrina because it was staffed by National Guardsmen, who were often pulled away from the machine to deal with other pressing issues.[13]

> The adequacy of the Emergency Alert System was much debated after a freight train crashed in Minot, North Dakota. Neither news broadcasters nor the government's alert system notified the community that a deadly cloud of anhydrous ammonia was heading their way.

Unlike in the case of a presidential alert, use of the system by broadcasters and other players for local incidents is voluntary. Although the FCC's Part 11 EAS rules require periodic testing of the EAS at the state and local level, there is no FCC requirement that local emergency personnel be involved in that testing (although state plans may require such participation). Closer coordination, regular training, and drills between broadcast media and state and local emergency authorities could better prepare EAS participants for actual emergencies.

Even if the EAS had been successful in Minot, however, it only would have reached those citizens who were listening to the radio or watching television. Those relying on mobile telephones or surfing the Internet would not have been notified. In an attempt to overcome such limitations, the federal, state, and local governments, along with industry groups have begun to coordinate their efforts to ensure that alerts go out by means of every communication medium available. Presidential Executive Order 13407 of 2006 (EO)[14] directs the federal government to create a comprehensive system to warn the American people in situations of war, terrorist attack, natural disaster, and other public hazards. The order vests overall responsibility with the Department of Homeland Security (DHS), which is tasked to establish a fully interoperable system, capable of delivering alerts through as many communication pathways as practicable, and to engage industry and government to ensure that all stakeholders are familiar with the system and trained in its use.[15]

The Federal Emergency Management Administration (FEMA) is developing the Integrated Public Alert and Warning System (IPAWS), the nation's next-generation infrastructure of alert and warning networks.[16] IPAWS is designed to ensure that government emergency alert systems—whether driven by local, state, or national governments—are able to notify the largest number of people possible, using a "system of systems" compatible with all types of communications technologies, both current and future. While Americans still rely on radio and TV for emergency information far more than any other medium,[17] today people are connected to a much wider variety of media. The IPAWS goal is to alert the 85 percent of the population that is connected to some form of media at any given moment within 10 minutes, whether through radio, television, mobile devices, personal computers, or any other communications device in use.

To help, FEMA has adopted a format known as Common Alerting Protocol, or CAP.[18] CAP is compatible with a wide variety of devices and systems and can be used to carry voice messages, digital images, audio, and video. It will work with programs that translate English messages into other languages, and it is compatible with devices used by the hearing- and sight-impaired. CAP also can incorporate security features to prevent the system from being hijacked. All emergency system participants must be able to receive CAP alerts by September 2011. On May 26, 2011 the FCC released a Notice of Proposed Rulemaking seeking comment on proposed rules by which EAS participants can receive CAP-based EAS alerts.[19]

> FEMA is developing the Integrated Public Alert and Warning System. Its goal is to alert much of the population within 10 minutes— through radio, television, mobile devices, personal computers, or any other communications device.

The widespread use of wireless devices, especially cell phones, has led to the creation of the Commercial Mobile Alert System (CMAS), or, as it will be presented to consumers, the Personal Localized Alerting Network (PLAN). The PLAN will enable mobile phone customers to receive local alerts about imminent danger (such as a tornado or a Minot-type event), presidential alerts, and abducted child (AMBER) alerts from commercial mobile service providers that choose to provide the service.[20] All major wireless carriers have elected to participate. FCC rules require that participating CMS providers develop, test, and deploy the PLAN no later than April 7, 2012.[21] On May 10, 2011, Mayor Michael Bloomberg, FCC Chairman Julius Genachowski, FEMA Administrator W. Craig Fugate, top executives from AT&T, Sprint, T-Mobile and Verizon and others gathered at the World Trade Center site to announce that PLAN will be available in New York City by the end of 2011.[22]

On the state and local level, a number of local emergency alert systems have begun adopting CAP-based systems. In Northern California's Contra Costa County, a map-based computer program generates a single alert message, which in turn triggers a broad array of warning delivery systems including sirens, telephone notification, broadcast EAS, low-power AM transmitters, Twitter and email notification, web displays, and in-building alerting systems. The CAP format allows additional new delivery systems to be added (and obsolete ones to be removed, if necessary) without affecting any of the others.[23]

Social Media

Social media also is becoming a more important factor during emergencies. A July 2010 opinion survey conducted for the American Red Cross found that Americans—especially those between the ages of 18 and 34—expect government agencies to use social media during emergencies.[24] A 2009 DHS Advisory Council survey of constituencies who work with emergency warning systems[25] found:

> "Warning systems for extreme events have long been designed in favor of a top-down, command and control model which relies heavily on experts for risk detection, decision making, and information dissemination. However, in the world of Web 2.0, communication modes and mechanisms are changing quickly. Members of the public are no longer reliant on information from public authorities, nor will they wait for official communications in times of need. Instead, they utilize social networks and networked communications to access information, to create and produce information, and to broadcast information to others."[26]

The DHS report says that new media must be integrated within any new emergency advisory system, and that involving the public through blogs and other systems that allow for public input is crucial to the success of any 21st-century risk communications strategy:[27]

> "Specific social media channels that can be utilized include wikis for collaborative information sharing about community risk, national risk, and protective actions; social networks such as Facebook or MySpace, using widgets linked to key protective action information; microblogs such as Twitter, which work as rapid or viral dissemination mechanisms for short text messages; and collaborative mapping for location-based information linked to key events or physical sites where help can be sought for evacuation, sheltering, decontamination, and other assistance. Videos or pictures demonstrating specific protective actions can be linked directly to alert and warning information via sites like YouTube or Flickr. Furthermore, educational campaigns can take advantage of multi-user online game technologies such as Second Life.

> "Now that these technologies exist, members of the public will come to expect that local, state and federal government will make use of them as effective means for communication."[28]

American Red Cross president and CEO Gail McGovern says, "The social web is creating a fundamental shift in disaster response—one that will ask emergency managers, government agencies and aid organizations to mix time-honored expertise with real-time input from the public."[29] The American Red Cross maintains an interactive presence on six social networks.[30]

In 2008, as Hurricanes Gustav and Ike approached the Gulf of Mexico, volunteers used the social-networking platform Ning to collect and organize hurricane information. Participants brought together news feeds from Twitter, Facebook, and blogs, and annotated maps with information about shelters, evacuation routes, and other resources.[31] While social media may seem chaotic, experts believe it can be an effective way to reach large numbers of people quickly. Dr. Jeannette Sutton, senior research scientist in the Trauma Health and Hazards Center at the University of Colorado at Colorado Springs, has concluded: "Social media is very organized. It just isn't organized through a central point." Government authorities have traditionally expressed concern about the reliability of reports from non-official sources, but Sutton argues that social media tends to be self-correcting: "Those who participate on sites like Wikipedia or are invested in a particular conversation have some sort of stake in making sure the information is correct. So they put out information to correct misinformation."

In Contra Costa County, a map-based computer program generates a single warning, which in turn triggers sirens, phone notifications, broadcast alerts, Twitter and email, and web displays.

American nongovernmental groups are also drawing on experiences in third-world countries, where residents without computers or Internet access use their mobile phones to transmit messages, and aid organizations are developing disaster assistance programs that work around cell phone technology. For example, Ushahidi ("testimony" in Swahili) is an open-source system (i.e., freely available to use or modify, without having to license the software) that allows users to construct a map of developments as they unfold in a given locale. Witnesses transmit information via text messages, tweets, and email reports, which is then placed on a map to allow aid workers and other volunteers to track where help is needed. Since its first use tracking post-election violence in Kenya in 2007, Ushahidi has helped such diverse efforts as targeting aid after the Haitian and Chilean earthquakes, tracking Swine Flu reports, and directing snowplows to road blockages in the snowstorms that closed much of the Washington, D.C., area in early 2010.[32]

Nonetheless, a 2009 American Public Health Association survey found that less than 20 percent of emergency managers use social media as anything other than a traditional, one-way broadcast tool aimed at educating the public or influencing public behavior. Most government agencies are playing catch-up with private businesses and nonprofits in the use of digital technology in times of crisis.[33]

Public broadcasters have begun to help all broadcasters use social media and other tools effectively during crises. They developed the SAFER (Station Action for Emergency Readiness) program, a set of online tools to help radio and television stations plan for staying on the air, online, and in touch with their audiences during emergencies.

CAP, PLAN, and IPAWS were conceived with broadband in mind. Further, the use of social media depends on the proliferation of broadband infrastructure, particularly at the state level. As recommended by the FCC's *National Broadband Plan*, in the spring of 2011 the FCC will launch a comprehensive next-generation alert system inquiry, exploring all issues for developing a broadband-based, next-generation alert system.[34]

American Red Cross CEO Gail McGovern: "The social web is creating a fundamental shift in disaster response—one that will ask emergency managers, government agencies and aid organizations to mix time-honored expertise with real-time input from the public."

18 Libraries

RATHER THAN BEING MADE OBSOLETE by new technologies, it appears that libraries are playing an increasingly important role in making sure communities get the information they need. Their importance was highlighted by the Knight Commission on the Information Needs of Communities in a Democracy: There are 9,198 public libraries in the United States, with over 16,500 outlets. Americans *use* them. Visits to public libraries totaled 1.4 billion in 2005. The circulation of materials topped two billion items.[1] Over three-quarters of all Americans used public libraries in the year leading up to a September 2009 survey.[2] A March 2010 survey conducted by the Institute of Museum and Library Services (IMLS) with funding from the University of Washington Information School and the Bill and Melinda Gates Foundation found that nearly half of all visitors use the Internet services at the library.[3]

> **44% of those in poverty used public library computers and Internet access.**

The IMLS survey also found that the three most common uses of library computers were to get information on education (42 percent), employment (40 percent), and health (37 percent).[4] One-third of those surveyed used library computers to learn about politics, news, and their community.[5] Many people turn to libraries for Internet access when their home service has been disrupted as well as during an emergency. In the aftermath of Hurricane Katrina, public libraries were among the last remaining places where people living in the Gulf region could search online for housing and FEMA aid.[6]

Today an Internet connection is often needed to complete school assignments, apply for jobs or college, and secure government services. According to the IMLS study, public libraries have become "extensions of the nation's education system. Librarians have begun serving as informal job coaches, college counselors, test monitors, and technology trainers."[7]

For less affluent populations, libraries have become especially important for the computer and Internet access they provide. Forty-four percent of people living in households below the federal poverty line used public library computers and Internet access, the IMLS survey found. Sixty-one percent of low-income young adults (ages 14 to 24) used them for educational purposes.[8] Many went to the library simply to learn how to use a computer:

> "At a time when access to technology and the Internet is becoming a necessary resource for full participation in society, public libraries provide an especially vital service to households in need. The study found that low income households, the elderly and English learners, were among the groups most likely to make use of computer training opportunities at local libraries. For these households, public libraries may provide the only low-cost entry point into an increasingly Internet-dependent world."[9]

About 35 percent of libraries offer formal technology classes and 53 percent offer informal assistance for patrons using library computers. In high-poverty areas, 97 percent of libraries offer classes in basic computer competencies, including mouse, keyboard, and general software use skills.[10]

The IMLS study found that adult learners most often use library computers and internet access to apply to vocational programs—to earn a professional license or certificates or a two-year degree. For instance, the study found that:

> "Chloe, a 50-year-old high school graduate from Baltimore, was one such user. Currently homeless, Chloe had been frustrated in her ability to find work because she lacked an email address—she explained, 'See, the jobs I used to get, you didn't need an email account for.' During her first visit to the library computer center, a librarian helped her set up an email account which she immediately began to use to send out job applications. Chloe eventually decided to pursue formal vocational education and

used the library's computers to find a nursing program: 'I looked it up last November for nursing on the Internet here, they told me everything, gave me the phone number; I called down there and started the school in November.' "[11]

In Chicago, the public library system's CyberNavigators program supplements staff librarians with young adult, part-time staffers who provide assistance with everything from basic computer instruction to advanced computer troubleshooting. CyberNavigators help people apply for unemployment insurance, write resumes, and set up new email accounts.[12] They also teach classes aimed at computer novices: Internet Basics, Mouse Skills, and Introduction to Email.[13] Begun as an experimental summer project, the CyberNavigators program is now a year-round effort funded through the Chicago Public Library Foundation by a grant from Bank of America.[14] "I haven't given up. I can't," a 69-year-old legal secretary said in a 2010 article about the program. "I have goals. I'm constantly doing searches on these job sites."[15] A principal at a low-income high school in Oakland, California, reported that most of his students use the Internet connection at the public library. "We work with largely disadvantaged and at-risk youth, and they don't have computers at home, so they come here to the library. They get support here. The librarians help them attain the online and print materials they need."[16]

Yet libraries are struggling to keep up with demand for Internet-based information services. Many visitors complain about the lines at the terminals and limits on how much time an individual can spend on the computer. More than 81 percent of libraries report that they have insufficient workstation availability some or all of the time, leading 94 percent to impose time limits on use of the workstations.[17]

The workstation shortage is particularly acute in high-poverty areas, which experienced the greatest decline in the number of workstations, falling from 27.2 per library in 2007/08 to 22 per library in 2008/09. In low-poverty areas, the number of workstations did not change much, falling from 11 per library to 10.4 per library in the same time period.[18]

About 60 percent of libraries consider their current connection speeds insufficient during at least part of the day.[19] For almost another quarter, higher speeds are just not affordable.[20]

"Chloe, a 50-year-old high school graduate from Baltimore, used the library's computers to find a nursing program: 'I looked it up... on the Internet here. They told me everything, gave me the phone number; I called down there and started the school in November.'"

In an effort to help expand library patrons' access to the Internet, the 1996 Telecommunications Reform Act included a provision that created the current "E-rate" program.[21] The program allocates approximately $2.25 billion a year to provide schools and libraries with discounts[22] on their purchases of Internet access, including internal connections.[23] To qualify, libraries must be eligible for assistance from a state library administrative agency under the Library Services and Technology Act, be nonprofit, and have budgets separate and independent of any school.[24]

More than 50 percent of U.S. libraries received E-rate discounts in the funding year 2008/09.[25] Over the last 10 years, libraries have received on average about $70 million per year.[26] The E-rate program seems to have helped enhance libraries' Internet access. During 2008/9, more than 44 percent of libraries reported connection speeds greater than 1.5 Mbps (compared with 25.7 percent in 2007/8), including about 64 percent of those in high-poverty locations.[27]

The American Library Association says that public demand for library Internet access is growing and is likely to surge with the advent of high-definition video streaming, the increasing prevalence of online job training and use of the Internet to submit employment applications, consumers' growing need for e-government services, and rising numbers of computer terminals and wireless laptop computer users.[28]

19 Schools

THE PREVIOUS CHAPTERS HAVE FOCUSED on the supply side of information—who produces it and how it is distributed. But what about the demand side—what kind of information do consumers seek? Ultimately, what citizens demand will affect not only democracy but the dynamics of the media market. If too many Americans do not care about or know how to find quality information, it is less likely to be produced.

Experts have focused on three related educational areas that schools (and other institutions) need to teach: "digital literacy" (how to use new technology), "media literacy" (how to assess online media in general), and "news literacy" (how to consume news in a sophisticated manner).

Digital Literacy

Conventional wisdom asserts that Americans born during the past three decades are naturally computer savvy and digitally literate, innately equipped to maneuver in the digital world more easily and successfully than older generations. In actuality, the young people who have grown up understanding how to utilize digital technology are generally those from socioeconomic elite families, with higher incomes and more education than most Americans. But even those who are technologically savvy often lack the skills required to conduct research online, or to discern the authenticity of the texts they are reading and the sources that provided them.[1] Genuine digital literacy requires more advanced skills and is essential to an informed citizenry's ability to explore and fulfill its information and educational needs in the 21st century. Cultural historian Siva Vaidhyanathan has written:

> "As a professor, I am in the constant company of 18-to-23-year-olds. I have taught at both public and private universities.… The levels of comfort with, understanding of, and dexterity with digital technology varies greatly within every class. Yet it has not changed in the aggregate in more than 10 years. Every class has a handful of people with amazing skills and a large number who can't deal with computers at all."[2]

In a recently published report for the Aspen Institute, media literacy scholar Renee Hobbs wrote:[3]

> "Many teens lack the ability to identify appropriate keywords for an online search activity, and many young adults cannot identify the author of a web page. These same children and young people often are convinced they are expert researchers because they can find information 'on Google.…'
>
> "People use a small number of research strategies in a repetitive way even when they do not get the information they are seeking. They don't take the time to digest and evaluate what they encounter. In many cases, students typically use information that finds them, rather than deciding what information *they* need."[4]

There is a broad consensus that substantive Internet skills should be incorporated into basic K–12 educational curricula. But few K–12 educational leaders are familiar with the pedagogy and core concepts of either digital or media literacy education.[5] Although all states incorporate some elements into their public education systems, many teachers report that they received little training or guidance from their school systems when drawing up lesson plans.[6]

Because of this, media scholars and education experts have begun recommending that states give greater attention to digital literacy skills. The Center for Media Literacy,[7] the National Association for Media Literacy Education (NAMLE),[8] Project New Media Literacies,[9] and the Media Education Lab[10] all have urged state educational systems to establish digital literacy curricula beginning at the primary school level, and to establish standards to ensure that their teaching staffs are equipped to teach these skills.

In the summer of 2009, U.S. Senators Rockefeller (West Virginia), Snowe (Maine), and Kerry (Massachusetts) introduced S. 1029, a bipartisan bill to establish a 21st Century Skills Incentive Fund that would provide $100 million annually in matching grants to public primary and secondary schools that establish digital and media literacy programs. The June 2009 press release announcing the bill noted: "74% of Americans believe proficiency in using computer technology should be a high school graduation requirement, ranking its importance just below that of reading (94%) and writing (84%); and 76% of the public support students learning to use computers at a young age."[11]

Media Literacy

Media literacy involves adapting critical thinking skills to a multimedia age. NAMLE describes media literacy as a system of "active inquiry and critical thinking about the messages we receive and create."[12]

More specifically, in a world in which students are constantly bombarded with messages, both negative and positive, media literacy supplies them with the tools they need to help make sense of all that information. "People today need sophisticated skills and competencies involving the ability to find information, comprehend it, and use it to solve problems. The growth of the knowledge economy is dependent upon workers who have these skills," writes NAMLE.[13] Children need to critically analyze and evaluate the quality of both entertainment and information.[14] That means, for instance, not assuming all websites that *look* professional are credible and knowing how to tell when a site about a product is created by its producer rather than an independent third party.[15]

> "Many teens lack the ability to identify appropriate keywords for an online search activity, and many young adults cannot identify the author of a web page."

Media literacy education aims to give students tools to learn not to take messages at face value, but to evaluate the reliability of their sources; and to understand not only what the message says, but also factors that might influence the source's viewpoint—whether it is something as basic as the date on which the information was transmitted (e.g., before or after September 11, 2001), a different cultural perspective (e.g., many countries are not familiar with the First Amendment values that Americans take for granted, and therefore accept censorship that would outrage Americans), or potential bias, whether deliberate or not.

Media literacy education also involves learning how to create effective messages, which among other things means becoming aware that different audiences require different approaches. For example, many young people who have grown up using the informal slang associated with text-messaging are often unprepared for and even unaware of the need to switch gears for the more formal communication styles required in school and business.

Media literacy can affect people's decisions about medical treatment or nutrition. As Renee Hobbs writes, "To get relevant health information, people need to be able to distinguish between a crackpot marketing ploy for nutritional supplements and solid information based on research evidence."[16] Since the 1990s, when the federal Office of National Drug Control Policy incorporated media literacy education into student substance-abuse programs targeting tobacco and alcohol advertising, most states have included aspects of media literacy education in their health education instruction segments, as part of an emphasis on helping students understand environmental influences on their health decisions.

Training can also help people protect themselves from the negative aspects of media. The American Academy of Pediatrics (AAP) has stated: "Particularly important are the effects of violent or sexual content, and movies or shows that glamorize alcohol and tobacco use. Studies have associated high levels of media use with school problems, attention difficulties, sleep and eating disorders, and obesity. And the Internet and cell phones have become important new sources and platforms for illicit and risky behaviors."[17] The AAP has endorsed widespread media literacy education.[18]

Common Sense Media, an independent nonprofit group, offers a Digital Literacy and Citizenship Curriculum to teach young children online safety and older kids "digital citizenship."[19] Components include:

"Students reflect on how to behave ethically online.

"Digital Life Unit: Students explore the positive and negative impact of digital media on their lives and communities, and define what it means to be a responsible digital citizen.

"Privacy and Digital Footprints Unit (middle school only): Students learn that the Internet is a very public space, and therefore they must carefully manage their information and respect the privacy of others online.

"Self-Expression and Identity Unit (middle school only): Students identify and explore different ways they can present themselves online while also learning to recognize when playing with identity crosses the line into deception.

"Connected Culture Unit: Students explore the ethics of online communities—both the negative behaviors to avoid, such as cyberbullying and hurtful behavior, and positive behaviors that support collaboration and constructive relationships. They also learn about how to clearly communicate by email.

"Respecting Creative Work Unit: Students learn about the value and responsibility of being a 21st-century creator: receiving credit for your own online work and giving others respect by properly citing their work."[20]

News Literacy

News literacy, a subset of media literacy, has been defined as "the ability to use critical thinking skills to judge the reliability and credibility of news reports and news sources."[21] One recent Pew study found that 31 percent of people aged 18 to 24 had not obtained news the day before (compared to 17 percent for the population as a whole).[22] News habits tend to be formed early; if young people turn away from the news, it may lead to a less informed citizenry and make it less likely that there will be a critical mass of news consumers to sustain the high-quality journalism and information production crucial to a healthy democracy.

Several former journalists—motivated in part by the assumption that *valuing quality journalism will spur its creation*—have moved to create news literacy programs to help insure that young people become well-informed, non-gullible adults. Rex Smith, editor of the *Albany Times-Union* explained: "There needs to be an audience that recognizes good journalism even when there's no longer a reflexive trust in the vendors of journalism."[23] Conversely, a public understanding of what constitutes good journalism would help police the excesses of the fourth estate. As explained by Howard Schneider, a former editor of *Newsday* and founder of the National Center for News Literacy at the Stony Brook University Journalism School:

> In one curriculum, "Students explore the ethics of online communities—both the negative behaviors to avoid, such as cyberbullying and hurtful behavior, and positive behaviors that support collaboration and constructive relationships."

"The ultimate check against an inaccurate or irresponsible press never would be just better-trained journalists, or more press critics and ethical codes. It would be a generation of news consumers who would learn how to distinguish for themselves between news and propaganda, verification and mere assertion, evidence and inference, bias and fairness, and between media bias and audience bias—consumers who could differentiate between raw, unmediated information coursing through the Internet and independent, verified journalism."[24]

News literacy efforts used to be a more common fixture in American education. According to Renee Hobbs, "In 1947, more than half of American high schools offered a course in Problems in Democracy that emphasized news and current events reading. Times have changed.... Today many K–12 educators believe it's not good for children to read or view the news. Research has shown that violent news content induces more fear reactions than violent fiction, creating persistent worrisome thoughts."[25] Moreover, many teachers are reluctant to bring news and current events into the classroom due to today's increasingly polarized political climate.[26]

Studies have shown that newspaper reading in high school contributes to reading and writing skill development.[27] According to the Growing Lifelong Readers study, "more than 60 percent of young adults with high exposure to newspapers in the classroom say they read a weekday paper regularly. Of those without exposure to newspapers in the classroom, the weekday readership is only 38 percent."[28]

Fortunately, some journalism organizations and foundations associated with journalism have stepped into this educational breach. Founded by former investigative reporter Alan C. Miller, the Bethesda, Maryland-based News Literacy Project is a two-year-old national educational program that mobilizes seasoned journalists to help middle school and high school students sort fact from fiction in the digital age. In 2009 through 2010, the News Literacy

Project worked with 21 teachers of English, history, and government in seven middle schools and high schools in New York City, Bethesda, and Chicago, reaching nearly 1,500 students. More than 75 journalists spoke to students and worked with them on projects. Among them:[29]

> Gwen Ifill of the PBS *NewsHour* and *Washington Week* explained how she handles bias: "I hope you never know what I think. I'm there to provide you the information so you can decide. I have to keep open the possibility that the other guy has a point.... I have to be an honest broker."

> Sheryl Gay Stolberg of the *New York Times* described how she spent the entire previous day nailing down a single name: that of the third gate-crasher at the infamous state dinner that President Barack Obama hosted for the prime minister of India at the White House in November 2009.

> Peter Eisler of *USA Today* discussed accountability: "Never trust anybody who doesn't admit they make a mistake. Never trust anyone in life who doesn't admit they make a mistake."

In one memorable presentation, Brian Rokus, a CNN producer, showed the students video excerpts from a report he did with Christiane Amanpour about the New York Philharmonic's trip to North Korea in 2008. The students got a glimpse of a country without First Amendment protections of free speech. They saw the minders who shadowed the tightly restricted American journalists. Rokus also passed around a copy of the *Pyongyang Times* with its full-page paeans to the nation's "Dear Leader." He then handed out an Associated Press report of a speech that President Obama had made to Congress and asked the students to cross out everything they would censor if they were the editor of the *Pyongyang Times* and Obama was the "Dear Leader."

Another journalism organization, the American Society of News Editors (ASNE), focuses on assisting high school journalism programs. ASNE offers an online toolkit to introduce the topic of news literacy[30] and also sponsors the High School Journalism Institute, an intensive two-week journalism training program for high school teachers. Since the Institute's 2001 founding, it has trained 1,603 high school teachers, most of whom continue to teach journalism and/or advise student media. One-third of those most recently trained teach at schools with minority-student populations of 50 percent or higher. ASNE also hosts an educational site at www.hsj.org and a high-school journalism website, which it touts as "the world's largest host of teen-generated news, connected to more than 3,000 student news outlets."[31]

"In 1947, more than half of high schools offered a course in Problems in Democracy that emphasized current events reading. Today many K–12 educators believe it's not good for children to read or view the news."

Digital and Media Literacy in the States

While U.S. school systems are generally aware that their students need to learn computer competency, digital and media literacy has not been implemented into the curricula in any consistent way throughout the country. Some school systems may offer stand-alone courses, while others incorporate aspects of digital and media literacy into various courses, including reading and language arts, library skills, and information technology. (Those who fear that "media literacy" curricula might be used to push a particular political agenda can be comforted that these efforts have popped up all over the country, in red, blue, and purple voting districts.)

The National Association of Media Literacy Education says that all 50 states include at least some components of media literacy in their education standards for public instruction. As of 2009, only 31 had instituted standards for media literacy curricula.[32] Of the 19 states that have not done so, 13 reported that they intend to do so in the future; the remaining six have no plans to do so.[33]

In Louisiana, media literacy is incorporated into school information literacy and library media programs. The guidelines declare:

"Interdisciplinary by nature, media literacy is concerned with helping students acquire the skills needed to comprehend the messages they receive through print and non-print media outlets—e.g., TV, radio, movies, Internet—and explore the impact of media and technology in our society. To become a successful student, responsible citizen, productive worker, or competent and conscientious consumer, individuals need to develop expertise with the increasingly sophisticated information and entertainment media that address us on a multi-sensory level, affecting the way we think, feel and behave."[34]

Missouri is one of the few states to have established specific criteria for integrating media literacy within the K–12 curriculum, setting out the following requirements for reading, listening and speaking, and information literacy:[35]

> During Grades K–4, schools are expected to teach students, with increasing degrees of sophistication and detail, how to "identify, with assistance, topics of messages conveyed through oral and visual media."

> During Grade 3, students are to be taught to "listen to distinguish fact from opinion."

> During Grade 4, students are to be taught to "use details from text to distinguish between fact and opinion, to identify and explain author's purpose," and to "identify and explain intended messages conveyed through oral and visual media."

> During Grade 5, students are to be taught to "analyze messages conveyed in various media (e.g., videos, pictures, websites, artwork, plays and/or news programs)."

> During Grade 6, students are to be taught to "use details from text to evaluate the accuracy of the information, to identify and interpret the author's purpose, slant, and bias," and to "identify and explain viewpoints conveyed in various media."

> During Grade 7, students are to be taught to "use details from the text to evaluate the accuracy of the information, analyze propaganda techniques" and "locate and use multiple sources to evaluate the reliability of information."

> During Grades 8–12, students are to be taught to incorporate appropriate media or technology into their discussions and presentations.

> During Grades 9–12, students are to be taught to locate and use multiple primary and secondary sources to select relevant and credible information; to evaluate the reliability of information; and to evaluate the reliability of sources."[36]

Noting the wide divergence in state curricula, state education leaders around the country have made digital and media literacy part of their 2010 Common Core State Standards Initiative, declaring that students who are college and career ready must be able to "use technology and digital media strategically and capably," employing technology "thoughtfully to enhance their reading, writing, speaking, listening, and language use." Students should be able to "tailor their searches online to acquire useful information efficiently," be able to "integrate what they learn using technology with what they learn offline," be "familiar with the strengths and limitations of various technological tools and mediums," and be able to "select and use those best suited to their communication goals."[37]

The process of adopting state standards depends on the laws of each state. Some states are adopting the standards through their state boards of education, while others are adopting them through their state legislatures.[38]

key cross-cutting issues

We have looked at the media landscape in terms of the traditional sectors that produce and/or disseminate news, information, and journalism. But the lines between these sectors are becoming increasingly blurred. In this world of converging media, TV is on the phone, the Internet is on the TV, and the newspaper is on the tablet. This section looks at the media landscape through different lenses. Rather than looking at individual market sectors—such as "newspapers" or "mobile"—it examines trends that cut across many platforms. In some cases, we draw on material that appeared in the first parts of this report; in others, we introduce new information. In all, we attempt to answer these questions: Overall, which parts of the media system are healthy and which are most vulnerable? How well is the media performing its most important functions? How have changes in the media world affected communities that have historically been underserved by mass media, such as ethnic minorities and people with disabilities?

If there is a vacuum in news, information, and journalism, how significant is it—and how likely is it that commercial markets alone will fill the void?

20 News Consumption

Consuming More Media

The media system has provided consumers with more choices with each passing decade. Cable and satellite TV dramatically increased the number of channels available, including many dedicated to national and business news, and the digital revolution seems to generate new options every time we blink.

Americans have responded to the proliferation of media choices by increasing their consumption. Looking at the full range—TV, radio, print, mobile devices, computers, video games, movies, recorded music—the average number of hours a typical American spends taking in some form of media rose from 7.4 hours per day in 1980 to 11.8 in 2008.[1]

The consumption of news has fluctuated in recent years. The average American spends 70 minutes a day taking in the news, according to the Pew Research Center for the People & the Press (although that number does not include news read on cell phones, iPads, or other digital devices).[2]

Americans have not abandoned traditional media (TV, radio, newspapers); they spend 57 minutes with those sources, roughly the same as in 2000.[3] But they spend an additional 13 minutes each day getting news online.[4]

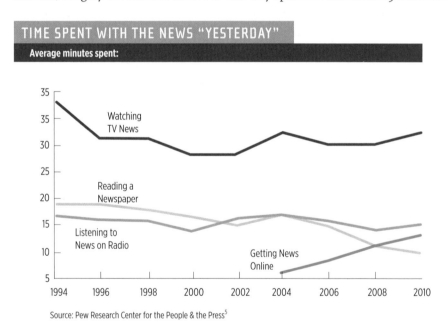

TIME SPENT WITH THE NEWS "YESTERDAY"

Average minutes spent:

Watching TV News

Reading a Newspaper

Listening to News on Radio

Getting News Online

Source: Pew Research Center for the People & the Press[5]

More Americans Are Skipping the News

But that robust overall number belies a small but worrisome trend. The percentage of Americans who reported that they had gone "newsless" the day before they were asked in a Pew survey rose from 14 percent in 1998 to 17 percent in 2009—and it was highest, 31 percent, among 18 to 24 year olds.

How can that be? After all, technology offers a stunningly wide variety of ways to get news, and young people are most facile with the newest technologies. It is possible that such surveys fail to include programs like the *Daily Show* that convey news but which respondents might not have thought to mention when surveyed. The most likely explanation is that while sources of news have increased, so have entertainment and sports choices. A study of 12 media markets in the 1980s, when cable TV was becoming more popular, showed that as consumers had more choices, they watched local news less frequently than those with broadcast TV only.[7] In addition, scholar Markus Prior conducted an experiment in which participants were randomly given one of two sets of choices and asked to make a decision:

1 Watch nightly broadcast network news or turn off television.

2 Watch broadcast network news, cable news, a comedy or sitcom, a drama, a science fiction program, a reality show, or a sports program, OR turn off the television.

When given choice set number one, 79.9 percent chose to watch news instead of turning off the set. When offered choice set number two, only 35.4 percent chose to watch broadcast network news, and an additional 8 percent chose cable news.[8]

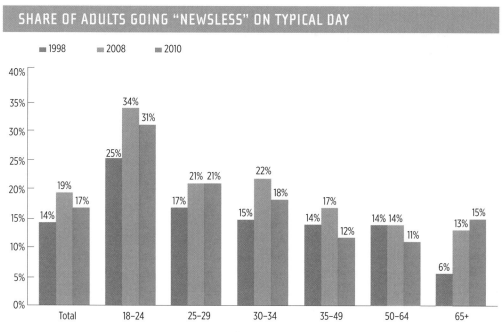

SHARE OF ADULTS GOING "NEWSLESS" ON TYPICAL DAY

■ 1998   ■ 2008   ■ 2010

Source: The Pew Research Center for the People and the Press[6]

In general, the increasing possibility that consumers can more easily avoid news has led some to fear that Americans' "incidental" exposure to news has declined. The traditional media, including TV and newspapers, in some ways thrust news on the unwilling and unexpecting. Sociologist Paul Starr testified at an FCC workshop:

> "Many people have bought and read their local paper primarily because of their interest in sports, stocks, the comics, or job opportunities, but they have nonetheless still scanned the front pages and learned something about their community. Online, however, anyone interested in sports, stocks, jobs, and so on can go to specialized, free sites that are typically better than what their local paper offers—except that those sites don't expose them, even minimally, to the news of their community. The incidental learning of a bundled metropolitan paper disappears, just as much of the incidental learning from exposure to local radio and television news is dropping with the fragmentation of television and audio audiences."[9]

This is not a black-and-white issue. Those using Internet portals like Yahoo!, MSN, and AOL to get sports scores may come across news headlines along the way. Facebook users will have news on various topics thrust before them by their friends. Indeed, news is so ubiquitous that one study concluded that those with a pre-existing interest in news are likely to stumble upon more and more of it, even when they are not trying.[10]

Both trends may be true at the same time: news junkies have more ways of finding news and everyone else has more ways of avoiding it.

Americans have not abandoned traditional media (TV, radio, newspapers). They spend 57 minutes with those sources, roughly the same as in 2000. But they spend an additional 13 minutes getting news online.

Americans Are Spending More on Media—and the Financial Beneficiaries Have Changed

From 2003 to 2008, the average annual spending per person on media and information rose from approximately $740 to $882[11]—an increase of 19 percent. This growth rate is greater than for other categories of consumer spending; for instance, spending on "apparel and services" rose only 9.8 percent during that period.[12] In terms of dollars, most of the increase can be attributed to rising consumer payments to satellite and cable TV service providers: the average spent on cable and satellite TV during this period was $294. In terms of percentage, spending on mobile phone service is growing the fastest.

ANNUAL MEDIA SPENDING PER CONSUMER[13]

Year	TV and Radio	Entertainment	Print	Pure Play Internet	Pure Play Mobile	Total
2003	$234.65	$244.20	$193.89	$60.39	$4.54	$737.67
2004	$257.58	$249.89	$193.85	$60.31	$7.54	$769.17
2005	$283.24	$234.41	$195.75	$57.88	$9.59	$780.87
2006	$313.34	$240.27	$193.25	$54.06	$12.33	$813.25
2007	$339.67	$241.67	$195.69	$55.45	$15.66	$848.14
2008	$366.72	$239.75	$189.17	$57.46	$18.55	$871.65

Source: U.S. Census Bureau[13]

Since consumers now get some material for free that they used to pay for—many online newspapers and magazines, for instance—it has been tempting to think that Americans are paying less for content. In reality, however, they are paying more than ever before. They may pay less for individual pieces of content, but they pay more for *access* to the content. The two-thirds of Americans with broadband at home, on average, pay $41 per month, and those with cell phones (86 percent of adults, nearly a third of whom own smartphones with online access) pay $92 per month.[14]

What has changed is not whether Americans are willing to pay—but to whom they are sending the cash. Much of the money Americans now spend on media goes to cable TV companies; Internet service providers (which often are cable companies); and mobile phone service providers. Pre-Internet and pre-cable, when most of what Americans spent on media went to newspapers—since TV and radio were free—the majority of the money went to the companies that created the content. Now, much of it goes to companies that do not create content.

Polarization

The Internet has given people tools to stitch together communities and connect with friends and strangers, locally as well as across vast distances. However, concern has grown that that the modern media landscape—specifically, its proliferation of media choices—has contributed to "polarization," with consumers gravitating toward shows or networks viewed by other people like themselves. The following Pew table charts ideological and partisan proclivities by show and network.

Academics have documented that when presented with a wide variety of choices, many Americans choose media outlets more in line with their views.[15] And the more people know about politics, the more likely they are to choose media that is also consumed by people like them. On the other hand, other studies have shown that people

In the Internet era, it has become conventional wisdom that Americans are less willing to pay for media than in the past. In reality, they are paying more than ever before.

Percentage of each audience who are . . .

■ Republican ■ Democrat ■ Independent

	Republican	Democrat	Independent
Rush Limbaugh	63	10	23
Hannity	62	6	29
O'Reilly Factor	54	10	32
Glenn Beck	53	9	33
Fox News	44	21	28
Wall Street Journal	36	22	41
USA Today	33	26	35
News blogs	28	34	34
Daily paper	28	34	33
Local TV news	25	35	32
TOTAL	25	33	34
Sunday shows	24	37	32
Network evening	24	35	34
Morning shows	23	43	30
News magazines	22	40	34
CNN	17	47	31
MSNBC	14	53	30
Daily Show	14	41	38
NPR	14	40	41
Colbert Report	14	39	44
Hardball	13	51	29
Rachel Maddow	12	50	34
New York Times	9	49	39
Countdown	3	60	29

■ Conservative ■ Moderate ■ Liberal

	Conservative	Moderate	Liberal
Hannity	80	15	3
Rush Limbaugh	80	13	2
Glenn Beck	74	19	2
O'Reilly Factor	72	21	3
Fox News	60	26	9
USA Today	46	41	11
Wall Street Journal	45	41	12
News blogs	41	33	24
Daily paper	40	40	17
Local TV news	39	41	14
Morning shows	36	42	16
Network evening	36	41	15
TOTAL	36	37	19
Sunday shows	35	40	18
MSNBC	30	38	30
News magazines	28	42	29
CNN	26	45	23
Hardball	25	39	33
NPR	22	45	29
Rachel Maddow	21	40	35
Daily Show	19	42	35
Colbert Report	19	41	35
Countdown	12	42	43
New York Times	11	47	38

Source: "Americans Spending More Time Following the News," by the Pew Research Center on The People & The Press (2010)

who look at their favorite ideological sites also look at other news sites.[16] Whether these patterns are worrisome or not continues to be debated widely, though it is not the focus of this report. Another question that could be studied in this regard: do polarization patterns make it harder for news models to take root that do not cater to one ideological perspective or another? If increasing numbers of people tend to gravitate toward more opinionated news, does that make it harder for more of the less-opinionated outlets to develop enough scale to create sustainable business models?

21 Types Of News

IN THE FIRST SEVERAL CHAPTERS, we saw media systems in flux. Fewer newspaper journalists but more websites, more hours of local TV news but fewer reporters, more "news/talk" radio but less local news radio, national cable news thriving, local cable news stalled.

But what matters most is not the health of a particular sector but how these changes net out, and how the pieces fit together. Here we will consider the health of the news media based on the region of coverage, whether neighborhood, city, state, country, or world.

Hyperlocal

The term "hyperlocal" commonly refers to news coverage on a neighborhood or even block-by-block level. The traditional media models, even in their fattest, happiest days could not field enough reporters to cover every neighborhood on a granular level.

As in all areas, there are elements of progress and retreat. On one hand, metropolitan newspapers have cut back on regional editions, which in all likelihood means less coverage of neighborhoods in those regions.

But the Internet has revolutionized the provision of hyperlocal information. The first wave of technology—LISTSERV® and other email groups—made it far easier for citizens to inform one another of what was happening with the neighborhood crime watch or the new grocery store or the death of a beloved senior who lived on the block for 40 years. More recently, social media tools have enabled citizens to self-organize, and connect in ever more dynamic ways. Citizens can now snap pictures of potholes and send them to city hall, or share with each other via Facebook, Twitter or email. New tools allow citizens to mine citywide information in ways that create hyperlocal stories: a database on restaurant health violations becomes a story about a diner down the block. Hyperlocal blogs—presenting a mix of reporting, commentary, and aggregation—are popping up throughout the country. They will not, for the most part, become successful businesses—*but they do not have to.* Volunteers can operate hyperlocal media just as volunteers organize clean-up days for the block.

> **Citizens can now snap picture of potholes and send to city hall, or share them with each other.**

These tools not only help the purely volunteer-based media but have given opportunities to commercial Internet ventures too. Many local TV stations have added hyperlocal areas to their websites. AOL's Patch, Examiner.com, and Everyblock each rely on community members to contribute content for free or for a small fee.

Two unknowns: so far, hyperlocal print weeklies have fared reasonably well in the new media economy (See Chapter 1, Newspapers.) But they will likely feel increasing pressure as online classifieds services, like Craigslist, and sites like Examiner.com and Patch, extend their reach into smaller communities and as locally originated sites are launched and/or expand.

Finally, recent legislation allowing for the growth of low-power FM may bring a wave of hyperlocal radio stations, especially in urban areas. These stations have only enough power to broadcast on a neighborhood basis, but it is unclear how they will be utilized. (See Chapter 11, Low Power FM.)

City and State

Local metropolitan and state-level coverage represent the areas of greatest concern— especially when it comes to how often and how thoroughly journalists report on powerful institutions such as city hall, the school board, the statehouse, and the local hospital. Almost every sector of media that covered these beats in the past has been shaken and transformed. Throughout Part One we looked at the positive and negative developments. To summarize:

> Newspapers, which had been the main source for this kind of reporting, have cut back staff. There are strong signs that these cutbacks have weakened coverage of schools, health care issues, city government, state legislatures, religion, and other important topics. Although many newspapers have become quite innovative online in the past couple of years, it generally has resulted in an increase in the ways news is presented, but not in the number of reporters gathering news. Even when beats have not been eliminated entirely, beat reporters have become responsible for covering more territory and "feeding the beast" by tweeting and writing blog posts in addition to their regular stories. These days, many newspapers reporters spend less time interviewing sources and more time producing copy. They have less time for enterprise journalism of the sort that anticipates problems and uncovers information that those in power want to conceal.

> Local radio has not stepped in to fill the void. In fact, the number of cities that had all-news radio stations dropped from 50 in the 1980s to 30 in 2010. Robert Papper, who surveys radio station news directors for the Radio Television Digital News Association, says:

"I can say this without a doubt—there are far fewer stations doing news than 10 years ago, there are far fewer people hired by commercial radio to work in the newsrooms, and the median number of people employed in a commercial radio newsroom has been 'one' for quite a few years." [1]

Although there are notable exceptions around the country, it's not realistic to expect that radio will counteract the loss of newspaper jobs.

> Local TV has, in some ways, expanded its role in the local news ecosystem. The number of hours of news aired has grown, and increasing numbers of stations are making full use of social media to enliven and enhance the quality of broadcasts. For instance, many stations now incorporate user videos, photos, and commentary to enhance coverage of natural disasters. Some stations continue to produce high-quality investigative journalism, as well. But on balance, stations have not increased their reportorial capacity, and in many cases they have cut it back. As a result, several long-standing maladies of local news have persisted, or even worsened, including: minimal coverage of local government, insufficient in-depth reporting, and a strong emphasis on crime coverage. Although they are not in the majority, a disturbing number of stations have allowed advertisers to dictate news content or in other ways blurred the lines between journalism and advertorial. In short, many stations are doing excellent work—and many more have the capacity to do even better—but, as yet, most stations have not been fielding enough reporters to fill the vacuum left by local newspapers.

"The tired idea that born-on-the-web news sites will replace traditional media is wrong-headed, and it's past time that academic research and news reports reflect that," said Michele McLellan after studying news websites.

> Cable TV, like radio, is thriving nationally (financially and in terms of audience), offering more national and business news programming than ever. But locally focused models have stalled, with local cable news efforts currently reaching only about 20 to 30 percent of the population. There are some hopeful signs—for instance, Time Warner and NBC/Comcast have announced plans to expand their local news efforts—but most other cable operators seem more inclined to freeze or cut back their local operations, as they are costly to maintain.

> Satellite TV has technological limitations and financial disincentives that make it an unlikely platform for increased local public affairs programming.

At first blush, it seems that there is more than enough exciting Internet-based activity to make up for the aforementioned gaps. But on closer inspection, it appears that in this one area—local accountability reporting—Internet-based properties have made insufficient progress. (See Chapter 4, Internet.)

Several studies—of Chicago, Baltimore, Philadelphia, and other cities—have found that Internet sites have not yet filled the gap. (See Chapter 4, Internet.)

Most of these hyperlocal blogs will not become successful businesses—but they do not have to. Volunteers can operate hyperlocal media just like volunteers organize clean-up days for the block.

A survey of 66 local news websites found that half of them had annual income of less than $50,000, and three-quarters had annual income of less than $100,000.[2] That is not enough to ensure these organizations' survival, much less finance labor-intensive journalism.

"The tired idea that born-on-the-web news sites will replace traditional media is wrong-headed, and it's past time that academic research and news reports reflect that,"[3] says Michele McLellan, who has done a comprehensive study of the new breed of news websites for the University of Missouri School of Journalism. While many of these organizations are providing services that never existed before—such as neighborhood-centric news—she makes clear that that does not compensate for the decrease in accountability reporting that was done by traditional newspapers.

What about national Internet companies that focus on local matters? These efforts *are* providing useful information on a wide range of topics, but, so far, they are not coming close to filling the gaps in accountability journalism. Examiner.com has hired thousands of local contributors, but its focus is on entertainment, sports, and shopping. Patch has hired 800 staff but has only one editor/reporter per community, and only covers small-to-medium-size affluent communities. At this point, Patch is more aptly seen as an element in the rise of hyperlocal information than as a solution to the deficiencies in municipal and state accountability reporting.

Some media companies have attempted to create "converged" models that use a combined newsroom to produce print, digital, and TV content. The hope is that by eliminating duplication and increasing reach, these entities will develop more robust business models. In Washington, Allbritton's combined newsroom launched a local TV station, a local all-news cable network, and a local website.[4] In Tampa, Media General has merged the operations of its newspaper and TV station. But while these efforts may have positive financial results for the companies, there is little evidence that they lead to the hiring of additional reporters. The merging of operations of the *Deseret Morning News*, KSL TV, and KSL Radio in Salt Lake City prompted media analyst Ken Doctor to note that both of these headlines could accurately describe the situation: "Salt Lake City Paper Axes 43% of its Staff" *and* "Deseret News a Model of Growth and Innovation for the Entire Industry." The mergers eliminate duplication, introduce efficiencies, and update technology—but have not necessarily led to more or better quality journalistic resources.[5]

Another collaborative model can be found in Ohio, where the eight largest newspapers joined forces to create the Ohio News Organization, which collectively fields reporters to cover the state.[6] They even produce some investigative projects—including an effort that found 32,000 public employees receiving pensions while still on the payroll.[7]

Is the nonprofit sector filling the gaps? Public TV stations do not do much in the way of local news: only 8 percent offer 30 minutes or more of local news per day. Public radio does a bit more and has tried in the past year to increase its investment in this area, but so far the scale is still small. (See Chapter 6, Public Broadcasting.)

In a handful states, state public affairs networks (SPANs) have played an important role, not only providing live coverage of legislative sessions but hosting candidate debates, issues forums, and other civically oriented types of coverage. But they exist only in 23 states. Some public, educational, and governmental access (PEG) channels have launched citizen journalism shows but most have not, and the PEG system in general faces funding challenges. be (See Chapter 7, Public Access Channels.)

Journalism schools have begun to have their students contribute to local reporting efforts, but their ability to sustain these efforts will depend greatly on whether they can raise the funds to hire additional permanent staff to manage the students.

Nonprofit websites, as noted above, have made great progress but are small in scale. For instance, the top 12 nonprofits represented at a recent conference on local journalism field only 88 reporters in total; they are making a useful contribution to be sure, but it is not nearly enough to fill the void left by the roughly 15,000 journalists who lost their jobs at newspapers in the last decade. (See Chapter 12, Nonprofit Websites.)

To be clear, the shortage is not in "news" or "information," per se, but in a very specific kind of journalism: labor-intensive reporting on civically important topics. Two surveys found that consumers are quite satisfied with some of their information choices while perceiving gaps in others. In a Pew Internet Project survey of residents of Philadelphia, Pennsylvania; Macon, Georgia; and San Jose, California, 62 percent said that they were very confident that they could find local information about medical and health problems. But only 24 percent said they were very confident that they could find information to "assess [whether] local politicians were doing their jobs."[8] In another study, 79 percent of Chicagoans surveyed said that they are "pretty well informed" about "issues affecting the Chicago area"—yet 51 percent said that they don't know enough about candidates or issues to vote, 48 percent "think local media does not do a good job keeping watch on state and local government," and 49 percent said "nobody covers what happens in my community very well." The study found that the gaps affected not only certain types of information but particular groups of citizens. The groups that had the most trouble "navigating the ecosystem" were those with less education or income and were Latino and African-American.[9]

> **Among the websites in Toledo, 56% were traditional national media (TV, newspapers)—and none were local Internet-only sites.**

There is an enormous caveat: These are snapshots of the landscape at a particular moment. A tremendous amount of creative energy is going into improving local reporting through a variety of models. There is much debate about whether the current obstacles will endure (See Chapter 25, How Big is the Gap and Who Will Fill It?) For now, all we can say is: local accountability reporting is down, and communities are likely suffering as a result. In another recent survey, while Americans reported that they were satisfied with the amount of press coverage they were getting in many areas, there was one they felt dissatisfied with: 53 percent said that they wanted more coverage of state and/or local news.[10]

The Advantages of Incumbency

When all of these media are assessed on a local level, something else becomes clear: for all the talk about new players, the legacy media—the long-standing newspaper and TV companies—still enjoy tremendous advantages. This matters for several reasons. Some had hoped that the shortcomings of the old media would be made up for by vibrant, newly created Internet companies. But as it turns out, much new media news content is being produced by the "old media." Staffing decisions at newspapers and TV stations no longer manifest themselves just in their print and on-air products. At this point, newspapers and TV stations are the primary sources of online news and information too, so their staffing decisions—not only how many people they hire but how they prioritize their time—affect not only the old media platforms but the new as well.

To determine the dominant sources of local news, FCC analysts studied web traffic in three randomly chosen sample markets.[11] First, we looked at Toledo, Ohio. Applying a variety of filters designed to find sites that were focused on local topics, we homed in on the five sites that appear to be the top destinations for local Toledo news.[12] Each of the sites, it turns out, is owned by a traditional media company, and not one is an Internet-based local news site.

> ToledoBlade.com, the website of the largest area newspaper, is owned by Block Communications Inc.

> WTOL.com, the CBS affiliate, is owned by Raycom Media Inc.

> 13ABC.com is owned by the Walt Disney Company.

> FOXToledo.com is owned by LIN TV Corp.

> lenconnect.com, run by the *Daily Telegram* of Adrian, Michigan, is owned by GateHouse Media Inc.

To account for the likelihood that some Toledoans might be getting news from national websites that provide a mix of national and local news, we also studied the full dataset of web traffic in the news and information category, which produced a slightly different list, with Yahoo! News drawing significant local traffic. It is impossible to know to what extent Toledoans went to Yahoo! News for national versus local news. But if they did go for local news, they would be reading material provided by the traditional media of the area. Yahoo! lists four primary sources for its

Toledo-centric content: the *Toledo Blade*, WTVG-TV, WTOL 11, and FOX Toledo. When it comes to news, Yahoo! is primarily an aggregator, relying on old media sources to provide the reporting. Thus, the reportorial health of the old media is determining the quality of the news consumed via the Internet.

We considered that while the top five news sites are dominated by traditional media players, a look farther down the list might reveal that Toledoans are actually getting news from a wider variety of new players. But the data indicates that traffic was heavily concentrated among the top sites. More than half of page views were on the websites of only six web entities, and nearly 75 percent of page views were on the websites of just 10 web entities.

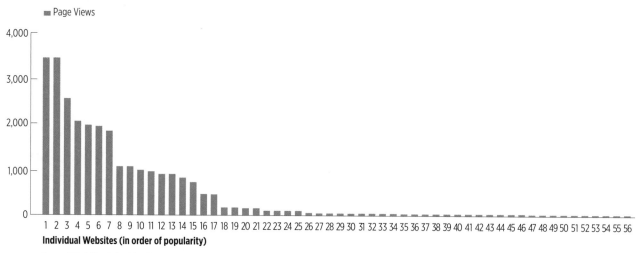

DISTRIBUTION OF NEWS AND INFORMATION WEB TRAFFIC IN TOLEDO (PAGE VIEWS—APRIL 2010)

Source: FCC staff analysis of ComScore, Local Market Internet Site Visitation Data, April 2010

If one looks at a different commonly used web metric—unique visitors, rather than page views—the same pattern is evident. Of the 56 websites visited by Toledoans for news, only four were estimated to have received more than 100,000 unique visitors per month, and approximately two-thirds were estimated to have received less than 20,000 monthly unique views. Again, traffic was concentrated among the traditional media companies' websites.

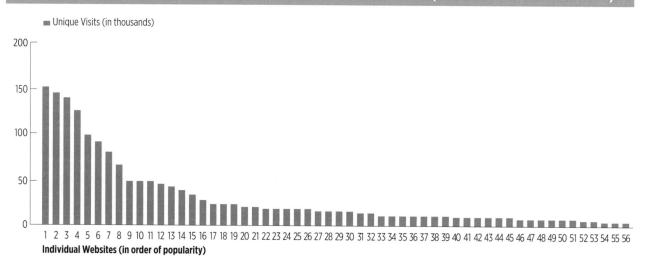

DISTRIBUTION OF NEWS AND INFORMATION WEB TRAFFIC IN TOLEDO (UNIQUE VISITS—APRIL 2010)

Source: FCC staff analysis of ComScore, Local Market Internet Site Visitation Data, April 2010

The pattern was the same in Richmond, Virginia. Most traffic observed in the local filter analysis went to just a few sites—all of which are run by traditional media companies.

> TimesDispatch.com, the main local daily newspaper, is owned by Media General Inc.
> NBC12.com, the NBC affiliate, is owned by Raycom Media Inc.
> WRIC.com, the ABC affiliate, is owned by Young Broadcasting Inc.
> Richmond.com, a lifestyle website, is owned by Media General Inc.
> Progress-Index.com, the newspaper of Petersburg, Virginia, is owned by Times-Shamrock Communications.

What about Seattle? It would seem that a web start-up would have the best chance in a well-educated, tech-savvy city like Seattle. Yet again our analysis found that most traffic was concentrated among a few sites, most of them owned by traditional media companies.

> SeattleTimes.com, the local newspaper, is owned by the Seattle Times Company.
> seattlepi.com, formerly a major print newspaper, is owned by Hearst Communications Inc.
> KOMOnews.com, the ABC affiliate, is owned by Fisher Communications Inc.
> TheNewsTribune.com, the newspaper of Tacoma, Washington, is owned by the McClatchy Company.
> HeraldNet.com, the *Everett (WA) Daily Herald* website, is owned by the Washington Post Company.

One of the top Seattle sites—seattlepi.com—is a web-only site, however, it is a bit of a special case, because it was originally the website of the former print publication, the *Seattle Post-Intelligencer*, and it is owned by a national media company, Hearst. If seattlepi.com succeeds, it could provide a model for struggling newspapers to ultimately run sustainable (albeit far smaller) web-only operations. The site receives about 4.2 million monthly page views, which may be enough to generate revenue to support a small reportorial staff, particularly if costs are borne by a large media company. On the other hand, seattlepi.com clearly has benefited from the brand established by the print paper over many years, and by being part of a large company. In other words, the success of a web-based arm of a national corporation does not necessarily offer much hope to newly created local websites.

Our findings in these three cities gibes with those of other studies. An analysis conducted in early 2010 by the Project for Excellence in Journalism and the Pew Internet & American Life Project concluded that the websites of "legacy" news organizations—mainly major newspapers and cable television stations—dominate online news space in both traffic and loyalty. "Of the top 199 sites in our analysis, 67 percent are from legacy media, and they account for 66 percent of the traffic. In all, 48 percent are from newspapers, and 19 percent from all other legacy media," the study reported.[13] A 2007 Free Press study of web traffic patterns in 11 cities found that local newspaper websites drew more than 9.4 million monthly unique visitors and local TV station websites drew 1.2 million—while and independent city-specific websites drew only 693,000.[14]

Given all the struggles newspapers and TV stations are facing under their old business models, how has it come to pass that they are dominating local online news? When there are many potential sources of news, strong brands have an advantage over start-ups in terms of marketing their sites, building traffic, and drawing advertisers. In local markets, TV stations and newspapers can use their existing platforms to promote their websites. They can use their standing in the community to create preferential business deals. They can afford state-of-the-art web designs and tools by sharing that cost with the larger corporation that runs them. They can use their capital to purchase search-based advertising. And they can use existing reporting pools to create robust content that attracts and retains audience.

Newspapers and TV stations are the primary sources of online news and information. So their staffing decisions affect not only the news on old media platforms but the new.

235

In part because the big regional newspapers have slashed Washington bureaus, most regulatory agencies—institutions whose job is to protect Americans from food poisoning, banking collapse and mine explosions—are receiving less coverage.

National News

On balance, we are more optimistic about the economic vitality of national news models than we are about local or international news. It is certainly not a uniformly encouraging picture—and everyone no doubt has their gripes about particular national news organizations and practices—but we found great dynamism in terms of innovation and business model development.

National Newspapers and Websites

Thirty years ago, there were no general interest national newspapers. *USA Today* didn't exist; *The New York Times* and *The Washington Post* were more locally focused; and *The Wall Street Journal* was primarily a business publication. Now, each offers a broad diet of news to a national audience. In addition, Bloomberg has become an important national force, too, having significantly increased its Washington and overseas bureaus. And now, the Huffington Post, the self-described "Internet newspaper," has reached massive scale and financial success, and the Daily Caller offers a mix of commentary and original reporting.

Despite all intimations two years ago that *The New York Times* might be a dying dinosaur, it arguably has greater reach than ever. In May 2010, NYTimes.com had 32 million unique visitors, equivalent to about a quarter of all the visits (123 million) to newspaper websites that month. By contrast, the weekday circulation of the newspaper from April through September that same year was 876,638 , which means the print paper represented less than 2 percent of overall newspaper circulation.[15]

The economics may work better for national media than local, because they can operate on a large enough scale to generate significant revenue. This factor has also made possible the growth of websites that cover niche topics but reach a national audience. Scores of subject-specific blogs—such as SCOTUSBlog, which covers the U.S. Supreme Court, and the *New England Journal of Medicine*'s The Health Care Blog, which covers health care policy—have brought meaty analysis to the blogosphere. Politico can reach a large scale by attracting political junkies from around the country.

National Investigative Reporting

There are no doubt fewer national newspapers and TV stations devoting resources to investigative reporting than there were in the past, but that contraction has been partly offset by a combination of two factors: the biggest newspapers have maintained their commitment to investigative reporting, and nonprofit organizations have increased their commitment to it.

Explaining the increase in *The New York Times*'s investigative staff, editor Matthew Purdy, said, "The whole notion is that we need to present people with stories they can't get elsewhere." The *Times* can do that, he acknowledges, because "we have the incredible luxury of talent, time and space."[16]

As a result of both the contraction of investigative reporting at local and regional newspapers and the renewed commitment of some national entities, the lion's share of Pulitzer Prizes now goes to a handful of nationally-oriented newspapers. "Until about 10 years ago, the honors were spread widely among papers throughout the country," the *American Journalism Review* reported in September 2010:

> "The *New York Times* or the *Washington Post* typically appeared only once—or not at all—as a winner or finalist for an investigative story each year. However, in the past decade, those two papers plus the *Los Angeles Times* have eclipsed all others combined, sometimes accounting for more than half of all investigative stories that were honored. Papers that once appeared with some frequency on the list seem now to have lost either the will or the wherewithal to mount major investigations."[17]

Several nonprofit organizations, buoyed by foundation money, have become significant players. (See Chapter 12, Nonprofit Websites.) Launched in 2008, ProPublica has now won two Pulitzers in two years. Other significant nonprofit investigative operations include the Center for Investigative Reporting and the Center for Public Integrity. National Public Radio (NPR) has created a new eight-person investigative unit.[18]

One of the most controversial new players is Wikileaks. While it clearly has many serious shortcomings, it is clear that this sort of web-based vessel for leaks and disclosures has become an important part of the news system. Media organizations of all shapes and sizes are still contemplating what role Wikileaks and organizations like it should play in newsgathering, but there is no debating that it has had a dramatic impact.

National Radio

The flip side of the de-localization of commercial radio is that there is more national news. The news-talk format has grown (See Chapter 2, Radio.) Meanwhile, NPR has increased its national and international bureaus, and in 2010 it deployed more than 1,400 reporters, editors, and producers in 21 domestic and 17 foreign bureaus.[19] As traditional media have struggled, NPR's audience has grown 56 percent since 1986, and its web audience is now a substantial 18 million visitors each month.[20] (See Chapter 6, Public Broadcasting.)

On the other hand, there are several national media areas of some concern.

Newsmagazines

Not long ago, newsmagazines helped set the agenda for national discourse and employed some of the best reporters in the country, staffing an elaborate system of bureaus around the world. In 1989, the big three newsmagazines (*Time, Newsweek,* and *U.S. News and World Report*) together sold almost 10 million copies a week.[21] Between 1994 and 2009 *Time* and *Newsweek* cut their staffs by about half.[22] In December 2010, *U.S. News & World Report* eliminated its regular print edition (limiting its print product to industry ranking guides), and in August 2010 *Newsweek* was sold for $1 after its corporate parent decided it no longer wanted to cover its massive financial losses.[23] By 2010, the combined circulation of the big three newsmagazines was down to around 6 million.[24]

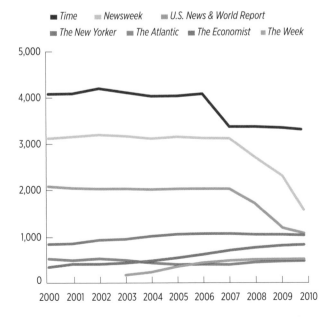

NEWS MAGAZINE CIRCULATION (2000–2010)

Average Circulation of *Time, The Economist, The Week, The Atlantic, The New Yorker* and *U.S. News* Over Time (in thousands)

■ Time ■ Newsweek ■ U.S. News & World Report
■ The New Yorker ■ The Atlantic ■ The Economist ■ The Week

Source: Pew Research Center's Project for Excellence in Journalism, 2011 State of the News Media[25]

In large part, because their weekly publication schedule meant that newsmagazines could not hope to be quite as current as TV or newspapers, they featured some of the best in-depth hard news reporting in the business. Often, their approach was to "flood the zone" by sending multiple correspondents into the field to cover various aspects of a single story. After 9/11, *Newsweek*'s Paris correspondent could address the exiled terrorist factions in Europe; the Mideast correspondent could listen for what was being said in Tehran, Jerusalem, Cairo, and Beirut; the correspondents in south Asia could send in details from Afghanistan, Pakistan, and India. The final article could pull together all these "threads" to show readers connections that would not necessarily be made, let alone analyzed, in the daily paper.[26]

Newsweeklies often undertook labor-intensive reporting projects that produced major scoops. In 2006, *Time* magazine broke the story of U.S. Marines deliberately killing 24 Iraqis in the town of Haditha, contradicting the military's initial reporting that they had been the victims of a roadside bomb. It took foreign correspondent Tim McGirk 10 weeks of reporting in Iraq and Washington to piece together the true story.[27] *Newsweek* magazine's investigative reporter Michael Isikoff is credited with breaking the Monica Lewinsky story, after years of relentless digging.[28]

As newsmagazines' finances have declined, the deepest cuts have impacted "correspondents," reporters in the field. At *Time* their numbers fell from 83 in 1998 to 35 in 2008, and the number of cities with bureaus went from 28 in 1998 to 18 in 2008.[29] *Time* and *Newsweek* reduced staff in bureaus (foreign and domestic) from 710 in 1983 to 297 in 2009.[30]

Still, *Time* and *Newsweek* (now combined with the website, TheDailyBeast.com) may well survive and devise compelling new formulas for readers—perhaps emphasizing provocative thought-pieces, or news-of-the-week summaries, or great photography. (The magazine industry oversaw a 2.6 percent increase in revenue during the first three-quarters of 2010 over that period the year before.)[31] But it is unlikely that these magazines will emphasize original reporting as much as they did in the past. "[*Time* magazine is] moving away from reporting and toward something else, something that is more commenting on the news rather than gathering it," says Tom Rosenstiel, director of the Pew Project for Excellence in Journalism.[32] Indeed, other print magazines that follow a similar model—some reporting but more commentary or aggregation—have succeeded. *The Economist*, *The Atlantic*, and *The Week* actually posted modest gains in circulation in 2010.[33] In several cases, it appears that magazines have succeeded when they have leveraged their brand to develop additional revenue streams rather than relying solely on advertising. *The Atlantic* turned a profit in 2010 for the first time in years, in part because it earns money by holding conferences on policy issues. *National Journal* has been hiring reporters aggressively—including for a free website—in part, because its limited-circulation publication charges high subscription prices to lobbyists and lawyers in Washington.

After an explosion killed 29 coal miners in West Virginia, journalists found that regulators had cited the mine for 1,342 safety violations. The problem: the stories came after the disaster.

Coverage of Regulatory Agencies

Cutbacks have also led many news companies to eliminate or reduce their Washington bureaus. As a result, fewer reporters cover regulatory agencies—institutions whose job is to protect Americans from food poisoning, banking collapse, mine explosions, and countless other hazards. In the *American Journalism Review*, Jodi Enda illustrated the consequences:

"After an explosion killed 29 coal miners in West Virginia in early April, the Washington Post and the New York Times quickly produced lengthy exposés detailing a plethora of safety breaches that preceded the nation's worst coal mining disaster in a quarter century. The Times reported that mining companies thwarted tough federal regulations enacted after a spate of deaths four years earlier simply by appealing citations. The Post wrote that federal regulators had cited the Upper Big Branch mine for a whopping 1,342 safety violations in the past five years, 50 times in the previous month alone."[34]

The problem is that these stories were published after the disaster, not before—even though many of the records had been there for inspection.

A similar pattern could be seen with the Toyota malfunctions that killed 19 people. After the tragedies, reporters discovered that more than 1,000 Toyota and Lexus owners had complained to the government. "'You simply need to have journalists who are willing to pull teeth,' [Clarence Ditlow of the Center for Auto Safety] says. 'Could Toyota have been discovered earlier? I think so...'"[35] Enda stated that not one newspaper now has a reporter working in the newsroom of the Department of Agriculture, which is in charge of farm policy and food safety:

"Newspaper reporters who remain in the capital tend to focus on the big issues of the moment (health care, Wall Street), their congressional delegations and politics. Scoops are measured in nanoseconds and posted online the moment they are secured (and sometimes prior to that)...

"'Dealing with agencies can be very time-consuming,' says Bill Lambrecht, the lone reporter remaining in the once-exalted Washington bureau of the St. Louis Post-Dispatch, a Lee Enterprises-owned newspaper. 'The kind of source work that you need to do—calling people at night, filing FOIAs [Freedom of Information Act requests]—to bird-dog the agencies that invariably try to put up obstructions to giving you what you should get takes a lot of time....' He has had to scale back on the type of hard-hitting stories he previously wrote about the Environmental Protection Agency, the Agriculture Department and the Food and Drug Administration, to name a few....

"'It's changed dramatically, and all for the worse,' George Condon, former Washington bureau chief for Copley News Service, says of Washington journalism. Condon was forced to close down the bureau in November two years after its reporters won a Pulitzer...for revealing that Rep. Randy 'Duke' Cunningham, a California Republican, had taken millions in bribes."[36]

Most newspapers cover the agencies only when particular issues burst to the surface but that approach leads to a paucity of what the *Washington Monthly* founder Charles Peters calls "preventive journalism"[37]: reportage that prevents tragedy.

Taken together, it appears that nationally oriented news producers have had greater success developing business models—and where they fall short, nonprofit media has stepped in and made significant contributions. That is not to say that national media is without problems. We have pointed to a few, and no doubt readers might offer their own concerns about the media. But compared with local news coverage, there are more reasons to be optimistic about national news evolving in a positive direction.

International News

As the nation fights two wars and suffers from a global recession, coverage of international news by most traditional media appears to have declined.

For newspapers, the greatest drop in foreign coverage has been at the big regional and city dailies. *The Philadelphia Inquirer* and *Newsday* won five Pulitzers for foreign coverage between 1979 and 2005, and by 2010 they had no overseas bureaus at all.[38] In a count of 28 newspapers, the total number of foreign newspaper bureaus fell from 145 in 1998[39] to 58 in 2010.[40] The *American Journalism Review* documented how these shifts rippled through a representative sample of newspapers—resulting in a 53 percent decline in foreign coverage since 1985 (see chart).

In 2008, nearly half (46 percent) of media managers reported cutting resources devoted to foreign coverage, and 64 percent said they devoted less space to foreign news.[42] The reason is obvious: The cost of fielding a single foreign correspondent—between $250,000 and $500,000, and more in a security-sensitive war zone—can equal the price of five hometown newsroom reporters.[43] And only 10 percent of editors said that they considered foreign coverage "very essential" to their audience.[44]

Network television news coverage of international affairs has waxed and waned according to external events. The initial coverage of the Iraq and Afghanistan wars was aggressive, but it faded over time.[45] In 2008, American fatalities for the year in both wars combined were about the same as in 2003 (469 and 534, respectively),[46] but network news coverage of the wars was 78 percent lower.[47] Though still nowhere near the coverage levels at the beginning of the Iraq war, overseas coverage

FOREIGN COVERAGE OVER TIME (1985 VS. 2010)						
■ 1985 ■ 2010	Total Stories		Staff-Written		Page 1	
Philadelphia Inquirer	101	62	26	2	15	6
Providence Journal	75	38	13	2	7	0
St. Louis Post-Dispatch	92	24	15	3	8	4
Cincinnati Enquirer	57	33	7	0	5	0
Dallas Morning News	75	59	18	4	6	6
Tampa Tribune	96	33	4	1	8	1
The Oregonian	115	41	11	2	8	1
Fresno Bee	78	31	8	0	6	1
Total	689	321	102	14	63	19

Source: "Shrinking Foreign Coverage," by Priya Kumar, *American Journalism Review*, 2011[84]

bounced back a bit after President Obama's decision to increase troops in Afghanistan, with most news operations increasing their coverage simply by shifting reporters from other parts of the world.

To make up for staffing cuts, some news operations have shifted away from expensive permanent bureaus, preferring to hire "MOJOs"—mobile journalists—who drop into an area when news breaks.[48] Andrew Tyndale, a TV news analyst, says this has been made possible by technology improvements, including light and tolerant cameras, directional microphones, easy uplinks, remote editing, online research, and social-network sourcing, among other advances. "Video newsgathering these days is so much more nimble, versatile and ubiquitous that ever so many fewer traditional bureaus need to be established as bases from which correspondents can be dispatched," Tyndale wrote.[49] For instance, in 2007, ABC News opened seven new bureaus, most in Asia, staffed with one employee each.[50] The staffer serves as both reporter and producer, and writes, shoots, edits, and feeds material from a laptop via a broadband Internet connection to New York. Other networks have adopted the same model.

Bright Spots

Although most news outlets have reduced their overseas presence, a few have increased it: Bloomberg now has a staff of 2,300 in 146 bureaus in 72 countries (more than half of Bloomberg's audience lives overseas).[51] The *Wall Street Journal*, the *New York Times*, the *Washington Post* and the *Los Angeles Times* continue to have large overseas bureaus.[52]

Cable news networks, especially CNN, have substantial overseas presence. In 2009, CNN had 33 foreign bureaus, FOX had nine, and MSNBC had 11. That year, CNN devoted 23 percent of its coverage to foreign news (18 percent to events involving the U.S. and 5 percent to strictly foreign stories), FOX News did 18 percent foreign news, and MSNBC offered 13 percent.[53]

Associated Press and Reuters continue to field thousands of overseas reporters. NPR has added 11 bureaus in 10 years[54] and now has reporters in London, Rome, Berlin, Moscow, Istanbul, Jerusalem, Cairo, Baghdad, New Delhi, Beijing, Shanghai, Dakar, Kabul, Nairobi, Islamabad, Jakarta, and Bogota.[55] In the television world, only CNN has more.[56] And there has been some extraordinary coverage when crisis strikes, as was seen in the aftermath of the Haiti earthquake.

Foundations and nonprofits, such as the Pulitzer Center on Crisis Reporting and the International Reporting Project (IRP), offer grants to fund overseas freelance projects. John Schidlovsky of IRP says he receives 300 applications for about 40 grants a year; the program has sent 174 reporters overseas to a total of 92 countries in the past dozen years. The Pulitzer Center, with a budget of $1.7 million, produces about 50 or 60 projects per year, usually in collaboration with national entities such as the *Washington Post, The Atlantic,* and *PBS NewsHour.*[57]

Just as important, the Internet has made it much easier for citizens who want more foreign information than TV or newspapers provide. Americans now have easy access to foreign media such as the BBC, the *Guardian, Haaretz, Le Monde,* and Al Jazeera, as well as to specialized sites like that of *Foreign Policy* magazine. In addition, those seeking a wider range of information on particular regions can turn to a myriad of international sites: GlobalVoices, a community of more than 300 bloggers and translators, delivers reports from blogs and citizen media worldwide with an emphasis on "voices that are not ordinarily heard in international mainstream media"[58] and GlobalPost.com, an online news outlet operating out of the United States, offers original reporting from about 50 journalists working in as many countries.[59]

> While professional photographers produced the searing images of Vietnam, it was an amateur Iranian doctor who drew American attention to the Iranian government crackdown with his cell phone video of a woman shot during protests.

The Internet also enables ordinary citizens around the world to report information to the rest of the planet. While professional photographers produced the searing images of Vietnam that shaped public perceptions, it was an amateur Iranian doctor who drew American attention to the Iranian government crackdown following elections in 2009 with his cell phone video of a woman who was shot during the protests. Coverage of the Egyptian protests was immeasurably enhanced by citizen reporting, as well as by U.S. access to foreign sources such as Al Jazeera. "The low cost of creation, transmission, and distribution means that a web user in the U.S. today has more raw data available on some foreign crises than a television producer for a network news program had ten years ago," writes James Hamilton of Duke University.[60]

The Nature of the Reporting

Still, many experts argue that these gains have not offset what has been lost—not just in volume but also in quality. The emphasis on crisis coverage has meant that large parts of the world are off the radar until disaster strikes. For example, in 2009, ABC and FOX News had no bureaus in Africa, and NBC had a presence only in Cairo. In Latin

America, although ABC, CBS, CNN, NBC, and MSNBC all listed bureaus in Havana, only ABC (with a Mexico City bureau) and CNN (with four more bureaus in Latin American countries) reported a broader presence in the region. FOX had no Latin American bureaus.[61]

If media outlets react only after a crisis hits, that coverage obviously cannot help *prevent* catastrophe. Roy Gutman, foreign editor for McClatchy, argues that failure to cover Afghanistan before 9/11 is "one of the great lapses in the modern history of the profession." He notes there had been almost no media reporting of the humanitarian crisis or Osama bin Laden's "fire-breathing threats" from his Afghan base prior to 9/11.[62]

Without trusted staff on the ground, news editors are hard put to detect, let alone highlight, an emerging situation before it turns into a crisis. Andrew Stroehlein, communications director of the International Crisis Group, a nonprofit, non-governmental organization,[63] noted that fewer media operations have a source on the ground who can call the newsroom and say, "In all my years in this country, I've never seen anything like this before," or "This is news: we need to cover it."[64]

Reporters who parachute into a region at the last minute rarely have as full an understanding of the area as do permanently stationed correspondents. Pew's *State of the News Media 2004* report found that much international network coverage was "actually camera work shot by freelancers with voiceover from a correspondent at the nearest bureau."[65] In other words, the reporters narrating the story did not observe the scenes they were describing and were not on scene to interview eyewitnesses and other important sources. In addition, if correspondents have not been on the ground long enough to build source relationships, they are that much more dependent on information the government puts out and on what they can observe with their own eyes.

"A web user in the U.S. today has more raw data available on some foreign crises than a television producer for a network news program had ten years ago."

The decline of overseas bureaus also has made Americans more dependent on foreign-owned news outlets. This has advantages and disadvantages. Foreign media may have deeper understanding of an area, more sources, and perhaps more clout with local citizens. During the unrest in Egypt, American journalists and citizens often found that some of the best coverage came from Al Jazeera. Blogger Jeff Jarvis started a campaign to get more U.S. cable operators to carry the service.[66] Meanwhile, the BBC's U.S. website draws more traffic than all but a few U.S newspapers.[67] On the other hand, some foreign-run news services are actually state owned and are more likely to offer a perspective that serves that country's interests. Steve Randall, a senior analyst at Fairness and Accuracy in Reporting (FAIR), a conservative group, notes with concern that millions of Americans are watching such channels as Russia Today, Al Jazeera, CCTV of China, and Press TV of Iran via cable and satellite.[68] These may offer valuable perspectives, he says, but they certainly should not be viewed as a complete replacement for American media coverage.

What are the repercussions? In his book *Uninhibited, Robust and Wide Open,* Columbia University president Lee Bollinger, argued, "The need for news about international and global issues is greater than ever," with America "at risk of intellectual isolationism, at least as grave a problem for the nation as economic protectionism."[69]

22 The Media Food Chain and the Functions of Journalism

TO GET AN ACCURATE READ on the current health of the media, it is important to recognize the roles historically played by different actors. While newspapers, TV, and radio all performed multiple functions in the pre-Internet age, they each had particular strengths and fed off each other in generally worthwhile ways. Newspapers tended to do the majority of accountability reporting. Because of the size of their staffs, the mobility of their reporters, and the many column inches they could dedicate to news, they could devote more time and resources to labor- and time-intensive projects, sustain ongoing beat reporting, and offer more in-depth explanation and analysis of complex issues.

The strengths of local TV flowed from the characteristics of the medium: The ability it affords to tell stories using moving images and sound, and to offer them live, has tended to make it the medium of choice for conveying a scene or a dramatic moment—whether the fall of the Berlin wall or a local traffic accident. TV was able to convey news more quickly than print, often airing a story the same day the event occurred. In terms of accountability journalism, television typically did not have sufficient staff to break as many stories as newspapers did, but it served another important function—amplifying, dramatizing, and legitimizing the accountability function of newspapers. Imagine if Watergate had never made it to network news.

Radio's role has been similar to TV's in the sense that it has usually amplified more than it has initiated original journalism. There are many exceptions to these generalities, of course, in which TV and radio stations scooped newspapers or, through their beat reporters, elevated the level of competition among reporters, improving everyone's game.

So the contraction of newspapers not only affects their readers, but the whole information food chain. In theory, TV and radio could have filled the vacuum left by newspapers, but our research indicates that they are not doing that. That means the ecosystem is missing a key element. Switching metaphors, Alex Jones of the Shorenstein Center on the Press, Politics, and Public Policy refers to the basic reporting newspapers have typically done as the "iron core" of journalism.[1] They bring forth the basic material from which other media craft their products. If too few people are mining the ore, the rest of media output becomes lower quality.

Can the new media create a new ecosystem that is better than what we have ever had? As we discussed in Chapter 4, Internet, we come away with both encouraging and sobering conclusions. There are many ways that today's media system improves accountability—both by citizens and journalists. On the other hand, in many communities TV and radio have not so far filled the reporting gaps created by the contraction of newspapers. In some ways, many news websites now play a similar role to that of TV and radio—offering speed, amplification, analysis, and commentary, often of extraordinary value but not exactly the same as labor-intensive reporting. Finally, many of the online entities that go beyond that model—those that attempt to mine the iron ore—are struggling mightily to find sustainable business models. To be sure, this is the situation at one particular moment; it is possible that over time different players will react to new needs and take on new roles. But so far, the deficits remain.

> Many reporters file continuously, do fewer interviews, and spend less time pressing for information. This has resulted in a shift in the balance of power—away from citizens, toward powerful institutions.

Functions of Journalism

So far, we have looked at the media system from two angles: by traditional sector (TV, newspapers, radio, etc.) and by region of coverage (hyperlocal, local, national, etc.). We now turn to one more perspective: the role the press plays in ensuring a healthy democracy and a well-served citizenry. One useful template was created by Tom Rosenstiel, head of the Pew Center's Project for Excellence in Journalism and author of *Blur: How to Know What's True in the Age of Information Overload*. He says that the 21st-century media have eight functions: Authentication, Watch Dog, Witness, Forum Leader, Sense Making, Smart Aggregation, Empowerment, and Role Model.[2]

How well are these functions being carried out in the new ecosystem?

Empowerment: In terms of their personal relationship to media, citizens have never been more empowered. They can publish their thoughts, observations, photographs, videos, treatises, and ideas, participating in a public dialogue previously restricted to a lucky or privileged few. Citizens can, as YouTube's motto urges: "broadcast yourself." They can also choose what information they want to consume, grabbing control from "gatekeepers," (a.k.a. the editors and publishers who had been deciding what the public saw), and they can customize information flow according to their interests and proclivities, producing what MIT media scholar Nicholas Negroponte first called "the Daily Me."[3] And, finally, they can be distributers of information. Any citizen can be reporter, publisher, and delivery boy or girl with just a few clicks. Although we see some countervailing power shifts (see below), there's no doubt that consumers in many ways have more control over what information they consume and share.

> One study found that 63% of the stories were initiated by government officials.

Smart Aggregation: The Internet offers endless volumes of information from countless sources—so anything that helps cull, curate, and package quality content to meet consumer needs and interests is invaluable. And because digitized information is so easy to manipulate (i.e., organize and reorganize, etc.) and affordable to publish (i.e., display/distribute), there is an abundance of smart aggregators that are finding and pushing out quality content quickly and inexpensively and making it available across multiple platforms. Whether the task is performed by editors, computer algorithms, crowd-sourcing, or social media, the media system has already created a variety of means for "smart aggregation."

Authentication: New media advocates argue that "the crowd" is usually more effective at authenticating something than an editor. Instead of having two smart reporters poring over the documents, have ten thousand citizens. And it is true that when someone posts inaccurate information on a blog, it does not take long for other people to point it out. One study by *Nature* found that Wikipedia had an average of 3.86 mistakes per entry, while *Encyclopedia Britannica* averaged 2.92 mistakes per entry.[4] The glass is both half full (a democratic, volunteer-based system has only a few errors per article) and half empty (Wikipedia had 32 percent more errors per article than the old-model encyclopedia).

Crowd-based fact-checking eventually works surprisingly well to correct inaccuracies. But most news is consumed when it breaks, not "eventually." Web culture places a bit less emphasis on getting it right the first time, since it relies on the speed of the post-and-correct process. Those who stay with a story as it plays out may eventually get the facts, but many people do not have the time, energy, or inclination to do that. In the old system, citizens had, in effect, outsourced that job to the editors at the newspapers they read; now they must take on more of the burden themselves.

Witness: Again, the picture is complex. In some ways, "witnessing" is the strength of the new media landscape. Whether the event is a tsunami or a press conference, coverage of news that transpires before our eyes, or our phone cameras, has gotten better. But in other ways, the current system is a step backward. No journalist was present in Bell City, California, to witness the Bell City Council raising the salaries of city officials again and again over the course of several years. Many parts of state and local government now go unobserved by the scrutinizing eyes of journalists. Moreover, witnessing has never been simply about watching something unfold; it also means observing situations over time, noticing slow-building crises—such as the rise in the number of soldiers with post-traumatic stress disorder. Reporting of that kind does not require someone to watch a single event but to follow, and draw together, hundreds of private agonies.

Sense Making: The returns here are mixed. We are awash in commentary, which is a form of "sense making": it looks at facts and attempts to clarify what is important and what is not. When a story breaks, its significance may not be readily apparent; commentators offer interpretation and opinion, helping to give a sense of context. Hearing a range of voices—both journalists and other experts—can allow for a richer, more nuanced understanding. Although the Internet clearly has many dubious sources, over time readers can determine for themselves who is most trustworthy. On the other hand, the speed of the Internet process is sometimes a liability. The rhythms of the newspaper and newsmagazine production cycle enabled, and required, reporters to spend time sorting through competing claims, connecting dots, and providing context. That extra time they spent was time saved for the reader, who did not have to review multiple sources to assess the relative wisdom or veracity of different parties.

Watchdog: On this function, the current media system appears to be worse than before, at least at the local level. To be sure, the move to put more government data online has enabled a mix of citizens and reporters to hold institutions accountable. But a crucial aspect of watchdog reporting is finding out information that someone wants covered up, or, less conspiratorially, pulling together threads of information that do not at first seem related. Newspapers, local TV stations, and local radio stations employ fewer reporters now than they used to, and many of those that have survived have become more like 1930s wire service reporters—filing rapidly and frequently, doing fewer interviews, and spending less time pressing for information. This has resulted in a shift in the balance of power—away from citizens, toward powerful institutions. The watchdog reporter hates a press release; the busy reporter often loves it.

> Bill Girdner of Courthouse News Service: "The court bureaucracy has gotten stronger and stronger.... When journalists don't have presence, others control the information process."

More government transparency will certainly help, enabling a wider range of reporters and citizens to look for problems, in a less costly way. (See Chapter 16, Government Transparency). But transparency without a critical mass of reporters will not be a panacea. The problem is human nature. People are naturally inclined to withhold information that makes them look bad. This is true for government, corporations, labor unions, universities, and any other type of institution, whether the information is in the form of handwritten scrawl on paper documents or digits in databases. Usually, dirty secrets must be "found out"—no easy task—and the people who are most likely to have the time, independence, and skills for the job are full-time professionals: police, prosecutors—and reporters.

Power Shifts

As noted above, the Internet has been a boon for democratic engagement and citizen empowerment in many ways. However, our on-the-ground research turned up numerous examples of a countervailing power shift, away from citizens and toward institutions. Since surveys reveal that Americans hold reporters in low esteem—and may associate them with rich and powerful TV personalities—some may be skeptical about the notion that a decline in the number of journalists could shift control away from citizens and toward the powerful. But this is what we have concluded. Reporters who have less time per story become more reliant on news doled out by press release or official statement, which means that they report the news powerful institutions want us to know rather than what has been concealed. That *is* a power shift.

Recall the Pew study of Baltimore, which concluded that governmental institutions, increasingly, were driving stories rather than reporters:

> "As news is posted faster, often with little enterprise reporting added, the official version of events is becoming more important. We found official press releases often appear word for word in first accounts of events, though often not noted as such . . . Government, at least in this study, initiates most of the news. In the detailed examination of six major storylines, 63% of the stories were initiated by government officials, led first of all by the police. Another 14% came from the press. Interest group figures made up most of the rest."[5]

Investigative reporter Mark Thompson says he has access to "a million times more stuff than [he] did 30 years ago" but that "now [he's] awash in the high tide of what the government wants [him] to see."[6] Bill Girdner, owner and editor of Courthouse News Service, says that as it gets harder for reporters to get information about cases, "the court bureaucracy has gotten stronger and stronger…. When journalists don't have presence, others control the information process."[7]

Some news organizations devote fewer resources to prying information from reluctant institutions. "As we lose resources, we lose our ability to fight Freedom of Information [law]suits," says Doug Guthrie, court reporter for the *Detroit News*. "We try to fake them out with stern letters, but they know we don't have it." When records are withheld, Guthrie says, there are more likely to be violations of citizens' rights:

> "I used to think public servants in the U.S. were over-criticized and under-appreciated. But dealing with state court officials reminds me of what people complained about in socialist economies…. These legions of apparatchiks that are interested in their turf, their petty domains of power and made-up rules, and have no understanding of and no interest in the principles of our nation or the need for a strong press."[8]

Caroline Smith DeWaal, food safety director at the Center for Science in the Public Interest, a consumer advocacy organization, says that the power shift stems in part from a lack of expertise. In the past, most major news outlets had reporters who focused primarily on food safety. Now, few do, DeWaal says. "One possible effect of this is that when the administration makes a major announcement, you don't have the quality of questions or the quality of analysis that you used to have."[9]

Many of these examples focus on government, but the same power shift bolsters the interests of any institution inclined to hide embarrassing information. Since private institutions—such as corporations, universities, labor unions, and hospitals—have few of the legal obligations to share information that government agencies do, it has always been much easier for them to withhold damaging information, especially when they have fewer reporters biting at their heels.

In some ways, the Internet has increased the influence of press releases. Wally Dean, a longtime TV news executive, says that stations often refer to people as "beat reporters" when really they are just the point person for press releases on a particular topic. "Frequently the so-called health reporter fronts the health news but is using handouts from the health industry or using material from one of the feeds coming into the TV station," Dean says.[10]

In the *Columbia Journalism Review*, Ryan Chittum described a company that put out a press release with a false claim about a new deal it had made with record labels. Major news outlets, such as the *Financial Times*, the *International Herald Tribune*, AP, and Reuters, among many others, published the story without verification. While most outlets followed up with corrections, few of them posted the correction along with their original article, and thus the "uncorrected version continued to proliferate on overseas news Websites…. And that can only lead to grief, thanks to the magic of Google caches and message boards, where original copies of the story can still be found." Chittum explained, "Events move so fast that there often seems to be little time to check facts, and announcement-based reporting is given too much prominence."[11]

One PR professional explained, "Newsrooms have been gutted and, particularly at the local level, journalists rely on press releases…to help them fill their ever-increasing news hole."

Amy Mengel, head of inbound marketing for public relations firm readMedia, wrote about this issue on a message board dedicated to public relations topics: "Newsrooms have been gutted and, particularly at the local level, journalists rely on press releases… to help them fill their ever-increasing news hole."[12] By one estimate, the ratio of public relations professionals to journalists is now four to one, compared with one to one just 30 years ago.[13]

In fact, public relations professionals increasingly use the Internet to get press releases directly into the hands of consumers, bypassing reporters entirely. Bernadette Morris, president and CEO of Black PR Wire, says that the press release "is no longer just a media relations tool; it is now widely read online, in addition to the eyes it attracts via traditional delivery inside the newsroom."[14] A survey of PR professionals conducted by PR News and PRWeb found that 24 percent now view the consumer as the direct target of press releases.[15]

There is nothing inherently wrong with a press release or with public relations efforts. These have always been a part of the news flow, and there was never a time when every press release was cross-checked by a reporter. But as the number of reporters declines, the balance shifts toward the institutions that call the press conference or issue the press release.

Consequences

Does any of this matter in a concrete way? We believe that an increase in local reporters would pay for itself many times over in terms of social value—through less corruption, better health information for citizens, less wasteful government spending, safer streets, ultimately better schools, and, most amorphous, a healthier democracy. Throughout the earlier chapters, there were examples of important topics that are receiving insufficient coverage. But can it be proven that this has negative repercussions for citizens or communities?

A comparison of what reporters used to do with what they now do helps to give a sense of what is being lost. When an editor at *The (Nashville) Tennessean* recounted how a story about the regulation of incompetent doctors was being held up, because his newspaper had eliminated one of its health reporters (see Chapter 1, Newspapers),[16] we cannot know for sure which incompetent doctors are continuing to practice. But we can reasonably expect that someone will be harmed. When experts in Michigan believe that parents are probably losing custody of their children as a result of insufficient coverage of family courts (see Chapter 1, Newspapers) we cannot know which parent is losing which child. But we can nonetheless imagine how we would feel if a broken justice system unfairly dismantled our family because no one was watching.

David Simon, formerly of the Baltimore Sun, told Senators: "It is going to be one of the great times to be a corrupt politician."

In the case of Bell, California—in which city officials paid themselves exorbitant salaries—if a reporter earning $50,000 had been regularly covering the city council, and salaries of those officials had therefore remained at the level of most other elected officials, taxpayers would have saved millions of dollars. Corruption costs taxpayers money, and it can continue much more easily when no one is watching. David Simon, a reporter turned screenwriter, said at a Senate hearing, "the next 10 or 15 years in this country are going to be a halcyon era for state and local political corruption. It is going to be one of the great times to be a corrupt politician."[17]

And by looking at some of the outstanding journalism that has been done after tragedies—such as mine collapses or auto defects (see Chapter 21, Types of News)—we can get a feel for how many lives might have been saved had coverage begun earlier.

Scholars have attempted to take things even further, studying whether the availability of news affects conditions in quantitative ways.

UNESCO's *Press Freedom and Development* survey of 194 countries[18] in 2008 found correlations between robust press freedom and higher levels of per capita GDP, higher percentages of GDP spent on health, and higher rates of primary and secondary education enrollment.[19] It is quite possible that these factors help generate a free press, rather than the reverse, but at a minimum these results indicate that a decline in the vigor of the press indicates *something* bad.[20]

Stronger evidence exists that the availability of news and information inhibits corruption. A 2003 international study found that the level of corruption in a country is largely influenced by how well informed the electorate is, as measured by the circulation of daily newspapers.[21] The study also showed that states that had a vibrant press were less corrupt than those that did not.[22]

Several studies have documented that voter turnout and the likelihood of competitive elections are higher when the electorate is well informed:

> A study of Spanish-language TV stations found that the presence of local Spanish-language newscasts increased voter turnout among Hispanics by an estimated 5 to 10 percent.[23]

> A study of more than 7,000 cities found that, in areas where voters had more information (through sample ballots and voter guides) or the presence of a local newspaper, fewer incumbents ran for or won re-election. As voters paid more attention, races became more competitive.[24]

> After the *Cincinnati Post* closed in 2007, researchers at Princeton University found that "the next year, fewer candidates ran for municipal office in the suburbs most reliant on the Post, incumbents became more likely to win re-election, and voter turnout and campaign spending fell."[25]

> Areas of Los Angeles not served by either daily or weekly newspapers exhibit lower rates of voter turnout than areas that have some access to local journalism."[26]

In short, social science research supports at least two hypotheses: 1) better-informed communities experience higher levels of governmental responsiveness, and 2) better-informed communities experience higher rates of political participation.

Unfortunately, reality is not as simple as "more media equals a better-informed public equals more accountability." A 2005 study found that the spread of television, "account[ed] for between a quarter and a half of the total decline in [voter] turnout since the 1950s." The study's author speculated that this was due to newspaper and radio covering civic matters more effectively than TV; so, at least in terms of election information, citizens had replaced a more-effective medium with a less effective one.[27]

The Knight Commission in 2009 observed that the mere presence of significant information within a local news environment does not guarantee its effective use. The Commission cited the example of Hurricane Katrina:

> "A front-page story in the June 8, 2004, *Times-Picayune*[28] in New Orleans detailed a near-stoppage in the work needed to shore up the city's levees. The mere revelation of that information in itself did not mobilize the effort that might have spared the city the worst ravages of Hurricane Katrina 14 months later. Interested or influential people did not engage with the information in timely, effective ways. Unless people, armed with information, engage with their communities to produce a positive effect, information by itself is powerless."[29]

While the presence of good journalism does not guarantee a healthy democracy, it is fair to say that the absence of good journalism makes a healthy democracy far less likely.

23 Diversity

THE CHANGING MEDIA LANDSCAPE presents both challenges and opportunities for minorities. In traditional media, minority ownership and employment has, in recent years, gone backward. But the openness of the Internet offers the promise of new opportunities for innovation and minority viewpoints that may not have flourished via traditional media platforms. Both rural and urban, English and foreign-language minority communities can now access a wealth of information and resources via their broadband connections. New technologies also offer opportunities to some minority entrepreneurs who have found the barriers for entry into traditional media too high to scale. This chapter explores how the traditional and digital media environments are performing in terms of programming, employment, and innovation.

Traditional Media

Radio

In 1948, WDIA in Memphis launched the first radio station designed to appeal to a black audience.[1] Although white-owned, this bold programming decision made the station a forerunner, and its example was widely followed by stations across the country wanting to reach this underserved audience. WDIA is also credited with breaking a color barrier in its employment of black announcers and station personnel, as well as in its programming content, which included public service announcements geared especially to a black audience. The nation's first black-owned radio station was WERD in Atlanta.[2] Purchased by Jesse B. Clayton Sr. in 1949, the financially successful station offered a mix of news, community announcements, information, and music that black audiences could not get elsewhere in the local market.[3] Other programming of interest could be found on the National Negro Network (NNN), a nationwide network of 40 stations that programmed news summaries, wire-copy, and music. NNN was launched in 1954 by a black ad executive from Chicago, Leonard Evans, who selected an interracial board of directors to help him reach his target audience.[4] During the 1950s, black-oriented programming could be found on numerous broadcast radio stations.

Following the social unrest of the 1960s, the Kerner Commission concluded that a new national policy was needed to facilitate greater minority ownership of media, which would allow for more balanced depictions of black people and create entrepreneurial and employment opportunities for minorities. Former CNN journalist Bernard Shaw summed up the conclusions of the Kerner Commission:

> "[I]t mattered mightily to other African-Americans. To read the byline, to read the copy written by people of color, and to see people of color on television, it confirms your vitality in this multiracial and multicultural society. It says we can do this too. It also mattered in the education of white people, in and out of government."[5]

The findings of the Kerner Commission greatly influenced regulatory policy at the FCC and other federal agencies and helped spawn an increase in the number of black-owned stations.[6]

Today, over 90 percent of black consumers ages 12 and over listen to radio each week, according to broadcast radio ratings company Arbitron's *Black Radio Today 2010* report.[7] Overall, the leading radio formats for blacks are urban adult contemporary (91.2 percent) and urban contemporary (78.9 percent).

All-news makes up 13.2 percent of programming formats.[8] James Winston, executive director and general counsel of the National Association of Black-Owned Broadcasters (NABOB), says that during the 1970s and 1980s, most black-owned stations had active local news departments and public service programming,[9] but they decreased news content to contain costs when the Commission relaxed its public interest requirements in the 1980s and 1990s.[10] The American Urban Radio Networks (AURN)[11] is the largest African-American-owned radio network company, providing news, sports, information, and entertainment programming to more than 300 affiliated broadcast stations.

AURN programs include *Black College Football Weekly, Healthwatch, NewsWorld This Morning,* and *White House Report.*[12] Additionally, Sirius XM recently announced plans to expand its portfolio of satellite radio programming aimed at minority audiences, adding music and talk shows created by Howard University and other historically black colleges and universities; Spanish-language music and talk programming from Eventus, National Latino Broadcasting, and WorldBand Media; and Korean-language music and talk programming.[13]

While commercial broadcasters offer an impressive array of national news programming for black consumers, it is less common on the local level. Lisa Fager Bediako, president and co-founder of the media advocacy group Industry Ears, noted at a Commission localism forum:

> "Over 75 percent of urban radio stations carry syndication and what this does is it limits our voices—it also limits jobs for people of color and others who want to work in radio, in urban radio. Syndication has not only caused a disproportionate loss of industry jobs, but more importantly, stifled news and information to local communities."[14]

For Hispanic audiences, media consumption is split between those Hispanics who prefer to speak Spanish in the home, rather than English, and those who are bilingual. For example, in Los Angeles, among Hispanic adults ages 18 to 49 who watch the 6:00 evening news, 29 percent of Spanish-dominant and 61 percent of non-Spanish-dominant viewers prefer to watch English-language news. By contrast, 86 percent of Spanish-dominant and 14 percent of non-Spanish dominant viewers prefer to watch Spanish-language news.[15]

Radio remains a vital medium for Hispanics too,[16] reaching 95 percent of Spanish-dominant Hispanics and more than 93 percent of English-dominant Hispanics.[17] Mexican regional is the most popular format, according to Arbitron's *Hispanic Radio Today 2010* report.[18] However, the news/talk/information and talk/personality formats attract 4.3 percent of Hispanic radio consumers, and, at four hours and 30 minutes, their time spent listening is the highest among listeners of any English-language format.[19] The Hispanic audience that listens to news/talk/information stations also has the highest rate of voter registration among listeners of any format assessed in the report (78 percent).[20]

Though Native American–owned stations' listenership is too small for Arbitron to measure, Loris Ann Taylor, executive director of Native Public Media (NPM), estimates that 90 percent of Native Americans on reservations listen to Native-owned radio stations.[21] "Native stations have programming that could work well on public broadcasting outlets and would provide some needed diversity, but those relationships have not flourished," Taylor says.[22] Shows oriented to Native Americans include: *Native Voice One*[23] and *National Native News,*[24] which can be streamed online, and national call-in talk shows like *Native America Calling,* heard on 52 stations in the U.S. and in Canada by an estimated 500,000 listeners each week.[25] The Indian Country News Bureau (ICBN), which was formed to produce news reports and long-form features for local, regional, and national use, has access to local tribal council and government meetings that would not be available to nontribal journalists.[26] The organization, however, has scaled back its operations and coverage due to funding constraints. NPM praised the Corporation for Public Broadcasting's Local Journalism Centers initiative, which will utilize newly hired, station-based reporters and editors.[27]

Television

African-Americans rely more on TV news than other ethnic groups.[28] Some 85 percent turn to local TV news, for instance, compared to 78 percent national average.

NEWS CONSUMPTION ON A TYPICAL DAY (BY RACE/ETHNICITY)

	Local TV News	National Cable or Network TV News	Internet	Radio	Print (Local Paper)	Print (National Paper)	Avg. Number of News Sources per Typical Day	Share "Newsless" on Typical Day
All	78%	73%	61%	54%	50%	17%	2.85	3%
Whites	79%	72%	61%	55%	52%	17%	2.87	3%
African-Americans	85%	85%	48%	57%	42%	22%	2.94	3%
Hispanics	75%	75%	67%	51%	46%	14%	2.79	3%

Source: Pew Research Center's Internet and American Life Project January 2010 (Survey included Spanish-language option.)

As the Hispanic population continues to grow in the U.S., so does the number of Hispanic television-owning households. Hispanic households comprised 40 percent of new TV households for the 2010/11 season, according to Nielsen—a 3 percent increase from the 2009/10 TV season and equal to approximately 400,000 homes.[29] The television networks with the highest Hispanic viewership are Univision, Telemundo, FOX, TeleFutura, and ABC.[30]

Univision, one of the top five television networks in America, provides network and local television, radio, and digital media for Hispanic consumers. Univision says that the top two reasons viewers watch its programming are: (1) it is in Spanish and (2) it is their preferred source for news.[31] KMEX-TV Univision 34 in Los Angeles often ranks as the number one station in late local news in Los Angeles. Its news feature, *El 15% de los Estados Unidos,* which focuses on the impact of Latinos on the United States, won a Peabody Award in 2006, and the station has won its share of Emmys and Golden Mics in the Los Angeles market.[32] A former *Los Angeles Times* reporter wrote in 2008:

> "The sharpest coverage of state and local issues—government, politics, immigration, labor, economics, health care—is now found on Spanish-language TV. They compete hard on serious stories. As a labor reporter for the Los Angeles Times in 2006, the only competitors I routinely saw at major union stories were reporters for KMEX, KVEA and La Opinion, a Spanish-language daily newspaper."[33]

Almost 12 million Americans, 4.2 percent of the population, identify themselves as being of Asian extraction. They identify with a range of countries of origin and speak languages and dialects specific to that nation or region. Today's Asian American community may comprise people of Chinese, Japanese, Korean, Filipino, Vietnamese, Laotian, South Asian, and Southeast Asian descent. Although Asian Americans possessed purchasing power of more than $397 billion in 2009, the variety of languages and dialects among them have proved a barrier to broadcasters being able to tailor media information and services to serve their needs. According to one study, 41 percent of first-generation Asian Americans, when given a choice, prefer to speak English, compared to 87 percent of second-generation Asian Americans.[34] According to a survey conducted in Manhattan's Chinatown, the most frequently used media for reading and accessing news are the web (64.7 percent), mobile media (64.7 percent), and television (52.9 percent).[35]

AsianMedia Group, which owns KSCI-TV Channel 18 (serving the Los Angeles and San Diego markets) and KIKU-TV Channel 20 (in Honolulu, Hawaii), has built a successful business model based on multilingual programming. "We're Chinese in the morning for about two hours of local news," says Peter Mathes, chairman of AsianMedia Group, which owns KSCI.[36] At around 11:30 a.m., the station airs Taiwanese news; Vietnamese news comes on at about 3:00 p.m., followed by Filipino informational programming at 4 p.m. Mathes tasks his three or four news crews with developing and producing local news content of interest to Chinese, Korean, and Filipino residents. In addition, an agreement with local NBC affiliate, KNBC, allows his station to insert Chinese (Mandarin-language) captioning into KNBC's 6:00 p.m. newscast and then air it at 11 p.m. on KSCI-TV.[37] Mathes says broadcast radio and TV are still the dominant information sources for the Asian community in his market, but he laments the paucity of advertising for his multilingual stations,[38] saying that the Asian market is the last to be added to advertisers' TV buys and the first to be dropped when there are cutbacks. Mathes also operates a suite of multilingual channels offering Korean, Armenian, Spanish, Vietnamese, and Japanese programming.[39] DISH and DirecTV provide Asian-focused channels on satellite television, but they are primarily international channels.

KMEX-TV Univision 34 often ranks as the number one station in late local news in Los Angeles. Nationally, Univision is the fifth largest network in America.

Although Asian Americans possessed purchasing power of more than $397 billion, the variety of languages and dialects have presented a barrier in media information available to this community.

New America Media (NAM), a national collaboration of some 2,000 ethnic news organizations,[40] provides additional news and information resources for many ethnic communities through a variety of media platforms. Founded in 1996 by Pacific News Service, NAM is a nonprofit headquartered in California. According to NAM, over 57 million ethnic adults "connect to each other, to home countries and to America" through more than 3,000 ethnic media.[41]

Ownership and Business Models

Minority ownership of traditional radio and television broadcast media has been low, relative to the size of the overall minority population.[42] When African-Americans comprised about 13 percent of the entire U.S. population, the group owned only six television stations (or 0.33 percent of total full-power television stations) and 240 radio stations (or 1.6 percent of total full-power radio stations).[43] Similarly, when Latinos comprised approximately 14 percent of the population, they owned only 1.11 percent of television stations and 2.9 percent of radio stations.[44] Asian Americans, who comprised 4 percent of the U.S. population, owned a total of six broadcast television stations (or .44 percent of all broadcast television stations).[45] A 2006 report by Free Press found that television stations owned by people of color reached only 21 percent of U.S. television households and only 30 percent of households occupied by minorities.[46] Latino-owned stations reached just 21.8 percent of Latino households, African-American-owned stations reached just 8.7 percent of African-American households, and Asian-owned stations reached just 10 percent of Asian households.[47]

African-Americans own only 6 TV stations, or less than one percent of the total. Latinos own 1.1 percent.

For the country's almost five million Native Americans, geography has often hindered the delivery of mass media. Most tribal lands are rural, and most broadcasters prefer to operate in densely populated areas, which are easier to monetize through advertising. Additionally, spectrum scarcity can limit the opportunities for new radio service in these areas.[48] The Commission recently concluded that Federally Administered Tribal Areas were insufficiently served by radio broadcast facilities.[49] The order explains that the nation's 563 federally recognized American tribes are served by approximately 41 full-power noncommercial educational FM radio stations, which are licensed to federally recognized tribes and affiliated groups.[50] (Some 14,547 radio stations are licensed in the United States.)[51] Loris Ann Taylor, of NPM, says that she would like to see the number of Native-owned radio stations "double…in the next three years," with new regulatory efforts to increase tribal broadcast ownership and Commission approval of pending station license applications.[52]

Bankruptcies have exacerbated problems for minority owners. In the past five years, some 500 broadcast stations have filed applications with the Commission to transfer their licenses to their equity lending partners or successor firms.[53] Washington, D.C., communications attorney Frank Montero, an expert in broadcast finance and FCC regulatory matters, predicts that more bankruptcies among minority owners "may be in the pipeline" because minority owners tend to be under-collateralized and therefore vulnerable to economic downturns.[54]

Minority broadcast owners and their advocates largely attribute low minority broadcast ownership levels to the Telecommunications Act of 1996, which relaxed the local broadcast ownership rules and led to increased consolidation in broadcast media.[55] On the one hand, the minority owners who sold their stations to larger chains likely benefited financially. On the other hand, the National Association of Hispanic Journalists and a number of media advocacy organizations have argued that media consolidation hurts small businesses in general, and minority-owned businesses in particular. They argue that NBC promised to enhance local programming when it acquired the prominent Hispanic broadcast entity Telemundo in 2002, but instead it closed news units at Telemundo stations and created regional news hubs.[56] As part of their 2011 merger deal, Comcast and NBCU committed to increasing local news programming on Telemundo stations and providing 10 new minority-oriented independent channels within eight years.[57]

Some minority advocacy groups have focused their criticism on what they call "no Urban, no Spanish" dictates, arguing that some stations have inappropriately restricted their ad spending to avoid minority-owned media.[58] In 2008, the Commission adopted policies banning "no Urban, no Spanish" dictates,[59] and the Media Bureau recently revised its renewal form for commercial broadcasters, now requiring broadcasters to certify that their advertising agreements do not discriminate on the basis of race or ethnicity and that all such agreements contain nondiscrimination clauses.[60]

Newspapers

In the early 1800s, America's black press arose out of a desire among free blacks to speak on their own behalf and from their own cultural perspective. In 1827, free black men in New York City founded *Freedom's Journal* to cover the political issues of the day, as well as community news, including births, deaths, and marriages.[61]

There are some 250 black-owned newspapers in the U.S. today, according to Danny Bakewell, chairman of the National Newspaper Publishers Association (NNPA).[62] Bakewell believes that black-owned newspapers rank high as a trusted source of news among African-Americans. "All stakeholders come to the black press when they want to get their message out to this community," Bakewell explained. The need for these news outlets to exist remains strong, in his view, due to the continuing lack of coverage of minority communities in mainstream media. "People want to see themselves reflected, warts and all," says Bakewell, arguing that most newspapers, even those serving large minority populations in urban centers, do not tend to cover or address the day-to-day issues in most communities of color.[63]

Black newspapers will continue to be relevant in the lives of African-Americans, even as these papers transition to online and new-media platforms, Bakewell says. He sees the traditional newsprint for-mat co-existing with digital newspapers for another 20 years or so, in part because African-Americans have lagged in broadband adoption on home computers. Bakewell says that most advertising that targets African-American consumers goes to mainstream media rather than to the black press.[64]

> Most tribal lands are rural; most broadcasters prefer densely populated areas, which are easier to monetize through advertising.

Newspapers targeted specifically to Hispanic consumers are also a vital source of information, particularly for recent Latino immigrants from Central America and the Caribbean. Often, these consumers need information on housing, education, citizenship and legal matters.[65] Aníbal Torres Jr. publishes the free weekly Spanish-language paper, *Mundo Hispánico*, which serves the Atlanta region.[66] He estimates that the paper has a regular readership of 190,000. *Mundo Hispánico* often addresses issues not covered by the local mainstream media, such as the Dream Act, immigration, and local politics.[67] Latino immigrants tend to have a strong cultural connection to their country of origin, Torres says, and Hispanic-owned newspapers help keep them informed about daily life and events in their countries. *Mundo Hispánico* does periodic investigative reporting on government and public institutions, and occasionally teams up with other Hispanic-oriented news media, including local Telemundo and Univision broadcast outlets.[68] The transition to web distribution for such newspapers has been hampered by a lack of financial resources and the difficulty of getting their readers to adapt to accessing the news online, as they tend to be older, less fluent in English, and lack Internet access.[69] Nonetheless, the Pew 2009 State of the Media report notes a growing trend of minority- and ethnic-oriented newspapers abandoning their costly print versions to become web-only publications.[70]

News Coverage

Several studies have indicated that mainstream media do not adequately cover African-American and other minority communities. Some experts believe that this is linked to hiring practices and a lack of minority voices at the editorial table.[71] Communications Workers of America has argued that "coverage of minority communities has been cut back substantially as reporters have been re-assigned to cover other general interest beats."[72]

A recent Pew study analyzing 67,000 national news stories between February 2009 and February 2010 found that only 643 stories (filling a mere 1.9 percent of the news hole) were related to African-Americans in some way.[73] Coverage that focused more generally on African-American life tended, according to Pew, to paint a "downbeat picture."[74] Mainstream outlets focused on difficult issues facing the African-American community, including the AIDS epidemic, the economic crisis, budget concerns at minority universities, employment disparities, and poverty and crime.[75] Pew also said there were some stories that presented a more positive outlook on the lives of African-Americans today, such as improved race relations, urban renewal, and minority entrepreneurship.[76] The amount of African-American-oriented coverage varied by type of media: 2.5 percent of cable's air time was devoted to such coverage; talk radio, 2.4 percent; online, 1.9 percent; evening TV network, 1.9 percent; morning network, 1.5 percent; newspaper, 1.5 percent and news radio, 0.9 percent.[77]

A recent Pew study found that only 643 news stories (a mere 1.9 percent of the news hole) related to African-Americans in some way.

For Hispanics, newspapers provide the most coverage of their issues and cable television the least, with just 1.9 percent of the total news time surveyed devoted to Hispanics or Hispanic concerns.[78]

As the number of Hispanics who consume television and media content grows, so do concerns about negative stereotyping.[79] The National Hispanic Media Coalition (NHMC), a media advocacy organization, has petitioned the Commission to conduct an inquiry on hate speech in the media emanating from hostile commentary about immigrants on broadcast media and the Internet.[80] The Commission has not officially responded, though it is clear that the First Amendment constrains its ability to limit even offensive speech. Despite NHMC's concerns about the rise of hate speech, it *is* cautiously optimistic about Internet media overall, noting that more people of color are going online "to tell their own stories fairly and accurately."[81]

Minority Journalists and Employment

Minority journalists have lost ground in terms of employment in recent years, and industry experts doubt that the trend will reverse any time soon. Roughly 5,300 minorities worked at newspapers in 2010 compared with 7,400 in 2007, according to the American Society of Newspaper Editors (ASNE). In the 2011 census, 441 newspapers had no minorities on full-time staff. Minorities made up about 12.8 percent of newsrooms. "At a time when the U.S. Census shows that minorities are 36 percent of the U.S. population, newsrooms are going in the opposite direction. This is an accuracy and credibility issue for our newsrooms," said Milton Coleman, former ASNE president.[82] UNITY: Journalists of Color, an alliance of four national minority journalism organizations, says that minority journalists are laid off disproportionately during hard economic times.[83]

One brighter spot: minorities are better represented online: according to the ASNE survey, nearly 18.72 percent of journalists working online are minorities.

Minority employment has been declining in broadcast too, according to the 2010 *RTDNA/Hofstra University Annual Survey*.[84] Robert Papper, the survey director, says, "We end the decade with no gains whatsoever for minorities in TV news, and the percentage of minorities in radio news is down substantially."[85] RTDNA data show that minorities comprise 35.3 percent of the U.S. population, but represent 20.2 percent and 5.0 percent, respectively, of the TV and radio workforce. RTDNA notes that in the last 20 years, the minority population in the U.S. has risen 9.4 percent, but the minority workforce in television news is up only 2.4 percent in that time, and the minority workforce in radio is "actually half what it was two decades ago."[86]

Roughly 5,300 minorities worked at newspapers in 2011 compared to 7,400 in 2007. In 2011, 441 newspaper reported having no minorities on fulltime staff.

Indeed, a consortium of three dozen diversity organizations wrote to the Commission in October 2010 requesting that it promptly collect and publish equal employment opportunity data for broadcast and cable companies and make the data publicly available in an "accessible and transparent format."[87] The groups noted that media firms were becoming less diverse in "an increasingly multicultural society."[88] Wade Henderson, president and CEO of the Leadership Conference for Civil Rights, has advocated for increased diversity in media employment:

> "If racial and ethnic minorities, people of color, women, older Americans, and persons with disabilities are not employed at news operations at all levels of management, there are few who can speak with authority about their condition in the community. This means less or less complete coverage of issues that are important to them. Issues like economic inclusion, the struggle for quality public education, immigration reform, and the prevention of violent hate crime."[89]

Since their implementation over forty years ago, the Commission's Equal Employment Opportunity rules have banned discrimination on the basis of race, color, religion, national origin or gender and originally sought to ensure employment opportunities for minorities and women in the communications industry.[90] Specifically, the Commission's current EEO rules and policies in effect since March 10, 2003, require broadcasters and multichannel video program distributors ("MVPDs") to conduct broad recruitment for new employees in all sectors of their communities.[91]

The Commission maintains two employment reporting forms which require broadcasters and MVPDs to annually collect and file with the agency the racial, ethnic origin and gender composition of their workforces. The Commission annually collects these data to assess industry trends, provide reports to Congress and respond to inquiries from Congress, and not to evaluate EEO rule compliance.[92] The annual employment reporting requirements were initially suspended in 2001 following judicial challenges to the Commission's EEO rules.[93] In 2004, the Commission re-instated the broadcast and cable annual employment reporting requirements.[94] The Commission simultaneously continued the suspension of the filing requirements until it resolves concerns about the confidentiality of the data and station identification in the employment forms.[95]

New Media

Digital media are presenting tremendous programming, employment, and ownership opportunities for minorities.[96]

A BET survey revealed that African-Americans are more likely to get news from the Internet than anywhere else.[97] Specifically, 65 percent of African-Americans demonstrate a propensity to consume online news compared with 47 percent other groups; and 47 percent of African-Americans use current event and political blogs compared with 33 percent of other groups.[98]

A March 2011 Pew study found that African-Americans, as compared with the general population, are more active in web 2.0 activities, such as social media[99] and are more likely to have created their own web content—by blogging, microblogging, and social networking—than members of other ethnic groups.[100] Almost a quarter (22 percent) of African-Americans created or worked on their own online journal or blog, compared with 14 percent of whites and 13 percent of Hispanics.[101]

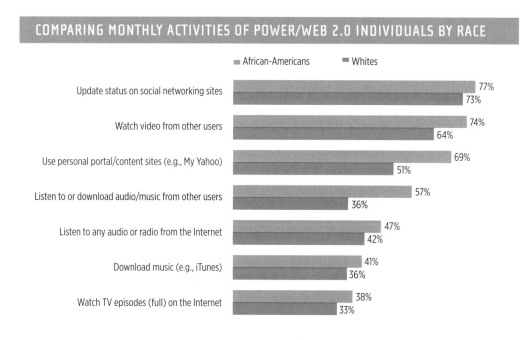

COMPARING MONTHLY ACTIVITIES OF POWER/WEB 2.0 INDIVIDUALS BY RACE

■ African-Americans ■ Whites

	African-Americans	Whites
Update status on social networking sites	77%	73%
Watch video from other users	74%	64%
Use personal portal/content sites (e.g., My Yahoo)	69%	51%
Listen to or download audio/music from other users	57%	36%
Listen to any audio or radio from the Internet	47%	42%
Download music (e.g., iTunes)	41%	36%
Watch TV episodes (full) on the Internet	38%	33%

Source: Forrester Research Technographics Q2 2010 Online Benchmark Study (n=26,749).[102]

An April 2010 Edison Media Research study found that nearly one-quarter of people on Twitter are African-American—"approximately double the percentage of African-Americans in the current U.S. population."[103] Researchers have found that minorities develop like-minded communities organically through their use of Twitter and other social media.[104] In 2010, 52 percent of African-Americans reported that they regularly or sometimes received news through social-networking sites, according to a Pew Research Center survey.[105] By contrast, 40 percent of white and 33 percent of Hispanic respondents did so.[106]

Social media and blogs may play a role in filling gaps left by traditional media. NPR's Michel Martin suggests, for example, that they brought national attention to the disappearance of Phylicia Barnes, an African-American high school honor student, whose disappearance had received limited local coverage in the mainstream media.[107]

African-Americans also appear to be using mobile devices at especially high rates. In July 2009, Pew Internet observed, "African-Americans are the most active users of the mobile internet—and their use of it is also growing the fastest."[108] Daily mobile Internet usage by African-Americans increased by 141 percent between 2007 (when it was 12 percent) and 2009 (when it was 29 percent), roughly double the rate of increase among the general population.[109]

On the other hand, minorities lag behind the rest of the population when it comes to *home* broadband. African-Americans not only trail whites in home broadband use, but they are less likely to own a desktop computer (51 percent of African-American adults do compared with 65 percent of whites).[110] English-speaking Latinos use the Internet and home broadband at almost the same rates as whites, but foreign-born and Spanish-dominant Latinos trail both whites and English-speaking Latinos in their use of the Internet and home broadband.[111]

For Native Americans, the growth of high-speed Internet connections may prove especially important. Because of the rural nature of tribal lands, Loris Ann Taylor, Executive Director of Native Public Media, recognizes that once broadband takes off in Native country, terrestrial broadcast stations may no longer be aggressively sought after.[112] When that occurs, she says, broadband will be the primary news and information facilitator on tribal lands.[113]

An increasing amount of news and information of relevance to minorities is finding its way onto the Internet, much of it flowing from traditional media, such as cable and broadcast TV.[114] For instance, TV One, a cable and satellite TV entertainment and lifestyle network geared toward black audiences,[115] operates a website with streaming video and hosts a news and information site for African-Americans: NewsOne for Blacks in America.[116] Other sites that provide national news for black Americans include TheRoot,[117] BlackAmericaWeb.com,[118] BlackVoices,[119] and Journal-isms.[120] David Wilson, managing editor of theGrio, says that while "news is at the center" of such online content, the real appeal is that, "it creates community…articles feed conversations."[121] His website's aggregated offerings—which include video, news articles, and blog posts on national politics, business, and entertainment—draw some 500,000 unique visitors each month. Because NBCUniversal owns the site, reporters that work for theGrio have a number of additional potential outlets for their stories, including NBC network news programs, MSNBC cable programs, and MSNBC.com.[122]

52% of African-Americans reported they regularly or sometimes received news through "social networking sites," compared to 40% of whites and 33% of Hispanics.

The Asian American Journalists Association (AAJA) launched the 2010/11 OurChinatown media demonstration project in New York City's Chinatown to test the efficiency of mobile devices as reporting tools.[123] AALJ envisions local residents using smartphones to capture images, text, and video, and teams of student journalists maintaining regular daily beats (culture, news, events) and fielding submissions from readers.[124] The project will provide "breaking newsflashes, events coverage, features, civic/political reminders, arts/food/shopping/cultural alerts; and on occasion notice for town hall meetings within the community."[125]

Cleveland Spears of iM4radio started his Internet radio network in reaction to the limitations of terrestrial radio formats.[126] Initially, he sought start-up funding from financial institutions, but was met with skepticism. Ultimately, he financed his venture with family loans and by liquidating his personal assets. Spears notes that while he could not afford to purchase an FCC radio license and construct a broadcast station, he did have enough money to launch an Internet channel.[127] Although Spears remains passionate about his web-based ventures, he admits that it has been challenging to attract investment, including advertising and foundation support. He has tapped into local advertising for small businesses in his Washington, D.C., market but says that national advertisers still "don't understand the business model" for Internet radio.[128]

AOL's Hispanic Cyberstudy report found that, compared with the general market, Hispanics are more sophisticated technology users, and that their use of a wide range of devices (from smartphones to gaming devices) illustrates "a high level of comfort" with and willingness to try new technologies.[129] Hispanics prefer English-language online media resources, though it is unclear whether that is just because there are more English-language websites: 27.3 percent of web content is created in English; 22.6 percent is created in Chinese; and 7.8 percent—a distant third—is created in Spanish.[130] Of those Hispanics who prefer English marketing, 57 percent say that they prefer sites that have pictures of "people who look like me."[131] Among Spanish or bilingual speakers, the most frequented websites are mostly English-language, but topically targeted for Hispanics.[132] The top sites are Univision,[133] Terra,[134] Yahoo! en Espanol,[135] MSN Latino,[136] and Batanga.[137] While it is clear that Hispanics are using web 2.0 technologies, the reported scope of usage varies among research entities. For example, according to Edison/Arbitron research data, Hispanics comprise 17 percent of Twitter users (Hispanics comprise 16 percent of the population).[138] But according to a July 2010 study by the Pew Hispanic Center, technology use by foreign-born Latinos lags significantly behind that of their U.S.-born counterparts.[139] Eighty-five percent of native-born Latinos ages 16 and older go online compared with just half (51 percent) of foreign-born Latinos.[140]

Pew Internet observed that "African-Americans are the most active users of the mobile Internet—and their use of it is also growing the fastest."

News and information sources in both Spanish and English flourish on websites such as Hispanic News[141] and MyLatino News.com.[142] Hispanic newspapers such as *El Diario*,[143] *La Prensa*,[144] *Hoy Nueva York*,[145] *La Opinion*,[146] and *El Nuevo Herald*[147] also have web presences. The owner of several of these newspapers, impreMedia, also provides Hispanic news content to MySpace.com, V-me TV, the McClatchy Company, AOL Latino, and ESPN Deportes.[148] *La Opinion*, published in Los Angeles, is the largest Spanish-language newspaper in the U.S. and the second-most-read newspaper in L.A., following the *L.A. Times*.[149] Many of the major topics of articles on *La Opinion*'s website are very similar to those on any major newspaper's website—news, sports, entertainment, and business, for example—but *La Opinion* also offers a channel on immigration.[150]

New media outlets appear to have a slightly better track record on minority hiring than traditional media. A census of online-only news sites shows that about one in five full-time journalists employed by the 27 responding news sites was a journalist of color, compared with about one of every seven in the annual ASNE census of daily paper newsrooms.[151] And that does not include part-time minority bloggers, some of whom are finding real audiences.[152] African-American blogger Nikki Peele launched East of the River in 2007, after becoming frustrated by the lack of online information about her new neighborhood, Anacostia, in Washington, D.C.[153] Her site attracts some 40,000 monthly page views, with posts ranging from the location of fresh food trucks to local civic information. Since she started blogging, Peele says that about 30 new blogs focused on the Anacostia neighborhood have launched.[154]

The web's lower barriers to entry are also enabling a range of minority ventures.

The web's lower barriers to entry are enabling a range of minority ventures. In 2004, Jonathan Moore, a longtime ad executive, launched Rowdy Orbit, a web destination for media content of interest to a multicultural audience.[155] Moore likens his site to the cable channels Sundance and IFC, which offer a platform for new, independent voices. Social media sites like Black Planet, MiGente, Twitter, and Facebook have allowed him to build an infinitely larger following than he could have with traditional media.[156]

Despite the opportunities, minorities still appear to be lagging behind in terms of web start-up creation. According to a recent report by CB Insights, African-Americans account for just one percent of Internet company founders nationally.[157] Eighty-seven percent of Internet company founders are white, and at 12 percent Asian/Pacific Islanders make up the second largest contingent of founders.[158] Venture capital has played an important role in technology entrepreneurship, but minorities may be at a disadvantage when it comes to attracting start-up funds. The report, which covers the period from January to June 2010, also found that the median amount of funding secured by an all-black founding team was $1.3 million, compared with $2.2 million for a racially mixed team, and $2.3 million for an all-white team. Asian/Pacific Islander teams, according to the report, secured the most funding with a median range of $4 million dollars.[159]

Retha Hill, director of the New Media Innovation Lab at the Walter Cronkite School of Journalism and Mass Communication,[160] emphasizes the importance of high schools and colleges obtaining the new media resources needed to foster entrepreneurial skills in students and not just consumption. Further, she hopes media professionals can do more to mentor tomorrow's journalists and innovators from diverse backgrounds. "We need new business models as well as varied people and institutions that will support innovation in local settings," she adds.

All in all, the digital media is providing new sources of news and information for minorities and spurring optimism about openings for minority entrepreneurs. But whether the digital age will end up better serving minorities than traditional media has remains to be seen. While it may be premature to give a full-throated endorsement to new media platforms as a substitute for traditional media in addressing the information needs of minorities, there are definite signs of progress—both in the diversity of content on the Internet and in the business opportunities now available to new and small entrants.

24 People with Disabilities

Traditional Media: Progress and Setbacks

More than 54 million Americans have disabilities; 35 million of them have severe disabilities.[1] Among Americans aged 65 and above, more than half have a disability, and nearly 37 percent have a severe disability.[2] About 15 percent of the population, or 34.5 million people, have hearing trouble, and 11 percent, or 25.2 million experience vision trouble.[3] The incidence of hearing trouble increases significantly with age, occurring in up to 27.8 percent of Americans ages 65 to 74, and 42.7 percent of those over 75.[4] Similarly, 14.3 percent of those between 65 and 74 have vision disabilities, as do 21.1 percent of individuals over 75.[5]

Newspapers/Printed Media

For most of the 20th century, the blind and visually impaired had little access to newspapers and other forms of printed media. In 1969, Radio Reading Services, a group of nonprofit enterprises, started enlisting volunteers to read newspapers and other printed materials over FM subcarriers called subsidiary communications authorizations (SCAs).[6] In the 1990s, this service grew into a broader program called Audio Information Services, which, in addition to these FM channels, has used the secondary audio program (SAP)—auxiliary audio channels on stereo TVs, telephones, and the Internet—for distribution of these audio materials.[7] In 1995, Newsline, a radio reading service run by the National Federation of the Blind, began making *USA Today*, the *Chicago Tribune*, and *The New York Times* available to people with vision loss by having these publications read aloud using a digitally synthesized voice over the telephone. NFB-Newsline now offers telephone access to over 300 newspapers, as well as an email service that transmits newspaper text in a computer format that is accessible to "screen readers" that convert text to speech.[8]

New legislation requires TV sets and other video devices to offer "interfaces" enabling those who cannot adequately see on-screen menus to receive audio prompts.

Unfortunately, while these services exist in various localities, there are huge gaps in their nationwide coverage. Most have threadbare budgets and are locally run, operated by universities, public radio stations, library systems, and nonprofit organizations.[9] In recent years, the transition from analog to digital radio and television has threatened the availability of Radio Reading Services and other forms of Audio Information Services. To begin with, efforts to increase power for poorly received high-definition (HD) radio signals have been interfering with SCA broadcasts over analog channels (SCAs used by reading services operating at 67kHz are marginally harmed, while those operating at 92kHz are rendered useless for analog transmission).[10] In addition, various radio reading services are reporting difficulty migrating to digital forms of radio because they have not been able to convince their FM main-channel hosts to carry their services over digital audio broadcasting radio stations, despite the greater bandwidth available to these stations.[11] According to those in the Audio Information Service field, the resistance seems to stem from two sources: confusion on the part of the digital channels over the copyright protections afforded materials that are translated from text to voice; and concerns by those channels about the use of profanity and vulgarity during on-air broadcasts, because reading services do not typically edit or censor the printed pages read aloud for listeners. As a result, at present, Audio Information Service providers report that only one or two radio reading services are being provided on digital radio subcarriers.[12]

Similarly, audio materials are less likely than before to be distributed via TV transmissions. Although these services originally used the SAP channel on analog television sets, they were eventually pushed off to make room for Spanish translations and, to a limited extent, video description.[13] After the transition to digital TV, providers of these services report that matters worsened because, like their digital radio counterparts, few stations were willing to give up the bandwidth needed to keep these services on the air.[14]

Television

It was not until the 1970s that people who were deaf and hard of hearing got access to national nightly news television programs, and not until the 1990s that such access was expanded to include local news programming. One of the first breakthroughs came in 1973, when PBS, working with WGBH/The Caption Center in Boston, began airing an open-captioned version of the *ABC Evening News* in three cities. As a result of pressure from the deaf community, distribution of the programming expanded to 190 stations the following year, though the show aired at 11 p.m., not at the dinner hour when the rest of the country was viewing it.[15] Closed captioning (which gives individual users the option to turn captions on and off) on television programming finally began in the 1980s, when the three major broadcast networks (ABC, NBC, and CBS) and PBS began airing some of their primetime programming with captions, supported in part by U.S. Department of Education grants. The Television Decoder Circuitry Act of 1990 required that all television sets with screens larger than thirteen inches have the capability to decode closed captions.[16] In 1997 the FCC set up benchmarks for video programming distributors[17] (broadcast, cable, and satellite providers) to closed caption an increasing number of hours of English- and Spanish-language programming over a 14-year period.[18]

At this time, *all* new, non-exempt English- and Spanish-language programming must be closed-captioned.[19] In 2011, the Twenty-First Century Communications and Video Accessibility Act (CVAA)[20] added a mandate for all television programs containing closed captions to retain those captions when re-shown on the Internet.[21]

Yet some disability advocates suggest that there are still problems. For instance, many stations generate captions for locally produced live news programs by using the text in the teleprompters.[22] Because teleprompter scripts are prepared in advance, the captions upon which they rely can miss live field interviews or late-breaking news stories.[23] In addition, many new Internet-based services offering monthly rental packages for movies and other programming do not routinely closed caption all of their offerings. The CVAA does not address Internet-originated programming or any other type of programming not first shown on television.

Emergencies present a special problem. While FCC rules require information about emergencies to be visually accessible to people who are deaf and hard of hearing, information that breaks into regularly scheduled television programming and is provided in "news flashes" that crawl along the bottom of the screen need only be accompanied by an aural tone to alert those who are blind or visually impaired to find another media source for the announcement.[24] Because these alerts contain critical emergency information about urgent situations—such as instructions for emergency response, the path of a dangerous hurricane or tornado, and evacuation orders—some consumers have argued that people who are blind or visually impaired are at risk of life and property loss.[25] The CVAA addressed this gap by requiring all televised emergency information to be accessible to this population.[26]

> Digital technology makes it easier to share information in multiple formats, so an online user can get text when audio is presented and audio when visual information is presented.

Access to television by people who are blind or visually impaired got its start when, in 2000, the FCC required a limited amount of video description, a service that adds audio narratives to fill the natural pauses of a program, by the top four commercial television broadcast networks and non-broadcast video programming distributors in the largest markets.[27] These rules were overturned by a federal court of appeals in 2002 for lack of Commission authority,[28] but have since been revived through a clear grant of authority by Congress to the FCC in the CVAA.[29] The new legislation also requires TV sets and other video programming devices to offer interfaces that allow people who cannot adequately see on-screen menus to receive audio prompts to help them select programming, change channels, and activate other controls.[30] Finally, the CVAA is the first federal law to require, if achievable, that programming guides and menus on navigation devices such as converter boxes be made accessible to people who are blind and visually impaired.[31]

Radio

New technologies may soon break new ground by making radio accessible to persons who are deaf and severely hard of hearing. On election night in 2008, NPR Labs, a nonprofit broadcast technology research and development center affiliated with National Public Radio, demonstrated a new captioned radio technology via its Internet radio channels in Boston, Maryland, Washington D.C., Denver, and Phoenix.[32] NPR Labs has also developed a car dashboard that provides passengers with real-time captioning of the audio being broadcast over the radio.[33]

NPR Labs has also developed the Personalized Audio Information Service (PAIS), which can direct standard radio HD receivers to proactively alert listeners to emergency messages, such as dangerous weather warnings.[34] For example, plans are in place for the PAIS receivers to incorporate "wake up on alert" signaling, as well as automatic storage of emergency messages for replay on command. This system is in its testing phase.

New Media: New Opportunities, New Gaps

Digital media hold great potential for people with disabilities for this simple reason: digital text is not inherently visual, audible, or tactile, but rather may be rendered in many different formats, including large print, speech, video, and Braille. Digital technology can make it much easier to share information in multiple, or "redundant," formats, so it is far more likely that an online user can get text when audio is presented and audio when visual information is presented. People with mobility disabilities may also benefit, as voice dictation and on-screen keyboards can eliminate the need to physically flip through pages or type.

Many websites offer material in both audio and visual formats but, crucially, even when they do not, new technologies, such as screen readers, can make sites accessible to people who are blind or visually impaired. This technology, which has been around since the 1980s, can translate written text into audio. There also is technology available that makes it possible for deaf-blind people to read Internet text through a Braille terminal connected to a screen reader. Such adaptive technologies have enabled many people with disabilities to become early adopters of digital and IP-based technologies. For example, the Coalition of Organizations for Accessible Technology (COAT), consisting of over 300 local and national disability organizations, has come to rely on new media (a hosted website, Facebook, Twitter, email groups, etc.) to distribute, receive, and share information. These delivery methods for news and information have allowed for an unprecedented level of interactivity by COAT members and other individuals with disabilities.[35]

> If a link to an article is depicted only graphically, without an accompanying text label or "alt tag" that can be voiced by a screen reader, then it is effectively inaccessible to a web surfer who is blind.

But while many websites are screen-readable, many are not—or they have subsets of content that are not. For people with disabilities to fully benefit from the web, content needs to be coded in ways that are compatible with assistive technologies. If a link to an article is depicted only graphically, without an accompanying text label or "alt tag" that can be voiced by a screen reader, then its content is effectively inaccessible to a web surfer who is blind. Similarly, if an article on a web page lacks organizational structure, such as section and article headings, it can become impossible for an assistive technology user to find the main content amidst surrounding, extraneous information, such as advertising or external links.

An October 2009 survey of 665 screen reader users suggests that web content is becoming more accessible, but the data is mixed: 46.3 percent said that web content had become more accessible; 33.3 percent thought its accessibility had not changed; and 20.4 percent believed it had become less accessible.[36] A little more than 8 percent found social-media sites to be "very accessible"; almost 53 percent found them "somewhat accessible"; and nearly 20 percent found that they were "somewhat inaccessible."[37] More than 35 percent of respondents found that flash technology, a popular way of streaming video, was very unlikely to be accessible, and 27.1 percent found that flash was somewhat unlikely to be accessible.[38] The most problematic sites were those requiring CAPTCHA (images presenting text used to verify that the user is human).[39]

In a survey of 1,121 screen reader users, conducted between December 2008 and January 2009, news sites ranked fifth among the 10-most-avoided types of websites due to accessibility issues.[40]

Newspaper and magazine sites—as well as the websites of news and entertainment shows—often create extra video clips that are available online only. More often than not, the video content on these sites is not accessible via closed captioning or via video description. Such barriers are compounded when the controls used to operate the video players, typically embedded in their web pages, are also not accessible to people with low or no vision.

These and other problems can be avoided if media sites comply with standards developed by the World Wide Web Consortium (W3C), including the Web Content Accessibility Guidelines and the Authoring Tool Accessibility Guidelines, which specify features that web creation software should have in order to produce accessible content.[41] When followed, these guidelines enable people who are blind to receive synthesized speech output using text-to-speech technology to get access to email, website content, SMS messages, and just about anything on the Internet that is in text.

While TV news has closed captions, online video content often does not.

People with disabilities seeking to obtain news and information via their mobile smartphone also confront difficulties. Section 255 of the Communications Act requires telecommunications equipment and services to be usable by people with disabilities to the extent it is readily achievable to make them so.[42] This requires manufacturers and service providers to identify accessibility barriers and ensure the usability and compatibility of equipment and services throughout their product design, development, and fabrication processes. For example, where visual information is necessary to use a phone, manufacturers are supposed to make it possible for people who are visually impaired to hear audio prompts.

But while section 255 covers telecommunications and interconnected voice over IP (voice communications over the Internet), its implementation has been erratic. Consumers complain that most mobile phones remain inaccessible to people who are visually impaired unless they also have expensive software, such as TALKS or Mobile Speak.[43] The CVAA includes measures to improve accountability and enforcement of section 255. In addition, it expands accessibility protections to advanced communication services on the Internet, including non-interconnected voice over IP (voice communications over the Internet that do not connect to the public switched telephone network), email, and instant messaging, as well as the products (such as smartphones) that are used to take advantage of those services.[44]

Although some e-Readers have a text-to-speech feature that could be a boon to people who are blind or visually impaired, the way these products were initially designed made it difficult for individuals who do not have sight to find and turn on this feature. After the blind community raised objections, manufacturers reconfigured them with audible prompts, enlarged type, and tactile bumps to make them more accessible to people unable to see the controls.[45]

As noted above, new legislation will address some of the accessibility problems that exist in new media,[46] and commercial and nonprofit sectors are developing technologies to help, too. In 2009, Google began providing tools for adding computer-generated closed captions to videos posted on YouTube.[47] Those tools have made it easier to automatically add (and time stamp) closed captions on videos. Some researchers are also exploring ways for people with disabilities to use applications in "the cloud" (i.e. hosted on the Internet at large rather than stored on a particular device), which might make it possible for people with disabilities to use screen readers even when they are not at their own computer.[48]

What about Americans with other physical disabilities? As towns set up Internet hot spots in parks, libraries, and schools, it is not clear how many will be accessible to people in wheelchairs or with other disabilities, despite the Americans with Disabilities Act's requirements that they be so equipped.[49] It is also unclear whether libraries and schools are providing material in accessible formats or offering sufficient digital literacy training to people with disabilities. This may be of particular concern to late-deafened adults and those with degenerative blindness who did not receive an education in assistive technologies during their childhood.

In short, there remain significant barriers to new media for people with disabilities. In the past, new technologies have tended to neglect this community until developers and manufacturers were forced to respond through compliance with statutes or regulations. There is evidence that new media technology may have inherent advantages that make it more disability friendly—if policymakers continue to address accessibility issues and companies incorporate accessible features into the designs of their products.

How Big Is the Local Reporting Gap and Who Will Fill It?

How Big Is the Gap?

There were about 13,400 fewer newspaper newsroom jobs in 2010 than there were in 2006, dropping from 55,000 positions to about 41,600.[1] Over the years, newsmagazines, local commercial radio, and local TV have reduced their newsgathering staffs, as well. At the same time, Internet sites, cable news, and public radio have *created* new journalism jobs. How does this net out? Is there some way of quantifying the gap between the current level of investment in journalistic activity by the public, private, and nonprofit sectors and the level of investment that would maximize the civic benefits of journalism?

It is an extremely difficult task. Weighing the value of "accountability journalism" compared with other kinds of reportage is a highly subjective endeavor. We have no expectation of calculating a definitive number, but we do believe it is important to get a sense of scale of the shortfall. We considered three different approaches: studying the drop in spending on news reporting at newspapers; estimating the change in journalists employed across different news media; and calculating an ideal staffing of accountability reporting beats and comparing that with media employment today.

Rick Edmonds of the Poynter Institute has studied the drop in reporting resources at newspapers. He calculates that with 2009 aggregate revenues of $37 billion, daily newspapers were spending $4.4 billion on news operations—an overall drop of about $1.6 billion in annual spending since 2006.[2]

Ava Seave, a management consultant and adjunct professor at the Columbia Business School and Journalism School, studied the same issue from another angle for this report. Looking both at jobs lost and new jobs created in the new media economy (such as by Patch and NPR), she concluded that there were between 7,000 and 10,820 fewer full-time journalists, and there was between $800 million and $1.3 billion less being spent on editorial salaries, in 2008 and 2009 than in an average year from 2001 to 2006.[3]

Edmonds and Seave approached the problem using entirely different methodologies and ended up with numbers that—even at their lowest estimates—reflect deep losses to the nation's journalistic capacity. Recognizing that neither of these analyses is definitive, it is nevertheless likely that, in terms of both employment levels and dollars spent, the media economy is spending less on full-time journalism today than it did before the Internet upended traditional business models.

This gives a rough sense of scale but leaves many questions unanswered.

First, we cannot conclude that our current gap is therefore $800 million or $1.6 billion. Some of the jobs and dollars cut eliminated duplication. A newsroom that once needed 12 production people may now need only three due to technological improvements. Some layoffs eliminated nice-to-have rather than have-to-have slots—for instance, scores of local newspapers had their own movie reviewers. Some reporters now work part-time, or produce more copy than they used to. Disruptive as these cuts were to the individuals involved, American journalism can safely survive them. What's more, a given reporter might be considerably more productive than his pre-Internet self, since some aspects of research take significantly less time than they used to.

Moreover, even before staffing cuts, many important stories were not being covered. So we cannot know with any precision if the $6 billion spending on news content by newspapers in 2006 was civically ideal—if only it had been allocated differently—or, for that matter, if it was still too little or was more than necessary. We do know from several studies of media ecosystems in particular cities that new media (though it adds value in myriad other ways) has not come close to replacing what old media lost in terms of basic reporting.

Another approach is to look at some of the basic beats that might need covering. According to 2007 census data, the U.S. contains 3,033 counties; 19,492 municipal governments; 16,519 townships. Each typically has a public safety function and other offices. There are also 14,561 public school systems; and 37,381 special districts—which oversee a wide range of municipal operations, including, hospitals, mass transit, airports, stadiums, solid waste disposal, and water supply.[4] There are many facets of community life that probably can be adequately covered by an ad hoc combination of bloggers, volunteers, and occasional journalism. But we also believe that communities and citizens are seriously harmed—including financially—if there is not a critical mass of full-time professional journalists watching over the key institutions, such as state and local government, local schools, state and local courts, police, environmental planning, land use, transportation, and public health.

Within particular jurisdictions, other beats will be essential. In West Virginia, a mine reporter is a necessity; in a university town, higher education must be covered. Covering all those units of government would take about 50,000 reporters.[5]

> The U.S. spends $560 billion a year on K–12 schools. It would cost about $231 million a year to ensure that every school system has at least a half-time reporter watching how the money is spent.

Of course, even at the peak of journalistic employment in local media, not all personnel were working on the most civically significant beats. How many were focused on accountability beats? During the 1990s, data from *Burrelle's Media Directory* indicates that only about 20 percent of reporters and editors at local newspapers worked on local news beats.[6] If, to be conservative, we assume that 20 percent of people currently working in newspaper newsrooms, local TV station news operations, and other outlets are working on accountability beats, this would yield a total of 20,000 journalists now on the local and state government accountability beats.[7] So, to get to the level of accountability journalism that likely existed in 2000, the media sector would need to hire roughly 5,000 reporters, costing about $265 million. To hire the 30,000 journalists that would bring the total working on local and state accountability beats to 50,000, it would cost $1.6 billion.

Trying to come up with a single number would give a false sense of precision. And we are pretty confident that merely replacing jobs lost, in the same configuration as before, would be truly misguided. Nonetheless, using what seem to be pretty conservative methodolgies, it appears that the cost to society (commercial and nonprofit sectors) of filling the gap in local accountability journalism would be somewhere between $265 million and $1.6 billion per year.

Would it be worth it? Having less reportorial journalism means that governments are apt to waste more money, citizens' rights are more likely to be infringed upon, and schools are more likely to underperform. The U.S. spends $560 *billion* a year on K–12 schools,[8] with increasingly discouraging results. It would cost about $231 million a year to ensure that every school system has at least a half-time reporter covering schools.[9] It is difficult to quantify the benefits foregone from a high school that could have been better or a river that could have been cleaner or a hospital that could have saved more lives. But we feel extremely confident in saying that the dollar value is orders of magnitude more than $1 billion.

How Fast Will Commercial Media Markets Evolve to Fill Gaps?

Will commercial media eventually fill these gaps? So far it has not, but we readily admit that we are only offering a snapshot of the media markets at a particular moment. Given the pace of change, might it be just a matter of minutes before someone will invent a new model that will solve the problems? Nonetheless, it would be a cop-out to throw up our hands and say we therefore cannot have any idea what is coming next. In this section, we assess the evidence related to a critical question: how likely is it that commercial markets will quickly address the existing problems in local media?

Signs That Commercial Markets May Fill Gaps Quickly

Positive Factors Affecting Advertising

BIA/Kelsey predicts that local advertising will double to $42.5 billion between now and 2015.[10] As local advertisers spend more online, digital businesses geared toward local news and information could grow.

Some already are succeeding. *The Batavian,* an online news website in upstate New York, reports revenue in the $100,000 to $150,000 range—enough to make the business sustainable, since its staff consists of only the founder and his wife.[11] A recent report on digital journalism by Columbia Journalism School described Baristanet, a site catering to affluent suburbs in New Jersey, as "one of the most successful local news sites in the country." The website is able to charge high ad rates to local businesses and "keeps costs radically low," making heavy use of free-lance and volunteer writers, photos, and community listings. "Everyone involved with the site has another job—even the two founders," the report concluded.[12] Other websites have gotten into the black by developing secondary revenue streams, such as creating consulting services that help local businesses use social media, reports Michele McLellan of the Missouri School of Journalism.[13]

Local advertising will double to $42.5 billion between now and 2015. As local advertisers spend more online, digital businesses targeted toward them may grow.

Ad rates on the iPad are higher than on websites, raising hope that the spread of tablets could increase digital ad revenue.[14] Gannett reports that it is currently charging Marriott a $50 CPM for Marriott ads embedded in its *USA Today* iPad application, more than five times the average CPM advertisers pay for ads placed on the *USA Today* website.[15] In March 2010, the *Wall Street Journal* reported that it had obtained $2.4 million in ad revenue from deals relating to its iPad app.[16]

Ad-serving technology has made it easier for advertisers to target their message, leading to the possibility of higher ad rates. Advertisers can target messages based on previous online consumer behavior and geographic location. If ad rates overall rose by even a few dollars it could make the difference between local news websites surviving or dying.

Yahoo! has created a service to help local newspapers benefit from targeting technology and the company's sales force. The effort involves 821 papers (with 22 million circulation, accounting for 52 percent of all U.S. Sunday circulation).[17] Yahoo! uses its aggregate data on what people read on the web, what they search for, and which ads and search results they click on to develop profiles of readers' likely interests in different product categories. When those Internet users visit the websites of papers that are part of the Newspaper Consortium, they are shown ads that are geared toward their likely product interests. Because these targeted ads are more likely to match consumer interests and get results, advertisers sometimes pay a premium for them.[18] Gary Pruitt, CEO of McClatchy, is encouraged: "We remain very pleased with the Yahoo! Consortium and believe it is helping to grow our retail online numbers at a substantial double-digit clip, 50 percent in the first half."[19]

Experimentation with Pay Models

"Quality journalism is not cheap, and an industry that gives away its content is simply cannibalizing its ability to produce good reporting," said News Corp.'s CEO Rupert Murdoch. "The digital revolution has opened many new and inexpensive distribution channels but it has not made content free."[20]

Efforts to charge users are taking many different forms: among them, putting all content behind a paywall, charging only for certain content, and charging those who use the most content. Payment strategies might involve monthly subscriptions, per issue charges, or per-article fees. Some content providers are experimenting with a single fee for access to the organization's content on all platforms.[21] And they are testing the possibility of charging on some platforms—phones, and tablets, for instance—but not others. (See Chapter 5, Mobile.)

New services and enterprises have arisen to helping publishers charge for content. Google and Apple have introduced new systems that allow publishers to sell subscriptions and charge in other ways. Firms, such as Journalism Online, help newspapers and other content creators determine and implement the best strategy for their particular needs. The *New York Times* set up a metered-paywall system, and News Corp. recently launched *The Daily,* a paid online newspaper. Some major newspapers have joined together to create Ongo, a paid service that provides premium journalism content for a flat subscription fee,[22] and major magazine publishers did the same with NextIssueMedia.[23] Many bundle together online and print products, or use one to subsidize the other.

On the local level, there are a handful of encouraging examples. The *Augusta Chronicle* saw no decline in web traffic in the first three months after it started charging for content.[24] The *Dallas Morning News* started charging in March 2011, an effort that will be closely watched, both because it is a metro newspaper (not a national entity) and because it has managed to hold on to a relatively large journalistic staff. A key question is whether that staff will provide reporting that is distinctive enough that subscribers will be willing to pay enough to support it.[25]

Several small news services have been created to cover state government, using a different kind of paid model: reaching a small, intensely interested audience and charging high subscription prices. The *Arizona Guardian* sustains its reporters on this beat through expensive subscriptions ($1,800 for a "professional subscription" per year; $1,440 for nonprofits; and $360 for individuals).[26]

New Forms of Bundling

As discussed in Chapter 4, Internet, the Internet can be seen as hostile to business models based on "bundles": it undermined the existing print business model that allowed newspapers to offer a variety of content for a single subscription price (thereby allowing certain types of content to subsidize others). The Internet tends to excel at offering only the content you absolutely want, and not making you pay for a word more. But that is not to say that the Internet is devoid of models that create "bundles." Netflix, Hulu, and Pandora offer a large variety of material for a single subscription price. On the iPad, magazines and newspapers are being sold more like they were in pre-Internet days, a single price allowing readers to access a variety of content. If this succeeds on a large scale, it might enable publications to re-establish the subsidy system that allowed for some forms of popular content to indirectly support costly forms of worthy reporting that generated less income.

Some national companies are experimenting with local content. The *Wall Street Journal* and the *New York Times* charge customers *and* now offer local content as part of targeted editions, available in print and online.[27] They already invest in the printing and other infrastructure cost, so the additional cost of creating local editions is limited largely to paying the salaries of local reporters and ad salespeople.

The Huffington Post is a general interest website in which popular content, such as entertainment news, in some ways subsidizes less popular content. In the wake of the merger with AOL, executives are pledging to increase their hiring of journalists. Founder Arianna Huffington has maintained that a major reason for her interest in this deal was to do more for local news and information AOL's Patch service has hired more local editor/reporters than any other media company in the last year. As of March 2011, there were 800 Patch sites, employing about 800 reporter/editors.[28] Patch engages in another form of subsidizing: it has built a single technology platform that can be used by content-creators throughout the country. Another company that has created a national infrastructure to enable the creation of local content is, Examiner.com, founded by entrepreneur Phillip Anschutz. It has sites in 233 cities and has recruited 67,000 (mostly part-time) "examiners" to write on local topics. In November 2010, Examiner.com sites drew 24 million unique readers and generated 68 million page views.[29]

"Quality journalism is not cheap, and an industry that gives away its content is simply cannibalizing its ability to produce good reporting," said Rupert Murdoch.

Technology Continues to Drive Down the Cost of Information Gathering

Capturing video, distributing it, researching, publishing text, transmitting photos, editing audio—all of these functions have become easier, cheaper, and accessible to a broader range of people due to less expensive cameras, new software, and many other technological advances. Will things continue in this direction?

Camera technology improves by the day, allowing video gathering to be done inexpensively. The cost of bandwidth and storage continue to drop, so journalists wanting to offer audio and video may eventually be able to do so without busting their budget. And Skype and other video streaming services allow for remote interviews that are infinitely less expensive than sending out crews, and they will only become more common as quality improves. Governments putting more data online will facilitate more data-driven research projects.

Open source code has become more varied, now providing entire content management systems for new websites—saving startups hundreds of thousands, if not millions, of dollars. The Journal Register newspaper chain recently asked its local papers to create websites using open source code only.[30]

Perhaps most important, the rise of cloud computing has lowered capital costs for start-ups. Rather than building an expensive technology infrastructure, web-based companies can rent a slice of the cloud for a fraction of the cost.

It Is Early

The collapse of newspapers spurred many journalists and entrepreneurs to try to create new models. But they have only been at it for a few years. It may take time to learn, from trial and error, what works best. In some cases, businesses that were started to perform one function have evolved toward performing another.

Cato Institute adjunct scholar Tim Lee argues that disruptive technologies often start off at the low-margin end of the market, but they eventually move toward products that can generate premium margins:

> "The most successful sites are getting tired of the thin margins at the lowest rungs of the ladder and have started looking upward. The *New York Times* alone generated $387.3 million in digital revenue last year. That might not seem like a lot of money to the grey lady, but it looks like a huge jackpot to a still-small company like the Huffington Post. They—and dozens of their competitors—are working hard to find ways to take a piece of that pie."[31]

It's hard to overstate how much mental and creative energy is going into solving these problems. Dan Gillmor, the director of the Knight Center for Digital Media Entrepreneurship wrote:

> "The entrepreneurial, startup culture has infiltrated journalism in a big way—because so many people are trying new things, mostly outside of big enterprises but also inside the more progressive ones; because Digital Age experimentation is so inexpensive; and because we can already see the outlines of what's emerging.… But the worriers appear to assume that we can't replace what we will lose. They have no faith in the restorative power of a diverse, market-based ecosystem, because they have little or no experience of being part of one.

> "The diversity that's coming—in fact, is already arriving—is breathtaking. As we all come to demand better from our information sources, and create trustworthy information ourselves, we'll have the choices we need at our fingertips."[32]

It may be that new models will be so fundamentally different, that it will take time for them to develop. Jeff Jarvis of CUNY's Graduate School of Journalism says, "The future is not the big, old, dumb company being replaced by the big, new, smart company."[33] Instead, a hundred individual local bloggers or small companies might join together to sell ads, never gathering in a single newsroom.

What is more, the first wave of local news start-ups were launched by journalists, many of whom had limited business skills. "Just because a bunch of journalists and civic minded folks can't figure out a business model for local news does not mean that business models aren't still to be invented," Michele McLellan says.[34]

Signs That the Commercial Media Will Not Fill the Gaps Soon

The Nature of News as a Public Good

As noted in Chapter 4, Internet, economists view news and information as "public goods" with big public benefits but a large "free rider" problem. People know they can get the news—and the benefits of reporters' work—without fully paying for it. We see nothing on the horizon that would change this attitude. In fact, free riding is easier than ever. For all the attention given to paid news apps on the iPad, the vast majority of news apps are free, so consumers know they will often have a free alternative. That doesn't make charging for content impossible, but it means that the material has to be truly unique and distinctive—while not being overly expensive to produce—and the uptake on pay schemes will be lower than it might be for other types of paid content.

By contrast, people have always been willing to pay more for entertainment programming than for news. Though there are problems with piracy, free riding is a much less significant problem when it comes to entertainment content than it is for news: If you don't pay for the movie, you will have a hard time being able to see it. If you don't pay for the news, there are many other ways you can get it. Hence the success of Netflix and Hulu as "bundled" business models probably does not tell us much about the likelihood that bundled models attempting to finance labor-intensive reporting will be successful.

Precision Metrics Encourage Managers to Shift Away from Low ROI Products

Just because a large company is generating a profit does not mean it will spend some of its earnings on local journalism. Indeed, publicly traded companies are under tremendous pressure to maximize profits. Justifying investment in expensive services with limited or negative return on investment (ROI) is difficult.

One factor that has contributed to the current situation is that managers now have much better information about the ROI a particular piece of content produces. Years ago, newspapers had a general sense that they were probably losing money on their overseas coverage, but it was more a hunch than a certainty since no one knew with any precision how many people actually read the foreign stories. Now, managers know in agonizing detail how many page views an article reported from, say, Rwanda receives, and therefore they can calculate exactly how much money they are losing by sending a reporter there. Companies can certainly decide to sustain losing propositions in the service of some greater corporate goal—improving prestige or brand, for instance—but each time the CEO or the finance department assesses the performance of its products, the ones that lose money will have bulls-eyes on their backs.

> Those attempting to earn revenue on a free, ad-supported model increasingly face a new problem: on the Internet one does not have to be a local content creator to be a venue for local advertising.

In fact, when we look again at the national entities that seem most likely to finance local journalism, we can see the pressures under which they operate. For instance, it is telling that the Huffington Post, which has news at its core, nonetheless decided that rather than funding investigative journalism it would create a foundation to do so. Former Huffington Post CEO Eric Hippeau says that they created (and later spun off) the Huffington Post Investigative Fund as a separate nonprofit, instead of making it part of the main company,[35] because that kind of journalism was just too expensive to support.[36] So far, the Huffington Post's local properties have followed the same model as its national news—heavily relying on aggregation, summarization, and unpaid bloggers. This formula may prove to be as popular on the local level, but, regardless, the company's financial success comes in part from its disciplined refusal to spend much money on original reporting. As previously noted, both Patch and Examiner have succeeded in part because they, too, avoid spending significant money on labor-intensive investigative journalism.

What about efforts by the *New York Times* and the *Wall Street Journal* to create local journalism? Though the *Journal's* New York City edition has been met with success, the paper has decided, at least for the next year, not to expand to other cities. The economics cannot sustain sinking significant reportorial resources into other cities.[37] And, tellingly, the *New York Times* has created its local editions in part by partnering with local nonprofits.[38] Again, the model works only by placing tight limits on how much one spends on local journalism.

Local Obstacles to Bundling

What about local media companies? Isn't it possible that their core mission—serving a particular community—might allow them to re-establish the subsidy model and finance the important-but-not-lucrative reporting that newspapers used to support?

Those attempting to do so on a free, ad-supported model will face all of the aforementioned forces that drive down Internet ad rates—plus a new one: On the Internet, one does not have to be a local content creator to be a venue for local advertising. For instance, in studying several cities, the FCC found that the top news destinations for local residents were national websites like Yahoo! News and AOL. It is impossible to know how much local versus national content residents are seeking on those sites, but, significantly, even if users in, say, Toledo go to Yahoo! News for *national* content, they are likely to see *local* advertising. Even though sites like Yahoo! News do not invest in creating local content, they are winning some of the local ad spend that used to go to newspapers and TV stations, and that might otherwise have gone to independent web start-ups.

On a local level, traffic is so fragmented that it is difficult for one site to garner large numbers of monthly page views; top local news sites are likely to generate only a few million. A typical site with two million page views generates $15,000 per month assuming an average effective CPM of $2.52 and three ads per page. The fourth ranking website in Toledo generated 73,408 page views. Even if it were to charge double or triple the average ad rates, it would be extremely difficult to sustain a newsroom on that kind of revenue.

What about models that combine advertising with charging for content, perhaps through tablets? While there have been some positive early returns for *national* media companies that charge—the *New York Times* and *The Daily*—the track record for local media is discouraging. *Editor & Publisher* magazine assessed the situation as of January 2011 as follows:

> "The late, though not necessarily lamented, 2010 was supposed to be the Year of the Paywall for newspapers. But consumers overwhelmingly repudiated the efforts of the few publishers who dared to demand payment for access to the news, leaving newspaper content about as widely and freely available on the Web at year's end as it has been for the past one-and-a-half decades....
>
> "As revealed in a survey of paywalls at three dozen newspapers by Belden Interactive, less than 1 percent of consumers on average were willing to subscribe. After experiencing alarming drops in readership at their websites, papers in places such as Harlingen, Texas, and Sonoma, Calif., quickly restored free access to their sites. With paywalls off the table, publishers now are moving toward hybrid systems that will let them charge some kinds of fees for some kinds of content under certain kinds of circumstances."[39]

PaidContent listed 13 local newspapers for which information was available about paywall performance. The newspapers' circulation totaled 883,000, with the circulation of the online-only paid products totaling 10,755.[40]

There are some in-between possibilities: It is possible that paywall experiments will eventually work, and yet still not lead to more funding of local accountability journalism. If history is any guide, consumers will be more willing to pay for financial, health, and entertainment content as well as other service content that materially and directly helps them in some way. Or, publishers may be able to add incremental revenue but not in a "game changing way." In looking at the *Augusta (GA) Chronicle*, for instance, one of the most successful paywall experiments to date, analyst Alan Mutter calculated:

> "Based on the experience to date and assuming a constant number of new subscribers on every day of the year for 12 months, the annual revenue from the pay system could range from about $43,000 (if two people subscribe each day) to $173,000 (if eight people subscribe each day). So long as the newspaper has enough page views to produce enough advertising inventory to satisfy demand, the subscription revenue would appear to be sufficient to support one to four additional bodies in the newsroom (although there can be no guarantee that this is where the windfall would land)."[41]

Local publishers contemplating a paywall model for mobile devices immediately have to reckon with the fact that their competitors are offering news content for free. While monopoly newspapers benefited from lack of competition, the local online space is actually quite competitive. A newspaper that wants to charge for its content, whether on its website or an iPad app, will have to do so with the knowledge that the local TV station will likely offer basic local news for free.

High-priced newsletters that serve relatively small groups of readers may well succeed financially.[42] The question here is whether democracy is served in the same way if the journalism is behind a prohibitively high paywall. It is possible that the mere reporting of unpleasant information might have an accountability effect even if the audience is relatively small, especially if the readers are influential. But politicians and CEOs tend ultimately to worry only when they think it will impact their re-election chances, so material that doesn't break through in popular media will have less impact. It is also possible that newsletters gear their coverage toward the interests of their readers. If those readers are mostly lobbyists, the coverage decisions may evolve toward topics of most interest to them.

Negative Advertising Trends

Many of the trends outlined in Chapter 4, Internet—that pushed toward lower ad rates—are likely to continue.

We noted, for instance, that advertising is increasingly less dependent on content. This phenomenon became apparent with the flood of advertising dollars going to search. But it is just as true of the ad vehicles growing most rapidly now—social media, coupons, and geotargeting. Currently only 20 percent of digital marketing spending goes to legacy media companies (TV, magazines, radio, billboards, etc.), and that amount is projected to decline to 13 percent

Managers have much better metrics about the Return on Investment of particular pieces of content. Each time the CEO assesses the performance of its products, the ones that lose money will have bullseyes on their backs.

by 2020. Media analyst Jack Myers estimates that 50 percent of digital marketing growth will go to social media, coupons, and other platforms that largely bypass content-based media.[43] Rafat Ali, founder of PaidContent.org, a leading analyst of online publishing, predicts that Facebook will become a major player in the *local* advertising space. Local advertisers will have more ways to reach customers without working with traditional content-creating media:

> "Facebook is blowing the lid off any kind of local advertising. Some of the savvier local businesses have figured that the way to reach people is directly through social [networks]. Will [traditional] media be an intermediary in that experience? Maybe. But why would local businesses want to add that layer?"[44]

There is much investment activity around efforts to geotarget ads directly on one's cell phone, again bypassing traditional media. "Very local, geotargeted [ad systems] are going to come in," Ali says. "Where is media? Nowhere. They're an afterthought of an afterthought."[45]

"Daily deal" oriented services, such as Groupon, have been popular with consumers, but it is not yet clear whether local media will benefit. On the one hand, local media are trying to create their own Groupon-like services or create affiliate arrangements where they might get a slice of revenue in exchange for marketing help. On the other, it means more ad dollars going into a mechanism that can bypass local media entirely. In general, private investment seems to be attracted to platforms that bypass content-based media to reach consumers directly.[46] Ali puts it even more provocatively: "All of the innovation is coming from people who don't need the news industry."[47]

Though there are reasons to believe that ad targeting can increase rates (see above), there is just as much evidence that its impact will be minimal. In the past, the benefits of targeting were washed out by the sheer growth of the Internet. The volume of page views grew so rapidly that advertisers had an abundance of choices and could insist upon lower and lower rates, even for targeted ads. In addition, although targeting might work well on a national level, it often falls apart on a local level. As a practical matter, a website that gets 500,000 monthly unique visitors and then starts slicing its community into advertisable chunks—say, middle-aged men ready to buy a car—ends up with an actual number of targetable customers too small to interest advertisers. In aggregate, these small, targeted audiences might be valuable, but most big national-brand advertisers have no interest in contracting with 1,000 small websites to reach their desired audience. Hence, the lion's share of advertising dollars now goes to the top few players, such as Yahoo! and AOL. This means that local news sites will have a harder time benefiting from hyper-targeting than big national sites.

Finally, privacy concerns have led both policymakers and companies to look for ways to restrict the ability of advertisers to gather information about consumers' online behavior.[48]

More Shoes to Drop for Traditional Media

Although increased broadband penetration has tremendous benefits (see Chapter 29, the Internet and Mobile) it will also create further dislocations for traditional media business models in the short run. Gordon Crovitz, former publisher of *The Wall Street Journal* and co-founder of Journalism Online, says his research over the years has shown an "inverse correlation between broadband penetration and newspaper profitability."[49] Broadband has not yet spread throughout the land. Twenty-two percent of Americans are not Internet users,[50] and 35 percent do not use broadband Internet at home.[51]

In other words, for people without easy access to the Internet, it still may be easier today to read and post classified newspaper ads and to clip coupons inserted in the local paper than to shop and sell on Craigslist. This, along with less competition from local TV news, may help explain why small-city newspapers and community newspapers have been faring better than their big-city brethren. Eventually, broadband should and will reach these audiences as well—and the old media business models in their towns will suffer, too.

Similarly, as Internet radio arrives in cars, traditional broadcast radio will suffer; and as IPTV (Internet TV) becomes a more common form of TV watching, local TV stations may suffer, too. In each case, the higher ad rates charged on traditional media will likely be undercut by the lower ad rates on the Internet. A recent survey of iPad users by the Donald W. Reynolds Journalism Institute at the University of Missouri found that 58 percent of print newspaper subscribers who also use their iPad a lot "said they were very likely to cancel their print subscriptions within the next six months."[52]

Of course, none of this is an argument against universal broadband, but it is an argument for realism about the inevitable by-products of this trend.

Another factor weighing against traditional media is human mortality. Media usage is generationally skewed. Seventeen percent of 18 to 24 year olds read a daily newspaper "regularly," whereas 40 percent of folks ages 40 to 49 do.[53] The same pattern can be seen with network TV, where the median age of the audience watching nightly newscasts is 62.3 and rising.[54] A generation that sustained the high-CPM business models of newspapers and television will gradually be replaced by a generation that prefers new technologies, which alas are the ones that rely on low-CPM business models. Finally, we can anticipate that one more leg of the traditional media advertising stool—advertising inserts in the Sunday paper—will also erode, as direct marketers shift to either deal-of-the-day sites like Groupon or web-, email-, and social-media-based direct marketing.

Separation of Distribution and Content

In the old system, media companies often acted as both content creators *and* distributors. Newspapers and TV created the content and invested in and profited from the distribution networks. They could use profits generated through distribution to subsidize content creation. In the modern system, most often those functions are performed by separate companies. Phone companies that provide Internet access, either through landlines or wireless pathways, earn tremendous revenue from consumers using the Internet to access content (and for other purposes). Yet the Internet service providers (ISPs) share none of that revenue with content creators.[55] Viewed in terms of spectrum resources, we can see a similar shift. Spectrum used to be held by entities that both distributed and created content: TV and radio stations. Now, spectrum is shifting toward wireless companies, which earn their revenue entirely through distribution.

In addition, a tremendous amount of the revenue that previously went to the content-creator/distributors now flows to search engines. Though not "distributions pipes" in the traditional sense, search engines create most of their value by directing people to content rather than creating it.

As publishers look to paid content models as a potential solution, they see the possibility that some of the savings generated by the lower cost of publishing online may be eaten up by the entities best positioned to distribute the content. Coincidentally, while a typical newspaper's costs of raw materials (e.g., paper, ink) and distributing the paper was 31 percent of revenues,[56] Apple keeps 30 percent of the revenue from publishers that sell subscriptions on iTunes.[57] In that sense, technology has not brought the anticipated drop in distribution costs for newspapers.

Interestingly, there have been few efforts aimed at getting ISPs to share the wealth with content creators, as there have been with cable service providers.[58] (See Chapter 27, Cable Television, for more on the battle between cable operators and programmers for "retransmission consent" fees.)

Corporate Structure Issues Remain Unchanged

Much of the debate about media concentration—whether a small number of companies own too many media outlets—has usually focused on whether it has reduced the diversity of voices.

While an important debate, our analysis indicates that the more significant risk of concentration may relate to its secondary effects: increasing percentages of media operations became subject to Wall Street pressure to focus on short-term profits over long term goals. Both TV stations and newspapers could have cut fewer core journalistic functions than they did in recent years, had their owners been willing or at the liberty to accept lower margins and had they been under less pressure to make debt payments. James Hamilton of Duke University did a provocative thought experiment for the Future of Media project:

1 If, in 2008, the newspaper industry had accepted a 9 percent cash margin instead of taking 13 percent, it could have generated enough additional cash to avoid virtually all of the layoffs that occurred around that period.[59]

2 If TV stations had been willing or able to reduce cash flow margins in 2009 by just two percentage points (e.g., accept 21 percent cash flow margins rather than 23), they could have increased newsroom spending by $269,070 per station, or 11 percent, and reduced pressure to fire staff.

We offer these estimates not to indicate bad faith on the part of those media managers. Indeed, it could be argued that they had a fiduciary *responsibility* to maximize profit. But this dynamic—the pressure to achieve short-term profit goals—is an important part of the story, and there is no reason to think that it will be any better in coming years. Andrew Lack, CEO of Bloomberg Media, described the huge investments Bloomberg is now making in hiring reporters around the globe to staff its now 127 bureaus. "The whole ambition is to have a civic impact," he said. Lack, a former executive at two publicly traded companies (Sony and NBC), then added, "I don't think we could execute this strategy as a public company." The pressures for short-term profit margins are too high, and the payback on journalistic investments take too long.[60] And that is the problem: the nature of being part of a large publicly traded media corporation makes investment in labor-intensive journalism difficult, because companies are not rewarded fully in the market for their longer-term or more journalistically ambitious choices.

Limits to How Much Technology Can Drive Down Accountability Journalism Costs

Technology has in some ways reduced workload, but it other ways it has increased it. In Chapter 3, TV, we heard one-man band TV reporters saying that, far from enabling them to do more reporting, having to serve as reporter-producer-cameraman has led them to be more scattered. And in Chapter 1, Newspapers, many reporters described themselves as having insufficient time to report and think, a state the *Columbia Journalism Review* referred to as "the hamster wheel."

> Andrew Lack, the CEO of Bloomberg Media, says his company can make huge journalistic investments in part because it is privately held. "I don't think we could execute this strategy as a public company."

In addition, financial incentives still drive companies to apply cost savings to the bottom line, rather than investing in low-ROI journalism. It may take 10 reporters to do the work it took 15 reporters to do a decade ago, but society has little to cheer about if newsroom managers mull that fact and decide to therefore employ only eight. Companies have seen their traditional revenue models collapse. Does it surprise anyone that they would apply cost savings to the bottom line?

Technology has created downward pressure on journalistic wages, which ultimately will reduce cost, but eventually you hit a floor: it costs far more to employ a full-time professional to work on a story for a few weeks than it does to reprint someone else's work.

Finally, the movement to make government data more available will certainly help, but it still requires a critical mass of full-time watchdogs to make it work. In one town, the decision to put court records online delayed their accessibility and slowed down their distribution.[61] The drive toward greater transparency in government will invariably run up against human nature: governments will never enjoy putting out data that makes them look bad. Full-time (read: costly) journalists will need to keep up the pressure.

A Shift in Thinking?

For all these reasons, even some of the biggest evangelists for new media now argue that there may be some gaps that commercial Internet players will not sufficiently fill.

No one is more ardent in his belief that the new media can replace and improve upon the old media systems than writer and professor Jeff Jarvis. Yet at a Future of Media workshop, Jarvis said, "There are areas the market will not support—most likely broccoli journalism,"[62] a reference to journalism that might be unpopular but good for society.

Clay Shirky, another highly respected new media advocate, believes most of the contraction of old media will be offset, and then some, by new media—yet he also says there is an important exception: "One function that's hard to replace is the kind of reporting that comes from someone going down to city hall again today, just in case. There are some in my tribe who think the web will solve that problem on its own, but that's ridiculous."[63]

Hal Varian, Google's chief economist, concluded that the "online world reflects offline: news, narrowly defined, is hard to monetize."[64]

Esther Dyson, an Internet pioneer and investor predicts that venture capital will gravitate toward social media and "service journalism—press release news, and consumer electronics. These are all things that provide good context for advertisers." But, when it comes to accountability journalism, she believes the *non*profit sector will need to play a bigger role.[65]

And then there is John Hood, president of the John Locke Foundation, a market-oriented think tank in North Carolina. The foundation's *Carolina Journal* finances nonpartisan investigative journalism, motivated, in part, by seeing the number of reporters covering the statehouse plummet over the years. "In North Carolina, several [out-of-town] TV stations had reporters. None has a bureau now. We were responding to changes in the market," Hood says. Although politically conservative, Hood is skeptical that commercial markets will sufficiently provide local accountability journalism. "When you get to the state and local level, the collapse of the traditional business models imperils the delivery of sufficient public interest journalism—and we do believe that donor driven journalism can be a very important model."[66]

> **Commercial media are getting help from nonprofit media for the functions that have been rendered cost-ineffective. This system can work well— but only if the nonprofits have healthy flow of funds from donors or other revenue.**

Given the speed and magnitude of change, anyone in the media or information technology space has to be pretty humble about making predictions. Strong arguments can be made on both sides. However, we conclude that at a minimum it is not a certainty that commercial markets alone will fill the reporting gaps—and that even if they eventually do, that transition period could be long and, for communities, quite painful.

The New Relationship Between the For-Profit and Nonprofit Sectors

We see the beginnings of a new paradigm in which the for-profit and nonprofit sectors work together more symbiotically than ever before.

The for-profit sector and nonprofit sectors realize that they need and can help each other. Throughout this report we have noted examples of such budding collaborations: the Texas Tribune working with the *New York Times*, ProPublica partnering with the *Washington Post*, the journalism school at Arizona State working with the local newspaper, the University of Missouri journalism school helping run the KOMU-TV station, the NBC station in San Diego working with voiceofsandiego.org, and California Watch providing investigative journalism for newspapers throughout the state. In each case, the commercial media entity benefits from a level of accountability reporting that the commercial model cannot sustain. The nonprofit media gets something extremely valuable, too: use of the massive distribution networks that the commercial media has built up over time. Nonprofit media simply could not pay to have that kind of distribution. Even better, in some cases, commercial media outlets are paying cold-hard cash, enabling nonprofits to create a new revenue stream through fee-for-service journalism.

In economic terms, commercial media are getting help from nonprofit media for the parts of their operation that have been rendered cost-ineffective by unbundling. In other words, they are outsourcing civically valuable journalism to the nonprofit sector, thereby creating a new bundle of sorts. This system can work well—but only if the nonprofits themselves have healthy flow of funds from foundations, donors, and other revenue lines.

The New Relationship Between Print, TV, and Radio

Unusual collaborations are sprouting not only between for-profit and nonprofit sectors, but also within the commercial sector. In some cases, entities have decided to collaborate in areas where competition among them was minimal anyway. In Ohio, newspapers around the state joined together to help finance statehouse coverage. This makes sense since these papers really don't compete much with each other for readers since they are in different parts of the state.

In other cases, media entities have decided to focus their limited resources on certain functions and rely on partnerships for others. For instance, Bloomberg now helps prepare the *Washington Post*'s business section.[67]

Such partnerships are not always easy. Each corporation has a different culture, style, set of standards, and business model. Beneficial collaborations often involve the melding of complementary rather than similar business models. As business models change, the types of companies that cooperate may change too. For instance, local TV stations and newspapers in some ways would have more reason than ever to cooperate, potentially pooling resources to maximize reporting efficacy. But in other ways, they now compete with each more directly than before, each trying to draw more readers online. Media executives also argue that ownership rules discourage collaboration.

The New Relationship Between New Media and Old

As the new media took off, traditional media felt threatened. Warring camps developed. Advocates for "traditional journalism" sometimes mocked and belittled the value of the new media. At the same time, some new media advocates minimized the implications of the newspaper collapse, and the value of professional full-time journalism.

We sense that the positions have become more nuanced in the past year, with most new media experts acknowledging that some functions are not, and will not be, adequately dealt with by the new media economy and that there is an important role for full-time, professional journalists. Meanwhile, most traditional media players have become far more respectful of the power and journalistic potential of new media, having now spent some time creating more dynamic web experiences for their readers or viewers, and using social media as a reporting tool.

The next step would seem to be embracing a fairly obvious idea: the old and new media improve each other's effectiveness. Crowds can pore through document dumps *and* reporters can find the source within the agency to describe the significance or reveal which documents were withheld. Citizens can offer Twitter updates from a scene, and reporters can look for patterns and determine which tweets might be self-serving or fraudulent. Traditional media may come up with a scoop, and new media can get it disseminated quickly and inexpensively; new media, may come up with a scoop, and traditional media can cast the information more broadly.

Parents or retirees can attend the school board meeting to write about what happened, and a well-sourced reporter can find out what went on behind the scenes—and then the parents can spread the word through social media and dog the issue after the reporter has moved on to other subjects. A block association can take pictures of potholes; a reporter can follow up to find out whether blocks in certain neighborhoods get their streets fixed faster than those in others.

Professional reporters can go where volunteers do not have the time or access to visit—for instance, prisons, war zones, the corridors of city hall—and citizen reporters can, through their numbers, be in many more places than reporters can hit.

Indeed, the combination of all these tools enables the news ecosystem to meet needs it has struggled with for centuries. Traditional mass media had to operate on a grand scale to reach a large enough audience to appeal to advertisers; but covering vast geographic areas with a relatively fixed number of reporters meant that very local matters were often neglected. Even at their peak, the accountability beats—schools, city hall, planning boards, hospitals, and the like—never had nearly enough reporters. Yet, if a community does not have a critical mass of full-time professional journalists, it will not harness the benefits of this new system. Indeed, it will be worse off than it has been in years. Full-time journalists are not just useful parts of this new machine. They are its essential components. New media elements—citizen journalism, crowdsourcing, public databases, blogs, and social media—are not just cool new bits of sizzle. They are at the heart of the new ecosystem. Without both, a community will not get the information it needs. With both, it can have the best media system it has ever had.

the policy and regulatory landscape

Since the beginning of the Republic, government policies have affected—sometimes profoundly—the evolution of the news media. What follows is a description and evaluation of FCC and other governmental policies that have shaped—and that continue to shape—the news media landscape and the provision of civically important information to citizens on a community level and nationwide. We focus on those policies that relate to the concerns raised in Part One, especially regarding the health of local information, news, and journalism.

We have tried to critically evaluate the FCC's own role. While some FCC policies have helped, some have not—and crafting sound policy going forward requires the Commission to understand why. Sociologist Paul Starr has argued that we are currently in a rare "constitutive moment," when today's decisions will shape media industry evolution for decades to come. Given the seismic nature of today's changes, it is imperative that we be conscious of what our policies are and what they are attempting to achieve.

In general, our review indicates that: 1. some current FCC policy is not in synch with the nature of modern media markets; and 2. many of the FCC's current policies are not likely to help communities and citizens get the information they need.

26 Broadcast Radio and Television

THERE IS NO DOUBT THAT FCC POLICIES have played a profound role in the development and growth of the modern broadcasting industry from its earliest days. Historically, some of the most significant Congressional and FCC policies were:

Promoting the creation of national radio networks: In 1928, the Federal Radio Commission, the FCC's predecessor, set aside national "clear channels" to allow for the creation of national radio networks. This allowed business models to develop more quickly since radio stations could attract national, not just local, advertising. These radio networks—the National Broadcasting Company and the Columbia Broadcasting System—later became the TV networks that set the course for the future of TV.

Licensing stations locally, creating a nationwide system: While allowing for the creation of national radio networks, Congress and the FCC decided to award TV licenses locally, not nationally (as has been done in many other countries). To do this, and ensure nationwide availability, FCC engineers worked for years to define the contours of local stations and resolve interference issues. Licensing stations locally was intended to promote the availability of locally oriented content, competition, and control.

Setting aside spectrum for noncommercial use: In 1952, the FCC set aside 242 television channels for educational use,[1] and historically the Commission has sought to reserve approximately 25 percent of television channels for noncommercial educational use.[2] Had it not, the public broadcasting systems might never have developed.

Ownership rules: While some argue that FCC ownership rules have led to massive consolidation with baneful results and others insist that they have facilitated greater market efficiencies with beneficial results for the public, few disagree that they have had a significant impact.

> Even though broadcasting was born with government help—based on a grant of airwaves from the public—once it took its first breath, it in some ways became "the press." Hence, government regulation of broadcasting is sometimes appropriate, yet circumscribed.

Must-carry rules: In general, Congress required major cable providers to set aside up to one-third of their channel capacity for local broadcast stations. This dramatically increased the leverage of broadcasters in the cable industry's early days, and probably protected the primacy of local TV news shows.

Digital and high-definition television: Between 1987 and 1997, the FCC adopted a series of decisions that began a transition from analog to digital television, paving the way for reallocation of 108 MHz of spectrum from television to other valuable uses.[3]

In addition to these decisions that shaped the *structure* of the broadcasting industry, a parallel track of regulations, in some form or another, has affected how content is developed and distributed. The government has played a greater role in shaping content in the broadcast industry than it has in the print industry for a simple reason: While the printing press belongs to private owners, the airwaves belong to the public. Because there is a finite amount of spectrum, and a much greater demand for licenses than can be accommodated, policymakers beginning in the 1920s had to decide who would get the spectrum and for what use. After all, if one broadcaster received a license it meant another could not have it, so it made sense to oblige those authorized "speakers" to meet broad community needs. Policymakers adopted a "trustee" model, in which, in exchange for public spectrum, broadcasters were required to serve public service goals. Companies that subsequently bought these stations did pay for them but that did not absolve them from having to fulfill the attendant public interest obligations.

Yet, even though broadcasting was born with government help—based on a grant of airwaves from the public—once it took its first breath, it in some ways became "the press." As such, broadcasters have, and should have, special protections under the First Amendment, although these protections are less rigorous than those afforded other media such as newspapers. Hence, government regulation of broadcasting is sometimes appropriate, yet always circumscribed. Courts and Congress have, at various points, reaffirmed the FCC's authority to consider program content in the exercise of its licensing function but to what extent and in what manner has been open to near constant debate. Over time, the combination of new court rulings and changing market forces have made policymakers less and less comfortable with highly prescriptive requirements. One court described the balancing act:

> "[T]he Commission walks a tightrope between saying too much and saying too little. In most cases it has resolved this dilemma by imposing only general affirmative duties—*e.g.,* to strike a balance between various interests of the community, or to provide a reasonable amount of time for the presentation of programs devoted to the discussion of public issues. The licensee has broad discretion in giving specific content to these duties, and on application for renewal it is understood the Commission will focus on his overall performance and good faith rather than on specific errors it may find him to have made."[4]

Questions abound. Among them: When, if ever, is it permissible or wise to regulate content? What are the limits? What governmental actions indirectly affect content? These questions have challenged media policymakers for decades. In some cases, governmental involvement is not appropriate; in others it may be unnecessary and unwise; and in yet other instances, it depends on the circumstances. We discuss three sets of rules that illustrate this point: We look at sponsorship identification and disclosure rules as an example of regulation that potentially promotes a vigorous and informative press by requiring transparency. We consider the Fairness Doctrine as an example of governmental action that would likely harm the development of a robust media. Finally, we delve even more thoroughly into the issue of the public interest obligations of broadcasters.

The Fairness Doctrine

The roots of the Fairness Doctrine go back to the Federal Radio Commission's 1929 *Great Lakes Broadcasting* decision, which denied licenses to a labor union-controlled radio station, on the grounds that "the public interest requires ample play for the free and fair competition of opposing views."[5] In 1940, the FCC went further and decided that, because the public interest required stations to present "all sides of important public questions fairly, objectively and without bias," stations must agree not to editorialize. The FCC stated that, "radio can serve as an instrument of democracy only when devoted to the communication of information and exchange of ideas fairly and objectively presented."[6] As a commenter has noted, "[l]icensees were thus put on notice that advocacy broadcasting would not be tolerated."[7] This speech-restrictive approach lasted eight years.

In order to ensure that broadcasters covered important issues in their programming, and did so in a balanced manner, in 1949 the Commission introduced what has become known as the Fairness Doctrine. In its Report on Editorializing By Broadcast Licensees, the Commission stated, "the public interest requires ample play for the free and fair competition of opposing views, and the commission believes that the principle applies to all discussion of importance to the public."[8]

It established a two-part obligation for broadcasters:

> provide coverage of vitally important controversial issues of interest in the community served by the station; *and*

> afford a reasonable opportunity for the presentation of contrasting viewpoints.

Stations were given wide latitude in deciding how they would present contrasting views; for instance, they might air segments during news or public affairs programs or broadcast distinct editorials. No particular party had a right to reply to an issue covered by the station. Rather, the station simply had to ensure that contrasting views on the issue were aired. But, a party that believed that a station had failed to honor this obligation could file a complaint with the Commission, which would be decided on a case-by-case basis. In time, two related rules were adopted: the "personal attack rule," which required that when an attack was made on someone's integrity during a program on a controversial issue of public importance, the station had to inform the subject of the attack and provide the opportunity to respond on the air; and the "political editorial rule," which required a station that had endorsed a particular candidate for political office to notify the other candidates for that office and offer them the opportunity to respond on the air.[9] These rules applied to broadcast TV and radio, but not to cable or satellite.

In 1969, in *Red Lion Broadcasting Co. v. FCC*, the Supreme Court ruled that the Fairness Doctrine was constitutional, concluding that the print and broadcast media were inherently different in terms of regulatory First Amendment considerations, especially given the scarcity of available broadcast spectrum.[10] The Court held, "[i]t is the right of the viewers and listeners, not the right of the broadcasters, which is paramount."[11]

As part of its 1980s deregulation of broadcasting, the Commission abolished the Fairness Doctrine, concluding after an inquiry that "the requirement that broadcasters provide balance in their overall coverage of controversial public issues in fact makes them more timid than they would otherwise be in airing programming that involves such issues."[12] The Commission's inquiry had provided numerous examples of this "chilling" effect, including Dan Rather's recollection of his time as a young reporter working at a radio station owned by the *Houston Chronicle*:

> "I became aware of a concern which I previously had barely known existed—the FCC. The journalists at the Chronicle did not worry about it: those at the radio station did. Not only the station manager but the news people as well were very much aware of the Government presence looking over their shoulders. I can recall newsroom conversations about what the FCC implications of broadcasting a particular report would be. Once a newsroom has to stop and consider what a Government agency will think of something he or she wants to put on the air, an invaluable element of freedom has been lost."[13]

Since that time, lawmakers have periodically attempted—unsuccessfully—to enact legislation to reinstate the Fairness Doctrine. Furthermore, in 2000, the Commission eliminated the "personal attack" and the "political editorial" rules after the D.C. Circuit Court of Appeals had issued a *writ of mandamus* directing it to do so.[14] All of the current commissioners are on record as opposing its reinstitution. For instance, Chairman Genachowksi told a Senate Committee in 2009: "I don't support reinstatement of the Fairness Doctrine. I believe strongly in the First Amendment. I don't think the FCC should be involved in censorship of content based on political speech or opinion."[15]

Although the Fairness Doctrine is not in effect, it is referenced in the FCC's written rules. *Section 73.1910 of the Commission's Rules states* that:

> The Fairness Doctrine is contained in section 315(a) of the Communications Act of 1934, as amended, which provides that broadcasters have certain obligations to afford reasonable opportunity for the discussion of conflicting views on issues of public importance.[16]

It is unclear why the Commission did not eliminate this when it repealed the Fairness Doctrine policy. The sentence has no force of law or policy import, but, it should be said, the language remains "on the books."

It is our view that its reinstatement would most likely chill the robust broadcast discussion of critical issues, because stations would simply avoid addressing controversial issues in their programming rather than risk Commission sanctions for their failure to have allowed all interested parties an opportunity to respond. With the growth of additional media sources, such as cable, satellite, and more recently the Internet, Commission regulation in this sensitive area seems particularly unnecessary and unwise.

Disclosure Rules and On-Air Deception

The FCC has established as a central principle that "listeners are entitled to know by whom they are being persuaded."[17] This concept is at the heart of several rules governing on-air disclosure.

Beginning with the Radio Act of 1927, Congress required broadcasters to identify their sponsors.[18] In 1969, the FCC applied similar disclosure rules to cable operators for programming they create.[19] Significantly, the rules do not prohibit the use of sponsored material; they only require identification of the sponsor.

Broadcasters and cable operators must identify sponsors and advertisers at the time of airing of any programming for which consideration has been received or promised. The relevant statute, section 317(a)(1) of the Communications Act, provides:

"All matter broadcast by any radio station for which any money, service or other valuable consideration is directly or indirectly paid, or promised to or charged or accepted by, the station so broadcasting, from any person, shall, at the time the same is so broadcast, be announced as paid for or furnished, as the case may be, by such person."[20]

The Commission only requires that the announcement occur once during the programming and remain on the screen long enough to be read or heard by an average viewer, although somewhat more rigorous identification rules apply to sponsored political speech.[21] Other decisions are left to the "reasonable, good faith judgment" of the licensee.[22]

Stations are not required to post the disclosure on their website.[23]

To make sure that broadcasters have the information necessary to decide whether sponsorship announcements are needed, station employees have a legal duty to notify the station management if they accept any gifts or compensation in exchange for agreeing to run programs. [24]

A particularly troubling development in recent years has been the rise of sponsored news stories, characterized by some as "fake news stories" or "pay for play." (See Chapter 3, Television.) In the Television chapter, we saw some cases in which broadcasters appear to have entered into agreements with sponsors to run news stories promoting the sponsors' products or services, without disclosing such agreements on the air.[25] The Enforcement Bureau recently entered into a consent decree with a broadcaster accused of airing particular news stories on behalf of a sponsor without appropriate sponsor identification.[26] "The evidence we've seen suggests that this is much more widespread than a few years ago," says Tom Rosensteil, director of the Pew Project on Excellence in Journalism. "That's what I'm hearing from news directors."[27]

A young Dan Rather stated: "Once a newsroom has to stop and consider what a Government agency will think of something he or she wants to put on the air, an invaluable element of freedom has been lost."

These cases often rely on the Enforcement Bureau getting written evidence of quid pro quo, which is hard to come by. The Bureau usually begins investigations on the basis of complaints filed. Those wanting to file a complaint can do so confidentially if they call the Enforcement Bureau, but the web-based complaint system currently has no way to ensure the confidentiality of emailed tips.

In addition, the penalties for such violations can be small. The base-level "forfeiture" per violation of the sponsorship-identification rules is $4,000.[28] Moreover, the pay-for-play disclosure rules do not apply to most programming on cable. The only exception is programming that is directly controlled by a cable operator, such as a local all-news station.

Sponsorship identification rules also govern the airing of video news releases (VNRs), described in Chapter 3, Television. With VNRs, sponsors create video clips that look like news stories, though they may use actors to play reporters.[29] Some studies have indicated that in many cases, stations do not identify the nature or provenance of the VNRs.[30] The FCC recently issued two Notices of Apparent Liability against TV stations for violating sponsorship identification rules—one for a station that had aired a VNR produced by General Motors and another for the airing of a VNR by the maker of a cold remedy. In both cases, the stations were fined $4,000.[31]

However, some argue that such enforcement actions violate First Amendment rights. FOX argued that its running VNRs did not violate sponsorship ID rules since it did not get paid to air them. FOX also objected "to the issuance of the Commission's Letter of Inquiry and to the Commission's attempt to encroach upon broadcasters' discretion in making editorial choices about what news to cover and how to produce local newscasts." FOX continued:

"[ne]ws content lies at the very heart of the First Amendment...intrusive inquiries tread heavily on the core constitutional principles of freedom of speech and freedom of the press...Faced with invasive inquiries into the newsgathering process, broadcasters likely will self-censor and eschew perfectly legitimate speech."[32] The Fox case remains pending.

Another type of disclosure rule attempts to force transparency regarding the origins of aired programming.[33] For instance, in 2007, the Enforcement Bureau issued a citation to the television personality Armstrong Williams and his production company for failing to disclose to TV stations that aired Williams' program that he had received compensation from the U.S. Department of Education in exchange for his favorable on-air comments about the No Child Left Behind law.[34] Though the Bureau concluded that the stations airing Williams' comments had not violated any FCC rules, stations do have an obligation to exercise "reasonable diligence" to learn of financial arrangements affecting the content[35] and disclose those arrangements to the public.[36]

Finally, FCC rules call for disclosure of any programming sponsorship, including "product placement" and "embedded advertising," that is done in exchange for money, service, or other forms of payment. A 2006 survey showed that out of 251 television news directors, 12.4 percent said they were either already doing or considering doing product placements within their newscasts.[37] FITM (Fairness and Integrity in Telecommunications Media) also provided research on embedded advertising (including references to McDonald's coffee being placed on local newscasts and Starbucks paying to have its products appear on an MSNBC cable newsmagazine show).[38] (See Chapter 3, Television.) The National Association of Broadcasters (NAB) and others responded that the public is not being deceived or misled because stations generally provide disclosures through on-air announcements and on-screen graphics.[39]

The "Public Interest" Standard

The notion of imposing a public interest obligation on broadcast station operators was first put forth officially by Herbert Hoover in 1924. As secretary of commerce for Republican President Calvin Coolidge, Hoover argued that radio "is not to be considered as merely a business carried on for private gain.... It is a public concern impressed with the public trust and is to be considered primarily from the standpoint of public interest to the same extent and upon the basis of the same general principles as our public utilities."[40] In 1925, the Fourth Radio Conference, a gathering of congressmen, government officials, radio industry professionals, academics, and private citizens, accepted Hoover's "public interest" concept, and recommended that licenses be issued only to those who will "render a benefit to the public; or are necessary in the public interest; or are contributing to the development of the [broadcast] art."[41] NAB supported the idea, declaring, "The test of the broadcasting privilege [must] be based on the needs of the public served by the proposed station."[42]

> Radio, Herbert Hoover argued, "is not to be considered as merely a business carried on for private gain... [It] is to be considered primarily from the standpoint of public interest."

In response to complaints about scarce spectrum, Hoover attempted to remedy interference problems by reallocating some of the spectrum and denying some license applications.[43] Court rulings blocked these remedial efforts.[44] At the same time, intolerable levels of interference were experienced in many major urban areas, in some cases making transmission virtually impossible. Under these circumstances, Congress passed the Radio Act of 1927, which created the Federal Radio Commission, giving it broad authority to classify stations, prescribe the nature of service to be provided, assign frequencies, determine transmitter power and location, and issue regulations to avoid interference.[45] What is more, it required that stations must serve "the public interest, convenience or necessity"—a phrase whose ambiguity would loom over communications policymaking for the next 80 years.[46]

Although the Radio Act did not provide a public interest definition, it established a clear—and dramatic—principle for policymakers: these were "the public's airwaves"—and no person or corporation could own the electromagnetic spectrum flowing through the air, any more than it could own the air itself.[47]

As a result, there would be a quid pro quo for the government's grant of spectrum use.[48] The public, with the government as its agent, would hand over—*gratis*—a license to use its airwaves to operate a radio station for a fixed period of time. In exchange, the lucky recipient of this extremely lucrative asset would operate the station as a trustee for the public that owned its spectrum, with the obligation to perform certain functions for the greater good beyond merely airing entertainment programming.[49] Congressman Wallace H. White, a sponsor of the Radio Act, commented, "If enacted into law, the broadcasting privilege will not be a right of selfishness. It will rest upon an assurance of public interest to be served."[50]

In 1933, Franklin Roosevelt's administration sought to remedy deficiencies in the Radio Act by enacting the Communications Act of 1934, which created the Federal Communications Commission. The Communications Act announced the "criterion governing the exercise of the Commission's licensing power" using, once again, the phrase "public interest, convenience and necessity."[51] The Act also contemplated the application of this "public interest" standard, beyond licensing and interference issues, to also govern programming issues and those of licensee conduct.[52]

Defining the Public Interest

During its early days, the Commission was quite prescriptive in defining how broadcasters should meet what came to be known as "public interest obligations." In a 1939 memorandum, the FCC listed 14 specific kinds of programming material or practices not deemed to be in the public interest, including defamation, racial or religious intolerance, obscenity, and excessive playing of recorded music to fill airtime.[53]

On March 7, 1946, the Commission issued one of its first major policy statements on broadcast programming: a 59-page internal document entitled *Public Service Responsibility of Broadcast Licensees*. This so-called Blue Book encouraged stations to air programming of local interest and that stimulated public discussion, noting in particular the importance of news and information programming:

> "American broadcasters have always recognized that broadcasting is not merely a means of entertainment, but also an unequaled medium for the dissemination of news, information, and opinion, and for the discussion of public issues…. Especially in recent years, such information programs and news and news commentaries have achieved a popularity exceeding the popularity of any other single type of program. The war, of course, tremendously increased listener interest in such programs; but if broadcasters face the crucial problems of the post-war era with skill, fairness, and courage, there is no reason why broadcasting cannot play as important a role in our democracy hereafter as it has achieved during the war years."[54]

The Commission concluded that it needed to look not only at technical issues but also "the broadcaster's service to the community"[55] and that "the principal ingredient of such obligation consists of a diligent, positive and continuing effort by the licensee to discover and fulfill the tastes, needs and desires of his service area."[56] The FCC emphasized the health of *local* media. Each station was licensed to a particular community and was required to provide service to that specific community. The process by which stations determined these local needs became known as "ascertainment."[57] The Commission outlined 14 "major elements" of programming that are generally necessary in the service of the public interest, but noted that they "are neither all-embracing nor constant:"

> "(1) opportunity for local self-expression, (2) the development and use of local talent, (3) programs for children, (4) religious programs, (5) educational programs, (6) public affairs programs, (7) editorialization by licensees, (8) political broadcasts, (9) agricultural programs, (10) news programs, (11) weather and market reports, (12) sports programs, (13) service to minority groups, (14) entertainment programs."[58]

A premise of all these rules is that the "trustee" obligations of broadcasters meant that they were required to provide programming beyond what the market would normally produce. Policymakers implicitly were taking the position that some types of programming ought to be provided—and are good for a community—even if there isn't a large enough consumer demand to lead to its provision in a pure free market.

"Ascertaining" Community Needs

Throughout the 1960s and 1970s, great emphasis was placed on prodding stations to *find out* community needs, so the stations themselves could then better serve them. The Commission's 1971 *Primer on Ascertainment of Community Problems by Broadcast Applicants* gave detailed instruction on how to determine community needs.[59] Notably, the *Primer* stated that the purpose of the ascertainment process was to help a station determine what the important issues were, which was different from determining what programming might be most popular.[60] The *Primer* got quite granular, requiring principals and management-level employees to personally speak with community leaders.[61] The goal was not for the FCC to determine what the significant local problems were, but rather to insure that the stations themselves were doing so, and then, at their discretion, producing relevant programming.

Beyond "ascertainment," the FCC ultimately tried to encourage a minimal level of non-entertainment programming. In 1973, the Commission revised its regulations in order to place initial determination of license renewal

The National Association of Broadcasters supported the idea of public interest obligations: "The test of the broadcasting privilege [must] be based on the needs of the public served by the proposed station."

applications of TV stations maintaining 10 percent or more of "non-entertainment" programming in the hands of the chief of the Commission's Broadcast Bureau, thereby avoiding a more time-consuming and complex analysis by the Commission itself.[62] So, if a station broadcast from 6:00 a.m. to midnight (18 hours), 10 percent would amount to one hour and 48 minutes per day. (The corresponding percentages were 8 percent for AM radio, 6 percent for FM.[63]) In 1976, the Commission amended these non-entertainment programming guidelines for commercial television, to require Commission action if the station had aired less than a total mix of 5 percent local and 5 percent informational (news and public affairs) programming per hour as part of its 10 percent non-entertainment programming.[64]

Throughout this period, some broadcasters bristled at the detailed nature of the guidelines, for instance being forced to meet with particular groups. And, in hindsight, it seems the government proffered jarringly detailed judgments about how a station's management ought to do its business, interact with its community, and cover stories.

On the other hand, some who worked in the industry at the time argue that the requirement that stations make affirmative efforts to "ascertain" community needs had a positive effect. Steve Schwaid, who has spent three decades in broadcast news and is currently director of news and digital content at WGCL-TV in Atlanta, says ascertainment lunches were valuable:

> "You listened to what people were talking about and hearing, what they wanted to discuss. That gave you an idea of what the stories were. The problem with newsrooms today is that we live in a bubble. We are in a newsroom all day long; we see the same sort of stuff all day long. Sometimes we try not to, but we worry more about what the other guy is covering. I think we have lost touch. Local stations as a whole can do a better job of being in touch with their communities. The ascertainment requirement forced them to do so."[65]

It is hard to conceive of it now, but media companies did not always expect news programs to turn a profit; they were viewed as part of the price of getting the license. Lee Giles, a 35-year broadcast pioneer who served as vice president and news director of WISH-TV in Indianapolis and is a member of both the Indiana Journalism Hall of Fame and the Indiana Associated Press Hall of Fame, puts it this way: "We all really felt that we were privileged to cover news for the public. I did operate in the public interest and necessity, and felt that was my mandate and charge to do so. Back then it made us conscious of our obligations. It kind of permeated all of what we were doing."[66]

Gayle Eichenthal, who spent nearly 35 years with all-news commercial radio station KNX-AM and public radio station KUSC in Los Angeles, describes the impact of the ascertainment rules, from her firsthand perspective:

> "We were so focused on the community. We were reporting every single aspect of the infrastructure of the city and surrounding cities…how do people live, what's happening with labor, what's happening with the arts, what's happening with housing, and every single aspect of the community. The assignment editor had a tremendous sense of responsibility in his position and he took it like it was a life's work to cover the people of the city and the city itself and to serve people by doing that."[67]

In the 1980s, the regulatory tide dramatically shifted, first under Jimmy Carter's FCC chairman, Charles Ferris, and then under Mark S. Fowler, appointed by Ronald Reagan. In 1981, Fowler argued that television was "just another appliance. It's a toaster with pictures. We've got to look beyond the conventional wisdom that we must somehow regulate this box."[68] In his view, the public interest would be determined by "the public's interest": if the public did not like the way a broadcaster was operating its station, people would stop watching or listening, and, without the sufficient numbers of eyes and ears, advertisers would stop providing the station revenue. The operation would fail without the need for government safeguards or intervention. By eliminating many broadcast regulatory requirements and instead providing licensees with flexibility, he believed that stations would experiment and innovate more. The Commission then initiated a series of changes, some of which went as far as Fowler's initial rhetoric, some of which did not.

Two broad exceptions to the deregulatory policies Commission rules regarding political programming and children's television. FCC guidelines provide that commercial broadcasters can satisfy their duty to serve the needs of their child audiences by offering at least three hours a week of programs that serve the educational and informational needs of children aged 16 and under.[69] Broadcasters must file quarterly reports describing the children's educational programming they offer.[70] FCC rules also limit the use of commercials during children's programming.[71]

Radio Deregulation

In 1981, led by Charles Ferris, the chairman appointed by Democratic President Jimmy Carter, the FCC deregulated radio.[72] It determined that the public interest would be served by eliminating what it characterized as "unnecessarily burdensome regulations of uniform applicability that fail to take into account local conditions, tastes or desires."[73] Specifically, the Commission moved to:

> eliminate the license-renewal guideline requiring that stations have a certain percentage of non-entertainment programming, while retaining a general licensee obligation that stations offer programming responsive to local issues.[74] It agreed that citizens needed to "be well informed on issues affecting themselves and their communities. It is with such information that the citizenry can make the intelligent, informed decisions essential to the proper functioning of a democracy."[75] But, it concluded, "stations will continue to present such programming as a response to market forces."[76]

> eliminate its formal ascertainment requirements, while stressing that "broadcasters should maintain contact with their community on a personal basis as when contacted by those seeking to bring community problems to the station's attention. What is not important is that each licensee follow the same requirements dictating how to do so."[77] Accordingly, in place of formal ascertainment, it required that new stations explain in their license application how they would carry out their obligation to determine issues facing their communities "by any means reasonably calculated to apprise them of the issues."[78] Thus, ascertainment changed its stripes but did not disappear.

In 1996, policymakers lengthened the license term from three years to eight and effectively eliminated competition for licenses between existing and would-be broadcasters as an important element.

> conclude that while all radio stations were expected to continue to air non-entertainment programming that addressed community needs, each station's programming need not be all things to all people. If station X was providing news, station Y need not:

"We do not expect broadcasters to fit their non-entertainment programming into a mold whereby each station has the same or similar amounts of programming. Other than issue responsive programming, stations need not, as a Commission requirement, present news, agricultural, etc., programming.

"We believe the record…demonstrates that stations will continue to present such programming as a response to market forces…. We do not expect radio broadcasters to attempt to be responsive to the particular problems of each group in the community in their programming in every instance. We do not expect radio broadcasters to be responsive to the Commission's choices of types of programs best suited to respond to their community. What we do expect, however, is that marketplace forces will assure the continued provision of news programs in amounts to be determined by the discretion of the individual broadcaster guided by the tastes, needs, and interests of its listenership. We do expect, and will require, radio broadcasters to be responsive to the issues facing their community.[79]

The Commission would defer to broadcasters' judgments about what actions best met community needs and limit itself to determining whether such judgments were 'reasonable':

"In other words, radio broadcasters will have what we believe to be the maximum flexibility under the public interest standard as regards their non-entertainment offerings."[80]

> eliminate its renewal guidelines on the maximum number of commercials that could be aired, again largely on the grounds that if a station went overboard with commercials, listeners would punish them it by changing the channel.[81]

> eliminate its requirement that licensees maintain and make available to the public and to the FCC detailed programming logs, which provided a comprehensive record of the amount, nature, and timing of every specified program type.[82] Broadcasters had complained that "the logs posed a tremendous record keeping burden…."[83] Instead, the Commission would require stations to file annual issues/programs lists, noting five to 10 issues that the licensee had covered, along with examples of the related programming it aired.

When a station failed to meet these stripped down obligations, members of the public would bring the station's shortcomings to the attention of the FCC in petitions to deny their renewal applications and by registering complaints with the Commission.

A number of parties, including the Office of Communication of the United Church of Christ, objected to the new rules. In 1983, the United States Court of Appeals for the D.C. Circuit largely upheld the Commission's order—but asserted that even the new deregulatory rules required stations to meet public interest goals. With regard to the elimination of the renewal application processing guidelines, it found that, "contrary to the dire intimations of some petitioners, the Commission has not effectively foresworn all regulation of non-entertainment programming in favor of total reliance on marketplace forces."[84] It concluded that the Commission had retained "an obligation to provide programming responsive to community issues," which it characterized as "a reasonable interpretation of the statutory public interest standard."[85] The court similarly found that the Commission was within its jurisdiction in eliminating ascertainment procedures and commercialization application processing guidelines.[86]

However, the Court did find fault with the Commission's elimination of the requirement that stations maintain programming logs and make them available to the public, especially given that the FCC was relying on private citizens to police the behavior of local stations:

"Th[e] proposed renewal scheme would place a near-total reliance on petitions to deny as the means to identify licensees that are not fulfilling their public interest obligations. That the Commission would simultaneously seek to deprive interested parties and itself of the vital information needed to establish a *prima facie* case in such petitions seems almost beyond belief."[87]

The court and the Commission went back and forth until the FCC ultimately modified its rule to require that radio licensees maintain "quarterly lists of programs, which in the exercise of the broadcaster's good faith judgment represent the most significant treatment by the station of the issues that the licensee believed to be a community concern."[88]

Television Deregulation

Mark Fowler, the FCC chairman appointed by President Reagan, sought to further the deregulatory efforts begun under Ferris. In 1984, the Commission deregulated TV in much the same manner it had radio: It eliminated programming guidelines, commercial limits, ascertainment, and the program logging requirement, replacing the latter with a quarterly issues/programs list requirement. As it had with radio, the Commission stressed that TV stations were still required to "provide programming that responds to issues of concern to the community."[89] However, as it had in the *Radio Deregulation Order*, it reiterated its belief "that the market demand for informational, local and non-entertainment programming will continue to be met as the video marketplace evolves."[90] In this regard, as it had for radio, the Commission held that not all TV stations had to offer a full complement of non-entertainment programming:

"[T]he failure of some stations to provide programming in some categories is being offset by the compensatory performance of other stations. In this respect, market demand is determining the appropriate mix of each licensee's programming…. We believe that licensees should be given the flexibility to respond to the realities of the marketplace by allowing them to alter the mix of their programming consistent with market demand. Such an approach not only permits more efficient competition among stations, but poses no real risk to the availability of these types of programming on a market basis. This is particularly true in view of the continuing obligation of all licensees to contribute issue-responsive programming and their responsibility to ensure that the strongly felt needs of all significant segments of their communities are met by market stations collectively."[91]

It added that the issues/programs lists would provide the public and the FCC with the information needed to assess licensees' performance under this new regulatory scheme, and that "procedures such as citizen complaints and petitions to deny will continue to function as important tools in this regard."[92] The FCC extended the same policy changes to public radio and TV broadcasters. (See Chapter 30, Nonprofit Media.)

Over the years, the FCC developed a "comparative renewal" system for when more than one party wanted a license.[93] In theory this added a healthy element of competition. But the process had its limitations. Incumbent licensees' *actual* performance records were being judged against the *non-binding promises* of prospective future license-holders. This led to concern that competing applicants were gaming the system to extract "greenmail" settlement payments from incumbent licensees.[94]

> Under the heading of "community involvement," one station listed, "America's Next Top Model Casting Call at Seven Sushi Ultralounge sponsored by Sunny's Hair and Wigs."

In the Telecommunications Act of 1996, Congress addressed license renewal issues by taking two important actions. First, it lengthened the license term from three years to eight years for both radio and television stations,[95] thus providing tremendous security and stability to incumbent licensees. Second, Congress eliminated the comparative license renewal process for commercial stations and formally required the Commission to consider competing applications only after first finding, pursuant to certain statutory factors, that the incumbent's license should not be renewed.[96] Through these actions, policymakers effectively *eliminated competition* for licenses between existing and would-be broadcasters.

Its license renewal application, FCC Form 303-S, asks applicants to certify that they filed their issues/programs lists as required,[97] but it does not ask for any programming information itself.

Enforcing "Public Interest" Rules: Theory and Practice

In reviewing the history of the public interest obligation, we found that the deregulatory principles espoused were not always put into practice.

Some Stations' "Issues/Programs" Lists Are Impressive, Some Are . . . Not

As noted above, after radio and television deregulation, all stations, even those that do not do news, have one concrete obligation. They are required to file an issues/programs list each quarter describing their "programs that have provided the station's most significant treatment of community issues during the preceding three month period."[98] In theory, the existence of this requirement might encourage stations to offer non-entertainment programming—such as news, public affairs, and governmental coverage—that is relevant to the local community.

But several factors have conspired to make this unlikely.

First, the FCC rarely sees these lists, which licensees *do not file with the FCC*. Stations are required to prepare and file them in their public inspection files, ostensibly so members of the public can review them. In its renewal application, a station must certify that its public file is in order, was updated in a timely manner, and contains all required materials, including the issues/programs lists.[99] If it checks that box, and no filings have been received from the public challenging the licensee's public interest performance, it is deemed to have met this basic obligation. In other words, in almost all cases, what FCC officials see is not the issues/programs list but a sheet saying that such a list exists.

And, in cases in which the box is not checked or someone complains or the licensee otherwise discloses that it has not included all of the required lists in the public file, a nominal monetary forfeiture is imposed and the renewal is then granted.

Second, in part because it almost never sees the lists, the FCC has given stations little ongoing guidance on what is supposed to be included in them.[100] As a result, the range of quantity and quality is absurdly broad.

Third, stations are not required to post these lists online.[101] Citizens can view them only if they drop by the station's main studio and ask to see the public file. Few do. And, the main studio can be a substantial distance from its community of license.

Stations that do not produce newscasts sometimes describe almost any local activity as constituting "programs that have provided the station's most significant treatment of community issues." For instance,[102] one Midwestern station included in its issues/programs file, under the heading "Community Involvement":

> "America's Next Top Model Casting Call…an open casting call for Cycle 14 of America's Next top Model on July 11th from 2–4 pm at Seven Sushi Ultralounge sponsored by Sunny's Hair and Wigs.

> "[C]reate a fun and innovative contest for our viewers to win an 8″ Dairy Queen ice cream cake from Dairy Queen for their birthdays.

> "[The local station]s and Little Caesars Pizza teamed up together and created a great way for viewers and their customers to join the Little Caesars text club.

> "The [station] and Spalon Montage teamed up together and created a great way for viewers and their customers to join the Spalon Montage text club."

When an FCC researcher asked a New England station for its issues/programs list, an employee provided copies of the station's programming schedule ("12:30 p.m., *Frasier*; 1:00 a.m., *That 70s Show*; 1:30 a.m., *Family Feud*…").

Some stations get creative by listing stories they happened to run under categories that sound as if they have to do with important community issues. For instance, in a filing otherwise full of substantive news mentions, a station in Texas created the category "High Tech education," which turns out to include only one piece—about Google considering the launch of a music service.

Some stations list stories of national importance as if they addressed issues of local importance. For instance, under the community-coverage "Crime" category, a station in New Hampshire, listed a story entitled "Authorities in Los Angeles revealed that crime rate in 2008 was the lowest in 40 years!"

Stations often list the public service ads (PSAs) they run. Many are worthwhile but many are not local in nature—and some do not appear to be charity related. For instance, in 2010 one station noted that it ran "Media Com Retran Notice (286591)" 84 times in one month—a PSA that turns out to be about a fight between broadcasters and a local cable operator over fees. Similar problems exist in radio. A New York radio station listed "a 15 second PSA furnished by the National Association of Broadcasters that discusses the harmful affects [sic] of a performance tax on local radio," clearly more of a priority issue for the station airing the PSAs than for its listeners.

In contrast, some stations take the reporting requirement quite seriously and detail news and public affairs programming addressing local issues. For instance, KNBC-TV in Los Angeles filed a 112-page report describing every minute of public affairs and news programming it broadcast during the third quarter of 2009, listing the date and time each program aired and the community issue addressed.[103]

The FCC Almost Never Denies License Renewals

A telling statistic: during the FCC's more than 75 years in existence, it has granted well over 100,000 license renewals; only in four cases was a renewal application denied because the licensee failed to meet its public interest programming obligation:[104]

> In 1965, a federal appeals court forced the FCC to deny a license renewal to a TV station in Jackson, Mississippi, that had been shown to give less coverage to African-Americans.[105]

> In 1970, the FCC denied a license to a radio station in Media, Pennsylvania, after a program host "made false and misleading statements and deliberate distortions of the facts relating to various public issues such as

race relations, religious unity, foreign aid" and failed to air a program on interfaith issues, even though the station had made a commitment to the FCC to do so.[106]

> In 1972, public TV stations in Alabama were denied license renewal because they excluded African-Americans from programming decisions and avoided programming oriented toward their community.[107]

> In 1980, in *West Coast Media, Inc.*, the FCC denied a license renewal to a San Diego radio station after finding that the station broadcast almost no public affairs, news, or other public service programming.[108]

In the last 30 years *not one* license renewal has been denied on the grounds of a station failing to serve the community with its programming.

Why?

It is not for lack of effort from citizens groups. Over the years, through petitions to deny license renewal applications, public interest groups have tried to make the case that particular stations did not merit renewals. But, in each case, the FCC either rejected the petition or declined to rule on the petition on procedural grounds. In some cases, the FCC has concluded that, when it comes to subjective judgments about appropriate quality or quantity, it is wise to defer to the discretion of the station. For example, various groups petitioned to deny six television stations (in 1990) and 10 radio stations (in 1993) serving Philadelphia, Pennsylvania,[109] arguing that the licensees had failed to provide a sufficient amount of general issue-responsive programming to address the concerns of minority groups and maintain the required issues/programs lists.[110] But the Commission held, "the stations have provided programming to the extent and in a manner well within their broad discretion."[111]

In 2004, the Chief of the Media Bureau's Audio Division denied the renewal application of WZFM in Narrows Virginia, after concluding that the station had violated section 312(g) of the Communications Act when it aired no programming from February 8, 1996 to February 8, 1997.[112] WZFM filed a petition for reconsideration, along with a Declaration from H. Edward Hale, Vice President of Old Dominion Communications, WZFM's parent company. Hale explained that on ten occasions between November 3, 1996 and June 3, 2003, he "turned on the transmitter and spoke into it." Hale further elaborated:

"On every occasion…, I broadcast the station's call sign, community of license and authorized frequency. On every occasion…, I broadcast my name and stated that Old Dominion was testing the facilities of WZFM. …In addition, on every occasion…, I broadcast additional remarks to the public, for example, commentary on the weather and view from the mountaintop and other observations. Sometimes I broadcast jokes. The broadcasts…typically lasted about fifteen minutes in duration.[113]

Old Dominion argued that these fifteen minute "broadcasts" satisfied the requirement of section 312(g) that it transmit a broadcast signal continuously for 12 months. Based on this record, the division granted WZFM's petition for reconsideration and renewed its license in a summary public notice that did not contain any discussion of whether the station served the community or met its public interest obligations.[114]

The most recent broadcast renewal cycles ran from 2003 to 2006 for radio stations and from 2004 to 2007 for television stations. A total of 1,772 television stations (1,389 commercial and 383 noncommercial educational), and 15,168 radio stations (12,360 commercial and 2,808 noncommercial educational), sought renewal of their licenses. Of the television stations, the Commission received 224 challenges to the license renewals of 213 stations (153 petitions to deny against 144 stations, and 71 informal objections to the renewals of 69 stations).

The Commission's staff has ruled on all but 45—and in every case has rejected the license challenges. In fact, in no case did the Commission even designate a challenge for hearing, the normal next step if there are concerns about the advisability of granting renewal.

The story is the same for radio. The Commission received 191 challenges to the renewal applications of radio stations (62 petitions to deny and 121 informal objections). Thirty-one of these challenges remain pending. Although 10 were granted in part, with the Commission assessing forfeitures for the violations, each license was renewed.

These results are consistent with the conclusions reached in a 2010 study conducted by Georgetown University Law Center's Institute for Public Representation, of the 2004 to 2007 television renewal application cycles. The study found that more than half of the challenges to applications either alleged that the station had failed to provide sufficient coverage of local issues in its programming or a sufficient amount of children's programming. It found that the Commission failed to act on a third of the filings and has denied all the others.[115]

In most cases, the FCC's Media Bureau denied the petition or objection by a brief letter to the filing party. Moreover, the Georgetown study concluded that it took the Commission a long time to render its decisions: from 114 to 1,543 days after a petition was filed (an average of 568 days). The study found that denial letters were relatively brief, disposing of the allegation of failure to air sufficient locally responsive programming by concluding that the petitioner had failed to show the station had shown "bad faith" in exercising its editorial discretion. Each letter typically closed by urging the petitioner to make any future concerns known directly to the station.

The Georgetown study concludes, "The fact that the FCC did not designate a single application for hearing during the entire renewal cycle suggests that relying on the public to bring license renewal challenges to ensure that television stations serve the public interest is not working well." It notes that the problem is not lack of public participation, but concludes that "[i]f the FCC is not going to do anything when citizens complain, then citizens will lack the incentive to monitor and participate." It also notes that the incentive for public participation is further reduced by the eight-year license term and delays in FCC action on petitions.[116] Accordingly, the study urges that stations be required to provide the public more information about their programming, reduce license terms, act more promptly on petitions, and take well-documented petitions more seriously. It suggests that "the Commission should also consider whether it is realistic to place so much reliance on public participation in meeting its statutory public interest obligations."

To be clear, this record does not result from negligence or lethargy on the part of career staff. The unwillingness to press license denials—which has characterized Democratic- and Republican-led commissions—likely stemmed from a growing discomfort with the FCC making content judgments and/or an uncertainty about the Commission's constitutional authority to do so. On top of that, some Commissioners no doubt feared denying licenses would trigger contentious battles with broadcasters.[117]

> In 1984, the FCC deregulated television as it had with radio, but stressed that television stations were still required to "provide programming that responds to issues of concern to the community."

Some Stations Do No Local News at All

The scores of unsuccessful petitions and other renewal challenges have sometimes involved the claim that particular existing news shows have done a poor job covering local communities in their news and other local programming. Worthy though that discussion is, the question of whether local newscasts do a good enough job may obscure an even more glaring issue: a large number of stations do not air news programming at all. A 2011 FCC staff analysis of data from Tribune Media Services found that there are 520 local stations that air no local news at all—258 commercial stations and 262 noncommercial stations. Adding in those stations that air less than 30 minutes of local news per day, 33 percent of commercial stations currently offer little or no local news. Most of those that do not offer local news are independent stations with no affiliation with a broadcast network. A separate analysis by the Media Bureau's Industry Analysis Division, based on reviewing public schedule listings, came to similar numbers: 42.6 percent of all television stations do not air any local news (30.2 percent of commercial stations and 81.9 percent of noncommercial educational stations).[118] (See Chapter 3, Television.)

Industry Self-Inspection

Prior to 1995, the FCC's Field Offices inspected broadcast stations as part of the commission's broadcast station license renewal process. After the FCC discontinued these routine licensing-related inspections, Field Offices conducted random inspections of broadcast stations to check for compliance with Commission rules. For staffing reasons, the Commission later shifted more of its inspection methodology to a complaint-based approach, whereby a complaint (e.g., from a competitor or a consumer) would trigger an inspection of the particular station at issue. Today, in addition to conducting complaint-based inspections and certain random inspections, the Commission utilizes the Alternative Broadcast Inspection Program (ABIP).

Under ABIP, a private party, usually a state broadcast association, enters into an agreement with the Enforcement Bureau to arrange inspections (and re-inspections, where appropriate) of participating broadcast stations to determine compliance with FCC regulations. ABIP was originally envisioned as a way for the Commission to focus its limited resources on other significant violations, rather than visiting all 30,000 broadcast stations. As the Commission noted in 1996, ABIP "allows private entities to perform inspections of broadcast stations and certify compliance with technical rules, obviating the need for random inspections by Commission staff and freeing them to focus on problem areas."[119] The inspectors assess technical issues, such as compliance with power limits and transmission control, as well as antenna painting, fencing and lighting, Emergency Alert System (EAS) compliance, and the completeness of the issues/programs and campaign advertising records.

The Enforcement Bureau executed ABIP agreements with each of the state broadcast associations in 2003, followed by a small number of agreements with individual inspectors in 2004 and 2006.[120] As of December 2010, about 26 percent of AM and FM radio stations and 48 percent of television stations participate in the program.[121] Under the agreement, the association or individual inspector has full discretion as to the rates it charges broadcast stations that choose to participate in ABIP. Inspectors are required to conduct a standard FCC Enforcement Bureau full-station inspection,[122] with very limited exceptions. The association or private inspector must then notify the local FCC District Office or Resident Agent Office, in writing, of those stations that pass the ABIP inspection and have been granted a Certificate of Compliance, which is then valid for three years.

They are not required to inform the FCC, however, if they find stations out of compliance. Rather, the inspectors work with stations to make improvements until they fulfill the rules.

Significantly, stations that have been certified compliant under ABIP are exempt from certain FCC inspections. During the period for which its compliance certificate is valid, a participating station is generally not subject to inspection, investigation, or audit by the FCC, except for tower safety issue investigations, complaint-driven inspections, and inspections involving EEO or political file issues.

Because the FCC has limited resources, ABIP continues to be a useful means to promote broadcaster compliance with FCC rules, while conserving agency resources to focus on other priorities. However, it is not clear whether ABIP inspections are always as detailed as the full-station inspections conducted by FCC staff, whether ABIP inspectors are sufficiently independent of the stations they inspect, and whether ABIP inspectors adequately confirm that stations have fixed noncompliance observed during inspections before issuing a Certificate of Compliance.

Moreover, the standard ABIP agreement raises other concerns, including its prohibition on audits of broadcast stations that participate in the program, making it difficult for the FCC to gauge the quality of ABIP inspections and the efficacy of the program. ABIP also appears to prohibit the Commission from including ABIP stations in "targeted inspections" that are part of broader Commission projects, for instance, to evaluate compliance with a specific Commission rule like the requirement for operational Emergency Alert System equipment.

Although ABIP appears to have many advantages, the Enforcement Bureau has not conducted a comprehensive review of the program since its inception. The ABIP agreements have three-year terms that automatically renew absent action by the Bureau or the other signatory party. The next agreements are set to expire in 2012. In the meantime, the Bureau is engaged in ongoing discussions with broadcasters, inspectors, and others about the program, and is examining ways to revise ABIP to improve broadcaster accountability and compliance.

Among other things, the Bureau is considering:

> measuring and improving the effectiveness of ABIP; for example, by implementing record-keeping requirements and/or auditing the program;

> ensuring the independence of ABIP inspectors: for example, by requiring disclosure of conflicts of interest;

> reserving the Commission's right to conduct certain "targeted inspections," as discussed above; and

> evaluating whether inspectors have sufficient guidance, binding and non-binding, regarding the Bureau's expectations about inspections, inspection follow-up, and re-inspections.

We expect that the Enforcement Bureau's continued outreach and examination, and resulting program changes, can enhance ABIP's reliability and effectiveness, while preserving its substantial benefits.

Reform Proposals

From among the many reform proposals that have been considered over the years,[123] we highlight the four that have been most discussed. (In Part Three, we suggest a fifth approach).

Spectrum Fees

In a February 1982 article titled "A Marketplace Approach to Broadcast Regulation," then-FCC Chairman Mark Fowler and Daniel Brenner, his legal advisor, proposed moving broadcast regulation in a new direction that was consistent with free-market principles. The Commission, they wrote, should "focus on broadcasters not as fiduciaries of the public, as their regulators have historically perceived them, but as marketplace competitors."[124]

In addition to proposing deregulation,[125] the authors also suggested two other ideas that might have more resonance today. First, recover and re-auction broadcast spectrum.[126] Second, charge broadcast licensees a spectrum usage fee in exchange for exclusive rights to use their assigned spectrum, which should be considered a property right.[127] The proposed spectrum fee could either be a percentage of the station's profits or a flat fee based upon bandwidth.[128] In Fowler's view, the fee would recognize that broadcasters receive something of value in the exclusivity that the government provides them, similar to government franchises for offshore oil rights or food concessions in public parks, and analogous to the franchise fees that cable operators pay to local authorities.[129]

Fowler proposed that these fees be applied, in part, to funding public broadcasting. In light of the value that public stations provide society in offering unique types of programming that commercial stations may decline to offer due to marketplace forces—such as cultural, locally oriented, and children's programming—he concluded that, although such value may not fit into his marketplace-oriented system, it is nevertheless desirable to have a source for such socially valuable alternative fare.[130]

> A Georgetown University study concluded that it took the Commission a long time to render its decisions: from 114 to 1,543 days after a petition was filed (an average of 568 days).

Noting the traditional opposition from broadcasters and others to the imposition of spectrum fees, Fowler observed, "Given the choice, many broadcasters might prefer the security of current regulation to true competition and a charge for their frequency exclusivity."[131]

President George W. Bush repeatedly proposed assessing "user fees." As his 2006 budget put it, "To continue to promote efficient spectrum use, the Administration also supports granting the FCC authority to set user fees on un-auctioned spectrum licenses based on public-interest and spectrum-management principles. Fee collections are estimated to begin in 2007 and total $3.1 billion in the first 10 years." Some conservatives prefer this approach because it is more market-oriented. Rather than proscribing certain behaviors, it simply acknowledges that TV stations have received something of value from the public and asks them to pay for it, and allows the funds to be targeted toward public purposes. They also believe that it would allow the market to drive spectrum toward the "highest and best use," which in some cases might mean low-performing stations putting spectrum up in an incentive auction, wherein they receive a cash payment and the spectrum can be applied toward broadband wireless use. Every White House budget proposal since 2006 has made this proposal.

Some liberal experts—who previously had been lukewarm to cool on the idea—have recently come around to join the conservatives. Henry Geller, general counsel at the FCC under President Kennedy and FCC Chairman Newt Minow—and formerly a strong supporter of the traditional public interest guidelines—now advocates giving up on that system and switching instead to a spectrum fee system, with proceeds going to public broadcasting. "The broadcast public trustee regulatory content system is anomalous in this century and will become more so in light of developments in electronic media, has difficult First Amendment strains if and when implemented quantitatively, has been very largely a failed regulatory scheme for seven decades," Geller stated at a Future of Media workshop.[132] Rather than forcing stations to do public affairs programming, he argued, let them pay a spectrum fee to do what they want, and use the revenue to fund those who are more committed to that kind of programming. "If you fund the organizations which *want* to do high-quality informational programming or children's programming, you now have the structure working for you. When you try to do behavioral content regulation to make somebody who's not interested in that, he's got an awful lot on his plate because of all this fierce competition. You're not going to get very far...."[133]

Norman Ornstein had co-chaired Advisory Committee on Public Interest Obligations of Digital Television Broadcasters in 1998, which recommended a series of public interest guidelines.[134] Recently he switched positions, saying that such guidelines would inevitably be watered down. He now supports assessing a spectrum fee and using the proceeds for public media.[135] Writing in the November/December 2009 issue of the *Columbia Journalism Review*, Steve Coll, president of the New American Foundation, endorsed a similar approach.[136]

Opposition to this approach comes from a few quarters. Commissioner Michael Copps has equated this with paying one's way out of the draft—in other words, avoiding obligations by paying a fee. And, tellingly, the broadcasters themselves have opposed this. Others argue that station owners have invested in the community by airing local news and should not have to pay additionally.

Enhanced Disclosure

On September 14, 2000, the Commission adopted a Notice of Proposed Rulemaking, entitled "Standardized and Enhanced Disclosure Requirements for Television Broadcast Licensee Public Interest Obligations."[137] It proposed replacing the issues/programs lists that television stations have to include in their public files with a standardized form seeking detailed programming information and requiring that the completed form be posted on the Internet, as well. On November 27, 2007, the Commission approved a Report and Order [adopting] these requirements.[138]

But this approach has not worked either. The form the Commission had proposed was eight pages long, with hundreds of programming-related data boxes that would need to be filled in.[139] It required broadcasters to list detailed information about "local civic affairs" as distinct from programming about "local electoral affairs," not to be confused with general "local news." And they would have to do this comprehensively, covering 365 days a year. "Form 355" drew complaints from broadcasters that it would be unnecessarily burdensome.[140] Beyond its being overly complex, there were other concerns, including that the rules did not require that the data be put in a format that would make it easy to analyze online, as advocates of government transparency recommend. Five parties appealed the action, and the FCC received nine petitions for reconsideration, including one from the National Association of Broadcasters— and it has not received the necessary approvals of the Office of Management and Budget under the Paperwork Reduction Act. As a result, these changes have not gone into effect.

Localism

In August 2003, FCC Chairman Michael Powell launched an inquiry into "broadcast localism" by explaining: "Fostering localism is one of this Commission's core missions and one of three policy goals, along with diversity and competition, which have driven much of our radio and television broadcast regulation during the past 70 years."[141] In the Notice of Inquiry, the Commission elaborated on why localism has been a policy emphasis:

> "The concept of localism derives from Title III of the Communications Act, and is reflected in and supported by a number of current Commission policies and rules. Title III generally instructs the Commission to regulate broadcasting as the public interest, convenience, and necessity dictate....[142] When the Commission allocates channels for a new broadcast service, its first priority is to provide general service to an area, but its next priority is for facilities to provide the first local service to a community....[143] Indeed, the Supreme Court has stated that '[f]airness to communities [in distributing radio service] is furthered by a recognition of local needs for a community radio mouthpiece....[144]

> "A station must maintain its main studio in or near its community of license to facilitate interaction between the station and the members of the local community it is licensed to serve.[145] For similar reasons, a station 'must equip the main studio with production and transmission facilities that meet the applicable standards, maintain continuous program transmission capability, and maintain a meaningful management and staff presence.'[146] The main studio also must house a public inspection file, the contents of which must include 'a list of programs that have provided the station's most significant treatment of community issues during the preceding three month period.'[147] The purpose of this requirement is to provide both the public

and the Commission with information needed to monitor a licensee's performance in meeting its public interest obligation of providing programming that is responsive to its community."[148]

Localism—specifically in terms of preserving the benefits of free, over-the-air local broadcast television—is one of the guiding principles of the must-carry rules.[149] Congress made the judgment that a broadcaster's duty to provide local news and public affairs programming was so critical that cable operators must be required to carry local channels; even though cable operators objected and fought all the way to the Supreme Court, the law was upheld.[150] In 1992, the Cable Act declared: "A primary objective and benefit of our Nation's system of regulation of television broadcasting is the local origination of programming. There is a substantial governmental interest in ensuring its continuation."[151]

Chairman Powell's 2003 effort came in response to complaints that many stations were not adequately addressing local needs and problems with their programming.[152] The Commission held six field public hearings and reviewed over 83,000 comments. On January 24, 2008, under Chairman Kevin Martin, the Commission released its *Report and Notice of Proposed Rulemaking*, which suggested that some rules and procedures could be changed to help encourage localism efforts by stations.[153] For example, it said that since the Commission relied on the public to scrutinize station behavior, stations ought to note on their websites when they have filed a renewal application.[154] While some of the recommendations made sense, others were overly bureaucratic. For instance, the Commission asked for comment on a proposal that would require stations to set up community advisory boards, and on one that would require staff to be on site whenever a station was on the air; and it inquired whether it should require licensees to provide reports on the quantity of local music played.[155]

The Copps Proposal

FCC Commissioner Michael Copps proposes creating a "public value" test that broadcasters would need to pass in order to get their licenses renewed. The test would include more disclosure of information about political ads, enhanced disclosure of information about broadcasters, greater efforts to promote diversity, greater broadcaster commitment to preparing for emergencies, and these programming related requirements:

> "*Meaningful Commitments to News and Public Affairs Programming*: These would be quantifiable and not involve issues of content interference. Increasing the human and financial resources going into news would be one way to benchmark progress. Producing more local civic affairs programming would be another. Our current children's programming requirements—the one remnant of public interest requirements still on the books—helped enhance kids' programming. Now it is time to put news and information front-and-center. At election time, there should be heightened expectations for debates and issues-oriented programming. Those stations attaining certain benchmarks of progress could qualify for expedited handling of their license renewals. This requirement would have, by the way, important spill-over effects in a media environment where many newspapers are owned by broadcast stations—although such cross-ownership is something I hope the Commission will put the brakes on.

> "*Community Discovery*: The FCC, back when stations were locally-owned and the license holder walked the town's streets every day, required licensees to meet occasionally with their viewers and listeners to see if the programs being offered reflected the diverse interests and needs of the community. Nowadays, when stations are so often owned by mega companies and absentee owners hundreds or even thousands of miles away—frequently by private equity firms totally unschooled in public interest media—we no longer ask licensees to take the public pulse. Diversity of programming suffers, minorities are ignored, and local self-expression becomes the exception. Here's some good news: Community Discovery would not be difficult to do in this Internet age, when technology can so easily facilitate dialogue.

> "*Local and Independent Programming*: The goal here is more localism in our program diet, more local news and information, and a lot less streamed-in homogenization and monotonous nationalized music at the expense of local and regional talent. Homogenized music and entertainment from huge conglomerates constrains creativity, suppresses local talent, and detracts from the great tapestry of our nation's cultural diversity. We should be working toward a solution wherein a certain percentage of prime-time programming—I have suggested 25 percent—is locally or independently-produced. Public Service Announcements should also be more localized and more of them aired in prime-time, too. And PEG channels—public, educational and government programming—deserve first-class treatment if we are to have a first class media."[156]

Copps argues that the main defect in our current system is an unwillingness to enforce the rules. With the emphasis on quantitative standards, he argues, regulators can avoid having to make subjective judgments about programming. Such an approach would set broad requirements but allow stations flexibility on coverage decisions. It would clearly re-establish and clarify the quid-pro-quo, and would lead to greater commitment of journalistic resources to local communities.

There are other ways of envisioning behavioral rules, too. For instance, one could say that for constitutional reasons it would be problematic to impose detailed behavioral rules on commercial broadcasters, but that is less true for public TV, as it receives public funds. One might therefore require each public TV station to have a few hours of local programming—news, public affairs, local entertainment, high school sports. This may have the added benefit of stimulating local journalistic activity, as public TV stations are likely to seek partnerships with nonprofit websites, public radio, and the local newspaper to produce the content.

Taking Stock of the Failure of the Public Interest Obligation System

As noted earlier, even during the peak period of deregulation, the basic requirement that all stations must serve the public interest endured. Instead of detailed formal ascertainment procedural and documentation requirements and preparation of programming logs, the Commission required stations to update their public files every quarter with issues/ programs lists that documented the "programs that have provided the station's most significant treatment of community issues during the preceding three month period."[157] So while the Commission—in deference to the First Amendment— did not prescribe detailed and specific guidance on the programs broadcasters had to air in order to meet their public interest obligation,[158] it never officially abandoned the concept that there needed to be some quid pro quo for the granting of the license—nor that providing "significant treatment of community issues" was part of the bargain.

Yet it is clear that the current system does not work.

It is entirely up to stations to define what it means to serve their community. Some produce news and public affairs programming, while others argue that sponsoring an America's Top Model event counts. Some believe that serving local communities means offering programming of relevance to the area; others have fulfilled their obligations entirely through occasional public service ads. It is tempting to ascribe cynical motives to some of the stations, but the truth is that the FCC has not made it clear, either through policy or enforcement, that any particular way is more desirable than any other.

The FCC relies on people in the community to challenge licenses—and yet has rejected those challenges in almost every case. Given that record, why should a community group or would-be broadcaster invest time and money in challenging a license?

In the last 30 years not one license renewal has been denied on the grounds of a TV station failing to serve the community with its programming.

What we have is neither a free market nor an effectively regulated market—but rather one that operates almost on auto-pilot to the benefit of current license holders. Sometimes that is good for a community; sometimes it is not.

Some argue that the deregulated system best advances the public interest because of the power of free markets, yet advocates of that position rarely grapple with the ways in which the current system *does not* resemble a free market. A true free market would operate more akin to the spectrum management system applied to newer technologies like mobile. That spectrum is auctioned off to the highest bidder, with proceeds going to taxpayers. Broadcast licenses initially were given, for free, to various companies. Over the years, other companies have purchased them, but the taxpayers have not seen any of that money. Moreover, broadcasters do not pay any ongoing rent to use the spectrum—another practice that free-market-oriented economists have recommended as a means to instill market principles. Finally, there is little opportunity for a competitive company to challenge licensure rights of an incumbent broadcaster.

But while it is not a free market, it is also not a sensibly regulated system. The FCC requires stations to keep lists of programs—but the regulators do not read those lists. The FCC invites community groups to challenges to licenses—and then rejects nearly 100 percent of those challenges. The FCC says that stations have an obligation to serve their communities but then offers no definition of what that means.

Part of the paralysis stems from some genuinely difficult constitutional issues. Yes, it is the case that the spectrum belongs to the public, and the public lent it to broadcasters. In that sense, taxpayers (through their governmental representatives) have every right to demand certain behavior—the quo that was supposed to be part of the original quid pro quo. But the challenge is this: once that spectrum becomes the property of a living, breathing broadcaster, how that broadcaster chooses to use it becomes, at least in part, an issue of free speech. Regardless of the origins of the license, once a broadcaster has it the broadcaster then becomes part of the fourth estate. When a slice of spectrum becomes an element of a "media operation" or "the press," the ability for the government to do much about it becomes much more limited—by the First Amendment--as it should. Monitoring to make sure that stations do an adequate amount of local news and public affairs would likely draw the FCC into difficult issues of defining what counts as "adequate," "local," and "news."

That does not mean the government cannot or should not do anything. Indeed, we believe the government can and should do better. But we should acknowledge that at least part of the disappointing history of the public interest obligations stems from the inherent difficulty of finding the right balance between constitutional principles and other public interest goals. One can both accept the idea that there *are* public interest obligations and still be vexed by the question of who, exactly, gets to decide how those goals are defined and met.

We are left with a difficult situation. The public has granted stations something of huge value—but because of the supreme importance of maintaining a free press, the public cannot actually use government to do all that much to make sure those licenses are well used.

This leads to another question: Does it matter? Some broadcasters argue that, by virtue of their commercially-driven need to produce popular programming, whatever the stations decide to do will be more attuned to local needs than any regulatory guideline. At the March 4, 2010 Future of Media Workshop, senior vice president of Legal and Strategic Affairs of Allbritton Communications Company, Jerald N. Fritz, who served as chief of staff to FCC Chairman Mark Fowler, testified that "broadcasters, as content creators, monitor what the public wants on a daily basis. We evaluate who they are, what they watch, where they watch, and how they watch. We even speculate on why they watch. The trick is to amalgamate large enough audiences that advertisers will pay to reach and offset the expenses necessary to provide that programming."[159] In his view, "broadcasters are following the public and attempting to serve it. Our sincere hope is that the Commission will have the considered, good sense to keep out of our way as we do."[160]

Other broadcasters, however, acknowledge that they have an obligation to provide services and programming beyond what might be most popular. Jane Mago, executive vice president of the National Association of Broadcasters (NAB) testified:

"Broadcasters have and will continue to take seriously their responsibility as broadcast licensees to serve the public interest…. Whatever specific elements have been in the regulatory spotlight, the essential core of the public interest obligation has remained constant. This core requirement focuses on whether a station is providing programming responsive to the local community. In NAB's view that core obligation should remain."

On balance, Mago argued, the system has worked well:

"The current public interest standards, other than a few tweaks for digital television broadcasting (such as the requirement that each multicast stream contain at least three hours per week of children's programming) have been in place for more than two decades. They have served both the public and the broadcast industry well….

"The fact that quantified regulatory public interest standards are suspect does not, however, imply that the public interest obligation has no real meaning or that broadcasters do not take them seriously. To the contrary, it is clear that radio and television stations fulfill their public interest obligation and serve their local listeners and viewers."[161]

NAB and other broadcasters offered numerous examples of excellent local programming (our own examples can be found in Chapter 3, Television.) They maintained that local broadcasters offer $10 billion worth of public interest value, largely calculated in the form of "lost" advertising revenue when they instead air public service announcements (PSAs).[162] And they note that local TV news is still the most popular source of local news, and that Americans give their local news teams higher favorability ratings than other media sources.[163]

Our view is that the "public interest obligation" system is broken, and it does matter.

First, we fully accept the idea that many, and perhaps most, TV stations serve their communities well, or at least adequately. But the implicit verdict of the FCC's track record on license renewals and of the NAB statement is that 100 percent of them do.

Second, though the lack of meaningful disclosure has made systematic study of local TV difficult, we have enough information from independent studies to believe that too many local TV stations are not serving their communities as well as they could. While many local broadcasters do an extraordinary job, some are letting advertisers pay to appear on-air as "expert guests," without informing viewers; some are airing video news releases from companies without identifying them as such; and many are doing minimal reporting on issues of local importance. And those indiscretions are occurring among local TV stations that are actually producing local programming and local news. Literally hundreds of local stations do not produce any local news. Some of them argue that they meet community needs by helping to promote a local modeling competition, for instance, or running PSAs—and that no additional programming about local communities is actually necessary.

Third, if a station has little interest in serving its community, there are now better uses for the scarce spectrum. It could be sold to another station or—if Congress so authorizes—stations could put the spectrum into an incentive auction, where it could be purchased by a wireless company to help make wireless high-speed Internet access more available. The station would get part of the proceeds and media system would benefit from greater availability of high-speed Internet.

Fourth, and most important, we believe that there is serious gap in some kinds of local reporting and information provision. TV stations are well positioned to fill that vacuum.

In the olden days (a few years ago), it might be said that when a local TV station did little to serve its community, it was a victimless crime. That is less true now. Contrary to the view of many old-time print journalists, we believe that local TV news can be great, often is great—and, in these times, needs to be great.

Commercial Radio

Many of the policies affecting radio are mentioned in other parts of this report, but to recap:

The licensing system for radio suffers from some of the same problems as that for TV. Stations are required to say how they serve the community but the FCC has not specified what serving the community means. The Working Group that produced this report did not comprehensively review radio issues/program lists, however, and so does not have as clear a sense of how stations fill those out.

As noted in Chapter 2, Radio, local news has become less voluminous on commercial radio. Many experts told us that the combination of license and ownership deregulation likely led to, accelerated, or allowed that to happen.

Other public policies, such as those that keep satellite radio from offering local programming (see Chapter 28, Satellite Television and Radio), have protected local broadcasters from threats to their advertising revenues but do not help encourage them to provide more local news and journalism.

Scholar Paul Starr proposed that radio broadcasters be required to offer a few minutes of news each hour, in part to ensure that those who are not news junkies would nonetheless be exposed to current events.[164] But such an approach could put radio at a competitive disadvantage, considering that the Internet and satellite radio have no such requirement.

Finally, the decline of news on commercial radio has been partly remedied by an increase in local efforts by public radio. (See Chapter 6, Public Broadcasting.)

Campaign Advertising Disclosures

Since broadcast regulation began, Congress has consistently recognized the critical importance of broadcast media as a platform for political discourse and campaigning—enacting laws "to give candidates for public office greater access to the media so that they may better explain their stand on the issues, and thereby more fully and completely inform the voters."[165] Congress viewed this function as an important requirement for holding a license. "The duty of broadcast licensees generally to permit the use of their facilities by legally qualified candidates…is inherent in the requirement that licensees serve the needs and interests of the [communities] of license."[166] The Supreme Court agreed that it "makes a significant contribution to freedom of expression by enhancing the ability of candidates to present, and the public to receive, information necessary for the effective operation of the democratic process."[167] The major laws governing TV stations' obligations during political campaigns include:

Lowest Unit Charge: Section 315(b)[168] requires broadcasters to sell political advertising time to all candidates at the "lowest unit charge" of the station—for the same class and amount of time—during the 45 days preceding primary elections and the 60 days preceding general elections. The provision also applies to cable,[169] satellite TV,[170] and satellite radio operators.[171]

Advertising Purchases: The Commission first required stations to maintain and make available records regarding requests to buy broadcast time on behalf of candidates in 1938.[172] By using these records, competing candidates can track their opponents' buying strategies and figure out what equal opportunities they can request. The files, kept at the station, are supposed to document every request made by or on behalf of a candidate for broadcast time and the outcome of that request, as well as a record of any free time provided to a candidate by the station.[173] Stations must also list the date and time of any non-candidate-sponsored broadcasts containing a positive candidate appearance of four seconds or more. As the Commission noted, "[w]ith this material as a guide, candidates are in a position to exercise the right to equal opportunities."[174] The Bipartisan Campaign Reform Act of 2002 (BCRA)[175] added section 315(e) to the Communications Act, which included a requirement that stations retain similar information concerning requests to purchase time for certain issue-oriented ads.[176] Stations must update the file "as soon as possible," which the Commission has held to mean immediately, absent extraordinary circumstances. Cable,[177] satellite TV,[178] and satellite radio operators are also required to keep these records in their political files for two years.[179]

In 2008, the Commission adopted policies that require television broadcast stations to place their public files on their website, if they have a website, or on their state association website, if available. The Commission, however, exempted the political component of the file from this requirement,[180] noting the multitude of requests, often on a daily basis, for political time and the resulting expenditure of station personnel resources and time to place the information on its website. The rules have not gone into effect.

Reasonable Access: The Communications Act requires broadcast stations "to allow reasonable access to or to permit the purchase of reasonable amounts of time...." by legally qualified candidates for federal elective office.[181] Stations may balance the needs of each candidate against such factors as the number of competing candidates and potential program disruption. These provisions also apply to satellite TV[182] and radio.[183]

The reasonable access provision does not apply to candidates for state and local elective offices. Prior to 1991, the Commission's policy had been that stations were "expected to devote time to campaigns of state and local candidates in proportion to the significance of the campaigns and the amount of public interest in them."[184] But in 1991 the Commission concluded that state and local candidates did not have an affirmative right of access to broadcast facilities.[185] In 2008, the Commission declined to take any further action, saying that it would be premature, given its decision at the time to move ahead with the Enhanced Disclosure Proceeding.[186] Alas, enhanced disclosure has not yet been implemented.

"Broadcasters are following the public and attempting to serve it. Our sincere hope is that the Commission will have the considered, good sense to keep out of our way as we do."

Equal Opportunities: Section 315 of the Communications Act prohibits broadcasters from favoring one candidate over another in terms of the use of broadcast facilities. It requires that "[i]f any licensee shall permit any person who is a legally qualified candidate for any public office to use a broadcasting station, he shall afford equal opportunities to all other such candidates for that office in the use of such broadcasting station."[187] The "equal opportunities" provision also applies to cable operators (section 76.205)[188] and direct broadcast satellite (DBS) providers.[189] The Commission also has held that these requirements apply to digital audio radio satellite operators.[190] Congress exempted from the equal opportunities requirements appearances by candidates in certain bona fide news programming—specifically, newscasts, news interviews, and on-the-spot coverage of news events, including debates and news documentaries.[191]

No Censorship: Section 315 of the Act also prohibits broadcasters from censoring candidates' advertisements.[192] This provision also applies to cable,[193] satellite TV,[194] and satellite radio operators.[195]

Origination Cablecasting: The rules for political programming on cable television, including the on-air disclosure requirements for political and issue ads, apply only to "origination cablecasting"[196] programming "subject to the exclusive control of the cable operator," such as a local news station run by the cable operator.[197] The Commission did not specify in 1972 whether these rules applied to cable news networks, as very few existed at the time. Given the intent of the law, it would seem that they should probably apply to cable too, but the FCC has never formally ruled on whether "origination cablecasting" includes national cable network programming.[198]

Free Time

In the 1990s, the Commission contemplated whether it should or could mandate that free airtime be provided to legally qualified candidates. The Commission ultimately rejected the idea on the grounds that it would be too burdensome because, under the equal opportunities provision, providing free time to one candidate would result in an obligation to provide free time, if requested, to all opponents. Instead, in 1996, the Commission found that various novel programming proposals involving candidate appearances—such as debates or candidate forums—qualified as on-the-spot coverage of *bona fide* news events and were, therefore, exempt from the equal opportunities provision under section 315(a)(4) of the Act.[199]

Recent Court Rulings

In the *Citizens United* decision in January 2010, the U.S. Supreme Court struck down restrictions on political ad spending, but—significantly—upheld BCRA's requirements for funding *disclosure* by eight to one. The Court found that disclosure does not prevent political expression and thus does not violate the First Amendment. In fact, Justice Kennedy's majority opinion held that funding limits could now be lifted only *because* the disclosure provisions of BCRA would serve as a counterbalance:

"A campaign finance system that pairs corporate independent expenditures with effective disclosure has not existed before today [and]…many of Congress' findings in passing BCRA were premised on a system without adequate disclosure. With the advent of the Internet, prompt disclosure of expenditures can provide shareholders and citizens with the information needed to hold corporations and elected officials accountable for their positions and supporters. Shareholders can determine whether their corporation's political speech advances the corporation's interest in making profits, and citizens can see whether elected officials are 'in the pocket' of so-called moneyed interests. The First Amendment protects political speech; and disclosure permits citizens and shareholders to react to the speech of corporate entities in a proper way. This transparency enables the electorate to make informed decisions and give proper weight to different speakers and messages."[200]

This opinion echoed the Court's decision when it upheld disclosure requirements in *Doe v. Reed*. Justice Scalia wrote:

"Requiring people to stand up in public for their political acts fosters civic courage, without which democracy is doomed. For my part, I do not look forward to a society which, thanks to the Supreme Court, campaigns anonymously and even exercises the direct democracy of initiative and referendum hidden from public scrutiny and protected from the accountability of criticism. This does not resemble the Home of the Brave."[201]

27 Cable Television

FCC POLICIES CONTRIBUTED IN SIGNIFICANT WAYS to the cable industry's evolution from a limited service that served rural areas to its current status as a major competitor to broadcasters.

Initially supportive of cable as a new communication medium, the FCC shifted its position in 1966 and began to regulate the cable industry due to its competition with over-the-air television broadcasters. In the mid-1970s, the FCC determined that cable was no longer a threat to broadcasting and eased up on the most restrictive regulations.[1]

Sometimes policy roads not taken are just as important as those that are. In previous chapters we have described how the breakup of the "bundle" in newspapers undercut the cross-subsidy model, which had allowed more profitable content to subsidize types of journalism that were more costly to produce or less popular. Cable TV currently bundles its offerings. Consumers pay a monthly rate for a basic collection and often premium rates for other packages, but do not have the option of picking only the shows or channels they want. Several FCC commissioners have proposed plans to introduce a la carte pricing that would allow consumers to pay only for the channels they want, but the Commission has never accepted this approach.[2] Geoffrey Cowan and David Westphal of the Annenberg School of Communication and Journalism argue that permitting bundling has had an important impact: "Cable news channels are the direct beneficiaries of FCC rules that allow cable operators to bundle services, requiring every cable subscriber to pay a fee to MSNBC, CNN and Fox News - whether they want them or not.[3]

Today, cable TV operators work under a complex set of rules regarding which broadcast programming they must carry and the process for securing rights to carry programming that is not required. Several of these rules have indirect, yet significant, effects on local news.

Must Carry and Retransmission Consent

Congress required major cable providers to set aside up to one-third of their channel capacity for local broadcast stations.[4] Broadcasters argued successfully that such a significant governmental intervention was required to protect them, insure more coverage of local issues, and promote broadcasters' ability to compete effectively against cable operators in their local markets. James B. Hedlund, head of the Association of Independent Television Stations, told Congress that failure to pass "must carry" would jeopardize "the number one source of news and information to the American public," namely local, over-the-air broadcasters.[5] Hedlund explained:

> "Why should the Congress care about the competitive relationship between cable operators and free off-air television? At stake is our long held national value of promoting a diverse and free information flow to all Americans. Studies confirm that local off-air television is the number one source of news and information to the American public. We may lose this lifeline in the next decade unless the unbridled power of cable is restrained today....

> "On the other hand, off-air broadcasting will provide this universal service. The economics of broadcasting—indirect payment through advertising—will insure that all citizens have access to information. Our responsibility as public trustees will insure that all citizens have access to programming that responds to the needs of the community. Absent free off-air television, government policy makers will be confronted with the costs of providing some form of lifeline service for those not connected to the wire, a cost which must be borne by the taxpayer or subscribers...."[6]

Edward O. Fritts, then-president and CEO of the National Association of Broadcasters, went one step further: "By accepting 'must-carry' rules, the public is guaranteed local news, weather, public service and programming in the local market."[7]

Yet, as noted earlier, many local broadcasters do little or no local programming. About 30 percent air no local news, and of those that do, about one-third are contracting it from other stations in town. Despite the lack of local programming, all of those stations have government-enforced carriage on cable TV.[8] In other words, the current must-carry system is *not* currently set up to favor stations that do local programming about their communities over those that do not. (See Chapter 3, Television.)

Cable systems with 12 or more channels must devote up to one-third of their channel capacity to the carriage of local commercial television stations that are located in the same designated market area (with some exceptions to avoid duplication of signals).[9] These stations are given the choice every three years of being carried pursuant to the Commission's must-carry rules or of entering into retransmission consent negotiations with local cable operators.[10]

The election of "must-carry" status prohibits a station from demanding payment for its carriage; however, the retransmission consent option allows a commercial station to engage in direct negotiations with cable companies, asking for payment in return for the cable company's right to "retransmit" the broadcast signal over cable lines. (In contrast, local noncommercial educational (NCE) stations have no retransmission consent rights and therefore cannot seek compensation for their carriage on local cable systems.)[11]

Changes in the marketplace have led to disputes over retransmission consent becoming more contentious and more public, and we recently have seen a rise in negotiation impasses that have affected millions of consumers.

While these retrans battles do not usually revolve around questions of news or local programming, some argue that their outcome may have indirect impact on local news. Most cable operators do not finance or carry local cable news operations, so local broadcasters provide almost all of the local news on cable. Broadcasters believe that if stations can increase the retrans revenue streams, they would be in a better financial position to invest in local news. Dave Lougee, president of Gannett's broadcast division, argues that if the FCC cares about local news it should disregard calls to arbitrate the

> Dave Lougee, president of Gannett's broadcast division, argues that the most under-compensated stations on the cable dial are the network affiliates. "If we can't use retransmission consent, local news will die," he said.

disputes between broadcasters and cable operators and instead let broadcasters bargain for more revenue. The most under-compensated stations on the cable dial, Lougee maintains, are the network affiliates. "If we can't use retransmission consent, local news will die," Lougee says.[12] On the other hand, should cable operators become more aggressive in providing local news and public affairs—through local cable news networks, state SPANS, or PEG operations—the broadcaster argument that only their local news teams are providing community reporting might weaken.

Leased Access

As cable grew in the 1980s, Congress feared that programming might be dominated by a handful of large media conglomerates.[13] In 1984, Congress began requiring cable operators to set aside up to 15 percent of their capacity for a "leased access" system designed to give access to independent programming.[14] In 1992, Congress broadened section 612's statutory scope to encourage "competition in the delivery of diverse sources of video programming," ostensibly allowing independent programmers (i.e., those not affiliated with major cable, satellite, or broadcast companies) to buy their way onto the cable dial, opening the door to a greater diversity of sources of information[15] and providing "public access to a wide variety of voices and viewpoints."[16]

Leased access has not worked as Congress intended. There has not been any significant independent programming on leased access channels.[17] A major obstacle is that prospective programmers seeking a national audience must reach agreements with thousands of separate cable systems. Independent programmers, such as the America Channel and members of the National Association of Independent Networks, have complained to Congress that they continue to face difficulties getting carriage on cable systems, and when they do get carriage they are placed on more expensive and less desirable tiers than networks controlled by cable operators.[18] In one case, a programmer estimated he would have had to pay $1 billion per year to reach 50 million customers.[19] At those rates, no programmer would be able to get off the ground. On average, cable systems carry 0.7 leased access channels, less than one percent of capacity (they are supposed to be setting aside 15 percent).[20]

If no programmers have applied successfully for leased access, then the cable operators may use the channels for whatever they want. So they may have a disincentive to make the leased access system work well. In addition, cable operators have stated that most leased access programming consists of infomercials and religious programs, although the FCC has limited information about the makeup of this programming or how the rest of the unused capacity is being used.[21]

Though the leased access rules have not been effective in promoting independent programming on a national scale, they do have the potential to be used to promote the growth of local programming, including possibly news and public affairs. For this to happen, the FCC may want to streamline its access rules for programmers and revise the structure to make leasing more affordable. We note that the Commission has its leased access rules under review in a pending proceeding.[22]

Public, Educational, and Government (PEG) Channels

In 1984, the Cable Communications Policy Act[23] declared that local franchising authorities (LFAs) could mandate channel capacity for public, educational, and governmental use:[24]

> "A requirement of reasonable third-party access to cable systems will mean a wide diversity of information sources for the public—the fundamental goal of the First Amendment—without the need to regulate the content of programming provided over cable.... Public access channels are often the video equivalent of the speaker's soapbox or the electronic parallel to the printed leaflet. They provide groups and individuals who generally have not had access to the electronic media with the opportunity to become sources of information in the electronic marketplace of ideas. PEG channels also contribute to an informed citizenry by bringing local schools into the home, and by showing the public local government at work."[25]

Though PEG channels could serve as an important means of enhancing the information flow to communities, numerous obstacles have prevented this from happening in many places.

First, PEG funding has been declining. In a survey of 165 PEG centers, half said their funding dropped from 2005 to 2010, and among those reporting a decline, the average drop was 40 percent. The survey stated that 100 community media centers shut down during that period.[26] For example, after the City of Dallas took over PEG funding in 2000, it reduced PEG allocations from $700,000 in 2001 to $246,000 in 2008, and in 2009 it cut the budget altogether for Dallas's public access system, which then had to shut down.[27] (See Chapter 7, Public Access Channels.) Many other LFAs are cutting PEG funding, pressed by economic realities, by state statutes that reorganize franchising, and by decreased franchise fees (from people cutting the cord or switching to satellite).

The current "must carry system" is not set up to privilege stations that do local programming about their communities over those that do not.

PEG advocates say that the increase in statewide franchising for cable companies has resulted in a significant downturn in funding for local PEG channels.[28] According to a 2008 survey of by the Alliance for Community Media (ACM), in which over 3,000 of its member PEG access center groups were interviewed, 17 communities in eight states have lost their PEG operations altogether; another nearly 25 percent have lost PEG channels or expect to lose them in the future; and 20 percent reported a decrease in PEG funding.[29] In 2011, ACM conducted an online survey with a smaller number of respondents (207) and found that PEG access stations in over 100 communities across the United States had closed since 2005, and hundreds more may be forced to close in the next three years.[30] Some examples:

> American Community Television estimates that by 2012, over 400 PEG channels could be lost in six states—Wisconsin, Florida, Missouri, Iowa, Georgia, and Ohio[31]—when funding ends.[32] In what the City of Pikeville, Kentucky, calls "a terrible blow to PEG funding in Kentucky," state franchising law forbids communities from requiring any in-kind payment of property or services from franchisees for PEG access.[33]

> A recent California state law allowing cable operators "the option of dropping their long-standing obligation to provide free studios, equipment, and training to the public," caused at least 45 PEG access centers across the state to shut down[34]—among them, at least 12 public access studios in Los Angeles alone.[35]

> Public access channels in Madison and West Allis Wisconsin shut down after a ban on PEG fees went into effect.[36]

> Kansas, South Carolina, Missouri, and Nevada do not require new cable TV entrants to provide any PEG support.[37]

PEG advocates also argue that cable and phone companies are making it harder and harder for viewers to find their channels. The FCC is currently considering whether AT&T should be permitted to locate all PEG outlets in a single media market on a single channel, for instance, channel 99.[38] AT&T argues that "U-verse TV is based on an all-IP architecture totally unlike that of traditional cable operators" and that the "[m]ethod of delivering PEG should not be frozen in time."[39] In some communities, this may amount to tens of channels that are accessible only through a drop-down menu. In addition, channels accessible through drop-down menus cannot be recorded for viewing at a later time.

New state laws are squeezing public access channels. American Community Television estimates that by 2012, over 400 PEG channels could be lost in six states.

Third, some states are increasingly mandating that PEG channels air a minimum number of hours of non-repeat programming per week. In Georgia, Texas, and Michigan, PEG channels are required to provide at least eight hours of non-repeat programming content daily.[40] On one hand, this seems like a reasonable minimum requirement. Since the point of PEG is to provide original local programming, if a station cannot provide that, perhaps a different group should be given a chance. But PEG operators are concerned that cable operators will seize on these requirements to unfairly eliminate PEG channels.[41] Indeed, in Texas, with the reduction of funding, some PEG channels "have dipped below the 8 hour programming requirement and were taken off the air."[42]

The FCC has no legal authority to require state or local governments to fund PEG channels, and many localities do not require disclosure of PEG funding either. As a result, there is no current national list of existing PEG channels, the nature of their franchising agreements, or what programming they air.

State Public Affairs Networks

Industry leaders often point to the creation of C-SPAN as the right way to achieve public interest goals. The industry voluntarily funded the creation of the network, and local operators pay C-SPAN a fee based on the number of subscribers to the overall cable system.[43] However, while 23 states and the District of Columbia have SPANs covering the operations of state government, in only four states have cable operators followed the C-SPAN pattern and funded the services. That has forced 12 of the SPANs to get funding from their state legislatures, making them less secure and more dependent on the institution they are ostensibly covering.[44] (See Chapter 8, State SPANs.)

At a minimum, states could help SPANs by allowing them to be part of the PEG system. In our view, section 611 of the Communications Act was not intended to entitle only "government access channels" operated by local governments to carriage as PEG channels. In providing for channel capacity for governmental use, Congress noted that "the governmental channel allows for a local 'mini-C-SPAN,' thus contributing to an informed electorate, essential to the proper functioning of government."[45] If SPANs qualified as legitimate forms of PEG programming, they might also then be eligible for fees from local franchising authorities. [46]

28 Satellite Television And Radio

THE GOVERNMENT PLAYED A MAJOR ROLE in the development of the satellite industry, as, over the course of several decades, NASA and the Defense Department invested tens of billions of dollars to develop the technology for satellites.[1] Congress also intervened mightily in 1992 by enacting the "program access" law that requires cable operators to make their programming available to their satellite competitors on non-discriminatory terms.[2] The FCC in 2007 extended those rules for five additional years.[3]

Set Asides

The Cable Television Consumer Protection and Competition Act of 1992 required the FCC to impose on satellite TV, also known as direct broadcast satellite (DBS), "public interest or other requirements for providing video programming."[4] Congress decreed that satellite TV operators must reserve between 4 and 7 percent of their channel capacity to carry "noncommercial programming of an educational or informational nature" at reduced rates.[5] Eligibility for this preferential access was limited to "any qualified noncommercial educational television station, other public telecommunications entities, and public or private educational institutions."[6]

With the flexibility to choose a noncommercial set aside of between 4 and 7 percent, in 1998 the Commission chose 4 percent on the grounds that the satellite industry was in its infancy and a larger set-aside requirement might "hinder DBS in developing as a viable competitor."[7]

Eligibility for set-aside channels is limited to nonprofit organizations that provide "noncommercial programming," defined largely by the absence of advertising.[8] The Commission envisioned that a wide variety of programming would be made available to DBS subscribers over the set-aside capacity, including distance learning, children's educational programming, and medical, historical, and scientific programming.[9] However, the satellite operators now reject most applicants because they already have hit the 4 percent mark. Among the stations rejected since 2007 because satellite companies had already hit their 4 percent quota were numerous religious stations (including CatholicTV, God TV, and Almavision Hispanic Network), the Connecticut Network (a public affairs network), The Documentary Channel, Classic Arts Showcase, Free Speech TV, New Abilities Television (a station for people with disabilities), TV Japan, CoLours TV, American Public Television, and California State University.[10] Although few satellite operators offer local programming, they do offer educational programming, programming for minorities and the disabled, and international programming.

Congress has left the FCC with leeway to reduce or eliminate fees for set-aside channels altogether. When determining reasonable prices, section 335(b)(4) instructs the Commission to take into account the nonprofit character of programming providers and any federal funds used to support the programming. It directs the FCC not to allow prices to exceed 50 percent of direct costs.[11] Educational programmers usually pay satellite operators significant monthly fees, in contrast to PEG channels, which do not pay cable operators and indeed earn fees from localities.]] (See Chapter 7, PEG.) In the past, some nonprofit broadcasters have suggested reducing or customizing fees, such as implementing a sliding scale for fees based on programmers' ability to pay.[12] DBS operators pushed for an expansive definition of "direct costs" that would include the cost of constructing and launching satellites. The Commission declined to adopt such a broad definition of "direct costs," arguing that to do so would go against Congressional intent:

> "If noncommercial educational or informational programmers are forced to share those expenses, the costs of leasing channels could keep many programmers out of the market, thus defeating Congress' desire to make noncommercial programming readily available."[13]

However, the FCC also decided that DBS operators should be given "flexible" regulatory treatment, and rather than agreeing to regulate rates the Commission decided to let DBS providers and noncommercial programmers negotiate rates themselves.[14]

Satellite providers are subject to disclosure requirements. They must maintain a file containing "quarterly measurements of channel capacity, yearly average calculations used to determine the four percent set aside, and a record of noncommercial programmers requesting and obtaining access to capacity."[15] However, they are not required to post these online.

Local Programming

Policymakers have considered increasing local programming, but so far have opted not to.

While section 335(a) directs the Commission to "examine the opportunities that the establishment of direct broadcast satellite service provides for the principle of localism…and the methods by which such principle may be served…." in 1998, the Commission noted that the statute provides no guidance on how to define "localism"—and that there were some technological limitations as to how much satellites could target local signals.[16]

But in 2004, the Commission revisited the issue, finding that "[m]any of the legal and technical impediments to the transmission of local television broadcasts are now eroding."[17] Indeed, by the middle of the last decade, increased satellite capacity, channel compression, and other technical advances had arisen to support the delivery of a limited number of local channels. In addition, a change in the law had removed the copyright obstacles to satellite carriage of local television broadcast signals.[18] In fact, the new law required DBS operators to carry the signals of *all* local broadcasters in any market that it chose to serve with *any* local signals.[19] At last count, DISH offered local-into-local service in 175 markets and DirecTV offered such service in all 210 markets.[20]

But provision of local coverage on satellites faces technical challenges. Local channels are carried on "spot beams" that focus coverage on a particular region of the country.[21] Satellite operators make this allocation in the satellite's design before it is launched (which typically happens every year or two). But in 2004 the FCC decided not to impose localism requirements "because it is not clear to what degree the satellite channel capacity may be limited by technical constraints, or whether market demand will result in local-to-local service in all parts of the country…."[22]

SPANs on Satellite

State SPANs report that the satellite companies have rejected their requests for carriage. (See Chapter 8, State SPANs.) Only one state SPAN channel is available through DBS—in Alaska.[23] In May 2010, President Obama signed into law the Satellite Television Extension and Localism Act of 2010, which permits satellite providers to reduce their public interest carriage obligations to 3.5 percent if they provide retransmission of the SPANs of at least 15 states.[24] However, officials at the National Association of Public Affairs Networks report that they do not expect this flexibility to increase carriage of SPANs.

Digital Audio Radio Services (Satellite Radio)

In 1997, the Commission granted licenses to American Mobile Radio Corporation (the predecessor of XM Radio) and Satellite CD Radio (the predecessor of Sirius Radio) to offer digital audio radio service by satellite (SDARS). (See Chapter 2, Radio.) The companies planned to use state-of-the-art satellite technology to provide CD-quality music and information to a nationwide audience.[25] Subsequently, both companies installed networks of terrestrial repeaters to retransmit information from the satellite in order to overcome signal blockage and reach subscribers who were not able to receive the satellite signal. Broadcasters, concerned that satellite operators would begin to provide locally originated programming and compete for local advertisers, urged the FCC to prevent them from airing locally originated programming. The satellite operators agreed, as a condition for authorization to use terrestrial repeaters, not to use them for locally originated programming that was not also carried on their satellites.

After XM and Sirius merged in 2008, the Commission adopted final rules for terrestrial repeaters, permitting the companies to use repeaters to transmit programming that they sent to all their subscribers by satellite, even if the programming was localized in nature (e.g., weather and traffic information in Los Angeles), but prohibiting them from using the repeaters to transmit locally *originated* programming that would reach only some of their subscribers.[26] In so doing, the Commission sided with the National Association of Broadcasters, which argued that allowing satellite radio to originate local programming would put them into competition with local broadcasters for listeners and local advertising dollars.

29 The Internet And Mobile

THE GOVERNMENT'S ROLE in creating the Internet started with the Pentagon's Advanced Research Project Agency (ARPA), which, in 1968 funded a network that would make it easier for researchers and computers at different locations and universities to share information.[1]

In 1985, ARPA transferred the network from the Pentagon to the National Science Foundation, which decided to open it up to commercial interests. In 1989, two European researchers, Tim Berners-Lee and Robert Cailliau, invented the World Wide Web, which allowed users to create locations on the Internet—what we now call websites—and link one piece of content on one site to another piece on another site.[2]

Several additional policy decisions helped foster and shape the Internet's development. The Communications Decency Act of 1996 immunized Internet service providers (through which you connect to the web) from liability for torts related to Internet content,[3] and the Internet Tax Freedom Act of 1998 decreed that products sold on the Internet would not be subject to state and local sales tax.[4]

One FCC decision that had a particularly profound effect came even earlier. In the 1940s and 1950s, the FCC had repeatedly supported prohibitions against any "foreign attachments" to phones. But in 1968 it ruled that the monopolistic AT&T could not ban such devices. In 1975, the Commission created the Part 68 rules, which entitled "any manufacturer to sell its wares to the public and demand cooperation from the telephone companies."[5] "[W]ithout Part 68," wrote FCC researcher Jason Oxman, "users of the public switched network would not have been able to connect their computers and modems to the network, and it is likely that the Internet would have been unable to develop."[6]

Current Policy Debates

The FCC has taken the lead on many issues related to the Internet. Rather than providing a comprehensive summary, we will focus on the aspects of FCC policy that are the most relevant to news, journalism, and civically important information.

Access

Some 55 percent of adult Americans now have a broadband Internet connection at home,[7] whereas almost all have access to TV.[8] If traditional media companies devote fewer resources to accountability journalism, it becomes more important for all Americans to have access to a full range of comparable resources online. Those that have low quality newspapers or TV and limited Internet access end up with less useful news. Conversely, greater broadband penetration will make it more likely that local digital media efforts will succeed. Whether digital media companies focus on drawing income from advertising or subscriptions, a significant increase in the pool of potential consumers can only generate more digital revenue opportunities.

> Those that have low quality newspapers or TV *and* limited Internet access end up with less useful news.

The FCC's 2010 *National Broadband Plan* sketched a strategy for providing high-speed access for 100 million Americans over the next decade.[9] A key element of the strategy is to move communities toward less dependence on the two platforms that dominate today—cable and telephone wires—by encouraging the growth of the wireless Internet sector. This will expand access and, by bringing competition to the existing ISPs, potentially lower consumer prices. The plan also set a long-term goal for the United States to lead the world in mobile innovation and have the fastest and most extensive wireless networks anywhere.[10] In early 2011, President Obama announced an initiative to make available fourth-generation high-speed wireless services to at least 98 percent of Americans.[11]

As news media migrate to the Internet, and wireless becomes an increasingly common way of accessing the Internet, it follows that a flourishing wireless ecosystem is essential to the future of the news. To the extent that wireless provides an open, affordable, and innovative platform for civic discourse, this will likely be to the benefit of news producers and consumers alike. Among the most important actions that can be taken to ensure this outcome is to ensure an abundant supply of spectrum to feed the enormous growth in wireless. A healthy mix of licensed and unlicensed spectrum will promote innovation without permission, a competitive marketplace, and affordable access—all preconditions of a robust wireless sector and all conducive to effectuating the recommendations of this report.

> A world without an open Internet would be one in which the very innovation we are depending on to save journalism would lose its oxygen before it had a chance to flourish.

Adoption

A murkier issue is how to deal with the substantial number of Americans, who live in communities with high-speed Internet service yet are not using it.[12] In some cases, this is because the service is too expensive. In other cases, people do not yet have a vivid sense of how the Internet can benefit them. For that reason, there is broad support for what is known as "digital literacy." (See pp. 174–178 of the *National Broadband Plan* and and Chapter 19 of this report.) A key part of the puzzle may be public libraries, which often provide Internet service for low income residents (See Chapter 18.)

Surprisingly, there may be a growing connection between digital literacy and public access channels. It turns out that the community media centers that arose as part of the public access system in the 1960s and 1970s have, in an effort to redefine their mission in the Internet age, increasingly taken on the role of training citizens in how to use the Internet and digital storytelling tools.[13] Whether training people to use the Internet for their own benefit or to shoot video as a professional skill or to become a citizen journalist who contributes occasionally, the net result will be a more robust local news and journalism ecosystem. (See Chapter 7, PEG.)

Openness

The effort to protect Internet freedom and openness, or "net neutrality," had been far more bipartisan traditionally than recent debates might indicate. Michael Powell, a Republican FCC Chairman, espoused "four freedoms" on the Internet.[14] In 2005, the FCC, under Chairman Kevin Martin, also a Republican, unanimously voted to build on Powell's framework by adopting principles to:

> "…preserve and promote the open and interconnected nature of public Internet: (1) consumers are entitled to access the lawful Internet content of their choice; (2) consumers are entitled to run applications and services of their choice, subject to the needs of law enforcement; (3) consumers are entitled to connect their choice of legal devices that do not harm the network; and (4) consumers are entitled to competition among network providers, application and service providers, and content providers.… All of these principles are subject to reasonable network management."[15]

Martin attempted several times to enforce the principles and in 2008, while chastising Comcast for possibly violating them, he asked:

"Would you be OK with the post office opening your mail, deciding they didn't want to bother delivering it, and hiding that fact by sending it back to you stamped 'address unknown—return to sender?' Or if they opened letters mailed to you, decided that because the mail truck is full sometimes, letters to you could wait, and then [they] hid both that they read your letters and delayed them?"[16]

While there is considerable disagreement about how to insure Internet openness—including what the government's role should be—there has been a relatively broad consensus that openness should persist.

In December 2010,the FCC adopted three rules codifying open Internet principles:

"Rule 1: Transparency: A person engaged in the provision of broadband Internet access service shall publicly disclose accurate information regarding the network management practices, performance, and commercial terms of its broadband Internet access services sufficient for consumers to make informed choices regarding use of such services and for content, application, service, and device providers to develop, market, and maintain Internet offerings.

"Rule 2: No Blocking: A person engaged in the provision of fixed broadband Internet access service, insofar as such person is so engaged, shall not block lawful content, applications, services, or non-harmful devices, subject to reasonable network management.

"A person engaged in the provision of mobile broadband Internet access service, insofar as such person is so engaged, shall not block consumers from accessing lawful websites, subject to reasonable network management; nor shall such person block applications that compete with the provider's voice or video telephony services, subject to reasonable network.

"Rule 3: No Unreasonable Discrimination: A person engaged in the provision of fixed broadband Internet access service, insofar as such person is so engaged, shall not unreasonably discriminate in transmitting lawful network traffic over a consumer's broadband Internet access service. Reasonable network management shall not constitute unreasonable discrimination."[17]

The Commission also noted that "pay for priority" arrangements—commercial arrangements between a broadband provider and a third party to favor some traffic over other traffic—were "unlikely to satisfy" the "no unreasonable discrimination" rule.[18] Although the rules were the subject of some political controversy, many in the technology sector supported them on the grounds that, as venture capitalist John Doerr put it, "maintaining an Open Internet is critical to our economy's growth."[19]

These rules have great significance for the development of news, information, and journalism. The rules forbid an ISP from blocking one news provider in favor of another with whom it might have a business relationship. By expressing skepticism that pay-for-priority arrangements would be acceptable under open Internet rules, the rules make it far harder for large, established news organizations to collaborate with ISPs to squelch competition from upstart news websites.

Whatever one's views on the mechanism for preserving openness, everyone can agree that the Internet has been an extraordinary gift to free speech, because the barriers to entry are low to non-existent. The ability to communicate freely online requires that those entities that control the infrastructure over which communications travel do not block or degrade particular traffic or pick winners and losers among content, applications, or services. But as the FCC's open Internet order noted, broadband providers have natural business incentives, and the demonstrated ability, to act as gatekeepers, favoring or disfavoring particular content, applications, and services that traverse their networks:

"The record and our economic analysis demonstrate, however, that the openness of the Internet cannot be taken for granted, and that it faces real threats. Indeed, we have seen broadband providers endanger the Internet's openness by blocking or degrading content and applications without disclosing their practices to end users and edge providers, notwithstanding the Commission's adoption of open Internet principles in 2005."[20]

That is why the conservative group, Christian Coalition, has backed open Internet rules:

"We believe that organizations such as the Christian Coalition should be able to continue to use the Internet to communicate with our members and with a worldwide audience without a phone or cable company snooping in on our communications and deciding whether to allow a particular communication to proceed, slow it down, or offer to speed it up if the author pays extra to be on the 'fast lane.'

"Simply put, free speech should not stop when you turn on your computer or pick up your cell phone. The Christian Coalition testified some time ago on this issue and many members of Congress promised to act if network operators blocked political speech. We are here today to say, 'network operators are blocking political speech.'"[21]

A healthy mix of licensed and unlicensed wireless broadband spectrum will promote "innovation without permission," a competitive marketplace, and affordable access.

In addition, ISPs may favor some types of content in more subtle ways not apparent to consumers—such as by transmitting some content more slowly or charging some content creators more to reach broadband subscribers, in effect disadvantaging less-well-capitalized operators. Would these practices become commonplace? It is hard to know. It would likely depend on how much competition there is in the market and how well-hidden the discrimination is. The fact that an ISP can prefer one entity over another without anyone noticing is one of the strongest arguments for the transparency rule passed by the FCC.

The open Internet debate has several implications for news. First, if the Internet were to evolve toward a tiered system in which preferred customers get better service, it could end up privileging certain types of content over others without regard to consumer demand. Public and nonprofit media would be particularly vulnerable, as it is likely that such a structure would reward established, well-heeled companies over less-well-capitalized start-ups, possibly commercial over nonprofits. It also is plausible that a broadband Internet provider with strong political views might wish to minimize the dissemination of antithetical viewpoints. On a local level, one could easily imagine that a cable provider that controls broadband distribution might discriminate against a news website that had published an investigative report presenting that company in an unfavorable light. This would happen not because the companies have naturally bad intent but because they will inherently seek ways to maximize their profit and/or market penetration.

These tendencies are particularly troublesome when it comes to the evolution of journalism, because we are in a moment when no business model has proven itself viable for the financing of labor-intensive, local accountability journalism. Some of the incipient optimism about media innovation comes from the emergence of small, independent, web-based news providers—precisely the sort that would be at a disadvantage in a tiered pricing system. A world without an open Internet would be one in which the very innovation we are depending on to save journalism would lose its oxygen before it had a chance to flourish.

More recently, some Internet companies have begun to call for "search neutrality," meaning search engines should not favor products or services offered by the company that owns the search engine. This newer idea comes in part from concerns about concentration and the potential for unfair discrimination in the online search market, where Google now accounts for 66 percent of U.S. searches.[22] Over time, Google has become more than a search engine, offering products that compete with other companies' services: Google Maps competes with MapQuest; Google owns YouTube, which competes with other video services; Google powers the Android phone, which competes with Apple's iPhone. This has led consumer watchdog groups to worry that Google skews its search results to advantage its own products and services over those of competitors.[23] In November 2010, the European Commission launched a formal investigation in order to look into that issue.[24]

> If the Internet were to evolve toward a tiered system in which preferred customers get better service, it could end up rewarding certain types of content over others—perhaps established, well-heeled companies over less-well-capitalized startups.

Aggregation, Summarizing and Revenue Sharing

Much criticism has been leveled at those who generate page views, and attract ad dollars, by summarizing the content created by others—as well as those who outright copy such content. (See Chapter 34, Copyright and Intellectual Property.) Less discussed is the role of Internet Service Providers. As noted in Chapter 20, News Consumption, Americans spend more money than in the past for access to content. In the case of cable, the holders-of-the-pipes share some of the revenue with content creators. There is debate about how exactly the revenue should be divided, but there is agreement that it should be shared. ISPs have a different relationship with content providers: they do not share revenues the websites people visit. There have been a few proposals to change this paradigm, though none have gained traction. The Writers Guild of Canada has proposed that ISPs pay content creators. Stephen Nevas of the Yale Law School Information Society Project argues, "Internet Service Providers (ISPs) sell access to free content but pay nothing for the privilege."[25] He suggests that every service provider and cell phone provider should collect content license fees, which would be passed on to a new division of the Copyright Office.[26]

However, even if there were agreement that ISPs should pay—and there is not—there is no agreement on how such funds would or could be distributed.

Licensing and Regulation of Mobile Services

Over the past two decades, mobile service has developed from a niche voice service offering to a mass-market voice and data service. During this time, the Commission's regulatory framework for mobile service generally has focused on fostering competition and establishing key public interest obligations unrelated to content regulation.

In recent years, the Commission has emphasized policies to expand deployment of mobile services, including broadband. The continued development of these policies likely will have a positive impact on the delivery of local information to communities, given that mobile service has become a major delivery mechanism for news, particularly among population groups that are less likely to have regular access to a PC.

In 1981, the FCC adopted a framework for licensing spectrum for mobile services in the cellular band—assigning one license in each market to the incumbent wireline company, and awarding another license in the market to a non-wireline applicant based on an FCC comparative review process .[27] Since 1993, after Congress authorized the FCC to award licenses through auctions, licenses for most commercial mobile services (including cellular, PCS, SMR, and paging) have been issued by auction.[28]

The Communications Act provides a regulatory framework for mobile services, requiring that commercial mobile radio service (CMRS) providers be regulated as common carriers under Title II of the Act,[29] and otherwise providing the Commission the authority to impose public interest obligations on mobile service providers that are spectrum licensees.[30] Under this framework, the FCC has adopted a variety of public interest obligations, including enhanced 911 location capability,[31] local number portability,[32] hearing aid compatibility,[33] roaming,[34] surveillance assistance for law enforcement,[35] and build-out of networks.[36] Because the Commission has regulated CMRS providers as common carriers, it generally has not imposed content-related public interest obligations on them, and policymakers have not viewed CMRS providers as having the same "trustee" obligations as broadcasters.[37]

Broadcasters have claimed that the inclusion of FM chips increased access to local information, particularly during emergencies. Mobile service providers argue, on the other hand, that an FM chip mandate would be costly to implement and is unnecessary.

The wireless industry has undertaken certain voluntary programs to provide particular types of information targeted to specific groups, often through partnerships with public interest organizations. For example, CTIA joined forces with parenting groups to develop text4baby, which provides free informational updates and reminders to pregnant women and new moms.[38] As yet, however, CTIA has not proposed partnerships geared toward providing civically important information on a local level.

The FCC has taken a number of steps to encourage the deployment of mobile service, including broadband, such as: providing "rules of the road" for an open Internet;[39] establishing requirements to promote the availability of data roaming arrangements;[40] removing obstacles to deployment of infrastructure for mobile networks;[41] modernizing the Universal Service Fund;[42] and other steps to make mobile service more available.[43] In addition, the Commission has recently taken steps to expand access to communications service, including mobile service, across the nation,[44] for low-income consumers,[45] Native Americans,[46] and persons with disabilities.[47]

As part of a strategy to make significant additional spectrum available for mobile broadband, the 2010 *National Broadband Plan* proposed a system of "incentive auctions" to encourage some broadcasters to put their spectrum back into auction in exchange for a piece of the proceeds.[48] The goal is to reallocate 120 MHz of spectrum from broadcast to wireless broadband usage, and the FCC has initiated some preliminary steps toward this goal, in the event that Congress provides the FCC with authority for incentive auctions.[49]

FM Chips on Mobile Phones

In addition to mobile Internet, applications, and messaging, discussed in Part One, another source of news and information for mobile subscribers is the FM chip—a small receiver placed in the phone that allows the headset to act as an antenna, so the phone can function as an FM radio.

This has been a topic of great controversy. Broadcasters have argued that American consumers have less access to the service than those in Europe and Asia.[50] An Insight Research Corporation report for NAB estimated that the penetration of broadcast radio capability in mobile phones was just 9.5 percent in the U.S. in 2009.[51] On the other hand, wireless companies and device manufacturers argue that numerous phones offer the service, and that the government should not get involved in what is a private marketplace issue.[52]

Putting aside the debate as to whether it is appropriate for government to force device manufacturers to include FM chips as opposed to the parties working out commercial deals, we recognize that FM chips in mobile devices can provide a number of benefits to consumers. For example, they could enhance the value of the Public Localized Alerting Network (PLAN) during disasters; after getting a short text about the emergency, they could tune into radio news broadcast for more information (particularly if congestion on mobile networks or power outages make it hard to get on the Internet). Moreover, given that both radio and mobile phone adoption are disproportionately high among minority populations, the FM chip could be a particularly effective way to broaden information dissemination in their communities. Further, public radio stations have argued that FM chips would make it possible for listeners to access their content on their phones without having to go through the Internet (which requires public radio stations to pay streaming costs).[53]

30 Ownership

HISTORICALLY, THE FCC'S CONCERN regarding media ownership has focused largely on how ownership affects the diversity of voices, localism, and competition—including the availability of news and information on a local level.

We will turn to those issues shortly but it is worth noting two other factors highlighted in Part One:

> the profit expectations that come with being part of a large, publicly-traded media corporation, and

> the debt levels incurred as a result of consolidation.

It is possible, in other words, that a transaction might meet the legal requirements related to diversity, localism, and competition—yet still not be in the best interest of local communities. As we saw in both the newspaper and local TV sections of Part One, some traditional media businesses have remained viable, and even relatively healthy, but pursued short-term cost-cutting strategies in order to keep profit levels high. The drive to maximize profit is so integral to the nature of the modern publicly-traded company, and policies that attempt to change that dynamic are destined to fail. That's why this report looks at not only at traditional ownership rules, but also at the potential of non-profits and "hybrid" corporate entities to better address the information needs of communities in those cases when commercial media is not doing so. (See Chapters 6–15.)

Now we turn to the more traditional focus of the FCC: broadcast ownership rules.

FCC Ownership Rules

Congress requires the FCC to review its media ownership rules every four years.[1] These rules seek to promote localism, diversity, and competition in broadcasting by limiting the number of broadcast stations a single party can own, both in a local market and nationally. "[T]he Commission has long acted on the theory that diversification of mass media ownership serves the public interest by promoting diversity of program and service viewpoints, as well as by preventing undue concentration of economic power."[2] The core goals of the ownership rules are:

Localism: Historically, the FCC has tried through regulation to ensure that broadcasters are responsive to "localism," or, the needs and interests of their local communities.[3] To measure localism in broadcasting markets, the Commission primarily had considered two measures: "the selection of programming responsive to local needs and interests, and local news quantity and quality."[4] *Diversity*: The FCC focuses in particular on viewpoint diversity (the availability of media content reflecting a variety of perspectives) and outlet diversity (the presence of independently owned outlets in a local broadcasting market).[5] To gauge viewpoint diversity, the Commission looks at news and public affairs programming: "Not only is news programming more easily measured than other types of content containing viewpoints, but it relates most directly to the Commission's core policy objective of facilitating robust democratic discourse in the media."[6] The idea behind outlet diversity is that because programming decisions are left to owners' discretion, a diversity of ownership will result in more diverse programming.[7] Critics, however, argue that consolidation better positions firms to achieve economies of scale and scope, which means that they are more likely to have the financial resources to provide more robust programming, not necessarily catering to the masses. A company that owns several stations might, for instance, have incentive to expand its reach by targeting each entity toward a different, narrower audience.

Competition: It has long been a basic tenet of communications policy that robust competition allows for more voices and a healthier media system.

The current ownership rules are:

Local Television Ownership Limit: An entity may own two television stations in the same designated market area (DMA) only if: (1) the Grade-B contours of the stations (as determined by 47 C.F.R. section 73.684) do not overlap, or (2) at least one of the stations in the combination is not ranked among the top four stations in terms of audience share, and at least eight independently owned-and-operated commercial or noncommercial full-power broadcast television stations would remain in the DMA after the combination.[8]

Local Radio Ownership Rule: A person or entity may own, operate, or control: (1) up to eight commercial radio stations, not more than five of which are in the same service (e.g., AM or FM) in a radio market with 45 or more radio stations; (2) up to seven commercial radio stations, not more than four of which are in the same service, in a radio market with between 30 and 44 (inclusive) radio stations; (3) up to six commercial radio stations, not more than four of which are in the same service, in a radio market with between 15 and 29 (inclusive) radio stations; and (4) up to five commercial radio stations, not more than three of which are in the same service, in a radio market with 14 or fewer radio stations, except that an entity may not own, operate, or control more than 50 percent of the stations in such a market unless the combination of stations comprises not more than one AM and one FM station.[9]

Newspaper/Broadcast Cross-Ownership Rule: The newspaper/broadcast cross-ownership rule generally prohibits common ownership of a full-service broadcast station and a daily newspaper if their coverage areas overlap.[10] But it allows for waivers of the rule if a combination is viewed as advancing the public interest.[11] The rule provides for a presumption in favor of a waiver where (i) a daily newspaper seeks to combine with a radio station in a top 20 DMA, or (ii) a daily newspaper seeks to combine with a television station in a top 20 DMA; and (a) the television station is not ranked among the top four stations in the DMA; and (b) at least eight independently owned and operating "major media voices" would remain in the DMA after the combination.[12]

For markets below the top 20 DMAs, the Commission presumes that a proposed combination would not be in the public interest. The Commission requires an applicant attempting to overcome a "negative presumption" to demonstrate that the merged entity will increase the diversity of independent news outlets and competition among independent news sources in the relevant market.[13] The Commission will reverse the negative presumption in two limited circumstances: (i) when the proposed combination involves a failed/failing station or newspaper, or (ii) when the proposed combination is with a broadcast station that was not offering local newscasts prior to the combination, and the station will initiate at least seven hours per week of local news after the combination.[14]

No matter which presumption applies, the Commission's analysis will consider four factors: "(1) the extent to which cross-ownership will serve to increase the amount of local news disseminated through the affected media outlets in the combination; (2) whether each affected media outlet in the combination will exercise its own independent news judgment; (3) the level of concentration in the DMA; and (4) the financial condition of the newspaper or broadcast station, and if the newspaper or broadcast station is in financial distress, the owner's commitment to invest significantly in newsroom operations."[15]

Radio/Television Cross-Ownership Rule: The radio/television cross-ownership rule allows a party to own up to two television stations (to the extent permitted under the local television ownership rule) and up to six radio stations (to the extent permitted under the local radio ownership rule) in a market where at least 20 independently owned media voices would remain post-merger.[16] In markets where parties may own a combination of two television stations and six radio stations, the rule allows a party alternatively to own one television station and seven radio stations. A party may own up to two television stations (where permitted under the current local television ownership rule) and up to four radio stations (where permitted under the local radio ownership rule) in markets where, post-merger, at least 10 independently owned media voices would remain. The rule allows a combination of two television stations (where permitted under the local television ownership rule) and one radio station regardless of the number of voices remaining in the market.[17] For purposes of this rule, media voices include television stations, radio stations, newspapers, and cable systems.[18]

The Dual Network Rule: The Commission's dual network rule permits common ownership of multiple broadcast networks, but prohibits a merger between or among the "top four" networks (that is, ABC, CBS, Fox, and NBC)."[19]

National TV Ownership: In 2004, Congress set the national television multiple ownership cap at 39 percent of television households.[20]

Attribution Rules: The broadcast attribution rules define which financial or other interests of a licensee must be counted in applying the broadcast ownership rules, and "seek to identify those interests in or relationships to licensees that confer on their holders a degree of influence or control such that the holders have a realistic potential to affect the programming decisions of licensees or other core operating functions."[21] At the same time, the attribution rules "permit arrangements in which a particular ownership or positional interest involves minimal risk of influence, in order to avoid unduly restricting the means by which investment capital may be made available to the broadcast industry."[22]

2010 Quadrennial Review

The Commission is in the midst of its 2010 "Quadrennial Review" of ownership rules.[23] A Notice of Proposed Rulemaking is expected within a few months of the release of this report, so we are reluctant to offer our own detailed analysis of ownership issues. We note, too, that the ownership review must consider a different set of factors than this report does. We therefore restrict ourselves to a few general observations:

The nature of the "diversity" calculus may have changed: In an earlier day, it was reasonable to assume that a diversity of media outlets indicated generalized media health. What we have seen in Part One of this report is that a media market can simultaneously have a diversity of news and information outlets and yet a scarcity of local reporting.

More is not necessarily better: Another assumption of past regulatory efforts is that more choices leads to greater benefits for consumers. We believe that the changes in the media market may sometimes call this assumption into question. For instance, it might be better to have nine TV stations in a market than 10, if consolidation leads the remaining stations to be economically healthier and therefore more able to invest in local news, information, and journalism.

Resources matter: As we have seen throughout the report, the new media system excels at creating more and cheaper ways of distributing content. This creates new challenges for regulators. In the past, the safest way to assess the health of a media market was through quantitative assessments of news output. Yet, these days, an increase in output—more stories, more shows, more channels, more websites—does not necessarily mean an increase in resources dedicated to such coverage. In some cases, the resources actually get spread thinner and quality declines. Given that it is extremely difficult—constitutionally and practically—to assess quality, regulators may need to consider looking at different measures. This is tricky business, too, as the station that devotes the most money to news might be the one that is the most committed—or it might just be inefficient in how it spends its money.

> The former tax certificate policy was generally lauded as an effective and nonintrusive tool to encourage media ownership diversity

Just because a merger could *lead to more journalism does not mean it will*: The FCC's ownership proceeding record includes comments from those who argue that relaxing the cross-ownership or other ownership rules would allow media companies more flexibility to create multiplatform business models that might help sustain local journalism in the long run. However, others argue that excessive deregulation in the 1980s and 1990s led to a reduction in news on the radio side, and that previous mergers have led to media layoffs, not staff increases. It is possible that both of these assessments can be true: savings and efficiencies produced by mergers could well lead the merged company to invest "significantly in newsroom operations"—or the money saved could flow to the bottom line, and lead to a *decline* in journalistic resources.

Though debates about ownership tend to focus on the ownership caps, these are not necessarily the only ways to influence ownership patterns. For instance, Ava Seave, an adjunct professor at the Columbia Business and Journalism schools and co-author of *Curse of the Mogul: What's Wrong with the World's Leading Media Companies*, has proposed what she calls a "flip tax"—a fee levied against media consolidations. Arguing that few media consolidations have worked out well for shareholders, Seave suggests that a merger tax would force the companies involved to internalize the true cost of the transaction and help to subsidize the media ecosystem in the communities or states where they are located, helping to insure that the net effect is positive. To explore the volume of deals and the amount of money involved, she looked at deals of more than $1 million from 2005 through the first quarter of 2010 and found an average of about $1 billion per year that closed. If those deals had been taxed at between .25 percent and .5 percent, the revenue raised would have been between $250 million and $500 million per year, nationwide.[24] A variant of Seave's idea would be to allow for more mergers on the condition that payments would be made to strengthen independent media in the community, perhaps by funding local nonprofit media.

Ownership Diversity

From the 1960s to the 1990s, the Commission sought to diversify broadcast ownership through a variety of policies, including: (1) adopting a tax certificate program that allowed broadcast and cable companies to defer capital gains on the sale of media and cable properties to minority-owned businesses;[25] and (2) allowing for the "distress sale" of a broadcast station, thereby permitting broadcasters to sell properties to minority owners at reduced rates as an alternative to losing the broadcast assets due to non-renewal or revocation of their licenses.[26] Today, however, as a result of the Supreme Court's decision in *Adarand Constructors, Inc. v. Pena*, which struck down race-based initiatives aimed at fostering ownership diversity, there are no race-specific policies in effect.[27] The Commission suspended the minority distress sale policy, and, in 1995, Congress repealed the tax certificate policy.[28] However, the Commission has continued to adopt policies to expand ownership opportunities for small businesses, including those owned by minorities and women. Some major areas of policy related to diversity include:

Data Collection: The Commission requires all commercial full-power AM, FM, TV, low-power TV, and Class-A broadcasters to submit ownership data, including information on the race, ethnicity, and gender of broadcast station owners. The data on race, ethnicity, and gender must be submitted every two years. The FCC revised the ownership form in 2009 to improve the quality and usability of this data and to collect minority and gender data from previously exempted broadcasters.[29] It made these changes in response to concerns expressed by researchers and the Government Accountability Office about inconsistencies in the data and difficulties users had experienced in aggregating the data.[30] Critics asserted that these shortcomings made it difficult for the Commission to promote the ownership of broadcast stations by women and minorities.[31] Broadcasters claimed that some aspects of the revised form would be burdensome and that one change in particular raised privacy concerns. The Commission delayed the initial filing deadline for the revised form and devised a temporary measure to address broadcasters' privacy concerns.[32] Broadcasters began using the new form in 2010 and reported ownership data as of November 1, 2009. The next filing deadline is November 1, 2011. In February, 2011, the Commission posted to its website the data broadcasters submitted in 2010 using the new form.[33]

Bidding credits: Since 1994, when new TV and radio licenses have become available, they have been awarded through auction. In 1997,[34] Congress added provisions designed to encourage participation by rural telephone companies, small, women- and minority-owned businesses:[35] Now, if an eligible party wins, it can reduce its bid amount. Also, companies that own no mass media facilities get a 35 percent discount; and companies that own no more than three mass media broadcast facilities get a 25 percent break.[36]

Tax Certificates: The Commission voted unanimously to reinstate the "tax certificate program."[37] Created in 1978, the "tax certificate" program attempted to encourage sale of TV and radio stations to minorities by allowing broadcast and cable companies to defer capital gains on the sale of media and cable properties to minority-owned businesses.[38] The entity receiving the tax certificate could roll over or defer the capital gains from the sale of the property, if the gain was reinvested in a similar broadcast or telecommunications property within two years of the sale. Prospective buyers could use the policy to attract equity investors. Subsequently, the Commission enhanced the tax certificate program, expanding it to cover sales of cable systems to minorities.[39] The Commission adopted further tax deferral measures to encourage the participation of small, minority-owned, and women-owned enterprises in the auction of broadband PCS and other spectrum-based services.[40] But this was repealed by Congress in 1995 to generate revenue for the Treasury.

The tax certificate policy was generally lauded as an effective and nonintrusive tool to encourage media ownership diversity. Many industry stakeholders consider it to have been the "single most effective program in lowering market entry barriers" to spur an increase in minority ownership of broadcast radio, television and other media properties.[41] From 1978 to its repeal in 1995, the tax certificate policy is credited with making possible minority acquisition of 288 radio stations, 43 television stations, and 31 cable systems.[42] As Commissioner Robert McDowell noted, "Changes in our ownership rules alone won't achieve much if the intended beneficiaries [small enterprises and new entrants, including minorities and women] can't obtain the financing they need to make their aspirations a reality."[43]

31 Nonprofit Media

THOUGH PUBLIC RADIO AND TV—NPR and PBS member stations—are perhaps the most recognized noncommercial outlets, the nonprofit media sector is far larger and more varied. It includes nonprofit websites, PEG channels, lower power FM stations, state public affairs networks, journalism schools, public radio networks unaffiliated with NPR, foundations, mobile news apps, and others. The public policy issues affecting nonprofit media organizations vary as well.

PUBLIC BROADCASTING

FCC Rules Governing Public TV and Radio

Since the 1930s, Congressional and FCC policies have mandated that spectrum be set aside for noncommercial use. The FCC first began reserving spectrum for noncommercial educational (NCE) radio broadcast use in 1938, selecting channels in the 41–42 MHz band[1] before moving the reserved band to 88–92 MHz in 1945.[2] In radio, the FCC continues to reserve the lowest 20 channels on the FM broadcast band for NCE use, as well as channel 200 (87.9 MHz) for class-D NCE stations.[3] The FCC has never reserved any AM channels for noncommercial use. In 1952, the FCC ruled that when more than three VHF channels were assigned to a city, one would be reserved for educational institutions. A total of 242 channels were reserved. By 2001, these had grown to more than 370 public TV stations.[4] The current estimated value of NCE television spectrum ranges from $1.96 billion to $26.8 billion.[5] There are currently 3,311 NCE FM stations in the U.S., approximately 23 percent of the total number of radio stations.[6] The FCC Media Bureau estimates that about 500 more NCE stations will be created over the next three years as a result of applications granted during the 2007 and 2010 filing windows. There are 391 noncommercial TV licensees.[7]

Noncommercial stations are generally subject to ordinary FCC broadcasting rules, with some exceptions.[8] The FCC requires certain governance structures of some noncommercial broadcasters. Noncommercial TV stations *not* affiliated with universities or governments are required to submit "evidence that officers, directors and members of the governing board are broadly representative of the educational, cultural, and civic groups in the community."[9] To meet this standard, a noncommercial TV station or applicant must show that a majority (over 50 percent) of its governing board is broadly representative of the community.[10]

Although this does not apply to stations run by universities or governments, some have suggested that it should.

Noncommercial television stations are issued licenses for an eight-year period. Eleven noncommercial TV renewal applications filed during the last renewal cycle remain pending due to the filing of an objection or because of indecency or EEO holds. In the FCC's history, we could find only two instances in which the Commission has denied the license renewal applications of public broadcasting licensees.[11]

Noncommercial television stations have the same FCC disclosure requirements as commercial. They compile issues/programs lists that ostensibly show how they have served the community.

FCC Programming Requirements

Noncommercial licenses are available only for "educational" purposes. TV stations must show that the licenses will be used "primarily to serve the educational needs of the community; for the advancement of educational programs; and to furnish a nonprofit and noncommercial television broadcast service."[12] This includes transmitting "educational, cultural, and entertainment programs."[13] FM radio licensees must be nonprofit educational organizations that advance "an educational program."[14]

In practice, though, the FCC has allowed the stations to determine for themselves whether they have produced programming of this sort. The Commission has intentionally left "educational programming" undefined, describing public broadcasting instead in terms of what it is not: Public stations "are not operated by profit-seeking organizations nor supported by on-the-air advertising," with their "positive dimensions" determined by "social, political, and economic forces outside the Commission."[15]

Because noncommercial stations have an educational mission, whose contours have been left unspecified, the FCC has never adopted public interest programming rules for noncommercial stations, such as requiring that a certain amount of airtime be dedicated to local news.

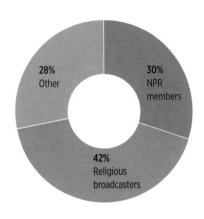

NONCOMMERCIAL FM RADIO LICENSES (2010)

28% Other

30% NPR members

42% Religious broadcasters

Source: BIA and NI

Religious Broadcasters

Forty-two percent of noncommercial educational radio stations broadcast in a primarily religious format. According to FCC regulations, stations may broadcast in this format, and a noncommercial license may be held by a religious entity, so long as the station is to "be used primarily to serve the educational needs of the community."[16] Here, too, section 326 of the Communications Act of 1934, as amended, precludes the Commission from favoring, censoring, or determining program choices, except for some narrow exceptions. The FCC has traditionally let the licensee determine whether it is serving educational purposes.[17]

FCC Rules and Public Broadcasting Business Models

Various rules and laws (including several by the FCC and CPB) restrict the ability of noncommercial broadcasters to generate revenue. In general, public broadcasters have accepted the restrictions, fearing that using commercial revenue-generation techniques would alienate donors and undercut the arguments for government or foundation funding.

Underwriting

There has always been tension between giving noncommercial TV and radio stations flexibility to raise revenue and preserving their character as "noncommercial" entities (i.e., operating on a not-for-profit basis and without commercials). Section 399(b) of the Communications Act prohibits the *broadcast* of advertisements on noncommercial stations.[18]

In 1984, the FCC granted stations more flexibility by adopting a policy of "enhanced underwriting,"[19] which permitted noncommercial stations to broadcast donor and underwriter acknowledgements from for-profit entities. These acknowledgments can include logograms and slogans that identify, but do not promote, sponsoring businesses. They may include business location information, value-neutral descriptions of a product line or service, and brand and trade names along with product or service listings.[20] That is why some underwriting messages resemble ads. Subjects that cannot be mentioned in underwriting announcements include price information, such as discounts, rebates, and interest rates; calls to action; inducements to buy, sell, rent, or lease; and any language that states or implies favorable comparisons to other like businesses or competitors.[21]

The underwriting policy has some gray areas. Sometimes it is difficult to distinguish between language and images that are descriptive and those that are promotional. Having too many shots of a product, or flashing or blinking features, has been considered promotional, although there are no quantitative boundaries defining what constitutes one image too many.[22] Describing a phone company's "quick connection and clear sound" has been prohibited on the grounds that it implies a comparative advantage over the company's competitors.[23] The FCC usually defers to broadcasters,[24] but in worrying about stepping over the line, licensees struggle to determine whether donor acknowledgments are descriptive, but not "comparative or qualitative,"[25] and whether slogans identify, but do not promote.[26] The FCC has said that "lengthy" or "verbose" announcements are more likely to be deemed promotional, but it has not said how many words or seconds constitute verbosity.[27]

In written comments filed with the FCC, most public broadcasters did not advocate for a significant loosening of the standards. Although they would welcome the ability to raise more revenue, public broadcasters fear that if their programming ends up seeming too commercial, they will lose their rationale for public and member funding. This concern, however, is not necessarily shared by the entire noncommercial broadcasting community. National Religious Broadcasters (NRB) has a different view: "NRB urges the FCC to both clarify, and to relax, the current rules that permit noncommercial broadcasters to give very short sponsorship mentions on the air as long as they 'identify' the sponsor but do not 'promote' the sponsor. The line-drawing here is confusing and inconsistent."[28] NRB argues that even if secular public broadcasters do not want this flexibility, religious broadcasters should have extra leeway, since they do not get federal money through CPB.[29]

Though the FCC publishes on its website enforcement actions related to underwriting, several parties have asked for clarifications on what is or is not allowed.[30] For instance, NPR wrote in 2010: "NPR and its public broadcasting colleagues work hard and carefully to comply with the FCC's rules, but uncertainties about particular language issues have made the task substantially more difficult, especially given the changing nature and expectations of underwriters."[31] National public radio identifies the following as "issues that arise routinely and that are not addressed by the FCC's formal guidance":

"1. Aspirational language, such as language describing an automobile tire as 'designed to extend mileage' or 'helping reduce energy loss.'

"2. References to technical specifications, such as language describing an air filter as '99.9 percent efficient and 100 percent covered in textured grip control.'

"3. References to third party standards, such as 'ENERGY STAR rated' appliances.

"4. Language referring to a funder's website for product specific information, such as 'where visitors can learn more about the importance of inspecting shocks and struts at fifty thousand miles.'

"5. Language describing an episode of a television program as 'all-new' or 'a sneak preview.'

"6. A reference to an award, such as an 'Academy Award' winning movie or actor.

"7. References to product ingredients, such as '130 calories or less per serving.'

"8. References to a funder's charitable endeavors, such as 'investing $100 million towards education each year.'

"9. Quantitative references to a funder's specific experience, such as 'thirty-five years of clinical experience.'

"10. References to arguably promotional website addresses, such as 'Trust the Check dot com.'"[32]

There has been some confusion as to whether underwriting rules apply to the websites created by public TV or radio stations. To be clear: the FCC rules do *not* restrict advertising or sponsorships on the websites in any way.[33] Guidelines on types of permissible sponsorship apply only on air. Of course, stations may decide to avoid ads on their websites, and the CPB is creating incentives for stations to apply broadcast underwriting standards to online advertising.[34]

Merchandising

Public broadcasters are allowed to generate ancillary revenue by selling merchandize related to their shows. The licensing of children's characters has been the most lucrative. But there are restrictions. Though the stations can allow for the creation of program-related merchandise, they cannot market any of it on air. And many broadcasters choose not to explore these options for fear of a backlash along the lines of what happened in the early 1990s when PBS forfeited the license fees from Barney, because it was under political pressure to remain noncommercial.[35]

Again, under FCC rules, while stations might be prohibited from marketing merchandise on air, they are allowed to do so on their websites.

There has been some confusion as to whether the FCC's underwriting restrictions apply to the websites created by public TV or radio stations. To be clear: they do not.

Retransmission Fees

Public TV stations have must-carry rights on cable TV, but, unlike commercial broadcasters, they are unable to get paid for their signals through "retransmission consent" fees.[36] Public TV leaders have been reluctant to ask for this authority, lest it undercut their status as noncommercial broadcast entities. It is not known how much additional revenue this could generate for local public TV stations.

Fundraising for Third Parties

Noncommercial broadcasters are generally prohibited from engaging in fundraising activities for other nonprofits.[37] This rule is intended to prevent the reserved noncommercial spectrum from being used as a barker platform for fundraising, taking time away from the provision of noncommercial service. The FCC has granted waivers in special circumstances, such as to permit on-air fundraising for Haiti relief and, to help restore a Washington, D.C. arts facility destroyed by fire.[38] NRB noted that WMIT-FM, in Asheville, North Carolina, used such a waiver to raise $272,250 in an on-air fundraiser in February 2010 for the Haiti relief project of nonprofit Samaritan's Purse—an amount projected to help "1,815 Haitian families with shelter, clean water, and medical supplies."[39]

The National Religious Broadcasters has proposed that noncommercial stations should be permitted to use up to one percent of their airtime to raise money for nonprofits. NRB's executive director suggests that among those that might benefit are "local rescue missions in their listening areas" and international relief organizations.[40] NRB argues that these fundraising-based shows would help raise awareness about important local and international issues such as hunger and global poverty. It also appears that the current waiver-based system puts the FCC in the position of deciding which human tragedy is most worthy of fundraising. It is not clear, for instance, why restoring an arts facility would be permissible but addressing persistent homeless in a community would not be.

Many secular public broadcasting officials do not want to have this flexibility because it would put them in the awkward position of deciding which worthy cause to support and which to reject. But at least one secular noncommercial broadcaster also endorses relaxation of the third-party fundraising rule. Joseph Bruns, a longtime public TV executive and currently COO of WETA in Washington, argues (in comments reflecting his personal views, not necessarily those of WETA) that relaxation would allow for more creative partnerships and enable broadcasters to highlight worthy charities in the community, thereby deepening the station's con-

> The National Religious Broadcasters has asked for the ability to do fundraising for "local rescue missions in their listening areas" and international relief organizations.

nection to the community.[41] Bruns notes that since they rely on donors, many public TV stations have the necessary infrastructure, including a "television production facility, and a backroom fundraising operation that can handle a large volume of call-in donations." The ability to participate in third-party fundraising, he argues, would allow noncommercial stations to expand their "community service mission" by "allowing us to work with social service nonprofit organizations and to lend to them our capability to allow them to extend their own community awareness and fundraising appeal." What Bruns imagines is "a kind of telethon in which we would bring in local celebrities, politicians, sports figures, music groups, and the like. We would allow the organizations an opportunity to do a presentation of what they do and why they are worthy of support."[42] A local public broadcasting station could partner with a nonprofit news web start-up in developing and distributing content. The station would gain access to additional local content, and the nonprofit might in turn benefit from increased distribution as well as further fundraising opportunities.

Digital Stations

Noncommercial television stations are entitled to carriage, through must-carry regulations, on local cable systems. Although public television stations are not legally entitled to carriage of their digital multicast signals, a private agreement between the National Cable Television Association and the Association of Public Television Stations in 2005 provides for cable carriage of up to four multicast programming streams from each public television station for a 10-year period.[43] All noncommercial television stations are required to use their digital capacity "primarily for a non-commercial, nonprofit, educational broadcast service,"[44] but they may also use some of it for commercial purposes, to generate income for the overall enterprise. In a controversial 2001 *Report and Order*, the Commission stated that noncommercial stations could accept traditional advertising on capacity that they are not using for broadcasting, even though they cannot do it on their primary channel.[45] If they do so, the noncommercial stations, like commercial licensees, must also pay the FCC a fee amounting to 5 percent of gross revenues generated.[46] In 2010, 88 full-power public TV stations reported revenues of $435,916.50 from ancillary and supplementary services and paid the FCC $21,795.83 in fees.[47]

The Corporation for Public Broadcasting

Although most public TV and radio funding comes from private sources, the money from the federal government is often quite important. It can provide seed funding for projects, which then get additional support from other sources such as universities, foundations, local governments, and viewers.[48] It also covers the mundane overhead ("keeping the lights on") that donors rarely want to support and that make station operations sustainable. This is particularly true in smaller markets where it is often difficult to attract sufficient membership dollars and other private donations.

The Corporation for Public Broadcasting (CPB) is the largest source of federal funding for public broadcasting. Its federal appropriations for 2009 were approximately $400 million and $420 million for 2010.[49] Public media advocates argue that the federal financial commitment to public broadcasting is insufficient. It is certainly far lower per-capita than that of many other western countries. U.S. taxpayers give about $1.35 each to public broadcasting per year, compared with $24.88 in Canada, $58.86 in Japan, $80.36 in the United Kingdom, and $101 in Denmark, based on appropriations (for the U.S.) and license fees (for the other countries) for 2007.[50]

Various rules and laws restrict the ability of noncommercial broadcasters to generate income. In general, public broadcasters have accepted the restrictions, fearing that using commercial revenue-generation techniques would alienate donors and undercut the arguments for government or foundation funding.

Perhaps even more important in the continually changing media environment, CPB is limited in how it can distribute funds allocated to it. By law, it must direct most of its annual budget (89 percent) to TV and radio stations, as well as to programming for those stations.[51] Seventy-five percent of its funds must go to television,[52] 25 percent to radio.[53] Most of those funds go to station support,[54] with only 25 percent of TV funding and 23 percent of radio funding going to programming.[55] In recent years, CPB has been receiving an additional appropriation earmarked for assisting TV (and to a lesser extent radio) stations with their digital transitions.[56] The mechanism CPB uses to direct funds to public television and radio stations is the Community Service Grant (CSG).[57] From 2009 to 2010, over 550 public TV and public radio stations received CSG disbursements, with approximately $212.2 million going to TV, and approximately $83.1 million to radio.[58] Stations must qualify for CSGs by meeting a set of eligibility requirements. For one thing, a substantial majority of the station's daily total programming hours must be devoted to "CPB-qualified programming, which is defined as general audience programming that serves demonstrated community needs of an educational, informational, and cultural nature."[59] This excludes programs that further political or religious philosophies, as well as those that are designed mainly for in-school audiences.[60]

In 2008, CSG funding constituted about 15.7 percent of the average public television station's budget and 10.1 percent of the average public radio station's budget.[61] Small and rural stations rely on CSG funding much more heavily than large urban stations do.[62] The amounts granted are based mainly on the size of the service area, but CPB also factors in considerations such as the amount of non-federal support the station receives, whether the station is the sole broadcaster in its area, whether it is the first CPB-funded licensee in its area, whether the station serves minority communities, and whether it is in a rural area. Because so much CPB funding is tied to statutory and CPB-created formulae, it is difficult for CPB to reward excellence or adapt to changing circumstances. Stations almost never lose CSG funding.[63]

In 2010, CPB conducted a review of CSG eligibility criteria. A panel of public media leaders recommended creating more financial incentives for stations to merge or collaborate and requiring stations to disclose information about local programming. But they declined to recommend that CPB require the production of local programming or other community service performance metrics as a condition of funding.[64]

Some want CPB to go farther. Bill Kling, president and CEO of American Public Media (APM), has long been an advocate for stricter CSG requirements that, for instance, mandate much more local content, larger full-time station staffs, and a governance structure for stations that makes them accountable to the community rather than to a university or other entity with diffuse interests.[65] Free Press has similarly argued that CSG funds should be tied to tougher performance standards for local stations.[66] The advocacy group Association of Independents in Radio (AIR) has urged the FCC to adopt local content rules for noncommercial stations that would prod stations to seek new voices, including independent producers.[67] CPB funding for independent programming now comes mostly through small programs, such as the Radio Program Fund, which has been responsible for funding Radio Bilingüe's national program service, public radio's principal source of Latino programming; Koahnik Public Media's Native Voice 1, public radio's principal source of Native American programming; and independent productions such as *StoryCorps* and *This I Believe*.[68]

As noted in chapters 6–12, the nonprofit media sector includes many players other than noncommercial TV and radio stations. In theory, CPB is permitted to fund these independent nonprofits;[69] however, due to statutory funding directives and the paucity of funds to disperse, CPB provides very little funding to them. In the past, adjustments to federal legislation have served to broaden CPB's pool of grantees. For example, in response to TV and film producers' complaints that they were being excluded from the public television schedule, in 1988 Congress made the Independent Television Service (ITVS) a mandatory CPB grantee in order to promote innovative content for underserved audiences.[70] AIR has argued that there should be a similar intervention on behalf of independent radio producers, who are generally not funded by CPB.[71]

Technology and Infrastructure Funding

There is a long tradition of federal funding (from various sources) going to public broadcasting infrastructure, as opposed to programming. For instance, CPB funds infrastructure through the satellite interconnection system, which made early use of satellites to network together programming among public television and radio stations nationwide.[72]

A Public Media Platform is currently under development. Public broadcasting stations and other media entities would contribute content, which could then be sliced, sorted, and redistributed to other public media entities.

What will "infrastructure" mean in the future? Basic infrastructure will no longer be limited to radio towers and satellite dishes, but will involve software, digital platforms, digital delivery systems, and applications. For example, a Public Media Platform is currently under development by NPR, PBS, the Public Radio Exchange (PRX), APM, and Public Radio International, with funding from CPB.[73] The plan is for public broadcasting stations and other media entities to contribute content, which could then be sliced, sorted, and redistributed to other public media entities. The prototype for this platform is the NPR API, which has fostered the sharing of radio and web-based content among public radio stations.

Another example of public media infrastructure not currently or systematically funded by the federal government is the "middle mile" infrastructure that connects public broadcasting entities to anchor institutions and other strategic points of access in local communities.[74] Initiatives such as National Public Lightpath,[75] which brings together members of the education, media, public broadcasting, and government sectors to build broadband networks, have called for increased federal funding to support universal access to broadband content that is in the public interest. The 2010 *National Broadband Plan* recommended that schools, hospitals, and other community institutions, including public broadcasting stations, function as anchor institutions for community access to broadband, especially in Tribal lands and rural areas.[76]

Government has also funded public broadcasting "software," as opposed to physical infrastructure. Between 1994 and 2004, the Technology Opportunities Program (TOP), run by the National Telecommunications and Information Administration (NTIA) within the Commerce Department, gave grants to support new telecommunications and information technologies aimed at providing education, health care, and public information. In the course of those ten years, TOP awarded 610 grants totaling $233.5 million and leveraging $313.7 million in local matching funds.[77] Only a small portion of TOP funds went to public media entities; among the public media grantees was PRX,[78] which curates over 20,000 independently produced noncommercial radio programs, making them available to all stations on an open online platform.[79] Also a CPB grantee, PRX developed what is currently one of public media's top innovations: the app that allows streaming of local radio stations on the iPhone.[80] One of the benefits of CPB, NTIA, and other operations existing within a broader public service media framework is that small investments can be leveraged in ways that connect innovators to each other and to the larger system.

Since the TOP program ended in 2005, and given the constraints on CPB funding, there is currently little federal support for technical innovation either in the existing public broadcasting community or among new entrants to the public service media world. Thus, entities and individuals that, for instance, want to develop noncommercial mobile apps for educational use have no obvious place to go for start-up grants. Foundations have provided some support,[81] but it remains to be seen whether their investments can be leveraged strategically to support widespread and follow-on innovation across communities and across the layers of public media activity, including distribution, applications, and content development.

Fundraising via New Technologies

Smartphone applications have been an area of extraordinary growth for public radio. But there is some controversy over whether all technology companies are doing enough to facilitate charitable transactions.[82]

The Problem of Rising Broadband Costs

As noted in Chapter 6, public broadcasters face a serious new challenge, which threatens to interfere with future innovation. As more people access their video and audio content online, the costs of streaming the material could skyrocket. Commercial broadcasters can often offset those costs through ad deals that pay them more as video plays increase, but given the commitment of public broadcasters to remaining noncommercial, they are left in a peculiar position: the more popular their video and audio streams, the deeper into the cost hole they go.

No current public policy attempts to address this issue.

Structural and Governance Issues

Station Ownership and Governance

In both radio and television, private nonprofit organizations own the bulk of NCE licenses. For television, the proportion is nearly half (approximately 46 percent) of total licenses; in radio, private nonprofits own roughly 62 percent of NCE licenses. A significant minority, however, are owned by governments or universities—a fact that may become more relevant if stations dive more deeply into the creation of local journalism. In TV, about 31 percent of licenses are owned by government (via boards, commissions, and authorities that are either directly or indirectly affiliated with city or states.) Colleges and universities own the remaining 23 percent. The numbers are slightly reversed in radio, with only 7 percent of NCE FM stations owned by entities affiliated with state and local governments and 31 percent owned by colleges and universities.

The composition of licensee types varies by state. For example, in states such as Georgia, Maryland, Alabama, Iowa, Arkansas, and South Dakota, all or nearly all of the NCE TV licenses are owned by state legislatures or government-affiliated entities. Private nonprofit organizations own all NCE TV licenses in Colorado, Connecticut, Hawaii, Massachusetts, Maine, Minnesota, New York, and North Dakota. Universities own nearly all television NCE licenses in Michigan and Utah.[84]

DISTRIBUTION OF TV AND RADIO NONCOMMERCIAL EDUCATIONAL LICENSES (2010)

	NCE TV Licenses	NCE Radio Licenses
Private nonprofit	46%	62%
State/local government	31%	7%
Colleges and universities	23%	31%

Source: FCC data[83]

There seems to be widespread agreement that good governance, including a professional, involved, and accountable board, is important to the productivity of NCE stations.[85] "Good governance is a combination of leadership structures, strong leadership at the top, vision, mission, strategy, a financial model that supports that core mission, and a sense of responsibility, accountability, and transparency to the community of service," says Terry Clifford, president of the Station Resources Group, a nonprofit public media consultancy.[86]

Community advisory boards, which are required for stations licensed to nonprofits, can provide some of this good governance.[87] However, they are in some cases merely ceremonial. APM president and CEO, Bill Kling, says, "In my experience, advisory boards are treated sort of like the old FCC-required ascertainment process. They come together and talk about things they care about relative to programming content and then they leave."[88] He contrasts this to "governing boards" which have the power to hire and fire, "decide how much financial risk they can take, open doors, raise money, approve and contribute to strategy and in even more ways, help move the vision of public media forward."[89]

Kling points to the example of KPCC in Los Angeles, which was licensed to Pasadena City College, and as such was not required to have a community advisory board, nor did it have a governing board that was focused uniquely on station operations. Instead, KPCC was governed by the elected board of trustees of the college, which managed the station along with all other college departments. The station had a budget of about $1 million, an annual deficit of $135,000, and an audience so small that it did not meet CPB audience minimums. The KPCC license was then leased to Southern California Public Radio, a nonprofit with a direct governing board (as well as a community advisory board, but that was not the game changer). It hired a new CEO, revised the program line-up, built a professional news department, added bureaus and offices in downtown L.A. and in Orange County, added a transmitter in the Inland Empire and Palm Springs, and brought in professionals for fundraising, marketing, and underwriting. Today, the station has the largest news audience of any public media company in L.A. (600,000), an aggressive digital media initiative, a balanced budget of $16 million, a new $27 million production center that has already been paid for, and a powerful, diverse board of directors, and it has become a "centering institution" for the diverse communities of Southern California.[90]

If CPB were to require all licensees to have a direct governing board as a condition of funding, public media could in many cases be strengthened.[91] In practice, this would mean that university and state licensees would appoint boards to run their stations. A direct governance requirement could help strengthen the already-strong university-run stations and nudge those university and state licensees that have little interest in managing a public media company to transfer control or operation of those facilities to other entities. Alternatively, they could appoint boards to oversee station performance. Bill Kling has urged that the FCC make the existence of a direct governing board a requirement of license renewal.[92]

Consolidation

As detailed in Chapter 6, there is some duplication of services among public TV stations in certain markets. For many years, CPB has tried to get multi-provider markets (also known as "overlap markets") to consolidate by offering financial incentives, but so far it has not achieved much change. A report on public media by the Aspen Institute recommended that the FCC take action to encourage consolidation: "The FCC should adopt policies that ease station acquisition, mergers and operating agreements."[93] The FCC permits stations to enter into shared services agreements, as long as control of the stations rests with the licensees, as required by the Communications Act.[94] One obstacle to consolidation may be the Commission's localism rules, which require stations to be controlled by a board that is broadly representative of the educational, cultural, and civic groups within the community.[95]

Consolidation could be spurred by the FCC's drive to reclaim unneeded broadcast spectrum for use in advancing wireless broadband connectivity. The FCC has proposed a voluntary incentive auction system in which broadcasters (commercial and noncommercial) could voluntarily put some of their spectrum up for auction and keep some of the proceeds from the sale. There may be some public TV stations that will go for the offer, leading to some elimination of duplication in the public media space.

Diversity

Reaching diverse audiences with diverse content is a core mission of public media. CPB and other public broadcasting organizations have invested in national public radio programs for ethnic media; CPB currently supports at least 75 stations governed by boards that are at least half minority.[96] CPB also supports the National Minority Consortia, which consist of the Center for Asian American Media, National Black Programming Consortium, Native American Public Telecommunications, Native Public Media, Pacific Islanders in Communications, and Latino Public Broadcasting.[97] The Consortia select, fund, develop, produce, and distribute radio and television programming about their ethnic communities, and also award grants for program production, training, exhibition, and outreach activities.[98]

Nevertheless, both public television and public radio have faced sharp criticism for failing to hire staff, and offer programming, reflecting the populations of the communities their stations serve.[99] There have been many calls to broaden their audience, improve programming and diversify management.[100]

The Latino Public Radio Consortium and the Native Public Media have worked to increase the number of noncommercial radio stations for Latino, tribal, and native entities.[101] CPB and PBS are making efforts to prioritize diversity. For instance, PBS recently established a Diversity and Innovation Fund to support programming that is of interest to diverse audiences.[102] CPB is also changing the TV Community Service Grant criteria to require that grantees formally adopt a goal having a diverse management staff and governing board reflective of their service area. They will also need to provide an annual report on hiring goals, guidelines, and employment statistics.[103] It has also proposed instituting diversity hiring training programs, better resourcing for minority stations, and establishing a new incentive for increased diversity in station leadership.

Public media leaders emphasize the need to incentivize stations to produce local content as a way of promoting diversity. The thinking is that if stations are compelled to produce local content, they will inevitably interact more with populations in their communities, and in turn will be more likely to produce programming that is reflective of it.[104] As one report put it: "If you seek to diversify the public media audience, understand that you must leave your office and go outside; you must find them and invite them to participate in telling the story of their lives and their community."[105]

Collaboration

Local commercial TV stations struggle to fill their airtime, while local websites struggle to get exposure for the content they produce. Public radio stations want to do more local reporting but have smaller staffs than local newspapers. Stations are free to collaborate, but neither CPB funding criteria, FCC licensing criteria, nor other national institutional strictures have incentivized them to do so. Indeed, some station managers seem to believe that collaboration will hurt their ability to distinguish themselves in the community and attract funding. In addition, there are often long-standing tensions and rivalries between leaders of nonprofit news and information providers within a community that deter them from collaboration.

The Political Firewall

CPB was intentionally established as a semi-private organization, rather than a government agency, to insulate it from political interference. Decisions about funding are made by a board of directors, composed of nine U.S. citizens "who are eminent in such fields as education, cultural and civic affairs, or the arts, including radio and television" and broadly represent "various regions of the Nation, various professions and occupations, and various kinds of talent and experience appropriate to" CPB's "functions and responsibilities."[106] The directors are appointed by the president with the consent of the Senate for six-year terms, with the proviso that a maximum of five directors may be "of the same political party."[107] There have been several instances in which the heat shield did not work optimally (See Chapter 6, Public Broadcasting), but by and large it has been effective at protecting editors from political pressure.

Free Press, a media advocacy group that believes public media funding should be significantly increased, also argues that the CPB governing structure needs reform. It suggests, for instance, that the chair and vice chair should be of different parties, and the board should be expanded to include leaders from major cultural institutions such as the Smithsonian and Library of Congress.[108]

Although even CPB has an effective firewall at the national level, it is unclear whether a local political firewall would work, particularly if public TV and radio begin to do more local investigative journalism. In one sense, the main form of protection against political interference on a local level is the fact that government funds come from the national government. If a public radio station owned by a community licensee were to criticize the mayor, His Honor would have a hard time finding a way to punish that station financially, since what government funding there is comes from the federal government by formula. Of course, ownership by local or state governmental entities makes it more likely that a local official would have the means to exercise disciplinary power.

For most public broadcasters, problems associated with their local watchdog role are not all that different from those faced by local commercial broadcasters: pressures from advertisers or sponsors. In that sense, the main issue may not be the fact that they receive government dollars, but rather the percentage of their budget that those dollars comprise. Just as a commercial station is better able to withstand pressure from, say, a car dealer that is providing 15 percent of the station's revenue than one who is providing 40 percent, noncommercial stations will be better positioned to preserve their independence if they have diverse revenue sources. Steve Coll, president of the New America Foundation and a Pulitzer Prize-wwinning journalist for the *Washington Post*, endorsed the idea of limiting the percentage of public media revenue that might come from the government, offering this general observation about how undue influence has been curbed in various institutions over the years:

"Firewalls are a daunting challenge, but they can be managed. Newspaper publishers, in their day, insulated their newsrooms from pressure from advertisers, for the most part; university presidents insulate their faculty from pressure from donors, for the most part. When they fail they are often exposed (typically by journalists) and held accountable. Conflicts of interest and the appearance of conflicts are inherent to professional activity in a free-market economy; law, medicine, accounting, and science all struggle with the problem. There is, in any event, no inherent moral difference between corporate advertising dollars and government dollars; both flow from institutions whose power over citizens journalists should be seeking to describe and challenge."[109]

Currently, CPB has political independence rules for its national governance, but at this time, there is no stipulation attached to CPB funding requiring that station personnel must have the leeway to make independent content decisions that are not subject to influence by local sponsors.

New Funding Sources and Strategies

Just how public broadcasting should be funded (e.g., where funds should come from, how funding should be structured, how much should be provided) has been a matter of continual debate. Over the decades, many have argued that alternatives to annual government appropriations would guarantee more sustainable, predictable, and politically insulated funding.

In 1967, the first Carnegie Commission advocated, unsuccessfully, for a permanent endowment, with the interest providing the annual funds for public broadcasting.[110] In early 1971, Congress considered a bill to establish a "public broadcasting trust fund" and to authorize a federal match of two dollars for every dollar of non-federal support over $50 million.[111] But the legislation did not pass. The Ford Foundation, in a report authored by former CBS News President Fred Friendly in 1966, proposed that a nonprofit corporation operate a new satellite system, lease capacity to commercial broadcast networks, and use the proceeds in part to fund educational television. In addition, the satellite would provide free interconnection to noncommercial stations. McGeorge Bundy, who publicly presented the report, characterized the financial support for noncommercial television as "a people's dividend, earned by the American nation from its enormous investment in space."[112]

In 1996, Republican Congressional leaders offered a plan to end all Congressional appropriations to CPB by 2000; it would endow a $1 billion trust fund, using proceeds from the auction of vacant noncommercial TV channels and setting aside $250 million annually from 1998 to 2000 to ensure there would be cash flow until the auction proceeds were available.[113] The bill stalled, however, when broadcasters concluded that Congress would not provide enough money.

The trust fund idea resurfaced as a recommendation in the 2010 *National Broadband Plan*—this time endowed by revenues from a voluntary auction of spectrum licensed to public television.[114] The *Broadband Plan* did not specify how this system would work or where precisely in "public media" the proceeds would go.

The 1998 Advisory Committee on Public Interest Obligations of Digital Television Broadcasters, also known as the "Gore Commission," considered a different approach to using spectrum to fund public media. Instead of imposing spectrum fees on commercial broadcasters or garnering funds from spectrum sales, the Gore Commission considered a "pay-or-play" proposal that would allow commercial broadcasters to buy their way out of public interest programming requirements on the digital channels, with the proceeds going to support public broadcasting in their markets.[115] The proposal was met with strong opposition by individual members of the Committee, however, who argued that it would damage the public trusteeship ethos of broadcasting and be administratively difficult to establish.[116]

In an October 2010 cover story for the *Columbia Journalism Review*, Steve Coll recommended that the FCC raise funds from a combination of spectrum auction proceeds and ongoing fees from holders of public spectrum.[117] In a more recent piece, Coll wrote, "Our public media system has achieved this extraordinary result despite being starved for public funds, in comparison to other industrialized countries."[118] He recommended a variety of reforms to make CPB more accountable, open to new media, and balanced, adding, "Any new funding regime should be measured by whether or not it will produce more serious, independent, diverse, public-minded reporting."[119]

> What will "infrastructure" mean in the future? Basic infrastructure will no longer be limited to radio towers and satellite dishes, but will involve software, digital platforms, digital delivery systems, and applications.

The Writers Guild of America East in 2010 proposed raising funds for public media by requiring a fee from commercial media companies that merge.[120]

Some have argued that the best way to fund public media is by taxing media services or devices. Again, the *Carnegie Commission Report* advocated for this early on, suggesting that the government tax new TV sets, as it had between 1950 and 1965, to finance public media.[121] This is a version of the license fee that television owners pay in Britain to fund the BBC.[122] Several other European nations have passed, or are considering, proposals to migrate the television device tax to a more general individual media tax or electronic device tax to support public service media (with the recipients generally being limited to the legacy broadcasters). In the U.S., contemporary device tax proposals focus on electronic devices, such as high-definition TVs, smartphones, and laptops.[123] Some have suggested levying a tax on commercial stations to have them share in the funding of public television.[124]

Another recent proposal involves taxing advertising expenditures or advertising revenue, or reducing the deductions businesses can take for advertising expenses and funneling the proceeds into a trust fund for public media.[125] With total U.S. spending on advertising expected to approach $310 billion this year, proponents estimate that taxing even 2 percent of advertising for 10 years could raise more than $45 billion total, amounting to a $2.25 billion annual budget by the end of the 10 years—which would exceed annual public broadcasting funding by governments, nonprofits, and corporate institutions combined.[126] An indirect tax, based on reducing or eliminating allowable deductions for advertising expenses, could feasibly fund a $61 billion trust in 10 years that would be self-sufficient by its 11th year.[127]

Of course, others argue that not only should we not be seeking new sources of funding for public media, but the time has come to eliminate taxpayers subsidies altogether. Randolph May, president of the Free State Foundation, has argued (not in connection with any specific de-funding proposal), "[T]oday's marketplace ought to provide as much 'quality' as the American public demands. Absent coercion, it is difficult to justify expenditure of taxpayer dollars trying to force-feed programming that the public does not want."[128]

Adam Thierer of the Progress and Freedom Foundation has argued that the revenue-raising ideas tend to be unfair. For instance, he says, extracting funds from broadcasters through spectrum fees is unfair, since they are generally not the ones that got the spectrum for free:

"Using spectrum fees as a reparations policy today fails to punish those who originally got their spectrum free-of-charge. The vast majority of broadcast spectrum licenses have traded hands in the secondary market for lucrative sums. In many cases, those television and radio properties have traded hands numerous times.

"Thus, the current spectrum-holders who would be taxed are generally not the beneficiaries of any "windfall," but have instead paid competitive market prices for the spectrum they use that should be roughly commensurate with the economic value of that spectrum (at least for the limited range of uses allowed by the FCC)."[129]

Taxing advertising, Thierer argues, is no better. "Advertising benefits society by subsidizing the creation of news, information, and entertainment," he says.[130] Efforts to fund public media by somehow taxing commercial media are, he says, strategically akin to "burn[ing] the village in order to save it."[131] Such proposals would channel taxpayer support to media entities the *proponents* favor, essentially destroying "the private provision of media in America" and the possibility of a truly free press.[132]

On a broader level, opponents argue that the government should not force taxpayers to subsidize media they may not want or find offensive, and assert that in an age of information abundance, consumers cannot be forced to watch, listen, finance, or read the "right" types of media.[133]

Over the years, there have been proposals to allow public broadcasting stations to enlarge their own revenue base, and new versions of those are now on the table. One such proposal would allow public television stations greater flexibility to lease excess digital capacity to commercial wireless service providers.[134] Though these proposals are designed to provide public broadcasting more security, there is often reluctance within the public broadcasting community to aggressively pursue revenue opportunities for fear that Congress will respond by cutting appropriations.

"Advertising benefits society by subsidizing the creation of news, information, and entertainment," writes Adam Thierer.

Until recently, it has been assumed that the incumbent noncommercial broadcasting stations would be the beneficiaries of any new fund or funding. But newer proponents of the trust fund model have suggested that proceeds could be used to assist new noncommercial media entities, such as nonprofit websites providing local news. And Eric Newton of the Knight Foundation has proposed creating a fund for technology innovation.[135] (See Chapter 12, Nonprofit News Websites.)

LOW POWER FM

The low power FM (LPFM) 100-watt radio service was created by the Commission in January 2000[136] to "create opportunities for new voices on the airwaves and to allow local groups, including schools, churches, and other community-based organizations, to provide programming responsive to local community needs and interests."[137] In order to be eligible for an LPFM license, an applicant must demonstrate that it is locally based, has no attributable interests in other media (broadcast or newspapers), and has no other LPFM stations.[138]

Like NCE stations, LPFMs cannot sell advertising, but can make underwriting announcements.[139]

Currently, there are about 860 LPFM stations. Further growth in the number of LPFM stations is likely as a result of two recent developments. First, the Local Community Radio Act (LCRA), signed into law on January 11, 2011, [140] removed the requirement, previously imposed by Congress in December 2000,[141] that LPFM stations protect nearby full power stations operating on third adjacent channels. LPFM advocates estimate it could double the number of LPFM stations,[142] including more in urban areas.[143]

Second, the FCC has taken steps to resolve the conflict between license applicants for LPFM and translator services (which take a radio station that operates on one frequency and rebroadcast it on another to expand the broadcaster's reach).[144] As secondary services, LPFMs and translators operate on an essentially co-equal basis, meaning that a first-filed LPFM or FM translator application is given priority over all subsequently filed LPFM and FM translator applications.[145] In 2003, the Commission witnessed what became known as the "Great Translator Invasion," in which

861 filers submitted 13,377 applications to operate translator stations.[146] Commission staff granted approximately 3,500 new station construction permit applications and then froze further processing in response to requests from the LPFM community, which feared that translators would use up all the frequencies, leaving little or no spectrum for future LPFM station licensing, particularly in larger markets.[147] The Commission agreed that processing the approximately 7,000 remaining translator applications would interfere with development of LPFM service and its efforts to promote localism. It instituted a cap of 10 applications per entity with regard to the remaining applications from the 2003 Auction No. 83 filing window.[148]

Although LPFM and translators are subject to similar prohibitions on interfering with other FM services, these stations could not be more different in terms of the service they provide. LPFMs not only are required to be locally based, but they are given points (under the LPFM comparative standard) if they produce local content.[149] Translators, on the other hand, are not legally authorized to originate local content (with a narrow exception for fundraising),[150] and they often rebroadcast satellite-distributed national programming.[151]

The Commission plans in the near future to initiate a rulemaking procedure to implement the LCRA. It is possible that the Commission will open the second LPFM window as early as 2012.

LOW POWER TV

The Commission created the low power television service—consisting of low power television (LPTV), TV translator, and Class-A television stations—in 1982.[152] Low power TV stations can be used to provide locally oriented service to small communities, both in rural areas and within large urban settings.[153] Class-A stations are former LPTV stations that have certain interference protection rights that are not available to LPTV stations; they operate at least 18 hours a day and air at least three hours a week of locally produced programming.[154] TV translator stations rebroadcast the programming of full-power broadcast stations to communities that are unable to receive their free over-the-air signals due to distance or interference from mountains and other geographic obstacles.[155] LPTV and TV translator stations have "secondary" frequency use status, which means they may not cause interference to, and must accept interference from, full-power TV stations, certain land mobile radio operations, and other primary services.[156]

Class-A stations must broadcast an average of at least three hours each week of programming produced within the media market area served by the station.[157]

As part of the FCC's efforts to assist stations making the transition to digital TV, the Commission in 2009 began issuing new digital low power television licenses in rural areas.[158]

NONPROFIT PROGRAMMING ON SATELLITE CABLE

State Public Affairs Networks (SPANs)

In most states, it is up to local cable providers to decide whether or not they want to carry state public affairs networks (SPANs). The Commission's FOM team counts 24 SPANs (in 23 states and the District of Columbia) that broadcast/multicast or cablecast varying amounts of live coverage of state government proceedings (with a primary focus on the legislative branch).[159] The National Association of Public Affairs Networks (NAPAN) has identified 16 of these states as having an "independent" SPAN—a network managed by a distinct operating unit and recognized by the national association of state SPANs.[160] In only four states do local cable operators follow the model set by national cable operators when C-SPAN was created, by passing along a portion of subscriber fees to state SPAN operations.[161] (As noted in Chapter 3, Television, some cable operators have been more cooperative than others.) In 12 states, SPANs receive funding from the state government,[162] but with budgets tightening, there has been little interest from lawmakers in other states to add a new budget line to accommodate SPANs. Furthermore, some SPAN advocates are averse to state funding because of its potential to undercut broadcast independence.[163] Although a few public TV stations have made deals with state SPANs, CPB does not currently provide direct funding to state SPANs.

There is typically no statewide entity with whom a network can contract for statewide carriage. Therefore, since SPAN channels are not must-carry channels, they must forge carriage agreements with each and every local cable operator in the state to get statewide coverage.[164] As we noted in Chapter 27, Cable Television, our reading of Section 611 of the Communications Act is that states or local franchising authorities can deem SPANs as eligible for inclusion in the PEG system. If they get carriage as part of a PEG arrangement, they could also potentially receive franchise fees.[165]

Satellite providers have offered virtually no assistance to state SPANs. The Alaska public affairs network is the only one currently carried on satellite.[166] Paul Giguere, president of NAPAN, has described the difficulties of obtaining carriage via satellite:

"The direct broadcast satellite providers would not even return our phone calls for many years and were not willing to negotiate carriage whatsoever until the Connecticut General Assembly began exerting pressure about the carriage of CT-N three years ago.… We have participated in that application process with no success to date, but the expense involved and the likelihood that a network designed to serve a single state would be selected for nationwide channel capacity makes this an untenable solution for one public affairs network, let alone 50 of them."[167]

Paying for carriage on satellite can cost as much as $10,000 per month or $120,000 per year, a figure that SPANs find prohibitive given their small budgets.[168] Most SPANs believe that some form of carriage assistance from satellite and telephone companies is needed if the system is the flourish.[169]

On May 12, 2010, Congress amended section 335 in the Satellite Television Extension and Localism Act of 2010 to reduce the set-aside requirement for satellite providers from 4 percent down to 3.5 percent if they carried state SPANs.[170] However, members of NAPAN argue that the amendment will not have the intended effect, because DBS operators that are already fulfilling their 4 percent obligation are unlikely to willingly replace channels they already carry with SPANs because of the disruption it would cause.[171]

NONPROFIT WEBSITES

By and large, nonprofit local news websites that have launched in the past few years operate without help or interference from government. Because of the openness of the Internet, and the low-cost of publishing online, hundreds of experiments have been launched.

However, relatively few have so far developed sustainable business models. It is certainly possible that revenue growth will come but the history of noncommercial broadcasting offers a cautionary lesson: public broadcasting (TV and radio) was created in the 1930s, but did not take off until 1967, when the Public Broadcasting Act was passed. Why was that such a stimulus? It provided a consistent, steady influx of federal funding with which broadcasters could build sustainable operations. The government funding started out as a higher percentage of public broadcasters' revenue and declined over time. Now the government essentially serves as a junior partner, providing a minority share of cash at all levels of public broadcasting.

There is no such base line of operating funds from the federal government to nonprofit websites. Budgetary constraints make the idea impossible. Even if money were available, many journalists wouldn't want it. They bristle at the idea of government funding when a big part of their job is investigating government.

But three ideas have surfaced that might help nonprofit websites without involving the government writing checks to news media.

First, foundations may be able to play an even bigger role than they already have (See Chapter 13, Foundations.)

Second, tax law changes may help nonprofits draw more private donations (See Chapter 30, Non Profit Media.)

Third, the government could invest in information technology in ways that would be content-neutral and pay significant dividends both for nonprofit and potentially commercial media. Eric Newton, senior advisor to the President of the Knight Foundation, has proposed that the government create a technology fund that would be available to nonprofit websites. Government can fund technology or software development that can help media in general and accountability reporting in particular. For instance, a new technology that makes it easier to scan handwritten public records will improve accountability journalism by websites covering the entire political spectrum. What is more, a technology fund could require that new innovations be made open to the public—meaning that they can be used by commercial ventures as well as nonprofits.

> "If a tech fund systematically unleashes open source software applications and the technology needed to operate them, and grants money for code, coders and computers to news organizations across the country, it could spread public media innovation faster into new groups and deeper into existing ones, and create nothing less than a news renaissance in America.

> "Everyone can win here. A local newspaper, a commercial or public broadcaster, ethnic and alternative media, citizen media, new web-based startups, all of them can use open source news technology. The technology does not care whether they are liberal or conservative, old or young, city dwellers or rural Americans, black or white or any color of the rainbow. People will still be free to choose what news they would like to consume; they will, in fact, have greater choice in a media ecosystem richer in local media."[172]

Technology development could help to lower the cost of reporting and enhance quality. But, to be clear, it would not directly address a website's short term revenue problems.

NONPROFIT TAX RULES

"Regardless of whether a paper is owned by a nonprofit organization or an unreconstructed capitalist, it has to take in more money than it spends—or it will perish," writes Alan Mutter, a media executive and investor. "The form of ownership doesn't change this fundamental truth."[173] And in today's shrinking publishing economy, both nonprofit and for-profit news organizations are searching for new sources of income.

Although being a nonprofit has many disadvantages for media—most important, the restrictions on raising capital—it also offers several advantages that are particularly relevant, considering the challenges media companies currently face. The nonprofit structure frees news outfits from the constant pressure to increase short-term profits that has sometimes distracted for-profit news organizations from their journalistic mission. The fact that donations to nonprofit media are tax deductible serves as an incentive for citizens to lend financial support to organizations whose missions they value. Unlike postal subsidies, which are only useful to newspapers, the nonprofit tax deduction "subsidy" is platform-neutral. For this and other reasons, tax attorney and Columbia Law School dean David M. Schizer has recommended that news organizations take better advantage of the opportunity to apply for nonprofit status, modeling themselves on universities and museums that rely largely on private philanthropy.[174] Schizer points out that unlike direct government subsidies, which empower the government to determine funding levels, "the charitable deduction allows the government to piggyback on the judgments of private donors about which charities to support." When it comes to charities, the IRS does not tell a citizen whether it is better to donate to the soup kitchen or the environmental group; it provides a deduction in either case. The donor makes the decision; the tax code gives them a reward for their efforts. The same is true for nonprofit media. The government doesn't choose what to subsidize, but makes it easier for private citizens who want to support nonprofit media.

Joel Kramer of MinnPost: "We ran an op-ed type piece.... And we got somebody who complained to us that running an article like this from a person in the community, was a violation of our 501(c)3 status."

Like museums and universities, most news organizations would fit into the 501(c)(3) "charitable organization" category if they advance "educational purposes," such as "the instruction of the public on subjects useful to individuals and beneficial to the community."[175] A wide range of media organizations that found ways to fit in the 501(c)(3) category, including the Associated Press, Mother Jones, The National Review Foundation, Wikipedia, The Washington Monthly, James O'Keefe's Project Veritas, NPR, and American Spectator. Their tax exempt status has enabled them to remain mission focused and attract tax deductible donations from individuals and foundations.

But there are regulatory complications that some experts fear may limit the ability of local news entities to thrive as nonprofit. For instance, some of the basic rules for 501(c)(3) entities seem an imperfect fit for some of the nonprofit websites that have arisen. A 1967 IRS ruling spelled out the four criteria an organization engaged in publishing must meet to qualify for section 501(c)(3) exemption:

"1. the content of the publication must be educational;

"2. the preparation of the material must follow methods generally accepted as educational in character;

"3. the distribution of the materials must be necessary or valuable in achieving the organization's exempt purpose; and

"4. the manner in which the distribution is accomplished must be distinguishable from ordinary commercial publishing practices."[176]

In 1977, the IRS denied tax-exempt status to a nonprofit newspaper on the grounds that its operations were "indistinguishable from ordinary commercial publishing practices. Accordingly, it is not operated exclusively for charitable and educational purposes."[177] While news content is clearly educational, and its distribution is clearly necessary or valuable in achieving the educational purpose, professional news organizations do not generally carry out their reporting duties following methods that are "generally accepted as educational in character."[178]

In May 2009, a dozen media lawyers, scholars, and editors wrote to the IRS with ideas for reforming the tax code to help newspapers.[179] First, they argued that even traditional newspapers satisfy the key mission criteria for nonprofit status: "By providing information to the general public about local, national, and international events, newspapers serve a critical educational function." Further, they are:

"'charitable' [because] maintaining the integrity of public institutions is an important obligation of government, and a vigilant press is the institution best positioned to assist in achieving tolerable levels of public integrity. In providing that assistance, the publication of a daily newspaper lessens the burdens of government. Further, by providing a convenient and comprehensive means for governments, businesses, and nonprofit organizations to convey information to each other and the general public regarding elections, public health services, and the availability of commercial goods and services, newspapers contribute importantly to the economic health and general welfare of the geographic areas they serve. Newspapers' coverage of public affairs issues particularly generates positive externalities through better informed voters."[180]

They cited various previous IRS rulings that they found discouraging, including conflicting rulings regarding the tax-exempt eligibility of various forms of news providers. Another area for re-thinking, they said, was the IRS's position regarding volunteer labor—namely that to avoid resembling commercial entities, nonprofit media should make heavy use of volunteer labor—noting, "in several important subsectors of the nonprofit world, hardly any volunteer labor is or can be used. Research hospitals and universities, for example, employ professional staff to execute their exempt functions...."[181]

Restrictions on political endorsements make some news executives reluctant to consider seeking nonprofit status. Some newspaper executives view the ability to endorse candidates as a central element of an independent press. "[P]olitical endorsements" are "an absolute no-no.... It's not even a gray area," says attorney Allen R. Bromberger,[182] whose practice focuses on nonprofits and social enterprise corporate philanthropy.

But the law doesn't merely restrict outright endorsements. It prohibits 501(c)(3) organizations from "publishing or distributing statements" of candidates.[183] In the case of all candidates, but particularly for incumbents, this prohibition clearly restrains the dissemination of information that a news organization would typically do. Ohio State University law professor and tax attorney Stephanie Hoffer points out that the restriction on political campaign involvement is absolute,[184] meaning that even a small amount can jeopardize the tax-exempt status of a 501(c)(3) organization.

More important, editors who have no interest in doing candidate endorsements nonetheless do want and need the freedom to publish commentaries on important issues or legislation. At a June 2010 hearing held by the Federal Trade Commission, Joel Kramer of MinnPost, a 501(c)(3) news organization, said:

"I don't think it's critical that we be able to do editorial endorsements, but I do think it's critical that it be clarified that when individuals write for us and take advocacy or political positions, that it doesn't endanger our status. We ran an op-ed type piece by somebody explaining why...after John Edwards dropped out of the race...she switched to Barack Obama instead of to Hillary Clinton. And we got somebody who complained to us that running an article like this from a person in the community, it was a violation of our 501(c)(3) status."[185]

Although section 501(c)(3) restrictions on seeking to influence legislation are less strict than campaign involvement restrictions, they present similar problems. Educational organizations are permitted to engage in some activity that seeks to influence legislation; however, determining which activities qualify and in what quantity they are permitted can be challenging under existing law. Section 501(h) of the Internal Revenue Code describes the permissible kind and scope of these activities by referring to section 4911 of the Code, which says that activities affected by the limitation include not only traditional lobbying activities, but also attempts to influence legislation through grass roots efforts. For instance, a news organization that attempts to influence public opinion on legislation and also provides the names of relevant legislators is deemed to have engaged in lobbying activity under the law. A special rule applies to news organizations that qualify as mass media outlets; for them, simply taking a position on publicized legislation is considered lobbying. Again, although this categorization seems fairly clear-cut on paper, it could prove difficult to monitor in practice. For instance, would speculating about potential benefits or detriments of pending legislation amount to stating a view on that legislation? Since news organizations regularly report on passed, pending, or needed legislation, as well as the legislators who draft it, the existing 501(c)(3) restriction would force editors and reporters to develop legal expertise on covered versus non-covered speech and to curtail their reports accordingly.

> In 1977, the IRS denied tax exempt status to a nonprofit newspaper on the grounds that its operations were "indistinguishable from ordinary publishing practices."

The ban on seeking to influence legislation is not absolute— meaning organizations have leeway to engage in some of the prohibited activities without losing their tax exempt status. Hoffer says that organizations do not jeopardize their tax exempt status if their expenses for these activities typically remain below 150 percent of a "non-taxable amount," as described in Internal Revenue Code section 4911. The non-taxable amount is calculated on a sliding scale. For instance, organizations can spend up to 20 percent of their first $500,000 of revenue on lobbying activities, and the non-taxable amount can never exceed $1 million. Many smaller organizations could stay below this limit but larger organizations would have to carefully monitor expenses associated with any speech that might qualify as an attempt to influence legislation (which, as described above, may be difficult, owing to the lack of easily applicable standards). Since the dollar amount of the applicable limitation must be calculated yearly under section 4911, the task would be continuous, requiring additional bookkeeping and accounting.[186] It is not unreasonable to think that some organizations will simply self-censor this speech in order to avoid the attendant costs, decreasing the range of political opinion and information available for inclusion in our vaunted marketplace of ideas. IRS investigations are lengthy, expensive, and worrisome to any organization's leadership. Experienced legal counsel would likely discourage nonprofit news organizations from publishing any sort of material that could raise a red flag to the IRS.[187]

Miles Maguire ran the Oshkosh Community News Network for five years before deciding to shut it down. "It was just going to be too hard to go to the next level in terms of revenue development, and my concerns were record-keeping and...that the IRS would decide to disallow our nonprofit status."

Advertising

A nonprofit publication is allowed to run advertising as long as the amount is considered insubstantial, but any profits that accrue as a result are subject to the unrelated business income tax (UBIT).[188] Smaller nonprofit organizations may struggle to understand what counts as unrelated income and what counts as "insubstantial." The *Raleigh Public Record* (www.RaleighPublicRecord.org) was set up as a nonprofit to fill a vacuum in local accountability journalism. "A lot of important decisions are made by the Planning Commission, and no reporter was covering them," explains Charles Duncan Pardo, the site's young reporter-founder. But as he struggles to bring in revenue, he says, he "could use some guidance" on how to acknowledge sponsors. "If a restaurant were to give a few thousand to post their company name, I don't know what we could do with it," he says. "I don't object to unrelated business income tax. I just need to know how to handle it with the IRS." Additional sponsor money would go a long way toward increasing the amount of news coverage the site can offer: "You sell a small ad for $100, it pays for one freelance story, and when we are publishing five to ten stories by paid freelancers each month that adds up. Right now, a lot of our content is volunteer-based."[189]

Miles Maguire, a University of Wisconsin professor, ran the Oshkosh Community News Network for five years before deciding to shut it down, in part because of concerns about tax law. "One of the reasons that we folded is that it was just going to be too hard to go to the next level in terms of revenue development, and my concerns were first of all record-keeping (for UBIT) and second of all that the IRS would decide to disallow our nonprofit status. (I could imagine complaints coming from the commercial media if we got to be successful in attracting ads/sponsorships of significant size)."[190]

One problem with the current IRS interpretation is that it ignores the centrality of advertising to media business models. Limiting the ability of nonprofits to take advertising could prove to be a significant impediment to the organizations fulfilling their basic missions. Some tax experts have pleaded for flexibility on the grounds that the advertisements themselves offer valuable information to consumers. In their letter to the IRS, the group of media lawyers, scholars, and editors wrote:

> "It would also be useful to have guidance on whether income from advertising—the primary source of income of most newspapers—is unrelated business income. We believe that it is not; a significant part of the function of newspapers in facilitating the operations of a local economy consists in the informational content provided by advertising."[191]

Legislation proposed by Senator Benjamin Cardin of Maryland would have allowed newspapers to become nonprofits, and made advertising revenue non-taxable.[192]

Although advertising income is taxable, organizations are allowed to deduct the cost of generating that ostensibly unrelated income. While that has traditionally covered expenses such as the ad sales team, in a web world many other costs are essential to the task of selling advertising: the technology that serves the site and the advertising, the personnel to sell the ads, and even the content around which the ads are placed. If the definition were more flexible and in tune with the realities of the Internet, it could reduce the odds that advertising revenue would become taxable for nonprofit media.

Facilitating Donations and Assistance to Nonprofit Entities

Nonprofit organizations could also benefit from the donation of certain kinds of services or goods from commercial enterprises. For instance, it could be hugely beneficial if an Internet service provider (ISP) could donate free Internet service to a nonprofit website or public radio station. But under current law, companies donating such services would likely not be able to take a charitable deduction for doing so, according to attorney Bruce Hopkins, who specializes in tax law concerning nonprofits.[193]

There may also be limits on the extent to which foundations can make "program-related investments" in news-oriented nonprofit media organizations. As the public tax lawyers wrote in their letter to the IRS:

> "Because the aims of the philanthropists who would provide support for these ventures are entirely altruistic, it would be appropriate to accord their support the usual tax advantages associated with charitable giving. It is far from clear under existing law, however, that charitable contributions made for these purposes would be deductible, or that grants or program-related investments made to advance such purposes would be 'qualifying distributions' under existing law."[194]

Other questions abound: If a TV station pays a nonprofit news website, under what circumstances would that revenue be taxable for the nonprofit media? And under what circumstances could the TV station take a tax deduction for making that donation? Ideally, a structure would be set up that would allow commercial entities that offer significant aid to nonprofit media in their communities a tax advantage for doing so.

A New 501(c) Classification?

Some have suggested that the difficulty nonprofit media companies have fitting in to the 501(c) educational category could be resolved if Congress were to create a separate 501(c) category for nonprofit media. There is much precedent for this. When presented with demonstrable needs, Congress has previously created new 501(c) categories for such diverse purposes as railroad retirees, black lung disease benefit trusts, and cemetery companies. Most recently, Congress enacted section 501(c)(29), which governs federal tax exemption of co-op health insurers.

Since section 501(c)(3) is intended to govern organizations whose mission and nature are much different from those of news organizations, Ohio State University's Stephanie Hoffer believes that, rather than adding to the complexity of section 501(c)(3), a new category of exemption would be a cleaner solution, allowing Congress to tailor benefits and costs specifically to news organizations while retaining the spirit of nonprofit law.[195] She is particularly concerned about the constraints in the 501(c)(3) section related to political expression:

"Unlike universities and other traditional educational organizations, news organizations have consistently had a political voice in our country's civic discourse. This role meaningfully distinguishes them from educational organizations, and has significant implications for their nonprofit classification. The benefits of federal tax exemption are unimportant to news organizations unable to make a profit."

On the other hand, David Schizer, dean of the Columbia Law School, argues that by issuing clarifying policy statements, the IRS could help nonprofit media tremendously without changing the law.[196]

Hybrids

Hybrids are for-profit companies that incorporate elements traditionally associated with nonprofits. The concept emerged out of a movement to bring greater social accountability to corporations, allowing their leadership to place "doing good" on an equal footing with "doing well." In a traditional for-profit organization, any decisions on the part of a company's board and management that would run contrary to the profit-making imperative, no matter how noble the aim, will be considered an abrogation of the duty to act in the owners'/stockholders' best interests. Thus, if the board of a thriving newspaper in a mid-size town were to turn down a purchase offer from an out-of-town corporation offering an above-market price, and shareholders wanted the sale to take place, board members would risk losing their positions and possibly even be subject to personal lawsuits for breach of their fiduciary duties. The fact that out-of-town ownership of a local newspaper might not be in the best interest of area residents would be beside the point. In contrast, the nonprofit form allows an organization to act in the best interest of its community. But nonprofit status has many limitations that most news organizations would wish to avoid, if at all possible.

Right now, most hybrids are still in their incubation period and have yet to prove themselves. Maryland has passed a law recognizing a new corporate entity called a "benefit corporation," a legal designation that allows corporations to pursue socially responsible purposes in addition to profits.[197] California is considering a similar bill that would create "flexible-purpose corporations," allowing businesses to codify their intent to pursue social or environmental good while also turning a profit.[198]," according to the following three-"tranche" formula:

"Equity tranche: highest risk, lowest return. Unlike most for-profit structures in which the first tranche investors with the highest risk want the highest return, foundations through the use of the PRI structure. can take this tranche. Since a PRI [Program Related Investment from a Foundation] is in lieu of a grant, no matter how risky the PRI, the potential return and income is still better than that from a grant.

"Mezzanine tranche: Because the high-risk portion has been taken care of, the mezzanine investor will ask for a lower rate of return since the risk is much lower. Individuals, banks under CRA [Community Reinvestment Act], corporations with dual objectives of investment return and corporate image are the types of investors who could occupy this tranche.

"Senior tranche: Whether there is real estate, equipment or whatever involved, most L3C transactions will have some hard assets which have value if the transaction fails. This makes the senior tranche very stable and hence investors in this tranche will ask for a lower return because of the low risk and could more likely be long-term-income directed investors. Pension funds and other large institutional investors are very possibly in this tranche."[199]

In theory, the L3C is an ideal way to combine business and philanthropic goals in one business structure. In practice, however, federal and state regulators are so accustomed to the established, binary system of handling for-profits and nonprofits that they are likely to have trouble determining appropriate ways to scrutinize the new entities.[200]

To help lead the way in minimizing such uncertainty, in March 2010 the Council of Foundations issued a position paper supporting the L3C structure. The Council contends that new business entities like the L3C will help loosen up new sources of funding, because at present IRS guidance "is either nonexistent or lags behind the pace of innovation," so that "definitely determining whether a project is charitable can be difficult."[201] The American Bar Association Section of Taxation has also made an effort to promote the use of program related investments (PRIs) by foundations to assist struggling newspapers.[202] In addition, Robert Lang has drafted a Congressional bill, the Philanthropic Facilitation Act of 2010, to make it easier for foundations to make PRI investments in L3Cs.[203]

32 Advertising Policy

GOVERNMENT POLICY GENERALLY does not address advertising, except when it comes to policing potential threats to consumers. Regulators have, often with good reason, worked to protect consumers from misleading health advertising, online privacy violations by advertisers, and some have suggested taxing advertising to raise money and discourage its use.

But those concerned about the state of news, information, and journalism, especially accountability reporting on the local level, need to face the fact that it has been advertising that has made possible much of the nation's accountability journalism. And it has been the drop in ad rates, especially online, that has undermined traditional media models and thwarted online ones. Consider a local news website that generates 1 million page views per month. With average online ad rates of $2.52 CPM (cost per 1,000 impressions), it earns $3,000 per month, not enough to pay a full-time journalist. If that rate were a few dollars higher, the website would earn $6,000 per month, turning its operation from a hobby into a job. The current low rates for online ads makes it less likely that local news start-ups will be able to survive. The health of news media, in other words, is very sensitive to fluctuations in advertising rates and spending.

So it is worth thinking of advertising spending through the lens of public policy. Are there public policies that will cause harm by further reducing ad dollars that go to local news efforts? Conversely, are there ways that we could encourage an increase in ad dollars to help support local news efforts?

Government as Advertiser

The U.S. government spends a substantial amount of money in advertising. Looking at spending in 2003, the Government Accountability Office found 137 contracts with advertising agencies, totaling $1.6 billion over three years, mostly spent by seven government departments: Commerce, Defense, Health and Human Services, Homeland Security, Interior, Treasury, and Veterans Affairs.[1] In 2005 alone, the federal government spent $1 billion, the GAO reported.[2]

The U.S. government spent $1 billion in 2005 on advertising.

The Commerce Department promoted the census and boating safety; Health and Human Services and the Centers for Disease Control promoted a variety of public health programs; Homeland Security launched campaigns to help people prepare for terrorist attacks and other emergencies; the Pentagon spent millions on recruitment; the Department of Interior did ad campaigns related to national park services, Indian affairs, and fish and wildlife; and the Treasury Department communicated information about taxes and marketed its coins.

Where is this money spent? In general, it is up to the government departments to contract with an advertising agency to design an ad campaign and decide where to run it.[3] In many cases, they spend it on national media platforms. For instance, in March 2010 the Census Bureau ran ads during some of the following shows: *The Amazing Race, E! News, Friends with Money* (starring Jennifer Aniston), Food Network's *Semi-Homemade Cooking With Sandra Lee,* and *The Da Vinci Code* on TNT.[4] They also ran a Super Bowl ad in 2010.[5]

In the past, government marketing managers may have erred on the side of national advertising purchases because that seemed to be a less expensive way to reach large numbers of people. But some have suggested that technological changes could now make it possible for the federal government to target their spending to local media more easily while maintaining or improving cost effectiveness. TVB, a company providing local TV stations ad support, has suggested that organizations such as theirs could enable the government to reach national audiences through local media outlets. TVB proposed that the federal government shift some of their spending to local entities. TVB president Steven Lanzano emphasized:

"…the significant benefits that the United States government could realize by focusing on *local media*, rather than exclusively on national media, in its advertising spending. In addition to conserving increasing scarce federal funds, U.S. government spending on local media could provide an important element of support for local journalism and the information needs of local communities."

The group argued that structural changes in the industry have made national buys through local stations easy—and that "local television can save advertisers, including the federal government, significant revenues for comparable advertising purchases because local television is more efficient than network television."[6]

Online ad networks make local targeting even easier on the Internet. The government could request placements on news websites in communities throughout the country, or targeted to specific demographics. And the Newspaper National Network allows advertisers to do national ad buys using local newspapers.

If a decision were made to direct federal ad dollars to local-oriented media, it would be imperative that policymakers come up with a system that would guarantee as much political neutrality as currently appears to exist -- unlike in the 19th century, when politicians would favor supportive newspapers with ad contracts. This seems doable. Ad networks would likely enable government managers to lay out the parameters and then turn over the specific ad buys to brokers. Federal official need never make decisions about actual specific media placements.

Public Notices

One way the government has indirectly helped media over the years is through the paid placement of public notices. Geoffrey Cowan and David Westphal of the Annenberg School of Communications describe the typical public notices:

"Typical public-notice laws apply to public budgets, public hearings, government contracts open for bidding, unclaimed property, and court actions such as probating wills and notification of unknown creditors. Public agencies have required paid publication of this kind of information for decades as a way to ensure that citizens are informed of critical actions. Historically, these fine-print notices have been a lucrative business for newspaper publishers, and have touched off heated bidding wars for government contracts. Legal notices have been especially important to weekly and other community newspapers. Their trade association, the National Newspaper Association, estimated in 2000 that public notices accounted for 5 percent to 10 percent of all community newspaper revenue."[7]

Some national news organizations have benefited. In a paper, "Public Policy & Funding the News, Cowan and Westphal in 2010 wrote:

"*The Wall Street Journal*, for example, has a contract with the government to print seized-property notices. In a four-week study, we discovered that the government was a top purchaser, by column inches, of ad space in the *Journal*. It's a business the newspaper would like to expand. In 2009 it was battling with Virginia-area papers to get its regional edition certified to print local legal notices."[8]

Increasingly, however, government agencies have been opting to put these notices on their own websites instead of in newspapers or other media outlets. In fact, legislation that has been introduced in 40 states to move public notices to the web, often specifies moving them to municipal sites.[9] It is eminently sensible for government agencies want to save money this way. But, at the same time it is potentially harmful to local news media, and it can leave those who lack Internet access out of the information loop.

Because public notices facilitate government transparency, apprising citizens of critical developments, hearings, and legislation under consideration can be important. The Public Notice Resource Center, a newspaper industry group, says that most states aspire to have "the greatest amount of people receive important information about the actions of

The Census Bureau in March 2010 spent ad dollars on The Amazing Race, E! News, Friends with Money starring Jennifer Aniston, Food Network's Semi Homemade with Sandra Lee, or the The Da Vinci Code on TNT.

their government."[10] Public notices can, in theory, improve accountability of powerful institutions. For example, one proposed bill, HR 2727 Financial Transparency Act, would require financial institutions to publish information about their financial conditions in newspapers.[11] Beth Grace, executive director of the North Carolina Press Association, says running public notices on municipal websites does not advance these accountability goals as much because they draw far fewer visitors than newspaper sites do, and, "Public notices need to be where the public notices."[12]

One possible solution that would benefit all parties would be for governments to save money by hosting public notices on their own websites and paying a lesser amount to run banner ads on other sites about the notices and linking back to the government site. The municipality would be able to spread information about the public notices to a broader range of audiences than they would by just publishing them in a particular newspaper. They would generate more traffic for their own websites, provide ad revenue for local news operations and advance the cause of government transparency.

Other Policies That Might Hurt Advertisers

Some have proposed taxing advertising as a way to pay for journalism. For example, Free Press has proposed a 2 percent sales tax on advertisers, to raise $45 billion for a public media trust fund.[13] This strikes us self-defeating: taxing a key revenue stream for journalism in order to help journalism. What this would actually do is shift revenue from commercial media to public media, which is not a defensible public policy goal.

Some have suggested restricting[14] the ability of businesses to deduct advertising expenses.[15] Though we appreciate the effort to raise revenue, this may be the wrong time to be penalizing advertising.

Finally, policymakers are looking at how to improve privacy for consumers online. We are highly sympathetic to this goal. Websites often collect information about consumers without the consumers knowing it. We would merely suggest, however that as policymakers wrestle with the nuances of crafting sound rules, they also consider that there is a countervailing interest: helping local news media. For instance, it might make sense for "do not track" policies to give more leeway to "first party" tracking than third party. This would give a relative advantage to publishers (the "first party") over ad networks.[16]

On the other hand, policies should also consider arrangements like the newspaper consortium created by Yahoo!. According to Yahoo!, 45 companies, involving 821 papers (with 22 million circulation, accounting for 52 percent of all U.S. Sunday circulation[17]) use Yahoo! data on what people read on the web, search for, what ads they click on, and what search results they click on to develop models of their likely interests in different product categories. When those Internet users show up on the websites of newspapers in the Newspaper Consortium, they see ads related to their likely product interests. Advertisers sometimes pay a premium for these targeted ads because they are more likely to match consumer interests and get results. The *New York Times* reported:

> "A similar sales blitz at The Ventura County Star, a small daily north of Los Angeles, netted nearly $1 million in sales in the run-up to Christmas, or roughly 40 percent of what the paper sold in online ads in 2008. The Naples Daily News in Florida did even better: The late-January blitz generated $2 million in sales, or more than half what the paper sold online in 2008. Some larger newspapers have had similar successes.
>
> " 'If we could do just shy of $1 million in two weeks in a horrible economy, what does it mean for us when the economy turns?' asked George H. Cogswell III, publisher of The Ventura County Star."

Again, we are not arguing that these sorts of efforts necessarily trump privacy concerns, but that a reasonable policy discussion would consider, as one factor, the impact of various approaches on content creators.

> **Technological improvements would enable local targeting in a way that would not cost the government more money—and in many cases could be more cost effective.**

33 Print

THE MOST FAMOUS FOUNDING FATHER QUOTATION about the press comes from Thomas Jefferson: "Were it left to me to decide whether we should have a government without newspapers, or newspapers without a government, I should not hesitate a moment to prefer the latter."

The full quote was written in a letter from Jefferson to Edward Carrington of Virginia, January 16, 1787.[1] Jefferson believed that Shays' Rebellion, an armed insurrection of economically frustrated farmers and merchants in Western Massachusetts, might have been prevented if only the people had been better informed. That led him to conclude that it was necessary to "give them full information of their affairs thro' the channel of the public papers, & to contrive that those papers should penetrate the whole mass of the people."[2]

How did Jefferson and the other Founders "contrive" for the papers to reach "the whole mass of the people"? They focused not on content but on distribution. First, they created a network of post offices, "reaching towns and villages deep in the interior and employing more than 8,700 postmasters, or just over three-fourths of the entire federal civilian workforce."[3] With the support of Washington, Jefferson, Madison, and others, the new government then subsidized postal rates, allowing newspapers to pay steeply discounted distribution rates that were far below the actual costs of fielding, feeding, and caring for that day's distribution technology (horses.) This changed the economics of newspapers, reducing publication costs and enabling papers to reach readers outside their hometown.

Though newspapers got a big boost from public policy, it would be misleading to give the impression that the press blossomed only because of government support. Early growth of the American press stemmed as much from the fact that newspapers in the Colonies were far *less* regulated than in Europe. Guild regulations did not limit who could become a printer, as they did in England, and for much of Colonial history, the Stamp Tax did not apply to the Colonial papers.[4]

Early efforts to help newspapers led to a closeness between politicians and the press that would today seem grossly inappropriate. In the early days of the Republic, each newspaper was usually aligned with a political faction. This did not mean they merely had ideological proclivities; it often meant they received money from and coordinated with political sponsors, usually through printing contracts or by placing "official notices" in the paper as advertisements. In 1830 in New York State, for example, 22 editors served as postmasters.[5] Parties and interest groups also used "gifts, donations, loans, and sometimes even outright ownership of papers to assure that the party's views were advanced."[6] Without support from political parties, many of the partisan newspapers would not have survived.

After the Civil War, under pressure from the magazine industry, government policy began to support periodicals as well. In 1863, it created "second-class mail" for regular publications and, to make sure that advertising circulars would not qualify, restricted the low-cost rate to materials that disseminated "information of a public character, or be devoted to literature, the sciences, arts, or some special industry." In 1885, Congress slashed second-class rates by two-thirds, "making them far cheaper than advertising circulars as a vehicle for marketing" and leading to the growth of the low-price, mass circulation magazine.[7]

For the next 115 years, government provided assistance to the newspaper and magazine industry in a variety of ways. The Newspaper Preservation Act of 1970 provided an exemption from antitrust law to newspapers that joined together, to keep from going out of business.[8] And the postal subsidy continues to this day. Professors Geoffrey Cowan and David Westphal of the Annenberg School of Communications estimate:

> "As recently as the late 1960s, the government was forgiving roughly three-fourths of print publications' periodical mailing expenses, at a cost of about $400 million annually (or, adjusted for inflation, about $2 billion today). Much of that disappeared with the Postal Reorganization Act of 1970 and in subsequent cutbacks. But the Post Office still discounts the postage cost of periodicals by about $270 million a year."[9]

As a result, magazines receive taxpayer aid. This has been particularly beneficial to opinion and political magazines which have forever struggled to attract advertisers.

Another postal policy, unknown to most Americans affects newspapers in an indirect but powerful way. The Postal Service charges one price—its standard mail "saturation rate"—to companies that send the same piece of marketing mail to everyone in a community. To compete with these bulk mailers, which reach everyone in a community, newspapers will put some advertisements in the paper as inserts and then, to ensure that advertisers reach all the customers in the community, mail the advertisements to residents who do not subscribe to the newspaper. For that mail, newspapers get charged the standard mail "high-density rate"—which is now 18 percent higher than the saturation rate. Newspapers believe that they are losing millions of dollars a year as advertisers take advantage of the lower postal rates to mail directly to consumers instead of working with the newspapers to do a combination insert-and-mail campaign. The gap between these two mailers—the mass marketing mail using the "saturation rate" and the "high-density rate" ads sent by newspapers—has been growing. Whether this rate differential is sensible public policy may depend on what the primary policy goal is. The Postal Service justifies giving the preferential rate to the everyone-gets-one saturation mail because it costs less to deliver, since no sorting is involved. But viewed through the prism of media policy, this differential makes no sense—as it incentivizes advertisers to do direct-to-the-mailbox solicitations instead of advertising through newspapers.

Added together, the government's current annual spending on postal subsidies, notices, and advertising is an amount several times the yearly budget of the Corporation for Public Broadcasting. We mention this not as an argument for added government subsidies for newspapers, which we do not recommend, but rather to point out the relative lack of controversy over these currently existing forms of government subsidy that benefit media.

We suspect these have been relatively noncontroversial because they are content neutral. To qualify for the postal subsidy, a periodical need only prove that it has content; no IRS inspector has to inspect or judge the quality of the articles. Of course, this is a blunt instrument: all sorts of inferior publications end up being subsidized by taxpayers. But the First Amendment stands uninjured, because once the government set the rules, it then put the disbursements on autopilot.

34 Copyright and Intellectual Property

IN 1790, CONGRESS PASSED the first Copyright Act giving copyright owners the right to control reproduction and distribution of their creative works for a limited time.[1] In the two centuries since, copyright law has evolved apace with technology. As all forms of media converge onto the Internet, online social and legal norms of conduct continue to change as well. In the early days of the web, it was not unheard of for websites to require permission before allowing other sites to link to their web pages.[2] Today, of course, most linking happens without permission. Tim Berners-Lee, one of the inventors of the World Wide Web, has said that a link is nothing more than a digital referral or footnote, and that the ability to refer to a document is a fundamental right of free speech.[3]

But as news organizations' revenue dwindles, major news publishers point fingers at the vast numbers of websites they see "scrap[ing], syndicat[ing] and monetize[ing]" their original news content "without fair compensation to those who produce, report and verify it,"[4] and they wonder if changes to federal copyright and related intellectual property law policies can help stem their monetary losses.

The very act of performing an Internet search implicates copyright law: in order to carry out a search, the search engine must copy some of other sites' content. Programs variously called "spiders," "robots," and "web crawlers" scour the Internet and perform searching, copying, and retrieving functions on billions of websites to collect the information that ultimately appears in the search results.[5] Although copying is one of the exclusive rights granted to a copyright owner, caching (storing data within a computer program) is not generally considered to be a violation of copyright law.[6]

In contrast, copying an entire news article to disseminate widely—whether by using the keyboard function keys to copy the web page, scanning the article into a PDF file, or simply manually typing the material—constitutes copyright infringement, regardless of whether the source is given attribution. And it appears to happen often. In one 30-day period in 2009, according to the news publisher group Fair Syndication Consortium, 112,000 unlicensed copies of articles were detected on 75,000 websites that featured advertising.[7] The Consortium says that most of the ads came from Google's and Yahoo!'s ad networks. "By running paid advertising alongside articles that have been copied and posted without first being licensed (which therefore infringe upon the owners' copyrights), these websites make money off news stories without compensating the originators of the stories."[8]

Many of these issues will be worked out by private companies, without government involvement. In response to complaints that aggregators and scrapers were benefiting from appearing prominently in search results, Google recently announced a series of steps that may make it easier for the creators of original content to tag their stories in ways that can improve their search rankings.[9]

Whether public policy changes are also needed—specifically a rethinking of copyright law—is tremendously controversial. Any attempts by publishers to use federal copyright policy to try to rein in widespread unpaid distribution of their stories would be constrained by two other principles: The First Amendment and the fair-use doctrine. Copyright, the First Amendment, and fair use overlap and coexist uneasily. Which of these takes precedence in any given instance depends on the particular facts of the case, as interpreted in the context of contemporaneous political and social circumstances.[10] Attorney Doug Rand wrote:

> "It is no overstatement to say that the Internet as we know it could not exist without the fair use defense.... Since it would be impossible for any search engine to get permission to copy and display this information from billions of websites, the concept of fair use underlies all search."[11]

"Fair use" allows other parties to use copyrighted materials in certain circumstances. The current generally accepted industry practice is to allow aggregators to excerpt a small part of a news story to give a sample of what the story is about, with attribution. News aggregators are presumed to be covered under fair use as long as they limit their copying to a credited excerpt with a linking headline that, when clicked on, brings up the original source. However, some news publishers contend that including enough of the story to enable readers to grasp the gist of the story without having to click through to the article devalues the original content, because many have no interest in reading past the initial sample.

In March 2010, Associated Press attorney Laura Malone told the audience at an FTC hearing that news-aggregation sites that take headlines and leads are taking "the heart of the story." "[C]opyright owners" should be able "to set the parameters by which people can republish our stuff. If people want to build sites based on the news that is published by any of the news organizations, that's great. We'll give them a license,"[12] she said. Bruce W. Sanford of Baker Hostetler, LLP, a law firm that represents news publishers, has written the same philosophy, proposing that Congress pass federal legislation that explicitly makes linking a form of copyright infringement.[13]

Others, including Google (which does have licensing agreements with the major news publishers), contend that linking increases the value of the content by bringing the story to the attention of readers interested in the topic who otherwise would not see it, who then click through to the original story.[14] Yet another viewpoint is that, given prevailing online habits for looking at news, the utility of the quote and link are in the public interest and outweigh any theoretical, unproven loss in value.

Opt-out versus Opt-in

Had the Internet been constructed by lawyers mindful of potential copyright infringement, it would be a very different place. Instead, it was originally constructed by academics and programmers who wanted primarily to communicate with one another. They established a default "opt-out" system that required webmasters to add certain code language to their systems in order to have their websites excluded from search engine copying, indexing, and caching. Some news publishers perceive this as the root of many of their copyright infringement problems. James W. Marcovitz, senior vice president and deputy general counsel for News Corp., explained:

> "What we would like to see is a permission-based economy where we could set the value for our content and people come to us and seek permission to use it.... If aggregators would like to build business based on the use of our content, they should come to us to seek permission to obtain it on terms that we would sell."[15]

However, James Boyle of Duke Law School responded by explaining how the Internet would have evolved if this approach had been taken:

> "[A]t the beginning of the Internet, had we been debating in this room, 'Hey, there's this web thingy, so should we be permissions based or should we be kind of opt-in, opt-in or opt-out?' We could have come up with great reasons why everyone should have permission. It's not that hard. You just have to write to the person and get permission to link. It's not that hard. If you want to create a match up on Google Maps, you just have to write to all the data sources that you're going to get, all million of them, and just get permissions, it's not that hard.

> "All that would have prevented is the World Wide Web, right, but of course people in this room wouldn't have cared because they didn't know what the World Wide Web was.... [W]e would have got it wrong, dramatically wrong, if we had gone permissions based.... This for me suggests humility as the guiding principle of intervention."[16]

The Robot Exclusion Standard, the most widely used "opt-out" program directing search engines to refrain from copying, indexing, and caching a website, requires that a webmaster add specific lines of HTML code known as Robot Exclusion Headers to the website, which instruct the search engine spider to ignore the site and not to archive the website via a cached link.[17] According to Google's Josh Cohen, Robots.txt allows a publisher great latitude: the ability to block an entire article, show only a snippet, or show the article without any of the artwork and photos.[18]

Take-Down Notices

The Copyright Act, as amended in 1998 by the Digital Millennium Copyright Act,[19] provides a fairly simple mechanism that allows any copyright owner to compel unlicensed material to be taken off a website. It also shields online service providers from their own acts of copyright infringement and those of others as long as they expeditiously remove any material alleged to be infringing, and maintain policies to deal with repeat infringers, up to and including terminating their accounts, if necessary.

The law was passed over the objections of content-industry groups that had lobbied for service providers to be held strictly liable for the acts of their users, meaning that they would have been held liable regardless of whether they were aware of the presence of infringing material. In return for being granted the safe harbor, service providers are obliged to disclose information about users who are alleged to be infringers.[20] (Internet privacy advocates have expressed concern about this aspect of the law.[21])

There is no requirement that the service provider investigate or try to ascertain whether the material actually does infringe copyright. The Fair Syndication Consortium was founded in 2009 to rally publishers around a new syndication model based on Attributor Corporation's freely available FairShare service. FairShare places digital "fingerprints" on online content and then tracks which sites are picking up the content. The Consortium hopes to track down unauthorized aggregators and negotiate a share of their ad revenue. If the negotiations fail, the Consortium will demand the removal of the advertising running alongside the copyright-protected material.[22] Between March and July 2010, Attributor contacted 107 unauthorized aggregators deemed "systematic infringers," for-profit sites that make a practice of running unlicensed original work and placing ads near the copied content.[23] Seventy-five percent of the sites removed the unlicensed content or started licensing discussions after receiving only one or two emails from Attributor—the second of which notified the site that if no response was forthcoming, Aggregator would contact search engines and request that the unauthorized copies be removed from their indexes and ad networks to request removal of the ads. The Fair Syndication consortium hopes that the trial results will help provide a new framework for enforcing copyright on the Internet. The Associated Press recently created the News Licensing Group, naming former ABC president David Westin CEO of the organization whose mission will be to help hundreds of publishers track and get payment for their content when it is used by other websites.[24]

"Hot News"

Journalists have always drawn on the work of other journalists to create news stories, and the U.S. Supreme Court has repeatedly asserted that there can be no copyright protection for facts: "The most fundamental axiom of copyright law is that 'no author may copyright his ideas or the facts he narrates.' "[25]

But a few publishers have filed lawsuits against businesses that repeatedly appropriate ideas and facts that others have researched, articulated, and published, citing their right to protection under the "hot-news misappropriation" doctrine. In 2008, the Associated Press (AP) filed suit in New York against All Headlines News Corp. (AHN), alleging, among other claims, that AHN was illegally copying, rewriting, and transmitting AP stories to paying clients, in violation of AP's quasi-property right to breaking news.[26] AP's claim relied on a long-neglected doctrine created by the U.S. Supreme Court during World War I when it ruled in *International News Service v. Associated Press* that INS's policy of rewriting AP's European war-coverage stories that were written for East Coast papers, then telegraphing them without attribution to papers farther west, violated AP's right to profit from its reporting efforts.[27] The practice did not violate any AP copyrights, because no direct plagiarism was involved, yet the U.S. Supreme Court wrote:

> "Stripped of all disguises, the process amounts to an unauthorized interference with the normal operation of [AP's] legitimate business precisely at the point where the profit is to be reaped, in order to divert a material portion of the profit from those who have earned it to those who have not...."[28]

While it is no longer binding federal law, the 1918 ruling established it as a common-law doctrine, granting news producers a pseudo-property right to the news stories they break. The right can only be asserted against competitors, and only for as long as the news has commercial value.[29] And it can only be applied in situations where another party rewrites the news without independent investigation and verification.[30] Because it is a common-law doctrine, each state's judicial system has the freedom to decide whether to recognize the validity of a hot-news claim. The doctrine is considered valid in the U.S. Court of Appeals for the Second Circuit, which has jurisdiction over New York, where most news publishers are based.[31]

The hot-news doctrine had lain dormant until 1997, when the National Basketball Association (NBA) resuscitated it in order to bring suit against Motorola for its subscription text messaging service, which provided immediate access to NBA scores on an ongoing basis.[32] The court ruled against the NBA, but the case gave legitimacy to a doctrine that had not been called on for 80 years.[33]

The doctrine gained further momentum in 2010, when it was invoked in *Barclays v. FlyOnTheWall.com*.[34] The plaintiffs were Wall Street research analysts who distributed stock tips through password-protected sites to paying clients, mostly large institutional investors whose licensing agreements forbade them to redistribute the information. The defendant, FlyOnTheWall.com, had obtained Barclays's information through leaks, and then sold it to its own clients. The trial judge found in favor of Barclays, declaring, "It is not a defense to misappropriation that a recommendation is already in the public domain by the time Fly reports it."[35] (The injunction was lifted once Fly filed its appeal.)

A major cross-section of the American media, including news services, publishers of major weekly and monthly news and opinion magazines, and major broadcasting chains, filed a brief in the Barclay's case supporting the continued existence of the doctrine.[36] Google and Twitter filed a brief urging the court to strike down the doctrine, as did the Electronic Frontier Foundation, Citizen Media Law Project, and Public Citizen.[37] It should be noted that this fight does not uniformly pit traditional media companies against digital companies. Many traditional media companies fear an expansion of copyright laws, too.[38]

Some have suggested that instead of tightening the "fair use" rules, policymakers should focus on ensuring that content creators get proper credit. Patricia Aufderheide and Peter Jaszi of American University's School of Communication note that their efforts to help develop codes of best practices in fair use for filmmakers, scholars, and online video makers have shown them that non-corporate creators are often primarily concerned with receiving credit whenever their work is used,[39] prioritizing "recognition, rather than monetary reward."[40] They therefore suggest a "limited general right of attribution," guaranteeing that content creators be properly credited, even if they are not financially compensated.

PART THREE

35 Recommendations

THE FOLLOWING FINDINGS from Parts One and Two should be considered by policymakers, business and nonprofit leaders, entrepreneurs, philanthropists and the FCC itself:

The media landscape is mostly vibrant. In many ways, today's media system is better than ever: faster and cheaper distribution networks; fewer barriers to entry; and more ways of consuming information. Americans not only have ways of expressing their opinions, they can help create and cover the news. Choice abounds.

But there are a few areas of serious concern. We face not a broad crisis of "the news" or "content"—but something much more specific: a shortage of local, professional accountability reporting. This is likely to lead to more government waste, more local corruption, worse schools, a less-informed electorate, and other serious problems in communities. In some cases, the loss of reporting capacity has meant a power shift away from citizens toward government and other institutions. Gaps created by the contraction of newspapers have—so far—not been fully filled by other media. Some local TV news shows are investing more in reporting about critical local issues, but many are not (and some are exhibiting alarming tendencies to allow advertisers to dictate content). Commercial radio, cable and satellite play a small and likely declining role in local news. Public TV does little local programming; local public radio is trying but has limited resources. Most important, Internet-native local news operations have so far not gained sufficient traction. In many cases, the result is more media outlets but less local reporting. An important caveat: Markets are evolving rapidly and it is certainly possible these gaps will be eventually filled by commercial markets. But so far it has not happened, and we cannot assume all reporting deficits will be solved this way.

In terms of public policy, many rules intended to advance public interest goals are ineffective—and out of sync with the information needs of communities and the nature of modern local media markets. In some cases, policies do not achieve their intended goals. In other cases, policies that might have once made sense have not kept up with changes in media markets. Several policies are not sufficiently oriented toward addressing the *local* information gap.

Technology has increased the potential potency of transparency as a policy tool. Properly formatted, data routinely produced by the government can now be sliced, diced, analyzed and spread around more rapidly and effectively. The effective dissemination of government-collected information can empower citizens, improve accountability, lower reporting costs, and stimulate entrepreneurship. This should drive us towards a reassessment both of what government does with the data it already collects and what information it gathers in the first place. The gathering and dissemination of information should be a far more important policy lever than it has been in the past.

Government is not the main player in this drama but it can remove obstacles confronting those working to solve the problems of providing robust local news and information. Most of the solutions to today's media problems will be found by entrepreneurs, reporters, and creative citizens, not legislators or agencies. Government cannot "save journalism." Indeed, the media landscape is evolving so rapidly that heavy-handed regulatory intervention dictating media company behavior could backfire, distorting markets in unhelpful ways. However, government can make it easier for citizens, communities and reporters—in both the for-profit and nonprofit sectors—to themselves create new information systems and forms of sustainable journalism.

When foundations, entrepreneurs, citizens or policy makers attempt to assess the information health of a community, they should look not only at abundance of media outlets, diversity of voices and competition, but also at reportorial resources, including full-time reporting, producing and editing staff. In the modern media landscape, many communities have both more media outlets and less full-time accountability reporting. The volume of news being disseminated has never been greater, obscuring shortfalls in the resources being committed to local reporting. In the past, a key civic focus was on insuring Americans had access to the public square. Now, anyone with an Internet connection has a megaphone—but certain types of information are nonetheless scarce.

Nonprofit media needs to be better understood, and play a bigger role. The nonprofit media sector includes: journalism schools that field reporters, concerned citizens who start a nonprofit website, community Low Power FM stations, anyone contributing to a Wikipedia page, state-based C-SPANs, software developers who write open source code in nonprofit settings, public access channels, newspapers run by foundations, religious broadcasters, citizens tweeting news from the scene of a disaster and public broadcasting. Some of these media providers get government funding but most do not. Government money should not, and need not, be the main driver of the growth, but the nonprofit sector will, in many cases, need to play a greater role in filling remaining media gaps.

Collaborations among media—including between for-profit and nonprofit media—will and should be an important ingredient in the new system. In private markets, companies routinely outsource certain specialized functions that another can do more effectively. One characteristic of the new media economy may be that large and/or for-profit media will rely on the work of small and/or nonprofit media for certain types of content that most would agree is civically-important but insufficiently supported by commercial media.

Great opportunities remain for TV and newspapers. Newspapers were supposed to be destroyed by radio which was supposed to be destroyed by TV which was supposed to be destroyed by the Internet. Each of these predictions has been only partly right. The new technologies did forever change the media landscape; the previously dominant medium never regained its previous stature. But many did adapt, survive and, in some cases, remain just as profitable as ever. It is now clear that in many communities the dominant online players in local news are the new media manifestations of old media companies, most notably the websites of local newspapers and TV newscasts. Policymakers should be mindful of this dynamic.

Philanthropists—individuals or foundations—should consider changing their approach to media. Without strong reporting, the issues that philanthropists care about—whether health, environment, children, fiscal responsibility—are all shortchanged. The public will be less well informed and institutions professing to solve the problems will be less accountable. Private individual donations will also need to play a bigger role, filling the civically-important gaps.

There is an opportunity to create the best news and information system in the nation's history. Citizen and professional reporters serve different but complementary functions. For instance, volunteer-based journalism has led to the flowering of "hyperlocal" neighborhood-based coverage—a form that traditional media always struggled with—while full-time professional reporting is essential for certain types of labor-intensive accountability reporting. The old and new media improve each other's effectiveness. For instance, online "crowds" can pore through government document dumps *and* professional reporters can find the particular source within the agency to describe which documents were withheld. If we can preserve the best attributes of both the old and new media—and fill the serious gaps in local reporting—our news and information system will offer a depth, breadth and speed of coverage never before seen in the U.S.

Beyond these conclusions, we were guided by one more fundamental principle: Congress shall make no law, and government agencies shall make no rule, abridging the freedom of speech or of the press. Any government policy has to live within and respect the essential constraints of the First Amendment.

We offer no magic bullet or magic app. Rather, government policy changes should focus on three primary goals: increasing transparency, making better use of the public's existing resources, and removing obstacles to innovation—or, in the words of the National Religious Broadcasters, "fertiliz[ing] the conditions under which the media does its work."[1] With a terrain more hospitable to local media innovation, the private sector—both for-profit and nonprofit entities—can increase the production of local programming, including accountability reporting. The resulting media system could be the best the nation has ever had.

With that ambition in mind, we recommend consideration of the following:

EMPHASIZE ONLINE DICLOSURE AS A PILLAR OF FCC MEDIA POLICY

Historically, the segment of media most directly affected by government policy has been broadcasting. Far from becoming obsolete, it appears that many local TV news operations are more important today than they have ever been. Not only are they the leading sources of news on air, they are emerging as key providers online. Government should make sure it places no unnecessary burdens on broadcasters that are attempting to cover their communities using a variety of media platforms.

Yet these *are* the public's airwaves on which broadcasters base their business. And since the earliest days of television there has been a quid pro quo: taxpayers permit broadcasters to license exclusive use of high-quality spectrum and protect them from interference; in return broadcasters serve the community with programming about significant community issues, in addition to entertainment. Even the FCC's deregulatory policies of the 1980s maintained this principle, which many broadcasters embrace to this day.

For many years, the FCC attempted to enforce this bargain through rules requiring local news and public affairs programming. Over time, and for various reasons, the FCC's license renewal process lost its rigor, permitting stations to retain their licenses regardless of whether they are investing heavily in local programming or doing none at all.

Past efforts to solve this dilemma have not worked. Broadcasters waste time filling out government paperwork, maintaining "issues/programs lists," that are often uninformative, and which few people read. This laborious system is largely useless to consumers, taxpayers and public interest groups, and does little to help make the local market for news work better. Efforts to strengthen the system—such as the "enhanced disclosure" rules and "localism" proceeding—would have been overly bureaucratic and unnecessarily burdensome to broadcasters.

The regulatory system for broadcasters is broken. And while this discouraging track record is due, in part, to muddy policy, it also reflects the reality that the important values embodied in the First Amendment rightly limit the Federal government's ability to take more aggressive action. Even though broadcasting was born thanks to a grant of spectrum from the taxpayers, it is unlike any other industry with a government benefit. While courts have viewed First Amendment protections afforded to broadcasters' speech as being somewhat more limited than for some other media, to aggressively intervene in the programming decisions of broadcasters could nonetheless be an affront to constitutionally protected free speech and free press. There invariably is a tension between two very legitimate goals: the First Amendment on the one hand and the requirement that broadcasters serve their communities in exchange for the use of public spectrum, on the other.

How might this policy riddle be solved? We believe the key is to a) improve transparency in ways that will better empower citizens and make markets work better and b) remove unnecessary burdens on broadcasters who aim to serve their communities.

We are proposing a shift in emphasis for the FCC. In the past, the FCC has tended to view the license renewal system as the only way of exerting leverage over broadcasters to ensure that they serve their communities. This has not been successful. Our proposed approach suggests a greater reliance on disclosure and information to lubricate local media markets. The point of revealing this information is not primarily so *regulators* can discipline or reward stations—but so *consumers* can, if they choose.

This approach is consistent with the FCC's efforts in the last year to put a wide variety of information online. The Internet has made it far more likely that transparency-based approaches can be effective than in the past. The FCC's public interest regime should move into the digital era.

Reduce Paperwork, Terminate Unnecessary Rules and Move Important Disclosure Online

Broadcasters should be spared make-work paperwork and be relieved of the threat of several potentially burdensome rules—*and* the genuinely useful information that is required to be disclosed should be moved online. (See below)

First, we propose that the FCC consider eliminating the longstanding requirement that TV broadcasters create, on a quarterly basis, a paper file detailing programming ostensibly responsive to issues of importance to their community of license. In addition, the *"enhanced disclosure" form adopted in 2007, but not yet approved by the Office of Management and Budget, should be replaced.* It is overly complex. Moreover, the Commission should *terminate the "localism" proceeding and withdraw the localism Notice of Proposed Rulemaking (NPRM).* While the existing NPRM attempts to advance the worthwhile goal of promoting local media—an aspiration of many of the recommendations in this report—that particular rulemaking includes several unworkable or unnecessarily burdensome ideas, such as a requirement that all stations have around-the-clock staffing.

We also share the view held by all of the current commissioners that the Fairness Doctrine should not be reinstituted for many reasons, including that we believe it could chill speech, undermine news gathering, and potentially violate the First Amendment. In the course of researching this report, we came to understand that while the Fairness Doctrine had been repealed as a policy, remnants of the rule remained on the books. To be clear: the policy is not in effect; restoring it would require a majority vote of the full commission, all of whose members currently oppose the Fairness Doctrine. Nonetheless, we should eliminate any outstanding uncertainty about our intentions—about the localism proceeding, about enhanced disclosure, and about the Fairness Doctrine. *We therefore recommend that the Commission consider cleaning up its books by repealing what's left of the Fairness Doctrine.* Similarly, the language related to the political editorial and personal attack rules should also be made consistent with current policy. We recognize that these changes have no actual policy import; these policies were already dead, and should remain so. But as a matter of common sense, it makes no sense to have dead policy in a living code of federal rules.

But while eliminating burdensome or ineffective paper disclosures, the FCC should return to the original purpose of the "public inspection file" rules, which was to allow the "public" to "inspect" important information. That rarely happens. Fortunately, the Internet allows for this concept to be far more meaningful than in the past. *As a general principle, the information already required to be disclosed by broadcasters should be, over time, put online, and the paper file should become a thing of the past.*[2]

Currently, broadcasters are required to disclose in their Public Inspection File a variety of different types of information such as:

> Ownership reports and related materials

> Material relating to FCC investigation or complaints

> Children's Television Programming Reports

> Political file

> Citizen agreements (noncommercial agreements between the broadcaster and citizen(s) groups)

> Lists of Donors (For noncommercial stations)

> License applications and related materials[3]

A transition to a digital system needs to be handled carefully and in a manner sensitive to the capacities of different broadcasters. The FCC should start with the current material that would be easiest to transition and with the most public benefit, and with broadcasters most able to implement it (for instance, it would make sense to focus on TV stations, rather than on radio stations). The FCC might consider creating and maintaining a database itself so TV stations would not have to update the information on their own websites. Taking this approach, and ensuring that as much data as possible is in a standardized, machine-readable format, could also enhance the usefulness and accessibility of the data as well. Online disclosure should be done according to the principles advocated by experts on transparency: in standardized, machine readable and structured formats.

In the cases listed above, our assumption is that what should be moved online is simply the information that is *currently already required* to be in the paper file. But there is one area we propose a change in what kind of material is collected and disclosed—the information that television broadcasters provide about their community-oriented programming, the disclosures designed to fulfill their "public interest obligation." This too should be put online but we recommend a different approach than used in the past. Instead of a detailed form requiring reporting on 365 days of programming (or the current, ineffective system of "issues/programs" lists) we propose a *streamlined, web-based form focused on a relatively short list of essential data.* The FCC should strongly consider *requiring information drawn from only a sample or "composite" week of programming on a quarterly basis, rather than requiring a comprehensive listing of all relevant programs throughout the year.*

As part of this new online form, the FCC should consider having TV broadcasters disclose:

> How much of their programming is about their local community, including some breakdown of types (for instance, reporting about local government).

> How they are using their extra "multicast" channels.

> News-sharing arrangements, staffing levels, and collaborations with other local news entities.

> The extent to which websites are accessible to the hearing and visually impaired.

> Sponsorship identification disclosures for 'pay-for-play' material appearing in news and information programming. (See below).

Since most stations now offer video clips on their websites, we recommend offering a voluntary spot where stations can link to examples of programming they think has especially served the community, including accountability reporting.

This system should be used by both commercial and public TV stations. A random audit system can help insure that the reporting is accurate, or the FCC could consider the viability of a system in which TV stations that have their programming online could post links to the videos about the community.

In most cases, the primary goal should not be to provide the FCC with tools for license-renewal denials, but to provide communities the data they need to understand what their local TV stations are doing and how they compare to others in the city, state, or nationwide. Broadcasters that demonstrably do the most to cover their communities can use this official data to market their commitment. Community leaders—whether the local newspaper media columnist or a citizens group or the Chamber of Commerce—should be able to use this data to highlight which stations are covering their communities most effectively and which are not. Disability groups should be able to highlight the stations whose websites are most accessible. National watchdog groups should be able to rank which TV station chains do the most local programming and which do the least—or which allow for significant numbers of pay-for-play advertising arrangements. Lawmakers making spectrum policy should have a more granular understanding of how broadcasters use their stations and serve the public.

Strengthen "Pay-for-Play" Disclosure Rules

Chapter 3 provided disturbing examples of "pay-for- play" arrangements at local TV stations, in which advertisers have been allowed to dictate, shape or sculpt news or editorial content. This trend, if not checked by the industry itself, will rot away the community's trust in local TV. Current "sponsorship identification" laws and rules already require that stations disclose during a broadcast whether content is paid for, furnished or sponsored by an outside party, but the Commission should make enforcement more effective by considering one simple but potentially potent additional step: when newscasts are required to provide sponsorship identification on air, they should also disclose it on the Internet. Specifically, when a show providing news identifies a pay-for-play arrangement or use of a video news release on air, it should also post that information online, perhaps as part of a unified online public file. This would create a permanent, searchable record of which stations use these arrangements and afford easy access by consumers, competitors and watchdog groups to this information.

Consider the Potential Effects of Newspaper-TV Station Mergers on Local News Ecosystems

The FCC is in the midst of its Congressionally mandated quadrennial ownership review. It will have the benefit of original research not available to this project at the point of publication. So rather than offering specific recommendations, we offer two broad observations.

First, it is easy to see how newspapers and TV stations merging operations could lead to efficiencies and improved business models that might result in more reporting resources and therefore help reach the policy goal of enhanced "localism." On the other hand, it is also easy to see how such mergers could simply improve the bottom line of a combined company *without* actually increasing the resources devoted to local newsgathering in a community. Therefore, we are not persuaded that relaxing ownership rules would *inevitably* lead to more local news, information or reporting or that it would *inevitably* lead to less.

Second, it goes without saying that in considering the cross-ownership rules, the FCC should consider the impact of its rules on local news and public affairs reporting in the community as a whole. The FCC should consider looking at shared services agreements with the same question in mind—whether the arrangements contribute to the overall media health of the community.

Improve Disclosure and Other Policies for Cable and Satellite Operators

The leased access system for cable television appears to be grossly ineffective. It was supposed to ensure that as much as 15 percent of cable capacity went to independent programming, including local material. Instead, less than one percent does. *The FCC should undertake a comprehensive study on the current state of leased access* and whether it fulfills the goals set out by Congress.

Another way that MVPDs could help communities is by offering local all-news cable shows. Some cable operators are already providing valuable local cable news operations, but many find them to be uneconomical. Congress might consider legislation to *reduce the leased access burdens for MVPDs that carry local cable news efforts* (whether created by the cable operator, a broadcaster, or other player). Moreover, we hope that if there are broadcasters or other organizations that want to fund all-news channels, MVPDs—especially those that do not already fund local cable news operations—they will seriously consider the tremendous potential benefits to communities of providing carriage to such channels.

As for Direct Broadcast Satellite companies, Congress gave the FCC the authority to set aside between 4 and 7 percent of their capacity for educational programming. In 1998, the FCC chose 4 percent on the grounds that DBS was a fledgling industry. It may now be worth another look at that requirement, as today the DBS industry is well-established and currently serving millions of Americans. Under the current set-aside program, satellite operators air valuable educational programming. However, they are also turning away additional educational programming—public affairs, religious and otherwise—on the grounds that they have no capacity. We recommend that the FCC more thoroughly *assess the effectiveness of the set-aside system*. In the meantime, *the information that satellite providers currently offer upon request should be put online, available to the public.* This should continue to include information about how they calculate the number of stations eligible under the set-aside; what those programmers are charged; what channels are being accepted and rejected, and why.

MAKE IT EASIER FOR CITIZENS TO MONITOR THEIR GOVERNMENT BY PUTTING MORE PROCEEDINGS, DOCUMENTS AND DATA ONLINE

Of course transparency is not only important for the FCC or broadcasters. Greater openness by government—at all levels—can make it easier for Americans to inform themselves and for both citizen and professional reporters to hold institutions accountable.

First, citizens should be able to more easily monitor the workings of state and local government. State government spending has risen substantially while the number of traditional news reporters watching over that spending has dropped by a third. Several state public affairs networks (SPANs) have showed that they can help provide some measure of accountability—simply by airing the proceedings of government. Some SPANs also provide venues for candidate debates, town halls and forums on critical state and local issues. Therefore, *every state should have a vibrant public affairs network, a state-based C-SPAN.*

The cable industry has long pointed with pride to its creation and support of C-SPAN, an effective way of meeting civic needs without government regulation. We agree—and believe all MVPDs should work toward the goal of insuring that state public affairs networks become as significant on the state level as C-SPAN has become on the national level.

There is no one-size-fits-all way to do this. We are partial to the model that has worked for C-SPAN, in which the cable industry itself provided the upfront capital and now pays the network annually through subscriber fees. This model has the advantage of reducing a network's dependence on the state legislature it is supposed to cover (a common funding source in the states in which the cable operators have not funded spans). But other models may work as well. For instance, in some states, the public TV stations air the SPANs; the Corporation for Public Broadcasting could further incentivize such collaborations. Or, Congress could consider *reducing the leased access requirements to cable operators that give carriage or financing to SPANs.* State legislatures should consider *looking at the PEG (Public, Education and Government access) system as a way of carrying and financing state SPANs.* Our reading of the 1992 Cable Act is that such efforts could qualify as appropriate PEG programming, which would also mean SPAN programming could be eligible for funding from local franchising authorities.

Second, and just as important, *governments at all levels should put far more data and information online, and do it in ways that are designed to be most useful.* Among the data most important to be disclosed are those related to: the integrity of political institutions (e.g., campaign contributions, financial disclosures and disclosures of outside employment by government employees), government agency performance (audits), public expenditures (e.g., budgets, expenditures), public health and safety (e.g., inspection reports for schools, hospitals, nursing homes, child care centers, bridges and buildings), and legal compliance by regulated entities (e.g., fictitious business name registrations, environmental citations, disciplinary actions against attorneys and physicians).

It matters greatly *how* this information organized. It needs to be put out in standardized, machine-readable, structured formats that make it easy for programmers to create new applications that can present the data in more useful formats, or combine one agency's information with another. *Data releases should include an Application Programming Interface (API) that allows the data to be shared easily with other computers and applications.* Rep. Darrell Issa's Government Information Transparency Act would require "a single data standard for the collection, analysis, and dissemination of business and financial information for use by private sector entities . . . for information required to be reported to the Federal Government, and a single data standard for use by agencies within the Federal Government for Federal financial information."[4] It would further require that the standard represent "a widely accepted, open source, non-proprietary, searchable, computer-readable format for business and financial data."[5] These are excellent ideas, and should guide the approaches of state and local governments as well. Ultimately, whenever possible, government documents should also be created in searchable, analyzable formats.

These approaches can make government more effective and efficient. For instance, the FCC recently undertook to document broadband speeds in different parts of the country. Instead of sending out, say, half a dozen researchers to report on variations, they built an application that allowed citizens to perform tests themselves and report the data to the FCC. Two million submissions resulted.

Putting more government data online will make it more likely that entrepreneurs can create new businesses and jobs based on distributing, shaping or analyzing this data. It will enable reporters to unearth stories in a day or two that might have previously taken two months. And it can make government more useful to citizens, and in so doing, encourage broadband adoption by making the Internet ever more relevant to people's everyday lives. (And, in a virtuous circle, increased broadband adoption will lead to a greater likelihood of success for digital news enterprises).

To make this strategy most effective, data should be archived so that information, once posted, does not disappear over time.

Policymakers should also consider ways to ensure that many of the companies and organizations that receive public funding or are regulated by government electronically file information so taxpayers could track the quality of their performance and the use of public dollars.

Legislatures should consider increasing the likelihood that the public gets maximum value from government transparency initiatives by creating, within each jurisdiction, two positions: a Senior Transparency Officer, who would audit the performance of individual agencies and coordinate training, and a public Information Ombudsperson, to mediate public information disputes promptly. Governments could consider maintaining a single online portal to facilitate access to public documents, whether those "documents" take the form of text, audio or video. The portal could give access to webcasts, both live and archived, of all public meetings and hearings, from sessions of Congress to town halls.[6] *We would also encourage legislative bodies to consider the proposal,* advocated by House Energy and Commerce Committee Subcommittee on Communications and Technology Chairman Greg Walden and others on the federal level, that such portals be used *to post all nonemergency legislation for at least 72 hours prior to a final vote, to facilitate public and media analysis.*

Public records law should carry a presumption in favor of releasing documents whose disclosure would not undermine national security, public safety, compelling privacy interests, trade secrets, or law enforcement. Those responsible for compliance with open records laws should be fully trained, so that they are aware of the relevant laws governing what counts as "confidential" versus "public" information. Agencies should post responses to information requests online to avoid duplication in requests and redundant compliance efforts.

The federal government can also play a helpful role by fostering technical advances in the cause of transparency. The National Archives and Records Administration, in collaboration with OMB, might convene a national working group of Chief Information and Technology Officers to discuss and decide upon technical and operational procedures. A computing "cloud" for the permanent storage of all government events could be created. The Library of Congress, National Science Foundation, Department of Homeland Security, Department of Defense (especially DARPA), and National Endowment for Humanities already support, to some extent, research into tools that can aid in the mining of text, audio, and/or video recordings. Such funding should be coordinated to assure it operates in ways that will facilitate accountability reporting.

Foundations and other nonprofit groups can help by developing apps and other software that make it easier for citizens and reporters to make use of the data that is put forward. The Apps for Communities programs run by

New York City, DC and the FCC's Apps for Inclusion programs might serve as models for other local governments and other foundations.

CONSIDER TARGETING CURRENT GOVERNMENT ADVERTISING MORE TOWARD LOCAL MEDIA

The government currently spends money on advertising to advance various public goals—such as military recruitment, census compliance, or park safety. In 2005, the amount spent was $1 billion, according to the General Accountability Office. Currently much of this spending goes to national entertainment media. Some local broadcasters have argued that this could be targeted to local news enterprises without undermining the cost effectiveness of the campaigns, and perhaps even *saving* taxpayers money. We agree. *Targeting existing federal advertising spending to local news media could help local news media models—both commercial and nonprofit, online and off-line—gain traction and help create local jobs, while potentially making taxpayer spending more cost-effective*. In the past, it may have been more cost effective to buy national rather than local but technological improvements have made it possible to easily buy local media placements on TV, in print and online—so that shifting ads to local news media could prove *more* cost-effective for taxpayers. To be clear, we have no opinion on how much the federal government ought to spend on advertising; but if it does spend money on marketing, it makes public policy sense to target it to a variety of local news media.

One critical point: with such an effort, it is imperative that this strategy be implemented in a way that is strictly non-political and not subject to political manipulation. This appears to be an achievable goal, as ad spending currently appears to be apolitical and new technology allows for the buying of ads in such a way that government entities need not be involved in the micro-decisions about which specific media entities get money. Targeting would need to be focused on broad industry-standard categories and quantitative measures.

Another important advertising-related policy issue is privacy. Regulators and consumers have an extremely legitimate concern that targeted advertising might invade the privacy of Internet users. However, ad targeting, since it commands higher prices, offers one possible way for local content creators to build sustainable business models that can help finance local journalism. When considering privacy rules, the policymakers should therefore also *consider the positive benefits of ad targeting for local news and journalism operations.*

In recognition that advertising is, and will always be, a crucial part of media business models, we also *recommend against proposals to raise money for public media by taxing advertising*. This would make it harder, not easier, for both commercial and nonprofit media entities to create sustainable business models. As scholar Adam Thierer has written, "Advertising benefits society by subsidizing the creation of news, information, and entertainment."[7]

MAKE IT EASIER FOR NONPROFIT MEDIA TO DEVELOP SUSTAINABLE MODELS

Some types of journalism are so costly, and provide such a poor short-term financial return on investment, that commercial media will likely under-finance their production. We therefore believe that the nonprofit sector, broadly defined, should play a greater role in filling the gaps in labor-intensive reporting.

Nonprofit media includes a wide range of players including large nonprofit media companies (such as the Associated Press and *Consumer Reports*), public TV and radio, nonprofit information or publishing websites (such as Wikipedia, Mozilla and Wordpress), local independent nonprofit websites, Low Power FM, PEG channels, state public affairs networks (SPANs), journalism schools and nonprofit programming on satellite TV. Some receive government funds; most do not, which is as it should be.

We estimate it would take somewhere between $265 million and $1.6 billion to fill the current gaps in local reporting each year. Some will hopefully be filled by the commercial sector in the coming years but, at least in the near term, a meaningful chunk of this missing accountability reporting will need to come from the nonprofit sector, broadly defined, including individual citizens, foundations and philanthropists donating to nonprofit media. The *main focus of government policy should not be providing the funds to sustain reporting but rather helping create conditions under which nonprofit news operations can gain traction*.

Obstacles in Tax Policy

Private donations to nonprofit media will be an important factor in the health of local media.

The tax code already indirectly subsidizes nonprofit media, along with many other types of nonprofits, by allowing Americans to deduct from their taxable income the amount that they contribute to charities. In the case of charities, the government does not decide to give particular subsidies to organizations it deems worthy; rather, it enables the decisions of American taxpayers. Within broad parameters, no one at the IRS decides whether a donation to the soup kitchen is more meritorious than one to the senior center. It currently works that way for nonprofit media, too. Someone who donates $100 gets the same deduction if she donates to a conservative magazine, a liberal radio station or a nonpartisan investigative website—as long as the recipients are all eligible nonprofit organizations. The government subsidy simply magnifies the impact of the individual's choice. The system works well.

However, some nonprofit media entrepreneurs and tax experts have expressed concerns that these rules were designed for a certain type of charity, and nonprofit media companies sometimes fit more awkwardly into those parameters than they should. Indeed, some nonprofit media entrepreneurs feel confused about the IRS approach. The agency allows numerous magazines, investigative reporting groups, and websites to be registered as nonprofit organizations—yet in 1977 it denied tax exempt status to a nonprofit newspaper on the grounds that its operations were "indistinguishable from ordinary commercial publishing practices. Accordingly, it is not operated exclusively for charitable and educational purposes."[8] Nonprofits currently face uncertainty, steep legal bills or the prospect of losing their nonprofit status if they make the wrong move.

In addition, the IRS code prohibits nonprofit charities from lobbying for legislation. While few (if any) nonprofit news websites want to lobby, some fear that even running a commentary for or against a piece of legislation might count as lobbying and jeopardize their tax status. This potentially chills free speech and makes it harder for a nonprofit media entity to do its job—covering important news and civic issues—and restricts development of sustainable business models.

Another issue raised by nonprofit web startups is advertising. A nonprofit website that wants to take advertising has to count it as unrelated business income—taxable like a for-profit business—even though in every other way the organization functions as a nonprofit.

In the past, when it became clear that a particular set of IRS rules did not fit an industry, lawmakers created a new 501c category that better reflected the realities of that group, e.g. railroad retirement funds (501c28) or cemetery companies (501c13). Some have suggested, therefore, the creation of a subsection of the tax code for nonprofit media. Other tax experts reject that idea, suggesting that the current tax code could work adequately if the IRS were to clarify some of its positions. Either way, it's important that tax ambiguities or restrictions do not stand in the way of essential nonprofit media innovation.

Finally, policymakers should consider finding ways of giving owners of dying newspapers, TV stations or radio stations a way to convert them to nonprofit status. We have seen over and over again that even financially embattled newspapers, including those in bankruptcy, still have tremendously valuable assets. In most communities, they produce the most popular news website so they are well positioned to transition to the digital age. But they may not be able to produce the profit margins demanded by publicly traded corporate chains. In other words, some newspaper-based media companies could survive as nonprofits even if they cannot as for-profits. But switching from commercial to nonprofit status is financially difficult, in part because creditors understandably want to be made whole. A bill by Senator Ben Cardin attempted to make such conversions easier, but there may be additional tax changes that could be considered.

This is a complex area. Some believe that the needed modifications are minor and could be done through IRS rulings. Others suggest statutory changes. The particulars are beyond our area of expertise so we make these two broad recommendations:

Policymakers should recognize *that cleaning up the ambiguities in the tax code for nonprofit media is potentially a crucial step toward enabling nonprofit entities to develop sustainable business models.*

A respected nonpartisan organization, such as the Council on Foundations, *should convene both nonprofit tax experts and nonprofit news entrepreneurs to study the question of what tax changes or clarifications could better enable nonprofit media to meet the information needs of communities and issue a report making recommendations about how to implement such changes.* The report could then serve as a roadmap to ensure an organized and focused sector-wide approach to the issue.

A Crucial New Role for Foundations, Philanthropists and Citizens

Several foundations have already played a crucially important role in stimulating innovation during this period of dramatic transformation of the media landscape. We recommend that more foundations, philanthropists and citizens consider thinking about news media differently than in the past.

In general, a growing but small percentage of foundation and philanthropic spending goes toward helping communities enrich and protect themselves through local reporting. No doubt foundations and philanthropists had until recently viewed the funding of journalism as unnecessary since the well-heeled commercial media sector seemed to be filling these needs. In addition, philanthropists and foundations pursue other worthy causes, many of which will seem, and often are, more immediately pressing than the quality of local reporting. It could seem hard to argue for a city hall reporter over money for local food banks.

But, in fact, society will be less equipped to solve pressing problems if it is ill informed. It is now clear that there are important gaps—not in the number of media outlets or the forms of media distribution but specifically in labor-intensive, professional reporting, especially on the local level. As demonstrated in Part One, these shortages have particularly worrisome consequences in the areas of education, health, government accountability, and crime. Ensuring that communities have a healthy media system is not in conflict with foundation efforts to other important goals; it's a prerequisite for them to meet those needs. Foundations or philanthropists that focus on particular issues should be conscious of the role of media in a) educating the public and b) holding officials and the institutions that oversee reforms accountable. Spending money on a cause without ensuring that there are reporters to analyze the problem, and the proposed solutions, makes it more likely the money will be wasted. For instance, it seems more than a little risky to devote billions to education reform when most communities do not have full-time education reporters working to make sure the reform is effective. Foundations focused on economic development or financials issues should fund business reporters; those concerned with religion should fund local religion reporters; etc. Alberto Ibargüen, the president of the Knight Foundation has said, "It is hard to succeed in the areas of environment, safety, education or health when the news and information system isn't working."

An especially important role will need to be played by the 650 local "community and place based" foundations, often formed by local business and other civic leaders, that spend $2.6 billion a year attempting to build healthy communities. These foundations have become crucial players in helping solve local problems. Terry Mazany, the president of the Chicago Community Trust put it well: "The success of nonprofit organizations depends on a strong media ecosystem." We applaud the interest expressed by a growing number of local foundations, for just as foreign countries without a robust press tend toward corruption and economic stagnation, communities without a healthy media will suffer.

Some may argue that relying so heavily on donations from foundations, nonprofits and individuals lets government off the hook. But we do not believe government should play the primary role in directly funding journalism, in part because it is difficult (though not impossible) for the state to fund accountability reporting against the state. Nonprofit media outlets are more likely to succeed if they draw money from a wide variety of different sources, including foundations and individual donations.

We hope that a critical mass of foundations and donors that do increase their commitment to this field approach it in a nonpartisan, non-ideological fashion. Foundations that invest in reporting need to have a basic faith in the ultimate societal value of objective reporting and let go of the notion that only journalism that advances a particular set of policies should be supported. At least some reporters need to be *reporters*, not propagandists. One inspiring model is the John Locke Foundation, a free-market foundation in North Carolina, which decided that the lack of nonpartisan statehouse reporting was harming the state. John Hood, the president of the Foundation, believes that since the commercial sector will not fill the gaps, foundations and other donors will need play a bigger role: "When you get to the state and local level, the collapse of the traditional business models imperils the delivery of sufficient public interest journalism—and we do believe that donor driven journalism can be a very important model."

Foundation leaders have been discussing many creative new ways of helping local media. In many cases they are working on their own, determining how local media fits in with their other missions. But there is increasing discussion about collaborations as well. For instance, foundations that fund controversial journalism directly will need to develop thick skins and a set of journalistic principles when local powers-that-be complain. Some have therefore suggested creating state-level foundation collaboratives. This would provide a level of political insulation, since a third body, one level removed, would be making the funding decisions rather than the individual local foundation. This could also create a mechanism for insuring that poorer communities lacking local foundations might benefit. Some state foundation collaboratives could consider creating a pool of funds to subsidize local nonprofit websites through a formula based on traffic growth or success in recruiting large number of donors, rather having than only a competitive grant system. This would reward success and help ensure that foundation money provides ongoing online operational support, not just seed capital. The collaborative structure might work for national foundations as well. For instance, foundations, philanthropists and individual donors might create a national organization for the funding of local school reporters on the Teach for America model. The financing could be split between national philanthropy and local community foundations; the reporters could be placed in either for-profit or nonprofit entities.

Foundations have already shown tremendous creativity in supporting journalism, not only funding nonprofit news websites but also journalism schools that do reporting and technology that helps local reporting flow. In that vein, we hope foundations will also consider ways they can help nonprofit groups make good use of data and information put out by local governments. Transparency will only work if there are mechanisms for organizing, analyzing and distributing the data. We also can envision a role for foundations in helping make the FCC's new transparency efforts effective as well. Having broadcasters disclose information about their programming will only improve the functioning of commercial markets if the data are well used.

Ordinary citizens are crucial, too. Most nonprofit websites that have been created in recent years rely heavily on individual contributions. Those who support veterans' organizations might consider whether there are any nonprofit media outlets that have paid special attention to the plight of veterans. Those who give to soup kitchens, might look for local media that has made a commitment to covering poverty. It is time for citizens to think of media as an important item on their menu of charitable choices.

We do not, by the way, express a preference for individuals to give donations to free nonprofit sites *over* paying a subscription for a commercial media product. Indeed, the more done by the commercial sector, the better. But labor-intensive, civically-valuable reporting will not flourish unless citizens spend more on it, whether through donations to nonprofits, subscriptions to commercial entities, or a combination of both.

Even a relatively small shift in behavior can have a significant impact on nonprofit media. If local "place based" and community foundations, which have a big stake in the health of communities, put 5 percent of their spending toward journalism it would generate $130 million annually to fulfill the local information, news and accountability journalism needs of communities. If the foundations of the top new media companies and their founders, which have benefited tremendously from the new media landscape, put 5 percent of their spending toward local accountability journalism, that would generate $220 million annually. If Americans spent one percent of their charitable giving on nonprofit media, that would generate $2.7 billion per year. To make it easier for individuals to give to local media, should they so choose, nonprofit groups and foundations should consider creating a database of nonprofit media, searchable by zip code and interest. We hope that the foundation sector will consider year-over-year increases in the funding of accountability reporting and we hope that each year more individuals will do the same.

A Crucial New Role for Journalism Schools

Journalism schools have begun playing a significant new role in the media ecosystem. Innovators in the profession are calling for schools to adopt a "medical residency" model, which is to say—have the students *do* journalism as they learn it. Given that in any year there are about 4,500 graduate students and 50,000 undergraduates earning journalism degrees, this has the potential to add meaningfully to the accountability journalism in many communities. Many journalism schools have created partnerships with other media entities and achieved great results. (See Chapter 14, Journalism Schools.) *We recommend that foundations and philanthropists help fund journalism-school "residencies" for recent graduates* who can help manage year-round efforts to produce significant journalism for the community, using journalism school students. This simple step could enable journalism schools to significantly increase their impact in communities, while improving the quality of their instruction at the same time.

Public Broadcasting and the Emerging Nonprofit Media

Give Non-Commercial Broadcasters, Including Religious Broadcasters, More Flexibility to Create Sustainable Nonprofit Business Models

Both supporters and opponents of government funding for public broadcasters should be able to agree that government rules should not hamstring the ability of noncommercial broadcasting to create sensible, responsive business models that make them less dependent on taxpayer funds.

There is some confusion, for instance, about whether FCC rules prohibit public TV and radio stations from accepting advertising or merchandizing products on their websites. They do not. According to FCC rules, the *restrictions on underwriting or merchandizing that govern on-air programming do not apply on the websites created by public media.* Stations or funders may have their own rules or policies leading them to not take advertising online but they should do so with the knowledge that FCC rules do give them flexibility.

The National Religious Broadcasters and others have argued that the FCC should allow noncommercial stations to devote a small amount of air time, up to one percent, to help fundraise for charities and other nonprofits. In some cases, having local charities on the air can be a useful way of informing residents about problems in their communities, and certainly allowing such efforts can help stations achieve their public service or religious missions. We recommend that the FCC consider allowing stations or programmers that are not grantees of the CPB, such as most religious broadcasters, *to spend up to one percent of their airtime doing fundraising for charities and other third-party nonprofits.* The broadcasters should *disclose how this time is used—including how much is helping charities in the local community—so the FCC can make an assessment about the efficacy of this experiment.*

Remove Obstacles That Prevent CPB From Emphasizing Local Content and Innovation

Public broadcasters need to continue to play an important role on the media landscape. They have done superb work in many areas, and this would be precisely the wrong time to defund the Corporation for Public Broadcasting.

But the system can be improved so that public TV and radio would be more likely to produce local programming and digital innovation.

Like commercial broadcasters, *public TV stations should be spared the paperwork burdens of the current disclosure system* and *required to offer the public clear information about how much local programming they are doing and other types of information that might promote accountability and improve quality.*

The leaders of the Corporation for Public Broadcasting have asked for more flexibility as they embrace a 21st century mission. We agree. For instance, it may not make sense to continue to stipulate that approximately 75 percent of funding go to public TV and 25 percent go to radio. In a converged world, radio stations are doing video on their websites; TV stations are producing for the Internet, and websites are doing multimedia for multiple platforms. Based on what public media leaders have told us, local communities would benefit if the CPB had more flexibility to award money to multimedia innovators, whether their original platforms were TV or radio or something else. *We especially hope that such flexibility would be used by CPB to incentivize public media players to provide more* local *content and services.*

We also would like to see public TV consider the potential of state public affairs networks (SPANs) as a possible form of programming on their multicast channels. Perhaps CPB could provide extra funding to public TV stations that provide carriage for such operations.

CPB should have more leeway to fund nonprofit media that do not hold an over-the-air TV or radio license. It makes little sense that a nonprofit children's program that runs on a broadcast station gets money from CPB but an equally good nonprofit children's program that runs on only satellite TV does not. CPB should consider funding educational programming across a broader range of platforms including: *nonprofit programming on satellite, PEG channels, Low Power FM stations, state public affairs networks and nonprofit websites.*

However, we recommend that *any non-broadcast nonprofit media outlet getting government funding should not be allowed to have more than 15 percent of its revenue come from the Corporation for Public Broadcasting.* Eliminating the possibility that government would become the dominant funding source would go a long way toward reducing the odds that the state could financially pressure media. The bulk of the money for local nonprofit news sites should come from users and philanthropy, not government. To further guard against political interference at the local level, stations should, if they don't already, *have clear policies assuring editorial independence from underwriting pressures.*

Encourage Collaboration between For-Profit and Nonprofit Sectors

One of the most intriguing developments has been the organic rise of partnerships between for-profit and nonprofit entities. The partnership between Channel 7 in San Diego and the nonprofit website Voice of San Diego was so promising that that Comcast decided to apply it to four other local NBC stations, a decision we endorse. We saw fruitful collaborations, too, when the Pulitzer Center on Crisis Reporting, a nonprofit, worked with the *Washington Post* and when the Texas Tribune and Chicago News Cooperative were hired by the *New York Times*. The idea of the commercial and nonprofit sectors working together is not brand new—newspapers for years have relied on a nonprofit, the Associated Press, for essential coverage—but this model may become more important over time. Commercial ventures will gravitate toward the more profitable lines of business, yet they cannot ignore labor-intensive accountability coverage. Nonprofit ventures can fill the gaps but will struggle to survive. In all of these partnerships, the commercial entity benefited by getting high quality and low cost coverage; the nonprofit benefited by getting exposure and, yes, cash for services. If nonprofits can reliably count on this additional revenue stream—fees for service—from the commercial sector, both sides benefit. Most of this will happen organically. But public policy may be able to remove obstacles. For instance, IRS changes may make it easier for nonprofit websites to thrive and grow into such partnerships. When the FCC creates a streamlined disclosure form for broadcasters, it should offer a field for stations to describe their partnerships, including with nonprofit news websites. In making funding decisions, CPB could consider assessing the willingness of public broadcasters to engage in partnerships and help the media ecosystem as a whole.

There is one public-private partnership we think would be a bad idea: some have suggested creating a federally-funded AmeriCorps program for journalists. Journalism should often be about challenging powerful institutions, which sometimes will draw political fire and controversy. AmeriCorps has grown and prospered by focusing on the forms of service on which most Americans can agree, such as tutoring, helping seniors, or working for Habitat for Humanity. Creating a government-financed AmeriCorps for reporters would potentially seriously harm AmeriCorps.

SPANs, PEGs and LPFMs

PEG channels are in a time of great flux. These stations, and related community media centers, need to evolve, and many are. The original mission of providing media access to a diversity of voices is somewhat less compelling today given the availability of such platforms online. We applaud the community media centers that have moved to become key venues to help train citizens in digital literacy. We recommend that community media centers explore ways to help increase digital literacy and broadband adoption, and that *policymakers consider community media centers as a resource that can aid in efforts in those areas.*

We also believe that *PEG channels should not necessarily resist local efforts to require a minimum amount of local programming.* If community media centers cannot provide a minimum amount of original programming, it is possible that some other nonprofit entity that can do so should take over. We also encourage community media centers to work collaboratively with other nonprofit media, and vice versa. For instance, in some cases PEG channels could be used to carry state public affairs networks—or as a venue for local nonprofit websites to create local news shows. *PEG channels should consider evolving into broader platforms for a broader range of nonprofit programming, including that created by local nonprofit websites, LPFMs, SPANs, public radio or independent video programmers.*

At the same time, if the PEG community is going to push itself to evolve, it needs to do so with the knowledge that its basic rights are not being degraded by MVPDs or local government. It would be extremely unfortunate to cut back on Community Media Centers at precisely the moment when the need for creativity in local nonprofit media is growing. Community Media should continue to improve but should be an important part of the local media solution in the years to come.

In a bipartisan move, Congress recently passed and President Obama signed a law making it easiewr for Low Power FM stations to proliferate. The FCC must now implement the law. In doing so, *the FCC should make sure that licensing "windows" are set up in such a way to give LPFMs a fair shot at getting traction throughout the nation. LPFMs have asked the Commission to require a minimum amount of local programming. We recommend that the Commission consider such a requirement.*

Finally, it's clear that these thousands of local content creators ought to be able to find audiences far-and-wide for some of their material. Some, of course, have been uploading audio or video online, where anyone can check them out. But *social entrepreneurs and foundations might also consider creating clearinghouse systems* akin to documentcloud.org or Internetarchive.org—or expanding those that already exist. This would allow these media institutions grounded in audio and video to use the Internet not only reach new users but learn from each other. Moreover, to the extent that they air material about local governments or other important institutions, creating such a platform would improve accountability as well.

ENSURE THAT BROADBAND IS WIDESPREAD ENOUGH TO FUEL DIGITAL MEDIA INNOVATION

Universal and Open Internet

The highly motivated, well-wired news consumer can find many different sources of information. But those who lose the services of a high quality local newspaper and do not have meaningful access to the Internet will end up worse off than ever before. Conversely, media models online often depend on scale, so some models will only work once Internet usage reaches a certain level in a local community. Whether digital news enterprises depend on advertising or subscription fees or some other model, they will be more likely to succeed as the number of Americans using high speed Internet increases. Increased broadband adoption will increase the audience for digital news enterprises as well as the pool of citizen journalists capable of generating digital news. In short, *universal broadband is an essential ingredient for enabling local media innovation to succeed and to improving the information health of communites.*

Many of the most promising developments involve concerned citizens who have attempted to fill a gap in the information needs of their communities by starting new ventures. We take for granted that such innovation can happen on the Internet and in the mobile sector, but we should keep in mind that it is only *the openness of the system that allows for small startups to rise up* so easily.

Strong Libraries

Rather than being rendered obsolete by the Internet, libraries are playing an ever more important role in the information life of their communities. Forty percent of those in poverty say their sole access to the Internet is through the library. Poor children who lack digital skills will stay poor; unemployed adults who cannot access job opportunities will stay unemployed. Insuring that libraries have enough terminals and fast enough speeds becomes a matter of both basic equity and economic necessity.

At a minimum, as government plans broadband deployment and adoption strategies, it should consider the central role of public libraries. Whether helping them to become Wi-Fi hotspots or providing more desktop terminals, a first order of business is to ensure that those who want Internet access should get it.

Local foundations and businesses may play a role, too. To the extent libraries are maxed out because of lack of equipment or technical expertise, *technology companies can and should help fill the gap by donating equipment and services.*

Encourage Broad-based Digital and Media Literacy

There is widespread agreement that more needs to be done to promote "digital literacy"—the basic 21st century skills of how to use the Internet and the latest information and communication technology. This is a matter of fairness and economic competitiveness. The National Broadband Plan offered many good ideas. We add one more: we have noticed that the community media centers that run Public, Educational and Government access stations have increasingly taken on the task of teaching digital skills. This is a very healthy development. *Community media centers should continue promoting digital literacy, and localities considering cutting PEG funding should re-assess those decisions in light of this new role.*

"Media literacy"—learning how to be a shrewd consumer of information online—is also crucial. Citizens all across the country deserve to have the tools to assess information about health, schools and other important facets of living. In addition, consumers who recognize and are thus empowered to demand quality programming, including journalism, will make it more likely that business models can develop to provide such news. *We oppose the creation of a mandatory national standard or curriculum*; as it should be a local matter to design such programs. But fortunately, a thousand flowers are already blooming on the local level, in red, blue and purple communities around the country.

Incentive Auctions and Public Broadcasters

In order to promote wireless broadband, the FCC has proposed a voluntary incentive auction allowing broadcasters to contribute some or all of their spectrum in exchange for a portion of the proceeds. Public television license holders may want to participate as well. Policymakers should take care to treat public TV spectrum in a way that is both fair to current public TV license-holders and in keeping with the original principles underlying the decision to set aside spectrum for educational broadcasting. Specifically, *public TV license holders who voluntarily contribute spectrum should be treated on a par with the commercial broadcasters*. Whatever portion of the auction proceeds that commercial broadcasters get to keep as an incentive, noncommercial broadcasters should get the same.

As some of that "noncommercial educational broadcasting" spectrum makes its way to the commercial wireless companies that purchase it, Congress may consider directing a portion of auction proceeds to educational purposes. If so, we recommend including technology efforts that help to ensure that the information needs of communities are well met. We have become particularly convinced that investment in this innovation infrastructure can have huge benefits for the development of local media, both nonprofit and commercial. Moreover, technology investment is content-neutral. One could imagine, for example, that funding for software that enables machine reading of handwritten or nonstandard documents could help citizens and reporters hold institutions accountable. Or, government could fund the creation of a "public meeting cloud" to provide a low-cost way to archive and share video of local, state and national government meetings. Eric Newton, vice president of the Knight Foundation, observed:

"If a tech fund systematically unleashes open source software applications and the technology needed to operate them, and grants money for code, coders and computers to news organizations across the country, it could spread public media innovation faster into new groups and deeper into existing ones, and create nothing less than a news renaissance in America."[9]

ENSURE THAT MODERN MEDIA POLICY WORKS FOR PEOPLE IN HISTORICALLY UNDERSERVED COMMUNITIES

People with Disabilities

The recently passed Twenty-First Century Communications and Video Accessibility (CVAA) Act made great strides toward achieving the goal of ensuring that people with disabilities have full access to new forms of media. The swift and effective implementation of this Act is critical to ensuring that consumers with disabilities are fully able to reap the benefits of new media technologies.

New technologies offer tremendous opportunities for people with disabilities, but only if websites, applications, and the devices used to access them are designed to be accessible. This means that Web content needs to be provided in ways that are directly accessible (e.g., with closed captioning and video description) and compatible with assistive technologies (e.g., screen readers). In addition, when possible, media sites should comply with web content and authoring tool accessibility guidelines that specify features that web creation software should have to produce accessible content. The federal government is required to comply with these accessibility objectives under Section 508 of the Rehabilitation Act. But it is just as important that private websites aspire to meet these standards. We therefore recommend that TV stations, as part of their online disclosure form, describe the extent to which their websites are accessible to people with disabilities. In addition, we recommend that manufacturers of mobile devices move swiftly in meeting their future obligations under the CVAA to provide accessible interfaces and Internet browsers on media-capable wireless devices so that people who are blind or visually impaired have full access to web-based functions on these devices.

In general, as technology continues to change rapidly, the FCC should be attentive to how these new developments—such as cloud computing and emerging applications—affect whether people with disabilities can get the news and information they seek.

Minorities and Small Businesses

In general, the Commission should consider the impact of broadcast media ownership policies on local programming, and the impact of spectrum licensing policies on small businesses and minority and women-owned businesses.

For instance, the FCC is currently assessing what should happen to spectrum currently occupied by TV channels 5 and 6 in the event the band were realigned after a voluntary incentive auction, if Congress authorizes such auctions. The FCC should consider whether, in areas where TV channels 5 and 6 are not currently utilized for TV broadcasting, there exists the potential to expand TV or radio opportunities to new small businesses, including minority- and women-owned businesses.

The FCC's original efforts to provide more Low Power FM licenses stemmed in part from a desire to open up more radio opportunities to minorities. The recently enacted Local Community Radio Act creates an opportunity potentially to open up hundreds of new LPFM stations in urban areas. *The FCC should administer the new statute to maximize that potential and should take extra steps to disseminate information about any availability of new local broadcast opportunities.*

Alarmingly, minority ownership in traditional media is declining. The "tax certificate" program that was initiated in 1978 appears to have stimulated genuine improvements in minority ownership, but perceived abuse of the program led Congress to delete the Commission's tax certificate authority in 1995. Moreover, courts have since blocked government agencies from using race-specific remedies without sufficient data to support the need for race-conscious measures. The Commission, in a bipartisan vote, has recommended to Congress that it *reinstate the tax certificate program with a focus on small enterprises and new entrants,* which may include minority and women-owned businesses. This would both stimulate local job creation and improve diversity.

Foundation efforts to assist journalism schools that adopt the teaching hospital models should *pay special attention to communications programs in historically black colleges and other schools with particular emphasis on reaching historically underserved communities.* Additionally, public broadcasters can perform a vital educational resource function in local communities and should be encouraged to adopt outreach efforts to support their local communities, including minorities.

Transparency is key. Policymakers, citizens and entrepreneurs need better information about media ownership by small businesses, and minorities. The Commission currently requires entities that hold broadcast television and radio licenses to submit data on minority and female ownership on a biennial basis, and recently made public the data filed for the first time on the recently revised ownership reporting form. *It should continue to do so on a regular basis.* The Commission suspended collecting data from broadcast licensees on racial, ethnic, and gender employment at broadcast stations and cable systems while it resolves whether station-specific data should be kept confidential. It should *resolve the confidentiality issue and resume the collection of such data.*

To ensure that the new media economy leads to all communities being served, the Commission can play a supporting role by educating would-be entrepreneurs on opportunities for financing. *The Commission might consider creating or participating in a Minority Capital Institute* or similar permanent office that could conduct seminars on auctions, private sector capital availability, broadcast expertise, and other financial issues.

* * *

These recommendations attempt to address some of the challenges facing us right now. But the media landscape is changing continually. As conditions evolve, policymakers should pay special attention to making sure that markets remain open and fluid, so new players can continue to challenge the status quo and invent new ways of providing citizens the news and information they want. When obstacles arise to competition, innovation or progress, policymakers should remove them.

These proposals strive to increase transparency, use taxpayer resources more effectively and foster innovation. This approach preserves the tremendous benefits that the digital media are bringing to communities, while trying to also address the serious shortfalls. Our hope is it will lead to more coverage of communities, and better accountability of powerful local institutions. If the strengths of the new and old media economies can be combined, Americans will have the best local media system they have ever had.

How This Report Was Put Together

THIS REPORT WAS PULLED TOGETHER by members of an ongoing, informal "working group"—including both FCC staff, scholars and consultants. In addition, other members of the talented FCC staff generously contributed their time and extensive expertise.

Almost all FCC staff did this on top of their regular responsibilities, so their efforts, wisdom and conscientiousness are deeply appreciated.

Often, the conclusions were arrived at by consensus. When there was disagreement, the Chairman of the working group decided. The views of this "white paper" do not necessarily represent the views of the Federal Communications Commission, its Commissioners or any individual Bureaus or Offices.

The group did over 600 interviews—with people representing a wide range of experiences and perspectives, including journalists, media executives, scholars, conservative and liberal public advocacy groups, entrepreneurs, labor leaders, communications lawyers, financial analysts, minority group representatives, journalism school deans, foundation leaders, local government officials, Internet company leaders, TV producers, mobile carriers, nonprofit news organizations, public broadcasting officials, community media experts, state public affairs network founders, radio executives, educators, gadflys, lobbyists, bloggers, techies, Tweeters and many more.

In addition, the FCC held two full-day workshops for this report, participated in several workshops on ownership, and received more than a thousand comments in response to a public notice. Staff also reviewed the extensive literature of other reports and studies on this topic.

This version, printed July 2011, includes copy-editing corrections on the version released online in June 2011.

Regular members of the Working Group included:

Steven Waldman (Chairman of the Working Group) is Senior Advisor to the FCC Chairman. He was Co-founder, CEO, and Editor-in-Chief of Beliefnet.com, a leading religious website, which was acquired by News Corp's Fox Network Group. Before that he was National Editor of *US News & World Report*, National Correspondent of *Newsweek* and a columnist for WSJ.com. His writings have appeared in *The Washington Post*, NationalReviewOnline, *HuffingtonPost*, *The Atlantic* and others. He's the author of *Founding Faith: The Birth of Religious Freedom in America*.

Elizabeth Biley Andrion (General Manager of the Working Group) is the Deputy Chief of the FCC's Office of Strategic Planning and Policy Analysis. She served previously as an advisor to then-Chairman Kevin Martin and as Vice President of Legal Affairs for Fox Television Stations.

Sherille Ismail (Senior Policy Advisor to the Working Group) is Senior Counsel in the FCC's Office of Strategic Planning and Policy Analysis. He has held several senior management positions at the FCC, including Deputy Chief of the Cable Bureau, since joining the agency in 1996. Before that, he served as Counsel on the Judiciary Committee, U.S. House of Representatives.

James T. Hamilton served as a distinguished visiting scholar with the Working Group and the Charles S. Sydnor Professor of Public Policy and Director of the DeWitt Wallace Center for Media and Democracy at Duke University. His research on public affairs journalism includes *"All The News That's Fit to Sell: How the Market Turns Information into News."*

Ellen P. Goodman served as a distinguished visiting scholar with the Working Group and is a Professor of Law at Rutgers University-Camden, specializing in information law and policy and publishing widely on such topics as spectrum policy, advertising, and public media. Goodman has advised domestic and international stakeholders on noncommercial media and public service technologies, and she is a Ford Foundation grantee. She was a partner with the law firm of Covington & Burling LLP.

Peter M. Shane served as a distinguished visiting scholar with the Working Group and is the Jacob E. Davis and Jacob E. Davis II Chair in Law at Ohio State University. He was Executive Director to the Knight Commission on the Information Needs of Communities in a Democracy. Recent books include Connecting Democracy: Online Consultation and the Flow of Political Communication (with Stephen Coleman), and Democracy Online: The Prospects for Political Renewal Through the Internet.

Cynthia Kennard served as a distinguished visiting scholar with the Working Group and is a Senior Fellow at The University of Southern California's Annenberg Center on Communication Leadership and Policy. She was a CBS News correspondent based in Los Angeles, London and Moscow and earlier worked nearly 15 years in local television news for WFAA-TV in Dallas, KHOU-TV in Houston and WANE-TV in Ft Wayne Indiana. She started her career in local radio news and more recently was managing director of National Public Radio West. She has authored several reports on broadcast journalism and for nine years served on the jury for the duPont Columbia University Awards for excellence in broadcast journalism.

Tamara Lipper Smith (Senior Advisor to the Group) and a special advisor in the FCC's Office of Strategic Planning and Policy Analysis. She was also a senior advisor to then-chairman of the FCC, Kevin Martin. She is a former broadcast and print journalist who covered national politics and the White House for *ABC News* and *Newsweek Magazine*. She has been a Special Assistant in the FCC's Office of Strategic Policy and Planning since 2006.

Elizabeth Sams is a writer and editor with experience in both old and new media. An Emmy-, Peabody-, and Dupont-award-winning documentary film producer, she most recently spent a decade as Executive Editor of Beliefnet. com, honored in 2007 with the National Magazine Award for online excellence.

Robert Ratcliffe is Deputy Chief of the FCC's Media Bureau. He has been at the FCC for 36 years and has held a variety of positions, from staff attorney in the original Cable Television Bureau in 1975, to interim media advisor to Chairman Sikes in 1989, to Acting Chief of the Media Bureau during the final stages of the DTV transition in 2009, and several jobs in between.

William Freedman is Associate Chief of the Consumer and Government Affairs Bureau. He has also worked at the FCC as Associate Chief of the Media Bureau, Deputy Chief of the Enforcement Bureau's Investigations and Hearings Division, and a media advisor to Commissioners Deborah Taylor Tate and Meredith Attwell Baker. He worked for over 20 years in private practice representing communications clients.

Jamila Bess Johnson is a Senior Attorney, Industry Analysis Division, Media Bureau.

J. Evan Shapiro is an attorney specializing in telecommunications and energy law.

Paige Gold practices media and entertainment law in Washington, D.C. and Los Angeles, California.

Simon Banyai is an Attorney Advisor in the FCC's Media Bureau, Policy Division.

Jeff Tignor is Special Counsel in the Broadband Division of the Wireless Telecommunications Bureau at the Federal Communications Commission. Previously, Mr. Tignor served as a Division Chief in the FCC's Consumer & Governmental Affairs Bureau. Prior to working at the FCC, Mr. Tignor was an associate at Dickstein Shapiro.

Jonathan Levy is Deputy Chief Economist at the FCC, specializing in media policy. Over the past 30 years at the agency, he has played a significant role in FCC proceedings on cable and satellite television issues, including must carry, retransmission consent, program access, encryption of satellite signals, media ownership rules, and the transition from analog to digital television.

Renee L. Roland is Senior Counsel in the Wireless Telecommunications Bureau of the FCC, having previously served as Deputy Bureau Chief in the Wireline Bureau and as a Senior Legal Advisor for Commissioners. Prior to the FCC, Ms. Roland worked in private practice for nearly a decade, specializing in media, wireline and wireless services.

Joel Taubenblatt is Senior Counsel in the Spectrum and Competition Policy Division of the FCC's Wireless Telecommunications Bureau. He has served in a number of roles at the Commission since 1996, including Deputy Bureau Chief of WTB and Chief of the Bureau's Broadband Division.

Mark S. Nadel is an Attorney Advisor in the Wireline Competition Bureau of the FCC. He has also taught and written law review articles on copyright economics, personalized news services, and interpreting the First Amendment in an Internet age, particularly protection of editorial freedom.

Gregory Cooke is the Associate Chief of the Policy Division in the FCC's Public Safety and Homeland Security Bureau. He focuses on emergency alerting issues, including the future national test of the Emergency Alert System and the upcoming comprehensive Notice of Inquiry on Broadband Alert and Warnings.

Irene S. Wu, Ph.D. is the International Bureau's Chief Data Officer (acting), and an adjunct professor in the Communications, Culture and Technology program at Georgetown University.

MK Guzda Struck has been a journalist and editor overseas for nearly 15 years with a variety of publications including *Pacific Stars and Stripes*, GlobalPost.com, and the *Baltimore Sun*. She is now managing editor of the *Lowell Sun* in Massachusetts.

Krista Witanowski is a Legal Advisor in the front office of the FCC's Media Bureau. She previously served as Acting Legal Advisor for media law issues for Commissioner Meredith Baker. Her first position at the Commission was working for then-Chairman Kevin Martin. She began her legal career in the Communications group at Wiley Rein.

In addition, special research and editorial assistance was provided by:

Mary Beth Murphy is Chief of the Policy Division of the FCC's Media Bureau. In this role, and in her prior positions at the FCC, she has led proceedings on a range of issues involving broadcasters and cable and satellite television providers.

Naomi Wax is a New York-based editor and editorial consultant.

Vincent Lisi is principal of Two Dogs Design in New York.

Karen Peltz Strauss is the FCC's Deputy Bureau Chief in the Consumer and Governmental Affairs Bureau, where she oversees the Commission's disability policies. She has over 25 years experience working on communications access issues concerning people with disabilities, and helped spearhead several federal laws to expand telephone and TV access. Before joining the FCC, she co-founded the Coalition of Organizations for Accessible Technology.

Natalie (Talia) Jomini Stroud is an Assistant Professor in the Department of Communication Studies and the Assistant Director of the Annette Strauss Institute for Civic Participation at the University of Texas at Austin. Her research on political news includes a recent book entitled "Niche News: The Politics of News Choice."

Dana Scherer is an analyst in the Industry Analysis Division of FCC's Media Bureau, where she analyzes trends in the media and telecommunications industries. She has worked on the Comcast-NBC Universal transaction, the Open Internet Proceeding, the Commission's Annual Reports on the State of Video Competition. She worked previously for Univision Communications.

Ava Seave is a Principal with consulting firm Quantum Media. She is an Associate Adjunct Professor at Columbia Business School and an Assistant Adjunct Professor at Columbia Journalism School.

Sherry Ricchiardi-Folwell is a contributing writer for American Journalism Review, specializing in international issues, and a professor at the Indiana University School of Journalism. She has been a media trainer and consultant in Pakistan, Yemen, former Soviet Union and other countries.

Anne Levine is a Policy Analyst in the Office of Strategic Planning and Policy Analysis at the FCC. Since 1997, she has worked on projects related to corporate ownership structure, individual firm performance, and technological developments in media, broadband, cable television, broadcast, and related industries. She has provided empirical analysis to on such issues as Program Access, Leased Access, Media Ownership, the DTV Transition, Open Internet, and the Future of Media Report.

Robert Baker serves as head of Media Bureau's political programming staff, Washington, DC. He travels extensively to speak to local and national broadcast and cable television associations about political programming rules. He also advises the Commissioners, the Office of General Counsel and the Media Bureau on all political programming issues.

Zemira Jones is President/CEO of All American Management Group, a media management consulting company. He is a 32 year radio veteran with 27 years of major market management experience including Fortune 100 companies. His career spans a wide range of broadcast platforms and companies, including ABC, Disney, ESPN, and Radio One, Inc.

Karen Archer Perry worked at the FCC on issues of broadband adoption, media literacy and libraries. She is currently a Senior Program Officer at the Bill and Melinda Gates Foundation, manages the access and advocacy portfolios for the U.S. Library program.

John Horrigan worked at the FCC as Director of Consumer Research for the National Broadband Plan and, from 2000–2009 as Associate Director, Research at the Pew Internet & American Life Project. He is currently Vice President for Policy Research for TechNet.

Jodi Enda is an award-winning journalist specializing in politics and policy. At the Philadelphia Inquirer and Knight Ridder Newspapers, she covered the White House, Congress, presidential campaigns and national news. She is a former president of Journalism & Women Symposium and a former member of the White House Correspondents' Association Board of Directors.

Fellows and Interns:

Monica Alba, Christopher Ali, Anne Chen, Christopher Clark, Sarah Erickson, Robert Grabow, Cara Haberman, Lili Hughes, Benjamin Jacobs, Tayla Janoff, Andrew Kaplan, Chad Kempen, David Hyun Kim, Laura Layton, Cater Lee, Andrew Lewandowski, Patrick Lucey, Alexandra McKinney, Kim Krzywy, Siddhartha Menon, Sade Oshinubi, Hauwa Otori, Michael Reiter, Kara Romagnino, Anya Schiffrin, Rebecca Shapiro, Kevin Smith, Matthew Starr, Keith Watson, Corinna Wu, Melissa Yeo, Jennifer Young, and Tracy Young.

Other FCC staff that gave us significant advice, research or brutally-frank criticism:

Jamie Barnett, Paul de Sa, Michelle Ellison, Terri Glaze, Joel Gurin, William Lake, Ruth Milkman, Thomas Reed, Steve Van Roekel, Lori Alexiou, Adele Andrews, Ty Bream, Amy Brett, Gray Brooks, Toby Brown, Robert Cannon, Rosalee Chiara, Hope Cooper, Katie Costello, William Davenport, Peter Doyle, Jack Erb, Amaryllis Flores, Katrina Kleinwachter Fortney, Marcia Glauberman, Noelle Green, Judith Herman, Tom Hutton, Leon Jackler, Rick Kanner, Vanessa Lemme, Lori Holy Maarbjerg, Kim Matthews, Betty Morris, Erica Porter, Mary Beth Richards, Chris Robbins, Arnett Rogiers, Holly Saurer, Daniel Shiman, Debbie Smoot, Priya Shrinivasan, Jennifer Tatel, Bonita Tingley, Haley Van Dyck, Michael Wagner, Sarah Whitesell, and George Williams.

This report relied heavily on the research conducted already by think tanks, foundations, scholars and journalists. Our knowledge would be pitiful if not for their extraordinary work, for which we are extremely grateful.

Overview

1 MG Siegler, *Eric Schmidt: Every 2 Days We Create As Much Information As We Did Up to 2003*, TECH CRUNCH, Aug 4, 2010, http://techcrunch.com/2010/08/04/schmidt-data/.

2 *Company History*, THOMSON REUTERS (*Company History*), http://thomsonreuters.com/about/company_history/#1890_1790 (last visited Feb. 8, 2011).

3 *Company History*. Reuter also used carrier pigeons to bridge the gap in the telegraph line then existing between Aachen and Brussels. Reuters Group PLC, http://www.fundinguniverse.com/company-histories/Reuters-Group-PLC-Company-History.html (last visited Feb. 8, 2011).

4 Reuters Group PLC (Reuters Group), http://www.fundinguniverse.com/company-histories/Reuters-Group-PLC-Company-History.html (last visited Feb. 8, 2011).

5 Reuters Group.

6 This calculation assumes that the bird carried about 1,000 words and that 64,782 Microsoft Word pages can fit per gigabyte. *How Many Pages in a Gigabyte?*, LEXISNEXIS, http://www.lexisnexis.com/applied-discovery/lawlibrary/whitePapers/ADI_FS_PagesInAGigabyte.pdf (last visited Feb. 8, 2011). If one assumes stripped down text files, then a 256 gigabyte flash drive could carry 86,779,264 times more than the pigeon. *Id.*

7 *See* WikiSource, Letter to Edward Carrington—January 16, 1787, http://en.wikisource.org/wiki/Letter_to_Edward_Carrington_-_January_16,_1787 (last visited Jan. 25, 2011).

8 THE KNIGHT COMMISSION, INFORMING COMMUNITIES: SUSTAINING DEMOCRACY IN THE DIGITAL AGE at XI (2010), *available at* http://www.knightcomm.org/read-the-report-and-comment/.

9 The Commission's statutory mandate includes responsibility for a wide range of media issues, including policy and licensing for the regulation of cable television, broadcast television and radio, and satellite services in the United States and its territories. *See* 47 U.S.C. Titles I, III and VI. *See also id.* at § 303(g) (requiring the FCC to "encourage the larger and more effective use of radio in the public interest"); *NBC v. United States*, 319 U.S. 190, 217 (1943) (Communications Act of 1934, as amended, confers on the FCC "comprehensive powers to promote and realize the vast potentialities of radio"). More specifically, the FCC's media regulatory responsibilities include, but are not limited to: broadcast television and radio station licensing, technical standards, ownership, localism, equal employment opportunity, children's programming, political programming, sponsorship identification, and indecency. *See* 47 U.S.C. §§ 301, 303a, 303b, 307–310, 315, 317, 334–336, 507; 18 U.S.C. § 1464 (1994); Telecommunications Act of 1996 § 202, Pub. L. No. 104-104, 110 Stat. 56 (1996). Additionally, cable television rates, technical standards, consumer protection and customer service, ownership, broadcast station signal retransmission and carriage, program access, wiring, equipment, and channel leasing are also included in the FCC's media regulatory responsibilities. *See* 47 U.S.C. §§ 611–617, 623, 624, 628, 632. Digital Broadcast Satellite licensing, ownership, broadcast station signal retransmission and carriage also fall under the purview of the FCC. *See* 47 U.S.C. §§ 335, 338–341. We believe effective performance of these responsibilities requires FCC Commissioners and staff to have an understanding of developments within the broader sphere where radio, television, cable and satellite media outlets operate. Accordingly, we do not confine the discussion in this report to those specific issues within the Commission's regulatory jurisdiction. Instead, we describe below a set of inter-related changes in the media landscape that provide the background for future FCC decision-making, as well as assessments by other policymakers beyond the FCC.

10 Founders' Constitution, James Madison, Report on the Virginia Resolutions, http://press-pubs.uchicago.edu/founders/documents/amendI_speechs24.html (last visited Feb. 7, 2011).

11 *Advertising Expenditures*, NEWSPAPER ASSOC. OF AM. (last updated Mar. 2010), http://www.naa.org/TrendsandNumbers/Advertising-Expenditures.aspx.

12 "Newspapers: News Investment" in PEW RESEARCH CTR.'S PROJ. FOR EXCELLENCE IN JOURNALISM, THE STATE OF THE NEWS MEDIA 2010 (PEW, STATE OF NEWS MEDIA 2010), http://stateofthemedia.org/2010/newspapers-summary-essay/news-investment/.

13 The editorial workforce for daily newspapers in 1971 was estimated to be 38,000. JOHN W.C. JOHNSTONE, EDWARD J.SLAWSKI, & WILLIAM W. BOWMAN, THE NEWS PEOPLE: A SOCIOLOGICAL PORTRAIT OF AMERICAN JOURNALISTS AND THEIR WORK 195 (University of Illinois Press, 1976). The American Society of Newspaper Editors put total newspaper newsroom employment in 2010 at 41,600. *Newsroom Employment Up Slightly, Minority Numbers Plunge for Third Year*, AM. SOC'Y OF NEWS EDITORS, Apr. 7, 2011, http://asne.org/article_view/articleid/1788/newsroom-employment-up-slightly-minority-numbers-plunge-for-third-year.aspx. This means that roughly the same number of journalists are working at newspapers today as in 1970, even though the population of the US has increased by more than 50 percent. The population in 1970 was 203,302,031, while the population in 2010 was 308,745,538. *Population, Housing Units, Area Measurements, and Density: 1790 to 1990*, U.S. CENSUS BUREAU, http://www.census.gov/population/www/censusdata/files/table-2.pdf; Press Release, U.S. Census Bureau, U.S. Census Bureau Announces 2010 Census Population Counts—Apportionment Counts Delivered to President (Dec. 21, 2010), http://2010.census.gov/news/releases/operations/cb10-cn93.html.

14 "Overview" in PEW, STATE OF NEWS MEDIA 2010, http://stateofthemedia.org/2010/overview-3/.

15 "Magazines: News Investment" in PEW, STATE OF NEWS MEDIA 2010, http://stateofthemedia.org/2010/magazines-summary-essay/news-investment/.

16 "News on the Radio" in PEW RESEARCH CTR.'S PROJ. FOR EXCELLENCE IN JOURNALISM, THE STATE OF THE NEWS MEDIA 2011 (PEW, STATE OF NEWS MEDIA 2011), http://stateofthemedia.org/2011/audio-essay (citing Arbitron Inc., Radio Today 2010 Edition); Email from Claudine Kinsley, Dir., Syndicated Standards & Analysis, Arbitron Inc., to Alexandra McKinney, FCC, Nov. 17, 2010. Arbitron provided aggregate data to the FCC but did not identify the stations that identified themselves as all-news stations.

17 ADAM LYNN, MARK COOPER & S. DEREK TURNER, NATIONAL OWNERS DOMINATE LOCAL CABLE NEWS: LOCAL CABLE NEWS CHANNELS DO NOT SIGNIFICANTLY CONTRIBUTE TO SOURCE OR VIEWPOINT DIVERSITY 1, 5 (Free Press) (2006) http://www.freepress.net/files/study_4_cable_local_news.pdf ("these stations serve about one-fifth of the total population…"). The number could be slightly higher. Our own FCC analysis, based on research in September 2010 by FOM team members Simon Banyai and Ava Seave (Banyai and Seave Research), we previously found there to be approximately 39 local or regional cable news channels that produced their own news. These channels serve subscribers on cable systems in approximately 71 out of the total 210 Designated Market Areas in the country, and many of these DMAs contain large metropolitan regions—New York, Boston, Chicago, or San Francisco—with multiple channels. Using 2010 data, out of the total of 54,335,000 TV households located in 71 DMAs, we found that 52.4 percent or 28,471,540 were cable subscribers. Therefore, we estimated that these 39 cable news channels were available to at least 24.6 percent of the 115.8 million total TV households in the country in 2010. Our cable news channel count incorporates only those channels that continue to utilize journalists to originate local or regional news. While Americans may receive news from a somewhat greater number of cable channels that merely rebroadcast or simulcast network news programming, we have omitted such channels from our tally. The "20 to 30 percent" figure also includes local cable news channels referenced in footnote 264 of Chapter 3, Television.

18 FCC staff analysis of data from Tribune Media Services for Nov. 1–Nov. 14, 2009 and May 6–May 12, 2010.

19 LEONARD DOWNIE JR. & MICHAEL SCHUDSON, COLUMBIA JOURNALISM REV., THE RECONSTRUCTION OF AMERICAN JOURNALISM, Oct. 19, 2009 (DOWNIE & SCHUDSON, RECONSTRUCTION OF AMERICAN JOURNALISM), http://www.cjr.org/reconstruction/the_reconstruction_of_american.php?page=all.

20 HOW NEWS HAPPENS: A STUDY OF THE NEW ECOSYSTEM OF ONE AMERICAN CITY, PROJECT FOR EXCELLENCE IN JOURNALISM 2 (2010), http://www.journalism.org/sites/journalism.org/files/Baltimore%20Study_Jan2010_0.pdf.

21 JAN SCHAFFER, J-LAB: THE INSTITUTE FOR INTERACTIVE JOURNALISM, EXPLORING A NETWORKED JOURNALISM: COLLABORATIVE IN PHILADELPHIA: AN ANALYSIS OF THE CITY'S MEDIA ECOSYSTEM WITH FINAL RECOMMENDATIONS 3, http://www.j-lab.org/publications/exploring-a-networked-journalism-collaborative-in-philadelphia.

22 JAMES T. HAMILTON, SUBSIDIZING THE WATCHDOG: WHAT WOULD IT COST TO SUPPORT INVESTIGATIVE JOURNALISM AT A LARGE METROPOLITAN DAILY NEWSPAPER? 3 (2009), http://sanford.duke.edu/nonprofitmedia/documents/dwchamiltonfinal.pdf; Fiona Morgan, *An Information Community Case Study: The Research Triangle, N.C.*, NEW AM. FOUND. (2011), at 12, http://mediapolicy.newamerica.net/sites/newamerica.net/files/policydocs/Triangle%20NC%20Case%20Study%20%28Version%202.0%29_0.pdf.

23 Jennifer Dorroh, *Statehouse Exodus*, AM. JOURNALISM REVIEW, Apr./May 2009 (*Statehouse Exodus*), http://www.ajr.org/article.asp?id=4721. *See also Summary of State and Local Government Finances by Level of Government: 2002–03*, U.S. CENSUS BUREAU, http://www.census.gov/govs/estimate/03sl00us.html (2003 figure); *State and Local Government Finances Summary: 2008*, U.S. CENSUS BUREAU, Apr. 2011, at Table 1, http://www2.census.gov/govs/estimate/08statesummaryreport.pdf (2008 figure).

24 *Statehouse Exodus*.

25 *Statehouse Exodus*.

26 *Statehouse Exodus*.

27 *Statehouse Exodus*.

28 Interview of Mark Horvit by M.K.Guzda Struck, FCC, Aug. 16, 2010.

29 Interview of Mary Walton by M.K.Guzda Struck, FCC, Aug. 29, 2010.

30 The total number of members has increased, with the bulk describing themselves as freelancers. They had 1,100 members in 2000 and 1,500 members now. Interview with Beth Parke, Executive Director, Society of Environmental Journalists, by M.K.Guzda Struck, FCC, Aug. 23, 2010.

31 PEW RESEARCH CENTER'S PROJECT FOR EXCELLENCE IN JOURNALISM, THE NEW WASHINGTON PRESS CORPS: AS MAINSTREAM MEDIA DECLINE, NICHE AND FOREIGN OUTLETS GROW (Feb. 11, 2009), http://www.journalism.org/analysis_report/new_washington_press_corps.

32 Email from Debra Mason, Religion Newswriters Association, to Steven Waldman, FCC, Feb. 18, 2011.

33 GARY SCHWITZER, KAISER FAMILY FOUNDATION, THE STATE OF HEALTH JOURNALISM IN THE U.S. 16 (Mar. 2009), http://www.kff.org/entmedia/upload/7858.pdf.

34 Email from Richard Colvin to Steven Waldman, FCC, Jan. 19, 2011.

35 Interview with Andrew Lack by Steven Waldman, FCC, Dec. 16, 2010.

36 Testimony of David Simon, former Baltimore Sun reporter and Creator, HBO series The Wire, Hearing on the Future of News and Journalism, U.S. Senate Subcommittee on Communications, Technology and the Internet, May 8, 2009, *available at* http://www.onthemedia.org/transcripts/2009/05/08/01.

37 Interview with Mark Silverman, (Nashville) Tennessean, by Steven Waldman, FCC, May 24, 2010.

38 Interview with Brian Hamlin, Senior Reporter, Vacaville (CA) Reporter, by M.K.Guzda Struck, FCC, June 2010. Hamlin provided an example of the distances he was required to drive in a single day to cover far-flung stories, due to staff reductions: Stockton to Vallejo, 65.7 mi.; Vallejo to Fairfield, 17 mi.; Fairfield to Sacramento, 43 mi.

39 Jodi Enda, *Capital Flight*, AM. JOURNALISM REV., June/July 2010, http://www.ajr.org/Article.asp?id=4877.

40 Interview of Vivek Sankaran by M.K.Guzda Struck, FCC, Aug. 17, 2010.

41 PEW RESEARCH CENTER'S PROJECT FOR EXCELLENCE IN JOURNALISM, HOW NEWS HAPPENS: A STUDY OF THE NEWS ECOSYSTEM OF ONE AMERICAN CITY (Jan. 11, 2010), http://www.journalism.org/analysis_report/how_news_happens.

42 Interview with Bill Girdner, Editor and Publisher, Courthouse News Service by M.K. Guzda Struck, FCC, July 2, 2010.

43 Dean Starkman, *The Hamster Wheel*, COLUMBIA JOURNALISM REV. (Oct. 2010), http://www.cjr.org/cover_story/the_hamster_wheel.php?page=all.

44 Interview with Matthew Zelkind, Station Mgr., WKRN-TV, by Steven Waldman, FCC, May 24, 2010.

45 Interview with Fred Young, former Vice President of Hearst Broadcasting, by Cynthia Kennard, FCC, June 2010.

46 MARTIN KAPLAN AND MATTHEW HALE, LOCAL TV NEWS IN THE LOS ANGELES MEDIA MARKET: ARE THE STATIONS SERVING THE PUBLIC INTEREST? 4–6 (USC Annenberg School of Communication & Journalism, 2010), http://www.learcenter.org/pdf/LANews2010.pdf.

47 THOMAS BALDWIN, DANIEL BERGIN, FRED FICO, STEPHEN LACY, & STEVEN WILDMAN, NEWS MEDIA COVERAGE OF CITY GOVERNMENTS IN 2009 4–5 (Michigan State Univ., 2010), http://quello.msu.edu/sites/default/files/pdf/PEJ_City_Govt_report-final.pdf.

48 Interview with Con Psarris, Vice President of Editorials and Special

Projects, KSL-TV, by Cynthia Kennard, FCC, July 20, 2010.

49 Interview with Reporter, KNTV ABC Las Vegas, Nevada, by Steven Waldman, FCC, Apr. 13, 2010.

50 Curtis Brainard, *News Director Quits over Hospital Deal*, COLUMBIA JOURNALISM REV., Jan. 25, 2008, http://www.cjr.org/the_observatory/news_director_quits_over_hospi.php.

51 Steph Gregor, *And Now a Word from our Sponsor*, THE OTHER PAPER (Columbus Ohio), Nov. 29, 2007.

52 Howard Kurtz, *TV Station Cashes in on Interview 'Guests,'* WASH. POST, Oct. 16, 2003, at C1.

53 The survey was conducted December 2009 through January 2010. *See News Leaders and the Future: News Executives, Skeptical of Government Subsidies, See Opportunity in Technology but are Unsure About Revenue and the Future*, PROJECT FOR EXCELLENCE IN JOURNALISM, AMERICAN SOCIETY OF NEWS EDITORS (ASNE), RADIO TELEVISION DIGITAL NEWS ASSOCIATION (RTDNA), Apr. 12, 2010, http://www.journalism.org/analysis_report/news_leaders_and_future.

54 Average recurring EBITDA from 2005 to 3Q 2010 is 36.64 percent, according to SNL Kagan data.

55 PEW RESEARCH CENTER'S PROJECT FOR EXCELLENCE IN JOURNALISM, HOW NEWS HAPPENS: A STUDY OF THE NEWS ECOSYSTEM OF ONE AMERICAN CITY 2 (Jan. 11, 2010), *available at* http://www.journalism.org/analysis_report/how_news_happens.

56 American Society of Newspaper Editors, Newsroom Employment Census, 2011, http://asne.org/article_view/articleid/1788/newsroom-employment-up-slightly-minority-numbers-plunge-for-third-year.aspx; "Newspapers: News Investment" in PEW, STATE OF NEWS MEDIA 2010, http://stateofthemedia.org/2010/newspapers-summary-essay/news-investment/.

57 *Meet the New Media Makers—and the Foundations that Make Their News Sites Possible*, KNIGHT CITIZEN NEWS NETWORK, http://www.kcnn.org/toolkit/funding_database/ (last visited Mar. 1, 2011).

58 Interview with Rick Blair, President, Examiner.com by Steven Waldman, FCC, Dec. 17, 2010.

59 Michele McLellan, *Debunking the Replacement Myth*, KNIGHT DIGITAL MEDIA CTR., July 26, 2010, http://www.knightdigitalmediacenter.org/leadership_blog/comments/20100726_the_replacement_myth/.

60 *Newspaper Websites (Nielsen)*, NEWSPAPER ASSOC. OF AM., http://www.naa.org/TrendsandNumbers/Newspaper-Websites-Nielsen.aspx/(last visited Jan. 20, 2011) (providing that in May 2009: 69,950,403 uniques, 2,995,584,721 page views, versus May 2005: 43,704,725 uniques 1,635,119,778 page views).

61 *Advertising Expenditures*, NEWSPAPER ASSOC. OF AM., http://www.naa.org/TrendsandNumbers/Advertising-Expenditures.aspx (last visited Nov. 18, 2010).

62 "Survey: Mobile News & Paying Online" in PEW, STATE OF NEWS MEDIA 2011, http://stateofthemedia.org/2011/mobile-survey/.

63 Research by FCC staff on May 27 (iPad) and May 31 (iPhone), 2011, counting all iPad and iPhone apps that appeared within the Apple iTunes App Store's pages displaying "All News iPad Apps—Paid," "All News iPad Apps—Free," "All News iPhone Apps—Paid," and "All News iPhone Apps—Free." At the time, Apple offered 537 paid iPad news apps, 2,388 free iPad news apps, 2,719 paid iPhone news apps, and 6,514 free iPhone news apps.

64 National Public Radio, Inc. Comments in re *FCC Launches Examination of the Future of Media and Information Needs of Communities in a Digital Age*, GN Docket No. 10-25, Public Notice, 25 FCC Rcd 384 (2010) (*FOM PN*), filed May 7, 2010 (NPR Comments) at 3.

65 NPR Comments at 7.

66 NPR Comments at 2.

67 *Local News Station Survey: Executive Summary*, NAT'L PUB. RADIO, http://www.localnewsinitiative.org/executive.cfm (last visited Feb. 11, 2010).

68 THE PEW RESEARCH CENTER FOR THE PEOPLE AND THE PRESS, AUDIENCE SEGMENTS IN A CHANGING NEWS ENVIRONMENT: KEY NEWS AUDIENCES NOW BLEND ONLINE AND TRADITIONAL SOURCES 5 (2008), http://people-press.org/reports/pdf/444.pdf (1998, 2008 data); THE PEW RESEARCH CENTER FOR THE PEOPLE AND THE PRESS, AMERICANS SPENDING MORE TIME FOLLOWING THE NEWS 14 (2010), http://people-press.org/reports/pdf/652.pdf (2010 data).

69 *Statistical Abstract of the United States: 2011*, at 711, http://www.census.gov/compendia/statab/2011/tables/11s1130.pdf.

70 Alan Mutter, *The State of Play for Paid Content, 2011*, EDITOR & PUBLISHER, Jan. 11, 2011.

71 Email from Clay Shirky to Steve Waldman, FCC, Apr. 2, 2010.

72 *Newspaper Economics: Online and Offline*, Presentation by Hal Varian, Chief Economist, Google, and Professor, Univ. of California, Berkeley, FTC Workshop, "From Town Criers to Bloggers: How Will Journalism Survive The Internet Age?" (Mar. 9, 2010), at 20, *available at* http://www.ftc.gov/opp/workshops/news/mar9/docs/varian.pdf.

73 MICHAEL R. FANCHER, OF THE PRESS: MODELS FOR TRANSFORMING AMERICAN JOURNALISM, A REPORT OF THE 2009 ASPEN INSTITUTE FORUM ON COMMUNICATIONS AND SOCIETY 16 (2009) (quoting Esther Dyson's statement about investments in new start-ups), *available at* http://www.knightcomm.org/wp-content/uploads/2010/04/Of-the-Press-Models-for-Transforming-American-Journalism.pdf.

74 Interview with Esther Dyson by Steven Waldman, FCC, Sept. 3, 2010.

75 National Religious Broadcasters Comments in re *FOM PN*, filed Feb. 18, 2010 (NRB Comments) at 12.

1 Newspapers

1 Newspaper Association of America, Advertising Expenditures, http://www.naa.org/TrendsandNumbers/Advertising-Expenditures.aspx (last visited Jan. 20, 2011) (NAA, Advertising Expenditures).

2 "Newspapers: News Investment" in PEW RESEARCH CTR.'S PROJ. FOR EXCELLENCE IN JOURNALISM, THE STATE OF THE NEWS MEDIA 2010 (PEW, STATE OF NEWS MEDIA 2010), http://www.stateofthemedia.org/2010/newspapers_news_investment.php.

3 American Society of News Editors, *Newsroom employment up slightly, minority numbers plunge for third year*, April 7, 2011, http://asne.org/article_view/articleid/1788/newsroom-employment-up-slightly-minority-numbers-plunge-for-third-year.aspx; *Newspapers: By the Numbers*, http://stateofthemedia.org/2011/newspapers-essay/data-page-6/.

4 According to sociologist Paul Starr, "A study of the subscription books of two small-town Ohio papers in the 1820s, the *Ashtabula Sentinel* and

the *Mansfield Gazette*, finds that a majority of subscribers to both papers lived out of town; indeed, 47 percent of the *Sentinel*'s subscribers and 34 percent of the *Gazette*'s lived more than 20 miles away.... In addition, postmasters collected and remitted subscription fees." PAUL STARR, THE CREATION OF THE MEDIA: POLITICAL ORIGINS OF MASS COMMUNICATION 89–90 (Basic Books) (2004) (STARR, CREATION OF THE MEDIA).

5 STARR, CREATION OF THE MEDIA at 90.

6 GERALD J. BALDASTY, THE COMMERCIALIZATION OF NEWS IN THE NINE-TEENTH CENTURY 20 (University of Wisconsin Press) (1992) (BALDASTY, COMMERCIALIZATION OF NEWS).

7 STARR, CREATION OF THE MEDIA at 93.

8 The ability of federal and state governments at the executive and legislative levels to fund patronage meant that diverse sources of funding generated political diversity in the partisan press. As Gerald Baldasty notes:

"During the last two years of the John Quincy Adams administration, federal patronage went to the three major political newspapers in the nation's capital: the executive patronage went to the *National Journal*, Adams' official organ; the House printing contracts went to Joseph Gales and William Seaton of the *National Intelligencer*, and the Senate printing contract to Duff Green of the *U.S. Telegraph*. Consequently, during the 1828 presidential campaign, federal patronage funds were supporting two papers that advocated the reelection of Adams and one newspaper that advocated the election of Andrew Jackson."

BALDASTY, COMMERCIALIZATION OF NEWS at 24–25.

9 FRANK LUTHER MOTT, AMERICAN JOURNALISM: A HISTORY OF NEWS-PAPERS IN THE UNITED STATES THROUGH 260 YEARS: 1690–1950 314 (Macmillan) (1950). As Frank Mott has pointed out (*id*):

"The large circulations of the cheap papers would have been impossible without the improvements in papermaking which reduced the price of newsprint paper, and the startling developments in fast printing presses. Improvements in the Fourdrinier papermaking machine continued; and prices, variable in the period, ranged from fourteen to eight cents a pound for the rag paper used in printing.

"More remarkable, however, were the improvements in presses. The penny papers of large circulation were printed on Napier presses built by Richard M. Hoe & Company, of New York. These were at first single-cylinder, flat-bed presses capable of about 2,000 impressions per hour and turned by cranks manned by stout laborers. As circulations expanded, they soon gave way to double-cylinder presses with two feeders and capable of 4,000 impressions an hour. In 1835 the New York *Sun* installed steam power, setting an example which was soon followed by the other successful penny papers."

10 STARR, CREATION OF THE MEDIA at 131.

11 STARR, CREATION OF THE MEDIA at 135. Starr observes (at 135):

"According to a study of sixty-seven daily and nondaily newspapers published between 1820 and 1860, news became more localized in two senses. First, an increasing proportion of news stories concerned events in a paper's hometown or state, while relatively fewer stories reported events taking place abroad or in Washington, D.C. Second, local editors and reporters, who wrote only 25 percent of news articles in their own papers during the years 1820 to 1832, increased their share of the total to 45 percent by 1847 to 1860, while the proportion clipped from other newspapers (or, in the later period, received by telegraph) fell from 54 percent to 38 percent. During the middle decades of the nineteenth century, newspapers added sections entirely devoted to local news, and 'city editor' often became the second most important position. In other ways, however, remarkably little changed. The survey of sixty-seven papers found no significant shift during the antebellum period in the general subjects of stories (there was no reduction in attention to politics) or in the level of readability."

12 JAMES T. HAMILTON, ALL THE NEWS THAT'S FIT TO SELL: HOW THE MARKET TRANSFORMS INFORMATION INTO NEWS 45 (Princeton University Press) (2004) (HAMILTON, ALL THE NEWS).

13 MENAHEM BLONDHEIM, NEWS OVER THE WIRES: THE TELEGRAPH AND THE FLOW OF PUBLIC INFORMATION IN AMERICA, 1844–1897 16 (Harvard University Press) (1994). Blondheim observes (at 16):

"In the period spanning 1820 and 1832, up to 28 percent of news items published in a sample of American papers reported events that had taken place a month or more previously, and only 21 percent of news items related to events that had occurred within the preceding three days. From 1833 to 1846, a corresponding sample indicated that only 13 percent of published news items concerned events more than a month old, and twice as many items (41 percent) were of events that had taken place within the three days prior to publication."

14 HAMILTON, ALL THE NEWS at 49.

15 HAMILTON, ALL THE NEWS at 48. As one editor noted in 1906:

"The immensely large capital now required for the conduct of a daily newspaper in a great city has had important consequences. It has made the newspaper more of an institution, less of a personal organ. Men no longer designate journals by the owner's or editor's name. It used to be Bryant's paper, or Greeley's paper, or Raymond's, or Bennett's. Now it is simply *Times, Herald, Tribune*, and so on." *Id.*

16 According to Inland Daily Press Association data, the breakdown of 1922 newspaper revenues was: circulation 21 percent, advertising 78 percent, and miscellaneous one percent. By 1933 that had changed to circulation 30 percent, advertising 69 percent, and miscellaneous one percent. In their own study of newspaper revenue in 1941, Borden, Taylor, and Hovde found that circulation accounted for a median of 29 percent of revenues among papers with circulation under 10,000, and a median of 36 percent of revenues at papers with circulation over 100,000. *See* NEIL H. BORDEN, MALCOLM D. TAYLOR, & HOWARD T. HOVDE, NATIONAL ADVERTISING IN NEWSPAPERS 5, 434, 435 (Harvard University Press) (1946).

17 DAVID HOLBROOK CULBERT, NEWS FOR EVERYMAN: RADIO AND FOR-EIGN AFFAIRS IN THIRTIES AMERICA 16 (Greenwood) (1976). *See also* GWENYTH L. JACKAWAY, MEDIA AT WAR: RADIO'S CHALLENGE TO THE NEWSPAPERS, 1924–1939 (Praeger) (1995).

18 OSWALD GARRISON VILLARD, THE DISAPPEARING DAILY 8 (Knopf) (1944).

19 Matthew Gentzkow, *Television and Voter Turnout*, 121 Q. J. ECON. 931–972 (2006), *available at* http://www.mitpressjournals.org/doi/pdf/10.1162/qjec.121.3.931.

20 Newspaper Association of America, Total Paid Circulation, http://www.naa.org/TrendsandNumbers/Total-Paid-Circulation.aspx; U.S. Census, Families and Living Arrangements, Table HH-1. Households, by Type: 1940 to Present, http://www.census.gov/population/www/socdemo/hh-fam.html#ht (each last visited Feb. 28, 2011).

21 LEO BOGART, PRESERVING THE PRESS: HOW DAILY NEWSPAPERS MOBI-LIZED TO KEEP THEIR READERS 40, 41 (Columbia University Press) (1991) (BOGART, PRESERVING THE PRESS).

22 In his 1991 book, PRESERVING THE PRESS: HOW DAILY NEWSPAPERS MOBILIZED TO KEEP THEIR READERS, Leo Bogart, longtime executive vice president and general manager of the Newspaper Advertising Bureau, explained:

"Zest and aptitude for a publishing career are not transmitted in the genes. Inheritance taxes sometimes forced extended families to liquidate properties whose multiple owners had other interests. These pressures to sell coincided with an incredible escalation in the market value of newspapers and television stations. Surviving dailies became all the more valuable as their competitors dropped by the wayside.

"The growth of the chains and giant media companies followed inexorably. A comparatively small number of these companies competed aggressively for the newspapers that became available in single-ownership markets at the same time that huge money-losing second papers in big cities scrambled to find new owners. The fantastic prices (up to $4,650 a unit of circulation) that Gannett, Times Mirror, and others were willing to pay in part reflected the bullish temper of the stock market, since most of these companies were publicly owned and in a number of cases concluded their deals in exchange for stock certificates rather than cash. In a business world where to stand still was to lose ground, expansion and acquisition were the essential rules of the game. Such activities required capital and propelled companies into public ownership."

BOGART, PRESERVING THE PRESS at 49.

23 Gene Roberts & Thomas Kunkel, *Leaving Readers Behind: The Age of Corporate Newspapering*, AMER. JOURNALISM REV. (May 2001), http://www.ajr.org/Article.asp?id=363.

24 Geneva Overholser, *State of the American Newspaper: Editor Inc.*, AMER. JOURNALISM REV. (Dec. 1998), http://www.ajr.org/Article.asp?id=3290.

25 ELI M. NOAM, MEDIA OWNERSHIP AND CONCENTRATION IN AMERICA 139 (Oxford University Press) (2009).

26 LAUREN RICH FINE, BAD PUBLIC RELATIONS OR IS THIS A REAL CRISIS?: YES 11 (Duke Conference on Nonprofit Media) (2009) (RICH, BAD PUBLIC RELATIONS), *available at* http://dewitt.sanford.duke.edu/images/uploads/About_3_Research_A_4_dwcrichfinefinal.pdf.

27 BOGART, PRESERVING THE PRESS at 53.

28 As Mary Walton describes this:

"These [hometown] newspapers are indispensable in another way—as local citizens, heading up annual United Way drives, championing local business, and generally lending their communities a sense of stability in an unstable world. Just about half the nation's 1,483 daily newspapers are under 13,000 circulation; they help form the backbone of an America seldom featured in glossy magazines or on the evening news.

"But deeply rooted as they may be, the nation's hometown papers are vulnerable to outside forces. And these days, they are changing hands like used cars at an auction. Of the 564 U.S. newspapers sold from January of 1994 through July of 2000, about two-thirds had circulations under 13,000. One hundred and eleven of these small papers were sold two, three, or even four times during this six-and-a-half year period.

"In one of the biggest shifts in newspaper ownership since chains began devouring independent papers more than a generation ago, big-city businessmen with deep pockets are flocking to the industry, lured by small papers with generous margins. These new owners are highly leveraged and itching to make money. Indeed, often built into their financial arrangements are 'exit strategies' that force the companies either to sell or go public, generally within five to seven years."

Mary Walton, *The Selling of Small-Town America*, in GENE ROBERTS, THOMAS KUNKEL, & CHARLES LAYTON, LEAVING READERS BEHIND: THE AGE OF CORPORATE NEWSPAPERING 19–20 (University of Arkansas Press) (2001).

29 RICH, BAD PUBLIC RELATIONS at 12.

30 "Newspaper—Summary Essay: Newsroom Cutbacks" in PEW, STATE OF NEWS MEDIA 2010, http://stateofthemedia.org/2010/newspapers-summary-essay/.

31 Katherine Q. Seelye, *Wall St. Journal to Shrink Page Size, Joining Trend to Cut Newsprint Costs,* N.Y. TIMES, Oct. 12, 2005, http://www.nytimes.com/2005/10/12/business/media/12paper.html.

32 BOGART, PRESERVING THE PRESS at 52–53.

33 BOGART, PRESERVING THE PRESS at 52.

34 PHILIP MEYER, THE VANISHING NEWSPAPER: SAVING JOURNALISM IN THE INFORMATION AGE (University of Missouri Press) 189–190 (2009).

35 Bogart, Preserving the Press at 52.

36 Geneva Overholser, *Editor Inc.* in LEAVING READERS BEHIND: THE AGE OF CORPORATE NEWSPAPERING at 169 (Gene Roberts, Thomas Kunkel, & Charles Layton, eds.) (Univ. of Arkansas Press) (2001).

37 John S. Carroll, *Last Call at the ASNE Saloon* (speech delivered at the 2006 American Society of Newspaper Editors convention, Seattle, Washington) (Apr. 26, 2006).

38 Mark G. Contreras, The E.W. Scripps Company, Presentation at The Aspen Institute Forum on Communications and Society (Aug. 16, 2010) (Contreras Presentation 8/16/10) at 5, *available at* www.knightcomm.org/.../FOCAS10_Mark_Contreras_Scripps_Presentation.pdfhttp://www.knightcomm.org/wpcontent/uploads/2010/08/FOCAS10_Mark_Contreras_Scripps_Presentation.pdf.

39 Rick Edmonds (The Poynter Institute), Emily Guskin, & Tom Rosensteil, "Newspapers: Missed the 2010 Media Rally" in *Pew, State of News Media 2011*, http://stateofthemedia.org/2011/newspapers-essay/.

40 Contreras Presentation 8/16/10 at 5.

41 NAA, Advertising Expenditures.

42 Newspaper Association of America, Newspaper Websites (Nielsen), http://www.naa.org/TrendsandNumbers/Newspaper-Websites-Nielsen.aspx (last visited Feb. 8, 2011).

43 NAA, Advertising Expenditures.

44 NAA, Advertising Expenditures.

45 Miriam Marcus, *The Best Way to Find (and Fill) a Job Online*, FORBES, May 26, 2009, http://www.forbes.com/2009/05/26/job-seeking-web-sites-entrepreneurs-human-resources-monster.html.

46 Top 10 Automotive-Classifieds Websites, MARKETING CHARTS QUARTERLY, July 2010, http://www.marketingcharts.com/interactive/top-10-automotive-classifieds-websites-july-2010-13754/.

47 Top 10 Real Estate Websites, MARKETING CHARTS QUARTERLY, Jan. 2010, http://www.marketingcharts.com/interactive/top-10-real-estate-websites-january-2010-11938/.

48 Kansas City Star, Online Self-Serve Order Entry, http://kansascitystar.adperfect.com/ (last visited Feb. 8, 2011).

49 A 2009 profile of the site in *Wired* provides estimates of the site's impact and profitability, including a projection that in 2009 revenues for the privately held company would top $100 million. Gary Wolf, *Why Craigslist is Such a Mess*, WIRED, Aug. 24, 2009, http://www.wired.com/entertainment/theweb/magazine/17-09/ff_craigslist?currentPage=all.

50 NAA, Advertising Expenditures (under "Quarterly Classified" tab).

51 NAA, Advertising Expenditures.

52 *See* Alan D. Mutter, *Newspaper Ad Sales Head to 25-Year Low*, REFLECTIONS OF A NEWSOSAUR, Sept. 7, 2010, http://newsosaur.blogspot.com/2010/09/newspaper-ad-sales-head-to-25-year-low.html; Alan D. Mutter, *Make No Mistake: Newspapers Are Still in Trouble,* REFLECTIONS OF A NEWSOSAUR, June 15, 2010, http://newsosaur.blogspot.com/2010/06/make-no-mistake-newspapers-are-still-in.html; Alan D. Mutter, *Newspapers Now Have Lost Half of Core Sales*, REFLECTIONS OF A NEWSOSAUR, May 28, 2010, http://newsosaur.blogspot.com/2010/05/newspapers-now-have-lost-half-of-core.html.

53 *See* David Phelps, *Star Tribune Files for Chapter 11 Bankruptcy*, MINNEAPOLIS STAR TRIBUNE, Jan. 16, 2009, http://www.startribune.com/business/37685134.html (*Star Tribune* positive earnings when declared bankruptcy); Mike Spector & Shira Ovide, *MediaNews Holding Company to Seek Bankruptcy Protection*, WALL ST. J., Jan. 15, 2010, http://online.wsj.com/article/SB10001424052748703657604575005813195786280.html (at time filed for bankruptcy, MediaNews indicated all but one of newspapers was profitable); Bob Lentz, *Top 2 Philadelphia Newspapers File for Bankruptcy*, USA TODAY, Feb. 23, 2009, http://www.usatoday.com/news/nation/2009-02-22-newspapers_N.htm.

54 Erica Smith, Closed Newspapers (2010 tab), PAPER CUTS, http://newspaperlayoffs.com/maps/closed/ (Closed Newspapers) (last visited Mar. 7, 2011).

55 "Newspaper—Summary Essay: Newsroom Cutbacks" in PEW, STATE OF NEWS MEDIA 2010.

56 The editorial workforce for daily newspapers in 1971 was estimated to be 38,000. JOHN W.C. JOHNSTONE, EDWARD J.SLAWSKI, AND WILLIAM W. BOWMAN, THE NEWS PEOPLE: A SOCIOLOGICAL PORTRAIT OF AMERICAN JOURNALISTS AND THEIR WORK, 195 (University of Illinois Press) (1976). The American Society of Newspaper Editors put total newspaper newsroom employment in 2010 at 41,600. American Society of News Editors, *Newsroom employment up slightly, minority numbers plunge for third year*, Apr. 7, 2011, http://asne.org/article_view/articleid/1788/newsroom-employment-up-slightly-minority-numbers-plunge-for-third-year.aspx. This means that roughly the same number of journalists are working at newspapers today as in 1970, even though the population of the US has increased by more than 50 percent. The population in 1970 was 203,302,031 (http://www.census.gov/population/www/censusdata/files/table-2.pdf), while the population in 2010 was 308,745,538 (http://2010.census.gov/news/releases/operations/cb10-cn93.html).

57 *Newspapers: By the Numbers*, http://stateofthemedia.org/2011/newspapers-essay/data-page-6/p; ASNE, *Newsroom employment up slightly* http://asne.org/article_view/articleid/1788/newsroom-employment-up-slightly-minority-numbers-plunge-forthird-year.aspx.

58 Rob Davis & Randy Dotinga, *Layoffs Hit Union-Tribune Newsroom*, VOICE OF SAN DIEGO, June 17, 2010, http://www.voiceofsandiego.org/environment/muck/article_f5f81632-7a7c-11df-ad0d-001cc4c002e0.html.

59 Michael R. Fancher, "Seattle: A New Media Case Study" in *Pew, State of News Media 2011*, http://stateofthemedia.org/2011/mobile-survey/seattle-a-new-media-case-study/.

60 Anick Jesdanun, *Star-Ledger Cuts Newsroom Staff by Nearly Half*, BREITBART.COM, Oct. 24, 2008, http://www.breitbart.com/article.php?id=d9415ac00&show_article=1.

61 Phil Rosenthal, *Chicago Tribune Reduces Newsroom Staff*, CHICAGO TRIBUNE, Apr. 22, 2009, http://newsblogs.chicagotribune.com/towerticker/2009/04/chicago-tribune-reduces-newsroom-staff.html.

62 Erica Smith, *2009 Layoffs and Buyouts at U.S. Newspapers*, PAPER CUTS, Dec. 31, 2009, http://newspaperlayoffs.com/maps/2009-layoffs.

63 *See Miami Herald Shedding Another 49 Jobs, Imposing Another Furlough*, EDITOR & PUBLISHER, Sept. 16, 2010, http://www.editorandpublisher.com/Headlines/miami-herald-shedding-another-49-jobs-imposing-another-furlough-62628-.aspx; *More News Outlets Instituting Furloughs*, REYNOLDS CENTER, Mar. 23, 2009, http://businessjournalism.org/2009/03/23/more-news-outlets-instituting-furloughs/; Emma Heald, *New York Times to Implement Across the Board Pay Cuts*, EDITORS WEBLOG, Mar. 27, 2009, http://www.editorsweblog.org/newspaper/2009/03/new_york_times_to_implement_across_the_b.php; and *Philly Newspapers Guild Agrees to Pay Cuts*, EDITOR & PUBLISHER, Aug. 25, 2010, http://www.editorandpublisher.com/Headlines/philly-newspapers-guild-agrees-to-pay-cuts-62397-.aspx.

64 NAA, Total Paid Circulation, http://www.naa.org/TrendsandNumbers/Total-Paid-Circulation.aspx; U.S. Census Bureau, Families and Living Arrangements, Table HH-1. (Households, by Type: 1940 to Present), http://www.census.gov/population/www/socdemo/hh-fam.html#ht, (each last visited March 8, 2011); *Newspapers: by the Numbers*, http://stateofthemedia.org/2011/newspapers-essay/data-page-6/.

65 Brian Steffens, *Annual Readership Study Shows Good News for Small Papers*, REYNOLDS JOURNALISM INSTITUTE, Oct. 6, 2009, http://www.rjionline.org/casr/reasearch-reports/nna/2009-oct-readership.php.

66 National Newspaper Association, Facts and Figures (last updated Dec. 23, 2009), http://www.nnaweb.org/?/nnaweb/community02/87 (last visited Mar. 8, 2011).

67 Inland Press Association, *Inland Clarifies Data From Its Five-Year Trend Analysis* (press release), July 21, 2009, http://www.inlandpress.org/articles/2010/12/08/about/press_releases/doc4a5665832e7d9957638950.txt (*Inland Clarifies Data*).

68 Joe Mahon, *News Flash: Small-Market Papers Prosper*, FEDGAZETTE, Jan. 2007, http://www.minneapolisfed.org/publications_papers/pub_display.cfm?id=1274.

69 Ken Doctor, *The Newsonomics of Reborn Newspaper Profit*, NIEMAN JOURNALISM LAB, May 2010, http://www.niemanlab.org/2010/05/the-newsonomics-of-reborn-newspaper-profit/.

70 Julia Boorstin, *2010 Surprise: Newspaper Stocks Q4 Surge*, MEDIA MONEY, Dec. 27, 2010, http://www.cnbc.com/id/40818403/ (*2010 Surprise*).

71 *2010 Surprise*.

72 "Newspapers: Missed the 2010 Media Rally" in *Pew, State of News Media 2011*.

73 Jennifer Dorroh, *Statehouse Exodus*, AMER. JOURNALISM REV. (April/May 2009), http://www.ajr.org/article.asp?id=4721.

74 Rotten Tomatoes, http://www.rottentomatoes.com (last visited Mar. 8, 2011).

75 PEW RESEARCH CTR., HOW NEWS HAPPENS: A STUDY OF THE NEWS ECOSYSTEM OF ONE AMERICAN CITY, (2010), http://www.journalism.org/analysis_report/how_news_happens, (PEW, HOW NEWS HAPPENS).

76 PEW, HOW NEWS HAPPENS.

77 The Pulitzer Prizes, Columbia Univ., Search results: Inquirer, Philadelphia, journalism, winner, http://www.pulitzer.org/faceted_search/results/taxonomy-5-2-philadelphia-inquirer (last visited Mar. 4, 2011).

78 Edgar Williams, *A History of the Inquirer*, PHILADELPHIA INQUIRER, June 20, 2003, http://web.archive.org/web/20070219044935/http:/www.philly.com/mld/inquirer/news/local/6135296.htm?1c.

79 Jodi Enda, *Retreating from the World*, AMER. JOURNALISM REV. (Dec. 2010/Jan. 2011), http://ajr.org/Article.asp?id=4985.

80 Katharine Q. Seelye & Andrew Ross Sorkin, *Newspaper Chain Agrees to a Sale for $4.5 Billion*, N.Y. TIMES, Mar. 13, 2006, http://www.nytimes.com/2006/03/13/business/media/13knight.html; Associated Press, *McClatchy Sells Philadelphia Newspapers for $562 Million*, USA TODAY, May 23, 2006, http://www.usatoday.com/money/media/2006-05-23-philadelphia-newspapers-sold_x.htm.

81 Steven Church & Greg Bensinger, *Philadelphia Inquirer's Bankruptcy Costs Owners Group (Update 2)*, BLOOMBERG, Feb. 23, 2009, http://www.bloomberg.com/apps/news?sid=aY33Ly.1UsnA&pid=newsarchive.

82 Bob Warner, *Daily News, Inquirer Sale Plan OK'd by Bankruptcy Judge*, PHILADELPHIA DAILY NEWS, June 29, 2010, http://article.wn.com/view/2010/06/29/Daily_News_Inquirer_sale_plan_OKd_by_bankruptcy_judge/.

83 JAN SHAFFER, EXPLORING A NETWORKED JOURNALISM COLLABORATIVE IN PHILADELPHIA (2010), http://www.j-lab.org/publications/philadelphia_media_project (SHAFFER, EXPLORING).

84 SHAFFER, EXPLORING.

85 LEONARD DOWNIE JR. & ROBERT G. KAISER, THE NEWS ABOUT THE NEWS: AMERICAN JOURNALISM IN PERIL 75 (Knopf) (2002).

86 James T. Hamilton, *Subsidizing the Watchdog: What Would It Cost to Support Investigative Journalism at a Large Metropolitan Daily Newspaper?* (2009), (Hamilton, *Subsidizing the Watchdog*) http://sanford.duke.edu/nonprofitmedia/documents/dwchamiltonfinal.pdf.

87 FIONA MORGAN, AN INFORMATION COMMUNITY CASE STUDY: THE RESEARCH TRIANGLE, N.C. 12 (New America Foundation) (2011), http://mediapolicy.newamerica.net/publications/policy/the_research_triangle_north_carolina.

88 Hamilton, *Subsidizing the Watchdog*.

89 Interview with Mark Silverman, (Nashville) Tennessean, by Steven Waldman, FCC (May 24, 2010) (Silverman Interview 5/24/10).

90 U.S. Census Bureau, Table 1: Summary of State and Local Government Finances by Level of Government: 2002–03, http://www.census.gov/govs/estimate/03sl00us.html (2003 figure); U.S. Census Bureau, Table 1: State and Local Government Finances by Level of Government and by State: 2007–08 (2008 figure), *available at* State and Local Government Finances by Level of Government, http://www.census.gov/govs/estimate/ (select US Summary & Alabama–Mississippi).

91 Jennifer Dorroh, *Statehouse Exodus*, AMER JOURNALISM REV. (Apr./May 2009) http://www.ajr.org/article.asp?id=4721 (*Statehouse Exodus*).

92 *Statehouse Exodus*.

93 *Statehouse Exodus*.

94 *Statehouse Exodus*.

95 Mark Lisheron, *Reloading at the Statehouse*, AMER. JOURNALISM REV. (Sept. 2010) (*Reloading at the Statehouse*), http://www.ajr.org/Article.

asp?id=4908.

96 Jeremy W. Peters, *As Newspapers Cut Costs, A Thinning of the Guard Among Albany's Press Corps*, N.Y. TIMES, Oct. 7, 2008, http://www.nytimes.com/2008/10/08/nyregion/08press.html.

97 Interview with Jeanette Krebs by M.K. Guzda Struck, FCC (Sept. 19, 2010).

98 John Miller, *News Sites Funded by Think Tanks Take Root*, BOSTON.COM, Apr. 13, 2010, http://www.boston.com/news/nation/articles/2010/04/13/news_sites_funded_by_think_tanks_take_root/.

99 Interview with Ed Vogel by M.K. Guzda Struck, FCC (Aug. 2010).

100 *Statehouse Exodus;* Rich Miller, *Newspaper Carnage Continues*, Aug. 18, 2008, http://capitolfax.com/2008/08/18/newspaper-carnage-continues/.

101 Interview with John Beck by M.K. Guzda Struck, FCC (Sept. 15, 2010).

102 *Statehouse Exodus*.

103 *AJR's 2009 Count of Statehouse Reporters*, AMER. JOURNALISM REV. (Apr./May 2009), http://www.ajr.org/article.asp?id=4722.

104 *See* Texas Tribune, http://www.texastribune.org/; California Watch at http://californiawatch.org/; NJSpotlight at http://www.njspotlight.com/ (each last visited Feb. 2, 2011).

105 *Reloading at the Statehouse*.

106 Interview with Rick Edmonds by Steven Waldman, FCC (Apr. 19, 2010).

107 Paul Pringle, Corinna Knoll, & Kim Murphy, *Rizzo's Horse Had Come In*, L.A. TIMES, Aug. 22, 2010, http://articles.latimes.com/2010/aug/22/local/la-me-rizzo-20100822.

108 Interview with Christina Garcia by M.K. Guzda Struck, FCC (July 28 2010) (Garcia Interview 7/28/10).

109 "If that's a number people choke on, maybe I'm in the wrong business," said Rizzo—who garnered the $787,637 salary—to the *Los Angeles Times*. "I could go into private business and make that money. This council has compensated me for the job I've done." "I would have to argue you get what you pay for," said assistant city manager, Angela Spaccia, casually, who made $376,288 annually. Jeff Gottlieb & Ruben Vives, *Is a City Manager Worth $800,000?*, L.A. TIMES, July 15, 2010 (*Is a City Manager Worth $800,000?*), http://articles.latimes.com/2010/jul/15/local/la-me-bell-salary-20100715; Corinna Knoll, *Residents of Bell Unhappy Over High Salaries for City Employees*, L.A. TIMES, July 16, 2010, http://articles.latimes.com/2010/jul/16/local/la-me-0716-bell-residents-20100716.

110 *Is a City Manager Worth $800,000?*.

111 *Is a City Manager Worth $800,000?*

112 *Is a City Manager Worth $800,000?*

113 Jeff Gottlieb & Ruben Vives, *Residents Irate as Bell Council Requests Report on Salaries*, L.A. TIMES, July 20, 2010, http://www.latimes.com/news/local/la-me-bell-20100720,0,6229042.story.

114 Jeff Gottlieb, Ruben Vives, & Jack Leonard, *Bell Leaders Hauled Off in Cuffs*, L.A. TIMES, Sept. 22, 2010, http://articles.latimes.com/2010/sep/22/local/la-me-bell-arrest-20100922.

115 Garcia Interview 7/28/10.

116 Brian Hews, *City of Bell: Why Cities Need a Community Newspaper*, LOS CERRITOS COMMUNITY NEWSPAPER GROUP, http://loscerritosnews.net/city-of-bell-why-cities-need-a-community-newspaper-p874-150.htm (last visited Jan. 24, 2011).

117 David Folkenflik, *How the L.A. Times Broke the Bell Corruption Story*, NATIONAL PUBLIC RADIO, Sept. 25, 2010, http://www.npr.org/templates/story/story.php?storyId=130108851.

118 Email correspondence from David Lauter to M.K. Guzda Struck, FCC (July 29, 2010).

119 Email from David Lauter to M.K. Guzda Struck, FCC (July 29, 2010).

120 James Spencer, *The Story of How the Bell Scandal Broke: An Account from LA Times Reporter Jeff Gottlieb*, PUBLICCEO.COM, Aug. 11, 2010, http://publicceo.com/index.php/local-governments/151-local-govern-ments-publicceo-exclusive/1843-the-story-of-how-the-bell-scandal-broke-an-account-from-la-times-reporter-jeff-gottlieb.

121 Interview of Jeff Gottlieb by M.K. Guzda Struck, FCC (July 29, 2010).

122 Terry Francke, *Why the Bell Scandal Happened and What Can Be Done*, VOICE OF OC, July 28, 2010, http://www.voiceofoc.org/article_a7d-8e4e2-9a78-11df-aefd-001cc4c03286.html.

123 Interview of Christine Garcia by M.K. Guzda Struck, FCC (July 28, 2010).

124 Testimony of Montana State Senator Jerry Black, Knight Commis-sion Forum on Meeting the Public's Information Needs in Montana (Oct. 25, 2008), *available at* http://www.knightcomm.org/files/flashplayer/251008/251008a.html.

125 Interview of Mark Thompson by M.K. Guzda Struck, FCC (July 15, 2010).

126 Interview of Brian Hamlin, Sr. Reporter, *Vacaville (CA) Reporter*, by M.K.Guzda Struck, FCC (Aug. 28, 2010) (Hamlin Interview 8/28/10). Tragically, since these interviews, Hamlin died of cancer.

127 Hamlin Interview 8/28/10. Hamlin provided an example of the distances he was required to drive in a single day to cover far-flung stories, due to staff reductions: Stockton to Vallejo, 65.7 mi.; Vallejo to Fairfield, 17 mi.; Fairfield to Sacramento, 43 mi.

128 Hamlin Interview 8/28/10.

129 Interview with Bill Girdner by M.K. Guzda Struck, FCC (July 6, 2010) (Girdner Interview 7/6/10).

130 Girdner Interview 7/6/10.

131 Girdner Interview 7/6/10. Girdner laments the closing of ranks on a federal level, as well, specifically in the Justice Department. Justice overseas FBI, DEA, Bureau of Prisons, U.S. Marshals, Executive Office for Immigration Review, Tax Division, Antitrust Division, Office of Profes-sional Responsibility, and numerous other branches. *See* U.S. Dept. of Justice, Dept. of Justice Agencies, http://www.justice.gov/agencies/index-org.html (last visited Jan. 24, 2011).

132 Interview with Steven Kaplan by M.K. Guzda Struck, FCC (Sept. 15, 2010).

133 Email from Jack Kresnak, former journalist, Pres. & CEO, Michigan's Children, to Steven Waldman, (Mar. 8, 2011).

134 Interview with Vivek Sankaran by M.K. Guzda Struck, FCC (Aug. 17, 2010) Sankaran Interview 8/17/10).

135 Professor Sankaran's research and policy interests center on improving outcomes for children in child abuse and neglect cases by empowering parents and strengthening due process protections in the child welfare system. Sankaran Interview 8/17/10.

136 Email from Paul Cates, Innocence Proj., to M.K. Guzda Struck, FCC (Sept. 20, 2010).

137 Tim Arango, *Death Row Foes See Newsroom Cuts as a Blow*, N.Y. TIMES, May 20, 2009, http://www.nytimes.com/2009/05/21/business/media/21innocent.html.

138 David Simon, *In Baltimore, No One Left to Press the Police*, WASH. POST, Mar.1, 2009, http://www.washingtonpost.com/wp-dyn/content/article/2009/02/27/AR2009022703591.html.

139 GARY SCHWITZER, THE STATE OF HEALTH JOURNALISM IN THE U.S. 16 (Kaiser Family Found.) (2009) (SCHWITZER, STATE OF HEALTH JOURNAL-ISM), *available at* http://www.kff.org/entmedia/upload/7858.pdf.

140 SCHWITZER, STATE OF HEALTH JOURNALISM at 16.

141 SCHWITZER, STATE OF HEALTH JOURNALISM at 3.

142 SCHWITZER, STATE OF HEALTH JOURNALISM at 3.

143 SCHWITZER, STATE OF HEALTH JOURNALISM at 3.

144 Ferrel Guillory, *Weaker Media, Weaker Health News Reporting*, 70 N.C. MED. J. 360 (July/Aug. 2009) (*Weaker Media*), *available at* http://www.ncmedicaljournal.com/wp-content/uploads/NCMJ/Jul-Aug-09/Guillory.pdf.

145 *Weaker Media*.

146 *Weaker Media*.

147 Silverman Interview 5/24/10.

148 MARYN MCKENNA, SUPERBUG: THE FATAL MENACE OF MRSA (Free Press) (2010).

149 Interview with Maryn McKenna by M.K. Guzda Struck, FCC (Aug. 22, 2010).

150 SCHWITZER, STATE OF HEALTH JOURNALISM at 10.

151 *See, e.g., PSA Test Cut-off Could Signal Low-Risk Prostate Cancer*, HEALTH NEWS REV., Feb. 16, 2011, http://www.healthnewsreview.org/review.html?review_id=3639.

152 Cristine Russell, The Observatory, *Science Reporting by Press Release*, COLUMBIA J. REV., Nov. 14, 2008, http://www.cjr.org/the_observatory/science_reporting_by_press_rel.php.

153 SURVEY OF AHCJ MEMBERS REPORT at 4.

154 Kaiser Health News, http://www.kaiserhealthnews.org/ (last visited Jan. 24, 2011) (Kaiser Health News).

155 Kaiser Health News.

156 Kevin Sack, *Foundation Starts Health Policy News Service*, N.Y. TIMES, Nov. 23, 2008 (*Foundation Starts Health Policy News Service*), http://www.nytimes.com/2008/11/24/business/media/24health.html?_r=1&scp=1&sq=kaiser%20health%20news%20and%202008&st=cse.

157 *Foundation Starts Health Policy News Service*.

158 Carol Guensburg, *Nonprofit News*, AMER. JOURNALISM REV. (Feb./Mar. 2008), http://www.ajr.org/Article.asp?id=4458.

159 DARRELL M. WEST, GROVER J. "RUSS" WHITEHURST & E.J. DIONNE JR., RE-IMAGINING EDUCATION JOURNALISM (Brookings Institution) (2010) (RE-IMAGINING EDUCATION JOURNALISM), *available at* http://www.brookings.edu/reports/2010/0511_education_journalism.aspx.

160 Email from Debbie Cafazzo to Jodi Enda, FCC (Nov. 19, 2010).

161 Email from Richard Colvin to Steven Waldman, FCC (Jan. 19, 2011).

162 RE-IMAGINING EDUCATION JOURNALISM.

163 Michael Petrilli, *Disappearing Ink*, 9 EDUCATION NEXT 83 (Fall 2009), http://educationnext.org/disappearing-ink/.

164 Interview with Jay Mathews by Jodi Enda, FCC (Nov. 20, 2010).

165 Interview with Dale Mezzacappa by Jodi Enda, FCC (Nov. 22, 2010).

166 Education News Colorado, http://www.ednewscolorado.org/ (last visited Jan. 25, 2011).

167 Interview with Alan Gottlieb by Jodi Enda, FCC (Nov. 20, 2010).

168 DARRELL M. WEST, GROVER J. "RUSS" WHITEHURST & E.J. DIONNE JR., AMERICANS WANT MORE COVERAGE OF TEACHER PERFORMANCE AND STUDENT ACHIEVEMENT (Brookings Institution) (2011), *available at* http://www.brookings.edu/reports/2011/0329_education_news.aspx.

169 Interview of Mark Horvit by M.K. Guzda Struck, FCC (Aug. 16, 2010).

170 Mary Walton, *Investigative Shortfall*, AMERICAN JOURNALISM REV., (Sept. 2010) (Walton, *Investigative Shortfall*), http://www.ajr.org/Article.asp?id=4904.

171 Interview of Mary Walton by M.K. Guzda Struck (Aug. 29, 2010).

172 Chelsea Ide & Kanupriya Vashisht, *Today's Investigative Reporters Lack Resources*, AZCENTRAL.COM, May 28, 2006, http://www.azcentral.com/specials/special01/0528bolles-stateofreporting.html.

173 Walton, *Investigative Shortfall*.

174 Walton, *Investigative Shortfall*.

175 Richard Pérez-Peña, *Group Plans to Provide Investigative Journalism*, N.Y. TIMES, Oct. 15,, 2007 http://www.nytimes.com/2007/10/15/business/media/15publica.html?oref=slogin.

176 ProPublica, About Us, http://www.propublica.org/about/ (ProPublica) (last visited Jan. 25, 2011).

177 ProPublica.

178 Richard Pérez-Peña, *In Chicago, An Ex-Editor Fights Back, N.Y. Times, Nov. 22, 2009*, http://www.nytimes.com/2009/11/23/business/media/23local.html.

179 Prepared Testimony of James O'Shea, Editor & Cofounder, Chicago News Cooperative, FCC Workshop on the Future of Media and the Information Needs of Communities: Public and Other Noncommercial Media in the Digital Era (Apr. 30, 2010) *available at* http://reboot.fcc.gov/futureofmedia/public-and-other-noncommercial-media-in-the-digital-era.

180 PEW RESEARCH CTR.'S PROJ. FOR EXCELLENCE IN JOURNALISM, THE NEW WASHINGTON PRESS CORPS: AS MAINSTREAM MEDIA DECLINE, NICHE AND FOREIGN OUTLETS GROW (last updated July 16, 2009), http://www.journalism.org/analysis_report/new_washington_press_corps.

181 Al Diamon, *Barely Covering Maine's Delegation*, DOWN EAST, July 19, 2010, http://www.downeast.com/media-mutt/2010/july/barely-maine-congressional-delegation.

182 Email from Debra Mason, Exec. Dir. of Religion Newswriters Assn., to Steven Waldman, FCC (Feb. 18, 2011).

183 Interview with Andrew Lack by Steven Waldman, FCC (Dec. 16, 2010).

184 THOMAS BALDWIN, DANIEL BERGIN, FRED FICO, STEPHEN LACY, & STEVEN S. WILDMAN, NEWS MEDIA COVERAGE OF CITY GOVERNMENTS IN 2009 (Michigan State Univ. & Nat'l Science Found.) (2010).

185 Interview of Michael Marizco by M.K. Guzda Struck, FCC (May 26, 2010).

186 The total number of members has increased, with the bulk describing themselves as freelancers. They had 1,100 members in 2000 and have 1,500 members now. Interview with Beth Parke, Executive Director, Society of Environmental Journalists, by M.K. Guzda Struck, FCC (Aug. 23, 2010) (Parke Interview 8/23/10).

187 Parke Interview 8/23/10.

188 Interview of Tim Wheeler by Jodi Enda, FCC (Dec. 15, 2010).

189 Dean Starkman, *The Hamster Wheel*, COLUMBIA J. REV. (Sept./Oct. 2010), http://www.cjr.org/cover_story/the_hamster_wheel.php?page=all.

190 "Nielsen Analysis" in PEW, STATE OF NEWS MEDIA 2010, http://stateofthemedia.org/2010/online-summary-essay/nielsen-analysis/.

191 "Newspaper Audiences" in Pew, *State Of News Media 2010*, http://stateofthemedia.org/2010/newspapers-summary-essay/audience/.

192 For evidence of newspaper experimentation, *see* Joseph Tartakoff, *Gannett Tries Out Paywalls at Three Papers*, PAID CONTENT, July 1, 2010, http://paidcontent.org/article/419-gannett-tries-out-paywalls-at-three-papers/; Nick Bilton, *iPad vs. Newspaper, Fly-Swatting Edition*, BITS: BUSINESS INNOVATION TECHNOLOGY SOCIETY (N.Y. Times), Sept. 10, 2010, http://bits.blogs.nytimes.com/2010/09/10/fly-swatting-the-ipad-versus-the-newspaper/?scp=1&sq=%22swatting%20the%20ipad%20versus%20the%20newspaper%22&st=cse; Jenna Wortham, *Betaworks and the Times Plan a Social News Service*, BITS: BUSINESS INNOVATION TECHNOLOGY SOCIETY (N.Y. Times), Sept. 9, 2010, http://bits.blogs.nytimes.com/2010/09/09/betaworks-and-the-times-develop-social-news-service/; David LaFontaine, *Mobile Advertising: The Next Big Thing Is Starting to Arrive (Part Two: Banners, Texts and Coupons)*, Apr. 2, 2010, NEWSPAPER ASSN. OF AMER., http://www.naa.org/Resources/Articles/Digital-Media-Moving-To-Mobile-Advertising-2/Digital-Media-Moving-To-Mobile-Advertising-2.aspx.

193 Bill Mitchell, *Pay Walls Debut at Three Gannett Papers Testing 'Journalism as a Service,'* THE POYNTER INSTITUTE, July 1, 2010, http://www.poynter.org/latest-news/business-news/newspay/104103/pay-walls-debut-at-three-gannett-papers-testing-journalism-as-a-service/; Jim Romenesko, *Gannett to Launch Page Design 'Hubs' in Five Cities*, THE POYNTER INSTITUTE, July 13, 2010, http://www.poynter.org/latest-news/romenesko/104296/gannett-to-launch-page-design-hubs-in-five-cities/.

194 Jenna Wortham, *Betaworks and the Times Plan a Social News Service*, BITS: BUSINESS INNOVATION TECHNOLOGY SOCIETY (N.Y. Times), Sept. 9, 2010, http://bits.blogs.nytimes.com/2010/09/09/betaworks-and-the-times-develop-social-news-service/; Richard Pérez-Peña, *The Times to Charge for Frequent Access to Its Website*, N.Y. TIMES, Jan. 20, 2010, http://www.nytimes.com/2010/01/21/business/media/21times.html.

195 Beth Lawton, *Mobilized: TBO Mobile*, NEWSPAPER ASSN. OF AMER., July 31, 2008, http://www.naa.org/Resources/Articles/Digital-Media-Moving-To-Mobile-TBO-Case-Study/Digital-Media-Moving-To-Mobile-TBO-Case-Study.aspx.

196 Damon Kiesow, *News of the World iPad App Highlights News Corp. Price Experiments*, THE POYNTER INSTITUTE, Dec. 22, 2010, http://www.poynter.org/latest-news/media-lab/mobile-media/111941/news-of-the-world-ipad-app-highlights-news-corp-price-experiments/.

197 *See* The Ben Franklin Project, What's the Ben Franklin Project, http://jrcbenfranklinproject.wordpress.com/about/ (last visited Mar. 8, 2011); Megan Garber, *Journal Register Company Joins with Outside.in for a Hyperlocal News/Ad Portal in Philadelphia*, NIEMAN JOURNALISM LAB, Sept. 22, 2010, http://www.niemanlab.org/2010/09/journal-register-company-joins-with-outside-in-for-a-hyperlocal-newsad-portal-in-philadelphia/; Mallary Jean Tenore, *Ben Franklin Project's 'Digital First, Print Last' Approach Produces First Products*, THE POYNTER INSTITUTE,

May 19, 2010, http://www.poynter.org/latest-news/top-stories/102741/ben-franklin-projects-digital-first-print-last-approach-produces-first-products/; Mark Fitzgerald, *Fireworks at Journal Register Co.: 'Ben Franklin Project' Successful at All 19 Dailies*, EDITOR & PUBLISHER, July 6, 2010, http://www.editorandpublisher.com/Headlines/fireworks-at-journal-register-co-'ben-franklin-project'-successful-at-all-18-dailies-61891-.aspx.

198 "Newspapers: Missed the 2010 Media Rally" in *Pew, State of News Media 2011*.

199 PEW RESEARCH CTR.'S PROJ. FOR EXCELLENCE IN JOURNALISM, NEWS LEADERS AND THE FUTURE: THE STATE OF JOURNALISM (2010), http://www.journalism.org/analysis_report/child.

2 Radio

1 HAROLD EVANS, THEY MADE AMERICA: FROM THE STEAM ENGINE TO THE SEARCH ENGINE: TWO CENTURIES OF INNOVATORS 219 (Little, Brown & Co.) (2004).

2 CHRISTOPHER H. STERLING & JOHN MICHAEL KITTROSS, STAY TUNED: A HISTORY OF AMERICAN BROADCASTING (THIRD EDITION) 32 (Routledge) (2001) (STERLING & KITTROSS, STAY TUNED). Even before this breakthrough Christmas Eve broadcast, Fessenden had gained notoriety for being the first to experimentally broadcast voice over the air. On December 23, 1900, Fessenden, stationed at Cobb Island on the Potomac River, successfully transmitted his voice, asking if it was snowing, to his assistant, in Arlington, Virginia. Fessenden's experiment in 1900 marked the first time that speech was broadcast over the air, even though, at this time, the experiment only involved point-to-point communication. *An Unsung Hero: Reginald Fessenden, the Canadian Inventor of Radio Telephony*, THE INSTITUTE OF ELECTRICAL AND ELECTRONICS ENGINEERS (reprinted from The Radioscientist), http://www.ieee.ca/millennium/radio/radio_unsung.html (last visited Mar. 6, 2011).

3 Lisa Sergio, *Marconi: Wizard of the Airwaves*, THE ROTARIAN 14, 18 (Sept. 1974).

4 TIM WU, THE MASTER SWITCH 33–34 (Knopf) (2010) (THE MASTER SWITCH).

5 THE MASTER SWITCH at 35, *quoting Voice Broadcasting the Stirring Progress of the 'Battle of the Century,'* WIRELESS AGE (Aug. 1921).

6 STERLING & KITTROSS, STAY TUNED at 63–69.

7 STERLING & KITTROSS, STAY TUNED at 86–87.

8 WILLIAM ALBIG, MODERN PUBLIC OPINION 447 (McGraw-Hill) (1956) (MODERN PUBLIC OPINION). In addition to music and variety programs (more than 70 percent), small amounts of drama programming, educational information, market reports, weather, sports, health exercises, church services, and women's and children's programming made up the other 22.5 percent of a typical station's programming.

9 STERLING & KITTROSS, STAY TUNED at 79–80, 93–97, 105, 207–208; *In re Great Lakes Broadcasting Co.*, Federal Radio Commission, 3 FRC Ann. Rep. 32 (1929), *rev'd on other grounds*, 37 F.2d 993 (D.C. Cir.), *cert. dismissed*, 281 U.S. 706 (1930); ROBERT W. MCCHESNEY, TELECOMMUNICATIONS, MASS MEDIA, AND DEMOCRACY 25 (Oxford Univ. Press) (1995); ROBERT L. HILLARD & MICHAEL C. KEITH, THE QUIETED VOICE: THE RISE AND DEMISE OF LOCALISM IN AMERICAN RADIO 1 (So. Ill. Univ. Press) (2005) (HILLARD & KEITH, THE QUIETED VOICE).

10 ENCYCLOPEDIA OF RADIO 291 (Christopher H. Sterling, ed.) (Museum of Broadcast Communications) (2004) (ENCYCLOPEDIA OF RADIO).

11 GWENYTH L. JACKAWAY, MEDIA AT WAR: RADIO'S CHALLENGES TO THE NEWSPAPERS 1924–1939 14 (Praeger) (1995) (JACKAWAY, MEDIA AT WAR).

12 STERLING & KITTROSS, STAY TUNED at 136–137.

13 JACKAWAY, MEDIA AT WAR at 20.

14 JACKAWAY, MEDIA AT WAR at 20.

15 JACKAWAY, MEDIA AT WAR at 23–24.

16 JACKAWAY, MEDIA AT WAR at 27–28.

17 STERLING & KITTROSS, STAY TUNED at 193.

18 *Newspaper-Radio Legislation Delayed*, BROADCASTING, Mar. 15, 1937, at 22; *Dailies Must Oppose Use of Radio to Impair Democracy*, EDITOR & PUBLISHER, Apr. 30, 1938, at 18; *Giving News to Radio Viewed as Menace to Newspapers by Many Editors*, EDITOR & PUBLISHER, Dec. 22, 1928.

19 STERLING & KITTROSS, STAY TUNED at 194.

20 STERLING & KITTROSS, STAY TUNED at 237.

21 In 1937, Edward R. Murrow sailed for London where he was to take up the post of chief CBS radio correspondent in Europe. At the time, Murrow had never written a news story in his life, and he had never made a scheduled radio broadcast. Mark Bernstein, *History of Edward R. Murrow: Inventing Broadcast Journalism, available at* Washington State Univ., The Edward R. Murrow College of Communication, Overview, http://communication.wsu.edu/overview/history/history.htm (last visited Mar. 22, 2011).

22 STERLING & KITTROSS, STAY TUNED at 241.

23 MODERN PUBLIC OPINION at 447; PAUL F. LAZARSFELD & FRANK N. STANTON, COMMUNICATIONS RESEARCH, 1948–1949 51–72 (Harper & Bros.) (1949).

24 STERLING & KITTROSS, STAY TUNED at 253–255 (400,000); HUGH R. SLOTTEN, RADIO AND TELEVISION REGULATION: BROADCAST TECHNOLOGY IN THE UNITED STATES, 1920–1960 199 (Johns Hopkins Univ. Press) (2000).

25 MITCHELL V. CHARNLEY, NEWS BY RADIO 238 (Furnas Press) (2007).

26 STERLING & KITTROSS, STAY TUNED at 179, 362.

27 ENCYCLOPEDIA OF RADIO at 61.

28 ENCYCLOPEDIA OF RADIO at 581; ZEMIRA JONES, RADIO AND THE PUBLIC INTEREST: WHERE WE ARE TODAY 10 (All-American Mgmt. Group) (2010) (JONES, RADIO AND THE PUBLIC INTEREST).

29 JONES, RADIO AND THE PUBLIC INTEREST.

30 JONES, RADIO AND THE PUBLIC INTEREST at 10 (interview with Jack Swanson, former WLS news anchor).

31 The FCC's freeze on issuing AM licenses lasted from 1968–1973. *Amendment of Part 73 of the Commission's Rules Regarding AM Station Assignment Standards and the Relationship Between the AM and FM Broadcast Services,* 39 F.C.C. 2d 645 (1973).

32 HILLARD & KEITH, THE QUIETED VOICE at 59.

33 STERLING & KITTROSS, STAY TUNED at 501–502, 526–527.

34 ENCYCLOPEDIA OF RADIO at 1020.

35 Vernon A. Stone, *Changing Profiles of News Directors of Radio and TV Stations, 1972–1986*, 64 JOURNALISM Q. 745 (1987).

36 *Deregulation of Radio*, Report and Order, 84 FCC 2d 968, 975–78 (1981).

37 Vernon A. Stone, *Deregulation Felt Mainly in Large-Market Radio and Independent TV,* RTDNA COMMUNICATOR 9 (Apr. 1987).

38 EDWARD BLISS JR., NOW THE NEWS: THE STORY OF BROADCAST JOURNALISM 197–198 (1991).

39 Michael L. McKean and Vernon A. Stone, *Deregulation and Competition,* 69 JOURNALISM Q. 715–717 (1992).

40 Sterling, ENCYCLOPEDIA OF RADIO at 1020–1021.

41 DAVID H. WEAVER, RANDAL A. BEAM, BONNIE J. BROWNLEE, PAUL S. VOAKES & CLEVELAND G. WILHOIT, THE AMERICAN JOURNALIST IN THE 21ST CENTURY: U.S. NEWS PEOPLE AT THE DAWN OF A NEW MILLENNIUM 2 (Lawrence Erlbaum) (2007). By another measure, the number of radio journalists declined from more than 0.08 per 100,000 people in 1982 to less than 0.04 per 100,000 people in 2008. ROBERT W. MCCHESNEY & JOHN NICHOLS, THE DEATH AND LIFE OF AMERICAN JOURNALISM: THE MEDIA REVOLUTION THAT WILL BEGIN THE WORLD AGAIN 256, Appendix 3 (Nation Books) (2010).

42 *See Amendment of Section 73.3555,* First Report and Order, 4 FCC Rcd 1723 (1989) (relaxing the "radio duopoly" rule), and *Revision of Radio Rules and Policies,* Report and Order, 7 FCC Rcd 2755 (1992)(increasing national and local ownership limits).

43 Lydia Polgreen, *The Death of Local Radio,* WASH. MONTHLY (Apr. 1999). *See also* STERLING & KITTROSS, STAY TUNED at 669.

44 TASNEEM CHIPTY, CRA INT'L INC., FCC MEDIA OWNERSHIP STUDY #5: STATION OWNERSHIP AND PROGRAMMING IN RADIO 1 (2007), *available at* http://hraunfoss.fcc.gov/edocs_public/attachmatch/DA-07-3470A6.pdf. Of Clear Channel's 1,183 radio stations, 821 are FM stations and 362 are AM stations. *Id* at 7.

45 Interview with John Hogan, CEO, Clear Channel, by Cynthia Kennard, FCC (Oct. 7, 2010).

46 JONES, RADIO AND THE PUBLIC INTEREST at 12–13.

47 JONES, RADIO AND THE PUBLIC INTEREST at 12–13.

48 Arbitron Inc., *Overall Radio Listeners Persons Aged 12 and Older Increases More Than 3.3 Million Year Over Year* (press release), Dec. 7, 2010, http://arbitron.mediaroom.com/index.php?s=43&item=731.

49 ARBITRON INC., RADIO TODAY 2010 EDITION (2010), *available at* www.arbitron.com/downloads/RadioToday_2010.pdf.

50 GEORGE WILLIAMS, REVIEW OF THE RADIO INDUSTRY 2007 10–12 (FCC) (2007), *available at* http://hraunfoss.fcc.gov/edocs_public/attachmatch/DA-07-3470A11.pdf.

51 MICHAEL C. KEITH, RADIO PROGRAMMING: CONSULTANCY AND FORMATICS 100 (Elsevier Science) (1987).

52 "News on the Radio" in PEW, STATE OF NEWS MEDIA 2011, http://stateofthemedia.org/2011/audio-essay (*citing* ARBITRON INC., RADIO TODAY 2010 EDITION); Email from Claudine Kinsley, Dir., Syndicated Standards & Analysis, Arbitron Inc., to Alexandra McKinney, FCC (Nov. 17, 2010). Arbitron provided aggregate data to the FCC but did not identify the stations that identified themselves as all-news stations.

53 Based on an estimate by Dr. Gary Heller, VP, Research & Audience Measurement, CBS Radio Corp., provided to Cynthia Kennard, FCC (Oct. 29, 2010) (CBS Email 10/29/10).

54 "Audio: News/Talk Continues to Be an Important Force in Radio" in PEW, STATE OF NEWS MEDIA 2011, http://stateofthemedia.org/2011/audio-essay/data-page/.

55 ARBITRON INC., RADIO TODAY 2010 EDITION (2010).

56 PEW RESEARCH CTR. FOR THE PEOPLE & THE PRESS, AMERICANS SPENDING MORE TIME FOLLOWING THE NEWS (2010) (PEW 2010 NEWS CONSUMPTION SURVEY), http://people-press.org/report/652/.

57 PEW 2010 NEWS CONSUMPTION SURVEY.

58 Interview with Mel Karmazin, CEO, Sirius XM Radio Inc., by Cynthia Kennard, FCC (Sept. 20, 2010).

59 Interview with Paul Jacobs, Jacobs Media, by Cynthia Kennard, FCC (Sept. 25, 2010).

60 Lee Hood, *Radio Reverb: The Impact of "Local" News Reimported to Its Own Community,* 51 J. BROAD. & ELEC. MEDIA 1 (Mar. 2007).

61 Interview with Lee Hood, Assist. Prof., Loyola Univ. Chicago, School of Communication, by Cynthia Kennard, FCC (Sept. 29, 2010).

62 Interview with John Hogan, CEO, Clear Channel, by Cynthia Kennard, FCC (Oct. 7, 2010).

63 Interview with J.P. Skelly, News Dir., KORN-AM, by Monica Alba, FCC (Sept. 24, 2010).

64 Interview with John Hogan, CEO, Clear Channel, by Cynthia Kennard, FCC (Oct. 7, 2010).

65 Interview with Robert Papper, Dir., RTDNA/Hofstra Univ. Annual Survey, by Cynthia Kennard, FCC (Sept. 30, 2010) (Papper Interview 9/30/10).

66 Papper Interview 9/30/10.

67 Papper Interview. *See Radio Staff Size 2009,* RTDNA, http://www.rtdna.org/media/PartIIIStaffing.pdf.

68 *Who Killed Black Radio News?,* BLACK COMMENTATOR, May 29, 2003, http://www.blackcommentator.com/44/44_cover.html.

69 Interview with Ed Perry, Station Owner, WATD-95.9 FM, by Corrina Wu, FCC (Sept. 2010).

70 Email from Ed Perry to Cynthia Kennard, FCC (Nov. 24, 2010).

71 Interview with Dan Dillion, News Dir., KFDI-FM, Wichita, KA, by Monica Alba, FCC (Sept. 2010) (Dillion Interview).

72 Dillion Interview.

73 Interview with Edward Esposito, VP, Information Media, Rubber City Radio Group (Akron, OH), by Cynthia Kennard, FCC (Sept. 14, 2010) (Esposito Interview 9/14/10).

74 Esposito Interview 9/14/10.

75 Interview of Harvey Nagler, VP, CBS Radio News, by Cynthia Kennard, FCC (April 20, 2011).

76 BIA Financial Network Inc., BIA/Kelsey Media Access Pro Radio Analyzer Database, May 26, 2011.

77 JONES, RADIO AND THE PUBLIC INTEREST at 12.

78 CBS Email 10/29/10.

79 Interview of Ron Gleason, News Dir., WBBM Radio, Chicago, by Corrina Wu, FCC (Sept. 2010).

80 Robert Philpot, *KRLD-AM Going All-News,* FORT WORTH STAR TELEGRAM, Sept. 24, 2010, http://www.dfw.com/2010/09/24/339603/krld-am-going-all-news.html.

81 Interview of Dan Mason, President and CEO, CBS Radio, by Cynthia Kennard, FCC (May 5, 2011).

82 Prepared Testimony of Barbara S. Cochran, Pres. Emeritus, Radio Television Digital News Association, FCC Workshop on the Future of Media

and the Information Needs of Communities: Serving the Public Interest in the Digital Era (Mar. 4, 2010), *available at* http://reboot.fcc.gov/futureofmedia/serving-the-public-interest-in-the-digital-era.

83 ARBITRON INC., RIDING OUT THE STORM: THE VITAL ROLE OF LOCAL RADIO IN TIMES OF CRISIS 2 (2005), *available at* http://www.arbitron.com/downloads/hurricane_summary.pdf. The study catalogued listener praise:

"Radio was far superior compared to any other media source."

"We couldn't have done without our radio. It was the only source of info we had."

"Radio personalities talked people through the crisis, helped to keep hopes alive and pulled the community together."

"If it had not been for radio, it would have been much more difficult to deal with the 2004 hurricanes. The connection with callers calling in and announcements made me feel people were out there who knew what was going on. This experience gave me a much greater appreciation for radio."

"[Some] stations were able to keep audiences aware of important public-service information such as shelter locations, emergency phone numbers, and other necessary info for our area. They all did a very good job."

Id. at 25.

84 *LPFM Activists Taking Their Case to the NAB*, RADIO & TELEVISION BUSINESS REPORT, Dec. 11, 2010, http://www.rbr.com/radio/lpfm-activists-taking-their-case-to-the-nab.html. *See also* WRAL TV (Raleigh, NC), Interview regarding amateur coverage of Hurricane Katrina by ham radio operators, *available at* http://www.youtube.com/watch?v=yC0u42MnMdM (last visited Mar. 23, 2011).

85 Email from Zemira Jones to Steven Waldman, FCC (Aug. 3, 2010).

86 "Audio: Talk Radio" in PEW RESEARCH CTR.'S PROJ. FOR EXCELLENCE IN JOURNALISM, THE STATE OF THE NEWS MEDIA (2010), (PEW, STATE OF NEWS MEDIA 2010), http://stateofthemedia.org/previous-reports/.

87 ARBITRON INC., RADAR® 103 (DEC. 7, 2009).

88 "Audio: Traditional Broadcast" in PEW, STATE OF NEWS MEDIA 2010, http://stateofthemedia.org/previous-reports/.

89 "Audio: News on the Radio," in PEW, STATE OF NEWS MEDIA 2011, http://stateofthemedia.org/2011/audio-essay (*citing* ARBITRON INC., RADIO TODAY 2010 EDITION).

90 "Audio: News on the Radio," in PEW, STATE OF NEWS MEDIA 2011, (*citing* ARBITRON INC., RADIO TODAY 2010 EDITION). http://stateofthemedia.org/2011/audio-essay/data-page/#fnref-5203-15.

91 The survey was conducted by Edison Media Research for the FCC in 2005 and 2006. *See* FCC, Media Ownership 2006 Research Studies Archive, 7/31/07, http://www.fcc.gov/ownership/2006-studies.html (at link "Edison Media Research Radio Recording Data") (Edison Media Research Radio Recording Data). Edison collected six separate 20-minute segments of airtime, totaling two hours all together. The 245 "news and talk" stations (a subset of the total of 1,128 stations in the survey) had 495 minutes daily of news programming, of which 80.6 percent was non-local and 13.5 percent was local. After Edison submitted its finding, FCC staff audited the data and found that some observations had been misclassified, with the result that some specific categories (e.g., public affairs) had been undercounted.

92 Edison Media Research Radio Recording Data.

93 Interview of Ken P. Stern, former CEO and EVP-COO, National Public Radio, by Cynthia Kennard, FCC (Sept. 12, 2010).

94 National Public Radio Comments in re *FOM PN* (*Comment Sought On FCC Launches Examination of the Future of Media and Information Needs of Communities in a Digital Age*, GN Docket No. 10-25, Public Notice, 25 FCC Rcd 384 (2010) (*FOM PN*)), filed May 7, 2010, at 2, 3, 7.

95 National Public Radio, Local News Station Survey: Executive Summary, http://www.localnewsinitiative.org/executive.cfm (last visited Feb. 11, 2010).

96 *See FCC Announces Auction Winners for Digital Audio Radio Service*, Public Notice, DA 97-656, 12 FCC Rcd 18727 (1997).

97 *See American Mobile Radio Corporation Application for Authority to Construct, Launch, and Operate Two Satellites in the Satellite Digital Audio Radio Service*, Order and Authorization, 13 FCC Rcd 8829 (IB 1997).

98 *Establishment of Rules and Policies for the Digital Audio Radio Satellite Service in the 2310–2360 MHz Frequency Band*, Report and Order, Memorandum Opinion and Order and Further Notice of Proposed Rulemaking, 12 FCC Rcd 5754, 5812 (1997); *see also Amendment of Part 27 of the Commission's Rules to Govern the Operation of Wireless Communications Services in the 2.3 GHz Band,* Notice of Proposed Rulemaking and Second Further Notice of Proposed Rulemaking, 22 FCC Rcd 22123, 22141 (2007).

99 *Application for Consent to Transfer of Control of Licenses, XM Satellite Radio to Sirius Satellite Radio*, Memorandum Opinion and Order, 23 FCC Rcd 12348, 12419–20 (2008). *See also* 47 C.F.R. § 25.144(e)(4), (5); *Amendment of Part 27 of the Commission's Rules to Govern Operation of Wireless Communications Services in the 2.3 GHz Band*, Report and Order and Second Report and Order, 25 FCC Rcd 11710, 11825–26 (2010).

100 "Audio: Satellite Radio Gains in 2010" in Pew, State of News Media 2011, http://stateofthemedia.org/2011/audio-essay/#news-on-the-radio.

101 "Audio: Satellite Radio Gains in 2010" in Pew, State of News Media 2011.

102 Sirius/XM Satellite Radio, Presentation at Bank of America/Merrill Lynch (NYSE: BAC) Media, Communications, and Entertainment Conference (Sept. 15, 2010), *available at* http://investor.sirius.com/events.cfm, http://investor.sirius.com/releasedetail.cfm?releaseid=437649 (webcast).

103 HILLARD & KEITH, THE QUIETED VOICE at 178.

104 "Audio: By the Numbers," in Pew, State of News Media 2011.

105 "Audio: By the Numbers," in Pew, State of News Media 2011.

106 TOM WEBSTER, EDISON RESEARCH, THE CURRENT STATE OF PODCASTING 5 (2010), *available at* http://www.edisonresearch.com/2010%20Edison%20Podcast%20Study%20Data%20Graphs%20Only.pdf.

107 "Audio: By the Numbers," in PEW, STATE OF NEWS MEDIA 2011.

108 *SNL Kagan on "The Future of Online Radio Revenue,"* RADIO NEWS, July 29, 2010, http://www.radiostreamingnews.com/2010/07/snl-kagan-on-future-of-online-radio.html

109 Podcastalley.com, as reported in "Audio: By the Numbers," in PEW, STATE OF NEWS MEDIA 2011.

110 Pandora, Company overview, http://blog.pandora.com/press/pandora-company-overview.html.

111 Stitcher, About Us, http://www.stitcher.com/about_us.php (last visited Mar. 6, 2011).

112 Testimony of William H. Kling, Pres. and CEO, American Public Media Group, FCC Workshop on the Future of Media and the Information Needs of Communities: Public and Other Noncommercial Media in the Digital Era (Apr. 30, 2010), Tr. at 384:15–385:7, *available at* http://reboot.fcc.gov/futureofmedia/public-and-other-noncommercial-media-in-the-digital-era.

113 *SNL Kagan on "The Future of Online Radio Revenue,"* RADIO NEWS, July 29, 2010, http://www.radiostreamingnews.com/2010/07/snl-kagan-on-future-of-online-radio.html.

114 HILLARD & KEITH, THE QUIETED VOICE at 170.

115 Interview of Harvey Nagler, VP, CBS Radio News, by Cynthia Kennard, FCC (Sept. 2010).

3 Television

1 CHRISTOPHER STERLING & JOHN KITTROSS, STAY TUNED: A HISTORY OF AMERICAN BROADCASTING 164–168 (Erlbaum) (2002) (STERLING & KITTROSS, STAY TUNED).

2 Television stations often relied upon the capital provided by established radio and newspaper firms to sustain themselves through their first few years of losses. Typically, after a short period of time, they became highly profitable for their owners. STERLING & KITTROSS, STAY TUNED at 283.

3 CRAIG ALLEN, NEWS IS PEOPLE: THE RISE OF LOCAL TV NEWS AND THE FALL OF NEWS FROM NEW YORK 3–6 (Iowa State Press) (2001) (ALLEN, NEWS IS PEOPLE).

4 Chicago's WBKB began a local newscast in 1947; later, its competitor WGN followed with *Chicagoland Newsreel*. In addition, Los Angeles stations KTLA and KTTV were constantly engaged in a battle for coverage of breaking events in Los Angeles. ALLEN, NEWS IS PEOPLE at 7–8.

5 Owned and operated stations are owned by, rather than simply affiliated with, a television network.

6 ALLEN, NEWS IS PEOPLE at 11.

7 ALLEN, NEWS IS PEOPLE at 12.

8 STERLING & KITTROSS, STAY TUNED at 295–297, 317, 840 App. C, 3-B.

9 Craig Chamberlain, *Rare "Hear It Now" Recordings Lend Insight on Murrow and News History*, ILLINOIS NEWS BUREAU, Sept. 26, 2007, http://news.illinois.edu/news/07/0926murrow.html.

10 STERLING & KITTROSS, STAY TUNED at 370.

11 STERLING & KITTROSS, STAY TUNED at 378–380.

12 STERLING & KITTROSS, STAY TUNED at 379–380.

13 STERLING & KITTROSS, STAY TUNED at 445.

14 ALLEN, NEWS IS PEOPLE at 58.

15 Ted Koppel, *Olbermann, O'Reilly and the Death of Real News*, WASH. POST, Nov. 14, 2010, http://www.washingtonpost.com/wp-dyn/content/article/2010/11/12/AR2010111202857.html?sid=ST2010111203190.

16 STERLING & KITTROSS, STAY TUNED at 378.

17 STERLING & KITTROSS, STAY TUNED at 445.

18 PHYLLIS KANISS, MAKING LOCAL NEWS 102 (Univ. of Chicago Press) (1997).

19 Craig Allen, *Television News*, in HISTORY OF MASS MEDIA IN THE UNITED STATES: AN ENCYCLOPEDIA 647–648 (Margaret A. Blanchard, ed.) (Fitzroy Dearborn) (1998).

20 CAB analysis of Nielsen Galaxy time period level data. Mon-Sat 8–11 p.m. & Sun 7–11 p.m.; LIVE + Same Day; 9/21/09–5/26/10 vs. prior years. Email from David Woolfson, SVP–Research & Insights, Cabletelevision Advertising Bureau, to Sherille Ismail, Mar. 13, 2011.

21 "Average Revenue Trends Down for News-Producing Stations" in PEW RESEARCH CTR.'S PROJ. FOR EXCELLENCE IN JOURNALISM, THE STATE OF THE NEWS MEDIA (2011) (PEW, STATE OF NEWS MEDIA 2011), http://stateofthemedia.org/2011/local-tv-essay/data-page-3/#local-tv-news-economics.

22 National Association of Broadcasters Comments in re *FOM PN* (*FCC Launches Examination of the Future of Media and Information Needs of Communities in a Digital Age, Comment Sought*, GN Docket No. 10–25, Public Notice, 25 FCC Rcd 384 (2010) (*FOM PN*), filed May 7, 2010 http://fjallfoss.fcc.gov/ecfs/document/view?id=7020450082

23 *See, e.g.,* NAT'L ASS'N OF BROADCASTERS, NAB TELEVISION FINANCIAL REPORT (2010), *available at* http://www.nabstore.com/nab-television-financial-report-2010.html.

24 "Local TV Economics" in PEW, STATE OF NEWS MEDIA 2011, http://stateofthemedia.org/2011/local-tv-essay/data-page-3.

25 Justin Nielson, T*V Station Revenue Growth Outlook Upbeat for 2010*, SNL KAGAN, Aug. 19, 2010.

26 "Local TV Economics" in PEW RESEARCH CTR.'S PROJ. ON EXCELLENCE IN JOURNALISM, THE STATE OF THE NEWS MEDIA (2010), (STATE OF NEWS MEDIA 2010), http://stateofthemedia.org/previous-reports/

27 "Local TV Economics" in PEW, STATE OF NEWS MEDIA 2010.

28 Lisa Phillips, *Trends in Consumers' Time Spent with Media*, EMARKETER, Dec. 28, 2010, http://www.emarketer.com/Article.aspx?R=1008138.

29 Steve McClellan, *Political Ad Spend to Soar*, ADWEEK, Aug. 23, 2010, http://www.adweek.com/aw/content_display/news/agency/e3i915ec0f-14ba05d6789c0e34796b8f7d4#.

30 "Political Advertising" in PEW, STATE OF NEWS MEDIA 2011 (*citing* estimates from Campaign Media Analysis Group/Television Bureau of Advertising), http://stateofthemedia.org/2011/local-tv-essay/#economics. According to Morgan Stanley total political ad spending across media platforms was estimated at $2.5–$3.5 billion in 2010, about 75 percent of which went to local TV stations. BENJAMIN SWINBURNE, DAVID GOBER, KRISTI BONNER, & MICAH NANCE, MORGAN STANLEY, FROM THE COUCH, WE SEE EARNINGS UPSIDE IN MEDIA 3, 21 (2010) (MORGAN STANLEY, FROM THE COUCH).

31 "Political Advertising" in PEW, STATE OF NEWS MEDIA 2011.

32 National Association of Broadcasters Comments in re *FOM PN* (*FCC Launches Examination of the Future of Media and Information Needs of Communities in a Digital Age, Comment Sought*, GN Docket No. 10–25, Public Notice, 25 FCC Rcd 384 (2010) (*FOM PN*), filed May 7, 2010. *See also* Michael Malone, *Local Broadcasters Bullish at SNL Kagan Conference: Broadcasters' retrans over $1 billion this year, but the networks want stations to share*, BROADCASTING & CABLE, June 16, 2010, http://www.broadcastingcable.com/article/453826-Local_Broadcasters_Bullish_at_SNL_Kagan_Conference.php.

33 "Retransmission Fees for Local Televisions Signals" in PEW, STATE OF NEWS MEDIA 2011 (*citing* data from Veronis Suhler Stevenson, 2010-2014 Communications Industry Forecast), http://stateofthemedia.org/2011/local-tv-essay/#economics.

34 KATIE PURCELL, ET. AL, PEW RESEARCH CTR., PEW INTERNET & THE AMERICAN LIFE PROJECT, PROJ. ON EXCELLENCE IN JOURNALISM, UNDERSTANDING THE PARTICIPATORY NEWS CONSUMER 3 (2010), *available at* http://www.pewinternet.org/Reports/2010/Online-News.aspx.

35 PEW RESEARCH CTR. FOR THE PEOPLE & THE PRESS, IDEOLOGICAL NEWS SOURCES: WHO WATCHES AND WHY, AMERICANS SPENDING MORE TIME FOLLOWING THE NEWS 25 (2010), *available at* http://people-press.org/report/652/. Interview with Michael Dimock, Assoc. Dir., Pew Research Ctr. for People & the Press, by Cynthia Kennard, FCC (Aug. 16, 2010). Mr. Dimmock says the viewers are looking for quality and substance. There is still a core of Americans who regularly schedule their news watching; it is part of a routine for them, and they still like getting news in the packaged traditional format, and that is where local news programs still fill an important niche.

36 "Nielsen Analysis" in PEW, STATE OF NEWS MEDIA 2010, http://stateofthemedia.org/previous-reports/

37 RTDNA/HOFSTRA UNIV. ANNUAL SURVEY 2010, TV AND RADIO NEWS STAFFING AND PROFITABILITY SURVEY (RTDNA) (2010), http://www.rtdna.org/pages/media_items/2010-tv-and-radio-news-staffing-and-profitability-survey1943.php?id=1943.

38 Radio Television Digital News Association Comments in re *FOM PN*, filed May 7, 2010 (RTDNA Comments), at 44.

39 Robert Feder, *ABC 7 to Join Early Birds with 4:30* A.M. *Newscast*, WBEZ 91.5 BLOG, July 26, 2010, http://blogs.vocalo.org/feder/2010/07/abc-7-to-join-early-birds-with-430-a-m-newscast/31271. In July 2010, the ABC-owned and operated station in Chicago, WLS, announced that it would add "early bird" morning news. The announcement came 10 days after WGN in Chicago had announced it would be starting its morning news block at 4:30 A.M. in mid-August. Chicago's WMAQ had been the first to move into the 4:30 A.M. time period, in 2007.

40 Interview with Brian Bracco, VP, News, Hearst Corporation, by Cynthia Kennard, FCC (July 2010) (Bracco Interview 7/10).

41 Interview with Deborah Collura, VP, News, Post-Newsweek Stations; former News Director, WDIV-TV, by Cynthia Kennard, FCC (July 22, 2010) (Collura Interview 7/22/10).

42 Interview with general manager at medium-market station in Kansas (asked not to be indentified), by Cynthia Kennard, FCC.

43 Interview with Steve Schwaid, Dir., News and Digital Content, WGCL-TV, by Cynthia Kennard, FCC, (June 30, 2010) (Schwaid Interview 6/30/10).

44 "Local TV: By the Numbers," in PEW, STATE OF NEWS MEDIA 2011, http://stateofthemedia.org/2011/local-tv-essay/data-page-3/.

45 RTDNA Comments at 46–47.

46 RTDNA Comments at 47–48.

47 RTDNA Comments at 46–47.

48 RTDNA Comments at 47.

49 Interview with Mike Devlin, Gen. Mgr., WFAA-TV, by Cater Lee, FCC (July 26, 2010) (Devlin Interview 7/26/10).

50 Interview with Matthew Zelkind, Station Mgr., WKRN-TV, by Steven Waldman, FCC (June 2010).

51 Barrington Broadcast Group, *et al*. Comments in re *FOM PN*, filed May 7, 2010, (Barrington Broadcast Group Comments), at 6–7.

52 Prepared Testimony of Jane E. Mago, FCC Workshop on the Future of Media and the Information Needs of Communities: Serving the Public Interest in the Digital Era (Mar. 4, 2010), at 5, *available at* http://reboot.fcc.gov/futureofmedia/serving-the-public-interest-in-the-digital-era.

53 Interview with Tom Planchet, Mgr., News and Operations, WWL-TV, by Cynthia Kennard, FCC (Feb. 14, 2011).

54 Columbia Univ. School of Journalism, Alfred I. duPont-Columbia University Awards for Excellence in Broadcast Journalism, Columbia University 2000–2010 (DuPont-Columbia University Awards 2000–2010), http://www.dupontawards.org/year/2001 (last visited Feb. 7, 2011). WWL-TV of New Orleans, LA, won in 2007.

55 Interview with Russell Banz, VP, Products, Desert Digital Media, by Cynthia Kennard, FCC (Mar. 18, 2011). *See also* Desert Digital Media, Why DDM?, http://deseretdigital.com/content/view/119/why-ddm (noting 3.8 million unique visitors in December 2009).

56 Bracco Interview 7/10.

57 Interview with Maria Barrs, news director of KDFW, June 3, 2011, by Steven Waldman

58 Interview with Susanna Schuler, VP, News, Raycom Media, by Cynthia Kennard, FCC (July 29, 2010) (Schuler Interview 7/29/10).

59 DataSphere, *Raycom and DataSphere to Launch Hundreds of Neighborhood Websites in 35 Cities* (press release), Mar. 3, 2010, http://datasphere.com/content/raycom-and-datasphere-launch-hundreds-neighborhood-websites-35-cities.

60 DataSphere, *Gannett Broadcasting and DataSphere to Launch Community Websites in 10 U.S. Cities* (press release), June 15, 2010, http://datasphere.com/content/gannett-broadcasting-and-datasphere-launch-community-web-sites-10-us-cities. These markets include: Atlanta, GA (WXIA/WATL); Washington, D.C. (WUSA); Tampa, FL (WTSP); Sacramento, CA (KXTV); Grand Rapids, MI (WZZM); Jacksonville, FL (WTLV/WJXX); Buffalo, NY (WGRZ); Little Rock, AR (KTHV); Portland, ME (WCSH); Macon, GA (WMAZ).

61 Broadcast Interactive Media, *Belo Corp Launches YouNews™ Social Media Platform on 16 Websites* (press release), Jan. 20, 2010, http://www.broadcast-interactive.com/news/82170542.html.

62 Deborah Potter, NewsLab, Katerina-Eva Matsa & Amy Mitchell, "Local TV: Good News After the Fall: Digital Revenue" in PEW, STATE OF NEWS MEDIA 2011, http://stateofthemedia.org/2011/local-tv-essay/.

63 Michael Malong, *Fox Embraces Underdog Status*, BROADCASTING & CABLE, Nov. 28, 2010, http://www.broadcastingcable.com/article/460334-Fox_Embraces_Underdog_Status.php.

64 Interview with Al Tompkins, Group Leader, Broadcast and Online, The Poynter Institute, by Cynthia Kennard, FCC, July 2010 (Tompkins Interview 7/10).

65 Engelhart, Becky, "Local Media Reach: November 2010," Jan. 6, 2011, http://www.ibsys.com/local-media-reach/november-2010/.

66 Radio Television Digital News Association, Comments in re *FOM PN,* filed May 7, 2010 (RTDNA Comments), at 31.

67 Interview with Richard Boehne, CEO of Scripps, by Steven Waldman, April 26, 2011.

68 Interview with Greg Dawson, News Dir., KNSD-TV, by Steven Waldman, FCC, Nov. 30, 2010.

69 Email from Scott Lewis, CEO, Voice of San Diego, to Steven Waldman, FCC (Oct. 11, 2010).

70 *Applications of Comcast Corp., General Electric Co. and NBC Universal,*

Inc., Memorandum Opinion and Order, FCC 11-4, 2011 FCC LEXIS 414 at *440–441, 52 Comm. Reg. (P & F) 249 (rel. Jan. 20, 2011) (Appendix A. Conditions, XI. Localism Conditions, 5.b.).

71 *See NBC Stations Seek Nonprofit News Partners in Nine Markets*, Communications Daily (May 24, 2011) at 10–11.

72 KING 5, *The Seattle Times and KING 5 Partner to Create Local Online Advertising Network* (press release), Oct. 25, 2010, http://www.king5.com/community/news-releases/The-Seattle-Times-and-KING-5-partner-to-create-local-online-advertising-network–105697913.html.

73 Open Mobile Video Coalition, *Mobile Digital TV Viewers Watching More Local News and Weather, Consumer Showcase Research Reveals* (press release), Sept. 14, 2010, *available at* http://www.openmobilevideo.com/_assets/docs/press-releases/2010/2010-09-14-omvc-press-release.pdf.

74 Columbia School of Journalism, Alfred I. duPont-Columbia University Awards for Excellence in Broadcast Journalism, 2011 Winners (2011 Winners of DuPont-Columbia University Awards for Excellence), http://www.journalism.columbia.edu/page/659/462 (last visited Feb. 7, 2011). DuPont Awards director, Abi Wright, says the jury was impressed by what they saw from local television news stations coverage in 2009—though at the same time, of the six prizes that were given, four went to TV stations that had won previously.

"They were repeat winners. WWL in New Orleans had won for Hurricane Katrina coverage in 2006, WTVF in Nashville had won for coverage of the Tennessee State House, and at KMGH in Denver, John Ferrugia had won before as well," Wright says. "But WCAX in Burlington, Vermont, had never won before. WCAX is a family-owned station, and I know the reporters at these stations thank the owner and managers of these stations for giving them the resources for the reporting to do what they needed to do."

Wright says the jury sees consistently strong work over the years from stations that have resources or make good, strong local journalism a priority. Already this year duPont has seen a big rise in entries—5 percent—and the bulk is from local entries. Interview with Abi Wright, Dir., Alfred I. duPont Awards for Excellence in Broadcast Journalism, Columbia Univ., by Cynthia Kennard, FCC (Aug. 17, 2010).

75 Barrington Broadcasting Group Comments at 6.

76 RTDNA Comments at 11.

77 RTDNA Comments at 9–10.

78 Interview with Marci Burdick, Sr. VP, Schurz Communications, by Cynthia Kennard, FCC (June 2010) (Burdick Interview 6/10).

79 Devlin Interview 7/26/10.

80 *See* WPLG—Miami, Ft. Lauderdale, Jeff Weinsler, http://www.justnews.com/station/269270/detail.html (describing investigative report and Florida law change) (last visited Mar. 5, 2011).

81 Al Tompkins, *What 2011 Holds for Investigative Reporting*, THE POYNTER INSTITUTE, Jan. 3, 2011, http://www.poynter.org/latest-news/als-morning-meeting/112043/what-2011-holds-for-investigative-reporting-imagine-a-julian-assange-in-every-state-and-major-city-in-the-us/#.

82 DuPont-Columbia University Awards 2000–2010Columbia School of Journalism, Alfred I. duPont-Columbia University Awards for Excellence in Broadcast Journalism, http://www.dupontawards.org/year/2001 (last visited Feb. 7, 2011). KBCI-TV of Boise, ID, won in 2004, KNOE-TV of Monroe, LA, won in 2008.

83 MARTIN KAPLAN & MATTHEW HALE, LOCAL TV NEWS IN THE LOS ANGELES MEDIA MARKET: ARE THE STATIONS SERVING THE PUBLIC INTEREST? 4–6 (USC Annenberg School of Communication & Journalism) (2010) (KAPLAN & HALE, LOCAL TV NEWS IN LOS ANGELES), *available at* http://www.learcenter.org/pdf/LANews2010.pdf.

84 THOMAS BALDWIN, DANIEL BERGIN, FRED FICO, STEPHEN LACY, & STEVEN WILDMAN, NEWS MEDIA COVERAGE OF CITY GOVERNMENTS IN 2009 4–5 (Michigan State Univ.) (2010) (BALDWIN, ET AL., COVERAGE OF CITY GOVERNMENTS IN 2009), *available at* http://quello.msu.edu/sites/default/files/pdf/PEJ_City_Govt_report-final.pdf.

85 *TV News Ignores Local Political Races*, POLITICS AND SOCIETY: A SPECIAL RESOURCE FOR JOURNALISTS (Univ. of Southern California), Feb. 17, 2005, http://politicsandsociety.usc.edu/2005/02/tv-news-ignores-local.html.

86 Dennis Chaptman, *Study: Political Ad Time Trumps Election Coverage on the Tube*, UNIV. OF WISCONSIN–MADISON NEWS, Nov. 21, 2006, http://www.news.wisc.edu/13213.

87 Walter Shapiro, *Nikki Haley and Rand Paul Races: Where Have All the Reporters Gone?*, POLITICSDAILY.COM, June 11, 2010, http://www.politicsdaily.com/2010/06/11/nikki-haley-and-rand-paul-races-where-have-all-the-reporters-go/.

88 Erica Fowler, Martin Kaplan, Kenneth Goldstein, & Matthew Hale, *Does Local News Measure Up?* 18 STAN. LAW. & POL. REV. 411, 419 (2007).

89 Prepared Testimony of Tom Rosenstiel, Dir., Pew Research Ctr. Proj. for Excellence in Journalism, FCC Workshop on the Future of Media and the Information Needs of Communities: Serving the Public Interest in the Digital Era (Mar. 4, 2010) (Rosenstiel Prepared Testimony 3/4/10), at 3, *available at* http://reboot.fcc.gov/futureofmedia/serving-the-public-interest-in-the-digital-era.

90 KRISTINE GLORIA & KARA HADGE, AN INFORMATION COMMUNITY CASE STUDY: WASHINGTON, D.C. 10–11 (New American Found.) (2010), *available at* http://mediapolicy.newamerica.net/sites/newamerica.net/files/policydocs/DC_Policy_Paper.pdf.

91 Interview with Wally Dean, Dir. Training, Committee of Concerned Journalists, by Cynthia Kennard, FCC (Aug. 2010) (Dean Interview).

92 Dean Interview.

93 Kathleen Hall Jamieson, Bruce W. Hardy, & David Romer, *The Effectiveness of the Press in Serving the Needs of American Democracy*, *in* THE ANNENBERG DEMOCRACY PROJECT, INSTITUTIONS OF AMERICAN DEMOCRACY: A REPUBLIC DIVIDED 21-51 (*Oxford University Press 2007*).

94 Interview with Matthew Zelkind, Station Mgr., WKRN-TV, by Steve Waldman, FCC (May 24, 2010) (Zelkind Interview 5/24/10).

95 For a decade, the number of contest entries from local TV news operations was consistently averaging around 100; in 2009, they got only 50 submissions. Ten-Year History: Contest Entries for IRE Awards in Local Television News: Year followed by number of entries: 1999: 119; 2001: 82; 2003: 100; 2005: 110; 2007: 100; 2009: 50. Data adapted from Mark Horvit, Exec. Dir., Investigative Reporters and Editors (July 23, 2010).

96 At the same time, broadcast membership in IRE dropped to its lowest level in a decade in 2010. Ten-Year History: Broadcast Membership in IRE: Year followed by membership number: 2000: 874; 2002: 750; 2004: 705; 2006: 733; 2008: 800; 2010: 648. Data adapted from Mark Horvit (July 23, 2010).

97 Interview with Fred Young, former VP, Hearst Broadcasting, by Cynthia Kennard, FCC (June 2010).

98 Lisa Anderson, *Can Local Television Afford Investigations?*, COLUMBIA JOURNALISM REV. (May/June, 2010), http://www.cjr.org/feature/can_local_television_afford_investigations.php.

99 Sheila Gibbons, *News Layoffs Aren't All Bad for Female Veterans*, WOMEN'S ENEWS, Mar. 30, 2009, http://www.womensenews.org/story/uncovering-gender/090330/news-layoffs-arent-all-bad-female-veterans/ (*News Layoffs*).

100 *News Layoffs*.

101 Interview with Roberta Baskin by Cater Lee, FCC (July 7, 2010).

102 Interview with Bill Lord, Station Mgr., WJLA, by Cater Lee, FCC (July 26, 2010) (Lord Interview 7/26/10). Lord, like other news managers, admits that not having a dedicated investigative unit hurts the quality of a station's news product. "I also think it serves a great public function, to have the world put on notice that if there is corruption, if there is any cutting of corners, if people are not being treated fairly, there's someone that's going to come ask them questions about it." *Id.*

103 Zelkind Interview 5/24/10.

104 Zelkind Interview 5/24/10.

105 Interview with Joe Bergantino, Dir., New England Ctr. for Investigative Reporting, by Cater Lee, FCC (July 2010) (Bergantino Interview 7/10).

106 Bergantino Interview 7/10.

107 Interview with Byron Harris, Investigative Reporter, WFAA-TV, by Cater Lee, FCC (June 2010).

108 Bergantino Interview 7/10.

109 Investigative News Network, About INN, http://investigativenewsnetwork.org/about/ (last visited Feb. 9, 2011).

110 Interview with Kevin Davis, CEO, Investigative News Network (INN) by Cater Lee, FCC (July 21, 2010).

111 KAPLAN & HALE, LOCAL TV NEWS IN LOS ANGELES at 4.

112 PEW PROJ. FOR EXCELLENCE IN JOURNALISM, HOW NEWS HAPPENS: A STUDY OF THE NEWS ECOSYSTEM OF ONE AMERICAN CITY 6–7 (2010), *available at* http://www.journalism.org/sites/journalism.org/files/Baltimore%20Study_Jan2010_0.pdf.

113 BALDWIN, ET AL., COVERAGE OF CITY GOVERNMENTS IN 2009 at 4–5.

114 Rosenstiel Prepared Testimony 3/4/10.

115 Interview with Steve Hertzke, former News Dir., KUTV-TV, by Cynthia Kennard, FCC (July 20, 2010).

116 Charles Gibson address to the Radio Television News Directors Association, April 24, 2006.

117 Tompkins Interview 7/10.

118 KAPLAN & HALE, LOCAL TV NEWS IN LOS ANGELES at 4.

119 RTDNA Comments at 38–40.

120 Interview with Robert Sullivan, VP, Content, Scripps Broadcasting, by Cater Lee, FCC (July 27, 2010) (Sullivan Interview 7/27/10).

121 Bracco Interview 7/10.

122 Sullivan Interview 7/27/10. While Phase One of the "Newsroom of the Future" initiative was driven by technology, Sullivan says, Phase Two is focused on the content, figuring out what works and what does not in order to create the best possible news product:

"As the processes get better, then we get back to working on the journalism, the storytelling.... The newsroom of the future, at least for Scripps stations, is a living, breathing, 24/7 entity…that has an insatiable appetite to understand the community they serve, and then use the skills we possess to help them stay informed by using the technologies that are available to us."

123 Interview with Susana Schuler, VP, Raycom Media, by Cynthia Kennard, FCC (July 29, 2010).

124 Interview with Andrew Vrees, News Dir., WCVB-TV, by Steven Waldman, FCC (Apr. 13, 2010).

125 Interview with Ben Winslow, Multimedia Journalist, KTSU-TV, by Cynthia Kennard, FCC (July 19, 2010) (Winslow Interview 7/19/10).

126 Interview with Con Psarris, VP, Editorials and Special Projects, KSL-TV, by Cynthia Kennard, FCC (July 20, 2010) (Psarris Interview 7/20/10).

127 Interview with Othello Richards, Reporter, KREM-TV, by Cater Lee, FCC (July 19, 2010).

128 Interview with Noah Cooper, News Dir., KREM-TV, by Cater Lee, FCC (July 19, 2010).

129 Deborah Potter, *How VJs Are Changing TV News*, NEWSLAB, July 22, 2010, http://www.newslab.org/2010/07/22/how-vjs-are-changing-tv-news/ (*How VJs Are Changing TV News*).

130 Interview with Mary Angela Bock, PhD Candidate, Annenberg School of Journalism, Univ. of Penn. & Faculty Member, Kutztown Univ., by Cynthia Kennard, FCC, June 2010.

131 *How VJs Are Changing TV News*.

132 Interview with Marco Villarreal, Reporter, KNTV ABC Las Vegas, Nevada, by Steven Waldman, FCC (Apr. 13, 2010).

133 Interview with Mike Daniels, Reporter, KESQ-TV, by Cater Lee, FCC (Sept. 6, 2010).

134 Winslow Interview 7/19/10.

135 Interview with Bill Lord, Station Mgr., WJLA-TV, by Cater Lee, FCC (July 25, 2010).

136 Interview with Jill Geisler, Sr. Faculty, Leadership and Management, The Poynter Institute, by Steve Waldman, FCC, (Apr. 18, 2010).

137 Interview with Stacey Woelfel, former Chair, RTDNA Ethics Committee, by Cynthia Kennard, FCC (Sept. 2010).

138 Curtis Brainard, *News Director Quits Over Hospital Deal*, COLUMBIA JOURNALISM REV., Jan. 25, 2008, http://www.cjr.org/the_observatory/news_director_quits_over_hospi.php.

139 Interview with Glen Mabie, former News Dir., WEAU-TV, by Cynthia Kennard, FCC (Jan. 2011).

140 Trudy Lieberman, *Epidemic: Phony Medical News Is on the Rise, Thanks to Dozens of Unhealthy Deals Between TV Newsrooms and Hospitals*, 45 COLUMBIA JOURNALISM REV. 38, 38 (2007).

141 Interview with Trudy Lieberman, Prof., Baruch College City Univ. of NY, by Cynthia Kennard, FCC (Aug. 6, 2010).

142 Interview with Pam Vaught, News Dir., KTBC-TV, by Cynthia Kennard, FCC (Jan. 2011).

143 Steph Gregor, *And Now a Word from Our Sponsor*, THE OTHER PAPER (Columbus, Ohio), Nov. 29, 2007. Ohio State University Medical Center is no longer doing the "Medical Breakthrough" segment, according to Lori Abshire, senior director of marketing for the OSU Medical Center. However, Abshire says that the medical center still makes agreements with stations to purchase time on the station in Columbus, but now OSU

supplies the story, talent, and production team. The segments are called "Medical Minutes," and Abshire says that if the medical center buys time within the newscast then they run during the newscast. Interview with Lori Abshire, Sr. Dir., Marketing, Ohio State Medical Center, by Cynthia C. Kennard, FCC, by telephone, Mar. 18, 2011.

144 Interview with Ike Walker, News Dir., WCMH-TV, by Cynthia Kennard, FCC (Jan. 2011).

145 Ass'n of Health Care Journalists & Society of Professional Journalists, *Journalism Groups Warn Newsrooms Against Unhealthy Alliances with Hospitals* (press release), Aug. 11, 2008, *available at* http://www.health-journalism.org/about-news-detail.php?id=59.

146 Interview with Forest Carr, former Ethics Fellow, The Poynter Institute, by Cynthia Kennard, FCC (Aug. 5, 2010).

147 Interview with Steve Hertzke, former News Dir., KUTV-TV, by Cynthia Kennard, FCC (June 20, 2010) (Hertzke Interview 6/20/10).

148 Howard Kurtz, *TV Station Cashes in on Interview 'Guests,'* WASH. POST, Oct. 16, 2003, at C1.

149 Email from Tom Rosenstiel, Dir., Pew Proj. on Excellence in Journalism, to Steven Waldman, FCC (Jan. 31, 2011).

150 Interview with Tom Rosenstiel by Steven Waldman, FCC, (Jan. 11, 2011).

151 James Rainey, *"The news is, that pitch was paid for: When spokespersons for hire promote products on local TV news shows,"* L.A. TIMES, September 15, 2010, http://articles.latimes.com/2010/sep/15/entertainment/la-et-onthemedia-20100915.

152 Psarris Interview 7/20/10.

153 Burdick Interview 6/10.

154 *See* Center for Media and Democracy Comments in re *Sponsorship Identification NOI & NPRM* (*Sponsorship Identification Rules and Embedded Advertising*, MB Docket No. 08-90, Notice of Inquiry and Notice of Proposed Rulemaking, 23 FCC Rcd 10682 (2008) (*Sponsorship Identification NOI & NPRM*)), filed Sept. 22, 2008, at 2 (*citing* BOB PAPPER, THE FUTURE OF NEWS: A STUDY BY THE RADIO TELEVISION NEWS DIRECTORS FOUNDATION 32–33 (2006) (Section 7: The business side)).

155 *See* Comments of Fairness and Integrity in Telecommunications Media in re *Sponsorship Identification NOI & NPRM*, filed Sept. 23, 2009, at 10–15.

156 *See, e.g.,* The National Association of Broadcasters Reply Comments in re *Sponsorship Identification NOI & NPRM*, filed Nov. 21, 2008, at 18–19; Reply Comments of The Walt Disney Company in re *Sponsorship Identification NOI & NPRM*, filed Nov. 21, 2008, at 14–20.

157 Stephanie Clifford, *A Product's Place is on the Set*, N.Y. TIMES, July 22, 2008, http://www.nytimes.com/2008/07/22/business/media/22adco.html (*A Product's Place*).

158 *A Product's Place*.

159 Michael Malone, *Your Ad Here… and Here*, BROADCASTING & CABLE, May 31, 2010 (*Your Ad Here*), http://www.broadcastingcable.com/article/453179-Your_Ad_Here_And_Here.php. KVVU went even further on its 9:00 A.M. live show, *More*, integrating a flat-screen TV sponsored by burger-chain Sonic and announced the sponsored Dasani Green Room. *More* does not feature breaking news. As product integration on *More* became increasingly common, the station "moved the show out of the newsroom and into its own division," in order to maintain a church-state wall. KVVU continues to develop innovative ways in which advertisers can reach desired markets, and now boasts that advertisers

can do so "by integrating KVVU.com web creative, video and content sponsorship with a targeted television schedule on KVVU." *Your Ad Here*. The station calls this a "convergence campaign" that "will both capture the attention of the marketplace and provide the details and interactivity to create new customers." FOX 5 News Las Vegas, Advertise With KVVU, http://www.fox5vegas.com/advertise/index.html (last visited Apr. 18, 2011).

160 *Your Ad Here*.

161 Robert Pear, *U.S. Videos, for TV News, Come Under Scrutiny*, N.Y. TIMES, Mar. 15, 2004, http://www.nytimes.com/2004/03/15/us/us-videos-for-tv-news-come-under-scrutiny.html. Following this initial article, the media continued to report on the Bush administration's aggressive use of video news releases. At least twenty federal agencies, including the State Department, Transportation Security Administration, the Agriculture Department, the Census Bureau, and the Defense Department, all created and disseminated videos resembling newscasts. Some of these videos included department officials who were posing as reporters and failed to mention that the individuals were in fact employees of government agencies. Of the videos, "many were subsequently broadcast on local stations across the country without any acknowledgement of the government's role in their production." David Barstow & Robin Stein, *Under Bush, a New Age of Prepackaged TV News,* N.Y. TIMES, Mar. 13 2005, http://www.nytimes.com/2005/03/13/politics/13covert.html. Over the following year, the media focused on examining the lengths to which the administration would go for good press. Eventually, it was reported that the Department of Education paid nearly a quarter of a million dollars to commentator Armstrong Williams for supporting the No Child Left Behind Act in his weekly newspaper column and televised news show. Greg Toppo, *Education Dept. paid commentator to promote law*, USA TODAY, Jan. 7, 2005, http://www.usatoday.com/news/washington/2005-01-06-williams-whitehouse_x.htm. The FCC's Enforcement Bureau cited the Graham Williams Group for violating the sponsorship identification rules. *The Graham Williams Group*, Citation, 22 FCC Rcd 18092 (Enf. Bur. 2007).

162 D.S. Haus, *Videobiz just gets bigger*, PR WEEK, Jan. 11, 1999, at 19.

163 DIANE FARSETTA & DANIEL PRICE, FAKE TV NEWS: WIDESPREAD AND UNDISCLOSED (Ctr. for Media and Democracy) (2006), http://www.prwatch.org/fakenews/execsummary. As a result, the FCC distributed official Letters of Inquiry to the documented seventy-seven television stations. The Radio-Television News Directors Association, now the Radio Television Digital News Association (RTDNA)—concerned that stations' First Amendment rights were being infringed upon and that the FCC was moving toward content regulation—filed official comments with the Commission, noting that the FCC instructed stations to "collect and turn over to the agency tapes and transcripts of newscasts, news outtakes, and VNRs; to answer detailed questions concerning the identification, selection, production, editing, and broadcasting of specific news stories; and to submit statements that are descriptive of news department practices and policies." Letter from Kathleen A. Kirby & Lawrence W. Secrest III, Wiley Rein & Fielding LLP, Counsel for the Radio-Television News Directors Ass'n, to Marlene H. Dortch, Secretary, FCC, MB Docket No. 05-171 (filed Oct. 5, 2006), at 1. In their comments, RTDNA pointed out flaws in CMD's report, noted that the FCC's actions departed from established precedent, warned of a potential "chilling effect," and described the adverse effect the FCC's actions might have on news agencies' ability to grant anonymity to sources. RTDNA amended their professional practices and ethics guideline to include stricter clauses about the need for television stations to disclose the creator of any VNR they air. *Id.* at 2, Appendix A (Memorandum from Wiley Rein & Fielding LLP, to RTDNA re: Critique of Center for Media and Democracy's "Fake TV News: Widespread and Undisclosed" Report (Sept. 29, 2006).

164 Harry Martin, *FCC Issues VNR Fines,* BROADCAST ENGINEERING, Dec. 1, 2007, http://broadcastengineering.com/news/broadcasting_fcc_issues_vnr/#.

165 "Fox News Fake News," by Joseph Loveland, April 5, 2011 http://thesamerowdycrowd.wordpress.com/2011/04/05/fox-newsfake-news/

166 *See* Radio-Television News Directors Association Comments in re, *Video News Release PN*, filed June 22, 2005, at 2–3.

167 Interview with Stacey Woelfel, News Dir., KOMU-TV (and former Chair, RTDNA Ethics Committee), by Cynthia Kennard, FCC (Aug. 5, 2010).

168 *Fox Television Stations, Inc., Licensee of Station KMSP-TV, Minneapolis, MN,* Notice of Apparent Liability for Forfeiture, File No. EB-06-IH-3709 (EB rel. Mar. 24, 2011); *Access 1 New Jersey License Company, LLC, Licensee of Station WMGM-TV, Wildwood, NJ,* Notice of Apparent Liability for Forfeiture, File No. EB-06-IH-3725 (EB rel. Mar. 24, 2011). http://www.fcc.gov/eb/Orders/2011/DA-11-521A1.html Transcripts of the two VNRs:

WMGM:

[Reporter] A national survey by Harris Interactive, shows only nine percent of travelers over the age of thirty say they feel very knowledgeable about how to treat the common cold. This is especially important as we begin the cold and flu season and one of the biggest travel times of the year.

[Voiceover] Nearly two-thirds of U.S. travelers [thirty] and over say they are somewhat or not at all knowledgeable about treating the common cold, according to the new Zicam Travel Well Survey conducted by Harris Interactive. Yet [two] out of [five] travelers surveyed say colds have negatively impacted their trips.

Allison Janse wrote Germ Freak's Guide to Outwitting Colds & Flu, she says being a mother of premature twins made her start researching how to avoid germs.

[Caption: Allison Janse, Author] You can do everything I say in my book. You can eat right, exercise, walk around in a bubble suit. But, eventually, you're gonna get sick. And in m[y] research, I found that homeopathic zinc products can shorten the duration of your illness.

[Voiceover] Travelers are at [an] increased risk of getting sick because of things like greater exposure to viruses, stress and other variables. The survey showed [four] in [five] of the U.S. travelers surveyed believe the worst time to catch the common cold is while traveling. Dr. Mark Siegel of New York University says that obtaining relief is possible, but that it's important to begin treatment as soon as symptoms occur.

[Caption: Dr. Marc Siegel, New York University] There is no cure for the common cold. But there are some things you can do to get better. Especially in the first 48 hours. You can take an intranasal zinc preparation, like Zicam. To cut down on the severity and duration of symptoms. You can also take a decongestant. Get more rest. Drink some chicken soup. And sleep.

[Voiceover] Nearly [ninety] percent of the U[.]S[.] travelers survey [sic] say reducing the duration of the common cold would be important or very important for treating the common cold, but only [thirty-three] percent of those travelers who typically use over-the-counter medications to treat the common cold, have used a zinc cold remedy.

[Allison Janse] I think the survey showed me that people really need help figuring out how to treat a common cold when they're on the go. For instance, most people don't know that zinc products are available to help them. I mean, yes, we'd like to avoid all germs and never get sick, but that's not gonna happen. If you do get sick, there are things you can do to fight back.

[Reporter] To see this report again or to find out more about zinc as a treatment for the common cold, go to our website

And KMSP:

Voiceover: Thinking of getting a convertible now that summer is here? Well think fast. The buzz around this year's convertibles, many brand-new and affordable, means there may not be many left.

[Caption: Bob Lutz, General Motors] "The Solstice is sold out. The Sky is sold out. The Pontiac G6 convertible is sold out."

Bob Lutz, who has worked at all three domestic manufacturers, is now the head of product development at General Motors. He was hired 5 years ago to revive GM's much criticized product line – and the hope is that the success he's had bringing these new convertibles to market will continue across the entire company.

[Caption: Jean Jennings, Automobile Magazine] "Does General Motors have the ability to make cars that people want? Yes they do. It's absolutely clear. This is the key to their survival and on top of that, I have seen, as many journalists have, cars that are scheduled for the next couple of years and I'll tell you that if those cars were on the road right now today, I don't think they'd be in this jam at all."

But Lutz knows [that] making higher quality automobiles is only part of the equation–changing a generation[']s worth of less-than-favorable opinions is the real battle.

"What we're seeing is the old beliefs about General Motors, which we probably earned over twenty, twenty-five years. The old beliefs of all our cars look the same, our quality isn't very good, the vehicles use a lot of gas, none of that stuff is true anymore but these perceptions linger."

However[,] the good looking convertibles coming from GM may be changing that perception, as well as the company's fortunes. America's largest manufacturing company actually turned a profit in the first quarter of '06.

169 *Fox Television Stations, Inc., Licensee of Station KMSP-TV, Minneapolis, MN,* Notice of Apparent Liability for Forfeiture, File No. EB-06-IH-3709 (EB rel. Mar. 24, 2011); *Access 1 New Jersey License Company, LLC, Licensee of Station WMGM-TV, Wildwood, NJ,* Notice of Apparent Liability for Forfeiture, File No. EB-06-IH-3725 (EB rel. Mar. 24, 2011). http://www.fcc.gov/eb/Orders/2011/DA-11-521A1.html

170 Interview with Fred Young, former VP, Hearst Broadcasting, by Cynthia Kennard, FCC (May 2010).

171 Interview with Kevin Benz, News Mgr., News 8 Austin, by Rebecca Shapiro, FCC (July 6, 2010) (Benz Interview 7/6/10).

172 Collura Interview 7/22/10.

173 Schwaid Interview 6/30/10.

174 Bracco Interview 7/10.

175 Interview with Renai Bodley, News Director, KSTU-TV, by Cynthia Kennard, FCC (July 19, 2010)

176 Synaptic Digital, Our Solutions, http://www.synapticdigital.com/what-we-do/solutions (last visited Feb. 10, 2011).

177 Interview with Brian Schwartz, Dir., Client Solutions, Synaptic Digital, by Cynthia Kennard, FCC (Sept. 3, 2010).

178 Email from Douglas Simon, Pres., D S Simon Productions, to Rebecca Shapiro, FCC (July 16, 2010).

179 Interview with Dave McAnally, Partner, Fusion Communications, by Cynthia Kennard, FCC (July 2010).

180 Multiple interviews with Robert Papper, Prof., Hofstra Univ., by Cynthia Kennard, FCC (May-Aug. 2010).

181 Communications Workers of America, *et al.* Comments in re *FOM PN*, filed May 7, 2010 (Communications Workers of Amer. Comments), at ii.

182 Communications Workers of Amer. Comments at 4.

183 *In the Matter of Media Council Hawai'i*, "Response to "Complaint and Request for Emergency Relief Regarding Shared Services Agreement," October 16, 2009.

184 Independent Network News (INN), What We Do, http://www.inn-news.net/whatwedo.html (last visited Apr. 18, 2011).

185 Dave McAnally, Owner, Fusion Communications, interview by Cynthia Kennard, FCC (July 15, 2010) (McAnally Interview 7/15/10).

186 McAnally Interview 7/15/10.

187 McAnally Interview 7/15/10. *See also* INN, Our History, http://www.inn-news.net/history.html (last visited Apr. 18, 2011).

188 WLTZ-38 News, News Team, http://www.wltz.com/Global/category.asp?C=205082 (last visited Apr. 18, 2011). Stefanie Tiso, WLTZ's news director, says the INN agreement has actually enabled the station do local news in an affordable way. Tiso says that they don't mention INN on the station website because WLTZ ABC 38 is a local news product and INN is just helping them with their newscast. Interview with Stefanie Tiso, by Cynthia Kennard, FCC (Mar. 18, 2011).

189 RTDNA Comments at 20.

190 David Lieberman, *NBC, Fox TV Stations to Share Camera Crews for Local News*, USA TODAY, Nov. 13, 2008 (*NBC, Fox TV Stations to Share Camera Crews*), http://www.usatoday.com/money/media/2008-11-13-fox-nbc-local-tv-news_N.htm.

191 Communications Workers of Amer. Comments at 11.

192 *NBC, Fox TV Stations to Share Camera Crews*.

193 Barrington Broadcast Group Comments at 13-14.

194 Eyewitness account of Cynthia Kennard, FCC.

195 Burdick Interview 6/10.

196 Lord Interview 7/26/10.

197 Lord Interview 7/26/10.

198 Interview with Rebecca Campbell by Steve Waldman, FCC (Apr. 13, 2010).

199 Lord Interview 7/26/10.

200 Collura Interview.

201 Communications Workers of Amer. Comments at iii, 2.

202 Communications Workers of Amer. Comments at iii.

203 Seventeen news directors noted another TV station that they're running on a second (or third) digital channel. A dozen noted news programming—just not all news. Seven noted weather radar. Four said informational programming, and four noted sports. Three said traffic; two said programming in another language; and one noted movies.

204 RTDNA Comments at 20-21.

205 Email from Larry Wert, President NBC Local Media, to Cinny Kennard (Apr. 26, 2011); John Eggerton, *NBCU Launching Three New Local News Nets*, Broadcasting & Cable, May 2, 2011, http://www.broadcastingcable.com/article/467514-NBCU_Launching_Three_New_Local_News_Nets.php

206 John Eggerton, *NBCU Launching Three New Local News Nets*, Broadcasting & Cable, May 2, 2011, http://www.broadcastingcable.com/article/467514-NBCU_Launching_Three_New_Local_News_Nets.php

207 Belo Corporation Comments in re *FOM PN*, filed May 7, 2010, at 6.

208 Interview with Robert Prather, COO and Dir., Gray Television, by Cynthia Kennard, FCC (July 2010).

209 Interview with Ann Arnold, Texas Ass'n of Broadcasters, by Cynthia Kennard, FCC (June 2010).

210 Interview with Susanna Schuler, VP, News, Raycom Media, by Cynthia Kennard, FCC (July 29, 2010) (Schuler Interview 7/29/10).

211 Schuler Interview 7/29/10.

212 FCC staff analysis of data from Tribune Media Services for Nov. 1–Nov. 14, 2009 and May 6–May 12, 2010.

213 Data come from Tribune Media Services during the time periods Nov. 1–Nov. 14, 2009 and May 6–May 12, 2010. Data averages include total scheduled news minutes on full-power broadcast television stations over the sample period. Includes all news minutes; no deductions are made for weather, sports, advertising, etc. Programs included in this count are those indicated as "News" or "Newsmagazine" (or their Spanish equivalents) in the "Genre" field, and those indicated by TMS as "Local" in the "Origination" field (possible values in this field are "Local", "Network", or "Syndicated").

214 Specifically, the Industry Analysis Division of the Media Bureau looked at week-long television station programming schedules from 12:00 a.m. Monday to 11:59 p.m. Sunday to determine if the station aired any news. The sources used to determine station programming were Zap2It.com, TV Guide, local station websites, and Wikipedia.org.

   If the station broadcast 30 minutes or more of news per week, that station was deemed to broadcast news. Notation was made if the station fell into any of the following categories: airing Local and National News, Local News Only, National News Only, or No News. Regional and Campus News programs were included in the local news category. Broadcasts of state legislature, public affairs, and public interest programs were not considered news.

   Once these determinations were made, percentages were calculated for the total markets. The total number of broadcast stations was 1,632. Of those, 1,239 stations were commercial stations, and 393 were noncommercial educational stations. There were 696 stations that broadcast no local news, and 248 stations did not broadcast news. Of the 393 noncommercial educational stations, 322 did not broadcast local news.

   Calculations were also made for the Top 100 DMAs in those categories. The Top 100 DMAs contained 1,100 stations. Of those, 842 were commercial stations and 258 were noncommercial educational stations. There were 496 stations in the top 100 markets that broadcast no local news, and 207 stations that broadcast no news. Of the 258 noncommercial educational stations, 199 did not broadcast local news.

215 This is a survey of news directors at 1,800 TV stations. Email from Bob Papper to Cynthia Kennard, FCC (Sept. 30, 2010). *See also* RTDNA, *RTDNA/Hofstra Survey Finds TV Doing More with Less, Optimism on*

Staffing (press release), Apr. 14, 2010, http://www.rtdna.org/pages/posts/rtdnahofstra-survey-finds-tv-doing-more-with-less-optimism-on-staffing920.php.

216 JESSICA DURKIN & TOM GLAISYER, AN INFORMATION COMMUNITY CASE STUDY: SCRANTON, 6 (New American Found.) (2010), http://mediapolicy.newamerica.net/sites/newamerica.net/files/policydocs/Scranton%20Case%20Study.pdf

217 Adam Jones, Sr. VP, NBC News, *The Cosmic Change in the News Business* (presentation at The Columbia Institute for Tele-Information at Columbia Business School), May 21, 2010, *available at* http://www4.gsb.columbia.edu/citi/events/transmedia.

218 Frazier Moore, *Legendary CBS Anchor Walter Cronkite Dies at 92*, ASSOCIATED PRESS, July 17, 2009, http://minnesota.publicradio.org/display/web/2009/07/17/walter_cronkite_death/.

219 MARC GUNTHER, THE TRANSFORMATION OF NETWORK NEWS: HOW PROFITABILITY HAS MOVED NETWORKS OUT OF HARD NEWS (Nieman Found. for Journalism at Harvard) (1999) (GUNTHER, THE TRANSFORMATION OF NETWORK NEWS), http://www.nieman.harvard.edu/reports/article/102153/The-Transformation-of-Network-News.aspx.

220 GUNTHER, THE TRANSFORMATION OF NETWORK NEWS.

221 Emily Guskin, Tom Rosenstiel & Paul Moore, "Network News: Durability & Decline: Evening News Audiences" in PEW, STATE OF NEWS MEDIA 2011, http://stateofthemedia.org/2011/network-essay/#audience; "Network TV: Audience" in PEW, STATE OF NEWS MEDIA 2010, http://stateofthemedia.org/previous-reports/..

222 "Network TV: Audience" in PEW, STATE OF NEWS MEDIA 2010.

223 Interview with Andrew Tyndall, The Tyndall Report, by Tamara Smith, FCC (July 23, 2010).

224 "As Ratings Fall Over Time, NBC Fairs [sic] Best" in PEW, STATE OF NEWS MEDIA 2011, http://stateofthemedia.org/2011/network-essay/data-page-5/#evening-news-demographics".

225 "Network TV: Audience" in PEW, STATE OF NEWS MEDIA 2010. http://stateofthemedia.org/previous-reports/..

226 "Network News Audience" in PEW, STATE OF NEWS MEDIA 2010.

227 "Network News: Durability & Decline: Evening News Audiences" in PEW, STATE OF NEWS MEDIA 2011.

228 "Network News: Durability & Decline: Evening News Audiences" in PEW, STATE OF NEWS MEDIA 2011.

229 The Walt Disney Co., Notice of *Ex-Parte* Presentation to FCC, GN Docket No. 10-25 (filed Oct. 18, 2010), at 7, *available at* http://fjallfoss.fcc.gov/ecfs/comment/view?id=6016059149.

230 "Overview" in PEW, STATE OF NEWS MEDIA 2010, http://stateofthemedia.org/previous-reports/..

231 Matea Gold, *ABC News President David Westin Promises that Cuts Will Not Impede 'First-Rate Journalism,'* L.A. TIMES: COMPANY TOWN BLOG, Feb. 23, 2010, http://latimesblogs.latimes.com/entertainmentnews-buzz/2010/02/abc-news-president-david-westin-promises-that-cuts-will-not-impede-firstrate-journalism.html.

232 "Network News: Durability & Decline: PBS: Audience" in PEW, STATE OF NEWS MEDIA 2011.

233 2011 Winners of DuPont-Columbia University Awards for Excellence.

234 "TV Summary Essay" in PEW, STATE OF NEWS MEDIA 2010, http://stateofthemedia.org/previous-reports/..

235 L.J. DAVIS, THE BILLIONAIRE SHELL GAME: HOW CABLE BARON JOHN MALONE AND ASSORTED CORPORATE TITANS INVENTED A FUTURE NOBODY WANTED 10–12 (Doubleday) (1998) (DAVIS, THE BILLIONAIRE SHELL GAME).

236 STEPHEN KEATING, CUTTHROAT: HIGH STAKES AND KILLER MOVES ON THE ELECTRONIC FRONTIER 39 (Big Earth) (1999) (KEATING, CUTTHROAT).

237 DAVIS, THE BILLIONAIRE SHELL GAME at 12–13.

238 By the late 1980s, Cooke cashed in, selling his entire stake to John Malone for $380 million. DAVIS, THE BILLIONAIRE SHELL GAME at 17, 116.

239 DAVIS, THE BILLIONAIRE SHELL GAME at 18.

240 KEATING, CUTTHROAT at 43.

241 *Rules and Regulations Relating to the Distribution of Television Broadcast Signals by the Community Antenna Television Systems*, Second Report and Order, 2 FCC 2d 725, 747–756 (1966).

242 KEATING, CUTTHROAT at 46.

243 KEATING, CUTTHROAT at 47.

244 THOMAS STREETER, SELLING THE AIR, 177 n.21 (Univ. of Chicago) (1996) n.21; ROBERT CRANDALL & HAROLD FURCHTGOTT-ROTH, CABLE TELEVISION: REGULATION OR COMPETITION 6 (Brookings Press) (1996).

245 DAVIS, THE BILLIONAIRE SHELL GAME at 26; KEATING, CUTTHROAT at 48.

246 *Annual Assessment of the Status of Competition in the Market for the Delivery of Video Programming,* Second Report & Order, 11 FCC Rcd 2060, 2069 nn.30–31 (1995) (*citing* Nat'l Cable Television Ass'n, *Viewing Shares: Broadcast Years 1983/1984–1993/1994*, CABLE TELEVISION DEVELOPMENTS (Spring 1995), at 5; Sixth Annual Report, 15 FCC Rcd 978, 991 nn.47–48 (2000) (*citing* NIELSEN MEDIA RESEARCH, NIELSEN TELEVISION INDEX: USAGE/VIEWING SOURCE SHARE TRENDS (1999)); Ninth Annual Report, 17 FCC Rcd 26901, 26913-14, nn.41–42 (2002) (*citing* NIELSEN MEDIA RESEARCH, TOTAL DAY 24 HOURS 6 A.M.–6 A.M: TOTAL US RATINGS BY VIEWING SOURCE JULY 2000–JUNE 2002 (2002)); *Annual Assessment of the Status of Competition in the Market for the Delivery of Video Programming,* Eleventh Annual Report, 20 FCC Rcd. 2755, 2772, nn.75–78 (2005) (*Eleventh Annual Report*) (*citing* NIELSEN MEDIA RESEARCH, BROADCAST CALENDAR (TV SEASON) SHARE OF AUDIENCE REPORT, PRIME TIME AND TOTAL DAY (2004)). According to NCTA, the 2003/2004 TV season (September 2003 to May 2004) was the first time that the combined nonbroadcast networks' share of prime-time viewing was greater than the combined national broadcast networks' share of prime-time viewing. *Eleventh Annual Report*, 20 FCC Rcd. at 2772 n. 80 (citing National Cable Television Association Comments in re *Delivery of Video Programming NOI* (*Annual Assessment of the Status of Competition in the Market for the Delivery of Video Programming*, Notice of Inquiry, 19 FCC Rcd 10909 (2004), filed July 23, 2004, at 46).

247 BEN BAGDIKIAN, THE NEW MEDIA MONOPOLY 45 (Beacon Press) (2004); Jane Hall, *News Channel Aims to Out-Fox Opponents*, L.A. TIMES–WASH. POST SERVICE, Oct. 5, 1996.

248 Microsoft and NBC created MSNBC, using Microsoft's technological expertise and NBC's existing news operations to provide news over multiple platforms. *Annual Assessment of the Status of Competition in the Market for the Delivery of Video Programming*, First Annual Report, 9 FCC Rcd 7442, 7591–2, App. G, Table 4 (1994).

249 KEATING, CUTTHROAT at 18.

250 SNL Kagan, SNL Interactive: Briefing Book Search Page, http://www.snl.com/interactivex/bbsearch.aspx?activeTabIndex=8 (visited Jan. 27, 2011).

251 Jesse Holcomb, Amy Mitchell & Tom Rosenstiel, "Cable: By the Numbers: Audience" in PEW, STATE OF NEWS MEDIA 2011, http://stateofthemedia.org/2011/cable-essay/.

252 "Cable TV Economics" in PEW, STATE OF NEWS MEDIA 2010, http://stateofthemedia.org/previous-reports/..

253 "Cable: By the Numbers: Audience" in PEW, STATE OF NEWS MEDIA 2011.

254 "Cable: By the Numbers: Economics" in PEW, STATE OF NEWS MEDIA 2011.

255 "Cable TV: Economics" in PEW, STATE OF NEWS MEDIA 2010, http://stateofthemedia.org/previous-reports/., and "Cable Profits Up Across the Board," in PEW PROJ. FOR EXCELLENCE IN JOURNALISM, STATE OF THE NEWS MEDIA (2011) (PEW, STATE OF THE NEWS MEDIA) (citing SNL Kagan, a division of SNL Financial LLC), http://stateofthemedia.org/2011/cable-essay/data-page-2/.

256 "Cable: By the Numbers: News Investment" in PEW, STATE OF NEWS MEDIA 2011.

257 "Cable: By the Numbers: News Investment" in PEW, STATE OF NEWS MEDIA 2011.

258 Joe Nocera, *Bland Menu if Cable Goes à la Carte*, N.Y. TIMES, Nov. 24, 2007, http://www.nytimes.com/2007/11/24/business/media/24nocera.html?_r=1&ex=1353560400&en=a362ab94b8687400&ei=5090&partner=rssuserland&emc=rss.

259 News 12 Long Island, About News 12, http://www.news12.com/news/aboutus_LI?news_type=About%20Us (last visited Jan. 27, 2011).

260 George Winslow, *Moving Beyond Local News, Channels Expand Base of Homes, Platforms*, MULTICHANNEL NEWS, June 12, 2006 (*Moving Beyond Local News*), http://www.multichannel.com/article/123850-Moving_Beyond_Local_News.php.

261 Adam Lynn, Mark Cooper, & S. Derek Turner, NATIONAL OWNERS DOMINATE LOCAL CABLE NEWS: LOCAL CABLE NEWS CHANNELS DO NOT SIGNIFICANTLY CONTRIBUTE TO SOURCE OR VIEWPOINT DIVERSITY 1, 5 (Free Press) (2006)

http://www.freepress.net/files/study_4_cable_local_news.pdf ("these stations serve about one-fifth of the total population…"). The number could be slightly higher. Our own FCC analysis, based on research in September 2010 by FOM team members Simon Banyai and Ava Seave (Banyai and Seave Research), we previously found there to be approximately 39 local or regional cable news channels that produced their own news. These channels serve subscribers on cable systems in approximately 71 out of the total 210 Designated Market Areas in the country, and many of these DMAs contain large metropolitan regions—New York, Boston, Chicago, or San Francisco—with multiple channels. Using 2010 data, out of the total of 54,335,000 TV households located in 71 DMAs, we found that 52.4 percent or 28,471,540 were cable subscribers. Therefore, we estimated that these 39 cable news channels were available to at least 24.6 percent of the 115.8 million total TV households in the country in 2010. Our cable news channel count incorporates only those channels that continue to utilize journalists to originate local or regional news. While Americans may receive news from a somewhat greater number of cable channels that merely rebroadcast or simulcast network news program ming, we have omitted such channels from our tally. The "20 to 30 percent" figure also includes local cable news channels referenced in footnote 264 below.

262 Banyai and Seave Research.

263 Tribune Co., Business Unites and Websites, http://corporate.tribune.com/pressroom/?page_id=2311 (last visited Apr. 18, 2011).

264 Press Release, "NBC Owned-and-Operated Stations to Expand New Locally_Produced News, Information and Public Affairs Programming, May 12, 2011, *available at* http://www.nbcuni.com/corporate/newsroom/nbc-owned-and-operated-stations-to-expand-new-locally-produced-news-information-and-public-affairs-programming. The new local cable news channels will expand the availability of local and regional news to an additional 5,419,208 cable subscribers, or an almost 4.7 additional percent of television households. FCC staff calculation.

265 Banyai and Seave Research.

266 RADIO & TELEVISION NEWS DIRECTORS FOUND., CABLE NEWS: A LOOK AT REGIONAL NEWS CHANNELS AND STATE PUBLIC AFFAIRS NETWORKS 2 (2004) (RTNDF, CABLE NEWS), *available at* http://www.rtdna.org/media/pdfs/bestpractices/cablenews/2004/cable.pdf. In addition to NY1, Time Warner operates NY1 Noticias, YNN ("Your News Now") Capital Region, YNN Central Region, YNN Southern Region, YNN Western Region, YNN Northern Region, and YNN Hudson Valley. *See* Banyai and Seave research.

267 RTNDF, CABLE NEWS AT 2.

268 Kevin Brass, *Can Austin's Little News Station That Could Survive the Grim Reapers at Time Warner?*, THE AUSTIN CHRONICLE, Sept. 3, 2004, http://www.austinchronicle.com/news/2004-09-03/227255/.

269 Benz Interview 7/6/10.

270 New England Cable News, About NECN, http://www.necn.com/pages/about (last visited Jan. 28, 2011); RTNDF, CABLE NEWS at 3.

271 RTNDF, CABLE NEWS at 4.

272 RTNDF, CABLE NEWS at 4–5. Similarly, Chicago-based CLTV had live reports and speeches from five campaign headquarters and, as has been the practice since the news channel was launched, Chicago Tribune writers and editors offered their analysis and insight during interviews from the television stage in the main newsroom of the newspaper. "Many races, especially those that aren't for statewide or congressional offices, are undercovered," says Steve Farber, CLTV's director of news and programming. "We make a difference by highlighting candidates and issues that broadcast stations don't cover." RTNDF, CABLE NEWS at 4–5.

273 RTNDF, CABLE NEWS at 8.

274 *Moving Beyond Local News*.

275 News 12 Long Island, Home Login, http://www.news12.com//Login/home_login (last visited Jan. 31, 2011).

276 Bay News 9, Tampa News, Weather, Traffic, Entertainment, Politics, http://www.baynews9.com (last visited Jan. 31, 2011).

277 Telephone interview of Alan Mason , VP and GM, News 14, Carolina, with Steve Waldman and Sherille Ismail (August 12, 2010); interview of Kevin Benz (news manager, News 8 Austin), Rebecca Shapiro, July 6, 2010.

278 SNL KAGAN, BROADBAND CABLE FINANCIAL DATABOOK: 2009 EDITION 4 (2009) ("KAGAN 2009 FACTBOOK").

279 CRAIG MOFFETT, NICHOLAS DEL DEO, REGINA POSSAVINO, & ANDREW WEISGALL, BERNSTEIN RESEARCH, THE LONG VIEW: BEYOND VIDEO… TAKING THE MEASURE OF THE BROADBAND-CENTRIC CABLE MSO 1 (2010); SNL Kagan, Custom Charts.

280 BENJAMIN SWINBURNE, DAVID GOBER, & RYAN FIFTAL, MORGAN STANLEY, CABLE/SATELLITE, BUILT FOR ROUGH WATERS, CONSTRUCTIVE ON GROUP FOR 2H10 1 (2010) (MORGAN STANLEY, CABLE/SATELLITE).

281 MORGAN STANLEY, CABLE/SATELLITE at 5. For comparison purposes, cable has over 60 million subscribers.

282 MORGAN STANLEY, CABLE/SATELLITE at 6.

283 KAGAN 2009 FACTBOOK at 8 (2009).

284 STERLING & KITTROSS, STAY TUNED at 717.

285 *Implementation of Section 3 of the Cable Television Consumer Protection and Competition Act of 1992, Statistical Report on Average Rates for Basic Service, Cable Programming Service, and Equipment*, Report on Cable Industry Prices, MM Docket No. 92-266, February 14, 2011, at 16.

286 KEATING, CUTTHROAT at 107–109.

287 *Development of Regulatory Policy in Regard to Direct Broadcast Satellites*, Report & Order, 90 FCC 2d 676, 680 (1982) (*Direct Broadcast Satellites Report*).

288 *Direct Broadcast Satellites Report*, 90 FCC 2d at 678–79; 698–706.

289 STERLING & KITTROSS, STAY TUNED at 573.

290 KEATING, CUTTHROAT at 115.

291 EDWARD COMOR, COMMUNICATION, COMMERCE, AND POWER 63 (McMillan Press) (1998) (COMOR, COMMUNICATION, COMMERCE, AND POWER).

292 COMOR, COMMUNICATION, COMMERCE, AND POWER at 168. Congress created a compulsory license, which permits satellite carriers to deliver network programming to unserved viewers without the copyright owner's permission. STUART BENJAMIN, DOUGLAS LICHTMAN, & HOWARD SHELANSKI, TELECOMMUNICATIONS LAW AND POLICY 549 (Carolina Academic Press) (2001).

293 DANIEL L. BRENNER, MONROE PRICE, & MICHAEL MEYERSON, CABLE TELEVISION AND OTHER NONBROADCAST VIDEO: LAW AND POLICY at 15–9 (Clark Boardman Callaghan) (2004).

294 KEATING, CUTTHROAT at 137.

295 However, a satellite company is not required to carry more than one local broadcast TV station within the DMA that is affiliated with a particular TV network in the same state FCC, Service Options for Satellite Television Subscribers, Fact Sheet, *available at* http://www.fcc.gov/cgb/consumerfacts/shvera.pdf (last visited Mar. 6, 2011).

296 DirecTV, Annual Report (Form 10-K) for Fiscal Year Ended 12/31/10, at 2 (Jan. 2011) (DirecTV 2010 Annual Report), *available at* http://www.sec.gov/Archives/edgar/data/1465112/000104746911001443/a2202196z10-k.htm.

297 DISH Network Corp., Quarterly Report for the Quarterly Period Ended 9/30/2010 (Form 10-Q) (Nov. 2010) at 4, *available at* http://www.sec.gov/Archives/edgar/data/1001082/000110465910056240/a10-19251_110q.htm.

298 DISH Network, English Packages, http://www.dishnetwork.com/packages/detail.aspx?pack=AEP (last visited Apr. 18, 2011).

299 DirecTV 2010 Annual Report at 34.

300 DISH Network Corp., Annual Report (Form 10-K) for the Fiscal Year Ended 12/31/10 (Feb. 2011), at 52, *available at* http://www.sec.gov/Archives/edgar/data/1001082/000110465911009436/a11-3040_110k.htm#Item6_SelectedFinancialData_141543.

301 The survey was conducted December 2009 through January 2010. News Leaders and the Future: News Executives, Skeptical of Government Subsidies, *See* Opportunity in Technology but are Unsure About Revenue and the Future, Project for Excellence in Journalism, American Society of News Editors (ASNE), Radio Television Digital News Association (RTDNA), 2010, http://www.journalism.org/analysis_report/news_leaders_and_future.

4 Internet

1 W3C, *Tim Berners-Lee Bio*, http://www.w3.org/People/Berners-Lee/ (last visited Mar. 1, 2011); Tim Berners-Lee, *Weaving the Web*, http://www.w3.org/People/Berners-Lee/Weaving/Overview.html (last visited May 20, 2011).

2 Tim Berners-Lee, *Long Live the Web: A Call for Continued Open Standards and Neutrality,* SCIENTIFIC AMERICAN, Dec. 2010, http://www.scientificamerican.com/article.cfm?id=long-live-the-web.

3 ANDREW METRICK & AYAKO YASUDA, VENTURE CAPITAL AND THE FINANCE OF INNOVATION 12 (John Wiley & Sons) (2006) (VENTURE CAPITAL AND THE FINANCE OF INNOVATION).

4 John Markoff, *With a Debut, a Test of On-Line Publishing,* N.Y. TIMES, Nov. 13, 1995, at D7 (providing that Salon Magazine was set to launch its first online issue in January 19 at www.salon1999.com); Laura M. Holson, *Healtheon Is Expected to Join Forces With Internet Provider,* N.Y. TIMES, May 15, 1999, at C14 (explaining that WebMd began in October 1998 and later merged with the Healtheon Corporation in 1999); Timothy Hanrahan, *CBS News, DBC Online Launch Financial News Web Site,* DOW JONES NEWS SERVICE, Oct. 30, 1997 (announcing the launch of CBS MarketWatch); Beliefnet, About Beliefnet, http://www.beliefnet.com/About-Us/About-Beliefnet.aspx (noting that Beliefnet was founded in 1999); Slate, *About Us,* http://www.slate.com/id/2147070/ (last visited Feb. 8, 2011); VENTURE CAPITAL AND THE FINANCE OF INNOVATION at 13.

5 *See, e.g.,* Andres Rueda, *The Hot IPO Phenomenon and the Great Internet Bust*, 7 FORDHAM J. CORP. & FIN. L. 21 (2001).

6 Ken Doctor, *The Newsonomics of Time-on-Site,* NIEMAN JOURNALISM LAB, Mar. 4, 2010, http://www.niemanlab.org/2010/03/the-newsonomics-of-time-on-site/.

7 Google News, http://news.google.c.com/intl/en_us/about_google_news.html (last visited June 3, 2011); *See also, e.g.,* CrunchBase, *Google News Profile*, http://www.crunchbase.com/product/google-news (last visited May 20, 2011); "Nielsen Analysis" in PEW RESEARCH CTR.'S PROJ. FOR EXCELLENCE IN JOURNALISM, THE STATE OF THE NEWS MEDIA (2010), http://stateofthemedia.org/previous-reports/.

8 PEW RESEARCH CTR. FOR THE PEOPLE & THE PRESS, AMERICANS SPENDING MORE TIME FOLLOWING THE NEWS (2010), *available at* http://people-press.org/2010/09/12/americans-spending-more-time-following-the-news/.

9 "Main News Source, By Age" in PEW RESEARCH CTR.'S PROJ. FOR EXCELLENCE IN JOURNALISM, THE STATE OF THE NEWS MEDIA (2011) (PEW, STATE OF THE NEWS MEDIA 2011), http://stateofthemedia.org/2011/online-essay-data-page-7/.

10 WordPress.com, *Stats*, http://en.wordpress.com/stats/ (last visited May 24, 2011).

11 CHRIS ANDERSON, THE LONG TAIL: WHY THE FUTURE OF BUSINESS IS SELLING LESS OF MORE (Hyperion) (2006).

12 *Newspaper Economics: Online and Offline*, Presentation by Hal Varian, Chief Economist, Google, and Professor, Univ. of California, Berkeley, Federal Trade Commission Workshop, "How Will Journalism Survive The Internet Age?" (Mar. 9, 2010) (Varian, *Newspaper Economics: Online and Offline*), at 3 (Mar. 9, 2010) (Varian, *Newspaper Economics: Online and Offline*), *available at* http://www.ftc.gov/opp/workshops/news/mar9/docs/varian.pdf (showing that, while core costs (promotion, editorial, administrative) and the costs of production, distribution and raw materials accounted for 87 percent of revenue, Internet distribution could cut production costs by at least half).

13 Chris Anderson & Michael Wolff, *The Web is Dead: Long Live the Internet*, WIRED MAGAZINE, Aug. 17, 2010, http://www.wired.com/magazine/2010/08/ff_webrip/.

14 Andrew Sullivan, *Campaign '04: A Blogger's Creed*, TIME, Sept. 27, 2004, http://www.time.com/time/magazine/article/0,9171,995196,00.html/.

15 *ACLU v. Reno*, 929 F. Supp. 825 (E.D. Pa. 1996), *aff'd*, 521 U.S. 844 (1997):

"It is no exaggeration to conclude that the Internet has achieved, and continues to achieve, the most participatory marketplace of mass speech that this country—and indeed the world—has yet seen. The plaintiffs in these actions correctly describe the "democratizing" effects of Internet communication: individual citizens of limited means can speak to a worldwide audience on issues of concern to them. Federalists and Anti-Federalists may debate the structure of their government nightly, but these debates occur in newsgroups or chat rooms rather than in pamphlets. Modern-day Luthers still post their theses, but to electronic bulletin boards rather than the door of the Wittenberg Schlosskirche. More mundane (but from a constitutional perspective, equally important) dialogue occurs between aspiring artists, or French cooks, or dog lovers, or fly fishermen…. [T]he Internet may fairly be regarded as a never-ending worldwide conversation. The Government may not, through the CDA, interrupt that conversation. As the most participatory form of mass speech yet developed, the Internet deserves the highest protection from governmental intrusion."

16 Reader comments counted on May 30, 2010. The Huffington Post, http://www.huffingtonpost.com/.

17 PEW RESEARCH CTR.'S PROJ. FOR EXCELLENCE IN JOURNALISM, HOW NEWS HAPPENS: A STUDY OF THE NEW ECOSYSTEM OF ONE AMERICAN CITY 3 (2010) (PEW, HOW NEWS HAPPENS), *available at* http://www.journalism.org/analysis_report/how_news_happens.

18 WASHINGTON POST MEDIA, 2010 CIRCULATION AND HOUSEHOLD COVERAGE (2010), *available at* http://www.washingtonpostads.com/adsite/_res/files/managed/2010%20Circ%20and%20HHLD%20Cov.pdf; Washington Post Digital Ad Center, *Audience Profiles*, http://advertising.washingtonpost.com/index.php/audience/page/audience_profiles#3, (last visited Sept. 30, 2010).

19 USA Ultimate, http://www.usaultimate.org/news/default.aspx (last visited May 20, 2011).

20 Geocaching: The Official Global GPS Cache Hunt, http://www.geocaching.com/press/default.aspx (last visited May 20, 2011).

21 Groundspeak, http://www.groundspeak.com/ (last visited May 20, 2011).

22 Howard Kurtz, *After Blogs Got Hits, CBS Got a Black Eye*, WASH. POST, Sept. 20, 2004, http://www.washingtonpost.com/ac2/wp-dyn/A34153-2004Sep19?language=printer.

23 AARON SMITH, PEW INTERNET & AMERICAN LIFE PROJ., MOBILE ACCESS 2010 at 2 (2010) (MOBILE ACCESS 2010), http://pewinternet.org/Reports/2010/Mobile-Access-2010.aspx.

24 SeeClickFix, *Citizens Get Started*, http://www.seeclickfix.com/citizens (last visited May 20, 2011).

25 Jay Rosen, *A Most Useful Definition of Citizen Journalism*, PRESSTHINK, July 14, 2008, http://archive.pressthink.org/2008/07/14/a_most_useful_d.html.

26 Clay Shirky, *How Cognitive Surplus Will Change the World* (oral presentation), TED: IDEAS WORTH THINKING, June 2010 (*Cognitive Surplus*), http://www.ted.com/talks/view/id/896.

27 *See Cognitive Surplus*.

28 Jason Jones, *End Times* (video excerpt), THE DAILY SHOW, June 10, 2009, http://www.thedailyshow.com/watch/wed-june-10-2009/end-times.

29 ARLnow.com—Arlington, Va.—Breaking News, Opinions & Community Happenings, http://www.arlnow.com/ (last visited May 18, 2011).

30 Universal Hub, Boston Crime, http://www.universalhub.com/crime/home.html (last visited Apr. 13, 2011).

31 EveryBlock, http://www.everyblock.com/; Topix, http://www.topix.com/; Outside.in, http://www.outside.in/; Placeblogger, http://placeblogger.com (each last visited May 20, 2011).

32 Joseph Tartakoff, *AOL's Patch Aims to Quintuple in Size by Year-End*, GUARDIAN, Aug. 17, 2010, http://www.guardian.co.uk/media/pda/2010/aug/17/aol-patch-local-journalism.

33 Irish Philadelphia, www.irishphiladelphia.com/ (last visited Apr. 13, 2011).

34 BikePortland, http://bikeportland.org/ (last visited Jan. 28, 2011).

35 HAROLD VOGEL, ENTERTAINMENT INDUSTRY ECONOMICS: A GUIDE FOR FINANCIAL ANALYSIS 343 (Cambridge University Press) (2007).

36 LEE RAINIE & KRISTEN PURCELL, PEW INTERNET AND AMERICAN LIFE PROJ., HOW THE PUBLIC PERCEIVES COMMUNITY INFORMATION SYSTEMS (2011), *available at* http://www.pewinternet.org/Reports/2011/08-Community-Information-Systems.aspx.

37 Testimony of Bill Allison, Sunlight Found., Federal Trade Commission Workshop, "From Town Criers to Bloggers: How Will Journalism Survive the Internet Age?" (Dec. 2, 2009), Tr. at 176: 17-177:5 (Allison Testimony 12/2/09), *available at* http://www.ftc.gov/opp/workshops/news/.

38 Allison Testimony 12/2/09, Tr. at 177:5–8.

39 Information and Reporting Services, Data Reporting, http://www.p12.nysed.gov/irs/data_reporting.html (last visited Jan. 20, 2011).

40 GreatSchools—Public and Private School Ratings, Reviews, and Parent Community, http://www.greatschools.org/ (last visited Jan. 20, 2011).

41 PEW, HOW NEWS HAPPENS.

42 PEW, HOW NEWS HAPPENS at 4.

43 PEW, HOW NEWS HAPPENS at 2.

44 PEW, HOW NEWS HAPPENS at 2.

45 THOMAS BALDWIN, DANIEL BERGIN, FRED FICO, STEPHEN LACY, & STEVEN WILDMAN, NEWS MEDIA COVERAGE OF CITY GOVERNMENTS IN 2009 4-5 (Michigan State Univ.) (2010) (BALDWIN, ET AL., COVERAGE OF CITY GOVERNMENTS IN 2009) (detailing a study of 389 news outlets in central cities, which provided 6,042 local stories, and 77 "suburban cities," which provided 769 local stories), *available at* http://quello.msu.edu/sites/default/files/pdf/PEJ_City_Govt_report-final.pdf.

46 BALDWIN, ET AL., COVERAGE OF CITY GOVERNMENTS IN 2009 at 12.

47 BALDWIN, ET AL., COVERAGE OF CITY GOVERNMENTS IN 2009 at 12.

48 BALDWIN, ET AL., COVERAGE OF CITY GOVERNMENTS IN 2009 at 12.

49 Nate Silver, *A Note to Our Readers on the Times Pay Model and the Economics of Reporting*, FIVETHIRTYEIGHT (N.Y. Times), Mar. 24, 2011, http://fivethirtyeight.blogs.nytimes.com/2011/03/24/a-note-to-our-readers-on-the-times-pay-model-and-the-economics-of-reporting/.

50 Jan Schaffer, *Exploring a Networked Journalism: Collaborative in Philadelphia: An Analysis of the City's Media Ecosystem with Final Recommendations*, J-LAB: THE INSTITUTE FOR INTERACTIVE JOURNALISM, Apr. 2010 (*Exploring a Networked Journalism*), http://www.j-lab.org/publications/philadelphia_media_project#kfb.

51 *Exploring a Networked Journalism*.

In its analysis, the Institute for Interactive Journalism found "both the number of stories and the space and airtime devoted to public affairs reporting has suffered in both daily newspapers and on commercial television newscasts over the last three years." It concluded that there were fewer column inches and stories in *The Philadelphia Inquirer* and fewer stories—albeit more column inches—in the *Daily News*. Further, "[p]ublic affairs news coverage on Philadelphia's four commercial television stations also decreased, but there was not a significant amount of coverage for either period measured." *Id.*

For daily news, J-Lab found that the number of stories declined 7.2 percent between August 2006 to August 2009, and yet "the amount of news space given to public affairs journalism increased by 5 percent… This means there were six additional columns of public affairs news in the Daily News for August 2009, equivalent to one additional full page plus one additional column for the month." *Id.*

Finally, for commercial television newscast, J-Lab found the number of stories and minutes devoted to public affairs stories declined on local Philadelphia evening newscasts from 2006 to 2009, adding "[i]t's hard to describe this decline as precipitous because there wasn't a great deal of public affairs reporting to begin with." *Id.* In conducting its research, J-Lab commissioned time logs and story-subject logs for the nightly newscasts of WCAU, WPVI, WTXF and KYW for May 1–7, 2006 and May 1–7, 2009. "From May 1 to 7, 2006, the four stations aired a total of 46 minutes, 30 seconds of public affairs stories about the broadcast market region during their nightly newscasts. For the same period in 2009 all four stations aired only 38 minutes, 58 seconds, a 16 percent drop. A larger discrepancy occurs for coverage aimed more specifically at Philadelphia and South Jersey. Of the 46.5 minutes devoted to public affairs coverage in May 2006, 32 minutes, or almost 69 percent, focused on local issues. For the same period in 2009, coverage of local issues dropped to 17 minutes, 22 seconds or only 44.5 percent, of the 38 minutes, 58 seconds aired." *Id.*

52 Jonathan Stray, *The Google/China Hacking Case: How Many News Outlets Do the Original Reporting on a Big Story*?, NIEMAN JOURNALISM LAB, Feb. 24, 2010 (*The Google/China hacking case*), http://www.niemanlab.org/2010/02/the-googlechina-hacking-case-how-many-news-outlets-do-the-original-reporting-on-a-big-story/.

53 *The Google/China Hacking Case*.

54 JAN SHAFFER, J-LAB: THE INSTITUTE FOR INTERACTIVE JOURNALISM, NEW VOICES: WHAT WORKS: LESSONS FROM FUNDING FIVE YEARS OF COMMUNITY NEWS STARTUPS (2010), *available at* http://www.j-lab.org/about/press_releases/newvoices_whatworks/.

55 Steven Waldman, *Why the Huffington Post Can't Replace the New York Times*, THE HUFFINGTON POST, Jan. 12, 2009, http://www.huffingtonpost.com/steven-waldman/the-case-against-huffingt_b_157075.html.

56 MinnPost, www.minnpost.com (last visited May 20, 2011).

57 VoiceofSanDiego.org, www.voiceofsandiego.org (last visited May 20, 2011).

58 Michele McLellan, *Niche News Sites*, DONALD W. REYNOLDS JOURNALISM INSTITUTE (updated June 7, 2010), http://umrji.prod.acquia-sites.com/news/micheles-list-promising-local-news-sites.

59 MICHELE MCLELLAN, DONALD W. REYNOLDS JOURNALISM INSTITUTE, BLOCK BY BLOCK: BUILDING A NEW ECOSYSTEM (2010), at Pt. 3 Revenue Streams, http://www.rjionline.org/fellows-program/mclellan/block-by-block/part-3.php.

60 Knight Citizen News Network, *Meet the New Media Makers—and the Foundations that Make Their News Sites Possible*, http://www.kcnn.org/toolkit/funding_database (last visited Mar. 1, 2011).

61 Rick Edmonds, *Shrinking Newspapers Have Created $1.6 Billion News Deficit*, Poynter, Oct. 10, 2009, http://www.poynter.org/latest-news/business-news/the-biz-blog/98784/shrinking-newspapers-have-created-1-6-billion-news-deficit/.

62 PEW RESEARCH CTR.'S PROJ. FOR EXCELLENCE IN JOURNALISM & PEW INTERNET & AMERICAN LIFE PROJECT, THE ECONOMICS OF ONLINE NEWS 4 (2010), *available at* http://www.pewinternet.org/~/media//Files/Reports/2010/The-economics-of-online-news.pdf.

63 MICHAEL R. FANCHER, OF THE PRESS: MODELS FOR TRANSFORMING AMERICAN JOURNALISM, A REPORT OF THE 2009 ASPEN INSTITUTE FORUM ON COMMUNICATIONS AND SOCIETY 16 (2009) (quoting Esther Dyson's statement about investments in new start-ups), *available at* http://www.knightcomm.org/wp-content/uploads/2010/04/Of-the-Press-Models-for-Transforming-American-Journalism.pdf.

64 Interview with Esther Dyson by Steven Waldman, FCC (Sept. 3, 2010).

65 Brett Pulley, *AOL's Huffington to Add News Staff in Local Site Revamp*, BLOOMBERG BUSINESSWEEK, Apr. 12, 2011, http://www.businessweek.com/news/2011-04-12/aol-s-huffington-to-add-news-staff-in-local-site-revamp.html.

66 Interview with Rick Blair, Pres., Examiner.com, by Steven Waldman, FCC (Dec. 17, 2010) (Blair Interview 12/17/10).

67 Blair Interview 12/17/10.

68 AOL Advertising, http://advertising.aol.com/environmentmatters/engagement (last visited May 20, 2011).

69 Patch.org, *About Us*, http://www.patch.com/about (last visited May 20, 2011).

70 Michele McLellan, *Debunking the Replacement Myth*, DONALD W. REYNOLDS JOURNALISM INSTITUTE, July 26, 2010, http://www.rjionline.org/projects/mclellan/stories/debunk/index.php.

71 KNIGHT COMMISSION ON THE INFORMATION NEEDS OF COMMUNITIES IN A DEMOCRACY, INFORMING COMMUNITIES, SUSTAINING DEMOCRACY IN THE DIGITAL AGE 15 (2010) (SUSTAINING DEMOCRACY IN THE DIGITAL AGE), *available at* http://www.knightcomm.org/wp-content/uploads/2010/02/Informing_Communities_Sustaining_Democracy_in_the_Digital_Age.pdf.

72 SUSTAINING DEMOCRACY IN THE DIGITAL AGE at 15.

73 SUSTAINING DEMOCRACY IN THE DIGITAL AGE at XI-XV.

74 *See* Sarah Ovaska, Joseph Neff, & David Raynor, *Probationers Kill,*

State Dawdles, NEWS & OBSERVER, Dec. 7, 2008, http://www.news-observer.com/2008/12/07/56083/probationers-kill-state-dawdles.html#storylink=misearch; Joseph Neff, Sarah Ovaska, & Anne Blythe, *Probation Bungles Raise Alarm*, NEWS & OBSERVER, Dec. 12, 2008, http://www.newsobserver.com/2008/12/12/58379/probation-bungles-raise-alarm.html#storylink=misearch; Joseph Neff, Sarah Ovaska, & Anne Blythe, *Probation Vacancies a Boon, a Burden*, NEWS & OBSERVER, Dec. 14, 2008, http://www.newsobserver.com/2008/12/14/36485/probation-vacancies-a-boon-a-burden.html#storylink=misearch.

75 *See* Joseph Neff & Anne Blythe, *Perdue Urges $28 Million Probation Fix*, NEWS & OBSERVER, Mar. 14, 2009, http://www.newsobserver.com/2009/03/14/58191/perdue-urges-28-million-probation.html#storylink=misearch; Sarah Ovaska, *Perdue Signs Probation Reform Bill*, NEWS & OBSERVER, July 30, 2009, http://www.newsobserver.com/2009/07/30/68970/perdue-signs-probation-reform.html#storylink=misearch.

76 *See* James T. Hamilton, *Subsidizing the Watchdog: What Would it Cost to Support Investigative Journalism at a Large Metropolitan Daily Newspaper?* (lecture) (May 4–5, 2009), *available at* http://dewitt.sanford.duke.edu/images/uploads/About_3_Research_A_7_Hamilton.pdf.

77 Brian Stetler, *Finding Political News Online, the Young Pass on It*, N.Y. TIMES, Mar. 27, 2008, http://www.nytimes.com/2008/03/27/us/politics/27voters.html?_r=1.

78 Richard Siklos, *Information Wants to be Free…and Expensive*, FORTUNE TECH, July 20, 2009, http://tech.fortune.cnn.com/2009/07/20/information-wants-to-be-free-and-expensive/.

79 Benjamin Compaine & Brendan Cunningham, *Scholars Help Answer John Wanamaker's Query. Which Half of My Advertising Is Wasted?*, 23 ECON. 1 (2010), http://www.informaworld.com/smpp/section?content=a920015172&fulltext=713240928 (membership required for access).

80 *See* Google, *Google Advertising Programs*, http://www.google.com/intl/en/ads/ (last visited Apr. 2, 2011).

81 Newspaper Association of America, Advertising Expenditures (NAA, Advertising Expenditures), http://www.naa.org/TrendsandNumbers/Advertising-Expenditures.aspx (last visited May 20, 2011). Between 2009 and 2010, newspaper print advertising revenue dropped again to less than $22.8 billion. *Id.*

82 Newspaper Association of America, Newspaper Websites (NAA, Newspaper Websites per Nielsen), http://www.naa.org/TrendsandNumbers/Newspaper-Websites-Nielsen.aspx/ (last visited Jan. 20, 2011). Specifically, in May 2009: 69,950,403 different people ("unique visitors") accessed newspaper websites and 2,995,584,721 pages were viewed by these visitors. In May 2005: 43,704,725 different people accessed newspaper websites and 1,635,119,778 pages were viewed by these visitors." *Id.*

83 NAA, Advertising Expenditures.

84 NAA, Advertising Expenditures.

85 NAA, Newspaper Websites per Nielsen.

86 Catherine P. Taylor, *Newspapers Online Traffic Is Strong, So Why Are Ad Rates Weak?*, BNET, June 29, 2010 (*Newspapers Online Traffic Is Strong*), http://www.bnet.com/blog/new-media/newspapers-online-traffic-is-strong-so-why-are-ad-rates-weak/5551.

87 comScore, *The New York Times Ranks as Top Online Newspaper According to May 2010 U.S. comScore Media Metrix Data* (press release),

June 16, 2010, http://www.comscore.com/Press_Events/Press_Releases/2010/6/The_New_York_Times_Ranks_as_Top_Online_Newspaper_According_to_May_2010_U.S._comScore_Media_Metrix_Data.

88 THE WASHINGTON POST MEDIA, *Daily Circulation and CPM – Lowest Retail Rate CPMs Among Major Dailies,* http://www.washingtonpostads.com/adsite/why/media/versus/cpm/page1449.html (last visited Jan. 20, 2011) (stating that the average CPM across the 14 newspapers compared by the *Washington Post* range from $11.55 to $27.79, with an average of $19.72).

89 Varian, *Newspaper Economics: Online and Offline* at 20.

90 *Newspapers Online Traffic Is Strong*.

91 JUPITER RESEARCH, MARKETING & BRANDING FORECAST: ONLINE ADVERTISING AND E-MAIL MARKETING THROUGH 2008 4 (2003) (JUPITER RESEARCH, MARKETING & BRANDING FORECAST), *available at* www.pe.com/mediakit/audience/industry_research/images/jupiter_2.pdf.

92 JUPITER RESEARCH, MARKETING & BRANDING FORECAST.

93 "Online: Key Questions Facing Digital News" in PEW, STATE OF THE NEWS MEDIA 2011, http://stateofthemedia.org/2011/online-essay/#digital-ad-spending.

94 Interactive Advertising Bureau, *Interactive Advertising Bureau (IAB) Reports Full-Year Internet Ad Revenues for 2010 Increase 15% to 26 Billion, a New Record* (press release), Apr. 23, 2001, http://www.iab.net/about_the_iab/recent_press_releases/press_release_archive/press_release/pr-041311.

95 *We Knew the Web Was Bi*g…, OFFICIAL GOOGLE BLOG, July 25, 2008 (*We Knew the Web Was Big*), http://googleblog.blogspot.com/2008/07/we-knew-web-was-big.html (last visited Dec. 21, 2010).

96 *We Knew the Web Was Big*.

97 Interactive Advertising Bureau, *Interactive Advertising Bureau (IAB) Reports $8.2 Billion Online Ad Revenue in the United States for Year 2000* (press release) (*IAB Reports $8.2 Billion Online Ad Revenue*), Apr. 23, 2001, http://www.iab.net/about_the_iab/recent_press_releases/press_release_archive/press_release/4422.

98 DAVID HALLERMAN, EMARKETER, US AD SPENDING: ONLINE OUTSHINES OTHER MEDIA (2010) (US AD SPENDING: ONLINE OUTSHINES OTHER MEDIA); Interactive Advertising Bureau, *Internet Ad Revenues Break Records, Climb to More than $12 Billion for First Half of '10* (*Internet Ad Revenues Break Records*) (press release), Oct. 12, 2010, http://www.iab.net/about_the_iab/recent_press_releases/press_release_archive/press_release/pr-101210.

99 *Internet Ad Revenues Break Records*.

100 KATHLEEN ANNE RUANE, CONGRESSIONAL RESEARCH SERVICE, PRIVACY LAW AND ONLINE ADVERTISING: LEGAL ANALYSIS OF DATA GATHERING BY ONLINE ADVERTISERS SUCH AS DOUBLE CLICK AND NEBUAD (2009), *available at* http://assets.opencrs.com/rpts/RL34693_20090116.pdf; FTC STAFF REPORT, SELF-REGULATORY PRINCIPLES FOR ONLINE BEHAVIORAL ADVERTISING, FEB. 2009, *available at* http://www.ftc.gov/os/2009/02/P085400behavadreport.pdf.

101 Google, *Google Privacy: Interest-based Advertising* (video presentation), Mar. 2, 2009, http://www.youtube.com/watch?v=aUkm_gKgdQc&feature=player_embedded.

102 *IAB Reporrts $8.2 Billion Online Ad Revenue*.

103 "Online: By the Numbers" in PEW STATE OF THE NEWS MEDIA, 2011, http://stateofthemedia.org/2011/online-essay/data-page-7/ (citing Kantar Media Display Ad Revenue 2010).

104 Varian, *Newspaper Economics: Online and Offline* at 19.

105 Robin Wauters, *Report: 44% of Google News Visitors Scan Headlines, Don't Click Through*, TECHCRUNCH, Jan. 19, 2010, http://techcrunch.com/2010/01/19/outsell-google-news/.

106 Jay Garmon, *Top 10 Google Chrome Extensions for Better, Faster Browsing*, NOTEBOOK REVIEW, Mar. 23, 2010, http://www.notebookreview.com/default.asp?newsID=5575&review=Top+10+Google+Chrome+Extensions+for+Better+Faster+Browsing.

107 "Nielsen Analysis" in PEW, STATE OF THE NEWS MEDIA 2010.

108 Michael Hastings, *The Runaway General*, ROLLING STONE, June 22, 2010, http://www.rollingstone.com/politics/news/the-runaway-general-20100622.

109 David Carr, *Heedlessly Hijacking Content*, N.Y. Times, June 27, 2010, at B1, *available at* http://www.nytimes.com/2010/06/28/business/media/28carr.html.

110 *See* Demand Media, www.demandmedia.com; Associated Content, www.associatedcontent.com.

111 *Demand Media Sets IPO Offering Size, Boosts Traffic*, SOCALTECH.COM, Oct. 19, 2010, http://www.socaltech.com/demand_media_sets_ipo_offering_size__boosts_traffic/s-0031991.html.

112 Lucian Parfeni, *Yahoo Buys 'Content Farm' Associated Content*, SOFTPEDIA, May 19, 2010, http://news.softpedia.com/news/Yahoo-Buys-Content-Farm-Associated-Content-142379.shtml.

113 Alex Pham, *Demand Media to Provide Travel Articles and Videos for USA Today Website*, LOS ANGELES TIMES, Apr. 8, 2010, http://articles.latimes.com/2010/apr/08/business/la-fi-ct-demand8-2010apr08.

114 NELLIE BRISTOL & JOHN DONNELLY, KAISER FAMILY FOUND., TAKING THE TEMPERATURE: THE FUTURE OF GLOBAL HEALTH JOURNALISM 7 (2011), *available at* http://www.kff.org/globalhealth/upload/8135.pdf.

115 NELLIE BRISTOL & JOHN DONNELLY, KAISER FAMILY FOUND., TAKING THE TEMPERATURE: THE FUTURE OF GLOBAL HEALTH JOURNALISM 7 (2011), *available at* http://www.kff.org/globalhealth/upload/8135.pdf.

116 Facebook, *Press Room*, http://www.facebook.com/press/info.php?statistics (last visited Nov. 18, 2010).

117 Edmund Lee, *Social Networks Sink Online-Ad Pricing: Facebook and Its Ilk Might be Reducing Overall Pricing of CPMs*, ADAGEDIGITAL, July 12, 2010, http://adage.com/article/digital/social-networks-sink-online-ad-pricing/144884/.

118 Attributor, *Success for the Graduated Response Trial* (press release), Nov. 8, 2010 (Attributor Study Press Release), http://attributor.com/blog/success-for-the-graduated-response-trial/.

119 Attributor Study Press Release. Although the content on these websites was initially unauthorized, 75 percent of the infringing sites agreed to either pursue licensing agreements with the content providers or remove content voluntarily during the first two steps of the "Graduated Response" process, namely after courtesy notices of unlicensed use were sent to the site owner, or after removal notices were sent to the search engines to remove the listing from results and to ad networks to remove ads on the page of the copied content. *Id.*

120 Clinton Boulton, Google Algorithm Change Targets Content Farms, EWEEK.COM, February 26, 2011, http://www.eweek.com/c/a/Search-Engines/Google-Algorithm-Change-Targets-Content-Farms-285369/.

121 Kent Walker, *Making Copyright Work Better*, GOOGLE PUBLIC POLICY BLOG, Dec. 2, 2010, http://googlepublicpolicy.blogspot.com/2010/12/making-copyright-work-better-online.html.

122 Email correspondence between Derek Slater, Policy Mgr., Google, and Steven Waldman, FCC (Dec. 2010 & Jan. 2011).

123 Based on estimates by Flatiron Media; *See also Newspapers Online Traffic Is Strong*.

124 IAB, REVENUE REPORT 2009 FULL YEAR RESULTS at 7-8; INTERACTIVE ADVERTISING BUREAU, IAB INTERNET ADVERTISING REVENUE REPORT, 2010 FIRST HALF-YEAR RESULTS 11 (2010), *available at* www.iab.net/media/file/IAB_report_1H_2010_Final.pdf.

125 Debra Aho Williamson, *Facebook Is Closing the Ad Revenue Gap with the Portals*, THE EMARKETER BLOG, June 23, 2010, http://www.emarketer.com/blog/index.php/facebook-revenue-portals-advertising-aol-google-yahoo/.

126 Nat Ives, *Mounting Web Woes Pummel Newspapers*, ADVERTISING AGE, June 28, 2010, http://adage.com/mediaworks/article?article_id=144684; David S. Evans, *The Online Advertising Industry: Economics, Evolution, and Privacy*, JOURNAL OF ECONOMIC PERSPECTIVES (forthcoming) (providing history of the online advertising market), *available at* http://www.intertic.org/Policy%20Papers/EvansEOAI.pdf.

5 Mobile

1 Nielsen has estimated that in 2010, 230 million Americans use mobile phones. See "Television, Internet and Mobile Usage in the US," THE NIELSEN CO., 8 THREE SCREEN REPORT 4 (TABLE 3) (2010). CTIA estimates that in December 2010, 96 percent of the U.S. population has used the devices, and that there were 302.9 million "wireless subscriber connections." CTIA-The Wireless Association, Wireless Quick Facts: Year-End Figures, http://www.ctia.org/media/industry_info/index.cfm/AID/10323 (last visited May 16, 2011). Pew has estimated that 82 percent of American adults "own a cell phone of some kind," and has concluded that "overall mobile phone ownership has not grown over the last year...." AARON SMITH, PEW INTERNET & AMERICAN LIFE PROJ. MOBILE ACCESS 2010 12 (2010) (PEW, MOBILE ACCESS 2010), http://pewinternet.org/Reports/2010/Mobile-Access-2010.aspx. Most of the findings reported in PEW, MOBILE ACCESS 2010 are based on a tracking survey of 2,252 individuals 18 years old or older in the U.S., conducted from April 29 through May 30, 2010. PEW, MOBILE ACCESS 2010, at 2, 4, 5. According to a recent Pew report, 40 percent of all adults in the U.S. "go online" (defined as using the Internet, email, or instant messaging) on mobile devices. Id. at 2. Moreover, 38 percent of cell phone owners use their cell phones to access the Internet. Id. These figures represent increases of 8 percent and 13 percent, respectively, for the 13-month period from April 2009 to May 2010. Id.

2 "Survey: Mobile News & Paying Online" in PEW RESEARCH CTR.'S PROJ. FOR EXCELLENCE IN JOURNALISM, THE STATE OF THE NEWS MEDIA (2011) (PEW, STATE OF NEWS MEDIA 2011), http://stateofthemedia.org/2011/mobile-survey/.

3 For a description of 2G technologies, see Implementation of Section 6002(b) of the Omnibus Budget Reconciliation Act of 1993, Annual

Report and Analysis of Competitive Market Conditions With Respect to Mobile Wireless, Including Commercial Mobile Services, Fourteenth Report, 25 FCC Rcd. 11407, 11638-40 (2010) (Fourteenth Mobile Wireless Competition Report).

4 FCC, CONNECTING AMERICA, THE NATIONAL BROADBAND PLAN 78 (2010) (NATIONAL BROADBAND PLAN), http://www.broadband.gov.

5 NATIONAL BROADBAND at 78 (citations omitted).

6 NATIONAL BROADBAND at 76–78.

7 NATIONAL BROADBAND at 84–85 (Exhibit 5-F).

8 NATIONAL BROADBAND at 77.

9 See FCC, Omnibus Broadband Initiative, OBI Technical Paper No. 6, Mobile Broadband: The Benefits of Additional Spectrum, at 9, Exhibit 4 (2010), http://transition.fcc.gov/Daily_Releases/Daily_Business/2010/db1021/DOC-302324A1.pdf. "35 times" is an average of projections by Cisco Systems, Coda Research, and the Yankee Group.

10 See Internet Access Services: Status as of June 30, 2010, Industry Analysis and Technology Division, Wireline Competition Bureau, Federal Communications Commission, 15, 30, March 2011, http://www.fcc.gov/Daily_Releases/Daily_Business/2011/db0321/DOC-305296A1.pdf.

11 Greg Sterling, Google: 50 Percent Of Those Exposed To Mobile Ads Took Action, SEARCHENGINELAND.COM, April 26, 2011 (Google: 50 percent), http://searchengineland.com/google-50-percent-of-smartphone-users-exposed-to-ads-took-action-74760.

12 Google: 50 percent.

13 Google: 50 percent.

14 "Survey: Mobile News & Paying Online" in PEW, STATE OF NEWS MEDIA 2011.

15 Fourteenth Mobile Wireless Competition Report at 11495.

16 The distinction between "smartphones" and "feature phones" is not absolute and is blurring as time passes. "[I]n terms of what users can do with their phones, the line between feature phones and smartphones has been blurring for some time. From the perspective of most mobile users, this difference may be becoming less important or meaningful." Amy Gahran, New Facebook App Shows Why Feature Phones Still Matter, CNNTECH, Jan. 25, 2011, http://articles.cnn.com/2011-01-25/tech/feature.phone.apps_1_feature-phones-app-data-charges?_s=PM:TECH (noting that feature phone users' preference for "simpler" technology "doesn't keep feature phone users away from the mobile Internet").

17 FCC, Chairman Julius Genachowski, Spectrum: American Competitiveness, Opportunity, Dollars and the Cost of Delay, Spectrum Fact Sheet (press release), Mar. 2011, available at http://www.fcc.gov/Daily_Releases/Daily_Business/2011/db0322/DOC-305309A2.doc.

18 Smartphones to Overtake Feature Phones in U.S. by 2011, NIELSENWIRE, March 26, 2010, http://blog.nielsen.com/nielsenwire/consumer/smartphones-to-overtake-feature-phones-in-u-s-by-2011/.

19 comScore, Mobile Internet Becoming a Daily Activity for Many Number of People Accessing News and Information On Their Mobile Device More Than Doubles in a Year (press release), Mar. 16, 2009 (Mobile Internet Becoming Daily Activity), http://ir.comscore.com/releasedetail.cfm?releaseid=370870.

20 For purposes of this section, "low-income earners" are defined as individuals who are members of a "family" with an annual household income below $30,000.

21 See, e.g., PEW, MOBILE ACCESS 2010 at 4; JOHN HORRIGAN, PEW INTERNET& AMERICAN LIFE PROJECT, WIRELESS INTERNET USE 3-4, 15, 18 (2009) (WIRELESS INTERNET USE), http://www.pewinternet.org/~/media//Files/Reports/2009/Wireless-Internet-Use-With-Topline.pdf; "Survey: Mobile News & Paying Online" in PEW, STATE OF NEWS MEDIA 2011.

22 See, e.g., Pew Research Ctr. for the People & the Press, Americans Spending More Time Following the News 16, 29, 90 (2010) (Pew 2010 News Consumption Survey), http://people-press.org/report/652/; Pew Research Ctr. for the People & the Press, Audience Segments in a Changing News Environment: Key News Audiences Now Blend Online and Traditional Sources, Pew Research Center Biennial News Consumption Survey 64 (2008) (Pew 2008 News Consumption Survey). It is noteworthy, however, that at least one study of which we are aware indicates that print news consumption by African-Americans may not be significantly different from that of white Americans. Pew Research Center's 2010 News Consumption Survey found that 43 percent of white Americans, and 37 percent of African-Americans, read "a daily newspaper" on a "regular" basis, while 25 percent of white Americans and 34 percent of African-Americans do so "sometimes." Pew 2010 News Consumption Survey at 90.

23 PEW, MOBILE ACCESS 2010 at 10.

24 PEW, MOBILE ACCESS 2010 at 10-11.

25 PEW, MOBILE ACCESS 2010 at 16.

26 PEW, MOBILE ACCESS 2010 at 18.

27 PEW, MOBILE ACCESS 2010 at 3; WIRELESS INTERNET USE at 3-4, 15, 18.

28 See, e.g., Among Mobile Phone Users, Hispanics, Asians Are Most-Likely Smartphone Owners in the U.S., NielsenWire, Feb. 1, 2011 (Hispanics, Asians Most-Likely Smartphone Owners), http://blog.nielsen.com/nielsenwire/?p=25901.

29 WIRELESS INTERNET USE at 4.

30 PEW, MOBILE ACCESS 2010 at 4.

31 James Fallows, How to Save the News, THE ATLANTIC, June 2010 (How to Save the News), quoting Eric Schmidt of Google, http://www.theatlantic.com/magazine/archive/2010/06/how-to-save-the-news/8095/6/.

32 How to Save the News, quoting Eric Schmidt of Google.

33 How to Save the News, quoting Eric Schmidt of Google.

34 See, e.g., Dan Nystedt, IDG, Folding Screen for Mobile Phones Unveiled, PC WORLD, Nov. 21, 2008, http://www.pcworld.com/article/154307/folding_screen_for_mobile_phones_unveiled.html; Richard Darrell, Sony Unveils Genius Roll-Up OLED Screen of the Future!, BIT REBELS, May 28, 2010, http://www.bitrebels.com/lifestyle/sony-unveils-genius-roll-up-oled-screen-of-the-future/; Mike Hanlon, Philips Roll-Up Large Screens and Electronic Books on the Way, GIZMAG, http://www.gizmag.com/go/2548/ (last visited May 16, 2011).

35 Kevin Parish, Verizon Says Smartphones Can Replace PCs, TOM'S HARDWARE, July 15, 2010 (Smartphones Can Replace PCs), http://www.tomshardware.com/news/Verizon-Smartphone-4G,10878.html.

36 Smartphones Can Replace PCs.

37 See, e.g., Jason Ankeny, Google Steers Mobile Advertising into Hyperlocal Relevance, FIERCEMOBILECONTENT, Sept. 30, 2010, http://www.fiercemobilecontent.com/story/google-steers-mobile-advertising-hyperlocal-relevance/2010-09-30; Ziplocal Debuts Affiliate-Based

Hyperlocal Mobile Advertising Solution, MOBILEMARKETINGWATCH, Nov. 5, 2010, http://www.mobilemarketingwatch.com/ziplocal-debuts-affiliate-based-hyperlocal-mobile-advertising-solution-10921/.

38 comScore, Social Networking Ranks as Fastest-Growing Mobile Content Category (press release), June 2, 2010 (Social Networking Ranks), http://www.comscore.com/Press_Events/Press_Releases/2010/6/Social_Networking_Ranks_as_Fastest-Growing_Mobile_Content_Category.

39 Social Networking Ranks.

40 Stuart Dredge, AP Mobile: 'There's Not a Lot of Money to Be Made from Ad-Supported Apps,' MOBILE ENTERTAINMENT, Nov. 10, 2009, http://www.mobile-ent.biz/news/read/ap-mobile-there-s-not-a-lot-of-money-to-be-made-from-ad-supporte.

41 In the past, most mobile sites eschewed the "busy" quality of standard websites—their high degree of detail and number of windows and demarcated areas. However, mobile website design is becoming more elaborate as wireless networks are able to provide faster download speeds to mobile users. Mobile websites have far more restrictive text limitations than those of standard websites. The "maximum page size for a mobile page is only 20 kilobytes." How to Design. Thus mobile site builders are advised to "make everything fit and if possibly use less than 10 Kb," keeping "in mind that the users usually get charged per Kb of mobile web data." How to Make a Mobile Website—6 Easy Tips, TEMPLATE MONSTER BLOG, http://blog.templatemonster.com/2010/05/11/how-make-mobile-website-6-easy-tips/ (last visited May 16, 2011). This limitation can result in design practices that condense content and thus facilitate the quick browsing and scanning of content. Thus, for example, a mobile website consultant advises his readers to "put all the most important information that you want mobile users to see on the top of the page" because "[i]t can be time consuming to browse through a mobile site, not to mention tedious to read through. Make your mobile site design convenient for your consumers." How to Design.

42 See, e.g., ABC News, http://abcnews.go.com/Technology/page?id=6481775; Associated Press, http://www.ap.org/mobile/; CBS News, http://wap.cbsnews.com/; CNN, http://edition.cnn.com/mobile/; FOX News, http://www.foxnews.com/mobile/; MSNBC, http://news.mobile.msn.com/en-us/; NPR, http://www.npr.org/services/mobile/; The New York Times, http://www.nytimes.com/services/mobile/index.html; Newsweek, http://mobile.newsweek.com/; Reuters, http://www.reuters.com/tools/mobile/news; Time Magazine, http://mobile.time.com/; USA Today, http://www.usatoday.com/mobile/index.htm; The Wall Street Journal http://online.wsj.com/public/page/mobile.html; and The Washington Post, http://mobile.washingtonpost.com/ (each last visited May 16, 2011).

43 AUDIT BUREAU OF CIRCULATIONS, EXECUTIVE SUMMARY: GOING MOBILE: HOW PUBLISHERS ARE SOLIDIFYING STRATEGIES AND ADAPTING TO THE MOBILE MARKET 7-8 (2010) (GOINGMOBILE), http://www.accessabc.com/pdfs/mobile2010.pdf.

44 GOING MOBILE at 8. Some small and medium city newspapers, and newspapers covering well-populated counties, have developed mobile websites. For example, the following papers have mobile sites: Orange County Register, http://m.ocregister.com/; Oregonian, http://www.oregonlive.com/mobile-device/; Memphis (TN) Commercial Appeal, http://www.commercialappeal.com/mobile/; Kansas City Star, http://www.kansascity.com/mobile/; Maine Today, http://m.mainetoday.com/; Charleston City Paper, http://m.charlestoncitypaper.com/; Miami Herald, http://m.miamiherald.com/; Sacramento Bee, http://m.sacbee.

com/; and Sandusky Register, http://m.sanduskyregister.com/ (each last visited May 16, 2011). Topix, an Internet news aggregator that focuses on providing access to local news, maintains a mobile website that consumers can customize to receive news and information specific to their locale. See http://www.topix.com/. In July 2010, 12 percent of Topix's audience came through mobile, compared to one percent in May 2009. Interview with Chris Tolles, CEO, Topix, by Jeffrey Tignor and Irene Wu, FCC (July 23, 2010). Prominent websites offering mobile sites include: the Huffington Post, http://www.huffingtonpost.com/blackberry/; Slate, http://mobile.slate.com/; the Drudge Report, http://www.idrudgereport.com/MobileFriendly.aspx; and Google News http://news.google.com/ (each last visited May 16, 2011). A few maintain a mobile website that limits access to consumers who enter into a subscription agreement. See, e.g., Try the WSJ.com Mobile Reader (concerning BlackBerry version of WSJ Reader software), http://online.wsj.com/public/page/0_0560.html (last visited May 16, 2011).

45 Natasha Lomas, Want to Build a Mobile App? Here's How to Convince the CFO, Silicon.com, Feb. 10, 2010, http://www.silicon.com/technology/mobile/2010/02/11/want-to-build-a-mobile-app-heres-how-to-convince-the-cfo-39745366/.

46 See Kimberly Hill, FTC May Probe iOS as War Over Mobile Customer Data Heats Up, MACNEWSWORLD, June 11, 2010, http://www.macnewsworld.com/story/70189.html?wlc=1279658396.

47 MORGAN STANLEY, THE MOBILE INTERNET REPORT 37 (2009) (MORGAN STANLEY REPORT), http://www.morganstanley.com/institutional/techresearch/mobile_internet_report122009.html.

48 MORGAN STANLEY REPORT at 37. The 13 categories ranked ahead of news were: games, entertainment, books, travel, utilities, education, lifestyle, reference, music, sports, navigation, productivity, and business. Id.

49 BlackBerry App World, http://appworld.blackberry.com/webstore/ (last visited May 16, 2010).

50 "Survey: Mobile News & Paying Online" in PEW, STATE OF NEWS MEDIA 2011.

51 "Survey: Mobile News & Paying Online" in PEW, STATE OF NEWS MEDIA 2011.

52 "Survey: Mobile News & Paying Online" in PEW, STATE OF NEWS MEDIA 2011.

53 THE NIELSEN CO., STATE OF MOBILE APPS 2 (2010) (STATE OF MOBILE APPS), http://blog.nielsen.com/nielsenwire/wp-content/uploads/2010/09/NielsenMobileAppsWhitepaper.pdf.

54 LSN Mobile, LSN Mobile Announces BlackBerry® App for Local Mobile News; First Company to Offer More Than 250 Local TV Mobile Apps (press release), June 3, 2010, http://www.lsnmobile.com/news_events/blackberryapp.html.

55 DoApp Wants to Dominate Mobile Apps for Local Media, MEDIASHIFT, May 7, 2010, http://www.pbs.org/mediashift/2010/05/doapp-wants-to-dominate-mobile-apps-for-local-media127.html.

56 "Newspapers: Alternative Weeklies" in Pew Research Ctr.'s Proj. for Excellence in Journalism, The State of the News Media (2010) (Pew, State of News Media 2010), http://stateofthemedia.org/previous-reports/.

57 See, e.g., Here's Your List of Local News Apps, BRAUBLOG, July 8, 2010, http://www.minnpost.com/braublog/2010/07/08/19546/heres_your_list_of_local_news_apps.

58 Newsy, Newsy for iPad: Multisource Video News Analysis, June 21,

2010, http://itunes.apple.com/us/app/newsy-for-ipad-multisource/id367718944?mt=8.

59 Francis Scardino, Review: Newsy App for Android, All the Latest News Right to Your Mobile, GEARDIARY, Mar. 9, 2010, http://www.geardiary.com/2010/03/09/review-newsy-app-for-android-all-the-latest-news-right-to-your-mobile/.

60 Josh Lowensohn, Browse the News in Tags with Zen News, CNET.COM, Oct. 15, 2009 (Zen News Review), http://news.cnet.com/8301-27076_3-10375909-248.html.

61 Zen News Review.

62 Clyde Bentley, The Road to 2013: A Timeline for Newspapers, REYNOLDS JOURNALISM INSTITUTE MOBILE BLOG, Feb. 6, 2010, http://mobile.rjiblog.org/2010/02/06/the-road-to-2013-a-timeline-for-newspapers/.

63 Jenny Dean, 4. Smartphone User Survey: A Glimpse into the Mobile Lives of College Students, in DIGITAL MEDIATEST KITCHEN, CU-BOULDER SCHOOL OF JOURNALISM & MASS COMMUNICATION, IN-DEPTH NEWS FOR SMARTPHONES (2010) (Smartphone User Survey, IN-DEPTH NEWS), http://testkitchen.colorado.edu/projects/reports/smartphone/smartphone-survey/.

64 Digital Media Test Kitchen, 7. Recommendations: Next Steps Forward with Mobile for News Providers, in IN-DEPTH NEWS (Recommendations, IN-DEPTH NEWS), http://testkitchen.colorado.edu/projects/reports/smartphone/smartphone-recommendations/.

65 Smartphone User Survey, IN-DEPTH NEWS.

66 The Poynter Institute, A Note from Dr. Garcia, Eyetracking the News: A Study of Print and Online Reading (Eyetracking the News), http://eyetrack.poynter.org/note.html (last visited May 16, 2011) (emphasis added).

67 The Poynter Institute, Key Findings, Reading Depth, Eyetracking the News (Poynter Eyetracking), http://eyetrack.poynter.org/keys_01.html (last visited May 16, 2011). Poynter also "measured whether a story was read from start to finish" and found that participants read to completion a greater percentage (63 percent) of online "story text" selected by subjects than that (40 percent) of the "broadsheet" (i.e., print, non-tabloid newspaper) "story text" similarly selected. Id. It is important to note that other research conducted by the Poynter Institute, and well-known research conducted by others, have established that individuals scan web pages on desktop screens rather than reading them word-for-word or even sentence for sentence. See, e.g., Jakob Nielsen, How Users Read on the Web, Oct. 1, 2010, http://www.useit.com/alertbox/9710a.html; The Poynter Institute, Eyetracking the News, Previous Studies, http://eyetrack.poynter.org/previous.html (last visited May 16, 2011).

68 Pew Internet & American Life Proj., Understanding the Participatory News Consumer: How Internet and Cell Phone Users Have Turned New into a Social Experience 34 (2010) (PEW, UNDERSTANDING THE PARTICIPATORY NEWS CONSUMER), http://www.pewinternet.org/Reports/2010/Online-News.aspx.

69 PEW, UNDERSTANDING THE PARTICIPATORY NEWS CONSUMER at 34.

70 Recommendations, IN-DEPTH NEWS.

71 See, e.g., Mitch Radcliffe, Kindle Books Come to the PC—a Nook Counterpunch, ZDNET, Oct. 22, 2009, http://www.zdnet.com/blog/ratcliffe/kindle-books-come-to-the-pc-a-nook-counterpunch/462.

72 PBN Staff, RI.gov goes mobile with iPhone app, PROVIDENCE BUSINESS-NEWS, Jul. 2, 2010, http://www.pbn.com/RIgov-goes-mobile-with-iPhone-app,50905.

73 Lauren Katims, Niche Apps Growing More Popular for Service Delivery, GOVTECH.COM, Nov. 4, 2010, (Niche Apps), http://www.govtech.com/e-government/Niche-Apps-Growing-More-Popular-for-Service-Delivery.html.

74 Niche Apps.

75 USAJOBS iPhone application, https://my.usajobs.gov/FeaturedArticle/FeaturedArticleContent.aspx?ArticleID=474&ArticleTypeID=1&count=5.

76 USA.gov Product Recalls application, http://apps.usa.gov/product-recalls-2/.

77 Smithsonian Institution Collections Search application, http://collections.si.edu/mobile.

78 FCC Mobile Broadband Test iPhone app, http://beta.fcc.gov/encyclopedia/measuring-mobile-broadband.

79 FBI's Most Wanted application, http://apps.usa.gov/fbis-most-wanted/.

80 Tablets and e-readers are distinguished in that tablets can serve as e-readers, but e-readers generally have more limited functionalities than tablets.

81 See Amazon.com, Kindle Store, http://www.amazon.com/kindle-store-ebooks-newspapers-blogs/b?ie=UTF8&node=133141011 (last visited May 16, 2011) (Kindle Store).

82 See Kindle Store.

83 See Kindle Store.

84 See Kindle Store.

85 Changewave Research, New ChangeWave Surveys Measure Future Consumer Demand and Reactions of New iPad Owners (press release), May 20, 2010, http://www.changewaveresearch.com/articles/2010/05/ipad_20100520.html. The Changewave Survey involved 3,714 owners of e-Readers; 62 percent owned Amazon Kindles; 16 percent owned Apple iPads; 7 percent owned the Sony Reader; 7 percent owned "a smartphone with eBook capability"; 3 percent owned Barnes & Noble Nooks; and 7 percent owned "Other" e-Readers. Id.

86 See Digital Publishing Alliance, iPad News Apps May Diminish Newspaper Print Subscriptions in 2011, DONALD W. REYNOLDS JOURNALISM INSTITUTE, Dec. 9, 2010, http://www.rjionline.org/news/dpa-ipad-research-project.

87 RALUCA BUDIU AND JAKOB NIELSEN, NIELSEN NORMAN GROUP, USABILITY OF IPAD APPS AND WEBSITES 16 (2010), http://www.nngroup.com/reports/mobile/ipad/ipad-usability.pdf.

88 "Local TV: Good News After the Fall" in PEW, STATE OF NEWS MEDIA 2011, http://stateofthemedia.org/2011/local-tv-essay/.

89 "Local TV: Good News After the Fall" in PEW, STATE OF NEWS MEDIA 2011.

90 See LIN TV Corp., GOOGLE FINANCE, http://www.google.com/finance?q=NYSE:TVL (last visited May 16, 2011).

91 Local TV: Digital: Content" in PEW, STATE OF NEWS MEDIA 2010, http://stateofthemedia.org/2010/local-tv-summary-essay/digital/.

92 "Local TV: Good News After the Fall" in PEW, STATE OF NEWS MEDIA 2011.

93 Stephen Lawson, IDG News, Broadcaster Group Signs on to Mobile TV, Nov. 19, 2010, http://www.pcworld.com/article/211269/broadcaster_group_signs_on_for_mobile_dtv.html.

94 Glen Dickson, Mobile DTV Rollout Continues, BROADCASTING & CABLE, July 12, 2010 (Mobile DTV), http://www.broadcastingcable.com/article/454654-Mobile_DTV_Rollout_Continues.php?rssid=20068.

95 See Mobile DTV.

96 Lauren Goode, Mobile TV's Uphill Climb, DIGITS (WALL ST. J.), Oct. 11, 2010 (Uphill Climb), http://blogs.wsj.com/digits/2010/10/11/going-local-with-mobile-tv/.

97 See, e.g., Uphill Climb; Glen Dickson, Special Report: Mobile TV Heats Up, BROADCASTING & CABLE, July 13, 2009, http://www.broadcasting-cable.com/article/314792-Special_Report_Mobile_DTV_Heats_Up.php (Mobile TV Heats Up).

98 See, e.g., Mobile TV Heats Up.

99 See generally The Infinite Dial 2011: Navigating Digital Platforms, Arbi-tron, Inc./Edison Research (2011), http://www.arbitron.com/downloads/infinite_dial_2011_presentation.pdf.

100 See "Audio: Summary Essay: More Options for Listeners, Less Advertis-ing Dollars for Producers" in PEW, STATE OF NEWS MEDIA 2010, http://stateofthemedia.org/2010/audio-summary-essay/.

101 About the Public Radio Player, PUBLICRADIOPLAYER.ORG, Oct. 31, 2008, http://www.publicradioplayer.org/?page_id=2.

102 Email from Rekha Murthy, Director of Projects and Partnerships, Public Radio Exchange (PRX), to Siddhartha Menon, FCC (Apr. 29, 2011).

103 Mobile Internet Becoming Daily Activity.

104 PEW, UNDERSTANDING THE PARTICIPATORY NEWS CONSUMER at 44.

105 Meeting of FCC staff (including Joel Taubenblatt, Elizabeth Andrion, Jeffrey Tignor, Ty Bream, and Leon Jackler) with Tim Sparapani, Dir., Public Policy, and Andrew Noyes, Mgr., Public Policy Communications, Facebook (June 9, 2010) (Facebook Meeting 6/9/10).

106 Citizen Tube, http://www.citizentube.com/ (last visited May 16, 2011).

107 Facebook Meeting 6/9/10.

108 Email from Professor Harry Dugmore, Rhodes University, to J. Evan Shapiro, FCC (Dec. 7, 2010).

109 Anne-Ryan Heatwole, Grocott's Mail, a Local Newspaper Embraces Mobile Phones, MOBILEACTIVE.ORG, July 14, 2010, http://mobileactive.org/grocotts-mail-newspaper-embraces-mobile-phones.

110 "Survey: Mobile News & Paying Online" in PEW, STATE OF NEWS MEDIA 2011, http://stateofthemedia.org/2011/mobile-survey/. The survey found that 35 percent of mobile local information consumers say they and others like them can have a "big" impact on their community, compared with 27 percent of those who do not connect with their communities on their mobile devices. Id. Furthermore, nearly two-thirds of mobile information connectors (65 percent) feel that it is easier today than five years ago to keep up with information about their community. Id.

111 AARON SMITH, PEW INTERNET & AMERICAN LIFE PROJ., NEIGHBORS ONLINE, ONE IN FIVE AMERICANS USE DIGITAL TOOLS TO COMMUNICATE WITH NEIGHBORS AND MONITOR COMMUNITY DEVELOPMENTS 2 (2010) (NEIGHBORS ONLINE), http://www.pewinternet.org/Reports/2010/Neighbors-Online.aspx.

112 See Prabhas Pokharel, How Mobile Voices Developed a Citizen Media Platform, MEDIA SHIFT IDEA LAB, Jan. 26, 2010 (Mobile Voices), http://www.pbs.org/idealab/2010/01/how-mobile-voices-developed-a-citizen-media-platform020.html.

113 VozMob: Voces Móviles, Mobile Voices, About Vozmob, http://vozmob.net/en/about (last visited May 16, 2011).

114 Mobile Voices.

115 A. Adam Glenn, Mobile Phone Gathering Outlines Successful Projects, MEDIA SHIFT IDEA LAB, June 22, 2010, http://www.pbs.org/ide-alab/2010/06/mobile-phone-gathering-outlines-successful-projects168.html.

116 See Twitter Vote Report, http://blog.twittervotereport.com/ (last visited May 16, 2011).

117 Jennifer 8. Lee Comments in re FOM PN (FCC Launches Examination of The Future of Media and the Contributions of Public Media to the Information Needs of America, Comment Sought, GN Docket No. 10-25, Public Notice (FOM PN)), filed September 13, 2010 at 5.

118 See See ClickFix, How it Works (SeeClickFix), http://www.seeclickfix.com/how_seeclickfix_works (last visited May 16, 2011).

119 Kenny Olmstead, Amy Mitchell, & Tom Rosenstiel, "Online: Key Ques-tions Facing Digital News" in PEW, STATE OF NEWS MEDIA 2011, http://stateofthemedia.org/2011/online-essay/.

120 Mobile Ad Spending Up Nearly 80% in 2010, EMARKETER, Oct. 19, 2010, http://www.emarketer.com/Article.aspx?R=1007992.

121 Interview with Nicole Perrin, Senior Editor, eMarketer, by Siddhartha Menon, FCC (Apr. 27, 2011).

122 "Online: Key Questions Facing Digital News" in PEW, STATE OF NEWS MEDIA 2011, http://stateofthemedia.org/2011/online-essay/.

123 Philip Elmer-DeWitt, AdAge: Apple's iAd is 'double dipping,' FORTUNE TECH, May 4, 2010, http://tech.fortune.cnn.com/2010/05/04/adage-apples-iad-is-double-dipping/. In May 2010, Fortune reported that "AdMob…charges $10 to $15 CPM on average, but doesn't add costs per click," and that advertisers "who want to reach iPhone, iPad and iPod touch users through iAds will have to pay [Apple] $10 per thousand impressions plus $2 per click." Id.

124 See, e.g., mobiThinking.com, The mobiThinking Guide to Mobile Adver-tising Networks 2010: Blind Networks, Nov. 2010, http://www.mobithink-ing.com/mobile-ad-network-guide/blind; mobiThinking.com, The Guide to Mobile Advertising Networks 2010: Premium Blind Networks, Nov. 2010, http://mobithinking.com/mobile-ad-network-guide/premium-blind; mobiThinking.com, The mobiThinking Guide to Mobile Advertising Networks 2010: Premium Networks, Nov. 2010, http://mobithinking.com/mobile-ad-network-guide/premium.

125 See, e.g., In iPad, Publishers See Hope for Ad Revenue: Newspapers, Magazines Getting up to 5 Times as Much for Ads Placed in iPad Appli-cations, CBS NEWS, June 3, 2010 (Ads Placed in iPad Apps), http://www.cbsnews.com/stories/2010/06/03/business/main6543926.shtml.

126 Ads Placed in iPad Apps.

127 Research by FCC staff on May 31, 2011, counting and reviewing all iPad apps that appeared within the Apple iTunes App Store's pages display-ing "All News iPad Apps—Paid" and "All News iPad Apps—Free."

128 GOING MOBILE at 11.

129 "Local TV: Good News After the Fall" in PEW, STATE OF NEWS MEDIA 2011, http://stateofthemedia.org/2011/local-tv-essay/.

130 Emily Steel, Apple to Charge a Premium to Put Ads in Mobile Apps, WALL ST. J., Apr. 29, 2010, http://online.wsj.com/article/SB10001424052748703648304575212411500983040.html.

131 Tony Bradley, Google and AdMob Ready to Take on Apple iAd, PC WORLD, May 30, 2010, http://www.pcworld.com/businesscenter/ar-ticle/197559/google_and_admob_ready_to_take_on_apple_iad.html.

132 See, e.g., Top 200 (Free) in News for iPhone, APPSHOPPER http://app-shopper.com/bestsellers/news/free/?device=iphone; Top 200 (Paid) in News for iPhone, APPSHOPPER, http://appshopper.com/bestsellers/news/paid/?device=iphone;News & Magazines, Top Paid/Top Free, GOOGLE, ANDROID MARKET, https://market.android.com/apps/NEWS_AND_MAGAZINES/ (each last visited May 16, 2011).

133 Jason D. O'Grady, My Favorite New Ipad App: Pulse News Reader, THE APPLE CORE (ZDNET), June 11, 2010, http://www.zdnet.com/blog/apple/my-favorite-new-ipad-app-pulse-news-reader/7163; See Apple, Pulse News Reader, http://itunes.apple.com/us/app/pulse-news-reader/id371088673?mt=8 (last visited May 31, 2011).

134 See Claire Cain Miller, App to Tailor News Streams Gets Boost, N.Y. TIMES, Nov. 14, 2010, http://www.nytimes.com/2010/11/15/technology/15pulse.html?_r=1&scp=1&sq=pulse%20free&st=cse.

135 Joel Johnson, Is Flipboard Legal?, GIZMODO, http://gizmodo.com/5594176/is-flipboard-legal; Joe Mullin, AP, WaPo, Other Big Media Companies Send Cease & Desist Over Zite App, PAID CONTENT, Mar. 30, 2011, http://paidcontent.org/article/419-media-companies-send-cease-desist-over-zite-app/.

136 Jenna Wortham, Apps Alter Reading on the Web, N.Y. TIMES, Jan. 31, 2011, http://www.nytimes.com/2011/02/01/technology/01read.html?_r=2&ref=technology.

137 See, e.g., Stuart Dredge, AP Mobile: 'There's Not a Lot of Money to Be Made from Ad-Supported Apps,' MOBILE ENTERTAINMENT, Nov. 10, 2009 (discussing the decision by AP to make its BlackBerry application free following an experiment selling it for $2.99), http://www.mobile-ent.biz/news/read/ap-mobile-there-s-not-a-lot-of-money-to-be-made-from-ad-supporte.

138 See BlackBerry App World, http://appworld.blackberry.com/webstore/ (last visited May 18, 2011).

139 Research by FCC staff on May 31, 2011, counting all iPhone apps that appeared within the Apple iTunes App Store's pages displaying "All News iPhone Apps—Paid" and "All News iPhone Apps—Free." At the time, Apple offered 2,719 paid news apps, compared to 6,514 free news apps.

140 See, e.g., CNN Mobile (review), APPADVICE, Dec. 5, 2009, http://appadvice.com/appnn/2009/12/review-cnn-mobile/.

141 CNN Launches New iPad App, CNN, Dec. 14, 2010, http://cnnpressroom.blogs.cnn.com/2010/12/14/cnn-launches-new-ipad-app/; See also Apple, iTunes Preview, CNN App for iPhone by CNN Interactive Group, Inc., http://itunes.apple.com/app/cnn-app-for-iphone-u-s/id331786748.

142 David Sarno, L.A. Times Releases iPhone App for Mobile News Reading, L.A. TIMES, June 21, 2010, http://latimesblogs.latimes.com/technology/2010/06/la-times-releases-iphone-app-for-real-time-news-reading.html.

143 See Apple, iTunes Preview, LA Times by Tribune Interactive, http://itunes.apple.com/us/app/la-times/id373238146.

144 Arthur Sulzberger Jr., A Letter to Our Readers: Times Begins Digital Subscriptions, N.Y. TIMES, Mar. 28, 2011 (Times Begins Digital Subscriptions), http://www.nytimes.com/2011/03/28/opinion/l28times.html.

145 See Public Radio Exchange, This American Life iPhone App: For Immediate Distribution! (press release), Feb. 1, 2010, http://blog.prx.org/2010/02/this-american-life-iphone-app-for-immediate-distribution/.

146 Interview with Wendy Turner, VP, Systems, Chicago Public Media, by J. Evan Shapiro, FCC (Dec. 7, 2010).

147 Research by FCC staff on May 31, 2011, counting and reviewing all iPhone apps that appeared within the Apple iTunes App Store's pages displaying "All News iPhone Apps—Paid" and "All News iPhone Apps—Free." At the time, Apple offered 2,719 paid news apps, compared to 6,514 free news apps.

148 See, e.g., Gartner, Gartner Says Worldwide Mobile Application Store Revenue Forecast to Surpass $15 Billion in 2011 (press release), Jan. 26, 2011, http://www.gartner.com/it/page.jsp?id=1529214; 80 percent of Developers Say 70 percent Revenue Share is Not Enough, INTOMOBILE, May 12, 2010, http://www.intomobile.com/2010/05/12/80-of-developers-say-70-revenue-share-is-not-enough/; Peter Dockrill, Why Developers Should Consider BlackBerry: RIM's Chris Smith Speaks to APC, APCMAG.COM, Jan. 17, 2011, http://apcmag.com/why-developers-should-consider-blackberry-rims-chris-smith-speaks-to-apc-.htm; John Markoff & Laura M. Holson, Apple's Latest Opens a Developers' Playground, N.Y. TIMES, July 10, 2008, http://www.nytimes.com/2008/07/10/technology/personaltech/10apps.html.

149 DISTIMO, Insights into Apple's App Ecosystem: Comparing Mac, iPad and iPhone, Mar. 18 2011, at 3 http://www.distimo.com/blog/2011_03_insights-into-apple's-app-ecosystem-comparing-mac-ipad-and-iphone/.

150 Research by FCC staff on May 27, 2011, counting all iPad apps that appeared within the Apple iTunes App Store's pages displaying "All News iPad Apps—Paid" and "All News iPad Apps—Free." At the time, Apple offered 537 paid news apps, compared to 2,388 free news apps.

151 Apple, iTunes Preview, NPR for iPad by NPR, http://itunes.apple.com/us/app/npr-for-ipad/id364183644?mt=8; Apple, iTunes Preview, BBC News by BBC Worldwide, http://itunes.apple.com/us/app/bbc-news/id364147881?mt=8; Apple, iTunes Preview, AP News by The Associated Press, http://itunes.apple.com/us/app/ap-news/id364677107?mt=8; Apple, iTunes Preview, Reuters News Pro for iPad by Thomson Reuters, http://itunes.apple.com/us/app/reuters-news-pro-for-ipad/id363274833?mt=8 (each last visited May 27, 2011).

152 DISTIMO, Distimo Report, July 2010, http://www.distimo.com/blog/2010_07_distimo-report-july-2010/. The popularity of the USA Today iPad app has since declined. In April, 2011, Distimo found the top ten were: (1) Angry Birds Rio HD; (2) Friendly for Facebook; (3) iBooks; (4) Bing for iPad; (5) Terra; (6) Atari's Greatest Hits; (7) The Weather Channel Max; (8) Contract Killer; (9) Crackle; and (10) Flipboard. DISTIMO, In-Depth View on Download Volumes in the Google Android Market, May 2011, http://www.distimo.com/publications.

153 Apple iTunes Preview, New York Post by NYP Holdings, Inc., http://itunes.apple.com/us/app/new-york-post/id378590820?mt=8; Applie iTunes Preview, 60 Minutes for iPad by CBS Interactive, http://itunes.apple.com/us/app/60-minutes-for-ipad/id403426652?mt=8;

154 Research by FCC staff on May 31, 2011, counting and reviewing all iPad apps that appeared within the Apple iTunes App Store's pages displaying "All News iPad Apps—Paid" and "All News iPad Apps—Free."

155 Apple, iTunes Preview, the Oklahoman by Oklahoma Publishing Company, http://itunes.apple.com/us/app/the-oklahoman/id397754521?mt=8; Apple, iTunes Preview, the Virginian-Pilot for iPad by Good.iWare Ltd., http://itunes.apple.com/us/app/the-virginian-pilot-for-ipad/id395579203?mt=8; Apple iTunes Preview, the Boston Pilot by Pedro Enrique Cifres, http://itunes.apple.com/us/app/the-boston-pilot/id386253491?mt=8 (each last visited May 27, 2011).

156 See Apple, iTunes Preview, Vanity Fair iPad Edition by Conde Naste Digi-

tal, http://itunes.apple.com/us/app/id427270716?mt=8# (last visited May 18, 2011).

157 Apple, iTunes Preview, TIME Magazine by Time, Inc., http://itunes.apple.com/us/app/time-magazine/id369021520?mt=8; Apple, iTunes Preview, Popular Science+ by Bonnier Corp., http://itunes.apple.com/us/app/popular-science/id364049283?mt=8; Apple, iTunes Preview, WIRED Magazine by Conde Nast Digital, http://itunes.apple.com/us/app/wired-magazine/id373903654?mt=8 (each last visited May 18, 2011).

158 D8 Conference Interview with Steve Jobs by Kara Swisher and Walt Mossberg, ALL THINGS DIGITAL, June 2, 2010 (Jobs Interview), http://video.allthingsd.com/video/d8-steve-jobs-on-the-iphone-origin/3BBFA695-DC39-4834-9E39-7097C9CE1243.

159 Times Begins Digital Subscriptions.

160 Staci Kramer, New York Times: More Than 100,000 Digital Subs In First Weeks of Paywall, PAIDCONTENT.ORG, Apr. 21, 2011, http://paidcontent.org/article/419-new-york-times-more-than-100k-digital-subs-in-first-weeks-of-paywall/.

161 See The Daily, http://www.thedaily.com/; Erick Schonfeld, One-Click Subscriptions Come to the iPad, TECHCRUNCH, Feb. 2, 2011, http://techcrunch.com/2011/02/02/one-click-subscriptions-come-to-the-ipad/#.

162 See, e.g., Brett Pulley & Adam Satariano, News Corp.'s Murdoch Unwraps Daily Digital Publication for Apple's iPad, BLOOMBERG, Feb. 2, 2011, http://www.bloomberg.com/news/2011-02-02/news-corp-unwraps-daily-digital-publication-for-apple-s-ipad.html (quoting News Corp.'s Rupert Murdoch as saying, "We have license to experiment, the ability to innovate.… We believe the Daily will be the model for how stories are told and consumed.").

163 See Kindle Store.

164 Interview of L. Gordon Crovitz, co-Founder, Journalism Online, by Steven Waldman, FCC (Oct. 5, 2010).

165 See Josh Halliday, No Longer the Apple of Every Publisher's Eye, GUARDIAN.CO.UK, Feb. 21, 2011, http://www.guardian.co.uk/media/pda/2011/feb/21/apple-newspaper-app-subscriptions (noting that Apple's new terms of service dictate that the company keeps 30 percent of revenue from the growing number of publishers in its App Store, while Google's One Pass, allows publishers to set their own payment plan, keep 90 percent of the revenue, and all of the lucrative customer information).

166 Sarah Rabil, Adam Satariano & Peter Burrows, Apple Said to Negotiate With Publishers Over Digital Newsstand, BLOOMBERG, Sept. 17, 2010, http://www.bloomberg.com/news/2010-09-17/apple-said-to-negotiate-with-publishers-over-digital-newsstand-for-ipad.html.

167 See Google Moving in on Apple's Digital Newsstand, PHYSORG.COM, Jan. 3, 2011, http://www.physorg.com/news/2011-01-google-apple-digital-newsstand.html (last visited May 18, 2011).

168 Anita Hamilton, Donating by Text: Haiti Fundraising Goes Viral, TIME, Jan. 13, 2010, http://www.time.com/time/business/article/0,8599,1953528,00.html.

169 See, e.g., Matt Ritchel, Wireless Companies Speed Up Texted Haiti Donations, BITS: BUSINESS INNOVATION TECHNOLOGY SOCIETY (N.Y. TIMES), Jan. 15, 2010, http://bits.blogs.nytimes.com/2010/01/15/verizon-speeds-up-text-message-donations-to-haiti/.

170 See, e.g. Stephanie From, Donations Ban on iPhone Apps Irritates Nonprofits, N.Y. TIMES, Dec. 8, 2010, http://www.nytimes.com/2010/12/09/technology/09charity.html; Jacqui Cheng, Public Radio Pushing iPhone Donation Requests: OK or Not?, ARS TECHNICA, http://arstechnica.com/apple/news/2010/05/public-radio-pushing-iphone-donation-requests-ok-or-not.ars; Jake Shapiro, Apple's No-Donation Policy for Apps is a Cop-Out, ARS TECHNICA, June 4, 2010, http://arstechnica.com/apple/news/2010/06/nonprofit-developer-apples-no-donation-policy-is-a-cop-out.ars; (each last visited May 16, 2011).

171 CTIA—The Wireless Association, Year-End 2010 Top Line Survey Results, http://files.ctia.org/pdf/CTIA_Survey_Year_End_2010_Graphics.pdf.

172 John C. Hodulik, et al., UBS Investment Research, US Wireless 411 (Ver. 38.0) 10 (2010).

6 Public Broadcasting

1 Ernest J. Wilson, Acceptance as Chair at Corp. for Public Broadcasting (CPB) Board of Directors (Sept. 16, 2009) at 1, *available at* http://www.ernestjwilson.com/uploads/Chairman_Wilsons_Remarks_-_Sept_16,_2009.pdf.

2 LEONARD DOWNIE JR. & MICHAEL SCHUDSON, THE RECONSTRUCTION OF AMERICAN JOURNALISM, COLUMBIA JOURNALISM REV. (2009) (DOWNIE & SCHUDSON, RECONSTRUCTION OF AMERICAN JOURNALISM) http://www.cjr.org/reconstruction/the_reconstruction_of_american.php?page=all.

3 *See, e.g.,* Ellen P. Goodman, *Public Service Media 2.0,* in…AND COMMUNICATIONS FOR ALL: A POLICY AGENDA FOR A NEW ADMINISTRATION 270 (Amit M. Schejter, ed.) (2009) (*Public Service Media 2.0,* AND COMMUNICATIONS FOR ALL) (arguing for a restructured CPB that is capable of supporting new media and platforms that may be independent of existing broadcasters).

4 STEVE COLL, REBOOT: AN OPEN LETTER TO THE FCC ABOUT A MEDIA POLICY FOR THE DIGITAL AGE, COLUMBIA JOURNALISM REV. (Nov/Dec 2010) at 33, http://www.cjr.org/cover_story/reboot.php?page=all (COLL, REBOOT: AN OPEN LETTER TO THE FCC); *see also,* BARBARA COCHRAN, RETHINKING PUBLIC MEDIA: MORE LOCAL, MORE INCLUSIVE, MORE INTERACTIVE (Aspen Institute) (Dec. 2010) (COCHRAN, RETHINKING PUBLIC MEDIA), *available at* http://www.knightcomm.org/wp-content/uploads/2010/12/Rethinking_Public_Media.pdf (proposing that the CPB become the Corporation for Public Media and that public broadcasting take on an expanded role in the production of journalism).

5 Randall Davidson, *9XM Talking: The Early History of WHA Radio,* WISCONSIN PUBLIC RADIO, http://web.archive.org/web/20080508184054/http://www.portalwisconsin.org/9xm.cfm (last visited Feb. 10, 2011) (explaining that after an experimental "first broadcast" in early 1917, 9XM (which later became WHA) made its first, clear undistorted transmission of human speech in 1999).

6 TV Acres: Children's Show Hosts: The Friendly Giant, http://www.tvacres.com/child_friendlygiant.htm (last visited Aug. 25, 2010) (stating that the children's show, The Friendly Giant, debuted in its original format in 1953 on WHA-AM Radio in Madison at the University of Wisconsin).

7 JOHN WITHERSPOON & ROSELLE KOVITZ, THE HISTORY OF PUBLIC BROADCASTING 4, 7 (Educational Broadcasting Corp.) (1987) (WITHERSPOON & KOVITZ, PUBLIC BROADCASTING). In the early 1920s, the Secretary of Commerce was the radio industry's sole licensing authority, which was then succeeded by the Federal Radio Commission, established in 1927 by the Dill-White Radio Act, and ultimately the Federal Communications

Commission in the Communications Act of 1934. *Id.* at 6.

8 S.E. FROST, EDUCATION'S OWN STATIONS 178 (Arno Press Inc.) (1971).

9 WITHERSPOON & KOVITZ, PUBLIC BROADCASTING at 8.

10 WITHERSPOON & KOVITZ, PUBLIC BROADCASTING at 7.

11 WITHERSPOON & KOVITZ, PUBLIC BROADCASTING at 8; RALPH ENGELMAN, PUBLIC RADIO AND TELEVISION IN AMERICA: A POLITICAL HISTORY 28-30 (Sage Publications) (1996) (ENGELMAN, PUBLIC RADIO AND TV).

12 ENGELMAN, PUBLIC RADIO AND TV at 36 (*citing* R.W. McChesney, *Free Speech and Democracy: The Debate in the American Legal Community over the Meaning of Free Expression on Radio, 1926-1939* (paper presented at the annual meeting of the Association for Education in Journalism and Mass Communication), 1987, at n. 68). Crane went on to add:

"The absurdity passes comprehension when we not only give up our public birthright but tax ourselves to support commissions, to protect private monopoly in the use and control of what belongs to the nation. The absurdity becomes tragic when the total values of radio communication to a democracy are considered."

ENGELMAN, PUBLIC RADIO AND TV at 36.

13 ENGELMAN, PUBLIC RADIO AND TV at 30-34 (describing the positions of the National Advisory Council on Radio in Education (NACRE), which advocated offering educational programming on commercial stations, and that of the National Committee on Education by Radio (NCER), which supported independent noncommercial stations and systems). These included not only educational groups, such as The National Association of Educational Broadcasters ("NAEB"), but also other citizen groups whose interests were not met by commercial broadcasters: Though not a completely uniform assembly—some of these organizations took diametrically opposed positions on how to respond to commercialization of the airwaves, leading to "separatist" and "collaborationist" ideologies that persist today.

14 ENGELMAN, PUBLIC RADIO AND TV at 34.

15 It selected channels in the 41-42 MHz band, far above the AM band that commercial stations used. In 1939, the FCC shifted the educational broadcasting allocation to 42-43 MHz, and stations were required to change from AM to the then-new FM mode.

16 *See Allocation of Frequencies to the Various Classes of Non-Governmental Services in the Radio Spectrum from 10 Kilocycles to 30,000,000 Kilocycles*, Report, 39 FCC 226 (1945).

17 *See* JOHN WITHERSPOON, ROSELLE KOVITZ, ROBERT AVERY, & ALAN G. STAVITSKY, THE HISTORY OF PUBLIC BROADCASTING (Current Publishing) (2000) (HISTORY OF PUBLIC BROADCASTING 2000).

18 *See* SUSAN L. BRINSON, PERSONAL AND PUBLIC INTERESTS: FRIEDA B. HENNOCK AND THE FEDERAL COMMUNICATIONS COMMISSION 120 (Praeger Publishers) (2002) (BRINSON, PERSONAL AND PUBLIC INTERESTS) (referencing *Notice of Further Proposed Rulemaking*, FCC 49-948, MIMEO 37460, July 11, 1949, which stated that the Notice "should include a provision for the reservation of a specified number of frequencies in the ultra-high frequency band for the establishment of a noncommercial educational television service.")

19 BRINSON, PERSONAL AND PUBLIC INTERESTS at 120.

20 Geneva Collins, *Public Television Got Its Kickstart 50 Years Ago*, CURRENT, May 12, 2003 (*Public TV Kickstart*), http://www.current.org/history/hist-0309houston.html.

21 *Public TV Kickstart*.

22 ENGELMAN, PUBLIC RADIO AND TV at 50; *see also id* at 44 (explaining that Lewis Hill, father of the Pacifica Radio Network, criticized university radio stations for not purposing to "form a cultural bridge between centers of learning and occupational classes," adding that station leadership was often "tied either to state legislatures or to boards of trustees which inevitably represent tendencies close to the commercial and conservative part of the community").

23 ENGELMAN, PUBLIC RADIO AND TV at 59, 65.

24 ENGELMAN, PUBLIC RADIO AND TV at 67.

25 ENGELMAN, PUBLIC RADIO AND TV at 149.

26 ENGELMAN, PUBLIC RADIO AND TV at 145.

27 WITHERSPOON & KOVITZ, PUBLIC BROADCASTING at 13.

28 CARNEGIE COMMISSION ON THE FUTURE OF PUBLIC BROADCASTING, THE REPORT AND RECOMMENDATIONS OF THE CARNEGIE COMMISSION ON EDUCATIONAL TELEVISION: PUBLIC TELEVISION, A PROGRAM FOR ACTION 92 (1967) (CARNEGIE I).

29 WITHERSPOON & KOVITZ, PUBLIC BROADCASTING at 15 ("No issue was more sensitive than the prospect of a partisan political tilt in public broadcasting programs…. [S]everal members of Congress were determined that any future system should be rigidly neutral"; ENGELMAN, PUBLIC RADIO AND TV at 88 (stating that "The CPB was designed to provide both political insulation and funds for public radio and TV").

30 ENGELMAN, PUBLIC RADIO AND TV at 159-60; Public Broadcasting Act of 1967, 47 U.S.C. § 396(c) (2000) (describing the functions and duties of the Corporation for Public Broadcasting Board of Directors).

31 Public Broadcasting Act of 1967, 47 U.S.C. § 396.

32 Corporation for Public Broadcasting *et. al* Comments in re *FOM PN* (*FCC Launches Examination of the Future of Media and Information Needs of Communities in a Digital Age*, Public Notice, 25 FCC Rcd 384 (2010) (*FOM PN*)), filed May 7, 2010 (CPB Comments), at 7.

33 ENGELMAN, PUBLIC RADIO AND TV at 91 (reporting 292 educational FM stations in 1966); WITHERSPOON & KOVITZ, PUBLIC BROADCASTING at 13 (reporting 124 educational TV stations in 1965).

34 WITHERSPOON & KOVITZ, PUBLIC BROADCASTING at 33.

35 CPB Comments at 7.

36 Vivian Schiller, *Why Online Won't Kill the Radio Star: Vivian Schiller of NPR on How Public Radio Can Thrive in the Digital Age*, WALL ST. J., June 7, 2010, http://online.wsj.com/article/SB10001424052748704764404575287070721094884.html.

37 CPB Comments at 11.

38 CPB Comments at 12.

39 Email from Jason Seiken, Sr. V.P., Interactive, PBS, to Ellen P. Goodman, FCC (Oct. 29, 2010) (Seiken Email 10/29/10).

40 Public Broadcasting Service, *New Research Confirms PBS the Most Trusted and Unbiased Source for News Ahead of Fox News Channel, CNN, and Other Commercial Networks* (press release), Feb. 18, 2010, http://www.pbs.org/roperpoll2010/.

41 CPB, PUBLIC BROADCASTING REVENUE FISCAL YEAR 2008 6 (2009) (PUBLIC BROADCASTING REVENUE FISCAL YEAR 2008), *available at* http://www.cpb.org/stations/reports/revenue/2008PublicBroadcastingRevenue.pdf. CPB Appropriation does not separate appropriation for digital transition or interconnection funds. "Other" includes revenue from subsidiaries, special fundraising activities, passive income, gains (losses) on sales of assets or securities, endowment revenue, and capital campaigns. *Id.* at 7.

42 PUBLIC BROADCASTING REVENUE FISCAL YEAR 2008 at 6.

43 PUBLIC BROADCASTING REVENUE FISCAL YEAR 2008 at 3.

44 PUBLIC BROADCASTING REVENUE FISCAL YEAR 2008 at 3, 6.

45 WHYY, Financial Statements: A Note from the Senior Vice President and Chief Financial Officer, *available at* http://www.whyy.org/about/inside-whyy/financials.html.

46 WETA Financial Report in Report to the Community at 20, available at http://www.weta.org/files/FY10_reportcommunity.pdf. These numbers seem to be representative of mid-size to larger stations over the past decade. For example, WMFE in Orlando has depended on individual donations for nearly 50 percent of its funding in the past ten years. WMFE (Orlando, Fla.) (reporting individual donations contributing to between 42 percent and 52 percent since 2000).

47 PUBLIC BROADCASTING REVENUE FISCAL YEAR 2008 at 6.

48 STATION RESOURCE GROUP (SRG), GROW THE AUDIENCE: CENSUS OF JOURNALISTS IN PUBLIC RADIO AND TELEVISION, DELIVERABLE #3—FINAL REPORT 8 (2010) (CENSUS OF JOURNALISTS IN PUBLIC RADIO AND TELE-VISION, DELIVERABLE #3).

49 David Sit, NewsHour's vice president for operations and technology. According to Sit, "most of NewsHour's funding, about $12 million for the 2010-11 season, comes from the federal government.... Corporate underwriting accounts for roughly $9 million of the 2010-2011 budget and foundations make up most of the remainder, about $6.5 million.... Despite decreases in funding, staffing levels remained stable at News-Hour in 2010." Emily *et. al*, "Network News: Durability & Decline" in PEW RESEARCH CTR.'S PROJ. FOR EXCELLENCE IN JOURNALISM, STATE OF THE NEWS MEDIA (2011) (PEW, STATE OF NEWS MEDIA 2011), http://stateofthe-media.org/2011/network-essay/.

50 "Network News: Durability & Decline" in PEW, STATE OF NEWS MEDIA 2011.

51 CORPORATION FOR PUBLIC BROADCASTING, PUBLIC BROADCASTING MEMBERSHIP FISCAL YEAR 2005-2009.

52 CORPORATION FOR PUBLIC BROADCASTING, APPROPRIATION REQUEST AND JUSTIFICATION, FY 2011 AND FY 2013 5 (2010) *available at* http://www.cpb.org/appropriation/justification_11-13.pdf. "Congress recognized this need by providing to CPB $25 million worth of station 'fiscal stabilization' grants in FY 2010."

53 Memorandum from Public Television CSG Review Panel to Pat Harrison, President & CEO, Corporation for Public Broadcasting, Final Report and Recommendations, Aug. 25, 2010, at 9.

54 CORPORATION FOR PUBLIC BROADCASTING, FEDERAL APPROPRIATION HISTORY, *available at* http://cpb.org/appropriation/history.html.

55 *Budget Agreement Cuts Three CPB Funds, Leaves NPR Intact*, Current (Apr. 12, 2011), http://currentpublicmedia.blogspot.com/2011/04/budget-agreement-cuts-three-cpb-funds.html

56 CORPORATION FOR PUBLIC BROADCASTING, FY2010 RADIO COMMUNITY SERVICE GRANT GENERAL PROVISIONS & ELIGIBILITY CRITERIA 4-10 (2010), *available at* http://www.cpb.org/stations/grants/radio/2010/cpb_10RadioCSG_GeneralProvisions.pdf; CORPORATION FOR PUBLIC BROADCASTING, FY2010 TELEVISION COMMUNITY SERVICE GRANT GEN-ERAL PROVISIONS & ELIGIBILITY CRITERIA 4-6 (2010), *available at* http://

www.cpb.org/stations/grants/tv/2010/cpb_10TV_CSG_GeneralProvi-sions.pdf.

57 CORPORATION FOR PUBLIC BROADCASTING, APPROPRIATION REQUEST AND JUSTIFICATION FY 2011 AND FY 2013, 12, 14 (2010), *available at* http://www.cpb.org/aboutcpb/financials/appropriation/justification_11-13.pdf. *See also, Ex parte* letter of Ellen P. Goodman to Blair Levin in FCC GN Docket No. 09-51, A National Broadband Plan for Our Future (Jan. 15, 2010) (discussing mandatory public broadcasting investments in broadcast infrastructure at the expense of broadband content and infrastructure investments).

58 *Budget Agreement Cuts Three CPB Funds, Leaves NPR Intact*, Current (Apr. 12, 2011), http://currentpublicmedia.blogspot.com/2011/04/budget-agreement-cuts-three-cpb-funds.html. *See also* U.S. OFFICE OF MANAGEMENT & BUDGET, FISCAL YEAR 2012 BUDGET OF THE U.S. GOV-ERNMENT (2011) (President's Proposed Budget for FY 2012), *available at* http://www.whitehouse.gov/sites/default/files/omb/budget/fy2012/assets/budget.pdf.

59 An Act To Prohibit Federal Funding of National Public Radio and the Use of Federal Funds To Acquire Radio Content, H.R. 1076, 112th Cong., *available at* http://www.gpo.gov/fdsys/pkg/BILLS-112hr1076eh/pdf/BILLS-112hr1076eh.pdf.

60 Economic theories for public service media have traditionally been rooted in public good theory and market failure. From an economic perspective, consumers lack the incentive to demand, and commercial media producers lack the market incentives to produce, the optimal amounts of socially valuable news, information, and content. This is particularly common in the case of public goods, which are by definition non-rivalrous (where consumption of the good does not diminish the good itself) and nonexclusive (with no exclusive rights of consump-tion). Because consumers know that they can benefit ("free ride") from the good without having to purchase them, they are not optimally motivated to demand them, and because producers cannot always control the consumption of public good products, they are not optimally motivated to produce them.

This mismatch between market production and public needs, the ratio-nale goes, leads to an under-production of content that is valuable for democratic and civic purposes—increasing political accountability, social solidarity, educational levels, or imaginative and expressive freedom, for example. Thus, the market may not provide socially optimal amounts of content that would produce positive externalities—social benefits that result from private transactions. Public subsidies and other forms of government support can, and do, therefore serve to motivate the production of public service media.

61 WITHERSPOON & KOVITZ, PUBLIC BROADCASTING at 3.

62 CPB Comments at 6–7; *See also* Corporation for Public Broadcasting, *Goals and Objectives*, http://www.cpb.org/aboutcpb/goals/goalsandob-jectives/goalsandobjectives_full.html (last visited July 11, 2010).

63 *See, e.g.,* Ellen P. Goodman & Anne H. Chen, *Modeling Policy for New Public Media Networks*, 24 HARV. J. LAW & TECH. 112, 136-163 (2010), *available at* http://jolt.law.harvard.edu/articles/pdf/v24/24HarvJLTech111.pdf; Ellen P. Goodman & Anne H. Chen, Digital Public Media Networks to Advance Broadband and Enrich Connected Communities, *A National Broadband Plan for Our Future*, GN Docket No. 09-51, filed Nov. 7, 2009 (Goodman & Chen, Digital Public Media Networks), at 5, available at http://ssrn.com/author=333377.

64 HISTORY OF PUBLIC BROADCASTING 2000 at 70.

65 JOHN SILVER, CANDACE CLEMENT, CRAIG AARON, & S. DEREK TURNER, FREE PRESS, NEW PUBLIC MEDIA: A PLAN FOR ACTION 10 (2010) (FREE PRESS, NEW PUBLIC MEDIA), *available at* http://www.freepress.net/files/New_Public_Media.doc.pdf.

66 PBS Children's Media, available at http://www.pbs.org/about/pbskids/ (last visited May 31, 2011).

67 CHILDREN NOW, EDUCATIONALLY/INSUFFICIENT? AN ANALYSIS OF AVAIL-ABILITY & EDUCATIONAL QUALITY OF CHILDREN'S E/I PROGRAMMING 9 (2008) (CHILDREN NOW, EDUCATIONALLY/INSUFFICIENT?), *available at* http://pbskids.org/lions/parentsteachers/pdf/childrennow_report.pdf.

68 PBS Kids, The Ready to Learn Initiative, http://pbskids.org/read/about/ (last visited Feb. 22, 2011).

69 Email from Jason Seiken, PBS, to Ellen P. Goodman, FCC (Feb. 21, 2011) (relying on Google analytics).

70 Email from Jason Seiken, PBS, to Ellen P. Goodman, FCC (Feb. 21, 2011) (relying on comScore's Video Metrix data from January 2011).

71 PBS, Program HH Demo Profile (reporting 29 percent viewership for *Clifford* from families with income less than $20,000 and 33 percent from families with an income above $60,000).

72 PBS, Program HH Demo Profile (reporting 11 percent viewership from families whose head of household has less than a four-year high school education but 34 percent viewership from families whose head of household has more than four years of college, and 24 percent viewership from families with less than $20,000 of family income but 38 percent with more than $60,000).

73 CPB, PUBLIC TELEVISION STATIONS: A TRUSTED SOURCE FOR EDUCATING AMERICA 9 (2008) (PUBLIC TELEVISION STATIONS), *available at* http://www.cpb.org/aboutpb/education/services2008/2008TVEducationReport.pdf.

74 PBS Educational Services, *About PBS*, http://www.pbs.org/aboutpbs/aboutpbs_corp_education.html (last visited June 29, 2010). *See also* Teacher's Domain, *About Teacher's Domain*, http://www.teachersdomain.org/about.html (last visited June 29, 2010). Teacher's Domain, created by WGBH Boston, is a free collection of over 1,000 standards-based multimedia resources for both students and teachers.

75 PBS, *PBS Programming Tops the List of Teacher Favorites for Second Consecutive Year* (press release), Aug. 25, 2004, http://www.pbs.org/aboutpbs/news/20040825_teacherfavorite.html.

76 PBS Digital Learning Library, http://www.pbsdigitallearninglibrary.org/ (last visited Sept. 2, 2010); PBS Teachers, *Introducing the PBS Digital Learning Library*, http://www.pbs.org/teachers/dll (last visited Sept. 2, 2010).

77 Email from Robert M. Lippincott, Sr. V.P., Education, Public Broadcasting Service, to Ellen P. Goodman, FCC (Aug. 30, 2010). Seven leading local stations began testing the Library in September 2010, with a focus on assessing the teacher's experience and the value of digital media in instruction. PBS anticipates providing DLL resources and other educational services through state portals, some supported by recent Department of Education "Race to the Top" grants. It has already entered agreements with Pennsylvania and Texas to deliver DLL resources.

78 Richard Somerset-Ward, *American Public Television: Programs—Now, and in the Future* in PUBLIC TELEVISION IN AMERICA 100 (Bertelsmann Foundation Publishers) (1999). *See also* PUBLIC TELEVISION STATIONS at 8 (reporting 68 percent of surveyed stations with an established partnership with universities; 61 percent with services for college or university students, and 52 percent with college or university instructors), *available at* http://www.cpb.org/aboutpb/education/services2008/2008TVEducationReport.pdf.

79 CHILDREN NOW, EDUCATIONALLY/INSUFFICIENT?.

80 FREE PRESS, NEW PUBLIC MEDIA at 9.

81 PBS Video, Austin City Limits, http://video.pbs.org/program/1273976454/ (last visited Mar. 15, 2011) (Austin City Limits).

82 Austin City Limits. PBS's forthcoming Arts Showcase is an online portal that will allow art enthusiasts to directly engage with young and established artists of all art genres.

83 *See* Chris Johnson, *Federal Support of Public Broadcasting: Not Quite What LBJ Had in Mind*, 8 COMMLAW CONSPECTUS 135, 138-40 (2000) (criticizing public television forpolitical bias and a failure to garner a larger audience); Howard White, *Fine Tuning the Federal Government's Role in Public Broadcasting*, 46 FED. COMM. L.J. 491, 501-03, 513 (1994) (discussing Congressional attempts to eliminate funding for public television and criticizing public broadcastings' overreliance on its most popular programming). The same critique has been leveled against public radio. *See also* Bill McKibben, *All Programs Considered*, N.Y. REV. OF BOOKS, Nov. 11, 2010, http://www.nybooks.com/articles/archives/2010/nov/11/all-programs-considered/.

84 Letter from Gregory A. Lewis, Assist. Gen. Counsel, National Public Radio, to Marlene H. Dortch, Secretary, FCC, GN Docket No. 10-25 (filed Dec. 3, 2010) (NPR *Ex Parte* 12/3/10), at 2.

85 FREE PRESS, NEW PUBLIC MEDIA at 9.

86 National Public Radio Comments in re *FOM PN*, filed May 7, 2010 (NPR Comments), at 12.

87 NPR Comments at 15.

88 NPR Comments at 14. American Public Media is the largest producer and distributor of classical music programming in the country.

89 From the Top, http://www.fromthetop.org/content/top, last visited (May 27, 2011).

90 Ellen P. Goodman, *Media Policy Out of the Box: Content Abundance, Attention Scarcity, and the Failures of Digital Markets*, 19 BERKELEY TECH. L.J. 1389, 1406 (2004) ("The hallmark of a civic republic, also known as a deliberative democracy, is rational deliberation among citizens, resulting in a consensus that drives public policy"). For a more in-depth discussion of theoretical rationales underlying public broadcasting, *see Id.* at 1400–19. Scholarly works, as early as Alexander Meiklejohn's FREE SPEECH AND ITS RELATION TO SELF-GOVERNMENT (Harper Brothers Publishers) (1948) and into Jürgen Habermas' THE STRUCTURAL TRANSFORMATION OF THE PUBLIC SPHERE (MIT Press)(1989), provided a theoretical framework for public broadcasting that called for a greater exchange of this sort of public and "counterpublic" discourse. *See also,* Patricia Aufderheide & Jessica Clark, American University School of Communication Center for Social Media Comments in re *FOM PN,* filed May 6, 2010 (American University Comments) at 3–4.

91 CARNEGIE I at 95.

92 THE CENTURY FOUNDATION, QUALITY TIME? REPORT OF THE TASK FORCE ON PUBLIC TELEVISION 14 (Century Press Found.) (1993).

93 Public Broadcasting Service News, *New Research Confirms PBS the Most Trusted and Unbiased Source for News Ahead of Fox News Channel, CNN,* *and Other Commercial Networks* (press release), Feb. 18, 2010, http://www.pbs.org/roperpoll2010.

94 Public Broadcasting System Comments in re *FOM PN*, filed May 7, 2010 (PBS Comments), at 14.

95 PBS Comments at 14.

96 FCC staff analysis of Tribune Media Services data, April 2011.

97 Data come from Tribune Media Services during the time periods Nov. 1-Nov.14, 2009 and May 6-May 12, 2010. Data averages include total scheduled news minutes on full-power broadcast television stations over the sample period. Includes all news minutes; no deductions are made for weather, sports, advertising, etc. Programs included in this count are those indicated as "News" or "Newsmagazine" (or their Spanish equivalents) in the "Genre" field, and those indicated by TMS as "Local" in the "Origination" field (possible values in this field are "Local", "Network", or "Syndicated").

98 Christopher Ali, *The Second Day Story: Re-imagining Public Broadcasting Through Community*, RIPE@2010 (Univ. of Tampere, Finland), 2010, at 15, n.2, *available at* http://ripeat.org/wp-content/uploads/tdomf/1281/Ali.pdf. Going state-by-state, the author looked at every listed station's website for mention of news and public affairs programs (examining program descriptions and program guides for everyday of a given week). For the 170 stations listed on PBS.org, the results were (not accounting for overlap): "77 stations produced no local newscasts; 79 stations produced a weekly newsmagazine; 6 stations produced a newscast that aired 1-3 times per week; and 14 stations produced a nightly local newscast (5 times per week or more)". *Id. at n. 2*. Determining local news programming was based on two criteria: local production and a focus on local issues. Here, the most obvious programs were the nightly local newscasts, as some newsmagazines may have been produced in house, but retained a national focus. In a more general study of local newscasts, the Commission drew data from secondary sources, such as the BIA/Kelsey database, Zap2It.com, and TV websites, to determine levels of local news programming on all 390 noncommercial educational (NCE) TV stations (not just PBS member stations). It found that 17 stations (4.3 percent) aired both national and local news, and 11 stations (2.8 percent) aired only local news. In total, just 28 stations (7.2 percent) out of the 390 examined aired some form of local news.

99 UNITED STATES GENERAL ACCOUNTING OFFICE, REPORT TO CONGRESSIONAL REQUESTERS, TELECOMMUNICATIONS ISSUES RELATED TO FEDERAL FUNDING FOR PUBLIC TELEVISION BY THE CORPORATION FOR PUBLIC BROADCASTING 47 (GAO-04-284) (2004) (GAO, REPORT TO CONGRESSIONAL REQUESTERS 2004), *available at* http://www.gao.gov/new.items/d04284.pdf.

100 PBS Comments at 15; *see also* GAO, REPORT TO CONGRESSIONAL REQUESTERS 2004 at 46, *available at* http://www.gao.gov/new.items/d04284.pdf.

101 William F. Baker & Evan Leatherwood, *Back to the Future: Here's A Way Public TV Can Ramp Up Local News*, CURRENT, Dec. 14, 2009, http://www.current.org/news/news0923pmmag.shtml.

102 COCHRAN, RETHINKING PUBLIC MEDIA at 32; *Public TV Kickstart*.

103 PBS Comments at i.

104 The Radio Television Digital News Association Comments in re *FOM PN*, filed May 7, 2010 (RTDNA Comments), at 8.

105 COCHRAN, RETHINKING PUBLIC MEDIA at 32.

106 PBS, Not in Our Town, http://www.pbs.org/niot/ (last visited June 29, 2010).

107 CPB, St. Louis is Facing the Mortgage Crisis, http://www.stlmortgagecrisis.org/ (last visited June 29, 2010).

108 CPB, Facing the Mortgage Crisis Final Report, http://www.fmcimpact.org/ (last visited June 29, 2010).

109 COCHRAN, RETHINKING PUBLIC MEDIA at 32.

110 Interview with Amy Shaw, Sr. V.P., Community Engagement, Nine Network of Public Media, by Cynthia Kennard, FCC (Jan.14, 2011).

111 Interview with Lynda Clarke, Dir., Television Programming Projects, PBS, by Cynthia Kennard, FCC (Jan. 21, 2011).

112 Interview with Amy Burkett, V.P., Production, WLVT, by Cynthia Kennard, FCC (Jan. 2011).

113 Email from Debbi Hinton, former CFO of KCET, to Cynthia Kennard, FCC (May 31, 2011).

114 Walker Interview 7/13/10.

115 ENGELMAN, PUBLIC RADIO AND TV at 205-06.

116 COCHRAN, RETHINKING PUBLIC MEDIA at 32.

117 PAT AUFDERHEIDE & JESSICA CLARK, PUBLIC BROADCASTING & PUBLIC AFFAIRS: OPPORTUNITIES AND CHALLENGES FOR PUBLIC BROADCASTING'S ROLE IN PROVISIONING THE PUBLIC WITH NEWS AND PUBLIC AFFAIRS 4 (Berkman Ctr. for Internet and Society at Harvard Univ.) (2008), *available at* http://cyber.law.harvard.edu/sites/cyber.law.harvard.edu/files/Public%20Broadcasting%20and%20Public%20Affairs_MR.pdf.

118 David Lumb & Patt Morrison, *KCET drops PBS, risks viewer loyalty to avoid $6.8M yearly dues*, 89.3 KPCC, Oct. 8, 2010, http://www.scpr.org/news/2010/10/08/kcet-drops-pbs-risks-viewer-loyalty-avoid-68-milli.

119 NPR's 2010 listenership was 3 percent higher than the 2009 total of 26.4 million. "Audio: Medium on the Brink of Major Change" in PEW, STATE OF NEWS MEDIA 2011, http://stateofthemedia.org/2011/audio-essay/.

120 NPR *Ex Parte* 12/3/10 at 5-6.

121 Samuel G. Freedman, *'Listener Supported' and 'NPR': All Things Considered*, N.Y. TIMES, July 17, 2005, http://www.nytimes.com/2005/07/17/books/review/17FREEDMA.html?_r=1&scp=1&sq=%22all%20things%20considered%22&st=cse; Bill Virgin, *'Morning Edition' Starts the Day Strong for NPR*, SEATTLE PI, Mar. 31, 2005, http://www.seattlepi.com/tv/218155_radiobeat31.html; JACK W. MITCHELL, LISTENER SUPPORTED: THE CULTURE AND HISTORY OF PUBLIC RADIO 175 (Praeger Publishing) (2005) (mentioning *Morning Edition* and *All Things Considered* as the second and third most listened-to radio programs in the United States).

122 CPB, PUBLIC RADIO IN THE NEW NETWORK AGE: WIDER USE, DEEPER VALUE, COMPELLING CHANGE—REPORT AND RECOMMENDATIONS OF THE PUBLIC RADIO AUDIENCE GROWTH TASK FORCE 22 (2010) (PUBLIC RADIO IN THE NEW NETWORK AGE), *available at* http://www.srg.org/GTA/Public_Radio_in_the_New_Network_Age.pdf.

123 NPR Comments at 2.

124 Of these 335, 314 were full time and 21 were part time. "Audio: Medium on the Brink of Major Change" in PEW, STATE OF NEWS MEDIA 2011.

125 NPR Comments at 3.

126 "Audio: Medium on the Brink of Major Change" in PEW, STATE OF NEWS MEDIA 2011.

127 CPB Comments at 12. "NPR also seems to have bucked the trend on podcasts, which showed just the smallest audience growth overall for the year. It has created more ways for users to consume its audio content online from streaming audio to podcasts. In December 2010, NPR reported 23.3 million downloads of its podcasts each month. That figure is up 58 percent from 2009." "Audio: Medium on the Brink of Major Change" in PEW, STATE OF NEWS MEDIA 2011.

128 "Audio: Medium on the Brink of Major Change" in PEW, STATE OF NEWS MEDIA 2011.

129 NPR Comments at 4.

130 NPR Comments at 5.

131 NPR Comments at 26.

132 Interview with Tom Thomas, C.E.O., Station Resource Group, by Cynthia Kennard, FCC (Jan. 2011) (Thomas Interview Jan. 2011).

133 NPR Comments at 7.

134 NPR Comments at 2, 6, 7, 8.

135 NPR Comments at 8.

136 Station Resource Group (SRG), *About Station Group,* http://www.srg.org/about.html (last visited Feb. 22, 2011).

137 Thomas Interview Jan. 2011.

138 NPR Comments at 8.

139 For more examples of local news and information programming produced by public radio stations, *see* NPR Comments at 8–11.

140 Local News Initiative, Local News Station Survey: Executive Summary, http://www.localnewsinitiative.org/executive.cfm (Local News Station Survey) (last visited Mar. 13, 2011).

141 Local News Station Survey.

142 Colorado Public Radio, Schedules & Links, http://www.cpr.org/article/legacy-cpr-86 (last visited Jan. 4, 2011).

143 Email from Erik Nycklemoe, Dir., Radio, Content & Media, American Public Media, to Ellen P. Goodman, FCC (Feb. 2, 2011).

144 NPR Comments at 18–19; *see also* Corporation for Public Broadcasting, *NPR Launches New Online Local Journalism Venture with CPB and Knight Foundation Funding* (press release), Oct. 2, 2009, http://www.cpb.org/pressroom/release.php?prn=776.

145 NPR Comments at 19.

146 For a complete list of examples, *see* NPR Comments at 19.

147 Email from Eric Newton, Knight Foundation, to Siddhartha Menon, FCC (May 11, 2011). The *Takeaway* was designed to attract a more diverse audience and has succeeded. It is syndicated in 60 markets, many of which are urban centers with diverse populations. The *Takeaway* has more African-American listeners, for example, than the national *Morning Edition*. COCHRAN, RETHINKING PUBLIC MEDIA at 36.

148 Elizabeth Jensen, *With Grant, NPR to Step Up State Government Reporting*, N.Y. TIMES, Oct. 17, 2010, http://www.nytimes.com/2010/10/18/business/media/18npr.html.

149 Karen Everhart, *Goal for Several Big-City Pubradio Newsrooms: 100 Reporters Each*, CURRENT, Oct. 20, 2010, http://www.current.org/news/news1019newsrooms.shtml.

150 Walker Interview 7/13/10; COCHRAN, RETHINKING PUBLIC MEDIA at 26.

151 "Audio: Traditional Broadcast & Broadcast Online, NPR" in PEW PROJ. FOR EXCELLENCE IN JOURNALISM, STATE OF THE NEWS MEDIA (2010) (PEW, STATE OF NEWS MEDIA 2010), http://stateofthemedia.org/2010/audio-summary-essay/traditional-broadcast/.

152 "Audio: Traditional Broadcast & Broadcast Online, NPR" in PEW, STATE OF NEWS MEDIA 2010.

153 New America Foundation *et al.* Comments in re *FOM PN*, filed May 7, 2010 (New America Found. Comments) at 64. While New America Foundation applauded the CPB for funding projects designed to expand local reporting, describing a "new commitment to journalism" from public broadcasting leadership, it notes that such initiatives are still not enough, and will not come close to filling the gap left by loss of nearly 13,500 newspaper jobs in the past three years. *Id.* at 93-94. Moreover, in their comments to the Commission, New America Foundation et al. recommend a "trust fund seeded with a large endowment and operated by the Corporation for Public Broadcasting (or better yet, a newly mandated Corporation for Public *Media*)." *Id.* at 95.

154 PBS Comments at 15; *see also* Karen Everhart, *CPB to Aid 7 'Local Journalism Centers:' About 50 New Employees Will Staff Stations' Specialized Regional Teams*, CURRENT, April 5, 2010, http://www.current.org/news/news1006localcenters.shtml (*CPB to Aid 7 Local Journalism Centers*).

155 *CPB to Aid 7 Local Journalism Centers*.

156 Native Public Media Comments in re *FOM PN*, filed May 7, 2010 (Native Public Media Comments) at 21; Healthy State Collaborative, http://healthystate.org/about (last visited Feb. 22, 2011); PBS Comments at 15.

157 Healthy State Collaborative, http://healthystate.org/about (last visited Feb. 22, 2011).

158 CPB Comments at 4. *See also* Native Public Media Comments at 21 (noting potential of the LJC's as collaborative partners with Native-owned stations and the National Native News, which airs from the Koahnic Broadcast Corporation and potential in expanding LJC's to include the Native American Journalism Association and Native American Public Telecommunications).

159 Katie Donnelly, *While Others Shrink, KQED Expands Cross-Platform News*, PBS MEDIA SHIFT, Aug. 25, 2010, http://www.pbs.org/mediashift/2010/08/while-others-shrink-kqed-expands-cross-platform-news237.html (*While Others Shrink*).

160 *While Others Shrink*.

161 In fact, in 2000, the Benton Foundation's report *Connecting Communities* observed that one the best practices for a public broadcaster was to partner with high-quality universities, bringing together "high-tech intellectual resources…with the digital firepower and community reach of experienced public broadcasters." BENTON FOUNDATION, CONNECTING COMMUNITIES 20 (2000), *available at* http://benton.org/sites/benton.org/files/archive_files/publibrary/pubmedia.pdf.

162 NPR Comments at 17.

163 CPB Comments at 10.

164 NPR Comments at 18.

165 STATION RESOURCE GROUP, PUBLIC RADIO AUDIENCE GROWTH TASK FORCE, PUBLIC RADIO IN THE NEW NETWORK AGE: WIDER USE, DEEPER VALUE, COMPELLING CHANGE 6 (2010) (PUBLIC RADIO IN THE NEW NETWORK AGE), *available at* http://www.srg.org/GTA/Public_Radio_in_the_New_Network_Age.pdf.

166 The Progress and Freedom Foundation Comments in re *FOM PN*, filed May 5, 2010, at 11.

167 Interview with Bill Davis, Pres. Southern California Public Radio, by Cynthia Kennard, FCC (Jan. 14, 2011).

168 *See generally Public Service Media 2.0.*

169 ALAN G. STAVITSKY & JEFFREY DVORKIN, OBJECTIVITY AND BALANCE: CONCEPTUAL AND PRACTICAL HISTORY IN AMERICAN JOURNALISM 18-19 (2008) (STAVITSKY & DVORKIN, OBJECTIVITY AND BALANCE, http://www.cpb.org/aboutcpb/goals/objectivity/whitepapers/cpb_ConceptualHistory_DvorkinStavitsky.pdf.

170 STAVITSKY & DVORKIN, OBJECTIVITY AND BALANCE at 18-19.

171 *Lauren J. Strayer, Corporation for Public Broadcasting: Building a Digital Democracy Through Public Media,* CTR. FOR AM. PROGRESS ACTION FUND 3, http://www.americanprogressaction.org/issues/2008/change-foramerica/pdf/pbs.pdf.

172 In setting forth the purposes and activities of CPB, Section 396(g)(1)(A) of the Public Broadcasting Act provides that CPB "is authorized to —

(A) facilitate the full development of public telecommunications in which programs of high quality, diversity, creativity, excellence, and innovation, which are obtained from diverse sources, will be made available to public telecommunications entities, *with strict adherence to objectivity and balance in all programs or series of programs of a controversial nature.*" (emphasis added) In 1992, Congress adopted measures to make CPB more accountable for advancing these goals. It directed CPB's Board to "review [its] existing efforts to meet its responsibility under section 396(g)(1)(A)" and, "after soliciting the views of the public, establish a comprehensive policy and set of procedures" to inform itself about the quality, diversity, creativity, excellence, innovation, objectivity, and balance of public broadcasting programming, as well as any needs not met by such programming. Pub. L. 102-356 §19. If that information reveals an unmet programming need or other area in which the programming falls short of the goals enumerated in Section 396(g)(1)(A), CPB should "take such steps in awarding programming grants… that it finds necessary to meet [its] responsibility under section 396(g)(1)(A), including facilitating objectivity and balance in programming of a controversial nature." *Id.*

The courts have held that the terms "objectivity and balance" must be viewed as "a guide to Congressional oversight policy and as a set of goals to which the Directors of CPB should aspire[,]… not a substantive standard, legally enforceable by agencies or courts." *Accuracy in Media, Inc. v. FCC*, 521 F.2d 288, 297 (D.C. Cir. 1975). In other words, Congress did not in 1992 make CPB a content police. Such a move would have been constitutionally suspect. Instead, it imposed procedural and reporting requirements designed to make it much harder for producers to make, and the networks to distribute, programming that is arguably not objective and balanced.

173 ENGELMAN, PUBLIC RADIO AND TV at 113.

174 Jeremy Egner, *The Probe: Unilateral Actions Exceeded Chair's Authority*, CURRENT, Nov. 21, 2005, http://www.current.org/cpb/cpb0521iig.shtml (*Unilateral Actions Exceeded Chair's Authority*). A six-month internal investigation found that Tomlinson had inappropriately meddled in programming decisions, made hiring decisions based on political considerations, and ignored contracting guidelines in his efforts to expunge a perceived liberal bias from public broadcasting.

175 Laura Leslie, *UNC-TV, Alcoa, and "The Don"*, NORTH CAROLINA PUBLIC RADIO—WUNC, Aug. 17, 2010, http://wunc.org/programs/news/Isaac-Hunters-Tavern/unc-tv-alcoa-and-the-don; *See, e.g.,* Dru Sefton,

Pubcasters Keep Funds in Some State Budgets, CURRENT, June 21, 2010, http://www.current.org/funding/funding1011state.shtml.

176 *See, e.g.,* Reed Irvine, *Give Up On Public Broadcasting*, WALL ST. J., Mar. 28, 1986 ("The entire public broadcasting bureaucracy is so insulated from the market, from public opinion and even from the legislators who vote its funding that there is little chance that it will be depoliticized"); STARR, AIR WARS at 30-31(recounting significant pressure and criticism for the "liberal bias" of PBS programming); ENGELMAN, PUBLIC RADIO AND TV, at 110–11 (describing heated criticisms during the Reagan administration accusing NPR of being too liberal); LAURENCE JARVIK, PBS: BEHIND THE SCREEN 198-201 (1997) (recounting criticisms in the 1980s that PBS programs had a liberal bias and were not open to other perspectives).

177 Bill O'Reilly, *Why is NPR Getting Our Money?*, BILLOREILLY.COM, Oct. 328, 2010, http://www.billoreilly.com/newslettercolumn?pid=30459.

178 David Brooks, *Campaign Cash*, PBS NEWSHOUR, Oct. 22, 2010 (transcript), http://www.pbs.org/newshour/bb/politics/july-dec10/shields-brooks_10-22.html.

179 Steve Coll, *Why Fox News Should Fund NPR*, WASH. POST, Oct. 29, 2010, http://www.washingtonpost.com/wp-dyn/content/article/2010/10/29/AR2010102904336.html.

180 Prepared Testimony of Randolph J. May, Pres., The Free State Foundation, FCC Workshop on the Future of Media and the Information Needs of Communities: Public and Other Noncommercial Media in the Digital Era (Apr. 30, 2010), at 2, *available at* http://reboot.fcc.gov/c/document_library/get_file?uuid=4df8b6fe-52a2-4a05-916c-fc74f4a9d7ec&groupId=101236.

181 CENSUS OF JOURNALISTS IN PUBLIC RADIO AND TELEVISION, DELIVERABLE #3 at 12.

182 PBS Comments at 14.

183 PBS Comments at 5.

184 PBS Comments at 14; "Network News: Durability & Decline" in PEW, STATE OF NEWS MEDIA 2011 NewsHour's website received an average of 669,000 unique monthly views in 2009. "In addition, NewsHour creates about 140 monthly podcasts that 1.1 million people download." *Id.*

185 PBS Comments at 19.

186 Seiken Email 10/29/10.

187 CPB Comments at 11.

188 CPB Comments at 4–5.

189 CPB Comments at 11.

190 PBS Comments at 19.

191 *See, e.g.*, New America Found. Comments (describing how the Commission's current decision not to include multicast signals in digital must-carry provisions will discourage investment on content, and dampen creative and innovative uses over, these secondary programming streams).

192 PBS Comments at 20.

193 NPR Comments at 36–37.

194 CPB Comments at 12.

195 NPR Comments at 22.

196 Public Insight Network, American Public Media, http://www.publicinsightnetwork.org/ (last visited May 11, 2011).

403

197 Testimony of William H. Kling, Pres. and C.E.O., American Public Media, Workshop on the Future of Media & Information Needs of Communities: Public and Other Noncommercial Media in the Digital Era (Apr. 30, 2010) (transcript), at 384:15-22; 385:1-7, *available at* http://reboot.fcc. gov/c/document_library/get_file?uuid=5272966f-441c-48dd-9c66-a6c8b1f8cc5d&groupId=101236.

198 Email from William H. Kling to Ellen P. Goodman and Steve Waldman, FCC (June 3, 2010).

199 Email from Roger LaMay, General Manager, WXPN Public Radio, to David Cohen, FCC (June 23, 2010) (LaMay Email 6/23/10).

200 LaMay Email 6/23/10 .

201 Email from Jon C. Brendsel, V.P., Product Development, PBS Interactive, to Ellen P. Goodman, FCC (June 14, 2010). Brendsel estimates that the average visitor to COVE, the PBS video streaming portal, watches approximately 3 videos per month, with an average viewing time of 1 hour per month. This translates to approximately 1.39-cents/hour in streaming costs incurred by PBS. For the month of May 2010, approximately 1.3 million hours of video were streamed, amounting to roughly $20,000 for video streaming.

202 Memorandum Summary of Trends in Online Delivery Costs, from Eric Wolf, Project Executive, PBS, to Jason Seiken, Sr. V.P., Interactive, PBS & John McCoskey, Chief Technology Officer, PBS (July 26, 2010) (Summary of Trends in Online Delivery Costs), at 3.

203 Summary of Trends in Online Delivery Costs at 3.

204 Summary of Trends in Online Delivery Costs at 2–3.

205 For discussion of these potential practices, *see Preserving the Open Internet*, Report & Order, 25 FCC Rcd 17905 (2010). As a general matter, it is unlikely that pay for priority [by a fixed broadband provider] would satisfy the 'no unreasonable discrimination' standard under the Commission's Open Internet Order. *Id.* at 76.

206 *See, e.g.*, Letter from William H. Kling, Pres. & C.E.O., American Public Media, to Julius Genachowski, Chairman, FCC, GN Docket No. 09-191 (filed Sept. 16, 2010), at 3–5.

207 *See* Stephanie Strom, *Donations Ban on iPhone Apps Irritates Nonprofits*, N.Y. TIMES, Dec. 8, 2010, http://www.nytimes.com/2010/12/09/technology/09charity.html; Jake Shapiro, *Apple's No-Donation Policy for Apps is a Cop-Out*, ARS TECHNICA, June 4, 2010, http://arstechnica.com/apple/news/2010/06/nonprofit-developer-apples-no-donation-policy-is-a-cop-out.ars.

208 CPB APPROPRIATION REQUEST AND JUSTIFICATION at 18-22.

209 CPB-defined multi-provider markets:

Atlanta, Georgia Public Broadcasting*, WPBA Philadelphia, WHYY*, WYBEChicago, WTTW*, WYCC, WYIN Salt Lake City, KUEN*, KBYU, KUED Denver, KRMA*, KBDI San Francisco, KQED*, KCSM, KRCB Los Angeles, KCET*, KLCS, KOCE, KVCR San Juan, WIPR*, WMTJ, Miami, WPBT*, WLRN Seattle/Tacoma, KCTS*, KBTC New Orleans, WYES*, WLAE Tampa, WEDU*, WUSF New York, WNET/WLIW*, WNYE Washington D.C., WETA*, WHUT, Orlando, WMFE*, WBCC, WCEU*Primary station

210 Email from Michael Levy, Exec. V.P., Corporate & Public Affairs, CPB, to Ellen P. Goodman, FCC staff (Jan. 11, 2010) (Levy Email 1/11/10).

211 Public Radio Capital Comments in re *FOM PN*, filed May 7, 2010 (Public Radio Capital Comments) at 2.

212 Email from William H. Kling, Pres. and C.E.O., American Public Media, to Ellen P. Goodman, FCC (July 28, 2010).

213 Levy Email 1/11/10.

214 CPB BOARD OF DIRECTORS, 2010 CSG REVIEW MANAGEMENT RECOMMENDATIONS AS REVISED BY THE CPB BOARD (2010), *available at* http://www.cpb.org/aboutcpb/leadership/board/resolutions/100922_TV_2010CSG_Recommendations.pdf.

215 Public Radio Capital Comments at 3.

216 COCHRAN, RETHINKING PUBLIC MEDIA at 46.

217 FCC analysis based on FCC database of license holders:

TELEVISION			
	Licensees	**Grantees**	**Stations**
Community	87	87	145
Local Authority	8	8	8
State	19	19	121
University	57	57	94
Total	171	171	368

RADIO			
	Licensees	**Grantees**	**Stations**
Community	160	171	367
Local Authority	29	29	46
State	12	15	79
University	187	199	442
Total	388	414	934

218 Email from Michael Levy, Exec. V.P., Corporate & Public Affairs, CPB, to Ellen P. Goodman, FCC (Feb. 2, 2011).

219 UNC-TV, licensed to the University of North Carolina, complied with a legislative request for reporters' notes, footage, etc. rather than use the state's journalist "shield law." *See, e.g.*, Greg Collard, *UNC-TV Endures Month of Controversy*, WFAE 90.7 FM, July 26, 2010, http://www.wfae.org/wfae/1_87_316.cfm?action=display&id=6336. Update: Mississippi Public Broadcasting made a controversial decision to remove (and then restore) *Fresh Air*. *See* Jim Romenesko, *Update: MPB Says It Dropped 'Fresh Air' Over Interviews of 'Explicit Sexual Nature'*, THE POYNTER INSTITUTE, July 15, 2010, http://www.poynter.org/column.asp?id=45&aid=186959.

220 STATION RESOURCE GROUP, GOVERNANCE: A FIRST REPORT (2002) (SRG, GOVERNANCE), http://www.srg.org/governance/report1.html; COCHRAN, RETHINKING PUBLIC MEDIA at 43-44.

221 *See, e.g.*, Email from Terry Clifford, Co-C.E.O., Station Resource Group (SRG), to Ellen P. Goodman, FCC (July 28, 2010) (Clifford Email 7/28/10) ("We know there are problems at many institutional licensees that consistently hold public media back. Personnel structures that are out of sync with media pay scales and do not allow for competitive hiring, union requirements designed for schools or other state agencies, bosses who place a much higher priority on the other departments they oversee, the unpredictability of new presidents and vice-presidents, and the challenge of providing a mass media community service inside of an institution whose core business is serving a very specific and limited demographic group.").

222 Public Radio News Directors Incorporated, PRNDI Awards, http://www. prndi.org/prndiWinners.html (last visited Apr. 10, 2011).

223 *See, e.g.,* SRG, GOVERNANCE (identifying the characteristics of good governance for NCE licensees). *See also* Email from Steven Bass, Pres., Oregon Public Broadcasting, to Ellen P. Goodman, FCC (July 28, 2010) (citing examples of governance changes that significantly improved performance at Nashville Public Television, which moved from school board to community licensee, and WNYC, which moved from municipal New York City ownership to community licensee).

224 Clifford Email 7/28/10.

225 Letter from William H. Kling, Pres. and C.E.O., American Public Media, to Steven Waldman, FCC (Nov. 1, 2010).

226 Interview with Rod Bates, General Manager, Nebraska Educational Telecommunications Network, by Ellen P. Goodman, FCC (Feb. 21, 2011).

227 PUBLIC RADIO IN THE NEW NETWORK AGE at 20.

228 BENTON FOUND., WHAT'S GOING ON IN COMMUNITY MEDIA 9 (2007) (BENTON, WHAT'S GOING ON), *available at* http://benton.org/sites/benton.org/files/CMReport.pdf.

229 CPB, National Minority Consortia, http://www.cpb.org/aboutpb/consortia.html (last visited Apr. 10, 2011).

230 FREE PRESS, NEW PUBLIC MEDIA at 34–38.

231 PUBLIC RADIO IN THE NEW NETWORK AGE at 13.

232 MICHAEL P. MCCAULEY, NPR: THE TRIALS AND TRIUMPHS OF NATIONAL PUBLIC RADIO 115 (Columbia University Press) (2005) (based on the *NPR Profile 2004* from the Mediamark Research Doublebase 2003/ Spring 2003/Fall 2003 MRI studies).

233 "Audio: Traditional Broadcast & Broadcast Online, NPR" in PEW, STATE OF NEWS MEDIA 2010.

234 PBS, What you Need to Know, Sept. 22, 2010, available at http://www. pbs.org/about/corporate-information/mission

235 *See* PBS, An Overview, July 2008, available at www-tc.pbs.org/teacherline/media/pdf/.../pbs_corporate_overview.pdf.

236 Email from Jason Seiken, PBS, to Ellen P. Goodman, FCC, (Sept. 2, 2010) (based on Quantcast data from May 2010, reporting an index of 118 and 141 for African-Americans visiting PBS.org and PBSkids.org, and an index of 122 and 210 for Hispanics visiting PBS.org and PBSkids.org, where 100 equals the average for U.S. web sites).

237 Quantcast, May 2010.

238 CENSUS OF JOURNALISTS IN PUBLIC RADIO AND TELEVISION, DELIVERABLE #3 at 10 (2010).

239 U.S. CENSUS BUREAU, 2010 CENSUS DATA, *available at* http://2010.census. gov/2010census/data/index.php. We came up with this figure by subtracting the "White alone" population count from 100 percent.

240 National Federation of Community Broadcasters Comments in re *FOM PN*, filed May 10, 2010 (NFCB Comments) at iv, 12.

241 NFCB Comments at 2, 12.

242 Corporation for Public Broadcasting, 47 U.S.C. Sec. 396 (6) ("it is in the public interest to encourage the development of programming that involves creative risks and that addresses the needs of unserved and underserved audiences, particularly children and minorities"); *see also* 47 U.S.C. Sec. 396 (8) ("public television and radio stations and public telecommunications services constitute valuable local community

resources for utilizing electronic media to address national concerns and solve local problems through community programs and outreach programs").

243 Association of Independents in Radio (AIR) & Jessica Clark of American University Center for Social Media Comments, *Spreading the Zing: Reimagining Public Media Through the Makers Quest 2.0,* in re *FOM PN,* filed May 11, 2010 (*Spreading the Zing*) at 1.

244 *Public Service Media 2.0,* AND COMMUNICATIONS FOR ALL at 270 (*citing* Chris Johnson, *Federal Support of Public Broadcasting: Not Quite What LBJ Had in Mind,* 8 COMMLAW CONSPECTUS 135, 138-40 (2000) (criticizing public television for political bias and a failure to garner a larger audience); Howard White, *Fine Tuning the Federal Government's Role in Public Broadcasting,* 46 FED. COMM. L.J. 491, 501-03, 513 (1994)).

245 *Spreading the Zing* at 1.

246 *Spreading the Zing* at 2. The Center for Social Media has said that these methods can only be developed with iterative and broad stakeholder input. It recommends that the Commission help develop standards for use by federal agencies involved in public service media work.

Public service media entities are currently working with Silicon Valley technologists to develop a dashboard that would map the transmission of public service media content, via social and other networks in the cloud. Some believe metrics should go farther to capture what further steps users take with content to measure engagement.

247 JESSICA CLARK & TRACY VAN SLYKE, INVESTING IN IMPACT: MEDIA SUMMITS REVEAL PRESSING NEEDS, TOOLS FOR EVALUATING PUBLIC INTEREST MEDIA 1(2010), *available at* http://www.centerforsocialmedia.org/sites/default/files/documents/pages/Investing_in_Impact.pdf (quoting Vince Lampone, *Listeners Take Action Based on What They Hear on NPR Stations,* Go Figure Blog (April 1, 2011, 9:00 AM), http://www.npr.org/blogs/gofigure/2010/03/31/125422530/listeners-take-action-based-on-what-they-hear-on-npr); *See also* Media Consortium Comments in re *FOM PN,* filed May 6, 2010, at 1.

248 CPB, Facing the Mortgage Financial Crisis, http://www.fmcimpact. org/?page_id=63 (last visited Feb. 17, 2011).

249 CHARLES P. GOLDFARB, CONGRESSIONAL RESEARCH SERVICE, PUBLIC, EDUCATIONAL AND GOVERNMENT (PEG) ACCESS CABLE TELEVISION CHANNELS: ISSUES FOR CONGRESS 1 (2008), *available at* http://www. millervaneaton.com/00142081.pdf (PEG CHANNELS: ISSUES FOR CONGRESS); American Community Television, Inc. Comments in re *FOM PN,* filed May 7, 2010 (Amer. Community TV Comments) at i, 3.

250 Email from Paul Giguere, Pres., NAPAN/President and C.E.O., The Connecticut Network, to Simon Banyai, FCC (Sept. 14, 2010) (Giguere Email 9/14/10). NAPAN identifies 16 states as having an "independent" SPAN in the sense that a distinct operating unit manages the network: Alaska, Arizona, California, Colorado, Connecticut, Florida, Illinois, Michigan, Montana, Nebraska, Ohio, Oregon, Pennsylvania, South Carolina, Washington, and Wisconsin. NAPAN identifies 12 of these SPANs as receiving state funding. These 12 SPANs are located in Alaska, Arizona, Colorado, Connecticut, Florida, Illinois, Montana, Nebraska, Ohio, Oregon, South Carolina, and Washington. *Id.*

Research by the FCC staff found that, as of December 20, 2010, 23 states and the District of Columbia—24 jurisdictions overall—broadcast/multicast or cablecast varying amounts of live coverage of their branches of government—with a primary focus on the legislative branch. In addition to the District of Columbia, the states in which such services are provided are: Alaska, Arizona, California, Colorado, Connecticut, Florida, Hawaii, Idaho, Illinois, Kentucky, Michigan, Minnesota, Montana, Nebraska, New Jersey, New York, Ohio, Oregon, Pennsylvania, Rhode Island, South Carolina, Washington, and Wisconsin. As noted above, NAPAN counts entities in only 16 of these states as SPANs.

251 National Association of Public Affairs Networks Comments in re *FOM PN*, filed June 30, 2010 (NAPAN Comments) at 14.

252 Interview with Paul Giguere by FCC staff (Sept. 7, 2010) (Giguere Interview 9/7/10).

253 *See, e.g.,* Goodman, *Public Service Media 2.0,* AND COMMUNICATIONS FOR ALL at 270; Goodman & Chen, Digital Public Media Networks (proposing amendment of Public Broadcasting Act to become Public Media Act); DOWNIE & SCHUDSON, RECONSTRUCTION OF AMERICAN JOURNALISM; COCHRAN, RETHINKING PUBLIC MEDIA; COLL, REBOOT: AN OPEN LETTER TO THE FCC at 33.

254 Testimony of Dr. Ernest Wilson III, Chair, CPB, Workshop on the Future of Media & Information Needs of Communities: Public and Other Noncommercial Media in the Digital Era (Apr. 30, 2010), Tr. at 32:8-17, *available at* http://reboot.fcc.gov/c/document_library/get_file?uuid=5272966f-441c-48dd-9c66-a6c8b1f8cc5d&groupId=101236.

7 PEG Access

1 N.E. FELDMAN, CABLE TELEVISION: OPPORTUNITIES AND PROBLEMS IN LOCAL PROGRAM ORIGINATION 10 (1970) (FELDMAN, CABLE TELEVISION), *available at* www.rand.org/pubs/reports/2006/R570.pdf.

2 FELDMAN, CABLE TELEVISION at 28-30.

3 Donna L. King & Christopher Mele, *Making Public Access Television: Community Participation, Media Literacy and the Public Sphere,* 43 J. OF BROADCASTING & ELECTRONIC MEDIA 608 (1999) (*Making Public Access Television*).

4 LAURA R. LINDER, PUBLIC ACCESS TELEVISION: AMERICA'S ELECTRONIC SOAPBOX 5 (Praeger) (1999) (LINDER, PUBLIC ACCESS TELEVISION).

5 LINDER, PUBLIC ACCESS TELEVISION at 5.; *Making Public Access Television.*

6 *Denver Area Educational Telecommunications Consortium v. FCC,* 518 U.S. 727, 788 (1996), *citing* Wally Mueller, Note, *Controversial Programming on Cable Television's Public Access Channels: The Limits of Governmental Response,* 38 DEPAUL L. REV. 1051, 1061 (1989).

7 PATRICIA AUFDERHEIDE, THE DAILY PLANET: A CRITIC ON THE CAPITALIST CULTURE BEAT 121-72 (Univ. of Minnesota Press) (2000) (AUFDERHEIDE, THE DAILY PLANET).; Email from Bunnie Riedel, Exec. Dir., Alliance for Community Media to Christopher Ali, FCC (June 15, 2010).

8 PEG CHANNELS: ISSUES FOR CONGRESS at 1.

9 Alliance for Community Media Comments in re *FOM PN*, filed May 21, 2010 (Alliance for Community Media Comments), at 14-17.

10 Interview with Rob McCausland, Dir., Information and Organizing Services, Alliance for Community Media, by Ellen P. Goodman, FCC (June 24, 2010).

11 Mapping Access, http://mappingaccess.org/ (last visited Apr. 10, 2011). Alabama does report two government access channels in Brewton and Gadsden, and Mississippi reports one, TV23, in Vicksburg.

12 Amer. Community TV Comments at 3, n.1 (explaining that because Massachusetts state law requires most of the franchises be used for PEG, there are about 106 access centers and 250 access channels in the state).

13 *See, e.g.,* Letter from John A. Rocco, Pres., American Community Television, Inc., to Marlene Dortch, Secretary, FCC, MB Docket No. 09-13 (filed Sept. 28, 2010).

14 Amer. Community TV Comments at 3 (including both capital and operating expenses, such as equipment and salaries, into the total budget).

15 *See, e.g.,* LINDER, PUBLIC ACCESS TELEVISION at 35 ("Most often public access television is managed in one of three ways: by the local government, by the cable operator, or by a nonprofit agency created for that purpose."). The governing New York State law, for example, requires that all "cable television franchisee[s] ... designate channel capacity for PEG access" and defines a "public access channel" as "a channel designated for noncommercial use by the public on a first-come, first-served, nondiscriminatory basis" provided prospective programmers meet certain competency and eligibility requirements. N.Y. COMP.CODES R. & REGS. tit. 9, §§ 595.4(b), 595.4(a)(1).

16 H.R. REP. NO. 98-934, *as reprinted in* 1984 U.S.C.C.A.N. 4655, 4667 (1984).

17 Amer. Community TV Comments at 3-5.

18 Alliance for Community Media Comments at 15.

19 In fact, Salem is reportedly the largest state capital community without local broadcast TV. Capital Community Television Comments in re *FOM PN*, filed May 5, 2010 (Capital Community TV Comments) at 2.

20 Capital Community TV Comments at 7.

21 Interview with Linda K. Ain, The Law Firm of Linda K. Ain (for Pikeville, KY), by FCC Staff (July 13, 2010).

22 Alliance for Communications Democracy Comments in re *FOM PN*, filed April 23, 2010 (Alliance for Communications Democracy Comments) at 4.

23 *See* BENTON FOUNDATION 17.

24 Saint Paul Neighborhood Network Comments in re *FOM PN*, filed May 7, 2010 (St. Paul Network Comments) at 9.

25 Cambridge Community Television Comments in re *FOM PN*, filed Apr. 28, 2010 at 2.

26 Media Bridges Cincinnati, Inc. Comments in re *FOM PN*, filed May 6, 2010 (Media Bridges Cincinnati Comments) at 3.

27 Amer. Community TV Comments at 7.

28 Amer. Community TV Comments at 20; Interview with Laurie Cirivello, Exec. Dir., Grand Rapids Community Media Center, by FCC staff (July 27, 2010) (Cirivello Interview 7/27/10).

29 Cirivello Interview 7/27/10; Reentry Resource Center, http://www.reentryhelp.org/ (last visited Feb. 11, 2010). Programs such as "Verified Resume" teach urban teens video production skills and "soft skills" such as responsibility, working with cultural diversity, acquiring and evaluating information, creativity, listening, and teamwork.

30 BENTON, WHAT'S GOING ON at 23; *see also* Grand Rapids Community Media Center, What is MoLLIE?, http://www.grcmc.org/education/mollie.php (last visited Feb. 11, 2010).

31 Media Bridges Cincinnati Comments at 1.

32 Email from Tom Bishop, Exec. Dir., Media Bridges Cincinnati, Inc., to Christopher Ali, FCC staff (July 29, 2010) (Bishop Email 7/29/10).

33 Alliance for Communications Democracy Comments at 2.

34 St. Paul Network Comments at 5; *see also* BENTON, WHAT'S GOING ON at 17.

35 Alliance for Communications Democracy Comments at 8.

36 Lewisboro (NY) Community Television Comments in re *FOM PN*, filed May 7, 2010, at 5.

37 Amer. Community TV Comments at 9.

38 Josh Goodman, *Unscripted Ending: The Picture Gets Blurry for Public Access Television,* GOVERNING, Jan. 31, 2008, http://www.governing.com/topics/technology/Unscripted-Ending.html (*Unscripted Ending*); *see also Making Public Access Television* at 604.

39 *See, e.g.,* LINDER, PUBLIC ACCESS TELEVISION at 11. The Klan subsequently sued the city for violating the First Amendment, with the court ruling in their favor. *See Missouri Knights of the Ku Klux Klan v. Kansas City, Mo.*, 723 F.Supp. 1347 (W.D. Mo. 1989).

40 Alliance for Communications Democracy Comments at 6. Many public access operations across the country require potential producers to attend courses and pay membership dues in order to have their programs aired by the station. While public access programming is protected under the First Amendment, most PEG programmers require that programs adhere to local standards and that adult material is properly labeled and can be scheduled from 10 p.m. to 6 a.m. and meet technical requirements such as tape or DVD formatting, length, sound quality, etc.

41 These bulletin boards provide information on such topics as school closings and lunch menus; local transportation alerts; health screenings; local resources for assistance (such as food banks and senior services); jobs postings; nonprofit services and events; government meeting schedules; recycling; and community sponsored events. Amer. Community TV Comments at 6–7.

42 For instance, the Charlotte, NC access center airs the local Radio Reading Service during its bulletin board programming from 2 p.m. to 3:30 p.m. on weekdays. Amer. Community TV Comments at 19.

43 *See, e.g.,* LINDER, PUBLIC ACCESS TELEVISION at 37.

44 Amer. Community TV Comments at 6–7.

45 Alliance for Communications Democracy Comments at 5.

46 City of Dallas, Texas, General Fund: Statement of Revenues and Expenditures 2009-2010, *available at* http://www.dallascityhall.com/Budget/adopted0910/FinancialSummaries.pdf; Prepared Testimony of Carole Post, Commissioner, Department of Information Technology and Telecommunications, New York City, before the New York City Council Committees on Land Use and Technology (Mar. 11, 2010), at 3, *available at* http://www.nyc.gov/html/doitt/downloads/pdf/doitt_prelim_budget_testimony_fy2011.pdf. These fees include fees from other retail services such as telephone and gas and electricity. General franchise fees were projected to raise more than $500 million in FY 2008 among Texas's 10 largest cities. BILL PEACOCK, TEXAS POLICY FOUND., FRANCHISE FEES: 2009-2010 LEGISLATOR'S GUIDE TO THE ISSUES 1 (2008), *available at* http://www.texaspolicy.com/pdf/2008-LegeEntry-FranchiseFees-bp.pdf.

47 47 U.S.C. § 542(h)(2)(i) ("Any Federal agency may not regulate the amount of the franchise fees paid by a cable operator, or regulate the use of funds derived from such fees, except as provided in this section.").

48 Alliance for Communications Democracy Comments at 11 (describing reduced support for public access from franchise fees, which can go instead to cities).

49 City and County of San Francisco Comments in re *FOM PN*, filed May

50 Email from Jennifer Gilomen, Dir., Public Media Strategies, Bay Area Video Coalition, to Ellen P. Goodman, FCC (July 1, 2010). The number is based on a revenue of $700,000 for capital costs and $170,000 for operating costs to public access, out of roughly $10 to $12 million of franchise fees per year to the City of San Francisco.

7, 2010 (San Francisco Comments) at 6–7; The Digital Infrastructure and Video Competition Act of 2006, CAL. PUB. UTIL. CODE § 5800 *et seq*. (2009). The Act codified local government authority to require operators to provide PEG channels and support fees, but adds no provisions for funding operating costs, such as salaries and benefits, and states only that those fees must be used in a way "consistent with federal law." CAL. PUB. UTIL. CODE § 5870(n). The provision thus reduces franchise fees only for capital costs, such as facilities and equipment.

51 Alliance for Communications Democracy Comments at 12.

52 *See, e.g.,* Reed Johnson, *Cable Flips Channel on Public Access TV*, L.A. TIMES, Jan. 5, 2009, http://articles.latimes.com/2009/jan/05/entertainment/et-publicaccess5 (*Cable Flips Channel*) (reporting the closing of 12 public access studios in Los Angeles as a bellwether of future PEG closings across the nation); *Unscripted Ending* (stating that in the aftermath of statewide franchises PEG channels are losing funding, studio space, or being shut down altogether, and adding that the future of public access TV as "more uncertain…than at any time since its inception in the 1970s").

53 THE BUSKE GROUP, ANALYSIS OF RECENT PEG ACCESS CENTER CLOSURES, FUNDING CUTBACKS AND RELATED THREATS 2 (2011) (prepared for the Alliance for Communications Democracy), *available at* http://theacd.org/uploaded_docs/2011_PEG_Access_study.pdf.

54 Amer. Community TV Comments at 15.

55 The Digital Infrastructure and Video Competition Act of 2006, CAL. PUB. UTIL. CODE § 5800 (2009); *Cable Flips Channel*.

56 Alliance for Communications Democracy Comments at 13.

57 PEG CHANNELS: ISSUES FOR CONGRESS at 6.

58 *Petition for Declaratory Ruling of the Alliance for Community Media et al.*, MB Docket No. 09-13 (filed Jan. 30, 2009), at 11–12.

59 Letter from James K. Smith, Assistant Vice President, Federal Regulatory, AT7T, to Marlene Dortch, FCC, June 11, 2009.

60 Amer. Community TV Comments at 10.

61 In January 2008, several Michigan communities filed a lawsuit against Comcast for its plan to move PEG channels from analog basic to digital basic. The parties settled the lawsuit, and Comcast will continue delivering PEG channels in Michigan in analog format on its basic cable package until the system goes all digital, or a particular community agrees to allow PEG channels to be provided in a digital programming tier. *See* Motion to Withdraw Petition For Declaratory Ruling of Dearborn, Michigan, *et al.,* in *Petition for Declaratory Ruling Regarding Primary Jurisdiction Referral in City of Dearborn et al. v. Comcast of Michigan III., Inc et al.*, MB Docket No. 09-13, filed Feb. 24, 2010, at 1–2.

62 Email from Jan Schaffer, Exec. Dir., J-lab, to Ellen P. Goodman, FCC (Nov. 2, 2010).

63 In Georgia, Texas and Michigan, PEG channels are required to provide at least eight hours of non-repeat programming content daily. PEG operators are concerned that cable operators will seize on these requirements to reallocate PEG channels and withhold funding. Indeed, in Texas, with the reduction of funding, some PEG channels "have dipped below the 8 hour programming requirement and were taken off the air." For instance, in 2006 Time Warner stopped airing San Antonio Public Access because the channel could no longer meet the 8-hour non-repeat daily programming requirement. CTR. FOR SCIENCE TECHNOLOGY & PUBLIC POLICY, HUBERT H. HUMPHREY INSTITUTE OF PUBLIC AFFAIRS, UNIV. OF MINNESOTA, STATEWIDE VIDEO FRANCHISING LEGISLATION: A COMPARATIVE STUDY OF OUTCOMES IN TEXAS, CALIFORNIA AND MICHIGAN 13, 21 (2009).

64 *See* BENTON, WHAT'S GOING ON at 12, 21 (noting the strategy of collaboration as a way to engage the breadth and diversity of a local community); *see also* RICHARD SOMERSET-WARD, BENTON FOUND., CONNECTING COMMUNITIES 18 (2000) (CONNECTING COMMUNITIES), *available at* http://www.benton.org/sites/benton.org/files/archive_files/publibrary/pubmedia.pdf (noting how alliances between community media providers and community institutions can create platforms of service to their communities).

65 Media Bridges Cincinnati Comments at 4.

66 Letter from Tom Glaisyer and Jessica Clark to Steven Waldman, FCC (October, 2010).

67 Interview with Gretjen Clausing, Exec. Dir., PhillyCAM by FCC staff (Aug. 6, 2010); Bishop Email 7/29/10; Cirivello Interview 7/27/10; Email from Bunnie Riedel, Exec. Dir., American Community Television to FCC (July 8, 2010); Interview with Rob McCausland, Dir., Information and Organizing Svcs., Alliance for Community Media, by FCC staff (June 24, 2010); Interviews with Bunnie Riedel; John Rocco, Exec. Dir., TV Access21 (Charlotte, NC); Mauro DePasquale, Exec. Dir. and Station Manager, WCCA-TV (Worcester, MA); Kathie Pohl, Director of Marketing and Community Relations Manager, Mentor Channel (Mentor, OH); Dennis Riggs, Dir., HEC-TV (St. Louis, MO); Barry Verrill, Exec. Dir., KLTV (Cowlitz County, WA); and Frank Bluestein, Exec. Producer, GHS-TV (Germantown, TN) by Christopher Ali, FCC (May 20, 2010).

68 *See, e.g.,* MARTHA FUENTES-BAUTISTA, BEYOND TELEVISION: THE DIGITAL TRANSITION OF PUBLIC ACCESS (2009); *Unscripted Ending*; PEG CHANNELS: ISSUES FOR CONGRESS; BENTON, WHAT'S GOING ON; S. Braman, *The Ideal vs. the Real in Media Localism: Regulatory Implications,* 12 COMM. LAW & POLICY 231 (2007); Kevin Howley, *Manhattan Neighborhood Network: Community Access Television and the Public Sphere in the 1990s,* 25 HISTORICAL JOURNAL OF FILM, RADIO & TELEVISION 119 (2005); Hillel Nossek, *Active Research as a Bridge between Theory and Practice: A Suggested Model for Playing an Active Role in Organizing Community Television as a Tool of Empowerment in the Community,* 28 EUROPEAN J. OF COMM. RESEARCH 305 (Sept. 2003); Elinor Rennie, *"Trespassers are Welcome": Access and Community Television Policy,* 10 JAVNOST-THE PUBLIC 49 (2003); Thomas Werner, *A Round "PEG" for a Round Hole: Advocating for the Town of Oyster Bay's Public Access Channel Restrictions,* 56 FED. COMM. L. J. 239 (2003); Anita Gallucci, *Making the Most of the Cable Television Franchise Renewal Process,* THE MUNICIPALITY 122, 126 (2002); Seung Kwan Ryu, *Reassessing Cable Access Channel Requirements Under Deregulation,* 24 COMM. & THE LAW Sept. 2002 at 47; John W. Higgins, *Community Television and the Vision of Media Literacy, Social Action and Empowerment,* 43 J. OF BROADCASTING & ELECTRONIC MEDIA 624 (1999); Randy Jacobs & William Yousman, *Understanding Cable Television Community Access Viewership,* 16 COMM. RESEARCH REPORTS 305 (1999); *Making Public Access Television.*

69 Grand Rapids Community Media Center, The Rapidian, http://therapidian.org/about (last visited Feb. 15, 2011).

70 Cirivello Interview 7/27/10.

71 Bay Area Video Coalition (BAVC), Proposal for Renaissance Journalism Center's Media Greenhouse Grant Program: n3 (neighborhood news network), Jan. 8, 2010 (Neighborhood News Network), at 2.

72 Neighborhood News Network at 2.

73 St. Paul Network Comments at 3.

74 Alliance for Communications Democracy Comments at 2.

75 Interview with Norris Chumley, Chair, and Dan Coughlin, Exec. Dir., Manhattan Neighborhood Network, by Steven Waldman, FCC (Sept. 28, 2010).

76 Alliance for Community Media Comments at 13.

77 J.H. SNIDER, NEW MEDIA AND DEMOCRATIC ACCOUNTABILITY: THE GROWTH OF GOVERNMENT ACCESS TV 4, 19 (1998) (SNIDER, NEW MEDIA AND DEMOCRATIC ACCOUNTABILITY), http://www.jhsnider.net/MyWritings/98-04—MPSA—NewMediaAndDemocraticAccountability—GrowthOfGovernmentAccessTV.pdf.

78 SNIDER, NEW MEDIA AND DEMOCRATIC ACCOUNTABILITY at 1.

79 NAPAN Comments at 6; Jessica Durkin, Tom Glaisyer & Kara Hadge, AN INFORMATION COMMUNITY CASE STUDY: SEATTLE 2.1 (Media Policy Initiative, New America Found.) (2010), *available at* http://mediapolicy.newamerica.net/sites/newamerica.net/files/policydocs/SeattleCaseStudy.pdf (SEATTLE CASE STUDY).

80 SEATTLE CASE STUDY.

81 Email from Bunnie Riedel, Exec. Dir., American Community Television to Christopher Ali, FCC (July 23, 2010); *see also* Alliance for Community Media Comments at 4.

82 SNIDER, NEW MEDIA AND DEMOCRATIC ACCOUNTABILITY at 21–22.

83 Howard Troxler, *With Less Cable Access, Door to Open Government Closes,* ST. PETERSBURG TIMES, Jan. 3, 2006, http://www.sptimes.com/2006/01/03/Columns/With_less_cable_acces.shtml (*With Less Cable Access*).

84 *With Less Cable Access.*

85 SNIDER, NEW MEDIA AND DEMOCRATIC ACCOUNTABILITY at 21.

86 SNIDER, NEW MEDIA AND DEMOCRATIC ACCOUNTABILITY at 19.

87 SNIDER, NEW MEDIA AND DEMOCRATIC ACCOUNTABILITY at 33 n.10.

88 Alliance for Communications Democracy Comments at 12.

89 Alliance for Communications Democracy Comments at 12.

90 San Francisco Comments at 8.

8 SPANs

1 *Annual Assessment of the Status of Competition in the Market for the Delivery of Video Programming*, Thirteenth Annual Report, 24 FCC Rcd 542, 710 n.4 (2009).

2 *See, e.g.,* David Corn, *Happy Birthday, C-SPAN!*, THE NATION, Mar. 11, 2004, http://www.thenation.com/blog/156075/happy-birthday-c-span.

3 C-SPAN, Frequently Asked Questions, http://legacy.c-span.org/about/viewer_info/faq.asp?code=ABOUT#funded (last visited May 24, 2011).

4 PEW RESEARCH CTR. FOR THE PEOPLE & THE PRESS, AMERICANS SPEND-

ING MORE TIME FOLLOWING THE NEWS 87 (2010), *available at* http://people-press.org/files/legacy-pdf/652.pdf.

5   C-SPAN, *C-SPAN at 30: Who's Watching? New Survey Details a Politically Active Audience Estimated at more than 39 Million Adults* (press release), Mar. 18, 2009, http://legacy.c-span.org/30Years/media-release.aspx. C-SPAN's mission from the beginning has been simply stated: "To provide C-SPAN's audience access to the live gavel-to-gavel proceedings of the U.S. House of Representatives and the U.S. Senate, and to other forums where public policy is discussed, debated and decided—all without editing, commentary or analysis and with a balanced presentation of points of view." C-SPAN, Company/Corporate Information: The C-SPAN Mission, http://legacy.c-span.org/about/company/index.asp (last visited Mar. 15, 2011).

6   American Historical Ass'n, 2004 Theodore Roosevelt–Woodrow Wilson Award Winner: Brian Lamb, C-SPAN, Aug. 13, 2007, http://www.historians.org/prizes/AWARDED/RooseveltWilsonWinner/04Lamb.cfm.

7   Research by FCC staff found that, as of December 20, 2010, 23 states and the District of Columbia—24 jurisdictions overall—broadcast/multicast or cablecast varying amounts of live coverage of their branches of government—with a primary focus on the legislative branch. In addition to the District of Columbia, the states in which such services are provided are: Alaska, Arizona, California, Colorado, Connecticut, Florida, Hawaii, Idaho, Illinois, Kentucky, Michigan, Minnesota, Montana, Nebraska, New Jersey, New York, Ohio, Oregon, Pennsylvania, Rhode Island, South Carolina, Washington, and Wisconsin. As noted above, NAPAN counts entities in only 16 of these states as SPANs. (Research by FOM staff); Email from Paul Giguere, Pres., NAPAN/Pres. and C.E.O., The Connecticut Network, to Simon Banyai, FCC (Sept. 14, 2010) (Giguere Email 9/14/10). NAPAN identifies 16 states as having an "independent" SPAN in the sense that a distinct operating unit manages the network: Alaska, Arizona, California, Colorado, Connecticut, Florida, Illinois, Michigan, Montana, Nebraska, Ohio, Oregon, Pennsylvania, South Carolina, Washington, and Wisconsin. *Id.*

8   National Conference of State Legislatures, Broadcasts and Webcasts of Legislative Floor Proceedings and Committee Hearings, http://www.ncsl.org/Default.aspx?TabId=13479 (last visited Mar. 15, 2011).

9   Research by FOM staff.

10 Giguere Email 9/14/10.

11 Meeting of National Association of Public Affairs Networks staff with FCC staff (Nov. 4, 2010) (NAPAN Meeting 11/4/10).

12 Connecticut Network, *Supreme Court Arguments on Rowlands Subpoena to Air Live on Connecticut Network* (press release), June 17, 2004, http://www.ctn.state.ct.us/press_2004.asp?pressID=12 (last visited Feb. 17, 2011).

13 As a result of these efforts, the base was kept open. *See* State of Connecticut, *BRAC Commission Votes 8/24/05 to Keep Sub Base Open* (press release), Aug. 24, 2005, http://www.ct.gov/governorrell/cwp/view.asp?a=1809&q=292820. CT-N has been honored with the 2007 Helen M. Loy Freedom of Information Award, the 2007 national Sunshine Award from the Society of Professional Journalists and the 2009 Open Government Award from the Connecticut Foundation for Open Government.

14 NAPAN Meeting 11/4/10 .

15 Wisconsin, 2009 Assembly Joint Resolution 76, at 2, *available at* legis.wisconsin.gov/2009/data/AJR-76.pdf.

16 *See* Washington State Public Affairs TV Network, Engaged: Students Becoming Citizens, http://www.tvw.org/modules/Articles/engaged.cfm?bhcp=1 (last visited Feb. 17, 2010).

17 Editorial, *TVW: Window to Washington*, THE SEATTLE TIMES, July 30, 2006, http://seattletimes.nwsource.com/html/editorialsopinion/2003159673_tvwed30.html.

18 NAPAN Meeting 11/4/10.

19 NAPAN Meeting 11/4/10.

20 Email from Christopher Long, President and CEO, WisconsinEye, to FCC staff (Sept. 16, 2010) (WisconsinEye Email 9/16/10).

21 Interview with Brian Lamb, Founder, C-SPAN by Steven Waldman, FCC (June 18, 2010) (Lamb Interview 6/18/10).

22 Giguere Email 9/14/10.

23 Giguere Email 9/14/10 (the 12 SPANs identified are in Arizona, Alaska, Colorado, Connecticut, Florida, Illinois, Montana, Nebraska, Ohio, Oregon, South Carolina, and Washington).

24 NAPAN Meeting 11/4/10.

25 National Association of Public Affairs Networks Comments in re *FOM PN*, filed June 30, 2010 (NAPAN Comments) at 4, 15.

26 NAPAN Comments at 4.

27 NAPAN Comments at 15.

28 NAPAN Comments at 4.

29 NAPAN Comments at 16.

30 NAPAN Comments at 4.

31 Interview with Lois Ewen, Office Manager, MGTV, by FCC staff (Sept. 9, 2010).

32 Interview with Dan Shellenbarger, Exec. Dir., The Ohio Channel, and Jerry Wareham, Pres. and C.E.O., ideastream/WVIZ by FCC staff (Sept. 10, 2010) (Shellenbarger/Wareham Interview).

33 Presently, ideastream—a multimedia partnership between Cleveland public television (WVIZ) and public radio (WCPN)—has been chosen by other Ohio PBS affiliates to administer these contracts in partnership with Ohio Government Telecommunication, the parent company of the Ohio Channel. Shellenbarger/Wareham Interview. *See also* Ideastream, http://www.ideastream.org/ideastream/about/about_ideastream/ (last visited Feb. 17, 2011).

34 Shellenbarger/Wareham Interview.

35 NAPAN Comments at 16.

36 WisconsinEye Email 9/16/10.

37 Email from Christopher Long, President and CEO, WisconsinEye, to FCC staff (Nov. 23, 2010) (WisconsinEye Email 11/23/10).

38 WisconsinEye Email 11/23/10; WisconsinEye Email 9/16/10.

39 NAPAN Comments at 15; *see also* 360 North, About 360 North, http://www.360north.org/about.php (last visited Feb. 17, 2011).

40 NAPAN Comments at 15.

41 WisconsinEye Email 9/16/10.

42 On July 7, 2005 at 2:00 am, the Pennsylvania General Assembly passed pay increases for state lawmakers, judges, and top executive-branch officials in a vote without public review or commentary. *See* Wikipedia, 2005 Pennsylvania General Assembly Pay Raise Controversy, http://en.wikipedia.org/wiki/2005_Pennsylvania_General_Assembly_pay_

raise_controversy (last visited Feb. 17, 2011). In the ensuing public controversy, one state judge's retention and several state legislators' primary elections were affected, and on November 16, 2005, Governor Rendell signed a repeal of the pay raise after a near unanimous vote for repeal. *See id.*

43 Interview with Brian Lockman, Pres. and C.E.O., Pennsylvania Cable Network by FCC staff (Nov. 19, 2010).

44 Interview with Paul Giguere by FCC staff (Sept. 10, 2010).

45 Email from Paul Giguere to Simon Banyai, FCC (Nov. 18, 2010) (Giguere Email 11/18/10).

46 Giguere Email 9/14/10. NAPAN identifies 16 states as having an "independent" SPAN in the sense that a distinct operating unit manages the network. The 16 SPANs identified as independent are: Arizona, Alaska, California, Colorado, Connecticut, Florida, Illinois, Michigan, Montana, Nebraska, Ohio, Pennsylvania, Oregon, South Carolina, Washington, and Wisconsin.

47 Meeting with NAPAN members with FCC staff (June 7, 2010).

48 Giguere Email 11/18/10.

49 Giguere Email 9/14/10.

50 47 U.S.C. § 335(b).

51 47 C.F.R. § 25.701(f).

52 47 C.F.R. § 25.701(f).

53 Giguere Email 11/18/10.

54 NAPAN Meeting 11/4/10.

55 NAPAN Meeting 11/4/10.

56 WisconsinEye Email 9/16/10.

57 Email from Paul Giguere to Simon Banyai, FCC (Sept. 7, 2010).

9 Satellite

1 *See Implementation of Section 25 of the Cable Television Consumer Protection and Competition Act of 1992, Direct Broadcast Satellite Public Interest Obligation*, Second Order on Reconsideration of First Report & Order, 19 FCC Rcd 5647 (2004).

2 *Matter of Implementation of Section 25 of the Cable Television Consumer Protection and Competition Act of 1992*, Report & Order, 13 FCC Rcd 23254, 23285 (1998) ("We choose four percent, instead of a higher number, because we find it in the public interest to put the minimum burden on this industry that currently has relatively little market power."). The FCC further added that "imposing the maximum set-aside percentage now might hinder DBS in developing as a viable competitor in the MVPD market and that this factor outweighs possible benefits in establishing a higher percentage." *Id.*

3 *See* 47 U.S.C. § 335(b); 47 C.F.R. § 25.701(f)(2).

4 Letter from Jeffrey Blum, Sr. V.P. and Deputy Gen. Counsel, DISH Network L.L.C., and Stacy Fuller, V.P., Regulatory Affairs, DIRECTV, Inc., to Marlene H. Dortch, Secretary, FCC, GN Docket No. 10-25 (filed Aug. 19, 2010) (DISH and DIRECTV *Ex Parte* 8/19/10), *available at* http://fjallfoss.fcc.gov/ecfs/document/view?id=7020709221.

5 DISH and DIRECTV *Ex Parte* 8/19/10.

6 DISH and DIRECTV *Ex Parte* 8/19/10.

7 For example, in addition to Almavision Hispanic Network, Brigham Young University Channel (BYU-TV), and the Catholic Eternal World Television Network (EWTN), Dish Network also carries self-designated Christian channels such as Christian Television Network, Kids & Teen Television, Three Angels Broadcasting Network, and Trinity Broadcasting Network. DirecTV carries many of the same programmers, as well as World Harvest Television, National Religious Broadcasters, The Word, Word of God Fellowship, GEM TV, the Hope Channel, and Jewish Life TV. DISH and DIRECTV *Ex Parte* 8/19/10.

8 Brigham Young University, BYUtv, http://www.byutv.org/(last visited Feb. 17, 2011); Eternal World Television Network, http://www.ewtn.com/ (last visited Feb. 17, 2011).

9 OnceTV México, http://www.oncemexico.tv/oncemexico/i_index.php (OnceTV México) (last visited Feb. 17, 2011).

10 OnceTV México.

11 DISH Network, English Packages, http://www.dishnetwork.com/packages/channel.aspx?channel=52107 (last visited Feb. 17, 2011).

12 Florida Education Channel, http://www.fec.tv/ (last visited Feb. 17, 2011).

13 Northern Arizona Univ., University House, http://extended.nau.edu/TelevisionServices.aspx (last visited Feb. 18, 2011). Similarly, the University of California Channel offers programming on "a broad spectrum of subjects of interest to a general audience including science, health and medicine, public affairs, humanities, arts and music, education issues and even gardening and agriculture." Univ. of California, University of California Television, http://www.uctv.tv/about/ (last visited Feb. 18, 2011).

14 *PRISA to Take Major Stake in V-me Media, Inc.: World's Largest Spanish-Language Media Company Joins With One of The Biggest US Hispanic Networks*, BLOOMBERG, Oct. 20, 2009, http://www.bloomberg.com/apps/news?pid=conewsstory&tkr=PRS%3ASM&sid=alqizMQHboyY.

15 V-me, http://www.vmetv.com/english_info (last visited Feb. 18, 2011).

16 CoLours TV, http://colourstv.org/ (last visited Feb. 18, 2011).

17 Free Speech TV, http://www.freespeech.org/ (last visited Feb. 18, 2011).

18 Link TV, http://www.linktv.org/ (last visited Feb. 18, 2011).

19 MHz Networks, http://www.mhznetworks.org/mhzworldview/programming/(last visited Feb. 18, 2011).

20 DISH Network, Channels & Packages, http://www.dishnetwork.com/downloads/Channel-Lineup/StandardHDChannelGuide.pdf (last visited Feb. 18, 2011).

21 DIRECTV, The Guide, http://www.directv.com/entertainment/guide (last visited Feb. 18, 2011).

22 These included God TV, El Sembrador Ministries, TCT Ministries, TV Japan (NHK) and Russia Today. *See* DISH and DIRECTV *Ex Parte* 8/19/10.

23 *See* DISH and DIRECTV *Ex Parte* 8/19/10.

24 "Ongoing" contracts were awarded only to those programmers who had been programming on Dish Network since 1996. These include only C-SPAN and NASA TV. *See* DISH and DIRECTV *Ex Parte* 8/19/10, Appendix A, 3.

25 Prepared Testimony, Jose Luis Rodriguez, Founder and C.E.O., Hispanic Information and Telecommunications Network, FCC Workshop on the Future of Media and the Information Needs of Communities: Public and Other Noncommercial Media in the Digital Era (Apr. 30, 2010)

(Rodriquez Testimony), at 2, *available at* http://reboot.fcc.gov/futureof-media/public-and-other-noncommercial-media-in-the-digital-era.

26 American University Comments, at 7–8 (*citing* AUFDERHEIDE, THE DAILY PLANET at 99–172).

27 Rodriguez Testimony at 1.

28 DISH and DIRECTV *Ex Parte* 8/19/10 at 1, 2.

29 DISH and DIRECTV *Ex Parte* 8/19/10 at 3.

30 *Implementation of the Satellite Home Viewer Improvement Act of 1999*, Report and Order, 16 FCC Rcd 1918, 1926 (2000).

31 *See* DISH Network, www.dishnetwork.com and DirecTV, www.directv.com.

32 Operators send up new satellites to expand capacity or to replace old ones. DirecTV has launched thirteen satellites since its inception in 1993 at the rate of one satellite every year or two. The newest DirecTV satellite, "DIRECTV 12," was launched on December 12th, 2009. DISH Network has launched a total of 12 satellites, starting with "EchoStar 1" on December 28, 1995. Like DirecTV, DISH Network has launched one satellite every year or two, with its latest, EchoStar14, having launched on March 20, 2010. Data provided by International Bureau, FCC.

33 47 U.S.C. § 335(b).

34 Giguere Interview 9/7/10; *see also* Email from Greg Lane, Pres. & C.E.O., TVW, to FCC staff (Aug. 13, 2010).

10 Low Power FM

1 *See Creation of Low Power Radio Service*, Report and Order, 15 FCC Rcd 2205, 2211-13 (2000). In the ten years since its inception, the Commission has revisited and revised the LPFM Rules in light of the experiences of LPFM applicants and licensees. *See Creation of a Low Power Radio Service*, Second Report and Order, 16 FCC Rcd 8026, 8028 (2001); *Creation of Low Power Radio Service*, Third Report and Order and Second Further Notice of Proposed Rulemaking, 22 FCC Rcd 21912 (2007).

2 *See* 47 C.F.R. § 73.811. The approximate service range of a 100-watt LPFM station is a 3.5 mile radius.

3 Prometheus Radio Project Comments in re *FOM PN*, filed June 8, 2010 (Prometheus Comments) at 4, 7.

4 Prometheus Comments at 3.

5 Prometheus Comments at 2.

6 WCIW-LP offers programming in Spanish, Haitian Creole and Mayan languages, providing human rights resources, social services, and a forum for civic dialogue. Prometheus Comments at 3.

Farm workers in Southwest Florida also depend on WCTI-LP, which offers music, information, and local women's rights shows in Spanish, Mexican, and Guatemalan languages. Free Press, Low Power FM Success Stories, http://www.freepress.net/lpfm/success (Low Power FM Success Stories) (last visited Feb. 18, 2011).

7 Prometheus Comments at 3.

8 Prometheus Radio Project, Low Power FM, *available at* http://www.prometheusradio.org/media/lpfm_factsheet_FP.pdf.

9 Prometheus Comments at 5.

10 Prometheus Comments at 4.

11 Prometheus Radio Project, Low Power FM.

12 Prometheus Comments at 6.

13 Prometheus Comments at 7.

11 Religious Broadcasting

1 BIA/Kelsey (listing 1,287 stations operating with a "religion" format).

2 Prepared Testimony of Craig Parshall, Sr. V.P. & Gen. Counsel of National Religious Broadcaster Association, FCC Workshop on the Future of Media and the Information Needs of Communities: Public and Other Noncommercial Media in the Digital Era (Apr. 30, 2010) (Parshall Testimony), at 1, *available at* http://reboot.fcc.gov/futureofmedia/public-and-other-noncommercial-media-in-the-digital-era.

3 47 C.F.R § 73.621 (2002).

4 *Applications of WQED Pittsburgh, Assignor, and Cornerstone TeleVision, Inc., Assignee*, Order, 15 FCC Rcd 202, 214 (1999) (*WQED Order I*).

5 *WQED Order I*, 15 FCC Rcd at 225 (citations omitted).

6 *Applications of WQED Pittsburgh, Assignor, and Cornerstone TeleVision, Inc., Assignee*, Order, 15 FCC Rcd. 2534, 2535 (2000). The "additional guidance" generated criticism from broadcasters, religious groups, and Members of Congress with respect to viewpoint discrimination and content regulation. In response, the FCC vacated the "additional guidelines" language and returned to a policy of deference to the editorial judgment of the licensee.

7 Parshall Testimony at 2.

8 Parshall Testimony at 3.

9 CORPORATION FOR PUBLIC BROADCASTING, RADIO COMMUNITY SERVICE GRANT GENERAL PROVISIONS & ELIGIBILITY CRITERIA 10 (2010), *available at* http://www.cpb.org/stations/grants/radio/2010/cpb_10RadioCSG_GeneralProvisions.pdf; CORPORATION FOR PUBLIC BROADCASTING, TELEVISION COMMUNITY SERVICE GRANT GENERAL PROVISIONS & ELIGIBILITY CRITERIA 6 (2010), *available at* http://www.cpb.org/stations/grants/tv/2010/cpb_10TV_CSG_GeneralProvisions.pdf.

10 Parshall Testimony at 8.

11 *See* 47 C.F.R. §§ 73.503(d), 73.621(e). *See also* Commission Policy Concerning the Noncommercial Nature of Educational Broadcast Stations, Memorandum Opinion and Order, 90 FCC 2d 895, 907 (1982).

12 Nonprofit News Websites

1 Ken Doctor, *The Newsonomics of a Single Investigative Story*, Nieman Journalism Lab, April 21, 2011, http://www.niemanlab.org/2011/04/the-newsonomics-of-a-single-investigative-story/.

2 Jim Romenesko, *Religion News Service becomes a nonprofit on June 1*, May 19, 2011, http://www.poynter.org/latest-news/romenesko/133091/newhouse-familys-religion-news-service-becomes-a-nonprofit-on-june-1.

3 Email from Michele McLellan, 2009-10 Reynolds Journalism Fellow at the Univ. of Missouri School of Journalism and Consultant, to Steven Waldman, FCC (Mar. 2, 2011).

4 Michele McLellan, *New Traditional News Sites*, UNIV. OF MISSOURI DONALD W. REYNOLDS JOURNALISM INSTITUTE, Apr. 9, 2010, http://www.rjionline.org/projects/mcellan/stories/community-news-sites/new-traditionals.php (*New Traditional Sites*).

5 MinnPost, The Best of MinnPost.com, http://www.minnpost.com/best/ (last visited Feb. 18, 2011).

6 Eric Schoenborn, *NJ Spotlight is Off to a Remarkable, Muckraking Start*, KNIGHT BLOG, May 18, 2010, http://www.knightblog.org/nj-spotlight-is-off-to-a-remarkable-muckraking-start.

7 Michele McLellan, *Community News Sites*, UNIV. OF MISSOURI DONALD W. REYNOLDS JOURNALISM INSTITUTE, June 8, 2010, http://www.rjionline.org/community-news-sites (*Community News Sites*).

8 *Community News Sites*.

9 *Community News Sites*; *see also* VT Digger, http://vtdigger.org/(last visited Feb. 22, 2011).

10 David Cohn (digidave), Comment to *The Pacific Garbage Patch: Published*, BLOG.SPOT.US (Nov. 10, 2009, 4:50 AM), http://blog.spot.us/2009/11/10/the-pacific-garbage-patch-published.

11 Email from David Cohn, Founder and Director, Spot.Us, to J. Evan Shapiro, FCC (Dec. 8, 2010).

12 *See* Spot.Us, Examples: Pioneering Community-Funded Reporting, http://spot.us/pages/examples (last visited Feb. 22, 2011).

13 Sunlight Foundation, Congress For Your Android Phone!, http://sunlight-foundation.com/android/congress/ (last visited Feb, 22, 2011).

14 Sunlight Foundation, The Fifty State Project, http://sunlightlabs.com/projects/FiftyStates/(last visited Feb. 22, 2011); Sunlight Foundation, National Data Catalog, http://sunlightlabs.com/projects/datacatalog/ (last visited Feb. 22, 2011).

15 Interview with John Hood by Steven Waldman, FCC (Apr. 2011)

16 Interview with Michael Stoll, Exec. Dir., SF Public Press, by Irene Wu, FCC (July 16, 2010).

17 Interview with Margaret Wolf Freivogel, Editor, St. Louis Beacon, by Irene Wu, FCC (July 16, 2010).

18 Email from Eric Newton, Knight Foundation, to Steven Waldman, FCC (Aug. 31, 2010) (Newton Email 8/31/10).

19 Mary Walton, *Investigative Shortfall,* AMER. JOURNALISM REV., Sept. 2010, http://www.ajr.org/article.asp?id=4904.

20 MINNPOST.COM 2010 YEAR END REPORT: A BREAKTHROUGH YEAR FOR MINNPOST (2010), http://www.minnpost.com/_asset/twc3tw/2010-End-of-Year-Report.pdf.

21 Interview with Jennifer Benka, VP Development, The Bay Citizen by FCC (Dec. 8, 2010).

22 Chris Rauber, *Bay Citizen Nonprofit News Producer Launches, Nabs $3.7M*, SF BUSINESS TIMES, May 26, 2010, http://www.bizjournals.com/sanfrancisco/stories/2010/05/24/daily39.html.

23 Staci D. Kramer, *Texas Tribune Raised Nearly $4 Million In 2009 But Can't Rest* , PAID CONTENT, Jan. 25, 2010, http://paidcontent.org/article/419-texas-tribune-raised-nearly-4-million-in-2009-but-cant-rest/$4m-in 2009.

24 Jim Barnett, *Nonprofits With a Perspective Hiring Journalists: A Sign of Things to Come?*, NIEMAN JOURNALISM LAB, Sept. 10, 2009, http://www.niemanlab.org/2009/09/nonprofits-with-a-perspective-hiring-journalists-a-sign-of-things-to-come/.

25 Rick Edmonds, *Shrinking Newspapers Have Created $1.6 Billion News Deficit*, THE POYNTER INSTITUTE, Oct. 10, 2009, http://www.poynter.org/column.asp?id=123&aid=171536.

26 Knight Citizen News Network, Project Archive, http://www.kcnn.org/toolkit/funding_database/ (last visited Feb. 22, 2011).

27 American Society of Newspaper Editors, Newsroom Employment Census, 2011, http://asne.org/article_view/articleid/1788/newsroom-employment-up-slightly-minority-numbers-plunge-for-third-year.aspx; "Newspapers: News Investment" in PEW, STATE OF NEWS MEDIA 2010, http://stateofthemedia.org/2010/newspapers-summary-essay/news-investment/.

28 Newton Email 8/31/10.

29 JAN SCHAFFER, NEW VOICES: WHAT WORKS, LESSONS FROM FUNDING FIVE YEARS OF COMMUNITY NEWS STARTUPS, 20 (Net Citizen News Network) (2010), *available at* http://www.kcnn.org/nv_whatworks/pdf.

30 Email from Joel Kramer, Editor and CEO, MinnPost, to Steven Waldman, FCC (Oct. 5, 2010) (Kramer Email 10/5/10).

31 Email from Nicole Hollway, General Manager, St. Louis Beacon, to J. Evan Shapiro, FCC (Dec. 9, 2010).

32 Kramer Email 10/5/10.

13 Foundations

1 Public Broadcasting Management Association (PBMA), State of the System Public Broadcasting Reporting FY2009 (presentation), June 2010, *available at* http://www.pbma.org/2010/Downloads/PBMA%20State%20of%20System%20Reporting%20Results%20Session%20-%20v6%2018%202010%20vFinal%20Presentation%20with%20Appendix.pdf.

2 PETER B. KAUFMAN & MARY ALBON, INTELLIGENT TELEVISION, FUNDING MEDIA, STRENGTHENING DEMOCRACY: GRANTMAKING FOR THE 21ST CENTURY (THE GFEM MEDIA FUNDING TRACKER) 4 (Grantmakers in Film + Electronic Media) (2010) (FUNDING MEDIA, STRENGTHENING DEMOC-RACY), *available at* http://gfem.org/node/873.

3 FUNDING MEDIA, STRENGTHENING DEMOCRACY at 20, 36.

4 Knight Citizen News Network, Project Archive, http://www.kcnn.org/toolkit/funding_database (last visited Feb. 22, 2011). That figure does not take into account public broadcasting grants, grants for documentary production, or support for student news services and journalism training.

5 STEVEN LAWRENCE & REINA MUKAI, FOUNDATION GROWTH AND GIVING ESTIMATES: CURRENT OUTLOOK (Found. Ctr.) (2010), *available at* http://foundationcenter.org/gainknowledge/research/pdf/fgge10.pdf. That figure does not take into account public broadcasting grants, grants for documentary production, or support for student news services and journalism training.

6 JAN SCHAFFER, NEW MEDIA MAKERS: A TOOLKIT FOR INNOVATORS IN COMMUNITY MEDIA AND GRANT MAKING 4 (J-Lab) (2009) (SCHAFFER,

NEW MEDIA MAKERS), *available at* http://www.j-lab.org/new_media_makers.pdf.

7 DOWNIE & SCHUDSON, RECONSTRUCTION OF AMERICAN JOURNALISM.

8 Newton Email 8/31/10.

9 Newton Email 8/31/10.

10 John S. and James L. Knight Found., Knight's Media Innovation Initiative, http://www.knightfoundation.org/mii/index.dot (last visited Feb. 22, 2011).

11 Newton Email 8/31/10.

12 FUNDING MEDIA, STRENGTHENING DEMOCRACY AT 27, 29.

13 Community Foundations, A Brief History, http://www.communityfoundations.net/page14094.html (last visited Feb. 22, 2011).

14 Dave Peters, *Who Tells the Story of a Place?*, MINNESOTA PUBLIC RADIO NEWS, Mar. 3, 2010, http://minnesota.publicradio.org/collections/special/columns/ground-level/archive/2010/03/who-tells-the-story-of-a-place.shtml.

15 SCHAFFER, NEW MEDIA MAKERS at 8–9.

16 Knight Citizen News Network: Introduction, http://www.kcnn.org/WhatWorks/introduction/ (last visited Feb. 22, 2011).

17 Interview with Kevin Harold, Publisher, New Jersey Spotlight, by Paige Gold, FCC (July 10, 2010).

18 JOHN S. AND JAMES L. KNIGHT FOUND. & FSG SOCIAL IMPACT ADVISORS, REPORT OF FINDINGS: THE STATE OF FUNDING TO ADDRESS COMMUNITY INFORMATION NEEDS AMONG COMMUNITY FOUNDATIONS 2 (2010) (STATE OF FUNDING TO ADDRESS COMMUNITY INFORMATION NEEDS), *available at* http://www.knightfoundation.org/dotAsset/376424.pdf.

19 STATE OF FUNDING TO ADDRESS COMMUNITY INFORMATION NEEDS at 3.

14 Journalism Schools

1 Letter from Deans of Journalism Schools to Julius Genachowski, FCC Chairman (Apr. 30, 2010).

2 Memo from Michael Schudson to Nick Lemann and Bill Grueskin (May 25, 2010).

3 Interview with Christopher Callahan, Founding Dean, Walter Cronkite School of Journalism and Mass Communication, Arizona State Univ., by Tamara Smith, FCC (Aug. 2010) (Callahan Interview Aug. 2010).

4 Christine Rogel, *As Economy Toppled, Seven AZ Congressmen Paid Staff Bonuses*, CRONKITE NEWS SERVICE, Dec. 21, 2009, http://www.tucsonsentinel.com/local/report/122109_cong_bonuses.

5 Callahan Interview Aug. 2010.

6 Interview with Steve Elliott, Dir. of Digital News, Cronkite News Service, by Tamara Smith, FCC (July 2010) (Elliot Interview July 2010).

7 KOMU, About, http://www.komu.com/about-komu-8 (last visited May 25, 2011).

8 Jennifer Epstein, *Reviving Local News,* INSIDE HIGHER ED, Oct. 7, 2009, http://www.insidehighered.com/layout/set/print/news/2009/10/07/berkeley.

9 CUNY Graduate School of Journalism, THE LOCAL, http://fort-greene.thelocal.nytimes.com (last visited Feb. 22, 2011).

10 Liza Eckert, *Community Garden Rally Tomorrow Morning*, THE LOCAL, Aug. 3, 2010, http://fort-greene.thelocal.nytimes.com/2010/08/03/community-garden-rally-tomorrow-morning; Soraya Batista, *Locals Confused by Bus Route Changes*, THE LOCAL, Aug. 3, 2010, http://fort-greene.thelocal.nytimes.com/2010/08/03/locals-confused-by-bus-route-changes.

11 *See Crowdsourcing: Broken Car Windows*, THE LOCAL, July 6, 2010, http://fort-greene.thelocal.nytimes.com/2010/07/06/crowdsourcing-broken-car-windows.

12 Lee B. Becker, Tudor Vlad & Devora Olin, *2008 Enrollment Report: Slow Rate of Growth May Signal Weakening of Demand*, JOURNALISM AND MASS COMMUNICATION EDUCATOR, (Autumn 2009), http://findarticles.com/p/articles/mi_7644/is_200910/ai_n55484758/?tag=content;col1.

13 Lee B. Becker, Tudor Vlad, Paris Desnoes & Devora Olin, ANNUAL SURVEY OF JOURNALISM & MASS COMMUNICATIONS GRADUATES 15 (James M. Cox Jr. Ctr. for Int'l Mass Communication Training and Research, Grady College of Journalism & Mass Communication, Univ. of Georgia) (2009), http://www.grady.uga.edu/annualsurveys/Graduate_Survey/Graduate_2009/Grad2009MergedB&W.pdf.

14 Steve Kolowich, *J-Schools to the Rescue?*, INSIDE HIGHER ED, Mar. 1, 2010, http://www.insidehighered.com/news/2010/03/01/journalism (*J-Schools to the Rescue?*).

15 *J-Schools to the Rescue?*.

16 Interview with Stephen Shepard, Dean, CUNY Graduate School of Journalism, by Tamara Smith, FCC (July 2010) (Shepard Interview July 2010).

17 Interview with George Stanley, Managing Editor, Milwaukee Journal Sentinel by Tamara Smith, FCC staff (May 2010).

18 Shepard Interview July 2010.

19 Callahan Interview Aug. 2010.

20 Faculty supervisors are critical to maintaining the program's relationships with the professional news outlets and serve as the hinge between them and the J schools. For example, stories from Northeastern's Walter V. Robinson investigative journalism class have run on the front page of the *Boston Globe*. Robinson who spent much of his career as a reporter for the *Globe* explained, "I have a very good association with the editor of the paper…You have to have that. There's gotta be trust. The newspaper has to have confidence that a journalism faculty has the experience and oversight capacity to make certain that students get it right." Elliot Interview.

21 Interview with Neil Henry, Dean, Graduate School of Journalism, Univ. of California at Berkeley, by Tamara Smith, FCC (August 2010) (Henry Interview Aug. 2010).

22 Callahan Interview Aug. 2010.

23 Jay Rosen, *Explaining The Local: East Village, NYU's collaboration with the New York Times*, PRESS THINK, Feb. 23, 2010, http://archive.pressthink.org/2010/02/23/the_local.html.

24 *Cronkite Lab's iPhone App Connects Citizens, Officials*, ARIZONA STATE UNIV. NEWS, June 3, 2010, http://asunews.asu.edu/20100601_newapp.

25 CRAIG NEWMAN, WHY LAW AND JOURNALISM SCHOOLS NEED TO WORK TOGETHER, COLUMBIA JOURNALISM REVIEW, (2011) May 16, 2011 http://www.cjr.org/behind_the_news/why_law_and_journalism_schools.php.

26 Amy Dunkin, *J-school Takes On Expanded Role On The Local Web Site With NYTimes.com*, CUNY GRADUATE SCHOOL OF JOURNALISM, Jan. 8,

2010, http://www.journalism.cuny.edu/2010/01/08/cuny-j-school-to-take-over-nytimes-coms-the-local-community-web-site.

27 Doug MacEachern, *ASU's Cash-Infused Cronkite Journalism School in Elite Company*, THE ARIZONA REPUBLIC, Aug. 24, 2008, http://www.azcentral.com/arizonarepublic/viewpoints/articles/2008/08/24/20080824vip-cronkite0824.html.

28 Henry Interview Aug. 2010.

15 Nonprofit Media Discussion

1 *See* FREE PRESS, CHANGING MEDIA: PUBLIC INTEREST POLICIES FOR THE DIGITAL AGE 221, 267 (2009), *available at* http://www.freepress.net/files/changing_media.pdf; SHAWN POWERS, Public Service Broadcasting: An Overview (Univ. of So. California Annenberg Center on Communication Leadership & Policy Public Policy & Funding the News Proj.) (2009), *available at* http://fundingthenews.usc.edu/related_research/3_Carnegie_PublicServiceBroadcasting.pdf.

2 David McCandless, *Information is Beautiful: The BBC-O-Gram*, GUARDIAN DATA BLOG, Mar. 1, 2010, http://www.guardian.co.uk/news/datablog/2010/mar/01/information-beautiful-bbc-o-gram-spending. The BBC had an operating expenditure of £4.26 billion in 2009-10. BBC, Financial Statements, http://www.bbc.co.uk/annualreport/exec/financial/fin_overview.shtml (last visited May 25, 2011).

3 *Why Online Won't Kill the Radio Star: Vivian Schiller of NPR on How Public Radio Can Thrive in The Digital Age*, WALL ST. J., June 7, 2010, http://online.wsj.com/article/SB10001424052748704764404575287070721094884.html.

4 Email from Michele McLellan to Steven Waldman, FCC (Mar. 1, 2011).

16 Government Transparency

1 KNIGHT COMMISSION ON THE INFORMATION NEEDS OF COMMUNITIES IN A DEMOCRACY, INFORMING COMMUNITIES: SUSTAINING DEMOCRACY IN THE DIGITAL AGE 37-38 (Aspen Institute) (2009).

2 LEONARD DOWNIE JR. & MICHAEL SCHUDSON, THE RECONSTRUCTION OF AMERICAN JOURNALISM (Columbia Law Rev.) (2009), http://www.cjr.org/reconstruction/the_reconstruction_of_american.php.

3 *See, e.g.*, Progress & Freedom Foundation Comments in re *FOM PN* (*FCC Launches Examination of the Future of Media and Information Needs of Communities in a Digital Age*, Public Notice, 25 FCC Rcd 384 (2010) (*FOM PN*)), filed May 5, 2010, at 75.

4 Now codified at 5 U.S.C. § 552.

5 Under FOIA, 5 U.S.C. § 552, government records are presumptively open to the public unless they fall within one of nine exempt categories. One of these categories, however—the so-called (b)(3) exemption—removes from mandatory disclosure any document authorized to be withheld under a statute other than FOIA. ProPublica recently reported that, over the last decade, federal agencies have relied on over 240 other statutes to withhold records under the (b)(3) exemption. In 2008-2009, for example, statutes other than FOIA were used to shield information about "watermelon handlers, avocado importers and caves." Jennifer LaFleur, *FOIA Eyes Only: How Buried Statutes Are Keeping Information Secret*, PROPUBLICA (Mar. 14, 2011), http://www.propublica.org/article/foia-exemptions-sunshine-law.

6 The Government in the Sunshine Act, Pub. L. No. 94-409, 90 Stat. 1241 (1976) (codified at 5 U.S.C. § 552b) (*Sunshine Act*).

7 President Barack Obama, Memorandum for the Heads of Executive Departments and Agencies re: Transparency and Open Government (Jan. 21, 2009), http://www.whitehouse.gov/the_press_office/Transparency_and_Open_Government (Presidential Memo on Transparency and Open Government 1/21/09).

8 Memorandum from Peter R. Orszag, Director, Office of Management and Budget, to the Heads of Executive Departments and Agencies re: Open Government Directive (Dec. 8, 2009) (OMB Open Government Directive Memo 12/8/09), *available at* http://www.whitehouse.gov/omb/assets/memoranda_2010/m10-06.pdf.

9 OMB Open Government Directive Memo 12/8/09.

10 OMB Open Government Directive Memo 12/8/09.

11 *See* DC.gov, eServices—Searchable Databases, http://app.dc.gov/more_services.asp?pagenum=1&tab=0&category=db (last visited Jan. 21, 2011).

12 NYC Stat enables users to connect easily to:

CPR, the Citywide Performance Reporting System, an interactive dashboard designed for user-friendly access to the most critical performance indicators for every City agency, with monthly updates and automatic evaluation of trends within specified program areas; The Mayor's Management Report, the public report card on City agency performance published twice a year;

The NYC*SCOUT web page, which maps street conditions such as potholes and catch basin defects, and allows users to track the progress of repairs;

My Neighborhood Statistics (MNS), which maps comparative performance data at the neighborhood level for approximately 50 selected performance measures;

Scorecard Cleanliness Ratings, updated monthly for streets and sidewalks throughout the five boroughs;

311 CustomerServiceCenter data, including basic operational statistics and community-level reports on the City's response to service requests from 311 callers;

Citywide Customer Survey Results, from the 2008 survey of New Yorkers' opinions on the delivery of city services;

NYCity Map, which lets users find information on transportation, education, public safety, resident services, neighborhood information, and City life;

Additional performance measures at the websites of 12 key City agencies.

See New York City Government, NYC Stat, http://www.nyc.gov/html/ops/nycstat/html/home/home.shtml (last visited Jan. 21, 2011).

Other examples of municipal data sites include:

Boston, MA—http://hubmaps1.cityofboston.gov/datahub/

Chicago, IL—http://opengovchi.pbworks.com/ and http://is.gd/d0XM1

San Francisco, CA—http://datasf.org/index.php

Portland, OR—http://www.civicapps.org/

Ann Arbor, Michigan—http://www.a2gov.org/data/Pages/default.aspx

Texas Tribune—http://www.texastribune.org/

Seattle—http://data.seattle.gov

Greater New Orleans—http://www.gnocdc.org/

New Orleans' Pre-Katrina Archive, broken down by neighborhood http://www.gnocdc.org/prekatrinasite.html.

13 PUBLIC TECHNOLOGY INSTITUTE, LOCAL GOVERNMENT USE OF WEB 2.0 AND SOCIAL NETWORKING TOOLS: TECHNOLOGY TRENDS IN LOCAL GOVERNANCE 2 (2009), *available at* http://www.pti.org/index.php/ptiee1/inside/C27 (PTI membership required for access to full report).

14 Dr. Alan R. Shark, *Turning Citizen Enragement into Citizen Engagement—Managing Expectations with Web 2.0 and Social Media* (Draft).

15 Michael Levenson, *Residents Use iPhone Application to Alert Officials of Street-Level Problems in the City's Neighborhoods*, BOSTON GLOBE, Feb. 2, 2010, http://www.boston.com/news/local/massachusetts/articles/2010/02/02/residents_use_iphone_to_report_street_level_woes/.

16 Mesa, Arizona, Capital Improvement Projects, http://gis.mesaaz.gov/CIP/ (last visited Jan. 21, 2011).

17 *More Than 8,000 People Using Pittsburgh's 'iBurgh' App*, WPXI.COM, Jan. 6, 2010, http://www.wpxi.com/news/22163491/detail.html.

18 San Jose Mobile City Hall, http://itunes.apple.com/us/app/san-jose-mobile-city-hall/id338029133?mt=8 (last visited Jan. 21, 2011).

19 Abbe Smith, *SeeClickFix Celebrates 50G Issues Reported*, NEW HAVEN REGISTER, Aug. 7, 2010, http://www.nhregister.com/articles/2010/08/07/news/aa3_neseeclickfix080710.txt.

20 Daniel E. Slotnik, *News Sites Dabble With a Web Tool for Nudging Local Officials*, N.Y. TIMES, Jan. 3, 2010, http://www.nytimes.com/2010/01/04/business/media/04click.html.

21 The researchers initially performed regressions of corruption scores against other measures of accountability, including various measures of democracy, media, and judicial independence. They found: "With the exception of government ownership of television, which is high in many developed countries, all the other measures of accountability influence corruption. Countries that are more democratic, have proportional representation, have party-specific voting, low government ownership of the press, and independent judiciaries all have lower levels of corruption." Then, controlling for these variables, they determined whether there was a correlation between corruption and the transparency variables. The one variable that made a significant difference—once other factors were controlled—was the public availability of financial disclosures. In other words, there was no evidence that the mandate for disclosure or its scope made a difference. Those countries that mandate disclosure to government agencies, but in which the disclosures remain inaccessible to the public, did not see any positive impact on their corruption levels. Likewise, assuming that the disclosure forms were identifiable to the public by the name of the legislator in question, it does not appear to make much difference how comprehensive the disclosure is, i.e., whether the disclosure is comprehensive as to personal assets, liabilities, expenditures, income, gifts, and potential conflicts of interest. What did appear to be significant was whether the public could see what was being disclosed. SIMEON DJANKOV, RAFAEL LA PORTA, FLORENCIO LOPEZ-DE-SILANES, & ANDREI SHLEIFER, TRANSPARENCY AND

ACCOUNTABILITY 11-14 (EDHEC Risk Instit., EDHEC Bus. School) (2008), http://www.edhec-risk.com/edhec_publications/all_publications/RISKReview.2008-07-01.0355/attachments/EDHEC Working Paper Transparency and accountability.pdf.

22 The remaining sets in the top 10 are viewable. Data.gov (U.S. Government), Top 10 Most Downloaded Data Sets in the Last 30 Days, http://www.data.gov/metric/visitorstats/top10datasetreport/Mostdownloaded30Days (last visited Jan. 21, 2011). Information on the top 10 visiting states in May 2010 may also be viewed. Data.gov, Top 10 Visiting States (May 2010), http://www.data.gov/metric/visitorstats/statestatistics/May-2010.

23 DataSF (San Francisco and San Francisco County, California), http://datasf.org (last visited Jan. 21, 2011).

24 Data.Seattle.gov (Seattle, Washington), http://data.seattle.gov/ (last visited Jan. 21, 2011).

25 DC.gov (Washington, DC), Data Catalog, http://data.dc.gov/ (last visited Jan. 21, 2011).

26 City of Ann Arbor, Michigan, Government Data Catalog, http://www.a2gov.org/data/Pages/default.aspx (last visited Jan. 21, 2011).

27 AARON SMITH, PEW INTERNET & AMERICAN LIFE PROJ., GOVERNMENT ONLINE: THE INTERNET GIVES CITIZENS NEW PATHS TO GOVERNMENT SERVICES AND INFORMATION 10 (2010) (PEW, GOVERNMENT ONLINE, *available at* http://www.pewinternet.org/~/media//Files/Reports/2010/PIP_Government_Online_2010.pdf.

Id. at 13–14.

28 PEW, GOVERNMENT ONLINE at 26.

29 DARRELL M. WEST & JENNY LU, BROOKINGS INSTITUTION, COMPARING TECHNOLOGY INNOVATION IN THE PRIVATE AND PUBLIC SECTORS 10-11 (2009), *available at* http://www.brookings.edu/~/media/Files/rc/papers/2009/06_technology_west/06_technology_west.pdf.

30 John Horrigan, "Wireless Internet Use" (Pew Internet and American Life Project, July 2009), http://pewinternet.org/Reports/2009/12-Wireless-Internet-Use.aspx.

31 NYC.gov (New York, New York), *Mayor Bloomberg Announces Winners of Inaugural NYC Bigapps Competition* (press release), Feb. 4, 2010, *available at* http://www.nyc.gov/portal/site/nycgov (follow links for Press Releases—Events Feb. 2010).

32 PEW, GOVERNMENT ONLINE at 9.

33 Apps for Democracy Community Edition, Application Directory, http://www.appsfordemocracy.org/application-directory (last visited Jan. 24, 2011).

34 http://sunlightlabs.com/about/.

35 http://sunlightlabs.com/blog/2009/and-winners-are/; http://sunlightfoundation.com/blog/2009/09/10/apps-for-america-2-winners/.

36 http://www.filibusted.us/.

37 http://legistalker.org/.

38 http://www.datamasher.org/.

39 http://govpulse.us/.

40 Clay Johnson, "Apps for Communities," FCC Blog (Apr. 11, 2011), http://www.fcc.gov/blog/apps-communities.

41 "Apps for Communities," Challenge.Gov, http://appsforcommunities.challenge.gov/.

42 Brad Bauman, Why You Need to Download the Real Time Congress App for iPhone now, Sunlight Found., Jan. 13, 2010, http://sunlightfoundation. com/blog/2010/01/13/why-you-need-to-download-the-real-time-congress-app-for-iphone-now/.

43 http://www.texastribune.org/library/data/.

44 Society of Professional Journalists, Open Doors, https://www.spj.org/opendoors5.asp (last visited Jan. 24, 2011).

45 Investigative Reporters and Editors, Database Library, http://data.nicar.org/node/61 (last visited Feb. 22, 2011).

46 Testimony of David M. Blaszkowsky, Dir., Office of Interactive Disclosure, U.S. Securities and Exchange Commission, Federal Trade Commission Workshop, "How Will Journalism Survive The Internet Age?" (Mar. 10, 2010), Tr. at 94: 5–13, *available at* http://www.ftc.gov/opp/workshops/news/; *Better Data, Better Reporting? How Interactive Data Might Affect Business Journalism…And Beyond*, Prepared Testimony of David M. Blaszkowsky, Federal Trade Commission Workshop, "How Will Journalism Survive The Internet Age?", Mar. 10, 2010, *available at* http://www.ftc.gov/opp/workshops/news/mar9/docs/blaszowsky.pdf.

47 Interview with Gar Joseph, City Editor, Philadelphia Daily News, by Tamara Smith, FCC (May 2010).

48 J. Todd Foster, *Reporter Daniel Gilbert's Natural Gas Series Underscores Vital Watchdog Role of Newspapers*, TRICITIES.COM, Dec. 6, 2009, http://www2.tricities.com/news/2009/dec/0w6/reporter_daniel_gilberts_natural_gas_series_unders-ar-239885/.

49 The capacity of reporters to exploit data for effective journalism is being fostered by new programs of professional training, including journalism-school courses for newly minted reporters and continuing education programs for mid-career journalists. The nonprofit Investigative Reporters and Editors, for example, holds conferences on computer-assisted journalism and offers short courses in statistics and the use of particular datasets, such as the census. Investigative Reporters and Editors, IRE and CAR Conferences, http://www.ire.org/training/conference/ (last visited Feb. 22, 2011).

50 Michael Powell, *Leery of Washington, Alaska Feasts on Its Dollars*, N.Y. TIMES, Aug. 18, 2010, http://www.nytimes.com/2010/08/19/business/19stimulus.html; Brian Naylor, *Political Pedigree No Longer Protects S.D. Rep.*, NATIONAL PUBLIC RADIO, Sept. 5, 2010, http://www.npr.org/templates/story/story.php?storyId=129662772; Tony Semerad, *Utah Takes in More Than $3B in Federal Stimulus Money*, SALT LAKE TRIBUNE, Sept. 28, 2010, http://www.sltrib.com/sltrib/news/50085161-78/stimulus-utah-state-money.html.csp; Lauren Russell, *Is It Working?*, BOZEMAN DAILY CHRONICLE, Aug. 22, 2010, http://www.bozemandaily-chronicle.com/news/article_1156d4b4-aca9-11df-897e-001cc4c03286.html.

51 Sunlight Foundation, Congrelate Alpha, http://congrelate (last visited Jan. 24, 2011).

52 Sunlight Foundation, Transparency Data, http://transparencydata.org/# (last visited Jan. 24, 2011).

53 Sunlight Foundation, Poligraft, http://poligraft.com/ (last visited Jan. 24, 2011).

54 Sunlight Foundation, Politiwidgets, http://politiwidgets.com/ (last visited Feb. 22, 2011).

55 Testimony of Bill Buzenberg, Exec. Dir., Center for Public Integrity, Federal Trade Commission Workshop, "How Will Journalism Survive The Internet Age?" (Dec. 2, 2009) (Buzenberg Testimony 12/2/09), Tr. at 158:1–10, *available at* http://www.ftc.gov/opp/workshops/news/index.shtml. Examples of stories using the CPE study include: Tom Abate, *California Had Most Subprime Loans, Study Says,* SAN FRANCISCO CHRONICLE, May 7, 2009, http://articles.sfgate.com/2009-05-07/news/17203711_1_subprime-lenders-mortgages; Neal St. Anthony, *Wells Fargo Listed Among Top Subprime Loan Makers; The Bank Is One of 25 Mortgage Originators a Report Blames As the Biggest Players in the Mortgage and Financial Mess*, STAR TRIBUNE, May 7, 2009; Robert Trigaux, *A Closer Look at Who Made This Mess,* ST. PETERSBURG TIMES, May 7, 2009, http://www.tampabay.com/news/business/banking/article998753.ece?ref=housingbubblenews.com.

56 Center for Public Integrity, Who's Behind the Financial Meltdown? http://www.publicintegrity.org/investigations/economic_meltdown/ (last visited Feb. 4, 2011); Buzenberg Testimony 12/2/09, Tr. at 158:11–17. The top five lenders were Countrywide Financial Corp., Ameriquest Mortgage Co., New Century Financial Corp., First Franklin Corp., and Long Beach Mortgage Co. Newspapers used these data to carry the story forward, drawing competing points of view from industry. For example, Scott Talbott, chief lobbyist for the Financial Services Roundtable, which represents some of the nation's largest lenders, was quoted by the Washington Post saying: "The report oversimplifies the problem and ignores the complexities of the market. To say we are victims is understating, and to say we are enablers is overstating." Dina ElBoghdady, *Major Banks Receiving Federal Aid Backed Subprime Lenders, Report Says,* WASH. POST, May 7, 2009, http://www.washingtonpost.com/wp-dyn/content/article/2009/05/06/AR2009050603365.html.

57 Exec. Order No. 13,489, 74 Fed. Reg. 4669 (Jan. 26, 2009).

58 Presidential Memo on Transparency and Open Government 1/21/09.

59 Pres. Barack Obama, Memorandum to the Heads of Executive Departments and Agencies re: Freedom of Information Act, 74 Fed. Reg. 4683 (Jan. 21, 2009) (Presidential Memo on FOIA 1/21/09).

60 Presidential Memo on FOIA 1/21/09.

61 U.S. Attorney General Eric Holder, Memorandum for Heads of Executive Departments and Agencies Concerning the Freedom of Information Act (Mar. 19, 2009) (Attorney General's FOIA Guidelines 3/19/09), *available at* http://www.usdoj.gov/ag/foia-memo-march2009.pdf.

62 Attorney General's FOIA Guidelines 3/19/09.

63 Martin Sieff, *Photo Ban on Iraq War Dead Lifted*, UPI.COM, Feb. 27, 2009, http://www.upi.com/news/issueoftheday/2009/02/27/Photo-ban-on-Iraq-war-dead-lifted/UPI-33241235755703/.

64 Executive Office of the President, *White House Voluntary Disclosure Policy Visitor Access Records* (press release), Sept. 4, 2009, http://www.whitehouse.gov/VoluntaryDisclosure.

65 Exec. Order No. 13,526, 75 Fed. Reg. 1013 (Jan. 8, 2010).

66 Alissa J. Rubin & Sangar Rahimi, *Bagram Detainees Named by U.S.*, N.Y. TIMES, Jan. 16, 2010, http://www.nytimes.com/2010/01/17/world/asia/17afghan.html.

67 *See, e.g.*, Clint Hendler, *Report Card: Obama's Marks at Transparency U.*, COLUMBIA JOURNALISM REV., Jan. 5, 2010, http://www.cjr.org/transparency/report_card.php.

68 Pub. L. No. 109-282, §§ 2(a)(2) and (b)(1), 120 Stat. 1186-87 (2006).

69 U.S. GOVERNMENT ACCOUNTABILITY OFFICE, ELECTRONIC GOVERNMENT: IMPLEMENTATION OF THE FEDERAL FUNDING ACCOUNTABILITY AND

TRANSPARENCY ACT OF 2006 (GAO 10-365) (2010) (GAO, ELECTRONIC GOVERNMENT), *available at* http://www.gao.gov/products/GAO-10-365.

70 *See* GAO, ELECTRONIC GOVERNMENT at 5. GAO randomly sampled 100 awards from the website and compared the data to information from the awarding agencies. Numerous inconsistencies were found. The most common discrepancies included the purpose of the award and the city where the award work was to be performed. The GAO also found that nine agencies had not reported awards to www.USAspending.gov. The GAO made several recommendations to the OMB to improve the website and the quality of available information. *See id.*

71 5 U.S.C. § 552(a)(6)(A)(1).

72 THE SUNSHINE IN GOVERNMENT INITIATIVE, THE WAIT FOR A FOIA RESPONSE, 2008 AND 2009 (2010) (SUNSHINE IN GOVERNMENT INITIATIVE, THE WAIT FOR A FOIA RESPONSE), *available at* http://www.sunshineingovernment.org/stats/2009/29agencies.pdf. The Sunshine in Government Initiative, a coalition of media groups including ASNE, the AP, and the NAB, among others, analyzed the 2008 and 2009 reports of the 29 largest federal agencies, which account for 97 percent of all FOIA requests. Data on average response time was available for 26 of those agencies. The Sunshine in Government Initiative, Waiting For Freedom of Information: Some Progress (2010) (Sunshine in Government Initiative, Some Progress 2010), http://www.sunshineingovernment.org/index.php?cat=224.

73 Sunshine in Government Initiative, Some Progress 2010.

74 SUNSHINE IN GOVERNMENT INITIATIVE, THE WAIT FOR A FOIA RESPONSE.

75 The reports are compiled at http://www.justice.gov/oip/reports-fy2011.html.

76 http://www.broadbandmap.gov/summarize.

77 Examples are easily found in the best online archive of Congressional Research Service reports, which is maintained by the Center for Democracy and Technology and appears at Open CRS, http://opencrs.com/ (last visited Feb. 4, 2011).

78 SOCIETY OF PROFESSIONAL JOURNALISTS, SUNSHINE WEEK 2009 SURVEY OF STATE GOVERNMENT INFORMATION ONLINE (2009) (SPJ, SURVEY OF STATE GOVERNMENT INFORMATION ONLINE), *available at* http://www.spj.org/pdf/sw09-surveyreport.pdf.

79 SPJ, SURVEY OF STATE GOVERNMENT INFORMATION ONLINE.

80 *See* The Pew Center on the States, Grading the States 2008 (Pew, Grading the States 2008), http://www.pewcenteronthestates.org/uploadedFiles/Information%20Performance.pdf.

81 Pew, Grading the States 2008.

82 Pew, Grading the States 2008.

83 Pew, Grading the States 2008.

84 Pew, Grading the States 2008.

85 Sunshine Review, States With Spending Online, http://sunshinereview.org/index.php/States_with_spending_online (last visited Feb. 4, 2011).

86 Sunshine Review, States With Spending Online.

87 Sunshine Review, Transparency Checklist, http://sunshinereview.org/index.php/The_Best_State_and_Local_Government_Websites_For_Transparency_Recognized,_March_10,_2010 (last visited Apr. 26, 2011).

88 *See, e.g.,* Sunshine Review, Sunny Awards recognize state, local governments with perfect transparency scores, http://sunshinereview.org/index.php/Best_transparency_scores (last visited Apr. 26, 2011).

89 *See, e.g.,* Sunshine Review, Sunny Awards recognize state, local governments with perfect transparency scores, http://sunshinereview.org/index.php/Best_transparency_scores (last visited Apr. 26, 2011).

90 David Cuillier, *Day 10: Police Agencies the Biggest Problem*, SOCIETY OF PROFESSIONAL JOURNALISTS ACCESS ACROSS AMERICA BLOG, May 7, 2010, http://blogs.spjnetwork.org/aaa/?p=184.

91 PACER, http://www.pacer.gov/ (last visited Jan. 24, 2011).

92 Reporters Committee For Freedom Of The Press, Electronic Access to Court Records, Spring 2007, http://www.rcfp.org/ecourt/index.html.

93 National Center for State Courts, Privacy/Public Access to Court Records FAQs, http://www.ncsc.org/topics/access-and-fairness/privacy-public-access-to-court-records/faq.aspx (last visited Feb. 4, 2011).

94 Duke Univ. School of Law Library & Technology, Court Records and Briefs, http://www.law.duke.edu/lib/researchguides/records_briefs (last visited Feb. 8, 2011).

95 The Reporters Committee for Freedom of the Press has created a summary of public access laws for police records in each state. The summaries include state policies on disclosing accident reports, the police blotter, 911 tapes, investigatory records, arrest records, criminal histories, victims, confessions, informants, police techniques and mug shots. *See* The Reporters Committee For Freedom of the Press, A Reporter's State-By-State Access Guide to Law Enforcement Records, http://www.rcfp.org/policerecords/index.html (last visited Jan. 24, 2011). The Society of Professional Journalists has created a similar database of state policies on accessing prison records, containing information on state policies governing media access, rules governing reporting tools, visitation list rules and execution witness policies. *See* The Society of Professional Journalists, Freedom of Information Covering Prisons, http://www.spj.org/prisonaccess.asp (last visited Jan. 24, 2011).

96 Sarah Klaper, *The Sun Peeking Around the Corner: Illinois' New Freedom of Information Act as a National Model*, 10 CONN. PUB. INT. L.J. 63 (Fall-Winter 2010) (*Sun Peeking Around the Corner*). As Sarah Klaper, an Instructor at DePaul University College of Law, explains:

"Pursuant to Section 9.5 of the Act, public requestors now have a new avenue of redress when a public body denies a request pursuant to FOIA, other than going straight into a lengthy and expensive court battle. Upon denial, a requestor may file a 'request for review' with the PAC within sixty days of the denial. The PAC will then determine whether further action is warranted on the case. The PAC will then either advise the requestor that the alleged violation is unfounded and take no further action or forward a copy of the request for review to the public body within seven days of receipt and request specific documents or records that the public body is required to furnish for the review. Both the public body and the requestor are also permitted to answer each other's claims in writing or supplement the review with additional affidavits or records.

"Within sixty days of the receipt of request for review, the PAC must take one of three actions: mediate the situation between the parties; issue a non-binding opinion; or make findings of fact and conclusions of law, and issue a binding opinion to resolve the matter. This binding opinion is considered to be a final decision of an administrative agency pursuant to Illinois' Administrative Review Law. If the PAC determines that a public body has violated FOIA, the public body is required to either immediately comply with the opinion, or to initiate administrative review."

10 CONN. PUB. INT. L.J. at 73 (citations omitted). Klaper further notes that:

"Only ten other states in the country, and the District of Columbia, have established public access counselors, or their equivalent, to review potential FOIA violations and issue binding opinions on these issues. However, Illinois is one of only three states in the country in which the PAC, or its equivalent, can issue binding decisions regarding FOIA violations and also seek enforcement of those binding decisions with the trial court."

Id at 76 (citations omitted).

97 *Sun Peeking Around the Corner*.

98 *Sun Peeking Around the Corner*.

99 Interview with Bill Girdner, Editor and Publisher, Courthouse News Service, by Kathleen Struck, FCC (July 2, 2010) (Girdner Interview 7/2/10).

100 Girdner Interview 7/2/10.

101 The suggestion has been made that law schools could help the cause of journalism by creating legal clinics through which students could assist in the pursuit of FOIA claims. Peter M. Shane, Statement at Ohio State Univ. Mortiz College of Law Symposium on Informing Communities: Sustaining Democracy in the Digital Age (Nov. 20, 2009). It appears that, as of late 2010, only the Georgetown University Law Center supports such a clinic. *Id.*

102 *See, e.g.,* Thomas Hargrove, *Sloppy Accounting Prevails for America's Unsolved Homicides*, SCRIPPSNEWS, June 7, 2010, http://www. scrippsnews.com/content/sloppy-accounting-prevails-americas-unsolved-homicides; *Homicide Rate, Police Procedures Questioned*, WBAL-TV, Feb. 14, 2006, http://www.wbaltv.com/news/7056945/detail. html.

103 Interview with Doug Guthrie, Court Reporter, Detroit News, by Kathleen Struck, FCC (July 1, 2010).

104 Interview with Kerry O'Brien, Dir., NYC School Survey, by Peter M. Shane, FCC (Aug. 31, 2010) (O'Brien Interview 8/31/10).

105 O'Brien Interview 8/31/10.

106 Email from Ira Chinoy, Assoc. Professor, Univ. of Maryland Philip Merrill College of Journalism, to Peter M. Shane, FCC (July 2, 2010).

107 Some grounds for resistance are appropriately built into the law. Under federal FOIA, categories of records exempt from mandatory disclosure include classified information, information relating to the pre-decisional processes of government agencies, records related to internal agency personnel practices, and certain records compiled for law enforcement purposes. The Government in the Sunshine Act, Pub. L. No. 94-409, 90 Stat. 1241 (1976) (codified at 5 U.S.C. § 552b).

108 U.S. Dep't of Transportation, Safety Complaints Search Engine, http://www-odi.nhtsa.dot.gov/complaints/index.cfm (last visited Feb. 22, 2011).

109 Similarly, Professor James T. Hamilton of Duke University has written about a variety of techniques available to journalists who want to use publicly available toxic release data to generate stories on pollution. For instance, to see which polluters report identical toxic information year after year—suggesting they are investing little time in actually monitoring their pollution. *See* James T. Hamilton, *Tracking Toxics When the Data Are Polluted: How Computational Journalism Can Uncover What Polluters Would Prefer to Hide*, NIEMAN REPORTS, Spring 2009, http://www.nieman.harvard.edu/reportsitem.aspx?id=100933.

110 Lawrence Lessig, *Against Transparency: The Perils of Openness in Government*, THE NEW REPUBLIC, Oct. 9, 2009, http://www.tnr.com/article/books-and-arts/against-transparency.

111 *See, e.g.,* Sharon Otterman & Robert Gebeloff, *Triumph Fades on Racial Gap in City, Schools*, N.Y. TIMES, Aug. 15, 2010, http://www.nytimes.com/2010/08/16/nyregion/16gap.html?_r=1&scp=1&sq=triumph%20fades&st=cse.

112 AARON SMITH, PEW RESEARCH CTR.'S INTERNET & AMERICAN LIFE PROJ., GOVERNMENT ONLINE: THE INTERNET GIVES CITIZENS NEW PATHS TO GOVERNMENT SERVICES AND INFORMATION 17 (2010), *available at* http://www.pewinternet.org/~/media//Files/Reports/2010/PIP_Government_Online_2010.pdf.

17 Emergency Information

1 National Association of Broadcasters Comments in re *FOM PN* (*FCC Launches Examination of the Future of Media and Information Needs of Communities in a Digital Age*, Public Notice, 25 FCC Rcd 384 (2010) (*FOM PN*)), filed May 7, 2010, at 23–26.

2 WORKING GROUP ON NATURAL DISASTER INFORMATION SYSTEMS SUBCOMMITTEE ON NATURAL DISASTER REDUCTION & NATIONAL SCIENCE AND TECHNOLOGY COUNCIL COMMITTEE ON ENVIRONMENT AND NATURAL RESOURCES, EFFECTIVE DISASTER WARNINGS 29 (2000), *available at* http://www.sdr.gov/NDIS_rev_Oct27.pdf.

3 *See, e.g.,* Federal Communications Commission, "Emergency Communications" (The FCC and its federal partners are working towards a comprehensive alerting system that utilizes multiple communications technologies to reach the public quickly and effectively.), http://www.fcc.gov/topic/emergency-communications (last visited May 27, 2011); Federal Emergency Management Agency, Integrated Public Alert and Warning System (IPAWS)(Transforming the national alert and warning system to enable rapid dissemination of authenticated alert information over as many communications channels as possible), http://www.fema.gov/emergency/ipaws/ (last visited May 27, 2011).

4 The precursor to the EAS was CONELRAD (Control of Electromagnetic Radiation), the first national emergency broadcasting system, established in 1951 by President Harry S. Truman, to warn the public of enemy attacks and supply emergency information. *See* Exec. Order No. 10,312, 51 Fed. Reg. 14,769 (Dec. 10, 1951). Under CONELRAD, designated AM radio stations operated on 640 or 1240 kHz during an emergency alert to prevent enemy missiles or bombers from using broadcast transmissions as a homing guide to enemy targets. *Id.* In 1963, President John F. Kennedy replaced CONELRAD with the Emergency Broadcast System (EBS), an analog transmission system that allowed all broadcast stations to continue operating on their assigned frequencies during an emergency. *See* Exec. Order No. 11,092, 63 Fed. Reg. 2216 (1963).

5 State and local emergency operations managers utilize local EAS entry points, such as the State Primary (SP) stations or LP-1s to relay local emergency messages to local areas. Local Primary sources also are responsible for coordinating the carriage of messages from the NWS or local emergency management offices as specified in EAS local area plans. The manner in which state and local EAS transmission systems vary from state to state, but can include over-the-air, telephone, links between emergency operations centers and broadcast facilities. A single station can play more than one role in the EAS, e.g. SP stations also monitor specifically-designated PEP stations and re-transmit the Presidential-level alert.

At present, the United States is divided into approximately 550 local EAS areas, each of which contains at least two Local Primary stations, designated "Local Primary One" (LP1), "Local Primary Two" (LP2), and so on. The LP stations must monitor at least two EAS sources for Presidential messages (including State Primary stations and in some cases a regional PEP station), and serve as the point of contact for state and local authorities and NWS to activate the EAS for localized events such as severe weather alerts. All other EAS Participants are designated Participating National (PN) stations and must monitor at least two EAS sources, including an LP1 and an LP2 station as specified in the state's EAS plan.

6 Jennifer Nislow, *The Wrong Time to Find Out That Emergency Alert System Doesn't Work*, SLATE, Mar. 15 & 31, 2003 (reprinted with permission from Law Enforcement News), http://www.slate.com/id/2157395/sidebar/2157437/.

7 KCJB was designated as the emergency broadcast station, but had no one on site at the time. Jack Shafer, *What Really Happened in Minot, N.D.?*, SLATE, Jan. 10, 2007, http://www.slate.com/id/2157395/. *See also* Eric Klinenberg, *Air Support*, N.Y. TIMES, Jan. 28, 2007, http://www.nytimes.com/2007/01/28/magazine/28WWLN_IdeaLab.t.html.

8 NAT'L TRANSPORTATION SAFETY BOARD, RAILROAD ACCIDENT REPORT: DERAILMENT OF CANADIAN PACIFIC RAILWAY FREIGHT TRAIN 292-16 AND SUBSEQUENT RELEASE OF ANHYDROUS AMMONIA NEAR MINOT, NORTH DAKOTA (RAILROAD ACCIDENT REPORT NTSB/RAR-04/01) 75 (2002) (NTSB MINOT ACCIDENT REPORT), *available at* http://www.ntsb.gov/publictn/2004/rar0401.pdf.

9 "Part VII Conclusions and Recommendations" in DR. M. MUSTOE, THE EMERGENCY ALERT SYSTEM: ITS VIABILITY IN THE NEW LOCALISM OF COMMERCIAL RADIO (2005), http://www.eou.edu/~mmustoe/easpaper.html.

10 NTSB MINOT ACCIDENT REPORT at 10.

11 *A synopsis of commercial radio's potential for delivering the EAS,* Memorandum from M. Mustoe, Geographer and Ph.D., Eastern Oregon Univ., to Paige Gold, FCC (Oct. 12, 2010).

12 M. Marion Mustoe, *Commentary: Reconsidering Minot and EAS*, RADIOWORLD, Jan. 18, 2006 (*Reconsidering Minot and EAS*), http://www.radioworld.com/article/2718; Interview with M. Marion Mustoe, Geographer and Ph.D., Eastern Oregon Univ., by Paige Gold, FCC (Oct. 2010) (Mustoe Interview Oct. 2010). Even in the incident where EAS was activated, that activation did not occur until about four hours after the incident. *Reconsidering Minot and EAS*; Mustoe Interview Oct. 2010.

13 *See* Jay Liotta, *You Can't Show Favoritism, Obviously, in This Industry*, KATRINA AND EMERGENCY RADIO BROADCASTING BLOG, Jan. 21, 2008, http://katrinaradioelon.wordpress.com.

14 Exec. Order No. 13407, 71 Fed. Reg. 36975 (June 26, 2006) (Exec. Order 13407).

15 Exec, Order 13407.

16 The IPAWS is being developed by FEMA, pursuant to Exec. Order 13407. According to FEMA, IPAWS objectives include to (1) "ensure that alert and warning messages can reach the public before, during and after a disaster, through as many means as possible"; (2) "diversify, and modernize the Emergency Alert System"; (3) "create an interoperability framework by establishing or adopting standards such as the Common Alert Protocol"; (4) "enable alert and warning to those with disabilities and those who do not understand the English language"; (5) "provide federal state and local alert and warning emergency communications officials access to multiple broadcast and other communications networks as a means for creating and activating alert and warning messages"; and (6) "partner with National Oceanic and Atmospheric Administration (NOAA) to enable seamless integration of message transmission through National Weather Radio (NWR) networks". Federal Emergency Management Agency, Integrated Public Alert and Warning System (IPAWS), http://www.fema.gov/emergency/ipaws/ (last visited Apr. 3, 2011).

17 Sixty-three percent of those responding to a 2010 Red Cross online survey said they use TV to get information about an emergency; 44 percent use radio and 37 percent use online news sites, far more than look at Facebook (14 percent) or Twitter (6 percent). *See* AMERICAN RED CROSS, SOCIAL MEDIA IN DISASTERS AND EMERGENCIES 5 (2010) (SOCIAL MEDIA IN DISASTERS AND EMERGENCIES), *available at* http://www.redcross.org/www-files/Documents/pdf/other/SocialMediaSlideDeck.pdf.

18 CAP employs an open, interoperable standard that incorporates XML (Extensible Markup Language), a language developed and widely used for web documents. The digital system is capable of incorporating links to voice, audio or data files, images, and multilingual translations of an alert, along with links to further information. ORGANIZATION FOR THE ADVANCEMENT OF STRUCTURED INFORMATION STANDARDS (OASIS), COMMON ALERTING PROTOCOL VERSION 1.2 (2010), http://docs.oasis-open.org/emergency/cap/v1.2/CAP-v1.2-os.html. *See also* COMMUNICATIONS SECURITY, RELIABILITY AND INTEROPERABILITY COUNCIL (CSRIC), WORKING GROUP 5A, CAP INTRODUCTION—FINAL REPORT (2010) *available at* http://www.fcc.gov/pshs/docs/csric/CSRIC%205A%20Working%20Group.pdf.

It is responsive to the requirement in Executive Order 13407 that DHS adopt a protocol to enable an interoperable alert system capable of delivering alerts to multiple communications pathways. CAP provides an alert initiator with a uniform manner of sending an alert to multiple media. CAP also is necessary for separate media to decode the alert targeted to them, without having to alter the substance of the alert to fit their format. CAP allows great flexibility in the construction of alerts (text, data, multi-media), geo-targeting of alerts, and the media to which alert are directed (TV, radio, mobile devices, highway signs).

19 *Review of the Emergency Alert System*, Third Further Notice of Rulemaking, May 26, 2011, http://transition.fcc.gov/Daily_Releases/Daily_Business/2011/db0526/FCC-11-82A1.pdf.

20 Warning, Alert, and Response Network Act, Pub. L. No. 109-347, tit. VI, § 602(a), 120 Stat. 1936 (2006) (codified at 47 U.S.C. §1201(a)).

21 *The Commercial Mobile Alert System*, First Report and Order, 23 FCC Rcd 6144, 6177 (2008).

22 *"New York City Unveils First-in-the-nation Public Safety System; Enabled Mobile Devices Will Receive Emergency Alerts at Critical Moments With Potentially Life-Saving Messages,* FCC News release, May 10, 2011, http://hraunfoss.fcc.gov/edocs_public/attachmatch/DOC-306417A1.doc.

23 E-mail from Art Botterell, Founding Trustee, Partnership for Public Warning and Research Associate, Centre for Policy Research in Science and Technology, Simon Fraser Univ., to Paige Gold, FCC (Oct. 4, 2010).

24 SOCIAL MEDIA IN DISASTERS AND EMERGENCIES at 15-18.

25 U.S. DEP'T OF HOMELAND SECURITY, HOMELAND SECURITY ADVISORY COUNCIL HSAS TASK FORCE STAKEHOLDER FEEDBACK (2009) (HOMELAND SECURITY ADVISORY COUNCIL HSAS TASK FORCE STAKEHOLDER FEEDBACK), *available at* http://www.dhs.gov/xlibrary/assets/hsas_task_

force_stakeholder_feedback.pdf. The report was the result of a 2009 Homeland Security Advisory System Task Force survey of a wide range of constituencies—state, local and tribal governments and community groups; federal agencies; the private sector; first responders; academics in the field of communications, and others working in media—concerning the effectiveness of present emergency warning systems.

26 HOMELAND SECURITY ADVISORY COUNCIL HSAS TASK FORCE STAKEHOLDER FEEDBACK at 43-44.

27 HOMELAND SECURITY ADVISORY COUNCIL HSAS TASK FORCE STAKEHOLDER FEEDBACK at 19, 25.

28 HOMELAND SECURITY ADVISORY COUNCIL HSAS TASK FORCE STAKEHOLDER FEEDBACK at 44.

29 American Red Cross, *Social Media in Disasters and Emergencies* (press release), Aug. 9, 2010, http://www.redcross.org/portal/site/en/menuitem.94aae335470e233f6cf911df43181aa0/?vgnextoid=6bb5a96d0a94a210VgnVCM10000089f0870aRCRD.

30 AMERICAN PUBLIC HEALTH ASS'N ET. AL, EXPERT ROUND TABLE ON SOCIAL MEDIA AND RISK COMMUNICATION DURING TIMES OF CRISIS: STRATEGIC CHALLENGES AND OPPORTUNITIES 4 (2009), *available at* http://www.apha.org/NR/rdonlyres/47910BED-3371-46B3-85C2-67EFB80D88F8/0/socialmedreport.pdf .

31 Jeanette Sutton, *Social Media Brings Together Resources, Creates More Resilient Communities*, EMERGENCY MANAGEMENT, July 31, 2009, http://www.emergencymgmt.com/training/Social-Media-Brings-Together-Resources.html.

32 Clay Shirky, *How Cognitive Surplus Will Change the World* (oral presentation), TED: IDEAS WORTH THINKING, June 2010, http://www.ted.com/talks/view/id/896.

33 Station Action for Emergency Readiness, About Us, http://saferstations.org/content/about.html (last visited Feb. 9, 2011). The site also notes that only one-third of all public radio stations in the U.S. have a functioning, tested, emergency readiness plan. *See id*. The project builds on the knowledge of stations in areas that have experienced disasters such as hurricanes, ice storms, floods, and wildfires. *See id*.

34 FCC, NATIONAL BROADBAND PLAN at 323 (2010) (NATIONAL BROADBAND PLAN).

18 Libraries

1 ADRIENNE CHUTE AND P. ELAINE KROE, U.S. NAT'L CTR. FOR EDUCATION STATISTICS, PUBLIC LIBRARIES IN THE UNITED STATES: FISCAL YEAR 2005 3 (2007), *available at* http://nces.ed.gov/pubs2008/2008301.pdf.

2 AMERICAN LIBRARY ASS'N, THE STATE OF AMERICA'S LIBRARIES 20 (2009), *available at* http://www.ala.org/ala/newspresscenter/mediapresscenter/presskits/2009stateofamericaslibraries/State%20draft_04.10.09.pdf.

3 SAMANTHA BECKER, MICHAEL D. CRANDALL, KAREN E. FISHER, BO KINNEY, CAROL LANDRY & ANITA ROCHA, OPPORTUNITY FOR ALL: HOW THE AMERICAN PUBLIC BENEFITS FROM INTERNET ACCESS AT U.S. LIBRARIES 186 (Institute of Museum and Library Sciences) (2010) (OPPORTUNITY FOR ALL), *available at* http://www.gatesfoundation.org/learning/Pages/us-libraries-report-opportunity-for-all.aspx.

4 OPPORTUNITY FOR ALL at 186.

5 OPPORTUNITY FOR ALL at 186.

6 OPPORTUNITY FOR ALL at 4.

7 OPPORTUNITY FOR ALL at 4.

8 OPPORTUNITY FOR ALL at 2.

9 OPPORTUNITY FOR ALL at 186.

10 DENISE M. DAVIS, JOHN CARLO BERTOT & CHARLES R. MCLURE, LIBRARIES CONNECT COMMUNITIES 3: PUBLIC LIBRARY FUNDING & TECHNOLOGY ACCESS STUDY 47-48 (American Library Ass'n) (revised 2010) (PUBLIC LIBRARY FUNDING & TECHNOLOGY ACCESS STUDY), *available at* http://www.ala.org/ala/research/initiatives/plftas/previousstudies/0809/librariesconnectcommunities3.pdf.

11 OPPORTUNITY FOR ALL at 64.

12 Catherine Ngai, *Chicago Job Seekers Move 'Offices' From Coffee Shops To Libraries,* MEDILL REPORTS—CHICAGO (Northwestern Univ.), Aug. 11, 2010 (*Chicago Job Seekers*), http://news.medill.northwestern.edu/chicago/news.aspx?id=168110.

13 FCC, CONNECTING AMERICA: THE NATIONAL BROADBAND PLAN 176 (2010) (NATIONAL BROADBAND PLAN). *available at* http://download.broadband.gov/plan/national-broadband-plan-chapter-9-adoption-and-utilization.pdf.

14 KATE WILLIAMS, THE CYBERNAVIGATORS OF CHICAGO PUBLIC LIBRARY AND THE 'INFORMATICS MOMENT': ON A BUDGET, DEMOCRATIZING INFORMATION FLOWS IN LOW-INCOME NEIGHBORHOODS 4 (Univ. of Illinois at Urbana Champaign) (2010), *available at* http://www.ifla.org/files/hq/papers/ifla76/140-williams-en.pdf.

15 *Chicago Job Seekers*.

16 OPPORTUNITY FOR ALL at 6.

17 PUBLIC LIBRARY FUNDING & TECHNOLOGY ACCESS STUDY at 34, 45.

18 PUBLIC LIBRARY FUNDING & TECHNOLOGY ACCESS STUDY at 33.

19 PUBLIC LIBRARY FUNDING & TECHNOLOGY ACCESS STUDY at 44.

20 PUBLIC LIBRARY FUNDING & TECHNOLOGY ACCESS STUDY at 44.

21 *See* 47 U.S.C. § 254 (h).

22 Universal Service Administrative Co., Questions and Answers About the E-rate, http://eratehotline.org/facts/quest.html (last visited Jan. 26, 2011) (Q & A re: E-rate Program). The discounts range between 20 and 90 percent, depending upon the poverty level of the community served.

23 Q & A re: E-rate Program. The E-rate program is governed by the rules provided in subpart F of 47 CFR 54, 47 C.F.R. §§ 54.500-54.523.

24 47 C.F.R. § 54.501(b).

25 Of those that did not apply, about a quarter found the process too complicated, more than 22 percent said the amount they would receive was not worth the effort and nearly 22 percent did not want to be subject to the CIPA filtering requirement. PUBLIC LIBRARY FUNDING & TECHNOLOGY ACCESS STUDY at 53.

26 *See* Universal Service Administrative Co., Schools and Libraries, http://www.usac.org/sl/tools/commitments-search/Default.aspx (last visited Jan. 26, 2011). Libraries and library consortium have received commitments representing about 3 percent of the amounts granted annually under the E-rate program. Combining the dollar totals for 2000–2009 with about 3 percent of the additional amount committed to consortiums that include both schools and libraries, produces a total of about $70 million/yr for libraries.

27 PUBLIC LIBRARY FUNDING & TECHNOLOGY ACCESS STUDY at 42.

28 JOHN WINDHAUSEN, JR. & MARIJKE VISSER, FIBER TO THE LIBRARY: HOW PUBLIC LIBRARIES CAN BENEFIT FROM USING FIBER OPTICS FOR THEIR BROADBAND INTERNET CONNECTION 3 (ALA Office For Information Technology Policy) (2009), *available at* http://www.pla.org/ala/aboutala/offices/oitp/PDFs/fiber%20brief_%20published.pdf.

19 Schools

1 RENEE HOBBS, DIGITAL AND MEDIA LITERACY: A PLAN OF ACTION (Aspen Institute) (2010) (DIGITAL AND MEDIA LITERACY), *available at* http://www.knightcomm.org/wp-content/uploads/2010/12/Digital_and_Media_Literacy_A_Plan_of_Action.pdf.

2 Seb Chan, *Siva Vaidhyanathan on the "Generational Myth,"* FRESH + NEW, Sept. 16, 2008, http://www.powerhousemuseum.com/dmsblog/index.php/2008/09/16/siva-vaidhyanathan-on-the-generational-myth/.

3 DIGITAL AND MEDIA LITERACY at 25, 32.

4 DIGITAL AND MEDIA LITERACY at 25, 32 (*citing*

Debora Cheney, Jeffrey Knapp, Robert Alan & Pamela Czapla, *Convergence in the Library's Newsroom: Enhancing News Collections and Services in Academic Libraries 1*, 67 COLLEGE AND RESEARCH LIBRARIES 395-417 (2006), *available at* http://crl.acrl.org/content/67/5/395.full.pdf).

5 DIGITAL AND MEDIA LITERACY at 40–41.

6 Sherri Hope Culver, Renee Hobbs & Amy Jensen, *Media Literacy in the United States*, INT'L MEDIA LITERACY RESEARCH FORUM, http://www.imlrf.org./united-states (last visited 02/08/11).

7 Center for Media Literacy, About CML, http://www.medialit.org/about-cml (last visited Apr. 4, 2011).

8 Nat'l Ass'n for Media Literacy Education, Expanding and Inspiring the Practice of MLE in the USA, http://namle.net/about-namle/vision-mission/ (last visited Jan. 26, 2011).

9 Univ. of Southern California Annenberg School for Communication and Journalism, Project New Media Literacies, http://www.newmedialiteracies.org/our-methods.php (last visited Jan. 26, 2011).

10 Temple Univ. School of Communications and Theater, Media Education Lab, http://mediaeducationlab.com/curriculum/materials (last visited Jan. 27, 2011).

11 U.S. Senators Jay Rockefeller, Olympia Snowe & John Kerry, *S. 1029—The 21st Century Skills Incentive Fund* (press release), June 10, 2009, *available at* http://www.p21.org/documents/2009-21st%20Century%20Skills%20PIFfactsheet_06-10.pdf.

12 National Association for Media Literacy Education Comments in re *Protecting Children in an Evolving Media Landscape NOI* (*Empowering Parents and Protecting Children in an Evolving Media Landscape*, Notice of Inquiry, 24 FCC Rcd 13171 (2009) (*Protecting Children in an Evolving Media Landscape NOI*)), filed Feb. 3, 2010 (NAMLE Comments in re *Protecting Children in an Evolving Media Landscape NOI*), at 12.

13 NAMLE Comments in re *Protecting Children in an Evolving Media Landscape NOI* at 12.

14 NAMLE Comments in re *Protecting Children in an Evolving Media Landscape NOI* at 12.

15 DIGITAL AND MEDIA LITERACY at 27.

16 DIGITAL AND MEDIA LITERACY at viii.

17 American Academy of Pediatrics, AAP News Room, http://www.aap.org/advocacy/releases/mediaeducation2010.htm (last visited Jan. 27, 2011).

18 American Academy of Pediatrics, *Media Education*, 104 PEDIATRICS 341–343 (1999).

19 COMMON SENSE MEDIA, DIGITAL LITERACY AND CITIZENSHIP IN THE 21ST CENTURY (2009) (DIGITAL LITERACY AND CITIZENSHIP), *available at* http://www.commonsensemedia.org/sites/default/files/DigitalLiteracy-andCitizenshipWhitePaper-Oct2009.pdf.

20 DIGITAL LITERACY AND CITIZENSHIP at 2.

21 Stonybrook Univ. School of Journalism, The Center for News Literacy at Stony Brook University Presents News Literacy: Setting a National Agenda, http://www.newsliteracyconference.com/content/?page_id=2 (last visited Jan. 27, 2011).

22 PEW RESEARCH CTR. FOR THE PEOPLE & THE PRESS, AMERICANS SPENDING MORE TIME FOLLOWING THE NEWS 18 (2010), *available at* http://people-press.org/report/?pageid=1792.

23 Megan Garber, *Leap of Faith*, COLUMBIA JOURNALISM REV. (July-Aug. 2009), http://www.cjr.org/feature/leap_of_faith_1.php.

24 Howard Schneider, *It's the Audience, Stupid!*, NIEMAN REPORTS, Fall 2007, http://www.nieman.harvard.edu/reports/article/100169/Its-the-emAudienceem-Stupid.aspx.

25 DIGITAL AND MEDIA LITERACY at 23-34.

26 DIGITAL AND MEDIA LITERACY at 34.

27 Jack Dvorak, *ERIC Digest D145-Journalism Student Performance In Language Arts*, Nov. 1999, http://www.ericdigests.org/2000-3/arts.htm.

28 CLARK, MARTIRE & BARTOLOMEO, INC., GROWING LIFELONG READERS: A STUDY OF THE IMPACT OF STUDENT INVOLVEMENT WITH NEWSPAPERS ON ADULT READERSHIP (The Newspaper Ass'n of America Found.) (2004), http://www.nieworld.com/lifelongreaders.htm (reprinted with permission).

29 Alan C. Miller, *Nieman Reports: News Literacy Project: Students Figure Out what News and Information to Trust*, THE NEWS LITERACY PROJECT, http://www.thenewsliteracyproject.org/press/news/nieman_reports_news_literacy_project_students_figure_out_what_news_and_info/ (last visited Mar. 14, 2011).

30 American Society of News Editors, News Literacy Resources, http://www.hsj.org/News_Literacy/index.cfm?menu_id=4 (last visited Jan. 28, 2011).

31 American Society of News Editors, About Us, http://www.hsj.org/content.cfm?CmsPagesID=192 (last visited Jan. 28, 2011).

32 NAMLE Comments in re *Protecting Children in an Evolving Media Landscape NOI* at 19.

33 NAMLE Comments in re *Protecting Children in an Evolving Media Landscape NOI* at 19.

34 CECIL J. PICARD, GUIDELINES FOR LIBRARY MEDIA PROGRAMS IN LOUISIANA SCHOOLS 69–70 (Louisiana State Dep't of Education) (2004), *available at* http://www.louisianaschools.net/lde/uploads/15303.pdf.

35 SUSAN ROGERS, MEDIALITERACY.COM, MEDIA LITERACY EDUCATION: WHERE TO INTEGRATE IT WITHIN MISSOURI STATE GRADE LEVEL EXPECTATIONS IN COMMUNICATION ARTS, HEALTH EDUCATION AND SOCIAL STUDIES (Nat'l Ass'n of Media Literacy Educators) (2004) (MEDIA LITERACY

EDUCATION), *available at* http://medialiteracy.com/documents/Missouri Grade Level Expectations re MLE.pdf.

36 MEDIA LITERACY EDUCATION.

37 The Common Core Standards are a state-led effort to devise common public education standards, coordinated by the National Governors Association Center for Best Practices and the Council of Chief State School Officers (the highest-level public school administrators). The standards were developed in collaboration with teachers, school administrators, and experts, to provide a clear and consistent framework to prepare our children for college and the workforce. Individual states choose whether or not to adopt these standards. The Common Core Standards declare that students ought to be able to:

"Gather relevant information from multiple print and digital sources, assess the credibility and accuracy of each source, and integrate the information while avoiding plagiarism."

"Explore a variety of digital tools to produce and publish writing, including in collaboration with peers."

"Make strategic use of digital media and visual displays of data to express information and enhance understanding of presentations."

"Evaluate the advantages and disadvantages of using different mediums (e.g., print or digital text, video, multimedia) to present a particular topic or idea."

"Make strategic use of digital media (e.g., textual, graphical, audio, visual, and interactive elements) in presentations to enhance understanding of findings, reasoning, and evidence and to add interest."

COUNCIL OF CHIEF STATE SCHOOL OFFICERS & THE NAT'L GOVERNORS ASS'N COMMON CORE STATE STANDARDS INITIATIVE, COMMON CORE STATE STANDARDS FOR ENGLISH LANGUAGE ARTS & LITERACY IN HISTORY/ SOCIAL STUDIES, SCIENCE, AND TECHNICAL SUBJECTS 18, 19, 22, 39 (2010), *available at* http://www.corestandards.org/assets/CCSSI_ELA%20Standards.pdf.

38 Common Core State Standards Initiative, Frequently Asked Questions, http://www.corestandards.org/frequently-asked-questions (last visited Jan. 28, 2011).

20 News Consumption

1 ROBERT E. BOHN & JAMES E. SHORT, HOW MUCH INFORMATION? REPORT ON AMERICAN CONSUMERS 7 (Global Information Industry Ctr., Univ. of California San Diego) (2009), *available at* http://hmi.ucsd.edu/pdf/HMI_2009_ConsumerReport_Dec9_2009.pdf.

2 PEW RESEARCH CTR. FOR THE PEOPLE & THE PRESS, AMERICANS SPENDING MORE TIME FOLLOWING THE NEWS 2 (2010) (PEW 2010 NEWS CONSUMPTION SURVEY), http://people-press.org/files/legacy-pdf/652.pdf.

3 PEW 2010 NEWS CONSUMPTION SURVEY at 2.

4 PEW 2010 NEWS CONSUMPTION SURVEY at 2.

5 PEW 2010 NEWS CONSUMPTION SURVEY at 19.

6 PEW RESEARCH CTR. FOR THE PEOPLE & THE PRESS, AUDIENCE SEGMENTS IN A CHANGING NEWS ENVIRONMENT: KEY NEWS AUDIENCES NOW BLEND ONLINE AND TRADITIONAL SOURCES, PEW RESEARCH CTR. BIENNIAL NEWS CONSUMPTION SURVEY 5 (2008) (PEW 2008 NEWS CONSUMP-

TION SURVEY), *available at* http://people-press.org/reports/pdf/444.pdf (1998, 2008 data); PEW 2010 NEWS CONSUMPTION SURVEY at 14.

7 James G. Webster, *Cable television's impact on audience for local news*, 61 JOURNALISM QUART. 419, 419-22 (1984).

8 MARKUS PRIOR, POST-BROADCAST DEMOCRACY: HOW MEDIA CHOICE INCREASES INEQUALITY IN POLITICAL INVOLVEMENT AND POLARIZES ELECTIONS 34-35 (Cambridge Univ. Press) (2007).

9 Prepared Testimony of Paul Starr, Woodrow Wilson School, Princeton Univ., FCC Workshop on the Future of Media and the Information Needs of Communities: Serving the Public Interest in the Digital Era (Mar. 4, 2010) at 3–4, *available at* http://reboot.fcc.gov/c/document_library/get_file?uuid=9d2b16ad-3bfb-4255-bdab-d6dcd4bad7d6&groupId=101236.

10 PEW 2010 NEWS CONSUMPTION SURVEY analysis. Among those going online to get news every day, 87 percent report coming across news when going online for a purpose other than to get the news. In contrast, among those going online to get the news less than once every few weeks, only 61 percent report coming across news when going online for a purpose other than to get the news. *Id.* at 28, 119.

11 U.S. CENSUS BUREAU, STATISTICAL ABSTRACT OF THE UNITED STATES: 2011 at 711 (U.S. CENSUS BUREAU STATISTICAL ABSTRACT 2011), *available at* http://www.census.gov/compendia/statab/2011/tables/11s1130.pdf.

12 When adjusted for inflation, using the 2003 BLS Inflation Calculator, media spending increased 1.8 percent while consumer spending for apparel declined 6.2 percent. The elements that make up this figure are: TV (mainly cable or satellite TV), home video, consumer books, pure-play internet services, recorded music, newspapers, consumer magazines, box office, video games, pure-play mobile, and broadcast and satellite radio. The adjustment for inflation is based on a Bureau of Labor Statistics Inflation Calculator (BLS Inflation Calculator), http://www.bls.gov/data/inflation_calculator.htm. Other consumer spending figures are from Bureau of Labor Statistics, "Table 4. Size of consumer unit: Average annual expenditures and characteristics" for 2003 (2003 BLS Consumer Unit Table), *available at* Bureau of Labor Statistics, Consumer Expenditure Survey, Expenditure Tables, http://www.bls.gov/cex/csxstnd.htm#2003.

13 U.S. CENSUS BUREAU STATISTICAL ABSTRACT 2011 at 711, *available at* http://www.census.gov/compendia/statab/2011/tables/11s1130.pdf. "Adults 18 and older were the basis for estimates for newspapers, consumer books, consumer magazines, in-flight entertainment, out-of-home media, yellow pages and home video. Persons 12 and older were the basis for the estimates for box office, broadcast TV, cable TV Internet, mobile, radio, recorded music and videogames." TV and radio" includes cable and satellite TV, broadcast TV, and broadcast and satellite radio. "Entertainment" includes home video, recorded music, box office, and videogames. "Print" includes consumer books, newspapers, and magazines.

14 JOHN B. HORRIGAN, BROADBAND ADOPTION AND USE IN AMERICA (OMNIBUS BROADBAND INITIATIVE PAPER SERIES NO. 1) 3, 24 (2010) (HORRIGAN, BROADBAND ADOPTION AND USE IN AMERICA), *available at* http://online.wsj.com/public/resources/documents/FCCSurvey.pdf.

15 NATALIE JOMINI STROUD, NICHE NEWS: THE POLITICS OF NEWS CHOICE (Oxford Univ. Press) (2011) (STROUD, NICHE NEWS); Diana C. Mutz & Paul S. Martin, *Facilitating Communication across Lines of Political Difference: The Role of Mass Media*, 95 AMER. POLIT. SCI. REV., 97, 107 (2001), *available at* www.polisci.upenn.edu/faculty/bios/Pubs/mutzAPSR2001.pdf. Shanto

Iyengar & Kyu S. Hahn, *Red Media, Blue Media: Evidence of Ideological Selectivity in Media Use*, 59 J. COMMUNICATION 19 (2009), *available at* http://pcl.stanford.edu/research/2009/iyengar-redmedia-bluemedia.pdf.

16 Based on analysis of online surfing habits, Gentzkow and Shapiro conclude that "the data clearly reject the view that liberals only get news from a set of liberal sites and conservatives only get news from a set of conservative sites." MATTHEW GENTZKOW & JESSE M. SHAPIRO, IDEOLOGICAL SEGREGATION ONLINE AND OFFLINE 17 (Chicago Booth and Nat'l Bureau of Econ. Research) (2010), *available at* http://faculty.chicagobooth.edu/jesse.shapiro/research/echo_chambers.pdf.

R. Kelly Garrett argues that "individuals are using control over their political information environment to increase their exposure to opinion-reinforcing information, but ... they are not using this control to systematically screen out other opinions." R. Kelly Garrett, *Politically Motivated Reinforcement Seeking: Reframing the Selective Exposure Debate*, 59 J. COMMUNICATION 676, 692 (2009); *see also* R. Kelly Garrett, *Echo Chambers Online? Politically Motivated Selective Exposure among Internet Users*, 14 J. COMPUTER-MEDIATED COMMUNICATION 265, 265-285 (2009).

The evidence of exposure to the other side, however, should not be overstated. Gentzkow and Shapiro's data do not let them examine (a) whether multiple users use the same computer, (b) how visitors perceive the sites they visit—perhaps Beck is more likely to direct readers to the New York Times to illustrate a ridiculous claim. Sunstein (2007) reviews research conducted by Eszter Hargittai and her colleagues: "On the 'blogrolls' referring readers to other blogs, conservatives are far more likely to list other conservatives, and liberals are far more likely to list other liberals. When blogs refer to discussions by other bloggers, they usually cite likeminded others. To be sure, there is a significant amount of cross-citation as well. But—and here is perhaps the most striking finding—a plurality of cross-citations simply cast contempt on the views that are being cited! Only a quarter of cross-ideological posts involve genuine substantive discussion." (p. 149). Although there is evidence to suggest that citizens are not repelled by information incongruent with their beliefs, more research is needed. CASS R. SUNSTEIN, REPUBLIC.COM 2.0 (Princeton Univ. Press) (2009) (*citing* Eszter Hargittai, Jason Gallo and Matt Kane, *Mapping the Political Blogosphere: Analysis of Large-Scale Online Political Discussion*, Unpublished manuscript, Northwestern University, 2006).

21 Types of News

1 Interview with Robert Papper, Dir., RTDNA/Hofstra Univ. Annual Survey, by Cynthia Kennard, FCC (Sept. 30, 2010) (Papper Interview 9/30/10).

2 MICHELE MCLELLAN, COMMUNITY NEWS SURVEY PART THREE—REVENUE STREAMS (Donald W. Reynolds Journalism Institute) (2010), http://www.rjionline.org/fellows-program/mclellan/block-by-block/part-3.php.

3 Michele McLellan, *Debunking the Replacement Myth*, DONALD W. REYNOLDS JOURNALISM INSTITUTE, July 26, 2010, http://www.rjionline.org/projects/mcellan/stories/debunk/index.php.

4 BILL GRUESKIN, AVA SEAVE, AND LUCAS GRAVES, THE STORY SO FAR: WHAT WE KNOW ABOUT THE BUSINESS OF JOURNALISM, COLUMBIA JOURNALISM REV 37 (2011), http://cjrarchive.org/img/posts/report/The_Story_So_Far.pdf (BILL GRUESKIN, AVA SEAVE, AND LUCAS GRAVES,

THE STORY SO FAR). The Columbia Journalism School report stated: "TBD.com ran into trouble right from the start. In February 2011, just six months after going live, the Washington, D.C. area's high-profile experiment in local online journalism announced that it would lay off half of its editorial staff, detach its site from its TV-station partner and reinvent itself as a culture-and-lifestyle site." *Id.*

5 Ken Doctor, *The Newsonomics of Less Is More, More or Less*, NEWSONOMICS, Sept. 3, 2010, http://newsonomics.com/the-newsonomics-of-less-is-more-more-or-less/.

6 Marion Geiger, *The AP and Ohio newspapers*, EDITORSWEBLOG, Apr. 22, 2009, http://www.editorsweblog.org/newspaper/2009/04/ap_and_ohio_newspapers.php.

7 Carole Wurzelbacher, *Ohio Newspapers Collaborate to Expose State Pension Scandal*, EDITORSWEBLOG, Jun. 22, 2010, http://www.editorsweblog.org/newsrooms_and_journalism/2010/06/ohio_newspapers_collaborate_to_expose_st.php.

8 *See* PEW RESEARCH CTR'S INTERNET & AMER. LIFE PROJ., HOW THE PUBLIC PERCEIVES COMMUNITY INFORMATION SYSTEMS (2011), http://www.pewinternet.org/Reports/2011/08-Community-Information-Systems.aspx under "Explore Survey Questions."

9 RACHEL MERSEY, VIVIAN VAHLBERG, & BOB LEBAILLY, NEWS THAT MATTERS: AN ASSESSMENT OF CHICAGO'S INFORMATION LANDSCAPE 10, 14-15, 19 (Chicago Community Trust) (2010), http://www.cct.org/impact/partnerships-initiatives/expanding-information-access/community-news-matters/summit.

10 PEW RESEARCH CTR'S INTERNET & AMER. LIFE PROJ., UNDERSTANDING THE PARTICIPATORY NEWS CONSUMER (2010) (PEW, UNDERSTANDING THE PARTICIPATORY NEWS CONSUMER), http://www.pewinternet.org/Reports/2010/Online-News.aspx; Email from Kristen Purcell, Pew, to Steven Waldman, FCC (May 3, 2010).

11 Analysis of News and Information Web Traffic in Sample Markets:

To conduct our analysis, we started with comScore's "Local Market Internet Site Visitation April 2010" data. To create this dataset, comScore tracks web usage among its local market research groups along a number of different categories. Whereas the conventional definition of "News and Information" may be broadly defined to include such topics as business and finance, community interest, conversational media such as blogs, directories and resources, entertainment, government, sports, or other periodical reports or announcements of broad interest, we decided to restrict our analysis to comScore's narrowly defined category entitled "News/Information" which comScore defines as "Sites that provide news and information regarding domestic and international issues. This category also contains sites with articles and periodicals on current events and weather. Examples: New York Times Digital, About.com."

Starting with the entirety of comScore's dataset for the top 100 markets, we separated the markets into thirds and selected one market at random from each third. We then extracted out the web traffic data for just the News/Information category. For each of the websites visited by six or more study participants, comScore provided the raw data (actual traffic metrics for the group), and projected data (traffic metrics scientifically weighted by comScore to project market-wide estimates of traffic) as well as their own measures of local and national "reach." For our base analysis, we sorted by various traffic metrics and observed the patterns.

For our ownership analysis, we overlaid comScore's data with our own original research, identifying the highest-level parent company to own each website or web entity. We then developed a categorization mechanism, to separate the websites and web entities into discernable and analytically useful groups pertaining to national versus local ownership, traditional media versus Internet-based media and private, public, or non-profit ownership. We counted the number of parent companies in each category and observed the patterns.

For our local filter analysis we took the universe of News and Information websites and filtered out the websites with a disproportionately national reach based on comScore's measurement called "Reach Index." This yielded a list of websites with a particularly local appeal, and thus more likely, though not exclusively, to fall into the local news category. It is possible that some of websites on this list are of national interest, but may have been of particular interest to the observed locale in the sample month. We observed this once in one of our sample markets. To analyze this list, we then sorted list by the measure comScore calls "Local Reach" to get an ordered list of the most popular News and Information websites within the local market. We observed the patterns in the resulting list.

It should be noted, that because of the way in which comScore collects and reports its granular-level website data, in order to avoid double counting of the traffic metrics for the universe of all News and Information websites visited by six or more comScore market-based research participants at some point during the month of April 2011, we actually look at the universe of all News and Information parent web entities with one or more websites each visited by six or more market-based research subjects at some point during the month of April 2010 and consider each group of websites owned by the same parent web entity, a single website.

12 If we take the universe of all News and Information websites visited by the Toledo research group and filter out the websites with a disproportionately national reach, we can get closer to identifying the websites with a particularly local appeal, and thus more likely, though not exclusively, fall into the local news category.

13 "Nielsen Analysis" in PEW, STATE OF NEWS MEDIA 2010, http://stateofthemedia.org/2010/online-summary-essay/nielsen-analysis/.

14 ADAM LYNN, S. DEREK TURNER, & MARK COOPER, NEW MEDIA AND LOCALISM: ARE LOCAL CABLE CHANNELS AND LOCALLY FOCUSED WEBSITES SIGNIFICANT NEW AND DIVERSE SOURCES OF LOCAL NEWS AND INFORMATION? AN EMPIRICAL ANALYSIS 13 (Freepress) (2007), *available at* http://www.policyarchive.org/handle/10207/bitstreams/8002.pdf.

15 Jeremy W. Peters, *Newspaper Circulation Falls Broadly but at Slower Pace*, N.Y. TIMES, Oct. 25, 2010, http://mediadecoder.blogs.nytimes.com/2010/10/25/newspaper-circulation-falls-broadly-but-at-slower-pace/ (explaining *The New York Times*' circulation was 876,638 from April through September, 2010, down 5.5 percent from 927,851 during the same time the year before); *See also* NEWSPAPER ASS'N OF AMERICA, TOTAL PAID CIRCULATION—NEWSPAPER CIRCULATION VOLUME (2010), http://www.naa.org/TrendsandNumbers/Total-Paid-Circulation.aspx (stating the overall weekday paid circulation in the U.S. in 2009 was 45,653,000).

16 Mary Walton, *Investigative Shortfall*, AMER. JOURNALISM REV.(Sept. 2010) (*Investigative Shortfall*), http://www.ajr.org/article.asp?id=4904.

17 *Investigative Shortfall.*

18 *Investigative Shortfall.*

19 National Public Radio Comments in re *FOM PN* (*FCC Launches Examination of The Future of Media and the Contributions of Public Media to the Information Needs of America, Comment Sought*, GN Docket No. 10-25, Public Notice (*FOM PN*)), filed May 7, 2010 (NPR Comments), at 3.

20 National Public Radio (NPR), *About NPR: Audience*, http://www.npr.org/about/aboutnpr/audience.html (last visited Ma y 24, 2011).

21 "Magazines: Audience" in PEW RESEARCH CTR.'S PROJ. FOR EXCELLENCE IN JOURNALISM, THE STATE OF THE NEWS MEDIA (2010) (PEW, STATE OF THE NEWS MEDIA 2010), http://stateofthemedia.org/2010/magazines-summary-essay/audience/.

22 "Magazines: News Investment" in PEW, STATE OF THE NEWS MEDIA 2010, http://stateofthemedia.org/2010/magazines-summary-essay/news-investment/.

23 Brett Pulley, *U.S. News to Discontinue Monthly Print Magazine, Shift Focus to Digital*, BLOOMBERG, Nov. 5, 2010, http://www.bloomberg.com/news/2010-11-06/u-s-news-to-discontinue-monthly-print-magazine-shift-focus-to-digital.html; Tanzina Vega & Jeremy W. Peters, *Audio Pioneer Buys Newsweek*, N.Y. TIMES, Aug. 3, 2010, at B1, available at http://www.nytimes.com/2010/08/03/business/media/03newsweek.html.

24 *See* "Magazines: By the Numbers" in PEW RESEARCH CTR.'S PROJ. FOR EXCELLENCE IN JOURNALISM, THE STATE OF THE NEWS MEDIA (2011) (PEW, STATE OF THE NEWS MEDIA 2011), http://stateofthemedia.org/2011/magazines-essay/data-page-4/. Data drawn from Audit Bureau of Circulation, FAS-FAX reports.

25 *See* "Magazines: By the Numbers" in PEW, STATE OF THE NEWS MEDIA 2011. Numbers prior to 2009 are rounded.

26 Interview with Alexis Gelber, Editorial Consultant, Adjunct Professor at New York Univ. Arthur L. Carter J. Institute, by M.K. Guzda Struck, FCC (Oct. 6, 2010).

27 Jeffrey Kluger, *How Haditha Came to Light*, TIME, June. 4, 2006, http://www.time.com/time/magazine/article/0,9171,1200780,00.html (stating "The Haditha killings occurred last November, but it wasn't until January that TIME first heard whispers about them. The initial account of the incident was published in March in the magazine and on TIME.com.").

28 *See, e.g.,* Alex Kuczynski, *Media Talk: Reporters Square Off Over Clinton Scandal*, N.Y. TIMES, Feb. 7, 2000, http://www.nytimes.com/2000/02/07/business/media-talk-reporters-square-off-over-clinton-scandal.html (calling Michael Isikoff "a scrappy reporter whose work ushered in the story about President Clinton's relationship with Monica S. Lewinsky").

29 Jeff Bercovici, *Number Crunch: Downsizing at the Newsweeklies*, MIXED MEDIA, Nov. 8, 2008, http://www.portfolio.com/views/blogs/mixed-media/2008/11/18/number-crunch-downsizing-at-the-newsweeklies.

30 "Magazines: News Investment" in PEW, STATE OF THE NEWS MEDIA 2010, http://stateofthemedia.org/2010/magazines-summary-essay/news-investment/ (noting that TIME's staff decreased from 362 in 1983 to 147 in 2009, while Newsweek's staff decreased from 348 to 150 in the same time period).

31 MPA—THE ASSOCIATION OF MAGAZINE MEDIA, PUBLISHERS INFORMATION BUREAU MAGAZINE AD REPORT: Q3 2010 (2010), http://www.magazine.org/advertising/revenue/by_ad_category/pib-3q-2010.aspx.

32 Rachel Smolkin, *Finding a Niche*, AMER. JOURNALISM REV. (April/May 2007), http://www.ajr.org/article.asp?id=4297.

33 Katerina-Eva Matsa, Tom Rosenstiel & Paul Moore, "Magazines: A Shake-Out for News Weeklies: News Magazines" in PEW, STATE OF THE NEWS MEDIA 2011, http://stateofthemedia.org/2011/magazines-essay/.

34 Jodi Enda, *Capital Flight*, AMER. JOURNALISM REV. (June/July 2010), http://www.ajr.org/Article.asp?id=4877 (Enda, *Capital Flight*).

35 Enda, *Capital Flight*.

36 Enda, *Capital Flight*.

37 Understanding Government, Preventive Journalism, http://understand-inggov.org/?cat=21 (last visited May 24, 2011).

38 The Pulitzer Prize, International Reporting, *available at* http://www.pulitzer.org/bycat/International-Reporting (last visited Feb 08, 2011); Pew Research Center's Project for Excellent Journalism, *The Changing Newsroom: Changing Content*, JOURNALISM, July. 21, 2008, *available at* http://www.journalism.org/node/11963.

39 Peter Arnett, *State of The American Newspaper Goodbye, World*, AMERI-CAN JOURNAL REVIEW (1998).

40 These 2010 figures were obtained by a telephone survey of the newspa-pers listed in Arnett, *State of The American Newspaper: Goodbye, World*.

41 Priya Kumar, *Shrinking Foreign Coverage*, AM. JOURNALISM REV. (Dec./Jan. 2011), http://www.ajr.org/article.asp?id=4998.

42 "The Changing Newspaper Newsroom" in PEW, STATE OF THE NEWS MEDIA 2008, http://stateofthemedia.org/2008/special-reports-the-future-of-advertising/the-changing-newspaper-newsroom/.

43 Diana Saluri Russo, *Is the Foreign News Bureau Part of the Past?*, GLOBAL JOURNALIST, Jan. 30, 2010, http://www.globaljournalist.org/stories/2010/01/30/is-the-foreign-news-bureau-part-of-the-past/.

44 "The Changing Newspaper Newsroom" in PEW, STATE OF THE NEWS MEDIA 2008, http://stateofthemedia.org/2008/special-reports-the-future-of-advertising/the-changing-newspaper-newsroom/.

45 *See* "The Changing Newspaper Newsroom" in PEW, STATE OF THE NEWS MEDIA 2008, http://stateofthemedia.org/2008/special-reports-the-future-of-advertising/the-changing-newspaper-newsroom/.

46 iCasualties.org: Iraq Coalition Casualty Count, http://icasualties.org/ (last visited May 31, 2011).

47 "War Coverage Declines in 2010" in PEW, STATE OF THE NEWS MEDIA 2011, http://stateofthemedia.org/2011/network-essay/data-page-5/.

48 *See* "Network TV: News Investment, in PEW, STATE OF THE NEWS MEDIA 2010, http://stateofthemedia.org/2008/network-tv-intro/news-invest-ment/.

49 Email from Andrew Tyndall, The Tyndall Report, to Tamara Smith, FCC (July 23, 2010).

50 *See* "Network TV: News Investment" in PEW, STATE OF THE NEWS MEDIA 2008, http://stateofthemedia.org/2008/network-tv-intro/news-invest-ment/.

51 Bloomberg, *Bloomberg Markets Magazine Relaunches with November 2010 Issue* (press release), October 4, 2010, http://www.businesswire.com/news/home/20101004006912/en/Bloomberg-Markets-Magazine-Relaunches-November-2010-Issue.

52 Jodi Enda, *Retreating from the World*, AMER. JOURNALISM R. (Dec./Jan. 2011) (*Retreating from the World*), http://www.ajr.org/Article.asp?id=4985.

53 "Content Analysis: A Year in the News" in PEW, STATE OF THE NEWS MEDIA 2010, http://stateofthemedia.org/2010/online-summary-essay/content-analysis/.

54 *Retreating from the World*.

55 *Foreign Correspondents: Who Covers What.*

56 *See* "Cable TV: News Investment" in PEW, STATE OF THE NEWS MEDIA 2010, http://stateofthemedia.org/2010/cable-tv-summary-essay/news-investment/.

57 *Retreating from the World.*

58 Global Voices, http://globalvoicesonline.org/about/, last visited (May 25, 2011).

59 Global Post, http://www.globalpost.com/, last visited (May 25, 2011).

60 James T. Hamilton, *The (Many) Markets for International News: How News from Abroad Sells at Home*, 11 (5) JOURNALISM STUDIES 650, 657 (2010).

61 "Network TV: News Investment, in PEW, STATE OF THE NEWS MEDIA 2010, http://stateofthemedia.org/2008/network-tv-intro/news-investment/; "Cable TV: News Investment" in PEW, STATE OF THE NEWS MEDIA 2010, http://stateofthemedia.org/2010/cable-tv-summary-essay/news-invest-ment/.

62 ROY GUTMAN, HOW WE MISSED THE STORY: OSAMA BIN LADEN, THE TALIBAN, AND THE HIJACKING OF AFGHANISTAN xii, 261 (U.S. Institute of Peace) (2008).

63 International Crisis Group, http://www.crisisgroup.org/en/about.aspx (last visited May 25, 2011).

64 Andrew Stroehlein, *Without Foreign Coverage We Miss More Than News*, INT'L CRISIS GROUP, May 18, 2009, http://www.crisisgroup.org/en/publication-type/commentary/without-foreign-coverage-we-miss-more-than-news.aspx.

65 "Network TV: News Investment" in PEW RESEARCH CTR.'S PROJ. FOR EXCELLENCE IN JOURNALISM, THE STATE OF THE NEWS MEDIA (2004) (PEW, STATE OF NEWS MEDIA 2004), http://stateofthemedia.org/2004/network-tv-intro-2/news-investment/.

66 Alex Weprin, *Al Jazeera English Leads Egypt Coverage, But Most Americans Still Can't Watch It*, TVNEWSER, Jan. 31, 2011, http://www.mediabistro.com/tvnewser/al-jazeera-english-leads-egypt-coverage-but-most-americans-still-cant-watch-it_b50751#.

67 "Online Essay", in PEW, STATE OF THE NEWS MEDIA 2011), http://stateofthemedia.org/2011/online-essay/data-page-7/.

68 Haider Rizvi, *Foreign News Channels Drawing U.S. Viewers*, INTER PRESS SERVICES NEWS AGENCY, Jan. 29, 2010, http://ipsnews.net/news.asp?idnews=50157.

69 LEE C. BOLLINGER, UNINHIBITED, ROBUST, AND WIDE-OPEN-A FREE PRESS FOR A NEW CENTURY 85 (Oxford Univ. Press) (2010).

22 The Media Food Chain

1 ALEX JONES, LOSING THE NEWS: THE FUTURE OF THE NEWS THAT FEEDS DEMOCRACY 1 (Oxford Univ. Press) (2009).

2 Lee Rainie, *The Future of Public Relations*, PRESS LIFT, Aug. 22, 2010, at 23, http://blog.presslift.com/post/1043498152/the-pew-research-centers-pew-internet-american.

3 *See* "Part 5: News gets personal, social, and participatory: The 'Daily Me' and the 'Daily Us'" in PEW, UNDERSTANDING THE PARTICIPATORY NEWS CONSUMER, http://www.pewinternet.org/Reports/2010/Online-News/Part-5/3-Daily-Me-and-Daily-Us.aspx.

4 Daniel Terdiman, *Study: Wikipedia as Accurate as Britannica*, CNET NEWS, Dec. 15, 2005, http://news.cnet.com/Study-Wikipedia-as-accurate-as-Britannica/2100-1038_3-5997332.html.

5 *See* PEW RESEARCH CTR'S INTERNET & AMER. LIFE PROJ., HOW NEWS HAPPENS: A STUDY OF THE NEWS ECOSYSTEM OF ONE AMERICAN CITY (2011), http://www.journalism.org/analysis_report/how_news_happens.

6 Interview with Mark Thompson, Time Magazine, by M.K. Guzda Struck, FCC (July 15, 2010).

7 Interview with Bill Girdner, Editor and Publisher, Courthouse News Service, by M.K. Guzda Struck, FCC (July 2, 2010).

8 Interview with Doug Guthrie, Court Reporter, Detroit News, by M.K. Guzda Struck, FCC (July 1, 2010).

9 Enda, *Capital Flight.*

10 Interview with Wally Dean, Dir., Training, Committee of Concerned Journalists, by Cynthia C. Kennard, FCC (Aug. 2010).

11 Ryan Chittum, *Free Tunes! Not: Business Press Stampedes into Qtrax Blunder*, COLUMBIA JOURNALISM REV., Feb. 7, 2008, http://www.cjr.org/the_audit/free_tunes_not.php.

12 Jeremy Porter, *Journalists Find Some News Releases Useful*, JOURNAL-ISTICS, July 14, 2010, http://blog.journalistics.com/2010/journalists-find-some-news-releases-useful/.

13 ROBERT MCCHESNEY & JOHN NICHOLS, THE DEATH AND LIFE OF AMERICAN JOURNALISM (Nation Books) (2010).

14 *What Type of Multimedia Content Will Broaden the Appeal of a Press Release*, ALLBUSINESS.COM, Jan. 20, 2010, http://www.allbusiness.com/technology/software-services-applications-internet-social/13762388-1.html.

15 *PRNews and PRWeb, Study Shows Big Shift in PR Pros' Perceptions and Use of Releases*, PR WEB, Dec. 10, 2009, http://www.prweb.com/releases/prweb3322454.htm.

16 Interview with Mark Silverman, Editor, Nashville Tennessean by Steven Waldman, FCC (May 24, 2010).

17 Testimony of David Simon, former Baltimore Sun reporter and Creator, HBO series The Wire, Hearing on the Future of News and Journalism, U.S. Senate Subcommittee on Communications, Technology and the Internet (May 8, 2009), *available at* http://www.onthemedia.org/transcripts/2009/05/08/01.

18 MARINA GUSEVA, ET AL., PRESS FREEDOM AND DEVELOPMENT: AN ANALYSIS OF CORRELATIONS BETWEEN FREEDOM OF THE PRESS AND THE DIFFERENT DIMENSIONS OF DEVELOPMENT, POVERTY, GOVERNANCE AND PEACE 15 (Ctr. for Peace and Security at Sciences Po Univ. & United Nations Educational Scientific and Cultural Organization) (2008) (PRESS FREEDOM AND DEVELOPMENT), *available at* http://unesdoc.unesco.org/images/0016/001618/161825e.pdf.

19 *See* PRESS FREEDOM AND DEVELOPMENT at 108–111. The study also found a correlation between press freedom and higher ratings on scales of good governance. *Id.* That was consistent with the earlier discussion in this paper of the importance of the press to government accountability.

20 KNIGHT COMMISSION ON THE INFORMATION NEEDS OF COMMUNITIES IN A DEMOCRACY, INFORMING COMMUNITIES: SUSTAINING DEMOCRACY IN THE DIGITAL AGE 12 (Aspen Institute) (2009) (KNIGHT COMMISSION, INFORMING COMMUNITIES), *available at* http://www.knightcomm.org/wp-content/uploads/2010/02/Informing_Communities_Sustaining_Democracy_in_the_Digital_Age.pdf.

21 KNIGHT COMMISSION, INFORMING COMMUNITIES at 14.

22 Alícia Adserà, Carles Boix & Mark Payne, *Are You Being Served? Political Accountability and Quality of Government*, 19 J. LAW, ECON. & ORGANIZATIONS 445, 457-469 (2003). For a similar conclusion resting on measures of press freedom, *see* Aymo Brunetti & Beatrice Weder, *A Free Press is Bad News for Corruption*, 87 J. PUBLIC ECON. 1801 (2003).

23 FELIX OBERHOLZER-GEE & JOEL WALDFOGEL, MEDIA MARKETS AND LOCALISM: DOES LOCAL NEWS EN ESPAÑOL BOOST HISPANIC VOTER TURNOUT? 12 (2006), *available at* http://www.hbs.edu/research/pdf/07-062.pdf.

24 JESSICA TROUNSTINE, INCUMBENCY AND RESPONSIVENESS IN LOCAL ELECTIONS 15, 23 (2010), *available at* http://faculty.ucmerced.edu/jtrounstine/low_info_draft4.pdf.

25 SAM SCHULHOFER-WOHL & MIGUEL GARRIDO, DO NEWSPAPERS MATTER? EVIDENCE FROM THE CLOSURE OF THE CINCINNATI POST (Nat'l Bureau of Economic Research) (2009), *available at* http://www.nber.org/papers/w14817.pdf.

26 Jackie Filla & Martin Johnson, *Local News Outlets and Political Participation*, 45 URBAN AFFAIRS REV. 688 (2010).

27 Matthew Gentzkow, *Television and Voter Turnout*, 121 QUART. J. ECON. 931 (2006), *available at* http://faculty.chicagobooth.edu/matthew.gentzkow/research/tv_turnout.pdf.

28 Sheila Grissett, *Shifting Federal Budget Erodes Protection from Levees; Because of Cuts, Hurricane Risk Grows*, TIMES PICAYUNE, June 4, 2004, at 1. In a quote from the *Times-Picayune* article Al Naomi, a Senior Project Manager at the Army Corps of Engineers, said, "I can't tell you exactly what that could mean this hurricane season if we get a major storm…It would depend on the path and speed of the storm, the angle that it hits us. But I can tell you that we would be better off if the levees were raised,…and I think it's important and only fair that those people who live behind the levee know the status of these projects." *Id.*

29 KNIGHT COMMISSION, INFORMING COMMUNITIES at 12.

23 Diversity

1 LOUIS CANTOR, WHEELIN' ON BEALE: HOW WDIA-MEMPHIS BECAME THE NATION'S FIRST ALL-BLACK RADIO STATION AND CREATED THE SOUND THAT CHANGED AMERICA (Pharos) (1992).

2 Auburn Avenue Research Library on African-American Culture and History, WERD Oral History Interviews, http://aafa.galileo.usg.edu/aafa/view?docId=ead/aarl90-008-ead.xml;query=;brand=default (last visited MAY 25, 2011).

3 Donna L. Halper, *The First African-American Radio Station Owner: Jesse B. Blayton Sr.*, LWF NETWORK & AFRICAN-AMERICAN RADIO, 2008, http://www.lwfaah.net/aaradio/1staa_radio.htm.

4 *Radio: New Net*, TIME, Dec. 28, 1953, www.time.com/time/magazine/article/0,9171,858419,00.html; *See also* World News Network, *National Negro Network*, http://wn.com/National_Negro_Network (last visited May 25, 2011).

5 NAT'L ADVISORY COMM'N ON CIVIL DISORDER, KERNER PLUS 40 REPORT 83 (Univ. of Pennsylvania Annenberg School for Communication and Ctr. for Africana Studies & The Institute for Advanced Journalism Studies at North Carolina A&T State Univ.) (2008), *available at* http://www.ifajs. org/events/spring08/Kerner40/Report.pdf.

6 *See. e.g., Petition for Rulemaking to Require Broadcast Licensees to Show Nondiscrimination in Their Employment Practices,* 13 FCC 2d 766 (1968); *see also Strategies for Advancing Minority Ownership Opportunities in Telecommunications* (The Final Report of the Advisory Committee on Alternative Financing for Minority Opportunities in Telecommunications to the Federal Communications Commission *("Rivera Report"); Commission Policy Regarding the Advancement of Minority Ownership in Broadcasting,* 92 FCC 2d 849 (1982); *Petition for Rulemaking to Require Broadcast Licensees to Show Nondiscrimination in Their Employment Practices,* 23 FCC 2d 430 (1970).

7 ARBITRON INC., BLACK RADIO TODAY 2 (2010) (BLACK RADIO TODAY), *available at* http://www.arbitron.com/downloads/BlackRadioToday_2010.pdf. The report tracks several radio formats, including Urban Adult Contemporary, Urban Contemporary, Rhythmic Contemporary Hit Radio ("CHR"), News/Talk/Information, Pop Contemporary Hit Radio, All Sports, Religious and Adult Contemporary. *Id.* at 5.

8 BLACK RADIO TODAY at 11.

9 Interview with James Winston, Executive Director, Nat'l Ass'n of Black Owned Broadcasters by FCC (Mar. 2010) (Winston Interview 3/10). Indeed, a recent Pew study noted that only 9 percent of African-Americans used radio to get their national and international news, as compared to 18 percent of whites and 12 percent of Hispanics. *See* "African-American Media: Evolving in the New Era" in PEW, STATE OF NEWS MEDIA 2011, http://stateofthemedia.org/2011/african-american/ (*citing* PEW RESEARCH CTR. FOR THE PEOPLE & THE PRESS, INTERNET GAINS ON TELEVISION AS PUBLIC'S MAIN NEWS SOURCE (2011), *available at* http://people-press.org/2011/01/04/internet-gains-on-television-as-publics-main-news-source/).

10 Winston Interview 3/10. NABOB and others advocated for Commission action to address concerns about discriminatory conduct in advertising on broadcast radio and television that impacted the flow of advertising revenue to minority owned broadcast stations. As part of a broader ownership diversity rulemaking proceeding, the Commission in 2007 adopted a ban on discrimination in advertising sales contracts designed to avoid "no Urban/no Spanish" dictates in broadcast advertising contracts. *Promoting Diversification of Ownership in the Broadcasting Services,* 2006 Quadrennial Review, 23 FCC Rcd 5922, 5941-42 (2008) (*Broadcast Diversity Order*).

11 American Urban Radio Networks, http://www.aurn.com/ (last visited May 25, 2011).

12 American Urban Radio Networks, http://www.aurn.com/ (last visited May 25, 2011).

13 FCC, *Sirius XM Implements Merger Condition That Provides Leased Channels to Diverse Programmers* (press release), Apr. 18, 2011, http://www.fcc.gov/Daily_Releases/Daily_Business/2011/db0418/DOC-305856A1.pdf.

14 Testimony of Lisa Fager Bediako, Pres. & Co-founder, Industry Ears, FCC Hearing on Localism (Oct. 31, 2007), Tr. at 80:21–81:6, at 30, *available at* http://www.fcc.gov/localism/.

15 Univision Presentation 12/13/10. Those trends are consistent among Hispanic viewers that watch the 11:00 pm newscast in those markets. *Id.* at 46.

16 UNIV. OF NORTH TEXAS CTR. FOR SPANISH LANGUAGE MEDIA, THE STATE OF THE SPANISH LANGUAGE MEDIA ANNUAL 2010 REPORT 1 (2011) (THE STATE OF THE SPANISH LANGUAGE MEDIA ANNUAL 2010 REPORT), *available at* http://www.spanishmedia.unt.edu/english/downloads/annualreport/Sofslm2010.pdf

17 ARBITRON INC., HISPANIC RADIO TODAY 4 (2010) (HISPANIC RADIO TODAY 2010), *available at* http://www.arbitron.com/downloads/hisp_radio_today_10.pdf.

18 HISPANIC RADIO TODAY 2010 at 6.

19 HISPANIC RADIO TODAY 2010 at 40–41. Time spent listening is an estimate of the amount of time the average listener spent with a station (or total radio) during a particular daypart. *Id.* at 9.

20 HISPANIC RADIO TODAY 2010 at 42.

21 Interview with Loris Ann Taylor, Exec. Dir., Native Public Media, by Jamila Bess Johnson, FCC (Mar. 11, 2010) (Taylor Interview 3/11/10). "The term 'Indian Tribe[s]' or 'Federally-Recognized Indian Tribes' means any Indian or Alaska Native tribe, band, nation, pueblo, village or community which is acknowledged by the federal government to constitute a government-to-government relationship with the United States and eligible for the programs and services established by the United States for Indians." *Establishing a Government-to-Government Relationship with Indian Tribes,* Policy Statement, 16 FCC Rcd 4078, 4080 (2000) (*citing* The Federally Recognized Indian Tribe List Act of 1994, Pub. L. No. 103–454. 108 Stat. 4791 (1994) (codified at 25 U.S.C. § 479a)).

22 Taylor Interview 3/11/10.

23 Native Voice One, http://www.nv1.org/about.html (last visited May 25, 2011).

24 Koahnic Broadcast Corp., National Native News: News for All Americans, http://www.nativenews.net/ (last visited May 25, 2011).

25 Koahnic Broadcast Corp., www.koahnicbroadcast.org/index.html (last visited May 25, 2011); *See also* Koahnic Broadcast Corp., Native America Calling: The National Electronic Talking Circle, www.nativeamericacalling.com/nac_about.shtml (last visited May 25, 2011). The 52 stations that air Native America Calling are in Alaska, Arizona, California, Colorado, Idaho, Montana, New Mexico, North Carolina, North Dakota, Oklahoma, Oregon, South Dakota, Utah, Washington, Wisconsin, and Wyoming. Koahnic Broadcast Corp., Native America Calling Affiliates, http://www.nativeamericacalling.com/nac_affiliates.shtml (last visited May 25, 2011). The program is available online. *Id.; See also* Native Voice One, www.nv1.org/ (last visited May 25, 2011).

26 Corporation for Public Broadcasting, Indian Country News Bureau, http://www.cpb.org/programs/program.php?id=429 (last visited May 25, 2011); Taylor Interview 3/11/10.

27 Native Public Media Comments in re *FOM PN (Comment Sought On FCC Launches Examination of the Future of Media and Information Needs of Communities in a Digital Age,* GN Docket No. 10-25, Public Notice, 25 FCC Rcd 384 (2010) (*FOM PN*)), filed May 7, 2010 (Native Public Media Comments), at 21–22.

28 Black Entertainment Television Networks, Presentation to FCC's Advisory Committee on Diversity re: African-American Media Consumption Trends, June 15, 2010, (BET Networks Presentation to FCC Advisory Comm. on Diversity 6/15/10), at 8, *available at* http://www.fcc.gov/DiversityFAC/061510/bet-trends-presentation-061510.ppt.

29 THE STATE OF THE SPANISH LANGUAGE MEDIA ANNUAL 2010 REPORT at 10; *See also* Melissa Guthrie, *Nielsen: Hispanic TV Homes Jump to*

40% This Season, BROADCASTING & CABLE, Sept. 3, 2010, http://www. broadcastingcable.com/article/456686-Nielsen_Hispanic_TV_Homes_ Jump_to_40_This_Season.php.

30 ADVERTISING AGE, HISPANIC FACT PACK: 2009 EDITION 33 (2009) (HISPANIC FACT PACK 2009), *available at* http://adage.com/images/random/0709/HispFP2009.pdf.

31 Univision, Presentation to FCC, GN Docket No. 10-25 (Dec. 13, 2010) (Univison Presentation 12/13/10), at 27.

32 Univision press release, 2006 http://corporate.univision.com/corp/en/ pr/Los_Angeles_06042006-1.html

33 Joe Mathews, *Switch to Español*, WASHINGTON POST, MAY 11, 2008, http://www.washingtonpost.com/wp-dyn/content/article/2008/05/09/ AR2008050902540.html?hpid=opinionsbox1.

34 Seventy-seven percent of the parents of second generation Asian Americans, also referred to as the "1.5" generation, prefer to speak English. *See* SIMMONS MARKET RESEARCH BUREAU, TEENS AND ADULT NATIONAL CONSUMER SURVEYS: PACKAGED FACTS 18 (2005).

35 Asian American Journalists Ass'n, Report to FCC Future of Media Team, GN Docket No. 10-25 (Dec. 6, 2010).

36 Interview with Peter Mathes, Chairman, AsianMedia Group, LLC, by FCC (July 15, 2010) (Mathes Interview 7/15/10).

37 Mathes Interview 7/15/10.

38 AsianMedia is financed with private equity resources, according to Mathes. Mathes Interview 7/15/10.

39 Mathes adds that he attempted to stream his TV signals online but found the enterprise too costly and with the lack of sufficient Internet-based advertising was forced to discontinue online streaming. Mathes Interview 7/15/10. Other commenters also raised concerns about the ability of the Internet to address the information needs of their communities. The Communications Workers of America states, "[w]hile the Internet continues to offer exciting new possibilities for dissemination of news and information, it is no substitute for print and broadcast media." Communications Workers of America Comments in re *FOM PN*, filed May 7, 2010 (Communications Workers of Amer. Comments), at 4.

40 New America Media, http://newamericamedia.org/ (last visited May 25, 2011).

41 In addition to aggregating news stories, NAM works to expand the creation of content for underserved populations through its partnership with journalism schools. New America Media, *About Us*, http://newamericamedia.org/about/ (last visited May 25, 2011). Additionally, the Asian American Justice Center (AAJC) advocates for media diversity on behalf of Asian Americans. As part of that effort, AAJC works with other media advocacy groups to achieve parity in the representation of Asian Americans on television and other media. *See, e.g.,* AAJC, The 2010 Asian Pacific American Media Coalition Report Card on Television Diversity & Statement by Karen K. Narasaki (President, AAJC and Chair, Asian Pacific American Media Coalition), http://advancingequality. org/2010-diversity-report-card/.

42 Alliance for Women in Media, Inc. surmises that women-owned stations account for only approximately five percent of full power television stations and six percent of radio stations. *See* Alliance for Women in Media, Inc. Comments in re *FOM PN*, filed May 7, 2010, at 2.

43 Reply of National Association of Black Owned Broadcasters in re *Comcast/NBC PN* (*Application of Comcast Corp., General Electric and NBC Universal, Inc. for Consent to Assign Licenses or Transfer Control of Licenses, Comment Sought*, MB Docket No. 10-56, Public Notice, 25 FCC Rcd 4407 (2010) (*Comcast/NBC PN*)), filed July 21, 2010, at 2. According to recent Commission data, there are 1,774 commercial and educational television stations and 14,728 commercial and educational radio stations in the U.S. as of March 31, 2011. FCC, *Broadcast Station Totals as of March 31, 2011* (press release), May 6, 2011 , *available at* http://hraunfoss.fcc. gov/edocs_public/attachmatch/DOC-302349A1.pdf.

44 National Hispanic Media Coalition *et al.* Comments in re *FOM PN*, filed May 7, 2010 (Nat'l Hisp. Media Coalition Comments) at 13–14 (citing S. DEREK TURNER & MARK COOPER, OUT OF THE PICTURE: MINORITY & FEMALE TV STATION OWNERSHIP IN THE UNITED STATES 3, 10 (Free Press) (2006) (TURNER & COOPER, OUT OF THE PICTURE), *available at* http:// www.freepress.net/files/out_of_the_picture.pdf; *See also* CATHERINE J.K. SANDOVAL, MINORITY COMMERCIAL RADIO OWNERSHIP IN 2009: FCC LICENSING AND CONSOLIDATION POLICIES, ENTRY WINDOWS, AND THE NEXUS BETWEEN OWNERSHIP, DIVERSITY AND SERVICE IN THE PUBLIC INTEREST 5 (2009) (MINORITY COMMERCIAL RADIO OWNERSHIP IN 2009), *available at* http://law.scu.edu/faculty/file/Minority%20Commercial%20 Radio%20Broadcasters%20Sandoval%20MMTC%202009%20final%20.pdf. According to Sandoval's study, 139 stations were Latino-owned. *Id.* at 8.

45 TURNER & COOPER, OUT OF THE PICTURE at 2.

46 TURNER & COOPER, OUT OF THE PICTURE at 4.

47 TURNER & COOPER, OUT OF THE PICTURE at 4.

48 *Policies to Promote Rural Radio Service and to Streamline Allotment and Assignment Procedures*, Notice of Proposed Rulemaking, 24 FCC Rcd 5239, 5248 (2009) (*Rural Radio NPRM*) (noting "the problem is most acute in the case of tribal lands that are near large Urbanized Areas, or where the suburbs of such Urbanized Areas have begun to encroach upon areas adjacent to tribal lands. In such instances, spectrum scarcity may limit the opportunities for new radio service.").

49 *Policies to Promote Rural Radio Service and to Streamline Allotment and Assignment Procedures*, First Report and Order and Further Notice of Proposed Rulemaking, 25 FCC Rcd 1583 (2010).

50 *Rural Radio NRPM*, 24 FCC Rcd at 5247–48.

51 In March 2011, the Commission adopted a further Report and Order that enhances opportunities for Tribal entities to provide broadcast radio service to Native communities. *See* FCC, *FCC Takes Action to Help Strengthen and Expand Broadband and Other Communications Services in Native Nations* (press release), Mar. 3, 2011, http://www.fcc.gov/ Daily_Releases/Daily_Business/2011/db0303/DOC-304981A1.pdf.

52 Taylor Interview 3/11/10.

53 FCC staff compiled the data on bankruptcies. Although the data do not reveal whether the owners were minority, anecdotal evidence suggests that minority broadcasters have been hit hard by the recent financial crisis. For example, Amador Bustos, former president and CEO of Bustos Media LLC filed applications to transfer control of 28 Spanish language television and radio stations to NAP Broadcast Holdings LLC. Bustos attempted to work through his financial difficulties brought on by a lack of advertising revenue, but was in default to his lenders. NAP stands for the initials of the three senior lenders, NewStart, Atalaya and Prudential. *Bustos Media Files to Transfer All Stations*, RADIO INK MAGAZINE, June 30, 2010, http://www.radioink.com/article. asp?id=1860408&spid=24698; *See generally* MINORITY COMMERCIAL RADIO OWNERSHIP IN 2009.

54 Interview with Francisco Montero, Co-Managing Partner, Fletcher, Heald & Hildreth, P.L.C., by FCC staff (May 25, 2010); S. Jennell Trigg, a Washington D.C. lawyer representing small- and minority-owned telecommunications businesses, believes that the U.S. Treasury should encourage community banks and financial institutions to provide small and micro-loans to local minority-owned communications firms. This type of financial lifeline, "can help keep the lights on" at minority firms and avoid job losses in local communities. Interview with S. Jennell Trigg, Chair, Intellectual Property and New Technology Group, Lerman Senter PLLC, by FCC staff (May 2010).

55 Communications Workers of America & Media Council Hawaii Comments in re *FOM PN*, filed May 7, 2010, at 4–7; Minority Media and Telecommunications Council Comments in re *FOM PN*, filed May 7, 2010 at 6–7.

56 Elena Shore, *Attention NBC Telemundo: Latinos Need Local News Too,* NEW AMERICA MEDIA, Nov. 1, 2006, http://news.newamericamedia.org/news/view_article.html?article_id=1d7944d313122e7ca7f9262bc4dcdb61. Iván Román, Executive Director of the National Association of Hispanic Journalists (NAHJ) states that not long after the consummation of the NBC/Telemundo merger, NBC eliminated Telemundo's local newscasts in five of the top 10 Hispanic markets—Houston, Dallas, San Antonio, San Jose and Phoenix—and replaced them with a regionally-produced newscast hub out of Fort Worth, Texas. NBC's action resulted in 700 employees being laid off, including NAHJ members. *See id.*

57 FCC, *FCC Grants Approval of Comcast-NBCU Transaction* (press release), Jan. 18, 2011, http://hraunfoss.fcc.gov/edocs_public/attachmatch/DOC-304134A1.pdf.

58 *See, e.g.,* KOFI ASIEDU OFORI, WHEN BEING NO. 1 IS NOT ENOUGH: THE IMPACT OF ADVERTISING PRACTICES ON MINORITY-OWNED AND MINORITY-FORMATTED BROADCAST STATIONS (Civil Rights Forum on Communications Policy) (1999); *see also* FCC Commissioner Robert M. McDowell, Remarks at FCC Diversity Advisory Committee Meeting (Dec. 2, 2010), at 20 (referring to the BMW-Mini Cooper "no urban" incident in the summer of 2009), http://www.fcc.gov/DiversityFAC/meeting120210.html.

59 *Broadcast Diversity Order,* 23 FCC Rcd at 5941–42. Another key issue in minority media: Ratings and audience measurement dictate the advertising rates that broadcasters are able to charge. Minority broadcasters have raised concerns about recent modifications to ratings methodologies that impact their ability to attract advertising. The PPM Coalition, a group of minority-owned broadcast entities and trade associations (consisting of the National Association of Black Owned Broadcasters, Spanish Radio Association, Minority Media and Telecommunications Council, American Hispanic Advertising Association, Border Media Partners, Entravision Communications Corporation, ICBC Broadcast Holdings, Inc., Spanish Broadcasting System, Inc., and Univision Communications Inc.) filed an Emergency Petition on September 2, 2008, asking the Commission to conduct a Section 403 inquiry into the PPM methodology, using its investigatory authority to issue subpoenas for the production of documents and to take testimony. Arbitron, Inc., a nationally recognized radio audience research firm that provides ratings data for radio stations, has been replacing its diary-based radio ratings with PPM-based ratings in major markets. The Portable People Meter ("PPM") is a mobile phone-sized device that consumers wear throughout the day. It automatically detects inaudible identification codes that are embedded in certain radio station programming to which the consumer is exposed. In May 2009, the Commission released a Notice of Inquiry which sought comment on allegations that PPMs undercount minority audiences and that such undercounting particularly affects the ratings of urban-formatted stations targeted to minority audiences, undermining the financial viability of those stations, and thereby potentially affecting diversity on the airwaves. *Impact of Arbitron Audience Ratings Measurements on Radio Broadcasters,* MB Docket 08-187, Notice of Inquiry, 24 FCC Rcd 6141 (2009). On April 22, 2010, Arbitron and PPMC announced that they had settled their outstanding disputes. On May 3, 2011, the Commission granted PPMC´s request to withdraw its emergency petition. *See Impact of Arbitron Audience Ratings Measurements on Radio Broadcasters Order*, MB Docket 08'187, FCC 11-70) *rel.* May 3, 2011. However concerns about ratings technologies and methodologies and their impact on minority audiences continues.

60 *See* Public Notice, *Media Bureau Announces Revisions to License Renewal Procedures and Form 303-S*, DA No. 11-489 (MB rel. Mar. 14, 2011). *See also* FCC Enforcement Advisory, *Non-Discrimination in Broadcast Advertising*, DA 11-500 (Enf. Bur. rel. Mar. 22, 2011).

61 Wisconsin Historical Society, African-American Newspapers and Periodicals: Freedom's Journal, Volume 1, http://www.wisconsinhistory.org/libraryarchives/aanp/freedom/volume1.asp (last visited May 25, 2011). *Freedom's Journal* was founded and edited by Samuel E. Cornish and John B. Russworm, free Black men, who envisioned the newspaper as a platform for the approximately 500,000 free persons of color in the U.S., stating, "From the press and the pulpit we have suffered much by being incorrectly represented." Several years later, the noted journalist and statesman Frederick Douglas continued the evolution of the Black press with his founding of the *The North Star* newspaper in December 1847. Public Broadcasting Service, Biographies: Frederick Douglass, http://www.pbs.org/blackpress/news_bios/douglass.html (last visited May 25, 2011).

62 National Newspaper Publishers Association (NNPA), http://www.nnpa.org/ (last visited May 25, 2011); Interview with Danny Bakewell, Chairman, National Newspaper Publishers Association, by FCC (Sept. 2010). Many Black papers publish once or several times a week (but seldom daily); and are available in public locations in neighborhoods populated by their readership or by subscription delivery. Included among NNPA's membership are such notable papers as *New York Amsterdam News*, *Afro-American* (Washington) and the *Chicago Defender*. For a listing of other Black-owned newspapers, *See* NNPA, *NNPA Member Papers*, http://www.nnpa.org/index.php?option=com_content&task=view&id=16&Itemid=45 (last visited May 25, 2011).

63 NNPA, http://www.nnpa.org/ (last visited Feb. 14, 2011); Interview with Danny Bakewell, Chairman, National Newspaper Publishers Association, by FCC (Sept. 2010) (Bakewell Interview 9/10).

64 These consumers, Bakewell asserts, have been disproportionately "de-valued" because the Black-owned newspapers that support the information needs of African-Americans do not traditionally receive the advertising revenue from companies seeking to reach that readership. Bakewell Interview 9/10. Other industry stakeholders have noted that "advertisers and agencies do not perceive a need" to spend their ad dollars with ethnic media when they assume that a general market buy will cover these consumers. *See, e.g.,* AMY KORZICK GARMER, UNMASSING AMERICA: ETHNIC MEDIA AND THE NEW ADVERTISING MARKETPLACE 15 (The Aspen Institute) (2006), *available at* http://www.aspeninstitute.org/sites/default/files/content/docs/communications%20and%20society%20program/C&SUnmassingAmerica.pdf.

65 Sally Lehrman, *The Danger of Losing the Ethnic Media*, BOSTON GLOBE, Mar. 5, 2009, http://www.boston.com/bostonglobe/editorial_opinion/oped/articles/2009/03/05/the_danger_of_losing_the_ethnic_media/ ("[D]ay after day, the various branches of ethnic media follow some of the most important and contentious issues, ones that grab the attention of the mainstream media only sporadically.").

66 Interview with Aníbal Torres Jr., Publisher, *MundoHispánico*, by FCC staff (Sept. 2010) (Torres Interview 9/10). Torres states that his newspaper has a wide readership, but its content is primarily aimed at dominant Spanish-speaking consumers. He adds that Hispanics that are more acculturated to the U.S. tend to read English language newspapers

67 Torres Interview 9/10.

68 Torres Interview 9/10.

69 "Hispanic Media" in PEW RESEARCH CTR.'S PROJ. FOR EXCELLENCE IN JOURNALISM, THE STATE OF THE NEWS MEDIA (2009) (PEW, STATE OF THE NEWS MEDIA 2009), http://stateofthemedia.org/2009/ethnic-intro/hispanic/.

70 *See* "Hispanic Media" in PEW, STATE OF THE NEWS MEDIA 2009. Pew cites as examples of this trend *Hoy New York*, a Spanish-language daily paper, which published its final print edition in December 2009 (*Id.*); *Asian-Week*, an English-language weekly that caters to Asian Americans and that published its last print edition in January 2009 ("Asian American Media" in PEW, STATE OF THE NEWS MEDIA 2009, http://stateofthemedia.org/2009/ethnic-intro/asian-american/); and *San Francisco Bay View*, which ceased publishing its weekly print version during the summer of 2009 (*see* "African-American Media" in PEW, STATE OF THE NEWS MEDIA 2009, http://stateofthemedia.org/2009/ethnic-intro/african-american/).

71 PAMELA NEWKIRK, WITHIN THE VEIL: BLACK JOURNALISTS, WHITE MEDIA (NYU Press) (2002).

72 Communications Workers of Amer. Comments at 3.

73 *See* PEW RESEARCH CTR.'S PROJ. FOR EXCELLENCE IN JOURNALISM & SOCIAL AND DEMOGRAPHIC TRENDS, MEDIA, RACE AND OBAMA'S FIRST YEAR: A STUDY OF AFRICAN-AMERICANS IN U.S. NEWS COVERAGE 1–2 (2010) (PEW, OBAMA'S FIRST YEAR), *available at* http://www.journalism.org/sites/journalism.org/files/African%20American%20Coverage%20FINAL.pdf. Pew's year-long study covered mainstream media outlets, including newspapers, cable and network television, radio and news websites. Pew's measurement is based on the news hole, which is the total time and space a story takes, not the number of stories.

74 PEW, OBAMA'S FIRST YEAR at 13.

75 PEW, OBAMA'S FIRST YEAR at 13–14.

76 PEW, OBAMA'S FIRST YEAR at 13–14.

77 PEW, OBAMA'S FIRST YEAR at 26.

78 *Hispanics in the News: Events Drive the Narrative*, PEW RESEARCH CTR.'S PROJ. FOR EXCELLENCE IN JOURNALISM, December 7, 2009, http://www.journalism.org/analysis_report/hispanics_news.

79 Nat'l Hisp. Media Coalition Comments at 15, 18. NHMC in its filed comments refers to various studies and analyses on the disparity in coverage of Latinos and issues of interest to that community. NHMC notes that of the estimated 12,600 stories aired on ABC, CBS and NBC network evening newscasts in 2005 only 105 or 0.83 percent were exclusively about Latinos. *Id.* at 16; *See also* NETWORK BROWNOUT REPORT 2006 at 19 (noting that, of 115 stories examined, four were exclusively about Latinos and two featured Latinos as news sources)..

80 Nat'l Hisp. Media Coalition Comments at 19–21.

81 Nat'l Hisp. Media Coalition Comments at 18.

82 *Newsroom Employment Up Slightly, Minority Numbers Plunge for Third Year*, AMERICAN SOCIETY OF NEWS EDITORS, April 7, 2011 (*Newsroom Employment Up Slightly*), http://asne.org/article_view/articleid/1788/newsroom-employment-up-slightly-minority-numbers-plunge-for-third-year.aspx.

83 Letter from Unity: Journalists of Color to Julius Genachowski, Chairman, FCC, GN Docket No. 10-25 (filed Mar. 5, 2010).

84 Radio Television Digital News Ass'n, *RTDNA/Hofstra University Survey: Number of Minority Journalists Down in 2009; Story Mixed for Female Journalists* (press release) (RTDNA, Minority Journalists Survey Press Release), Sept. 22, 2010, http://www.rtdna.org/pages/posts/rtdnahofstra-survey-number-of-minority-journalists-down-in-2009-story-mixed-for-female-journalists1083.php. Kathy Chow, Executive Director of the Asian American Journalists Association (AAJA), notes that the number of Asian American journalists is shrinking, with membership declining from over 2,000 to 1,400 members over the past year. Interview with Kathy Chow by FCC staff (June 29, 2010).

85 RTDNA, Minority Journalists Survey Press Release.

86 BOB PAPPER, NUMBER OF MINORITY JOURNALISTS DOWN IN 2009: STORY MIXED FOR FEMALE JOURNALISTS 1 (Radio Television Digital News Association/Hofstra Univ.) (2009), *available at* http://www.rtdna.org/media/women_minorities_survey_final.pdf. Papper has observed that since the FCC discontinued collecting employment data from broadcast licensees several years ago, the overall percentages in radio have dropped steadily, but less so in television. *Id.; See also* RTDNA, Minority Journalists Survey Press Release.

87 NHMC, *Over Three Dozen Diverse Organizations Urge the FCC to Reinstate Collection of Equal Employment Opportunity Data* (press release), Oct. 21, 2010 (NHMC, *Collection of Equal Employment Opportunity Data*), http://www.nhmc.org/content/media-ownership; *see also* Letter from NHMC, *et al.* to Marlene H. Dortch, Secretary, FCC, MB Docket No. 10-103 (filed Oct. 21, 2010). According to the U.S. Bureau of Labor Statistics (BLS), annual data collected in 2009 show a disparity among minorities as compared to the overall population in media-related fields. For example, in 2009 BLS reported that 80,000 Americans worked as news analysts, reporters and correspondents, of which 93.8 percent are White, 1.8 percent are Black or African-American, .9 are Asian and 4.0 are Hispanic or Latino. *See* U.S. DEP'T OF LABOR & U.S. BUREAU OF LABOR STATISTICS, LABOR FORCE CHARACTERISTICS BY RACE AND ETHNICITY 17 (Office of Employment and Unemployment Statistics, Division of Labor Force Statistics) (2009), *available at* http://www.bls.gov/cps/cpsrace2009.pdf.

88 *See* NHMC, *Collection of Equal Employment Opportunity Data*.

89 Testimony of Wade Henderson, Pres. & C.E.O., Leadership Conference for Civil Rights, FCC Hearing on Localism, Oct. 31, 2007, Tr. at 95:17–96:4, at 35, *available at* http://hraunfoss.fcc.gov/edocs_public/attachmatch/DOC-278750A1.pdf.

90 *Petition for Rulemaking to Require Broadcast Licenses to Show Nondiscrimination in Their Employment Practices*, Report and Order, 18 FCC 2d 240 (1969); *see also Nondiscrimination in the Employment Policies and Practices of Broadcast Licensees,* 54 FCC 2d 354 (1975) (adopting a Model EEO Program to ensure that minorities and women are given equal and full consideration for job opportunities). *See* 47 C.F.R. §

73.2080 (broadcast EEO rule). EEO regulations for cable television operators stem from a 1972 proceeding. *See Report and Order,* 34 F.C.C. 2d 186 (1972). [Cable rules started with this 1972 ruling.] The Commission's EEO rules for multichannel video program distributors ("MVPDs"), 47 C.F.R. § 76.71, *et seq.*, were implemented pursuant to Section 634 of the Cable Communications Policy Act of 1984, Pub. L. No. 98-549, 98 Stat. 2779 (1984), that applied to cable operators, and the Cable Television Consumer Protection and Competition Act of 1992, Pub. L. No. 102-385, 106 Stat. 1460 (1992), that extended the rules to other MVPDs. *See also* 47 C.F.R. §§ 21.920, 25.601, 74.996, 76.1702, 76.1802, and 100.51.

91 *Review of the Commission's Broadcast and Cable Equal Employment Opportunity Rules and Policies,* Second Report and Order and Third Notice of Proposed Rule Making, MM Docket No. 98-204, 17 FCC Rcd 24018 (adopted new broadcast and MVPD rules).

92 *Review of the Commission's Broadcast and Cable Equal Employment Opportunity Rules and Policies,* Third Report and Order and Fourth Notice of Proposed Rule Making, MM Docket No. 98-204 19 FCC Rcd 9973, 9975-77 ¶¶ 4–9 (2004) (*Third Report and Order*).

93 47 C.F.R. § 73.2080 (c). The Commission's current EEO rules stem from its efforts to comply with the court decisions in *Lutheran Church* decision and subsequent court decisions regarding the constitutionality of provisions of its EEO rules, including *Lutheran Church—Missouri Synod v. FCC*, 141 F.3d 344 (D.C. Cir. 1998), and *MD/DC/DE Broadcasters Association v. FCC*, 236 F.3d 13, (D.C. Cir. 2001), *cert. denied*, 122 S.Ct. 920 (2002)). *See also Suspension of the Broadcast and Cable Equal Employment Opportunity Program Requirements,* 16 FCC Rcd 2872, n.1 (2001).

94 *Third Report and Order*.

95 The Commission sought public comment on, among other things, the impact of the Confidential Information Protection and Statistical Efficiency Act of 2002 (CIPSEA) on the collection and public availability of its employment reporting forms. *See* Pub. L. 107-347, 116 Stat 2962, Dec. 17, 2002, codified in note to 44 U.S.C. § 3501; *see also Third Report and Order,* 19 FCC Rcd 9973, 9978 ¶14. Although the 2004 Order re-instated the annual employment report Forms 395-A and 395-B, the filing requirement remains suspended until a final order is released concerning the confidentiality of the forms. 73 FR 62992, October 22, 2008.

96 *See* JON P. GANT, NICOL E. TURNER-LEE, YING LI & JOSEPH S. MILLER, NATIONAL MINORITY BROADBAND ADOPTION: COMPARATIVE TRENDS IN ADOPTION, ACCEPTANCE AND USE (Joint Ctr. for Political and Economic Studies) (2010) *available at* http://www.jointcenter.org/publications1/publication-PDFs/MTI_BROADBAND_REPORT_2.pdf (examining the activities of African-Americans who utilize broadband technology). The Joint Center Report notes that a higher percentage of African-Americans (78 percent) and Hispanics (64 percent) use the Internet to look online for information about jobs as compared to 48 percent of White Internet users. *Id.* at 20. Additionally, African-American Internet users are also more likely than White and Hispanic users to look online for religious or spiritual information (52 percent) and ideas about starting an online business (28 percent). *Id.*

97 BET Networks Presentation to FCC Advisory Comm. on Diversity 6/15/10.

98 BET Networks Presentation to FCC Advisory Comm. on Diversity 6/15/10, at 8.

99 BET Networks Presentation to FCC Advisory Comm. on Diversity 6/15/10, at 7–9; *See also* "African-American Media: Evolving in the New Era" in PEW, STATE OF THE NEWS MEDIA 2011.

100 "African-American Media: Evolving in the New Era" in PEW, STATE OF THE NEWS MEDIA 2011.

101 "African-American Media: Evolving in the New Era" in PEW, STATE OF THE NEWS MEDIA 2011.

102 Web 2.0/Power Users are those proficient among the top three rungs of their Social Technographics Ladder: Critics, Conversationalists, & Critics.

103 TOM WEBSTER, EDISON RESEARCH, TWITTER USAGE IN AMERICA 4 (2010) (TWITTER USAGE IN AMERICA), http://www.edisonresearch.com/home/archives/2010/04/twitter_usage_in_america_2010_1.php. *See also* "African-American Media: Evolving in the New Era" in PEW, STATE OF THE NEWS MEDIA 2011 (citing a Pew Internet & American Life study released in December 2010 which found that non-Hispanic Blacks are more than twice as likely to use Twitter compared to White Internet users).

104 Farhad Manjoo, *How Black People Use Twitter,* SLATE, Aug. 10, 2010 (*How Black People Use Twitter*), http://www.slate.com/id/2263462/; Virginia Heffernan, *Making a Hashtag of It*, N.Y. TIMES, MAY 22, 2011, http://opinionator.blogs.nytimes.com/2011/05/22/making-a-hashtag-of-it/?hp.

105 PEW 2010 NEWS CONSUMPTION SURVEY at 93.

106 PEW 2010 NEWS CONSUMPTION SURVEY at 93.

107 Michel Martin, *Can I Just Tell You? Missing Girls Shouldn't Be Missing From The Media*, NATIONAL PUBLIC RADIO, Jan. 24, 2011, http://www.npr.org/2011/01/24/133182895/The-Media-And-The-Missing-Does-Race-Influence-Coverage.

108 *See* JOHN HORRIGAN, PEW RESEARCH CTR.'S INTERNET & AMERICAN LIFE PROJ., WIRELESS INTERNET USE 4 (2009) (PEW, WIRELESS INTERNET USE), *available at* http://www.pewinternet.org/~/media//Files/Reports/2009/Wireless-Internet-Use-With-Topline.pdf.

109 PEW, WIRELESS INTERNET USE at 19. Handheld Internet use on the average day grew by 73 percent for the general population from the end of 2007 to the beginning of 2009. *Id.* Pew's figures indicate that Hispanics in the U.S. were more likely to have been early adopters of mobile Internet access than other racial/ethnic demographics. In 2007, 18 percent of Hispanic Americans stated that they accessed the Internet on their mobile device on the average day—compared with 9 percent of White Americans, and 12 percent of African-Americans. PEW, WIRELESS INTERNET USE at 18.

110 AARON SMITH, PEW RESEARCH CTR'S INTERNET & AMERICAN LIFE PROJ., TECHNOLOGY TRENDS AMONG PEOPLE OF COLOR (2010) (PEW, TECHNOLOGY TRENDS AMONG PEOPLE OF COLOR), http://www.pewinternet.org/Commentary/2010/September/Technology-Trends-Among-People-of-Color.aspx.

111 PEW, TECHNOLOGY TRENDS AMONG PEOPLE OF COLOR.

112 Taylor Interview 3/11/10. Taylor indicated that there was no 911-Emergency access on reservations and tribal lands.

113 Native Public Media Comments in *FOM PN* at 2, 6, 7, 23–24 (stating "increasing the access of Native terrestrial radio stations to digital communications and technology, while at the same time making it possible for stations to enhance the already vital programming and services provided to their respective communities would provide an enormous opportunity to begin to bridge the historical, yet persistent, digital and media divide").

114 "African-American Media: Evolving in the New Era" in PEW, STATE OF THE NEWS MEDIA 2011.

115 TV One is a venture of Radio One, Inc., the largest minority-controlled radio broadcast firm primarily targeting African-American and urban listeners, and Comcast Corporation, the largest cable operator in the U.S. along with Bear Stearns, Constellation Ventures, Syndicated Communications and Opportunity Capital Partners. TV One, Inside TV One, http://www.tvoneonline.com/inside_tvone/ (last visited May 26, 2011).

116 News One for Black America, http://newsone.com/ (last visited May 26, 2011).

117 The Root, http://www.theroot.com/ (last visited May 26, 2011).

118 BlackAmericaWeb.com, http://www.blackamericaweb.com/ (last visited May 26, 2011).

119 AOL Black Voices, http://www.blackvoices.com/ (last visited May 26, 2011).

120 Maynard Institute, Richard Prince's Journal-isms, http://mije.org/richard-prince (last visited May 26, 2011).

121 Interview with David Wilson, Managing Editor, theGrio.com, by Jeffrey Tignor and J. Evan Shapiro, FCC (Aug. 2010) (Wilson Interview).

122 Wilson Interview.

123 Interview with Sharon Pian Chan, Nat'l Pres., Asian American Journalists Ass'n, by FCC staff (November 30, 2010) (Pian Chan Interview 11/30/10).

124 Email from Sharon Pian Chan to Jeffrey Tignor, FCC (Dec. 6, 2010); Interview with Sharon Pian Chan by FCC staff (Dec. 6, 2010) (Pian Chan Interview 12/6/10).

125 Pian Chan Interview 12/6/10.

126 Interview with Cleveland Spears, General Manager/Program Director, im4radio.com, by FCC staff (May 21, 2010) (Spears Interview 5/21/10).

127 Spears Interview 5/21/10.

128 Interview with Cleveland Spears by FCC staff (March 8, 2011).

129 HISPANIC CYBERSTUDY, MARKETING TO THE WEB'S MOST RAPIDLY GROWING POPULATION 15 (AOL Advertising & Cheskin) (2009) (HISPANIC CYBERSTUDY, WEB MARKETING), available at http://advertising.aol.com/sites/default/files/HispanicCyberStudy-2010.pdf.

130 HISPANIC CYBERSTUDY, WEB MARKETING at 27-29 (citing Internet World Stats, World Languages by Country, http://www.internetworldstats.com/stats7.htm (last visited May 26, 2011)). Additionally, the U.S. Hispanic population is very diverse in terms of income, national origin and English fluency, thus, it is difficult to reach broad conclusions about media and information needs and consumption. See, e.g., GRETCHEN LIVINGSTON, PEW HISPANIC CTR., THE LATINO DIGITAL DIVIDE: THE NATIVE BORN VERSUS THE FOREIGN BORN (2010) (PEW, THE LATINO DIGITAL DIVIDE), available at http://pewhispanic.org/reports/report.php?ReportID=123 (noting "[t]echnology use among foreign-born Latinos continues to lag significantly behind that of their U.S.-born counterparts" and that "nativity differences are especially pronounced when it comes to internet use.").

131 HISPANIC CYBERSTUDY, WEB MARKETING 2009 at 34.

132 ADVERTISING AGE, HISPANIC FACT PACK: 2010 EDITION 26 (2010) (HISPANIC FACT PACK 2010), available at http://www.adagewhitepapers.com/adage/hispanicfactpack2010#pg1.

133 Univision, http://www.univision.com/portal.jhtml (last visited May 26, 2011).

134 Terra, http://www.terra.com/ (last visited May 26, 2011).

135 Yahoo! en Espanol, http://espanol.yahoo.com/ (last visited May 26, 2011).

136 MSN Latino, http://latino.msn.com/ (last visited May 26, 2011).

137 Batanga, http://www.batanga.com/es/?nolang=true (last visited May 26, 2011).

138 TWITTER USAGE IN AMERICA at 23; See also HISPANIC FACT PACK 2010 at 27. Advertising Age also notes the Hispanics comprise 17.6 percent of MySpace users. Id.

139 PEW, THE LATINO DIGITAL DIVIDE.

140 PEW, THE LATINO DIGITAL DIVIDE.

141 The Jon Garrido Network, Hispanic News, http://hispanic.cc/ (last visited May 26, 2011).

142 Latino News, http://mylatinonews.com/latinonews.php (last visited May 26, 2011).

143 El Diario, http://www.impre.com/eldiariony/ (last visited May 26, 2011).

144 La Prensa, http://www.laprensatoledo.com/ (last visited May 26, 2011).

145 Hoy Nueva York, http://www.impre.com/hoynyc/home.php (last visited May 26, 2011).

146 La Opinión, http://www.impre.com/laopinion/ (last visited May 26, 2011).

147 El Nuevo Herald, http://www.elnuevoherald.com/ (last visited May 26, 2011).

148 Impremedia, http://www.impremedia.com/ (last visited May 26, 2011).

149 Wikipedia, La Opinión, http://en.wikipedia.org/wiki/La_Opinion (last visited May 26, 2011).

150 La Opinión, http://www.impre.com/laopinion/ (last visited May 26, 2011).

151 ASNE Completes Second Census of Online-Only News Sites, Finds Increasing Diversity, AMERICAN SOCIETY OF NEWS EDITORS, July 29, 2010, http://asne.org/article_view/articleid/833/asne-completes-second-census-of-online-only-news-sites-finds-increasing-diversity.aspx. ASNE is aiming for better response rates for future surveys and stated that some of the largest online-only news sites, such as Yahoo! News and The Huffington Post, failed to return the diversity questionnaire. Id.

152 Chris L. Jenkins, With Rent Strike Settled, Raft of Changes in Store for Marbury Plaza in Anacostia, WASH. POST., Sept. 19, 2010, http://www.washingtonpost.com/wp-dyn/content/article/2010/09/18/AR2010091803235.html (noting "[a] handful of community bloggers regularly chide [Anacostia] city leaders about quality-of-life issues.").

153 Interview with Nikki Peele, East of the River Blog, by FCC staff (Peele Interview 12/8/10) (Dec. 8, 2010); See River East D.C. Blogs, http://www.redcblogs.com/ (last visited May 26, 2011).

154 Peele Interview 12/8/10.

155 Rowdy Orbit, http://www.rowdyorbit.com/ (last visited May 26, 2011). Interviews with Jonathan Moore by FCC staff (July 2010; Oct. 2010) (Moore Interview 2010).

156 MiGente is the Hispanic website hosted by Black Planet. MiGente.com, http://www.migente.com/ (last visited May 26, 2011). Black Planet is owned by Radio One, a minority-controlled media firm. See Radio One, Fact Sheet, http://www.radio-one.com/properties/fact_sheet.asp?ID=9 (last visited May 26, 2011).

157 CB INSIGHTS, VENTURE CAPITAL HUMAN CAPITAL REPORT: VENTURE CAPITAL ACTIVITY REPORT (Part 1) 5 (Jan.—June 2010) (VENTURE CAPITAL ACTIVITY REPORT), available at http://www.cbinsights.com/blog/venture-capital/venture-capital-human-capital-report.

158 VENTURE CAPITAL ACTIVITY REPORT at 5.

159 VENTURE CAPITAL ACTIVITY REPORT at 8.

160 Interview with Retha Hill, Dir., New Media Innovation Lab, Walter Cronkite School of Journalism and Mass Communication, Arizona State Univ., by Jamila Bess Johnson, FCC (Mar. 9, 2011.)

24 People with Disabilities

1 MATTHEW W. BREAULT, AMERICANS WITH DISABILITIES: 2005 3 (U.S. Dep't of Commerce, U.S. Census Bureau) (2008) (AMERICANS WITH DISABILITIES), *available at* http://www.census.gov/prod/2008pubs/p70-117.pdf. "People with disabilities" is an umbrella term to include people who are blind or have low vision, people who are deaf, hard of hearing or have speech disabilities, those with physical or cognitive disabilities, and persons with multiple disabilities.

2 AMERICANS WITH DISABILITIES at 4. Census data from 2005 indicates that the chances of having a disability increase significantly with age. By 2030, 20 percent of the population will be over 65 years old. Frank B. Hobbs, The Elderly Population, U.S. Census Bureau, http://www.census.gov/population/www/pop-profile/elderpop.html (noting "[a]bout 1 in 8 Americans were elderly in 1994, but about 1 in 5 would be elderly by the year 2030.")

3 Centers for Disease Control and Prevention, Disability and Functioning (Adults), http://www.cdc.gov/nchs/fastats/disable.htm (last visited Feb. 4, 2011) (citing U.S Dep't of Health and Human Services Centers for Disease Control and Prevention & National Center, *Health Statistics Summary Health Statistics for U.S. Adults: National Health Interview Survey*, VITAL HEALTH STATISTICS SERIES 10, NO. 242 (2008) (*Health Statistics for U.S. Adults 2008*), at 36 (Table 11) and 38 (Table 12), *available at* http://www.cdc.gov/nchs/data/series/sr_10/sr10_242.pdf); *See also* AMERICANS WITH DISABILITIES 2008 at 5–7.

4 *See Health Statistics for U.S. Adults 2008* at 124 (TABLE IX).

5 *See Health Statistics for U.S. Adults 2008* at 124 (TABLE IX).

6 Radio Reading Services and FM Subcarriers, SCA History and Technical Details (*SCA History and Technical Details*), http://reader.ku.edu/oldsite/scatech.htm (last visited May 26, 2011). A subcarrier, also known as a Subsidiary Communications Authority (SCA), is a separate broadcasting radio signal that allows the carriage of additional voice or data information to be carried on the extra space available on FM signals, typically at 67 kHz and 92 kHz. In order to access radio reading services broadcast over a subcarrier, an individual needs a specially equipped receiver that is pre-tuned to pick up the closed circuit broadcast. *See id*. These services were facilitated by a Commission policy that required any noncommercial educational FM station utilizing subcarrier channels to provide one channel to a radio reading service upon request. 47 C.F.R. § 73.593 (1983). *See generally In re Allowable Costs for Noncommercial FM Licensees to Charge Radio Reading Services,* Policy Statement, 3 FCC Rcd 6323 (1988) (for a discussion on the permissible costs for the provision of station subcarriers for this purpose).

7 *See generally SCA History and Technical Details*. Radio Reading Services is one form of Audio Information Services, the latter being the umbrella term for audio access to print media such as newspapers and magazines.

8 National Fed'n of the Blind, NFB-Newsline, http://www.nfb.org/nfb/ Newspapers_by_Phone.asp (last visited May 26, 2011). This is accomplished using the DAISY (Digital Accessible Information System) digital format, which enables people who cannot access regular printed media to read and navigate printed information. *See* DAISY Consortium, http://www.daisy.org/ (last visited May 26, 2011).

9 *SCA History and Technical Details*; The Int'l Ass'n of Audio Information Services, http://iaais.org/findservices.html (last visited Feb. 4, 2011) (providing comprehensive information on the availability of these services).

10 Interview with David Noble, Chair, Government Relations & HD Radio Taskforce, Int'l Ass'n of Audio Information Svcs., by Karen Peltz Strauss, FCC (Aug. 18, 2010) (Noble Interview). There are currently no Commission policies or regulations prohibiting digital carriers from causing damage to analog SCA channels as these are generally self-imposed.

11 In the analog world, the Commission required non-commercial FM radio stations to provide a subcarrier channel to radio reading services upon request, but there is no similar policy for digital channels. *See generally SCA History and Technical Details*. As a result, the digital radio stations are turning down these requests without any consequences. Noble Interview.

12 The only existing radio reading service being broadcast over digital audio broadcasting is Sun Sounds of Arizona. Sun Sounds has four broadcast outlets in Arizona (Tempe, Tucson, Flagstaff, and Yuma) and serves approximately 49,000 people across the state. This service is atypical, in that most reading services do not have the ongoing and stable support of a college-owned public radio station. An Illinois subcarrier is expected to also begin providing radio reading services later this year. *See* Noble Interview; Email from David Noble to FCC staff (September 8, 2010) (Noble Email 9/8/10).

13 Video description is a service for people who are blind and visually impaired that employs narratives in the natural pauses of video programming to fill in the gaps when a program has no audio.

14 Noble Email 9/8/10.

15 KAREN PELTZ STRAUSS, A NEW CIVIL RIGHT: TELECOMMUNICATIONS EQUALITY FOR DEAF AND HARD OF HEARING AMERICANS 208 (Gallaudet Univ. Press) (2006).

16 Television Decoder Circuitry Act of 1990, 47 U.S.C. § 303(u). In 2010, the language of § 303(u) was amended to state that, where technically feasible, all televisions must come equipped with built-in closed caption decoder circuitry, but that televisions smaller than 13 inches must meet the requirements "only if the requirements of such subparagraphs are achievable." Id.; See also 47 U.S.C. § 330b ("No person shall ship in interstate commerce, manufacture, assemble, or import from any foreign country into the United States, any apparatus described in section 303(u)…except in accordance with rules prescribed by the Commission pursuant to the authority granted by that section.").

17 *Closed Captioning and Video Description of Video Programming, Implementation of Section 305 of the Telecommunications Act of 1996, Video Programming Accessibility,* Report and Order, MM Docket No. 95-176, 13 FCC Rcd 3272 (1997), *recon. granted in part,* Order on Reconsideration, 13 FCC Rcd 19973 (1998).

18 47 C.F.R. § 79.1(b) (1997). For example, the effective date for all nonexempt, new programming to be captioned was January 1, 2006 for English language programming, and January 1, 2010 for Spanish language programming. 47 C.F.R. § 79.1(b)(1)(iv) (English); 47 C.F.R. § 79.1(b)(3)(iv) (Spanish).

19 Certain programs, as listed at 47 C.F.R. § 79.1(d), are exempted from the captioning rules.

20 Twenty-First Century Communications and Video Accessibility Act of 2010, Pub. L. No. 111-260, 124 Stat. 2751 (2010) (CCVA).

21 CVAA § 202(b), 124 Stat. at 2770, 2771 (amending 47 U.S.C. § 613(c)) ("Not later than 6 months after the submission of the report to the Commission required by subsection (e)(1) of the Twenty-First Century Communications and Video Accessibility Act of 2010, the Commission shall revise its regulations to require the provision of closed captioning on video programming delivered using Internet protocol that was published or exhibited on television with captions after the effective date of such regulations.").

22 Specifically under existing rules, all local television stations must provide captions on their news programming, but most may meet this obligation by using a captioning method called "electronic newsroom technique" (ENT). 47 C.F.R. § 79.1(e)(3) (2010). Only the major national broadcast television networks (ABC, NBC, CBS and Fox), the affiliates of these networks in the top 25 television markets, and the national non-broadcast networks serving at least 50 percent of all homes subscribing to video programming services must use real-time captioning for such live news programming.

23 The lack of full captions on local news prompted consumer groups representing persons with hearing loss to file a petition in 2004 asking the Commission to re-evaluate the benefits of allowing the use of ENT as a captioning option in favor of requirements for real-time captioning of all local live news programming. *See Closed Captioning of Video Programming, Telecommunications for the Deaf, Inc.,* Petition for Rulemaking, Notice of Proposed Rulemaking, 20 FCC Rcd 13211 (2005) (*Closed Captioning* NPRM). The Commission responded with a notice of proposed rulemaking, still pending, to address this issue along with other captioning-related concerns. *Id.* In addition, some advocates have charged that certain exemptions to the Commission's captioning rules may be restricting the ability of people with hearing disabilities to access other information provided over television. These include exemptions for advertisements that are shorter than five minutes, including political advertisements (47 C.F.R. § 79.1(a)(1) (2009)); for certain programming involving candidates for public office (*Id.* at (e)(9)); and for certain commercial leased access, public access, and governmental and educational access programming (*Id.*). Advocates claim that such exemptions hinder the ability of deaf and hard of hearing individuals to fully participate in civic affairs, and suggest that the Commission give these exemptions a fresh look in light of the transition to media in a digital age. Coalition of Organizations for Accessible Technology Comments in re *FOM PN*, filed May 4, 2010 (COAT Comments) at 7; *See also* Rehabilitation Engineering Research Center on Telecommunications Access Comments in re *FOM PN*, filed March 31, 2010 (Rehabilitation Engineering Comments), at 3. Other commenters have urged making television and radio license renewals contingent in part on the extent to which these licensees make their programming accessible to people with disabilities. *See* Rehabilitation Engineering Comments at 3.

24 47 C.F.R. § 79.2(b)(1)(iii) (2005).

25 COAT Comments at 4; Rehabilitation Engineering Comments at 2–3.

26 CVAA § 203, 124 Stat. at 2772 (amending 47 U.S.C. § 303(u)(1)(C)) (stating the Commission shall require that, if technically feasible, "apparatus designed to receive or play back video programming transmitted simultaneously with sound, if such apparatus is manufactured in the United States or imported for use in the United States and uses a picture screen of any size…have the capability to decode and make available emergency information…in a manner that is accessible to individuals who are blind or visually impaired").

27 *Implementation of Video Description of Video Programming*, Report and Order, 15 FCC Rcd 15230 (2000), *recon. granted in part and denied in part*, 16 FCC Rcd 1251 (2001) (codified at 47 C.F.R. § 79.3(a)(3) (2009) (defining "video description" as "insertion of audio narrated descriptions of a television program's key visual elements into natural pauses between the program's dialogue").

28 *Motion Picture Ass'n of Am. v. FCC*, 309 F.3d 796, 805–07 (D.C. Cir. 2002).

29 CVAA, Title II, § 202(a), 124 Stat. at 2767–70 (amending 47 U.S.C. § 713(f)). *See also Video Description: Implementation of the Twenty-First Century Communications and Video Accessibility Act of 2010*, MM Docket No. 11-43, Notice of Proposed Rulemaking, 76 Fed. Reg. 14856 (Mar. 18, 2011).

30 CVAA § 204, 124 Stat. at 2773–74 (adding subsection (aa) after subsection (z) to 47 U.S.C. § 303).

31 CVAA § 205(a), 124 Stat. at 2774–75 (adding subsection (bb) after subsection (aa) to 47 U.S.C. § 303) (stating the Commission shall require that, "if achievable (as defined in section 716), that the on-screen text menus and guides provided by navigation devices (as such term is defined in section 76.1200 of title 47, Code of Federal Regulations) for the display or selection of multichannel video programming are audibly accessible in real-time upon request by individuals who are blind or visually impaired, except that the Commission may not specify the technical standards, protocols, procedures, and other technical requirements for meeting this requirement"); *See also* 47 C.F.R. 76.1200(c) (2010) (defining "navigation devices" as "[d]evices such as converter boxes, interactive communications equipment, and other equipment used by consumers to access multichannel video programming and other services offered over multichannel video programming systems.").

32 *NPR Pioneers Captioned Radio,* HEARING SPARKS, Aug. 2, 2010, http://hearingsparks.blogspot.com/2010/08/npr-pioneers-captioned-radio.html.

33 The driver cannot see the passenger's screen view for safety reasons. On July 19, 2010, a live demonstration of this technology, using a prototype car dashboard containing a digital captioned-radio display, was presented in honor of the 20th anniversary of the Americans with Disabilities Act at an event jointly coordinated by the White House, the Commission, and the Department of Commerce. *See* National Public Radio, *NPR to Demonstrate New Technologies at Celebration of the 20th Anniversary of the Americans with Disabilities Act* (press release), July 19, 2010 (*NPR New Technologies*), http://www.npr.org/about/press/2010/071910.CaptionedRadioDemo.html; *Captioned-Radio Initiative Paves Way for Deaf to Experience Radio*, ABILITY MAGAZINE, http://www.abilitymagazine.com/news/npr.html (last visited May 26, 2011).

34 *NPR New Technologies*. The technology uses XML tags that are capable of being transmitted in the comment title field of an HD radio channel. *Id.*

35 COAT Comments at 9.

36 WEB ACCESSIBILITY IN MIND, SCREEN READER USER SURVEY RESULTS (Utah State Univ. Ctr. for Persons With Disabilities) (2009) (WEB ACCESSIBILITY IN MIND), http://www.webaim.org/projects/screenreadersurvey2/.

37 WEB ACCESSIBILITY IN MIND.

38 WEB ACCESSIBILITY IN MIND.

39 WEB ACCESSIBILITY IN MIND.

40 WEB ACCESSIBILITY IN MIND, SURVEY OF PREFERENCES OF SCREEN READERS USERS (Utah State Univ. Ctr. for Persons With Disabilities) (2009). The question asked "What are a few web sites or types of web sites that you would like to visit, but avoid because of accessibility issues?" The top ten were: (1) Flash-based sites; (2) Shopping sites; (3) Amazon; (4) Facebook; (5) News sites; (6) MySpace; (7) Yahoo; (8) eBay; (9) YouTube; and (10) Travel sites.

41 *See* Web Accessibility Initiative, WAI Guidelines and Techniques, http://www.w3.org/wai/ (last visited May 26, 2011).

42 47 U.S.C. § 255(c) (1996) (codified at 47 C.F.R. Parts 6 and 7).

43 *See generally* Nuance Communications, *Nuance Talks: Convenient Audio Access to Mobile Phones*, http://www.nuance.com/talks/ (last visited May 26, 2011) (providing overview of the Nuance TALKS&ZOOMS software application); CodeFactory, Introducing Mobile Speak, http://www.codefactory.es/en/products.asp?id=316 (last visited May 26, 2011) (describing the Mobile Speak software application). On July 19, 2010, the Wireless Telecommunications Bureau and the Consumer and Governmental Affairs Bureau issued a Public Notice seeking comment on the extent to which mobile phones are accessible to people who are blind, deaf-blind, and have low vision in order to examine this problem in more depth. *Wireless Telecommunications Bureau and Consumer and Government Affairs Bureau Seek Comment on Accessible Mobile Phone Options for People who are Blind, Deaf-blind, or Have Low Vision*, CG Docket No. 10-145, Public Notice, 25 FCC Rcd 9228 (2010).

44 CVAA § 104, 124 Stat. at 2755–62; *Implementation of Sections 716 and 717 of the Communications Act of 1934, as Enacted by the Twenty-First Century Communications and Video Accessibility Act of 2010*, CG Docket No. 10-213, Notice of Proposed Rulemaking, 76 Fed. Reg. 13800 (rel. Mar. 3, 2011).

45 Lawsuits brought by the National Federation of the Blind and the American Council of the Blind against universities intending to use Amazon's Kindle DX in their classes first resulted in U.S. Department of Justice intervention, and eventually prompted Amazon to release a Kindle with audible menus, text-to-speech, tactile bumps on certain buttons, and extra large fonts for people who are blind or have low vision, in July, 2010. *See* Leslie Katz, *DOJ, Schools Settle Over Kindle's Blind Access*, CNET NEWS CRAVE, Jan. 13, 2010, http://news.cnet.com/8301-17938_105-10434512-1.html; Rachel Pryzgoda, *Amazon Debuts Blind-Accessible Kindle*, MARYLAND BUSINESS, July 30, 2010, http://mddailyrecord.com/maryland-business/2010/07/30/amazon-debuts-blind-accessible-kindle/; *Kindle Blind Accessible in 2010—Audible Menu, Supersize Font*, KINDLE REVIEW, Dec. 7, 2009, http://ireaderreview.com/2009/12/07/kindle-blind-accessible-in-2010-audible-menu-supersize-font/.

46 For example, long form video programming imported to the web from TV will be required to carry closed captioning, though videos created originally for the web will not.

47 YouTube, *Automatic Captions in YouTube Demo*, http://www.youtube.com/watch?v=kTvHIDKLFqc (last visited May 26, 2011).

48 Cloud computing is now being discussed as an exciting new prospect to enable people with vision disabilities to obtain accessibility features on any computer or Internet-connected device. Potentially this could allow such users to access screen reader, text-to-speech, or large print applications from the web in order to make Internet-based content accessible to them whenever and wherever they need it. In September 2010, the Interagency Committee on Disability Research brought together more than 65 researchers, government representatives, and industry participants in a symposium to explore the potential of cloud computing to enable "auto-personalization," a term used to describe the automatic adaptation of interfaces and materials to meet individual user needs. *See* COAT, *COAT Affiliates Look At Cloud Computing to Facilitate Accessibility*, http://www.coataccess.org/node/9849 (last vistied Mar. 18, 2011).

49 *See generally Nondiscrimination on the Basis of Disability in State and Local Government Services*, 28 C.F.R. Part 35 (July 23, 2010), and *Nondiscrimination on the Basis of Disability by Public Accommodations and in Commercial Facilities*, 28 C.F.R. Part 36 (July 23, 2010), both *available at* http://www.ada.gov/regs2010/ADAregs2010.htm.

25 How Big Is the Gap?

1 *Newsroom Employment Up Slightly*; Rick Edmonds, Emily Guskin & Tom Rosenstiel, *Newspapers: By the Numbers* in PEW, STATE OF NEWS MEDIA 2011, http://stateofthemedia.org/2011/newspapers-essay/data-page-6.

2 *See* "Newspapers: News Investment" in PEW, STATE OF NEWS MEDIA 2010, http://stateofthemedia.org/2010/newspapers-summary-essay/news-investment.

3 In brief, the numbers were developed by tracking down information about hiring and firing in the following news operations: newspaper newsrooms, new media news foundation projects, local TV news, AOL and other local news websites, public broadcast radio, ABC, NBC, CBS, national cable news, regional cable systems' news operations, and news magazines. We then made broad estimates about how much these translated into.

4 U.S. Census Bureau, Local Governments and Public School Systems by Type and State: 2007, http://www.census.gov/govs/cog/GovOrgTab03ss.html. For a description of special district functions by state, *see* U.S. CENSUS BUREAU, GOVERNMENTS—INDIVIDUAL STATE DESCRIPTIONS, *available at* http://www2.census.gov/govs/cog/all_ind_st_descr.pdf (last visited Feb. 17, 2011).

5 Proposing an "ideal" number of full-time reporters to cover these beats is utterly subjective. But as a thought experiment, one could imagine that a reasonable minimum might look something like:

> an average of one full-time journalist watching over any county, municipal, and township government—whose beat would include city hall and the courts

> an average of one half-time reporter per school system

> an average of one reporter per 10 special districts

> a national average of 11 full-time journalists per state capitol (with large states having more, and smaller states having fewer)

Calculated as such, the minimum number of full-time reporters covering these beats would be about 50,000. That number does not include dedicated reporters for entertainment, sports, local business affairs, health care, or the capacity to investigate business matters and financial institutions.

6 George and Waldfogel estimate based on 1993 and 1999 Burrelle data that the share of reporters and editors at local newspapers working on particular beats was 18 percent for local news, 14 percent for business, 12 percent for entertainment, and 12 percent for special issues and features. *See* Lisa M. George & Joel Waldfogel, *The "New York Times" and the Market for Local Newspapers*, 96(1) AMER. ECON. REV. 435, 446 (Mar. 2006). In another article using data from *Burrelle's Media Directory 2000*, they estimate that, on average, about 60 percent of newspaper reporters and editors in a local newspaper market worked on hard news beats such as news, business, and government. *See* Lisa George & Joel Waldfogel, *Who Affects Whom in Daily Newspaper Markets?*, 111 J. OF POLITICAL ECONOMY 765, 769 (2003).

7 Note that 20 percent of the 2009 newspaper newsroom workforce of 41,500, and of the 27,000 total local television newsroom employment in 2009, yields 14,000 accountability journalists on local beats. *See* "Newspapers: Summary" in PEW, STATE OF THE NEWS MEDIA 2010; BOB PAPPER, STAFFING AND PROFITABILITY—TV AND RADIO NEWS STAFFING AND PROFITABILITY SURVEY (Radio Television Digital News Association & Hofstra Univ.) (2010), *available at* http://www.rtdna.org/pages/media_items/2010-tv-and-radio-news-staffing-and-profitability-survey1943.php?id=1943. Adding in 355 reporters covering state capitols, and including other reporters likely covering local and state government at non-daily newspapers (which number more than 7,000) publications, radio, online, wire, and business media yields a generous estimate of 20,000 reporters covering local and state governments in 2009. National Newspaper Association, Facts and Figures, http://www.nnaweb.org/?/nnaweb/community02/87 (last visited Feb, 7, 2011). If 50,000 were an ideal figure, then 30,000 additional reporters would ideally be on these beats. Using an average salary of $44,000 (based on $43,270 2009 Bureau of Labor Statistics mean annual salary estimate for reporters and correspondents) and an added benefits factor of 20 percent, you arrive at a figure of ($44,000 per journalist*1.2 (benefits factor)* 30,000 journalists) $1.6 billion. U.S. Bureau of Labor Statistics, Occupational Employment and Wages May 2009, http://www.bls.gov/oes/2009/may/oes273022.htm (last visited May 27, 2011). To estimate those working on accountability beats in 2000, we used a similar methodology, with a newspaper newsroom workforce number of 56,400, total local television TV news employment figure of 35,061 and a state capitol reporting total of 543. *See Newspapers: Summary* in PEW, STATE OF NEWS MEDIA 2010; BOB PAPPER & MICHAEL GERHARD, NEWS, STAFF AND MAKING MONEY 1 (Radio Television News Directors Association/Ball State Univ.) (2000), *available at* http://www.bobpapper.com/attachments/File/RTDNA_reports/staff2001.pdf; *See AJR's 2009 Count of Statehouse Reporters*, AMER. JOURNALISM REV., Apr./May 2009, http://www.ajr.org/article.asp?id=4722. This yielded an estimate of 25,000 journalists working on accountability beats in 2000. To hire 25,000 additional reporters to close the gap would cost $1.3 billion. To hire 5,000 additional reporters to bring up today's accountability reporting ranks to the level in 2000, it would cost (5,000*$44,000*1.2)=$264 million.

8 Total expenditures for public elementary and secondary education, by function and state or jurisdiction: 2006-07, Digest of Education Statistics, http://nces.ed.gov/programs/digest/d09/tables/dt09_178.asp (last visited May 18, 2011).

9 A half-time reporter covering each of the 14,561 public school systems would yield a need for 7,281 journalists. At an average salary of $44,000 and benefits of 20 percent, this would mean the cost of starting from scratch would be (7,281*$44,000*1.2) = $384,436,800. However, since our estimates indicate that roughly 40 percent of the nation's needed

accountability reporting is already provided, the incremental cost to reach adequate coverage of the public schools would be 60 percent of that total—or $ 231 million.

10 David Kaplan, *BIA/Kelsey: Local Online Ad Revenues Will Double By 2015*, PAID CONTENT, Mar. 21, 2011, http://paidcontent.org/article/419-biakelsey-local-online-ad-revenues-will-double-by-2015-.

11 *See* Michele McLellan, "Emerging Economics of Community News" in PEW, STATE OF NEWS MEDIA 2011, http://stateofthemedia.org/2011/mobile-survey/economics-of-community-news (McLellan, *Emerging Economics of Community News*).

12 BILL GRUESKIN, AVA SEAVE, AND LUCAS GRAVES, THE STORY SO FAR.

13 Michele McLellan, "Emerging Economics of Community News" in PEW, STATE OF THE NEWS MEDIA 2011, http://stateofthemedia.org/2011/mobile-survey/economics-of-community-news/.

14 *See, e.g., In iPad, Publishers See Hope for Ad Revenue*, June 3, 2010, http://www.cbsnews.com/stories/2010/06/03/business/main6543926.shtml (*Ads Placed in iPad Apps*).

15 *Ads Placed in iPad Apps.*

16 *See* Joe Pompeo, *The Wall Street Journal's iPad App Is Killing It, So Far*, THE WIRE (Business Insider), June 2, 2010, http://www.businessinsider.com/the-wall-street-journals-ipad-app-is-killing-it-so-far-2010-6.

17 Panelist Presentation of Lem Lloyd, Vice President, Channel Sales, Yahoo!, U.S. Federal Trade Comm. (FTC) Workshop, "From Town Criers to Bloggers: How Will Journalism Survive the Internet Age?" (Dec. 1, 2009) (Yahoo FTC Presentation 12/1/09), at 4, *available at* http://www.ftc.gov/opp/workshops/news/index.shtml.

18 Miguel Helft, *Yahoo Teams with Newspapers to Sell Ads*, N.Y. TIMES, Feb. 27, 2009, http://www.nytimes.com/2009/02/28/technology/internet/28yahoo.html.

19 Yahoo FTC Presentation 12/1/09 at 7.

20 David Carr, *For Murdoch, It's Try, Try Again*, N.Y. TIMES, Aug. 10, 2009, http://www.nytimes.com/2009/08/10/business/media/10carr.html.

21 Joseph Tartakoff, *Taking the Plunge: How Newspaper Sites That Charge Are Faring*, PAID CONTENT, Sept. 2, 2009, http://paidcontent.org/article/419-taking-the-plunge-how-newspaper-sites-that-charge-are-faring/; Jeff Sonderman, *Newspapers: 180 Years of Not Charging for Content*, NEWS FUTURIST, July 18, 2009, http://www.newsfuturist.com/2009/07/newspapers-180-years-of-not-charging.html.

22 *See* Ongo…, Ongo Is…, http://www.ongo.com (last visited Apr. 7, 2011).

23 Lucia Moses, *Next Issue Consortium Falls Down to Earth*, ADWEEK, Feb. 13, 2011, http://www.adweek.com/news/press/next-issue-consortium-falls-down-earth-126595.

24 Alan Mutter, *Paper Erects Pay Wall—and Traffic Goes Up!*, REFLECTIONS OF A NEWSOSAUR , Mar. 14, 2011, http://newsosaur.blogspot.com/2011/03/paper-erects-pay-wall-and-traffic-goes.html (*Paper Erects Pay Wall—and Traffic Goes Up!*).

25 Ken Doctor, *Nine Question on the Dallas Morning News' New Paywall*, KEN DOCTOR'S INSTABLOG, Mar. 23, 2011, http://seekingalpha.com/instablog/391381-ken-doctor/148010-nine-questions-on-the-dallas-morning-news-new-paywall?source=kizur.

26 The Arizona Guardian, *Subscription Plans*, http://www.arizonaguardian.com/azg/index.php?option=com_jcs&view=jcs&layout=form&Itemid=108 (last visited Apr. 7, 2011).

27 *See, e.g.,* Kenneth Li & Andrew Edgecliffe-Johnson, *NY Times Eyes Local Editions in WSJ Clash*, FINANCIAL TIMES, Apr. 25, 2010, http://www.ft.com/cms/s/0/7aca2caa-5080-11df-bc86-00144feab49a.html#axzz1NZxTLbfr.

28 Brett Pulley, *AOL's Huffington to Add News Staff in Local Site Revamp*, BLOOMBERG BUSINESSWEEK, Apr. 12, 2011, http://www.businessweek.com/news/2011-04-12/aol-s-huffington-to-add-news-staff-in-local-site-revamp.html.

29 Interview with Rick Blair, President, Examiner.com by Steven Waldman, FCC (Dec. 17, 2010).

30 Curt Hopkins, *Major Newspaper Chain Goes Open Source*, READWRITE-WEB, July 4, 2010, http://www.readwriteweb.com/archives/major_newspaper_chain_goes_open_source.php.

31 Timothy B. Lee, *Online News As Disruptive Technology*, BOTTOM UP, Mar. 30, 2011, http://timothyblee.com/2011/03/30/online-news-as-a-disruptive-technology.

32 Dan Gillmor, *Mediactive,* 2010, http://mediactive.com/8-1-a-prescient-warning-and-unheeded-advice.

33 Testimony of Jeff Jarvis, Assoc. Professor & Director of the Interactive Program, CUNY Graduate School of Journalism, FCC Workshop on the Future of Media and the Information Needs of Communities: Serving the Public Interest in the Digital Era (Mar. 4, 2010), Tr. at 213:15-17, *available at* http://reboot.fcc.gov/c/document_library/get_file?uuid=57c2b1d8-4ecb-49b8-ad8e-bb30d794b784&groupId=19001 (Jarvis Testimony 3/4/10).

34 Email from Michele McLellan to Steven Waldman, FCC (Mar. 1, 2011).

35 The Huffington Post Investigative Fund, *About Us,* http://huffpostfund.org/about-us (last visited Feb. 3, 2011).

36 Interview with Eric Hippeau, former CEO of Huffington Post, by Steven Waldman, FCC (Nov. 22, 2010).

37 Interview with Alan Murray, Wall Street Journal's executive editor, by Steven Waldman, FCC (Mar. 21, 2011).

38 *See, e.g.,* Richard Pérez-Peña, *Naming Leaders, a Nonprofit News Outlet Takes Shape in San Francisco*, N.Y. TIMES, Jan. 10, 2010, http://www.nytimes.com/2010/01/22/business/media/22bay.html.

39 Alan Mutter, *The State of Play for Paid Content, 2011*, Jan. 11, 2011, EDITOR & PUBLISHER, http://www.editorandpublisher.com/Headlines/ep-exclu-sive-the-state-of-play-for-paid-content-2011-64184-.aspx.

40 *Local and Metro Newspapers With Pay Walls*, PAID CONTENT, http://paid-content.org/table/whos-charging (last visited Mar. 17, 2011).

41 *Paper Erects Pay Wall—and Traffic Goes Up!*

42 Email from Jovonda Howard, News Service of Florida to Steven Wald-man, FCC (Mar. 14, 2011).

43 *See* Jack Meyers, *Legacy Media's Slice of the Social Commerce Economy*, MEDIA ADVISORY GROUP, Mar. 21, 2011, http://www.jackmyers.com/commentary/jackmyers-think-tank/Legacy-Medias-Slice-of-the-Social-Commerce-Economy---Jack-Myers.html.

44 Interview with Rafat Ali, Paid Content, by Steven Waldman, FCC, Nov. 22, 2010 (Ali Interview 11/22/10).

45 Ali Interview 11/22/10.

46 Ali Interview 11/22/10.

47 Ali Interview 11/22/10.

48 Michael J. Miller, *Online Privacy and "Do Not Track" Proposals: Only the Beginning*, FORWARD THINKING… (PC Magazine), Jan. 26, 2011, http://blogs.pcmag.com/miller/2011/01/online_privacy_and_do_not_trac.php.

49 Interview with Gordon Crovitz by Steven Waldman, FCC (Oct. 5, 2010.)

50 HORRIGAN, BROADBAND ADOPTION AND USE IN AMERICA at 13, 27–29.

51 HORRIGAN, BROADBAND ADOPTION AND USE IN AMERICA at 24.

52 *See* Will Sullivan, *RJI iPad Research Shows Tablet Subscriptions Will Cannibalize Print Subscriptions*, DONALD W. REYNOLDS JOURNALISM INSTITUTE, Dec. 9, 2010, http://www.rjionline.org/blog/rji-ipad-research-shows-tablet-subscriptions-will-cannibalize-print-subscriptions.

53 *See* PEW 2010 NEWS CONSUMPTION SURVEY at 90.

54 "Network TV Audience" in PEW, STATE OF NEWS MEDIA 2010, http://stateofthemedia.org/2010/network-tv-summary-essay/audience/.

55 *See Copyright, Competition and Publishers' Pursuit of Online Compensa-tion*, Univ. of So. California Annenberg Ctr. on Communication Leader-ship & Policy, Comment No. 544505-00022 in re FTC File No. P091200: *From Town Criers to Bloggers: How Will Journalism Survive the Internet Age?* (filed Nov 6, 2009) (Annenberg Ctr., *Copyright, Competition and Publishers' Pursuit of Online Compensation*), *available at* http://www.ftc.gov/os/comments/newsmediaworkshop/544505-00022.pdf (stating "[o]nline readers are usually not paying for their news, and are often reading their news away from the content originator's site. Online ad-vertisers pay less for placement than they did in the traditional printed papers.").

56 HAROLD VOGEL, ENTERTAINMENT INDUSTRY ECONOMICS: A GUIDE FOR FINANCIAL ANALYSIS 343 (Cambridge University Press) (2007).

57 Apple, *Apple Launches Subscriptions on the App Store* (press release), Feb 15, 2011, http://www.apple.com/pr/library/2011/02/15appstore.html.

58 *See* Annenberg Ctr., *Copyright, Competition and Publishers' Pursuit of Online Compensation.*

59 Estimate for cash flow margin and employment reductions:

Calculations by Prof. James Hamilton (Duke Univ.) for the Future of Media Project, based on discussions with Rick Edmonds of the Poynter Institute. Analyzing the impact of reductions in newsroom reporting staff, Edmonds estimates that annual spending on newsroom expenses declined about $1.6 billion between 2006 and 2009. *See* "Newspapers: News Investment" in PEW, STATE OF THE NEWS MEDIA 2010, http://stateofthemedia.org/2010/newspapers-summary-essay/news-invest-ment/. He estimates that newspaper industry revenues were $47 billion in 2008 and $37 billion in 2009, which means that the $1.6 billion reduc-tion in annual newsroom expenses would be equivalent to 3.4 percent of industry revenues in 2008 and 4.3 percent in 2009. Examining cash flows as a percentage of firm revenues, Lauren Rich Fine calculated the cash flow margins of selected newspaper companies in 2008 was 13 percent. See LAUREN RICH FINE, BAD PUBLIC RELATIONS OR IS THIS A REAL CRISIS? YES 11 (Duke Conference on Nonprofit Media) (2009), *available at* http://sanford.duke.edu/nonprofitmedia/documents/dwcrichfinefinal.pdf. This implies that if newspaper firms had been willing to accept a 9 percent cash flow margin rather than 13 percent in 2008, then newsroom expenditures could go back up by more than $1.6 billion, and staffing could go back to 2006 newsroom employment levels (or even higher, since the original $1.6 billion estimate included cuts not made until 2009). Edmonds notes that about 80–90 percent of newsroom spending goes for salaries and the rest is spent on items such as travel, wire service, or freelance work. Survey data from NAB's Television Financial Report: 2010 show that in 2009 local television stations had average net revenues of $13,453,516, and average cash flow (defined as net revenues minus total expenses) of $3,071,955. Average news expenses at local TV stations in 2009 were $2,537,814. For a local television station with these average finances, this translates into a cash flow margin of 23 percent. If the station had reduced its cash margin by two percentage points (i.e., accepted a 21 percent cash margin), it could have increased newsroom spending by $269,070 or 11 percent, reducing the pressure to fire staff.

60 Interview with Andrew Lack, C.E.O., Multimedia Group, Bloomberg LP, by Steven Waldman, FCC (Dec. 16, 2010).

61 Interview with Bill Girdner, Editor and Publisher, Courthouse News Service, by Kathleen Struck, FCC (July 2, 2010).

62 Jarvis Testimony 3/4/10, Tr. at 216:3–4.

63 Email from Clay Shirky to Steve Waldman, FCC (Apr. 2, 2011).

64 *Newspaper Economics: Online and Offline*, Presentation by Hal Varian, Chief Economist, Google, and Professor, Univ. of California, Berkeley, FTC Workshop, "From Town Criers to Bloggers: How Will Journalism Survive The Internet Age?" (Mar. 9, 2010) (Varian, *Newspaper Economics: Online and Offline*), at 20, *available at* http://www.ftc.gov/opp/workshops/news/mar9/docs/varian.pdf.

65 Interview with Esther Dyson by Steven Waldman, FCC (Sept. 3, 2010).

66 Interview with John Hood by Steven Waldman, FCC (April, 2011)

67 Howard Kurtz, *Washington Post Will Pair With Bloomberg*, WASH. POST, Oct. 2, 2009, http://www.washingtonpost.com/wp-dyn/content/article/2009/10/01/AR2009100104226.html.

26 Broadcast, Radio and Television

1 *See Amendment of Section 3.606 Of The Commission's Rules and Regulations*, Report and Order, 41 FCC 148 (1952) ("*Sixth Report and Order*"); *see also Applications of WQED PITTSBURGH (Assignor) et al.*, Memorandum Opinion and Order, 15 FCC Rcd 202, 212 (1999) ("*WQED*").

2 Federal Communications Commission (FCC), 34th Annual Report for Fiscal Year 1968, at 28; *Deletion of Noncommercial Educational Reservation of Channel *16, 482-488 MHZ, Pittsburgh, Pennsylvania*, 11 FCC Rcd 11700, 11707-08 (1996).

3 *See, e.g., Advanced Telecommunications Systems and Their Impact on the Existing Television Broadcast Service* (*Advanced Television Systems*), Second Inquiry, 3 FCC Rcd 6520, 6525, 6530 (1988); *Advanced Television Systems*, First Order, 5 FCC Rcd 5627, 5627-5629 (1990); *Advanced Television Systems,* Notice of Proposed Rulemaking, 6 FCC Rcd 7024 (1991); *Advanced Television Systems,* Fourth Report and Order, 11 FCC Rcd 17771, 17787 (1996).

4 *Banzhaf v. FCC*, 405 F.2d 1082, 1095 (D.C. Cir. 1968), *cert. denied sub nom., Tobacco Inst. v. FCC*, 396 U.S. 842 (1969). *See also Turner Broadcasting System v. FCC*, 512 U.S. 622, 650-51 (1994) (discussing limited nature of FCC oversight responsibilities in light of First Amendment constraints, Court noted that "our cases have recognized that Govern-

ment regulation over the content of broadcast programming must be narrow, and that broadcast licensees must retain abundant discretion over programming choices.") (internal citations omitted). One study that documents the chilling effect: Thomas W. Hazlett and David W. Sosa, *Was the Fairness Doctrine A 'Chilling Effect'? Evidence from the Postderegulation Radio Market*, 26 J. LEGAL STUD. 279-301(1997).

5 *Great Lakes Broadcasting*, 3 F. R. C. Ann. Rep. 32 (1929), *rev'd on other grounds*, 59 App. D. C. 197, 37 F.2d 993, *cert. dismissed*, 281 U.S. 706 (1930). *See generally* Mark A. Conrad, *The Demise of the Fairness Doctrine: A Blow for Citizen Access*, 41 FED. COMM L.J. 161 (1989).

6 *Mayflower Broadcasting Corp.*, 8 FCC 333, 340 (1940).

7 Mark A. Conrad, *The Demise of the Fairness Doctrine: A Blow for Citizen Access*, 41 FED. COMM L.J. 161, 166 (1989).

8 *Report on Editorializing by Broadcast Licensees*, 13 FCC 1246 (1949).

9 *See, e.g., Repeal or Modification of the Personal Attack and Political Editorial Rules*, Proposed Rule, 48 Fed. Reg. 28295 (June 21, 1983).

10 As the Court noted, "Where there are substantially more individuals who want to broadcast than there are frequencies to allocate, it is idle to posit an unabridgeable First Amendment right to broadcast comparable to the right of every individual to speak, write, or publish." *Red Lion Broadcasting Co. v. FCC*, 395 U.S. 367, 388 (1969).

11 *Red Lion Broadcasting Co. v. FCC*, 395 U.S. 367, 390 (1969).

12 *Inquiry into Section 73.1910 of the Commission's Rules and Regulations Concerning the General Fairness Doctrine Obligations of Broadcast Licensees*, Report, 102 FCC 2d 145, 170 (1987) (*Fairness Doctrine Report 1987*).

13 *Fairness Doctrine Report 1987*, FCC 77-643, 102 FCC 2d at 171. For other examples of such chilling, *see id.* at 169–188, *passim*.

14 *Repeal or Modification of the Personal Attack and Political Editorial Rules*, 15 FCC Rcd 20697 (2000); *Radio-Television News Directors Ass'n v. FCC*, 229 F.3d 269 (D.C. Cir. 2000).

15 Congressional testimony for the Senate Commerce Committee, June 16, 2009. *Federal Communications Commission Chairman Nomination*, C-SPAN, June 16, 2009, http://www.c-spanvideo.org/program/287044-1.

16 47 C.F.R. § 73.1910.

17 *See Applicability of Sponsorship Identification Rules*, Public Notice, 40 FCC 141, 141 (1963).

18 See Radio Act of 1927, Pub. L. No. 69-632, § 19, 44 Stat. 1162, 1170 (1927); Communications Act of 1934, Pub. L. No. 73-416, § 317, 48 Stat. 1064, 1089 (1934) (codified as amended at 47 U.S.C. § 317); Communications Act Amendments, Pub. L. No. 86-752, § 8(b), 74 Stat. 889, 896 (1960). In 1960, Congress amended Section 317 to add this proviso to subsection (a) as well as to add subsections (b) through (e) of Section 317. *See* Communications Act Amendments, Pub. L. No. 86-752, § 8(a), 74 Stat. 895.

19 47 C.F.R. § 76.1615.

20 47 U.S.C. § 317(a)(1).

21 See Application of Sponsorship Identification Rules to Political Broadcasts, Teaser Announcements, Governmental Entities and Other Organizations, Public Notice, 66 FCC 2d 302 (1977).

22 See Codification of the Commission's Political Programming Policies, Opinion and Order, 7 FCC Rcd 678, 687 (1991).

23 Online disclosure would increase the ability of private parties to monitor compliance with the rules. Ellen P. Goodman, *Stealth Marketing and*

Editorial Integrity, 85 TEX. L. REV. 83, 151-152 (2006).

24 For instance, Section 507(a) of the Communications Act of 1934 (Communications Act), 47 U.S.C. § 508(a), requires that each station employee who has accepted consideration for the airing of the material, or any person who has paid an employee, must disclose that fact to the station prior to the airing of the matter. Section 507(b) imposes a similar duty of disclosure upon any person involved in the preparation of the story. The disclosure must be made to each payee's employer, the person for whom the material is being produced, or the licensee. These obligations do not apply to cable operators. See 47 U.S.C. § 508(a), (b), (c).

25 See Access Humboldt et al. Joint Comments in re FOM PN (FCC Launches Examination of The Future of Media and Information Needs of Communities in a Digital Age, Comment Sought, GN Docket No. 10-25, Public Notice, 25 FCC Rcd 384 (2010) (FOM PN)), filed May 7, 2010 (Humboldt Comments) at 75.

26 *ACC Licenses, Inc.,* Order and Consent Decree, 2010 WL 3806284 (Enf. Bur. rel. Sept. 29, 2010).

27 Interview with Tom Rosensteil, by Steven Waldman, FCC, (Jan. 11, 2011).

28 Fines can be increased above the base level for: "(1) Egregious misconduct; (2) Ability to pay/relative disincentive; (3) Intentional violation; (4) Substantial harm; (5) Prior violations of any FCC requirement; (6) Substantial economic gain; (7) Repeated or continuous violation." 47 CFR 1.80. *See, The Commission's Forfeiture Policy Statement and Amendment of Section 1.80 of the Rules to Incorporate the Forfeiture Guidelines*, Report and Order, 12 FCC Rcd 17087 (1997), *recon denied*, 15 FCC Rcd 303.

29 *Commission Reminds Broadcast Licensees, Cable Operators and Others of Requirements Applicable to Video News Releases and Seeks Comment on the Use of Video News Releases by Broadcast Licensees and Cable Operators*, MB Docket No. 05-171, Public Notice, 20 FCC Rcd 8593, 8593 (2005) (*Video News Release PN*)).

30 See Center for Media and Democracy & Free Press Comments in re *Video News Release PN*, filed June 22, 2005 (Ctr. for Media and Democracy Comments in re *Video News Release PN*) , at 2.

31 *Fox Television Stations, Inc., Licensee of Station KMSP-TV, Minneapolis, MN,* Notice of Apparent Liability for Forfeiture, File No. EB-06-IH-, 2011 WL 1099542 (EB rel. Mar. 24, 2011), *available at* http://www.fcc.gov/eb/Orders/2011/DA-11-521A1.html; *Access 1 New Jersey License Company, LLC, Licensee of Station WMGM-TV, Wildwood, NJ,* Notice of Apparent Liability for Forfeiture, File No. EB-06-IH-3725 , 2011 WL 1099543 (EB rel. Mar. 24, 2011), *available at* http://transition.fcc.gov/eb/Orders/2011/DA-11-523A1.html.

32 Letter from John C. Quale, Esq., Skadden, Arps, Slate, Meagher & Flom LLP, counsel for Fox Television Holdings, Inc., and Fox Television Stations, Inc., to Marlene H. Dortch, Secretary, Federal Communications Commission, dated June 25, 2007, at 1–2.

33 47 U.S.C. § 508(b)-(c).

34 *Graham Williams Group,* Letter, 22 FCC Rcd 18092 (Enf. Bur., Inv. & Hearings Div. 2007).

35 47 U.S.C. § 317(c). *See also* 47 C.F.R. §§ 73.1212(b), 76.1615(b).

36 47 U.S.C. § 317(b). *See also* 47 C.F.R. § 73.1212(c). Cable operators do not have a comparable reporting requirement. *Compare* 47 C.F.R. § 76.1615.

37 *See* Center for Media and Democracy Comments in *Sponsorship Identification Rules and Embedded Advertising*, MB Docket No. 08-90,

Notice of Inquiry and Notice of Proposed Rulemaking, 23 FCC Rcd 10682 (2008) (*Sponsorship Identification NOI & NPRM*)), filed Sept. 22, 2008, at 2 (*citing* BOB PAPPER, THE FUTURE OF NEWS: A STUDY BY THE RADIO TELEVISION NEWS DIRECTORS FOUNDATION 32-33 (2006))

38 *See* Comments of Fairness and Integrity in Telecommunications Media in re *Sponsorship Identification NOI & NPRM*, filed Sept. 23, 2009, at 10–15.

39 *See, e.g.,* The National Association of Broadcasters Reply Comments in re *Sponsorship Identification NOI & NPRM*, filed Nov. 21, 2008, at 18–19; Reply Comments of The Walt Disney Company in re *Sponsorship Identification NOI & NPRM*, filed Nov. 21, 2008, at 14-20.

40 Hearings on H.R. 7357 before the House Comm. on Merchant Marine & Fisheries, 68th Cong., 1st Sess. 10 (1924). *See also In the Matter of Policy Regarding Character Qualifications in Broadcast Licensing*, Notice of Inquiry, 87 FCC 2d 836 (1981).

41 EarlyRadioHistory.us, HTML Reproduction of Photocopy of Proceedings of the Fourth National Radio Conference and Recommendations for Regulation of Radio, November 9–11, 1925 (Fourth Nat'l Radio Conference Recommendations), http://earlyradiohistory.us/1925conf.htm (last visited Dec. 30, 2010); *see also* Thomas H. White, United States Early Radio History, Early Government Regulation (1903-1946), EARLYRADIOHISTORY.US, http://earlyradiohistory.us/sec023.htm (stating that the four National Radio Conferences held in 1922 through 1925 "brought together representatives from the government and the radio industry, plus private citizens, in order to provide guidance to Commerce Secretary Herbert Hoover on the future of radio") (last visited Feb. 2, 2010).

42 Fourth Nat'l Radio Conference Recommendations.

43 *See, e.g.,* LUCAS A. POWE, JR., AMERICAN BROADCASTING AND THE FIRST AMENDMENT 58 (Univ. of California Press) (1987).

44 *See, e.g., Hoover v. Intercity Radio Co.,* 286 F. 1003 (D.C. Cir. 1923).

45 Radio Act of 1927, Pub. L. No. 69-632, 44 Stat. 1162. The Act granted the FRC licensing authority for one year only, with the authority reverting thereafter to the Commerce Secretary.

46 In 1943, the Supreme Court approved the "public interest, convenience or necessity" standard as applied to the regulatory authority of the Federal Communications Commission. *See NBC v. United States*, 319 U.S. 190 (1943).

47 Reed E. Hundt, *The Public's Airwaves: What Does the Public Interest Require of Television Broadcasters?* 45 DUKE L.J. 1089 (1996).

48 One commentator wrote shortly after the passage of the Radio Act of 1927 that the inclusion of the phrase, "public interest, convenience, and necessity" was of enormous consequence, since it meant that "licenses are no longer for the asking. The applicant must pass the test of public interest. His wish is not the deciding factor." STEPHEN DAVIS, THE LAW OF RADIO COMMUNICATIONS 61 (McGraw Hill, 1927), NOTED IN ERWIN G. KRASNOW & LAWRENCE D. LONGLEY, THE POLITICS OF BROADCAST REGULATION 16 (St. Martin's Press) (1973).

49 This is not to suggest that entertainment programming was not "in the public interest." It was, in fact, one of 14 categories of programming identified by the Commission as being so. *See infra* at 12 & n.55. Rather, entertainment material was not generally the focus of regulatory efforts because its promotion was well regulated by market forces alone.

50 67 Cong. Rec. 5479 (1926).

51 *NBC v. United States*, 319 U.S. 190, 215 (1943), *citing* 47 U.S.C. §§ 307(a), (d), 309(a), 310, 312.

52 *See, e.g.,* 47 U.S.C. §§ 303, 307(a), 309(a).

53 STERLING & KITTROSS, STAY TUNED at 189.

54 See FCC, *Public Service Responsibility of Broadcast Licensees* (1946), *reprinted in* DOCUMENTS OF AMERICAN BROADCASTING (4TH EDITION) (Frank J. Kahn ed.) 148-63 (1984), at 39.

55 *Report and Statement of Policy res: Commission en banc Programming Inquiry*, 44 FCC 2303, 2310 (1960) (*1960 Programming Report*).

56 *1960 Programming Report*, 44 FCC at 2312.

57 *1960 Programming Report,* 44 FCC at 2314.

58 *1960 Programming Report*, 44 FCC at 2314.

59 *See Primer on Ascertainment of Community Problems by Broadcast Applicants*, Report and Order, 27 FCC 2d 650 at Appendix B (1971) (*Primer on Ascertainment of Community Problems*). The *Primer* instructed applicants to (1) determine the composition of the population falling with a station service area with respect to, among other factors, race and ethnicity; (2) interview leaders of significant groups within the community regarding community needs and problems; (3) randomly survey the general public regarding such needs and problems; (4) evaluate the relative importance of the needs and problems so disclosed, the timeliness of the comments, and the extent to which it can provide programming to meet each; and (5) formulate programs that addressed those issues deemed, in the good faith discretion of the applicant, to merit such on-air treatment. *See id.*

60 *Primer on Ascertainment of Community Problems* at Appendix B.

61 *Primer on Ascertainment of Community Problems* at Appendix B.

62 See *Amendment of Part 0 of the Commission's Rules- Commission Organization- With Respect to Delegation of Authority to the Chief, Broadcast Bureau, Order*, 43 FCC 2d 638, 640 (Appendix) (1973). If the applicant had failed to meet such limits or if the programming varied from the licensee's prior representations to the FCC (the so-called "promise-versus-performance" review), the application would be subject to review by the Commission itself, which would be a less expeditious and potentially more risky process than delegated Bureau action.

63 See *Amendment of Part 0 of the Commission's Rules- Commission Organization- With Respect to Delegation of Authority to the Chief, Broadcast Bureau, Order*, 43 FCC 2d at 640 (Appendix) (1973).

64 *Amendment of Section 0.281 of the Commission's Rules- Delegation of Authority to the Chief, Broadcast Bureau, Order*, 59 FCC 2d 491, 493 (1976).

65 Interview with Steve Schwaid, Director of News and Digital Content, WGCI Atlanta, by Cynthia C. Kennard, FCC (June 30, 2010).

66 Interview with Lee Giles, former V.P. and Director, News, WISH-TV Indianapolis, by Cynthia C. Kennard, FCC, (June 27, 2010).

67 Interview with Gayle Eichenthal, Program Director KUSC Radio, Los Angeles, by Cynthia Kennard, FCC (Sept. 25, 2010); *see also* Ken Reich, *Gail Eichenthal Leaves KNX, As Station Under New Management Gets Softer*, TAKE BACK THE TIMES BLOG, Jan. 20, 2005, http://takebackthetimes. blogspot.com/2005/01/gail-eichenthal-leaves-knx-as-station.html.

68 *Reason Interview: Mark S. Fowler*, REASON, Nov. 1, 1981, *excerpt available at* http://findarticles.com/p/articles/mi_m1568/is_1998_Dec/ ai_53260535/pg_4/?tag=content;col1.

69 47 C.F.R. § 73.671. *See also Policies and Rules Concerning Children's Television Programming*, Report and Order, 11 FCC Rcd 10,660, 10,662 (1996).

70 47 C.F.R. § 73.673.

71 47 C.F.R. § 73.670 (no more than 10.5 minutes per hour during weekends and 12 minutes per hour during the week).

72 *Deregulation of Radio*, Report and Order, 84 FCC 2d 968 (1981) (*Deregulation of Radio 1981*), *recon. granted in part*, 87 FCC 2d 797 (1981), *remanded sub nom. Office of Communication of the United Church of Christ v. FCC*, 707 F.2d 1413 (D.C. Cir. 1983), *on remand*, Second Report and Order, 96 FCC 2d 930 (1984), *remanded sub nom. Office of Communication of the United Church of Christ v. FCC*, 779 F.2d 702 (D.C. Cir. 1985), *on remand*, Memorandum Opinion and Order, 104 FCC 2d 505 (1986).

73 *Deregulation of Radio 1981*, 84 FCC 2d at 968-69.

74 *Deregulation of Radio 1981*, 84 FCC 2d at 971.

75 *Deregulation of Radio 1981*, 84 FCC 2d at 977.

76 *Deregulation of Radio 1981*, 84 FCC 2d at 978.

77 *Deregulation of Radio 1981*, 84 FCC 2d at 998.

78 *Deregulation of Radio 1981*, 84 FCC 2d at 971.

79 *Deregulation of Radio 1981*, 84 FCC 2d at 978. Notably the Commission applied a different analysis to stations in smaller communities "where few alternatives are available to listeners." *Id.* Such stations were required to "be more broadly based in their programming," something which the Commission believed to be dictated by "good business sense" anyway, as "stations in smaller communities must broadly base all of their programming to attract, hold and serve a large audience." *Id.*

80 *Deregulation of Radio 1981*, 84 FCC 2d at 979.

81 *Deregulation of Radio 1981*, 84 FCC 2d at 1002-08.

82 *Deregulation of Radio 1981*, 84 FCC 2d at 1008-1011.

83 *Deregulation of Radio 1981*, 84 FCC 2d at 1008.

84 *Office of Commc'n of the United Church of Christ v. FCC,* 707 F.2d 1413, 1426 (D.C. Cir. 1983).

85 *Office of Commc'n of the United Church of Christ v. FCC,* 707 F.2d at 1427.

86 *Office of Commc'n of the United Church of Christ v. FCC,* 707 F.2d at 1435-38.

87 *Office of Commc'n of the United Church of Christ v. FCC,* 707 F.2d at 1441 (internal citation omitted).

88 *Deregulation of Radio,* Memorandum Opinion and Order, 104 FCC 2d 505, 507 (1986).

89 *Revision of Programming and Commercialization Policies, Ascertainment Requirements, and Program Log Requirements for Commercial Television Stations*, Report and Order, 98 FCC 2d 1076, 1984 WL 251255 at *2 (Aug. 21, 1984) (*Television Deregulation Order*).

90 *Television Deregulation Order*, 1984 WL 251255 at *7.

91 *Television Deregulation Order*, 1984 WL 251255 at *8.

92 *Television Deregulation Order* at 1984 WL 251255 at *2.

93 Between 1934 and 1952, Section 307(d) of the Act provided that action on license renewal applications should be governed by the same considerations and practices as the granting of the original applications, including application of traditional comparative factors such as integration of ownership and management and diversification of media ownership. *See* ch. 652, Title III, Part I, § 307, 48 Stat. 1083 (June 19, 1934). Nevertheless, in 1951, the Commission acknowledged it had given some consideration to the past broadcast records of incumbent licensees in the renewal application process, and would continue to do so alongside the traditional comparative factors. *See Hearst Radio, Inc. (WBAL)*, 15 FCC 1149 (1951). In so doing, the Commission reasoned that a literal reading of Section 307(d) would effectively eliminate consideration of the incumbent's past broadcast record, which would not be in the public interest. The Commission's reasoning gave rise to the "renewal expectancy" preference, which was granted to the incumbent depending on the Commission's review of the incumbent's program performance. If the Commission's determination that the incumbent's past program service had been meritorious in meeting the needs and interests of listeners or viewers in its community of license or service area, renewal expectancy was warranted and was given significant weight when evaluated against the traditional structural factors. The Commission believed that Congress had to some extent confirmed the existence of such an expectancy when it amended Section 307(d) to delete the language subjecting renewal applicants to "the same considerations and practice" as original applicants and substituted the present language subjecting all applications to the standard of "public interest, convenience, and necessity." *See* 82 P.L. 554, ch 879, § 5, 66 Stat. 71447 (July 16, 1952).

The renewal expectancy preference was applied on an *ad hoc* basis, without guidelines concerning comparative criteria or the weights to be assigned to particular factors, until 1965. In that year, the Commission adopted a *Policy Statement* to deal with situations involving comparative proceedings between non-incumbent applicants according to the following principles:.

"Decisional significance will be accorded only to material and substantial differences between applicants' proposed program plans. Minor differences in the proportions of time allocated to different types of programs will not be considered. Substantial differences will be considered to the extent that they go beyond ordinary differences in judgment and show a superior devotion to public service."

Policy Statement on Comparative Broadcast Hearings, 1 FCC 2d 393, 397 (1965) (internal citations omitted) (*1965 Policy Statement*). Since the Commission didn't enforce the implementation of the program proposals of winning applicants, few were crazy enough to under-propose, warranting comparative consideration with their opponents' proposals. However, the *1965 Policy Statement* did not attempt to address the interplay between these comparative factors and the "renewal expectancy" preference adopted in the *Hearst Radio* decision.

In 1970, the Commission adopted a second policy statement specifically tailored for comparative hearings. *Policy Statement Concerning Comparative Hearings Involving Regular Renewal Applicants*, Public Notice, FCC-70-62, 22 FCC 2d 424 (1970) (*1970 Policy Statement*), *rev'd, Citizens Communications Center v. FCC*, 447 F.2d 1201 (1971). Under the *1970 Policy Statement*, a renewal applicant would be preferred over any competing applicant if the incumbent could show in a hearing that its programming during the license term had been "substantially attuned" to meeting the needs and interests of its service area, and that its operation had otherwise been characterized by "serious deficiencies." *1970 Policy Statement*, 22 FCC 2d at 425. If the presiding judge determined that the renewal applicant's record of service met that test, it was to halt the proceeding and grant the renewal application. *Id.* at 428.

The *1970 Policy Statement* lasted one year before it was overturned by the Court of Appeals for the District of Columbia Circuit. The Court held that the bifurcated procedure adopted in the *1970 Policy Statement* violated Section 309 of the Act as interpreted by the Supreme Court in

Ashbacker Radio Corp. v. FCC., 326 U.S. 327 (1945), by depriving qualified challenging applicants of the right to a full comparative hearing on the merits of their proposals. *Citizens Communication Center v. FCC*, 447 F.2d 1201 (D.C. Cir. 1971) (*CCC*), *clarified,* 463 F.2d 822 (D.C. Cir. 1972). However, the Court did note that prior cases had established a presumption—or, as the court referred to it, an "operational bias" that created an "insuperable advantage"—in favor of license renewal when the licensee's service record was satisfactory. *CCC*, 447 F.2d at 1207-08.

The Commission then returned to processing comparative renewal proceedings under the standards in the *1965 Policy Statement*, with the renewal expectancy typically being the dispositive factor, while also pursuing a rulemaking in the wake of the *CCC* decision. In the leading comparative license renewal case from this era, the D.C. Circuit court upheld the Commission's grant of the incumbent's renewal application against a competing application. *Cowles Florida Broadcasting, Inc.,* Decision, 60 FCC 2d 372 (1976) (*Cowles*), *recon. denied and clarified*, 62 FCC 2d 953 (1977), *further recon. denied*, 40 RR 2d 1627 (1977), *remanded sub nom. Central Florida Enterprises, Inc. v. FCC*, 598 F.2d 37 (D.C. Cir. 1978), *on remand, Cowles Broadcasting, Inc.*, 86 FCC 2d 993 (1981), *aff'd sub nom. Central Florida Enterprises, Inc. v. FCC*, 683 F.2d 503 (D.C. Cir. 1982). In granting the renewal, the Commission held that, for significant "public interest" reasons, an incumbent licensee's 'meritorious' record could outweigh a challenging applicant's advantages under the structural criteria of diversification and integration. *Cowles*. In affirming that decision, the D.C. Circuit held that so long as the Commission did not raise the renewal expectancy preference to an "irrebuttable presumption" in favor of the incumbent, and so long as it weighed all factors at the same time, the Commission could permissibly attribute renewal expectancies of varying strength and weight. *Central Florida Enterprises, Inc. v. FCC*, 683 F.2d 503, 506 (D.C. Cir. 1982). The court restated and affirmed the three-part justification underlying the renewal expectancy preference:

there is no guarantee that a challenger's paper proposals will, in fact, match the incumbent's proven performance;

the likelihood of renewal encourages licensees to make investments to ensure quality service which would not be made if their dedication to service is not rewarded; and

the comparing of challengers and incumbents on the same basis as new applicants are compared could lead to an undesirable haphazard restructuring of the broadcast industry, i.e., could lead to licensees owning more than one station being displaced by challengers with no or fewer stations.

Central Florida Enterprises, Inc., 683 F.2d at 507, *quoting Cowles*, 86 FCC 2d at 1013.

94 *See WWOR-TV, Inc.*, Decision, 7 FCC Rcd 636, 638 (1992), *aff'd sub nom. Garden State Broadcasting L.P. v. FCC*, 966 F.2d 386 (D.C. Cir. 1993) (in disqualifying a party for filing a competing application for purposes of obtaining a settlement payment from the incumbent licensee, the Commission states that "incentives and mechanisms for abuse…have been inherent in the licensing process").

95 Telecommunications Act of 1996, P.L. 104; § 203 110 Stat. 56, 112 (1996) (Telecom Act). The Omnibus Budget Reconciliation Act of 1981 had extended radio station license terms from the original three years to seven years and extended television station license terms from three years to five years. *See Omnibus Budget Reconciliation Act of 1996*, Pub. L. No. 35, Sub. B, ch. 2, 95 Stat. 357, 736 (1981).

96 Telecom Act § 204, 110 Stat. 56, 112-13. Passage of the Act, however, did not alter the Commission's longstanding policy of considering time-sharing proposals to accommodate competing demand for limited NCE-FM spectrum. *See, e.g., Nassau Community College*, File No. BMLED-951024KA, Memorandum Opinion and Order, 12 FCC Rcd 12234, 12234-5 (1997); *Comparative Standards for Noncommercial Educational Applicants,* Memorandum Opinion and Order, 16 FCC Rcd 5074, 5100-01 (2001) (affirming use of time sharing as tie-breaker of last resort in selecting among competing applicants for new NCE stations).

97 *See* FCC, *Instructions for FCC 303-S Application for Renewal of Broadcast Station License* (FCC Form 303-S Attached) (updated Sept. 2009) (*Instructions for FCC Form 303-S*) at 25, 34, *available at* www.fcc.gov/Forms/Form303-S/303s.pdf.

98 47 C.F.R. § 73.3527(e)(8)(i).

99 *See Application for Renewal of Broadcast Station License* at 25, 34.

100 Commission regulations do provide the following language with respect to the list: "The list shall include a brief narrative describing what issues were given significant treatment and the programming that provided the treatment. The description of the programs shall include, but shall not be limited to, the time, date, duration, and title of each program in which the issue was treated." *See, e.g.*, 47 C.F.R. § 73.3526(e)(12); and 47 C.F.R. § 73.3527(e)(8)(i) (containing identical language).

101 As discussed in Chapter 26, Broadcast Radio and Television, in its Enhanced Disclosure proceeding, the Commission imposed such a requirement on television licensees, *Standardized and Enhanced Disclosure Requirements for Television Broadcast Licensee Public Interest Obligations*, Report and Order, 23 FCC Rcd 1274 (2007), but this rule has not yet become effective.

102 These findings are based on FOM staff's review of the quarterly issues/programs lists that several stations have prepared and placed in their public inspection files.

103 KNBC-TV, Quarterly Issues/Program Report, third quarter of 2009.

104 It should be noted that renewal applications denied on grounds other than failure to meet public interest obligations were not included in this tally. Such grounds include misrepresentations, character matters or other disqualification involving the licensee or its principals, non-operation of the station in violation of Section 312 of the Communications Act, 47 U.S.C. § 312, or situations in which a competing applicant in a comparative renewal proceeding was deemed to be superior to the incumbent licensee.

105 During its initial administrative review of the petition of a coalition of church and civil rights groups to deny the renewal application of Lamar Life Broadcasting Company for Station WLBT-TV, the Commission concluded that the coalition lacked standing to protest the application. *See Lamar Life Broadcasting Co.*, 38 FCC 1143 (1965) (*Lamar Life 1965*), *rev'd and remanded sub nom. Office of Commc'n of the United Church of Christ v. FCC*, 359 F.2d 994 (D.C. Cir. 1966) (*UCC I*), *accepting remand*, 3 FCC2d 784 (1966); *renewing license again*, 14 FCC2d 495 (*ALJ 1967*); *aff'd*, 14 FCC2d 431 (1968) (*Lamar Life 1968*); *rev'd and vacated sub nom. Office of Commc'n of the United Church of Christ v. FCC*, 425 F.2d 543 (D.C. Cir. 1969) (*UCC II*). While nonetheless acknowledging that the petition raised serious questions about the Lamar Life's compliance with the public interest standard, the Commission noted its view that a licensee who had failed to comply with the standard in the past should be granted renewal upon its agreement to cease all operations which the Commission finds contrary to the public interest. *See Lamar Life 1965*. The DC Circuit reversed the Commission's decision, finding that the petitioners did have standing. *See UCC I*. On remand, the Commission granted the renewal application notwithstanding the petition after holding an evidentiary hearing. *See Lamar Life 1968*. The DC Circuit reversed, directing the Commission to cancel the renewal and noting that the FCC hearing examiner had displayed a "profound hostility to the participation of the Public Intervenors and their efforts." *UCC II*, 425 F.2d at 549–50.

106 *Brandywine-Main Line Radio, Inc. v. FCC*, 473 F.2d 16, 20 (D.C. Cir. 1972); *see also Brandywine-Main Line Radio, Inc.*, Decision, 24 FCC 2d 18 (1970), *recon. denied*, 27 FCC 2d 565 (1971).

107 See, e.g., *Applications of the Alabama Educational Television Commission For Renewal Of Licenses For Station Waiq (Ed-Tv), Montgomery, Ala.*, Memorandum Opinion and Order, 33 FCC 2d 495 (1972) (rescinding the Commission's grant of renewal applications to the Alabama stations and designated them for hearing); *Applications of Alabama Educational Television Comm'n*, 50 FCC 2d 461, 483 (1975) (overturning ALJ decision and denying renewal applications).

108 *West Coast Media, Inc.*, Decision, 79 FCC 2d 610 (1980).

109 *SeeLicense Renewal Applications of Certain Commercial Television Stations Serving Philadelphia, Pennsylvania*, Memorandum Opinion and Order, 5 FCC Rcd 3847 (1990), *recon. denied*, 6 FCC Rcd 4191 (1991) (*Philadelphia Television Cases*); *License Renewal Applications of Certain Commercial Radio Stations Serving Philadelphia, Pennsylvania*, Memorandum Opinion and Order, 8 FCC Rcd 6400 (Com. Car. Bur. 2003) (*Philadelphia Radio Cases*).

110 *See Philadelphia Television Cases*, 5 FCC Rcd at 3847 n.5.

111 *See Philadelphia Television Cases,* 5 FCC Rcd at 3847. The proceeding raised serious issues about the Commission's public file requirements. One of the television stations whose license was renewed admitted in papers that it had been "inadvertently" deficient in maintaining its public file. *License Renewal Applications of Certain Commercial Television Stations Serving Philadelphia, Pennsylvania*, Memorandum Opinion and Order, 6 FCC Rcd 4191, 4191 (1991). Evidence suggested that another such station had attempted to forestall review of its file. *See id.* at 4194 (Duggan, Ervin S., Commissioner, concurring). Although the Commission affirmed the renewal decisions on reconsideration, Commissioner Ervin S. Duggan, issued a Separate Statement in order to question whether the Commission was "taking its public file requirements serious enough today." *See id.* Duggan noted that the issues/programs list "is one of our most important requirements, for such lists [ ] provide the only real means for monitoring station compliance with the public interest standard of the Communications Act." *Id.* He concluded that, with the elimination of quantitative programming guidelines, if the public file requirement "is not vigorously enforced, does the public interest standard today mean anything at all?" *Id.*

112 WZFM (FM), Narrows, Va., *Application to Renew Station License, Operational Status Inquiry,* Letter from Peter Doyle, Chief, Audio Services Division, Media Bureau, to Old Dominion Communications, Inc., April 7, 2004. Under section 312(g), a station forfeits its license if it fails to broadcast signals for 12 consecutive months. 47 U.S.C. Section 312(g).

113 Old Dominion Communications, Inc., *Petition for Reconsideration*, Declaration of H. Edward Hale, at 1, Apr. 19, 2004.

114 Old Dominion Communications, Inc., *Petition for Reconsideration Granted, Application Reinstated,* June 9, 2004, http://hraunfoss.fcc.gov/edocs_public/attachmatch/DOC-262186A1.pdf.

115 ANGELA J. CAMPBELL, PUBLIC PARTICIPATION AT THE FEDERAL COMMUNICATIONS COMMISSION (2010) (unpublished study available upon request). The author is Director of Georgetown Law's Institute for Public Representation, which operates as clinic for law students and provides *pro bono* legal assistance to non-profit organizations. Kate Aishton and Niko Perazich provided research assistance.

116 These delays are often the result of processing holds that are placed on renewal applications by the Enforcement Bureau to preserve its right to issue notices of apparent liability in pending matters, most commonly indecency cases. Because Section 503(b)(6) of the Act imposes a statute of limitations of one year from the violation, postponing the renewal preserves the Commission's ability to propose a forfeiture. *See* 47 U.S.C. § 503(b)(6).

117 It should be noted that there were two cases in recent years in which the Commission did take major action—but, significantly, they involved mergers, not the normal license renewal process. One case involved the transfer of the Tribune Company to Sam Zell, the other, the sale of Univision. In both cases, it was necessary for the Commission to grant renewal applications to the stations before it could approve their sale. In the Univision case, the Commission confronted concerns over Univision's reliance on telenovas to satisfy its children's programming obligations. Rather than designating the applications for hearing, the Commission entered into a consent decree with Univision that required the licensee to pay $24 million to the U.S. Treasury. The sale was then approved.*See Shareholders of Tribune Company*, Memorandum Order and Opinion, 22 FCC Rcd. 21266 (2007); *Shareholders of Univision Communications Inc.*, Memorandum Order and Opinion, 22 FCC Rcd. 5842 (2007) (*Univision*).

118 Specifically, the Industry Analysis Division of the Media Bureau looked at week-long television station programming schedules from 12:00 a.m. Monday to 11:59 p.m. Sunday to determine if the station aired any news. The sources used to determine station programming were Zap2lt.com, TV Guide, local station websites, and Wikipedia.org.

If the station broadcast 30 minutes or more of news per week, that station was deemed to broadcast news. Notation was made if the station fell into any of the following categories: airing Local and National News, Local News Only, National News Only, or No News. Regional and Campus News programs were included in the local news category. Broadcasts of state legislature, public affairs, and public interest programs were not considered news.

Once these determinations were made, percentages were calculated for the total markets. The total number of broadcast stations was 1,632. Of those, 1,239 stations were commercial stations, and 393 were noncommercial educational stations. There were 696 stations that broadcast no local news, and 248 stations did not broadcast news. Of the 393 noncommercial educational stations, 322 did not broadcast local news.

Calculations were also made for the Top 100 DMAs in those categories. The Top 100 DMAs contained 1100 stations. Of those, 842 were commercial stations and 258 were non-commercial educational stations. There were 496 stations in the top 100 markets that broadcast no local news, and 207 stations that broadcast no news. Of the 258 non-commercial educational stations, 199 did not broadcast local news.

119 *See Improving Commission Processes*, Notice of Inquiry, 11 FCC Rcd 14006, 14017 (1996).

120 Absent action by the private party or the FCC, ABIP agreements automatically renew for subsequent three-year periods.

121 Far fewer stations in other broadcast services (e.g. Class A, Low Power TV) participate in ABIP. For example, as of December 2010, less than one percent of Low Power TV stations participate in ABIP.

122 The FCC's self-inspection checklists include information on assessing compliance with the most frequently violated broadcast regulations. *See* FCC, Broadcast Self Inspection-Checklists, http://www.fcc.gov/eb/bc-chklsts/.

123 For example, the Advisory Committee on Public Interest Obligations of Digital Television Broadcasters issued q comprehensive report, Charting the Digital Broadcasting Future, in December 1998. http://benton.org/archive/publibrary/piac/report.html. The Advisory Committee's major recommendations concerned the following topics: 1) improving the quality of public discourse, 2) disaster warnings, 3) disability access to digital programming and 4) diversity in broadcasting. See Letter from Vice President Al Gore to FCC Chairman William Kennard, October 20, 1999. http://benton.org/archive/publibrary/piac/vpltr.html.

124 Mark Fowler & Daniel Brenner, *A Marketplace Approach to Broadcast Regulation*, 60 TEX. L. REV. 207, 210 (1982) (*A Marketplace Approach to Broadcast Regulation*).

125 *A Marketplace Approach to Broadcast Regulation*, 60 TEX. L. REV. at 211–12. (1982). They also advocated the elimination of any restrictions on the alienation of licenses, including the ownership rules, maintaining that such rules serve to restrict growth by existing participants and create barriers to the entry of new ones, thus retarding program diversity. *Id.* at 245–47.

126 *A Marketplace Approach to Broadcast Regulation*, 60 TEX. L. REV. at 242–44 (1982). He alternatively proposed that current licensees retain "squatter's rights" to their authorizations, and be free to sell them to parties that would have flexibility to decide how to use the spectrum. *Id.* at 244.

127 *A Marketplace Approach to Broadcast Regulation*, 60 TEX. L. REV. at 247–48.

128 *A Marketplace Approach to Broadcast Regulation*, 60 TEX. L. REV. at 247–48.

129 *A Marketplace Approach to Broadcast Regulation*, 60 TEX. L. REV. at 248–49.

130 *A Marketplace Approach to Broadcast Regulation*, 60 TEX. L. REV. at 252–54.

131 *A Marketplace Approach to Broadcast Regulation*, 60 TEX. L. REV. at 255.

132 Prepared Testimony of Henry Geller, FCC Workshop on the Future of Media and the Information Needs of Communities: Serving the Public Interest in the Digital Era (Mar. 4, 2010), at 7, *available at* http://reboot.fcc.gov/futureofmedia/serving-the-public-interest-in-the-digital-era.

133 Testimony of Henry Geller, FCC Workshop on the Future of Media and the Information Needs of Communities: Serving the Public Interest in the Digital Era (Mar. 4, 2010), Tr. at 74:3–10, *available at* http://reboot.fcc.gov/c/document_library/get_file?uuid=57c2b1d8-4ecb-49b8-ad8e-bb30d794b784&groupId=19001.

134 SEE ADVISORY COMMITTEE ON PUBLIC INTERNET OBLIGATIONS OF DIGITAL TELEVISION BROADCASTERS, CHARTING THE DIGITAL BROADCASTING FUTURE (FINAL REPORT) (1998), http://benton.org/archive/publibrary/piac/report.html.

135 *See, e.g.,* Paul Taylor & Norm Ornstein, *The Case for Free Air Time: A Broadcast Spectrum Fee for Campaign Finance Reform (Spectrum*

Series Working Paper # 4), New America Foundation Public Assets Program, June 2002, at 8, http://www.newamerica.net/publications/policy/the_case_for_free_air_time.

136 Steve Coll, *Reboot: An open letter to the FCC about a media policy for the digital age*, COLUMBIA JOURNALISM REV. (Nov./Dec. 2010) (*Coll Open Letter*), http://www.cjr.org/cover_story/reboot.php.

137 *See Standardized and Enhanced Disclosure Requirements for Television Broadcast Licensee Public Interest Obligations*, Notice of Proposed Rule Making, 15 FCC Rcd 19816 (2000).

138 *See Standardized and Enhanced Disclosure Requirements for Television Broadcast Licensee Public Interest Obligations*, Report and Order, 23 FCC Rcd 1274 (2007).

139 *See Standardized and Enhanced Disclosure Requirements for Television Broadcast Licensee Public Interest Obligations*, Report and Order, 23 FCC Rcd 1274, Appendix B (2007).

140 *See, e.g., Heavy compliance burden of Enhanced Disclosure Order exceeds OMB threshold, NAB says*, BROADCASTENGINEERING.COM, May 14, 2008, http://broadcastengineering.com/eng/heavy_compliance_burden_enhanced_disclosure_order_0514/; David Oxenford, *Will the FCC Back off on its TV Enhanced Disclosure Requirements?*, BROADCAST LAW BLOG, Sept. 15, 2008, http://www.broadcastlawblog.com/2008/09/articles/public-interest-obligationsloc/will-the-fcc-back-off-on-its-tv-enhanced-disclosure-requirements/#discussion.

141 *Broadcast Localism*, Notice of Inquiry, 19 FCC Rcd 12425, 12445 (2004) (*Localism NOI*) (Powell, Michael K., Chairman, concurring).

142 47 U.S.C. § 307(b).

143 *See Revision of FM Assignment Policies and Procedures*, 90 FCC 2d 88, 92 (1982) (*FM Allocation Priorities Order*), *on recon.*, 56 Rad. Reg. 2d (P&F) 448 (1984); *Amendment of Section 3.606 of the Commission's Rules and Regulations*, 41 FCC 148, 167 (1952) (*TV Allocation Priorities Order*). The Commission's first FM allocation priority is first-time aural service, followed by second full-time aural service and first local service; the latter two have "co-equal status." *See FM Allocation Priorities Order*, 90 FCC 2d at 92. The Commission's first television allocation priority is "[t]o provide at least one television service to all parts of the United States"; its second is "[t]o provide each community with at least one television broadcast station." *TV Allocation Priorities Order*, 41 FCC at 167. Although AM stations are not allotted, where mutually exclusive AM applications are filed, they are first evaluated under similar section 307(b) criteria.

144 *FCC v. Allentown Broadcasting Corp.*, 349 U.S. 358, 362 (1955).

145 *Localism NOI* (citing 47 C.F.R.§ 73.1125).

146 *Localism NOI* (citing *Amendment of Sections 73.1125 and 73.1130 of the Commission's Rules, the Main Studio and Program Origination Rules for Radio and Television Broadcast Stations*, Memorandum Opinion and Order, 3 FCC Rcd 5024, 5026 (1988)).

147 *Localism NOI* (citing 47 C.F.R. §§ 73.3526(e)(11)(i) (commercial TV issues/program list), 73.3526(e)(12) (commercial AM and FM issues/program list)). "These lists must be retained until final action has been taken on the station's next renewal application." *Id.* (citing 47 C.F.R. §§ 73.3526(e)(1)(i), 73.3526(e)(12)).

148 *Localism NOI* (citing *Standardized and Enhanced Disclosure Requirements for Television Broadcast Licensee Public Interest Obligations*, Notice of Proposed Rulemaking, 15 FCC Rcd 19816, 19821 (2000) (*Enhanced Disclosure NPRM*) (citing *Commercial TV Deregulation Order*, 98 FCC

2d at 1076, 1107-11 (explaining the purpose of issues/programs lists for commercial television))).

149 *See* Cable Television Consumer Protection and Competition Act of 1992, Pub. L. 102-385, § 2(a)(11), 106 Stat. 1460 (1992) (1992 Cable Act). The Commission has stated its promotion of localism has a statutory basis in the "Congressional Findings and Policy" Section of the 1992 Cable Act. *2002 Biennial Regulatory Review—Review of the Commission's Broadcast Ownership Rules and Other Rules adopted Pursuant to Section 202 of the Telecommunications Act of 1996*, Notice of Proposed Rulemaking, 17 FCC Rcd 18503 (2002) (citations omitted).

150 *See Turner Broadcasting System v. FCC*, 520 U.S. 180, 225 (1997)

151 1992 Cable Act, 106 Stat. at 1461.

152 *See* FCC, Localism Task Force Archives, http://www.fcc.gov/localism/taskforce-archive.html (last visited Jan. 6, 2011).

153 *See Broadcast Localism*, Report on Broadcast Localism and Notice of Proposed Rulemaking, 23 FCC Rcd 1324 (2008) (*Localism Report & NPRM*), http://hraunfoss.fcc.gov/edocs_public/attachmatch/FCC-07-218A1.pdf.

154 *See Localism Report & NPRM*, 23 FCC Rcd at 1335-36.

155 *See Localism Report & NPRM*, 23 FCC Rcd at 1336-38, 1369.

156 Michael C. Copps, Commissioner, FCC, Getting Media Right: A Call to Action, Address Before the Columbia University Graduate School of Journalism (Dec. 2, 2010), *available at* http://www.journalism.columbia.edu/system/documents/347/original/Copps_speech_final.pdf.

157 47 C.F.R. § 73.3526(e)(12).

158 The uncertainty engendered by such ambiguity was apparent even to the Commission itself. *See Deregulation of Radio 1981*, 84 FCC 2d at 971 (stating, in response to concerns expressed by some commenters that its deregulatory actions would make even more unclear precisely what the public interest standard was, "The Commission was not created solely to provide certainty"). Moreover, the ambiguity raised such heightened concern that the National Association of Broadcasters, which itself had initially proposed the elimination of the application processing guidelines that the Commission embraced in the Radio Deregulation Order, asked the Commission to reconsider the elimination on the ground that it left broadcasters without "reasonably specific guidance. . .on those matters upon which his performance is to be judged- a judgment which will determine the licensee's fitness for continued broadcast service." *Deregulation of Radio*, Memorandum Opinion and Order, 87 FCC 2d 797, 813 (1981); *see also id.* at 815 (discussing NAB's initial proposals).

159 Testimony of Jerald N. Fritz, FCC Workshop on the Future of Media and the Information Needs of Communities: Serving the Public Interest in the Digital Era (Mar. 4, 2010) (Fritz Testimony 3/4/10), Tr. at 131:14-21, *available at* http://reboot.fcc.gov/futureofmedia/serving-the-public-interest-in-the-digital-era.

160 Fritz Testimony 3/4/10, Tr. at 138:15-18.

161 Prepared Testimony of Jane Mago, Exec. V.P. and Gen. Counsel, National Ass'n of Broadcasters, FCC Workshop on the Future of Media and the Information Needs of Communities: Serving the Public Interest in the Digital Era (Mar. 4, 2010), at 1-2, 4, *available at* http://reboot.fcc.gov/futureofmedia/serving-the-public-interest-in-the-digital-era.

162 National Ass'n of Broadcasters, *Broadcasters Generate $10.3 Billion in 2005 Public Service* (press release), June 12, 2006, http://www.nab.org/documents/newsroom/pressRelease.asp?id=1220.

163 National Association of Broadcasters Comments in re *FOM PN*, filed Oct. 13, 2010, at 52.

164 Testimony of Paul Starr, Professor of Communication and Public Affairs, Princeton Univ., FCC Workshop on the Future of Media and the Information Needs of Communities: Serving the Public Interest in the Digital Era (Mar. 4, 2010), Tr. at 75, *available at* http://reboot.fcc.gov/futureofmedia/serving-the-public-interest-in-the-digital-era.

165 S. REP. NO. 229, 92nd Cong., 1st Sess. at 1 (1971). The legislative history of Title I of the Federal Election Campaign Act of 1971 ("FECA"), Pub. L. No. 92-225, 86 Stat. 3 (1971), included provisions regarding reasonable access for federal candidates and lowest unit charge for all candidates.

166 S. REP. NO. 96, 92nd Cong., 1st Sess. at 15 (1971). This quote refers to the reasonable access obligation adopted in Title I of FECA. The FCC has also stressed the importance of political broadcasting: "In short, the presentation of political broadcasting, while only one of many elements of service to the public…is an important facet, deserving the licensee's closest attention, because of the contribution broadcasting can thus make to an informed electorate—in turn so vital to the proper functioning of our Republic." *Licensee Responsibility as to Political Broadcasts*, 15 FCC 2d 94 (1968) (citations omitted). The FCC emphasized that "the provision of time for [political broadcasts] is an essential element of the public interest obligations of broadcasters." *Id.*

167 *CBS, Inc. v. FCC*, 453 U.S. 367, 396 (1981).

168 Pub. L. No. 92-225, 86 Stat. 3 (1971); 47 U.S.C. § 315(b); 47 C.F.R. § 73.1942.

169 47 C.F.R. § 76.206.

170 47 C.F.R. § 25.701(c). *See* 47 U.S.C. § 335(a).

171 *DARS R&O*, 12 FCC Rcd at 5792.

172 3 Fed. Reg. 1692, 1693 (1938).

173 47 C.F.R. § 73.1943.

174 *Amendment of the Commission's Rules to Require Stations to Notify Opposing Candidates of Gifts of Time For Use Within 72 Hours Prior to Day of Election*, 60 FCC 2d 884, 886 (1976).

175 Pub. L. No. 107-155, 116 Stat. 81 (2002).

176 47 U.S.C. § 315(e). This is defined as "a message relating to any political matter of national importance including (i) a legally qualified candidate; (ii) any election to Federal office; or (iii) a national legislative issue of public importance." The information to be retained includes all requests for particular schedules of time, including rates and classes, and the actual broadcaster disposition of those requests.

177 47 U.S.C. § 315(c)(1). 47 C.F.R. § 76.1701.

178 47 U.S.C. § 335(e). *See* 47 C.F.R § 25.701(d).

179 47 C.F.R. §§ 73.3526 and 73.3527.

180 *Enhanced Disclosure Requirement for Television Broadcast Licensee Public Interest Obligations*, 23 FCC Rcd 1274, 1281-82 (2008) (*Enhanced Disclosure Proceeding*). We note that the rules adopted in this proceeding have not yet taken effect.

181 47 U.S.C. § 312(a)(7) (added in 1972 by Title I of FECA); 47 C.F.R. § 73.1944. In 1974, the FCC in effect repealed the provision applying the reasonable access provisions to cable.

182 47 C.F.R. § 25.701(b)(3). *See* 47 U.S.C. § 335(a).

183 *DARS R&O*, 12 FCC Rcd at 5792.

184 *The Law of Political Broadcasting and Cablecasting: A Political Primer 1984 Edition*, 100 FCC 2d 1476, 1522 (*1984 Primer*).

185 *Codification of the Commission's Political Programming Policy*, Report and Order, 7 FCC Rcd 678, 682 (1991). In the Commission's *1999 NOI on Public Interest Obligations*, however, the Commission requested comment on, among other things, several proposals to require broadcasters to provide time for state and local candidates, and whether there were "steps the Commission can take to promote voluntary efforts to enhance political debate and information that the public receives concerning candidates." *Public Interest Obligations of TV Broadcast Licensees*, Notice of Inquiry, 14 FCC Rcd 21633, 21648 (1999). In 2008, the Commission declined to take any further action, saying it would be premature given its decision at the time to move ahead with the *Enhanced Disclosure Proceeding. Review of the Commission's Broadcast Ownership Rules and Other Rules Adopted Pursuant to Section 202 of Telecommunications Act of 1996*, Report and Order and Order on Reconsideration, 23 FCC Rcd 2010, 2085 (2008). The Commission indicated, however, that to the extent circumstances changed, it would revisit its decision and initiate appropriate proceedings. As discussed above, the enhanced disclosure rules have not gone into effect.

186 *Review of the Commission's Broadcast Ownership Rules and Other Rules Adopted Pursuant to Section 202 of Telecommunications Act of 1996*, Report and Order and Order on Reconsideration, 23 FCC Rcd 2010 (2008).

187 47 U.S.C. § 315(b); 47 C.F.R. § 73.1941.

188 47 C.F.R. § 76.205.

189 47 C.F.R. § 25.701(b)(4). *See* 47 U.S.C. § 335(a).

190 *Establishment of Rules and Policies for the Digital Audio Radio Satellite Service in the 2310-2360 MHz Frequency Band,* Report and Order, Memorandum Opinion and Order & Further Notice Of Proposed Rulemaking, 12 FCC Rcd 5754, 5792 (1997) (*DARS R&O*).

191 *See* S. Rep. No. 562, 86th Cong., 1st Sess. 1959, 1959 U.S.C.C.A.N. 2564, 2572. *See also* Conf. Rep. No. 1069, 86th Cong., 1st Sess. 1959, 1959 U.S.C.C.A.N. 2564.

192 Specifically, these include advertisements where the candidate—on whose behalf the time is purchased—makes a positive, identifiable appearance, including by voice or picture, for at least four seconds (referred to as a candidate "use" in Section 315.) 47 U.S.C. § 315(a); 47 C.F.R. § 73.1941.

193 47 C.F.R. § Section 76.205(a).

194 47 C.F.R. § Section 25.701(b)(4)(i). *See* 47 U.S.C. § 335(a).

195 *DARS R&O*, 12 FCC Rcd at 5792.

196 47 U.S.C. § 315(c).

197 47 C.F.R. § 76.5(p) (emphasis added). Similarly, Section 25.701(b)(2) defines "DBS origination programming" as "programming (exclusive of broadcast signals) carried on a DBS facility over one or more channels and subject to the exclusive control of the DBS provider." 47 C.F.R. § 25.701(b)(2).

198 The issue was referenced in a 2000 Mass Media Bureau Staff Ruling responding to a request for declaratory ruling filed by A&E Television Networks ("AETN"). In that Ruling, the Bureau stated that "[t]he Commission has not considered whether cable network programming such as the programming produced by AETN could, under any circumstances, be deemed cablecast origination material and will not address this issue

here." *Request of A&E Television Networks for Declaratory Ruling*, Ruling, 15 FCCR 10796, 10796 (MMB 2000). *See, e.g., Emergency Complaint of Dennis J. Kucinich v. Cable News Network and Time Warner, Inc.*, Memorandum Opinion and Order, 23 FCC Rcd 482 (MB 2008) (because the Bureau denied the complaint on other grounds, it found "it unnecessary to consider whether the equal opportunities requirements set forth in Section 315 apply to cable programming aired by CNN").

199 *Requests of Fox Broadcasting Co., et al. for a Declaratory Ruling*, Declaratory Ruling, 11 FCC Rcd. 11,101 (1996); *Request of A.H. Belo Corp. for a Declaratory Ruling*, Staff Ruling, 11 FCC Rcd. 12,306 (MMB 1996).

200 *Citizens United v. Federal Election Commission*, 130 S.Ct. 876, 916 (2010) (internal footnotes omitted).

201 *John Doe No. 1 v. Reed*, 130 S.Ct. 2811, 2837 (2010) (Scalia, J., concurring in the judgment).

27 Cable Television

1 *Rules and Regulations Relating to the Distribution of Television Broadcast Signals by the Community Antenna Television Systems,* Second Report and Order, 2 FCC 2d 725 (1966). *See also* Stanley M. Besen & Robert W. Crandall, The Deregulation of Cable Television, 44 LAW & CONTEMP. PROBS. 77, 88-89 (1981).

2 *See, e.g.,* Scott M. Fulton, *FCC abandons its 'a la carte' cable programming plan*, BETANEWS.COM, Nov. 28, 2007 http://www.betanews.com/article/FCC-abandons-its-a-la-carte-cable-programming-plan/1196283815.

3 GEOFFREY COWAN & DAVID WESTPHAL, PUBLIC POLICY AND FUNDING THE NEWS 10 (Univ. of Southern California Annenberg School of Communication) (2010), http://fundingthenews.usc.edu/report/ (PUBLIC POLICY AND FUNDING THE NEWS).

4 *See* 1992 Cable Act §§ 4-5, 106 Stat. 1460 (codified at 47 U.S.C. §§ 534-535).

5 Statement and written testimony of James B. Hedlund, Ass'n of Independent Television Stations, Inc., Cable TV Consumer Protection Act of 1991: Hearing on S.12 Before the Subcommittee on Communications of the Committee on Commerce, Science and Transportation, 102nd Cong. 205 (1991) (*Hedlund Testimony*) (footnote omitted).

6 *Hedlund Testimony* at 205–6.

7 Statement of Edward O. Fritts, President and CEO, National Ass'n of Broadcasters Cable Television Regulation: Hearings on H.R. 1303 and H.R. 2546 Before the Subcommittee on Telecommunications and Finance of the Committee on Energy and Commerce of the House of Representatives, 102nd Cong. 753 (1991).

8 According to a study by the Industry Analysis Division of the Media Bureau in connection with this Report, discussed more fully, *supra*, at Chapter 3, Television.

9 *See* 47 C.F.R. § 76.56(b)(2) (smaller systems are required to carry fewer channels). *See also* 47 C.F.R. § 76.55(c), (e). A Designated Market Area or DMA is a geographic market designation that defines each television market exclusive of others, based on measured viewing patterns. Essentially, each county in the United States is allocated to a market based on which home-market stations receive a preponderance of total viewing

hours in the county. For purposes of this calculation, both over-the-air and cable television viewing are included. *See* Nielsen Media Research, Nielsen Station Index: Methodology Techniques and Data Interpretation.

10 *See* 47 C.F.R. § 76.64(f)(2); *see also* 47 C.F.R. § 76.56.

11 *See* 47 C.F.R. § 76.55(b)(1), (b)(2).

12 Interview of Dave Lougee, President, Gannett Broadcast Division, by Steven Waldman, FCC, (Feb. 16, 2011).

13 *See, e.g.,* House Committee on Energy and Commerce, H.R. REP. NO 934, 98th Cong., 2d Sess. at 48 (1984).

14 Pub. L. No. 98-549, 98 Stat. 2780, 2782-83 (1984). The purposes behind the Act (and Section 612) were "to promote competition in the delivery of diverse sources of video programming and to assure that the widest possible diversity of information sources are made available to the public from cable systems in a manner consistent with growth and development of cable systems." 47 U.S.C. § 532(a) (codifying Section 612 of the Act).

15 *Implementation of Sections of the Cable Television Consumer Protection and Competition Act of 1992*, Second Report and Order and Second Order on Reconsideration of the First Report and Order, 12 FCC Rcd 5267, 5269 (1997) (*Cable TV Consumer Protection & Competition Second Report & Order*) (citations omitted).

16 *Cable TV Consumer Protection & Competition Second Report & Order*, 12 FCC Rcd at 5273–74, *quoting* House Committee on Energy and Commerce, H.R. Rep. No. 628, 102d Cong., 2d Sess., at 40 (1992).

17 Independent programmers do get carried on cable systems, even if not on the leased access channels. Comcast, for example, says it has carriage agreements with 50 independent programming networks. *Annual Assessment of the Status of Competition in the Market for the Delivery of Video Programming*, Thirteenth Annual Report, 24 FCC Rcd 542, para 201 (2009).

18 Letter from Senator Herb Kohl, Chairman, Subcommittee on Antitrust, Competition Policy, and Consumer Rights, to Kevin Martin, Chairman, FCC, June 23, 2008.

19 *See* Letter Comment from Doron Gorshein, President and C.E.O., The America Channel, LLC, to Marlene H. Dortch, Secretary, FCC, MB Docket No. 07-42 (filed Sept. 11, 2007), at 13; Appendices B & C. *See Annual Assessment of the Status of Competition in the Market for the Delivery of Video Programming*, Thirteenth Annual Report, 24 FCC Rcd 542, para 215 (2009).

20 Overall, 0.7 channels were used for leased access programming out of an average number of 24.8 basic service tier channels as of January 1, 2006, or out of an average of 26.7 basic service tier channels as of January 1, 2008. *See Implementation of Section 3 of the Cable Television Consumer Protection and Competition Act of 1992: Statistical Report on Average Rates for Basic Service, Cable Programming Service, and Equipment*, Report on Cable Industry Prices, 24 FCC Rcd 259, 283 (MB 2009).

21 For instance,

"leased access programming on TWC systems falls primarily into three general categories: religious (often over 40 percent), infomercials promoting real estate sales, automobile dealers, and tourism, among other things (about one-third of total leased access programming), and international/foreign language programs (typically accounting for 10–15 percent). The remaining leased access programming usually consists of community programs featuring local news and sporting events, segments devoted to hobbies such as fishing and cooking, as well as educational, home shopping and entertainment programs."

Time Warner Cable Inc. Comments in re *Leased Commercial Access NPRM* (*Leased Commercial Access,* Notice of Proposed Rulemaking, 22 FCC Rcd 11222 (2007) (*Leased Commercial Access NPRM*), filed Sept. 11, 2007, at 14–15. Comcast reports that approximately half of the leased access time on its systems is used for infomercials or home shopping. *See* Comcast Corp. Comments in re *Leased Commercial Access NPRM*, filed Sept. 11, 2007, at 17.

22 *See, e.g., Leased Commercial Access NPRM; Leased Commercial Access,* Report and Order and Further Notice of Proposed Rulemaking, 23 FCC Rcd 2909 (2008).

23 Cable Communications Policy Act of 1984, Pub. L. No. 98-549, 98 Stat. 2779 (codified at 47 U.S.C. §§ 521-529).

24 47 U.S.C. § 531.

25 H.R. REP. NO. 98-934, *as reprinted in* 1984 U.S.C.C.A.N. 4655, 4667 (1984) (adding that the Act "continues the policy of allowing cities to specify in cable franchises that channel capacity and other facilities be devoted to such use").

26 THE BUSKE GROUP, ANALYSIS OF RECENT PEG ACCESS CENTER CLOSURES, FUNDING CUTBACKS AND RELATED THREATS (2011) (prepared for the Alliance for Communications Democracy), *available at* theacd.org/uploaded_docs/2011_PEG_Access_study.pdf.

27 Alliance for Communications Democracy Comments in re *FOM PN*, "Media: Public, Educational, and Government (PEG) Access by Laura Linder, Ph.D. and Gary Kenton, M.A.", filed Apr. 23, 2010 (Linder Kenton Comments), at 12.

28 *See, e.g.*, Reed Johnson, *Cable Flips Channel on Public Access TV*, L.A. TIMES, Jan. 5, 2009, http://articles.latimes.com/2009/jan/05/entertainment/et-publicaccess5 (reporting the closing of 12 public access studios in Los Angeles as a bellwether of future PEG closings across the nation); Josh Goodman, *Unscripted Ending: The Picture Gets Blurry for Public Access Television*, GOVERNING.COM, Jan. 31, 2008, http://www.governing.com/topics/technology/Unscripted-Ending.html (stating that in the aftermath of statewide franchises PEG channels are losing funding, studio space, or being shut down altogether, and adding that the future of public access TV as "more uncertain…than at any time since its inception in the 1970s").

29 *See* Alliance for Community Media, *Assessing the Damage: Survey shows that state video franchise laws bring no rate relief while harming public benefits* (press release), 2008, *available at* www.cantv.org/keepusconnected/Harm-Survey-Report.pdf.

30 Alliance for Community Democracy, *"Analysis of Recent PEG Access Center Closures, Funding Cutbacks, and Related Threats,"* at 3 (Benton Foundation, April 8, 2011), http://benton.org/sites/benton.org/files/2011%20PEG%20Access%20study.pdf.

31 American Community Television, Inc. Comments in re *FOM PN*, filed May 7, 2010 (American Community TV Comments), at 15. In Ohio, this only applies to the community service fees that are over and above the franchise fee. *See* Linder Kenton Comments at 13.

32 American Community TV Comments at 15.

33 City of Pikeville, Kentucky, Comments in re *FOM PN*, filed Apr. 29, 2010, at 6, *citing* KY. REV. STAT. ANN. § 136.660 (2010).

34 Linder Kenton Comments at 13.

35 Reed Johnson, *Cable Flips Channel on Public Access TV*, L.A. TIMES, Jan. 5, 2009, http://articles.latimes.com/2009/jan/05/entertainment/et-publicaccess5; *see also* the Digital Infrastructure and Video Competition Act of 2006, CAL. PUB. UTIL. CODE § 5800 (2010).

36 Alliance for Community Democracy, *"Analysis of Recent PEG Access Center Closures, Funding Cutbacks, and Related Threats,"* Appendix 2 (Benton Foundation, April 8, 2011), http://benton.org/sites/benton.org/files/2011%20PEG%20Access%20study.pdf.

37 CHARLES P. GOLDFARB, CONGRESSIONAL RESEARCH SERVICE, PUBLIC, EDUCATIONAL, AND GOVERNMENTAL (PEG) ACCESS CABLE TELEVISION CHANNELS: ISSUES FOR CONGRESS 6 (2008).

38 Petition for Declaratory Ruling of the Alliance for Community Media et al., File No. CSR-8126, MB Docket No. 09-13 (filed Jan. 30, 2009), at 7–8.

39 Letter from James K. Smith, Assistant Vice President, Federal Regulatory, AT7T, to Marlene Dortch, FCC, June 11, 2009.

40 GA. CODE ANN., § 36-76-8(b)(5); TEX. UTIL. CODE § 66.009(d); MICH. COMP. L. ANN. § 484.3304(2).

41 Interview with Bunnie Riedel, Executive Director, American Community Television; John Rocco, Executive Director, TV Access21 (Charlotte, NC); Mauro DePasquale, Executive Director and Station Manager, WCCA-TV (Worcester, MA); Kathie Pohl, Director of Marketing and Community Relations Manager, Mentor Channel (Euclid, OH); Dennis Riggs, Director, HEC-TV (St. Louis, MI); Barry Verrill, Executive Director, KL-TV (Cowlitz County, WA); and Frank Bluestein, Executive Producer, GHS-TV (Germantown, TN), by Christopher Ali, FCC (May 21, 2010).

42 For instance, in 2006 Time Warner stopped airing San Antonio Public Access because the channel could no longer meet the 8-hour non-repeat daily programming requirement. UNIV. OF MINNESOTA, HUBERT H. HUMPHREY INSTITUTE OF PUBLIC AFFAIRS, CENTER FOR SCIENCE TECHNOLOGY & PUBLIC POLICY, STATEWIDE VIDEO FRANCHISING LEGISLATION: A COMPARATIVE STUDY OF OUTCOMES IN TEXAS, CALIFORNIA AND MICHIGAN 13, 21 (2009).

43 *See* C-Span, About C-Span, http://www.c-span.org/About/About-C-SPAN/ (last visited Feb. 3, 2011).

44 Email from Paul Giguere, President, Nat'l Ass'n of Public Affairs Networks (NAPAN), to Simon Banyai, FCC (Sept. 7, 2010) (Giguere Email 9/7/10).

45 Cable Television Consumer Protection and Competition Act of 1992, SENATE REP. NO. 102-92, at 52–53, (1991), *reprinted in* 1992 U.S.C.C.A.N. 1133, 1185-86.

46 Section 541 of the Act allows a franchise authority to "require adequate assurance that the cable operator will provide adequate [PEG]…financial support." 47 U.S.C. § 541(a)(4)(B).

28 Satellite Television and Radio

1 *See Comsat Study—Implementation of Section 505 of the International Maritime Satellite Telecommunications Act*, Final Report and Order, 77 FCC 2d 564, 583-584 (1980) ("NASA embarked on experimental programs to develop information useful to an active commercial communications satellite system with the objective of testing the feasibility of communications via satellite, and providing information on the reliability and longevity of critical components in space."); EDWARD A. COMOR, COMMUNICATION, COMMERCE AND POWER: THE POLITICAL ECONOMY OF AMERICA AND THE DIRECT BROADCAST SATELLITE, 1960-2000 (Palgrave Macmillan) (1998).

2 Section 628 of the Communications Act, codified at 47 U.S.C. § 548).

3 *Review of the Commission's Program Access Rules and Examination of Programming Tying Arrangements*, Report and Order, 22 FCC Rcd 17791 (2007).

4 1992 Cable Act (codified at 47 U.S.C. § 335).

5 47 U.S.C. § 335(b); 47 U.S.C. § 335(b)(4) (requiring that prices not exceed 50 percent of total direct costs of making such a channel available).

6 47 U.S.C. § 335(b)(5)(B).

7 *Implementation of Section 25 of the Cable Television Consumer Protection and Competition Act of 1992*, Report and Order, 13 FCC Rcd 23254, 23285 (1998) (*1998 Order*).

8 *1998 Order*, 13 FCC Rcd at 23290 ("We conclude that the term 'national educational programming supplier' in Section 335(b)(5)(B) includes only noncommercial entities with an educational mission…[W]e believe that the eligibility of a programming supplier under the statute should depend on its noncommercial character, not merely whether its programming contains commercials").

9 *1998 Order*, 13 FCC Rcd at 23256. Initially, in 1998, the Commission concluded that although it had the authority to impose other public interest programming requirements, it would refrain given the relatively new status of the DBS industry. *Id.* at 23279-80. In 2004, the Commission ordered DBS providers adhere to limits on the commercialization of children's programming. *See Implementation of Section 25 of the Cable Television Consumer Protection and Competition Act of 1992*, Second Order and Reconsideration of First Report and Order, 19 FCC Rcd 5647, 5666-68 (2004) (*2004 Second Order and Reconsideration*).

10 *See* DISH Network and DirecTV Filings for 2007, 2008 and 2009.

11 47 U.S.C. §335(b)(4). The *1998 Order* further delineates direct costs to be those that "are directly related to making the capacity available to noncommercial programmers," such as incremental compression equipment and backhaul costs to transmit the noncommercial educational or informational programming. *1998 Order*, 13 FCC Rcd at 23308.

12 *See, e.g.,* Denver Area Education Telecommunication Consortium, et al. Comments in re *DBS-Public Interest PN* (*Comments Sought in DBS Public Interest Rulemaking*, MM Docket 93-25, Public Notice (Jan. 31, 1997) (*DBS-Public Interest PN*)), at 13–14, filed Apr. 28, 1997; Comments of the Alliance for Community Media and the National Ass'n of Telecommunications Officers and Advisers in re *DBS-Public Interest PN*, filed Apr. 28, 1997, at 15.

13 *1998 Order*, 13 FCC Rcd at 23308.

14 *1998 Order*, 13 FCC Rcd at 23308–09.

15 47 C.F.R. § 25.701(f)(6).

16 *1998 Order*, 13 FCC Rcd at 23276.

17 *2004 Second Order and Reconsideration*, 19 FCC Rcd at 5663.

18 *See* 17 U.S.C. § 119 (codifying the 1999 Satellite Home Viewer Improvement Act, Pub. L. No. 106-113 (S. 1948), 113 Stat. 1501 (Nov. 29, 1999), which permits satellite carriers to offer subscribers local-into-local service in markets across the country).

19 *Implementation of the Satellite Home Viewer Improvement Act of 1999*, Report and Order, 16 FCC Rcd 1918, 1926 (2000).

20 *Annual Assessment of the Status of Competition in the Market for the Delivery of Video Programming*, Thirteenth Annual Report, 24 FCC Rcd 542, 585 (2009).

21 Still, the local tailoring is rough, which means that regional and national capacity is "wasted" on local content transmitted far beyond its area of interest. Most subscribers are able to access far fewer channels than the satellite beams to their area—typically only the in-market local channels and the national channel package to which they have subscribed.

22 2004 Second Order and Reconsideration, 19 FCC Rcd at 5664.

23 Email from Paul Giguere, President, National Association of Public Affairs Networks ("NAPAN")/President and CEO, The Connecticut Network, to Simon Banyai, FCC (Sept. 14, 2010).

24 The Satellite Television Extension and Localism Act of 2010 § 209, Pub. L. No. 111-175, 124 Stat. 1218 (2010).

25 See American Mobile Radio Corp. Application for Authority to Construct, Launch, and Operate Two Satellites in the Satellite Digital Audio Radio Service, Order and Authorization, 13 FCC Rcd 8829 (IB 1997).

26 Specifically, the Commission reaffirmed that:

"SDARS terrestrial repeaters are restricted to the simultaneous retransmission of the complete programming, and only that programming, transmitted by the SDARS licensee's satellite directly to the SDARS licensee's subscribers' receivers, and may not be used to distribute any information not also transmitted to all subscribers' receivers."

"Operators of SDARS terrestrial repeaters are prohibited from using those repeaters to retransmit different transmissions from a satellite to different regions within that satellite's coverage area."

47 C.F.R.§ 25.144(e)(4),(5). See Amendment of Part 27 of the Commission's Rules to Govern Operation of Wireless Communications Services in the 2.3 GHz Band, Report and Order, 25 FCC Rcd 11710, 11825-26 (2010).

29 The Internet and Mobile

1 The system connected the Pentagon to researchers at MIT, the University of California-Berkeley, a consulting firm called the System Development Corporation, and the Rand Corporation. *See* COMMITTEE ON INNOVATIONS IN COMPUTING AND COMMUNICATIONS: LESSONS FROM HISTORY & NAT'L RESEARCH COUNCIL, FUNDING A REVOLUTION: GOVERNMENT SUPPORT FOR COMPUTING RESEARCH 101, 172 (Nat'l Academies Press) (1999).

2 *See, e.g.,* CERN: European Organization for Nuclear Research, 1990: Tim Berners-Lee invents the Web, http://public.web.cern.ch/public/en/About/History90-en.html (last visited Jan. 18, 2011); LivingInternet.com, Tim Berners-Lee, Robert Cailliau, and the World Wide Web, http://www.livingInternet.com/w/wi_lee.htm (last visited Jan. 18, 2011).

3 *See* Communications Decency Act, Pub. L. No. 104-104, 110 Stat. 56 (1996).

4 *See* Internet Tax Freedom Act, Pub. L. No 105-277, 112 Stat. 2681-719 (1998).

5 *See* JONATHAN E. NUECHTERLEIN & PHILIP J. WEISER, DIGITAL CROSSROADS: AMERICAN TELECOMMUNICATIONS POLICY IN THE INTERNET AGE 58-59 (MIT Press) (2005). "The Part 68 rules supplanted AT&T's last-gasp efforts to discriminate against equipment manufacturing rivals by forcing them to purchase, from AT&T, various 'protective coupling devices.'"

6 Jason Oxman, FCC, *The FCC and the Unregulation of the Internet* (OPP Working Paper, July 1999) at 14, *available at* http://www.fcc.gov/osp/workingp.html.

7 JOHN B. HORRIGAN, PEW INTERNET & AMERICAN LIFE PROJ, HOME BROADBAND ADOPTION: ADOPTION STALLS FOR LOW-INCOME AMERICANS EVEN AS MANY BROADBAND USERS OPT FOR PREMIUM SERVICES THAT GIVE THEM MORE SPEED (2008) (HOME BROADBAND ADOPTION), *available at* http://www.pewinternet.org/~/media/Files/Reports/2008/PIP_Broadband_2008.pdf.

8 See TELEVISION BUREAU OF ADVERTISING, INC., TV BASICS: A REPORT ON THE GROWTH AND SCOPE OF TELEVISION 2 (2011), *available at* http://www.tvb.org/media/file/TV_Basics.pdf (Television penetration of U.S. households is up to 98.9 percent in 2011).

9 FCC, NATIONAL BROADBAND PLAN at XIV (2010) (NATIONAL BROADBAND PLAN).

10 NATIONAL BROADBAND PLAN at XIV.

11 *See* President Barack Obama, *State of the Union 2011: Winning the Future* (speech) (Jan. 25, 2011), *available at* http://www.whitehouse.gov/state-of-the-union-2011. The details of the "Wireless Innovation and Infrastructure Initiative" were laid out in the President's February 10, 2011 speech at Northern Michigan University, including freeing up spectrum through incentive auctions, spurring innovation, and creating a nationwide, interoperable wireless network for public safety. *See* Exec. Office of the President, *President Obama Details Plan to Win the Future through Expanded Wireless Access* (press release), Feb. 10, 2011, http://www.whitehouse.gov/the-press-office/2011/02/10/president-obama-details-plan-win-future-through-expanded-wireless-access. See also National Broadband Plan at XIV.

12 According to a Pew survey, 10 percent of Americans are dial-up users and 62 percent of them are not interested in giving up their current connection to switch over to broadband. HOME BROADBAND ADOPTION at 1.

13 *See, e.g.,* Colin Rhinesmith, *Community Media and Information Literacy in the Digital Age*, SUSTAINING DEMOCRACY IN A DIGITAL AGE (New America Foundation Media Policy Initiative), June 22, 2010, http://mediapolicy.newamerica.net/blogposts/2010/community_media_and_information_literacy_in_the_digital_age-33433.

14 Michael K. Powell, *"The Digital Broadband Migration: Toward a Regulatory Regime for the Internet Age,"* Remarks at the Silicon Flatirons Symposium, University of Colorado School of Law, Boulder, Colorado, February 8, 2004, http://hraunfoss.fcc.gov/edocs_public/attachmatch/DOC-243556A1.pdf.

15 FCC, *FCC Adopts Policy Statement: New Principles Preserve and Promote the Open and Interconnected Nature of Public Internet* (press release), Aug. 5, 2005, *available at* http://hraunfoss.fcc.gov/edocs_public/attachmatch/DOC-260435A1.pdf; *see also Appropriate Framework for Broadband Access to the Internet over Wireline Facilities*, Policy Statement, 20 FCC Rcd 14986 (2005).

16 FCC, *Commission Orders Comcast To End Discriminatory Network Management Practices: FCC Affirms Its Authority to Protect Vibrant and Open Internet* (news report), 2008 FCC LEXIS 5790, at *7–*8 (Aug. 1, 2008); *see also Formal Complaint of Free Press and Public Knowledge Against Comcast Corporation for Secretly Degrading Peer-to-Peer Ap-*

plications, Memorandum Opinion and Order, 23 FCC Rcd 13028, 13065 (2005) (Martin, Kevin J., Chairman, concurring).

17 FCC, *FCC Acts To Preserve Internet Freedom And Openness; Action Helps Ensure Robust Internet For Consumers, Innovation, Investment, Economic Prosperity* (press release), 2010 FCC LEXIS 7415 at *7–*8 (rel. Dec. 23, 2010) (*Open Internet Press Release*); *see also Preserving the Open Internet*, Report and Order, 25 FCC Rcd 17905 (2010) (*Open Internet Report & Order 2010*).

18 *Open Internet Press Release*, 2010 FCC LEXIS 7415 at *9–*11.

19 "TechNet Leadership Comments on FCC's Draft Open Internet Framework, December 1, 2010. TechNet is an association of technology companies and leaders focused on innovation.

20 *Open Internet Report & Order 2010*, 25 FCC Rcd at 17907.

21 Written Statement of Michele Combs, Vice President of Communications, Christian Coalition of America, Hearing on Net Neutrality and Free Speech on the Internet before the Committee on the Judiciary, Task Force on Competition Policy and Antitrust Laws, 110th Cong. (2008), *available at* http://www.openInternetcoalition.org/files/CCA_Testimony.pdf

22 comScore, *Score Releases November 2010 U.S. Search Engine Rankings* (press release), Dec. 15, 2010, http://www.comscore.com/Press_Events/Press_Releases/2010/12/comScore_Releases_November_2010_U.S._Search_Engine_Rankings.

23 *See* Consumer Watchdog's Inside Google, *Google using search engine to muscle into Internet businesses, study finds* (press release), June 2, 2010, http://insidegoogle.com/2010/06/google-using-search-engine-to-muscle-into-Internet-businesses-study-finds-2/.

24 *See, e.g.,* James Kanter, *European Antitrust Inquiry Into Google Is Broadened*, N.Y. TIMES, Dec. 15, 2010, http://www.nytimes.com/2010/12/18/technology/18google.html.

25 Stephen Nevas Comments in re *FOM PN*, filed Apr. 19, 2010 (Nevas Comments), at 4.

26 "Copyright owners who elect to participate would be required to periodically submit records of their digitized download records to the Copyright Office, records to be cleansed in advance of information that personally identifies those who use that content." To "prevent gaming the system," organizations such as Nielson would be commissioned to conduct "market-by-market sampling" to "cross-check [ ] download records." Nevas Comments at 5.

27 See Use of the Bands 825-845 MHz and 870-890 MHz for Cellular Communications Systems, Report and Order (Proceeding Terminated), 86 FCC 2d 469 (1981).

28 *See* Wireless Telecommunications Bureau, FCC, Auctions Summary, http://wireless.fcc.gov/auctions/summary.html (listing auction completion dates and amounts) (last updated Dec. 15, 2010) (last visited Jan. 19, 2011).

29 47 U.S.C. § 332(c)(1). "Commercial mobile service" is defined to mean "any mobile service…that is provided for profit and makes interconnected service available (A) to the public or (B) to such classes of eligible users as to be effectively available to a substantial portion of the public." 47 U.S.C. § 332(d)(1). CMRS providers are subject to certain common carrier obligations such as providing service upon reasonable request and ensuring that charges and practices are just, reasonable, and not unreasonably discriminatory, 47 U.S.C. §§ 201, 202, though the

Commission has forborne from applying certain elements of common carrier regulation to CMRS providers. *See Implementation of Sections 3(n) and 332 of the Communications Act, Regulatory Treatment of Mobile Services*, Second Report and Order, 9 FCC Rcd 1411 (1994). *See also* 47 U.S.C. § 332(c)(1).

30 *See, e.g.,* 47 U.S.C. §§ 301, 303, 307(a), 316.

31 *See, e.g.*, Revision of the Commission's Rules to Ensure Compatibility with Enhanced 911 Emergency Calling Systems, CC Docket No. 94-102, Report and Order and Further Notice of Proposed Rulemaking, 11 FCC Rcd 18676 (1996). *See also* 47 C.F.R. § 20.18.

32 See. e.g., Telephone Number Portability, CC Docket No. 95-116, First Report and Order and Further Notice of Proposed Rulemaking, 11 FCC Rcd 8352 (1996); Telephone Number Portability, CC Docket No. 95-116, First Memorandum Opinion and Order on Reconsideration, 12 FCC Rcd 7236 (1997). See also 47 C.F.R. § 52.31.

33 See, e.g., Section 68.4(a) of the Commission's Rules Governing Hearing Aid-Compatible Telephones, WT Docket No. 01-309, Report and Order, 18 FCC Rcd 16753, 16764-65 ¶ 26 (2003)); Erratum, 18 FCC Rcd 18047 (2003). See also 47 C.F.R. § 20.19.

34 See, e.g., Reexamination of Roaming Obligations of Commercial Mobile Radio Service Providers, WT Docket No. 05-265, Report and Order and Further Notice of Proposed Rulemaking, 22 FCC Rcd 15817 (2007); Order on Reconsideration and Second Further Notice of Proposed Rulemaking, 25 FCC Rcd 4181 (2010); Second Report and Order, FCC 11-52 (rel. Apr. 7, 2011) (Commercial Data Roaming Second Report and Order). See also 47 C.F.R. § 20.12.

35 See, e.g., Communications Assistance for Law Enforcement Act, CC Docket No. 97-213, Second Report and Order, 15 FCC Rcd 7105 (2000).

36 See, e.g., 47 C.F.R. §§ 24.203, 27.14.

37 Presentation of Christoper Guttman-McCabe, V.P. Regulatory Affairs, CTIA-The Wireless Association, FCC Workshop on the Future of Media and the Information Needs of Communities: Serving the Public Interest in the Digital Era (Mar. 4, 2010), at 4, available at http://reboot.fcc.gov/c/document_library/get_file?uuid=f20f4ad8-e082-443c-a4fe-6672df61b4e4&groupId=101236.

38 Id.

39 See Open Internet Report & Order 2010, 25 FCC Rcd at 17956-17962, 17992-17993 (2010) (requiring mobile broadband providers to disclose the network management practices, performance characteristics, and terms and conditions of their broadband services; prohibiting mobile broadband providers from blocking lawful websites or blocking applications that compete with their voice or video telephony services, subject to reasonable network management).

40 See Commercial Data Roaming Second Report and Order (requiring facilities-based providers of commercial mobile data services to offer data roaming arrangements to other such providers on commercially reasonable terms and conditions, subject to certain limitations).

41

42 See Connect America Fund, WC Docket No. 10-90, Notice of Proposed Rulemaking and Further Notice of Proposed Rulemaking, FCC 11-13 (rel. Feb. 9, 2011) (proposing to fundamentally modernize the Commission's Universal Service Fund and intercarrier compensation system by eliminating waste and inefficiency and reorienting these programs to meet the nation's broadband availability challenge); Universal Service Reform, Mobility Fund, Notice of Proposed Rulemaking, 25 FCC Rcd 14716 (2010) (seeking comment on using reserves accumulated in the Universal Service Fund to create a new Mobility Fund to significantly improve coverage of current-generation or better mobile voice and Internet service for consumers in areas where such coverage is currently missing).

43 See, e.g., Amendment of Part 27 of the Commission's Rules to Govern the Operation of Wireless Communications Services in the 2.3 GHz Band, Report and Order and Second Report and Order, 25 FCC Rcd 11710 (2010) (modifying technical rules to facilitate the provision of mobile broadband service in 25 megahertz of spectrum in the 2.3 GHz band); Unlicensed Operation in the TV Broadcast Bands, Second Memorandum Opinion and Order, 25 FCC Rcd 18661 (2010) (finalizing rules to make the unused spectrum in the TV bands available for unlicensed broadband wireless devices); Fixed and Mobile Services in the Mobile Satellite Service Bands at 1525-1559 MHz and 1626.5-1660.5 MHz, 1610-1626.5 MHz and 2483.5-2500 MHz, and 2000-2020 MHz and 2180-2200 MHz, ET Docket No. 10-142, Report and Order, FCC 11-57 (rel. Apr. 6, 2011) (taking steps to remove regulatory barriers to terrestrial use of 90 megahertz of spectrum allocated to the Mobile Satellite Service).

44 See FCC, FCC Chairman Genachowski Takes Steps to Increase Access to Broadband and Telecommunications Services for All Americans (news release), Mar. 3, 2011 (announcing that the FCC approved several items to strengthen and improve access to broadband and telecommunications services for persons with disabilities, Native Americans, low-income consumers and small businesses), available at http://www.fcc.gov/Daily_Releases/Daily_Business/2011/db0303/DOC-305005A1.doc.

45 See Lifeline and Link Up Reform and Modernization, WC Docket No. 11-42, Notice of Proposed Rulemaking, 26 FCC Rcd 2770 (2011) (systematically reexamining the Commission's Lifeline/Link Up, which historically has provided assistance to Americans to afford basic telephone service, in light of technological, market, and regulatory changes).

46 *See, e.g., Improving Communications Services for Native Nations*, CG Docket No. 11-41, Notice of Inquiry, 26 FCC Rcd 2672 (2011) (seeking government-to-government consultation and coordination with federally recognized Tribes and the input of inter-Tribal government associations, Native representative organizations, and the public on modifications to the Commission's rules and policies to provide greater economic, market entry, and adoption opportunities and incentives for Native Nations); *Improving Communications Services for Native Nations by Promoting Greater Utilization of Spectrum over Tribal Lands*, WT Docket No. 11-40, Notice of Proposed Rulemaking, 26 FCC Rcd 2623 (2011) (seeking comment on a range of specific proposals and issues with the objective of promoting greater use of spectrum over Tribal lands).

47 *See, e.g., Implementation of Sections 716 and 717 of the Communications Act of 1934, as Enacted by the Twenty-First Century Communications and Video Accessibility Act of 2010*, CG Docket No. 10-213, Notice of Proposed Rulemaking, 26 FCC Rcd 3133 (2011) (seeking comment on ways to help promote access by persons with disabilities to advanced communications services through manufacturing requirements, enhanced enforcement efforts, and expanded access to mobile broadband services); *Contributions to the Telecommunications Relay Services Fund*, CG Docket No. 11-47, Notice of Proposed Rulemaking, 26 FCC Rcd 3285 (2011) (seeking comment on whether participation and contribution to the Telecommunications Relay Service Fund should be extended to non-interconnected voice over Internet Protocol (VoIP) service providers).

48 NATIONAL BROADBAND PLAN at 81–82.

49 NATIONAL BROADBAND PLAN at 88. *See also Innovation in the Broadcast Television Bands: Allocations, Channel Sharing and Improvements to VHF*, Notice of Proposed Rulemaking, 25 FCC Rcd 16498 (2010) (initiating preliminary steps to enable the repurposing of a portion of the UHF and VHF frequency bands that are currently used by the broadcast television service, which in later actions the Commission expects to make available for flexible use by fixed and mobile wireless communications services, including mobile broadband).

50 *See, e.g.,* Nat'l Ass'n of Broadcasters, *Equipping Mobile Phones with Broadcast Radio Capability for Emergency Preparedness* (issue paper), *available at* http://www.nab.org/advocacy/issue.asp?id=2354&issueid=1082; Nat'l Ass'n of Broadcasters, *NAB Statement on CTIA's Anti-Radio Letter to Lawmakers* (press release), Aug. 23, 2010, *available at* http://www.nab.org/documents/newsroom/pressRelease.asp?id=2351; CNET News, *Broadcasters defend push for mandatory FM tuners*, Aug. 27, 2010, *available at* http://news.cnet.com/8301-13578_3-20014874-38.html.

51 INSIGHT RESEARCH CORP., STUDY OF FM RADIO-ENABLED HANDSETS IN THE U.S. 4 (2010), *available at* http://www.nabfastroad.org/.

52 *See,* Letter from Brian Josef, Assistant Vice President, CTIA, to Marlene Dortch, Secretary, FCC, GN Docket No. 10-25 (filed Mar. 31, 2011). *See, e.g.,* Letter from Steve Largent President and CEO CTIA-The Wireless Association, et al. to The Honorable Patrick Leahy, Chairman Senate Judiciary Committee, et al., dated Aug. 23, 2010, *available at* http://files.ctia.org/pdf/Leahy_Conyers_Letter.pdf; Consumer Electronics Assoc'n, *CEA Survey Shows Americans Oppose Mandatory Fm Tuners In Cell* Phones (press release), *available at* http://www.ce.org/Press/Current-News/press_release_detail.asp?id=11964.

53 Testimony of William H. Kling, Pres. and CEO, American Public Media Group, FCC Workshop on the Future of Media and the Information Needs of Communities: Public and Other Noncommercial Media in the Digital Era (Apr. 30, 2010), Tr. at 384:15–385:7, *available at* http://reboot.fcc.gov/futureofmedia/public-and-other-noncommercial-media-in-the-digital-era.

30 Ownership

1 *See* Telecom Act § 202(h), 110 Stat. 56, 111-12.

2 *Prometheus Radio Project v. FCC*, 373 F.3d 372, 383 (2004), *quoting FCC v. Nat'l Citizens Comm. for Broadcasting*, 436 U.S. 775, 780, (1978).

3 *Localism NOI*, 19 FCC Rcd at 12426. As the Commission explained in the *2002 Biennial Order*, in the Communications Act, Congress directed the Commission to distribute licenses, as follows:

"'among the several States and communities as to provide a fair, efficient, and equitable distribution of radio service to each of the same.' In the earliest government regulation of radio, the Commission embraced localism. In the Federal Radio Commission's 1927 Report to Congress, it wrote: 'The Commission found it possible to reassign the allocated stations to frequencies which would serve as many communities as possible to ensure those communities had at least one station that would serve as a basis for the development of good broadcasting to all sections of the country.... New York and Chicago stations were not allowed to dominate the situation.'

"When the Commission created the Table of Allotments in 1952 pursuant to the Communications Act, localism was the organizing principle of the plan. In announcing the allotments, the Commission explained that dispersed allotments 'protect[] the interests of the public residing in smaller cities and rural areas more adequately than any other system.' In the legislative history of the 1996 Act, Congress strongly reaffirmed the importance of localism: 'Localism is an expensive value. We believe it is a vitally important value, however [and] should be preserved and enhanced as we reform our laws for the next century.'

"The courts too have long viewed localism as an important public interest objective of broadcast regulation. In NBC v. United States, the Supreme Court wrote: 'Local program service is a vital part of community life. A station should be ready, able, and willing to serve the needs of the local community.'"

2002 Biennial Review Order, 18 FCC Rcd at 13643–44 (internal citations omitted).

4 *2002 Biennial Review Order*, 18 FCC Rcd at 13644.

5 *2002 Biennial Review Order*, 18 FCC Rcd at 13632.

6 *2002 Biennial Regulatory Review—Review of the Commission's Broadcast Ownership Rules and Other Rules Adopted Pursuant to Section 202 of the Telecommunications Act of 1996*, Report and Order and Notice of Proposed Rulemaking, 18 FCC Rcd 13620, 13631 (2003) (*2002 Biennial Review Order*), *aff'd in part and remanded in part*, *Prometheus Radio Project. v. FCC*, 373 F.3d 372 (2004).

7 *See, e.g.*, DAVID PRITCHARD, MEDIA OWNERSHIP WORKING GROUP ("MOWG") STUDY NO. 2: VIEWPOINT DIVERSITY IN CROSS-OWNED NEWSPAPERS AND TELEVISION STATIONS: A STUDY OF NEWS COVERAGE OF THE 2000 PRESIDENTIAL CAMPAIGN (FCC) (2002) (examining to what extent commonly owned newspapers and TV stations in a community speak with a single voice about important political matters), *available at* http://www.fcc.gov/ownership/materials/already-released/viewpoint090002.pdf; TASNEEM CHIPTY, MOWG STUDY NO. 5: STATION OWNERSHIP AND PROGRAMMING IN RADIO (FCC) (2007) (studying the effects of radio ownership structure on content diversity), http://www.fcc.gov/ownership/studies.html.

8 47 C.F.R. § 73.3555(b). Currently, the local television ownership rule employs analog broadcast contours to determine compliance with the rule. Now that the transition to digital television is complete, analog contours are no longer relevant.

9 47 C.F.R. § 73.3555(a).

10 It's deemed to overlap if (1) a television station's Grade A service contour completely encompassed the newspaper's city of publication, (2) the predicted or measured 2 mV/m contour of an AM station completely encompassed the newspaper's city of publication, or (3) the predicted 1 mV/m contour for an FM station completely encompassed the newspaper's city of publication. 47 C.F.R. § 73.3555(d)(1)(i)-(iii).

11 47 C.F.R. § 73.3555(d)(3).

12 *2006 Quadrennial Regulatory Review—Review of the Commission's Broadcast Ownership Rules and Other Rules Adopted Pursuant to Section 202 of the Telecommunications Act of 1996*, Report and Order and Order on Reconsideration, 23 FCC Rcd 2010, 2042-43 (2008) (*2006 Quadrennial Regulatory Review Order*).

13 47 C.F.R. § 73.3555(d)(6).

14 47 C.F.R. § 73.3555(d)(7).

15 *2006 Quadrennial Regulatory Review Order*, 23 FCC Rcd at 2042–43.

16 47 C.F.R. § 73.3555(c).

17 47 C.F.R. § 73.3555(c).

18 47 C.F.R. § 73.3555(c)(3).

19 The rule provides that "[a] television broadcast station may affiliate with a person or entity that maintains two or more networks of television broadcast stations *unless* such dual or multiple networks are composed of two or more persons or entities that, on February 8, 1996, were 'networks' as defined in [section] 73.3613(a)(1) of the Commission's regulations.... " 47 C.F.R. § 73.658(g) (emphasis in original).

20 Appropriations Act, 118 Stat. at 100, amending Section 202(h) of the Telecommunications Act of 1996.

21 *Regulations Governing Attribution of Broadcast and Cable/MDS Interests*, 14 FCC Rcd 12559, 12560 (1999) (*1999 Broadcast Attribution Order*), *recon. granted in part*, *Review of the Commission's Regulations Governing Attribution of Broadcast and Cable/MDS Interests*, 16 FCC Rcd 1097 (2001), *stayed*, 16 FCC Rcd 22310 (2001).

22 *See 1999 Broadcast Attribution Order*, 14 FCC Rcd at 12562–63. The broadcast attribution rules are detailed in Note 2 of Section 73.3555 of the Commission's rules. *See* 47 C.F.R. § 73.3555 Note 2. The broadcast attribution rule attributes corporate voting stock interests of five percent or more. *See Corporate Ownership Reporting and Disclosure by Broadcast Licensees, Amendment of Sections 73.35, 73.240 and 73.636 of the Commission's Rules Relating to Multiple Ownership of Standard, FM and Television Broadcast Stations*, Report and Order, 97 FCC 2d 997, 1005-06 (1984) (*1984 Broadcast Attribution Order*), *recon. in part*, 58 R.R.2d 604 (1985), *further recon. granted in part*, 1 FCC Rcd 802 (1986); *see also* 47 C.F.R. § 73.3555 Note 2(a). For specified "passive" institutional investors (as defined by 15 U.S.C. § 80a-3), voting stock interests of 20 percent or more are attributable. 47 C.F.R. § 73.3555 Note 2(b). Non-voting stock interests, options, warrants, and debt are not attributable, subject to the equity/debt plus (EDP) rule, discussed below. 47 C.F.R. § 73.3555 Notes 2(e) and (i).

The broadcast attribution rule includes a single majority shareholder exemption, which provides that a minority shareholder's corporate voting interests will not be attributed where a single corporate shareholder owns more than 50 percent of the outstanding voting stock. *See* former 47 C.F.R. § 73.3555 Note 2(b). The Commission justified the exemption, which it first adopted in 1984, on the grounds that without the agreement or assistance of any other shareholder, a minority shareholder cannot ordinarily direct the activities of a company when a single person or entity can outvote all other shareholders. *See 1984 Broadcast Attribution Order*, 97 FCC 2d at 1008–09 (1984).

In 1995, the Commission initiated a broad review of its broadcast attribution rules, culminating in the *1999 Broadcast Attribution Order*. *See* 14 FCC Rcd at 12561. In that *Order*, the Commission adopted the Equity/Debt Plus ("EDP") attribution rule. Under the EDP attribution rule, where an investor is either (1) a major program supplier (supplying over 15 percent of a broadcast station's total weekly broadcast programming hours); or (2) a same-market media entity subject to the broadcast multiple ownership rules, its interest in a licensee or other media entity will be attributed if that interest, aggregating both debt and equity holdings, exceeds 33 percent of the total assets (equity plus debt) of the licensee or media entity. 47 C.F.R. § 73.3555 Notes 2(a) & (i). In other words, attribution results where the financial interest exceeds 33

percent and there is a triggering relationship, i.e., either the investor is a major program supplier or a same-market media entity subject to the broadcast multiple ownership rules. The EDP rule was intended to operate "in addition to other attribution standards and would attempt to increase the precision of the attribution rules, address our concerns about multiple nonattributable relationships, and respond to concerns about whether the single majority shareholder and nonvoting stock attribution exemptions were too broad." *1999 Broadcast Attribution Order*, 14 FCC Rcd at 12573. The Commission targeted its remedy to address its concerns. *Id.* at 12580. The EDP attribution rule narrows the availability of the single majority shareholder exemption and the exemptions for nonvoting stock and debt. *See id.* at 12579.

In the 2008, the Commission modified the EDP rule to allow an interest holder to exceed the 33 percent threshold without triggering attribution if the investment would enable an "eligible entity" to acquire a broadcast station provided that "(1) the combined equity and debt of the interest holder in the eligible entity is less than 50 percent, or (2) the total debt of the interest holder in the eligible entity does not exceed 80 percent of the asset value of the station being acquired by the eligible entity and the interest holder does not hold any equity interest, option, or promise to acquire an equity interest in the eligible entity or any related entity." *Promoting Diversification of Ownership in the Broadcasting Services*, Report and Order and Third Further Notice of Proposed Rulemaking, 23 FCC Rcd 5922, 5936 (2008). An "eligible entity" is defined as any entity that would qualify as a small business consistent with Small Business Administration standards for its industry groupings on revenue. *Id.* at 5925–26.

23 See *2010 Quadrennial Regulatory Review—Review of the Commission's Broadcast Ownership Rules and Other Rules Adopted Pursuant to Section 202 of the Telecommunications Act of 1996*, Notice of Inquiry, 25 FCC Rcd 6086 (2010).

24 SNLKagan Database for a five year + period—2005 to 2009 and Q.1 2010, deals of $1 million+. Closed deals only for an average year during this period was $503 billion, or a little more than $1 billion per year.

25 *Commission Policy Regarding the Advancement of Minority Ownership in Broadcasting*, 92 FCC 2d 849 (1982). From 1978 to 1995, the government offered "a tax certificate" program to encourage minority ownership. It allowed broadcast and cable companies to defer capital gains on the sale of media and cable properties to minority-owned businesses. Under Section 1071 of the Internal Revenue Code, the Commission could permit sellers of broadcast or cable properties to defer capital gains taxation on a sale whenever it was deemed "necessary or appropriate to effectuate a change in a policy of, or the adoption of a new policy by, the Commission with respect to the ownership and control of radio broadcasting stations." Prospective buyers could also use the policy to attract equity investors.

26 *1978 Policy Statement* at 983. Previously, the Commission had limited distress sales to circumstances where the licensee is bankrupt or physically or mentally disabled.

27 *Adarand Constructors, Inc. v. Pena*, 515 U.S. 200, 229-230 (1995). Gender-based classifications need only satisfy intermediate scrutiny. *United States v. Virginia*, 518 U.S. 515, 531-33 (1996).

28 *See* Deduction for Health Insurance Costs of Self-Employed Individuals, Pub. L. No. 104-7, § 2, 109 Stat 93 (1995).

29 For example, the Commission created data entry fields for corporate structure information that previously had been filed in exhibits that were not machine-readable, added internal checks to minimize the entry of incorrect data, and adopted measures to improve data users' ability to aggregate and cross-reference multiple forms involving the same owners or stations. *See Promoting Diversification of Ownership in the Broadcasting Services*, Report and Order and Fourth Further Notice of Proposed Rulemaking, 24 FCC Rcd 5896 (2009), *order on reconsideration*, Memorandum Opinion & Order and Fifth Further Notice of Proposed Rulemaking, 24 FCC Rcd 13040 (2009).

30 The Commission's orders adopting these changes, cited above, explain these concerns in more detail. *See also* U.S. GOVERNMENT ACCOUNTABILITY OFFICE, MEDIA OWNERSHIP: ECONOMIC FACTORS INFLUENCE THE NUMBER OF MEDIA OUTLETS IN LOCAL MARKETS, WHILE OWNERSHIP BY MINORITIES AND WOMEN APPEARS LIMITED AND IS DIFFICULT TO ASSESS (2008) (GAO-08-383) (GAO, MEDIA OWNERSHIP), *available at* http://www.gao.gov/products/GAO-08-383.

31 For more information on these concerns, see the orders cited above. The Commission is also considering a proposal to collect minority and female ownership information from noncommercial broadcasters. *See Promoting Diversification of Ownership in the Broadcasting Services*, Report and Order and Fourth Further Notice of Proposed Rulemaking, 24 FCC Rcd 5896 (2009).

32 Although the Commission had previously required broadcasters to identify the race, ethnicity, and gender of officers, directors, and individuals holding an ownership interest, the new form also required these individuals to obtain a unique FCC identification number, or FRN, to enable users to better aggregate forms involving the same owners and to more reliably determine whether multiple forms listing someone with the same name in fact referred to the same person. To obtain an FRN, individuals must submit their Social Security number to the Commission (the Commission does not make these Social Security numbers available to the public). The Commission already required companies who own broadcast stations to obtain an FRN and to submit their taxpayer identification number in order to get an FRN. In response to broadcasters' concerns, the Commission adopted a temporary means of allowing individuals to obtain an FRN without submitting their Social Security number.

33 *See* Public Notice, *Media Bureau Announces Availability of 2009 Biennial Ownership Data Set for Commercial Broadcast Licensees*, DA 11-334, 26 FCC Rcd 2024 (MB 2011), *available at* http://www.fcc.gov/document/media-bureau-announces-availability-2009-biennial-ownership-data-set-commercial-broadcast-l.

34 Pub. L. No. 105-33, 111 Stat 251 (1997).

35 As part of the Telecommunications Act of 1996, Congress directed the FCC to identify and eliminate market entry barriers for entrepreneurs and other small businesses in the provision and ownership of telecommunications services and information services. *See* Telecom Act; *see also* 47 U.S.C. § 257 (a-b).

36 47 C.F.R. §73.5007(a); *see also* 47 C.F.R. § 73.5008. Generally, media interests will be attributable for purposes of the new entrant bidding credit to the same extent that such other media interests are considered attributable for purposes of the broadcast multiple ownership rules. Further, any bidder asserting new entrant status must have de facto as well as de jure control of the entity claiming the bidding credit. *See* 47 C.F.R. § 73.5007. Typically, de jure control is evidenced by ownership of at least 50.1 percent of an entity's voting stock or equivalent level of interest

in cases where the bidder is not a corporate parent. De facto control is determined on a case-by-case basis. *See, e.g., Auction of FM Broadcast Construction Permits Rescheduled for April 27, 2011, Notice and Filing Requirements, Minimum Opening Bids, Upfront Payments, and Other Procedures for Auction 91*, Public Notice, DA 10-2253, 25 FCC Rcd 16787, 16805 n.90 (MB rel. Dec. 3, 2010).

37 Former FCC Chairman Michael Powell worked closely with the Diversity Advisory Committee, which he established, on tax deferral proposals. *See, e.g.,* Fifth Meeting of the Federal Advisory Committee on Diversity for Communications in the Digital Age (Dec. 10, 2004), Tr. at 10–11, *available at* http://www.fcc.gov/DiversityFAC/041210/transcript121004.doc.

38 To qualify as a minority-owned business, over 50 percent of the voting shares or over 20 percent of the total equity in a limited partnership must be owned by African-Americans, Hispanic Americans, Asian Americans or Native Americans.

39 The tax certificate program for the purchase of cable systems to minorities was available in those instances where a minority general partner holds more than 20 percent interest in the broadcast or cable facility, and where shareholders in a minority-controlled media entity seek to sell their shares. *Commission Policy Regarding the Advancement of Minority Ownership in Broadcasting*, Policy Statement and Notice of Proposed Rulemaking, 92 FCC 2d 849 (1982).

40 *See, e.g., Implementation of Section 309(j) of the Communications Act—Competitive Bidding*, Fifth Report and Order, 9 FCC Rcd 5532 (1994).

41 GAO, MEDIA OWNERSHIP at 25–26.

42 Erwin Krasnow and Lisa M. Fowlkes, *The FCC's Minority Tax Certificate Program: A Proposal for Life After Death*, 51 FED. COMM. L.J. 665, 670 (1999), *available at* http://www.law.indiana.edu/fclj/pubs/v51/no3/kramac9.PDF.

43 Remarks of FCC Commissioner Robert M. McDowell, FCC Media Bureau Workshop on Media Ownership and Diversity (Jan. 27, 2009), *available at* http://hraunfoss.fcc.gov/edocs_public/attachmatch/DOC-295992A1.pdf.

31 Nonprofit Media

1 *Reexamination of the Comparative Standards for Noncommercial Educational Applicants*, Second Further Notice of Proposed Rulemaking, 17 FCC Rcd 3833, 3834 n.3 (2002) (*NCE SFNPRM 2002*), *citing* 3 Fed. Reg. 364 (Feb. 9, 1938).

2 *See Allocation of Frequencies to the Various Classes of Non-Governmental Services in the Radio Spectrum from 10 Kilocycles to 30,000,000 Kilocycles*, Opinion, 39 FCC 165, 222, 226 (1945).

3 *NCE SFNPRM 2002*, 17 FCC Rcd at 3833–34.

4 Sterling and Kittross, STAY TUNED, 328; Sixth R&O at ¶ 38, in Pike and Fisher, Radio Regulation, Vol. 1, Part 3, at 91:612–91:613 (1952).

5 This valuation assumes that (1) the value of over-the-air (OTA) broadcast television spectrum is approximately $8.9 to $12.2 billion; (2) the value of broadcast television spectrum without broadcast restrictions (akin to spectrum currently used for mobile broadband) is approximately ten times that amount ($89 to 122 billion); and (3) NCE TV licenses constitute 22 percent of total TV allocated licenses. *See* OMNIBUS BROADBAND INITIATIVE, SPECTRUM ANALYSIS: OPTIONS FOR BROADCAST SPECTRUM 7

(2010) (calculating the $8.9-$12.2 valuation of OTA broadcast television spectrum and explaining a ten-fold gap in market value between mobile broadband and the more regulated OTA air television broadcasting); Broadcast Station Totals as of December 31, 2009, *available at* FCC, Broadcast Station Totals (Index)1990 to Present, http://www.fcc.gov/mb/audio/BroadcastStationTotals.html. The valuation range was calculated by taking 22 percent of the lowest ($8.9 billion) and highest ($122 billion) range valuation of OTA spectrum with and without broadcast restrictions, respectively.

6 FCC, Broadcast Station Totals as of December 31, 2010, Feb. 11, 2011 (Broadcast Station Totals), *available at* http://www.fcc.gov/mb/audio/BroadcastStationTotals.html.

7 Broadcast Station Totals.

8 While required to air children's programming, they do not have to submit children's television reports. Compare 47 C.F.R. § 73.671 (children's programming rules) with 47 C.F.R. § 3526(e)(11)(iii) (reports to be filed by commercial stations). Multiple ownership rules, which govern the ownership of more than one AM, FM, or television station by a single entity or company, are not applicable to noncommercial educational FM and TV stations. See 47 C.F.R. § 73.3555. In addition, NCE licensees have limited obligations in the area of political broadcasting. NCE FM radio licensees have some specific operating requirements. They must operate at least 36 hours per week, with at least 5 operating hours per day on at least 6 days of the week. Stations licensed to educational institutions are exempt from this schedule and are not required to operate during weekends or official school vacation or recess periods. Stations that operate less than 12 hours per day may be required to share their frequencies (an extremely rare occurrence). 47 C.F.R. § 73.561. In contrast, noncommercial educational AM and TV stations are not required to operate on a regular schedule and have no minimum hours of operation. However, the number of actual operating hours during a license period is a factor in determining the renewal of noncommercial educational AM and TV broadcast licenses. 47 C.F.R. § 73.621 (non-commercial TV).

9 *Applications of WQED PITTSBURGH (Assignor) and CORNERSTONE TELEVISION, INC. (Assignee); For Consent to the Assignment of License of Noncommercial Educational Station WQEX(TV), Channel *16, Pittsburgh, Pennsylvania*, Memorandum Opinion and Order, 15 FCC Rcd 202, 228 (1999) (*WQED*), *quoting* FCC, Form 340, Section II, Para. 11(a).

10 *See. e.g., Reexamination of the Comparative Standards for Noncommercial Educational Applicants,* Report and Order, 15 FCC Rcd 7386, 7409 n.38 (2000). The traditional list of ascertainment categories or elements is contained in the Community Leader Checklist that was adopted by the Commission in 1976 in connection with developing ascertainment standards. *See Ascertainment of Community Problems by Broadcast Applicants*, Primer, 41 Fed. Reg. 1372, 1384 (Jan. 7, 1976).

11 In 1975, the Commission denied applications for renewal or licensing of nine Alabama stations operated by the Alabama Educational Television Commission ("AETC"), based on its finding that racially discriminatory policies permeated AETC's programming practices. *See Applications of Alabama Educational Television Commission for Renewal of Licenses for: Station WAIQ (ED-TV), Montgomery, Ala., et al.*, 50 FCC 2d 461 (1975). In 1991, the Commission affirmed a Review Board decision denying the renewal application for KQEC(TV), San Francisco, based upon a finding that the licensee of the station committed serious misconduct by lacking candor and misrepresenting the reasons why it had deactivated the station. *See Application of KQED, INC. San Francisco, California for renewal of licenses of noncommercial stations KQED–FM KQED–TV, and KQEC(TV)*, 6 FCC RCd 625 (1991).

12 47 C.F.R. § 73.621(a).

13 47 C.F.R. § 73.621(c).

14 47 C.F.R. § 73.503(a).

15 *Revision of Programming Policies and Reporting Requirements Related to Public Broadcasting Licensees*, Notice of Proposed Rulemaking, 87 FCC 2d 716, 732 (1981).

16 47 C.F.R. § 73.621 (requiring nonprofit educational organizations to use their NCE broadcast stations "primarily to serve the educational needs of the community"). The Commission has clarified "primarily" to mean "substantial majority" of a station's entire digital capacity, as measured on a weekly basis. *See Ancillary or Supplementary Use of Digital Television Capacity by Noncommercial Licensees*, Report and Order, 16 FCC Rcd 19042, 19048 (2001).

17 *WQED*, 15 FCC Rcd at 214.

18 47 U.S.C. § 399(b)(2) ("No public broadcast station may make its facilities available to any person for the broadcasting of any advertisement").

19 See *Commission Policy Concerning the Noncommercial Nature of Educational Broadcasting Stations,* Memorandum Opinion and Order, 97 FCC 2d 255, 265-66 (1984); *Commission Policy Concerning the Noncommercial Nature of Educational Broadcasting Stations*, Public Notice (1986), *republished*, 7 FCC Rcd 827 (1992) (*citing* examples of the more liberal or "enhanced" underwriting policy) (*Commission Policy Concerning the Noncommercial Nature of EBS PN*).

20 *Commission Policy Concerning the Noncommercial Nature of EBS PN.*

21 *Commission Policy Concerning the Noncommercial Nature of EBS PN.*

22 *Minority Television Project, Inc.*, Notice of Apparent Liability for Forfeiture, 17 FCC Rcd 15646, 15649-52 (2002).

23 Letter from the Chief, Mass Media Bureau to WNYE-TV, 7 FCC Rcd 6864 (rel. Oct. 16, 1992) (WNYE-TV Letter).

24 *Commission Policy Concerning the Noncommercial Nature of EBS PN* ("It continues to be our view that the public broadcaster's good faith judgment must be the key element in meeting Congress' determination that the service should remain free of commercial and commercial-like matter."); *Petition of Xavier University, Licensee of Noncommercial Radio Station WVXU(FM), Cincinnati, OH for Reconsideration of Letter of Admonition*, 5 FCC Rcd 4920, 4921 (1990), *quoting Commission Policy Concerning the Noncommercial Nature of Educational Broadcast Stations*, Memorandum Opinion and Order, 90 FCC 2d 895, 911 (1982), *recon. granted*, 97 FCC 2d 255, 264-65 (1984) (*Commission Policy Concerning the Noncommercial Nature of EBS 1982*) ("We recognize that it may be difficult to distinguish at times between announcements that promote and those that identify. We only expect our public broadcast licensees to exercise their reasonable, good faith judgments in this regard.").

25 *Commission Policy Concerning the Noncommercial Nature of Educational Broadcasting Stations,* Memorandum Opinion and Order, 97 FCC 2d 255, 263 (1984) (*Commission Policy Concerning the Noncommercial Nature of EBS 1984*).

26 *Commission Policy Concerning the Noncommercial Nature of EBS 1984*, 97 FCC 2d at 263.

27 WNYE-TV Letter, 7 FCC Rcd 6864, 6865 (Oct. 16, 1992) ("[W]hile the Commission has not adopted any quantitative guidelines on underwriting announcements, the longer an announcement takes to identify the underwriter, the more likely it is to be promotional.").

28 Prepared Testimony of Craig Parshall Senior Vice-President and General Counsel National Religious Broadcasters, FCC Workshop on Future of the Media: Public and Other Noncommercial Media in the Digital Era (Apr. 30, 2010) (Parshall Prepared Testimony 4/30/10), at 8, *available at* http://reboot.fcc.gov/futureofmedia/public-and-other-noncommercial-media-in-the-digital-era.

29 National Religious Broadcasters Comments in re *FOM PN*, filed Feb. 18, 2010 (NRB Comments), at 13–15.

30 *See, e.g.,* Public Radio Capital Comments in re *FOM PN*, filed May 7, 2010, at 4 (recommending that "the Commission not regard announcements concerning fundraising events that a station conducts with other entities to be an 'interruption' of its regular programming"); Public Broadcasting System Comments in re *FOM PN*, filed May 7, 2010, at 24 (seeking, *inter alia*, a clarification that underwriting rule proscribing sponsorship messages that include a "call to action" in terms of selling a product do not prohibit public broadcasters from airing sponsorship messages that "using the common verbiage 'visit www.[site].com'"); NRB Comments at 14–15 (requesting that the Commission reject the distinction it has previously drawn between permissible promotional language constituting part of a pre-existing corporate *slogan*, and non-slogan-based promotional language by corporate sponsors that failed to have developed such slogans, on the grounds of 'manifest unfairness').

31 Memo from Vivian Schiller, President and C.E.O., National Public Radio, sent by email to Steven Waldman, FCC (Dec. 22, 2010) (Schiller Memo 12/22/10).

32 Schiller Memo 12/22/10.

33 The relevant Commission rules, Section 73.503(d) and 73.621(e), apply to noncommercial broadcast service.

34 The Community Service Grant ("CSG") Review Panel has recommended, for example, that while online advertising revenues cannot be counted toward the minimum non-Federal financial support ("NFFS") stations need to be eligible for Community Service Grants, online messages that are underwriting credits can. CORPORATION FOR PUBLIC BROADCASTING (CPB), SUMMARY OF TELEVISION CSG REVIEW PANEL MEETING #7 12-13 (2010); *see also* Memorandum from Public Television CSG Review Panel to Pat Harrison, President & CEO, CPB, Final Report and Recommendations (Aug. 25, 2010), at 15 (affirming that any underwriting revenue included in NFFS generated by websites must meet the current underwriting requirements stated in CPB's financial reporting guidelines).

35 *See* Ellen Edwards, *PBS Missing Out on 'Barney' Bucks; Tie-Ins Reap Millions for Creators*, WASH. POST, Sept. 13, 1993, at A1; Steve Behrens, *What Did Barney Earn, and Why Didn't PBS Get More?*, CURRENT, Mar. 6, 1995, http://www.current.org/funding/funding504barney.shtml.

36 47 U.S.C. § 325(b)(2)(A).

37 *See, e.g., Daystar Public Radio, Inc.*, Memorandum Opinion and Order, 17 FCC Rcd 13297, 13297-98 (2002) (*citing Commission Policy Concerning the Noncommercial Nature of EBS 1982*, 90 FCC 2d at 907; *Ohio State University*, Opinion, 62 FCC 2d 449 (1976)).

38 *See, e.g.,* FCC, *Media Bureau Announces Procedures for Obtaining Commission Approval for NCE Station Fundraising to Aid Haiti Relief Efforts* (press release), Jan. 13, 2010, *available at* http://www.fcc.gov/mb/haiti_relief_efforts.pdf; *Commission Policy Concerning the Noncommercial Nature of EBS 1982*, 90 FCC 2d at 907 n.29 (*citing* FCC 82-198 (Apr. 22, 1982), in which the

Commission granted a waiver of 47 C.F.R. § 73.621 to Greater Washington Educational Telecommunications Ass'n, Inc. (licensee of noncommercial educational television Station WETA-TV, Washington, D.C.), allowing it to conduct a three-hour fundraiser for the Wolf Trap Foundation after determining that unique circumstances warranted the waiver.

39 NRB Comments at 13.

40 Parshall Prepared Testimony 4/30/10 at 8. Asked what types of non-profits might benefit from such a rule change, Craig Parshall, executive director of NRB suggests, (1) Local rescue missions in their listening areas, most of which would provide food, shelter and sometimes clothing and employment assistance. (2) Seasonal charities, like Operation Christmas Child, which provide toys and necessities to needy children and their families. (3) International relief organizations (e.g. Compassion International, World Vision) that provide on-going world relief to needy nations and communities, not just the massive Haiti/ Katrina type situation. (4) Wycliffe Bible Translators, [for] their work in translating the Bible into indigenous languages, and international Christian radio broadcasters like HCJB Global and Trans World Radio, which have equipment needs in order to get radio transmissions to places like West Africa, and international cooperative efforts between American Christian broadcasters and fledgling Christian broadcasting stations in places like republics in the former Soviet Union. Email from Craig Parshall, Exec. Dir., NRB, to Steven Waldman, FCC (Nov. 4, 2010).

41 Interview with Joseph Bruns and Sharon Percy Rockefeller, President and C.E.O., WETA by Steven Waldman, FCC, (Aug. 4, 2010).

42 Email from Joseph Bruns, WETA, to Steven Waldman, FCC (Aug. 6, 2010). (Bruns noted that he was making his suggestion in his personal capacity and not as a representative of WETA).

43 *See, e.g.,* Bill McConnell, *Noncoms to Get Multicasting DTV Carriage*, BROADCASTING & CABLE, Jan. 31, 2005, http://www.broadcastingcable.com/article/156009-Noncoms_to_Get_Multicasting_DTV_Carriage.php.

44 47 C.F.R. § 73.621 (requiring nonprofit educational organizations to use their NCE broadcast stations "primarily to serve the educational needs of the community"). The Commission has clarified "primarily" to mean "substantial majority" of a station's entire digital capacity, as measured on a weekly basis.

45 *Ancillary or Supplementary Use of Digital Television Capacity by Noncommercial Licensees*, Report and Order, 16 FCC Rcd 19042, 19051-52 (2001) (*Digital Television Capacity R&O 2001*).

46 *Digital Television Capacity R&O 2001*, 16 FCC Rcd at 19059 (amending 47 C.F.R. § 73.624(g) to require NCE licensees to "remit fees of five percent of their gross revenues received for feeable ancillary or supplementary services provided on their digital bitstreams").

47 Email from Hossein Hashemzadeh, FCC, to Sherille Ismail, FCC (Mar. 8, 2011).

48 CORPORATION FOR PUBLIC BROADCASTING, APPROPRIATION REQUEST AND JUSTIFICATION FY 2011 AND FY 2013 13 (2010) (CPB FY2011 AND 2013 REQUEST), *available at* http://www.cpb.org/aboutcpb/financials/appropriation/justification_11-13.pdf.

49 CPB, Federal Appropriation History (CPB, Federal Appropriation History), http://www.cpb.org/aboutcpb/financials/appropriation/history.html (last visited Jan. 20, 2011).

50 *See* FREE PRESS, CHANGING MEDIA: PUBLIC INTEREST POLICIES FOR THE DIGITAL AGE 266-67 (2010) (CHANGING MEDIA), *available at* http://www.freepress.net/files/changing_media.pdf.

51 47 U.S.C. § 396(l). The remaining 11 percent goes towards system support and CPB operations. *Id.*; *see also* CPB FY2011 AND 2013 REQUEST at 17 (illustrating the breakdown of CPB federal appropriations for 2010).

52 47 U.S.C. § § 396(k)(3)(A)(i)(III), (k)(3)(A)(ii)(I).

53 47 U.S.C. § § 396(k)(3)(A)(i)(IV), (k)(3)(A)(ii)(II).

54 47 U.S.C. § 396(k)(3)(A)(ii)(II).

55 CPB, Proposed FY 2009 Operating Budget for the CPB and Cover Memo dated Sept. 23, 2008, at 4 (first page of FY 2009 Operating Budget), *available at* http://www.cpb.org/aboutcpb/leadership/board/resolutions/080923_fy09OperatingBudget.pdf. They are disbursed to public television programs such as the National Program Service (assembled by PBS), the Independent Television Service ("ITVS"), the Minority Consortia, a discretionary General Program Fund, and voluntary grants to PBS. CPB FY2011 AND 2013 REQUEST at 5–6. With PBS, CPB also jointly manages the Program Challenge Fund, which supports high-visibility, high-impact limited series and feature-length documentaries. CPB, Program Challenge Fund, http://www.cpb.org/grants/07challengefund/ (last visited Jan. 28, 2011).

56 *See, e.g.,* APT Action Inc., *Funding Brief: CPB Digital*, http://www.apts.org/legislative/policy-issues/cpb-digital (last visited Jan. 21, 2011) ("Congress, recognizing that the federally mandated transition to digital broadcast would place a hardship on public television's limited resources, has provided public television stations with more than $300 million in CPB digital funds since 2001.").

57 *See, e.g.,* CPB, *CPB Welcomes Additional Nine Radio Stations to the Community Service Grant Program* (press release), Aug. 23, 2007, http://www.cpb.org/pressroom/release.php?prn=614.

58 Email (and attachments thereto) from Eben Peck, Corporate and Public Affairs, CPB to Anne Chen, FCC (Aug. 20, 2010).

59 CPB, FY2010 RADIO COMMUNITY SERVICE GRANT GENERAL PROVISIONS & ELIGIBILITY CRITERIA 7 (2010) (CPB FY2010 RADIO CSG), *available at* http://www.cpb.org/stations/grants/radio/2010/ ; CPB, FY2010 TELEVISION COMMUNITY SERVICE GRANT GENERAL PROVISIONS & ELIGIBILITY CRITERIA 5 (2010) (CPB FY2010 TV CSG), *available at* http://www.cpb.org/stations/grants/tv/2010/.

60 CPB FY2010 RADIO CSG at 7; CPB FY2010 TV CSG at 6.

61 CPB FY2011 and 2013 Request at 13, 14.

62 CPB also imposes additional operating, use, and reporting requirements on CSG recipients. For example, FM stations must have an operating power of 100 watts or greater, and AM stations must broadcast at 250 watts or greater. CPB FY2010 RADIO CSG at 7. CSG radio stations must also operate at least 18 consecutive hours per day, 7 days per week, 52 weeks per year; have professionally equipped on-air and production facilities; be capable of simultaneous local production and origination; and offer sufficient office space for station operators. CPB FY2010 RADIO CSG at 7. Both radio and television stations must meet minimum staffing requirements. CPB FY2010 RADIO CSG at 7-8; CPB FY2010 TV CSG at 6. Stations eligible are also required to show significant and measurable listening relative to coverage area, and must have non-federal financial support. CPB FY2010 RADIO CSG at 8; CPB FY2010 TV CSG at 6. In general, these requirements are designed to ensure that stations provide a robust signal to their communities, have a significant amount of non-federal funding, and achieve a certain amount of scale.

63 *See* CPB, CORPORATION FOR PUBLIC BROADCASTING FY2011 RADIO COMMUNITY SERVICE GRANT GENERAL PROVISIONS & ELIGIBILITY CRITERIA,

available at http://www.cpb.org/stations/grants/radio/generalprovisions/cpb_11RadioCSG_GeneralProvisions.pdf (last visited Feb. 11, 2011); CPB, CORPORATION FOR PUBLIC BROADCASTING FY2010 TELEVISION COMMUNITY SERVICE GRANT GENERAL PROVISIONS AND ELIGIBILITY CRITERIA, *available at* http://www.cpb.org/stations/grants/tv/2010/cpb_10TV_CSG_GeneralProvisions.pdf (last visited Feb. 11, 2011).

64 Memorandum from Public Television CSG Review Panel to Pat Harrison, President & CEO, CPB, Final Report and Recommendations (Aug. 25, 2010) at 8–9, 12.

65 American Public Media Comments in re *FOM PN*, filed May 7, 2010 (American Public Media Comments), at 6–9.

66 JOSH SILVER ET AL., NEW PUBLIC MEDIA: A PLAN FOR ACTION 33-34 (Free Press) (2010) (NEW PUBLIC MEDIA), *available at* http://www.freepress.net/files/New_Public_Media.doc.pdf.

67 Email correspondence between Sue Schardt, Exec. Dir., Ass'n of Independents in Radio, Inc. and Ellen P. Goodman, FCC (Jan. 26, 2011); Association of Independents in Radio, Inc. Comments in re *FOM PN*, filed May 7, 2010 (AIR Comments), at 6.

68 Email from Terry Clifford, Station Resource Group, to Ellen P. Goodman, FCC (Mar. 16, 2011).

69 Its mandate is broad, and includes the ability to "contract with or make grants to public telecommunications entities, national, regional, and other systems of public telecommunications entities, and independent producers and production entities, for the production or acquisition of public telecommunications services to be made available for use by public telecommunications entities…" 47 U.S.C. §396(g)(2)(B).

70 Public Telecommunications Act of 1988, Pub. L. No. 100-626, 102 Stat. 3207, 3210-11 (1988) (codified at 47 U.S.C. § 396(k)(3)(B)(iii)) (requiring a portion of television programming grants to be set aside for an "independent production service" to "expand the diversity and innovativeness of programming available to public broadcasting").

71 Email correspondence between Sue Schardt, Exec. Dir., Ass'n of Independents in Radio, Inc. and Ellen P. Goodman, FCC (Jan. 26, 2011); AIR Comments at 6.

72 *See* 47 U.S.C. § 396. According to the Public Broadcasting Act, CPB is required to cover at least a portion of satellite interconnection costs. 47 U.S.C. § 396(k)(10) (2000) (establishing a Satellite Interconnection Fund for the maintenance, "replacement, refurbishment, or upgrading of [public radio and television's] national satellite interconnection systems"). Congress has funded public television satellite interconnection systems in the past, sponsoring the second interconnection system in 1989-91 for $150 million and a total of $418.3 million on interconnection capital since 1991. *See* Dan Odenwald, *Satellite Bill Coming Due as DTV Request Languishes*, CURRENT, June 24, 2002, http://www.current.org/tech/tech0211sat.html (second interconnection system in 1989-91); CPB, Federal Appropriation History (interconnection capital since 1991); Email (and attachements thereto) from Edward Coltman, Sr. Dir. Communications, CPB, to Anne Chen, FCC (Oct. 8, 2009). The Satellite Program Distribution Fund, which existed in the early to mid-1980s, also funded start-up projects to fill the then-largely unused capacity of satellite channels that interconnected public radio stations. AIR Comments at 7-8.

73 Karen Everhart, *Radio Nets and PBS Propose 'Public Media Platform' Based on API*, CURRENT, Mar. 1, 2010, *available at* http://www.current.org/web/web1004platform.shtml.

74 American Public Media Comments at 3–4.

75 *See, e.g.,* Bay Area Video Coalition, What if there was a high-speed fiber optic network that served the public interest?, http://www.bavc.org/index.php?Itemid=718&id=551&option=com_content&task=view (last visited Feb. 4, 2011).

76 NATIONAL BROADBAND PLAN at 10, 153, 239.

77 U.S. Nat'l Telecommunications and Information Administration (U.S. Dep't of Commerce), Technology Opportunities Program, Grants, http://www.ntia.doc.gov/top/grants/grants.htm (last visited June 29, 2010).

78 *See, e.g.,* Public Radio Exchange, *PRX receives major NTIA grant*, Oct. 13, 2003, http://www.prx.org/.

79 *See* Clea Simon, *Cambridge nonprofit wins MacArthur award*, BOSTON GLOBE, Apr. 11, 2008, *available at* Public Radio Exchange, Boston Globe on PRX, http://blog.prx.org/2008/04/boston-globe-on-prx-2; JOSH SILVER, PUBLIC MEDIA'S MOMENT 15 (Free Press) (2009).

80 *See, e.g., New, improved Public Radio Player now live in iTunes*, Public Radio Exchange Blog, Mar. 2, 2010, http://blog.prx.org/2010/03/new-improved-public-radio-player-now-live-in-itunes/.

81 *See, e.g.,* John D. and Catherine T. MacArthur Foundation & Humanities, Arts, Science, and Technology Advanced Collaboratory, Reimagining Learning (Digital Media and Learning Competition), http://dmlcompetition.net/reimagining_learning.php (last visited Feb. 11, 2011).

82 *See* Stephanie From, *Donations Ban on iPhone Apps Irritates Nonprofits*, N.Y. TIMES, Dec. 8, 2010, http://www.nytimes.com/2010/12/09/technology/09charity.html. Jake Shapiro, *Apple's No-Donation Policy for Apps is a Cop-Out*, ARS TECHNICA, June 4, 2010, http://arstechnica.com/apple/news/2010/06/nonprofit-developer-apples-no-donation-policy-is-a-cop-out.ars.

83 Based on research by Ben Jacobson, FCC, Summer 2010, using FCC Broadcast Station Totals, which are *available at* http://www.fcc.gov/mb/audio/BroadcastStationTotals.html.

84 Based on research by Ben Jacobson, FCC (Summer 2010).

85 *See, e.g.,* STATION RESOURCES GROUP (SRG), STATION RESOURCES GROUP REPORT ON GOVERNANCE (2002), http://www.srg.org/governance/report1.html (identifying the characteristics of good governance for NCE licensees). *See also* Email from Steven Bass, President, Oregon Public Broadcasting to Ellen P. Goodman (July 28, 2010) (*citing* examples of governance changes that significantly improved performance at Nashville Public Television, which moved from school board to community licensee, and WNYC, which moved from municipal New York City ownership to community licensee).

86 Email from Terry Clifford, co-C.E.O., SRG, to Ellen P. Goodman, FCC (July 28, 2010) (Clifford Email 7/28/10).

87 *See, e.g.,* SRG, STATION RESOURCES GROUP REPORT ON COMMUNITY ADVISORY BOARDS 2004 (2004) (identifying the characteristics of successful community advisory boards), http://www.srg.org/governance/CAB/CAB.html.

88 Email from William H. Kling, President and CEO, American Public Media Group, to Ellen P. Goodman, FCC (July 28, 2010) (Kling Email 7/28/10).

89 Kling Email 7/28/10.

90 Kling Email 7/28/10.

91 Terry Clifford recommends focusing the efforts to improve governance at CPB, noting:

"CPB has invested in several large-scale efforts to build organizational capacity at public television and radio stations that want to become stronger. The more a station engages in high-level fundraising (CPB's Leadership for Philanthropy), the more an organization forms community partnerships (CPB's National Center for Community Engagement and Harwood Institute projects), and the more an organization sets goals for growth in its audience (the CSG audience service criteria), the more that organization will move toward effective and substantive governance structures—mainly because they can't succeed in becoming a significant and valued organization without strong, connected leadership at the top."

Clifford Email 7/28/10.

92 *See* Letter from William H. Kling to Steven Waldman, FCC (Nov. 1, 2010).

93 BARBARA COCHRAN, THE ASPEN INSTITUTE, RETHINKING PUBLIC MEDIA: MORE LOCAL, MORE INCLUSIVE 48-49 (2010).

94 47 U.S.C. § 310(d).

95 For example, in 2008, the FCC dismissed an application by WXEL-TV, based in West Palm Beach, Florida, to assign its license to WXEL Public Broadcasting Corporation, which was based in New York and whose board was not representative of the licensee's community. *See* http://licensing.fcc.gov/cgi-bin/ws.exe/prod/cdbs/pubacc/prod/app_det.pl?Application_id=1155667.

96 CPB, PUBLIC RADIO IN THE NEW NETWORK AGE: WIDER USE, DEEPER VALUE, COMPELLING CHANGE—REPORT AND RECOMMENDATIONS OF THE PUBLIC RADIO AUDIENCE GROWTH TASK FORCE 20 (2010), http://www.srg.org/GTA/GTAReports.html.

97 THE BENTON FOUND., WHAT'S GOING ON IN COMMUNITY MEDIA 9 (2007), http://benton.org/node/6172.

98 CPB, National Minority Consortia, http://www.cpb.org/aboutpb/consortia.html (last visited June 29, 2010).

99 NEW PUBLIC MEDIA at 35-38.

100 *See, e.g.,* National Federation of Community Broadcasters Comments in re *FOM PN*, filed May 7, 2010 (NFCB Comments), at 3; PUBLIC RADIO AUDIENCE GROWTH TASK FORCE, PUBLIC RADIO IN THE NEW NETWORK AGE 12-18 (2010), *available at* http://www.srg.org/GTA/GTAReports.html; Native Public Media Comments in re *FOM PN*, filed May 7, 2010, at 4, 6 (Native Public Media Comments); NEW PUBLIC MEDIA at 34-38; African-American Public Radio Consortium et al., An Open Letter to Our Public Media Colleagues, May 2009, *available at* http://www.nativepublicmedia.org/images/stories/documents/OpenLetter.pdf.

101 NFCB Comments at 2–3.

102 NEW PUBLIC MEDIA at 35; *see also* Public Broadcasting Service (PBS), CPB/PBS Diversity & Innovation Fund, http://www.pbs.org/difund/ (last visited Jan. 21, 2011).

103 *See* Memorandum from Public Television CSG Review Panel to Pat Harrison, President & CEO, CPB, Final Report and Recommendations (Aug. 25, 2010).

104 *See, e.g.,* AIR Comments at 13.

105 *Spreading the Zing: Reimagining Public Media*, Comments of Association of Independents in Radio (AIR) & Jessica Clark, Center for Social Media, in re *FOM PN*, filed May 12, 2010.

106 47 U.S.C. § 396(c)(2).

107 47 U.S.C. § § 396(c)(1), (c)(5).

108 *See* CHANGING MEDIA 271-73. Free Press proposes that the CPB Board

Chair and Vice Chair should be affiliated with different political parties, and expanding the Board along the lines proposed by the Association of Public Television Stations with some caveats. *See id.* This would entail growth to 13 directors, five of which would include "leaders from both the major cultural institutions—the Library of Congress, the Smithsonian Institution, the National Science Foundation and the National Endowments for the Arts and Humanities." *Id.* at 273. Representation of PBS and NPR on the Board would be increased, but also ensured would be "representation from noncommercial media makers who are not part of PBS and NPR and from leaders in the field of journalism such as a representative from the Association for Education in Journalism and Mass Communication." *Id.* Under this proposal, the White House would only be involved in the nomination of eight directors, only four of which would be allowed to be of the same political party; however, it would have consultation rights vis-a-vis represented organizations with respect to the non-appointed directors. *Id.*

109 *Coll Open Letter*.

110 CARNEGIE COMMISSION ON THE FUTURE OF PUBLIC BROADCASTING, THE REPORT AND RECOMMENDATIONS OF THE CARNEGIE COMMISSION ON EDUCATIONAL TELEVISION: PUBLIC TELEVISION, A PROGRAM FOR ACTION at 68–73 (Harper & Row) (1967) (Carnegie I); RALPH ENGELMAN, PUBLIC RADIO AND TELEVISION IN AMERICA 88 (Sage) (1996).

111 JOHN WITHERSPOON & ROSELLE KOVITZ, THE HISTORY OF PUBLIC BROADCASTING 52-53 (Current) (1987) (WITHERSPOON & KOVITZ, HISTORY OF PUBLIC BROADCASTING)

112 Excerpt from RALPH ENGELMAN, FRIENDLYVISION: FRED FRIENDLY AND THE RISE AND FALL OF TELEVISION JOURNALISM (Columbia Univ. Press) (2009), *available at* http://www.current.org/history/hist0909friendly.shtml.

113 *See* Public Broadcasting Self-Sufficiency Act of 1996, H.R. 2979, 104th Cong. (1996), *available at* http://www.current.org/pbpb/legislation/fields96.html; *see also* Steve Behrens, *Field Proposes Trust Fund, But Caps Its Size At $1 Billion*, CURRENT, Mar. 11, 1996, http://www.current.org/mo/mo605.html.

114 NATIONAL BROADBAND PLAN at 304.

115 THE BENTON FOUND., CHARTING THE DIGITAL BROADCASTING FUTURE: FINAL REPORT OF THE ADVISORY COMMITTEE ON PUBLIC INTEREST OBLIGATIONS OF DIGITAL TELEVISION BROADCASTERS 65 (1998) (CHARTING THE DIGITAL BROADCASTING FUTURE), *available at* http://govinfo.library.unt.edu/piac/piacreport.pdf.

116 CHARTING THE DIGITAL BROADCASTING FUTURE at 65. Ultimately, the Commission came to no consensus of a specific alternative model of public interest obligations.

117 *Coll Open Letter*.

118 Steve Coll, *Why Journalists Shouldn't Resist Public Funds*, ZOCAL PUBLIC SQUARE, Jan. 8, 2011 (*Why Journalists Shouldn't Resist Public Funds*), http://zocalopublicsquare.org/thepublicsquare/2011/01/08/why-journalists-shouldnt-resist-public-funds/read/nexus/.

119 *Why Journalists Shouldn't Resist Public Funds*.

120 Writers Guild of America East Comments in re *2010 Quadrennial Review NOI* (*2010 Quadrennial Regulatory Review—Review of the Commission's Broadcast Ownership Rules and Other Rules Adopted Pursuant to Section 202 of the Telecommunications Act of 1996*, MB Docket No. 09-182, Notice of Inquiry, 75 Fed. Reg. 33227 (June 11, 2010) (*2010 Quadrennial Review NOI*)), filed July 8, 2010, at 1–2.

121 Carnegie I at 8.

122 *See* Christian M. Bron, *Financing and Supervision of Public Service Broadcasting*, IRIS PLUS 2010-4, 7, 11 (2010).

123 NEW PUBLIC MEDIA at 28.

124 WITHERSPOON & KOVITZ, HISTORY OF PUBLIC BROADCASTING at 51-52.

125 NEW PUBLIC MEDIA at 24–27.

126 NEW PUBLIC MEDIA at 24–25. This estimate assumes a taxable base of $190 billion in 2010 with a 3 percent growth rate per year, and exemptions from certain industries (e.g. newspapers, online advertising) that will increase from 38 percent to 49 percent in 2019 because of a greater shift to online advertising. *Id.* at 24. The estimate also assumes continued federal appropriations to the CPB at a growth rate of 3 percent per year, and that federal sources also include 10 percent of the amount collected from the advertising tax; the remainder would be deposited in a trust fund. *Id.*

127 NEW PUBLIC MEDIA at 26-27. This estimate also assumes a 3 percent annual increase in advertising spending and in federal appropriations for public media, though with no exemptions to the deduction for any particular industry. The estimate also assumes a tax law change allowing businesses to deduct 80 percent of advertising costs in the year ads are placed, with the remaining 20 percent amortized over the next four years. *Id.* at 27.

128 Prepared Testimony of Randolph May, FCC Workshop on the Future of Media and the Information Needs of Communities: Public and Other Noncommercial Media in the Digital Era (Apr. 30, 2010), at 6, *available at* http://reboot.fcc.gov/futureofmedia/public-and-other-noncommercial-media-in-the-digital-era.

129 Adam Thierer, *The* Wrong *Way to Reinvent Media, Part 2: Broadcast Spectrum Taxes to Subsidize Public Media*, THE PROGRESS & FREEDOM FOUNDATION: PROGRESS ON POINT, vol. 17, issue 2 (Mar. 2010), at 5 (*The* Wrong *Way to Reinvent Media, Part 2*).

130 Adam Thierer, *Unappreciated Benefits of Advertising and Commercial Speech*, MERCATUS ON POLICY No. 86 (Mercatus Ctr. at George Mason Univ.) (Jan. 2011), *available at* http://mercatus.org/sites/default/files/publication/unappreciated-benefits-of-advertising-and-commercial-speech_0.pdf.

131 *Why Expansion of the FCC's Public Interest Regulatory Regime is Unwise, Unneeded, Unconstitutional, and Unenforceable*, Prepared Testimony of Adam Thierer, President, The Progress & Freedom Foundation, FCC Workshop on the Future of Media and the Information Needs of Communities: Serving the Public Interest in the Digital Era (Mar. 4, 2010), at 11–12 (Thierer Prepared Testimony 3/4/10), *available at* http://reboot.fcc.gov/futureofmedia/serving-the-public-interest-in-the-digital-era.

132 Progress & Freedom Foundation Comments in re *FOM PN*, filed May 5, 2010 (PFF Comments), at 18; *The* Wrong *Way to Reinvent Media, Part 2*.

133 Thierer Prepared Testimony 3/4/10 at 4–5.

134 CPB Comments at 18–19.

135 Eric Newton Comments in re *FOM PN*, filed May 7, 2010.

136 *See Creation of Low Power Radio Service*, Report and Order, 15 FCC Rcd 2205, 2211-12 (2000) (*Low Power Radio Svc. Order 2000*).

137 *See Low Power Radio Svc. Order 2000*, 15 FCC Rcd at 2213.

138 47 C.F.R. § 73.853 (licensing requirement); 47 C.F.R. § 73.855 (ownership limits). In addition, former pirate radio operators are not eligible to hold an LPFM license. *See* 47 C.F.R. § 73.854. At one point, a single entity could own up to ten LPFM stations, but the Rules were revised in 2007 to restrict ownership of more than one LPFM station, with the notion that it would further protect localism and foster greater diversity of programming. *See Creation of a Low Power Radio Service*, Third Report and Order and Second Further Notice of Proposed Rulemaking, 22 FCC Rcd 21912, 21922 (2007) (*Low Power Radio Svc. Order 2007*); 47 C.F.R. § 73.855(a). An LPFM license may not be transferred or assigned for three years from the date of issue, and the transferee/assignee must satisfy all eligibility criteria that apply to an LPFM licensee. *See* 47 C.F.R. § 73.865. LPFM construction permits are non-transferrable. *Id.*

139 47 C.F.R. § 73.801 (incorporating restrictions in 47 C.F.R. § 73.503).

140 Pub. L. No. 111-371, 124 Stat. 4072 (2011).e

141 2001 District of Columbia Appropriations Act ("2001 DC Appropriations Act" or "Act").

142 See, e.g., Paul Riismandel, *Breaking down the House's new LPFM bill*, RADIO SURVIVOR, Dec. 18, 2010, http://www.radiosurvivor.com/tag/local-community-radio-act-of-2009/;Hayley Tsukayama, *Advocates rejoice as Obama signs Local Community Radio Act*, Post Tech (Wash. Post), Jan. 7, 2011 .

143 *See, e.g.,* Future of Music Coalition, Low Power FM, Dec. 8, 2010, http://futureofmusic.org/article/fact-sheet/low-power-fm.

144 Antenna Vision, http://www.antennavision.net/70111.html (last visited Dec. 27, 2010).

145 *Low Power Radio Svc. Order 2007*, 22 FCC Rcd at 21929–30; *see also* Local Community Radio Act of 2010, Pub. L. No. 111-371, § 5(3), 124 Stat. 4072,—(mandating that translators and LPFM stations remain "equal in status").

146 *Low Power Radio Svc. Order 2007*, 22 FCC Rcd at 21934.

147 *See Low Power Radio Svc. Order 2007*, 22 FCC Rcd at 21930, *citing Creation of Low Power Radio Service*, Second Order on Reconsideration and Further Notice of Proposed Rulemaking, 20 FCC Rcd 6763, 6776-78 (2005). Indeed, nearly two-thirds of all non-reserved band translator authorizations were issued out of the 2003 translator window. *See Amendment of Service and Eligibility Rules for FM Broadcast Translator Stations*, Report and Order, 24 FCC Rcd 9642, 9651 (2009).

148 *Low Power Radio Svc. Order 2007*, 22 FCC Rcd at 21934–35.

149 *Low Power Radio Svc. Order 2000*, 15 FCC Rcd at 2219–2220.

150 *See* 47 C.F.R. § 74.1231(b) ("An FM translator may be used for the purpose of retransmitting the signals of a primary AM or FM radio broadcast station or another translator station the signal of which is received directly through space, converted, and suitably amplified, and originating programming to the extent authorized in paragraphs (f), (g), and (h) of this section."); *Id.* at § 74.1231(g) ("Originations concerning financial support are limited to a total of 30 seconds an hour.").

151 Connolly-Ahern, C., Schejter, A., Obar, J., & Martinez-Carrillo, N. (September 2009). A slice of the pie: Examining the state of the Low Power FM Radio Service in 2009. Presented at the 37th TPRC Conference on Communication, Information and Internet Policy, Arlington, VA.

152 *See, e.g.,* FCC, Low Power Television (LPTV) Service: FCC Consumer Facts (FCC, LPTV Facts), http://www.fcc.gov/cgb/consumerfacts/lptv.html (last visited Dec. 27, 2010).

153 FCC, LPTV Facts.

154 FCC, Consumer Advisory: The DTV Transition and LPTV/Class A/Translator Stations (FCC, DTV Transition & LPTV/Class A/Translator Stations), http://www.fcc.gov/cgb/consumerfacts/DTVandLPTV.html (last visited Dec. 27, 2010).

155 FCC, DTV Transition & LPTV/Class A/Translator Stations.

156 *See, e.g.*, 47 C.F.R. §§ 74.703, 74.709, 90.303.

157 47 C.F.R. § 73.3580(d)(5)(i)(A). *See also In the Matter of Establishment of a Class A Television Service*, Report and Order, 15 FCC Rcd 6355 (2000).

158 *See Commencement of Rural, First-Come, First-Served Digital Licensing for Low Power Television and TV Translators Beginning August 25*, Public Notice, DA 09-1487, 24 FCC Rcd 8911 (MB, rel. June 29, 2009). The initiation of nationwide first-come, first-served digital licensing for low power television and TV translators was postponed to July 26, 2010. *See Initiation of Nationwide First-Come, First-Served Digital Licensing for Low Power Television and TV Translator Services Postponed to July 26, 2010*, Public Notice, DA 09-2611, 24 FCC Rcd 14614 (MB rel. Dec. 22, 2009).

159 These 24 are Alaska, Arizona, California, Colorado, Connecticut, the District of Columbia, Florida, Hawaii, Idaho, Illinois, Kentucky, Michigan, Minnesota, Montana, Nebraska, New Jersey, New York, Ohio, Oregon, Pennsylvania, Rhode Island, South Carolina, Washington, and Wisconsin.

160 These 16 are: Arizona, Alaska, California, Colorado, Connecticut, Florida, Illinois, Michigan, Montana, Nebraska, Ohio, Pennsylvania, Oregon, South Carolina, Washington, and Wisconsin. Giguere Email 9/14/10.

161 These states are California, Michigan, Wisconsin, and Pennsylvania. Giguere Email 9/14/10.

162 Giguere Email 9/14/10 (the 12 SPANs identified are in Arizona, Alaska, Colorado, Connecticut, Florida, Illinois, Montana, Nebraska, Ohio, Oregon, South Carolina, and Washington).

163 Email from Christopher Long, President and CEO, WisconsinEye, to Simon Banyai, FCC (Sept. 16, 2010).

164 Meeting of NAPAN with Steven Waldman and additional staff members, FCC (June 7, 2010).

165 47 U.S.C. § 531(a) (providing that franchising authorities "may establish requirements in a franchise with respect to the designation or use of channel capacity for public, educational, or governmental use" to the extent provided in section 531).

166 Giguere Email 9/14/10.

167 Email from Paul Giguere, President, NAPAN/President and CEO, The Connecticut Network, to Simon Banyai, FCC (Nov. 16, 2010).

168 Meeting of NAPAN with Steven Waldman and other staff members, FCC (Nov. 4, 2010) (NAPAN Meeting 11/4/10).

169 NAPAN Meeting 11/4/10.

170 *See* Satellite Television Extension and Localism Act of 2010 § 209, Pub. L. No. 111-175, 124 Stat. 1218, 1254-1255 (2010) (codified at 47 U.S.C. § 335(b)).

171 Email from Greg Lane, President & C.E.O., TVW (Washington State Public Affairs TV Network) to Sherille Ismail, FCC (Aug. 13, 2010); Interview of Paul Giguere by Simon Banyai, FCC (Sept. 7, 2010).

172 Letter from Eric Newton, V.P., Journalism Program, John S. and James L. Knight Foundation, to Steven Waldman, FCC (May 7, 2010).

173 Alan Mutter, *Bridge to Nowhere: Non-profit Press Ownership*, REFLECTIONS OF A NEWSOSAUR, Mar. 24, 2009, http://newsosaur.blogspot.com/2009/03/bridge-to-nowhere-non-profit-press.html.

174 David M. Schizer, *Subsidizing the Press*, JOURNAL OF LEGAL ANALYSIS (forthcoming) (2010) (*Schizer*), *available at* http://lsr.nellco.org/columbia_pllt/9191/ (abstract only).

175 MARION R. FREEMONT-SMITH, CAN NONPROFITS SAVE JOURNALISM? LEGAL CONSTRAINTS AND OPPORTUNITIES 16 (Joan Shorenstein Ctr. on the Press, Politics and Public Policy) (2009), (CAN NONPROFITS SAVE JOURNALISM?), *available at* http://www.npjhub.org/academics/academic-research, (*citing* Treas. Reg. § § 1.501(c)(3)⊠l(d)(3)).

176 CAN NONPROFITS SAVE JOURNALISM? at 18 (*citing* Rev. Rul. 67-4, 1967-1 C.B. 121).

177 Rev. Rul. 77-4, 1977-1 C.B. 141.

178 CAN NONPROFITS SAVE JOURNALISM? at 18.

179 Richard Schmalbeck, James T. Hamilton, Edward Skloot, et al., *Guidance Suggestions: Newspapers and Nonprofit Organizations* (letter to U.S. Internal Revenue Service), May 28, 2009 (*Guidance Suggestions: Newspapers and Nonprofit Organizations*), *available at* http://dewitt.sanford.duke.edu/images/uploads/dwcirsguidancefinal.pdf.

180 *Guidance Suggestions: Newspapers and Nonprofit Organizations.*

181 *Guidance Suggestions: Newspapers and Nonprofit Organizations* at 3.

182 Testimony of Allen R. Bromberger, Partner, Perlman & Perlman, LLP, Federal Trade Commission (FTC) Workshop, "From Town Criers To Bloggers: How Will Journalism Survive The Internet Age?" (Mar. 9, 2010), Tr. at 188:9–11, *available at* http://www.ftc.gov/opp/workshops/news/index.shtml.

183 26 U.S.C. § 501(c)(3).

184 IRS, The Restriction of Political Campaign Intervention by Section 501(c)(3) Tax-Exempt Organizations, http://www.irs.gov/charities/charitable/article/0,,id=163395,00.html (last reviewed June 16, 2010) ("Under the Internal Revenue Code, all section 501(c)(3) organizations are absolutely prohibited from directly or indirectly participating in, or intervening in, any political campaign on behalf of (or in opposition to) any candidate for elective public office.").

185 Testimony of Joel Kramer, FTC Workshop, "From Town Criers To Bloggers: How Will Journalism Survive The Internet Age?" (June 15, 2010), Tr. at 54, *available at* http://www.ftc.gov/opp/workshops/news/index.shtml.

186 Hoffer Memo.

187 The experience of a Pasadena, California church concerning speech issues and Section 501(c)(3) status provides helpful insight into the type of problems a Section 501(c)(3) news organization might face.

In 2005, the All Saints Episcopal Church found itself under investigation by the IRS, threatened with an audit of its finances and loss of its tax-exempt status, after a guest pastor gave a sermon shortly before the 2004 presidential election that presented a hypothetical debate about the Iraq conflict among Jesus, George Bush, and John Kerry. *See* All Saints Episcopal Church, *All Saints Church, Pasadena Demands Correction and Apology From the IRS* (press release), Sept. 23, 2007, http://www.allsaintspas.org/documents/IRS_Press_Release_Sept_23__2007.pdf?docID=2521. As the Church explained in a press release, the sermon "addressed the moral and religious implications of various social issues facing our country today" without "tell[ing] the congregation how to vote." *See id.* The Church eventually received a letter from the IRS concluding that the sermon in question constituted "prohibited political campaign intervention," but also informing the Church, paradoxically and without explanation, that the IRS would not challenge the Church's tax-exempt status or institute an audit. *See id.*

188 *See, e.g.,* Corinne Antley, *Intentionally Nonprofit Journalism: A Tax Lawyer's Perspective*, DOW LOHNES PLLC, Aug. 2010, at 3–4, www.dowlohnes.com/files/upload/section501(c)(3).pdf.

189 Interview with Charles C. Duncan Pardo, Editor, Raleigh Public Record, by Paige Gold, FCC, (June 23, 2010).

190 Email from Miles Maguire to Steven Waldman, April 3, 2011.

191 *Guidance Suggestions: Newspapers and Nonprofit Organizations* at 3.

192 Larry Margasak, *Cardin proposes nonprofit status for newspapers*, ASSOCIATED PRESS, Mar. 24, 2009, http://www.baltimoresun.com/news/nation-world/politics/bal-cardin-newspapers0324,0,7631327.story.

193 Interview with Bruce Hopkins, Sr. Partner, Polsinelli Shughart PC (Kansas City, MO), by Paige Gold, FCC (Dec. 22, 2010).

194 *Guidance Suggestions: Newspapers and Nonprofit Organizations* at 1.

195 Hoffer Memo.

196 David Schizer, Subsidizing the Press 26 *et seq.* (Columbia Law And Economics Working Paper No. 376) (2010), *available at* lsr.nellco.org/cgi/viewcontent.cgi?article=1083&context=columbia_pllt.

197 *See* Senate Bill No. 690, 2010 Md. ALS 97, 2010 Md. Laws 97 (codified at MD. CORP. & ASS'N CODE ANN. § 5-6C-01).

198 *See* Corporate Flexibility Act Of 2010/Flexible Purpose Corporation, Cal. Senate Bill 1463 (DeSaulnier) (Apr. 5, 2010).

199 ROBERT LANG, COMMUNITY FOUNDATIONS AND THE L3C (Americans for Community Development) (2008), http://www.americansforcommunitydevelopment.org/whitepapers.php.

200 For example, at a March 2010 FTC workshop, Elizabeth Grant, Attorney-in-Charge of the Oregon Department of Justice's Charitable Activities Section, said:

"[W]hen I think about how I'm going to be doing my job, it gets complicated in this hybrid realm because traditionally, one thing I know about nonprofit corporations, there's a whole body of law established, and there aren't equity interest...[b]ut with these hybrid forms, I hear... some amount of distribution is appropriate, but I'm not really sure what amount is appropriate, and when can you say they're distributing too much and not really furthering the charitable objective of the organization any more?"

Testimony of Elizabeth Grant, FTC Workshop, "From Town Criers To Bloggers: How Will Journalism Survive The Internet Age?" (Mar. 9, 2010), Tr. at 196:5–18, *available at* http://www.ftc.gov/opp/workshops/news/index.shtml.

201 Council on Foundations, *Program Related Investments (PRIs) Promotion Act* (position statement), Mar. 2010, http://www.cof.org/files/Bamboo/programsandservices/publicpolicy/documents/pris.pdf. "Under current procedure, foundations are understandably reluctant to enter into otherwise promising ventures because of the risks." *Id.* Such risks include steep financial penalties if the IRS later determines that an investment did not qualify as a PRI. There are two ways a foundation can determine whether an investment satisfies IRS requirements for PRIs, both of which are resource-intensive. A foundation can obtain a private legal opinion, the outcome of which will depend on the interpretation of the lawyer preparing it. It can also seek an IRS determination, a process that is costly, takes a great deal of time, and cannot be relied upon as precedent by any other groups. To help remedy this, the Council on

Foundations' position paper states, "A process that encourages foundations to request IRS guidance will promote transparency and consistency in the way that the legal rules surrounding PRI's are being interpreted and applied." *Id.*

202 *See* American Bar Ass'n Section of Taxation, Comments to Hon. Douglas Shulman, Internal Revenue Service Commissioner, Concerning Proposed Additional Examples on Program Related Investments, Mar. 3, 2010, *available at* http://www.abanet.org/tax/pubpolicy/2010/Comments_Concerning_Proposed_Additional_Examples_on_Program_Related_Investments.pdf.

203 *See* Americans for Community Development, Proposal for Philanthropic Facilitation Act, Nov. 9, 2010, http://www.americansforcommunitydevelopment.org/proposedfedlegislation.php.

32 Advertising Policy

1 U.S. GOVERNMENT ACCOUNTABILITY OFFICE, MEDIA CONTRACTS: ACTIVITIES AND FINANCIAL OBLIGATIONS FOR SEVEN FEDERAL DEPARTMENTS (2006) (GAO-06-305), *available at* http://www.gao.gov/products/GAO-06-305.

2 U.S. GOVERNMENT ACCOUNTABILITY OFFICE, FEDERAL ADVERTISING: ESTABLISHED PROGRAMS WERE LARGELY USED TO ADDRESS EXECUTIVE ORDER TO ENSURE SMALL AND MINORITY-OWNED BUSINESS PARTICIPATION (2007) (GAO-07-877), *available at* http://www.gao.gov/products/GAO-07-877. *See also,* U.S. GOVERNMENT ACCOUNTABILITY OFFICE, MEDIA CONTRACTS: ACTIVITIES AND FINANCIAL OBLIGATIONS FOR SEVEN FEDERAL DEPARTMENTS, (2006) (GAO-06-305) *available at* http://www.gao.gov/products/GAO-06-305.

3 U.S. GOVERNMENT ACCOUNTABILITY OFFICE, FEDERAL ADVERTISING: ESTABLISHED PROGRAMS WERE LARGELY USED TO ADDRESS EXECUTIVE ORDER TO ENSURE SMALL AND MINORITY-OWNED BUSINESS PARTICIPATION (2007) (GAO-07-877), *available at* http://www.gao.gov/products/GAO-07-877.

4 *See* U.S. Census Bureau, *2010 Census: Media Highlights Week 8: 3/6–3/12*, *available at* http://dola.colorado.gov/dlg/demog/census2010/publications/media_highlights_mar6.pdf; U.S. Census Bureau, *2010 Census: Media Highlights Week 6: 2/20–2/26*, *available at* http://dola.colorado.gov/dlg/demog/census2010/publications/media_highlights_feb20.pdf.

5 *See, e.g.,* U.S. Census Bureau, *Census Bureau Launches 2010 Census Advertising Campaign* (press release), Jan. 14, 2010, http://2010.census.gov/news/releases/operations/ad-campaign-release.html.

6 Letter from Steven Lanzano, President of TVB to Steven Waldman, April 15, 2011.

7 GEOFFREY COWAN & DAVID WESTPHAL, PUBLIC POLICY AND FUNDING THE NEWS 10 (Univ. of Southern California Annenberg School of Communication) (2010), http://fundingthenews.usc.edu/report/ (PUBLIC POLICY AND FUNDING THE NEWS).

8 Geoffrey Cowan & David Westphal, *American government: It's always subsidized commercial media*, ONLINE JOURNALISM REV., Nov. 30, 2009, http://www.ojr.org/ojr/people/davidwestphal/200911/1801/.

9 See, e.g., Public Notice Resource Center, Inc. (PNRC), c (last visited Feb. 11, 2011) (listing latest such legislation, proposed in New Jersey and Nebraska).

10 PNRC, Defining Characteristics, http://www.pnrc.net/about-public-notices/what-is-a-public-notice/defining-characteristics/ (last visited Jan. 25, 2011); PNRC, Where Do I Find A Public Notice?, http://www.pnrc.net/about-public-notices/where-do-i-find-a-public-notice/ (last visited Jan. 25, 2011).

11 Financial Transparency Restoration Act, H.R. 2727, 111th Cong., § 3(b).

12 Emery P. Dalesio, *Move to online public notices looms over papers*, USA TODAY, May 22, 2009, http://www.usatoday.com/tech/news/2009-05-22-online-notices_N.htm.

13 Prepared Testimony of Craig Aaron, Managing Director, Free Press, FCC Workshop on the Future of Media and the Information Needs of Communities: Public and Other Noncommercial Media in the Digital Era, (Apr. 30, 2010), at 6, *available at* http://reboot.fcc.gov/futureofmedia/public-and-other-noncommercial-media-in-the-digital-era. This estimate assumes inclusion of exemptions from the advertising tax for small businesses, newspapers or online advertising. *See id.* Free Press has proposed a "gross receipts tax on recipients of advertising revenue or via a 'sales tax' on advertisers" at 2 percent, which it estimates could raise "over $45 billion for a public media trust fund after a 10-year period, which would equate to a $2.25 billion annual budget in the 11th year." *Id.* Free Press also proposes "changing the tax code to allow only 80 percent of the advertising expense to be deducted in the year it was purchased, 'amortizing' the remaining expense over time." *Id.* at 6. Such change would cause the taxable base of each advertiser to rise, and thus lead to greater tax revenues, which "could be earmarked for a public media trust fund." *Id.* Free Press estimates that "in little more than a decade" a $61 billion media trust fund would be created, one that would "net[] a continued annual operating budget exceeding $3 billion." *Id.*

14 American Advertising Fed'n, *Alert: Threat to Advertising Deductibility Renewed* (member government affairs alert), Sept. 15, 2009, http://www.aaf.org/default.asp?id=1045.

15 U.S. Internal Revenue Service, 11. Other Expenses, http://www.irs.gov/publications/p535/ch11.html (under caption, "Miscellaneous Expenses") (last visited Jan. 25, 2011).

16 Ken Doctor, *The Newsonomics of Do Not Track*, NIEMAN JOURNALISM LAB, Dec. 9, 2010, http://www.niemanlab.org/2010/12/the-newsonomics-of-do-not-track/#.

17 Panelist Presentation of Lem Lloyd, Vice President, Channel Sales, Yahoo!, FTC Workshop, "From Town Criers To Bloggers: How Will Journalism Survive the Internet Age?" (Dec. 1, 2009), at 4, *available at* http://www.ftc.gov/opp/workshops/news/index.shtml.

33 Print

1 *See* WikiSource, Letter to Edward Carrington—January 16, 1787 (Letter to Edward Carrington), http://en.wikisource.org/wiki/Letter_to_Edward_Carrington_-_January_16,_1787 (last visited Jan. 25, 2011).

2 *See* Letter to Edward Carrington.

3 PAUL STARR, THE CREATION OF THE MEDIA: POLITICAL ORIGINS OF MODERN COMMUNICATIONS 87-88 (Basic Books) (2004) (STARR, CREATION OF THE MEDIA).

4 STARR, CREATION OF THE MEDIA at 57. In addition, newspapers in the colonies were published by printers who were focused on newspapers that carried information about public debate, in contrast to printers in Britain who were either more focused on the book trade or on publishing newspapers whose high price after taxes severely limited their circulation to elites.

5 GERALD J. BALDASTY, THE COMMERCIALIZATION OF NEWS IN THE NINE-TEENTH CENTURY 20 (Univ. of Wisconsin Press) (1992) (Baldasty).

6 BALDASTY, THE COMMERCIALIZATION OF NEWS IN THE NINETEENTH CENTURY at 23.

7 STARR, CREATION OF THE MEDIA at 261. "The number of periodicals with 100,000 circulation quadrupled from 21 to 85 between 1885 and 19000 and then nearly doubled again to 159 in 1905; the first magazine to hit a circulation of 1 million was the Ladies' Home Journal in 1903." Id.

8 15 U.S.C. § § 1801 et seq.

9 Geoffrey Cowan & David Westphal, Reality Check. Shrinking government support contributes to news media economic decline, UNIV. OF SOUTH-ERN CALIFORNIA ANNENBERG CENTER ON COMMUNICATION LEADERSHIP & POLICY BLOG, Nov. 30, 2009, http://communicationleadership.usc.edu/blog/government_action/cowan_westphal_reality_check_s.html.

34 Copyright and Intellectual Property

1 Copyright law protects "original works of authorship fixed in any tangible medium of expression," including pictorial and graphic works, audiovisual works and sound recordings. 17 U.S.C. § 102 (a). Among other exclusive rights, the copyright owner has the right to control reproduction and distribution of copies. 17 U.S.C. § 106.

2 Farhad Manjoo, Public Protests NPR Link Policy, WIRED, June 20, 2002, www.wired.com/techbiz/media/news/2002/06/53355.

3 TIM BERNERS-LEE, WEAVING THE WEB: THE ORIGINAL DESIGN AND ULTI-MATE DESTINY OF THE WORLD WIDE WEB (Harper) (2000).

4 Zachary M. Seward, Here's the AP document we've been writing about, NIEMAN JOURNALISM LAB, Aug. 13, 2009, http://www.niemanlab.org/2009/08/heres-the-ap-document-weve-been-writing-about/ (citing Associated Press, Protect, Point, Pay—An Associated Press Plan for Reclaiming News Content Online (internal memorandum), July 2009).

5 Nicole Bashor, The Cache Cow: Can Caching And Copyright Co-Exist?, 6 J. MARSHALL REV. INTELL. PROP. L. 101 (2006) (The Cache Cow) (citing Google Guide: How Google Works, http://www.googleguide.com) (last visited Jan. 31, 2011).

6 See, e.g., Jonathan Bailey, Why RSS Scraping Isn't O.K., PLAGIARISM TODAY, Aug. 29, 2006, http:www.plagiarismtoday.com/2006/08/29/why-rss-scraping-isnt-ok.

7 David Kaplan, Fair Syndication Consortium: Google Responsible For Over Half Of Unlicensed Newspaper Articles, PAID CONTENT, Dec. 1, 2009 (Fair Syndication Consortium), http://paidcontent.org/article/419-fair-syndication-consortium-google-responsible-for-over-half-of-unlicen/#.

8 Fair Syndication Consortium.

9 Eric Weigle, Credit where credit is due, GOOGLE NEWS BLOG, Nov. 16, 2010, http://googlenewsblog.blogspot.com/2010/11/credit-where-credit-is-due.html.

10 American Univ. Ctr. for Social Media, Documentary Filmmakers' State-ment of Best Practices in Fair Use, http://www.centerforsocialmedia.org/fair-use/best-practices/documentary/documentary-filmmakers-statement-best-practices-fair-use (last visited Jan. 26, 2011).

11 Doug Rand, Memo from the Edge: Legal Analysis and Practical Recom-mendations for Newspapers in Crisis (paper presented at Conference on "Journalism & The New Media Ecology: Who Will Pay the Messenger?," Yale Law School Nov. 13-14, 2009), at 3, available at http://www.law.yale.edu/intellectuallife/09mediapapers.htm.

12 Testimony of Laura Malone, Associate General Counsel, Intellectual Prop-erty, The Associated Press, FTC Workshop, "From Town Criers To Blog-gers: How Will Journalism Survive The Internet Age?" (Mar. 9, 2010), Tr. at 67, available at http://www.ftc.gov/opp/workshops/news/index.shtml.

13 Bruce W. Sanford, Revamped Legal Structure is Key to the Future of Journalism, SPEAKING FREELY, July 2010, available at http://www.tjcenter.org/wp-content/uploads/Spkng%20Frly%20Sanford%207-1-10%5B1%5D%281%29.pdf.

14 James Fallows, How to Save the News, THE ATLANTIC, June 2010, http://www.theatlantic.com/magazine/print/2010/06/how-to-save-the-news/8095.

15 Testimony of James W. Marcovitz, Sr. V.P. and Deputy Gen. Counsel, News Corp., FTC Workshop, "From Town Criers To Bloggers: How Will Journalism Survive The Internet Age?" (Mar. 9, 2010), Tr. at 65:8–10; 12-14, available at http://www.ftc.gov/opp/workshops/news/index.shtml.

16 Testimony of James Boyle, William Neal Reynolds Professor of Law, Duke Univ. Law School, FTC Workshop, "From Town Criers To Bloggers: How Will Journalism Survive The Internet Age?" (Mar. 9, 2010), Tr. at 86:4–18, 87:1–6, available at http://www.ftc.gov/opp/workshops/news/index.shtml.

17 The Cache Cow, 6 J. Marshall Rev. Intell. Prop. L. at 108 (citing Robots Exclusion, http://www.robotstxt.org/wc/exclusion.html (last visited Jan. 26, 2011)).

18 Danny Sullivan, Josh Cohen of Google News on Paywalls, Partnerships and Working with Publishers, SEARCHENGINELAND.COM, Nov. 15, 2009, http:searchengineland.com/josh-cohen-of-google-news-on-paywalls-partnerships-working-with-publishers-29881.

19 Digital Millennium Copyright Act, Title II, Online Copyright Infringement Liability Limitation Act, Pub L. 105-304, 112 Stat. 2877-2886 (1998) (amending 17 U.S.C. § 512).

20 See 17 U.S.C. § 512(h).

21 See, e.g., Chilling Effects Clearinghouse, Frequently Asked Questions (and Answers) About DMCA Subpoenas, http://www.chillingeffects.org/dmca-sub/faq.cgi ("Question: How is Internet anonymity affected by Section 512(h) subpoenas?…Answer: Since anyone who has ever written or typed something is a copyright holder, it is possible that any of these people might misuse the Section 512(h) subpoena to discover identity for purposes other than vindicating copyright rights. In some instances, the fear of improper discovery of their identity will intimidate or silence online speakers even though they were engaging in protected expression under the First Amendment.")

22 Fair Syndication Consortium, Content Syndication and Management Guidelines 0.9, http://www.fairsyndication.org/guidelines/Content_Syn-dication_and_Management_Guidelines_v0.9.html (last visited Jan. 26, 2011). Under the Fair Syndication Consortium plan, if a publisher

chooses to charge for full copy use, ad networks will act as royalty collectors/distributors. Publishers can choose the sites they want to publish their content, ruling out disreputable ones such as hate sites and pornography. Infringers will be dealt with using a "graduated escalation" enforcement path. The Consortium stresses the importance of considering the frequency and extent of reuse that is occurring, and does not consider it in publishers' best interest to expend resources going after casual, incidental, or unintentional re-users.

23 *See Graduated Response Trial Unmasks a Cooperative Internet*, FAIR SYNDICATION CONSORTIUM BLOG, Nov. 8, 2010, http://www.fairsyndication.org/blog/2010/graduated-response-trial-unmasks-a-cooperative-Internet/.

24 "*AP board approves independent agency to license digital news*," press release, Associated Press, Feb. 3, 2011, http://www.ap.org/pages/about/pressreleases/pr_020311a.html.

25 *Feist Publications, Inc. v. Rural Tel. Serv. Co.*, 499 U.S. 340, 344-45 (1991), *quoting Harper & Row Publishers, Inc. v. Nation Enterprises*, 471 U.S. 539, 556 (1985).

26 See *Associated Press v. All Headline News Corp. et al.*, 608 F. Supp. 2d 454 (S.D.N.Y. 2009) (*All Headline News*).

27 *Int'l News Service v. Associated Press*, 248 U.S. 215 (1918).

28 *Int'l News Service,* 248 U.S. at 240.

29 *Int'l News Service*, 248 U.S. at 245.

30 *Int'l News Service*, 248 U.S. at 245.

31 *Nat'l Basketball Ass'n v. Motorola, Inc.*, 105 F.3d 841 (2d Cir. 1997).

32 The NBA wanted to stop Motorola because it had negotiated a similar deal with a company called SportsSticker. Although the court ultimately ruled against the NBA, it held that similar forms of legal actions concerning intellectual property were not preempted by the Copyright Act if they met the following requirements:

(1) a plaintiff gathers information at a cost;

(2) the information is time-sensitive;

(3) the defendant's use of the information is "free-riding";

(4) the defendant is offering a service in direct competition with the plaintiff's;

(5) the ability to free ride on the plaintiff's efforts "would so reduce the incentive to produce the product or service that the existence or quality would be substantially threatened."

See Nat'l Basketball Ass'n, 105 F.3d at 845.

33 *Nat'l Basketball Ass'n*, 105 F.3d at 845. Based on this precedent, in 2008 the Second Circuit federal judge overseeing *All News Headlines* upheld AP's right to proceed to trial.

The Second Circuit ruling came as a shock to many media commentators. TechCrunch's Erick Schonfeld asked:

"But what constitutes "hot news" in an age of instant communications? And how long does it last. In 1918, "hot news" traveled by mail and telegraph. It could last hours or even days. Today, a true scoop lasts for about a minute. The AP would have to show instances of articles where not only the AP broke the news, but was the only outlet to get the original story—something rare and rarer when anyone can publish news over the Internet…. Hot news is a concept best left in the twentieth century."

Erick Schonfeld, *Hot News: The AP Is Living In The Last Century*, TECH-

CRUNCH.COM, Feb. 22, 2009, http://techcrunch.com/2009/02/22/hot-news-the-ap-is-living-in-the-last-century/.

34 *Barclays Capital, Inc. v. TheFlyOnTheWall.com*, 700 F. Supp. 2d 310 (S.D.N.Y. 2010) (*TheFlyOnTheWall.com*).

35 *TheFlyOnTheWall.com*, 700 F. Supp. 2d at 337.

36 Brief Amici Curiae of Advance Publications, Inc., *et al.*, *Barclays Capital Inc., et al. v. TheFlyOnTheWall.com*, Second Circuit Court of Appeals, No. 10-1372, June 21, 2010 (*News Organization Barlcays Amici Brief*), *available at* http://www.rcfp.org/newsitems/docs/20100623_163140_amicus_brief.pdf.

37 *See, e.g.,* Melissa Lipman, *Google, Twitter Back Removal Of 'Hot News' Injunction*, LAW 360, June 22, 2010, http://www.law360.com/topnews/articles/176629/google-twitter-back-removal-of-hot-news-injunction.

38 A Future of Media submission from the Corporation for Public Broadcasting, PBS, NPR and the Association of Public Television Stations reminded the Commission that "the public interest in continued access to information, education and enlightenment calls for a fair and reasonable balance" between the "sometimes competing interests" of copyright owners and users. CPB Comments at 20.

Native Public Media, an association of tribal radio stations, cautioned that any congressional amendments providing copyright exemptions to public broadcasting organizations for online distribution of public media should afford protection to the "intellectual property rights of Native Americans regarding information about tribal history, culture, and other information deemed proprietary by individual Tribal Nations." Native Public Media Comments at 7.

Patricia Aufderheide and Peter Jaszi sent a reminder that "Copyright and creativity are tightly linked. All cultural expression everywhere, including all media, draws upon existing culture; otherwise, it would be incomprehensible." Aufderheide/Jaszi Comments at 1.

New Media Rights, a San Diego-based group offering education and discussion about new media technologies and the law and policies affecting users of new media, wrote to voice its support for efforts to ensure that fair use protects incidental uses of content and personal, noncommercial uses of content. New Media Rights Comments in re *FOM PN*, filed May 7, 2010, at 4–5.

Comments submitted on behalf of two dozen community public interest groups by the New America Foundation, Free Press, and the Media Access Project brought up their concern with restrictive interpretations of fair use and misuse of the DMCA's notice-and-takedown process against non-infringing works, which they say threaten both the availability of source material and the persistent availability of citizen journalism and nonprofit media content.

"Innovators in digital news distribution, the builders of feed-readers, aggregators, podcasters and -catchers, and social discovery services also depend on the limits of copyright to bring media to news consumers in novel ways…We anticipate that the Commission will receive recommendations for the expansion of copyright protections. We recommend that you consider those critically, in light of the unintended negative consequences of previous copyright expansions."

Access Humboldt Joint Comments at 116.

39 Aufderheide/Jaszi Comments at 2.

40 Patricia Aufderheide & Peter Jaszi Comments in re *FOM PN*, filed Apr. 27, 2010 (Aufderheide/Jaszi Comments), at 3.

35 Recommendations

1 National Religious Broadcasters. Comments in re *FOM PN* (FCC Launches Examination of the Future of Media and Information Needs of Communities in a Digital Age, GN Docket No. 10-25, Public Notice, 25 FCC Rcd 384 (2010) (*FOM PN*), filed Febuary 18, 2010 (NRB Comments) at 12.

2 The Commission has recently taken a number of steps to move its processes away from reliance on paper and to being more reliant on digital technology. For instance the Commission has reduced the number of paper copies of pleadings that must be filed and moved towards electronic notification of docket filings and fees."

3 H.R. 2392, § 2(a), 111th Cong., 1st Sess. (2009), available at http://www. govtrack.us/congress/billtext.xpd?bill=h111-2392.

4 Id., at § 2(b).

5 Federal Trade Commission Staff. 2010. "Discussion Draft: Potential Policy Recommendations to Support the Reinvention of Journalism," at 31. Accessed Dec. 1, 2010. http://www.ftc.gov/opp/workshops/news/jun15/docs/new-staff-discussion.pdf.

6 *Unappreciated Benefits of Advertising and Commercial Speech*, by Adam Thierer, Mercatus on Policy, Mercatus Center, George Mason University, January 2011, available at http://mercatus.org/sites/default/files/publication/unappreciated-benefits-of-advertising-and-commercial-speech_0.pdf.

7 Rev. Rul. 77-4, 1977-1 C.B. 141.

8 Letter from Eric Newton, V.P., Journalism Program, John S. and James L. Knight Foundation, to Steven Waldman, FCC (May 7, 2010).

9 Letter from Eric Newton, V.P., Journalism Program, John S. and James L. Knight Foundation, to Steven Waldman, FCC (May 7, 2010).